АВТОРИТЕТНЫЙ СПРАВОЧНИК

Вот недорогой
русско-английский
англо-русский
словарь — лучший из когда-либо
вышедших из печати

Предназначенный для широкого круга лиц, интересующихся обоими языками, этот словарь будет особенно выгодным и ценным справочником как для учащихся и учителей, так и в частных и конторских библиотеках. Он содержит более 35 000 заглавных слов в алфавитном порядке с указанием правильного произношения, таблицы флексий, списки географических названий, сокращений, имен числительных, мер веса и длины и т. д.

Русско-английский/англо-русский словарь Романова подготовлен сотрудниками фирмы Лангеншейдта, самого известного в мире издательства двуязычных словарей. Он отличается сжатостью и достоверностью и является необходимым справочником исключительной ценности.

The above text appears in English on the back cover

А. С. РОМАНОВ

Карманный

РУССКО-АНГЛИЙСКИЙ

и

АНГЛО-РУССКИЙ

словарь

с учетом
американского произношения и правописания

Обе части в одном томе

Составили:

д-р Э. Ведель (ч. 1)

А. С. Романов (ч. 2)

WASHINGTON SQUARE PRESS
PUBLISHED BY POCKET BOOKS NEW YORK

ROMANOV'S Pocket RUSSIAN-ENGLISH ENGLISH-RUSSIAN Dictionary

With special emphasis on American English

Two Volumes in One

Part I by E. Wedel, Ph. D.

Part II by A. S. Romanov

WSP

WASHINGTON SQUARE PRESS
PUBLISHED BY POCKET BOOKS NEW YORK

A Washington Square Press Publication of
POCKET BOOKS, a Simon & Schuster division of
GULF & WESTERN CORPORATION
1230 Avenue of the Americas, New York, N.Y. 10020

Published by arrangement with Langenscheidt KG, Publishing House

ISBN: 0-671-44506-5

First Pocket Books printing August, 1964

20 19 18 17 16 15 14 13

Printed in the U.S.A.

Contents

Оглавление

Preface

This Russian-English dictionary has been compiled with the same care and diligence as all other publications of Langenscheidt Publishers, which have been appreciated as standard works for many decades.

The dictionary is meant to be used in all walks of life and at school. In its two parts it contains more than 35,000 vocabulary entries with many translations and idioms as well as their phonetic transcriptions. Americanisms have received special consideration, and in the Russian-English part cases of particular American usage are even cited in the first place, being followed by their respective British semantic (or orthographic) equivalents.

English pronunciation follows that laid down by Daniel Jones in his *An English Pronouncing Dictionary* (1953). In the Russian-English part pronunciation is only given after those Russian words and parts of words which deviate from the basic rules of pronunciation. Generally speaking, Russian words can be pronounced properly if the place of the accent is known. Therefore every Russian word has been given its stress. Shift of stress, as far as it takes place within the inflection, is also indicated. A detailed account of Russian pronunciation with the help of the symbols of I. P. A.'s phonetic transcription can be found on pages 21—27.

References to full-length inflection tables in the supplement to the dictionary, as given after nouns, adjectives and verbs, enable the user to employ the words in question in all their modifications.

In addition to the vocabulary this dictionary contains lists of geographical names (American and British), abbreviations, numerals, measures and weights and a survey of the most important differences between British and American spelling and pronunciation.

Publishers and editors hope of this book that it may contribute to the mutual understanding between nations and thus help to deepen their cultural relations.

Предисловие

Настоящий словарь русского и английского языков составлен с такой же тщательностью и аккуратностью, как и все издания Лангеншейдта, зарекомендовавшие себя образцовыми трудами на протяжении многих десятков лет.

Словарь предназначается преимущественно для работников разных профессий и учащихся. Он содержит в обеих частях более 35000 заглавных слов в алфавитном порядке, с указанием произношения, переводом и устойчивыми оборотами речи, причём учитываются в должной мере особенности американского варианта английского языка.

Английское произношение даётся по словарю Daniel Jones, An English Pronouncing Dictionary (1953).

К словнику прилагаются: списки географических названий (американских и английских), сокращений, имён числительных, мер длины и веса, грамматические таблицы, а также перечень важнейших различий между языком британцев и американцев в отношении правописания и произношения.

Издательство и сотрудники надеются изданием настоящего словаря способствовать взаимопониманию и укреплению культурных связей между народами.

Предисловие

[illegible]

[illegible]

[illegible]

[illegible]

[illegible]

ROMANOV'S
POCKET

Russian-English
English-Russian

DICTIONARY

Careful reading and observation of the following preliminary notes will both facilitate the use and help to open up the full value of the dictionary.

Preliminary Notes

1. Arrangement. Material in this dictionary has been arranged in alphabetical order. In the Russian-English part, proper names (Christian, geographical, etc.) as well as abbreviations appear in their individual alphabetical order within the vocabulary itself. In the case of a number of prefixed words, especially verbs, not explicitly listed because of the limited size of the dictionary, it may prove useful to drop the prefix, which is often but a sign of the perfective aspect (see below), and look up the primary (imperfective) form thus obtained.

Compounds not found in their alphabetical places should be reduced to their second component in order to find out their main meaning, e. g.: **термоя́дерный → я́дерный** = nuclear.

To save space with the aim of including a maximum of material, compounds, derivatives, and occasionally just similar words, have, wherever possible, been arranged in groups, the vertical stroke (|) in the first entry word of such a group separating the part common to all following items of the group, and the tilde (**~**) in the run-on words replacing the part preceding the vertical stroke in the first entry and consequently not repeated in the other articles of the group. The tilde may also stand for the whole first entry, which then has no separation mark since it is entirely repeated in the run-on items of the group.

Besides the bold-faced tilde just mentioned, the same mark in standard type (~) is employed within a great number of entries to give phrases and idioms of which the entry word or any component of its inflection system forms part.

A tilde with circlet (~̊) indicates a change in the initial letter (capital to small and vice versa) of a run-on word.

Examples: **Аме́рик|а ...; ~̊а́нский = америка́нский**
англи́|йский ...; '~̊я = 'Англия (for stress see below, 3).

Within brackets: square [ ], round ( ), acute-angled ⟨ ⟩, instead of the tilde a hyphen (-) with the same function (mark of repetition) has been used, e. g.:

то́лстый [14; толст, -á, -o] = [14; толст, толстá, то́лсто]
брать [беру́, -рёшь; брал, -á, -o] = [беру́, берёшь; брал, бралá, бра́ло]
весели́ть ...; (**-ся**) = **весели́ться**
cf. **убира́ть** ..., ⟨убра́ть⟩ ...; **-ся** = **убира́ться**, ⟨убра́ться⟩
проси́ть ..., ⟨по-⟩ = ⟨попроси́ть⟩.

Of the two main aspects of a Russian verb the imperfective form appears first, in boldface type, followed, in acute-angled brackets ⟨ ⟩ and in standard type, by its perfective counterpart. Verbs occurring only as perfective aspects (or whose imperfective or iterative aspect is hardly ever used) bear the mark *pf.*; those used only in the imperfective aspect have no special designation at all; verbs whose perfective aspect coincides with the imperfective are marked thus: *(im)pf.*

If in a certain meaning (or meanings) only one member of an aspect pair may be used, the cases concerned are preceded by the abbreviations *impf.* or *pf.* respectively and thus separated from the meanings to which both aspects apply, these latter being always given in the first place. Similarly in a noun the abbreviation *pl.* (or *sg.*) after one or more translation items designates the word(s) following it as referring only to the plural (or singular) form of the entry otherwise used in both numbers. Number differences between a Russian entry and its English counterpart(s) are indicated by adding the abbreviation *pl.* or *sg.* behind the latter, whereas a noun used only in the plural bears the mark *pl.* right after the entry itself, i. e. where usually the gender is given (see below).

In the English equivalents of Russian verbs the particle 'to' of the infinitive has been omitted for reasons of space economy.

Also, a number of quite similar international words, particularly nouns terminating in **-áция, -и́ция** or **-и́зм, -и́ст** = -ation, -ition, -ism, -ist, or likewise obvious cases such as **тайфу́н** 'typhoon' have not been included in the dictionary, especially since there are no stress or inflectional peculiarities about the Russian nouns in question nor is there, on the whole, any difficulty in deducing their semantic values.

Moreover, English adjectives used as nouns (and nouns used as adjectives) alike have, in connection with successive pertinent entries, been given but once, whereas the Russian words naturally appear in their different forms, i. e. parts of speech; e. g.:

америк|áнец *m* ..., **\~áнка** *f* ..., **\~áнский** ... = American (i. e. man, woman, *adj.*)
квадрáт *m* ..., **\~ный** ... square = square (*su.*) & square (*adj.*)
cf. **лими́т** *m* ..., **\~и́ровать** ... *(im)pf.* = limit (*su.*) & limit (*vb.*).

Otherwise the adjectival use of an English noun (and occasionally other parts of speech) corresponding to a Russian adjective has as a rule been noted by adding dots (...) to the noun, etc. form concerned, irrespective of the mode of its orthographic combination with another noun, i. e. whether they are spelled in one word, hyphenated or written separately.

2. Pronunciation. As a rule pronunciation in individual Russian entry words has been given only in cases and places that differ from the standard pronunciation of Russian vowel and consonant letters (for this cf. pp. 21—27), e. g.:

г = g, but in лёгкий = (-x-)
ч = tʃ, but in что = (ʃ-)
не = ɲɛ, but in (the loan word) пенснé = (-'nɛ)

To transcribe Russian sounds and (Cyrillic) letters, the alphabet of the International Phonetic Association (I.P.A.) has been used.

3. Stress. The accent mark (ʹ) is placed above the stressed vowel of a Russian entry (or any other) word having more than one syllable and printed in full, as well as of run-on words, provided their accentuated vowel is not covered by the tilde or hyphen (= marks of repetition), e. g.:

дока́з|ывать, ⟨~а́ть⟩ = ⟨доказа́ть⟩. Since ё is always stressed the two dots over it represent implicitly the accent mark.

Wherever the accent mark precedes the tilde ('~) the last syllable but one of the part for which the tilde stands is stressed.

Examples: **уведом|ля́ть** ..., ⟨'~ить⟩ = ⟨уве́домить⟩.
выполн|я́ть ..., ⟨'~ить⟩ = ⟨вы́полнить⟩.

An accent mark over the tilde (~́) implies that the last (or sole) syllable of the part replaced by the tilde is to be stressed.

Examples: **наход|и́ть** ...; ~́ка = **нахо́дка**
прода|ва́ть ..., ⟨~́ть⟩ = ⟨прода́ть⟩
по́езд ...; ~́ка = **пое́здка**
труб|а́ ...; ~́ка = **тру́бка**.

In special cases of phonetic transcription, however, the accent mark precedes the stressed syllable, cf. **анте́нна** [-ˈtɛn-], this usage being in accordance with I.P.A. rules.

Two accents in a word denote two equally possible modes of stressing it, thus:

и́на́че = **ина́че** *or* **и́наче**
загр|ужа́ть ..., ⟨~узи́ть⟩ [... -у́зи́шь] = [... загру́зишь *or* загрузи́шь]
нали|ва́ть ..., ⟨~́ть⟩ [... на́ли́л ...] = [... на́лил *or* нали́л ...].

Quite a number of predicative (or short) adjectives show a shift, or shifts, of stress as compared with their attributive forms. Such divergences are recorded as follows:

хоро́ший [17; хоро́ш, -а́] = [17; хоро́ш, хороша́, хорошо́ (*pl.* хороши́)]
плохо́й [16; плох, -а́, -о] = [16; плох, плоха́, пло́хо (*pl.* пло́хи)]
до́брый [14; добр, -а́, -о, до́бры́] = [14; добр, добра́, до́бро (*pl.* до́бры *or* добры́)].

The same system of stress designation applies, by the way, to accent shifts in the preterite forms of a number of verbs, e. g.:

да|ва́ть ..., ⟨~ть⟩ [... дал, -а́, -о; ...(дан, -а́)] = [... дал, дала́, да́ло (*pl.* да́ли); ... (дан, дана́, дано́, даны́)].

Insertion of "epenthetic" o, e between the two last stem consonants in masculine short forms has been noted in all adjectives concerned.

Examples: **лёгкий** [16; лёгок, легка́; *a.* лёгки] = [16; лёгок, легка́, легко́ (*pl.* легки́ *or* лёгки)]
бе́дный [14; -ден, -дна́, -о; бе́дны́] = [14; бе́ден, бедна́, бе́дно (*pl.* бе́дны *or* бедны́)]
больно́й [14; бо́лен, больна́] = [14; бо́лен, больна́, больно́ (*pl.* больны́)]
по́лный [14; по́лон, полна́, по́лно́] = [14; по́лон, полна́, по́лно *or* полно́ (*pl.* по́лны *or* полны́)].

If the stress in all short forms conforms to that of the attributive adjective the latter is merely provided with the abbreviation *sh.* (for *short form*) that indicates at the same time the possibility of forming such predicative forms, e. g.:

> **бога́тый** [14 *sh.*] = [14; бога́т, бога́та, бога́то, бога́ты]
> **паху́чий** [17 *sh.*] = [17; паху́ч, паху́ча, паху́че, паху́чи]
> **сво́йственный** [14 *sh.*] = [14; сво́йствен, сво́йственна, сво́йственно, сво́йственны].

4. Inflected forms. All Russian inflected parts of speech appearing in the dictionary are listed in their respective basic forms, i. e. nominative singular (nouns, adjectives, numerals, certain pronouns) or infinitive (verbs). The gender of Russian nouns is indicated by means of one of three abbreviations in italics (*m*, *f*, *n* — cf. list, pp. 487—488) behind the entry word.* Each inflected entry is followed, in square brackets [ ], by a figure, which serves as reference to a definite paradigm within the system of conjugation and declension as tabulated at the end of the book, pp. 483—491. Any variants of these paradigms are stated after the reference figure of each entry word in question.

Examples: **ло́жка** *f* [5; *g*/*pl.*: -жек], like **ло́жа** *f* [5], is declined according to paradigm 5, except that the former example inserts in the genitive plural "epenthetic" e between the two last stem consonants: ло́жек; cf. **ло́дка** *f* [5; *g*/*pl.*: -док] = [*g*/*pl.*: ло́док]. **кусо́к** *m* [1; -ска́] = "epenthetic" o is omitted in the oblique cases of the singular and in all cases of the plural; cf. **коне́ц** *m* [1; -нца́] = [конца́, концу́, etc.].

го́род *m* [1; *pl.*: -да́, *etc. e.*] = the example stresses its stem in the singular, but the endings in the plural, the nominative plural being in -а́ (instead of in -ы́): города́, городо́в, etc.

край *m* [3; в -аю́; *pl.*: -ая́, *etc. e.*] = declined after paradigm 3, but the ending of the prepositional singular, with prepositions в, на, is in -ю́ (stressed); as for the plural, see го́род, above. Cf. also **печь** *f* [8; в -чи́; *from g*/*pl e.*], where, in addition to the stressed ending of the prepositional singular (after в, на), the accent shifts onto the ending in the genitive plural and all following cases of that number.

кури́ть [13; курю́, ку́ришь] = conjugated after paradigm 13, except that stress shifts onto the stem syllable in the 2nd and all following persons (singular and plural).

As the prefixed forms of a verb follow the same inflection model and (with the exception of perfective aspects having the stressed prefix вы́-) mode of accentuation as the corresponding unprefixed verb, differences in stress, etc. have in cases of such aspect pairs been marked but once, viz. with the imperfective form.

---

* For users of part II: Any Russian noun ending in a consonant *or* -й is of masculine gender;
those ending in -а *or* -я are of feminine gender;
those ending in -о *or* -е are of neuter gender.
In case of deviation from this rule, as well as in nouns terminating in -ь, the gender is indicated.

5. Government. Government, except for the accusative, is indicated with the help of Latin and Russian abbreviations (cf. list, pp. 33—35). Emphasis has been laid on differences between the two languages, including the use of prepositions. Whenever a special case of government applies only to one of several meanings of a word, this has been duly recorded in connection with the meaning concerned. To ensure a clear differentiation of person and thing in government, the English and Russian notes to that effect show the necessary correspondence in sequence.

6. Semantic distinction. If a word has different meanings and, at the same time, different forms of inflection or aspect, such significations have been differentiated by means of figures (e. g. бить, коса́, коси́ть); otherwise a semicolon separates different meanings, a comma mere synonyms. Italicized additions serve to specify individual shades of meaning, e. g. **поднима́ть** ... take up (*arms*); hoist (*flag*); set (*sail*); give (*alarm*); make (*noise*); scare (*game*); **приёмный** ... reception (*day*; *room* ...); ... office (*hours*); entrance (*examination*); foster (*father* ...). For further definitions with the help of illustrative symbols and abbreviations cf. list below, pp. 33—35.

In a number of Russian verbs the perfective aspect indicated (particularly with the prefixes ⟨за-⟩ and ⟨по-⟩) has, strictly speaking, the connotations "to begin to do s. th." (the former) and "to do s. th. a (little) while" (the latter); but since these forms are very often rendered into English by means of the equivalent verb without any such additions they have occasionally been given as simple aspect counterparts without further indication as to their aforesaid semantic subtlety.

7. Orthography. In both the Russian and English parts newest spelling standards have been applied, and in the latter differences between American and British usage noted wherever possible and feasible.

A hyphen at the end of a line and at the beginning of the next one denotes a hyphenated word.

In parts of words or additions given in brackets a hyphen is placed within the respective bracket.

Полноценное пользование словарём возможно лишь при точном соблюдении нижеследующих указаний!

Предварительные замечания

1. Порядок. Все заглавные слова, включая и неправильные производные формы отдельных частей речи, расположены в алфавитном порядке, напр.: *bore, born, borne* от *bear*; *men* от *man*; в русско-английской части: лучше, лучший от хороший.

Американские и английские географические названия, а также сокращения даны в особых списках на стр. 493—505.

Тильда (~ ~) служит в гнёздах слов знаком повторения. Жирная тильда (~) заменяет или всё заглавное слово или же его составную часть, стоящую перед вертикальной чертой (|). Светлая тильда (~) заменяет: а) непосредственно предыдущее заглавное слово, которое уже само может быть образовано посредством жирной тильды; б) в указании произношения произношение всего предыдущего заглавного слова. Чёрточка (-) в указании произношения даётся вместо повторения неизменяемой части заглавного слова.

При изменении начальной буквы (прописной на строчную или наоборот) вместо простой тильды ставится соответствующая тильда с кружком £ (£).

Примеры: abandon [əˈbændən], ~ment [-mənt = əˈbændənmənt]; certi|ficate, ~fication, ~fy, ~tude.

2. Произношение. Произношение сложных английских слов как правило не указывается, если каждая из их составных частей приводится в алфавитном порядке как самостоятельное заглавное слово с указанием произношения.

3. Дополнения *курсивом* служат только для уточнения отдельных английских значений.

Дальнейшие пояснения даны в виде условных знаков и сокращений (см. стр. 33—35).

4. Точка с запятой отделяет различные оттенки значений; синонимы даны через запятую.

5. Прибавление (**~ally**) к английскому имени прилагательному означает, что его наречие образуется посредством добавления ~ally к заглавному слову, напр.: dramatic (~ally = dramatically).

6. Переносный знак в конце строчки и в начале последующей означает, что данное английское слово пишется через чёрточку, напр.: air-conditioned = air-
-conditioned.

The Russian Alphabet

Printed	Written	Russian name	Transcribed	Printed	Written	Russian name	Transcribed
А а	А а	а	a	П п	П п	пэ	pɛ
Б б	Б б	бэ	bɛ	Р р	Р р	эр	ɛr
В в	В в	вэ	vɛ	С с	С с	эс	ɛs
Г г	Г г	гэ	gɛ	Т т	Т т	тэ	tɛ
Д д	Д д д	дэ	dɛ	У у	У у	у	u
Е е	Е е	е	jɛ	Ф ф	Ф ф	эф	ɛf
Ё ё	Ё ё	ё	jɔ	Х х	Х х	ха	xa
Ж ж	Ж ж	жэ	ʒɛ	Ц ц	Ц ц	цэ	tsɛ
З з	З з з	зэ	zɛ	Ч ч	Ч ч	че	tʃ̡e
И и	И и	и	i	Ш ш	Ш ш	ша	ʃa
Й й	Й й	и[1])		Щ щ	Щ щ	ща	ʃ̡tʃ̡a
К к	К к	ка	ka	Ъ ъ	- ъ	[2])	
Л л	Л л	эль	ɛl̡	Ы ы	- ы	ы[3])	ɨ
М м	М м	эм	ɛm	Ь ь	- ь	[4])	
Н н	Н н	эн	ɛn	Э э	Э э	э[5])	ɛ
О о	О о	о	ɔ	Ю ю	Ю ю	ю	ju
				Я я	Я я	я	ja

[1]) и кра́ткое short i [2]) твёрдый знак hard sign, jer [3]) *or* еры́
[4]) мя́гкий знак soft sign, jer̡ [5]) э оборо́тное reversed e
Until 1918 in addition the following letters were used in Russia:
і, ѵ = и, ѣ = е, ѳ = ф.

Explanation of Russian Pronunciation with the Help of Phonetic Symbols

Объяснение русского произношения при помощи фонетических знаков

I. Vowels

1. All vowels in stressed position are half-long in Russian.
2. In unstressed position Russian vowels are very short, except in the first pretonic syllable, where this shortness of articulation is less marked. Some vowel letters (notably о, е, я), when read in unstressed position, not only differ in length (quantity), but also change their timbre, i. e. acoustic quality.

Russian letter	Explanation of its pronunciation		Transcription symbol
а	stressed	= a in 'father': ма́ма ('mamə) 'mamma, mother'	a
	unstressed	1. = a in the above examples, but shorter – in first pretonic syllable: каза́к (ka'zak) 'Cossack'	a
		2. = a in 'ago, about' – in post-tonic or second, etc. pretonic syllable(s): ата́ка (a'takə) 'attack' абрико́с (əbȥi'kɔs) 'apricot'	ə
		3. = i in 'sit' – after ч, щ in first pretonic syllable: часы́ (tʆɪ'sɨ) 'watch, clock' щади́ть (ʆ[t]ʆɪ'ɖiţ) 'spare'	ɪ
е	Preceding consonant (except ж, ш, ц) is soft, i. e. palatalized.		
	stressed	1. = ye in 'yet' – in initial position, i. e. at the beginning of a word, or after a vowel, ъ, ь (if not ё) before a hard consonant: ем (jɛm) '[I] eat' бытие́ (bɨţi'jɛ) 'being' съел (sjɛɫ) 'ate [up]' премье́р (pȥɪ'mjɛr) 'premier'	jɛ
		2. = e in 'set' – after consonants, soft or hard (ж, ш, ц), before a hard consonant, as well as in final position, i. e. at the end of a word, after consonants: нет (ɳɛt) 'no' шест (ʃɛst) 'pole' цел (tsɛɫ) 'whole, sound' в стране́ (fstra'ɳɛ) 'in the country' на лице́ (nəli'tsɛ) 'on the face'	ɛ
		3. = ya in 'Yale' (but without the i-component) – in initial position or after a vowel, ъ, ь, both before a soft consonant: ель (jeḷ) 'fir' бие́ние (ɓi'jeɲe) 'palpitation, throb' съесть (sjeşţ) 'to eat [up]'	je

Russian letter	Explanation of its pronunciation		Transcription symbol
		4. = a in 'pale' – after consonants, soft or hard (ж, ш, ц), before a soft consonant: петь (p̡et̡) 'to sing' сесть (s̡es̡t̡) 'to sit down' шесть (ʃest̡) 'six' цель (tsel̡) 'aim'	e
	unstressed	**1.** = i in 'sɪt', but preceded by (j) – in initial position, i. e. also after a vowel: ещё (jɪ'ʃ̡[t]ʃ̡ɔ) 'still, yet' знáет ('znajɪt) '[he, she, it] knows'	jɪ
		2. = i in 'sɪt' – after soft consonants: рекá (r̡ɪ'ka) 'river'	ɪ
		3. = ы (cf.) after ж, ш, ц: женá (ʒɨ'na) 'wife' пшенó (pʃɨ'nɔ) 'millet' ценá (tsɨ'na) 'price'	ɨ
ё	**Preceding consonant (except ж, ш, ц) is soft.**		
	only stressed	**1.** = ya in 'yacht' or yo in 'beyond' – in initial position, i. e. also after a vowel, ъ, ь, before a hard consonant, or in final position: ёлка ('jɔłkə) 'Christmas tree' даёт (da'jɔt) '[he, she, it] gives' подъём (pad'jɔm) 'rise' бельё (b̡ɪ'l̡jɔ) 'linen'	jɔ
		2. = o in 'cost' – after both soft and hard consonants before hard consonants: лёд (l̡ɔt) 'ice' шёлк (ʃɔłk) 'silk'	ɔ
и	**Preceding consonant (except ж, ш, ц) is soft.**		
	stressed	= ee in 'seen': и́ва ('ivə) 'willow' юри́ст (ju'r̡ist) 'lawyer'	i
		Note: In the instr/sg. of он/онó and the oblique forms of они́ initial и- may be pronounced (ji-): их (ix *or* jix) 'of them'.	i/ji
	unstressed	**1.** = ee in 'seen', but shorter – in **first pretonic** syllable: минýта (m̡i'nutə) 'minute'	i
		2. = i in 'sɪt' – in **post-tonic** or **second**, etc. **pretonic** syllable(s): хóдит ('xɔd̡ɪt) '[he, she, it] goes' приписáть (p̡r̡ɪp̡i'sat̡) 'to ascribe'	ɪ
	stressed & unstressed	= ы (cf.) after ж, ш, ц: жить (ʒɨt̡) 'to live' ши́рма ('ʃɨrmə) 'screen' цили́ндр (tsɨ'l̡indr) 'cylinder'	ɨ
о	**stressed**	= o in 'cost': том (tɔm) 'volume'	ɔ

Russian letter	Explanation of its pronunciation	Transcription symbol
	unstressed 1. = a in 'father', but shorter – in first pretonic syllable: водá (va'da) 'water' Москвá (ma'skva) 'Moscow'	a
	2. = a in 'ago', 'about' – in post-tonic or second, etc. pretonic syllable(s): гóрод ('gɔrət) 'town, city' огорóд (əga'rɔt) 'kitchen garden'	ə
	Note: In foreign words unstressed о is pronounced (ɔ) in final position, cf.: рáдио ('raḑiɔ) 'radio', какáо (ka'kaɔ) 'cocoa' as against Russian (native) мáсло ('masłə) 'butter'.	ɔ
у	stressed & unstressed = oo in 'boom': бýду ('budu) '[I] will (*Brt.* shall) be'	u
ы	stressed & unstressed a retracted variety of i, as in 'hill'; no English equivalent: вы (vɨ) 'you' рóзы ('rɔzɨ) 'roses'	ɨ
э	stressed & unstressed 1. = e in 'set' – before a hard consonant: э́то ('ɛtə) 'this' эпóха (ɛ'pɔxə) 'epoch'	ɛ
	2. resembles the English sound a in 'pale' (but without the i-component) or é in French 'été' – before a soft consonant: э́ти ('eţı) 'these' элемéнт (eļı'm̡ɛnt) 'element'	e
ю	Preceding consonant is soft.	
	stressed & unstressed 1. like yu in 'yule', but shorter – in initial position, i. e. also after a vowel, and after ь: юг (juk) 'south' знáю ('znaju) '[I] know' вьюга ('v̡jugə) 'snowstorm'	ju
	2. = u in 'rule' – after consonants: рю́мка ('r̡umkə) 'wineglass' люблю́ (ļu'bļu) '[I] like, love'	u
я	Preceding consonant is soft.	
	stressed 1. = ya in 'yard', but shorter – in initial position, i. e. also after a vowel and ъ, as well as after ь: я́ма ('jamə) 'pit' мая́к (ma'jak) 'lighthouse' изъя́н (iz'jan) 'defect' статья́ (sta'ţja) 'article' рья́ный ('r̡janɨj) 'zealous'	ja
	2. = a in 'father' – after a consonant and before a hard consonant: мя́со ('m̡asə) 'meat; flesh'	a
	3. = a in 'bad' – in interpalatal position, i. e. between soft consonants: пять (p̡æţ) 'five'	æ

Russian letter	Explanation of its pronunciation	Transcription symbol
	unstressed 1. = i in 'sit', but preceded by (j) – in initial position, i. e. also after a vowel and ъ: язы́к (jɪ'zɨk) 'tongue; language' та́ять ('tajɪţ) 'to thaw' изъяви́ть (ɪzjɪ'ɣiţ) 'to express, show'	jɪ
	2. = i in 'sit' – after soft consonants: мясни́к (mɪʂ'ɲik) 'butcher' Ряза́нь (ɽɪ'zaɲ) 'Ryazan [town]'	ɪ
	3. = a in 'ago' (preceded by j after vowels) – in final position: ня́ня ('ɲaɲə) '(wet) nurse' а́рмия ('armɟijə) 'army'	(j)ə
	II. Semivowel	
й	1. = y in 'yet' – in initial position, i. e. also after a vowel, in loan words: (Нью-)Йо́рк (jɔrk) '(New) York' майо́р (ma'jɔr) 'major'	j
	2. in the formation of diphthongs as their second element:	j
ай	= (ɪ) of (aɪ) in 'time': май (maj) 'May'	aj
ой	= [stressed] oi in 'noise': бой (bɔj) 'fight', большо́й (baʎ'ʃɔj) 'big'	ɔj
	= [first pretonic] i in 'time': война́ (vaj'na) 'war'	aj
	= [post-tonic] a in 'ago' + y in 'yet': но́вой ('nɔvəj) 'of/to the new'	əj
уй	= u in 'rule' + (j): бу́йвол ('bujvəɫ) 'buffalo'	uj
ый	= ы (cf.) + (j): вы́йти ('vɨjţɪ) 'to go out', кра́сный ('krasnɨj) 'red'	ɨj
ий	= и (cf.) + (j): кий (ķij) 'cue', си́ний ('ʂiɲɪj) 'blue'	ij ɪj
ей	(j +) a in 'pale' ей (jej) 'to her', пей (ɒej) 'drink!', нейтро́н (ɲej'trɔn) 'neutron'	(j)ej
юй	= ю (cf.) + (j): плюй (pʎuj) 'spit!'	(j)uj
яй	= [stressed] (j +) a in bad + (j): я́йца ('jæjtsə) 'eggs'	(j)æj
	= [unstressed] yi in Yiddish: яйцо́ (jɪ'tsɔ) 'egg'	jɪ

III. Consonants

1. As most Russian consonants may be palatalized (or 'softened') there is, beside the series of normal ('hard') consonants, a nearly complete set of 'soft' parallel sounds. According to traditional Russian spelling, in writing or printing this 'softness' is marked by a combination of such palatalized consonants with the vowels е, ё, и, ю, я or, either in final position or before a consonant, the so-called 'soft sign' (ь). In phonetic transcription palatalized

consonants are indicated by means of a small hook, or comma, attached to them. As a rule a hard consonant before a soft one remains hard; only з, с may be softened before palatalized з, с, д, т, н.

2. Always hard are ж, ш, ц.
3. Always soft are ч, щ.
4. The voiced consonants б, в, г, д, ж, з are pronounced voicelessly (i. e. = п, ф, к, т, ш, с) in final position.
5. The voiced consonants б, в, г, д, ж, з, when followed by (one of) their voiceless counterparts п, ф, к, т, ш, с, are pronounced voicelessly (regressive assimilation) and vice versa: voiceless before voiced is voiced (except that there is no assimilation before в).
6. The articulation of doubled consonants, particularly those following a stressed syllable, is marked by their lengthening.

Russian letter	Explanation of its pronunciation	Transcription symbol
б	hard = b in 'bad': бок (bɔk) 'side'	b
	soft as in 'Albion': бéлка ('b̡ɛłkə) 'squirrel'	b̡
в	hard = v in 'very': вóдка ('vɔtkə) 'vodka'	v
	soft as in 'view': вéра ('v̡ɛrə) 'faith, belief'	v̡
г	hard = g in 'gun': горá (ga'ra) 'mountain'	g
	soft as in 'argue': гимн (g̡imn) 'anthem'	g̡
	Note: 1. = (v) in endings -ого, -его: больнóго (bal̡'nɔvə) 'of the sick, ill' рабóчего (ra'bɔtʃɪvə) 'of the worker'	v
	2. = (x) in бог (bɔx) 'God' and in the combinations -гк-, -гч-: мя́гкий ('m̡axk̡ɪj) 'soft' мя́гче ('m̡axtʆɪ) 'softer'	x
д	hard = d in 'door': дáма ('damə) 'lady'	d
	soft as in 'dew': дя́дя ('d̡æd̡ə) 'uncle'	d̡
	-здн- – in this combination д is mute: пóздно ('pɔznə) 'late'	
ж	hard = s in 'measure', but hard: жáжда ('ʒaʒdə) 'thirst'	ʒ
	-жж- may also be soft: вóжжи ('vɔʒ̡ʒ̡ɪ) 'reins'	ʒ̡ʒ̡
	-жч- = щ: мужчи́на (mu'ʆ[t]ʆinə) 'man'	ʆ[t]ʆ
з	hard = z in 'zoo': зал (zał) 'hall'	z
	soft as in 'presume': зéркало ('z̡ɛrkələ) 'mirror'	z̡
	-зж- = hard or soft doubled ж: пóзже ('pɔʒʒɛ *or* 'pɔʒ̡ʒ̡ɛ) 'later'	ʒʒ/ʒ̡ʒ̡
	-зч- = щ: извóзчик (iz'vɔʆ[t]ʆɪk) 'coachman'	ʆ[t]ʆ
к	hard = c in 'come': как (kak) 'how, as'	k
	soft like k in 'key': кирпи́ч (k̡ir'p̡itʆ) 'brick'	k̡
л	hard = ll in General American 'call': лáмпа ('łampə) 'lamp'	ł
	soft = ll in English 'million': ли́лия ('l̡il̡ijə) 'lily'	l̡
м	hard = m in 'man': мак (mak) 'poppy'	m
	soft as in 'mute': мир (m̡ir) 'world; peace'	m̡

Russian letter	Explanation of its pronunciation	Transcription symbol
н	hard = n in 'noise': нос (nɔs) 'nose' soft = n in 'new': нет (ņɛt) 'no'	n ņ
п	hard = p in 'part': пол (pɔł) 'floor' soft as in 'scorpion': пить (p̧iţ) 'to drink'	p p̧
р	hard = trilled r: рот (rɔt) 'mouth' soft as in 'Orient': ряд (ŗat) 'row'	r ŗ
с	hard = s in 'sad': сад (sat) 'garden' soft as in 'assume': сюда́ (şu'da) 'hither, here' -сч- = щ: сча́стье ('ʆ[t]ʆæşţjı) 'happiness; luck'	s ş ʆ[t]ʆ
т	hard = t in 'tent': там (tam) 'there' soft as in 'tune': тюльпа́н (ţuļ'pan) 'tulip' -стн-, -стл- – in these combinations -т- is mute: ле́стница ('ļeşņıtsə) 'staircase' счастли́вый (ʆ[t]ʆıs'ļivɨj) 'happy; lucky'	t ţ
ф	hard = f in 'far': фа́брика ('fabŗıkə) 'factory' soft as in 'few': фильм (fiļm) 'film'	f f̧
х	hard = ch in Scotch 'loch': холм (xɔłm) 'hill' soft like ch in German 'ich'; no English equivalent: хи́мия ('x̧imịjə) 'chemistry'	x x̧
ц ч	hard = ts in 'tsar': царь (tsaŗ) 'tsar, czar' soft = ch in 'cheek': час (tʆas) 'hour'	ts tʆ
ш щ	hard = sh: шум (ʃum) 'noise' soft = sh + ch in 'cheek', cf. fresh cheeks, or = doubled (ʆʆ) as in 'sure': щека́ (ʆ[t]ʆı'ka) 'cheek', щи (ʆ[t]ʆi) 'cabbage soup'	ʃ ʆ[t]ʆ

IV. 'Surds'

Russian letter	Explanation of its pronunciation	Transcription symbol
ъ	The *jer* or 'hard sign' separates a hard (final) consonant of a prefix and the initial vowel, preceded by (j), of the following root, thus marking both the hardness of the preceding consonant and the distinct utterance of (j) before the vowel: предъяви́ть (pŗıdjı'v̧iţ) 'to show, produce' съезд (sjɛst) 'congress'. *Note*: Until 1918 the 'hard sign' was also used at the end of a word terminating in a hard consonant: братъ (brat) 'brother'.	

Russian letter	Explanation of its pronunciation	Transcription symbol
ь	The *jeŗ* or 'soft sign' serves to represent the palatal or soft quality of a (preceding) consonant in final position or before another consonant, cf.:	,
	брат (brat) 'brother' and брать (braţ) 'to take' по́лка ('pɔłkə) 'shelf' and по́лька ('pɔʝkə) 'polka, Pole (= Polish woman)'.	
	It is also used before vowels to indicate the softness of a preceding consonant as well as the pronunciation of (j) with the respective vowel, e. g.:	
	семья́ (şıɱ'ja) 'family' – *cf.* се́мя ('şeɱə) 'seed',	j
	and in foreign words, such as батальо́н (bəta'ʝjɔn) 'battalion'.	j

Объяснение английского произношения при помощи фонетических знаков

Explanation of English Pronunciation with the Help of Phonetic Symbols

А. Гласные и дифтонги

В английском языке существуют краткие и долгие гласные, независимо от ударения.

[ɑ:] — долгий, глубокий и открытый звук «а», как в слове «мама».

[ʌ] — краткий, неясный звук, похожий на русский неударный звук «о», который слышится в слове «Москва», или «а» в слове «варить».
Английский звук [ʌ] встречается главным образом в ударном слоге.

[æ] — звонкий, не слишком краткий звук, средний между «а» и «э», более открытый, чем «э». При произнесении рот широко открыт.

[ɛə] — дифтонг, напоминающий не слишком долгий открытый звук, близкий к русскому «э» (в слове «этот»), за которым следует неясный гласный [ə] (примерно эа).

[ai] — этот дифтонг похож на русское «ай»; его первый элемент близок к русскому «а» в слове «два». Второй элемент — очень краткий звук [i].

[au] — этот дифтонг похож на русское «ау» (в слове «пауза»). Его первый элемент тот же, что и в [ai]; однако этот звук переходит постепенно в очень краткий звук [u].

[ei] — дифтонг, напоминающий русское «эй». Он состоит из звука [e] и очень краткого звука [i].

[e] — краткий звук, напоминающий «э» в слове «эти», но короче.

[ə] — нейтральный, неясный, безударный гласный звук, напоминающий русский беглый гласный в словах: «комната», «водяной» (в первом слоге).

[i:] — долгий гласный звук, похожий на русское протяжное «и» в словах: «ива», «вижу».

[i] — короткий открытый гласный, напоминающий средний звук между «и» и «ы», похожий на «и» в слове «шить».

[iə] — дифтонг, состоящий из полуоткрытого, полудолгого звука [i] и неясного звука [ə].

[ou] — дифтонг, напоминающий русское «оу». Первый его элемент — полуоткрытый звук «о» — переходит в слабое «у», причём губы слегка округляются, а язык остается неподвижным.

[ɔ:] — открытый, долгий гласный, похожий на протяжное русское «о» в слове «бор».
При произнесении этого гласного губы округлены (но не выпячены), положение рта почти как при русском «а», однако язык отодвинут назад.

[ɔ] — краткий открытый звук, похожий на русское «о».
При произнесении этого звука надо открыть рот как при «а» и, отодвигая язык назад, не выпячивая губ, произнести «о».

[o] — закрытый, краткий (близкий к «у») звук «о» в безударных слогах.

[ə:] — В русском языке нет звука, похожего на [ə:]. При его произнесении надо рот приоткрыть только слегка, губы растянуть, а язык оставить в нейтральном положении.
В закрытом слоге этот гласный орфографически представлен сочетаниями -er, -ir и -ur.

[ɔi] — дифтонг, состоящий из звука [ɔ] и очень краткого [i].

[u:] — долгий гласный, напоминающий протяжно произнесенное русское «у» под ударением, напр.: сук, губка.

При произнесении этого звука губы вперёд не выдвигаются.

[uə] — дифтонг, состоящий из звука [u] и неясного гласного [ə].

[u] — краткий звук, похожий на русский неударный звук «у» в словах: «тупой», «сума».
При произнесении этого звука губы не выдвигаются.

Б. Согласные

Согласные: [b] — б, [f] — ф, [g] — г, [k] — к, [m] — м, [p] — п, [s] — с, [v] — в, [z] — з почти не отличаются от соответствующих русских.

Английские звонкие согласные, в противоположность русским, сохраняют на конце слова свою звонкость и произносятся чётко и энергично.

[r] — произносится только перед гласными, в конце слова только, если следующее слово начинается с гласного.
При произнесении этого звука кончик языка поднят к нёбу и только слегка прикасается к нему выше альвеол.
Английское [r] произносится, в отличие от соответствующего русского звука «р», без раскатистой вибрации языка.

[ʒ] — звук, похожий на смягченное русское «ж».

[ʃ] — звук, похожий на смягченное русское «ш».

[θ] — аналогичного звука в русском языке нет.
Для получения этого согласного пропускается струя воздуха между кончиком языка и краем верхних зубов; этот звук приближается к русскому «с» в слове «сын», если его произнести с чуть высунутым языком.

[ð] — отличается от [θ] только присутствием голоса. Следует избегать звука, похожего на русское «з».

[s] — соответствует русскому «с».

[z] — соответствует русскому «з».

[ŋ] — носовой заднеязычный согласный. В русском языке аналогичного звука нет.
(Чтобы научиться произносить этот звук, надо с открытым ртом задней частью спинки языка попробовать произнести «м» так, чтобы воздух проходил не через рот, а через нос.)

[ŋk] — согласный звук, отличающийся от [ŋ] только присутствием [k].

[w] — согласный, похожий на очень краткое русское «у». При произнесении этого звука воздух проходит между губами, которые сначала слегка вытягиваются вперёд, а затем быстро занимают положение, нужное для следующего гласного звука.

[h] — простой, безголосный выдох.

[j] — звук, похожий на русский «й».

[f] — соответствует русскому согласному «ф».

[v] — соответствует русскому согласному «в».

Ударение в английских словах обозначается знаком (ˈ) и ставится перед ударным слогом, напр.: onion (ˈʌnjən).

В английском языке, кроме слов с ударением на одном слоге, бывают слова с одинаково сильным ударением на двух слогах, напр.: unsound (ˈʌnˈsaund), а также (длинные слова) с главным и побочным ударением, напр.: conglomeration (kənˈglɔməˈˈreiʃn).

Две точки (:) обозначают **долготу звука**, напр.: ask (ɑːsk), astir (əsˈtəː).

Английский алфавит

a (ei), b (biː), c (siː), d (diː), e (iː), f (ef), g (dʒiː), h (eitʃ), i (ai), j (dʒei), k (kei), l (el), m (em), n (en), o (ou), p (piː), q (kjuː), r (ɑː, *Am.* ɑːr), s (es), t (tiː), u (juː), v (viː), w (ˈdʌbljuː), x (eks), y (wai), z (zed, *Am.* ziː).

Американская орфография

отличается от британской главным образом следующим:

1. Вместо **...our** пишется **...or**, напр.: hon*or* = honour, lab*or* = labour.
2. Окончанию **...re** соответствует **...er**, напр.: cent*er* = centre, theat*er* = theatre, meag*er* = meagre; исключения представляют og*re* и слова, оканчивающиеся на ...cre, напр.: massa*cre*, na*cre*.
3. Вместо **...ce** пишется **...se**, напр.: defen*se* = defence, licen*se* = licence.
4. Во всех словах, производных от глаголов, оканчивающихся на **...l** и **...p**, согласная на конце не удваивается, напр.: travel — trave*l*ed — trave*l*er — trave*l*ing, worship — worshi*p*ed — worshi*p*er — worshi*p*ing. Также и в некоторых других словах вместо двойной пишется одна согласная, напр.: wagon = waggon, woo*l*en = woollen.
5. В некоторых случаях немое **e** опускается, напр.: abrid*gm*ent = abridg*e*ment, acknowled*gm*ent = acknowledg*e*ment, jud*gm*ent = judg*e*ment, ax = ax*e*, good-by = good-by*e*.
6. В некоторых словах написанию приставки **en...** предпочитается **in...**, напр.: *in*close = enclose, *in*snare = ensnare.
7. Написания æ и œ часто заменяются простым e, напр.: an*e*mia = anæmia, diarrh*ea* = diarrhœa.
8. Немой конечный слог в словах французского происхождения часто опускается, напр.: catalog = catalog*ue*, program = program*me*, prolog = prolog*ue*.
9. Особые случаи:
   st*a*nch = staunch, m*o*ld = mould, m*o*lt = moult, gr*a*y = grey, pl*ow* = plough, ski*ll*ful = skilful, t*i*re = tyre.

Американское произношение

отличается от английского главным образом следующим:

1. ɑ: произносится как протяжное æ: в словах ask (æ:sk = ɑ:sk), castle (kæ:sl = kɑ:sl), grass (græ:s = grɑ:s), past (pæ:st = pɑ:st) и т. д.; так же в словах branch (bræ:ntʃ = brɑ:ntʃ), can't (kæ:nt = kɑ:nt), dance (dæ:ns = dɑ:ns) и т. д.
2. ɔ произносится как ɑ в таких словах: common ('kɑmən = 'kɔmən), not (nɑt = nɔt), on (ɑn = ɔn), rock (rɑk = rɔk), bond (bɑnd = bɔnd) и во многих других.
3. ju: произносится как u:, напр.: due (du: = dju:), duke (du:k = dju:k), new (nu: = nju:).
4. r произносится между предшествующим гласным и последующим согласным звонко, коротко, причём кончик языка оттягивается назад и касается твёрдого нёба несколько выше альвеол, напр.: clerk (klə:rk = klɑ:k), hard (hɑ:rd = hɑ:d); так же и в конце слова, напр.: far (fɑ:r = fɑ:), her (hə:r = hə:).
5. Глухие p, t, k в начале безударного слога (следующего за ударным слогом) произносятся звонко, т. е. как b, d, g, напр.: property, water, second.
6. Разница между слогами с сильным и слабым ударением выражена гораздо меньше; в более длинных словах слышится ясно второстепенное ударение, напр.: dictionary (''dikʃə'nɛri = 'dikʃənri), ceremony (''serə'mouni = 'seriməni), inventory (''inven'touri = 'invəntri), secretary (''sekrə'tɛri = 'sekrətri).
7. Перед, а часто также и после носовых согласных (m, n, ŋ) гласные и дифтонги произносятся с носовым оттенком, напр.: stand, time, small.

Symbols and Abbreviations

Условные знаки и сокращения

1. Symbols — Знаки

□ после английского имени прилагательного или причастия указывает на возможность правильного образования от них наречий путем прибавления суффикса *...ly* или изменения *...le* на *...ly* или *...y* на *...ily*, напр.: rich □ = *richly*; acceptable □ = *acceptably*; happy □ = *happily*.

□ after an English adjective or participle means that from it an adverb may be formed regularly by adding *...ly*, or by changing *...le* into *...ly* or *...y* into *...ily*; as: rich □ = *richly*; acceptable □ = *acceptably*; happy □ = *happily*.

F *familiar* = *colloquial language* разгово́рный язы́к.

P *popular* простоpе́чие.

⚒ *rare, little used* ре́дко, малоупотреби́тельно.

† *obsolete* устаре́вшее сло́во, выраже́ние.

🕮 *scientific term* нау́чный те́рмин.

⚘ *botany* бота́ника.

⊕ *handicraft, engineering* те́хника.

⚒ *mining* го́рное де́ло.

⚔ *military term* вое́нное де́ло.

⚓ *nautical term* судохо́дство.

☨ *commercial term* торго́вля.

🚂 *railroad, railway* железнодоро́жное де́ло.

✈ *aviation* авиа́ция.

✉ *postal affairs* по́чта.

♪ *musical term* му́зыка.

△ *architecture* архитекту́ра.

⚡ *electrical engineering* электроте́хника.

⚖ *jurisprudence* юриспруде́нция.

⚹ *mathematics* матема́тика.

⚘ *farming* се́льское хозя́йство.

⚗ *chemistry* хи́мия.

⚕ *medicine* медици́на.

& *and* и.

= *equal to* равно́.

2. Abbreviations — Сокращения

a. *also* та́кже.

abbr. *abbreviation* сокраще́ние.

acc. *accusative* (*case*) вини́тельный паде́ж.

adj. *adjective* и́мя прилага́тельное.

adv. *adverb* наре́чие.

Am. *Americanism* американи́зм.

anat. *anatomy* анато́мия

art. *article* арти́кль, член.

ast. *astronomy* астроно́мия.

attr. *attributively* атрибути́вное употребле́ние (т. е. в ка́честве определе́ния).

biol. *biology* биоло́гия.

Brt. *British* (*English*) *usage* брита́нское (англи́йское) словоупотребле́ние.

b. s. *bad sense* в дурно́м смы́сле.

cap. *capitalized* с большо́й бу́квы.

cf. *compare* сравни́.

ch. *chess* ша́хматы.

cj. *conjunction* сою́з.

co. *comic(ally)* шутли́во.

coll. *collective (noun)* собира́тельное и́мя (существи́тельное).

com. *commonly* обыкнове́нно.

comp. *comparative (degree)* сравни́тельная сте́пень.

compd(s). *compound(s)* сло́жное сло́во (сло́жные слова́).

cond. *conditional* усло́вное наклоне́ние.

contp. *contemptuously* пренебрежи́тельно.

cook. *cookery* кулина́рия.

dat. *dative (case)* да́тельный паде́ж.

dem. *demonstrative pronoun* указа́тельное местоиме́ние.

dim. *diminutive* уменьши́тельная фо́рма.

e. *endings stressed (throughout)* ударе́ние (сплошь) на оконча́ниях.

eccl. *ecclesiastical term* церко́вное выраже́ние.

econ. *economy* эконо́мика.

educ. *education* шко́ла, шко́льное де́ло, педаго́гика.

e. g. *for example* наприме́р.

esp. *especially* осо́бенно.

etc. *et cetera (and so on)* и т. д. (и так да́лее).

f *feminine (gender)* же́нский род.

fenc. *fencing* фехтова́ние.

fig. *figuratively* в перено́сном значе́нии.

form. *formerly* пре́жде.

f/pl. *feminine plural* мно́жественное число́ же́нского ро́да.

fr. *French* францу́зское сло́во, выраже́ние.

ft. *future (tense)* бу́дущее вре́мя.

gen. *genitive (case)* роди́тельный паде́ж.

geogr. *geography* геогра́фия.

geol. *geology* геоло́гия.

geom. *geometry* геоме́трия.

ger. *gerund* геру́ндий.

g/pl. *genitive plural* роди́тельный паде́ж мно́жественного числа́.

g. pr. *(pt.) present (past) gerund* дееприча́стие настоя́щего (проше́дшего) вре́мени.

gr. *grammar* грамма́тика.

hist. *history* исто́рия.

hunt. *hunting* охо́та.

imp. *imperative* повели́тельное наклоне́ние.

impers. *impersonal (form), -ly* безли́чная фо́рма, безли́чно.

impf. *imperfective (aspect)* несоверше́нный вид.

(im)pf. *imperfective and perfective (aspect)* несоверше́нный и соверше́нный вид.

ind(ecl). *indeclinable word* несклоня́емое сло́во.

inf. *infinitive* инфинити́в, неопределённая фо́рма глаго́ла.

instr. *instrumental (case)* твори́тельный паде́ж.

int. *interjection* междоме́тие.

interr. *interrogative(ly)* вопроси́тельная фо́рма, вопроси́тельно.

iro. *ironically* ирони́чески.

irr. *irregular* непра́вильный.

iter. *iterative, frequentative (aspect)* многокра́тный вид.

ling. *linguistics* лингви́стика, языкозна́ние.

lit. *literary* кни́жное выраже́ние.

m *masculine (gender)* мужско́й род.

metall. *metallurgy* металлу́ргия.

min. *mineralogy* минерало́гия.

mot. *motoring* автомобили́зм.

m/pl. *masculine plural* мно́жественное число́ мужско́го ро́да.

mst *mostly* бо́льшей ча́стью.

n *neuter (gender)* сре́дний род.

no. *number* но́мер.

nom. *nominative (case)* имени́тельный паде́ж.

n/pl. *neuter plural* мно́жественное число́ сре́днего ро́да.

npr. *proper name* (or *noun*) и́мя со́бственное.

o. a. one another друг дру́га, друг дру́гу.

obj. *objective* (*case*) объе́ктный паде́ж.

obl. *oblique* (*cases*) ко́свенные падежи́.

oft. *often* ча́сто.

once *semelfactive* (*aspect*) однокра́тный вид.

op. *opposite* противополо́жно.

opt. *optics* о́птика.

o. s. oneself себя́, себе́, -ся.

p. *participle* прича́стие.

p. person лицо́.

P. *person* челове́к.

paint. *painting* жи́вопись.

parl. *parliamentary term* парла́ментское выраже́ние.

part. 1. *particle* части́ца; 2. *particular*(*ly*) осо́бенно.

part. g. *partitive genitive* роди́тельный раздели́тельный.

pers. *pers. person*(*al form*) лицо́ (ли́чная фо́рма).

pf. *perfective* (*aspect*) соверше́нный вид.

pharm. *pharmacy* фармаце́втика.

phon. *phonetics* фоне́тика.

phot. *photography* фотогра́фия.

phys. *physics* фи́зика.

pl. *plural* мно́жественное число́.

poet. *poetic* поэти́ческое сло́во, выраже́ние.

pol. *politics* поли́тика.

poss. *possessive* (*form*) притяжа́тельная фо́рма.

p. pr. a. (*p.*) *present participle active* (*passive*) действи́тельное (страда́тельное) прича́стие настоя́щего вре́мени.

p. pt. a. (*p.*) *past participle active* (*passive*) действи́тельное (страда́тельное) прича́стие проше́дшего вре́мени.

pr. *present* (*tense*) настоя́щее вре́мя.

pred(*ic.*) *predicative* предикати́вное употребле́ние (т. е. в ка́честве именно́й ча́сти сказу́емого).

pref. *prefix* приста́вка.

pr(*e*)*s.* *present* (*tense*) настоя́щее вре́мя.

pron. *pronoun* местоиме́ние.

prov. *proverb*(*ial saying*) посло́вица, погово́рка.

prp. *preposition* предло́г.

prpos. *prepositional* (*case*) предло́жный паде́ж.

psych. *psychology* психоло́гия.

pt. *preterite, past* (*tense*) проше́дшее вре́мя.

rad. *radio* ра́дио.

refl. *reflexive* (*form*) возвра́тная фо́рма.

rel. *relative* (form) относи́тельная фо́рма.

rhet. *rhetoric* рето́рика.

s. *see* смотри́.

s. b. somebody кто́- (кого́-, кому́-) -нибудь.

s. b.'s somebody's че́й-нибудь.

sg. *singular* еди́нственное число́.

sh. *short* (*predicative*) *form* кра́ткая фо́рма.

sl. *slang* жарго́н.

Sov. *Soviet term* выраже́ние сове́тского пери́ода.

st. *stem stressed* (*throughout*) ударе́ние (сплошь) на осно́ве.

s. th. something что́-либо.

su. *substantive* и́мя существи́тельное.

sup. *superlative* превосхо́дная сте́пень.

surv. *surveying* топогра́фия.

tel. *telegraphy* телегра́ф.

teleph. *telephony* телефо́н.

text. *textiles* тка́ни.

th. *thing* вещь, предме́т.

thea. *theater* теа́тр.

typ. *typography* типогра́фское де́ло.

univ. *university* университе́т.

usu. *usually* обы́чно.

v/aux. *auxiliary verb* вспомога́тельный глаго́л.

vb. *verb* глаго́л.

vet. *veterinary* ветерина́рия.

v/i. *verb intransitive* неперехо́дный глаго́л.

voc. *vocative* (*case*) зва́тельный паде́ж.

v/refl. *verb reflexive* возвра́тный глаго́л.

v/t. *verb transitive* перехо́дный глаго́л.

zo. *zoology* зооло́гия.

Russian Abbreviations — Русские сокращения

И **имени́тельный паде́ж** nominative (case).

Р **роди́тельный паде́ж** genitive (case).

Д **да́тельный паде́ж** dative (case).

В **вини́тельный паде́ж** accusative (case).

Т **твори́тельный паде́ж** instrumental (case).

П **предло́жный паде́ж** prepositional *or* locative (case).

и т. д. (и так да́лее) *etc.* (*et cetera*).

и т. п. (и тому́ подо́бное) *and the like*.

лат. **лати́нский язы́к** Latin.

тж. **та́кже** *also*.

PART ONE

RUSSIAN-ENGLISH VOCABULARY

A

а 1. *cj.* but, and; а то or else; а что? why so?; **2.** *int.* ah!; **3.** *part.* F eh?
аб|ажу́р *m* [1] lamp shade; **~ба́т** *m* [1] abbot; **~ба́тство** *n* [9] abbey; **~за́ц** *m* [1] paragraph; **~онеме́нт** *m* [1] subscription; **~оне́нт** *m* [1] subscriber; **~орда́ж** ⚓ *m* [1] grappling, boarding; **~о́рт** *m* [1] abortion; **~рико́с** *m* [1] apricot; **~солю́тный** [14; -тен, -тна] absolute; **~стра́ктный** [14; -тен, -тна] abstract; **~су́рд** *m* [1] absurdity; **~су́рдный** [14; -ден, -дна] absurd; **~сце́сс** *m* [1] abscess.
аван|га́рд *m* [1] advance guard; vanguard; **~по́ст** *m* [1] outpost; **∠с** *m* [1] advance(d money); **∠сом** (*payment*) in advance; **~тю́ра** *f* [5] adventure; **~тюри́ст** *m* [1] adventurer; **~тюри́стка** *f* [5; *g/pl.*: -ток] adventuress.
авар|и́йный [14] emergency...; **∠ия** *f* [7] accident; wreck.
а́вгуст *m* [1] August.
авиа|ба́за *f* [5] air base; **~бо́мба** *f* [5] air bomb; **~констру́ктор** *m* [1] aircraft designer; **~ли́ния** *f* [7] airline; **~ма́тка** *f* [5; *g/pl.*: -ток], **~но́сец** *m* [1; -сца] aircraft carrier; **~по́чта** *f* [5] air mail; **~тра́сса** *f* [5] air route; **~ци́онный** [14] air(craft)...; **∠ция** *f* [7] aviation; aircraft *pl.*; **~шко́ла** *f* [5] flying school.
аво́сь F perhaps, maybe; на ~ at random.
австр|али́ец *m* [1; -и́йца], **~али́йка** *f* [5; *g/pl.*: -и́ек], **~али́йский** [16] Australian; **♀а́лия** *f* [7] Australia; **~и́ец** *m* [1; -и́йца], **~и́йка** *f* [5; *g/pl.*: -и́ек], **~и́йский** [16] Austrian; **'♀ия** *f* [7] Austria.
автобиогр|афи́ческий [16], **~афи́чный** [14; -чен, -чна] autobiographic(al); **~а́фия** *f* [7] autobiography.
авто́бус *m* [1] (motor) bus.
авто|го́нки *f/pl.* [5; *gen.*: -нок] (car) race; **∠граф** *m* [1] autograph; **~жи́р** *m* [1] autogiro; **~заво́д** *m* [1] car factory, automobile plant; **~кра́тия** *f* [7] autocracy; **~магистра́ль** *f* [8] highway; **~ма́т** *m* [1] automaton; slot machine; submachine gun; **~мати́ческий** [16], **~мати́чный** [14; -чен, -чна] automatic; **~ма́тчик** *m* [1] submachine gunner; **~маши́на** *f* [5] *s.* ~моби́ль; **~мобили́ст** *m* [1] motorist; **~моби́ль** *m* [4] (motor-)car; го́ночный ~моби́ль *m* racing car, racer; **~но́мия** *f* [7] autonomy.
а́втор *m* [1] author; **~изова́ть** [7] (*im*)*pf.* authorize; **~ите́т** *m* [1] authority; **~ский** [16] author's; ~ское пра́во *n* copyright; **~ство** *n* [9] authorship.
авто|ру́чка *f* [5; *g/pl.*: -чек] fountain pen; **~стра́да** *f* [5] (motor, super)highway.
ага́ (a'ha) aha!; (oh,) I see!
Ага́фья *f* [6; *g/pl.*: -фий] Agatha.
аге́нт *m* [1] agent; **~ство** *n* [9], **~у́ра** *f* [5] agency.
агит|ацио́нный [14] agitation..., propaganda...; **~и́ровать** [7], ⟨с-⟩ agitate; **∠ка** F *f* [5; *g/pl.*: -ток] (agitation) leaflet; **~про́п** (агитацио́нно-пропаганди́стский отде́л) *m* [1] *pol.* agitation and propaganda department; **~пу́нкт** *m* [1] (*local*) agitation center (*Brt.* -tre).
агра́рный [14] agrarian.
агресс|и́вный [14; -вен, -вна] agressive; **∠ия** *f* [7] aggression.
агрикульту́ра *f* [5] agriculture.
агро|но́м *m* [1] agriculturist; **~номи́ческий** [16] agronomi(cal); **~но́мия** *f* [7] agronomy.
ад *m* [1; в -у́] hell.
Ада́м *m* [1] Adam.
ада́птер (-ter) ⚡ *m* [1] pickup.
адвока́т *m* [1] lawyer; attorney (at law), *Brt.* barrister; solicitor; **~у́ра** *f* [5] ⚖ bar.
адми|нистрати́вный [14] administrative; **~нистра́ция** *f* [7] administration; **~ра́л** *m* [1] admiral; **~ралте́йство** *n* [9] admiralty.
а́дрес *m* [1; *pl.*: -á, *etc. e.*] address (не по Д at wrong); **~а́т** *m* [1], **~а́тка** *f* [5; *g/pl.*: -ток] addressee; consignee; **~ный** [14]: ~ный стол *m* register-office; **~ова́ть** [7] (*im*)*pf.* address, direct.
адриати́ческий [16] Adriatic...
а́дский [16] hellish, infernal.
адъюта́нт *m* [1] aide-de-camp.
аз *m* [1 *e.*]: **~ы́** *pl.* elementaries; F с ~о́в from scratch.
аза́рт *m* [1] passion, vehemence; hazard; войти́ в ~ get excited; **~ный** [14; -тен, -тна] hot-tempered, hazardous; venturesome.
а́збу|ка *f* [5] alphabet; **~чный** [14] alphabetic(al); ~чная и́стина *f* truism.
азербайджа́н|ец *m* [1, -нца] Azerbaijanian; **~ский** [16] Azerbaijan.
ази|а́т *m* [1], **~а́тка** *f* [5; *g/pl.*: -ток], **~а́тский** [16] Asian; Asiatic; **'♀я** *f* [7] Asia; Ма́лая '♀я Asia Minor.
азо́вский [16] Asov...

азо́т *m* [1] nitrogen; **~ный** [14] nitric.
а́ист *m* [1] stork; **~овый** [14] stork...
ай ah!, oh!
айва́ *f* [5] quince.
акаде́м|ик *m* [1] academician; graduate; **~и́ческий** [16] academic; **~ия** *f* [7] academy; **2ия** нау́к Academy of Sciences; **2ия** худо́жеств Academy of Arts.
ака́ция *f* [7] acacia.
акваре́ль *f* [8] water colo(u)r.
акклиматизи́ровать [7] (*im*)*pf.* acclimatize.
аккомпан|еме́нт ♪ *m* [1] accompaniment; **~и́ровать** ♪ [7] accompany.
акко́рд ♪ *m* [1] chord; **~ный** [14]: **~ная** рабо́та *f* piecework.
аккредит|и́в *m* [1] letter of credit; **~ова́ть** [7] (*im*)*pf.* accredit.
аккура́тный [14; -тен, -тна] accurate, punctual; tidy, neat.
акт *m* [1] act(ion); *thea.* act; document; *parl.* bill; **~ёр** *m* [1] actor.
акти́в *m* [1] asset(s); body of active functionaries; **~ный** [14; -вен, -вна] active.
актри́са *f* [5] actress.
актуа́льный [14; -лен, -льна] topical.
аку́ла *f* [5] shark.
аку́ст|ика *f* [5] acoustics; **~и́ческий** [16] acoustic(al).
акуше́р|ка *f* [5; *g*/*pl.*: -рок] midwife; **~ство** *n* [9] midwifery.
акце́нт *m* [1] accent; stress.
акцептова́ть ✝ [7] (*im*)*pf.* accept.
акци|оне́р *m* [1] stockholder, *Brt.* shareholder; **~оне́рный** [14] joint-stock (*company*); **'~я** *f* [7] share; *pl. a.* stock.
алба́н|ец *m* [1; -нца], **~ка** *f* [5; *g*/*pl.*: -нок], **~ский** [16] Albanian.
а́лгебра *f* [5] algebra.
алеба́стр *m* [1] alabaster.
Алексе́й *m* [3] Alexis.
але́ть [8] blush, grow crimson; glow.
Алжи́р *m* [1] Algeria; Algiers.
алиме́нты *m*/*pl.* [1] alimony.
алкого́л|ик *m* [1] alcoholic; **~ь** *m* [4] alcohol.
аллегори́ческий [16] allegorical.
алле́я *f* [6; *g*/*pl.*: -е́й] avenue, alley.
алма́з *m* [1], **~ный** [14] diamond.
алта́рь *m* [4 *e.*] altar.
алфави́т *m* [1] alphabet; **~ный** [14] alphabetical.
а́лчн|ость *f* [8] greed(iness); **~ый** [14; -чен, -чна] greedy (of, for к [Д]).
а́лый [14 *sh.*] crimson.
альбо́м *m* [1] album; sketchbook.
альмана́х *m* [1] almanac.
альпини́|зм *m* [1] mountain climbing, Alpinism; **~ст** *m* [1], **~стка** *f* [5; *g*/*pl.*: -ток] climber, Alpinist.
'Альпы *f*/*pl.* [5] Alps.
альт *m* [1 *e.*] alto.
а́льф|а *f* [5]: от **~ы** до оме́ги from beginning to end.
алюми́ний *m* [3] aluminium.
Аля́ска *f* [5] Alaska.
амба́р *m* [1] barn; granary.
амбразу́ра *f* [5] embrasure.
амбулато́р|ия *f* [7] ambulance station, dispensary; **~ный** [14]: **~ный** больно́й *m* outpatient.
Аме́рик|а *f* [5] America; **2а́нец** *m* [1; -нца], **2а́нка** *f* [5; *g*/*pl.*: -нок], **2а́нский** [16] American.
ами́нь amen.
амнист|и́ровать [7] (*im*)*pf.*, **'~ия** *f* [7] amnesty.
амортиз|а́ция *f* [7] amortization; **~и́ровать** [7] (*im*)*pf.* amortize, pay off.
а́мпула *f* [5] ampoule.
ампут|а́ция *f* [7] amputation; **~и́ровать** [7] (*im*)*pf.* amputate.
амуни́ция *f* [7] ammunition.
амфи́бия *f* [7] amphibian.
амфитеа́тр *m* [1] amphitheater (*Brt.* -tre); *thea.* circle.
ана́лиз *m* [1] analysis; **~и́ровать** [7] (*im*)*pf.*, ⟨про-⟩ analyze (*Brt.* -se).
ана|логи́чный [14; -чен, -чна] analogous, similar; **~ло́гия** *f* [7] analogy; **~на́с** *m* [1] pineapple; **'~рхия** *f* [7] anarchy.
анатом|и́ровать [7] (*im*)*pf.* anatomize; **~и́ческий** [16] anatomical; **'~ия** *f* [7] anatomy.
анга́р *m* [1] hangar.
а́нгел *m* [1] angel.
анги́на *f* [5] quinsy, tonsillitis.
англи́|йский [16] English; **~ча́нин** *m* [1; *pl.*: -ча́не, -ча́н] Englishman; **~ча́нка** *f* [5; *g*/*pl.*: -нок] Englishwoman; **'2я** *f* [7] England.
Андре́й *m* [3] Andrew.
'Анды *f*/*pl.* [5] Andes.
анекдо́т *m* [1] anecdote.
ане|ми́я *f* [7] anemia; **~стези́я** (-neste-) *f* [7] anesthesia.
ани́с *m* [1] anise.
Анкара́ *f* [5] Ankara.
анке́та *f* [5] questionnaire; form.
аннекс|и́ровать [7] (*im*)*pf.* annex; **'~ия** *f* [7] annexation.
аннули́ровать [7] (*im*)*pf.* annul.
ано́д *m* [1] anode; **~ный** [14] anodic.
анома́лия *f* [7] anomaly.
аноні́мный [14; -мен, -мна] anonymous.
анса́мбль *m* [4] ensemble.
антагони́зм *m* [1] antagonism.
Антаркт|и́да *f* [5] Antarctica; **'~ика** *f* [5], **2и́ческий** [16] Antarctic.
анте́нна (-'tɛn-) *f* [5] aerial; *zo.* antenna.
антиква́р *m* [1] antiquary; dealer in antiquarian goods; **~ный** [14] antiquarian.
антило́па *f* [5] antelope.
анти|пати́чный [14; -чен, -чна] antipathetic; **~па́тия** *f* [7] antipathy; **~санита́рный** [14] insani-

tary; ~се́птика *f* [5] antisepsis; antiseptic; ~те́за *f* [5] antithesis.
анти́чн|ость *f* [8] antiquity; **~ый** [14] antique.
антоло́гия *f* [7] anthology.
Анто́н *m* [1] Anthony; **~и́на** *f* [5] Antonia.
антра́кт *m* [1] intermission, *Brt.* interval; interlude.
антропо́л|ог *m* [1] anthropologist; **~о́гия** *f* [7] anthropology.
анчо́ус *m* [1] anchovy.
апат|и́чный [14; -чен, -чна] apathetic; **∠ия** *f* [7] apathy.
апелл|и́ровать [7] (*im*)*pf.* appeal (to к Д); **~яцио́нный** [14] (*court*) of appeal; ~яцио́нная жа́лоба *f* = **~я́ция** ⚖ *f* [7] appeal.
апельси́н *m* [1] orange.
аплоди́|ровать [7], ⟨за-⟩ applaud; **~сме́нты** *m/pl.* [1] applause.
апоге́й *m* [3] apogee.
аполити́чн|ость *f* [8] indifference toward(s) politics; **~ый** [14; -чен, -чна] indifferent to politics.
апологи́ческий [16] apologetic.
апопле́ксия *f* [7] apoplexy.
апо́стол *m* [1] apostle.
апофео́з *m* [1] apotheosis.
аппара́т *m* [1] apparatus; camera.
аппе́нд|икс *m* [1] *anat.* appendix; **~ици́т** *m* [1] appendicitis.
аппети́т *m* [1] appetite; прия́тного ~а! bon appétit!; **~ный** [14; -и́тен, -и́тна] appetizing.
апре́ль *m* [4] April.
апте́ка *f* [5] drugstore, *Brt.* chemist's shop; **~рь** *m* [4] druggist, *Brt.* (pharmaceutical) chemist.
ара́|б *m* [1], **~бка** *f* [5; *g/pl.*: -бок] Arab; **~бский** [16] (*a.* **~ви́йский** [16]) Arabian, Arabic; Arab (*Ligue, etc.*); **~п** † *m* [1] Moor, Negro.
арби́тр *m* [1] arbiter; umpire; **~а́ж** † *m* [1] arbitration.
арбу́з *m* [1] watermelon.
Аргенти́н|а *f* [5] Argentina; **♀ец** *m* [1; -нца], **♀ка** *f* [5; *g/pl.*: -нок], **♀ский** [16] Argentine.
арго́ *n* [*indecl.*] argot.
аргуме́нт *m* [1] argument; **~и́ровать** [7] (*im*)*pf.* argue.
аре́на *f* [5] arena; sphere.
аре́нд|а *f* [5] lease, rent; сдава́ть (брать) в ~у lease (rent); **~а́тор** *m* [1] lessee; tenant; **~ова́ть** [7] (*im*)*pf.* rent.
аре́ст *m* [1] arrest; **~а́нт** *m* [1], **~а́нтка** *f* [5; *g/pl.*: -ток] prisoner; **~о́вывать** [1], ⟨~ова́ть⟩ [7] arrest.
аристокра́тия *f* [7] aristocracy.
арифме́т|ика *f* [5] arithmetic; **~и́ческий** [16] arithmetic(al).
а́рия *f* [7] aria; air.
а́рка *f* [5; *g/pl.*: -рок] arc; arch.
арка́да *f* [5] arcade.
'Аркти|ка *f* [5] Arctic (Zone); **♀ческий** (-'ţi-) [16] arctic.
армату́ра *f* [5] fittings, armature.
Арме́ния *f* [7] Armenia.
а́рмия *f* [7] army.
армя́н|и́н *m* [1; *pl.*: -мя́не, -мя́н], **∠ка** *f* [5; *g/pl.*: -нок], **∠ский** [16] Armenian.
арома́т *m* [1] aroma, perfume, fragrance; **~и́ческий** [16], **~ный** [14; -тен, -тна] aromatic, fragrant.
арсена́л *m* [1] arsenal.
арте́ль *f* [8] workmen's cooperative association.
арте́рия *f* [7] artery.
артилле́р|ия *f* [7] artillery; **~и́ст** *m* [1] artilleryman; **~и́йский** [16] artillery...
арти́ст *m* [1] artist(e); actor; **~ка** *f* [5; *g/pl.*: -ток] artist(e); actress.
артишо́к *m* [1] artichoke.
а́рфа *f* [5] harp.
археолог *m* [1] archeologist; **~и́ческий** [16] archeologic(al); **∠ия** *f* [7] archeology.
архи́в *m* [1] archives *pl.*
архиепи́скоп *m* [1] archbishop.
архипела́г *m* [1] archipelago.
архите́кт|ор *m* [1] architect; **~у́ра** *f* [5] architecture; **~у́рный** [14] architectonic.
арши́н *m* [1; *g/pl.*: арши́н] arshine (†, = *0.711 m.* = *2 ft. 4 in.*).
арьерга́рд *m* [1] rear guard.
асбе́ст *m* [1] asbestos.
асе́птика (-'sɛ-) *f* [5] asepsis.
аспира́нт *m* [1] candidate (*for university teacher's/researcher's career*).
ассамбле́я *f* [6; *g/pl.*: -ле́й]: Генера́льная ♀ Организа́ции Объединённых На́ций United Nations, General Assembly.
ассигнова́|ть [7] (*im*)*pf.* assign, allocate, allot; **~ние** *n* [12] assignment, allocation, allotment.
ассимил|и́ровать [7] (*im*)*pf.* assimilate (-ся o. s.); **~я́ция** *f* [7] assimilation.
ассисте́нт *m* [1], **~ка** *f* [5; *g/pl.*: -ток] assistant.
ассортиме́нт *m* [1] assortment.
ассоци|а́ция *f* [7] association; **~и́ровать** [7] (*im*)*pf.* associate.
АССР (Автоно́мная Сове́тская Социалисти́ческая Респу́блика *f*) Autonomous Soviet Socialist Republic.
а́стра *f* [5] aster.
астроно́м *m* [1] astronomer; **~и́ческий** [16] astronomic(al); **~ия** *f* [7] astronomy.
асфа́льт *m* [1] asphalt.
ата́к|а *f* [5] attack, charge; **~ова́ть** [7] (*im*)*pf.* attack, charge.
атама́н *m* [1] hetman.
ателье́ (-tɛ-) *n* [*indecl.*] studio, atelier.
атланти́ческий [16] Atlantic...
а́тлас[1] *m* [1] atlas.
атла́с[2] *m* [1] satin.
атле́т *m* [1] athlete; **~ика** *f* [5] athletics; **~и́ческий** [16] athletic.
атмосфе́р|а *f* [5] atmosphere; **~ный** [16] atmospheric.
а́том *m* [1] atom; **~ный** [14] atomic.

аттеста́т *m* [1] certificate.
ауди|е́нция *f* [7] audience; **\~то́рия** *f* [7] lecture hall; audience.
аукцио́н *m* [1] auction (by с P).
Афана́сий *m* [3] Athanasius.
Афганиста́н *m* [1] Afghanistan.
афе́р|а *f* [5] speculation, fraud, shady deal; **\~и́ст** *m* [1], **\~и́стка** *f* [5; *g/pl.*: -ток] speculator, swindler.
Афи́ны *f/pl.* [5] Athens.
афи́ша *f* [5] playbill, poster.
афори́зм *m* [1] aphorism.
'**Африка** *f* [5] Africa.
африка́н|ец *m* [1; -нца], **\~ка** *f* [5; *g/pl.*: -нок], **\~ский** [16] African.
ах ah!; **∠ать** [1], *once* ⟨∠нуть⟩ [20] groan, lament; be amazed.
ацетиле́н *m* [1] acetylene.
аэро|дина́мика *f* [5] aerodynamics; **\~дро́м** *m* [1] airdrome (*Brt.* aero-); **\~навига́ция** *f* [7] aerial navigation; **\~пла́н** *m* [1] airplane (*Brt.* aero-); **\~по́рт** *m* [1] airport; **\~по́чта** *f* [5] air mail; **\~сни́мок** *m* [1; -мка] aerial view; **\~ста́т** *m* [1] balloon; **\~(фото)съёмка** *f* [5; *g/pl.*: -мок] aerial photography.

Б

б *s.* бы; б. *abbr.*: бы́вший.
ба́б|а *f* [5] (country)woman; peasant's wife; *fig.* milksop; сне́жная \~а snowman; **\~а-яга́** *f* [5] old witch, hag; **\~ий** [18] womanish, effeminate; **\~ье** ле́то *n* Indian summer; **\~ьи** ска́зки *f/pl.* old wives' tales; **\~ка** *f* [5; *g/pl.*: -бок] grandmother; повива́льная \~ка midwife; *pl.* knucklebones; **\~очка** *f* [5; *g/pl.*: -чек] butterfly; **\~ушка** *f* [5; *g/pl.*: -шек] grandmother; granny; вот тебе́ \~ушка и 'Юрьев день! a pretty business this!
бага́ж *m* [1*e.*] baggage, *Brt.* luggage; ручно́й \~ small baggage; сдать в \~ check one's baggage, *Brt.* register one's luggage; **\~ный** [14]: \~ный ваго́н *m* baggage car, *Brt.* luggage van.
багров|е́ть [8], ⟨по-⟩ become purple, redden; **∠ый** [14 *sh.*] purple.
бадья́ *f* [6] bucket, pail, tub.
ба́за *f* [5] base, basis, foundation.
база́р *m* [1] market, bazaar; F revel, row; **\~ный** [14] market...; *fig.* vulgar, cheap.
ба́зис *m* [1] basis.
байда́рка *f* [5; *g/pl.*: -рок] canoe.
ба́йка *f* [5] baize.
Байка́л *m* [1] (Lake) Baikal.
бак *m* [1] ⚓ forecastle; container, receptacle; tank; boiler.
бакал|е́йный [14]: \~е́йный магази́н *m*, \~е́йная ла́вка *f* grocery, grocer's store (*Brt.* shop); \~е́йные това́ры *m/pl.* = \~е́я; **\~е́йщик** *m* [1] grocer; **\~е́я** *f* [6] groceries *pl.*
ба́к|ен *m* [1] beacon; **\~енба́рды** *f/pl.* [5], **\~и** *m/pl.* [1; *gen.*: бак] whiskers.
баклажа́н *m* [1] eggplant.
баклу́ш|а *f* [5]: бить \~и F idle, dawdle, fool (away).
бактерио́лог *m* [1] bacteriologist; **\~и́ческий** [16] bacteriological; **∠ия** *f* [7] bacteriology.
бакте́рия *f* [7] bacterium.
бал *m* [1; на -у́; *pl. e.*] ball (at на П).
бала́ган *m* [1] booth, show.
балагу́р F *m* [1] joker; **\~ить** F [13] joke, crack jokes.
балала́йка *f* [5; *g/pl.*: балала́ек] balalaika.
баламу́тить F [15], ⟨вз-⟩ trouble, stir up.
бала́нс *m* [1] balance (*a.* ✝); торго́вый \~ balance of trade; **\~и́ровать** [7] balance; **\~овый** [14] balance...
балбе́с *m* [1] simpleton, booby.
балда́ *m/f* [5] blockhead, dolt.
балдахи́н *m* [1] canopy.
бале|ри́на *f* [5] (female) ballet dancer; **∠т** *m* [1] ballet.
ба́лка *f* [5; *g/pl.*: -лок] beam; hollow.
балка́нский [16] Balkan...
балко́н *m* [1] balcony.
балл *m* [1] grade, mark; point.
балла́да *f* [5] ballad.
балла́ст *m* [1] ballast.
баллисти́ческий [16] ballistic.
балло́н *m* [1] balloon.
баллоти́р|овать [7] ballot; **\~о́вка** *f* [5; *g/pl.*: -вок] vote, poll.
бало́в|анный F [14 *sh.*] spoilt; **\~а́ть** [7] (*a.* -ся) be naughty; trifle; ⟨из-⟩ spoil, coddle; '**\~ень** *m* [4; -вня] darling, pet; **\~ни́к** *m* [1 *e.*] urchin, brat; **\~ни́ца** *f* [5] tomboy; **\~ство́** *n* [9] naughtiness, spoiling, trifling.
балти́йский [16] Baltic...
бальза́м *m* [1] balm; **\~и́ровать** [7], ⟨на-⟩ embalm.
балюстра́да *f* [5] balustrade.
бамбу́к *m* [1] bamboo.
бана́ль|ность *f* [8] banality; commonplace; **\~ный** [14; -лен, льна] banal, trite.
бана́н *m* [1] banana.
ба́нда *f* [5] gang.
банда́ж *m* [1*e.*] bandage; truss.
бандеро́ль *f* [8] (postal) wrapper.
банди́т *m* [1] bandit, gangster.
банк *m* [1] bank; **∠а** *f* [5; *g/pl.*: -нок] jar; can, *Brt.* tin.
банке́т *m* [1] banquet.
банки́р *m* [1] banker.
банкно́т *m* [1], **\~а** *f* [5] bank note.

банкрóт *m* [1] bankrupt; **~иться** [15], ⟨о-⟩ go bankrupt; **~ство** *n* [9] bankruptcy.
бант *m* [1] bow.
бáнщ|ик *m* [1], **~ица** *f* [5] attendant (at baths).
бáня *f* [6] bath(s).
бар *m* [1] saloon, (snack) bar.
барабáн *m* [1] drum; **~ить** [13], ⟨про-⟩ (beat the) drum; **~ный** [14]: **~ный** бой *m* beat of the drum; **~ная** перепóнка *f* eardrum; **~щик** *m* [1] drummer.
барáк *m* [1] barracks, hut.
барáн *m* [1] wether; ⚔ ram; **~ий** [18] wether...; согнýть в **~ий** рог bully, intimidate; **~ина** *f* [5] mutton; **~ка** *f* [5; *g/pl.*: -нок] (*kind of*) round cracknel.
барахлó *n* [9] junk, *Brt.* lumber.
барáхтаться F [1] flounce, flounder.
барáшек *m* [1; -шка] lamb(skin).
барбарúс *m* [1] barberry.
барельéф *m* [1] bas-relief.
Бáренцово [19]: ~ мóре *n* Barents Sea.
бáржа *f* [5] barge.
бáрий *m* [3] barium.
бáрин *m* [1; *pl.*: бáре *or* бáры, бар] nobleman; landlord; master; sir.
баритóн *m* [1] baritone.
бáрка ⚓ *f* [5; *g/pl.*: -рок] bark, barque; **~с** ⚓ *m* [1] launch.
барóметр *m* [1] barometer.
баррикáда *f* [5] barricade.
барс *m* [1] panther.
бáр|ский [16] lordly; manorial; жить на **~скую** нóгу live in grand style; **~ство** *n* [9] the noble class; gentility; idleness; haughtiness.
барсýк *m* [1*e.*] badger.
бáрхат *m* [1] velvet; **~ный** [14] velvet(y).
бáрщина *f* [5] statute labo(u)r, corvée.
бáрын|я *f* [6] lady; mistress; madam, ma'am.
барыш *m* [1*e.*] profit, gain(s); **~ник** *m* [1] forestaller; horsedealer; **~ничать** [1] buy up, practise usury; **~ничество** *n* [9] forestallment.
бáрышня *f* [6; *g/pl.*: -шень] young lady; miss.
барьéр *m* [1] barrier.
бас ♪ *m* [1; *pl. e.*] bass.
баск *m* [1] Basque.
баскетбóл *m* [1] basketball.
басно|пúсец *m* [1; -сца] fabulist; **~слóвный** [14; -вен, -вна] fabulous, incredible.
бáсня *f* [6; *g/pl.*: -сен] fable.
басóн *m* [1] galloon, lace.
бассéйн *m* [1] basin; region; ~ для плáвания swimming-pool.
бáста that will do; no more of this!
бастáрд *m* [1] bastard; hybrid.
бастиóн *m* [1] bastion.
бастовáть [7], ⟨за-⟩ (be ⟨go⟩ on) strike.
батальóн *m* [1] battalion; **~ный** [14] battalion...; **~ный** (командúр) battalion commander.
батарé|йка *f* [5; *g/pl.*: -рéек] flashlight (*Brt.* torch, pocket lamp); **~я** ⚡, ⚔ *f* [6; *g/pl.*: -éй] battery.
батúст *m* [1] cambric; **~овый** [14] of cambric.
батрáк *m* [1 *e.*] day labo(u)rer, farm hand.
бáтюшк|а *m* [5; *g/pl.*: -шек] father, papa; priest; (F *address*) dear friend, old boy; как вас по **~е**? what's your father's name?; **~и** (мой)!, **~и** свéты! good gracious!, o(h) dear!
бахвáл P *m* [1] braggart; **~иться** [13] boast, brag; **~ьство** *n* [9] brag(ging), vaunt.
бахромá *f* [5] fringe.
бахчевóдство *n* [9] melon-growing.
бацúлла *f* [5] bacillus.
бáшенка *f* [5; *g/pl.*: -нок] turret.
башкá P *f* [5] head, noddle.
башлык *m* [1 *e.*] (*kind of*) hood.
башмáк *m* [1 *e.*] shoe; clog; drag; быть под **~óм** be henpecked.
бáшня *f* [6; *g/pl.*: -шен] tower; ⚔ turret, cupola.
баюкать [1], ⟨у-⟩ lull.
баян *m* [1] (*kind of*) accordion.
бдéние *n* [12] wake(fulness); care.
бдúтель|ность *f* [8] vigilance; **~ный** [14; -лен, -льна] vigilant, watchful.
бег *m* [1; на бегý] run(ning); *pl.* [бегá, *etc. e.*] race(s); escape; барьéрный ~ hurdle race; эстафéтный ~ relay race; на **~ý** while running; *s.* бегóм.
бéганье *n* [12] running (*a. for. s. th., on business*); ~ на конькáх skating.
бéгать [1], ⟨по-⟩ run (around); F shun (*a.* p. от P); *fig.* run after (*a* p. за T); ~ взáпуски F race, vie in a run.
бегемóт *m* [1] hippopotamus.
беглéц *m* [1 *e.*] runaway.
бéгл|ость *f* [8] fluency, agility; cursoriness; **~ый** [14] fluent, agile; cursory; fugitive.
бег|овóй [14] race...; **~óм** in full career; **~отня́** F *f* [6] running about, bustle; **~ство** *n* [9] flight (put to обратúть в B), escape, stampede.
бегýн *m* [1 *e.*] runner; trotter.
бед|á *f* [5; *pl.*: бéды] misfortune, disaster, mischief; что за **~á**? what does it matter?; не **~á** it doesn't matter; **~á** не великá there's no harm in that; в тóм-то и **~á** that's the trouble; на **~ý** F unluckily; **~á** как F awfully; **~ненький** [16] poor, pitiable; **~нéть** [8], ⟨о-⟩ grow (become) poor; **~ность** *f* [8] poverty; **~нотá** *f* [5] the poor *coll.*; **~ный** [14; -ден, -днá, -днo] poor (in T); **~ня́га** F [5], **~ня́жка** *m/f* [5; *g/pl.*: -жек] poor fellow, wretch; **~ня́к** *m* [1 *e.*] poor man, pauper; small farmer.

бедро́ *n* [9; *pl.*: бёдра, -дер, -драм] thigh; hip; loin.
бе́дств|енный [14 *sh.*] disastrous, miserable; **~енное** положе́ние *n* distress, emergency; **~ие** *n* [12] distress, disaster; **~овать** [7] suffer want, live in misery.
бежа́ть [4; бегу́, бежи́шь, бегу́т; беги́!; бегу́щий], ⟨по-⟩ (be) run (-ning, *etc.*); flee; avoid, shun (*a.* p. от P); ~ сломя́ го́лову F run for one's life *or* head over heels.
бе́жевый [14] beige.
бе́жен|ец *m* [1; -нца], **~ка** *f* [5; *g*/*pl.*: -нок] refugee.
без, ~о (P) **1.** without, ...less; out of (*work*); **2.** less (*with quantities*); **3.** to (*with time*): ~о всего́ without anything; ~ вас ... *a.* ... while you were out.
безала́берный F [14; -рен, -рна] slovenly, disorderly.
безалкого́льный [14] nonalcoholic.
безапелляцио́нный [14; -о́нен, -о́нна] unappealable; peremptory.
безбе́дный [14; -ден, -дна] well off.
безбиле́тный [14]: ~ пассажи́р *m* [1] stowaway.
безбо́ж|ие *n* [12], **~ность** *f* [8] atheism, ungodliness; **~ник** *m* [1], **~ница** *f* [5] atheist; **~ный** [14; -жен, -жна] atheistic, godless, impious; unscrupulous; F awful.
безболе́зненный [14 *sh.*] painless.
безборо́дый [14] beardless.
безбоя́зненный [14 *sh.*] fearless.
безбра́ч|ие *n* [12] celibacy; **~ный** [14; -чен, -чна] unmarried.
безбре́жный [14; -жен, -жна] shoreless, boundless.
безве́рие *n* [12] unbelief.
безве́стный [14; -тен, -тна] unknown.
безве́тр|енный [14 *sh.*] **~ие** *n* [12] calm.
безви́нный [14; -и́нен, -и́нна] guiltless, innocent.
безвку́с|ие *n* [12], **~ица** *f* [5] tastelessness, bad taste; **~ный** [14; -сен, -сна] tasteless, insipid.
безвла́стие *n* [12] anarchy.
безво́дный [14; -ден, дна] arid.
безвозвра́тный [14; -тен, -тна] irretrievable.
безвозду́шный [14] void of air.
безвозме́здный [-mezn-) [14] gratuitous; without compensation.
безволо́сый [14] hairless, bald.
безво́льный [14; -лен, -льна] lacking willpower, weak-willed.
безвре́дный [14; -ден, -дна] harmless.
безвре́менный [14] premature.
безвы́ездный [14] (-jiznyj) permanent.
безвы́ходный [14; -ден, -дна] **1.** continual; **2.** desperate, hopeless.
безголо́вый [14] headless; stupid; forgetful.
безгра́мотн|ость *f* [8] illiteracy, ignorance; **~ый** [14; -тен, -тна] illiterate; faulty.
безграни́чный [14; -чен, -чна] boundless, unlimited.
безда́рный [14; -рен, -рна] untalented, dull; bungling.
безде́йств|ие *n* [12] inactivity; **~овать** [7] be inactive, idle.
безде́л|ица *f* [5], **~ка** *f* [5; *g*/*pl.*: -лок], **~у́шка** *f* [5; *g*/*pl.*: -шек] trifle; (k)nick-(k)nack.
безде́ль|е *n* [12] idleness; **~ник** *m* [1], **~ница** *f* [5] idler; good-for-nothing; **~ничать** [1] idle, lounge.
безде́нежье *n* [10] want of money.
безде́тный [14; -тен, -тна] childless.
безде́ятельный [14; -лен, -льна] inactive.
бе́здна *f* [5] abyss; *fig.* F lots (of).
бездо́мный [14; -мен, -мна] homeless.
бездо́нный [14; -до́нен, -до́нна] bottomless; *fig.* unfathomable.
бездоро́ж|ье *n* [12] impassability; **~ный** [14; -жен, -жна] impassable.
бездохо́дный [14; -ден, -дна] unprofitable.
безду́шный [14; -шен, -шна] soulless; heartless.
безжа́лостный (biʒʒ-sn-) [14; -тен, -тна] ruthless.
безжи́зненный (biʒʒ-) [14 *sh.*] lifeless; *fig.* dull.
беззабо́тный [14; -тен, -тна] careless; carefree.
беззаве́тный [14; -тен, -тна] unselfish; unreserved.
беззако́н|ие *n* [12] lawlessness; anarchy; **~ность** *f* [8] illegality; **~ный** [14; -о́нен, -о́нна] illegal; lawless.
беззасте́нчивый [14 *sh.*] shameless; impudent; unscrupulous.
беззащи́тный [14; -тен, -тна] defenseless; unprotected.
беззвёздный (-zn-) [14; -ден, -дна] starless.
беззву́чный [14; -чен, -чна] soundless; silent; mute.
безземе́льный [14] landless.
беззло́бный [14; -бен, -бна] good-natured.
беззу́бый [14] toothless.
безли́чный [14; -чен, -чна] impersonal.
безлю́дный [14; -ден, -дна] deserted, uninhabited.
безме́рный [14; -рен, -рна] immeasurable; immense.
безмо́зглый F [14] brainless, stupid.
безмо́лв|ие *n* [12] silence; **~ный** [14; -вен, -вна] silent.
безмяте́жный [14; -жен, -жна] quiet, calm; undisturbed.
безнадёжный [14; -жен, -жна] hopeless.
безнадзо́рный [14; -рен, -рна] uncared for.

безнака́занный [14 *sh.*] unpunished, with impunity.
безнали́чный [14]: ~ расчёт *m* † cashless settlement.
безнра́вственный [14*sh.*] immoral.
безоби́дный [14; -ден, -дна] inoffensive; harmless.
безо́блачный [14; -чен, -чна] cloudless; serene.
безобра́з|ие *n* [12] ugliness; deformity; mess; disgrace; **~ие!** scandalous!, shocking!; **~ничать** [1] behave in an improper *or* mischievous manner; **~ный** [14; -зен, -зна] ugly; deformed; shameful, disgusting, abominable; indecent, mischievous.
безоговоро́чный [14; -чен, -чна] unconditional.
безопа́с|ность *f* [8] safety; security; Сове́т ♀ности Security Council; **~ный** [14; -сен, -сна] safe, secure (from от Р); ~ная бри́тва *f* safety razor.
безору́жный [14; -жен, -жна] unarmed; defenseless.
безостано́вочный [14; -чен, -чна] continuous; nonstop...
безотве́тный [14; -тен, -тна] without response; humble; dumb.
безотве́тственный [14 *sh.*] irresponsible.
безотлага́тельный [14; -лен, -льна] undelayable, urgent.
безотра́дный [14; -ден, -дна] desolate, wretched.
безотчётный [14; -тен, -тна] unaccountable; unconscious, involuntary.
безоши́бочный [14; -чен, -чна] faultless.
безрабо́т|ица *f* [5] unemployment; **~ный** [14] unemployed.
безразли́ч|ие *n* [12] (к Д) indifference (to, toward); **~ный** [14; -чен, -чна] indifferent; э́то мне ~но it is all the same to me.
безрассу́дный [14; -ден, -дна] thoughtless, reckless, rash.
безрезульта́тный [14; -тен, -тна] futile, vain.
безро́потный [14; -тен, -тна] humble, meek, submissive.
безрука́вка *f* [5; *g/pl.:* -вок] sleeveless jacket, waistcoat.
безуда́рный [14; -рен, -рна] unstressed.
безу́держный [14; -жен, -жна] unrestrained; impetuous.
безукори́зненный [14 *sh.*] irreproachable, unobjectionable.
безу́м|ец *m* [1; -мца] madman, lunatic; madcap; **~ие** *n* [12] madness, folly; **~ный** [14; -мен, -мна] mad, insane; nonsensical, absurd; rash.
безумо́лчный [14; -чен, -чна] incessant, uninterrupted.
безу́мство *n* [9] folly.
безупре́чный [14; -чен, -чна] blameless, irreproachable.
безусло́в|но certainly, surely; **~ный** [14; -вен, -вна] absolute, unconditional.
безуспе́шный [14; -шен, -шна] unsuccessful.
безуста́нный [14; -а́нен, -а́нна] incessant; indefatigable.
безуте́шный [14; -шен, -шна] disconsolate, inconsolable.
безуча́стный [14; -тен, -тна] indifferent.
безымя́нный [14] anonymous; ~ па́лец *m* ring finger.
безыску́сственный [14 *sh.*] unaffected, unsophisticated.
безысхо́дный [14; -ден, -дна] hopeless, desperate.
бейсбо́л *m* [14] baseball.
бека́с *m* [1] snipe.
белёсый [14] whitish.
беле́ть [8], ⟨по-⟩ grow *or* turn white; *impf.* (*a.* **-ся**) appear *or* show white.
белизна́ *f* [5] whiteness.
бели́ла *n/pl.* [9] ceruse.
бели́ть [13; белю́, бе́лишь; белённый] **1.** ⟨вы́-⟩ bleach; **2.** ⟨на-⟩ paint (white); **3.** ⟨по-⟩ whitewash.
бе́лка *f* [5; *g/pl.:* -лок] squirrel.
беллетри́стика *f* [5] fiction.
бело|бордый [14] white-bearded; **~брысый** F [14] flaxen-haired.
белова́тый [14 *sh.*] whitish.
бело|ви́к *m* [1 *e.*], **~во́й** [14]: **~вой** экземпля́р *m* fair copy; **~воло́сый** [14] white-haired; **~гварде́ец** *m* [1; -е́йца] White Guard (*member of troops fighting against the Red Guards and the Red Army in the Civil War 1918-1920*); **~голо́вый** [14] white-headed.
бело́к *m* [1; -лка́] albumen; white (*of egg or eye*).
бело|кали́льный [14] white hot; **~кро́вие** *n* [12] leukemia; **~ку́рый** [14 *sh.*] blond, fair; **~ру́с** *m* [1], **~ру́ска** *f* [5; *g/pl.:* -сок] Byelorussian, White Russian; ♀ру́ссия *f* [7] Byelorussia, White Russia; **~ру́сский** [16] Byelorussian; **~сне́жный** [14; -жен, -жна] snow-white; **~шве́йка** *f* [5; *g/pl.:* -шве́ек] seamstress.
белу́га *f* [5] sturgeon.
бе́л|ый [14; бел, -а́, -о] white; light, fair; secular; ~ый свет *m* (wide) world; ~ые стихи́ *m/pl.* blank verse; средь ~а дня F in broad day-light.
бель|ги́ец *m* [1; -ги́йца], **~ги́йка** *f* [5; *g/pl.:* -ги́ек], **~ги́йский** [16] Belgian; '♀гия *f* [7] Belgium.
бельё *n* [12] linen; ни́жнее ~ underwear.
бельм|о́ ⚕ *n* [9; *pl.:* бе́льма, бельм] wall-eye; *pl.* goggle-eyes; вы́пучить ~а F stare; он у меня́ как ~о́ на глазу́ he is an eyesore to me.
бельэта́ж *m* [1] *thea.* dress circle; second (*Brt.* first) floor.

бемо́ль ♪ *m* [4] flat.
бенефи́с *m* [1] benefit(-night).
бензи́н *m* [1] benzine; gasoline, *Brt.* petrol.
бензо|ба́к *m* [1] gasoline *or* petrol tank; **~коло́нка** (*a.* ~запра́вочная коло́нка) *f* [5; *g/pl.:* -нок] filling station; **~л** *m* [1] benzol.
бенуа́р *m* [1] *thea.* parterre box.
бе́рег *m* [1; на -гу́; *pl.*: -га́, *etc. e.*] bank, shore, coast; land; вы́йти (вы́ступить) из ~о́в overflow the banks; приста́ть к ~у land; **~ово́й** [14] coast(al), shore... ~ово́е судохо́дство *n* coasting.
бережли́вый [14 *sh.*] economical.
бе́режный [14; -жен, -жна] cautious, careful.
берёза *f* [5] birch.
берёзовый [14] birch(en).
бере́йтор *m* [1] horse-breaker.
бере́мен|ная [14] pregnant; **~ность** *f* [8] pregnancy.
бере́т *m* [1] cap, beret.
бере́чь [26 г/ж: берегу́, бережёшь] **1.** ⟨по-⟩ guard, watch (over); **2.** ⟨по-, с-⟩ spare, save, take care of; **3.** ⟨с-⟩ [сбережённый] keep; preserve; **-ся** take care (of o. s.); береги́сь! take care!, look out!, attention!
Бе́рингов [19]: ~ проли́в *m* Bering Strait; ~о мо́ре *n* Bering Sea.
берло́га *f* [5] bear's lair; den.
берцо́|вый [14]: ~вая кость *f* shinbone.
бес *m* [1] demon.
бесе́д|а *f* [5] conversation, talk; conference, discussion; **~ка** *f* [5; *g/pl.*: -док] arbo(u)r, summerhouse; **~овать** [7] converse.
бесёнок *m* [2; -нка; *pl.*: бесеня́та] imp.
беси́ть F [15], ⟨вз-⟩ [взбешённый] enrage, madden; **-ся** (fly into a) rage; romp.
бесконе́ч|ность *f* [8] infinity; до ~ности endlessly; **~ный** [14; -чен, -чна] endless, infinite; unlimited, boundless; eternal; ~но ма́лый 𝔄 infinitesimal.
бескоры́ст|ие *n* [12] unselfishness; **~ный** [14; -тен, -тна] disinterested.
бескро́в|ие *n* [12] an(a)emia; **~ный** [14; -вен, -вна] an(a)emic; bloodless.
бесновá|тый [14] possessed, demoniac; **~ться** [7] rage, rave.
бесо́вщина *f* [5] devilry.
беспа́мят|ность *f* [8] forgetfulness; **~ный** [14; -тен, -тна] forgetful; unconscious; **~ство** *n* [9] unconsciousness, swoon.
беспарти́йный [14] (*pol.*) independent; non-party (man).
беспербо́йный [14; -бо́ен, -бо́йна] uninterrupted, smooth.
беспереме́нный [14] invariable; unalterable.
беспереса́дочный [14] through...
беспе́ч|ность *f* [8] carelessness; **~ный** [14; -чен, -чна] careless.
беспла́т|ный [14; -тен, -тна] free (of charge), gratuitous; ~но gratis.
беспло́д|ие *n* [12] sterility; **~ный** [14; -ден, -дна] sterile; fruitless, vain.
беспоборо́тный [14; -тен, -тна] unalterable, irrevocable.
бесподо́бный [14; -бен, -бна] incomparable, matchless.
беспозвоно́чный [14] invertebrate.
беспок|о́ить [13], ⟨(п)о-⟩ upset, worry; disturb, bother, trouble; **-ся** worry, be anxious (about о П); **~о́йный** [14; -ко́ен, -ко́йна] restless; uneasy; **~о́йство** *n* [9] unrest; trouble; anxiety; прости́те за ~о́йство sorry to (have) trouble(d) you.
бесполе́зный [14; -зен, -зна] useless.
беспо́мощный [14; -щен, -щна] helpless.
беспоро́чный [14; -чен, -чна] blameless, irreproachable.
беспоря́до|к *m* [1; -дка] disorder, mess; *pl.* disorders; **~чный** [14; -чен, -чна] disorderly, incoherent.
беспоса́дочный [14]: ~ перелёт nonstop flight.
беспо́шлинный [14] duty-free.
беспоща́дный [14; -ден, -дна] pitiless, ruthless, relentless.
беспреде́льный [14; -лен, -льна] boundless, infinite, unlimited.
беспрекосло́вный [14; -вен, -вна] absolute, unquestioning, implicit.
беспрепя́тственный [14 *sh.*] unhampered, unhindered.
беспреры́вный [14; -вен, -вна] uninterrupted, continuous.
беспреста́нный [14; -а́нен, -а́нна] incessant, continual.
беспри́быльный [14; -лен, -льна] unprofitable.
беспризо́рн|ик *m* [1] waif, stray; **~ый** [14; -рен, -рна] homeless, uncared-for.
бесприме́рный [14; -рен, -рна] unprecedented, unparalleled.
беспринци́пный [14; -пен, -пна] unprincipled, unscrupulous.
беспристра́ст|ие *n* [12] impartiality; **~ный** (-sn-) [14; -тен, -тна] impartial, unprejudiced, unbias(s)ed.
беспричи́нный [14; -и́нен, -и́нна] groundless; unfounded.
бесприю́тный [14; -тен, -тна] homeless.
беспробу́дный [14; -ден, -дна] deep (*about sleep*); unrestrained.
беспро́волочный [14] wireless.
беспросве́тный [14; -тен, -тна] pitch-dark; *fig.* hopeless.
беспроце́нтный [14] without charge for interest.
беспу́тный [14; -тен, -тна] dissolute.

бессвя́зный [14; -зен, -зна] incoherent, rambling.
бессерде́чный [14; -чен, -чна] heartless, unfeeling, callous.
бесси́|лие *n* [12] debility; impotence; **~льный** [14; -лен, -льна] weak, powerless, impotent.
бессла́вный [14; -вен, -вна] infamous, disgraceful, inglorious.
бессле́дный [14; -ден, -дна] without leaving a trace, entire.
бесслове́сный [14; -сен, -сна] speechless, dumb; taciturn.
бессме́рт|ие *n* [12] immortality; **~ный** [14; -тен, -тна] immortal.
бессмы́сл|енный [14 *sh.*] senseless; dull; **~ица** *f* [5] nonsense.
бессо́вестный [14; -тен, -тна] unscrupulous.
бессодержа́тельный [14; -лен, -льна] empty, insipid, dull.
бессозна́тельный [14; -лен, -льна] unconscious.
бессо́нн|ица *f* [5] insomnia; **~ый** [14] sleepless.
бесспо́рный [14; -рен, -рна] indisputable; doubtless, certain.
бессро́чный [14; -чен, -чна] termless, not limited in time.
бесстра́ст|ие *n* [12] dispassionateness, calmness; **~ный** [14; -тен, -тна] dispassionate, composed.
бесстра́ш|ие *n* [12] fearlessness; **~ный** [14; -шен, -шна] fearless, intrepid.
бессты́д|ный [14; -ден, -дна] shameless, impudent; indecent; **~ство** *n* [9] impudence, insolence.
бессчётный [14] innumerable.
беста́ла́нный [14; -а́нен, -а́нна] 1. untalented; 2. ill-fated.
бе́стия *f* [7] brute, beast; artful dodger.
бестолко́в|щина *f* [5] nonsense; mess; confusion; **~ый** [14 *sh.*] absurd, confused.
бестре́петный [14; -тен, -тна] intrepid, undaunted.
бесхи́тростный [14; -тен, -тна] artless, naïve, ingenuous, unsophisticated.
бесхозя́йствен|ность *f* [8] mismanagement; **~ный** [14] thriftless.
бесцве́тный [14; -тен, -тна] colo(u)rless.
бесце́льный [14; -лен, -льна] aimless.
бесце́н|ный [14; -е́нен, -е́нна] invaluable, priceless; **~ок**: за **~ок** F for a song *or* a trifling sum.
бесцеремо́нный [14; -о́нен, -о́нна] unceremonious, bold, inconsiderate.
бесчелове́ч|ие *n* [12], **~ность** *f* [8] inhumanity; **~ный** [14; -чен, -чна] inhuman, cruel.
бесче́ст|ный [14; -тен, -тна] dishonest; dishono(u)rable; **~ье** *n* [10] dishono(u)r, disgrace.
бесчи́нство *n* [9] excess, outrage; **~вать** [7] behave outrageously.
бесчи́сленный [14 *sh.*] innumerable, countless.
бесчу́вств|енный (bi'ʃtʃustv-) [14 *sh.*] insensible, callous, hard-hearted; **~ие** *n* [12] insensibility; unconsciousness, swoon.
бесшаба́шный F [14; -шен, -шна] reckless, careless; wanton.
бесшу́мный [14; -мен, -мна] noiseless, quiet.
бето́н *m* [1] concrete; **~и́ровать** [7], ⟨за-⟩ concrete; **~ный** [14] concrete...
бечёвка *f* [5; *g/pl.*: -вок] string.
бе́шен|ство *n* [9] 1. ⚕ hydrophobia; 2. fury, rage; **~ый** [14] 1. rabid; 2. furious, frantic, wild; 3. enormous.
библе́йский [16] Biblical; Bible...
библиографи́ческий [16] bibliographic(al).
библиоте́|ка *f* [5] library; **~карь** *m* [4] librarian; **~чный** [14] library...
би́блия *f* [7] Bible.
бив(у)а́к *m* [1] bivouac; стоя́ть **~ом** *or* на **~ах** bivouac.
би́вень *m* [4; -вня] tusk.
бидо́н *m* [1] can.
бие́ние *n* [12] beat, throb.
бизо́н *m* [1] bison.
биле́т *m* [1] ticket; card; note, bill; обра́тный ~ round-trip ticket, *Brt.* return-ticket.
биллио́н *m* [1] billion, *Brt.* milliard.
билья́рд *m* [1] billiards.
бино́кль *m* [4] binocular(s); glass; театра́льный ~ opera glasses; полево́й ~ field glass.
бинт *m* [1 *e.*] bandage; **~ова́ть** [7], ⟨за-⟩ bandage, dress.
био́граф *m* [1] biographer; **~и́ческий** [16] biographic(al); **~ия** *f* [7] biography.
био́лог *m* [1] biologist; **~и́ческий** [16] biological; **~ия** *f* [7] biology.
биохи́мия *f* [7] biochemistry.
бипла́н *m* [1] biplane.
би́ржа *f* [5] (stock) exchange; ~ труда́ labor registry office, *Brt.* labour exchange.
бирже|ви́к *m* [1 *e.*], stockbroker; **~во́й** [14]: **~во́й** ма́клер = **~ви́к**.
Би́рм|а *f* [5] Burma; **2а́нец** *m* [1; -нца], **2а́нка** *f* [5; *g/pl.*: -нок], **2а́нский** [16] Burmese.
бирюза́ *f* [5] turquoise.
бис encore!
би́сер *m* [1] *coll.* (glass) beads *pl.*
бискви́т *m* [1] sponge cake.
би́тва *f* [5] battle.
бит|ко́м *s.* наби́тый; **~о́к** *m* [1; -тка́] (mince)meat ball.
бить [бью, бьёшь; бей!; би́тый] 1. ⟨по-⟩ beat; churn (*butter*); 2. ⟨про-⟩ [про́бил, -би́ла, про́би́ло] strike (*clock*); 3. ⟨раз-⟩ [разобью́, -бьёшь] break, smash; 4. ⟨у-⟩ shoot, kill; trump (*card*); 5. *no pf.* spout; ~ в глаза́ strike the eye; ~ в наба́т,

~ тревóгу sound the alarm (bell) (отбóй the retreat); ~ ключóм 1. bubble; 2. boil over; 3. sparkle; 4. abound in vitality; прóбил егó час his hour has struck; би́тый час *m* one solid hour; **-ся** fight; beat (*heart*); drudge, toil; -ся головóй о(б) стéну dash against the rock; -ся об заклáд bet; он бьётся как ры́ба об лёд he exerts himself in vain.

бифштéкс *m* [1] (beef)steak.

бич *m* [1 *e.*] whip; *fig.* scourge; **~евáть** [7] lash, scourge.

благови́дный [14; -ден, дна] attractive; *fig.* seemly.

благово|лéние *n* [12] benevolence, goodwill; **~ли́ть** [13] wish (a. p. к Д) well, be kind (to a. p.); deign.

благовóн|ие *n* [12] fragrance; **~ный** [14] fragrant.

благовоспи́танный [14 *sh.*] well-bred.

благогo|вéйный [14; -вéен, -вéйна] devout, reverent, respectful; **~вéние** *n* [12] awe (of), reverence, respect (for) (пéред Т); **~вéть** [8] (пéред Т) worship, venerate.

благодар|и́ть [13], ‹по-, от-› (В/за В) thank (a p. for s. th.); **∠ность** *f* [8] gratitude; thanks; не стóит ∠ности you are welcome, *Brt.* don't mention it; **∠ный** [14; -рен, -рна] grateful, thankful (to a p. for s. th. Д/за В); **~я́** (Д) thanks *or* owing to.

благодáт|ный [14]; -тен, -тна] blessed; **~ь** *f* [8] blessing.

благодéтель *m* [4] benefactor; **~ница** *f* [5] benefactress; **~ный** [14; -лен, -льна] beneficent; beneficial.

благодея́ние *n* [12] benefit.

благоду́ш|ие *n* [12] good nature, kindness; **~ный** [14; -шен, -шна] kindhearted, benign.

благожелáтель|ность *f* [8] benevolence; **~ный** [14; -лен, -льна] benevolent.

благозву́ч|ие *n* [12], **~ность** *f* [8] euphony, sonority; **~ный** [14; -чен, -чна] sonorous, harmonious.

благонадёжный [14; -жен, -жна] reliable, trustworthy.

благонамéренный [14 *sh.*] well-meaning, well-meant.

благонрáвный [14; -вен, -вна] well-mannered, modest.

благообрáзный [14; -зен, -зна] attractive, comely, sightly.

благополу́ч|ие *n* [12] well-being, prosperity, happiness; **~ный** [14; -чен, -чна] happy; safe.

благоприя́т|ный [14; -тен, -тна] favo(u)rable, propitious; **~ствовать** [7] (Д) favo(u)r, promote.

благоразу́м|ие *n* [12] prudence, discretion; **~ный** [14; -мен, -мна] prudent, judicious.

благорóд|ный [14; -ден, -дна] noble; high-minded, distinguished; lofty; precious; **~ство** *n* [9] nobility.

благосклóнный [14; -óнен, -óнна] favo(u)rable, well-disposed (to [-ward(s)] a p. к Д).

благосло|вéние *n* [12] benediction, blessing; **~вля́ть** [28], ‹**~ви́ть**› [14 *e.*; -влю́, -ви́шь] bless.

благосостоя́ние *n* [12] prosperity.

благотвори́тельный [14] beneficent, charitable.

благотвóрный [14; -рен, -рна] wholesome, salutary.

благоустрóенный [14 *sh.*] well-furnished, comfortable.

благоухá|ние *n* [12] fragrance, odo(u)r; **~ть** [1] scent, exhale fragrance.

благочести́вый [14 *sh.*] pious.

блажéн|ный [14 *sh.*] blissful; **~ство** *n* [9] bliss; **~ствовать** [7] enjoy felicity.

блаж|и́ть P [16 *e.*; -жу́, -жи́шь] be capricious, cranky; **~нóй** P [14] capricious; preposterous; **~ь** F *f* [8] caprice, whim, freak, fancy; folly.

бланк *m* [1] form; letterhead.

блат P *m* [1] profitable connections; по ∠у on the quiet, illicitly, through good connections; **~нóй** P [14] trickster, rogue; ~нóй язы́к *m* thieves' slang, cant.

бледнéть [8], ‹по-› turn pale.

бледно|вáтый [14 *sh.*] palish; **~ли́цый** [14 *sh.*] with a pale face.

блéд|ность *f* [8] pallor; **~ный** [14; -ден, -днá, -о] pale.

блёк|лый [14] faded, withered; **~нуть** [21], ‹по-› fade, wither.

блеск *m* [1] luster, shine, brilliance, glitter, splendo(u)r.

блест|éть [11; *a.* блéщешь], *once* ‹блесну́ть› [20] shine, glitter; flash; не всё то зóлото, что ~и́т all is not gold that glitters; **~ки** ('bʎɔski) *f/pl.* [5; *gen.*: -ток] spangle; **~я́щий** [17 *sh.*] brilliant.

блеф *m* [1] bluff.

блéять [27], ‹за-› bleat.

ближ|áйший [17] (*s.* бли́зкий) the nearest, next; **∠е** nearer; **∠ний** [15] near(-by); *su.* fellow creature.

близ (Р) near, close; **∠иться** [15; *3rd p. only*], ‹при-› approach (a p. к Д); **∠кий** [16; -зок, -зкá, -о; *comp.*: бли́же], (к Д) near, close; ∠кие *pl.* folk(s), one's family, relatives; ∠ко от (Р) close to, not far from; **~лежáщий** [17] nearby, neighbo(u)ring.

близнéц *m* [1 *e.*] twin.

близору́кий [16 *sh.*] short-sighted.

бли́зость *f* [8] nearness, proximity; intimacy.

блин *m* [1 *e.*] pancake.

блистáтельный [14; -лен, -льна] brilliant, splendid, magnificent.

блистáть [1] shine, beam.

блок *m* [1] 1. bloc, coalition; 2. pulley.
блок|áда *f* [5] blockade; **~и́ровать** [7] (*im*)*pf.* blockade, block up.
блокно́т *m* [1] notebook.
блонди́н *m* [1] blond; **~ка** *f* [5; *g/pl.*: -нок] blonde.
блоха́ *f* [5; *nom/pl. st.*: бло́хи] flea.
блуд *m* [1] licentiousness; **~и́ть** P 1. [15] roam, wander; 2. [15 *e.*; -жу́, -ди́шь] debauch; **~ли́вый** [14 F *sh.*], **∠ный** [14] wanton; **∠ный сын** *m* prodigal son.
блужда́|ть [1], ⟨про-⟩ roam, wander; **~ющий огонёк** *m* will-o'-the-wisp; **~ющая по́чка** *f* floating kidney.
блу́з|а *f* [5] blouse, smock; **~ка** *f* [5; *g/pl.*: -зок] (ladies') blouse.
блю́дечко *n* [9; *g/pl.*: -чек] saucer.
блю́до *n* [9] dish; course.
блю́дце *n* [11; *g/pl.*: -дец] saucer.
блюсти́ [25], ⟨со-⟩ observe, preserve, maintain; watch; **~тель** *m* [4], **~тельница** *f* [5] keeper, guardian.
бля́ха *f* [5] metal plate, badge.
боа́ [*indecl.*] 1. *m zo.* boa; 2. *n* boa (*wrap*).
боб *m* [1 *e.*] bean; haricot; оста́ться на **~а́х** have one's trouble for nothing.
бобёр *m* [1; -бра́] beaver (*fur*).
боби́на *f* [5] bobbin, spool, reel.
бобо́в|ый [14]: **~ые расте́ния** *n/pl.* legumes.
бобр *m* [1 *e.*], **~о́вый** [14] beaver.
бо́бслей *m* [3] bobsleigh.
бобы́ль *m* [4 *e.*] landless peasant; *fig.* solitary man, (old) bachelor.
бог (bɔx) *m* [1; *voc.*: бо́же; *from g/pl. e.*] God; god, idol; ~ весть, ~ (его́) зна́ет F God knows; бо́же (мой)! oh God!, good gracious!; дай ~ God grant; I (let's) hope (so); ей ∠у! by a God!; ра́ди ∠а for God's (goodness') sake; сохрани́ (не дай, изба́ви, упаси́) ~ (бо́же) God forbid!
богат|е́ть [8] ⟨раз-⟩ grow (become) rich; **∠ство** *n* [9] wealth; **∠ый** [14 *sh.*; *comp.*: бога́че] rich (in T), wealthy.
богаты́рь *m* [4 *e.*] hero; athlete.
бога́ч *m* [1 *e.*] rich man.
Боге́м|ия *f* [7] Bohemia; **♀ский** [16] Bohemian.
боги́ня *f* [6] goddess.
богома́терь *f* [8] the Blessed Virgin.
бого|мо́лец *m* [1; -льца], **~мо́лка** *f* [5; *g/pl.*: -лок] devotee; pilgrim; **~мо́лье** *n* [10] prayer; pilgrimage.
богоотсту́пник *m* [1] atheist.
богоро́дица *f* [5] the Blessed Virgin, Our Lady.
богосло́в *m* [1] theologian; **~ие** *n* [12] theology, divinity; **~ский** [16] theological.
богослуже́ние *n* [12] divine service.
боготвори́ть [13] adore, deify.
богоху́ль|ник *m* [1] blasphemer; **~ничать** [1] blaspheme; **~ный** [14] blasphemous; **~ство** *n* [9] blasphemy; **~ствовать** [7] = богоху́льничать.
бода́ть [1], ⟨за-⟩, *once* ⟨бодну́ть⟩ [20] (*a.* **~ся**) butt, gore (*a. o.a.*).
бо́др|ость *f* [8] vivacity, sprightliness; **~ствовать** [20] be awake; **~ый** [14; бодр, -á, -о] awake; sprightly, vivacious, brisk; vigorous.
боеви́к *m* [1 *e.*] hit, draw.
боево́й [14] battle..., fighting, war-..., military; live (*shell, etc.*); pugnacious, militant; ~ па́рень *m* dashing fellow; ~ поря́док *m* battle array.
бое|припа́сы *m/pl.* [1] ammunition; **~спосо́бный** [14; -бен, -бна] effective.
бое́ц *m* [1; бойца́] soldier, fighter.
бо́же *s.* бог; **~ский** [16] godlike, divine; **∠ственный** [14 *sh.*] divine; **~ство́** *n* [9] deity, divinity.
бо́жий [18] God's, divine.
божи́ться [16 *e.*; -жу́сь, -жи́шься], ⟨по-⟩ swear.
бой *m* [3; бо́я, в бою́; *pl.*: бои́, боёв, *etc. e.*] battle, combat, fight; брать (взять) бо́ем *or* с бо́ю take by assault (storm); рукопа́шный ~ close fight; ~ часо́в the striking of a clock; **∠кий** [16; бо́ек, бойка́, бо́йко; *comp.*: бо́йч(é)е] brisk, lively, busy; smart, quick, sharp; voluble, glib; **∠кость** *f* [8] liveliness, smartness.
бойкоти́ровать [7] (*im*)*pf.* boycott.
бойни́ца *f* [5] loophole, embrasure.
бо́йня *f* [6; *g/pl.*: бо́ен] slaughterhouse; *fig.* massacre, slaughter.
бок *m* [1; на боку́; *pl.*: бока́, *etc. e.*] side; на́ ~, ∠ом sideways; ~ о ~ side by side; по́д ∠ом F close by; бара́ний ~ leg of mutton.
бока́л *m* [1] wineglass.
боково́й [14] lateral.
бокс *m* [1] boxing; **~ёр** *m* [1] boxer; **~и́ровать** [7] box.
болва́н *m* [1] dolt, blockhead.
болга́р|ин *m* [4; *pl.*: -ры, -р] Bulgarian; **♀ия** *f* [7] Bulgaria; **~ка** *f* [5; *g/pl.*: -рок], **~ский** [16] Bulgarian.
бо́лее (*s.* бо́льше) more (than P); ~ высо́кий higher; ~ и́ли ме́нее more or less; не ~ at (the) most.
боле́зненный [14 *sh.*] sickly, ailing, morbid; painful.
боле́знь *f* [8] sickness (on the score of по Д), illness; disease; (*mental*) disorder; sick (*leave* ... по Д).
боле́льщик *m* [1] *sport*: fan.
боле́ть 1. [8] be sick, ill (with T); be anxious (for, about за В о П), apprehensive; 2. [9; *3rd p. only*] hurt, ache; у меня́ боли́т голова́ (зуб, го́рло) I have a headache (a toothache, a sore throat).
боло́т|истый [14 *sh.*] boggy

swampy; ~ный [14] bog..., swamp-...; ~о *n* [9] bog, swamp.
болт *m* [1 *e.*] bolt.
болта́ть [1] **1.** ⟨вз-⟩ shake up; **2.** (-ся) dangle; **3.** F ⟨по-⟩ [20] chat (-ter); ~ся F loaf *or* lounge about.
болтли́вый [14 *sh.*] talkative.
болтовня́ F *f* [6] idle talk, gossip.
болту́н *m* [1; -на́], ~ья *f* [6] babbler, chatterbox.
боль *f* [8] pain, ache.
больни́|ца *f* [5] hospital; **~чный** [14] hospital...; ~чная ка́сса *f* sick-fund; ~чный листо́к *m* medical certificate.
бо́льн|о painful(ly); P very; мне ~о it hurts me; глаза́м ~о my eyes smart; **~о́й** [14; бо́лен, больна́] sick, ill (*a. su.*), sore; patient, invalid; *fig.* delicate, burning; tender.
бо́льше bigger; more; ~ всего́ most of all; above all; ~ не ... no more *or* longer; как мо́жно ~ as much as possible; **~ви́зм** *m* [1] Bolshevism; **~ви́к** *m* [1 *e.*], **~ви́чка** *f* [5; *g/pl.*: -чек] Bolshevik; **~ви́стский** (-ˈvis-skij) [16] Bolshevist(ic).
бо́льш|ий [17] bigger, greater; **~инство́** *n* [9] majority; most; **~о́й** [16] big, large, great; grownup.
бо́мб|а *f* [5] bomb; **~ардирова́ть** [7] bomb, shell; bombard (*a. fig.*); **~ардиро́вка** *f* [5; *g/pl.*: -вок] bombardment, bombing; **~ардиро́вщик** *m* [1] bomber; **~ёжка** F *f* [5; *g/pl.*: -жек] = ~ардиро́вка; **~и́ть** [14 *e.*; -блю́, -би́шь; (раз-) бомблённый], ⟨раз-⟩ bomb.
бомбо|во́з *m* [1] = бомбардиро́вщик; **~убе́жище** *n* [11] air-raid shelter.
бонбонье́рка *f* [5; *g/pl.*: -рок] bonbonnière, box for candies.
бо́нда́рь *m* [4 & 4 *e.*; *pl. a.* -ря́, *etc. e.*] cooper.
бор *m* [1] **1.** [в бору́] pine wood *or* forest; **2.** ⚗ boron.
бордо́ *n* [*indecl.*] claret.
бордю́р *m* [1] border, trimming.
боре́ц *m* [1; -рца́] fighter; wrestler; *fig.* champion, partisan.
бор|зо́й [14] swift, fleet (*dog*); ~за́я (соба́ка) *f* borzoi, greyhound.
бо́рзый [14; борз, -а́, -о] brisk, swift.
Бори́с *m* [1] Boris (*masc. name*).
бормота́ть [3], ⟨про-⟩ murmur, mutter.
бо́ров *m* [1; *from g/pl. e.*] boar.
борода́ *f* [5; *ac/sg.*: бо́роду; *pl.*: бо́роды, боро́д, -да́м] beard.
борода́вка *f* [5; *g/pl.*: -вок] wart.
борода́|тый [14 *sh.*] bearded; **~ч** *m* [1 *e.*] bearded man.
боро́дка *f* [5; *g/pl.*: -док] small beard; bit (*key*).
борозд|а́ *f* [5; *pl.*: бо́розды, боро́зд -да́м] furrow; **~и́ть** [15 *e.*; -зжу́ -зди́шь], ⟨вз-⟩ furrow.
боро|на́ *f* [5; *ac/sg.*: бо́рону; *pl.*: бо́роны, боро́н, -на́м] harrow; **~ни́ть** [13], **~нова́ть** [7], ⟨вз-⟩ harrow.
боро́ться [17; боря́сь] fight, struggle (for за В); wrestle.
борт *m* [1; на -ту́; *nom/pl.*: -та́] **1.** braid, lace; border; **2.** board; на ~у́ су́дна on board a ship; бро́сить за́ ~ throw overboard; челове́к за ~ом! man overboard!; **~ово́й** [14] board...
борщ *m* [1 *e.*] borsch(t), red-beet soup.
Бо́ря *m* [6] *dim. of* Бори́с.
босико́м barefoot.
босо́й [14; бос, -а́, -о] barefooted; на бо́су но́гу = босико́м.
босоно́гий [16] = босо́й.
Босфо́р *m* [1] Bosporus.
бося́к *m* [1 *e.*] tramp, vagabond.
бота́ни|к *m* [1] botanist; **~ка** *f* [5] botany; **~ческий** [16] botanic(al).
боти́нок *m* [1; *g/pl.*: -нок] shoe, *Brt.* (lace-)boot.
ботфо́рты *m/pl.* [1] jackboots.
бо́ты *m/pl.* [1; *g/pl. a.* бот] overshoes.
бо́цман *m* [1] boatswain.
боча́р *m* [1 *e.*] cooper.
бо́чка *f* [5; *g/pl.*: -чек] cask, tun.
бочко́м sideway(s), sidewise.
бочо́но|к *m* [1; -нка] (small) barrel; **~чный** [14]: ~чное пи́во *n* draught beer.
боязли́вый [14 *sh.*] timid, fearful.
боя́знь *f* [8] fear, dread.
боя́р|ин *m* [4; *pl.*: -ре, -р], **~ыня** *f* [6] boyar(d) (*member of old nobility in Russia*).
боя́рышник *m* [1] hawthorn.
боя́ться [бою́сь, бои́шься; бо́йся, бо́йтесь!], ⟨по-⟩ be afraid (of P), fear; бою́сь сказа́ть I don't know exactly, I'm not quite sure.
бра́вый [14] brave, courageous.
бразды́ *f/pl.* [5] *fig.* reins.
брази́|лец [1; -льца] Brazilian; **⁀лия** *f* [7] Brazil; **~льский** [16], **~лья́нка** *f* [5; *g/pl.*: -нок] Brazilian.
брак *m* [1] **1.** marriage; matrimony; **2.** (*no pl.*) defective articles, spoilage.
бракова́ть [7], ⟨за-⟩ scrap, reject.
бракосочета́ние *n* [12] wedding.
брани́ть [13], ⟨по-, вы́-⟩ scold, rebuke, abuse; -ся quarrel, wrangle; swear, curse.
бра́нный [14] **1.** abusive; **2.** battle-..., military.
бранчли́вый [14 *sh.*] quarrelsome.
брань *f* [8] **1.** abuse, quarrel([l]ing); invective; **2.** battle, fight.
брасле́т *m* [1] bracelet.
брат *m* [1; *pl.*: бра́тья, -тьев, -тьям] brother; (*address:*) old boy!; ваш ~ F of your kind; наш ~ F (such as) we.
брата́|ние *n* [12] fraternization; **~ться** [1], ⟨по-⟩ fraternize.
бра́тец *m* [1; -тца] dear brother; (*address:*) old fellow!, dear friend!

бра́тия *f* [7] fraternity; friary; ни́щая ~ beggary.
брато|убийство *n* [9], **~убийца** *m/f* [5] fratricide.
бра́т|ский [16; *adv.*: (по-)бра́тски] brotherly, fraternal; **~ство** *n* [9] brotherhood, fraternity, fellowship.
брать [беру́, -рёшь; брал, -á, -о; '...бранный], ⟨взять⟩ [возьму́, -мёшь; взял, -á, -о; взя́тый (взят, -á, -о)] take; ~ напрока́т hire; ~ приме́р (с Р) take (a p.) for a model; ~ верх над (Т) be victorious over, conquer; ~ на пору́ки be (-come) bail (for B); ~ сло́во take (have) the floor; ~ (с Р) сло́во make (s. o.) promise; ~ (свой слова́) обра́тно withdraw (one's words); ~ себя́ в ру́ки *fig.* collect o.s., pull o.s. together; ~ на себя́ assume; ~ за пра́вило make it a rule; его́ взяла́ охо́та писа́ть he took a fancy to writing; он взял да сказа́л F he said it without further consideration; возьми́те напра́во! turn (to the) right!; *s. a.* взима́ть; **-ся** [бра́лся, -ла́сь, -ло́сь], ⟨взя́ться⟩ [взя́лся, -ла́сь, взя́ло́сь, взя́ли́сь] (за В) undertake; set about; take hold of seize; ~ за́ руки join hands; ~ за кни́гу (рабо́ту) set about *or* start reading a book (working); отку́да э́то берётся? where does that come from?; отку́да у него́ де́ньги беру́тся? wherever does he get his money from?; отку́да ни возьми́сь all of a sudden.
бра́чный [14] matrimonial, conjugal.
брев|е́нчатый [14] log...; **~но́** *n* [9; *pl.*: брёвна, -вен, -внам] log; beam.
бред *m* [1] delirium; **~ить** [15], ⟨за-⟩ rave, talk deliriously (about Т); **~ни** *f/pl.* [6; *gen.*: -ней] nonsense, fantasies; raving.
бре́зг|ать [1] (Т) disdain; **~ли́вость** *f* [8] squeamishness, disgust; **~ли́вый** [14 *sh.*] squeamish, fastidious (in к Д).
брезе́нт *m* [1] tarpaulin.
бре́зжить [16], **-ся** glimmer; dawn.
бре́мя *n* [13; *no pl.*] burden, load.
бренча́ть [4*e.*; -чу́, -чи́шь], ⟨за-, про-⟩ clink, jingle; strum.
брести́ [25], ⟨по-⟩ drag, lag; grope.
брешь *f* [8] breach; gap.
брига́|да *f* [5] brigade (*a.* ⚔), team, group of workers; уда́рная **~да** shock brigade; **~ди́р** *m* [1] brigadier; foreman.
бри́джи *pl.* [*gen.*: -жей] breeches.
бриллиа́нт *m* [1], **~овый** [14] brilliant.
брита́н|ец *m* [1; -нца] Briton, Britisher; **Ⓑия** *f* [7] Britain; **~ский** [16] British; **Ⓑская Импе́рия** *f* British Empire; **Ⓑские острова́** *m/pl.* British Isles.

бри́т|ва *f* [5] razor; **~венный** [14]: **~венный** прибо́р *m* shaving things.
брить [бре́ю, бре́ешь; бре́й(те)!; бре́я; брил; бри́тый], ⟨вы́-, по-⟩ shave; **-ся** *v/i.* get shaved, (have a) shave; **~ё** *n* [10] shaving.
бров|ь *f* [8; *from g/pl. e.*] eyebrow; хму́рить **~и** frown; он и **~ью** не повёл F he did not turn a hair; попа́сть не в **~ь**, а в глаз F hit the nail on the head.
брод *m* [1] ford.
броди́ть [15] **1.** ⟨по-⟩ wander, roam; **2.** (*impers.*) ferment.
бродя́|га *m* [5] tramp, vagabond; **~жничать** F [1] stroll, tramp; **~жничество** *n* [9] vagrancy; **~чий** [17] vagrant.
броже́ние *n* [12] fermentation; *fig.* agitation, unrest.
бром *m* [1] bromine.
броне|ви́к *m* [1 *e.*] armo(u)red car; **~во́й** [14] armo(u)red; **~но́сец** *m* [1; -сца] battleship; **~по́езд** *m* [1] armo(u)red train; **~та́нковый** [14]: **~та́нковые** ча́сти *f/pl.* armo(u)red troops.
бро́нз|а *f* [5] bronze; **~овый** [14] bronzy, bronze...
брони|рова́ть[1] [7], ⟨за-⟩ armo(u)r; **~ровать**[2] [7], ⟨за-⟩ reserve secure.
бро́нх|и *m/pl.* [1] bronchi *pl.* (*sg.* ~ bronchus); **~и́т** *m* [1] bronchitis.
броня́[1] *f* [6; *g/pl.*: -не́й] armo(u)r.
бро́ня[2] *f* [6; *g/pl.*: -ней] reservation.
броса́ть [1], ⟨бро́сить⟩ [15] throw, (*a.* ⚓) cast, fling (*a.* out) (s. th. at B *or* Т/в В); leave, abandon, desert; give up, quit, leave off; (*impers.*) break into, be seized with (в В); lay down (*one's arms*); F waste, squander; брось(те) ...! F (oh) stop ...!; **-ся** dash, rush, plunge, dart (off -ся бежа́ть); fall (up)on (на В); go to (в В); **-ся в глаза́** strike the eye.
бро́со|вый [14] catchpenny; under (*price*); **~вый** э́кспорт *m* dump.
бросо́к *m* [1; -ска́] hurl, throw.
бро́шка *f* [5; *g/pl.*: -шек] brooch.
брошю́|ра *f* [5] brochure, pamphlet; **~рова́ть** [7], ⟨с-⟩ stitch.
брус *m* [1; *pl.*: бру́сья, бру́сьев, бру́сьям] (square) beam; bar; *pl.* (*a.* паралле́льные **~ья**) (*gymnastics*) parallel bars; **~ко́вый** [14] bar...
бруснн́ка *f* [5] red bilberry, -ries *pl.*
бруco̍к *m* [1; -ска́] **1.** bar; **2.** (*a.* точи́льный ~) whetstone.
бру́тто [*indecl.*] gross (weight).
бры́з|гать [1 *or* 3] *once* ⟨**~**нуть⟩ [20] splash, spatter, sprinkle; gush; **~ги** *f/pl.* [5] splash, spray.
брык|а́ть [1], *once* ⟨**~**ну́ть⟩ [20] (*a.* **-ся**) kick.
брюз|га́ F *m/f* [5] grumbler, griper, grouch; **~гли́вый** [14 *sh.*] morose, sullen, peevish, grouchy; **~жа́ть**

[4 *e.*; -жу́, -жи́шь], ⟨за-⟩ grumble, growl, grouch.
брю́ква *f* [5] turnip.
брю́ки *f/pl.* [5] trousers, pants.
брюне́т *m* [1] brunet; **~ка** *f* [5; *g/pl.:* -ток] brunette.
Брюссе́ль *m* [4] Brussels; **2ский** [16]: **2ская** капу́ста *f* Brussels sprouts.
брю́хо P *n* [9] belly, paunch.
брюш|и́на *f* [5] peritoneum; **~но́й** [14] abdominal; **~но́й тиф** *m* typhoid fever.
бря́кать [1], *once* ⟨бря́кнуть⟩ [20] **1.** *v/i.* clink; **2.** *v/t.* plump.
бряца́ть [1] clank, jingle; rattle.
БССР (Белору́сская Сове́тская Социалисти́ческая Респу́блика *f*) Byelorussian Soviet Socialist Republic.
бу́бен *m* [1; -бна; *g/pl.:* бу́бен] (*mst pl.*) tambourine; **~е́ц** *m* [1; -нца́], **~чик** *m* [1] jingle, small bell.
бу́блик *m* [1] (round) cracknel.
бу́бн|ы *f/pl.* [5; *g/pl.:* бубён, -бна́м] (*cards*) diamonds.
буго́р *m* [1; -гра́] hillock.
Будапе́шт *m* [1] Budapest.
бу́дет (*s.* быть) (*impers.*) (it's) enough!, that'll do!
буди́льник *m* [1] alarm clock.
буди́ть [15] **1.** ⟨раз-⟩ (a)wake, waken; **2.** ⟨про-⟩ [пробуждённый] *fig.* (a)rouse.
бу́дка *f* [5; *g/pl.:* -док] booth, box.
бу́дни *m/pl.* [1; *gen.:* -дней] weekdays; everyday life, monotony; **~чный** [14] everyday; humdrum.
будора́жить [16], ⟨вз-⟩ excite.
бу́дто as if, as though (*a.* ~ бы, ~ б); that; allegedly.
бу́дущ|ее *n* [17] future; **~ий** [17] future (*a. gr.*); **~ность** *f* [8] futurity, future.
бу́ер *m* [1; *pl.:* -pá, *etc. e.*] iceboat.
буза́ P *f* [5] row, shindy.
бузина́ *f* [5] elder.
буй *m* [3] buoy.
бу́йвол *m* [1] buffalo.
бу́йный [14; бу́ен, буйна́, -o] impetuous, violent, vehement; unbridled; exuberant.
бу́йство *n* [9] mischief, rage, outrage, violence; **~вать** [7] behave outrageously, rage.
бук *m* [1] beech.
бу́к|ва *f* [5] letter; прописна́я (строчна́я) **~ва** capital (small) letter (with c P); **~ва́льный** [14] literal, verbal; **~ва́рь** *m* [4 *e.*] ABC book, primer; **~вое́д** *m* [1] pedant.
букини́ст *m* [1] second-hand bookseller
бу́ковый [14] beechen, beech...
букс *m* [1] box(wood).
букси́р *m* [1] tug(boat); tow; взять на ~ take in tow; **~ный** [14] tug...; **~овать** [7] tow, tug.
була́вка *f* [5; *g/pl.:* -вок] pin; англи́йская ~ safety pin.
була́ный [14] dun (*horse*).
була́т *m* [1] Damascus steel; **~ный** [14] steel...; damask...
бу́лка *f* [5; *g/pl.:* -лок] small loaf; roll.
бу́лоч|ка *f* [5; *g/pl.:* -чек] roll; bun; **~ная** *f* [14] bakery; **~ник** *m* [1] baker.
булы́жник *m* [1] cobblestone.
бульва́р *m* [1] boulevard, avenue; **~ный** [14] boulevard...; **~ный** рома́н *m* dime novel, *Brt.* penny dreadful; **~ная** пре́сса *f* gutter press.
бу́лькать [1] gurgle.
бульо́н *m* [1] broth, bouillon.
бума́|га *f* [5] paper; document; **~жка** *f* [5; *g/pl.:* -жек] slip of paper; P note (*money*); **~жник** *m* [1] wallet; **~жный** [14] **1.** paper...; **2.** cotton...; **~зе́я** *f* [6] fustian.
бунт *m* [1] **1.** revolt, mutiny, insurrection, uprising; **2.** bale, pack; **~а́рь** *m* [4 *e.*] = **~овщи́к**.
бунтов|а́ть [7] rebel, revolt; ⟨вз-⟩ instigate; **~ско́й** [14] rebellious, mutinous; **~щи́к** *m* [1 *e.*] mutineer, rebel.
бура́ *f* [5] borax.
бура́в *m* [1 *e.*] drill, auger; **~ить** [14], ⟨про-⟩ bore, drill.
бура́н *m* [1] snowstorm, blizzard.
бурда́ F *f* [5] wash, wish-wash.
бурдю́к *m* [1 *e.*] wineskin.
буреве́стник *m* [1] (stormy) petrel.
буре́ние *n* [12] drilling, boring.
буржуа́ *m* [*indecl.*] bourgeois; **~зи́я** *f* [7] bourgeoisie; **~зный** [14] bourgeois...
буржу́й *contp.* P *m* [3], **~ка** *f* [5; *g/pl.:* -жу́ек] *s.* буржуа́.
бури́ть [13], ⟨про-⟩ bore.
бу́рка *f* [5; *g/pl.:* -рок] felt, cloak.
бурла́к *m* [1 *e.*] (barge) hauler.
бурли́ть [13] rage; seethe.
бурми́стр *m* [1] steward; mayor.
бу́рный [14; -рен, -рна] stormy, storm...; violent, boisterous.
буру́н *m* [1 *e.*] surf.
бурча́|нье *n* [12] grumbling; rumbling; **~ть** [4 *e.*; -чу́, -чи́шь] mumble; grumble; rumble.
бу́ры *m/pl.* [1] Boers.
бу́рый [14] brown, fulvous; ~ у́голь *m* brown coal, lignite.
бурья́н *m* [1] wild grass (*steppe*).
бу́ря *f* [6] storm, tempest.
бу́сы *f/pl.* [5] *coll.* (glass)beads.
бутафо́рия *f* [7] *thea.* properties *pl.*
бутербро́д (-tɛr-) *m* [1] sandwich.
буто́н *m* [1] bud.
бу́тсы *f/pl.* [5] football boots.
буты́л|ка *f* [5; *g/pl.:* -лок] bottle; **~очка** *f* [5; *g/pl.:* -чек] small bottle; **~ь** *f* [8] large bottle; carboy.
буф *m* [1] (*mst pl.*) puff; рука́в (вздү́тый) **~ом** puffed sleeve.
бу́фер *m* [1; *pl.:* -pá, *etc. e.*] buffer.
буфе́т *m* [1] sideboard; bar, lunch-

room, refreshment room; ~чик *m* [1] barkeeper; ~чица *f* [5] barmaid.
буффо́н *m* [1] buffoon.
бух bounce!, plump!
Бухара́ *f* [5] Bokhara.
Бухаре́ст *m* [1] Bucharest.
буха́нка *f* [5; *g/pl.:* -нок] loaf.
бу́хать [1], *once* ⟨бу́хнуть⟩ plump.
бухга́лтер (bu'ha-) *m* [1] bookkeeper; ∠ия *f* [7] bookkeeping; ~ский [16] bookkeeper('s)..., bookkeeping...
бу́хнуть [21] 1. ⟨раз-⟩ swell; 2. *s.* бу́хать.
бу́хта *f* [5] 1. bay; 2. coil.
бушева́ть [7; бушу́ю, -у́ешь] roar, rage, storm.
бушла́т *m* [1] (sailor's) jacket.
бушпри́т *m* [1] bowsprit.
буя́н *m* [1] brawler, rowdy, ruffian; ~ить [13] brawl, riot, kick up a row.
бы, *short* б, *is used to render subjunctive and conditional patterns:* a) *with the preterite, e.g.* я сказа́л ~, е́сли ~ (я) знал I would say it if I knew it; (*similarly: should, could, may, might*); b) *with the infinitive, e.g.:* всё ~ ему́ знать he would like to know everything; не вам ~ говори́ть you had better be quiet.
быва́лый [14] experienced; former; common; *cf.* быва́ть.
быва́|ть [1] 1. occur, happen; как ни в чём не ~ло as if nothing had happened; он, ~ло, гуля́л he would (*or* used to) go for a walk; бо́ли как не ~ло F the pain had (*or* has) entirely disappeared; 2. ⟨по-⟩ (у Р) be (at), visit, stay (with).
бы́вший [17] former, late, ex-...
бык *m* [1 *e.*] 1. bull; 2. abutment.
були́на *f* [5] Russian epic.
были́нка *f* [5; *g/pl.:* -нок] blade of grass.
бы́ло (*s.* быть) (*after verbs*) already: я уже́ заплати́л ~ де́ньги ... I had already paid the money, (but) ...; almost nearly, was (were) just going to ...; я чуть ~ не сказа́л I was on the point of saying, I nearly said.
был|о́й [14] bygone, former; ~о́е *n* past; ~ь *f* [8] true story *or* ocurrence; past.
быстро|но́гий [16] swift(-footed); ~та́ *f* [5] quickness, swiftness, rapidity; ~хо́дный [14; -ден, -дна] fast.
бы́стрый [14; быстр, -а́, -о] quick, fast, swift.
быт *m* [1; в быту́] way of life, manners *pl.*; ~ие́ *n* [12] existence, being; *Bibl.* Genesis; ∠ность *f* [8] stay; в мою ∠ность в (П) during my stay in, while staying in; ~ово́й [14] of manners, popular, genre; common, everyday.
быть (*3rd p. sg. pr.:* есть, *cf.*; *3rd p. pl.:* † суть; *ft.:* бу́ду, -дешь; будь[те]!; бу́дучи; был, -а́, -о; не́ был, -о, -и) be; (*cf.* бу́дет, быва́ть, бы́ло); ~ (Д) ... will (inevitably) be *or* happen; мне бы́ло (бу́дет) ... (го́да *or* лет) I was (I'll be) ... (years old); как (же) ~? what is to be done?; так и ~! I don't care; будь что бу́дет come what may; будь по-ва́шему have it your own way!; бу́дьте до́бры (любе́зны), ... be so kind as ..., would you please ...
бюва́р *m* [1] writing case.
бюдже́т *m* [1], ~ный [14] budget.
бюллете́нь *m* [4] bulletin; ballot, *Brt.* voting paper; medical certificate.
бюро́ *n* [*indecl.*] office, bureau; спра́вочное ~ inquiry office; information; ~ путеше́ствий travel bureau, *Brt.* tourist(s') office.
бюрокра́т *m* [1] bureaucrat; ~и́зм *m* [1] red tape; ~и́ческий [16] bureaucratic; ~ия *f* [7] bureaucracy.
бюст *m* [1] bust; ~га́льтер (-'haltər) *m* [1] bra(ssière).
бя́зь *f* [8] cheap cotton goods.

В

в, во 1. (В): (*direction*) to, into; for; в окно́ out of (in through) the window; (*time*) in, at, on, within; в сре́ду on Wednesday; в два часа́ at two o'clock; (*measure, price, etc.*) at, of; в день a *or* per day; длино́й в четы́ре ме́тра four meters long; чай в два рубля́ килогра́мм tea at 2 roubles a kilo(gram); в де́сять раз бо́льше ten times as much; (*promotion*) to the rank of; идти́ в солда́ты become a soldier; 2. (П): (*position*) in, at, on; (*time*) in; в конце́ (нача́ле) го́да at the end (beginning) of the year; (*distance*) в пяти́ киломе́трах от (Р) five kilometers from.
в. *abbr.*: век.
Вавило́н *m* [1] Babylon.
ваго́н 🚋 *m* [1] car(riage, *Brt.*); ~-рестора́н *m* dining car; ~е́тка *f* [5; *g/pl.*: -ток] lorry, trolley, truck; ~овожа́тый *m* [14] streetcar (*Brt.* tram) driver.
ва́жн|ичать [1] put on (*or* give o.s.) airs; ~ость *f* [8] importance; conceit; ~ый [14; ва́жен, -жна́, -о, ва́жны́] important, significant; haughty; F не~о rather bad; э́то не~о that doesn't matter *or* is of no importance.
ва́за *f* [5] vase, bowl.
вака́н|сия *f* [7] vacancy; ~тный [14; -тен, -тна] vacant.

вакса *f* [5] (shoe) polish, blacking.
вакцина *f* [5] vaccine.
вал *m* [1; на -ý; *pl. e.*] **1.** rampart; bank; wall; **2.** billow; **3.** ⊕ shaft, axle.
валежник *m* [1] brushwood.
валенок *m* [1; -нка] felt boot.
валерьян|ка F *f* [5], **~овый** [14]: ~овые капли *f/pl.* valerian.
валет *m* [1] (*cards*) knave.
валик *m* [1] **1.** ⊕ roller **2.** bolster.
вал|ить [13; валю, валишь; валенный], ⟨по-, с-⟩ **1.** overturn, tumble (down; *v/i.* -ся), fell; heap (up), dump; **2.** [*3rd p. only*: -ит] flock, throng; снег ~ит it is snowing heavily.
валовой [14] gross, total.
валун *m* [1 *e.*] boulder.
вальдшнеп *m* [1] woodcock.
вальс *m* [1] waltz; **~ировать** [7], ⟨про-⟩ waltz.
вальцевать [7] ⊕ roll.
валют|а *f* [5] (foreign) currency; золотая ~а gold standard; **~ный** [14] currency..., exchange...; ~ный курс *m* rate of exchange.
валять [28], ⟨по-⟩ roll; knead; full; P валяй! go!; ~ дурака idle; play the fool; -ся wallow, loll; lie about (in disorder).
ваниль *f* [8] vanilla.
ванн|а *f* [5] tub; bath; солнечная ~а sun bath; принять ~у take a bath; **~ая** *f* [14] bath(room).
Ванька *m* [5] **1.** *s.* Ваня; **2.** ~-встанька *m* [5] tumbler (*toy*).
Ваня *m* [6] *dim. of* Иван John.
варвар *m* [1] barbarian; **~ский** [16] barbarous; **~ство** *n* [9] barbarity.
Варвара *f* [5] Barbara, Babette.
варежка *f* [5; *g/pl.*: -жек] mitten.
вар|ение *n* [12] = варка; **~еник** *m* [1] (*mst pl.*) boiled pieces of paste enclosing curd *or* fruit; **~ёный** [14] cooked, boiled; **~енье** *n* [10] jam, preserves *pl.*
Варенька *f* [5] *dim. of* Варвара.
вариант *m* [1] variant, version.
варить [13; варю, варишь; варенный], ⟨с-⟩ **1.** cook, boil (*v/i.* **-ся**); brew; **2.** digest.
варка *f* [5] cooking, boiling.
Варшава *f* [5] Warsaw.
варьете *n* (-ˈtɛ) [*indecl.*] vaudeville, *Brt.* variety (*show & theater, -tre*).
варьировать [7] vary.
Вар|я *f* [6] *dim. of* ~вара.
варяг *m* [1] Varangian.
василёк *m* [1; -лька] cornflower.
Василий *m* [3] Basil.
вассал *m* [1] vassal.
Вася [6] *dim. of* Василий.
ват|а *f* [5] absorbent cotton, *Brt.* cotton wool; wadding; на ~е wadded.
ватага *f* [5] gang, band, troop.
ватер|линия (-tɛr-) *f* [7] water line; **~пас** *m* [1] level.
ватный [14] cotton(-wool)...; wadded.
ватрушка *f* [5; *g/pl.*: -шек] curd *or* jam patty.
вафля *f* [6; *g/pl.*: -фель] waffle, wafer.
вахт|а ⚓ *f* [5] watch; стоять на ~е keep watch; **~енный** [14] sailor on duty; **~ер** (*a.* ~ёр) *m* [1] guard, watchman.
ваш *m*, **~а** *f*, **~е** *n*, **~и** *pl.* [25] your; yours; по-~ему in your opinion (*or* language); (пусть будет) по-~ему (have it) your own way, (just) as you like; как по-~ему? what do you think?; *cf.* наш.
Вашингтон *m* [1] Washington.
вая|ние *n* [12] sculpture; **~тель** *m* [4] sculptor; **~ть** [28], ⟨из-⟩ form, cut, model.
вбе|гать [1], ⟨~жать⟩ [4; -гу, -жишь, -гут] run *or* rush in.
вби|вать [1], ⟨~ть⟩ [вобью, вобьёшь; вбей(те)!; вбил; вбитый] drive (*or* hammer) in; ~ть себе в голову take it into one's head; **~рать** [1], ⟨вобрать⟩ [вберу, -рёшь] absorb, imbibe.
вблизи nearby; close (to P).
вброд: переходить ~ ford.
вв. *or* **в. в.** *abbr.*: века.
ввал|ивать [1] ⟨~ить⟩ [13; ввалю, ввалишь; вваленный] throw (in[to]), dump; **-ся** fall *or* tumble in; flock in.
введение *n* [12] introduction.
ввезти *s.* ввозить.
вверг|ать [1], ⟨~нуть⟩ [21] fling *or* cast (into в B); plunge (*v/i.* **-ся**); ~ать в отчаяние drive to despair.
вверять [14], ⟨~ить⟩ entrust, commit, give in charge.
ввёртывать [1], ⟨ввертеть⟩ [11; вверчу, ввертишь], *once* ⟨ввернуть⟩ [20; ввёрнутый] screw in; *fig.* put in (*a word, etc.*).
вверх up(ward[s]); ~ по лестнице upstairs; ~ дном (*or* ногами) upside down; ~ тормашками F headlong; руки ~! hands up!; **~у** above; overhead.
ввести *s.* вводить.
ввиду in view (of P), considering; ~ того, что as, since, seeing that.
ввин|чивать [1], ⟨~тить⟩ [15 *e.*; -нчу, -нтишь] screw in.
ввод|ить [15], ⟨ввести⟩ [25] introduce; bring *or* usher (in); ~ить в курс дела acquaint with an affair; ~ить в строй (*or* действие, эксплуатацию) ⊕ put into operation; **~ный** [14] introductory; ~ное слово *or* предложение *n gr.* parenthesis.
ввоз *m* [1] import(s); importation; **~ить** [15], ⟨ввезти⟩ [24] import; **~ный** [14] import...
вволю (P) F plenty of; to one's heart's content.
ввяз|ываться [1], ⟨~аться⟩ [3] meddle, interfere (with в B); get involved (in).
вглубь inward(s), deep (into).

вглядывать|ся [1], ⟨~éться⟩ [11] (в В) peer (into), look narrowly (at).
вгоня́ть [28], ⟨вогна́ть⟩ [вгоню́, вго́нишь; вогна́л, -á, -о; во́гнанный (во́гнан, -ана)] drive in(to).
вдава́ться [5], ⟨вда́ться⟩ [вда́мся, вда́шься, *etc. s.* дать] jut out; press in; indulge (in в В), plunge *or* go (into). [in.
вда́в|ливать [1], ⟨~и́ть⟩ [14] press
вдал|екé, ~и́ far off, far (from от Р); ~ь into the distance.
вдви|га́ть [1], ⟨~нуть⟩ [20] put *or* push in.
вдво́|е twice (as..., *comp.*: ~е бо́льше twice as much *or* many); *vb.* + ~е *a.* double; ~ём both *or* two (of us, *etc.*, *or* together); ~йнé twice (as much, *etc.*), doubly.
вде|ва́ть [1], ⟨~ть⟩ [вдéну, вдéнешь; вдéтый] (в В) thread.
вдéл|ывать, ⟨~ать⟩ [1] set (in).
вдоба́вок in addition (to); into the bargain, to boot.
вдов|á *f* [5; *pl. st.*] widow; ~éц *m* [1; -вца́] widower. [of.
вдо́воль (Р) F quite enough; plenty
вдо́вый [14 *sh.*] widowed.
вдого́нку after, in pursuit of.
вдоль (Р, по Д) along; lengthwise; ~ и поперёк throughout, far and wide.
вдохнов|éние *n* [12] inspiration; ~ённый [14; -вéнен, -вéнна] inspired; ~ля́ть [28], ⟨~и́ть⟩ [14 *e.*; -влю́, -ви́шь] inspire; **-ся** get inspired (with *or* by Т).
вдрéбезги into smithereens.
вдруг suddenly, all of a sudden.
вду|ва́ть [1], ⟨~ть⟩ [18] blow in.
вду́м|чивый [14 *sh.*] thoughtful; ~ываться, ⟨~аться⟩ [1] (в В) ponder (over), reflect ([up]on), dive (into). [hale; *fig.* inspire (with).
вдыха́ть [1], ⟨вдохну́ть⟩ [20] in-
вегета|риа́нец *m* [1; -нца] vegetarian; ~ти́вный [14] vegetative.
вéд|ать [1] **1.** † know; **2.** (Т) be in charge of, manage; ~éние *n* [12] running, directing; ~éние книг bookkeeping; ~ение *n* [12] knowledge, lore; authority, charge, competence; ~омо known; без моегó ~ома without my knowledge; ~омость *f* [8; *from g/pl. e.*] list, roll; bulletin; ~омство *n* [9] department, administration.
ведро́ *n* [9; *pl.*: вёдра, -дер, -драм] bucket, pail; ~ для му́сора garbage can, *Brt.* dust-bin.
вёдро † *n* [9] serene weather.
веду́щий [17] leading; basic.
ведь indeed, sure(ly); why, well; then; you know!; ~ ужé по́здно it is late, isn't it?
вéдьма *f* [5] witch, hag.
вéер *m* [1; *pl.*: -рá, *etc. e.*] fan.
вéжлив|ость *f* [8] politeness; ~ый [14 *sh.*] polite.
вездé everywhere.
везти́ [24], ⟨по-, с-⟩ *v/t.* drive (be driving, *etc.*), transport; pull; ему́ (не) везёт F he is (un)lucky.
век *m* [1; на веку́; *pl.*: векá, *etc. e.*] **1.** century; age; **2.** life(time); срéдние ~á *pl.* Middle Ages; на моём ~у́ in my life(time); ~ с тобо́й мы не вида́лись we haven't met for ages.
вéко *n* [9; *nom/pl.*: -ки] eyelid.
векової́ [14] secular.
вéксель *m* [4; *pl.*: -ля́, *etc. e.*] bill of exchange, promissory note.
велéть [9; вéленный] (*im*)*pf.*; *pt. pf. only* order, tell (p. s. th. Д/В).
велика́н *m* [1] giant.
вели́к|ий [16; вели́к, -á] great; (too) large *or* big; от ма́ла до ~а everybody, young and old; ~ая пя́тница *f* Good Friday; Пётр ♀ий Peter the Great.
Велико|брита́ния *f* [7] Great Britain; ♀ду́шие *n* [12] magnanimity; ♀ду́шный [14; -шен, -шна] magnanimous, generous; ♀лéпие *n* [12] splendo(u)r, magnificence; ♀лéпный [14; -пен, -пна] magnificent, splendid; ♀ру́с *m* [1], ♀ру́сский [16] (Great) Russian.
велича́|вый [14 *sh.*] sublime, majestic, lofty; ~ть [1] praise, glorify; style.
вели́ч|ественный [14 *sh.*] majestic, grand, stately; ~ество *n* [9] Majesty; ~ие *n* [12] grandeur; ~ина́ *f* [5; *pl. st.*: -чи́ны] size; quantity; celebrity; ~ино́й в *or* с (В) ... big *or* high.
вело|го́нки *f/pl.* [5; *gen.*: -нок] cycle race; ~дро́м *m* [1] cycling ground.
велосипéд *m* [1] bicycle; éздить на ~е cycle; ~и́ст *m* [1] cyclist; ~ный [14] (bi)cycle..., cycling...
вельмо́жа *m* [5] magnate.
вéна *f* [5] **1.** *anat.* vein; **2.** ♀ Vienna.
венгéр|ец *m* [1; -рца] ~ка *f*, [5; *g/pl.*: -рок], ~ский [16] Hungarian.
Вéнгрия *f* [7] Hungary.
венери́ческий [16] venereal.
Венесуэ́ла *f* [5] Venezuela.
венéц *m* [1; -нца́] wreath, garland; crown; halo; идти́ под ~ † marry.
венеци|а́нский [16] Venetian; ′♀я (-′ŋɛ-) *f* [7] Venice.
вéнзель *m* [4; *pl.*: -ля́] monogram.
вéник *m* [1] broom, besom.
вено́к *m* [1; -нкá] wreath, garland.
вентил|и́ровать [7], ⟨про-⟩ ventilate, air; ~я́тор *m* [1] ventilator, fan.
венча́|льный [14] wedding...; ~ние *n* [12] wedding (ceremony); ~ть [1] **1.** ⟨у-⟩ wreathe, crown; **2.** ⟨об-, по-⟩ marry; **-ся** get married (in church).
вéра *f* [5] **1.** faith, belief, trust (in в В); religion; **2.** ♀ Vera.

ве́рба *f* [5] willow.
верблю́|д *m* [1] camel; **~жий** [18]: ~жья шерсть *f* camel's hair.
ве́рбн|ый [14]: ~ое воскресе́нье *n* Palm Sunday.
вербов|а́ть [7], ⟨за-, на-⟩ enlist, recruit; engage, hire; **~ка** *f* [5] enlistment; hire; **~щик** *m* [1] enlister; hirer.
верёв|ка *f* [5; *g/pl.*: -вок] rope; **~очка** *f* [5; *g/pl.*: -чек] string, cord; **~очный** [14] rope...
верени́ца *f* [5] file, chain, line.
ве́реск *m* [1] heather.
веретено́ *n* [9; *pl. st.*: -тёна] spindle.
верещáть [16 *e.*; -щу́, -щи́шь] chirp.
верзи́ла F *m* [5] big (stupid) fellow, spindlelegs.
ве́рить [13], ⟨по-⟩ believe (in в В); believe, trust (*acc.* Д); ~ на́ слово take on trust; -ся (*impers.*) (мне) не ве́рится one (I) can hardly believe (it).
вермише́ль *f* [8] *coll.* vermicelli.
ве́рно *adv.* 1. & 2. *s.* ве́рный 1. & 2.; 3. probably; **~сть** *f* [8] 1. faith (-fulness), fidelity, loyalty; 2. correctness, accuracy.
верну́ть(ся) [20] *pf.*, *s.* возвраща́ть(ся).
ве́рн|ый [14; -рен, -рна́, -о] 1. faithful, true; loyal; 2. right, correct; accurate, exact; 3. safe, sure, reliable; 4. inevitable, certain; **~ée** (сказа́ть) or rather.
ве́ро|вание *n* [12] faith, belief; **~вать** [7] believe (in в В).
вероисповéдание *n* [12] creed.
вероло́м|ный [14; -мен, -мна] perfidious, treacherous; **~ство** *n* [9] perfidy, treachery.
вероотсту́пник *m* [1] apostate.
веротерпи́мость *f* [8] toleration.
вероя́т|ие *n* [12] likelihood; **~ность** *f* [8] probability; по всей ~ности in all probability; **~ный** [14; -тен, -тна] probable, likely.
ве́рсия *f* [7] version.
верста́ *f* [5; *pl. st.*: вёрсты] verst (= *3500 ft.*); **~к** *m* [1 *e.*] workbench; **~ть** [1], ⟨с-⟩ [свёрстанный] *typ.* make up.
ве́рт|ел *m* [1; *pl.*: -ла́] spit; **~е́ть** [11; верчу́, ве́ртишь], ⟨по-⟩ turn; twist; (-ся) 1. turn, revolve; 2. fidget; 3. loaf; 4. make subterfuges; -ся на языке́ be on the tip of one's tongue; **~ика́льный** [14; -лен, -льна] vertical; **~ля́вый** [14 *sh.*] fidgety, restless; **~олёт** *m* [1] helicopter; **~у́н** *m* [1 *e.*] fidget; **~у́шка** [5; *g/pl.*: -шек] light-minded woman.
ве́рующий [17] pious; believer.
верфь *f* [8] dockyard.
верх *m* [1; на -у́; *pl. e.*] 1. top, upper part; 2. right side (*fabric, clothes*); *fig.* 1. summit, apex, pink; 2. upper hand; **~и́** *pl.* 1. heads, leaders; ... в ~а́х summit ...; 2. ♪ high notes; 3. surface; superficial knowledge; **~ний** [15] upper.
верхо́в|ный [14] supreme, high; ~ная власть *f* supreme power; ~ный суд *m* supreme court; **~о́й** [14] riding...; rider, horseman; ~а́я езда́ *f* riding; **~ье** *n* [10; *g/pl.*: -ьев] upper (course).
верхо́м *adv.* astride; on horseback; е́здить ~ ride, go on horseback.
верху́шка *f* [5; *g/pl.*: -шек] top, crest; the highest ranks.
верши́на *f* [5] peak, summit.
верши́ть [16 *e.*; -шу́, -ши́шь; -шённый], ⟨за-, с-⟩ 1. (re)solve, decide; 2. direct (T); 3. accomplish.
вершо́к *m* [1; -шка́] vershok (†, = *4.45 cm.* = *1.75 in.*).
вес *m* [1] weight; на ~ by weight; уде́льный ~ *phys.* specific gravity; по́льзоваться больши́м **~ом** enjoy great credit; **~ом** в (В) weighing...
вес|ели́ть [13], ⟨раз-⟩ amuse, divert (-ся o. s., enjoy o. s.); **~ёлость** *f* [8] gaiety, mirth; **~ёлый** [14; ве́сел, -а́, -о] gay, merry, cheerful; как **~ело**! it's such fun!; ему́ **~ело** he enjoys himself, is of good cheer; **~е́лье** *n* [10] merriment, merrymaking, fun; **~ельча́к** *m* [1 *e.*] merry fellow.
весе́нний [15] spring...
ве́с|ить [15] *v/i.* weigh; **~кий** [16; ве́сок, -ска] weighty.
весло́ *n* [9; *pl.*: вёсла, -сел] oar.
весн|а́ *f* [5; *pl.*: вёсны, вёсен] spring (in [the] T); **~у́шка** *f* [5; *g/pl.*: -шек] freckle.
весов|о́й [14] 1. weight...; balance-...; 2. sold by weight; **~щи́к** *m* [1 *e.*] weigher.
вести́ [25], ⟨по-⟩ 1. (be) lead(ing, *etc.*), conduct, guide; 2. carry on; 3. keep; 4. drive; ~ (своё) нача́ло spring (from от Р); ~ себя́ behave (o.s.); **~сь** be conducted *or* carried on; так уж у нас ведётся that's a custom among us.
вестибю́ль *m* [4] entrance hall.
Вест-'Индия *f* [7] West Indies.
ве́ст|ник *m* [1] messenger; bulletin; **~ово́й** ⚔ *m* [14] orderly; **~ь** *f* [8; *from g/pl. e.*] 1. news, message; 2. gossip, rumo(u)r.
весы́ *m/pl.* [1] scales, balance.
весь *m*, вся *f*, всё *n*, *pl.*: все [31] 1. *adj.* all, the whole; full, life (*size*; at в В); 2. *su. n* all over; everything, *pl. a.* everybody; лу́чше всего́ (всех) best of all, the best; при всём том *or* со всем тем for all that; во всём ми́ре all over the world; по всей стране́ throughout the country; всего́ хоро́шего! good luck!; во всю F *s.* си́ла; 3. всё *adv.* always, all the time; only, just; всё

(ещё) не not yet; всё бо́льше (и бо́льше) more and more; всё же nevertheless, yet.
весьма́ very, extremely; ~ веро́ятно most probably.
ветв|и́стый [14 *sh.*] branchy; **~ь** *f* [8; *from g/pl. e.*] branch.
ве́тер *m* [1; -тра] wind; встре́чный ~ contrary *or* head wind; попу́тный ~ fair wind; броса́ть де́ньги (слова́) на ~ waste money (words); держа́ть нос по ве́тру be a timeserver.
ветерина́р *m* [1], **~ный** [14]: **~ный** врач *m* veterinarian.
ветеро́|к [1; -рка́], **~чек** [1; -чка] *m* light wind, breeze, breath.
ве́тка *f* [5; *g/pl.*: -ток] branch(let), twig; 🚂 branch line.
ве́то *n* [*indecl.*] veto; наложи́ть ~ veto; **~шь** *f* [8] rags, tatters *pl.*
ве́тр|еный [14 *sh.*] windy (*a. fig.* = flippant); **~яно́й** [14] wind...; **~яна́я** ме́льница *f* windmill; **~яный** [14]: **~яная** о́спа *f* chicken pox.
ве́тх|ий [16; ветх, -á, -о; *comp.*: ве́тше] old, dilapidated; worn-out, shabby; decrepit; **~ость** *f* [8] decay, dilapidation; приходи́ть в **~ость** fall into decay.
ветчина́ *f* [5] ham.
ветша́ть [1], ⟨об-⟩ decay, dilapidate, weaken.
ве́ха *f* [5] landmark; ⚓ spar buoy.
ве́чер *m* [1; *pl.*: -pá, *etc. e.*] **1.** evening; **2.** evening party; soiree; **~ом** in the evening; сего́дня **~ом** tonight; вчера́ **~ом** last night; по́д ~ toward(s) the evening; **~е́ть** [8; *impers.*] decline (*of the day*); **~и́нка** *f* [5; *g/pl.*: -нок] = ве́чер **2.**; **~ко́м** F = **~ом**; **~ний** [15] evening..., night...; **~ня** *f* [6; *g/pl.*: -рен] vespers *pl.*, evensong; **~я** *f* [6]: та́йная **~я** *or* **~я** госпо́дня the Lord's Supper.
ве́чн|ость *f* [8] eternity; (це́лую) **~ость** F for ages; **~ый** [14; -чен, -чна] eternal, everlasting; perpetual.
ве́ша|лка *f* [5; *g/pl.*: -лок] hanger, tab; peg, rack; cloakroom; **~ть** [1], **1.** ⟨пове́сить⟩ [15] hang (up); **-ся** hang o. s.; **2.** ⟨взве́сить⟩ [15] weigh.
вещево́й [14]: ~ мешо́к *m* knapsack.
вещ|е́ственный [14] corporeal, real, material, substantial; **~ество́** *n* [9] matter, substance; **~и́ца** *f* [8] knickknack; piece; **~ь** *f* [8; *from g/pl. e.*] thing; object; work, piece, play; *pl.* belongings; baggage, *Brt.* luggage.
ве́я|лка *f* [5; *g/pl.*: -лок] winnowing machine; **~ние** *n* [12] waft; 🌾 winnowing; *fig.* trend; influence; **~ть** [27] **1.** *v/i.* breathe; spread; **2.** ⟨про-⟩ *v/t.* winnow.
вжи|ва́ться [1], ⟨**~ться**⟩ [-ву́сь, *etc. s.* жить] accustom o.s. (to в B).
взад back(ward[s]); ~ и вперёд back and forth, to and fro; up and down.
взаи́мн|ость *f* [8] reciprocity; **~ый** [14; -мен, -мна] mutual, reciprocal; спаси́бо, **~о** F thanks, the same to you.
взаимо|де́йствие *n* [12] interaction; coöperation; **~де́йствовать** [7] interact; cooperate; **~отноше́ние** *n* [12] mutual (*or* inter-, cor)relation; **~по́мощь** *f* [8] mutual aid; **~понима́ние** *n* [12] mutual understanding.
взаймы́ on credit *or* loan; брать ~ borrow (from у, от P); дава́ть ~ lend.
вза|ме́н (P) instead of, in exchange for; **~перти́** locked up, under lock and key; **~пра́вду** P = впра́вду.
взба́л|мошный F [14; -шен, -шна] extravagant; **~тывать**, ⟨взболта́ть⟩ [1] shake *or* stir up.
взбе|га́ть [1], ⟨**~жа́ть**⟩ [4; взбегу́, -жи́шь, -гу́т] run up.
взбива́ть [1], ⟨взбить⟩ [взобью́, -бьёшь; взбил, -а; взби́тый] fluff; whip, froth.
взбира́ться [1], ⟨взобра́ться⟩ [взберу́сь, -рёшься; взобра́лся, -ла́сь, -ло́сь] climb (s. th. на B).
взболта́ть *s.* взба́лтывать.
взбудора́живать [1] = будора́жить.
взбух|а́ть [1], ⟨**~нуть**⟩ [21] swell.
взва́ливать [1], ⟨взвали́ть⟩ [13; взвалю́, -а́лишь; -а́ленный] load, charge (with на B).
взвести́ *s.* взводи́ть.
взве́|шивать [1], ⟨**~сить**⟩ [15] weigh; **-ся** weigh o. s.
взви|ва́ть [1], ⟨**~ть**⟩ [взовью́, -вьёшь, *etc. s.* вить] whirl up; **-ся** soar up, rise.
взви́зг|ивать [1], ⟨**~нуть**⟩ [20] squeak, scream.
взви́н|чивать [1], ⟨**~ти́ть**⟩ [15 *e.*; -нчу́, -нти́шь; -и́нченный] excite; raise (*prices*).
взвить *s.* взвива́ть.
взвод *m* [1] platoon.
взводи́ть [15], ⟨взвести́⟩ [25] lead up; lift; impute (s. th. to a p. B/на B); ~ куро́к cock (*firearm*).
взволно́|ванный [14 *sh.*] excited; uneasy; **~ва́ть(ся)** *s.* волнова́ть.
взгля|д *m* [1] look; glance; gaze; stare; *fig.* view, opinion; на ~д in appearance, by sight; на мой ~д in my opinion; на пе́рвый ~д at first sight; с пе́рвого **~да** on the face of it; at once; **~дывать** [1], *once* ⟨**~ну́ть**⟩ [19] (на B) (have a) look, glance (at).
взгромо|жда́ть [1], ⟨**~зди́ть**⟩ [15 *e.*; -зжу́, -зди́шь; -мождённый] load, pile up; **-ся** clamber, perch (on на B).
вздёр|гивать [1], ⟨**~нуть**⟩ [20] jerk up; **~нутый** нос *m* pug nose.

вздор *m* [1] nonsense; **∠ный** [14; -рен, -рна] foolish, absurd; F quarrelsome.
вздорожá|ние *n* [12] rise of price(s); **~ть** *s.* дорожáть.
вздох *m* [1] sigh; испусти́ть послéдний ~ give up the ghost; **~нýть** *s.* вздыхáть.
вздрáгивать [1], *once* ⟨вздрóгнуть⟩ [20] start, wince; shudder.
вздремнýть F [20] *pf.* nap.
взду|вáть [1], ⟨~ть⟩ [18] **1.** whirl up; **2.** *v/i.* **-ся** inflate; **3.** F thrash; **∠тие** *n* [12] swelling.
вздýма|ть [1] *pf.* conceive the idea, take it into one's head; **-ся:** емý ~лось = он ~л; как ~ется at one's will.
взды|мáть [1] raise, whirl up; **~хáть** [1], *once* ⟨вздохнýть⟩ [20] sigh; ~хáть (по, о П) long (for); *pf.* F draw breath, breathe again.
взи|мáть [1] levy, raise (from с Р); **~рáть** [1] (на В) look (at); не взирáя на without regard to, notwithstanding.
взлáмывать [1], ⟨взломáть⟩ [1] break *or* force open.
взлез|áть [1], ⟨~ть⟩ [24 *st.*] (на В) climb up.
взлёт *m* [1] ascent, rise.
взлет|áть [1], ⟨~éть⟩ [11] fly up, soar.
взлом *m* [1] breaking in; **~áть** *s.* взлáмывать; **∠щик** *m* [1] burglar.
взмах *m* [1] stroke; sweep; **∠ивать** [1], *once* ⟨~нýть⟩ [20] swing.
взмет|áть [3], *once* ⟨~нýть⟩ [20] whirl *or* throw up; flap.
взмóрье *n* [10] seashore, seaside.
взнос *m* [1] payment; fee.
взнýзд|ывать [1], ⟨~áть⟩ bridle.
взобрáться *s.* взбирáться.
взойти́ *s.* восходи́ть & всходи́ть.
взор *m* [1] look; gaze; eyes *pl.*
взорвáть *s.* взрывáть.
взрóслый [14] grown-up, adult.
взрыв *m* [1] explosion; detonation; *fig.* outburst; **~áтель** *m* [4] fuse; **~áть** [1], ⟨взорвáть⟩ [-вý, -вёшь; взóрванный] blow up; *fig.* enrage; **-ся** explode; **~нóй** [14], **∠чатый** [14] explosive (*su.*: ∠чатое вещество).
взрыхля́ть [28] *s.* рыхли́ть.
взъе|зжáть [1] ⟨∠хать⟩ [взъéду, -дешь; взъезжáй(те)!] ride *or* drive up; **~рóшивать** [1], ⟨~рóшить⟩ [16 *st.*] dishevel, tousle; **-ся** bristle up.
взывáть [1], ⟨воззвáть⟩ [-зовý, -зовёшь; -звáл, -á, -о] cry, call; invoke; appeal (to к Д).
взыск|áние *n* [12] **1.** levy, collecting; **2.** punishment, reprimand: **~áтельный** [14; -лен, -льна] exacting, exigent; **∠ивать** [1], ⟨~áть⟩ [3] (с Р) **1.** levy, exact; collect; recover (from); **2.** call to account; impose a penalty (on); не взыщи́(те)! no offence!
взя́т|ие *n* [12] seizure, capture; **~ка** *f* [5; *g/pl.*: -ток] **1.** bribe; дать ~ку bribe, P grease; **2.** trick (*cards*); **~очник** *m* [1] bribe taker, corrupt official; **~очничество** *n* [9] bribery; **~ь** *s.* брать.
вибр|áция *f* [7] vibration; **~и́ровать** [7] vibrate.
вид *m* [1] **1.** look(s), appearance, air; **2.** sight, view; **3.** kind, sort; species; **4.** *gr.* aspect; в ∠е (Р) in the form of, as, by way of; при ∠е at the sight of; на ~ý (у Р) in sight; visible (to); с (*or* по) ∠у by sight; judging from one's appearance; ни под каки́м ∠ом on no account; у негó хорóший ~ he looks well; дéлать *or* покáзывать ~ pretend; (не) терять *or* выпускáть из ∠у lose sight of (keep in view); стáвить на ~ reproach (a p. with Д/В); **∠ы** *pl.* prospects (for на В).
видáть F [1], ⟨у-; по-⟩ егó давнó не ~ I *or* we haven't seen him for a long time; **-ся** (*iter.*) meet, see (o. a.; a p. с Т).
видéние *n* [12] vision.
ви́деть [11 *st.*], ⟨у-⟩ see; catch sight of; ~ во сне dream (of В); ви́дишь (-ите) ли? you see?; **-ся** = видáться (*but a. once*).
ви́дим|о apparently, evidently; ~о-не~о F lots of, immense quantity; **~ость** *f* [8] **1.** visibility; **2.** appearance; **~ый 1.** [14 *sh.*] visible; **2.** [14] apparent.
видн|éться [8] appear, be seen; **∠о** it can be seen; it appears; apparently; (мне) ничегó не ∠о I don't *or* can't see anything; **∠ый 1.** [14; -ден, -днá, -о] visible; **2.** [14] outstanding, eminent, prominent; F stately, portly.
видоизмен|éние *n* [12] variation; variety; **~я́ть** [1], ⟨~и́ть⟩ [13] alter, change.
видоискáтель *m* [4] (view) finder.
ви́за *f* [5] visa.
визант|и́ец *m* [1; -и́йца], **~и́йка** *f* [5; *g/pl.*: и́ек], **~и́йский** [16] Byzantine; **~и́я** *f* [7] Byzantium.
виз|г *m* [1] scream, shriek; yelp; **~гли́вый** [14 *sh.*] shrill, squeaky; **~жáть** [4 *e.*; -жý, -жи́шь], ⟨за-⟩ shriek; yelp.
визи́ровать [7] (*im*)*pf.* visa.
визи́т *m* [1] visit, call; **~ный** [14]: ~ная кáрточка *f* calling card.
ви́ка *f* [5] vetch.
ви́л|ка *f* [5; *g/pl.*: -лок] **1.** fork; **2.** (штéпсельная) ~ка ⚡ plug; **~ы** *f/pl.* [5] pitchfork.
виля́ть [28], ⟨за-⟩, *once* ⟨вильнýть⟩ [20] wag (one's tail хвостóм); *fig.* prevaricate, shuffle.
вин|á *f* [5] **1.** guilt; fault; **2.** reason; вменя́ть в ~ý impute (to Д); свáливать ~ý lay the blame (on на В); э́то не по моéй ~é it's not my fault.

винегрéт *m* [1] vinaigrette (salad).
винит|ельный [14] *gr.* accusative (*case*); **~ь** [13] blame (for за В), accuse (of в П).
вин|ный [14] wine...; **~ный кáмень** *m* tartar; **~ная ягода** *f* (dried) fig; **~ó** *n* [9; *pl. st.*] wine; F vodka.
виновáт|ый [14 *sh.*] guilty (of в П); **~!** sorry!, excuse me!; (I beg your) pardon!; вы в э́том (не) **~ы** it's (not) your fault; я **~** пéред вáми I must apologize to you, (*a.* кругóм **~**) it's all my fault.
винóв|ник *m* [1] **1.** culprit; **2.** originator, author; **~ный** [14; -вен, -вна] guilty (of в П).
виногрáд *m* [1] **1.** vine; **2.** *coll.* grapes *pl.*; сбор **~а** vintage; **~арство** *n* [9] winegrowing; **~арь** *m* [4] winegrower; **~ник** *m* [1] vineyard; **~ный** [14] (of) grape(s).
вино|дéлие *n* [12] winemaking; **~кýренный** [14]: **~кýренный завóд** *m* distillery; **~торгóвец** [1; -вца] wine merchant.
винт *m* [1 *e.*] screw; **~ик** *m* [1] small screw; у негó **~ика** не хватáет F he has a screw loose; **~óвка** *f* [5; *g/pl.*: -вок] rifle; **~овóй** [14] screw...; spiral; **~овáя лéстница** *f* spiral (winding) stairs.
виньéтка *f* [5; *g/pl.*: -ток] vignette.
виолончéль *f* [8] (violon)cello.
вирáж *m* **1.** [1 *e.*] bend, curve; **2.** [1] *phot.* toning solution.
виртуóз *m* [1] virtuoso.
ви́селица *f* [5] gallows, gibbet.
висéть [11] hang.
ви́ски *n* [*indecl.*] whisk(e)y.
вискóза *f* [5] viscose.
Ви́сла *f* [5] Vistula.
ви́смут *m* [1] bismuth.
ви́снуть F [21], ⟨по-⟩ *v/i.* hang, be suspended.
висóк *m* [1; -скá] *anat.* temple.
високóсный [14]: **~** год *m* leap year.
вися́чий [17] hanging; suspension-...; **~** замóк *m* padlock.
витами́н *m* [1] vitamin.
вит|áть [1] **1.** stay, linger; **2.** soar; **~невáтый** [14] affected, bombastic.
витóк *m* [1; -ткá] coil.
витри́на *f* [5] shopwindow; show-case.
вить [вью, вьёшь; вéй(те)!; вил, -á, -о; ви́тый (вит, -á, -о)], ⟨с-⟩ [совью, совьёшь] wind, twist; build (*nests*); **-ся 1.** wind; spin, whirl; **2.** twine, creep; curl; **3.** hover.
ви́тязь *m* [4] hero.
вихóр *m* [1; -хрá] forelock.
вихрь *m* [4] whirlwind.
ви́це-... (*in compds.*) vice-...
вишн|ёвый [14] cherry...; **~я** *f* [6; *g/pl.:* -шен] cherry.
вишь P look, there's; you see.
вкáпывать [1], ⟨вкопáть⟩ dig in; drive in; *fig* как вкóпанный stock-still, transfixed.
вкáт|ывать [1], ⟨**~и́ть**⟩ [15] roll in, wheel in.
вклад *m* [1] deposit; *fig.* contribution (to в В); **~ка** [5; *g/pl.:* -док] insert; **~чик** *m* [1] depositor; **~ывать** [1], ⟨вложи́ть⟩ [16] put in, insert, enclose; invest; deposit.
вклé|ивать [1], ⟨**~ить**⟩ [13] glue *or* paste in; **~йка** *f* [5; *g/pl.:* -éек] gluing in; sheet, *etc.*, glued in.
вкли́ни|вать(ся) [1], ⟨'**~ть(ся)**⟩ [13; *a. st.*] (be) wedge(d) in.
включ|áть [1], ⟨**~и́ть**⟩ [16 *e.*; -чý, -чи́шь; -чённый] include; insert; ⚡ switch *or* turn on; **-ся** join (s. th. в В); **~áя** including; **~éние** *n* [12] inclusion; insertion; ⚡ switching on; **~и́тельно** included.
вкол|áчивать [1], ⟨**~оти́ть**⟩ [15] drive *or* hammer in.
вконéц F completely, altogether.
вкопáть *s.* вкáпывать.
вкорен|я́ться [28], ⟨**~и́ться**⟩ [13] take root; **~и́вшийся** established, (deep-)rooted.
вкось askew, aslant, obliquely; вкривь и **~** pell-mell; amiss.
ВКП(б) = Всесою́зная Коммунисти́ческая пáртия (большевикóв) C.P.S.U.(B.) = Communist Party of the Soviet Union (Bolsheviks); (*since 1952*: КПСС, *cf.*).
вкрá|дчивый [14 *sh.*] insinuating, ingratiating; **~дываться** [1], ⟨**~сться**⟩ [25] creep *or* steal in; *fig.* insinuate o.s.
вкрáтце briefly, in a few words.
вкрутýю: яйцó **~** hard-boiled egg.
вкус *m* [1] **1.** taste; flavo(u)r; **2.** style; прия́тный на **~** savo(u)ry; прия́тно на **~** = **~но**; быть *or* прийти́сь по **~у** be to one's taste, relish (*or* like) s. th.; имéть **~** (P) taste (of); **~ный** [14; -сен, -снá, -о] tasty; (э́то) **~но** it tastes well *or* nice.
вку|шáть [1], ⟨**~си́ть**⟩ [15; вкушённый] **1.** taste; **2.** enjoy, experience.
влáга *f* [5] moisture.
владé|лец *m* [1; -льца] owner, proprietor, possessor; **~ние** *n* [12] possession (of T); **~тель** *m* [4] **1.** owner; **2.** ruler; **~ть** [8], ⟨за-, о-⟩ (T) own, possess; rule, govern; master, manage; **~ть собóй** control o.s.
Влади́мир *m* [1] Vladimir.
влады́|ка *m* [5] **1.** lord, sovereign; **2.** archbishop; **~чество** *n* [9] rule, sway.
влáжн|ость *f* [8] humidity; **~ый** [14; -жен, -жнá, -о] humid, damp.
влáмываться [1], ⟨вломи́ться⟩ [14] break in.
влáст|вовать [7] rule, dominate; **~ели́н** *m* [1] sovereign; **~и́тель** *m* [4] master, ruler; **~ный** [14; -тен, -тна] imperious, commanding; в э́том я не **~ен** I have no power

over it; **~ь** *f* [8; *from g/pl. e.*] authority, power; rule, regime; control; *pl.* authorities.

влачи́ть [16 *e.*; -чу́, -чи́шь] drag; eke out.

вле́во (to the) left.

влез|а́ть [1], ⟨**~ть**⟩ [24 *st.*] climb *or* get in(to); climb up.

влет|а́ть [1], ⟨**~е́ть**⟩ [11] fly in; rush in.

влеч|е́ние *n* [12] inclination; **~ь** [26], ⟨по-, у-⟩ drag, pull; *fig.* attract, draw; **~ь** за собо́й involve, entail.

вли|ва́ть [1], ⟨**~ть**⟩ [волью́, -льёшь; вле́й(те)!; влил, -а́, -о; вли́тый (-та́, -о)] pour in; **-ся** flow *or* fall in; **~я́ние** *n* [12] influence; **~я́тельный** [14; -лен, -льна] influential; **~я́ть** [28], ⟨по-⟩ (have) influence.

ВЛКСМ (Всесою́зный Ле́нинский Коммунисти́ческий Сою́з Молодёжи) Leninist Young Communist League of the Soviet Union.

вложи́ть *s.* вкла́дывать.

вломи́ться *s.* вла́мываться.

влюб|лённость *f* [8] amorousness; **~ля́ться** [28], ⟨**~и́ться**⟩ [14] fall in love (with в В); **~лённый** enamo(u)red; lover; **~чивый** [14 *sh.*] amorous.

вмен|я́емый ⚖ [14 *sh.*] responsible, accountable; **~я́ть** [28], ⟨**~и́ть**⟩ [13] consider (as в В), impute; **~я́ть** (себе́) в обя́занность pledge s. o. (o. s.) (to *inf.*).

вме́сте together, along with; **~** с тем at the same time.

вмести́|мость *f* [8] capacity; **~тельный** [14; -лен, -льна] capacious, spacious; **~ть** *s.* вмеща́ть.

вме́сто (Р) instead, in place (of); as.

вмеш|а́тельство *n* [9] interference, intervention; ⚕ operation; **~ивать** [1], ⟨**~а́ть**⟩ [1] (В/в В) mingle (with); involve (in); **-ся** interfere, intervene, meddle (with в В).

вме|ща́ть [1], ⟨**~сти́ть**⟩ [15 *e.*; -ещу́, -ести́шь; -ещённый] **1.** put, place; **2.** hold, contain, accomodate; **-ся** find room; hold.

вмиг in an instant, in no time.

внаём *or* **внаймы́**: отда́ть (сдать) ~ rent, *Brt.* let; взять ~ rent, hire.

внача́ле at first, at the beginning.

вне (Р) out of, outside; beyond; быть ~ себя́ be beside o. s.

внебра́чный [14] illegitimate.

внедр|е́ние *n* [12] introduction; **~я́ть** [28], ⟨**~и́ть**⟩ [13] inculcate; introduce; **-ся** take root.

внеза́пный [14; -пен, -пна] sudden, unexpected.

внекла́ссный [14] out-of-class.

внеочередно́й [14] extra(ordinary).

внес|е́ние *n* [12] entry; **~ти́** *s.* вноси́ть.

внешко́льный [14] nonschool.

вне́шн|ий [15] outward, external; foreign; **~ость** *f* [8] appearance; exterior.

вниз down(ward[s]); **~у́** **1.** (Р) beneath, below; **2.** down(stairs).

вник|а́ть [1], ⟨**~нуть**⟩ [19] (в В) penetrate (into), fathom.

внима́|ние *n* [12] attention; care; приня́ть во ~ние take into consideration; принима́я во ~ние in view of, with regard to; оста́вить без ~ния disregard; **~тельность** *f* [8] attentiveness; **~тельный** [14; -лен, -льна] attentive; **~ть** [1], ⟨внять⟩ [*inf. & pt. only*; внял, -а́, -о] (Д) hear *or* listen (to); follow, watch; comply with.

вничью́: сыгра́ть ~ draw (*game*).

вновь **1.** again; **2.** newly.

вноси́ть [15], ⟨внести́⟩ [24 -с-: -су́, -сёшь; внёс, внесла́] carry *or* bring in; enter, include; pay (in); contribute; make (*correction*).

внук *m* [1] grandson; *cf.* внуча́та.

вну́тренн|ий [15] inner, inside, internal, interior; inland...; home...; **~ость** *f* [8] interior; (*esp. pl.*) internal organs, entrails.

внутр|и́ (Р) in(side); within; **~ь** (Р) in(to), inward(s), inside.

внуч|а́та *m/f pl.* [2] grandchildren; **~ка** *f* [5; *g/pl.*: -чек] granddaughter.

внуш|а́ть [1], ⟨**~и́ть**⟩ [16 *e.*; -шу́, -ши́шь; -шённый] (Д/В) suggest; inspire (a p. with); inculcate (upon); **~е́ние** *n* [12] suggestion; infusion; reprimand; **~и́тельный** [14; -лен, -льна] imposing, impressive; **~и́ть** *s.* **~а́ть**.

вня́т|ный [14; -тен, -тна] distinct; intelligible; **~ь** *s.* внима́ть.

вобра́ть *s.* вбира́ть.

вовл|ека́ть [1], ⟨**~е́чь**⟩ [26] drag in; *fig.* involve.

во́время in *or* on time, timely.

во́все quite; ~ не(т) not at all.

вовсю́ F with all one's might.

во-вторы́х second(ly).

вогна́ть *s.* вгоня́ть.

во́гнутый [14 *sh.*] concave.

вод|а́ *f* [5; *ac/sg.*: во́ду; *pl.*: во́ды, вод, во́дам] water; на ~е́ и на су́ше by sea and by land; в му́тной ~е́ ры́бу лови́ть fish in troubled waters; вы́йти сухи́м из ~ы́ come off clear; толо́чь ~у (в сту́пе) beat the air.

водвор|я́ть [28], ⟨**~и́ть**⟩ [13] settle; install; (re)establish.

водеви́ль *m* [4] musical comedy.

води́тель *m* [4] driver.

вод|и́ть [15], ⟨по-⟩ **1.** lead, conduct, guide; **2.** drive; **3.** move (Т); **4.** breed; ~и́ть дру́жбу be on friendly terms; **-ся** be (found), live; be customary *or* the custom; (у Р, за Т) have; (с Т) associate

(with); это за ним ⁓ится F that's in his way, to be sure!
во́дка *f* [5; *g/pl.:* -док] vodka (*kind of whisky*); дать на во́дку tip.
водо|боя́знь *f* [8] hydrophobia; **⁓во́з** *m* [1] water carter; **⁓воро́т** *m* [1] whirlpool, eddy; **⁓ём** *m* [1] reservoir; **⁓измеще́ние** ⚓ *n* [12] displacement, tonnage; **⁓ка́чка** *f* [5; *g/pl.:* -чек] waterworks.
водо|ла́з *m* [1] diver; **⁓лече́ние** *n* [12] hydropathy, water cure; **⁓напо́рный** [14]: ⁓напо́рная ба́шня *f* water tower; **⁓непроница́емый** [14 *sh.*] watertight; **⁓но́с** *m* [1] water carrier; **⁓па́д** *m* [1] waterfall; **⁓по́й** *m* [3] watering place; watering (*of animals*); **⁓прово́д** *m* [1] water pipe; **⁓разде́л** *m* [1] divide, *Brt.* watershed; **⁓ро́д** *m* [1] hydrogen; **⁓ро́дный** [14]: ⁓ро́дная бо́мба *f* hydrogen bomb; **'⁓росль** *f* [8] alga, seaweed; **⁓снабже́ние** *n* [12] water supply; **⁓сто́к** *m* [1] drain(age), drainpipe; **⁓сто́чный** [14]: ⁓сто́чная труба́ *f* gutter; **⁓храни́лище** *n* [11] reservoir.
водру|жа́ть [1], ⟨⁓зи́ть⟩ [15 *e.*; -ужу́, -узи́шь; -ужённый] set up; hoist.
вод|яни́стый [14 *sh.*] watery; **⁓я́нка** *f* [5] dropsy; **⁓яно́й** [14] water...
воева́ть [14], wage *or* carry on war, be at war.
воеди́но together.
военача́льник *m* [1] commander.
воениз|а́ция *f* [7] militarization; **⁓и́ровать** [7] (*im*)*pf.* militarize.
военно|-возду́шный [14]: ⁓-возду́шные си́лы *f/pl.* air force; **⁓-морско́й** [14]: ⁓-морско́й флот *m* navy; **⁓пле́нный** [14] prisoner of war; **⁓-полево́й** [14]: ⁓-полево́й суд *m* court-martial; **⁓слу́жащий** [17] military man, soldier.
вое́нн|ый [14] **1.** military, war...; **2.** military man, soldier; ⁓ый врач *m* medical officer; ⁓ый кора́бль *m* man-of-war, warship; ⁓ое положе́ние *n* martial law (under на П); поступи́ть на ⁓ую слу́жбу enlist, join; ⁓ые де́йствия *n/pl.* hostilities.
вож|а́к [1 *e.*] guide; leader; **⁓а́тый** [14] leader, guide; streetcar (*Brt.* tram) driver; **⁓дь** *m* [4 *e.*] chief (-tain); leader; **⁓жи** *f/pl.* [8; *from g/pl. e.*] reins.
воз *m* [1; на -у́; *pl. e.*] cart(load).
возбу|ди́мый [14 *sh.*] excitable; **⁓ди́тель** *m* [4] exciter; **⁓жда́ть** [1], ⟨⁓ди́ть⟩ [15 *e.*; -ужу́, -уди́шь] excite, stir up; arouse; incite; raise; bring, present; **⁓жда́ющий** [17] stimulating; ⁓жда́ющее сре́дство *n* stimulant; **⁓жде́ние** *n* [12] excitement; **⁓ждённый** [14] excited.
возвели́ч|ивать [1], ⟨⁓ить⟩ [16] exalt, praise, glorify.
возвести́ *s.* возводи́ть.
возве|ща́ть [1], ⟨⁓сти́ть⟩ [15 *e.*; -ещу́, -ести́шь; -ещённый] (В/Д *or* о П/Д) announce.
возв|оди́ть [15], ⟨⁓ести́⟩ [25] (в *or* на В) lead up; raise, elevate; erect; make.
возвра́|т *m* [1] **1.** = ⁓ще́ние **1.** & **2.**; **2.** ⚕ relapse; **⁓ти́ть(ся)** *s.* ⁓ща́ть (-ся); **⁓тный** [14] back...; relapsing; *gr.* reflexive; **⁓ща́ть** [1], ⟨⁓ти́ть⟩ [15 *e.*; -ащу́, -ати́шь; -ащённый] return; give back; restore, reimburse; recover; **-ся** return, come back (from из *or* с Р); revert (to к Д); **⁓ще́ние** *n* [12] **1.** return; **2.** restitution.
возв|ыша́ть [1], ⟨⁓ы́сить⟩ [15] raise, elevate; **-ся** rise; tower (over над Т); **⁓ыше́ние** *n* [12] rise; elevation; **⁓ы́шенность** *f* [8] **1.** sublimity, loftiness; **2.** hill (range); **⁓ы́шенный** [14] elevated, lofty.
возгл|авля́ть [28], ⟨⁓а́вить⟩ [14] (be at the) head.
во́згла|с *m* [1] exclamation, (out-) cry; **⁓ша́ть** [1], ⟨⁓си́ть⟩ [15 *e.*; -ашу́, -аси́шь; -ашённый] proclaim.
возд|ава́ть [5], ⟨⁓а́ть⟩ [-да́м, -да́шь, *etc. s.* дава́ть] reward; show, do; ⁓а́ть до́лжное do justice (to Д).
воздвиг|а́ть [1], ⟨⁓нуть⟩ [21] erect, construct, raise.
возде́йств|ие *n* [12] influence, impact; **⁓овать** [7] (*im*)*pf.* (на В) influence; act upon, affect.
возде́л|ывать, ⟨⁓ать⟩ [1] till.
воздержа́ние *n* [12] abstinence; abstention.
возде́рж|анный [14 *sh.*] *s.* ⁓ный; **⁓иваться** [1], ⟨⁓а́ться⟩ [4] abstain (from от Р); при двух ⁓а́вшихся *pol.* with two abstentions; **⁓ный** [14; -жен, -жна] abstemious, temperate.
во́здух *m* [1] air; на (откры́том *or* све́жем) ⁓е in the open air, outdoors; **⁓опла́вание** *n* [12] aeronautics.
возду́ш|ный **1.** [14] air...; ⁓ная трево́га *f* air-raid warning; ⁓ные за́мки *m/pl.* castles in the air; **2.** [14; -шен, -шна] airy.
воззва́|ние *n* [12] appeal; proclamation; **⁓ть** *s.* взыва́ть.
вози́ть [15] drive, transport; **-ся** (с Т) busy o.s. (with), mess (around with); dawdle; fidget; romp, frolic.
возл|ага́ть [1], ⟨⁓ожи́ть⟩ [16] (на В) lay (on); entrust (with); ⁓ага́ть наде́жды на (В) rest one's hopes upon.
во́зле (Р) by, near, beside.
возложи́ть *s.* возлага́ть.
возлю́блен|ный [14] beloved; *m* lover; ⁓ная *f* mistress, sweetheart.
возме́здие *n* [12] requital.
возме|ща́ть [1], ⟨⁓сти́ть⟩ [15 *e.*; -ещу́, -ести́шь; -ещённый] com-

pensate, recompense; **～щéние** *n* [12] compensation, indemnification.
возмóжн|о it is possible; possibly; óчень ～о very likely; **～ость** *f* [8] possibility; chance; по (мéре) ～ости as ... (far) as possible; **～ый** [14; -жен, -жна] possible; сдéлать всё ～ое do one's utmost.
возмужáлый [14] mature, virile.
возму|тúтельный [14; -лен, -льна] revolting, shoking; **～щáть**, ⟨**～тúть**⟩ [15 *e.*; -щý, -утúшь] revolt; **-ся** be shocked *or* indignant (at T); **～щéние** *n* [12] indignation; revolt; **～щённый** [14] indignant.
вознагра|ждáть [1], ⟨**～дúть**⟩ [15 *e.*; -ажý, -адúшь; -аждённый] reward, recompense, indemnify; **～ждéние** *n* [12] reward, recompense.
вознамéри|ваться [1], ⟨**～ться**⟩ [13] intend, decide.
вознес|éние *n* [12] ascension; **～тú(сь)** *s.* возносúть(ся).
возник|áть [1], ⟨**∠нуть**⟩ [21] arise, originate, emerge; **～новéние** *n* [12] rise, origin.
возн|осúть [15], ⟨**～естú**⟩ [24 -с-: -сý, -сёшь; -нёс, -неслá; -несённый] raise, elevate; exalt; **-ся**, ⟨**-сь**⟩ **1.** rise; **2.** become haughty.
вознá *f* [6] **1.** fuss, bustle, romp; **2.** trouble, bother.
возобнов|лéние *n* [12] renewal; resumption; **～лáть** [28], ⟨**～úть**⟩ [14 *e.*; -влю, -вúшь; -влённый] renew; resume.
возра|жáть [1], ⟨**～зúть**⟩ [15 *e.*; -ажý, -азúшь] **1.** object (to прóтив P); **2.** return, retort (to на B); (я) не ～жáю I don't mind; **～жéние** *n* [12] objection; rejoinder.
вóзраст *m* [1] age (at в П); **～áние** *n* [12] growth, increase; **～áть** [1], ⟨**～ú**⟩ [24 -ст-: -растý; -рóс, -лá; -рóсший] grow up; increase, rise.
возро|ждáть [1], ⟨**～дúть**⟩ [15 *e.*; -ожý, -одúшь; -ождённый] revive, regenerate (*v/i.:* **-ся**); **～ждéние** *n* [12] rebirth, revival; эпóха **Ѳ**ждéния Renaissance.
вóзчик *m* [1] wag(g)oner, carter.
вóин *m* [1] warrior, soldier; **～ский** [16] military; ～ская обязанность († повúнность) *f* conscription; **∠ственный** [14] martial, bellicose.
воúстину truly, really.
вой *m* [3] howl(ing), wail(ing).
вóйло|к *m* [1] **～чный** [14] felt.
войн|á *f* [5; *pl. st.*] war (at на П); warfare; идтú на ～ý take the field; поджигáтель ～ы warmonger; вторáя мировáя ～á World War II.
вóйск|о *n* [9; *pl. e.*] host; army; *pl.* troops, (*land, etc.*) forces.
войтú *s.* входúть.
вокзáл *m* [1] railroad (*Brt.* railway) station, depot.
вокрýг (P) (a)round; вертéться ～ да óколо F beat about the bush.
вол *m* [1 *e.*] ox.
Вóлга *f* [5] Volga.
волдырь *m* [4 *e.*] blister, swelling.
волейбóл *m* [1] volleyball.
вóлей-невóлей willy-nilly.
вóлжский [16] (on the) Volga...
волк *m* [1; *from g/pl. e.*] wolf; смотрéть ∠ом F scowl.
волн|á *f* [5; *pl. st., from dat. a. e.*] wave; ⚡ длúнные, срéдние, корóткие ∠ы long, medium, short waves; **～éние** *n* [12] agitation, excitement, unrest; *pl.* troubles, riots; **～úстый** [14 *sh.*] wavy, undulating; **～овáть** [7], ⟨вз-⟩ (**-ся** be) agitate(d), excite(d); worry; **～ýющий** [17] exciting, thrilling.
волóвий [18] ox...
Волóдя *m* [6] *dim. of* Владúмир.
волокúт|а F [5] **1.** *f* red tape; a lot of fuss and trouble; **2.** *m* lady-killer, ladies' man; **～ство** *n* [9] flirtation.
волокн|úстый [14 *sh.*] fibrous; **～ó** *n* [9; *pl.*: -óкна, -óкон, *etc. st.*] fiber, *Brt.* fibre.
волонтёр *m* [1] volunteer.
вóлос *m* [1; *g/pl.*: -лóс; *from dat. e.*] (*a. pl.*) hair; **～áтый** [14 *sh.*] hairy; **～óк** *m* [1; -скá] (small) hair; ⚡ filament; быть на ～óк (*or* на ～кé) от смéрти F be on the verge (within a hair's breadth *or* ace) of death; висéть (*or* держáться) на ～кé hang by *or* on a thread.
вóлость *f* [8; *from g/pl. e.*] district.
волосянóй [14] hair...
волочúть [16], ⟨по-⟩ drag, pull, draw; **-ся** drag o.s., crawl along; F (за T) run after, court.
волхв *m* [1 *e.*] magician, wizard.
вóлчий [18] wolfish; wolf('s)...
волчóк *m* [1; -чкá] top (*toy*).
волчóнок *m* [2] wolf cub.
волшéб|ник *m* [1] magician; **～ница** *f* [5] sorceress; **～ный** [14] magic, fairy...; [-бен, -бна] *fig.* enchanting; **～ствó** *n* [9] magic, witchery.
волынка *f* [5 *g/pl.*; -нок] bagpipe.
вольно|дýмец *m* [1; -мца] freethinker; **～слýшатель** *m* [4] auditor, irregular student.
вóльн|ость *f* [8] liberty; freedom; **～ый** [14; -лен, -льнá, -о] free, easy, unrestricted; ⚔ ～о! at ease!
вольт *m* [1] volt.
вольфрáм *m* [1] wolframite.
вóл|я *f* [6] **1.** will; сúла ～и will power; **2.** liberty, freedom; ～я вáша (just) as you like; по дóброй ～е of one's own will; отпустúть на ～ю set free; дать ～ю give free rein.
вон 1. F there; ～ там over there; **2.** ～! get out!; пошёл ～! out *or* away (with you)!; вы́гнать ～ turn out; ～ (онó) что! F you don't say!; oh, that's it!
вонз|áть [1], ⟨**～úть**⟩ [15 *e.*; -нжý,

-зи́шь; -зённый] thrust, plunge, transfix.

вон|ь *f* [8] stench, stink; **~ю́чий** [17 *sh.*] stinking; **~ю́чка** *f* [5; *g/pl.*: -чек] skunk; **~я́ть** [28] stink (of T).

вообра|жа́емый [14 *sh.*] imaginary, supposed; **~жа́ть** [1], ⟨**~зи́ть**⟩ [15 *e.*; -ажу́, -ази́шь; -ажённый] (*a.* ~жа́ть себе́) imagine, fancy; ~жа́ть себя́ imagine o.s. (s.b. T); ~жа́ть о себе́ be conceited; **~же́ние** *n* [12] imagination; fancy; **~зи́мый** [14 *sh.*] imaginable.

вообще́ generally, in general; at all.

воодушев|ле́ние *n* [12] enthusiasm; **~ля́ть** [28], ⟨**~и́ть**⟩ [14 *e.*; -влю́, -ви́шь; -влённый] (**-ся** feel) inspire(d by T).

вооруж|а́ть [1], ⟨**~и́ть**⟩ [16 *e.*; -жу́, -жи́шь; -жённый] **1.** arm, equip (with T); **2.** stir up (against про́тив P); **~е́ние** *n* [12] armament, equipment.

воо́чию with one's own eyes.

во-пе́рвых first(ly).

вопи́|ть [14 *e.*; -плю́, -пи́шь], ⟨**за-**⟩ cry out, bawl; lament, wail; **~ю́щий** [17] crying, flagrant.

вопло|ща́ть [1], ⟨**~ти́ть**⟩ [15 *e.*; -ощу́, -оти́шь; -ощённый] embody, personify; ~щённый *a.* incarnate; **~ще́ние** *n* [12] embodiment, incarnation.

вопль *m* [4] outcry, clamo(u)r; wail.

вопреки́ (Д) contrary to; in spite of.

вопро́с *m* [1] question; под ~ом questionable, doubtful; ~ не в э́том that's not the question; спо́рный ~ point at issue; что за ~! of course!; **~и́тельный** [14] interrogative; ~и́тельный знак *m* question mark.

вор *m* [1; *from g/pl. e.*] thief.

ворва́ться *s.* врыва́ться.

ворко|ва́ть [7], ⟨за-⟩ coo; **~тня́** F *f* [6] grumble.

вороб|е́й *m* [3 *e.*; -бья́] sparrow; ста́рый (*or* стре́ляный) ~е́й F cunning fellow; **~ьи́ный** [14] sparrow('s)...

ворова́|ть [7], ⟨F с-⟩ steal; **~ка** *f* [5; *g/pl.*: -вок] (female) thief; **~ско́й** [16] thievish; thieves'...; **~ство́** *n* [9] theft, larceny.

ворожи́ть [16 *e.*; -жу́, -жи́шь], ⟨по-⟩ tell fortunes.

во́рон *m* [1] raven; **~а** *f* [5] crow; воро́н счита́ть F stand gaping about.

воро́нка *f* [5; *g/pl.*: -нок] **1.** funnel; **2.** crater.

вороно́й [14] black; *su. m* black horse.

во́рот *m* [1] **1.** collar; **2.** windlass; **~а** *n/pl.* [9] gate; **~и́ть** [15] **1.** (*pf.*) F *cf.* возвраща́ть; **2.** (*impf.*) P move, roll; turn off, round; **3.** *s.* воро́чать **2.**; **~ни́к** *m* [1 *e.*] collar; **~ничо́к** *m* [1; -чка] (small) collar.

во́рох *m* [1; *pl.*: -ха́, *etc. e.*] pile, heap.

воро́|чать [1] **1.** *s.* ~ти́ть **2.**; **2.** F manage, boss (T); **-ся** toss; turn; stir; **~ши́ть** [16 *e.*; -шу́, -ши́шь; -шённый] turn (over).

ворч|а́ние *n* [12] grumbling, growl; **~а́ть** [4 *e.*; -чу́, -чи́шь], ⟨за-, п(р)о-⟩ grumble, growl; **~ли́вый** [14 *sh.*] grumbling, surly; **~у́н** F *m* [1 *e.*], **~у́нья** *f* [6] grumbler.

восвоя́си F home.

восемна́дца|тый [14] eighteenth; **~ть** [35] eighteen; *s.* пять, пя́тый.

во́семь [35; восьми́, *instr.* восемью́] eight; *cf.* пять & пя́тый; **~десят** [35; восьми́десяти] eighty; **~со́т** [36; восьмисо́т] eight hundred; **~ю** eight times.

воск *m* [1] wax.

воскл|ица́ние *n* [12] exclamation. **~ица́тельный** [14] exclamatory; ~ица́тельный знак *m* exclamation mark *or* point; **~ица́ть** [1], ⟨**~и́кнуть**⟩ [20] exclaim.

восково́й [14] wax(en)...

воскр|еса́ть [1], ⟨**~е́снуть**⟩ [21] rise (from из P); recover; Христо́с ~е́с(е)! Christ has arisen! (*Easter greeting*); (*reply*:) вои́стину ~е́с(е)! (He has) truly arisen!; **~есе́ние** *n* [12] Resurrection; **~есе́нье** *n* [10] Sunday (on: в В, *pl.* по Д); **~еша́ть** [1], ⟨**~еси́ть**⟩ [15 *e.*; -ешу́, -еси́шь; -ешённый] resuscitate, revive.

воспал|е́ние *n* [12] inflammation; ~е́ние лёгких (по́чек) pneumonia (nephritis); **~ённый** [14 *sh.*] inflamed; **~и́тельный** [14] inflammatory; **~я́ть** [28], ⟨**~и́ть**⟩ [13] inflame (*v/i.* **-ся**).

воспе|ва́ть [1], ⟨**~ть**⟩ [-пою́, -поёшь; -пе́тый] sing of, praise.

воспит|а́ние *n* [12] education, upbringing; **~анник** *m* [1], **~анница** *f* [5] foster child; pupil; **~анный** [14 *sh.*] well-bred; пло́хо ~анный ill-bred; **~а́тель** *m* [4] educator; (private) tutor; **~а́тельный** [14] educational, pedagogic(al); **~ывать** [1], ⟨**~а́ть**⟩ bring up; educate.

воспламен|я́ть [28], ⟨**~и́ть**⟩ [13] inflame (*v/i.* **-ся**).

восполн|я́ть [28], ⟨**~ить**⟩ [13] fill (up); make up (for).

воспо́льзоваться *s.* по́льзоваться.

воспомина́ние *n* [12] remembrance, recollection, reminiscence; *pl. a.* memoirs.

воспре|ща́ть [1], ⟨**~ти́ть**⟩ [15 *e.*; -ещу́, -ети́шь; -ещённый] prohibit, forbid; вход ~щён! no entrance!; кури́ть ~ща́ется! no smoking!; **~ще́ние** *n* [12] interdiction, prohibition.

воспри|и́мчивый [14 *sh.*] sensitive; susceptible (to к Д); **~нима́ть** [1], ⟨**~ня́ть**⟩ [-приму́, -и́мешь; -и́нял, -а́, -о; -и́нятый] take (up); conceive; **~я́тие** *n* [12] perception.

воспроизв|еде́ние *n* [12] reproduction; ~**оди́ть** [15], ⟨~**ести́**⟩ [25] reproduce.
воспря́нуть [20] *pf.* rise, jump up; ~ ду́хом cheer up.
воссоедин|е́ние *n* [12] reun(ification); ~**я́ть** [28], ⟨~**и́ть**⟩ [13] reunite.
восста|ва́ть [5], ⟨~**ть**⟩ [-ста́ну, -ста́нешь] (a)rise; revolt.
восстан|а́вливать [1], ⟨~**ови́ть**⟩ [14] **1.** reconstruct, restore; **2.** stir up, dispose. ~**ие** *n* [12] insurrection, revolt; ~**ови́ть** *s.* ~а́вливать; ~**овле́ние** *n* [12] reconstruction, restoration.
восто́к *m* [1] east; ♀ the East, Orient; Бли́жний (Да́льний) ♀ the Near (Far) East; на ~ (to[ward] the) east, eastward(s); на ~е in the east; с ~а from the east; к ~у от (P) (to the) east of.
восто́р|г *m* [1] delight, rapture; я в ~ге I am delighted (with от P); приводи́ть (приходи́ть) в ~г = ~**га́ть(ся)** [1] *impf.* (be) delight(ed) (with T); ~**женный** [14 *sh.*] enthusiastic, exalted.
восто́чный [14] east(ern, -erly); oriental.
востре́бова|ние *n* [12]: до ~ния poste restante; ~**ть** [7] *pf.* call for.
восхвал|е́ние *n* [12] praise, eulogy; ~**я́ть** [28], ⟨~**и́ть**⟩ [13; -алю́, -а́лишь] praise, extol.
восхи|ти́тельный [14; -лен,-льна] delightful; ~**ща́ть** [1], ⟨~**ти́ть**⟩ [15 *e.*; -ищу́, -ити́шь; -ищённый] delight, transport; -ся (T) be delighted (with), admire; ~**ще́ние** *n* [12] admiration, delight; приводи́ть (приходи́ть) в ~ще́ние *s.* ~ща́ть(ся).
восхо́|д *m* [1], ~**жде́ние** *n* [12] rise; ascent; ~д со́лнца sunrise; ~**ди́ть** [15], ⟨взойти́⟩ [взойду́, -дёшь; взошёл, -шла́; взоше́дший] rise, ascend.
восше́ствие *n* [12] ascent; ~ на престо́л accession to the throne.
восьм|ёрка *f* [5; *g/pl.*: -рок] eight (*cf.* двойка); ~**еро** [37] eight (*cf.* дво́е).
восьми|деся́тый [14] eightieth; *cf.* пят(идеся́т)ый; ~**ле́тний** [14] of eight, aged 8; ~**со́тый** [14] eight hundredth; ~**часово́й** [14] eight-hour...
восьм|о́й [14] eighth; *cf.* пя́тый; ~**у́шка** *f* [5] eighth of lb.; octavo.
вот here (is); there; now; well; that's ...; ~ и всё F that's all; ~ (оно́) как *or* что! you don't say!, is that so?; ~ те(бе) ра́з *or* на́! there you are!; a pretty business this!; ~ како́й ... such a ...; ~ челове́к! what a man!; ~-~! yes, indeed; ~-~ every *or* (at) any moment.
воткну́ть *s.* втыка́ть.
во́тум *m* [1] vote.
во́тчина *f* [5] patrimony (*estate*).
воцар|я́ться [28], ⟨~**и́ться**⟩ [13] **1.** accede to the throne; **2.** set in; be restored.
вошь *f* [8; вши; во́шью] louse.
вощи́ть [16 *e.*], ⟨на-⟩ wax.
вою́ющий [17] belligerent.
впа|да́ть [1], ⟨~**сть**⟩ [25; впал, -а] (в В) fall (flow, run) in(to); ~**де́ние** *n* [12] flowing into; mouth, confluence; ~**дина** *f* [5] cavity, socket; ~**лый** [14] hollow, sunken; ~**сть** *s.* [~да́ть.
впервы́е for the first time.
вперего́нки́ F *s.* наперего́нки́.
вперёд forward, ahead (of P), on (-ward); in future; in advance, beforehand; *s. a.* зад.
впереди́ in front, ahead (of P) before.
впереме́жку F alternately.
впер|я́ть [28], ⟨~**и́ть**⟩ [13] fix (one's eyes on взор в В).
впечатл|е́ние *n* [12] impression; ~**и́тельный** [14; -лен, льна] sensitive.
впи|ва́ть [1], ⟨~**ть**⟩ [вопью́, -пьёшь; впил, -а́, -о] suck in, imbibe; -ся (в В) cling to; seize; stick; fix. [insert.
впи́с|ывать [1], ⟨~**а́ть**⟩ [3] enter,
впи́т|ывать [1], ⟨~**а́ть**⟩ soak up *or* in; absorb, imbibe; ~**ь** *s.* впива́ть.
впи́х|ивать [1], *once* ⟨~**нуть**⟩ [20] push *or* squeeze in(to) (в В).
вплавь by swimming.
вплe|та́ть [1], ⟨~**сти́**⟩ [25 -т-: вплету́, -тёшь] interlace, braid.
вплот|ну́ю (к Д) (quite) close(ly) by, (right) up to; *fig.* F seriously; ~**ь** (к Д) (right) up to; even (till).
вполго́лоса in a low voice.
вполз|а́ть [1], ⟨~**ти́**⟩ [24] creep *or* crawl in(to), up.
вполне́ quite, fully, entirely.
впопа́д F to the point, relevantly.
впопыха́х *s.* второпя́х.
впо́ру: быть ~ fit.
впосле́дствии afterward(s), later.
впотьма́х in the dark.
впра́вду F really, indeed.
вправ|ля́ть [28], ⟨~**ить**⟩ [14] set.
впра́ве: быть ~ have the right.
впра́во (to the) right.
впредь henceforth, in future.
впро́голодь starv(el)ing.
впрок **1.** for future use; **2.** to a p.'s benefit; э́то ему́ ~ не пойдёт he won't profit by it.
впро́чем by the way; however.
впры́г|ивать [1], *once* ⟨~**нуть**⟩ [20] jump in(to) *or* on; (в, на В).
впры́с|кивание *n* [12] injection; ~**кивать** [1], *once* ⟨~**нуть**⟩ [20] inject.
впря|га́ть [1], ⟨~**чь**⟩ [26 г/ж; *cf.* напря́чь] harness, put to (в В).
впус|к *m* [1] admission; ~**ка́ть** [1], ⟨~**ти́ть**⟩ [15] let in, admit.
впусту́ю F in vain, to no purpose.
впу́т|ывать [1], ⟨~**ать**⟩ entangle,

involve (in в В); **-ся** become entangled.
впя́тер|о five times (*cf.* вдвóе); **~óм** five (together).
враг *m* [1 *e.*] enemy; † devil.
враж|дá *f* [5] enmity; **~дéбность** *f* [8] animosity; **~дéбный** [14; -бен, -бна] hostile; **~довáть** [7] be at enmity (with с Т); **∠еский** [16], **∠ий** [18] (the) enemy('s)...
вразбрóд F separately, scatteringly.
вразрéз: идтú ~ be contrary (to с Т).
вразум|úтельный [14; -лен, -льна] intelligible, clear; **~ля́ть** [1], ⟨**~úть**⟩ [13] bring to reason; instruct, make wise.
врá|ль F *m* [4 *e.*] liar; tattler; **~ньё** *n* [12] lies, fibs *pl.*, idle talk.
врас|плóх unawares, by surprise; **~сыпнýю:** брóситься ~сыпнýю disperse.
враст|áть [1], ⟨**~ú**⟩ [24 -ст-: -стý; врос, -лá] grow in(to); settle *or* subside.
вратáрь *m* [4 *e.*] goalkeeper.
врать F [вру, врёшь; врал, -á, -о], ⟨со-⟩ [сóвранный], lie; make a mistake; be inaccurate; tell (tales).
врач *m* [1 *e.*] doctor, physician; **~éбный** [14] medical.
вращ|áть [1] (В *or* Т) turn, revolve, rotate (*v/i.* **-ся**; -ся в П associate with); **~áющийся** revolving, rotatory; **~éние** *n* [12] rotation.
вред *m* [1 *e.*] harm, damage; detriment; **~úтель** *m* [4] ✓ pest; saboteur; **~úтельство** *n* [9] sabotage; **~úть** [15 *e.*; -ежý, -едúшь], ⟨по-⟩ (do) harm, (cause) damage (to Д); **∠ный** [14; -ден, -днá, -о] harmful, injurious (to Д *or* для Р).
врез|áть [1], ⟨**∠ать**⟩ [3] (в В) cut in(to); lay *or* put in(to); **-ся** run in(to); project into; impress (on).
врéмен|ный [14] temporary, transient, provisional; **~щúк** *m* [1 *e.*] favo(u)rite, minion.
врéм|я *n* [13] time; *gr.* tense; weather; ~я гóда season; во ~я (Р) during; в настоя́щее ~я at (the) present (moment); от ~ени до ~ени, по ~енáм, ~енáми from time to time, (every) now and then, sometimes; в скóром ~ени soon; в то (же) ~я at that (the same) time; в то ~я как whereas; за послéднее ~я lately, recently; на ~я for a (certain) time, temporarily; in (*the long*) run; со ~енем in the course of time; тем ~енем meanwhile; скóлько ~ени? how long?; what's the time?; хорошó провестú ~я have a good time; **~ясчислéние** *n* [12] chronology; **~я(пре)провождéние** *n* [12] pastime.
врóвень even, abreast (with с Т).
врóде like; such as; kind of.
врождённый [14 *sh.*] innate.

врóз(н)ь separately, apart.
врун F *m* [1 *e.*], **∠ья** F *f* [6] lier.
вруч|áть [1], ⟨**~úть**⟩ [16] hand over; entrust.
вры|вáть [1], ⟨**~ть**⟩ [22] dig in; **-ся**, ⟨ворвáться⟩ [-вýсь, -вёшься; -вáлся, -лáсь] rush in(to); enter (by force).
вряд: ~ ли hardly, scarcely.
всáдни|к *m* [1] horseman; **~ца** *f* [5] horsewoman.
всá|живать [1], ⟨**~дúть**⟩ [15] thrust *or* drive in(to), hit; **~сывать** [1], ⟨всосáть⟩ [-сý, -сёшь] suck in *or* up, imbibe.
всё, все *s.* весь.
все|вéдущий [17] omniscient; **~возмóжный** [14] of all kinds *or* sorts.
всегдá always; **~шний** [15] constant, habitual.
всегó (-'vɔ) altogether, in all; sum total; ~ (тóлько, лишь, -нáвсего) only, merely; прéжде ~ above all.
всел|éнная *f* [14] universe, world; **~я́ть** [28], ⟨**~úть**⟩ [13] settle, move in(to) (*v/i.* **-ся**); *fig.* inspire.
все|мéрный every (*or* all) ... possible; **~мéрно** in every possible way; **~мúрный** [14] world..., universal; **~могýщий** [17 *sh.*] = **~сúльный**; **~нарóдный** [14; -ден, -дна] national, nation-wide; *adv.:* ~нарóдно in public; **∠нощная** *f* [14] vespers *pl.*; **~óбщий** [17] universal, general; **~объéмлющий** [17 *sh.*] universal; **~россúйский** [16] All-Russian.
всерьёз F in earnest, seriously.
все|сúльный [14; -лен, -льна] omnipotent, almighty; **~сою́зный** [14] All-Union, ... of the U.S.S.R.; **~сторóнний** [15] all-round.
всё-таки nevertheless, (but) still.
всеуслы́шание: во ~ in public.
всецéло entirely, wholly.
вскá|кивать [1], ⟨вскочúть⟩ [16] jump *or* leap (up/on на В); start (from с Р); F rise *or* swell; **~пывать**, ⟨вскопáть⟩ [1] dig up.
вскарáбк|иваться, ⟨**~аться**⟩ [1] (на В) climb (up).
вскáрмливать [1], ⟨вскормúть⟩ [14] raise, rear *or* bring up.
вскачь at full gallop.
вскип|áть [1], ⟨**~éть**⟩ [10 *e.*; -плю́, -пúшь] boil (up); *fig.* fly into a passion.
вскló(кó)|чивать [1], ⟨**~чить**⟩ [16] tousle; ~ченные *or* ~чившиеся вóлосы *m/pl.* dishevel(l)ed hair.
всколы́х|ивать [1], ⟨**~áть**⟩ [3 *st.* & 1], *once* ⟨**~нýть**⟩ [20] stir up, rouse.
вскользь in passing, cursorily.
вскопáть *s.* вскáпывать.
вскóре soon, before long.
вскормúть *s.* вскáрмливать.
вскочúть *s.* вскáкивать.
вскрú|кивать [1], ⟨**~чáть**⟩ [4 *e.*

-чу́, -чи́шь], *once* ⟨~кнуть⟩ [20] cry out, scream.

вскружи́ть [16; -жу́, -у́жи́шь] *pf.*; ~ (Д) го́лову turn a p.'s head.

вскры|ва́ть [1], ⟨~ть⟩ [22] **1.** open; reveal; **2.** dissect; **-ся 1.** open; be disclosed; **2.** break (up); **∠тие** *n* [12] **1.** opening; disclosure; **2.** dissection, autopsy; **3.** breaking up.

вспасть F to one's heart's content.

вслед (за Т; Д) (right) after, behind, following; **∠ствие** (Р) in consequence of, owing to; ∠ствие э́того consequently.

вслепу́ю F blindly, at random.

вслух aloud.

вслу́ш|иваться [1], ⟨~аться⟩ (в В) listen attentively (to).

всма́триваться [1], ⟨всмотре́ться⟩ [9; -отрю́сь, -о́тришься] (в В) peer, look narrowly (at).

всмя́тку: яйцо́ ~ soft-boiled egg.

всо́|вывать [1], ⟨всу́нуть⟩ [20] put, slip (into в В); **~са́ть** *s.* вса́сывать.

вспа́|хивать [1], ⟨~ха́ть⟩ [3] plow (*Brt.* plough) *or* turn up; **~шка** *f* [5] tillage.

всплес|к [1] splash; **∠кивать** [1], ⟨~ну́ть⟩ [20] splash; ~ну́ть рука́ми throw up one's arms.

всплы|ва́ть [1], ⟨~ть⟩ [23] rise to the surface, emerge.

всполоши́ть F [16 *e.*; -шу́, -ши́шь; -шённый] *pf.* startle (*v/i.* **-ся**).

вспом|ина́ть [1], ⟨∠нить⟩ [13] (В *or* о П) remember, recall; (Д + **-ся** = И + *vb.*); **~ога́тельный** [14] auxiliary; **~яну́ть** Р [19] = ∠нить.

вспорхну́ть [20] *pf.* fly up.

вспры́г|ивать [1], *once* ⟨~нуть⟩ [20] jump *or* spring (up/on на В).

вспры́с|кивать [1], ⟨~нуть⟩ [20] sprinkle; wet; inject.

вспу́г|ивать [1], *once* ⟨~ну́ть⟩ [20] start, frighten away.

вспух|а́ть [1], ⟨∠нуть⟩ [21] swell.

вспыл|и́ть F [13] *pf.* get angry; **∠ьчивость** *f* [8] irascibility; **∠ьчивый** [14 *sh.*] quick-tempered.

вспы́|хивать [1], ⟨~хнуть⟩ [20] **1.** flare up, flash; blush; **2.** burst into a rage; break out; **~шка** *f* [5; *g/pl.*: -шек] flare, flash, outburst, outbreak.

вста|ва́ть [5], ⟨~ть⟩ [вста́ну, -нешь] stand up; get up, rise (from с Р); arise; **∠вка** *f* [5; *g/pl.*: -вок] setting in, insertion, inset; **~вля́ть** [28], ⟨∠вить⟩ [14] set *or* put in, insert; **~вно́й** [14] (to be) put in; ~вны́е зу́бы *m/pl.* false teeth.

встрепену́ться [20] *pf.* start, shudder, shake up.

встрёпк|а Р *f* [5] reprimand; зада́ть ~у (Д) Р bowl out, blow up (a p).

встре́|тить(ся) *s.* ~ча́ть(ся); **~ча** *f* [5] meeting, encounter; reception; тёплая ~ча warm welcome; **~ча́ть** [1], ⟨~тить⟩ [15 *st.*] **1.** meet (*v/t.*, with В), encounter; come across; **2.** meet, receive, welcome; ~ча́ть Но́вый год celebrate the New Year; **-ся 1.** meet (*v/i.*, o. a., with с Т); **2.** (*impers.*) occur, happen; there are (were); **~чный** [14] counter..., (coming from the) opposite (direction), (s. b. *or* s. th.) on one's way; пе́рвый ~чный the first comer.

встря́|ска *f* [5; *g/pl.:* -сок] **1.** F shock; **2.** Р = встрёпка; **~хивать** [1], *once* ⟨~хну́ть⟩ [20] shake (up); stir (up); (**-ся** *v/i.*, o. s.).

вступ|а́ть [1], ⟨~и́ть⟩ [14] (в В) enter, join; set one's foot, step (into); begin, enter *or* come into, assume; ~и́ть в брак contract marriage; ~и́ть на трон accede to the throne; **-ся** (за В) intercede (for), protect; take a p.'s side; **~и́тельный** [14] introductory; opening; entrance...; **~ле́ние** *n* [12] entry, entrance; accession; beginning; introduction.

всу́|нуть *s.* всо́вывать; **~чивать** F [1], ⟨~чи́ть⟩ [16] foist (s.th. on В/Д).

всхлип *m* [1], **∠ывание** *n* [12] sob(bing); **∠ывать** [1], *once* ⟨∠нуть⟩ [20 *st.*] sob.

всход|и́ть [15], ⟨взойти́⟩ [взойду́, -дёшь; взошёл, -шла́; взоше́дший; *g. pt.*: взойдя́] **1.** go *or* climb ([up]on на В), ascend, rise; come up, sprout; **2.** = входи́ть; **∠ы** *m/pl.* [1] standing *or* young crops.

всхрапну́ть F [20] *pf.* nap.

всып|а́ть [1], ⟨∠ать⟩ [2 *st.*] pour *or* put (into в В); Р thrash (a p. Д).

всю́ду everywhere, all over.

вся́|кий [16] **1.** any, every; any-, everybody (*or* -one); **2.** = **~ческий** [16] all kinds *or* sorts of, sundry; every possible; ~чески in every way; ~чески стара́ться take great pains; **~чина** F *f* [5]: ~кая ~чина whatnot(s), hodgepodge.

вта́|йне in secret; **~лкивать** [1], ⟨втолкну́ть⟩ [20] push *or* shove in(to); **~птывать** [1], ⟨втопта́ть⟩ [3] tramp(le) in(to); **~скивать** [1], ⟨~щи́ть⟩ [16] pull *or* drag in, up.

вте|ка́ть [1], ⟨~чь⟩ [26] flow in(to).

втере́ть *s.* втира́ть.

вти|ра́ть [1], ⟨втере́ть⟩ [12; вотру́, -рёшь; втёр] rub in; worm; ~ра́ть очки́ (Д) throw dust in (p.'s) eyes; **-ся** F worm into; **∠скивать** [1], ⟨∠снуть⟩ [20] press *or* squeeze in.

втихомо́лку F on the quiet.

втолкну́ть *s.* вта́лкивать.

втоптать *s.* вта́птывать.

втор|га́ться [1], ⟨∠гнуться⟩ [21] (в В) intrude, invade, penetrate; meddle (with); **~же́ние** *n* [12] invasion, incursion; **∠ить** [13] ♪ sing (*or* play) the second part; echo, repeat; **~и́чный** [14] second, repeated; secondary; ~и́чно once more,

for the second time; **∠ник** *m* [1] Tuesday (on: во В, *pl.*: по Д); **~óй** [14] second; upper; из **~ы́х** рук second hand; *cf.* пéрвый & пя́тый; **~окýрсник** *m* [1] sophomore.
второпя́х in a hurry, being in a great haste, hastily.
второстепéнный [14; -éнен, -éнна] secondary, minor.
в-трéтьих third(ly).
втри́дорога F very dearly.
втрó|е three times (as ..., *comp.*; *cf.* вдвóе); *vb.* + **~е** *a.* treble; **~ём** three (of us, *etc.*, *or* together); **~йнé** three times (as much, *etc.*), trebly.
втуз *m* [1] (вы́сшее техни́ческое учéбное заведéние *n*) technical college, institute of technology.
втýлка *f* [5; *g/pl.*: -лок] plug.
втýне in vain; without attention.
втыкáть [1], ⟨воткнýть⟩ [20] put *or* stick in(to).
втя́|гивать [1], ⟨**~**нýть⟩ [19] draw *or* pull in(to), on; envolve, engage; **-ся** (в В) fall in; enter; (become) engage(d) in; get used (to).
вуáль *f* [8] veil.
вуз *m* [1] (вы́сшее учéбное заведéние *n*) university, college; **∠овец** *m* [1; -вца] college student.
вулкáн *m* [1] volcano; **~и́ческий** [16] volcanic.
вульгáрный [14; -рен, -рна] vulgar.
вход *m* [1] entrance; плáта за **~** entrance *or* admission fee.
входи́ть [15], ⟨войти́⟩ [войдý, -дёшь; вошёл, -шлá; вошéдший; *g. pt.*: войдя́] (в В) enter, go, come *or* get in(to); go in(to), have room *or* hold; run into (*debts, etc.*); penetrate into; be included in; **~** во вкус (Р) take a fancy to; **~** в довéрие (ми́лость) к (Д) gain a p.'s confidence (favo[u]r); **~** в положéние (Р) appreciate a p.'s position; **~** в привы́чку *or* быт (послóвицу) become a habit (proverbial); **~** в (состáв [Р]) form part (of), belong (to).
входнóй [14] entrance..., admission...
вцеп|ля́ться [28], ⟨**~**и́ться⟩ [14] (в В) grasp, catch hold of.
ВЦСПС (Всесою́зный Центрáльный Совéт Профессионáльных Сою́зов) the All-Union Central Council of Trade Unions.
вчерá yesterday; **~шний** [15] yesterday's, (of) yesterday.
вчернé in the rough; in a draft.
вчéтверо four times (as ..., *comp.*; *cf.* вдвóе); **∠м** four (of us, *etc.*).
вчи́т|ываться [1], ⟨**~**áться⟩ (в В) become absorbed in *or* familiar with s.th. by reading.
вшéстеро six times (*cf.* вдвóе).
вши|вáть [1], ⟨**~**ть⟩ [вошью́, -шьёшь; *cf.* шить] sew in(to); **∠вый** [14] lousy; **~ть** *s.* **~**вáть.
въе|дáться [1], ⟨**∠**сться⟩ [*cf.* есть[1]] eat (in[to]).
въе|зд *m* [1] entrance, entry; ascent; разрешéние на **~**зд entry permit; **~зжáть** [1], ⟨**∠**хать⟩ [въéду, -дешь; въезжáй(те)!] enter, ride *or* drive in(to), up/on (в, на В); move in(to); **∠сться** *s.* **~**дáться.
вы [21] you (*polite form a.* ♀); **~** с ним you and he; у вас (был) ... you have (had) ...
выб|áлтывать F [1], ⟨**∠**олтать⟩ blab *or* let out; **~егáть** [1], ⟨**∠**ежать⟩ [4; вы́бегу, -ежишь] run out; **~ивáть** [1], ⟨**∠**ить⟩ [вы́бью, -бьешь, *etc.*, *cf.* бить] **1.** beat *or* knock out; break; smash; drive out; hollow out; **2.** stamp, coin; **-ся** break out *or* forth; -ся из сил be(come) exhausted, fatigued; -ся из колей come off the beaten track; **~ирáть** [1], ⟨**∠**рать⟩ [вы́беру, -решь; -бранный] choose, pick out; elect; take out; find; **-ся** get out; move (out); **∠ить** *s.* **~**ивáть.
вы́бор *m* [1] choice, selection; на **~** (*or* по **~**у) at a p.'s discretion; random (*test*); *pl.* election(s); всеóбщие **~**ы *pl.* general election; дополни́тельные **~**ы by-election; **~ка** *f* [5; *g/pl.*: -рок] selection; *pl.* excerpts; **~ный** [14] electoral; *su.* delegate.
выбр|áсывать [1], ⟨**~**осить⟩ [15] throw (out *or* away); thrust (out); discard *or* dismiss; exclude, omit; strand; **~**áсывать (зря) дéньги waste money; **-ся** throw o. s. out; **~ать** *s.* выбирáть; **~ить** [-ею, -еешь; -итый] *pf.* shave clean; (*v/i.* **-ся**); **~осить** *s.* **~**áсывать.
выб|ывáть [1] ⟨**∠**ыть⟩ [-уду, -удешь] leave, withdraw, drop out.
выв|áливать [1], ⟨**∠**алить⟩ [13] discharge, throw out; P stream; **-ся** fall out; stream out; **~áривать** [1], ⟨**∠**арить⟩ [13] extract; boil down; **~éдывать**, ⟨**∠**едать⟩ [1] find out, (try to) elicit; **∠езти** *s.* **~**ози́ть; **~ёртывать** [1], ⟨**∠**ернуть⟩ [20] unscrew; tear out; dislocate; turn (inside out); *v/i.* **-ся**; slip out, extricate o. s.
вы́вес|ить *s.* вывéшивать; **~ка** *f* [5; *g/pl.*: -сок] sign(board); **~ти** *s.* выводи́ть.
выв|éтривать [1], ⟨**∠**етрить⟩ [13] (remove by) air(ing); **-ся** weather; **~éшивать** [1], ⟨**∠**есить⟩ [15] hang out *or* put up; **~и́нчивать** [1], ⟨**∠**интить⟩ [15] unscrew.
вы́вих *m* [1] dislocation; **~нуть** [20] *pf.* dislocate, sprain (one's ... себé В).
вы́вод *m* [1] **1.** withdrawal; **2.** breeding, cultivation; **3.** derivation, conclusion; сдéлать **~** draw a conclusion; **~и́ть** [15], ⟨вы́вести⟩ [25] **1.** take, lead *or* move (out, to);

2. derive, conclude; 3. hatch; cultivate; 4. construct; 5. remove, extirpate; 6. write *or* draw carefully; 7. depict; ~ить (В) из себя make s. b. lose his temper; **-ся**, ⟨-сь⟩ disappear; **~ок** *m* [1; -дка] brood.

вывоз *m* [1] export(s); **~ить** [15], ⟨вывезти⟩ [24] remove, get *or* take *or* bring out; export; **~ной** [14] export...

выв|орачивать F [1], ⟨∠оротить⟩ [15] = вывёртывать, вывернуть.

выг|адывать, ⟨∠адать⟩ [1] gain *or* save (s. th. from В/на П).

выгиб *m* [1] bend, curve; **~ать** [1], ⟨выгнуть⟩ [20] arch, curve.

выгля|деть [11 *st.*] *impf.* look (s. th. Т, like как); как она ~дит? what does she look like?; он ~дит моложе своих лет he doesn't look his age; **∠дывать** [1], *once* ⟨~нуть⟩ [20 *st.*] look *or* peep out (of в В, [из Р).

выгнать *s.* выгонять.

выгнуть *s.* выгибать.

выгов|аривать [1], ⟨'~орить⟩ [13] 1. pronounce; utter; 2. F stipulate; 3. *impf.* F (Д) rebuke; **'~ор** *m* [1] 1. pronunciation; 2. reproof, reprimand.

выгод|а *f* [5] profit; advantage; **~ный** [14; -ден, -дна] profitable; advantageous (to Д, для Р).

выгон *m* [1] pasture; **~ять** [28], ⟨выгнать⟩ [выгоню, -нишь] turn *or* drive out; expel *or* fire.

выгор|аживать [1], ⟨'~одить⟩ [15] enclose; P exculpate, free from blame; **~ать** [1], ⟨'~еть⟩ [9] 1. burn down; 2. fade; 3. F click, come off.

выгр|ужать [1], ⟨∠узить⟩ [15] unload; discharge; disembark; (*v/i.* **-ся**); **∠узка** [5; *g/pl.*: -зок] unloading; disembarkation.

выдавать [5], ⟨выдать⟩ [-дам, -дашь, *etc. cf.* дать] 1. give (out), pay (out); distribute; 2. draw *or* issue; 3. betray; 4. extradite; ~ (себя) за (В) [make] pass (o.s. off) for; ~ (замуж) за (В) give (*a girl*) in marriage to; **-ся** 1. stand out; 2. F happen *or* turn out.

выд|авливать [1], ⟨∠авить⟩ [14] press *or* squeeze out; **~албливать** [1], ⟨∠олбить⟩ [14] hollow out.

выда|ть *s.* ~вать; **~ча** *f* [5] 1. distribution; delivery; payment; 2. issue; grant; 3. betrayal; 4. extradition; день ~чи зарплаты payday; **~ющийся** [17; -щегося, *etc.*] outstanding, distinguished.

выдви|гать [1], ⟨'~нуть⟩ [20] 1. pull out; 2. put forward, propose, promote; **-ся** 1. step forth, move forward; 2. project; 3. advance; 4. *impf.* *s.* ~жной; **~женец** *m* [1; -нца] promoted worker; **~жной** [14] pull-out..., sliding.

выд|еление *n* [12] separation, detachment; discharge, secretion; **∠елка** *f* [5; *g/pl.*: -лок] manufacture; workmanship; **~елывать**, ⟨∠елать⟩ [1] work, make; elaborate; curry (*leather*); **~елять** [28], ⟨∠елить⟩ [13] 1. separate, detach; 2. mark (out); emphasize; 3. ⚖ allot; satisfy (*coheirs*); 4. ⚕ secrete; 5. ⚘ evolve; **-ся** *v/i.* 1,4; stand out, come forth; rise above, excel; **~ёргивать**, ⟨∠ернуть⟩ [20] pull out.

выдерж|ивать [1], ⟨'~ать⟩ [4] stand, bear, endure; pass (*exam.*); observe (*size, etc.*); '~ать характер be firm; '~анный self-restrained; consistent; mature; **'~ка** *f* [5; *g/pl.*: -жек] 1. self-control; 2. extract, quotation 3. *phot.* exposure; на '~ку at random.

выд|ирать F [1], ⟨∠рать⟩ [-деру, -ерешь] tear out; pull; *pf.* thrash; **∠олбить** *s.* ~албливать; **∠охнуть** *s.* ~ыхать; **∠ра** *f* [5] otter; **∠рать** *s.* ~ирать; **∠умка** *f* [5; *g/pl.*: -мок] invention; **~умывать**, ⟨∠умать⟩ [1] invent, contrive, devise.

выд|ыхать [1], ⟨∠охнуть⟩ [20] breathe out; **-ся** become stale; *fig.* exhaust o.s.

выезд *m* [1] departure; drive, ride; exit; gateway; visit.

выезжать[1] [1], ⟨выехать⟩ [выеду, -едешь; -езжай(те)!] *v/i.* (из, с Р) 1. leave, depart; 2. drive *or* ride out, on(to); 3. (re)move (from); 4. (begin to) visit (*social affairs, etc.*); ~[2] *a.* **выезживать** [1], ⟨выездить⟩ [15] *v/t.* break in (*a horse*).

выемка *f* [5; *g/pl.*: -мок] excavation; hollow.

выехать *s.* выезжать.

выж|ать *s.* ~имать; **~дать** *s.* ~идать; **~ивать** [1], ⟨~ить⟩ [-иву, -ивешь; -итый] survive; go through; stay; F oust; ~ить из ума be in one's dotage; **~игать** [1], ⟨~ечь⟩ [26 г/ж: -жгу, -жжешь, -жгут; -жег, жгла; -жженный] burn out, down *or* in; brand; **~идать** [1], ⟨~дать⟩ [-жду, -ждешь; -жди(-те)!] (Р *or* В) wait for *or* till (after); **~имать** [1], ⟨~ать⟩ [-жму, -жмешь; -жатый] squeeze, press *or* wring out; *sport* lift; **~ить** *s.* ~ивать.

вызвать *s.* вызывать.

выздор|авливать [1], ⟨'~оветь⟩ [10] recover; **~авливающий** [17] convalescent; **~овление** *n* [12] recovery.

выз|ов *m* [1] call; summons; invitation; challenge; **~убривать** [1] = зубрить; **~ывать** [1], ⟨~вать⟩ [-ову, -овешь] 1. call (to; for *thea.*; up *tel.*; [up]on *pupil*); send for; 2. summon (to к Д; before a court в суд); 3. challenge (to на В); 4. rouse, cause; evoke; **-ся** undertake *or* offer; **~ывающий** [17] defiant, provoking.

вы́игр|ывать, ⟨′**~ать**⟩ [1] win (from у P), gain, benefit; **′~ыш** *m* [1] win(ning[s]), gain(s); prize; profit; быть в ′~ыше have won (profited); **′~ышный** [14] advantageous, profitable; lottery...
вы́йти *s.* выходи́ть.
вык|а́зывать F [1], ⟨**~азать**⟩ [3] show, prove; display; **~а́лывать** [1], ⟨**~олоть**⟩ [17] put out; cut out; **~а́пывать,** ⟨**~опать**⟩ [1] dig out *or* up; **~ара́бкиваться,** ⟨**~арабкаться**⟩ [1] scramble *or* get out; **~а́рмливать** [1], ⟨**~ормить**⟩ [14] bring up, rear, breed; **~а́тывать** [1] **1.** ⟨**~атать**⟩ [1] mangle; roll; **2.** ⟨**~атить**⟩ [15] push *or* move out; ~атить глаза́ P stare.
вы́ки́|дывать [1], *once* ⟨′**~инуть**⟩ [20] **1.** throw out *or* away, discard; omit; strand; stretch (out); **2.** hoist (up); **3.** miscarry; **4.** F play (*trick*); **′~идыш** *m* [1] miscarriage, abortion.
вы́кл|адка *f* [5; *g/pl.*: -док] laying out, spreading; exposition; border, trimming; computation, calculation; ⚔ outfit; **~а́дывать** [1], ⟨вы́ложить⟩ [16] **1.** take *or* lay out, spread; set forth; **2.** border; **3.** brick *or* mason; **4.** compute.
выклика́ть [1] call up(on *or*, F, out).
выключ|а́тель *m* [4] ⚡ switch; **~а́ть** [1], ⟨′**~ить**⟩ [16] **1.** switch *or* turn off; stop; **2.** exclude; **~е́ние** *n* [12] switching off, stopping.
вык|о́вывать [1], ⟨**~овать**⟩ [7] forge; *fig.* mo(u)ld; **~ола́чивать** [1], ⟨**~олотить**⟩ [15] beat *or* knock out; dust; P exact (*debts, etc.*); **~олоть** *s.* ~а́лывать; **~опать** *s.* ~а́пывать; **~ормить** *s.* ~а́рмливать; **~орчёвывать** [1], ⟨**~орчевать**⟩ [7] root up *or* out.
выкр|а́ивать [1], ⟨**~оить**⟩ [13] cut out; F hunt (up), spare; **~а́шивать** [1], ⟨**~асить**⟩ [15] paint, dye; **~и́кивать** [1], *once* ⟨**~икнуть**⟩ [20] cry *or* call (out); **~оить** *s.* ~а́ивать; **~ойка** *f* [5; *g/pl.*: -оек] pattern.
выкр|ута́сы F *m/pl.* [1] flourishes, scrolls; dodges, subterfuges; **~у́чивать** [1], ⟨**~утить**⟩ [15] twist; wring (out); F unscrew; **-ся** F slip out.
вы́куп *m* [1] redemption; ransom; **~а́ть¹** [1], ⟨**~ить**⟩ [14] redeem; ransom; **~ать²** *s.* купа́ть.
выку́р|ивать [1], ⟨′**~ить**⟩ [13] **1.** smoke (out); **2.** distill.
выл|а́вливать [1], ⟨**~овить**⟩ [14] fish out *or* up; **~азка** *f* [5; *g/pl.*: -зок] **1.** ⚔ sally; **2.** excursion, outing; **~а́мывать,** ⟨**~омать**⟩ [1] break out.
выл|еза́ть [1], ⟨**~езть**⟩ [24] climb *or* get out; fall out (*hair*); **~епля́ть** [28], ⟨**~епить**⟩ [14] model.
вы́лет *m* [1] ✈ start, taking off; flight; **~а́ть** [1], ⟨**~еть**⟩ [11] fly out; ✈ start, take off (for в B); rush out *or* up; fall out; slip (a p.'s memory ~еть из головы́).
выл|е́чивать [1], ⟨**~ечить**⟩ [16] cure, heal (*v/i.* **-ся**); **~ива́ть** [1] ⟨**~ить**⟩ [-лью, -льешь; *cf.* лить] pour (out); **~итый** [14] poured out; ⊕ cast; F just like (s.b. И).
вы́л|овить *s.* ~авливать; **~ожить** *s.* выкла́дывать; **~омать** *s.* ~а́мывать; **~упля́ть** [28], ⟨**~упить**⟩ [14] shell; **-ся** hatch.
вым|а́зывать [1], ⟨**~азать**⟩ [3] smear; soil (**-ся** o.s.) (with T); **~а́ливать** [1], ⟨**~олить**⟩ [13] get *or* obtain by entreaties; **~а́нивать** [1], ⟨**~анить**⟩ [13] lure (out of из P); coax *or* cheat (a p. out of s. th. у P/B); **~а́ривать** [1], ⟨**~орить**⟩ [13] extirpate; ~а́ривать го́лодом starve (out); **~а́рывать,** ⟨**~арать**⟩ [1] **1.** soil; **2.** delete, cross out; **~а́чивать** [1], ⟨**~очить**⟩ [16] drench, soak *or* wet; **~а́щивать** [1], ⟨**~остить**⟩ [15] pave; **~е́нивать** [1], ⟨**~енять**⟩ [28] exchange (for на B); **~ереть** *s.* ~ира́ть; **~ета́ть** [1], ⟨**~ести**⟩ [25 -т- *st.*: -ету, -етешь] sweep (out); **~еща́ть** [1], ⟨**~естить**⟩ [15] avenge o.s. (on Д); vent (on p. на П); **~ира́ть** [1], ⟨**~ереть**⟩ [12] die out, become extinct.
вымога́т|ельство *n* [9] blackmail, extortion; **~ь** [1] extort (s.th. from B *or* P/у P).
вым|ока́ть [1], ⟨**~окнуть**⟩ [21] wet through, get wet; **~олвить** [14] *pf.* utter, say; **~олить** *s.* ~а́ливать; **~орить** *s.* ~а́ривать; **~остить** *s.* ~а́щивать; **~очить** *s.* ~а́чивать.
вы́мпел *m* [1] pennant, pennon.
вым|ыва́ть [1], ⟨**~ыть**⟩ [22] wash (out, up); ~ыть го́лову (Д) F bawl out, blow up; **~ысел** *m* [1; -сла] invention; falsehood; **~ыть** *s.* ~ыва́ть; **~ышля́ть** [28], ⟨**~ыслить**⟩ [15] invent; **~ышленный** *a.* fictitious.
вы́мя *n* [13] udder.
вын|а́шивать [1], ⟨**~осить**⟩ [15] **1.** wear out; **2.** evolve, bring forth; **3.** train; **4.** nurse; **~ести** *s.* ~оси́ть.
вын|има́ть [1], ⟨**~уть**⟩ [20] take *or* draw out, produce.
вын|оси́ть¹ [15], ⟨**~ести**⟩ [24 -с-: -су, -сешь; -с, -сла] **1.** carry *or* take out (away), remove; transfer; **2.** endure, bear; **3.** acquire; **4.** submit; express (*gratitude*); pass (*a.* ⚖); **~осить²** *s.* ~а́шивать; **~оска** *f* [5; *g/pl.*: -сок] marginal note, footnote; **~о́сливость** *f* [8] endurance; **~о́сливый** [14 *sh.*] enduring, sturdy, hardy, tough.
вын|ужда́ть [1], ⟨**~удить**⟩ [15] force, compel; extort (s. th. from B/у *or* от P); **~ужденный** [14 *sh.*] forced; of necessity.

вы́нырнуть [20] *pf.* emerge.
вы́па|д *m* [1], **~де́ние** *n* [12] falling out; *fenc.* lunge; *fig.* thrust, attack; **~да́ть** [1], ⟨**~сть**⟩ [25] **1.** fall *or* drop (out); slip out; **2.** fall (to Д, *a.* на до́лю to a p.'s share *or* lot), devolve on; **3.** lunge.
вып|а́ливать [1], ⟨**~алить**⟩ [13] blurt out; F shoot (with из P); **~а́лывать** [1], ⟨**~олоть**⟩ [17] weed (out); **~а́ривать** [1], ⟨**~арить**⟩ [13] steam; evaporate.
вып|ека́ть [1], ⟨**~ечь**⟩ [26] bake; **~ива́ть** [1], ⟨**~ить**⟩ [-пью, -пьешь; *cf.* пить] drink (up); F booze; **~ить** (ли́шнее) F overdrink o.s.; **~ить** ча́шку ча́ю have a cup of tea; **~ивка** F *f* [5; *g/pl.*: -вок] booze; **~ивший** [17] drunk; tipsy.
вы́п|иска *f* [5; *g/pl.*: -сок] **1.** writing out, copying; **2.** extract; ✝ statement (of account из счёта); **3.** order, subscription; **4.** discharge; notice of departure; **~и́сывать** [1], ⟨**~исать**⟩ [3] **1.** write out (*or* down); copy; **2.** *s.* выводи́ть 6.; **3.** order, subscribe; **4.** discharge, dismiss; **-ся** register one's departure; **-ся** из больни́цы leave hospital.
вы́пла|вка *f* [5] smelting; **~кать** [3] *pf.* weep (one's eyes глаза́) out; F obtain by weeping; **~та** *f* [5] payment; **~чивать** [1], ⟨**~тить**⟩ [15] pay (out *or* off).
выпл|ёвывать [1], *once* ⟨**~юнуть**⟩ [20] spit out; **~ёскивать** [1] ⟨**~ескать**⟩ [3], *once* ⟨**~еснуть**⟩ [20] dash *or* splash (out).
выпл|ыва́ть [1], ⟨**~ыть**⟩ [23] emerge, come out, appear.
выпол|а́скивать [1], ⟨**'~оскать**⟩ [3] rinse; gargle; **~за́ть** [1], ⟨**'~зти**⟩ [24] creep or crawl out; **~не́ние** *n* [12] fulfil(l)ment, execution, realization; **~ня́ть** [1], ⟨**'~нить**⟩ [13] carry out, fulfil(l); make (up); **'~оть** *s.* выпа́лывать.
вы́пр|авка *f* [5; *g/pl.*: -вок] **1.** correction; **2.** carriage (*of a soldier*); **~авля́ть** [28], ⟨**~авить**⟩ [14] set right *or* straight; correct; **~а́шивать** [1], ⟨**~осить**⟩ [15] (try to) obtain by request; **~ова́живать** F [1], ⟨**~оводить**⟩ [15] see out; **2.** turn out; **~ы́гивать** [1], ⟨**~ыгнуть**⟩ [20] jump out *or* off; **~яга́ть** [1], ⟨**~ячь**⟩ [26 г/ж: -ягу, -яжешь; -яг] unharness; **~ямля́ть** [28], ⟨**~ямить**⟩ [14] straighten; **-ся** erect o.s.
вы́пуклый [14] convex; prominent; *fig.* expressive, distinct.
вы́пуск *m* [1] letting out; omission; ⊕ output; ✝ issue; publication; instal(l)ment; (age) class of graduates; **~а́ть** [1], ⟨вы́пустить⟩ [15] let out (*or* go); ⚖ release; ⊕ produce; issue; publish; omit, leave out; graduate; **~а́ть** в прода́жу put on sale; **~ни́к** *m* [1 *e.*] graduate; **~но́й** [14] graduate ..., graduation ..., final, leaving; ⊕ discharge-...; outlet ...
вып|у́тывать, ⟨**~утать**⟩ [1] disentangle *or* extricate (o. s. **-ся**); **~у́чивать** [1], ⟨**~учить**⟩ [16] **1.** bulge; **2.** P *s.* тара́щить.
вып|ы́тывать, ⟨**~ытать**⟩ [1] find out, (try to) elicit.
выпя́|ливать P [1], ⟨**'~лить**⟩ [13] *s.* тара́щить; **~чивать** F [1], ⟨**'~тить**⟩ [15] protrude.
выраб|а́тывать, ⟨**'~отать**⟩ [1] manufacture, produce; elaborate, work out; develop; earn, make; **'~отка** *f* [5; *g/pl.*: -ток] manufacture, production; output, performance; elaboration.
выр|а́внивать [1], ⟨**~овнять**⟩ [28] level, ⊕ plane; smooth (*a. fig.*); **-ся** straighten; ⚔ dress; develop, grow up.
выра|жа́ть [1], ⟨**'~зить**⟩ [15] express, show; **~жа́ть** слова́ми put into words; **~же́ние** *n* [12] expression; **~зи́тельный** [14; -лен, -льна] expressive; F significant.
выр|аста́ть [1], ⟨**~асти**⟩ [24 -ст-: -асту; *cf.* расти́] **1.** grow (up); increase; develop into; **2.** emerge, appear; **~а́щивать** [1], ⟨**~астить**⟩ [15] grow; breed; bring up; *fig.* train; **~вать 1.** *s.* **~ыва́ть**[1]; **2.** *s.* рвать 3.
вырез|а́ть [1], ⟨**'~ать**⟩ [15] **1.** cut out, clip; **2.** carve; engrave; **3.** slaughter; **'~ка** *f* [5; *g/pl.*: -зок] cutting (out), clipping; carving; engraving; tenderloin; **~но́й** [14] carved.
вы́ро|док *m* [1; -дка] degenerate; monster; **~жда́ться** [1], ⟨**~диться**⟩ [15] degenerate; **~жде́ние** *n* [12] degeneration.
вы́ро|нить [13] *pf.* drop; **~сший** [17] grown.
выр|уба́ть [1], ⟨**~убить**⟩ [14] **1.** cut down *or* fell; **2.** cut out *or* carve; **~уча́ть** [1], ⟨**~учить**⟩ [16] **1.** help, rescue, relieve; redeem; **2.** ✝ gain; **~учка** *f* [5] rescue, relief, help (to на В); ✝ proceeds.
выр|ыва́ть[1] [1], ⟨**~вать**⟩ [-ву, -вешь] **1.** pull out; tear out; **2.** snatch away; extort (s.th. from a p. В/у Р); **-ся** break away, rush (out); escape; **~ыва́ть**[2], ⟨**~ыть**⟩, [22] dig out, up.
вы́с|адка *f* [5; *g/pl.*: -док] disembarkation, landing; **~а́живать** [1], ⟨**~адить**⟩ [15] **1.** land, disembark; **2.** help out; make *or* let a p. get out; **3.** (trans)plant; **-ся** = **1.** *v/i.*; *a.* get out, off.
выс|а́сывать [1], ⟨**~осать**⟩ [-осу, -осешь] suck out; **~ве́рливать** [1], ⟨**~верлить**⟩ [13] bore, drill; **~вобожда́ть** [1], ⟨**~вободить**⟩ [15] free.

выс|ева́ть [1], ⟨**ҁеять**⟩ [27] sow; **~ека́ть** [1], ⟨**ҁечь**⟩ [26] **1.** hew, carve; strike (*fire*); **2.** *s.* сечь[2]; **~еле́ние** *n* [12] expulsion, eviction; transfer; **~еля́ть** [28], ⟨**ҁелить**⟩ [13] expel, evict; transfer, move; **ҁеять** *s.* **~е́ивать**; **~а́живать** [1], ⟨**ҁидеть**⟩ [11] sit (out), stay; hatch.

выск|а́бливать [1], ⟨**ҁоблить**⟩ [13] scrub clean; erase; **~а́зывать** [1], ⟨**ҁазать**⟩ [3] express, tell, give; **-ся** express o.s.; express one's opinion, thoughts, *etc.* (about о П); declare o.s. (for за В; against про́тив Р); **~а́кивать** [1], ⟨**ҁочить**⟩ [16] jump, leap *or* rush out; **~а́льзывать, ~ользá́ть** [1], ⟨**ҁользнуть**⟩ [20] slip out; **ҁоблить** *s.* **~а́бливать**; **ҁочить** *s.* **~а́кивать**; **ҁочка** *m/f* [5; *g/pl.*: -чек] upstart; F forward pupil; **~реба́ть** [1], ⟨**ҁрести**⟩ [25 -б-; *cf.* скрести́] scrub clean; scratch out.

вы́сл|ать *s.* высыла́ть; **~е́живать** [1], ⟨**~едить**⟩ [15] track down; **~у́живать** [1], ⟨**~ужить**⟩ [16] F serve; obtain by *or* for service; **-ся** advance, rise; insinuate o.s.; **~у́шивать**, ⟨**~ушать**⟩ [1] listen (to), hear; ⚕ auscultate.

высм|е́ивать [1], ⟨**ҁеять**⟩ [27] deride, ridicule.

выс|о́вывать [1], ⟨**ҁунуть**⟩ [20 *st.*] put out; **-ся** lean out.

высо́кий [16; высо́к, -á, -со́ко́; *comp.*: вы́ше] high; tall (*a.* ~ ро́стом); *fig.* lofty.

высоко|благоро́дие *n* [12] (Right) Hono[u]r(able); **~ка́чественный** [14] (of) high quality; **~квалифици́рованный** [14] highly skilled; **~ме́рие** *n* [12] haughtiness; **~ме́рный** [14; -рен, -рна] haughty, arrogant; **~па́рный** [14; -рен, -рна] bombastic, high-flown; **~превосходи́тельство** *n* [9] Excellency; **~уважа́емый** [14] dear (*polite address*).

вы́сосать *s.* выса́сывать.

высо|та́ *f* [5; *pl.*: -о́ты, *etc. st.*] height; (✈, *astr.*, *geogr.*) altitude; hill; level; *fig.* climax; **~то́й** в (В) ... *or* ... в **~ту́** ... high.

вы́сох|нуть *s.* высыха́ть; **~ший** [17] dried up, withered.

выс|оча́йший [17] highest; supreme, imperial; **~о́чество** *n* [9] Highness; **ҁпаться** *s.* высыпа́ться.

вы́спренний [15] bombastic.

выстав|ить *s.* **~ля́ть**; **~ка** *f* [5; *g/pl.*: -вок] exhibition, show; **~ля́ть** [28], ⟨**~ить**⟩ [14] **1.** put (take) out, put forward (*a. fig.*); **2.** exhibit, display, expose; (re)present (o.s. себя́); **3.** mark, provide (*with date, no.*); ⚔ post; P turn out; **~ля́ть** напока́з show off; **-ся** come out, emerge; **~очный** [14] (of the) exhibition, show...

выстр|а́ивать(ся) [1] *s.* стро́ить (-ся); **ҁел** *m* [1] shot; (*noise*) report; на (расстоя́ние, -ии) **ҁел(а)** within gunshot; **ҁелить** *s.* стреля́ть.

выссту́к|ивать, ⟨**'~ать**⟩ F [1] strike, [tap; ⚕ percuss.

вы́ступ *m* [1] projection; **~а́ть** [1], ⟨**~ить**⟩ [14] **1.** step forth, forward; come *or* stand out; appear; **2.** set out, march off; **3.** speak (sing, play) in public; **~а́ть** с ре́чью (в пре́ниях) deliver a speech (take the floor); **~а́ть** в похо́д ⚔ take the field; **~ле́ние** *n* [12] **1.** appearance; **2.** departure; *pol.* speech, declaration; *thea.* performance, turn.

вы́сунуть(ся) *s.* высо́вывать(ся).

высу́ш|ивать [1], ⟨**'~ить**⟩ [16] dry (up); drain, *fig.* exhaust.

вы́сш|ий [17] highest, supreme; higher (*a. educ.*), superior; **~ая** ме́ра наказа́ния supreme penalty, capital punishment.

выс|ыла́ть [1], ⟨**ҁлать**⟩ [вы́шлю, -лешь] send forward; send out, away; banish; **ҁылка** *f* [15] dispatch; exile; **~ыпа́ть** [1], ⟨**ҁыпать**⟩ [2] pour out *or* in, on; *v/i.* swarm forth, out; **~ыпа́ться** [1], ⟨вы́спаться⟩ [-сплюсь, -спишься] sleep one's fill (*or* enough), have a good night's rest; **~ыха́ть** [1], ⟨**ҁохнуть**⟩ [21] dry up, wither; **~ь** *f* [8] height.

выт|а́лкивать, F ⟨**ҁолкать**⟩ [1], *once* ⟨**ҁолкнуть**⟩ [20 *st.*] push out; **~а́пливать** [1], ⟨**ҁопить**⟩ [14] **1.** heat; **2.** melt (down); **~а́скивать** [1], ⟨**ҁащить**⟩ [16] take *or* pull out; F pilfer.

выт|ека́ть [1], ⟨**ҁечь**⟩ [26] flow out; *fig.* follow, result; **ҁереть** *s.* **~ира́ть**; **ҁерпеть** [14] *pf.* endure, bear; F не **ҁерпел** couldn't help; **~есня́ть** [28], ⟨**ҁеснить**⟩ [13] force, push out; oust, expel; **ҁечь** *s.* **~ека́ть**.

выт|ира́ть [1], ⟨**ҁереть**⟩ [12] dry, wipe (o.s. -ся); wear out.

вы́точенный [14] well-turned.

вы́тр|ебовать [7] *pf.* ask for, demand, order, summon; obtain on demand; **~яса́ть** [1], ⟨**ҁясти**⟩ [24 -с-] shake out.

выть [22], ⟨вз-⟩ howl.

выт|я́гивать [1], ⟨**ҁянуть**⟩ [20 *st.*] draw, pull *or* stretch (out); drain; F elicit; endure, bear; **-ся** stretch, extend (o.s.); ⚔ come to attention; F grow (up); **ҁяжка** *f* [5] drawing, stretching (out); ⚕ extract; на **ҁяжку** ⚔ at attention.

выу́|живать [1], ⟨**'~дить**⟩ [15] fish out (*a. fig.*).

выу́ч|ивать [1], ⟨**'~ить**⟩ [16] learn, memorize; (В + *inf.* *or* Д) teach (a p. to ... *or* s.th.); **-ся** learn (s.th. from Д/у Р).

вых|а́живать F [1], ⟨**ҁодить**⟩ [15] **1.** rear, bring up; nurse, restore to

health; 2. go (all) over, through; **~вáтывать** [1], ⟨**~ватить**⟩ [15] snatch away, from, out; snap up, off.
вы́хлоп *m* [1] exhaust; **~нóй** [14] exhaust...; **~отать** [1] *pf.* obtain.
вы́ход *m* [1] 1. exit; way out (*a. fig.*); outlet; 2. departure; withdrawal, retirement; 3. appearence, publication; *thea.* entrance (*on the stage*), performance; 4. yield, output; ~ зáмуж marriage (*of women*); ~ в отстáвку retirement, resignation; **~ец** *m* [1; -дца] immigrant, native of; come *or* originate from.
выходи́ть[1] [15], ⟨**вы́йти**⟩ [вы́йду, -дешь; вы́шел, -шла; вы́шедший; вы́йдя] 1. go *or* come out, leave; get out, off; withdraw, retire; 2. appear, be published *or* issued; 3. come off; turn out, result; happen, arise, originate; 4. spend, use up, run out of; † become due; F вы́шло! it's clicked!; вы́йти в офицéры rise to the rank of an officer; ~ в отстáвку (на пéнсию) retire, resign; ~ за предéлы (P) transgress the bounds of; ~ (зáмуж) за (B) marry (*v/t.*; *of women*); ~ из себя́ be beside o.s.; ~ из терпéния lose one's temper (patience); окнó выхóдит на у́лицу the window faces the street; ~ из стрóя fall out, be out of action; из негó вы́шел ... he has become ...; из э́того ничегó не вы́йдет nothing will come of it.
вы́ход|ить[2] *s.* выхáживать; **~ка** [5; *g/pl.:* -док] trick, prank; excess; **~нóй** [14] exit...; outlet...; holiday-...; festive; ~нóй день *m* holiday, day off; (have one's быть T).
вы́холенный [14] well-groomed.
выцве|тáть [1], ⟨**'~сти**⟩ [25 -т-: -ету] fade, wither.
выч|ёркивать [1], ⟨**~еркнуть**⟩ [20] strike out, obliterate; **~éрпывать**, ⟨**~ерпать**⟩ [1], *once* ⟨**~ерпнуть**⟩ [20 *st.*] scoop; dredge (out); **~есть** *s.* ~итáть; **~ет** *m* [1] deduction.
вычисл|éние *n* [12] calculation; **~я́ть** [1], ⟨**'~ить**⟩ [13] calculate, compute.
вы́чи|стить *s.* ~щáть; **~тáемое** *n* [14] subtrahend; **~тáние** *n* [12] subtraction; **~тáть** [1], ⟨**вы́честь**⟩ [25 -т-: -чту; -чел, -чла; *g. pt.*: вы́чтя] deduct; ⅍ subtract; **~щáть** [1], ⟨**~стить**⟩ [15] clean, scrub, brush, polish.
вычýрный [14; -рен, -рна] ornate, flowery; fanciful.
вы́швырнуть [20 *st.*] *pf.* turn out.
вы́ше higher; above; beyond; он ~ меня́ he is taller than I (am); э́то ~ моегó понимáния that's beyond my reach.
вы́ше... above..., afore...
выш|ибáть F [1], ⟨**~ибить**⟩ [-бу, -бешь; -б, -бла; -бленный] knock *or* throw out; **~ивáние** *n* [12] embroidery; **~ивáть** [1], ⟨**~ить**⟩ [-шью, -шьешь] embroider; **~ивка** *f* [5; *g/pl.:* -вок] embroidery.
вышинá *f* [5] height; *cf.* высотá.
вы́шка *f* [5; *g/pl.:* -шек] tower.
выяв|ля́ть [28], ⟨**'~ить**⟩ [14] discover, uncover, reveal.
выясн|éние *n* [12] clarification; **~я́ть** [28], ⟨**'~ить**⟩ [13] clear up, find out, ascertain; **-ся** turn out; come to light.
вью|га *f* [5] snowstorm; **~к** *m* [1] pack, bale, load; **~н** *m* [1 *e.*] loach (*fish*); **~чить** [16], ⟨на-⟩ load; **~чный** [14] pack...; **~щийся** [17] curly; ~щееся растéние *n* creeper.
вя́жущий [17] astringent.
вяз *m* [1] elm.
вязáн|ка *f* [5; *g/pl.:* -нок] fag(g)ot; **'~ый** [14] knitted; **~ье** *n* [10] (*a.* ~ие *n* [12]) knitting; crochet.
вяз|áть [3], ⟨с-⟩ 1. tie, bind (together); 2. knit; (крючкóм) crochet; **-ся** *impf.* match, agree, be in keeping; F make sense; work (well), get on; **~кий** [16; -зок, -зкá, -о] viscous, sticky; swampy, marshy; **~нуть** [21], ⟨за-, у-⟩ sink in, stick.
вя́лить [13], ⟨про-⟩ dry, sun.
вя́|лый [14 *sh.*] withered, faded; flabby; *fig.* sluggish; dull (*a.* †); **~нуть** [20], ⟨за-, у-⟩ wither, fade; droop, flag.

Г

г *abbr.*: грамм.
г. *abbr.:* 1. год; 2. гóрод; 3. господи́н.
га 1. ha(h)!; 2. *abbr.*: гектáр.
Гаа́га *f* [5] The Hague.
Гавáнна *f* [5] 1. Havana; 2. ♀ Havana cigar.
гáвань *f* [8] harbo(u)r.
Гаври|и́л *m* [1], P **~ла** [5] Gabriel.
гáга *f* [5] *zo.* eider.
гад *m* [1] reptile (*a. fig.*).
гадá|лка *f* [5; *g/pl.:* -лок] fortuneteller; **~ние** *n* [12] fortunetelling; guessing, conjecture; **~ть** [1] 1. ⟨по-⟩ tell fortunes; (by cards на кáртах); 2. *impf.* guess, conjecture.
гáд|ина F *f* [5] = гад; **~ить** [15] 1. ⟨на-, за-⟩ F soil; (Д) P harm; 2. ⟨из-⟩ P spoil, botch; **~кий** [16; -док, -дкá, -о] nasty, ugly, disgusting, repulsive; **~ли́вый** [14 *sh.*] squeamish; **~ость** F *f*[8] vermin; villainy, ugly thing (act, word); **~ю́ка** *f* [5] *zo.* viper (*a.*, P, *fig.*), adder.
газ *m* [1] 1. gas; свети́льный ~

coal gas; дать ~ *mot.* step on the gas; на по́лном ~е (~у́) at full speed (throttle); *pl.* ⚕ flatulences; **2.** gauze.

газе́ль *f* [8] gazelle.

газе́т|а *f* [14] newspaper; **~ный** [14] news...; ~ный кио́ск *m* newsstand, *Brt.* news stall; **~чик** *m* [1] newsman, newsboy.

газиро́ван|ный [14]: **~ная вода́** *f* soda water.

га́з|овый [14] **1.** gas...; **~овый** счётчик *m* = ~оме́р; ~овая педа́ль *f* *mot.* accelerator (pedal); **2.** gauze...; **~оме́р** *m* [1] gas meter; **~о́метр** *m* [1] gasometer.

газо́н *m* [1] lawn.

газо|обра́зный [14; -зен, -зна] gaseous; **~прово́д** *m* [1] gas pipe line.

га́йка *f* [5; *g/pl.:* га́ек] ⊕ nut.

галантер|е́йный [14]: **~е́йный** магази́н *m* notions store, *Brt.* haberdashery; ~е́йные това́ры *m/pl.* = **~е́я** *f* [6] notions *pl.*, dry goods *pl.*, *Brt.* fancy goods *pl.*

галд|ёж P *m* [1 *e.*] row, hubbub; **~е́ть** P [11], ⟨за-⟩ clamo(u)r, din.

гал|ере́я *f* [6] gallery; **~ёрка** F *f* [5] *thea.* gallery.

галифе́ *pl. indecl.* ⚔ breeches.

га́лка *f* [5; *g/pl.:* -лок] jackdaw.

гало́п *m* [1] gallop; ~ом at a gallop; **~и́ровать** [7] gallop.

гало́ши *f/pl.* [5] galoshes, rubbers.

га́лстук *m* [1] (neck)tie.

галу́н *m* [1 *e.*] galloon, braid.

гальван|изи́ровать [7] *(im)pf.* galvanize; **~и́ческий** [16] galvanic.

га́лька *f* [5; *g/pl.:* -лек] pebble.

гам F *m* [1] din, row, rumpus.

гама́к *m* [1 *e.*] hammock.

гама́ши *f/pl.* [5] gaiters.

га́мма *f* [5] ♪ scale; range.

ган|гре́на ⚕ *f* [5] gangrene; **~дика́п** *m* [1] handikap; **~те́ли** (-ˈtɛ-) *f/pl.* [8] dumbbells.

гара́ж *m* [1 *e.*] garage.

гарант|и́ровать [7] *(im)pf.*, **∠ия** *f* [7] guarantee, warrant.

гардеро́б *m* [1] wardrobe; (*a.* **~ная** *f* [14]) check-, cloakroom; **~щик** *m* [1], **~щица** *f* [5] cloakroom attendant.

гарди́на *f* [5] curtain.

гармо́|ника *f* [5] (*kind of*) accordion; губна́я ~ника mouth organ, harmonica; **~ни́ровать** [20] harmonize, be in harmony (with с T); **~ни́ст** *m* [1] accordionist; harmonist; **~ни́ческий** [16] harmonic; *a.* = **~ни́чный** [14; -чен, -чна] harmonious; **~ния** *f* [7] harmony; F *a.* = **~нь** F *f* [8], **~шка** *f* [5; *g/pl.:* -шек] = ~ника.

гарни|зо́н *m* [1] garrison; **∠р** *m* [1], **∠ровать** [7] *(im)pf., cook.* garnish; **~ту́р** *m* [1] set.

гарпу́н *m* [1 *e.*], **~ить** [13] harpoon.

гарцева́ть [7] prance.

гарь *f* [8] (s. th.) burnt, char.

гаси́ть [15], ⟨по-, за-⟩ extinguish, put *or* blow out; slake.

га́снуть [21], ⟨по-, у-⟩ go out, die away; *fig.* fade, wither.

гастрол|ёр *m* [1] guest actor *or* artist, star; **~и́ровать** [7] tour, give performance(s) on a tour; **∠ь** *f* [8] starring (performance).

гастроно́м *m* [1] **1.** gastronome(r); gourmet; **2.** *a.* = ~и́ческий магази́н *m* delicatessen, (dainty) food store *or* shop; **~и́ческий** [16] gastronomic(al); *cf.* ~ 2.; **~ия** *f* [7] gastronomy; dainties, delicacies *pl.*

гауптва́хта *f* [5] guardhouse.

гвалт F *m* [1] rumpus, din.

гвард|е́ец *m* [1; -е́йца] guardsman; **∠ия** *f* [7] Guards *pl.*

гво́зд|ик *dim. of* ~ь, *cf.*; **~и́ка** *f* [5] carnation, pink; (*spice*) clove; **~ь** *m* [4 *e.*; *pl.:* гво́зди, -де́й] nail; *fig.* main feature, hit.

гг. *or* **г.г.** *abbr.:* **1.** го́ды; **2.** господа́.

где where; F *s.* куда́ F; ~-~ = ко́е-где́, *cf.*; *cf.* ни; ~ F = **∠-либо, ∠-нибудь, ∠-то** any-, somewhere; ∠-то здесь hereabout(s).

ГДР *cf.* герма́нский.

гей! F heigh!

гекта́р *m* [1] hectare.

гектоли́тр *m* [1] hectoliter.

ге́ли|й *m* [3] helium; **~копте́р** (-ˈtɛ) *m* [1] *s.* вертолёт; **~отерапи́я** *f* [7] heliotherapy.

генеало́гия *f* [7] genealogy.

генера́|л *m* [1] general; ~л-майо́р *m* major general; **~льный** [14] general; ~льная репети́ция *f* dress rehearsal; **~тор** *m* [1] generator.

ген|иа́льный [14; -лен, -льна] of genius; ingenious; **∠ий** *m* [3] genius.

гео́|граф *m* [1] geographer; **~графи́ческий** [16] geographic(al); **~гра́фия** *f* [7] geography; **~лог** *m* [1] geologist; **~ло́гия** *f* [7] geology; **~ме́трия** *f* [7] geometry.

Гео́рг|ий *m* [3] George; **♀и́н(а** *f* [5]) *m* [1] dahlia.

гера́нь *f* [8] geranium.

Гера́сим *m* [1] Gerasim (*m. name*).

герб *m* [1 *e.*] (coat of) arms; emblem; **∠овый** [14] stamp(ed).

Герма́н|ия *f* [7] Germany; Федерати́вная Респу́блика ~ии (ФРГ) Federal Republic of Germany; **♀ский** [16] German; ~ская Демократи́ческая Респу́блика (ГДР) German Democratic Republic (*Eastern Zone of Germany*).

гермети́ческий [16] hermetic.

геро|и́зм *m* [1] heroism; **~и́ня** *f* [6] heroine; **~и́ческий** [16] heroic; **∠й** *m* [3] hero; **∠йский** [16] heroic.

ге́тры *f/pl.* [5] gaiters.

г-жа *abbr.:* госпожа́.

гиаци́нт *m* [1] hyacinth.

ги́бель *f* [7] ruin, destruction; loss;

⚓ wreck; death; P immense number, lots of; **~ный** [14; -лен, -льна] disastrous, fatal.
ги́бк|ий [16; -бок, -бка́, -о] supple, pliant, flexible (*a. fig.*); **~ость** *f* [8] flexibility.
ги́б|лый P [14] ruinous; **~нуть** [21], ⟨по-⟩ perish.
Гибралта́р *m* [1] Gibraltar.
гига́нт *m* [1] giant; **~ский** [16] gigantic, huge.
гигие́н|а *f* [5] hygiene; **~и́ческий** [16], **~и́чный** [14; -чен, -чна] hygienic.
гид *m* [1] guide.
гидравли́ческий [16] hydraulic.
гидро|пла́н, ~самолёт *m* [1] seaplane, hydroplane; **~(электро)ста́нция** *f* [7] hydroelectric power station.
гие́на *f* [5] hyena.
гик *m* [1], **∠анье** *n* [10] whoop(ing).
ги́льза *f* [5] (*cartridge*) case; shell.
Гимала́и *m/pl.* [3] The Himalayas.
гимн *m* [1] hymn; anthem.
гимна|зи́ст *m* [1] pupil *of* **∠зия** *f* [7] high school, *Brt.* grammar school; **∠ст** *m* [1] gymnast; **~стёрка** *f* [5; *g/pl.*: -рок] ⚔ blouse, *Brt.* tunic; **∠стика** *f* [5] gymnastics; **~сти́ческий** [16] gymnastic.
гипе́рбол|а *f* [5] hyperbole; ⅍ hyperbola; **~и́ческий** [16] hyperbolic, exaggerated.
гипно́|з *m* [1] hypnosis; **~тизи́ровать** [7], ⟨за-⟩ hypnotize.
гипо́теза *f* [5] hypothesis.
гиппопота́м *m* [1] hippopotamus.
гипс *m* [1] *min.* gypsum; ⊕ plaster of Paris; **∠овый** [14] gypsum..., plaster...
гирля́нда *f* [5] garland.
ги́ря *f* [6] weight.
гита́ра *f* [5] guitar.
глав|а́ [5; *pl. st.*] **1.** *f* head; top, summit; cupola; chapter (*in books*); (быть, стоя́ть) во **~е́** (be) at the head; lead (by с T); **2.** *m/f* head, chief; **~а́рь** *m* [4 *e.*] (ring) leader, chieftain.
главе́нство *n* [9] priority, hegemony; **~вать** [7] (pre)dominate.
главнокома́ндующий *m* [17]: ~ commander in chief; Верхо́вный ~ Commander in Chief; Supreme Commander.
гла́вн|ый [14] chief, main, principal, central; head...; ... in chief; **~ая** кни́га *f* ✝ ledger; **~ое** (де́ло) *n* the main thing; above all; **~ый** го́род *m* capital; **~ым** о́бразом mainly, chiefly.
глаго́л *m* [1] *gr.* verb; † word, speech; **~ьный** [14] verb(al).
глад|и́льный [14] ironing; **∠ить** [15] **1.** ⟨вы́-⟩ iron, press; **2.** ⟨по-⟩ stroke, caress; F **∠ить** по голо́вке treat with indulgence *or* favo(u)r; **∠кий** [16; -док, -дка́, -о] smooth (*a. fig.*); lank (*hair*); plain (*fabric*); P well-fed; **∠кость, ~ь** *f* [8] smoothness.
глаз *m* [1; в -у́; *pl.*: -а́, глаз, -а́м] eye; look; (eye)sight; F heed, care; в **~а́** (Д) to s.b.'s face; (*strike*) the eye; в мои́х **~а́х** in my view *or* opinion; за **~а́** in s.b.'s absence, behind one's back; plentifully; на ~ approximately, by eye; на **~а́х** (*poss. or* у P) in s.b.'s presence, sight; с **∠у** на ~ privately, tête-à-tête; просты́м (невооружённым) **∠ом** with the naked eye; темно́, хоть ~ вы́коли F it is pitch-dark; **~а́стый** F [14 *sh.*] goggle-eyed; sharp-sighted; **~е́ть** P [8] stare *or* gape (around); **~но́й** [14] eye..., optic; **~но́й** врач *m* oculist; **~о́к** *m* [1; -зка́] **1.** [*pl. st.*: -зки, -зок] *dim. of* ~; аню́тины **∠ки** *pl.* pansy; **2.** [*pl. e.*: -зки́, -зко́в] ⚘ bud; *zo.* ocellus, eye; peephole.
глазоме́р *m* [1]: на ~ estimate(d) by the eye; (*sure, etc.*) eye.
глазу́нья *f* [6] fried eggs *pl.*
глазур|ова́ть [7] (*im*)*pf.* glaze; **∠ь** *f* [8] glaze.
гла|си́ть [15 *e*; *3. p. only*] say, read, run; **∠сность** *f* [8] public(ity); **∠сный** [14] public; (*a. su.*) vowel; *su.* council(l)or; **~ша́тай** *m* [3] town crier; *fig.* herald.
гле́тчер *m* [1] glacier.
гли́н|а *f* [5] loam; clay; **~истый** [14 *sh.*] loamy; **~озём** *m* [1] *min.* alumina; **~яный** [14] earthen; loamy.
глист *m* [1 *e.*], **~а́** *f* [5] (intestinal) worm; (ле́нточный) ~ tapeworm.
глицери́н *m* [1] glycerine.
гло́бус *m* [1] globe.
глода́ть [3], ⟨об-⟩ gnaw (at, round).
глот|а́ть [1], ⟨про**~и́ть**⟩ [15], *once* ⟨**~ну́ть**⟩ [20] swallow; F devour; **∠ка** *f* [5; *g/pl.*: -ток] throat; во всю **∠ку** *s.* го́лос; **~о́к** *m* [1; -тка́] draught, gulp (at T).
гло́хнуть [21] **1.** ⟨о-⟩ grow deaf; **2.** ⟨за-⟩ fade, die away, out; go out; grow desolate.
глуб|ина́ *f* [5] depth; remoteness (*past*); *fig.* profundity; *thea.* background; T/в (B) ..., *or* ... в B ... deep; **~о́кий** [16; -бо́к, -бока́, -бо́ко́] deep; low; remote; *fig.* profound; complete; great (*age*); **~о́кой** зимо́й (но́чью) in the dead of winter (late at night).
глубоко|мы́сленный [14 *sh.*] thoughtful, sagacious; **~мы́слие** *n* [12] thoughtfulness; **~уважа́емый** [14] dear (*polite address*).
глубь *f* [8] *s.* глубина́.
глум|и́ться [14 *e.*; -млю́сь, -ми́шься] sneer, mock, scoff (at над T); **~ле́ние** *n* [12] mockery.
глуп|е́ть [8], ⟨по-⟩ become stupid; **~е́ц** *m* [1; -пца́] fool, blockhead; **~и́ть** F [14 *e.*; -плю́, -пи́шь] fool; **∠ость** *f* [8] stupidity; foolery; non-

sense; ∠ый [14; глуп, -á, -o] foolish, silly, stupid.
глух|áрь *m* [4 *e.*] capercailie, wood grouse; ~óй [14; глух, -á, -o; *comp.*: глу́ше] deaf (*a. fig.*; к Д to; *cf.* слепóй); dull, vague; desolate, wild; out-of-the-way; ⚠ tight, solid, blind; late, the dead of; *gr.* voiceless; ~онемóй [14] deaf-mute; ~отá *f* [5] deafness.
глуш|и́тель ⊕ *m* [4] muffler; ~и́ть [16 *e.*; -шу́, -ши́шь; -шённый] **1.** ⟨о-⟩ deafen, stun; **2.** ⟨за-⟩ deafen; deaden; muffle; smother, suppress (*a.* ♀); ⊕ switch off, throttle; ⚡ jam; ~ь *f* [8] thicket; wilderness; solitude, lonely spot, nook.
глы́ба *f* [5] lump, clod; block.
гля|дéть [11; гля́дя], ⟨по-⟩, *once* ⟨∠нуть⟩ [20] look, glance (at на В); F look after, take care of (за Т); peep (out of, from из Р); F ~ди́ very likely; look out!; тогó и ~ди́ ... may + *inf.* (unexpectedly); куда́ глаза́ ~дя́т at random; after one's nose.
гля́н|ец *m* [1; -нца] polish; luster; ~цев(и́т)ый [14 (*sh.*)] glossy, lustrous; glazed *paper*; ~уть *s.* глядéть.
г-н *abbr.*: господи́н.
гнать [гоню́, гóнишь; гони́мый; гнал, -á -o; '...гнанный], ⟨по-⟩ **1.** *v/t.* (be) drive (-ving, *etc.*); F send; float; **2.** distil; **3.** pursue, chase; (*a.* -ся за Т; *fig.* strive for); **4.** *v/i.* speed along.
гнев *m* [1] anger; ∠аться [1], ⟨раз-, про-⟩ be(come) angry (with на В); ∠ный [14; -вен, -вна́, -o] angry.
гнедóй [14] sorrel, chestnut (*horse*).
гнезд|и́ться [15] nest; ~ó *n* [9; *pl.*: гнёзда, *etc. st.*] nest, aerie.
гнёт *m* [1] press(ure); oppression.
гни|éние *n* [12] putrefaction; ~лóй [14; гнил, -á, -o] rotten, putrid; wet; ~ль *f* [8] rottenness; ~ть [гнию́, -ёшь; гнил, -á, -o], ⟨с-⟩ rot, putrefy.
гно|éние *n* [12] suppuration; ~и́ть (-ся) [13] fester; ~й *m* [3] pus; ∠и́ный [14] purulent.
гнуса́вить [14] snuffle, twang.
гну́сн|ость *f* [8] meanness; ~ый [14; -сен, -сна́, -o] vile, mean, base.
гнуть [20], ⟨со-⟩ bend, curve; bow; F drive (at к Д); *fig.* bully.
гнуша́ться [1], ⟨по-⟩ (Р *or* Т) scorn, despise, disdain.
говé|нье *n* [12] fast; ~ть [1] fast.
гóвор *m* [1] talk, hum, murmur; rumo(u)r; accent; dialect, patois; ~и́ть [13], ⟨по-; сказа́ть⟩ [3] speak *or* talk (about, of о П, про В; to *or* with p. с Т); say, tell; ~я́т, ~я́тся they say, it is said; ~и́ть по-ру́сски speak Russian; ина́че ~я́ in other words; не ~я́ ужé о (П) let alone; по пра́вде (сóвести) ~я́ to tell the truth; что вы ~и́те! you don't say!; что (как) ни ~и́ whatever you (one) may say; что и ~и́ть, и не ~и́(те)! yes, of course, sure!; ~ли́вый [14 *sh.*] talkative.
говя́|дина *f* [5], ~жий [18] beef.
гóгот *m* [1], ~а́ть [3], ⟨за-⟩ cackle; P roar (with laughter).
год *m* [1; *pl.*: -ды & -да́, *from g/pl. e.* & лет, *etc.* 9 *e.*] year (в ~ a *or* per year); в э́том (прóшлом) ~у́ this (last) year; из ∠а в ∠ year in year out; ∠ óт ~у year by year; кру́глый ~ all the year round; (с) ~а́ми for (after a number of) years; *cf.* пят(и-десят)ый.
годи́т|ься [15 *e.*; гожу́сь, годи́шься], ⟨при-⟩ be of use (for для Р, к Д, на В), do; fit; *pf.* come in handy; э́то (никуда́) не ~ся that's no good (for anything), that won't do, it's (very) bad.
годи́чный [14] annual.
гóдный [14; -ден, -днá, -o, гóдны́] fit, suitable, useful, good, ⚔ able(-bodied) (to, *a.* + *inf.*, for для Р, к Д, на В); ни на чтó не ~ good-for-nothing.
годов|óй [14] annual; one year (old); ~щи́на *f* [5] anniversary.
гол *m* [1] goal; заби́ть ~ score.
гол|ени́ще *n* [11] bootleg; ∠ень *f* [8] shank.
голла́нд|ец *m* [1; -дца] Dutchman; ♀ия *f* [7] Holland; ~ка *f* [5; *g/pl.*: -док] Dutchwoman; ~ский [16] Dutch.
голов|á [5; *pl.*: гóловы, голóв, -ва́м] **1.** *f* [*ac/sg.*: '~у] head; **2.** *m* head, chief; ~á са́хару sugar loaf; как снег нá ~у all of a sudden; с ~ы́ до ног from head to foot; в ~áх at the head; на свою́ '~у F to one's own harm; повéсить '~у become discouraged *or* despondent; ~á идёт кру́гом (у Р s.b.'s) thoughts are in a whirl; ∠ка *f* [5; *g/pl.*: -вок] small head; head (*pin, nail, etc.*); bulb, clove (*onion, garlic*); ~нóй [14] head...; ⚔ advance...; ~ная боль *f* headache.
голово|кружéние *n* [12] giddiness; ~кружи́тельный [14] dizzy, giddy; ~лóмка *f* [5; *g/pl.*: -мок] puzzle; ~мóйка *f* [5; *g/pl.*: -мóек] F blowup; ~рéз F *m* [1] daredevil; cutthroat, thug; ~тя́п F *m* [1] booby, bungler.
гóлод *m* [1] **1.** hunger; **2.** *s.* ~óвка; ~áть [1] starve; ∠ный [14; гóлоден, -днá, -o, гóлодны́] hungry; starv(el)ing; ~óвка *f* [5; *g/pl.*: -вок] starvation; famine; hunger strike.
гололéдица *f* [5] ice-crusted ground.
гóлос *m* [1; *pl.*: -cá, *etc. e.*] voice; vote; пра́во ~а suffrage; во весь ~ at the top of one's voice; в оди́н ~ unanimously; ~á зá и прóтив the yeas (ayes) & noes; ~и́ть P [15 *e.*; -ошу́, -оси́шь] bawl; ~лóвный

[14; -вен, -вна] unfounded; empty; **~ова́ние** *n* [12] voting, poll(ing); закры́тое ~ова́ние secret vote; **~ова́ть** [7], ⟨про-⟩ vote; **~ово́й** [14] vocal (cords свя́зки *f/pl*).

голуб|е́ц *m* [1; -бца́] stuffed cabbage; **~о́й** [14] (sky) blue; **∠(уш)ка** *f* [5; *g/pl.*: -бок (-шек)], **∠чик** *m* [1] (F *address*) (my) dear; **'~ь** *m* [4] pigeon; **~я́тня** *f* [6; *g/pl.*: -тен] dovecote.

го́л|ый [14; гол, -á, -о] naked, nude; bare (*a. fig.*); poor, miserable; **~ь** *f* [8] poverty; waste (land).

гомеопа́тия *f* [7] homeopathy.

гомин(ь)да́н *m* [1] Kuomintang.

го́мон F *m* [1] din, hubbub.

гондо́ла *f* [5] gondola (*a.* ✈).

гон|е́ние *n* [12] persecution; **~е́ц** *m* [1; -нца́] courier; **∠ка** *f* [5; *g/pl.*: -нок] rush; chase; F haste; ⚗ distil(l)ment; *pl.* race(s), ⚓ regatta; F blowup; ∠ка вооруже́ний arms race.

Гонко́нг *m* [1] Hong Kong.

го́нор *m* [1] airs *pl.*; **~а́р** *m* [1] fee.

го́ночный [14] race..., racing.

гонт *m* [1] *coll.* shingles.

гонча́р *m* [1 *e.*] potter; **~ный** [14] potter's; ~ные изде́лия *n/pl.* pottery.

го́нчая *f* [17] (*a.* ~ соба́ка) hound.

гоня́ть(ся) [1] drive, *etc.*, *s.* гнать.

гор|а́ *f* [5; *ac/sg.*: го́ру; *pl.*: го́ры, гор, гора́м] mountain; heap, pile; (*a. pl.*) (toboggan) slide; в ∠у *or* нá ~у uphill; *fig.* up(ward); по́д ~у *or* с ~ы́ downhill; под ~о́й at the foot of a hill (*or* mountain); не за ~а́ми not far off; пир ~о́й F sumptuous feast; стоя́ть ~о́й (за В) defend s.th. *or* s.b. with might & main; у меня́ ~а́ с плеч свали́лась F a load's been (*or* was) taken off my mind.

гора́здо *used with the comp.* much, far; P quite.

горб *m* [1 *e.*; на -у́] hump, hunch; **~а́тый** [14 *sh.*] humpbacked; curved; aquiline (*nose*); **∠ить** [14], ⟨с-⟩ stoop, bend, curve (*v/i.* **-ся**); **~у́н** *m* [1 *e.*] hunchback; **~у́шка** *f* [5; *g/pl.*: -шек] top crust, heel (*bread*).

горд|ели́вый [14 *sh.*] haughty, proud; **~е́ц** *m* [1 *e.*] proud man; **~и́ться** [15 *e.*; горжу́сь, горди́шься], ⟨воз-⟩ be(come) proud (of T); **∠ость** *f* [8] pride; **∠ый** [14; горд, -á, -о] proud (of T).

го́р|е *n* [10] grief, distress; trouble; misfortune, disaster; с ~я out of grief; ~е мне! woe is me!; ему́ и ~я ма́ло F he doesn't care a bit; с ~ем попола́м F hardly, with difficulty; **~ева́ть** [6], ⟨по-⟩ grieve; regret (s. th. о П).

горе́л|ый [14] burnt. **~ка** *f* [5; *g/pl.*: -лок] burner;

горемы́ка F *m/f* [5] poor wretch.

го́рест|ный [14; -тен, -тна] sad, sorrowful; **~ь** *f* [8] *cf.* го́ре.

гор|е́ть [9], ⟨с-⟩ burn (*a. fig.*), be on fire; glow, gleam; не ~и́т F there's no hurry; де́ло ~и́т (в рука́х у P) F the matter is top urgent (makes good progress).

го́рец *m* [1; -рца] mountaineer.

го́речь *f* [8] bitter taste (*or* smell); *fig.* bitterness; grief, affliction.

горизо́нт *m* [1] horizon; **~а́льный** [14; -лен, -льна] horizontal, level.

гори́стый [14 *sh.*] mountainous; hilly.

го́рка *f* [5; *g/pl.*: -рок] *dim. of* горá, *s.*; hill; whatnot, small cupboard.

горла́нить P [13], ⟨за-, про-⟩ bawl.

го́рл|о *n* [9] throat; gullet; (*vessel*) neck (*a.* **~ышко** *n* [9; *g/pl.*: -шек]); по ~о F up to the eyes; я сыт по ~о F I've had my fill (*fig.* I'm fed up with [T]); во всё ~о *s.* го́лос.

горн *m* [1] **1.** ⊕ (*a.* **~и́ло** *n* [9]) furnace, forge; crucible (*a. fig.*); **2.** ♪ horn, bugle; **~и́ст** *m* [1] bugler.

го́рничная *f* [14] parlo(u)rmaid.

горно|заво́дский [16], **~промы́шленный** [14] mining, metallurgical; **~рабо́чий** *m* [17] miner.

горноста́й *m* [3] ermine.

го́рн|ый [14] mountain(ous), hilly; *min.* rock...; ⊕ mining; ~ый про́мысел *m*, ~ое де́ло *n* mining; ~ое со́лнце *n* sun lamp; **~я́к** *m* [1 *e.*] miner.

го́род *m* [1; *pl.*: -дá, *etc. e.*] town; city (*large town*; F *down town*); зá ~(ом) *go* (*live*) out of town; **~и́ть** P [15], ⟨на-⟩ (вздор, *etc.*) talk nonsense; **~о́к** *m* [1; -дкá] small town; quarter; **~ско́й** [14] town..., city..., municipal; *s. a.* горсове́т.

горожа́н|ин *m* [1; *pl.*: -жа́не, -жа́н] townsman; *pl.* townspeople; **~ка** *f* [5; *g/pl.*: -нок] townswoman.

горо́|х *m* [1] pea (*plant*); *coll.* peas (*seeds*) *pl.*; **~ховый** [14] pea(s)...; pea green; чу́чело ~ховое *n*, шут ~ховый *m* F *fig.* scarecrow; boor, merry-andrew; **~шек** *m* [1; -шка] *coll.* (small) peas *pl.*; **~шин(к)а** *f* [5 (*g/pl.*: -нок)] pea; dot.

горсове́т (городско́й сове́т) *m* [1] city *or* town soviet (council).

го́рст|очка *f* [5; *g/pl.*: -чек] *dim.* of **~ь** *f* [8; *from g/pl. e.*] hollow (*hand*); handful (*a. fig.*).

горта́н|ный [14] guttural; **~ь** *f* [8] larynx.

горчи́ца *f* [5] mustard.

горшо́к *m* [1; -шкá] pot.

го́рьк|ий [16; -рек, -рькá, -о; *comp.*: го́рче] bitter (*a. fig.*); *f su.* vodka, bitters *pl.*; ~ий пья́ница *m* dipsomaniac.

горю́ч|ее *n* [17] (engine) fuel; gasoline, *Brt.* petrol; **~ий** [17 *sh.*] combustible; P bitter (*tears*).

горя́ч|ий [17; горя́ч, -á] hot (*a. fig.*); fiery, hot-tempered; ardent, passionate; violent; warm (*scent*); cordial; hard, busy; **~и́ть** [16 *e.*;

-чу́, -чи́шь], ⟨раз-⟩ heat (*a. fig.*); **-ся** get *or* be excited; **~ка** *f* [5] fever (*a. fig.*); **~ность** *f* [8] vehemence, hot temper.

гос = госуда́рственный state... (*of the U.S.S.R.*); **2ба́нк** *m* [1] State Bank; **2изда́т** (2уда́рственное изда́тельство) *m* [1] State Publishing House; **2пла́н** (2уда́рственный пла́новый комите́т) *m* [1] State Planning Committee.

го́спиталь *m* [4] ⚔ hospital.

господ|и́н *m* [1; *pl.*: -пода́, -по́д, -да́м] gentleman; master (*a. fig.*); Mr. (*with name or title*); (ladies &) gentlemen (*a. address*); *pl.* (*servants*:) master & mistress; уважа́емые **~а́** dear Sirs (*in letters, a.* †); я сам себе́ **~и́н** I am my own master; **~ский** [16] seignorial, (land)lord's, master's; manor (house); **~ство** *n* [9] rule; supremacy; **~ствовать** [7] rule, reign; (pre)dominate, prevail (over над T); command (*region*); **~ь** *m* [го́спода, -ду; *voc.*: -ди] Lord, God (*a. as int., cf.* бог).

госпожа́ *f* [5] lady; mistress; Mrs. *or* Miss (*with name*).

гостеприи́м|ный [14; -мен, -мна] hospitable; **~ство** *n* [9] hospitality.

гост|и́ная *f* [14] drawing room; **~и́нец** *m* [1; -нца] present, gift; **~и́ница** *f* [5] hotel; inn; **~и́ть** [15 *e.*; гощу́, гости́шь] be on a visit, stay with (у P); **~ь** *m* [4; *from g/pl. e.*] guest; visitor (*f* **~ья** [6]); идти́ (е́хать) в **~и** go to see (s.b. к Д); быть в **~я́х** (у P) = и́ть.

госуда́рственный [14] state...; national; ⚖ public; high (*treason*); ~ переворо́т *m* coup d'état; ~ стро́й *m* political system, regime; *s. a.* ГПУ.

госуда́р|ство *n* [9] state; **~ь** *m* [4] sovereign; Czar; ми́лостивый **~ь** (dear) Sir (*a. pl., in letters, a.* †).

готова́льня *f* [6; *g/pl.*: -лен] (case of) drawing utensils *pl.*

гото́в|ить [14] **1.** ⟨при-⟩ prepare (o.s. *or* get ready for **-ся** к Д); **2.** ⟨под-⟩ prepare, train; **3.** ⟨за-⟩ store up; lay in (*stock*); **~ность** *f* [8] readiness; willingness; **~ый** [14 *sh.*] ready (for к Д *or inf.*), on the point of; finished; willing; ready-made (*clothes*); будь **~**! — всегда́ **~**! be ready! — always ready! (*slogan of pioneers, cf.* пионе́р).

ГПУ (Госуда́рственное полити́ческое управле́ние) G.P.U. = Political State Administration (*predecessor, 1922—35, of* НКВД, *cf.*).

гр. *abbr.*: граждани́н.

граб *m* [1] hornbeam.

граб|ёж *m* [1 *e.*] robbery; **~и́тель** *m* [4] robber; **~ить** [14], ⟨о-⟩ rob, plunder.

гра́бли *f/pl.* [6; *gen.*: -бель & -блей] rake.

грав|ёр *m* [1] engraver; **~ий** *m* [3] gravel; **~ирова́ть** [7], ⟨вы́-⟩ engrave; **~иро́вка** *f* [5; *g/pl.*: -вок] engraving, etching, print (*a.* **~ю́ра** *f* [5]).

град *m* [1] hail (*a. fig.* = shower); ~ идёт it is hailing; **~ом** thick & fast, profusely.

гра́дус *m* [1] degree (of в B); под **~ом** F tipsy; **~ник** *m* [1] thermometer.

гражд|ани́н *m* [1; *pl.*: гра́ждане, -ан], **~а́нка** *f* [5; *g/pl.*: -нок] citizen (*U.S.S.R. a.* = [wo]man, & *in address, mst. without name*); **~а́нский** [16] civil (*a. war*); civic (*a. right*); **~а́нство** *n* [9] citizenship; citizens *pl.*; дать (получи́ть) пра́во **~а́нства** (be) accept(ed) (in public); приня́ть ... **~а́нство** become a ... citizen.

грамза́пись *f* [8] recording.

грамм *m* [1] gram(me).

граммат|ика *f* [5] grammar; **~и́ческий** [16] grammatical.

граммофо́н *m* [1] gramophone.

гра́мот|а *f* [5] reading & writing; document; patent; diploma; † letter; вери́тельная **~а** credentials; э́то для меня́ кита́йская **~а** F it's Greek to me; **~ность** *f* [8] literacy; **~ный** [14; -тен, -тна] literate; trained, expert.

грана́т *m* [1] pomegranate; *min.* garnet; **~а** *f* [5] shell; grenade.

грандио́зный [14; -зен, -зна] mighty; grand.

гранёный [14] facet(t)ed; cut.

грани́т *m* [1] granite.

грани́|ца *f* [5] border, frontier; boundary; *fig.* limit, verge; за **~цу** (**~цей**) *go* (*be*) abroad; из-за **~цы** from abroad; **~чить** [16] border *or* verge ([up]on с T).

гра́н|ка *f* [5; *g/pl.*: -нок] *typ.* galley (proof); **~ь** *f* [8] *s.* грани́ца; ⅊ plane; facet; edge; *fig.* verge.

граф *m* [1] earl (*Brt.*); count.

граф|а́ *f* [5] column; **~ик** *m* [1] diagram, graph; **~ика** *f* [5] graphic arts.

графи́н *m* [1] decanter, carafe.

графи́ня *f* [6] countess.

графи́|т *m* [1] graphite; **~ть** [14 *e.*; -флю, -фи́шь; -флённый], ⟨раз-⟩ line *or* rule (*paper*), draw columns; **~ческий** [16] graphic(al).

граци|о́зный [14; -зен, -зна] graceful; **'~я** *f* [7] grace(fulness).

грач *m* [1 *e.*] rook.

греб|ёнка *f* [5; *g/pl.*: -нок] comb; стри́чь(ся) под **~ёнку** (have one's hair) crop(ped); **~ень** *m* [4; -бня] comb; crest; **~е́ц** *m* [1; -бца́] oarsman; **~ешо́к** *m* [1; -шка́] *s.* **~ень**; **~ля** *f* [6] rowing; **~но́й** [14] row(ing)...

грёз|а *f* [5] (day)dream; **~ить** ('grе-) [15] *impf.* dream (of о П); ⚘

rave; **-ся**, ⟨по-, при-⟩: мне гре́зится (И) I dream (of *or v/t.*).
грек *m* [1] Greek.
гре́лка *f* [5; *g/pl.*: -лок] hot-water bottle; электри́ческая ~ heating pad.
грем|е́ть [10 *e.*; гремлю́, **-ми́шь**], ⟨про-, за-⟩ thunder, peal (*a. voice, bell, etc.*); rattle, clank, tinkle (*sword, chains, keys*); clatter (*dishes*); *fig.* ring; be famous (for, as); **~у́чий** [17] rattling; ⚗ oxyhydrogen; fulminating; ~у́чая змея́ *f* rattlesnake; **~у́шка** *f* [5; *g/pl.*: -шек] rattle (*toy*).
гренки́ *m/pl.* [1 *e.*] toast (*sg.*: **-но́к**).
Гренла́ндия *f* [7] Greenland.
грести́ [24 -б-: гребу́; грёб, гребла́], ⟨по-⟩ row; scull; rake; scoop.
греть [8; ...гре́тый], ⟨со-, на-, разо-, обо-, подо-⟩ warm (o.s. **-ся**) (up); heat; -ся на со́лнце sun.
грех *m* [1 *e.*] sin; fault; F = грешно́; с ~о́м попола́м F so-so; *cf.* го́ре; есть тако́й ~ F well, I own it; как на ~ F unfortunately.
Гре́|ция *f* [7] Greece; **2цкий** [16]: 2цкий оре́х *m* walnut; **2ча́нка** *f* [5; *g/pl.*: -нок], **2ческий** [16] Greek.
греч|и́ха, **∠ка** *f* [5] buckwheat; **∠невый** [14] buckwheat...
греш|и́ть [16 *e.*; -шу́, **-ши́шь**], ⟨со-⟩ sin (*a.* against про́тив Р); **∠ник** *m* [1], **∠ница** *f* [5] sinner; **~но́** (it's a) shame (on Д); **∠ный** [14; -шен, -шна́, -о]; sinful; F *sh.*: sorry.
гриб *m* [1 *e.*] mushroom; **~о́к** [1; -бка́] *dim. of* ~; fungus.
гри́ва *f* [5] mane.
гри́венник F *m* [1] ten-kopeck coin.
Григо́рий *m* [3] Gregory.
грим *m* [1] *thea.* make-up.
грима́с|а *f* [5] grimace; **~ничать** [1] make faces *or* grimaces.
гримирова́ть [7], ⟨за-, на-⟩ make up (*v/i.* **-ся**).
грипп *m* [1] influenza.
гри́фель *m* [4] slate pencil.
Гри́ш(к)а *m* [5] *dim. of* Григо́рий.
гр-ка *abbr.*: гражда́нка.
гроб *m* [1; в -у́; *pl.*: -ы́ & -а́, *etc. e.*] coffin; † grave; **~ни́ца** *f* [5] tomb; **~ово́й** [14] coffin...; tomb...; deadly; **~овщи́к** *m* [1 *e.*] coffin maker.
гроза́ *f* [5; *pl. st.*] (thunder)storm (*a fig.*); disaster; danger, menace; terror.
грозд|ь *m* [4; *pl.*: -ди, -де́й, *etc. e.*, & -дья, -дьев] bunch (*grapes*); cluster.
грози́ть [15 *e.*; грожу́, **-зи́шь**], ⟨по-⟩ threaten (a p. with Д/Т) (*a.* **-ся**).
гро́з|ный [14; -зен, -зна́, -о] menacing; formidable; P severe, cruel; Ива́н 2ный Ivan the Terrible; **~ово́й** [14] storm(y).
гром *m* [1; *from g/pl.*: *e.*] thunder (*a. fig.*); ~ греми́т it thunders; как ∠ом поражённый *fig.* thunderstruck.
грома́д|а *f* [5] giant, colossus; mass, heap; **~ный** [14; -ден, -дна] huge, tremendous.
громи́|ть [14 *e.*; -млю, -ми́шь; -млённый], ⟨раз-⟩ smash, crush; rout.
гро́мк|ий [16; -мок, -мка́, -о; *comp.*: гро́мче] loud; noisy; *fig.* famous, great, noted; notorious; (*words, etc.*) pompous; **~оговори́тель** *m* [4] loud-speaker.
громо|во́й [14] thunder..., thunderous; **~гла́сный** [14; -сен, -сна] roaring; *mst. adv.* in public; **~зди́ть** **(-ся)** [15 *e.*; -зжу́, -зди́шь] *cf.* взгромозжда́ть(ся); **∠здкий** [16; -док, -дка] bulky, cumbersome; **~отво́д** *m* [1] lightning rod *or* conductor.
громыха́ть F [1] rattle.
грот *m* [1] grotto.
гро́х|нуть F [20] *pf.* crash, tumble (*v/i.* **-ся**); **~от** *m* [1] rumble; **~ота́ть** [3], ⟨за-⟩ rumble; P roar.
грош *m* [1 *e.*] half-kopeck; piece; ни ~а́ not a stiver *or* farthing; ~ цена́ *or* ~а́ ло́маного не сто́ит not worth a pin; ни в ~ не ста́вить not care a straw (for В); **~о́вый** [14] worth 1 ~; *fig.* (dirt-)cheap, paltry.
груб|е́ть [8], ⟨за-, о-⟩ harden, become callous; **~и́ть** [14 *e.*; -блю́, -би́шь], ⟨на-⟩ say rude things; **~ия́н** F *m* [1] rude fellow; **∠ость** *f* [8] rudeness; **∠ый** [14; груб, -а́, -о] coarse; rough; rude; gross (*error, etc.*).
гру́да *f* [5] pile, heap, mass.
груд|и́нка *f* [5; *g/pl.*: -нок] brisket; bacon; **~но́й** [14]: ~на́я клётка *f* thorax, chest; **~ь** *f* [8; в, на -ди́; *from g/pl. e.*] breast; bosom; стоя́ть **∠ью** (за В) defend bravely.
груз *m* [1] load, freight; ⚓ cargo.
грузи́н *m* [1; *g/pl.*: грузи́н], **~ка** *f* [5; *g/pl.*: -нок] Georgian; **~ский** [16] Georgian.
грузи́ть [15 & 15 *e.*; -ужу́, -у́зи́шь], ⟨на-, за-, по-⟩ load, embark.
Гру́зия *f* [7] Georgia (*Caucasus*).
гру́з|ный [14; -зен, -зна́, -о] massive, heavy; **~ови́к** *m* [1 *e.*] truck, *Brt.* lorry; **~ово́й** [14] freight..., goods..., ⚓ cargo...; ~ово́й автомоби́ль *m* = ~ови́к; **~оподъёмность** *f* [8] carrying capacity, ⚓ tonnage; **~чик** *m* [1] loader, ⚓ stevedore.
грунт *m* [1] soil; ground (*a. paint.*); **~ово́й** [14] ground...; unpaved.
гру́пп|а *f* [5] group; **~ирова́ть** **(-ся)** [7], ⟨с-⟩ (form a) group.
груст|и́ть [15 *e.*; -ущу́, -сти́шь], F ⟨взгрустну́ть⟩ [20] grieve; long (for) (по П); **∠ный** [14; -тен, -тна́,

-о] sad, sorrowful; dreary; F deplorable; мне ˏно I feel sad; ˷ь *f* [8] sadness, grief, melancholy.
гру́ша *f* [5] pear (*a. tree*).
гры́жа *f* [5] hernia, rupture.
грыз|ня́ F *f* [6] squabble; ˷ть [24; *pt. st.*], ⟨раз-⟩ gnaw (*a. fig.*), nibble; bite; crack (*nuts*); -ся bite o. a.; F squabble; ˷у́н *m* [1 *e.*] *zo.* rodent.
гряд|а́ *f* [5; *nom/pl. st.*] ridge, range (*a. fig.* = line); ⚒ bed (*a.* ˏка *f* [5; *g/pl.*: -док]).
гряду́щий [17] future, coming; на сон ˷ for a nightcap.
гряз|ево́й [14] mud...; ˷езащи́тный [14]: ˷езащи́тное крыло́ *n* fender, mudguard; ˷елече́бница *f* [5] mud bath; ˏи *f/pl.* [8] (curative) mud; ˷ни́ть [13], ⟨за-⟩ soil (*a. fig.*); -ся get dirty; ˏнуть [20], ⟨по-⟩ sink (*mud, etc., & fig.*); ˏный [14; -зен, -зна́, -о, гря́зны́] dirty (*a. fig.*); muddy; slop... (*pail*); ˷ь *f* [8; в -зи́] dirt; mud (*street, etc.*); в ˷и́ dirty; не уда́рить лицо́м в ˷ь save one's face.
гря́нуть [19 *st.*] *pf.* crash, thunder, (re)sound, ring, roar; break out, burst, start.
губ|а́ *f* [5; *nom/pl. st.*] lip; bay; gulf; ˏа не ду́ра (у P p.'s) taste isn't bad.
губерн|а́тор *m* [1] governor; ˏия *f* [7] government, province.
губи́т|ельный [14; -лен, -льна] pernicious; ˷ь [14], ⟨по-, F с-⟩ destroy, ruin; waste (*time*).
гу́б|ка *f* [5; *g/pl.*: -бок] 1. *dim. of* ˷а́; 2. sponge; ˷но́й [14] labial; ˷на́я пома́да *f* lipstick.
гуверн|а́нтка *f* [5; *g/pl.*: -ток] governess; ˷ёр *m* [1] tutor.
гуд|е́ть [11], ⟨за-⟩ buzz; honk, hoot, whistle; ˷о́к *m* [1; -дка́] honk, hoot, signal; horn; siren, whistle.
гул *m* [1] boom, rumble; hum; ˏкий [16; -лок, -лка́, -о] booming, loud; resonant.
гуля́|нье *n* [10] walk(ing); revel(ry), open-air merrymaking, (popular) festival; ˷ть [28], ⟨по-⟩ [20] go for a walk (*a.* идти́ ˷ть), stroll; *fig.* sweep (*wind, etc.*); make merry.
ГУМ (госуда́рственный универма́г) *m* [1] state department store.
гума́нн|ость *f* [8] humanity, humaneness; ˷ый [14; -а́нен, -а́нна] humane.
гумно́ *n* [9; *pl. st., gen.*: -мен & -мён] ⚒ floor.
гур|т *m* [1 *e.*] drove (*cattle*); ˷то́м F wholesale; ˷ьба́ F *f* [5] crowd (in T).
гу́сеница *f* [5] caterpillar (*a.* ⊕).
гуси́ный [14] goose (*a.* flesh ко́жа *f*).
густ|е́ть [8], ⟨за-⟩ thicken; ˷о́й [14; густ, -а́, -о] thick, dense; deep, rich (*colo[u]r, sound*); ˷ота́ *f* [5] thickness; density; depth.
гус|ь *m* [4; *from g/pl. e.*] goose; *fig.* хоро́ш ˷ь F a fine fellow indeed!; как с ˏя вода́ F like water off a duck's back, thick-skinned; ˷ько́м in single file.
гу́ща *f* [5] grounds *pl.*; sediment; thicket; *fig.* center (*Brt.* -tre), middle.
ГЭС *abbr.*: гидро(электро)ста́нция.

Д

д. *abbr.*: 1. дере́вня; 2. дом.
да 1. *part.* yes; oh (yes), indeed (*a. interr.*); (oh) but, now, well; *imp.* do(n't) ...!; *tags:* aren't, don't, *etc.*; may, let; 2. *cj.* (*a.* ˷ и) and; but; ˷ и то́лько continually; ˷ что́ вы! you don't say!
дабы́ † (in order) that *or* to.
да|ва́ть [5], ⟨˷ть⟩ [дам, дашь, даст, дади́м, дади́те, даду́т ('...-) дал, -а́, -о; ('...)да́нный (дан, -а́)] give; let; bestow; take (*oath*), pledge; make (*way*); ˷ва́й(те)! come on!; *with vb.* (*a.* ˏй[те]) let us (me); ни ˏть ни взять exactly like; ˷ва́ть ход де́лу set s.th. going *or* further it; -ся let o.s. (*be caught. cheated* в В); (turn out to) be (*e.g. hard*, for Д); (can) master (s. th. И); *pt.* F take to.
дави́ть [14] 1. ⟨на-⟩ press; squeeze (⟨вы́-⟩ out); 2. ⟨за-, раз-⟩ crush; run over, knock down; 3. ⟨по-⟩ oppress; suppress; 4. ⟨при-, с-⟩ press (down *or* together), jam, compress; throng, crowd; 5. ⟨у-⟩ strangle; -ся choke; F hang o.s.
да́в|ка F *f* [5] throng, jam; ˷ле́ние *n* [12] pressure (*a. fig.*).
да́вн|(и́шн)ий [15] old; ˷о́ long ago; for a long time, long since; ˷опроше́дший [17] long past; ˷опроше́дшее вре́мя *n. gr.* past *or* pluperfect; ˷ость *f* [8] remoteness; ⚖ limitation; ˷ы́м-˷о́ F (a) very long (time) ago.
да́же (*a.* ˷ и) even; ˷ не not even.
да́л|ее *s.* да́льше; и так ˷ее and so on (*or* forth); ˷ёкий [16; -лёк, -лека́, -леко́ & -лёко; *comp.*: да́лее, да́льше], far, distant (from от P); long (*way*); *fig.* wide (of); strange (to); F smart, clever; ˷еко́, ˷ёко far (off, away); a long way (to до P); (Д) ˷еко́ до (P) F can't match with; ˷еко́ не F by no means; ˷еко́ за (В) long after; (*age*) well over; ˷ь *f* [8; в -ли́] distance; open (space); ˷ьне́йший [17] further;

в ~ьнейшем later *or* further on; **~ьний** [15] distant (*a. relative*); remote; *s. a.* ~ёкий; **~ьневосточный** [14] Far Eastern.

дально|бойный ⚔ [14] long range; **~видный** [14; -ден, -дна] clear-sighted; **~зоркий** [16; -рок, -рка] far-, long-sighted; **'~сть** *f* [8] remoteness; ⚔, ⊕ (long) range.

дальше farther; further(more); then, next; (читайте) ~! go on (reading); не ~ как *or* чем this very; only.

дам|а *f* [5] lady; partner (*dance*); queen (*card*); **~ский** [16] ladies', women's; **~ба** *f* [5] dam, dike; **~ка** *f* [5; *g/pl.*: -мок] king (*draughts*).

Дани|ил [1], P **∠ла** *m* [5] Daniel.

Дания *f* [7] Denmark.

дан|ный [14] given, present, this; **~ная** *f* ♣ quantity; **~ные** *pl.* data, facts; statistics.

дантист *m* [1] dentist.

дань *f* [8] tribute (*a. fig.*).

дар *m* [1; *pl. e.*] gift (*a. fig.*); **~ить** [13], ⟨по-⟩ give (a p. s.th. Д/В), present (a p. with В/Т); **~моед** F *m* [1] sponger; **~ование** *n* [12] gift, talent; **~овитый** [14 *sh.*] gifted, talented; **~овой** [14] gratis, free.

даром *adv.* gratis, for nothing; in vain; ~ что (al)though; это ему ~ не пройдёт F he will smart for it.

Дарья *f* [6] Darya (*first name*).

дат|а *f* [5] date; **~ельный** [14] *gr.* dative (*case*); **~ировать** [7] (*im*)*pf.* (задним числом ante)date.

дат|ский [16] Danish; **~чанин** *m* [1; *pl.*: -чане, -чан], **~чанка** *f* [5; *g/pl.*: -нок] Dane.

дать(ся) *s.* давать(ся).

дач|а *f* [5] giving; cottage, summer residence, villa; на ~е out of town, in the country; **~ник** *m* [1] summer resident; **~ный** [14] suburban; country...; garden (city посёлок).

Даш([ень]к)а *f* [5] *dim. of* Дарья.

два *m*, *n*, две *f* [34] two; *cf.* пять & пятый; в ~ счёта F in a jiffy.

двадцат|илетний [15] twenty-years-old, of 20; **∠ый** [14] twentieth; *cf.* пят(идесят)ый; **'~ь** [35; -ти] twenty; *cf.* пять.

дважды twice; ~ два ♣ two by two; как ~ два (четыре) as sure(ly) as two & two makes four.

двенадцат|и... (*in compds.*) twelve-...; dodec(a)...; duodecimal, -denary; **~ый** [14] twelfth; *cf.* пятый; **~ь** [35] twelve; *cf.* пять.

двер|ной [14] door...; **∠ца** *f* [5; *g/pl.*: -рец] *dim. of* **~ь** *f* [8; в -ри; *from g/pl. e.*; *instr. a.* -рьми] door (*a. pl.* ∠и).

двести [36] two hundred.

дви|гатель *m* [4] engine, motor; **~гать** [1 & 3], ⟨~нуть⟩ [20] (В & Т) move, push, drive (on); stir; **-ся** move, advance; set out, start; **~жение** *n* [12] movement (*a. pol.*); stir; *phys.* motion; traffic; *fig.* emotion; *pl.* (light) gymnastics; приводить (приходить) в ~жение set going (start [moving]); **~жимый** [14 *sh.*] movable; **~нуть** *s.* ~гать.

двое [37] two (*in a group, together*); нас было ~ we (there) were two (of us); **~брачие** *n* [12], **~жёнство** *n* [9] bigamy; **~точие** *n* [12] colon.

двоиться [13], ⟨раз-⟩ bifurcate.

двой|ка *f* [5; *g/pl.*: двоек] two (*a. boat*; *team*; P *bus, etc., no. 2*; *cards, a.* deuce); pair; F (*mark*) = плохо, *cf.*; **~ник** *m* [1 *e.*] double(ganger); **~ной** [14] double (*a. fig.*); **~ня** *f* [6; *g/pl.*: двоен] twins *pl.*; **~ственный** [14 *sh.*] double, twofold, -faced; dual (*a. gr.* number число).

двор *m* [1 *e.*] (court)yard; farm(-stead); court; на ~е outside, outdoors; **~ец** *m* [1; -рца] palace; **∠ник** *m* [1] janitor, (yard &) street cleaner; F *mot.* windshield (*Brt.* windscreen) wiper; **∠ня** *f* [6] *coll.*, † servants, domestics *pl.*; **~няга** F *f* [5], **~няжка** F *f* [5; *g/pl.*: -жек] mongrel; watchdog; **~овый** [14] yard-..., house...; servant...; **~цовый** [14] court...; palace...; **~янин** *m* [1; *pl.*: -яне, -ян] nobleman; **~янка** *f* [5; *g/pl.*: -нок] noblewoman; **~янский** [16] n ble; **~янство** *n* [9] nobility.

двоюродн|ый [14]: ~ый брат *m*, ~ая сестра *f* cousin.

двояк|ий [16 *sh.*] double, twofold; **~о** in two ways.

дву|бортный [14] double-breasted; **~главый** [14] double-headed; **~гласный** [14] diphthong(al); **~жильный** P [14] sturdy, tough; **~колка** *f* [5; *g/pl.*: -лок] cart; **~кратный** [14] double; done twice; **~личие** *n* [12] duplicity; **~личный** [14; -чен, -чна] double-faced; **~рушник** *m* [1] double-dealer; **~рушничество** *n* [9] double-dealing; **~смысленный** [14 *sh.*] ambiguous; **~стволка** *f* [5; *g/pl.*: -лок] double-barrel(l)ed gun; **~ствольный** [14]: ~ствольное ружьё *n* = ~стволка; **~створчатый** [14]: ~створчатая дверь *f* folding doors; **~сторонний** [15] bilateral; two-way (*traffic*); reversible (*fabric*).

двух... (*cf. a.* дву...): **~дневный** [14] two days'; **~колейный** 🚂 [14] double-track; **~колёсный** [14] two-wheel(ed); **~летний** [15] two-years-old; two years'; **~местный** [14] two-seat(ed); **~месячный** [14] two months' *or* two-months-old; **~моторный** [14] twin-engine(d); **~недельный** [14] two weeks', *Brt. a.* a fortnight's; **~сотый** [14] two hundredth; **~этажный** [14] two-storied (*Brt.* -reyed).

двуязы́чный [14; -чен, -чна] bilingual.
дебат|и́ровать [7] debate; **~ы** *m/pl.* [1] debate.
дебе́лый F [14 *sh.*] plump, fat.
де́бет † *m* [1] debit; занести́ в ~ = **~ова́ть** [7] *(im)pf.* debit (*sum* against *or* to a p. В/Д).
дебито́р *m* [1] debtor.
дебо́ш *m* [1] riot, row.
де́бри *f/pl.* [8] thicket; wilderness.
дебю́т *m* [1] debut; opening.
де́ва *f* [5]: (ста́рая) ~ (old) maid.
девальва́ция *f* [7] devaluation.
дева́ть [1], ⟨деть⟩ [де́ну, -нешь] put; place; leave, mislay; куда́ ~ *a.* what to do with, how to spend; **-ся** go, get; *vb.* + И = put, leave + *obj.*; be (*pr.*); куда́ мне ~ся? where shall I go *or* stay? куда́ он де́лся? what has become of him?
де́верь *m* [4; *pl.:* -рья́, -ре́й, -рья́м] (*wife's*) brother-in-law.
деви́з *m* [1] motto.
дев|и́ца *f* [5] maid, girl; **~и́чий** [18] maiden, girl's; ~и́чий монасты́рь *m* nunnery; **~ка** *f* [5; *g/pl.:* -вок] wench; P maid; P whore; **~очка** *f* [5; *g/pl.:* -чек] (little) girl; **~ственный** [14 *sh.*] maiden; virgin...; primeval; **~ушка** *f* [5; *g/pl.:* -шек] (grown-up) girl; † parlo(u)rmaid; **~чо́нка** F *f* [5; *g/pl.:* -нок] slut; girl.
девя|но́сто [35] ninety; **~но́стый** [14] ninetieth; *cf.* пят(идеся́т)ый; **~тисо́тый** [14] ninehundredth; **~тка** *f* [5; *g/pl.:* -ток] nine (*cf.* дво́йка); **~тна́дцатый** [14] nineteenth; *cf.* пять & пя́тый; **~тна́дцать** [35] nineteen; *cf.* пять; **~тый** [14] ninth; *cf.* пя́тый; **'~ть** [35] nine; *cf.* пять; **~тьсо́т** [36] nine hundred; '~тью nine times.
дегенера́т *m* [1] degenerate.
дёготь *m* [4; -гтя] tar.
де́д|(ушка *m* [5; *g/pl.:* -шек]) *m* [1] grandfather; old man; *pl.* ~ы *a.* forefathers; ♀ Моро́з *m* Jack Frost; Santa Claus, Father Christmas.
деепричა́стие *n* [12] *gr.* gerund.
дежу́р|ить [13] be on duty; sit up, watch; **~ный** [14] (p.) on duty; **~ство** *n* [9] duty; (night) watch.
дезерти́р *m* [1] deserter; **~овать** [7] *(im)pf.* desert; **~ство** *n* [9] desertion.
дезинф|е́кция *f* [7] disinfection; **~ици́ровать** [7] *(im)pf.* disinfect.
дезорганиз|ова́ть [7] *(im)pf.*, *impf. a.* **~о́вывать** [1] disorganize.
де́йств|енный [14 *sh.*] efficient; **~ие** *n* [12] action; activity; ⚔, ⊕, ⅍ operation; *thea.* act; effect; efficacy; influence, impact; ме́сто ~ия scene; свобо́да ~ий free play; **~и́тельно** really; indeed; **~и́тельность** *f* [8] reality; validity; **~и́тельный** [14; -лен, -льна] real, actual; valid; ⚔, *gr.* active (*service*; *voice*); **~овать** [7], ⟨по-⟩ act, work (*a.* upon на В); operate, function; apply; have effect (on на В); get (*on one's nerves*); **~ующий** [17] active; acting; ⚔ field...; ~ующее лицо́ *n* character, personage.
дека́брь *m* [4 *e.*] December.
дека́н *m* [1] dean.
декла|ми́ровать [7], ⟨про-⟩ declaim; **~ра́ция** *f* [7] declaration.
декольт|е́ (dɛ-; -'tɛ) *n* [*indecl.*] décolleté; **~иро́ванный** [14 *sh.*] low-necked.
декора́|тор *m* [1] decorator; **~ция** *f* [7] decoration; *thea.* scenery.
декре́т *m* [1] decree, edict; **~и́ровать** [7] *(im)pf.* decree.
де́ла|нный [14 *sh.*] affected, forced; **~ть** [1], ⟨с-⟩ make, do; ~ть не́чего F it can't be helped; **-ся** (Т) become, grow, turn; happen (with, to с Т), be going on; что с ним сде́лалось? what has become of him?
делега́|т *m* [1] delegate; **~ция** *f* [7] delegation.
дел|ёж F *m* [1 *e.*] distribution, sharing; **~е́ние** *n* [12] division (*a.* ⅍); partition; point (*scale*).
деле́ц *m* [1; -льца́] (sharp) businessman, moneymaker.
делика́тн|ость *f* [8] tact(fulness), delicacy; **~ый** [14; -тен, -тна] delicate.
дели́|мое *n* [14] ⅍ dividend; **~тель** *m* [4] ⅍ divisor; **~ть** [13; делю́, де́лишь] **1.** ⟨раз-, по-⟩ (на В) divide (in[to]), *a.* ⅍ (by); **2.** ⟨по-⟩ share (*a.* **-ся** [Т/с Т s.th. with s. b.], exchange; confide [s.th. to], tell; ⅍ be divisible).
дели́шки F *n/pl.* [9; *gen:* -шек] [business.]
де́л|о *n* [9; *pl. e.*] affair, matter, concern; work, business (on по Д), line; art *or* science; deed, act(ion); ⚖ case, (*a. fig.*) cause; file; ⚔ action, battle; говори́ть ~о F talk sense; де́лать ~о *fig.* do serious work; то и ~о continually, incessantly; в чём ~о? what's the matter?; в том то и ~о F that's just the point; что вам за ~о? *or* э́то не ва́ше ~о that's no business of yours; на ~е in practice; на (*or* в) са́мом ~е in reality, in fact; really, indeed; по ~а́м on business; как ~а́? F how are you?; ~о идёт *cf.* идти́.
делов|и́тый [14 *sh.*], **~о́й** [14] businesslike; expert; ~о́й *a.* business...; work(ing).
делопроизводи́тель *m* [4] secretary.
де́льный [14] competent; sensible.
демаго́г *m* [1] demagogue; **~и́ческий** [16] demagogic(al).
демаркацио́нный [14] (of) demarcation.
демилитаризова́ть [7] *(im)pf.* demilitarize.
демобилизова́ть [7] *(im)pf.* demobilize.

демокра́т *m* [1] democrat; **~и́ческий** [16] democratic; **~ия** [7] democracy.
демонстр|а́ция *f* [7] demonstration; **~и́ровать** [7] (*im*)*pf*., *a*. ⟨про-⟩ demonstrate; show, project (*film*).
демонта́ж *m* [1] dismantling.
де́нежный [14] money..., monetary, pecuniary; currency...; F rich.
день *m* [4; дня] day; в ~ a *or* per day; в э́тот ~ (on) that day; ∠ за́ ~ day after day; изо дня́ в ∠ day by day; ∠ ото дня́ from day to day; весь ~ all day (long); на (э́тих) днях the other day; one of these days; три часа́ дня 3 p.m., 3 o'clock in the afternoon; *cf*. днём.
де́ньги *f*/*pl*. [*gen*.: де́нег; *from. dat. e*.] money.
департа́мент *m* [1] department.
депе́ша *f* [5] dispatch, wire(less).
депози́т ✝ *m* [1] deposit.
депута́т *m* [1] deputy, delegate; member of the Supreme Soviet.
дёр|гать [1], *once* ⟨~нуть⟩ [20] pull, tug (*a*. за B at), jerk, twist; F press a p. hard, importune.
дерев|ене́ть [8], ⟨за-, о-⟩ stiffen; grow numb; **~е́нский** [16] village-..., country..., rural, rustic; **~е́нский жи́тель** *m* villager; **∠ня** *f* [6; *g*/*pl*.: -ве́нь, *etc*. *e*.] village; country(side); **'~о** *n* [9; *pl*.: -е́вья, -е́вьев] tree; *sg*. wood; кра́сное '~о mahogany; чёрное '~о ebony; резьба́ по ~у wood engraving; **~я́нный** [14] wooden (*a*. *fig*.).
держа́ва *f* [5] power; *hist*. orb.
держа́ть [4] hold; keep; support; have (*a*. ✝ in stock; *a*. *exam*.); read (*proofs*); ~ сто́рону side with; ~ себя́ (кого́-либо) в рука́х (have) control (over) o.s. (a p.); ~ себя́ conduct o.s., behave = -ся 1.; 2. ⟨у~ся⟩ (за B; P) hold (on[to]); *fig*. stick (to); keep; hold out, stand.
дерз|а́ть [1], ⟨~ну́ть⟩ [20] dare, venture; **∠кий** [16; -зок, -зка́, -о; *comp*.: -зче] impudent, insolent; bold, daring, audacious; (*a*. = † **~нове́нный** [14; -е́нен, -е́нна] & **∠остный** [14; -тен, -тна]); **∠ость** *f* [8] impudence, cheek.
дёрн *m* [1] turf; **~уть** *s*. дёргать.
дес|а́нт *m* [1] landing; troops *pl*. landed (авиа... airborne...); **~е́рт** *m* [1] dessert; **~на́** *f* [5; *pl*.: дёсны, -сен, *etc*. *st*.] gum; **∠пот** *m* [1] despot.
десяти|дне́вный [14] ten days'; **~кра́тный** [14] tenfold; **~ле́тие** *n* [12] decade; tenth anniversary; **~ле́тка** *f* [5; *g*/*pl*.: -ток] ten-grades (*or* -forms) standard school (*leading to maturity*) (*U.S.S.R.*); **~ле́тний** [15] ten years'; ten-years-old.
десят|и́на *f* [5] †, = *approx*. $2^3/_4$ *acres*; tithe; **~и́чный** [14] decimal; **∠ка** *f* [5; *g*/*pl*.: -ток] ten (*cf*. дво́йка); **∠ник** *m* [1] foreman; **∠ок** *m* [1; -тка] ten; *pl*. dozens of, many; *s*. идти́; не ро́бкого ∠ка F not a craven; **∠ый** [14] tenth (*a*., *f*, part; 3,2 — *read*: три це́лых и две ∠ых = 3.2); *cf*. пя́т(идеся́т)ый; из пя́того в ∠ое discursively, in a ramblingmanner; **'~ь** [35 *e*.] ten; *cf*. пять & пя́тый; **'~ью** ten times.
дета́ль *f* [8] detail; ⊕ part; **~но** in detail; **~ный** [14; -лен, -льна] detailed, minute.
дет|вора́ *f* [5] *coll*. F = ∠и; **~ёныш** *m* [1] young one; cub, *etc*.; **∠и** *n*/*pl*. [-е́й, -ям, -ьми́, -ях] children, kids; дво́е, (тро́е, че́тверо, *etc*.) ~е́й two (three, four) children; *sg*.: дитя́ (*a*. ребёнок), *cf*.; **∠ский** [16] child(ren)'s, infant(ile); childlike; childish; ∠ский дом *m* (orphan) boarding school; ∠ский сад *m* kindergarten; ∠ская *f* nursery (room); **∠ство** *n* [9] childhood.
де́ть(ся) *s*. дева́ть(ся).
дефе́ктный [14] defective.
дефици́тный [14; -тен, -тна] unprofitable; scarce.
деш|еве́ть [8], ⟨по-⟩ cheapen, become cheaper; **~еви́зна**, F **~ёвка** *f* [5] cheapness, low price(s); **~ёвый** [14; дёшев, дешева́, дёшево; *comp*.: деше́вле] cheap (*a*. *fig*.); low (*price*).
де́ятель *m* [4] man; representative; госуда́рственный ~ statesman; нау́чный ~ scientist; обще́ственный ~ public man; полити́ческий ~ politician; **~ность** *f* [8] activity, -ties *pl*.; work; **~ный** [14; -лен, -льна] active.
джу́нгли *f*/*pl*. [*gen*.: -лей] jungle.
диа́|гноз *m* [1] diagnosis; **~гона́ль** *f* [8] diagonal; **~ле́кт** *m* [1] dialect; **~ле́ктный** [14] dialectic(al); **~ле́ктика** *f* [5] dialectic(s); **~лекти́ческий** [16] dialectic(al); **~ло́г** *m* [1] dialogue; **~ма́т** *m* [1] dialectical materialism; **~метр** *m* [1] diameter; **~пазо́н** *m* [1] ♪ diapason (*a*. *fig*.); ⊕ range; **~позити́в** *m* [1] (lantern) slide; **~фра́гма** *f* [5] diaphragm.
дива́н *m* [1] divan, sofa.
диверс|а́нт *m* [1] saboteur; **∠ия** *f* [7] sabotage; ⚔ diversion.
диви́зия ⚔ *f* [7] division.
див|и́ться [14 *e*.], ⟨по-⟩ wonder (at Д *or* на B); **∠ный** [14; -вен, -вна] wonderful; delightful; **∠о** *n* [9] wonder, miracle, marvel (*a*. it is a ...); на ∠о excellently; что за ∠о! (most) wonderful!; no wonder.
дие́т|а (-'ɛta) *f* [5] diet; **~и́ческий** [16] dietetic(al).
дизентери́я *f* [7] dysentery.
дик|а́рь *m* [4 *e*.] savage (*a*. *fig*.); F shy person; **∠ий** [16; дик, -á, -о] wild, savage (*a*. *fig*.); odd, bizarre; shy, unsociable; drab; ⚘ proud

(*flesh*); dog (*rose*);**⁓ость** *f* [8] wildness, savagery, -geness; absurdity.

дикт|áнт *m* [1] *s.* ⁓óвка; **⁓áтор** *m* [1] dictator; **⁓áторский** [16] dictatorial; **⁓атýра** *f* [5] dictatorship; **⁓овáть** [7], ⟨про-⟩ dictate; **⁓óвка** *f* [5; *g/pl.:* -вок] dictation; **⁓ор** *m* [1] (radio) announcer.

дилетáнт *m* [1] dilettante; **⁓ский** [16] dilettant(e)ish.

динáм|ика *f* [5] dynamics; **⁓и́т** *m* [1] dynamite; **⁓и́ческий** [16] dynamic; **⁓о(-маши́на** *f* [5]) *n* [*indecl.*] dynamo.

динáстия *f* [7] dynasty.

диплóм *m* [1] diploma; F thesis to degree.

диломáт *m* [1] diplomat; **⁓и́ческий** [16] diplomatic; **⁓ия** *f* [7] diplomacy.

дирек|ти́ва *f* [5] directive; **⁓тор** *m* [1; *pl.:* -рá, *etc. e.*] manager, director; (*school*) principal, *Brt.* headmaster; **⁓ция** *f* [7] management, directorate.

дириж|áбль *m* [4] airship; **⁓ёр** *m* [1] ♪ conductor; **⁓и́ровать** [7] (T) ♪ conduct.

дисгармóния *f* [7] discord.

диск *m* [1] disk; **⁓óнт** *m* [1], **⁓онти́ровать** [7] (*im*)*pf.* discount; **⁓ýссия** *f* [7] discussion.

дисп|ансéр (-ˈsɛr) *m* [1] dispensary; **⁓éтчер** *m* [1] dispatcher; 🚂 traffic superintendent; **⁓ут** *m* [1] dispute, disputation.

дис|сертáция *f* [7] dissertation, thesis; **⁓сонáнс** *m* [1] dissonance, discord; **⁓тáнция** *f* [7] distance; 🚂 section; **⁓тилли́ровать** [7; -óванный] (*im*)*pf.* distil(l); **⁓циплúна** *f* [5] discipline.

дитя́ *n* [-я́ти ⚒; *pl.* дéти, *cf.*] child.

диф|ирáмб *m* [1] dithyramb; **⁓тери́т** *m* [1], **⁓тери́я** *f* [7] diphtheria; **⁓фамáция** *f* [7] defamation.

дифференц|иáл *m* [1], **⁓иáльный** [14] ℞, ⊕ differential; **⁓и́ровать** [7] (*im*)*pf.* differentiate.

дич|áть [1], ⟨о-⟩ run wild; *fig.* grow (**⁓и́ться** F [16 *e.*; -чýсь, чи́шься] be) shy, unsociable; shun (a p. P); **⁓ь** *f* [8] game, wild fowl; F wilderness; F nonsense, bosh.

длин|á *f* [5] length; в ⁓ý (at) full length, lengthwise; ⁓óй в (В) ... *or* в ⁓ý ... long; **⁓но...** (*in compds.*) long...; **⁓ный** [14; -и́нен, -иннá, -и́нно] long; too long; F tall.

дли́т|ельный [14; -лен, -льна] long; protracted, lengthy; **⁓ься** [13], ⟨про-⟩ last.

для (P) for, to; because of; ⁓ тогó, чтóбы (in order) to, that ... may; ⁓ чегó? wherefore?; я́щик ⁓ пи́сем mail (*Brt.* letter) box.

Дми́трий *m* [3] Demetrius (*name*).

днев|áльный [14] ⚔ orderly; p. on duty; **⁓áть** [6] spend the day; have a day of rest; **⁓ни́к** *m* [1 *e.*] journal, diary (*vb.:* вести́ keep); **⁓нóй** [14] day('s), daily; day(light свет *m*).

днём by day, during the day.

Днепр *m* [1 *e.*] Dnieper; **⁓óвский** [16] Dnieper...

дн|о *n* [9; *pl.:* дóнья, -ньев] bottom; золотóе ⁓о *fig.* gold mine; вы́пить до ⁓а drain, empty; идти́ ко ⁓у *v/i.* (пусти́ть на ⁓о *v/t.*) sink.

до (P) *place:* to, as far as, up (*or* down) to; *time:* till, until, to; before; *degree:* to, up (*or* even) to; *age:* under; *quantity:* up to; about; ⁓ тогó so (much); (Д) не ⁓ F not be interested in *or* disposed for, *or* have no time, *etc.*, for, to.

добáв|ить *s.* ⁓ля́ть; **⁓лéние** *n* [12] addition; supplement; **⁓ля́ть** [28], ⟨⁓ить⟩ [14] add; **⁓очный** [14] additional, extra; supplementary.

добе|гáть [1], ⟨⁓жáть⟩ [-егý, -ежи́шь, -егýт] run up to (до P).

доб|ивáть [1], ⟨⁓и́ть⟩ [-бью́, -бьёшь; -бéй(те)!; -би́тый] beat completely *or* utterly, smash; kill, finish; **-ся** (P) (try to) get, obtain *or* reach; strive for; find out (about); он ⁓и́лся своегó he gained his end(s); **⁓ирáться** [1], ⟨⁓рáться⟩ [-берýсь, -рёшься] get to, reach.

дóблест|ный [14; -тен, -тна] valiant, brave; **⁓ь** *f* [8] valo(u)r.

добрó[1] *n* [9] good; F property; **⁓м** F kindly, amicably; ⁓[2] F well; ⁓ бы if only; ⁓ пожáловать! welcome!; please; **⁓вóлец** *m* [1; -льца] volunteer; **⁓вóльный** [14; -лен, -льна] voluntary; **⁓дéтель** *f* [8] virtue; **⁓дéтельный** [14; -лен, -льна] virtuous; **⁓дýшие** *n* [12] good nature; **⁓дýшный** [14; -шен, -шна] good-natured; **⁓желáтельный** [14; -лен, -льна] benevolent; **⁓желáтельство** *n* [9] benevolence; **⁓кáчественный** [14 *sh.*] (of) good (quality); ⚕ benign; **⁓сердéчный** [14; -чен, -чна] good-hearted; **⁓сóвестный** [14; -тен, -тна] conscientious; **⁓сосéдский** [16] good neighbo(u)rly; **⁓м** *s.* ⁓[1].

добр|отá *f* [5] kindness; **⁓óтный** [14; -тен, -тна] (very) good, solid; **⁓ый** [14; добр, -á, -о, дóбры́] kind; good; F solid; ⁓ое ýтро *n* (⁓ый день *m*, вéчер *m*)! good morning (afternoon, evening)!; в ⁓ый час!, всегó ⁓ого! good luck!; чегó ⁓ого after all; бýдь(те) ⁓(ы́) will you be so kind.

добы|вáть [1], ⟨⁓ть⟩ [-бýду, -дешь; дóбы́л, -á, дóбы́ло; дóбы́тый (дóбы́т, добы́та, дóбы́то)] get, obtain, procure; ⚒ extract, mine; *hunt.* bag; **⁓ча** *f* [5] procurement; ⚒ extraction, mining; booty, spoil; (*animals'*) prey (*a. fig.*); *hunt.* bag.

довезти́ *s.* довози́ть.

довéр|енность *f* [8] (на В) ⚖ letter of attorney; † = ~ие; **~енный** [14] deputed; proxy, agent; **~ие** *n* [12] confidence, trust (in к Д); **~ить** *s.* ~я́ть; **~чивый** [14 *sh.*] trusting, trustful; confidential; **~ша́ть** [1], ⟨~ши́ть⟩ [16 *e.*; -шу́, -ши́шь] finish; complete; **~ше́ние** *n* [12] completion; в ~ше́ние *or* к ~ше́нию (Р) to complete *or* crown (s.th.); **~я́ть** [28], ⟨~ить⟩ [13] trust (a p. Д); confide *or* entrust (s.th. to В/Д); entrust (a p. with Д/В); **-ся** (Д) *a.* trust, rely (on).

дов|ести́ *s.* ~оди́ть; **´од** *m* [1] argument; **~оди́ть** [15], ⟨~ести́⟩ [25] (до Р) see (a p. to); lead ([up] to); bring (to); drive (to), make.

довое́нный [14] prewar.

дов|ози́ть [15], ⟨~езти́⟩ [24] (до Р) take *or* bring ([right up] to).

дово́ль|но enough, sufficient; rather, pretty, fairly; **~ный** [14; -лен, -льна] content(ed), satisfied (with Т); **~ствие** ⚔ *n* [12] ration, allowance; **~ство** *n* [9] contentment, satisfaction; F prosperity; **~ствоваться** [7] content o.s. (with Т).

довы́боры *m/pl.* [1] by-election.

догад|а́ться *s.* ´ываться; **´ка** *f* [5; *g/pl.*: -док] guess, conjecture; **´ливый** [14 *sh.*] quick-witted; **´ываться**, ⟨~а́ться⟩ [1] (о П) guess, surmise.

до́гма *f* [5], **~т** *m* [1] dogma.

догна́ть *s.* догоня́ть.

догов|а́ривать [1], ⟨~ори́ть⟩ [13] finish (speaking), speak; **-ся** (о П) agree (upon), arrange; ~а́ривающиеся сто́роны *f/pl.* contracting parties; **~о́р** *m* [1] contract; *pol.* treaty; **~ори́ть(ся)** *s.* ~а́ривать(ся); **~о́рный** [14] contract(ual).

дог|оня́ть [28], ⟨~на́ть⟩ [-гоню́, -го́нишь, *cf.* гнать] catch up (with), overtake; drive *or* bring to; *impf. a.* pursue, try to catch up, be (on the point of) overtaking; **~ора́ть** [1], ⟨~оре́ть⟩ [9] burn down; *fig.* fade, die out.

дод|е́лывать, ⟨~е́лать⟩ [1] finish, complete; **~у́мываться**, ⟨~у́маться⟩ [1] (до Р) find, reach *or* hit upon (s. th., by thinking).

доезжа́|ть [1], ⟨дое́хать⟩ [-е́ду, -е́дешь] (до Р) reach; не ~я short of.

дожд|а́ться *s.* дожида́ться; **~еви́к** F *m* [1 *e.*] raincoat; **~ево́й** [14] rain(y); ~ево́й зо́нтик *m* umbrella; ~ево́й червь *m* earthworm; **~ли́вый** [14 *sh.*] rainy; **~ь** *m* [4 *e.*] rain (in под Т, на П); ~ь идёт it is raining.

дож|ива́ть [1], ⟨~и́ть⟩ [-живу́, -вёшь; до́жил, -а́, -о; до́житый (до́жит, -а́, -о)] *impf.* live one's last years, *etc.*; (до Р) *pf.* live (till *or* up to); (live to) see; come to; **~ида́ться** [1], ⟨~да́ться⟩ [-ду́сь, -дёшься; *cf.* ждать] (Р) wait (for, till); *pf. a.* see.

до́за *f* [5] dose.

дозво|ля́ть [28], ⟨´лить⟩ [13] permit, allow; ´ленный *a.* licit; **~ни́ться** F [13] *pf.* reach (a p. by phone до Р), ring till the door *or* phone is answered.

дозна́ние ⚖ *n* [12] inquest.

дозо́р ⚔ *m* [1], **~ный** ⚔ [14] patrol.

дои́ск|иваться F [1], ⟨~а́ться⟩ [3] (Р) (try to) find (out).

дои́ть(ся) [13], ⟨по-⟩ (give) milk.

дойти́ *s.* доходи́ть.

док *m* [1] ⚓ dock.

доказ|а́тельство *n* [9] proof, evidence; **´ывать** [1], ⟨~а́ть⟩ [3] prove; argue.

док|а́нчивать [1], ⟨~о́нчить⟩ [16] finish, end.

докла́д *m* [1] report; lecture (on о П); **~на́я** [14] (*a.* записка *f*) memorandum, report; **~чик** *m* [1] lecturer; reporter; **~ывать** [1], ⟨доложи́ть⟩ [16] report (s.th. В *or* on о П); announce (a p. о П).

доко́нчить *s.* дока́нчивать.

до́ктор *m* [1; *pl.* -ра́, *etc. e.*] doctor.

доктри́на *f* [5] doctrine.

докуме́нт *m* [1] document.

докуча́ть F [1] = надоеда́ть.

долби́ть [14 *e.*; -блю́, -би́шь; -блённый] **1.** ⟨вы́-, про-⟩ hollow (out); peck (*bird*); chisel; *impf.* F strike; **2.** P ⟨в-⟩ inculcate; cram.

долг *m* [1; *pl. e.*] debt; *sg.* duty; (last) hono(u)rs *pl.*; в ~ = взаймы́; в ~у́ indebted (*a. fig.*, to у Р, пе́ред Т); **´ий** [16; до́лог, долга́, -о] long; **´о** long, (for) a long time *or* while.

долго|ве́чный [14; -чен, -чна] perennial (*a.* ⚘), durable; **~во́й** [14]: ~во́е обяза́тельство *n* promissory note; **~вре́менный** [14] (very) long; **~вя́зый** F [14 *sh.*] lanky; **~игра́ющий** [17]: ~игра́ющая пласти́нка *f* long-playing record; **~ле́тие** *n* [12] longevity; **~ле́тний** [15] longstanding; of several years; **~сро́чный** [14] long-term; **~та́** *f* [5; *pl.*: -го́ты, *etc. st.*] length; *geogr.* longitude; **~терпели́вый** [14 *sh.*] long-suffering.

до́л|ее = ~ьше, *cf.*; **~ета́ть** [1], ⟨~ете́ть⟩ [11] (до Р) fly ([up] to), reach; *a.* = доноси́ться.

до́лж|ен *m*, ~на́ *f*, ~но́ *n* (*cf.* ~но́[2]), ~ны́ *pl.* **1.** must [*pt.*: ~ен был, ~на́ была́, *etc.* had to]; **2.** (Д) owe (a p.); **~ни́к** *m* [1 *e.*] debtor; **~но**[1] one (it) must *or* ought to (be ...); proper(ly); **~но́**[2] P = ~но́ быть probably, apparently; **~ностно́й** [14] official; **~ность** *f* [8] post; office; **~ный** [14] due (*a. su.* ~ное *n*), proper; ~ным о́бразом duly.

доли|ва́ть [1], ⟨´ть⟩ [-лью́, -льёшь; *cf.* лить] fill (up), add.

доли́на *f* [5] valley.

до́ллар *m* [1] dollar.
доложи́ть *s.* докла́дывать.
доло́й F off, down; ~ ... (B)! down *or* off with ...!; с глаз ~! out of my sight!
долото́ *n* [9; *pl. st.*: -ло́та] chisel.
до́льше (*comp. of* до́лгий) longer.
до́ля *f* [6; *from g/pl. e.*] lot, fate; grain (*of truth*), spark (*of wit, etc.*); в восьму́ю (четвёртую) до́лю листа́ octavo (quarto), in 8vo (4to).
дом *m* [1; *pl.*: -а́, *etc. e.*] house; home; family; household; вы́йти и́з ~у leave (one's home), go out; на́ ~ = ~о́й; на ~у́ = ~а at home; как ~а at one's ease; (у P) не все ~а (be) a bit off (one's head), nutty; **~а́шний** [15] home..., house(hold)-...; private; domestic; *pl. su.* folks; ~а́шний стол *m* plain fare; **~енный** [14]: ~енная печь *f* = ~на; **~ик** *m* [1] *dim. of* дом.
домин|ио́н *m* [1] (*Brt.*) dominion; **~и́ровать** [7] (pre)dominate; **~о́** *n* [*indecl.*] domino(es).
домкра́т *m* [1] (lifting) jack.
до́мна *f* [5; *g/pl.*: -мен] blast furnace.
дом|ови́тый [14 *sh.*] thrifty, careful; notable (*housewife*); **~овладе́лец** *m* [1; -льца] house owner; **~о́вый** [14] house...
домога́ться [1] (P) strive for, solicit.
домо́|й home; **~ро́щенный** [14] homebred; **~се́д** *m* [1] stay-at-home; **~управле́ние** *n* [12] house management; **~ча́дцы** *m/pl.* [1] folks; inmate.
домрабо́тница *f* [5] housemaid.
до́мысел *m* [1; -сла] conjecture.
Дон *m* [1; на -ну́] Don; **~ба́сс** (= Доне́цкий бассе́йн) ⚒ *m* [1] Donets Basin.
доне|се́ние *n* [12] report; **~сти́(сь)** *s.* доноси́ть(ся); **~цкий** [14] *s.* Донба́сс.
до́н|изу to bottom; **~има́ть** F [1], ‹~я́ть› [дойму́, -мёшь; *cf.* заня́ть] press, exhaust (with T).
доно́с ⚖ *m* [1] denunciation, information (against на B); **~и́ть** [15], ‹донести́› [24; -су́, -сёшь] carry *or* bring ([up] to); report (s.th., about, on о П); denounce, inform (against на B); ~и́ть *pf.* wear out; *a.* **-ся** (до P) waft (to), reach, (re-) sound; **~чик** *m* [1] informer.
донско́й [16] (*adj. of* Дон) Don...
доны́не to this day, till now.
доня́ть *s.* донима́ть.
допи|ва́ть [1], ‹~ть› [-пью́, -пьёшь; *cf.* пить] drink up.
допла́|та *f* [5] additional payment, extra (*or* sur)charge; **~чивать** [1], ‹~ти́ть› [15] pay in addition.
допо́длинный F [14] true, real.
дополн|е́ние *n* [12] addition; supplement; *gr.* object; **~и́тельный** [14] additional, supplementary; extra; *adv. a.* in addition; more; **~я́ть** [28], ‹~ить› [13] add, supply, complete, fill up; enlarge (*edition*).
допото́пный [14] antediluvian.
допр|а́шивать [1], ‹~оси́ть› [15] ⚖ interrogate, examine; *impf.* question; **~о́с** *m* [1] ⚖ interrogation, examination; F questioning; **~оси́ть** *s.* ~а́шивать.
до́пу|ск *m* [1] access, admittance; **~ска́ть** [1], ‹~сти́ть› [15] admit (*a.* of), concede; allow; tolerate; suppose; make (*mistake*); **~сти́мый** [14 *sh.*] admissible, permissible; **~ще́ние** *n* [12] admission.
допы́т|ываться [1], ‹~а́ться› F (try to) find out.
дореволюцио́нный [14] pre-revolutionary, before the revolution.
доро́г|а *f* [5] road, way (*a. fig.*); passage; trip, journey; больша́я ~а highroad; желе́зная ~а railroad, *Brt.* railway; ~ой *or* в (по) ~е on the way; туда́ ему́ и ~а F that serves him right; *cf. a.* путь.
дорого|ви́зна *f* [5] dearness, high price(s); **~й** [16; до́рог, -а́, -о; *comp.*: доро́же] dear (*a. fig.*), expensive.
доро́дный [14; -ден, -дна] stout, burly.
дорож|а́ть [1], ‹вз-, по-› become dearer, rise in price; **~и́ть** [16 *e.*; -жу́, -жи́шь] (T) esteem (highly), (set a high) value (on).
доро́ж|ка *f* [5; *g/pl.*: -жек] path; беговая́ ~ка race track (*Brt.* -way); лётная ~ка ✈ runway; **~ный** [14] road...; travel(l)ing.
доса́|да *f* [5] vexation; annoyance, fret; F кака́я ~да! how annoying!, what a pity!; **~ди́ть** *s.* ~жда́ть; **~дливый** [14 *sh.*] fretful, peevish; **~дный** [14; -ден, -дна] annoying, vexatious; deplorable; (мне) ~дно it is annoying (annoys me); **~довать** [7] feel *or* be annoyed, vexed (at, with на B); **~жда́ть** [1], ‹~ди́ть› [15 *e.*; -ажу́, -ади́шь] vex, annoy (a p. with Д/T).
доск|а́ *f* [5; *ac/sg.*: до́ску; *pl.*: до́ски, досо́к, доска́м] board, plank; (*a.* кла́ссная ~а́) blackboard; plate; гри́фельная ~а́ slate; от ~и́ до ~и́ (*read*) from cover to cover; на одну́ ~у on a level.
доскона́льный [14; -лен, -льна] thorough.
досло́вный [14] literal, verbal.
досм|а́тривать [1], ‹~отре́ть› [9; -отрю́, -о́тришь] see up to *or* to the end (до P); watch, look after (за T); не ~отре́ть overlook; **~о́тр** *m* [1] supervision; (customs) examination; **~отре́ть** *s.* ~а́тривать.
доспе́хи *m/pl.* [1] armo(u)r; outfit.
досро́чный [14] preschedule.
дост|ава́ть [5], ‹~а́ть› [-ста́ну, -ста́нешь] take (out, *etc.*); get; procure; ([до] P) touch; reach (to); F (P) suffice, have enough; **-ся** (Д)

fall to a p.'s share; (turn out to) be, cost (*fig.*); F catch it; **~áвить** *s.* **~авля́ть**; **~áвка** *f* [5; *g/pl.*: -вок] delivery; conveyance; с ~áвкой (нá дом) carriage paid; free to the door; **~авля́ть** [28], ‹~áвить› [14] deliver, hand; bring; *fig.* procure, cause, give; **~áток** *m* [1; -тка] prosperity, (good) fortune; F sufficiency; **~áточно** considerably; (P) (be) enough, sufficient; suffice; **~áточный** [14; -чен, -чна] sufficient.

дости|гáть [1], ‹~гнуть›, ‹~чь› [21 -г-: -сти́гну, -гнешь] (P) reach, arrive at, attain (*a. fig.*); (*prices*) amount *or* run up (to); **~же́ние** *n* [12] attainment; achievement; **~жи́мый** [14 *sh.*] attainable.

достове́рный [14; -рен, -рна] authentic, reliable; positive.

достó|инство *n* [9] dignity; merit, advantage; (*money, etc.*) worth, value; **~йный** [14; -óин, -óйна] worthy (*a.* of P); well-deserved; **~пáмятный** [14; -тен, -тна] memorable, notable; **~примечáтельность** *f* [8] (*mst. pl.*) sight(s); **~примечáтельный** [14; -лен, -льна] remarkable, noteworthy; **~я́ние** *n* [12] property (*a. fig.*), fortune.

дóступ *m* [1] access; **∠ный** [14; -пен, -пна] accessible (*a. fig.*); approachable, affable; comprehensible; susceptible; moderate (*price*).

досу́г *m* [1] leisure; на ~е at leisure, during one's leisure hours.

дóс|уха (quite) dry; **∠ы́та** one's fill.

дот ⚔ *m* [1] pillbox.

дотлá completely, utterly; to the ground.

дотр|áгиваться [1], ‹~óнуться› [20] (до P) touch.

дóх|лый [14] dead; **~ля́тина** *f* [5] carrion; **~нуть** [21], ‹из-, по-› die; P croak, kick off; **~ну́ть** *s.* дышáть.

дохóд *m* [1] income, revenue; proceeds *pl.* **~и́ть** [15], ‹дойти́› [дойду́, -дёшь; *cf.* идти́] (до P) go *or* come (to), arrive (at), reach: *hist.* come down to; (*price*) rise, run up to; **~ный** [14; -ден, -дна] profitable.

доцéнт *m* [1] lecturer, instructor.

дóчиста (quite) clean; F completely.

дочи́т|ывать, ‹~áть›, [1] finish (*book, etc.*) *or* read up to (до P).

дóч|ка *f* [5; *g/pl.*: -чек] F = **~ь** *f* [дóчери, *etc.* = 8; *pl.*: дóчери, -рéй, *etc. e.*; *instr.*: -рьми́] daughter.

дошкóльный *m* [1] preschool.

дощ|áтый [14] of boards, plank...; **~éчка** *f* [5; *g/pl.*: -чек] *dim. of* доскá.

доя́рка *f* [5; *g/pl.*: -рок] milkmaid.

драгоцéнн|ость *f* [8] jewel, gem (*a. fig.*); precious thing *or* possession; **~ый** [14; -цéнен, -цéнна] precious (*a. stone*), costly, valuable.

дразни́ть [13; -ню́, дрáзнишь] **1.** ‹по-› tease, banter; nickname; **2.** ‹раз-› excite.

дрáка *f* [5] scuffle, fight.

дракóн *m* [1] dragon.

дрáма *f* [5] drama; **~ти́ческий** [16] dramatic; **~ту́рг** *m* [1] playwright, dramatist.

драп|ировáть [7], ‹за-› drape; **∠овый** [14] (of thick) cloth (драп).

дра|ть [деру́, -рёшь; драл, -á, -о; '... дранный], ‹со-› (*cf.* сдирáть) pull (off); tweak (p.'s *ear* B/за B; F *cf.* выдирáть & раздирáть; **-ся**, ‹по-› scuffle, fight, struggle; **~чли́вый** [14 *sh.*] pugnacious.

дребе|дéнь F *f* [8] trash; **'~зг** F *m* [1] clash; *cf.* вдрéбезги; **~зжáть** [4; -зжи́т], ‹за-› rattle.

древ|еси́на *f* [5] wood substance *or* material(s); **~éсный** [14] tree...; wood(y); ~éсный спирт *m* methyl alcohol; ~éсный у́голь *m* charcoal; **∠ко** *n* [9; *pl.*: -ки, -ков] flagpole.

дрéвн|ий [15; -вен, -вня] ancient (*a. su.*), antique; (very) old; **~ость** *f* [8] antiquity (*a. pl.* = -ties).

дрейф ⚓, ✈ *m* [1], **~овáть** [7] drift.

дрем|áть [2], ‹за-› doze (off), slumber; **~óта** *f* [5] drowsiness; slumber, doze; **~у́чий** [17] dense; ~у́чий лес *m* primeval forest.

дрессировáть [7], ‹вы́-› train.

дроб|и́ть [14 *e.*; -блю́, -би́шь; -блённый], ‹раз-› break to pieces, crush; dismember, divide *or* split up; *impf.* F drum; **∠ный** [14; -бен, -бна] fractional; rolling; drumming; **~ь** *f* [8] *coll.* (small) shot; (*drum*) roll; ⅋ [*from g/pl. e.*] fraction; decimal.

дров|á *n/pl.* [9] (fire)wood; **∠ни** *m/pl.* [4; *a. from g/pl. e.*] peasant's sled(ge); **~осéк** *m* [1] lumberman, *Brt.* woodcutter.

дрó|ги *f/pl.* [5] dray; **~гнуть 1.** [21], ‹про-› shiver *or* shake (*with cold*), chill; **2.** [20 *st.*] *pf.* start; waver, falter; shrink, flinch; **~жáть** [4 *e.*; -жу́, -жи́шь], ‹за-› tremble, shake, shiver (with от P); flicker, glimmer; dread (s.th. пéред T); be anxious (about за B); guard, save (над T); **~жжи** *f/pl.* [8; *from gen. e.*] yeast, barm; **~жки** *f/pl.* [5; *gen.*: -жек] droshky; **~жь** *f* [8] trembling, shiver; vibration; ripples *pl.*

дро|зд *m* [1 *e.*] thrush; **~к** *m* [1] ♀ broom; **∠тик** *m* [1] dart, javelin; **~фá** *f* [5; *pl. st.*] *zo.* bustard.

друг[1] *m* [1; *pl.*: друзья́, -зéй, -зья́м] friend; (*address a.*) dear; **~**[2]: ~ ∠а each (one an)other; ~ за ∠ом one after another; ~ с ∠ом with each other; **~óй** [14] (an)other, different; else, next, second; (н)и тóт (н)и ~óй both (neither); на ~óй день the next day.

дру́ж|ба *f* [5] friendship; **\~елю́бный** [14; -бен, -бна] amicable, friendly; **\~еский** [16], **\~ественный** [14 *sh.*] friendly; **\~и́на** *f* [5] bodyguard, retinue; militia; troop, (*fire*) brigade; **\~и́ть** [16; -жу́, -у́жи́шь] be friends, be on friendly terms (with с T); **\~и́ще** *m* F [11] old chap *or* boy; **\~ка** [5; *g/pl.*: -жек] **1.** *f* F = друг²; **2.** *m* best man; **\~ный** [14; -жен, -жна́, -о, дру́жны́] friendly, on friendly terms; harmonious, concurrent, unanimous; ⚘, ⚔ vigorous; *adv. a.* hand in hand, together; at once.

дря́|блый [14; дрябл, -á, -о] limp, flabby; **\~зги** F *f/pl.* [5] squabbles; **\~нно́й** P [14] wretched, mean, trashy; **\~нь** F *f* [8] rubbish, trash (*a. fig.*); P rotten, lousy (thing, p.); **\~хлый** [14; дряхл, -á, -о] decrepit; F dilapidated.

дуб *m* [1; *pl. e.*] oak; **\~и́льный** [14] tan...; **\~и́льня** *f* [6; *g/pl.*: -лен] tannery; **\~и́на** *f* [5] club, cudgel; P boor, dolt; **\~и́ть** [14 *e.*; -блю́, -би́шь], ⟨вы́-⟩ tan; **\~лёр** *m* [1] *thea.* understudy, double; **\~ова́тый** F [14 *sh.*] dull; **\~о́вый** [14] oak(en); *fig.* dull; **\~ра́ва** *f* [5] (oak) wood, forest.

дуг|á *f* [5; *pl. st.*] arc (*a.* ⚡); (shaft) bow (*harness*); \~о́й arched; **\~ово́й** [14]: \~ова́я ла́мпа *f* arc light.

ду́дк|а *f* [5; *g/pl.*: -док] pipe; F \~и! fudge!, rats!; пляса́ть под \~у *or* по \~е dance to s.b.'s tune *or* piping.

ду́ло *n* [9] muzzle; barrel (*gun*).

ду́ма *f* [5] **1.** thought; meditation; **2.** (*Russia, prior to 1917*) duma = council; elective legislative assembly; **\~ть** [1], ⟨по-⟩ think (about, of о П); reflect, meditate (on над T, о П); (+ *inf.*) intend, be going to; care (for о П); F suspect (на B); как ты \~ешь? what do you think?; мно́го \~ть о себе́ be conceited; не до́лго \~я without hesitation; **-ся** seem, appear; ([one, you] must, can) think.

Дуна́й *m* [3] Danube.

дун|ове́ние *n* [12] waft, breath; **∠уть** *s.* дуть.

Ду́ня *f* [6] *dim. of* Евдоки́я.

дупло́ *n* [9; *pl. st.*: ду́пла, -пел, -плам] hollow (*tree*); cavity (*tooth*).

ду́р|а *f* [5] silly woman; **\~а́к** *m* [1 *e.*] fool, simpleton; \~а́к \~ако́м arrant fool; **\~а́цкий** [16] foolish, silly; fool's; **\~а́чество** F *n* [9] tomfoolery; **\~а́чить** F [16], ⟨о-⟩ fool, hoax; **-ся** fool, play tricks; **\~е́ть** F [8], ⟨о-⟩ grow stupid; become stupefied; **\~и́ть** F [13] *s.* \~а́читься; be naughty *or* obstinate.

дурма́н *m* [1] jimson weed, thorn apple; *fig.* narcotic; **\~ить** [13], ⟨о-⟩ stupefy.

дурн|е́ть [8], ⟨по-⟩ grow plain *or* ugly; **\~о́й** [14; ду́рен, -рна́, -о] bad; plain, ugly; P stupid; мне ∠о I feel (am) sick *or* unwell; **\~ота́** F *f* [5] giddiness, sickness.

дурь F *f* [8] folly, caprice; trash.

ду́т|ый [14] blown (*glass*); *fig.* inflated; false; **\~ь** [18], ⟨по-⟩, *once* ⟨ду́нуть⟩ [20] blow; ду́ет there is a draught (draft); **-ся**, ⟨на-⟩ swell; F sulk, be angry with (на B); P give o.s. airs.

дух *m* [1] spirit; mind; courage; ghost; F breath; P scent; (не) в ∠е in a good (bad) temper *or* in high (low) spirits, ([+ *inf.*] in no mood to); в моём ∠е to my taste; на \~у́ at the confession; P ∠ом in a jiffy *or* trice; at one draught; во весь \~ *or* что́ есть ∠у at full speed, with all one's might; **\~и́** *m/pl.* [1 *e.*] perfume.

духов|е́нство *n* [9] *coll.* clergy; **∠ка** *f* [5; *g/pl.*: -вок] oven; **\~ни́к** *m* [1 *e.*] (father) confessor; **∠ный** [14] spiritual; mental; ecclesiastical, clerical, religious, sacred; **∠ная** *f* (*form.*) testament, will; ∠ный оте́ц *m* = \~ни́к; ∠ное лицо́ *n* clergyman; **\~о́й** [14] ♪ wind (*instrument*); **\~о́й** орке́стр *m* brassband.

духота́ *f* [5] sultriness, sultry air.

душ *m* [1] shower (bath); douche.

душ|á *f* [5; *ac/sg.*: ду́шу; *pl. st.*] soul; mind, disposition; temper (-ament); feeling, emotion; person; *hist.* serf; F *address*: dear, darling; \~á в ∠у in perfect harmony; в глубине́ \~и́ in one's heart of hearts; от (всей) \~и́ from (with all) one's heart; по \~а́м heart-to-heart; \~а́ в пя́тки ушла́ have one's heart in one's mouth.

душ|евнобольно́й [14] mentally sick *or* deranged (person); **\~е́вный** [14] mental, psychic(al); sincere, hearty; **∠енька** F *f* [5] darling; **\~ераздира́ющий** [17] heart-rending.

душ|и́стый [14 *sh.*] fragrant; sweet (*peas*); **\~и́ть** [16] **1.** ⟨за-⟩ strangle, choke (*a. fig.*); **2.** ⟨на-⟩ perfume (o.s. **-ся**); **∠ный** [14; -шен, -шна́, -о] stuffy; sultry.

дуэ́|ль *f* [8] duel; **\~т** *m* [1] duet.

ды́б|ом (*stand*) on end (*hair*); **\~ы́:** (встать, *etc.*) на \~ы́ rear (*a.* up, *fig.*), prance.

дым *m* [1] smoke; **\~и́ть** [14 *e.*; -млю́, -ми́шь], ⟨на-⟩ *or* **\~и́ться** smoke; steam; **∠ка** *f* [5] haze; gauze; **∠ный** [14] smoky; **\~ово́й** [14] smoke...; **\~о́к** *m* [1; -мка́] small stream *or* puff of smoke; **\~охо́д** *m* [1] flue.

ды́ня *f* [6] muskmelon.

дыр|á *f* [5; *pl. st.*], **∠ка** *f* [5; *g/pl.*: -рок] hole; **\~я́вый** [14 *sh.*] having a hole *or* full of holes; (*clothes, shoes*)

tattered; F bad (*memory*); ~ая голова́ F forgetful person.
дыха́|ние *n* [12] breath(ing); **~тельный** [14] respiratory; ~тельное го́рло *n* windpipe.
дыша́ть [4], ⟨по-⟩, F (*a. once*) ⟨дохну́ть⟩ [20] breathe (s. th. T); *a.* devote o.s. to, indulge in; foam with; ~ све́жим во́здухом take the air; е́ле ~ *or* ~ на ла́дан F have one foot in the grave.
ды́шло *n* [9] (*wagon, cart*) pole.
дья́вол *m* [1] devil; **~ьский** [16] devilish.
дья|к, ~чо́к *m* [1; -чка́] clerk & chanter, sexton; **~кон** *m* [1] deacon.
дю́жий P [17; дюж, -á, -е] sturdy.
дю́жин|а *f* [5] dozen; ~ами, по ~ам by the dozen; **~ный** [14] common (-place), mediocre.
дю|йм *m* [1] inch; **~на** *f* [5] dune.
дюралюми́ний *m* [3] duralumin.
дя́д|ька *m* [5; *g/pl.*: -дек] F & *contp.* = ~я; † tutor, instructor; **~я** *m* [6; *g/pl.*: -дей] uncle (*a. in* F *address*); F (strong) fellow, guy.
дя́тел *m* [1; -тла] woodpecker.

Е

'Ева *f* [5] Eve (*name*).
Ева́нгелие *n* [12] Gospel (♀ *fig.*).
Евге́ни|й *m* [3] Eugene; **~я** *f* [7] [Eugenia.
Евдоки́я *f* [7] Eudoxia.
евре́й *m* [3] Jew; **~ка** *f* [5; *g/pl.*: -ре́ек] Jewess; **~ский** [16] Jewish.
Евро́п|а *f* [5] Europe *n*; **♀е́ец** *m* [1; -пе́йца], **♀е́йка** *f* [5; *g/pl.*: -пе́ек], **♀е́йский** [16] European.
е́герь *m* [4; *pl.*: *a.* -ря́, *etc. e.*] hunter; ⚔ chasseur.
Еги́п|ет *m* [1; -пта] Egypt; **♀етский** [16] Egyptian; **♀тя́нин** *m* [1; *pl.*: -я́не, -я́н], **♀тя́нка** *f* [5; *g/pl.*: -нок] Egyptian.
его́ (ji'vɔ) his; its; *cf.* он.
Его́р P *m* [1] George.
еда́ *f* [5] food; meal.
едва́ (*a.* ~ ли) hardly, scarcely; *s. a.* е́ле; no sooner; ~ не almost, nearly; ~ ли не perhaps.
един|е́ние *n* [12] unity, union; **~и́ца** *f* [5] ♄ one; digit; unit; F (*mark*) very bad; *pl.* (a) few; **~и́чный** [14; -чен, -чна] single, isolated.
едино... (*cf. a.* одно...): **~бо́рство** *n* [9] (single) combat, duel; **~вла́стие** *n* [12] autocracy; **~вре́менный** [14] single; † simultaneous; **~гла́сие** *n* [12] unanimity; **~гла́сный** [14; -сен, -сна] unanimous; ~гла́сно unanimously; **~ду́шие** *n* [12] unanimity; **~ду́шный** [14; -шен, -шна] unanimous; **~ли́чный** [14] individual (*a.* peasant ~ли́чник *m*), personal; **~мы́слящий** [17] like-minded; **~мы́шленник** *m* [1] like-minded p., associate, confederate; **~обра́зный** [14; -зен, -зна] uniform; **~ро́г** *m* [1] unicorn.
еди́нствен|ный [14 *sh.*] only, single, sole; ~ный в своём ро́де unique; ~ное число́ *n gr.* singular.
еди́н|ство *n* [9] unity; unanimity; **~ый** [14 *sh.*] one, single; only (one), sole; one whole; united; (one and the) same; все до ~ого all to a man.
е́дкий [16; е́док, едка́, -о] caustic.
едо́к *m* [1 *e.*] (F good) eater.
её her; its; *cf.* она́.
ёж *m* [1 *e.*] hedgehog.
ежеви́ка *f* [5] blackberry, -ries *pl.*
еже|го́дный [14] annual; **~дне́вный** [14] daily; everyday; **~ме́сячный** [14] monthly; **~мину́тный** [14] (occuring) every minute; continual; **~неде́льный** [14] weekly; **~ча́сный** [14] hourly.
ёжиться [16], ⟨съ-⟩ shrink; be shy.
ежо́в|ый [14]: держа́ть в ~ых рукави́цах rule with a rod of iron.
езд|а́ *f* [5] ride, drive; **~ить** [15], go (by T), ride, drive; come, visit; travel; **~о́к** *m* [1 *e.*] rider, horseman.
ей: ~(-~) P, ~-бо́гу F really, indeed.
Екатери́на *f* [5] Catherine.
е́ле (*a.* ~-~) hardly, scarcely, barely; slightly; with (great) difficulty.
еле́й *m* [3] (holy) oil; *fig.* unction; **~ный** [14] unctuous.
Еле́на *f* [5] Helen.
Елизаве́та *f* [5] Elizabeth.
ёлка *f* [5; *g/pl.*: ёлок] fir; (рожде́ственская, новогóдняя) ~ Christmas (*Sov.*: New Year's) tree *or* (children's) party (на В to, for; на П at).
ел|о́вый [14] fir(ry); **~ь** *f* [8] fir; **~ьник** *m* [1] fir wood (*or* greens *pl.*).
ёмк|ий [16; ёмок, ёмка] capacious; **~ость** *f* [8] capacity; ме́ра ~ости cubic measure.
Енисе́й *m* [3] Yenisei (*Siber. river*).
ено́т *m* [1] raccoon.
епи́скоп *m* [1] bishop.
ерала́ш F *m* [1] mess, muddle, jumble.
е́ре|сь *f* [8] heresy; **~ти́к** *m* [1 *e.*] heretic.
ёрзать F [1] fidget; slip.
еро́шить [16] = взъеро́шивать, *s.*
ерунда́ F *f* [5] nonsense; trifle(s).
е́сли if, in case; once (*a.* ~ уж[е́]); а *or* и ~ if ever; whereas; ~ и *or*

(да́)же even though; ах *or* о, ~ б(ы) ... oh, could *or* would ...; ~ бы не but for; ~ то́лько provided.
есте́ств|енный [14 *sh.*] natural; **~о́** *n* [9] nature; **~ове́д** *m* [1] naturalist, scientist; **~ове́дение, ~озна́ние** *n* [12] natural science; **~оиспыта́тель** *m* [4] *s.* **~ове́д.**
есть[1] [ем, ешь, ест, еди́м, еди́те, едя́т; ешь(те)!; ел; ...е́денный] **1.** ⟨съ-, по-⟩ eat (*pf. a.* up), have; **2.** ⟨разъ-⟩ eat away (*rust*); corrode; bite; **3.** F ⟨по-, разъ-⟩ bite, gnaw, sting; P torment.
есть[2] *cf.* быть; am, is, are; there is (are); у меня́ ~ ... I have ...; так и ~ indeed!; ~ тако́е де́ло! F O.K.; ~! yes, sir!
ефре́йтор *m* [1] private first class, *Brt.* lance-corporal.
е́ха|ть [е́ду, е́дешь; поезжа́й!], ⟨по-⟩ (be) go(ing, *etc.*) (by T), ride, drive (in, on T *or* в, на П); come; run; (в, на В) leave (for), go (to); (за T) go for, fetch; по~ли! *s.* идти́.
ехи́д|ный [14; -ден, -дна] spiteful, malignant; **~ство** *n* [9] spite, malice.
ещё (не) (not) yet; (всё) ~ still (*a. with comp.*); another, more (& more ~ и ~); ~ раз once more; else; already; as early (late, *etc.*) as; possibly, probably; more or less, somewhat; ~ бы! (to be) sure!, I should think so!, of course!; it would be worse still if ...

Ж

ж *s.* же.
жа́б|а *f* [5] toad; грудна́я **~а** angina pectoris; **~ра** *f* [5] gill.
жа́воронок *m* [1; -нка] (sky)lark.
жа́дн|ичать F [1], ⟨по-⟩ be greedy *or* avaricious; **~ость** *f* [8] greed(-iness), avarice; **~ый** [14; -ден, -дна́, -о] greedy (of на В, до Р, к Д), avaricious.
жа́жда *f* [5] thirst (*a. fig.* for P, *or inf.*); **~ть** [-ду, -дешь] thirst, crave (for P, *or inf.*).
жаке́т *m* [1], F **~ка** *f* [5; *g/pl.*: -ток] jacket.
жале́ть [8], ⟨по-⟩ **1.** pity; (о П) regret; **2.** (Р *or* В) spare; grudge.
жа́лить [13], ⟨у-⟩ sting, bite.
жа́лк|ий [16; -лок, -лка́, -о; *comp.*: жа́льче] pitiable; miserable, wretched; **~о** *s.* жаль.
жа́ло *n* [9] sting (*a. fig.*).
жа́лоб|а *f* [5] complaint; action; **~ный** [14; -бен, -бна] mournful, plaintive; (of) complaint(s).
жа́лова|нье *n* [10] pay, salary; reward; **~ть** [7], ⟨по-⟩ (T) reward, award; give; appoint (в И *pl.*); F like; come (to see a p. к Д); **-ся** (на В) complain (of); F inform (against); sue, go to law.
жа́лост|ливый F [14 *sh.*] compassionate; sorrowful; **~ный** F [14; -тен, -тна] mournful; compassionate; **~ь** *f* [8] pity, compassion.
жаль it is a pity (как ~ what a pity); unfortunately; (Д ~ В): мне ~ его́ I am sorry for (*or* pity) him; *a.* regret; grudge.
жар *m* [1; в -у́] heat; fever; *fig.* ardo(u)r; **~а́** *f* [5] heat, hot weather; **~еный** [14] fried; roast(ed); *s. a.* **~ко́е**; **~ить** [13], ⟨за-, из-, P с-⟩ roast; fry; F (*sun*) burn; **~кий** [16; -рок, -рка́, -о; *comp.*: жа́рче] hot; *fig.* ardent, vehement, intense; мне **~ко** I am hot; **~ко́е** *n* [16] roast meat.
жа́т|ва *f* [5] harvest; crop; **~венный** [14] reaping.
жать[1] [жму́, жмёшь; ...жа́тый], ⟨с-⟩, *cf.*, & ⟨по-⟩ press, squeeze (*a.* out); shake (hands with ру́ку Д); pinch (*shoes, etc.*); F *fig.* oppress; **-ся** shrink (with от Р); crowd; snuggle; F vacillate; **~**[2] [жну, жнёшь; ... жа́тый], ⟨с-⟩ [сожну́], ⟨по-⟩ reap, harvest.
жва́ч|ка *f* [5] rumination; cud; P chewing gum (*or* tobacco); **~ный** [14]: **~ные** (живо́тные) *n/pl.* ruminants.
жгут *m* [1 *e.*] strap.
жгу́чий [17 *sh.*] burning; poignant.
ж. д. *abbr.*: желе́зная доро́га; *cf.* R. R., Ry.
ждать [жду, ждёшь; ждал, -а́, -о], ⟨подо-⟩ wait (for P); expect, await; вре́мя не ждёт time presses; ~ не дожда́ться wait impatiently (for P).
же 1. *conj.* but, and; whereas, as to; **2.** = ведь, *cf.*; *a.* do + *vb.*; the (this) very, same (*a.* place, time, *etc.*); just; too; *interr.* ever, on earth; for goodness' sake.
жева́|ть [7 *e.*; жую, жуёшь] chew; **~тельный** [14] masticatory; chewing.
жезл *m* [1 *e.*] staff, rod, wand.
жела́|ние *n* [12] wish, desire; по (согла́сно) **~нию** at, by (as) request(ed); **~нный** [14; -а́нен, -а́нна] desired, long wished for; welcome; beloved; **~тельный** [14; -лен, -льна] desirable; desired; мне **~тельно** I am anxious to; **~ть** [1], ⟨по-⟩ wish (a p. s.th. Д/Р), desire; love; **~ющие** *pl.* [17] p.s wishing to ...
желе́ *n* [*indecl.*] jelly (*a. fish, meat*).
железа́ *f* [5; *pl.*: же́лезы, желёз, железа́м] gland.

желез|нодоро́жник *m* [1] railroad (*Brt.* railway-) man; **~нодоро́жный** [14] railroad..., *Brt.* railway...; **~ный** [14] iron...; rail...; **~о** *n* [9] iron; кро́вельное ~о sheet iron; куй ~о, пока́ горячо́ strike while the iron is hot; **~обето́н** *m* [1] reinforced concrete.

жёлоб *m* [1; *pl.:* -бá, *etc. e.*] gutter.

желт|е́ть [8], ⟨по-⟩ grow *or* turn yellow; *impf.* (*a.* **-ся**) appear *or* show yellow; **~изна́** *f* [5] yellow (-ness); **~ова́тый** [14 *sh.*] yellowish; **~о́к** *m* [1; -ткá] yolk; **~у́ха** *f* [5] jaundice.

жёлтый [14; жёлт, -á, -o] yellow.

желу́до|к *m* [1; -дка] stomach; **~чный** [14] gastric, stomachic(al).

жёлудь *m* [4; *from g/pl. e.*] acorn.

жёлч|ный [14] gall...; [жёлчен, -чна, -o] bilious (*a. fig.*); **~ь** *f* [8] bile, gall (*a. fig.*); grief.

жема́н|иться F [13] mince; be prim; **~ница** F *f* [5] prude; **~ный** [14; -áнен, -áнна] affected, mincing, prim; **~ство** *n* [9] primness, prudery.

же́мчуг *m* [1; *pl.:* -гá, *etc. e.*] *coll.* pearls *pl.*; **~у́жина** *f* [5] pearl; **~у́жный** [14] pearl(y).

жен|а́ *f* [5; *pl. st.:* жёны] wife; † woman; **~а́тый** [14 *sh.*] married (*man*; to a p. на П); **~и́ть** [13; женю́, же́нишь] (*im*)*pf.* marry (*a man* to на П); **-ся** marry (*v/t.* на П; *of men*); **~и́тьба** *f* [5] marriage (to на П); **~и́х** [1 *e.*] fiancé; bridegroom; suiter; F marriageable young man; **~олю́б** *m* [1] lady-killer, ladies' man; **~оненави́стник** *m* [1] woman hater **~оподо́бный** [14; -бен, -бна] womanlike; **~ский** [16] female, woman('s) *or* women's; girls'; *gr.* feminine; **~ственный** [14 *sh.*] womanly; womanish, effeminate; **~щина** *f* [5] woman.

жердь *f* [8; *from g/pl. e.*] pole.

жереб|ёнок *m* [2] foal, colt; **~е́ц** *m* [1; -бцá] stallion.

жерло́ *n* [9; *pl. st.*] crater; aperture, mouth; muzzle (*gun, etc.*).

жёрнов *m* [1; *pl. e.:* -вá] millstone.

же́ртв|а *f* [5] sacrifice; (*p.:*) victim; **~овать** [7], ⟨по-⟩ (T) sacrifice (*v/t.*; o.s. собо́й); (B) give; **~оприноше́ние** *n* [12] offering.

жест *m* [1] gesture; **~икули́ровать** [7] gesticulate.

жёсткий [16; -ток, -ткá, -o; *comp.:* -тче] hard; rough, rude, coarse, harsh (*a. fig.*); tough; stiff, rigid, severe, rigorous; ~ ваго́н (ordinary) passenger car, *Brt.* second-class carriage.

жесто́к|ий [16; жесто́к, -á, -o] cruel; terrible, dreadful, fierce, grim; rigorous, violent; **~осе́рдие** *n* [12] hard-heartedness; **~ость** *f* [8] cruelty; severity.

жест|ь *f* [8] tin (plate); **~я́нка** *f* [5; *g/pl.:* -нок] can, *Brt.* tin; **~яно́й** [14] tin...; **~я́нщик** *m* [1] tinsmith.

жето́н *m* [1] counter; medal; token.

жечь, ⟨c-⟩ [26 г/ж: (со)жгу́, -жжёшь, -жгу́т; (с)жёг, (со)жглá; сожжённый] burn (*a. fig.*); torment.

живи́т|ельный [14; -лен, -льна] vivifying; crisp (*air*); **~ь** [14 *e.*; живлю́, -ви́шь], ⟨о-⟩ vivify, animate.

жив|о́й [14; жив, -á, -o] living; alive (*pred.*); lively, vivid, vivacious; quick, nimble; real, true; в **~ы́х** alive; ~ и здоро́в safe & sound; ни ~ ни мёртв more dead than alive; заде́ть за **~о́е** sting to the quick; **~опи́сец** *m* [1; -сца] painter; **~опи́сный** [14; -сен, -сна] picturesque; **~опись** *f* [8] painting; **~ость** *f* [8] vivacity; vividness.

живо́т *m* [1 *e.*] P belly; stomach; † life; **~во́рный** [14; -рен, -рна] vivifying; **~новóдство** *n* [9] cattle breeding; **~ное** *n* [14] animal; **~ный** [14] animal; *fig.* brutal.

жив|отрепе́щущий [17] living (*fish*); *fig.* burning; **~у́чий** [17 *sh.*] hardy, tough; enduring; **~ьём** P alive.

жи́дк|ий [16; -док, -дкá, -o; *comp.:* жи́же] liquid, fluid; watery, weak, thin; sparse, scanty; **~ость** *f* [8] liquid; scantiness.

жи́ж|а, ~ица F *f* [5] slush; broth.

жи́зне|нность *f* [8] viability; vitality; vividness; **~нный** **1.** [14 *sh.*] (of) life('s), worldly; vivid; living; **2.** [14] vital; **~описа́ние** *n* [12] biography; **~ра́достный** [14; -тен, -тна] cheerful, merry; **~спосо́бный** [14; -бен, -бна] viable.

жизн|ь *f* [8] life; practice; в **~ь** (**~и**) не ... never (in one's life); при **~и** in a p.'s lifetime; alive; не на **~ь**, а на смерть of life & death.

жи́л|а *f* [5] F sinew, tendon; vein (*a.* ⚒); **~е́т** *m* [1], **~е́тка** *f* [5; *g/pl.:* -ток] vest, *Brt.* waistcoat; **~е́ц** *m* [1; -льцá] lodger, roomer; inmate; † = жи́тель; **~истый** [14 *sh.*] sinewy, stringy (*a. meat*), wiry; **~и́ще** *n* [11] dwelling, lodging(s); **~и́щный** [14] housing; **~ка** *f* [5; *g/pl.:* -лок] *dim. of* **~а**; veinlet; vein (*leaf, wing, marble, & fig.*); **~о́й** [14] dwelling; inhabited; living, *cf.* **~пло́щадь** *f* [8] living space; **~ьё** *n* [10] habitation; F dwelling.

жир *m* [1; в -у́; *pl. e.*] fat; grease; ры́бий ~ cod-liver oil; **~е́ть** [8], ⟨о-, раз-⟩ grow fat; **~ный** [14; -рен, -рнá, -o] fat; (of) grease, greasy; ♀ fleshy; *fig.* rich; *typ.* bold -(-faced); **~о** † *n* [*indecl.*] endorsement; **~ово́й** [14] fat(ty).

жит|е́йский [16] worldly, (of) life('s); everyday; **~ель** *m* [4], **~ельница** *f* [5] inhabitant, resident;

~ельство *n* [9] residence; вид на ~ельство residence (*or* stay) permit; **~ие́** *n* [12] life (*a. of a saint*).
жи́тница *f* [5] granary.
жить [живу́, -вёшь; жил, -а́, -о; не́ жил(и)] live (Т, на В [up]on; Т *a.* for); reside, lodge; exist, be; как живёте? how are you (getting on)?; жи́л(и)-бы́л(и) ... once upon a time there was (were) ... (*in fairy tales*); **~ся:** ему́ хорошо́ живётся he is well off; **~ё(-бытьё)** F *n* [10] life, living; residence, stay; (Д) be well off.
жму́рить [13], ⟨за-⟩ screw up *or* contract (one's eyes **-ся**; blink).
жн|е́йка *f* [5; *g/pl.:* -е́ек], **~ея́** *f* [6] reaping machine, harvester; **~ец** *m* [1 *e.*] reaper; **~ивьё** *n* [10; *pl.*: жни́вья, -вьев] stubble(s); **~и́ца** *f* [5] reaper.
жо́л..., **жо́р...** *s.* жёл..., жёр...
жрать P [жру, жрёшь; жрал, -а́, -о], ⟨со-⟩ eat; devour, gorge, gobble.
жре́бий *m* [3] lot (*a. fig.* = destiny); броса́ть (тяну́ть) ~ cast (draw) lots; ~ бро́шен the die is cast.
жрец *m* [1 *e.*] (*pagan*) priest (*a. fig.*).
жужжа́|ние *n* [12], **~ть** [4 *e.*; жужжу́, -и́шь] buzz, hum.
жу|к *m* [1 *e.*] beetle; ма́йский ~к cockchafer; P = **~ли́к** F *m* [1] swindler, cheat(er), trickster; filcher, pilferer; **~льни́чать** F [1], ⟨с-⟩ cheat, trick.
жу́пел *m* [1] bugaboo, bugbear.
жура́вль *m* [4 *e.*] (*zo., well*) crane.
жури́ть F [13], ⟨по-⟩ scold, rebuke.
журна́л *m* [1] magazine, periodical, journal; diary; ⚓ log(book); **~и́ст** *m* [1] news(paper)man, journalist; **~и́стика** *f* [5] journalism.
журча́|ние *n* [12], **~ть** [-чи́т] purl, murmur.
жу́т|кий [14; -ток, -тка́, -о] weird, uncanny, dismal, sinister; мне ~ко I am terrified; **~кость**, F **~ь** *f* [8] dismay, dread(ful P *pred.*).
жюри́ *n* [*indecl.*] jury (*prizes*).

З

за 1. (В): (*direction*) behind; over, across, beyond; out of; (*distance*) at; (*time*) after; over, past; before (*a.* ~ ... до Р); (with)in, for, during; (*object*[*ive*], *favo*[*u*]*r, reason, value, substitute*) for; ~ то, что because; ~ что? what for?, why?; **2.** (Т): (*position*) behind; across, beyond; at, over; after (*time & place*); because of; with; ~ мной ... *a.* I owe ...; ко́мната ~ мной I take (reserve) the room.
заба́в|а *f* [5] amusement, entertainment; **~ля́ть** [28], ⟨(по)~ить⟩ [13] amuse (-ся o.s., be amused at Т); **~ник** F *m* [1] joker, wag; **~ный** [14; -вен, -вна] amusing, funny.
забасто́в|ка *f* [5; *g/pl.*: -вок] strike, walkout; **~очный** [14] strike ...; **~щик** *m* [1] striker.
забве́ние *n* [12] oblivion.
забе|га́ть [1], ⟨~жа́ть⟩ [4; забегу́, -ежи́шь, -егу́т; -еги́!] run in(to), get; run off, away; F drop in (on к Д); **~га́ть** вперёд forestall.
заб|ива́ть [1], ⟨~и́ть⟩ [-бью́, -бьёшь; *cf.* бить] drive in; nail up; stop up, choke (up); block (up); F outdo, beat; (*fountain*) spout forth; sound (*alarm*); F stuff (*head*); take (*into one's head*); **-ся** F hide, get; *pf.* begin to beat.
заб|ира́ть [1], ⟨~ра́ть⟩ [-беру́, -рёшь; *cf.* брать] take (*a.*, F, away); capture, (*a. fig.*) seize; arrest; put (into); turn, steer; (Т) close, partition (off); **-ся** climb *or* creep (in, up); steal in, penetrate; hide; get (far off).
заби́|тый [14] browbeaten, cowed, (in)timid(ated); **~ть** *s.* ~ва́ть; **~я́ка** F *m/f* [5] bully, squabbler.
заблаго|вре́менно in (due) time, beforehand; **~вре́менный** [14] preliminary; timely; **~рассу́диться** [15; *impers., with* Д] think fit.
забл|уди́ться [15] *pf.* lose one's way, go astray; **~у́дший** [17] lost; stray; **~ужда́ться** [1] be mistaken, err; **~ужде́ние** *n* [12] error, mistake; ввести́ в ~ужде́ние mislead.
забол|ева́ть [1], ⟨~е́ть⟩ [8] fall sick *or* ill (of Т), be taken ill with; ache; *su.*: **~ева́ние** *n* [12] *a.* = боле́знь.
забо́р *m* [1] fence; **~ный** [14] fence...; *fig.* vulgar, trashy.
забо́т|а *f* [5] care (about, of о П), concern, anxiety, worry, trouble; без ~ careless; carefree; **~иться** [15], ⟨по-⟩ (о П) care (for), take care of, look after; worry, be anxious (about); **~ливый** [14 *sh.*] careful, provident; attentive; anxious, solicitous.
забр|а́сывать [1] **1.** ⟨~оса́ть⟩ (Т) fill up; heap (*a. fig.* = overwhelm); pelt (*stones*); bespatter (*dirt*); **2.** ⟨~о́сить⟩ [15] throw, fling, (*a. fig.*) cast; neglect, give up; **~а́ть** *s.* забира́ть; **~еда́ть** [1], ⟨~ести́⟩ [25] wander *or* get ([in]to, far); **~оса́ть**, **~о́сить** *s.* ~а́сывать; **~о́шенный** [14] deserted; unkempt.
забры́згать [1] *pf.* splash, sprinkle.
заб|ыва́ть [1], ⟨~ы́ть⟩ [-бу́ду, -дешь] forget (*o.s.* **-ся**; *a.* nap, doze); **~ы́вчивый** [14 *sh.*] forgetful; **~ытьё** *n* [12; в -тьи́] unconscious-

ness, swoon; drowsiness; slumber; reverie; frenzy.

зава́л *m* [1] heap, drift; obstruction, abatis; **~ивать** [1], ⟨~и́ть⟩ [13; -алю́, -а́лишь] fill *or* heap (up); cover; block, obstruct, close; F overburden (*with work, etc.*); **-ся** fall; sink; collapse.

зава́р|ивать [1], ⟨~и́ть⟩ [13; -арю́, -а́ришь] boil (*a.* down), make (*tea*); scald; P *fig.* concoct.

зав|еде́ние *n* [12] establishment, institution; (закры́тое) учёбное ~еде́ние (boarding) school; **~е́довать** [7] (T) be in charge *or* the head (chief) of, manage; **~е́домый** [14] notorious, indubitable; ~е́домо knowingly; admittedly, certainly; **~е́дующий** [17] (T) chief, head; director; **~ести́** *s.* ~ози́ть.

зав|ере́ние *n* [12] assurance; **~е́рить** *s.* ~еря́ть; **~ерну́ть** *s.* ~ёртывать; **~ерте́ть** [11; -ерчу́ -е́ртишь] *pf.* start turning (*v/i.* **-ся**); **~ёртывать** [1], ⟨~ерну́ть⟩ [20] wrap (up); turn (*a.* up; off, screw up); F drop in; **~ерша́ть** [1], ⟨~ерши́ть⟩ [16 *e.*; -шу́, -ши́шь; -шённый] finish, complete, accomplish; crown; **~ерше́ние** *n* [12] conclusion, end; completion; **~еря́ть** [28], ⟨~е́рить⟩ [13] assure (a p. of В/в П); attest, authenticate.

заве́|са *f* [5] curtain; screen (*a.* ⚔); *fig.* veil; **~сить** *s.* ~шивать; **~сти́** *s.* заводи́ть.

заве́т *m* [1] legacy; precept, maxim; vow; *Bibl.* (Ве́тхий Old, Но́вый New) ~ Testament; **~ный** [14] sacred; dear, precious; fond; cherished; intimate; † forbidden.

заве́|шивать [1], ⟨~сить⟩ [15] cover, hang with, curtain.

завеща́|ние *n* [12] testament, will; **~ть** [1] (*im*)*pf.* bequeath; instruct, leave as precept.

завзя́тый F [14] inveterate; enthusiastic; true, genuine.

зав|ива́ть [1], ⟨~и́ть⟩ [-вью́, -вьёшь; *cf.* вить] wave, curl; wind round; **~и́вка** *f* [5; *g/pl.:* -вок] waving; холо́дная (шестиме́сячная) ~и́вка water (permanent) wave.

зави́д|ный [14; -ден, -дна] enviable, desirable; envious (of Д/И); **~овать** [7], ⟨по-⟩ envy (a p. a th. Д/в П), be envious (of).

зави́н|чивать [1], ⟨~ти́ть⟩ [15 *e.*; -инчу́, -инти́шь] screw up.

зави́с|еть [11] depend (on от Р); **~имость** *f* [8] dependence; в ~имости от (Р) depending on; **~имый** [14 *sh.*] dependent.

зави́ст|ливый [14 *sh.*] envious, jealous; **′~ь** *f* [8] envy (of, at к Д).

зави|то́й [14] curly; **~то́к** *m* [1; -тка́] curl, ringlet; flourish; **∠ть** *s.* **~ва́ть.**

завко́м *m* [1] (заводско́й комите́т) works council.

завлад|ева́ть [1], ⟨~е́ть⟩ [8] (T) take possession *or* hold of, seize.

завл|ека́тельный [14; -лен, -льна] enticing, tempting; **~ека́ть** [1], **~е́чь** [26] (al)lure, entice, tempt; involve; carry away.

заво́д[1] *m* [1] works, factory, plant (at/to на П/В); stud (*a.* ко́нский ~); **~**[2] winding mechanism; *typ.* edition; **~и́ть** [15], завести́⟩ [25] take, bring, lead; put; establish, set up, found (*business, etc.*); form, contract (*habit, friendship, etc.*); get, procure, acquire (*things*); start (*a. motor*), begin (*talk, dispute, etc.*; *a.* to keep [*animals*]); wind up (*watch, etc.*); **-ся**, ⟨завести́сь⟩ appear; nest; get, have; **~но́й** [14] ⊕ starting; mechanical (*toy*); **~ский**, **~ско́й** [16] works..., factory...; stud...

заво|ева́ние *n* [12] conquest; *fig.* (*mst pl.*) achievement(s); **~ева́тель** *m* [4] conqueror; **~ёвывать** [1], ⟨~ева́ть⟩ [6] conquer; win, gain.

зав|ози́ть [15], ~езти́⟩ [24] take, bring, drive; leave, F deliver.

завол|а́кивать [1], ⟨~о́чь⟩ [26] cover, overcast; get cloudy.

завор|а́чивать [1], ⟨~оти́ть⟩ [15] turn (in, up, down, about); direct.

завсегда́тай *m* [3] habitué.

за́втра tomorrow; **~к** *m* [1] breakfast (at за Г; for на В, к Д); (второ́й ~к) lunch; **~кать** [1], ⟨по-⟩ (have, take) breakfast (lunch); **~шний** [15] tomorrow's; ~шний день *m* tomorrow; *fig.* (near) future.

завыва́ть [1], завы́ть⟩ [22] howl.

зав|яза́ть[1] [3], ~я́знуть⟩ [21] sink in, stick; F *fig.* get stuck *or* involved in; **~яза́ть**[2] *s.* ~я́зывать; **~я́зка** *f* [5; *g/pl.:* -зок] string, tie; beginning, starting point; entanglement, plot; **~я́зывать** [1], ⟨~яза́ть⟩ [3] tie (up), bind, fasten; *fig.* begin, start; entangle, knit (*plot*); **∠язь** ⚘ *f* [8] ovary; **~я́нуть** *s.* вя́нуть.

заг|ада́ть *s.* ~а́дывать; **~а́дить** *s.* ~а́живать; **~а́дка** *f* [5; *g/pl.:* -док] riddle, enigma; **~а́дочный** [14; -чен, -чна] enigmatic(al); mysterious; **~а́дывать** [1], ⟨~ада́ть⟩ [1] propose (*a riddle*); try to find out (*by a guess, fortunetelling, etc.*); F fix upon; plan; **~а́живать** F [1], ⟨~а́дить⟩ [15] soil, befoul.

зага́р *m* [1] sunburn, tan.

загво́здка F *f* [5; *g/pl.*: -док] hitch, trouble.

заги́б *m* [1] bend; dog-ear (*page*); *pol.* deviation; **~а́ть** [1], ⟨загну́ть⟩ [20] bend, fold (over), turn (up).

загла́в|ие *n* [12] title (*book, etc.*); **~ный** [14] title...; ~ная бу́ква *f* capital letter.

загла́|живать [1], ⟨~дить⟩ [15] smooth; press, iron; *fig.* make up (*or* amends) for, expiate.

загл|óхнуть *s.* глóхнуть 2.; **~óхший** [17] deserted, desolate; **~ушáть** [1], ⟨~ушить⟩ [16] *s.* глушить 2.
загля́|дывать [1], ⟨~нýть⟩ [19] glance; peep; look (through, up); have a look (at); F drop in *or* call (on к Д); **~дываться** [1], ⟨~дéться⟩ [11] (на В) gaze, gape *or* stare (at), feast one's eyes *or* gloat ([up]on).
заг|нáть *s.* ~онять; **~нýть** *s.* ~ибáть; **~овáривать** [1], ⟨~оворить⟩ [13] **1.** *v/i.* begin, start (*or* try) to talk *or* speak; **2.** *v/t.* tire with one's talk; exorcise; **3. -ся** F drivel, talk nonsense; be(come) confused; talk (too) long, much; **~овор** *m* [1] conspiracy, plot; exorcism; составлять ~овор conspire, plot; **~оворить** *s.* ~овáривать; **~овóрщик** *m* [1] conspirator.
заголóвок *m* [1; -вка] heading, title.
загóн *m* [1] enclosure; быть в ~е F suffer neglect; **~я́ть** [28], ⟨загнáть⟩ [-гоню, -гóнишь; *cf.* гнать] drive (in, off); exhaust, fatigue.
загор|áживать [1], ⟨~одить⟩ [15 & 15 *e.*; -рожý, -рóдишь] enclose, shut in; block (up), bar (*way*); **-ся** fence, protect; **~áть** [1], ⟨~éть⟩ [9] become sunburnt; **-ся** catch *or* take fire; light up, kindle, flash; blush, blaze up; *fig.* (get) inflame(d); break out; **~éлый** [14] sunburnt; **~одить** *s.* ~áживать; **~óдка** F *f* [5; *g/pl.*: -док] fence, enclosure; partition; **'~одный** [14] country (*house, etc.*); out-of-town.
загот|áвливать [1] & **~овлять** [28], ⟨~óвить⟩ [14] prepare; store up; lay in (*stock*); **~óвка** *f* [5; *g/pl.*: -вок], **~овлéние** *n* [12] storage, laying in (*stocks, supplies*).
загра|дительный [14] ⚔ curtain (*fire*), barrage (*a. balloon*); **~ждáть** [1], ⟨~дить⟩ [15 *e.*; -ажý, -адишь; -аждённый] block (up), bar; **~ждéние** *n* [12] block(ing), obstruction; прóволочное ~ждéние wire entanglement.
заграни|чный [14] foreign; ... abroad.
загре|бáть [1], ⟨~сти⟩ *s.* грести.
загрóбн|ый [14] sepulchral (*voice*); ~ый мир *m* the other world; ~ая жизнь *f* the beyond.
загромо|ждáть [1], ⟨~здить⟩ [15 *e.*; -зжý, -здишь; -мождённый] block (up), (en)cumber, crowd; overload; **~ждéние** *n* [12] blocking; overloading.
загрубéлый [14] callous, coarse.
загр|ужáть [1], ⟨~узить⟩ [15 & 15 *e.*; -ужý, -ýзишь] (T) load; ⊕ charge; F busy, assign work to; be occupied (*or* taken) by work (*time*); **~ýзка** *f* [5] load(ing, *etc.*), charge; **~ызáть** [1], ⟨~ы́зть⟩ [24; *pt. st.*; загры́зенный] bite (*fig.* worry) to death, kill.
загрязн|éние *n* [12] soiling; pollution; infection; **~я́ть** [28], ⟨~ить⟩ [13] (**-ся** become) soil(ed), pollute(d) (*water, etc.*), infect(ed) (*air*).
загс *m* [1] (*abbr.*: отдéл зáписей áктов граждáнского состоя́ния) registrar's (registry) office.
зад *m* [1; на -ý; *pl. e.*] back, rear *or* hinder part; posterior(s), rump; *pl.* F things already (well-)known *or* learned; ~ом наперед back to front.
зад|áбривать [1], ⟨~óбрить⟩ [13] (B) insinuate o.s. (with), gain upon.
зад|авáть [5], ⟨~áть⟩ [-дáм, -дáшь, *etc.*, *cf.* дать; зáдал, -á, -о; зáданный (зáдан, -á, -о)] set, assign (*task*); give (*a.* ♪ *keynote*), F dress (down); ask (*question*); **-ся** [*pt.*: -дáлся, -лáсь] цéлью (мы́слью) take it into one's head, set one's mind on doing s.th.; F happen to be.
задáв|ливать [1], ⟨~ить⟩ [14] crush; run over, knock down; *fig.* suppress; P strangle, kill.
задáние *n* [12] assignment, task; (com)mission (*a.* ⚔); домáшнее ~ homework.
задáток *m* [1; -тка] earnest money; deposit; *pl.* rudiments.
задá|ть *s.* ~вáть; **~ча** *f* [5] problem (*a.* ♞); task; object(ive), aim, end; **~чник** *m* [1] book of problems.
задв|игáть [1], ⟨~инуть⟩ [20] push (into, *etc.*); shut (*drawer*); draw (*curtain*); slide (*bolt*); **~и́жка** [5; *g/pl.*: -жек] bolt; **~ижнóй** [14] sliding (*door*); sash (*window*).
задвóрки *f/pl.* [*gen.*: -рок] backyards.
зад|евáть [1], ⟨~éть⟩ [-éну, -éнешь; -éтый] be caught (by за B), brush against, touch (*a. fig.*, [up]on); excite; hurt, wound; ⚕ affect; **~éлывать**, ⟨~éлать⟩ [1] stop up, choke (up); wall up.
задёр|гать [1] *pf.* overdrive; F harrass; **~гивать** [1], ⟨~нуть⟩ [20] draw (*curtain*); cover.
задержáние *n* [12] arrest.
задéрж|ивать [1], ⟨~áть⟩ [4] detain, hold back *or* up, stop; delay, check; arrest; slow down; **-ся** stay; be delayed; linger; stop; be late; **~ка** *f* [5; *g/pl.*: -жек] delay; (*a.* ⊕) trouble, break.
задёрнуть *s.* задёргивать.
задéть *s.* задевáть.
зад|ирáть F [1], ⟨~рáть⟩ [-дерý, -рёшь; *cf.* драть] lift *or* pull (up); stretch; *impf.* provoke, vex, pick a quarrel (with); ~(и)рáть нос be haughty, turn up one's nose.
зáдний [15] back, hind(er); reverse (*gear*).
задóлго (до P) long before.
зад|олжáть F [1] *pf.* run into debt; owe (money); **~óлженность** *f* [8] debts *pl.*, indebtedness.
зáдом backward(s); *cf.* зад.
задóр *m* [1] fervo(u)r; quick temper;

provocative tone *or* behavio(u)r; **~ный** [14; -рен, -рна] fervent; provoking, teasing; frolicsome.
задрáть *s.* задирáть.
зад|увáть [1], ⟨**~ýть**⟩ [18] blow out; F begin to blow; *impf.* blow (in).
задý|мать *s.* **~мывать**; **~мчивый** [14 *sh.*] thoughtful, pensive; **~мывать** [1], ⟨**~мать**⟩ conceive; resolve, decide; plan, intend; **-ся** think (about, of о П); reflect, meditate (on над Т); begin to think, (be) engross(ed, lost) in thought(s); hesitate; **~ть** *s.* **~вáть**.
задушéвный [14] heart-felt, warm-hearted, affectionate; intimate, in(ner)most.
зад|ыхáться [1], ⟨**~охнýться**⟩ [21] gasp, pant; choke (*a. fig.*, with от Р).
заéз|дить F [15] *pf.* fatigue, exhaust; **~жáть** [1], ⟨заéхать⟩ [-éду, -éдешь; -езжáй!] call on (*on the way*), drive, go *or* come (to [see, *etc.*] к Д *or* into в В); pick up, fetch (за Т); get; **~жий** [17] visitant.
заём *m* [1; зáйма] loan.
за|éхать *s.* **~езжáть**; **~жáть** *s.* **~жимáть**; **~жéчь** *s.* **~жигáть**.
заж|ивáть [1], ⟨**~ить**⟩ [-ивý, -вёшь; зáжил, -á, -о] **1.** heal (up); close, skin (over); **2.** *pf.* begin to live.
зáживо alive.
зажигá|лка *f* [5; *g/pl.*: -лок] (cigarette) lighter; **~ние** *n* [12] lighting; ignition; **~тельный** [14] incendiary (*bomb, & fig.*); **~ть** [1], ⟨зажéчь⟩ [26 г/ж: -жгý, -жжёшь; *cf.* жечь] light, kindle (*a. fig.*); (*match a.*) strike; turn on (*light*); **-ся** light (up), kindle.
зажи́м *m* [1] ⊕ clamp; *fig.* suppression; **~áть** [1], ⟨зажáть⟩ [-жмý, -жмёшь; -жáтый] press, squeeze; clutch; *fig.* F (sup)press; stop (*mouth*), hold (*nose*), close (*ears*).
зажи́|точный [14; -чен, -чна] prosperous; **~точность** *f* [8] prosperity; **~ть** *s.* **~вáть**.
заздрáвный [14] (to s.b.'s) health.
зазевáться F [1] gape (at на В); be(-come) heedless, absent(-minded).
зазем|лéние *n* [12], **~ля́ть** [28], ⟨**~ли́ть**⟩ [13] ⚡ ground, *Brt.* earth.
зазна|вáться F [5], ⟨**~ться**⟩ [1] be(-come) presumptuous, put on airs.
заз|óрный †, P [14; -рен, -рна] shameful, scandalous; **~рéние** *n* [12]: без **~рéния** (сóвести) without remorse *or* shame.
зазýбр|ивать [1] *s.* зубри́ть; **~ина** *f* [5] notch.
заи́грывать F [1], (с Т) flirt, coquet (with), make advances (to); ingratiate o.s. (with).
заи́к|а *m/f* [5] stutterer; **~áние** *n* [12] stutter; stammer; **~áться** [1], *once* ⟨**~нýться**⟩ [20] stutter; stammer; F (give a) hint (at о П), suggest, mention; stir; *pf.* stop short.
заи́мствова|ние *n* [12] borrowing, taking; loan word (*a.* **~нное** слóво); **~ть** [7] (*im*)*pf.*, *a.* ⟨по-⟩ borrow, take (over).
заи́ндевелый [14] frosty.
заинтересóв|ывать(ся) [1], ⟨**~ать** (-ся)⟩ [7] (be[come]) interest(ed in Т), rouse a p.'s interest (in в П); я **~ан(а)** I am interested (in в П).
заи́скивать [1] ingratiate o.s. (with у Р).
зайти́ *s.* заходи́ть.
зáйчик *m* [1] *dim. of* заяц; F speck(le).
закабал|я́ть [28], ⟨**~и́ть**⟩ [13] enslave.
закавкáзский [16] Transcaucasian.
закады́чный F [14] bosom (*friend*).
закáз *m* [1] order; дать **~** (на В/Д) ✝ place an order (for ... with); **~áть** *s.* **~ывать**; на **~** = **~нóй** [14] made to order; **~нóй** лес (p)reserve; **~нóе** (письмó) *n* registered (letter); **~чик** *m* [1] customer; **~ывать** [1], ⟨**~áть**⟩ [3] order (o.s. себé); † forbid.
закáл *m* [1], **~ка** *f* [5] ⊕ tempering; *fig.* hardening; endurance, hardiness; breed, kind; **~я́ть** [28], ⟨**~и́ть**⟩ [13] ⊕ temper; *fig.* harden; **~ённый** tempered (*metal*); *fig.* hardened, tried, experienced.
зак|áлывать [1], ⟨**~олóть**⟩ [17] kill, slaughter; stab; pin (up); у меня́ **~олóло** в бокý I have a stitch in the side; **~áнчивать** [1], ⟨**~óнчить**⟩ [16] finish, conclude; **~áпывать** [1], ⟨**~опáть**⟩ [1] bury; fill up.
закáт *m* [1] sunset; *fig.* decline; end; **~ывать** [1] **1.** ⟨**~áть**⟩ [1] roll up; **2.** ⟨**~и́ть**⟩ [15] roll (into, under, *etc.* в, под В); turn up (*eyes*); **-ся** roll; set (*sun, etc.*); *fig.* end; F burst (out laughing *or* into tears).
заквá|ска *f* [5] ferment; leaven; *fig.* F breed; **~шивать** [1], ⟨**~сить**⟩ [15] sour.
заки́|дывать [1] **1.** ⟨**~дáть**⟩ [1] F fill up, cover; *fig.* ply, assail, pelt (with Т); **2.** ⟨**~нуть**⟩ [20] throw (in [-to], on, over, behind, *etc.* в, на, за ... В; *a.* out [*net*], back [*head*]); fling, (*a. fig.*) cast.
зак|ипáть [1], ⟨**~ипéть**⟩ [10; -пи́т] begin to boil; *cf.* кипéть; **~исáть** [1], ⟨**~и́снуть**⟩ [21] turn sour.
заклáд *m* [1] † = залóг; *s. a.* би́ться; **~ка** *f* [5; *g/pl.*: -док] laying; walling (up); harnessing, putting to; bookmark; **~нóй** [14] pawn...; **~нáя** mortgage (bond); **~чик** *m* [1] pawner; pawnbroker; **~ывать** [1], ⟨заложи́ть⟩ [16] put (*a.* in, *etc.*), lay (*a.* out [*garden*], the foundation [stone] of, found), place; F mislay; heap, pile (with Т); wall up; pawn, pledge; harness, put (*horse*[*s*]) to, get ready (*carriage*); mark, put in (*bookmark*); *impers.* F obstruct (*hearing, nose*), press (*breast*).

закл|ёвывать [1], ‹~евать› [6 *e.*; -клюю, -юёшь] peck to death *or* wound (badly) (by pecking); F wreck, ruin; **~ёнвать** [1], ‹~е́ить› [13] glue *or* paste up (over); **~ёпка** *f* [5; *g/pl.*: -пок], **~ёпывать**, ‹~епать› [1] rivet.

заклина́|ние *n* [12] conjuration, incantation; exorcism; **~тель** *m* [4] conjurer, exorcist; (*snake*) charmer; **~ть** [1] conjure, adjure.

заключ|а́ть [1], ‹~и́ть› [16 *e.*; -чу́, -чи́шь; -чённый] enclose, put; confine, imprison; conclude (= finish, with T; = infer, from из P, по Д — что; *v/t.*: *treaty*, [= make] *peace, etc.*); *impf.* (*a.* в себе́) contain; **~а́ться** [1] consist (in в П); end (with T); **~е́ние** *n* [12[confinement, imprisonment (*a.* тюре́мное); conclusion; **~ённый** [14] prisoner; **~и́тельный** [14] final, concluding.

закля́тый [14] implacable; sworn.

зако́в|ывать [1], ‹~а́ть› [7 *e.*; -кую́, куёшь] put in (irons), chain; *fig.* freeze; prick (*horse*).

закол|а́чивать F [1], ‹~оти́ть› [15] drive in; nail up; board up; *fig.* beat to death; thrash; **~до́вывать** [1], ‹~дова́ть› [7] enchant; bewitch, charm; **~до́ванный** круг *m* vicious circle; **~оти́ть** *s.* **~а́чивать**; **~о́ть** *s.* зака́лывать.

зако́н *m* [1] law; rule; ~ бо́жий (God's) Law; religion (*form. school subject*); объяви́ть вне ~а outlaw; по (вопреки́) ~у according (contrary) to law; охраня́емый ~ом ✝/⚖ registered; **~ность** *f* [8] legality; law; **~ный** [14; -о́нен, -о́нна] legal, lawful, legitimate.

законо|ве́д *m* [1] jurist, jurisprudent; **~да́тель** *m* [4] legislator; **~да́тельный** [14] legislative; **~да́тельство** *n* [9] legislation; **~ме́рность** *f* [8] regularity; **~ме́рный** [14; -рен, -рна] regular; **~положе́ние** *n* [12] regulation(s); **~прое́кт** *m* [1] bill, draft.

зако́|нчить *s.* зака́нчивать; **~па́ть** *s.* зака́пывать; **~пте́лый** [14] smoky; **~рене́лый** [14] deep-rooted, inveterate,in grained; **~рю́чка** F *f* [5; *g/pl.*: -чек] flourish; trick, ruse; hitch; **~сне́лый** [14] = ~рене́лый; **~у́лок** *m* [1; -лка] alleyway, (*Brt.*) (narrow) lane; nook; **~чене́лый** [14] (be)numb(ed), stiff.

закра́|дываться [1], ‹~сться› [25; *pt. st.*] creep in; **~шивать** [1], ‹~сить› [15] paint over.

закреп|ле́ние *n* [12] fastening; strengthening; securing; (за T) assignment (*a.* ⚖); ⚔ fortification; **~ля́ть** [28], ‹~и́ть› [14 *e*; -плю́, -пи́шь; -плённый] fasten, (*a. phot.*) fix; strengthen, consolidate, fortify (*a.* ⚔); secure; assign (to за T, *a.* ⚖); ⚒ strut.

закрепо|ща́ть [1], ‹~сти́ть› [15 *e.*; -ощу́, -ости́шь; -ощённый] enslave; **~ще́ние** *n* [12] enslavement.

закро́йщи|к *m* [1], **~ца** *f* [5] cutter.

закругл|е́ние *n* [12] rounding (off); curve; **~я́ть** [28], ‹~и́ть› [13] round (off).

закру́|чивать [1], ‹~ти́ть› [15] turn (round, off, up); twist.

закр|ыва́ть [1], ‹~ы́ть› [22] shut, close; lock (up); cover, hide; turn off (*tap*); **~ыва́ть** глаза́ (на В) shut one's eyes (to); **~ы́тие** *n* [12] closing, close; **~ы́ть** *s.* **~ыва́ть**; **~ы́тый** [14] closed; secret; boarding (*school*); high-necked (*dress*); в **~ы́**том помеще́нии indoor(s).

закули́сный [14] (lying *or* passing) behind the scenes; secret.

закуп|а́ть [1], ‹~и́ть› [14] buy (*a.* in), purchase; **∠ка** *f* [5; *g/pl.*: -пок] purchase.

заку́пор|ивать [1], ‹~ить› [13] cork (up), (*cask*) bung (up); **~ка** *f* [5; *g/pl.*: -рок] corking; ⚕ embolism; constipation.

заку́пщик [1] purchasing agent, buyer.

заку́р|ивать [1], ‹~и́ть› [13; -урю́, -у́ришь] light (*cigar, etc.*), begin to smoke; F (blacken with) smoke; **~и́**(те)! have a cigar(ette)!

заку́с|ка *f* [5; *g/pl.*: -сок] snack, lunch; hors d'oeuvres; на ~ку *a.* for the last bit; **~о́чная** *f* [14] lunchroom, snackbar; **~ывать** [1], ‹~и́ть› [15] bite (*a. one's lip*[*s*]); take *or* have a snack, lunch; eat (s.th. [with, after a drink] T); **~и́ть** язы́к stop short, hold one's tongue.

заку́т|ывать, ‹~ать› [1] wrap up.

за́л *m* [1], † **~а** *f* [5] hall; room.

зал|ега́ние *n* [12] *geol.* deposit(ion); **~ега́ть** [1], ‹~е́чь› [26; -ля́гу, -ля́жешь] lie (down); hide; *fig.* root; ⚕ be obstructed (with phlegm).

заледене́лый [14] icy; numb.

зал|ежа́лый [14] stale, spoiled (by long storage); **~ежа́лый** това́р *m* drug; **~ёживаться** [1], ‹~ежа́ться› [4 *e.*; -жу́сь, -жи́шься] lie (too) long (*a. goods, & spoil thus*), stale; **∠ежь** *f* [8] *geol.* deposit; ⚘ fallow.

зал|еза́ть [1], ‹~е́зть› [24 *st.*] climb up, in(to), *etc.*; hide; steal *or* get in(to); **~епля́ть** [28], ‹~епи́ть› [14] stop, close; glue *or* paste up; stick over; **~ета́ть** [1], ‹~ете́ть› [11] fly in(to), up, far off, beyond; come, get; **~ётный** [14] stray(ing); migratory (*bird*); F visitant.

зале́ч|ивать [1], ‹~и́ть› [16] heal; F cure to death; **~ь** *s.* **~ега́ть**.

зал|и́в *m* [1] gulf, bay; **~ива́ть** [1], ‹~и́ть› [-лью́, -льёшь; за́лил, -а́, -о; за́литый] (T) flood, overflow; pour (all) over, cover; fill; extinguish; **-ся** break into *or* shed (*tears* слеза́ми), burst out (laughing сме́хом); trill, warble, roll, quaver;

~ивной [14] floodable, flooded; jellied; resonant; **~и́ть** *s.* ~ива́ть.
зал|о́г *m* [1] pledge (*a. fig.*); pawn; security; *gr.* voice; дать в ~о́г pawn, pledge; **~ожи́ть** *s.* закла́дывать; **~о́жник** *m* [1], **~о́жница** *f* [5] hostage.
залп *m* [1] volley; ~ом F (*drink*) at one draught; (*smoke, etc.*) at a stretch; (*read*) at one sitting; blurt out.
зама́|зка *f* [5] putty; **~зывать** [1], ‹~зать› [3] smear, soil; paint over; putty; F *fig.* veil, hush up; **~лчивать** F [1], ‹замолча́ть› [4 *e.*; -чу́, -чи́шь] conceal, keep secret; **~нивать** [1], ‹~ни́ть› [13; -маню́, -ма́нишь] lure, decoy, entice; **~нчивый** [14 *sh.*] alluring, tempting; **~хиваться** [1], *once* ‹~хну́ться› [20] lift one's arm (*etc.* against T/на B), threaten (with); **~шка** F *f* [5; *g/pl.*: -шек] habit, manner.
замедл|е́ние *n* [12] delay; **~я́ть** [28], ‹~ить› [13] slow down, reduce; delay, retard (*a.* с T); не ~я́ть с (T) (do, *etc.*) soon.
заме́|на *f* [5] substitution (of/for T/P), replacement (by T); ⚖ commutation; substitute; **~ни́мый** [14 *sh.*] replaceable, exchangeable; **~ни́тель** *m* [4] substitute; **~ня́ть** [28], ‹~ни́ть› [13; -меню́, -ме́нишь; -менённый] replace (by T), substitute (p., th. for T/B); ⚖ commute (for, into); (И/В) (be) follow(ed).
замере́ть *s.* замира́ть.
замерза́|ние *n* [12] freezing; то́чка ~ния freezing point; **~ть** [1], ‹замёрзнуть› [21] freeze, congeal; be frozen (to death, *a.* F = feel very cold).
за́мертво (as if) dead, unconscious.
замести́ *s.* замета́ть.
замести́|тель *m* [4] deputy, assistant, vice-...; **~ть** *s.* замеща́ть.
заме|та́ть [1], ‹~сти́› [25 -т-: -мету́] sweep (up); drift, cover; block up (*roads*); wipe out (*tracks*).
заме́|тить *s.* ~ча́ть; **~тка** *f* [5; *g/pl.*: -ток] mark; note; paragraph, (brief) article, item; **~тный** [14; -тен, -тна] noticeable, perceptible; marked, remarkable; ~тно *a.* one (it) can (be) see(n), notice(d); **~ча́ние** *n* [12] remark, observation; *pl.* criticism; reproof, rebuke; досто́йный ~ча́ния worthy of notice; **~ча́тельный** [14; -лен, -льна] remarkable, outstanding; wonderful; noted (for T); **~ча́ть** [1], ‹~тить› [15] notice; mark; observe, remark; reprove.
замеша́тельств|о *n* [9] confusion, embarrassment; в ~е confused, disconcerted, embarrassed.
зам|е́шивать, ‹~еша́ть› [1] involve, entangle; ~е́шан(а) в (П) *a.* mixed up with; (-ся be) mingle(d) in, with (в B *or* П, ме́жду T); supervene; **~е́шкаться** F [1] *pf.* be delayed, tarry; **~еща́ть** [1], ‹~ести́ть› [15 *e.*; -ещу́, -ести́шь; -ещённый] replace; substitute; act for, deputize; fill (*vacancy*); **~еще́ние** *n* [12] substitution (*a.* ⚗, ⚘); replacement; deputizing; filling.
зам|ина́ть F [1], ‹~я́ть› [-мну́, -мнёшь; -мя́тый] crumple; smother, hush up; **-ся** falter, halt, stick, be(come) confused, stop short; flag; **~я́нка** *f* [5; *g/pl.*: -нок] halt, hitch; **~ира́ть** [1], ‹~ере́ть› [12; за́мер, -рла́, -о] be(come) *or* stand stockstill, transfixed (with от P); stop; fade, die away; у меня́ се́рдце ~ерло my heart stood still.
за́мкнутый [14 *sh.*] closed; secluded; reserved; *cf.* замыка́ть.
за́м|ок[1] *m* [1; -мка] castle; **~о́к**[2] *m* [1; -мка́] lock; америка́нский ~о́к springlock; на ~ке́ *or* под ~ко́м under lock & key.
замо́л|вить [14] *pf.*: ~вить сло́в(е́чк)о F put in a word (for a p. за B, о П); **~ка́ть** [1], ‹~кнуть› [21] become silent, stop (speaking, *etc.*), cease, break off; die away *or* off; **~ча́ть** [4 *e.*; -чу́, -чи́шь] *pf.* **1.** *v/i.* *s.* ~ка́ть; **2.** *v/t.* *s.* зама́лчивать.
замор|а́живать [1], ‹~о́зить› [15] freeze, congeal; **'~озки** *m/pl.* [1] (light morning *or* night) frost; **~ский** [16] (from) oversea; foreign.
за́муж *s.* выдава́ть & выходи́ть; **~ем** married (to за T, *of women*); **~ество** *n* [9] marriage (*of women*); **~ний** [15]: ~няя (же́нщина) married (woman).
замуро́в|ывать [1], ‹~а́ть› [7] immure; wall up.
заму́ч|ивать [1], ‹~ить› [16] torment to death; fatigue, exhaust.
за́мш|а *f* [5], **~евый** [14] chamois, suede.
замыка́|ние *n* [12]: коро́ткое ~ние ⚡ short circuit; **~ть** [1], ‹замкну́ть› [20] (en)close; † lock (up); **-ся** isolate o.s. (in в B *or* T); -ся в себе́ become unsociable.
за́м|ысел *m* [1; -сла] intention, plan, design; conception; **~ы́слить** *s.* ~ышля́ть; **~ыслова́тый** [14 *sh.*] intricate, ingenious; fanciful; **~ышля́ть** [28], ‹~ы́слить› [15] plan, intend; resolve; conceive.
замя́ть(ся) *s.* замина́ть(ся).
за́нав|ес *m* [1] curtain (*a. thea.*); желе́зный ~ес *pol. a.* iron curtain; **~е́сить** *s.* ~е́шивать; **~е́ска** *f* [5; *g/pl.*: -сок] (*window*) curtain; **~е́шивать** [1], ‹~е́сить› [15] curtain.
зан|а́шивать [1], ‹~оси́ть› [15] soil; wear out; **~емо́чь** [26 г/ж: -могу́, -мо́жешь; *cf.* мочь[1]] *pf.* fall sick, *Brt.* ill; **~ести́** *s.* ~оси́ть 1.
занима́|ние *n* [12] borrowing; **~тельный** [14; -лен, -льна] interesting, entertaining, amusing; engaging, captivating; **~ть** [1], ‹за-

ня́ть⟩ [займу́, -мёшь; за́нял, -á, -o; заня́вший; за́нятый (за́нят, -á, -o)] **1.** borrow (from y P); **2.** (T) occupy, (*a. time*) take; employ, busy; reserve, secure (*place*); interest, engross, absorb; entertain; ~ть дух y (P) F take one's breath away; **-ся** [заня́лся́, -ла́сь] **1.** *v/t.* (& T) occupy *or* busy o.s. (with); (*a. sport*) engage in; attend (to); learn, study; set about, begin to (read, *etc.*); **2.** *v/i.* blaze *or* flare up; break, dawn; *s. a.* заря́.

за́ново anew, afresh.

зано́|за *f* [5] splinter; **~зи́ть** [15 *e.*; -ожу́, -ози́шь] *pf.* run a splinter (into B).

зано́с *m* [1] drift; **~и́ть** [15] **1.** ⟨занести́⟩ [24 -c-: -су́, -сёшь] bring; carry; note down, enter, register; (*a. impers.*) (be) cast, get; drift, cover, block up; lift, raise (*arm, etc.*), set (*foot*); **2.** *pf., s.* зана́шивать; **~чивый** [14 *sh.*] arrogant, presumptuous.

заня́т|ие *n* [12] occupation, work, business; exercise (of T); *pl.* F lessons, school, lecture(s) (to на B, at на П); ⚔ capture; **~ный** [14; тен, -тна] F = занима́тельный; **~ь** (**-ся**) *s.* занима́ть(ся); **~о́й** [14] busy; **'~ый** [14; за́нят, -á, -o] occupied, busy, engaged.

заодно́ conjointly; together; at one; F at the same time, besides, too.

заостр|я́ть [28], ⟨**~и́ть**⟩ [13] point, sharpen (*a. fig.*); **-ся** taper.

заочн|ик [1] student of a correspondence school, college, *etc.*; **~ый** [14] in a p.'s absence; behind one's back; ~ое обуче́ние *n* instruction by correspondence; ~ое реше́ние *n* ⚖ judg(e)ment by default.

за́пад *m* [1] west; ♀ the West, Occident; *cf.* восто́к; **~а́ть** [1], ⟨запа́сть⟩ [25; -па́л, -a] fall in, sink; impress (*a.* on на *or* в B); **~ник** *m* [1] *hist.* Westerner; **~ный** [14] west(ern, -erly); occidental.

западня́ *f* [6; *g/pl.*: -не́й] trap.

запа́|здывать, ⟨запозда́ть [1] be late (for на B), be tardy (with c T); **~ивать** [1], ⟨**~я́ть**⟩ [28] solder (up); **~ко́вывать** [1], ⟨**~кова́ть**⟩ [7] pack (up); wrap up.

запа́л *m* [1] ⚔, ⚒ fuse; touchhole; (*horse*) heaves; F fit, passion; **~ьный** [14] touch...; ~ьный шнур *m* match; ~ьная свеча́ *f* ⚡ spark(ing) plug; **~ьчивый** [14 *sh.*] quick-tempered, irascible; provoking.

запа́с *m* [1] stock (*a. fig., of words, etc.* = store, fund), supply, (*a.* ⚔) reserve; в ~e in stock, on hand; про ~ in store *or* reserve; **~а́ть** [1], ⟨**~ти́**⟩ [24 -c-: -су́, -сёшь]; **-ся,** ⟨**~ти́сь**⟩ provide o.s. (with T); **~ливый** [14 *sh.*] provident; **~но́й, ~ный** [14] spare (*a.* ⊕); reserve... (*a.* ⚔; *su.* reservist), emergency..., side... (*a.* 🚂); **~ть** *s.* запада́ть.

за́п|ах *m* [1] smell, odo(u)r, scent; **~а́хивать** [1] **1.** ⟨**~аха́ть**⟩ [3] plow (*Brt.* plough) *or* turn up, in; **2.** ⟨**~ахну́ть**⟩ [20] lap (over), wrap (o.s. **-ся**) up (in в B, T); F slam; **~а́шка** *f* [5] tillage; **~ая́ть** *s.* **~а́ивать.**

запе|ва́ла *m/f* [5] precentor, (*a. fig.*) leader; **~ва́ть** [1] lead (*chorus*); **~ка́нка** *f* [5; *g/pl.*: -нок] baked pudding; spiced brandy; **~ка́ть** [1], ⟨**~чь**⟩ [26] bake (in); **-ся** clot, coagulate (*blood*); crack (*lips*); **~ре́ть** *s.* запира́ть; **~ть** *pf.* [-пою́, -поёшь; -пе́тый] start singing, strike up.

запеча́т|ать *s.* **~ывать; ~лева́ть** [1], ⟨**~ле́ть**⟩ [8] embody, render; impress (on в П), retain; mark, seal; **~ывать,** ⟨**~ать**⟩ [1] seal (up); close, glue up.

запе́чь *s.* запека́ть.

запи|ва́ть [1], ⟨**~ть**⟩ [-пью́, -пьёшь; *cf.* пить] wash down (with T), drink *or* take after, thereupon; F take to drink.

зап|ина́ться [1], ⟨**~ну́ться**⟩ [20] stumble (over, against за *or* o B), falter; pause, hesitate; **~и́нка** *f* [5]: без ~и́нки fluently, smoothly.

запира́|тельство *n* [9] disavowal, denial; **~ть** [1], ⟨запере́ть⟩ [12; за́пер, -ла́, -o; за́пертый (за́перт, -á, -o)] lock (up; *a.* ~ть на ключ, замо́к); ⚔, ⚓ blockade; **-ся** *impf.* F (в П) deny, disavow.

запис|а́ть *s.* **~ывать; ~ка** *f* [5; *g/pl.*: -сок] note, slip; (brief) letter; memorandum, report; *pl.* notes, memoirs, reminiscences; transactions, proceedings; **~но́й** [14] note...; F inveterate; **~ывать** [1], ⟨**~а́ть**⟩ [3] write down, note (down); record (*a. on tape, etc.*); enter, enrol(l), register; ⚖ transfer (to Д, на B, за T), deed; **-ся** enrol(l), register, matriculate; subscribe (to; for в, на B), book; make an appointment (with a doctor к врачу́); **'~ь** *f* [8] entry; enrol(l)ment; registration; record (-ing); subscription; ⚖ deed.

запи́ть *s.* запива́ть.

запи́х|ивать F [1], ⟨**~а́ть**⟩ [1], *once* ⟨**~ну́ть**⟩ [20] push in; cram, stuff.

запла́ка|нный [14 *sh.*] tearful, in tears, tear-stained; **~ть** [3] *pf.* begin to cry.

запла́та [5] patch.

запле́сневелый [14] mo(u)ldy.

запле|та́ть [1], ⟨**~сти́**⟩ [25 -т-: -плету́, -тёшь] braid, plait; **-ся** F: но́ги ~та́ются totter, stagger; язы́к ~та́ется slur, mumble.

заплы|ва́ть [1], ⟨**~ть**⟩ [23] swim (far), get (*by swimming*); (T) be covered *or* closed (*a. by swelling, with fat*); swell, bloat, puff up.

запну́ться *s.* запина́ться.
запове́д|ник *m* [1] reserve; nursery; **~ный** [14] forbidden, reserved; secret; dear; intimate, inmost; **~овать** [7], ⟨~ать⟩ [1] command; **~ь** ('za-) *f* [8] *Bibl.* commandment.
запод|а́зривать († -о́зр-) [1], ⟨~о́зрить⟩ [13] suspect (of в П).
запозда́|лый [14] (be)late(d), tardy; out-of-date; **~ть** *s.* запа́здывать.
запо́|й *m* [3] hard drinking; пить ~ем booze, tipple, be a hard drinker.
заполз|а́ть [1], ⟨~ти́⟩ [24] creep (in).
заполн|я́ть [28], ⟨∠ить⟩ [13] fill (up); (*form*) fill out (*Brt.* in).
запом|ина́ть [1], ⟨∠нить⟩ [13] remember, keep in mind; memorize; **-ся** (Д) remember, stick to one's memory.
за́понка *f* [5; *g/pl.*: -нок] cuff link; collar button (*Brt.* stud).
запо́р *m* [1] bar, bolt; lock; ⚕ constipation; на ~е bolted.
запор|а́шивать [1], ⟨~оши́ть⟩ [16 *e.*; *3rd p. only*] powder *or* cover (with *snow* T).
запоте́лый F [14] moist, sweaty.
заправ|и́ла *m* F [5] boss, chief; **~ля́ть** [28], ⟨∠ить⟩ [14] put, tuck (in); (T) dress, season (*meals* with); get ready; tank, refuel (*car, plane*); **∠ка** *f* [5; *g/pl.*: -вок] refuel(l)ing; seasoning, condiment; **∠очный** [14]: ∠очная коло́нка *f* filling (gas) station; **∠ский** F [16] true, real.
запр|а́шивать [1], ⟨~оси́ть⟩ [15] ask, inquire (with/about у Р/о П); (*a.* Р) request; charge, ask (*excessive price*; с Р).
запре́|т *m* [1] = ~ще́ние; **~ти́тельный** [14] prohibitive; **~ти́ть** *s.* ~ща́ть; **~тный** [14] forbidden; ~тная зо́на *f* prohibited area; **~ща́ть** [1], ⟨~ти́ть⟩ [15 *e.*; -ещу́, -ети́шь; -ещённый] forbid, prohibit, interdict; **~ще́ние** *n* [12] prohibition, interdiction.
заприхо́довать [7] *pf.* enter, book.
запроки́|дывать [1], ⟨~нуть⟩ [20] F throw back; P overturn.
запро́с *m* [1] inquiry (about о П, *esp.* ⚓ на В); *pl.* demands, requirements, claims, interests; F overcharge; ⚓ цена́ без ~а fixed price; **~и́ть** *s.* запра́шивать; **'~то** plainly, unceremoniously.
запру́|да *f* [5] dam(ming); **~живать** [1], ⟨~ди́ть⟩ **1.** [15 & 15 *e.*; -ужу́, -у́ди́шь] dam up; **2.** [15 *e.*; -ужу́, -уди́шь] F jam, crowd.
запр|яга́ть [1], ⟨~я́чь⟩ [26 г/ж: -ягу́, -яжёшь; *cf.* напря́чь harness; put (*horse[s]*) to (в В); yoke (*oxen*); get ready (*carriage*); **~я́жка** *f* [5; *g/pl.*: -жек] harness(ing); team; **~я́тывать** F [1], ⟨~я́тать⟩ [3] hide, conceal; put (away); P confine; **~я́чь** *s.* запряга́ть.
запу́г|ивать, ⟨~а́ть⟩ [1] intimidate; ~анный (in)timid(ated).
за́пус|к *m* [1] start; **~ка́ть** [1], ⟨~ти́ть⟩ [15] **1.** neglect; disregard; let grow (*beard*); leave untilled (*land*); **2.** ⊕ start, set going; fly (*kite*); F (*a.* Т / в В) fling, hurl (s. th. at); put, slip, thrust, drive (into); **~те́лый** [14] desolate; **~ти́ть** *s.* ~ка́ть.
запу́|тывать, ⟨~тать⟩ [1] (**-ся** become, get) tangle(d, *etc.*); *fig.* confuse, perplex; complicate; F entangle, involve (in в В); ~танный *a.* intricate; **~щенный** [14] deserted, desolate; neglected, uncared-for, unkempt.
запыха́ться F [1] pant.
запя́стье *n* [10] wrist; † bracelet.
запята́я *f* [14] comma; F hitch, fix.
зараб|а́тывать, ⟨~о́тать⟩ [1] earn; **-ся** F overwork o.s.; **'~отный** [14]: '~отная пла́та *f* wages *pl.*; salary; pay; **'~оток** *m* [1; -тка] earnings *pl.*; job; на '~отки in search of a job; ... to hire o.s. out.
зара|жа́ть [1], ⟨~зи́ть⟩ [15 *e.*; -ражу́, -рази́шь; ражённый] infect (*a. fig.*); **-ся** become infected (with T), catch; **~же́ние** *n* [12] infection; ~же́ние кро́ви blood poisoning.
зара́з F at once; at the same time.
зара́|за *f* [5] infection; contagion; pest; **~зи́тельный** [14; -лен, -льна] infectious; **~зи́ть** *s.* ~жа́ть; **~зный** [14; -зен, -зна] infectious, contagious; infected.
зара́нее beforehand, in advance.
зара|ста́ть [1], ⟨~сти́⟩ [24; -сту́, -стёшь; *cf.* расти́] be overgrown.
за́рево *n* [9] blaze, glow, gleam.
заре́з *m* [1] slaughter; P ruin; до ~у F (*need s.th.*) very badly.
заре|ка́ться [1], ⟨∠чься⟩ [26] forswear, abjure; **~комендова́ть** [7] *pf.* recommend; ~комендова́ть себя́ (T) show o. s., prove.
заржа́вленный [14] rusty.
зарисо́вка *f* [5; *g/pl.*: -вок] drawing, sketch.
зарни́ца *f* [5] sheet (heat) lightning.
зар|оди́ть(ся) *s.* ~ожда́ть(ся); **~о́дыш** *m* [1] embryo, germ (*a. fig.*); в ~о́дыше in the bud; **~ожда́ть** [1], ⟨~оди́ть⟩ [15 *e.*; -ожу́, -оди́шь; -ождённый] *fig.* engender; † bear; (**-ся**) arise; (be) conceive(d); **~ожде́ние** *n* [12] origin, rise; conception.
заро́к *m* [1] vow, pledge, promise.
зарони́ть [13; -роню́, -ро́нишь] *pf.* rouse; infuse; F drop, cast; **-ся** impress (on в В).
за́росль *f* [8] underbrush; thicket.
зар|пла́та *f* [5] F *s.* ∠аботный.
заруб|а́ть [1], ⟨~и́ть⟩ [14] kill, cut down; notch, cut in; ~и́(те) на носу́ (на лбу, в па́мяти)! mark it well!
зарубе́жный [14] foreign.

зар|уби́ть *s.* ~уба́ть; **~у́бка** *f* [5; *g/pl.:* -бок] incision, notch; **~убцева́ться** [7] *pf.* cicatrize.
заруч|а́ться [1], ⟨**~и́ться**⟩ [16 *e.*; -учу́сь, -учи́шься] (T) secure.
зар|ыва́ть [1], ⟨**~ы́ть**⟩ [22] bury.
зар|я́ *f* [6; *pl.*: зо́ри, зорь, заря́м & зо́рям] (у́тренняя) ~я́ (*a. fig.*) dawn (⚔ [*acc.* зо́рю] reveille); вече́рняя ~я́ evening glow; (⚔ tattoo, retreat); на ~е́ at dawn, daybreak (*a.* с ~ёй); *fig.* at the earliest stage *or* beginning; от ~и́ до ~и́ from morning to night, all day (night); ~я́ занима́ется it dawns.
заря́|д *m* [1] charge (⚔, ⚡); shot; shell, cartridge; *fig.* store; **~ди́ть** *s.* ~жа́ть; **~дка** *f* [5] ⚔ loading; ⚡ charge, -ging; *sport:* gymnastics *pl.*, bodily exercise; **~дный** [14] charge..., loading; ~дный я́щик *m* ammunition wag(g)on; **~жа́ть** [1], ⟨~ди́ть⟩ [15 & 15 *e.*; -яжу́, -я́ди́шь; -я́женный & -яжённый] ⚔, *phot.* load; ⚡ charge; *fig.* inspire, imbue; *pf.* F (set in &) reiterate *or* go on & on.
заса́|да *f* [5] ambush; попа́сть в ~ду be ambushed; **~живать** [1], ⟨~ди́ть⟩ [15] plant; F confine; compel to (*do s. th.*); **-ся** F, ⟨засе́сть⟩ [25; -ся́ду, -дешь; -се́л] sit down; settle, retire, stay; hide, lie in ambush; (за В) set *or* begin to, bury o.s. in (*work*).
заса́л|ивать [1] **1.** ⟨~ить⟩ [13] grease, smear; **2.** ⟨засоли́ть⟩ [13; -олю́, -о́ли́шь; -о́ленный] salt; corn (*meat*).
зас|а́ривать [1] & **засоря́ть** [28], ⟨~ори́ть⟩ [13] litter, soil; stop (up), obstruct (*a. fig.*); ⚕ constipate; be(come) weedy; ~ори́ть глаз(а́) have (get) s.th. in(to) one's eye(s).
зас|а́сывать [1], ⟨~оса́ть⟩ [-су́, -сёшь; -о́санный] suck in; engulf, swallow up.
заса́харенный [14] candied, sugared.
за́свет|ло by daylight; **~и́ть(ся)** [13; -све́тится] *pf.* light (up).
засвиде́тельствовать [7] *pf.* testify; attest, authenticate.
засе́|в *m* [1] sowing; **~ва́ть** [1], ⟨~ять⟩ [27] sow.
заседа́|ние *n* [12] session (⚖, *parl.*); meeting; (*prp.*: in, at на П); **~тель** *m* [4] assessor; **~ть** [1] **1.** be in session; sit; meet; **2.** ⟨засе́сть⟩ [-ся́ду, -дешь; -се́л] stick.
засе|ка́ть [1], ⟨~чь⟩ [26] **1.** [-се́к, -ла́; -сечённый] notch, mark; stop (*time with stop watch*); **2.** [-се́к, -се́кла; -се́ченный] flog to death.
засел|е́ние *n* [12] colonization; **~я́ть** [28], ⟨~и́ть⟩ [13] people, populate; occupy, inhabit.
засе́|сть *s.* заса́живаться & ~да́ть 2.; **~чь** *s.* ~ка́ть; **~ять** *s.* ~ва́ть.
заси́|живать [1], ⟨~де́ть⟩ [11] (~женный [му́хами]) flyblow(n); **-ся** sit, stay *or* live (too) long; sit up late.
заскору́злый [14] hardened.
засло́н|ка *f* [5; *g/pl.:* -нок] (stove, *etc.*) door, screen, trap; **~я́ть** [28], ⟨~и́ть⟩ [13] protect, screen; shut off, take away (*light*); repress, oust.
заслу́|га *f* [8] merit, desert; он получи́л по ~гам (it) served him right; **~женный** [14] merited, (well-)deserved, just; meritorious, worthy; hono(u)red (*a. in Sov. titles*); **~живать** [1], ⟨~жи́ть⟩ [16] merit, deserve (*impf. a.* P); F earn.
заслу́ш|ивать, ⟨~ать⟩ [1] hear; **-ся** listen (to T, P) with delight.
засм|а́триваться [1], ⟨~отре́ться⟩ [9; -отрю́сь, -о́тришься] (на В) feast one's eyes *or* gloat ([up]on), look (at) with delight.
засну́ть *s.* засыпа́ть 2.
зас|о́в *m* [1] bar, bolt; **~о́вывать** [1], ⟨~у́нуть⟩ [20] put, slip, tuck; F mislay; **~оли́ть** *s.* ~а́ливать 2.
засор|е́ние *n* [12] obstruction; ⚕ constipation; **~я́ть, ~я́ть** *s.* заса́ривать.
засоса́ть *s.* заса́сывать.
засо́х|ший [17] dry, dried up; ⚘ dead; **~нуть** *s.* засыха́ть.
за́спанный F [14] sleepy.
заста́|ва *f* [5] *hist.* (toll)gate, turnpike; ⚔ frontier post; outpost; **~ва́ть** [5], ⟨~ть⟩ [-а́ну, -а́нешь] find, meet with; surprise; take ...; **~вля́ть** [28], ⟨~вить⟩ [14] **1.** compel, force, make; ~вить ждать keep waiting; ~вить замолча́ть silence; **2.** (T) block (up); fill; **~ре́лый** [14] inveterate, chronic; **~ть** *s.* ~ва́ть.
заст|ёгивать [1], ⟨~егну́ть⟩ [20; -ёгнутый] button (one's coat, *etc.*, *a.* **-ся**, up); buckle, clasp, hook (up); **~ёжка** *f* [5; *g/pl.*: -жек] clasp.
застекл|я́ть [28], ⟨~и́ть⟩ [13] glaze.
засте́н|ок *m* [1; -нка] torture chamber; **~чивый** [14 *sh.*] shy, timid.
засти|га́ть [1], ⟨~гнуть⟩, ⟨~чь⟩ [21 -г-: -и́гну, -и́гнешь; -и́г, -и́гла; -и́гнутый] surprise, catch; take...
заст|ила́ть [1], ⟨~ла́ть⟩ [-телю́, -те́лешь; за́стланный] cover; cloud.
засто́|й *m* [3] standstill, deadlock; stagnation; **~йный** [14] stagnant; chronic; ✝ unsalable; **~льный** [14] table...; drinking; **~я́ться** [-ою́сь, -ои́шься] *pf.* stand *or* stay too long; be(come) stagnant, stale.
застр|а́ивать [1], ⟨~о́ить⟩ [13] build on; build up, encumber; **~ахо́вывать** [1], ⟨~ахова́ть⟩ [7] insure; *fig.* safeguard; **~ева́ть** [1], ⟨~я́ть⟩ [-я́ну, -я́нешь] stick; F come to a standstill; be delayed; be lost; **~е́ливать** [1], ⟨~ели́ть⟩ [13; -елю́, -е́лишь; -е́ленный]

shoot, kill; **~е́льщик** *m* [1] ⚔ skirmisher; *fig.* instigator; initiator; **~бить** *s.* ~а́ивать; **~о́йка** *f* [5; *g/pl.*: -о́ек] building (on); **~я́ть** *s.* ~ева́ть.
за́ступ *m* [1] spade.
заступ|а́ть [1], ‹~и́ть› [14] take (*s. b.'s place*), relieve; F start (*work* на В); **-ся** (за В) take s. b.'s side; protect; intercede for; **~ник** *m* [1] protector, patron; advocate; **~ница** *f* [5] protectress, patroness; **~ничество** *n* [9] intercession.
засты|ва́ть [1], ‹~ть› [-ы́ну, -ы́нешь] cool down, congeal; stiffen, be(come) *or* stand stockstill; (*a. blood*) freeze (F to death), chill.
засу́нуть *s.* засо́вывать.
за́суха *f* [5] drought.
засу́ч|ивать [1], ‹~и́ть› [16] turn *or* tuck up.
засу́ш|ивать [1], ‹~и́ть› [16] dry (up); F make arid; **~ливый** [14 *sh.*] droughty.
засчи́т|ывать, ‹~а́ть› [1] reckon, (ac)count; credit.
зас|ыпа́ть [1] **1.** ‹~ы́пать› [2] (Т) fill up; cover, drift; *fig.* heap, ply, overwhelm; F pour, strew; **2.** ‹~ну́ть› [20] fall asleep; **~ыха́ть** [1], ‹~о́хнуть› [21] dry up; wither.
зата́|ивать [1], ‹~и́ть› [13] conceal, hide; hold (*breath*); bear (*grudge*); ~ённый *a.* secret.
зат|а́пливать [1] & **~опля́ть** [28], ‹~опи́ть› [14] **1.** light (make) a fire; **2.** flood; sink; **~а́птывать** [1], ‹~опта́ть› [3] trample, tread (down); **~а́скивать** [1] **1.** F, ‹~аска́ть› [1] wear out; ~а́сканный worn, shabby; hackneyed; **2.** ‹~ащи́ть› [16] drag, pull (in, *etc.*); mislay.
затв|ердева́ть [1], ‹~ерде́ть› [8] harden; **~е́рживать** [1], ‹~ерди́ть› [15 *e.*; -ржу́, -рди́шь; -ржённый] memorize, learn (by heart).
затво́р *m* [1] bolt, bar; (*a.* ⚔) lock; gate; *phot.* shutter; **~я́ть** [28], ‹~и́ть› [13; -орю́, -о́ришь; -о́ренный] shut, close; **-ся** shut o.s. up.
зат|ева́ть F [1], ‹~е́ять› [27] start, undertake; conceive; resolve; **~е́йливый** [14 *sh.*] fanciful; ingenious, intricate; **~ека́ть** [1], ‹~е́чь› [26] flow (in, *etc.*); swell; be(come) numb, asleep (*limbs*), bloodshot (*eyes*).
зате́м then; for that purpose, that is why; ~ что́бы in order to (*or* that); ~ что † because.
затемн|е́ние *n* [12] ⚔ blackout; obscuration; **~я́ть** [28], ‹~и́ть› [13] darken, overshadow, (*a. fig.*) obscure; ⚔ black out.
затер|е́ть *s.* затира́ть; **~я́ть** F [28] *pf.* lose; **-ся** get *or* be lost; disappear; lie in the midst of.
зате́|чь *s.* затека́ть; **~я** *f* [6] plan, undertaking; invention, freak; diversion; trick; **~ять** *s.* ~ва́ть.
зат|ира́ть [1], ‹~ере́ть› [12] wipe *or* blot out; jam, block (up); F wear out; efface, stunt; **~иха́ть** [1], ‹~и́хнуть› [21] become silent *or* quiet, stop (speaking, *etc.*); die away *or* off; calm down, abate; **~и́шье** *n* [10] lull, calm; shelter, quiet spot, nook.
заткну́ть *s.* затыка́ть.
затм|ева́ть [1], ‹~и́ть› [14 *e.*; *no 1st. p. sg.*; -ми́шь], **~е́ние** *n* [12] eclipse.
зато́ but (then, at the same time), instead, in return, on the other hand; therefore.
затова́ривание † *n* [12] glut.
затоп|и́ть, ~ля́ть *s.* зата́пливать; **~та́ть** *s.* зата́птывать.
зато́р *m* [1] jam, block, obstruction.
заточ|а́ть [1], ‹~и́ть› [16 *e.*; -чу́; -чи́шь; -чённый] confine, imprison; exile; **-е́ние** *n* [12] confinement, imprisonment; exile.
затра́|вливать [1], ‹~ви́ть› [14] bait (*a. fig.* F), course, chase down; **~гивать** [1], ‹затро́нуть› [20] touch (*a. fig.*, [up]on); affect; hurt.
затра́|та *f* [5] expense, expenditure; **~чивать** [1], ‹~тить› [15] spend.
затро́нуть *s.* затра́гивать.
затрудн|е́ние *n* [12] difficulty, trouble; embarrassment; в ~е́нии *a.* at a loss; **~и́тельный** [14; -лен, -льна] difficult, hard, straitened; ~и́тельное положе́ние *n* predicament; **~я́ть** [28], ‹~и́ть› [13] embarrass, (cause) trouble; render (more) difficult, inconvenience; aggravate, complicate; **-ся** *a.* be at a loss (for в П, Т).
зату|ма́нивать(ся) [1], ‹~ма́нить (-ся)› [13] fog; dim; **~ха́ть** F [1], ‹~хнуть› [21] die out; (*a. radio*) fade; **~шёвывать** [1], ‹~шева́ть› [6] shade; *fig.* F smooth over; **-ся** efface; **~ши́ть** F [16] *s.* туши́ть.
за́тхлый [14] musty, fusty.
зат|ыка́ть [1], ‹~кну́ть› [20] stop (up), (про́бкой) cork (up); F tuck, slip; **~ы́лок** *m* [1; -лка] back of the head; nape (of the neck).
заты́чка *f* F [5; *g/pl.*: -чек] bung, plug.
затя́|гивать [1], ‹~ну́ть› [19] tighten, draw tight; gird, lace, enclose, press; draw in, *etc.*; involve; cover; *impers.*: sink; close, skin (over); protract, delay; begin (to sing); **~жка** *f* [5; *g/pl.*: -жек] drawing tight; protraction; inhalation (*smoking*); **~жно́й** [14] long, lengthy, protracted.
зау|ны́вный [14; -вен, -вна] sad, mournful, melancholy; **~ря́дный** [14; -ден, -дна] common(place), ordinary, mediocre; **~се́ница** *f* [5] agnail.
зау́треня *f* [6] matins *pl.*
зау́ч|ивать [1], ‹~и́ть› [16] memorize.

захва́т *m* [1] seizure, capture; usurpation; **~ывать** [1], ‹**~и́ть**› [15] grasp, grip(e); take (along [with one, *a.* с собо́й]); seize, capture; usurp; absorb, captivate; F catch, snatch, take (away [*breath*], up, *etc.*); **~нический** [16] aggressive; **~чик** *m* [1] invader, aggressor; **~ывать** *s.* **~и́ть.**

захвора́ть F [1] *pf.* fall sick, ill.

захл|ёбываться [1], ‹**~ебну́ться**› [20] choke, stifle (with T, от P); *fig.* be beside o.s.; ⚔, ⊕ break down, stop; **~ёстывать** [1], ‹**~естну́ть**› [20; -хлёстнутый] lash (round, on [-to], together); swamp (*boat, etc.*); *fig.* seize; **~о́пывать(ся)** [1], ‹**~о́пнуть(ся)**› [20] slam, bang.

захо́д *m* [1] (со́лнца sun)set; call (*at a port*); ✈ approach; **~и́ть** [5], ‹зайти́› [зайду́, -дёшь; *g. pt.*: зайдя́; *cf.* идти́] go *or* come in *or* to (see, *etc.*), call *or* drop in (on, at к Д, в В); pick up, fetch (за Т); ⚓ call *or* touch at, enter; get, advance; pass, draw out; (*a.* ✈) approach; ⚔ outflank; turn, disappear, go behind (за В); *ast.* set; речь зашла́ о (П) (we, *etc.*) began (came) to (*or* had a) talk (about).

захолу́ст|ный [14] out-of-the-way, provincial, country...; rustic, boorish; **~ье** *n* [10] solitude, lonely *or* dreary spot (suburb).

захуда́лый [14] down & out; mean.

зацеп|ля́ть [28], ‹**~и́ть**› [14] (*a.* за В) catch, hook on, grapple; fasten; F & **-ся** *s.* задева́ть.

зачаро́в|ывать [1], ‹**~а́ть**› [7] [charm.]

зачасту́ю F often, frequently.

зача́|тие *n* [12] conception; **~ток** *m* [1; -тка] germ; *pl.* rudiments; **~точный** [14] rudimentary; **~ть** [-чну́, -чнёшь; зача́л, -а́, -о; зача́тый (зача́т, -а́, -о)] conceive.

заче́м why, wherefore, for what (*or* what for); **~-то** for some purpose (reason) (or other).

зач|ёркивать [1], ‹**~еркну́ть**› [20; -чёркнутый] strike out, obliterate; **~ёрпывать** [1], ‹**~ерпну́ть**› [20; -чёрпнутый] scoop, dip; **~ерстве́лый** [14] stale; *fig.* unfeeling; **~е́сть** *s.* **~и́тывать**[1]; **~ёсывать** [1], ‹**~еса́ть**› [3] comb (back); **~ёт** *m* [1] examination, test; F *educ.* credit.

зач|и́нщик *m* [1] instigator; **~исля́ть** [28], ‹**~и́слить**› [13] enrol(l), enlist, engage; ✝ enter; **~и́тывать**[1] [1], ‹**~е́сть**› [25 -т-: -чту́, -чтёшь; *cf.* проче́сть] reckon, charge, account; *educ.* credit; **~и́тывать**[2], ‹**~ита́ть**› [1] read (to, aloud); F thumb, wear out, tear; not return (*borrowed book*); **-ся** be(come) absorbed (in T); read (too) long.

зачумлённый [14 *sh.*] infected with pestilence.

заш|ива́ть [1], ‹**~и́ть**› [-шью́, -шьёшь; *cf.* шить] sew up; **~нуро́вывать** [1], ‹**~нурова́ть**› [7] lace (up); **~то́панный** [14] darned.

защёлк|ивать [1], ‹**~нуть**› [20] snap, catch.

защем|ля́ть [28], ‹**~и́ть**› [14 *e.*; -емлю́, -еми́шь; -емлённый] squeeze (in), pinch, jam; *impers. fig.* oppress with grief.

защи́|та *f* [5] defense (*Brt.* -nce), protection, cover; maintenance; **~ти́ть** *s.* **~ща́ть**; **~тник** *m* [1] defender; protector; ⚖ advocate (*a. fig.*), counsel([l]or) for the defense; *sport*: back; **~тный** [14] protective; safety...; khaki ...; crash (*helmet*); **~ща́ть** [1], ‹**~ти́ть**› [15 *e.*; -ищу́, -ити́шь; -ищённый] (от P) defend (from, against); protect (from); vindicate, advocate, (*a. thesis*) maintain, support; *impf.* ⚖ defend, plead (for).

заяв|и́ть *s.* **~ля́ть**; **~ка** *f* [5; *g/pl.*: -вок] application (for на В); claim; request; **~ле́ние** *n* [12] declaration, statement; petition, application (for о П); **~ля́ть** [28], ‹**~и́ть**› [14] (*a.* о П) declare, announce, state; claim, present; enter, lodge; notify, inform; show, manifest.

зая́длый F [14] = завзя́тый.

за́я|ц *m* [1; за́йца] hare; F speck(le); P stowaway; **~чий** [18] hare('s)...; F cowardly; **~чья губа́** *f* harelip.

зва́|ние *n* [12] rank; title; class; standing; **~ный** [14] invited; **~ный обе́д** (ве́чер) *m* dinner (evening) party; **~тельный** [14] *gr.* vocative (*case*); **~ть** [зову́, зовёшь; звал, -а́, -о; ('...)зва́нный (зван, -а́, -о)] **1.** ‹по-› call; invite (to [*a.* **~ть** в го́сти] к Д, на В); **2.** ‹на-› (Т) F (be) call(ed); как вас зову́т? what is your (first) name?; меня́ зову́т Петро́м *or* Пётр my name is Peter.

звезда́ [5; *pl.* звёзды, *etc. st.*] star (*a. fig.*); морска́я **~** *zo.* starfish.

звёзд|ный [14] star..., stellar; starry (*sky*); starlit (*night*); **~очка** *f* [5; *g/pl.*: -чек] starlet; *print.* asterisk.

звен|е́ть [9], ‹за-, про-› ring, jingle, clink; у меня́ **~и́т** в уша́х my ears ring.

звено́ *n* [9; *pl.*: зве́нья, -ьев] link; *fig.* part, branch; ✈ flight; squad.

звери́н|ец *m* [1; -нца] menagerie; **~ый** [14] animal; feral; *s.* зве́рский.

зверо|бо́й *m* [3] (*seal, walrus, etc.*) hunter; **~ло́в** *m* [1] trapper; hunter.

зве́р|ский [16] *s.* звери́ный; *fig.* brutal, atrocious; F beastly, awful, dog(-*tired*); **~ство** *n* [9] brutality; *pl.* atrocities; **~ь** *m* [4; *from g/pl. e.*] (wild) animal, beast; *fig.* brute.

звон *m* [1] ring, jingle, peal, chime; **~а́рь** *m* [4 *e.*] bell ringer, sexton; **~и́ть** [13], ‹по-› ring (*v/t.* в В), chime, peal; (Д) telephone, call up; **~́кий** [16; зво́нок, -нка́, -о; *comp.*:

зво́нче] sonorous, clear; resonant; *gr.* voiced; hard (*cash*); **~о́к** *m* [1; -нка́] bell; ring; the bell rings.
звук *m* [1] sound; tone (*a.* ♪); tune; **~ово́й** [14] sound...; talking (*picture*); **~онепроница́емый** [14] soundproof; **~оподража́ние** *n* [12] onomatopoeia; **~оподража́тельный** [14] onomatopoe(t)ic.
звуч|а́ние *n* [12] sounding; **~а́ть** [4 *e.*; *3rd p. only*], ⟨про-⟩ (re)sound; ring; clang; **∠ный** [14; -чен, -чна́, -о] sonorous, clear; resonant.
звя́к|ать [1], ⟨**~нуть**⟩ [20] clink.
зги: (ни) зги́ не вида́ть *or* не ви́дно it is pitch-dark.
зда́ние *n* [12] building.
зде|сь here; local (*on letter*); **~сь!** present!; **∠шний** [15] local; я не **∠шний** I am a stranger here.
здоро́в|аться [1], ⟨по-⟩ (с T) greet *or* salute (o. a.), welcome; wish good morning, *etc.*; **~аться** за́ руку shake hands; **~о**[1] P hi!, hello!; **'~о**[2] P awfully; well done, dandy; **~ый** [14 *sh.*] healthy (*a. su.*), sound (*a. fig.*); wholesome, salubrious; P strong; in good health; бу́дь(те) **~**(ы)! good-by(e)!, good luck!; your health!; **~ье** *n* [10] health; ка́к ва́ше **~ье**? how are you?; за ва́ше **~ье**! your health!, here's to you!; на **~ье**! good luck (health)!; е́шь(те) на **~ье**! help yourself (-ves), please!
здра́в|ие *n* [12] † = здоро́вье; **~ия** жела́ю (-ла́ем) ⚔ good morning (*etc.*), sir!; **~ица** *f* [5] toast; **~ница** *f* [5] sanatorium; sanitarium; **~омы́слящий** [17] sane, sensible; **~оохране́ние** *n* [12] public health service; **~ствовать** [7] be in good health; **~ствуй(те)!** hello!, hi!, good morning! (*etc.*); how do you do?; да **~ствует** ...! long live ...!; **~ый** [14 *sh.*] † = здоро́вый; *fig.* sound, sane, sensible; **~ый** смысл *m* common sense; в **~ом** уме́ in one's senses; **~** и невреди́м safe & sound.
зев *m* [1] throat, gullet, *anat.* pharynx; † jaws *pl.*; **~а́ка** F *m*/*f* [5] gaper; **~а́ть** [1], *once* ⟨**~ну́ть**⟩ [20] yawn; F gape (at на B); **~а́ть** по сторона́м stand gaping around; F dawdle; не **~а́й!** look out!; **~о́к** *m* [1; -вка́] yawn; **~о́та** *f* [5] yawning.
зелен|е́ть [8], ⟨за-, по-⟩ grow, turn *or* be green; *impf.* (*a.* -ся) appear *or* show green; **~но́й** [14] greengrocer's; **~ова́тый** [14 *sh.*] greenish; **~щи́к** *m* [1 *e.*] greengrocer.
зелёный [14; зе́лен, -а́, -о] green (*a. fig.*), verdant; **~** теа́тр open-air stage; **~** юне́ц F greenhorn.
зе́л|ень *f* [8] verdure; green; potherbs, greens *pl.*; **~ье** *n* [10] herb; poison.
земе́льный [14] land...; landed.
землевладе́|лец *m* [1; -льца] landowner; **~ние** *n* [12] (кру́пное great) landed property, (real) estate.
земледе́л|ец *m* [1; -льца] farmer; **~ие** *n* [12] agriculture, farming; **~ьческий** [16] agricultural.
земле|ко́п *m* [1] digger; *Brt.* navvy; **~ме́р** *m* [1] (land) surveyor; **~трясе́ние** *n* [12] earthquake; **~черпа́лка** [5; *g*/*pl.*: -лок] dredge.
земли́стый [14 *sh.*] earthy; ashy.
земл|я́ *f* [6; *ac*/*sg.*: зе́млю; *pl.*: зе́мли, земе́ль, зе́млям] earth (*as planet* **♁я́**); land; ground, soil; † country; на **∠ю** to the ground; **~я́к** *m* [1 *e.*] (fellow) countryman; **~яни́ка** *f* [5] (wild) strawberry, -ries *pl.*; **~я́нка** *f* [5; *g*/*pl.*: -нок] (*a.* ⚔) dugout; (mud) hut; **~яно́й** [14] earth(en), mud...; land...; ashy; **~яно́й** opе́х *m* peanut; **~яна́я** гру́ша *f* (Jerusalem) artichoke.
земново́дный [14] amphibian.
земно́й [14] (of the) earth, terrestrial; earthly; *fig.* earthy.
зе́м|ский [16] *hist.* State...; county-...; ⚔ Territorial (*Army*); **~ский** собо́р *m* diet; **~ский** нача́льник *m* sheriff, bailiff; **~ство** *n* [9] zemstvo, county council (*1864—1917*).
зени́т *m* [1] zenith (*a. fig.* = climax); **~ный** ⚔ [14] anti-aircraft...
зени́ц|а *f* [5] † pupil, eye; бере́чь как **~у** о́ка cherish like the apple of one's eye.
зе́ркал|о *n* [9; *pl. e.*] looking glass, (*a. fig.*) mirror; **∠ьный** [14] *fig.* (dead-)smooth; plate (*glass*).
зерн|и́стый [14 *sh.*] grainy, granular; **~о́** *n* [9; *pl.*: зёрна, зёрен, зёрнам] grain (*a. coll.*), corn, (*a. fig.*) seed; **~ово́й** [14] grain...; *su. pl.* cereals.
зигза́г *m* [1], **~ообра́зный** [14; -зен, -зна] zigzag.
зим|а́ *f* [5; *ac*/*sg.*: зи́му; *pl. st.*] winter (in [the] T; for the на B); **∠ний** [15] winter..., wintry; **~ова́ть** [7], ⟨за-, пере-⟩ winter; hibernate; **~о́вка** *f* [5; *g*/*pl.*: -вок], **~о́вье** *n* [10] wintering; hibernation; winter hut.
зия́|ние *n* [12] gaping; *ling.* hiatus; **~ть** [28] gape.
злак *m* [1] herb; grass; *pl.* ♣ gramineous plants; хле́бные **~и** *pl.* cereals.
злато... † *poet.* gold(en).
злить [13], ⟨обо-, разо-⟩ vex, anger *or* make angry, irritate; **~ся** be (-come) *or* feel angry (with на B); *fig.* rage.
зло *n* [9; *pl. gen.* зол *only*] evil.
зло́б|а *f* [5] spite; rage; **~а** дня topic of the day; **~ный** [14; -бен, -бна] spiteful, malicious; **~одне́вный** [14; -вен, -вна] topical, burning; **~ствовать** [7] *s.* зли́ться.
злов|е́щий [17 *sh.*] ominous, ill-boding; **~о́ние** *n* [12] stench; **~о́нный** [14; -о́нен, о́нна] stinking, fetid; **~ре́дный** [14; -ден, -дна] malicious, malign(ant).

злоде́|й *m* [3] malefactor, evildoer; criminal; villain; **~йский** [16] vile, villainous, outrageous; malicious; **~йство** *n* [9], **~я́ние** *n* [12] misdeed, outrage, villainy, crime.
злой [14; зол, зла, зло] wicked, (*a. su. n*) evil; malicious, spiteful; angry (with на В); fierce; severe; bad; mordant; ⚕ malignant.
зло|ка́чественный [14 *sh.*] malignant; **~ключе́ние** *n* [12] misfortune; **~наме́ренный** [14 *sh.*] malevolent; **~нра́вный** [14; -вен, -вна] ill-natured; **~па́мятный** [14; -тен, -тна] vindictive; **~полу́чный** [14; -чен, -чна] unfortunate, ill-fated; **~ра́дный** [14; -ден, -дна] mischievous.
злосло́ви|е *n* [12], **~ть** [14] slander.
зло́ст|ный [14; -тен, -тна] malicious, spiteful; malevolent; **~ь** *f* [8] spite; rage.
зло|сча́стный [14; -тен, -тна] *s.* ~полу́чный.
злоумы́шленн|ик *m* [1] plotter; malefactor; **~ый** [14] malevolent.
злоупотреб|ле́ние *n* [12], **~ля́ть** [28], ⟨~и́ть⟩ [14 *e.*; -блю́, -би́шь] (Т) abuse; (make) excessive use.
зме|и́ный [14] snake('s), serpent('s), -tine; **~и́ться** [13] meander, wind (o.s.); **~й** *m* [3] dragon; (*a.* бума́жный ~й) kite; †, P = **~я́** *f* [6; *pl. st.:* зме́и, змей] snake, serpent (*a. fig.*).
знак *m* [1] sign, mark, token; symbol; omen; badge; signal; ~и *pl.* препина́ния punctuation marks; в ~ (P) in (*or* as a) token (sign) of.
знако́м|ить [14], ⟨по-⟩ introduce (a p. to В/с Т); *a.* ⟨о-⟩) acquaint (with с Т); **-ся** (с Т) *p.*: meet, make the acquaintance of, (*a. th.*) become acquainted with; *th:* familiarize o.s. with, go into; **~ство** *n* [9] acquaintance (-ces *pl.*); **~ый** [14 *sh.*] familiar, acquainted (with с Т); known; *su.* acquaintance; бу́дьте ~ы = ~ьтесь, ..., meet ...
знамена́тель *m* [4] denominator; **~ный** [14; -лен, -льна] memorable, remarkable; significant, suggestive; *gr.* notional.
знаме́н|ие *n* [12] †, *s.* знак; **~и́тость** *f* [8] fame, renown; *p.:* celebrity; **~и́тый** [14 *sh.*] famous, renowned, celebrated (by, for Т).
знам|ено́сец *m* [1; -сца] standard bearer; **~я** *n* [13; *pl.:* -мёна, -мён] banner, flag; ⚔ standard; colo(u)rs.
зна́ни|е *n* [12] (*a. pl.* ~я) knowledge; со ~ем де́ла with skill *or* competence.
зна́т|ный [14; -тен, -тна́, -о] noble; distinguished, notable, eminent; **~о́к** *m* [1 *e.*] expert; connoisseur.
знать[1] **1.** [1] know; дать ~ (Д) let know; дать себя́ (о себе́) ~ make o.s. felt (send news); то и знай = то и де́ло; кто́ его́ зна́ет goodness knows; **-ся** F associate with (с Т); (get to) know; **2.** P apparently, probably; **~**[2] *f* [8] nobility, notables.
знач|е́ние *n* [12] meaning, sense; significance, importance (*vb.*: име́ть be of); **~и́тельный** [14; -лен, -льна] considerable; large; important; significant, suggestive; **~ить** [16] mean, signify; matter; ~ит consequently, so; well (then); **-ся** be registered; *impers.* (it) say(s); **~о́к** *m* [1; -чка́] badge; sign.
зноби́т|ь: меня́ ~ I feel chilly.
зной *m* [3] heat, sultriness; **~ный** [14; зно́ен, зно́йна] sultry, hot.
зоб *m* [1] crop, craw; ⚕ goiter, -tre.
зов *m* [1] call; F invitation.
зо́дчество *n* [9] architecture.
зол|а́ *f* [5] ashes *pl.*; **~о́вка** *f* [5; *g/pl.:* -вок] sister-in-law (*husband's sister*).
золоти́|стый [14 *sh.*] golden; **~ть** [15 *e.*; -очу́, -оти́шь], ⟨по-, вы́-⟩ gild.
зо́лот|о *n* [9] gold; на вес ~а worth its weight in gold; **~оиска́тель** *m* [4] gold digger; **~о́й** [14] gold(en) (*a. fig.*); dear; ~ы́х дел ма́стер *m* † jewel(l)er.
золоту́|ха F *f* [5] scrofula; **~шный** F [14; -шен, -шна] scrofulous.
золочёный [14] gilt, gilded.
зо́н|а *f* [5] zone; **~а́льный** [14] zonal.
зонд *m* [1], **~и́ровать** [7] sound.
зонт, ~ик *m* [1] umbrella; sunshade.
зоо́|лог *m* [1] zoölogist; **~логи́ческий** [16] zoölogical; **~ло́гия** *f* [7] zoölogy; **~па́рк, ~са́д** *m* [1] zoo (-logical garden).
зо́ркий [16; зо́рок, -рка́, -о; *comp.:* зо́рче] sharp-sighted (*a. fig.*); observant, watchful, vigilant.
зрачо́к *m* [1; -чка́] *anat.* pupil.
зре́л|ище *n* [11] sight; spectacle; show; **~ость** *f* [8] ripeness, maturity; **~ый** [14; зрел, -а́, -о] ripe, mature; deliberate.
зре́ни|е *n* [12] (eye)sight; по́ле ~я range of vision, eyeshot; *fig.* horizon; то́чка ~я point of view, standpoint, angle (*prp.*: с то́чки ~я = под угло́м ~я from ...).
зре́ть 1. [8], ⟨со-, вы́-⟩ ripen, mature; **2.** † [9], ⟨у-⟩ see; look.
зри́тель *m* [4] spectator, onlooker, looker-on; **~ный** [14] visual, optic; ~ный зал *m* hall, auditorium; ~ная труба́ spyglass.
зря F in vain, to no purpose, (all) for nothing; it's no good (use) ...ing.
зря́чий [17] seeing (*one that can see*).
зуб *m* [1; *from g/pl. e.*; ⊕ зу́бья, зу́бьев] tooth; ⊕ *a.* cog, dent; до ~о́в to the teeth; не по ~а́м too tough (*a. fig.*); сквозь ~ы through clenched teeth; (*mutter*) indistinctly; име́ть *or* точи́ть ~ (на В) have a grudge against; **~а́стый** [14 *sh.*]

large-, sharp-toothed; *fig.* sharp--tongued; **~éц** *m* [1; -бцá] ⊕ = зуб; ⚔ battlement; **~úло** *n* [9] chisel; **~нóй** [14] tooth...; dental; **~нóй** врач *m* dentist; **~нáя** боль *f* toothache; **~очúстка** *f* [5; *g/pl.*: -ток] toothpick.
зубр *m* [1] bison; *fig.* fossil.
зубр|ёжка F *f* [5] cramming; **~úть** **1.** [13], ⟨за-⟩ notch; зазу́бренный jagged; **2.** F [13; зубрю́, зу́бришь], ⟨вы́-, за-⟩ [зазу́бренный] cram, learn by rote.
зубчáтый [14] ⊕ cog(wheel)..., gear...; indented.
зуд *m* [1], **~éть** F [9] itch (*a. fig.*).
зы́б|кий [16; зы́бок, -бкá, -o; *comp.*: зы́бче] loose; shaky; unsteady, unstable; swelling, rippled; vague; **~у́чий** [17 *sh.*] = **~кий**; **~ь** *f* [8] ripples *pl.*; swell; † wave.
зы́чный [14; -чен, -чна; *comp.*: -чнée] ringing.
зя́б|кий [16; -бок, -бкá, -o] chilly; **~левый** [14] winter...; **~лик** *m* [1] chaffinch; **~нуть** [21], ⟨(пр)о-⟩ feel chilly; freeze; **~ь** *f* [8] winter tillage.
зять *m* [4; *pl. e.*: зятья́, -ьёв] son- *or* brother-in-law (*daughter's or sister's husband*).

И

и **1.** *cj.* and; and then, and so; but; (even) though, much as; (that's) just (what ... is, *etc.*), (this) very *or* same; **2.** *part.* oh; too, (n)either; even; и ... и ... both ... and ...
и́бо because, since, as.
и́ва *f* [5] willow.
Ивáн *m* [1] Ivan; John.
и́волга *f* [5] oriole.
игл|á *f* [5; *pl. st.*] needle (*a.* ⊕, ⛏, *min.*, ⚘); thorn, prickle; quill, spine, bristle; **~и́стый** [14 *sh.*] prickly, thorny; spiny; crystalline.
Игнá|тий *m* [3], F **~т** [1] Ignatius.
игнори́ровать [7] (*im*)*pf.* ignore.
и́го *n* [8] *fig.* yoke.
игóл|ка *f* [5; *g/pl.*: -лок] *s.* иглá; как на **~ках** on tenterhooks; с **~(оч)ки** brand-new, spick-and--span; **~ьный** [14] needle('s)...
игóрный [14] gambling; card...
игрá *f* [5; *pl. st.*] play; game (of в В); effervescense; sparkle; ~ слов play on words, pun; ~ не стóит свеч it isn't worth while *or* doesn't pay; **~лище** *n* [11] sport, plaything; **~льный** [14] playing (*card*); **~ть** [1], ⟨по-, сыгрáть⟩ play (*sport, cards, chess, etc.*, в В; ♪ на П); gamble; (*storm, etc.*) rage; (*a. wine, etc.*) sparkle; *thea. a.* act.
игри́|вый [14 *sh.*] playful, sportive; equivocal, immodest; **~стый** [14 *sh.*] sparkling.
игрóк *m* [1 *e.*] player, gambler.
игру́шка *f* [5; *g/pl.*: -шек] toy, plaything.
игу́мен *m* [1] abbot, superior.
идеáл *m* [1] ideal; **~и́зм** *m* [1] idealism; **~и́ст** *m* [1] idealist; **~исти́ческий** [16] idealistic; **~ьный** [14; -лен, -льна] ideal.
идéйный [14; -éен, -éйна] ideologic(al); ideal; high-principled.
идеóлог *m* [1] ideologist; **~и́ческий** [16] ideologic(al); **~ия** [7] ideology.
идéя *f* [6] idea.
иди́лл|ия *f* [7] idyl(l); **~и́ческий** [16] idyllic.
идиомáт|ика *f* [5] stock of idioms; idiomology; **~и́ческий** [16] idiomatic(al).
идиóт *m* [1] idiot; **~и́зм** *m* [1] idiocy; **~ский** [16] idiotic.
и́дол *m* [1] idol; *contp.* blockhead.
идти́ [иду́, идёшь; шёл, шла; шéдший; идя́, F и́дучи; ...дённый], ⟨пойти́⟩ [пойду́, -дёшь; пошёл, -шлá] (be) go(ing, *etc.*; *a. fig.*), walk; come; run, pass, drive, sail, fly, *etc.*; (за Т) follow, *a.* go for, fetch; leave; move (*a. chess*, Т), flow, drift, blow; (в, на В) enter (*school*), join (*army, etc.*), become; proceed, be in progress, take place; be on (*thea., film*); lead (*road*; *a. card* с Р); (на В) attack; spread (*rumo[u]r*); (be) receive(d); ✝ sell; ⊕ work; (в, на, под В) be used, spent (for); (в В) be sent to; ([к] Д) suit; (за В) marry; ~ в счёт count; ~ на вёслах row; ~ по отцу́ take after one's father; идёт! all right!, done!; пошёл (пошли́)! (let's) go!; дéло (речь) идёт о (П) the question *or* matter is (whether), it is a question *or* matter (of); ... is at stake; ему́ идёт *or* пошёл шестóй год (деся́ток) he is over *or* past five (fifty).
иезуи́т *m* [1] Jesuit (*a. fig.*).
иерóглиф *m* [1] hieroglyph(ic).
Иерусали́м *m* [1] Jerusalem.
иждивéн|ец *m* [1; -нца] dependent; **~ие** *n* [12]: на **~ии** (Р) (*live*) at s.b's. expense, depend on.
из, ~о (Р) from, outof; of; for, through; with; in; by; что ж ~ э́того? what does that matter?
избá *f* [5; *pl. st.*] (peasant's) house, hut, cottage; room (*therein*); **~-читáльня** *f* [5/6] village reading room.
избав|и́тель *m* [4] rescuer, saver, deliverer; **~и́ть** *s.* **~ля́ть**; **~лéние** *n* [12] deliverance, rescue; **~ля́ть** [28], ⟨**~и́ть**⟩ [14] (от Р from) deliver,

free; save; relieve; redeem; **-ся** (от P) escape, get rid of.
избало́ванный [14] spoilt.
избе|га́ть [1], ⟨**~жа́ть**⟩ [4; -егу́, -ежи́шь, -егу́т], ⟨**~́гнуть**⟩ [21] (P) avoid, shun; escape, evade; **~жа́ние** *n* [12]: во ~жа́ние (P) (in order) to avoid.
изб|ива́ть [1], ⟨**~и́ть**⟩ [изобью́, -бьёшь; *cf.* бить] beat, thrash; † slaughter, extirpate; F damage; **~ие́ние** *n* [12] beating; extermination, massacre.
избира́тель *m* [4] voter, elector; *pl. a.* electorate; constituency; **~ный** [14] electoral; election...; **~ный** уча́сток *m* polling place; ~ное пра́во *n* franchise; ~ное собра́ние *n* caucus, *Brt.* electoral assembly.
изб|ира́ть [1], ⟨**~ра́ть**⟩ [-беру́, -рёшь; *cf.* брать] choose; elect (В/в И *pl.* or /Т); **~́ранный** *a.* select(ed).
изби́|тый [14] *fig.* beaten (*path, etc.*); hackneyed, trite; **~ть** *s.* **~ва́ть**.
избра́|ние *n* [12] election; **~нник** *m* [1] the elect; **~ть** *s.* избира́ть.
избы́т|ок *m* [1; -тка] superfluity, surplus; abundance, plenty; в ~ке, с ~ком in plenty, plentiful(ly); **~очный** [14; -чен, -чна] superfluous, surplus...
извая́ние *n* [12] statue; *s.* вая́ть.
изве́д|ывать, ⟨**~ать**⟩ [1] learn, (come to) know, see; experience.
и́звер|г *m* [1] monster; **~га́ть** [1], ⟨**~́гнуть**⟩ [21] cast out (*a. fig.*); vomit; erupt; **~же́ние** *n* [12] ejection, eruption.
извернýться *s.* изворáчиваться.
извести́ *s.* изводи́ть.
изве́ст|ие *n* [12] news *sg.*; information; *pl. a.* bulletin; после́дние ~ия *rad.* news(cast); **~и́ть** *s.* извеща́ть.
извёстк|а *f* [5], **~о́вый** [14] lime.
изве́стн|ость *f* [8] notoriety; reputation, fame; по́льзоваться (мирово́й) ~остью be (world-)renowned or famous or well known; ста́вить (В) в ~ость bring to a p.'s notice (s. th. о П); **~ый** [14; -тен, -тна] known (for Т; as как, P за В), familiar; well-known, renowned, famous; notorious; certain; ~ое (P ~о) де́ло of course; (мне) ~о it is known (I know); (ему́) э́то хорошо́ ~о it is a well-known fact (he is well aware of this).
извест|ня́к *m* [1 *e.*] limestone; [′**~ь** *f* [8] lime.]
изве|ща́ть [1], ⟨**~сти́ть**⟩ [15 *e.*; -ещу́, -ести́шь; -ещённый] inform (of о П); notify; † *a.* advise; **~ще́ние** *n* [12] notification, information, notice; ⚖ summons, writ.
изви|ва́ться [1] wind, twist, wriggle, meander; **~́лина** *f* [5] bend, curve; turn; **~́листый** [14 *sh.*] winding, tortuous.
извин|е́ние *n* [12] pardon; apology, excuse; **~и́тельный** [14; -лен, -льна] pardonable; [*no sh.*] apologetic; **~я́ть** [28], ⟨**~и́ть**⟩ [13] excuse, pardon; forgive (a p. a th. Д/В); ~и́(те)! excuse me!, (I'm) sorry!; нет, (уж) ~и́(те)! oh no!, on no account!; **-ся** apologize (to/for пе́ред Т/в П); beg to be excused (on account of Т); ~я́юсь! P = ~и́(те)!
извл|ека́ть [1], ⟨**~е́чь**⟩ [26] take or draw out; extract (*a.* ⚗); derive (*a. profit*); **~ече́ние** *n* [12] extract(ion).
извне́ from outside or without.
изводи́ть F [15], ⟨**извести́**⟩ [25] use up; exhaust, ruin. [cab.]
изво́зчик *m* [1] cabman, cab driver;
изво́л|ить [13] please, deign; † want (*or just polite form of respect*); **~ь(те)** + *inf.* (would you) please + *vb.*; *a. order, admonition:* (if you) please; *discontent*: how can one ...; F **~ь(те)** all right, O. K.; please; *cf.* уго́дно.
извор|а́чиваться [1], ⟨**изверну́ться**⟩ [20] F dodge; shift; (try to) wriggle out; **~о́тливый** [14 *sh.*] nimble (*a. fig.*), elusive; shifty.
извра|ща́ть [1], ⟨**~ти́ть**⟩ [15 *e.*; -ащу́, -ати́шь; -ащённый] distort; pervert.
изги́б *m* [1] bend, curve, turn; *fig.* shade; **~а́ть** [1], ⟨**изогну́ть**⟩ [20] bend, curve, crook (*v/i.* **-ся**).
изгла́|живать [1], ⟨**~дить**⟩ [15] (**-ся** be[come]) efface(d), erase(d); smooth out.
изгна́|ние *n* [12] expulsion, banishment; exile; **~нник** *m* [1] exile; **~ть** *s.* изгоня́ть.
изголо́вье *n* [10] head (*bed*); bolster.
изг|оня́ть [28], ⟨**~на́ть**⟩ [-гоню́, -го́нишь; -гна́л, -ла́, -о; и́згнанный] drive out; oust; expel; exile, banish.
и́згородь *f* [8] fence; hedge(row).
изгот|а́вливать [1], **~овля́ть** [28], ⟨**~о́вить**⟩ [14] make, produce, manufacture; F prepare (*food*); **~овле́ние** *n* [12] production, manufacture; making.
изда|ва́ть [5], ⟨**~́сть**⟩ [-да́м, -да́шь, *etc.*, *cf.* дать; и́зданный (и́здан, -а́, -о)] publish; edit; (*order*) issue; (*law*) enact; (*sound*) utter, emit.
и́зда|вна at all times; from of old; long since; **~лека́**, **~лёка**, **~ли** from afar; afar off.
изда́|ние *n* [12] publication; edition; issue; **~тель** *m* [4] publisher; editor (*of material*); **~тельство** *n* [9] publishing house, publishers *pl.*; **~ть** *s.* издава́ть.
издева́т|ельство *n* [9] derision (of над Т), scorn, scoff; **~ься** [1] jeer, sneer, mock (at над Т); bully.
изде́лие *n* [12] make; product(ion), article; (needle)work; *pl. a.* goods.

издéрж|ивать [1], ‹**~ать**› [4] spend; use up; **-ся** F spend much (*or* run short of) money; **~ки** *f/pl.* [5; *gen.*: -жек] expenses; ⚖ costs.
издыхá|ть [1] *s.* дóхнуть; **~ние** *n* [12] (last) breath *or* gasp.
изж|ивáть [1], ‹**~ить**› [-живý, -вёшь; -жи́тый, F -тóй (изжи́т, -á, -o)] eliminate, extirpate; complete, end (*life, etc.*); endure; **~и́ть** себя́ be(come) outdated, have had one's day; **~óга** *f* [5] heartburn.
из-за (P) from behind; from; because of; over; for (the sake of); ~ чегó? what for?; ~ э́того therefore.
излагáть [1],‹изложи́ть› [16] state, set forth, expound, expose.
излеч|éние *n* [12] cure, (medical) treatment; recovery; **∠ивать** [1], ‹**~и́ть**› [16] cure; **~и́мый** [14 *sh.*] curable.
изл|ивáть [1], ‹**~и́ть**› [изолью́, -льёшь; *cf.* лить] shed; **~и́ть** дýшу, мы́сли unbosom o.s.; *anger*: vent ... on (на В).
изли́ш|ек *m* [1; -шка] surplus, (*a.* **~ество** *n* [9]) excess, & = избы́ток; **~ний** [15; -шен, -шня, -не] superfluous, excessive; needless.
изл|ия́ние *n* [12] outpouring, effusion; **~и́ть** [28] = **~ивáть**.
изловчи́ться F [16 *e.*; -чýсь, -чи́шься] *pf.* contrive.
излож|éние *n* [12] exposition, statement; **~и́ть** *s.* излагáть.
излóманный [14] broken; angular; spoilt, deformed, unnatural.
излуч|áть [1], ‹**~и́ть**› [16 *e.*; -чý, -чи́шь; -чённый] radiate.
излýчина *f* [5] *s.* изги́б.
излю́бленный [14] favo(u)rite.
измéн|а *f* [5] (Д to) treason; unfaithfulness; **~éние** *n* [12] change, alteration, modification; впредь до **~éния** until further notice; **~и́ть** *s.* **~я́ть**; **~ник** *m* [1] traitor; **~чивый** [14 *sh.*] changeable, variable; fickle; **~я́ть** [28], ‹**~и́ть**› [13; -еню́, -éнишь] **1.** *v/t.* change (v/i. **-ся**), alter; modify; vary; **2.** *v/i.* (Д) betray; be(come) unfaithful (to); break, violate (*oath, etc.*); fail (*memory, etc.*), desert.
измер|éние *n* [12] measurement; Ⓐ dimension; **~и́мый** [14 *sh.*] measurable; **~и́тель** *m* [4] meter, measure, measuring instrument; **~я́ть** [28], ‹**∠ить**› [13] measure; fathom (*a. fig.*).
измождённый [14 *sh.*] exhausted.
измóр: взять **~ом** ⚔ starve (out).
и́зморозь *f* [8] rime; mist.
и́зморось *f* [8] drizzle.
измýчи|вать [1], ‹**~ть**› [16] (**-ся** be[come]) fatigue(d), exhaust(ed), wear (worn) out; *refl. a.* pine.
измышл|éние *n* [12] invention; **~я́ть** [28], ‹измы́слить› [13; -ы́шленный] invent; contrive, devise.
изнáнка *f* [5] back, inside; (*fabric*) wrong side; *fig.* seamy side.
изнáшивать [1], ‹износи́ть› [15] wear out (by use); *v/i.* **-ся.**
изнéженный [14] coddled; effeminate.
изнем|огáть [1], ‹**~óчь**› [26 г/ж: -огý, -óжешь, -óгут] be(come) exhausted *or* enervated; collapse; **~ожéние** *n* [12] exhaustion, weariness.
изнóс *m* [1] wear and tear; **~и́ть** *s.* изнáшивать.
изнур|éние *n* [12] exhaustion, fatigue; **~и́тельный** [14; -лен, -льна] wearisome, wasting; **~я́ть** [28], ‹**~и́ть**› [13] (**-ся** be[come]) fatigue(d), exhaust(ed), waste(d).
изнутри́ from within; within.
изны|вáть [1], ‹**∠ть**› [22] pine (for по Д); *impf. a.* (от P) die of, be wearied *or* bored to death.
изоби́л|ие *n* [12] abundance, plenty (of P, *a.* в П); **~овать** [7] abound (in T); **~ьный** [14; -лен, -льна] rich, abundant (in T).
изоблич|áть [1], ‹**~и́ть**› [16 *e.*; -чý, -чи́шь; -чённый] convict (of в П); unmask; *impf.* reveal, show.
изобра|жáть [1], ‹**~зи́ть**› [15 *e.*; -ажý, -ази́шь; -ажённый] represent (*a. impf.* + собóю), depict; describe; express; **~жáть** из себя́ (B) F act, set up for; **~жéние** *n* [12] representation; description; image, picture; **~зи́тельный** [14; -лен, -льна] graphic, descriptive; (*no sh.*) fine (*arts*).
изобре|сти́ *s.* **~тáть**; **~тáтель** *m* [4] inventor; **~тáтельный** [14; -лен, -льна] inventive, resourceful; **~тáть** [1], ‹**~сти́**› [25 -т-: -бретý, -тёшь] invent; **~тéние** *n* [12] invention.
изогнýть *s.* изгибáть.
изóдранный [14] F = изóрванный.
изол|и́ровать [7] (*im*)*pf.* isolate; ⚡ *a.* insulate; **~я́тор** *m* [1] ⚡ insulator; ⚕ isolation ward; cell *or* jail (for close solitary confinement); **~я́ция** *f* [7] isolation; ⚡ insulation.
изóрванный [14] torn, tattered.
изощр|ённый [14] refined, subtle; **~я́ть** [28], ‹**~и́ть**› [13] (**-ся** become) refine(d), sharpen(ed); *refl. impf. a.* exert o.s., excel (in в П *or* T).
из-под (P) from under; from; from the vicinity of; буты́лка ~ молокá milk bottle.
изразéц *m* [1; -зцá] (Dutch) tile.
Изрáиль *m* [4] Israel.
и́зредка occasionally; here & there.
изрéз|ывать [1], ‹**~ать**› [3] cut up.
изре|кáть [1], ‹**∠чь**› pronounce; **~чéние** *n* [12] aphorism, maxim.
изруб|áть [1], ‹**~и́ть**› [14] chop, mince; cut (up, down); saber (-bre).
изря́дный [14; -ден, -дна] (fairly) good *or* big, fair (*amount*).
изувéр *m* [1] fanatic; monster.
изувéч|ивать [1], ‹**~ить**› [16] mutilate.

изум|и́тельный [14; -лен, -льна] amazing, wonderful; **~и́ть(ся)** *s.* ~ля́ть(ся); **~ле́ние** *n* [12] amazement; **~ля́ть** [28], ⟨~и́ть⟩ [14 *e*; -млю́, -ми́шь; -млённый] (**-ся** Д be) amaze(d), astonish(ed), surprise(d at, wonder).
изумру́д *m* [1] emerald.
изу́стный [14] oral.
изуч|а́ть [1], ⟨~и́ть⟩ [16] study, learn; familiarize o. s. with, master; scrutinize; **~е́ние** *n* [12] study.
изъе́з|дить [15] *pf.* travel (all) over, through; **~женный** [14] beaten; bumpy (*road*).
изъяв|и́тельный [14] *gr.* indicative; **~ля́ть** [28], ⟨~и́ть⟩ [14] express, show; (*consent*) give.
изъя́н *m* [1] defect; stain; loss.
изыма́ть [1], ⟨изъя́ть⟩ [изыму́, изы́мешь] withdraw; seize.
изыска́ние *n* [12] investigation, research; survey; ⚒ prospect.
изы́сканный [14 *sh.*] refined, elegant; choice, exquisite; far-fetched.
изы́ск|ивать [1], ⟨~а́ть⟩ [3] find.
изю́м *m* [1] *coll.* raisins *pl.*
изя́щн|ый [14; -щен, -щна] graceful, elegant, (*a.*, †, *arts*) fine; **~ое** *n su.* the beautiful; **~ая** литерату́ра *f* belles-lettres *pl.*
Иису́с *m* [1; *voc.*: -у́се] Jesus.
ик|а́ть [1], ⟨~ну́ть⟩ [20] hiccup.
ико́|на *f* [5] icon; **~та** *f* [5] hiccup.
икра́ *f* [5] (hard) roe, spawn; caviar; *mst. pl.* [*st.*] calf (*leg*).
ил *m* [1] silt.
и́ли or; or else; ~ ... ~ either ... or.
иллю|зия *f* [7] illusion; **~мина́ция** *f* [7] illumination; **~минова́ть** [7] (*im*)*pf.* illuminate; **~стра́ция** *f* [7] illustration; **~стри́ровать** [7] (*im*)*pf.* illustrate.
Ил|ья́ *m* [6], F *dim.* **~ю́ша** [5] Elias.
им. *abbr.*: и́мени, *s.* и́мя.
имби́рь *m* [4 *e.*] ginger.
име́ние *n* [12] estate.
имени́|ны *f/pl* [5] name day; **~тельный** [14] *gr.* nominative; **~тый** [14 *sh.*] eminent, notable.
и́менно just, very (*adj.*), exactly, in particular; (*a.* а ~, и ~) namely, to wit, that is to say; (*a.* вот ~) F indeed.
именова́ть [7], ⟨на-⟩ call, name.
име́ть [8] have, possess; ~ де́ло с (Т) have to do with; ~ ме́сто take place; ~ в виду́ have in view, mean, intend; remember, bear in mind; **-ся** be at, in *or* on hand; (у Р) have; there is, are, *etc.*
иммигра́нт *m* [1] immigrant.
иммуните́т *m* [1] immunity.
импера́т|ор *m* [1] emperor; **~ри́ца** *f* [5] empress.
империали́|зм *m* [1] imperialism; **~ст** *m* [1] imperialist; **~сти́ческий** [16] imperialist(ic).
импе́рия *f* [7] empire.
и́мпорт *m* [1], **~и́ровать** [7] (*im*)*pf.* import.
импровизи́ровать [7] (*im*)*pf.* & ⟨сымпровизи́ровать⟩ improvise.
и́мпульс *m* [1] impulse.
иму́щ|ество *n* [9] property; belongings *pl.*; (не)движи́мое ~ество ⚖ (im)movables *pl.*; **~ий** [17] well-to-do.
и́мя *n* [13] (*esp.* first, Christian) name (*a. fig.* & *gr.*; *parts of speech*: = *Lat.* nomen); и́мени: шко́ла им. Че́хова Chekhov school; и́менем, во ~; от и́мени (*all 3*) in the name of (P); на ~ addressed to, for; по и́мени named; in name (only); (*know*) by name.
и́на́че differently; otherwise, (or) else; не ~, как just; та́к и́ли ~ one way or another, anyhow.
инвали́д *m* [1] invalid; ~ труда́ (войны́) disabled worker (veteran, *Brt.* ex-serviceman).
инвент|ариза́ция *f* [7] inventory, stock-taking; **~а́рь** *m* [4 *e.*] inventory; (живо́й live)stock; implements, fittings *pl.*
инд|е́ец *m* [1; -е́йца] (*Am.* Red) Indian; **~е́йка** *f* [5; *g/pl.*: -е́ек] turkey; **~е́йский** [16] (Red) Indian; ~е́йский пету́х *m* = ~ю́к; **~иа́нка** *f* [5; *g/pl.*: -нок] *fem. of* ~е́ец & ~и́ец.
индиви́д, ~уум *m* [1] individual; **~уа́льный** [14; -лен, -льна] individual.
инди́|ец *m* [1; -и́йца] (East) Indian, Hindu; **~йский** [16] Indian (*a.* Ocean: Ώйский океа́н *m*), Hindu.
'Индия *f* [7] India.
Индо|кита́й *m* [3] Indo-China; **~не́зия** *f* [7] Indonesia; **~ста́н** *m* [1] Hindustan.
инду́с *m* [1], **~ка** *f* [5; *g/pl.*: -сок], **~ский** [16] Hindu.
индустриализ|а́ция *f* [7] industrialization (*Brt.* -sa-); **~(и́р)ова́ть** [7] (*im*)*pf.* industrialize (*Brt.* -se).
инд|устриа́льный [14] industrial; **~у́стрия** *f* [7] industry.
индю́к *m* [1 *e.*] turkey cock.
и́ней *m* [3] (white *or* hoar)frost.
ине́р|тный [14; -тен, -тна] inert; **~ция** *f* [7] inertia; по ~ции mechanically.
инжене́р *m* [1] engineer; ~-строи́тель *m* [1/4] civil engineer; **~ный** [14] (*a.* ⚔ & ~ное де́ло *n*) engineering.
инициа́|лы *m/pl.* [1] initials; **~ти́ва** *f* [5] initiative; **~тор** *m* [1] initiator.
иногда́ sometimes, now and then.
иногоро́дний [15] nonresident, foreign.
инозе́м|ец *m* [1; -мца] foreigner; **~ный** [14] foreign.
ино́|й [14] (an)other, different; some, many a; ~й раз sometimes; не кто ~й (не что ~е), как ... nobody (nothing) else but ...

иносказа́тельный [14; -лен, -льна] allegorical.
иностра́н|ец *m* [1; -нца], **~ка** *f* [5; *g/pl.*: -нок] foreigner; **~ный** [14] foreign; *s. a.* министе́рство.
инста́нция *f* [7] ⚖ instance; *pl.* (official) channels; hierarchy.
инсти́нкт *m* [1] instinct; **~и́вный** [14; -вен, -вна] instinctive.
институ́т *m* [1] institute; (*a.* ⚖) institution; *form.* (girls') boarding school (**~ка** *f* [5; *g/pl.*: -ток] pupil *thereof*).
инструме́нт *m* [1] instrument.
инсцени́р|овать [7] (*im*)*pf.* stage, screen; *fig.* feign; **~о́вка** *f* [5; *g/pl.*: -вок] staging, *etc.*; direction; dramatization.
интегра́л *m* [1] integral; **~ьный** [14; *fig.* -лен, -льна] integral.
интеллектуа́льный [14; -лен, -льна] intellectual.
интеллиге́н|т *m* [1] intellectual; **~тность** *f* [8] intelligence; **~тный** [14; -тен, -тна] intelligent; intellectual; **~ция** *f* [7] intelligentsia, intellectuals *pl.*
интенда́нт *m* [1] ⚔ commissary; **~ство** *n* [9] commissariat.
интенси́вный (-tɛn-) [14; -вен, -вна] intense, (*a. econ.*) intensive.
интерва́л *m* [1] interval.
интерве́нция *f* [7] intervention.
интервью (-tɛr-) *n* [*indecl.*], **~и́ровать** (-tɛr-) [7] (*im*)*pf.* interview.
интере́с *m* [1] interest (in к *D*; be of/to име́ть ~ для Р; in the/of в **~ах** Р); F use; **~ный** [14; -сен, -сна] interesting; F handsome, attractive; **~ова́ть** [7], ⟨за-⟩ (-ся be[come]) interest(ed, take an interest in Т).
интерна́т *m* [1] boarding school; hostel.
Интернациона́л *m* [1] International(e); **&ьный** [14; -лен, -льна] international.
интерни́рова|ние (-tɛr-) *n* [12] internment; **~ть** (-tɛr-) [7] (*im*)*pf.* intern.
инти́мн|ость *f* [8] intimacy; **~ый** [14; -мен, -мна] intimate.
интри́г|а *f* [5] intrigue; **~а́н** *m* [1] intriguer; **~а́нка** *f* [5; *g/pl.*: -нок] intrigante; **~ова́ть** [7], ⟨за-⟩ intrigue.
интуити́вный [14; -вен, -вна] intuitive.
Интури́ст *m* [1] (*Sov.*) State bureau of foreign tourism.
инфе́кция *f* [7] infection.
инфля́ция *f* [7] inflation.
информ|а́ция *f* [7] information; **&бюро́** *n* [*indecl.*] (Communist) Information Bureau, Cominform; **~и́ровать** [7] (*im*)*pf.* & ⟨про-⟩ inform.
и. о. = исполня́ющий обя́занности.
ипподро́м *m* [1] race track (course).
и пр(оч). *abbr.*: и про́чее, *s.* про́чий.
Ира́|к *m* [1] Iraq; **~н** *m* [1] Iran.
ири́дий *m* [3] iridium.
и́рис *m* [1] iris (⚘, *anat.*).
ирла́нд|ец *m* [1; -дца] Irishman; **~ка** *f* [5; *g/pl.*: -док] Irishwoman; **~ский** [16] Irish (*a.* Sea: **&ское** мо́ре); **&ия** *f* [7] Ireland; Eire.
ирон|изи́ровать [7] mock, sneer (at над Т); **~и́ческий** [16] ironic(al), derisive; **~ия** *f* [7] irony.
иск ⚖ *m* [1] suit, action.
иска|жа́ть [1], ⟨**~зи́ть**⟩ [15 *e.*; -ажу́, -ази́шь; -ажённый] distort, disfigure; **~же́ние** *n* [12] distortion.
иска́ть [3], ⟨по-⟩ (В) look for; (*mst.* Р) seek; ⚖ sue (a p. for с Р/В).
исключ|а́ть [1], ⟨**~и́ть**⟩ [16 *e.*; -чу́, -чи́шь; -чённый] exclude, leave out; expel; **~а́я** (Р) except(ing); **~ено́** impossible; **~е́ние** *n* [12] exclusion; expulsion; exception (with the за Т; as an в ви́де Р); **~и́тельный** [14; -лен, -льна] exceptional; exclusive; extraordinary; F excellent; *adv. a.* solely, only; **~и́ть** *s.* **~а́ть**.
иско́мый [14] sought, looked for;
иск|они́ † = и́здавна; **~о́нный** [14] (ab)original, native; arch...
ископа́ем|ый [14] (*a. fig.* & *su. n*) fossil; mined; *pl. su.* minerals; поле́зные **~ые** treasures of the soil.
искорен|я́ть [28], ⟨**~и́ть**⟩ [13] extirpate.
и́скоса askance, asquint.
и́скра *f* [5] spark(le); spangle.
и́скренн|ий [15; -ренен, -ренна, -е & -о, -и & -ы] sincere, frank, candid; **~о** пре́данный Вам Sincerely (*or* Respectfully) yours; **~ость** *f* [8] sincerity, frankness.
искрив|ля́ть [28], ⟨**~и́ть**⟩ [14 *e.*; -влю́, -ви́шь; -влённый] (-ся become) bend (-t), crook(ed); distort(ed), disfigure(d).
искр|и́стый [14 *sh.*] sparkling; **~и́ться** [13] sparkle, scintillate.
искуп|а́ть [1], ⟨**~и́ть**⟩ [14] (В) atone for, expiate; **~ле́ние** *n* [12] atonement, expiation.
иску́с *m* [1] trial (*fig.*); **~и́тель** *m* [4] tempter; **~и́ть** *s.* искупа́ть
иску́с|ный [14; -сен, -сна] skil(l)ful, skilled; **~ственный** [14 *sh.*] artificial; false (*tooth, etc.*), imitation (*pearls, etc.*); **~ство** *n* [9] art; skill.
иску|ша́ть [1], † ⟨**~си́ть**⟩ [15 *e.*; -ушу́, -уси́шь] tempt; **~ше́ние** *n* [12] temptation; **~шённый** [14] tried; versed, (*a.* **~ённый** о́пытом) experienced.
исла́м *m* [1] Islam.
Исла́ндия *f* [7] Iceland.
испа́н|ец *m* [1; -нца], **~ка** *f* [5; *g/pl.*: -нок] Spaniard; **&ия** *f* [7] Spain; **~ский** [16] Spanish.
испар|е́ние *n* [12] evaporation; *pl. a.* vapo(u)r(s); **~я́ть** [28], ⟨**~и́ть**⟩ [13] evaporate (*v/i.* -ся, *a. fig.*).
испе|пеля́ть [28], ⟨**~пели́ть**⟩ [13] burn to ashes; **~стря́ть** F [28],

⟨~стри́ть⟩ [13], ~щря́ть [28], ⟨~щри́ть⟩ [13] mottle, speckle, variegate; stud; interlard.

испи́с|ывать [1], ⟨~а́ть⟩ [3] write (*sheet, etc.*), write upon (*on both sides, etc.*), fill (up, *book*); ~сан full of notes, *etc.*; F use up; **-ся** F write o.s. out; be(come) used up (by writing).

испито́й F [14] emaciated.

испове́д|ание *n* [12] confession; creed; **~ать** [1] † = ~овать; **~ник** *m* [1] confessor; **~овать** [7] (*im*)*pf.* confess (*v/i.* **-ся**, to a p. пе́ред T; s.th. в П); profess (*religion*); F interrogate; **~ь** ('is-) *f* [8] confession (*eccl.* [*prp.*: на В/П to/at] & *fig.*).

и́спод|воль F gradually; **~ло́бья** frowningly; **~тишка́** F on the quiet.

испоко́н: ~ ве́ку (веко́в) = и́здавна.

исполи́н *m* [1] giant; **~ский** [16] gigantic.

исполко́м *m* [1] (исполни́тельный комите́т) executive committee.

исполн|е́ние *n* [12] execution; fulfil(l)ment, performance; приводи́ть в ~е́ние = ~я́ть; **~и́мый** [14 *sh.*] realizable; practicable; **~и́тель** *m* [4] executor; *thea.*, ♪ performer; ⚖ (court) bailiff; **~и́тельный** [14] executive; [-лен, -льна] industrious; **~я́ть** [28], ⟨~́ить⟩ [13] carry out, execute; fulfil(l), do (*duty*); hold, fill (*office, etc.*); keep (*promise*); *thea.*, ♪ perform; **-ся** come true; (*age*) be: ему́ ~́илось пять лет he is five; (*period*) pass (since [с тех пор] как).

испо́льзова|ние *n* [12] use, utilization; **~ть** [7] (*im*)*pf.* use, utilize.

испо́р|тить *s.* по́ртить; **~ченный** [14 *sh.*] spoilt, broken; depraved.

исправ|до́м F *m* [1] (~и́тельный дом) reformatory, reform school; **~и́тельный** [14] correctional; *s.* ~дом; **~ле́ние** *n* [12] correction; improvement; reform; **~ля́ть** [28], ⟨~́ить⟩ [14] correct; improve; reform; repair; *impf.* hold (*office*); **-ся** reform.

испра́вн|ость *f* [8] intactness; accuracy; в ~ости = **~ый** [14; -вен, -вна] intact, in good order; accurate, correct; diligent, industrious.

испражн|е́ние *n* [12] ⚕ evacuation; *pl.* f(a)eces; **~я́ться** [28], ⟨~и́ться⟩ [13] ⚕ evacuate.

испу́г *m* [1] fright; **~а́ть** *s.* пуга́ть.

испус|ка́ть [1], ⟨~ти́ть⟩ [15] utter; emit; exhale; give up (*ghost*).

испыт|а́ние *n* [12] test, (*a. fig.*) trial; examination (at на П); **~́анный** [14] tried; **~а́тельный** [14] test...; **~у́ющий** [17] searching; **~́ывать**, ⟨~а́ть⟩ [1] try (*a. fig.*), test; experience, undergo, feel.

иссле́дова|ние *n* [12] investigation, research; exploration; examination; ⚗ analysis; treatise, paper, essay (on по Д); **~тель** *m* [4] research worker, researcher; explorer; **~тельский** [16] research... (*a.* нау́чно-~тельский); **~ть** [7] (*im*)*pf.* investigate; explore; examine (*a.* ⚕); ⚗ analyze; ⚓ sound.

иссо́хнуть *s.* иссыха́ть.

и́сстари = и́здавна, *cf.*

исступл|е́ние *n* [12] ecstasy, frenzy; rage; **~ённый** [14] frantic.

исс|уша́ть [1], ⟨~уши́ть⟩ [16] *v/t.*, **~ыха́ть** [1], ⟨~о́хнуть⟩ [21] *v/i.* & **~яка́ть** [1], ⟨~я́кнуть⟩ [21] *v/i.* dry (*v/i.* up); *fig. a.* exhaust, wear out (*v/i.* o.s. *or* become ...).

ист|ека́ть [1], ⟨~е́чь⟩ [26] flow out; *impf.* spring; elapse (*time*), expire, become due (*date*); dissolve (in *tears* T); ~ека́ть кро́вью bleed to death; **~е́кший** [17] past, last.

исте́р|ика *f* [5] hysterics *pl.*; **~и́ческий** [16], **~и́чный** [14; -чен, -чна] hysterical; **~и́я** *f* [7] hysteria.

исте́ц *m* [1; -тца́] plaintiff.

истече́ни|е *n* [12] expiration (*date*), lapse (*time*); ⚕ discharge; ~е кро́ви bleeding; по ~и (P) at the end of.

исте́чь *s.* истека́ть.

и́стин|а *f* [5] truth; **~ный** [14; -инен, -инна] true, genuine; right (*way, fig.*); plain (*truth*).

истл|ева́ть [1], ⟨~е́ть⟩ [8] mo(u)lder, rot, decay; die away.

и́стовый [14] true; grave; zealous.

исто́к *m* [1] source (*a. fig.*).

истолк|ова́ние *n* [12] interpretation; **~о́вывать** [1], ⟨~ова́ть⟩ [7] interpret, expound, (*a.* себе́) explain (to o.s.).

исто́м|а *f* [5] languor; **~ля́ть** [28], ⟨~и́ть⟩ [14 *e.*; -млю́, -ми́шь; -млённый] (**-ся** be[come]) tire(d), fatigue(d), weary (-ied).

истоп|ни́к *m* [1 *e.*] stoker; **~та́ть** F [3] *pf.* trample; wear out.

исторг|а́ть *m* [1], ⟨~́нуть⟩ [21] wrest; draw; deliver, save.

исто́р|ик *m* [1] historian; **~и́ческий** [16] historical; **~ия** *f* [7] history; story; F affair, thing; ве́чная ~ия! always the same!

источ|а́ть [1], ⟨~и́ть⟩ [16 *e.*; -чу́, -чи́шь] draw; shed; exhale, emit; **~́ник** *m* [1] spring; (*a. fig.*) source.

истощ|а́ть [1], ⟨~и́ть⟩ [16 *e.*; -щу́, -щи́шь; -щённый] (**-ся** be[come]) exhaust(ed), use(d) up.

истра́чивать [1] *s.* тра́тить.

истреб|и́тель *m* [4] destroyer (*a.* ⚓); ✈ pursuit plane, fighter; **~и́тельный** [14] destructive; fighter...; **~и́ть** *s.* ~ля́ть; **~ле́ние** *n* [12] destruction; extermination; **~ля́ть** [28], ⟨~и́ть⟩ [14 *e.*; -блю́, -би́шь; -блённый] destroy, annihilate; exterminate.

истука́н *m* [1] idol; dolt; statue.

и́стый [14] true, genuine; zealous.

истяза́|ние *n* [12], **~ть** [1] torment.
исхо́д *m* [1] end, outcome, result; way out, outlet, vent; † exit; *Bibl.* Exodus; быть на ~е come to an end; run short of; **~и́ть** [15] (из Р) come, emanate; originate, proceed; start from; † depart; *pf.* F go all over; *s. a.* истека́ть; **~ный** [14] initial, of departure.
исхуда́лый [14] emaciated, thin.
исцара́пать [1] *pf.* scratch (all over).
исцел|е́ние *n* [12] healing; recovery; **~я́ть** [28], ⟨~и́ть⟩ [13] heal, cure; **-ся** recover.
исчез|а́ть [1], ⟨∠нуть⟩ [21] disappear, vanish; **~нове́ние** *n* [12] disappearance; ∠нуть *s.* ~а́ть.
исче́рп|ывать, ⟨~ать⟩ [1] exhaust, use up; settle (*dispute, etc.*); **~ывающий** exhaustive.
исчисл|е́ние *n* [12] calculation; ⅍ calculus; **~я́ть** [28], ⟨∠ить⟩ [13] calculate.
ита́к thus, so; well, then, now.
Ита́лия *f* [7] Italy.
италья́н|ец *m* [1; -нца], **~ка** *f* [5; *g/pl.*: -нок]; **~ский** [16] Italian; ~ская забасто́вка *f* sit-down strike.
и т. д. *abbr.*: и так да́лее.
ито́г *m* [1] sum, total; result; в ~е in the end; подвести́ ~ sum up; **~о́** (-'vɔ) altogether; in all, total.
и т. п. *abbr.*: и тому́ подо́бное.
итти́ *s.* идти́.
их (*a.* jix) their (*a.*, Р, ∠ний [15]); *cf.* они́.
ишь Р (just) look, listen; there; oh; now.
ище́йка *f* [5; *g/pl.*: -е́ек] bloodhound, sleuthhound.
ию́|ль *m* [4] July; **~нь** *m* [4] June.

Й

йод *m* [1] iodine.
йо́т|а *f* [5]: **ни на ~у not a jot.**

К

к, ко (Д) to, toward(s); *time a.* by; for.
к. *abbr.*: копе́йка, -ки, -е́ек.
-ка F (*after vb.*) just; will you.
каба́к *m* [1 *e.*] tavern, pub; mess.
кабала́ *f* [5] serfdom, bondage.
каба́н *m* [1 *e.*] (*a.* wild) boar.
ка́бель *m* [4] cable.
каби́н|а *f* [5] cabin, booth; ✈ cockpit; **~е́т** *m* [1] study; office; ⚕ (consulting) room; *pol.* cabinet.
каблу́к *m* [1 *e.*] heel; быть под ~о́м *fig.* be henpecked.
каб|ота́ж *m* [1] coasting; **~ы́** Р if.
кавале́р *m* [1] cavalier; knight; **~и́йский** [16] cavalry...; **~и́ст** *m* cavalryman; **~ия** *f* [7] cavalry, horse.
ка́верз|а F *f* [5] intrigue; trick; **~ный** [14] trick(s)y.
Кавка́з *m* [1] Caucasus (*prp.*: на В/П to/in); 2**ец** *m* [1; -зца] Caucasian; 2**ский** [16] Caucasian.
кавы́чк|и *f/pl.* [5; *gen.*: -чек] quotation marks; в ~ах *iron.* so-called.
кади́|ло *n* [9] cencer; **~ть** [15 *e.*; кажу́, кади́шь] cence.
ка́дка *f* [5; *g/pl.*: -док] tub, vat.
ка́дмий *m* [3] cadmium.
кадр *m* [1] (*mst. pl.*) cadre, key group, van(guard); skilled workers; (*film*) shot; close-up; **∠овый** [14] ⚔ regular, active; commanding; skilled.
кады́к F *m* [1 *e.*] Adam's apple.
каждодне́вный [14] dayly.
ка́ждый [14] every, each; either (*of two*); *su.* everybody, everyone.
ка́ж|ется, **~ущийся** *s.* каза́ться.
каза́к *m* [1 *e.*; *pl. a.* 1] Cossack.
каза́рма ⚔ *f* [5] barracks *pl.*
каза́|ться [3], ⟨по-⟩ (Т) seem, appear, look; мне ка́жется (~лось), что ... it seems (seemed) to me that; он, ка́жется, прав he seems to be right; *a.* apparently; ка́жущийся seeming; ~лось бы one would think.
каза́х *m* [1], **~ский** [16] Kazak(h); 2ская ССР Kazak Soviet Socialist Republic; 2**ста́н** *m* [1] Kazakstan.
каза́|цкий [16], **~чий** [18] Cossack('s)...
каз|ённый [14] state..., government...; official, public; formal, perfunctory; commonplace; на ~ённый счёт *m* gratis; **~на́** *f* [5] treasury, exchequer; **~наче́й** *m* [3] treasurer; ⚔ paymaster.
казн|и́ть [13] (*im*)*pf.* execute, put to death; *impf. fig.* scourge; **~ь** *f* [8] execution; (*a. fig.*) punishment.
Каи́р *m* [1] Cairo.
каймá *f* [5; *g/pl.*: каём] border.
как how; as; (as) like; what; but; since; F when, if; (+*su.*, *adv.*) very (much), awfully; (+ *pf. vb.*) suddenly; я ви́дел, как он шёл ... I saw him going ...; ~ бу́дто, ~ бы as if, as it were; ~ бы мне (*inf.*) how am I to ...; ~ ни however; ~ же! sure!; ~ (же) так? you don't say!;

~ ..., так и ... both ... and ...; ~ когдá, *etc.* that depends; ~ не (+ *inf.*) of course ...; ~ мóжно (нельзя́) скорéе (лу́чше) as soon as (in the best way) possible.
какáо *n* [*indecl.*] cocoa.
кáк-нибу́дь somehow (or other); anyhow; sometime.
какóв [-вá, -ó] how; what; what sort of; (such) as; ~! just look (at him)!; ~ó? what do you say?; **~óй** [14] which.
какóй [16] what, which; such as; F any; that; ещё ~! and what ... (*su.*)!; какóе там! not at all!; **~-либо, ~-нибудь** any, some; F no more than, (only) about; **~-то** some, a.
кáк-то 1. *adv.* somehow; somewhat; F (*a.* ~ раз) once, one day; **2.** *part.* [such as.]
каламбу́р *m* [1] pun.
каланчá *f* [5; *g/pl.*: -чéй] watchtower; F maypole.
калáч *m* [1 *e.*] small (*padlock-shaped*) white loaf; тёртый ~ *fig.* F cunning fellow.
калéка *m/f* [5] cripple.
календáрь *m* [4 *e.*] calendar.
калёный [14] red-hot; roasted.
калéчить [16], ⟨ис-⟩ cripple, maim.
кáлий *m* [3] potassium.
кали́на *f* [5] snowball tree.
кали́тка *f* [5; *g/pl.*: -ток] gate, wicket.
кали́ть [13] **1.** ⟨на-, рас-⟩ heat, incandesce; roast; **2.** ⟨за-⟩ ⊕ temper.
калóрия *f* [7] calorie.
калóши *s.* галóши.
кáльк|а *f* [5; *g/pl.*: -лек] tracing; tracing paper; *fig.* loan translation; **~и́ровать** [7], ⟨с-⟩ trace.
калькул|и́ровать [7], ⟨с-⟩ ☤ calculate; **~я́ция** *f* [7] calculation.
кальсóны *f/pl.* [5] drawers, underpants.
кáльций *m* [3] calcium.
кáмбала *f* [5] flounder.
камен|éть [8], ⟨о-⟩ turn (in)to stone, petrify; **~и́стый** [14 *sh.*] stony; **~ноугóльный** [14] coal (mining)...; **'~ный** [14] stone...; *fig.* stony; rock (*salt*); **'~ный у́голь** *m* (pit) coal (*hard & soft*); **~олóмня** *f* [6; *g/pl.*: -мен] quarry; **~отёс** *m* [1] stonemason; **'~щик** *m* [1] bricklayer, (*a. hist.*) mason; **'~ь** *m* [4; -мня; *from g/pl. e.* (*a.*, ⚒, -мéнья, -мéньев)] stone; rock; ⚕ *a.* calculus, gravel; *fig.* weight; кáмнем like a stone; **'~ь** преткновéния stumbling block.
кáмер|а *f* [5] (*prison*) cell; ⚕ ward; 🚂 (cloak)room, office; *parl.* (†), ⚖, ⊕, ⚔ chamber; *phot.* camera; bladder (*ball*); tube (*wheel*); **~ный** [14] ♪, ⊕ chamber...
ками́н *m* [1] fireplace.
камкá *f* [5] damask (*fabric*).
камóрка *f* [5; *g/pl.*: -рок] closet, small room.
кампáния *f* [7] ⚔, *pol.* campaign.
камфарá *f* [5] camphor.
Камчáт|ка *f* [5] Kamchatka; **♀-(н)ый** [14] damask...
камы́ш *m* [1 *e.*], **~óвый** [14] reed.
канáва *f* [5] ditch; gutter; drain.
Канáд|а *f* [5] Canada; **♀ец** *m* [1; -дца], **♀ка** *f* [5; *g/pl.*: -док]; **♀ский** [16] Canadian.
канáл *m* [1] canal; (*a. fig.*) channel; pipe; **~изáция** *f* [7] canalization; (*town*) severage.
канарéйка *f* [5; *g/pl.*: -éек] canary.
канáт *m* [1], **~ный** [14] rope, cable.
канвá *f* [5] canvas; *fig.* basis; outline. [les.]
кандалы́ *m/pl.* [1 *e.*] fetters, shack-]
кандидáт *m* [1] candidate; *a. lowest Sov. univ. degree, approx.* = master.
кани́кулы *f/pl.* [5] vacation, *Brt. a.* holidays (during на П, в В).
канитéль F *f* [8] fuss; trouble; humdrum, monotony.
канон|áда *f* [5] cannonade; **~éрка** *f* [5; *g/pl.*: -рок] gunboat.
кану́н *m* [1] eve.
кáнуть [20] *pf.* sink, fall; как в вóду ~ disappear without leaving a trace; ~ в вéчность pass into oblivion.
канцеля́р|ия *f* [7] (secretary's) office, secretariat; **~ский** [16] office...; writing; clerk's; **~щина** *f* [5] red tape.
кáп|ать [1 & 2], *once* ⟨~нуть⟩ [20] drip, drop, trickle; leak; **~елька** *f* [5; *g/pl.*: -лек] droplet; *sg.* F bit, grain.
капитáл *m* [1] ☤ capital; stock; **~и́зм** *m* [1] capitalism; **~и́ст** *m* [1] capitalist; **~исти́ческий** [16] capitalist(ic); **~овложéние** *n* [12] investment; **~ьный** [14] capital; dear, expensive; main; thorough.
капитáн *m* [1] ⚔, ⚓ captain.
капитул|и́ровать [7] (*im*)*pf.* capitulate; **~я́ция** *f* [7] capitulation.
капкáн *m* [1] trap (*a. fig.*).
кáпл|я *f* [6; *g/pl.*: -пель] drop; *sg.* F bit, grain; ~ями by drops; как две ~и воды́ (as like) as two peas.
капóт *m* [1] dressing gown; overcoat; ⊕ hood, *Brt.* bonnet.
каприз *m* [1] whim, caprice; **~ничать** F [1] be capricious; **~ный** [14; -зен, -зна] capricious, whimsical.
кáпсюль ⚔ *m* [4] percussion cap.
капу́ста *f* [5] cabbage; ки́слая ~ sauerkraut.
капу́т P *m* [*indecl.*] ruin, end.
капюшóн *m* [1] hood.
кáра *f* [5] punishment.
караби́н *m* [1] carbine.
карáбкаться [1], ⟨вс-⟩ climb.
каравáй *m* [3] (big) loaf.
каравáн *m* [1] caravan.
карáемый [14 *sh.*] ⚖ punishable.
карáкул|ь *m* [4], **~евый** [14] astrakhan; **~я** *f* [6] scrawl.

каран|да́ш *m* [1 *e.*] pencil; **\~ти́н** *m* [1] quarantine.
карапу́з F *m* [1] tot; hop-o'-my--thumb.
кара́сь *m* [4 *e.*] crucian (*fish*).
кара́|тельный [14] punitive; **\~ть** [1], ⟨по-⟩ punish.
карау́л *m* [1] sentry, guard; взять (сде́лать) на \~! present arms!; стоя́ть на \~е stand sentinel; F \~! help!, murder!; **\~ить** [13], ⟨по-⟩ guard, watch (F *a.* for); **\~ьный** [14] sentry... (*a. su.*); \~ьная *f* (*su.*) = **\~ьня** *f* [6; *g/pl.*: -лен] guardroom.
карбо́ловый [14] carbolic (*acid*).
карбу́нкул *m* [1] carbuncle.
карбюра́тор *m* [1] carburet(t)or.
каре́л *m* [1] Karelian; **2ия** *f* [7] Karelia; **\~ка** *f* [5; *g/pl.*: -лок] Karelian.
каре́та *f* [5] carriage, coach.
ка́рий [15] (dark) brown; bay.
карикату́р|а *f* [5] caricature, cartoon; **\~ный** [14] caricature...; [-рен, -рна] comic(al), funny.
карка́с *m* [1] frame(work), skeleton.
ка́рк|ать [1], *once* ⟨\~нуть⟩ [20] croak (*a.*, F, *fig.*), caw.
ка́рлик *m* [1] dwarf, pygmy; **\~овый** [14] dwarf...; dwarfish.
карма́н *m* [1] pocket; э́то мне не по \~у F I can't afford that; э́то бьёт по \~у that makes a hole in my (*etc.*) purse; держи́ \~ (ши́ре) that's a vain hope; он за сло́вом в \~ не ле́зет he has a ready tongue; **\~ный** [14] pocket...; note(*book*); **\~ный вор** *m* pickpocket; *cf.* фона́рик.
карнава́л *m* [1] carnival.
карни́з *m* [1] cornice.
Карпа́ты *f/pl.* [5] Carpathian Mts.
ка́рт|а *f* [5] map; ⚓ chart; (playing) card; menu; ста́вить (всё) на \~у stake (have all one's eggs in one basket); **\~а́вить** [14] jar (*or* mispronounce) *Russ.* r &/*or* l (*esp. as uvular* r *or* u, v); **\~ёжник** *m* [1] gambler (*at cards*); **\~е́ль** (-'tɛl) *f* [8] cartel; **\~е́чь** *f* [8] case shot.
карти́н|а *f* [5] picture (in на П); movie, image; painting; scene (*a. thea.*); **\~ка** *f* [5; *g/pl.*: -нок] (small) picture, illustration; **\~ный** [14] picture...; picturesque, vivid.
карто́н *m* [1] cardboard, pasteboard; † = **\~ка** *f* [5; *g/pl.*: -нок] (cardboard) box; hatbox.
картоте́ка *f* [5] card index.
карто́фель *m* [4] *coll.* potatoes *pl.*
ка́рточ|ка *f* [5; *g/pl.*: -чек] card; F ticket; photo; menu; **\~ный** [14] card(s)...; \~ная систе́ма *f* rationing system; \~ный до́мик *m* house of cards.
карто́шка P *f* [5; *g/pl.*: -шек] potato(es).
карту́з *m* [1 *e.*] cap; † pack(age).
карусе́ль *f* [8] merry-go-round.
ка́рцер *m* [1] dungeon; lockup.
карье́р *m* [1] full gallop (at T); с ме́ста в \~ on the spot; **\~а** *f* [5] career; fortune; **\~и́ст** *m* [1] careerist.
каса́|тельная ⩘ *f* [14] tangent; **\~тельно** ([† до] P) concerning; **\~ться** [1], ⟨косну́ться⟩ [20] ([до †] P) touch (*a. fig.*); concern; F be about, deal *or* be concerned with; де́ло \~ется *a.* = де́ло идёт о, *s.* идти́; что \~ется ..., то as for (to).
ка́ска *f* [5; *g/pl.*: -сок] helmet.
каспи́йский [16] Caspian.
ка́сса *f* [5] pay desk *or* office; (*a.* биле́тная \~) 🚂 ticket window, *Brt.* booking office; *thea.* box office; bank; fund; cash; cash register; money box *or* chest, safe.
кассац|ио́нный [14] *s.* апелляцио́нный; **\~ия** ⚖ *f* [7] reversal.
кассе́та *f* [5] *phot.* plate holder.
касси́р *m* [1], **\~ша** F *f* [5] cashier.
ка́ста *f* [5] caste (*a. fig.*).
касто́ровый [14] castor (*oil*; *hat*).
кастри́ровать [7] (*im*)*pf.* castrate.
кастрю́ля *f* [6] saucepan; pot.
катало́г *m* [1] catalogue.
ката́нье *n* [10] driving, riding, skating, *etc.* (*cf.* ката́ть[ся]).
катастро́ф|а *f* [5] catastrophe; **\~и́ческий** [16] catastrophic.
ката́ть [1] roll (*a.* ⊕); mangle; ⟨по-⟩ (take for a) drive, ride, row, *etc.*; **-ся** (go for a) drive, ride (*a.* верхо́м, *etc.*), row (на ло́дке); skate (на конька́х); sled(ge) (на саня́х), *etc.*; roll.
катег|ори́ческий [16] categorical; **\~о́рия** *f* [7] category.
ка́тер ⚓ *m* [1; *pl.*: -pа́, *etc. e.*] cutter; торпе́дный \~ torpedo boat.
кати́ть [15], ⟨по-⟩ roll, drive, wheel (*v/i* **-ся**; sweep; move, flow; *cf. a.* ката́ться).
като́д *m* [1] cathode; **\~ный** [14] cathodic.
като́к *m* [1; -тка́] (skating) rink; mangle; ⊕ roll.
като́л|ик *m* [1], **\~и́чка** *f* [5; *g/pl.*: -чек], **\~и́ческий** [16] (Roman) Catholic.
ка́тор|га *f* [5] hard labo(u)r in (*Siberian*) exile; place of such penal servitude; *fig.* drudgery, misery; **\~жа́нин** *m* [1; *pl.*: -а́не, -а́н], **\~жник** *m* [1] (exiled) convict; **\~жный** [14] hard, penal; *s.* \~га; *su.* = \~жник.
кату́шка *f* [5; *g/pl.*: -шек] spool; [⚡ coil.]
Катю́ша [5], **Ка́тя** *f* [6] (*dim. of* Екатери́на) Kitty, Kate.
каучу́к *m* [1] caoutchouc, rubber.
кафе́ (-'fɛ) *n* [*indecl.*] café.
ка́федра *f* [5] platform, pulpit, lecturing desk; chair, cathedra.
ка́фель *m* [4] (Dutch) tile.
кача́|лка *f* [5; *g/pl.*: -лок] rocking chair; **\~ние** *n* [12] rocking; swing(-ing); pumping; **\~ть** [1] 1. ⟨по-⟩, *once* ⟨качну́ть⟩ [20] rock; swing;

shake (*a.* one's head головой), toss; ⚓ roll, pitch; (**-ся** *v/i.*; stagger, lurch); **2.** ⟨на-⟩ pump.
качели *f/pl.* [8] swing.
качеств|енный [14] qualitative; **~о** *n* [9] quality; в ~е (Р) as, in one's capacity as in the capacity of.
кач|ка ⚓ *f* [5] rolling (бортовая *or* боковая ~ка); pitching (килевая ~ка); **~нуть(ся)** *s.* ~ать(ся).
каш|а *f* [5] mush, *Brt.* porridge; gruel; pap; F slush; *fig.* mess, jumble; **~евар** ⚔ *m* [1] cook.
кашл|ель *m* [4; -шля], **~лять** [28], *once* ⟨~лянуть⟩ [20] cough.
кашне (-ˈnɛ) *n* [*indecl.*] neckscarf.
каштан *m* [1], **~овый** [14] chestnut.
каюта ⚓ *f* [5] cabin, stateroom.
каяться [27], ⟨по-⟩ (в П) repent.
кв. *abbr.*: **1.** квадратный; **2.** квартира.
квадрат *m* [1], **~ный** [14] square.
квак|ать [1], *once* ⟨~нуть⟩ [20] croak.
квалифи|кация *f* [7] qualification(s); **~цированный** [14] qualified, competent; skilled, trained.
квартал *m* [1] quarter (= district; 3 months); block, F building (*betw.* 2 *cross streets*); **~ьный** [14] quarter(ly); district... (*a., su., form.*: district inspector).
квартир|а *f* [5] apartment, *Brt.* flat; ~а в две комнаты two-room apt./flat; lodgings *pl.*; ⚔ quarter(s); billet; ~а и стол board and lodging; **~ант** *m* [1], **~антка** *f* [5; *g/pl.*: -ток] lodger, roomer, subtenant; **~ный** [14] housing, house-...; ~ная плата = **квартплата** *f* [5] rent.
квас *m* [1; -а & -у; *pl. e.*] quass (*Russ. drink*); **∠ить** [15], ⟨за-⟩ sour.
квасц|овый [14] aluminous; **~ы** *m/pl.* [1] alum.
квашеный [14] sour, leavened.
кверху up, upward(s).
квит|анция *f* [7] receipt; check, ticket; ∠(ы) F quits, even, square.
квота *f* [5] quota, share.
квт(ч) *abbr.* = kw. (K.W.H.)
кег|ельбан *m* [1] bowling alley; **∠ля** *f* [6; *g/pl.*: -лей] pin (*pl.*: ninepins), *Brt.* skittle(s).
кедр *m* [1] cedar; **сибирский ~** cembra pine.
кекс *m* [1] cake.
Кёльн *m* [1] Cologne.
кельт *m* [1] Celt; **∠ский** [16] Celtic.
келья *f* [6] *eccl.* cell.
кем = Т *of* кто, *cf.*
кенгуру *m* [*indecl.*] kangaroo.
кеп|и *n* [*indecl.*], **~ка** *f* [5; *g/pl.*: -пок] cap.
керам|ика *f* [5] ceramics; **~иковый** [14], **~ический** [16] ceramic.
керосин *m* [1], **~овый** [14] kerosene.
кета *f* [5] Siberian salmon.
кефир *m* [1] kefir.
кибитка *f* [5; *g/pl.*: -ток] tilt cart (*or* sledge).
кив|ать [1], *once* ⟨~нуть⟩ [20] nod; beckon; point (to на В); **∠ер** *m* [1; *pl.*: -ра, *etc. e.*] shako; **~ок** *m* [1; -вка] nod.
кида|ть(ся) [1], *once* ⟨кинуть(ся)⟩ [20] *s.* бросать(ся); меня ~ет в жар и холод I'm hot and cold all over (have a shivering fit).
Киев *m* [1] Kiev; **♀лянин** *m* [1; *pl.*: -яне, -ян], **♀лянка** *f* [5; *g/pl.*: -нок] Kiever; **♀ский** [16] Kiev...
кий *m* [3; кия; *pl.*: кии, киёв] cue.
кило *n* [*indecl.*] = ~грамм; **~ватт**-(**-час**) *m* [1; *g/pl.*: -ватт] kilowatt(-hour); **~грамм** *m* [1] kilogram (-me); **~метр** *m* [1] kilometer (*Brt.* -tre).
киль *m* [4] keel; **~ватер** (-tɛr) *m* [1] wake; **∠ка** *f* [5; *g/pl.*: -лек] sprat.
КИМ *m* [1] *abbr.*: Communist Youth International (*1919—1943*).
кинематогр|аф *m* [1] cinema(tograph), movie theater; **~афия** *f* [7] cinematography.
кинжал *m* [1] dagger.
кино *n* [*indecl.*] movie, motion picture, *Brt.* the pictures, cinema (to/at в В/П); *coll.* screen, film; **~актёр** *s.* ~артист; **~актриса** *s.* ~артистка; **~артист** *m* [1] screen (*or* film) actor; **~артистка** *f* [5; *g/pl.*: -ток] screen (*or* film) actress; **~ателье** (-tɛ-) *n* [*indecl.*] (film) studio; **ʹ~варь** *f* [8] cinnabar; **~журнал** *m* [1] newsreel; **~звезда** F *f* [5; *pl.*: -звёзды] filmstar; **~картина** *f* [5] film; **~лента** *f* [5] reel, film (copy); **~оператор** *m* [1] cameraman; **~плёнка** *f* [5; *g/pl.*: -нок] film (strip); **~режиссёр** *m* [1] film director; **~сеанс** *m* [1] show, performance; **~сценарий** *m* [3] scenario; **~съёмка** *f* [5; *g/pl.*: -мок] shooting (of a film), filming; **~театр** *m* [1] movie theater, cinema; **~хроника** *f* [5] newsreel.
кинуть(ся) *s.* кидать(ся).
киоск *m* [1] kiosk, stand, stall.
киот *m* [1] *eccl.* image case, shrine.
кипа *f* [5] pile, stack; bale, pack.
кипарис *m* [1] cypress.
кипе|ние *n* [12] boiling; точка ~ния boiling point; **~ть** [10 *e.*; -плю, -пишь], ⟨за-, вс-⟩ boil; seethe; surge (up), rage, overflow, teem with; be in full swing (*work, war*).
Кипр *m* [1] Cyprus.
кипучий [17 *sh.*] seething; lively, vigorous, exuberant, vehement; busy.
кипят|ить [15 *e.*; -ячу, -ятишь], ⟨вс-⟩ boil (up; *v/i.* **-ся**); F be(come) excited; **~ок** *m* [1; -тка] boiling *or* boiled (hot) water.
киргиз *m* [1], **~ский** [16] Kirghiz.
Кирилл *m* [1] Cyril; **♀ица** *f* [5] Cyrillic alphabet.

кирка́ *f* [5; *g/pl.*: -ро́к] pick(ax[e]), mattock.
кирпи́ч *m* [1 *e.*], **~ный** [14] brick.
кисе́ль *m* [4 *e.*] (*kind of*) jelly.
кисе́т *m* [1] tobacco pouch.
кисея́ *f* [6] muslin.
кисл|ова́тый [14 *sh.*] sourish; **~оро́д** *m* [1] oxygen; **~ота́** *f* [5; *pl. st.*: -о́ты] acid; **∠ый** [14; -сел, -сла́, -о] sour, (*a.* ⚗) acid...
ки́снуть [21], ⟨с-, про-⟩ turn sour; F *fig.* get rusty.
ки́ст|очка *f* [5; *g/pl.*: -чек] (*paint, shaving*) brush; tassel; *dim. of* **~ь** *f* [8; *from g/pl. e.*] brush; tassel; cluster, bunch; hand.
кит *m* [1 *e.*] whale.
кита́|ец *m* [1; -та́йца], Chinese; **Ωй** *m* [3] China; **~йский** [16] Chinese; Ωйская Наро́дная Респу́блика (КНР) Chinese People's Republic; **~я́нка** *f* [5; *g/pl.*: -нок] Chinese.
ки́тель *m* [4; *pl.* -ля́, *etc. e.*] jacket.
китобо́й *m* [3], **~ный** [14] whaler.
кич|и́ться [16 *e.*; -чу́сь, -чи́шься] put on airs; boast (of T); **~ли́вый** [14 *sh.*] haughty, conceited.
кише́ть [киши́т] teem, swarm (with T; *a.* кишмя́ ~).
киш|е́чник *m* [1] bowels, intestines *pl.*; **~е́чный** [14] intestinal, enteric; digestive (*tract*); **~ка́** *f* [5; *g/pl.*: -шо́к] intestine (small то́нкая, large то́лстая), gut; *pl.* F bowels; hose.
кла́виш *m* [1], **~а** *f* [5] ♪, ⊕ key.
клад *m* [1] treasure (*a. fig.*); **∠бище** *n* [11] cemetery; **∠ка** *f* [5] laying, (*brick-, stone*)work; **~ова́я** *f* [14] pantry, larder; stock- *or* storeroom; **~овщи́к** *m* [1 *e.*] stockman, storekeeper; **~ь** *f* [8] freight, load.
кла́ня|ться [28], ⟨поклони́ться⟩ [13; -оню́сь, -о́нишься] (Д) bow (to); greet; **~йтесь** ему́ от меня́ give him my regards; F cringe (to пе́ред T); present (a p. s. th. Д/T).
кла́пан *m* [1] ⊕ valve; ♪ key, stop.
класс *m* [1] class; *shool*: grade, *Brt.* form; classroom; **∠ик** *m* [1] classic; **~ифици́ровать** [7] (*im*)*pf.* class(ify); **~и́ческий** [16] classic(al); **∠ный** [14] class(*room, etc.*); **∠овый** [14] class (*struggle, etc.*).
класть [кладу́, -дёшь; клал] **1.** ⟨положи́ть⟩ [16] (в, на, *etc.*, В) put, lay (down, on, *etc.*), deposit; apply, spend; take (*as a basis* в В); F fix; rate; make; leave (*mark*); **2.** ⟨сложи́ть⟩ [16] lay (down); erect.
клева́ть [6 *e.*; клюю́, клюёшь], *once* ⟨клю́нуть⟩ [20] peck, pick; bite (*fish*); ~ но́сом F nod.
кле́вер *m* [1] clover, trefoil.
клевет|а́ *f* [5], **~а́ть** [3; -вещу́, -ве́щешь], ⟨о-⟩ *v/t.*, ⟨на-⟩ (на В) slander; **~ни́к** *m* [1 *e.*] slanderer; **~ни́ческий** [16] slanderous.
клевре́т *m* [1] accomplice.
клеён|ка *f* [5], **~чатый** [14] oilcloth.
кле́|ить [13], ⟨с-⟩ glue, paste; **-ся** stick; F work, get on *or* along; **~й** *m* [3; на клею́] glue, paste; ры́бий **~й** isinglass; **~йкий** [16; клеёк, клейка] sticky, adhesive.
клейм|и́ть [14 *e.*; -млю́, -ми́шь], ⟨за-⟩ brand; *fig. a.* stigmatize; **~о́** *n* [9; *pl. st.*] brand; *fig.* stigma, stain; фабри́чное ~о́ trademark.
клён *m* [1] maple.
клепа́ть [1], ⟨за-⟩ rivet; hammer.
клёпка *f* [5; *g/pl.*: -пок] riveting; stave.
кле́т|ка *f* [5; *g/pl.*: -ток] cage; square, check; *biol.* (*a.* ~очка) cell; в ~(оч)ку (~[оч]ками) check(er)ed, *Brt.* chequered; **~ча́тка** *f* [5] cellulose; cellular tissue; **~чатый** [14] checkered (*Brt.* chequered); cellular.
кле|шня́ *f* [6; *g/pl.*: -не́й] claw (*of the crayfish*); **∠щи́** *f/pl.* [5; *gen.*: -ще́й, *etc. e.*] pincers.
клие́нт *m* [1] client.
кли́зма *f* [5] enema.
клик *m* [1] cry, shout; shriek; **∠а** *f* [5] clique; **∠ать** [3], *once* ⟨∠нуть⟩ [20] shriek; P call.
кли́мат *m* [1] climate; **~и́ческий** [16] climatic.
клин *m* [3; *pl.*: кли́нья, -ьев] wedge; gusset; ∠ом pointed (*beard*); свет не ∠ом сошёлся the world is large; there is always a way out.
кли́ника *f* [5] clinic.
клино́к *m* [1; -нка́] blade.
клич *m* [1] call; cry; **∠ка** *f* [5; *g/pl.*: -чек] (*dog's, etc.*) name; nickname.
клише́ *n* [*indecl.*] cliché (*a. fig.*).
клок *m* [1 *e.*; *pl.*: -о́чья, -ьев & клоки́, -ко́в] tuft; shred, rag, tatter, piece, frazzle.
клокота́ть [3] seethe, bubble.
клон|и́ть [13; -оню́, -о́нишь], ⟨на-, с-⟩ bend, bow; *fig.* incline; drive (*or* aim) at (к Д); † cast down; меня́ ∠ит ко сну I am (feel) sleepy; (**-ся** *v/i.*; *a.* decline; approach).
клоп *m* [1 *e.*] bedbug, *Brt.* bug.
кло́ун *m* [1] clown.
клочо́к *m* [1; -чка́] wisp; scrap.
клуб[1] *m* [1; *pl. a. e.*] cloud, puff (*smoke, etc.*); *s. a.* ~о́к; ~[2] [1] club (-house); **∠ень** *m* [4; -бня] tuber, bulb; **~и́ть** [14 *e.*; *3rd p. only*] puff (up), whirl, coil (*v/i.* **-ся**).
клубни́ка *f* [5] strawberry, -ries *pl.*
клубо́к *m* [1; -бка́] clew; tangle.
клу́мба *f* [5] (flower) bed.
клык *m* [1 *e.*] tusk; canine, fang.
клюв *m* [1] beak, bill.
клюка́ *f* [5] crutch(ed stick), staff.
клю́ква *f* [5] cranberry, -ries *pl.*
клю́нуть *s.* клева́ть.
ключ *m* [1 *e.*] key (*a. fig.*, clue; *a.* ⊕ [га́ечный ~] = wrench; англи́йский ~ monkey wrench); ♪ clef; spring, source; ⚠ keystone; **~и́ца** *f* [5] clavicle, collarbone; **∠ница** *f* [5] housekeeper.

клю́шка *f* [5; *g/pl.*: -шек] club.
кля́кса *f* [5] blot.
кля́нчить F [16] beg for.
кляп *m* [1] gag.
кля|сть [-яну́, -нёшь; -ял, -á, -о] = проклинáть, *cf.*; **-ся**, ⟨покля́сться⟩ swear (s. th. в П; by Т); **∠тва** *f* [5] oath; дать ∠тву (*or* ∠твенное обещáние) take an oath, swear; **~твопреступлéние** *n* [12] perjury.
кля́уза *f* [5] intrigue, denunciation; † captious suit; pettifoggery.
кля́ча *f* [5] jade.
кни́г|а *f* [5] book (*a.* ✝); *teleph.* directory; register; **~опечáтание** *n* [12] (book) printing, typography; **~опродáвец** *m* [1; -вца] bookseller; **~охрани́лище** *n* [11] archives, storerooms *pl.*; library.
кни́ж|ка *f* [5; *g/pl.*: -жек] book (-let); notebook; passport; **~ный** [14] book...; bookish; **~óнка** *f* [5; *g/pl.*: -нок] trashy book.
кни́зу down, downward(s).
кнóпка *f* [5; *g/pl.*: -пок] thumbtack, *Brt.* drawing pin; ⚡ (push) button; patent (*or* snap) fastener.
кнут *m* [1 *e.*] whip, knout, scourge.
княгиня *f* [6] princess (*prince's consort*; *daughter*: **~жнá** *f* [5; *g/pl.*: -жóн]); **~зь** *m* [4; *pl.*: -зья́, -зéй] prince; вели́кий ~зь grand duke.
коа|лициóнный [14] coalition ...; **~ли́ция** *f* [7] coalition.
кóбальтовый [14] cobaltic.
кобурá *f* [5] holster; saddlebag.
кобы́ла *f* [5] mare; *sport:* horse.
кóваный [14] wrought (*iron*).
ковáр|ный [14; -рен, -рна] artful, guileful, insidious; **~ство** *n* [9] craft, guile, wile.
ковáть [7 *e.*; кую́, куёшь] **1.** ⟨вы́-⟩ forge; **2.** ⟨под-⟩ shoe (*horse*).
ковёр *m* [1; -врá] carpet, rug.
ковéркать [1], ⟨ис-⟩ distort, deform; mutilate; murder (*fig.*).
кóв|ка *f* [5] forging; shoeing; **~кий** [16; -вок, -вкá, -о] malleable.
коври́жка *f* [5; *g/pl.*: -жек] gingerbread.
ковчéг *m* [1] ark; Нóев ~ Noah's Ark.
ковш *m* [1 *e.*] scoop; bucket; haven.
ковы́ль *m* [4 *e.*] feather grass.
ковыля́ть [28] toddle; stump, limp.
ковыря́ть [28], ⟨по-⟩ pick, poke.
когдá when; F if; ever; sometimes; *cf.* ни; **~-либо, ~-нибудь** (at) some time (or other), one day; *interr.* ever; **~-то** once, one day, sometime.
кó|готь *m* [4; -гтя; *from g/pl. e.*] claw; **~д** *m* [1] code.
кóе|-гдé here & there, in some places; **~-кáк** anyhow, somehow; with (great) difficulty; **~-какóй** [16] some; any; **~-когдá** off & on; **~-ктó** [23] some(body); **~-кудá** here & there, (in)to some place(s), somewhere; **~-чтó** [23] something, some things.
кóж|а *f* [5] skin; leather; из ~и (вóн) лезть F do one's utmost; **~аный** [14] leather...; **~éвенный** [14] leather...; ~éвенный завóд *m* tannery; **~éвник** *m* [1] tanner; **~ица** *f* [5] peel; rind (*a.* **~урá** *f* [5]); cuticle.
коз|á *f* [5; *pl. st.*] (she-)goat; **~ёл** *m* [1; -злá] (he-)goat; **∠ий** [18] goat...; **~лёнок** *m* [2] kid; **∠лы** *f/pl.* [5; *gen.*: -зел] (coach) box; trestle.
кóзни *f/pl.* [8] intrigues, plots.
козу́ля *f* [6] roe (deer).
коз|ырёк *m* [1; -рькá] peak (*cap*); **∠ырь** *m* [4; *from g/pl. e.*] trump; **~ыря́ть** F [28], *once* ⟨~ырну́ть⟩ [20] trump; boast; ⚔ salute.
кóйка *f* [5; *g/pl.*: кóек] cot; bed.
кокéт|ка *f* [5; *g/pl.*: -ток] coquette; **~ливый** [14 *sh.*] coquettish; **~ничать** [1] coquet, flirt; **~ство** *n* [9] coquetry.
коклю́ш *m* [1] whooping cough.
кóкон *m* [1] cocoon.
кок|óс *m* [1] coco; **~óсовый** [14] coco(nut)...; **~с** *m* [1] coke.
кол *m* **1.** [1 *e.*; *pl.*: кóлья, -ьев] stake, pale; **2.** [*pl.* 1 *e.*] P *s.* едини́ца; ни ~á ни дворá neither house nor home.
колбасá *f* [5; *pl. st.*: -áсы] sausage.
колд|овáть [7] conjure; **~овствó** *n* [9] magic, sorcery; **~у́н** *m* [1 *e.*] sorcerer, magician, wizard; **~у́нья** *f* [6] sorceress, enchantress.
колеб|áние *n* [12] oscillation; vibration; *fig.* vacillation, hesitation; (*a.* ✝) fluctuation; **~áть** [2 *st.*: -éблю, *etc.*; -éбли(те)!; -éбля], ⟨по-⟩, *once* ⟨~ну́ть⟩ [20] shake (*a. fig.*); **-ся** shake; (*a.* ✝) fluctuate; waver, vacillate, hesitate; oscillate, vibrate.
колéн|о *n* [*sg.*: 9; *pl.*: 4] knee; стать на ~и kneel; [*pl.*: -нья, -ьев] ⚘ joint, knot; [*pl. a.* 9] bend; ⊕ crank; [*pl.* 9] degree, branch (*pedigree*); P ♪ pas(sage); trick; **~чатый** [14] *biol.* geniculate; ⊕ crank(*shaft*).
колес|и́ть F [15 *e.*; -ешу́, -еси́шь] travel (much); take a roundabout way; **~ни́ца** *f* [5] chariot; **~ó** *n* [9; *pl. st.*: -лёса] wheel; кружи́ться как бéлка в ~é fuss, bustle about; вставля́ть пáлки в колёса (Д) put a spoke in a p.'s wheel; нóги ~óм bowlegged.
колея́ *f* [6; *g/pl.*: -лéй] rut, (*a.* 🚃) track (*both a. fig.*).
коли́бри *m/f* [*indecl.*] hummingbird.
кóлики *f/pl.* [5] colic, gripes.
коли́честв|енный [14] quantitative; *gr.* cardinal (*number*); **~о** *n* [9] quantity; number; amount; по ~у quantitatively.
кóлка *f* [5] splitting, chopping.
кóлк|ий [16; кóлок, колкá, -о]

prickly; biting, pungent; **~ость** *f* [8] sarcasm, gibe.
коллéг|а *m* /*f* [5] colleague; **~ия** *f* [7] board, staff; college.
коллекти́в *m* [1] collective, group, body; **~иза́ция** *f* [7] collectivization; **~ный** [14] collective.
коллéк|тор *m* [1] ⚡ collector; **~ционéр** *m* [1] (*curiosity*) collector; **~ция** *f* [7] collection.
колóд|а *f* [5] block; trough; pack, deck (*cards*); **~ец** [1; -дца] well; shaft, pit; **~ка** *f* [5; *g/pl.*: -док] last; (foot) stock(s); ⊕ (*brake*) shoe; **~ник** *m* [1] convict (*in stocks*).
кóлок|ол *m* [1; *pl.*: -лá, *etc. e.*] bell; **~óльня** *f* [6; *g/pl.*: -лен] bell tower, belfry; **~óльчик** *m* [1] (little) bell; ✿ bellflower.
колони|а́льный [14] colonial; **~за́ция** *f* [7] colonization; **~з(и́р)ова́ть** [7] (*im*)*pf.* colonize; **'~я** [7] colony.
колóн|ка *f* [5; *g/pl.*: -нок] *typ.* column; (*gas*) station; water heater, *Brt.* geyser; *a. dim. of* **~на** *f* [5] column (⌂ *a.* pillar; *typ.* †).
кóлос *m* [1; *pl.*: -лóсья, -ьев], **~и́ться** [15 *e.*; *3rd p. only*] ear; **~ни́к** *m* [1 *e.*] grate.
колоти́ть [15] knock (at, on в В, по Д).
колóть [17] **1.** ‹рас-› split, cleave; break (*sugar*); crack (*nuts*); **2.** ‹на-› chop (*firewood*); кóлотый lump (*sugar*); **3.** ‹у-›, *once* ‹кольну́ть› [20] prick, sting; *fig.* F taunt; **4.** ‹за-› stab; kill, slaughter (*animals*); *impers.* have a stitch; ~ глаза́ (Д) be a thorn in one's side.
колпа́к *m* [1 *e.*] cap; shade; bell glass.
колхóз *m* [1] collective farm, kolkhoz; **~ный** [14] kolkhoz...; **~ник** *m* [1], **~ница** *f* [5] collective farmer.
колча́н *m* [1] quiver.
колчеда́н *m* [1] pyrites.
колыбéль *f* [8] cradle; **~ный** [14]: ~ная (пéсня) *f* lullaby.
колых|а́ть [3 *st.*: -ы́шу, *etc.*, *or* 1], ‹вс-›, *once* ‹~ну́ть› [20] sway, swing; stir; heave; flicker; **-ся** *v/i.*
кóлышек *m* [1; -шка] peg.
кольну́ть *s.* колóть 3. *& impers.*
коль|цевóй [14] ring...; circular; **~цó** *n* [9; *pl. st., gen.*: колéц] ring; circle; **~чу́га** *f* [5] mail.
колю́ч|ий [17 *sh.*] thorny, prickly; barbed (*wire*); *fig. s.* кóлкий; **~ка** *f* [5; *g/pl.*: -чек] thorn, prickle; barb.
Кóля *m* [6] (*dim. of* Никола́й) Nick.
коля́ска *f* [5; *g/pl.*: -сок] carriage, victoria; baby carriage, *Brt.* perambulator.
ком *m* [1; *pl*: кóмья, -ьев] lump, clod; снéжный ~ snowball.
кома́нд|а *f* [5] command; detachment; ⚓ crew; *sport:* team; (*fire*) company (*or* department), *Brt.* brigade; F gang.
команди́р *m* [1] commander; **~ова́ть** [7] (*im*)*pf.*, *a.* ‹от-› send (on a mission); detach; **~óвка** *f* [5; *g/pl.*: -вок] mission; sending.
кома́нд|ный [14] command(ing); team...; **~ование** *n* [12] command; **~овать** [7] ([над] T) command (*a.* = [give] order, ‹с-›); F domineer; **~ующий** [17] (T) commander.
кома́р *m* [1 *e.*] mosquito, gnat.
комба́йн ⚘ *m* [1] combine.
комбин|а́т *m* [1] combine of complementary industrial plants (*Sov.*); **~а́ция** *f* [7] combination; **~и́ровать** [7], ‹с-› combine.
комéдия *f* [7] comedy; F farce.
коменда́|нт *m* [1] commandant; superintendent; **~ту́ра** *f* [5] commandant's office.
комéта *f* [5] comet.
ком|и́зм *m* [1] comicality; **∠ик** *m* [1] comedian, comic (actor).
Коминтéрн *m* [1] (Third) Communist International (*1919—1943*).
комисса́р *m* [1] commissar (*Sov.*); commissioner; **~иа́т** *m* [1] commissariat.
коми|ссиóнный [14] commission (*a.* ✝; *pl. su.* = *sum*); **∠ссия** *f* [7] commission (*a.* ✝), committee; **~тéт** *m* [1] committee
коми́ч|еский [16], **~ный** [14; -чен, -чна] comic(al), funny.
кóмкать [1], ‹ис-, с-› crumple.
коммент|а́рий *m* [3] comment(ary); **~а́тор** *m* [1] commentator; **~и́ровать** [7] (*im*)*pf.* comment (on).
коммер|са́нт *m* [1] (wholesale) merchant; **∠ческий** [16] commercial.
коммýн|а *f* [5] commune; **~а́льный** [14] municipal; **~и́зм** *m* [1] communism; **~ика́ция** *f* [7] communication (*pl.* ⚔); **~и́ст** *m* [1], **~и́стка** *f* [5; *g/pl.*: -ток], **~исти́ческий** [14] communist (*a. cap.*, *cf.* КПСС).
коммута́тор *m* [1] commutator; *teleph.* switchboard; operator(s' room).
кóмнат|а *f* [5] room; **~ный** [14] room...; ✿ indoor.
комó|д *m* [1] bureau, *Brt.* chest of drawers; **~к** *m* [1; -мка́] lump, clod.
компа́н|ия *f* [7] company (*a.* ✝); води́ть ~ию с (T) associate with; **~ьóн** *m* [1] ✝ partner; F companion.
компа́ртия *f* [7] Communist Party.
кóмпас *m* [1] compass.
компенс|а́ция *f* [7] compensation; **~и́ровать** [7] (*im*)*pf.* compensate.
компетéн|тный [14; -тен, -тна] competent; **~ция** *f* [7] competence; line.
кóмплек|с *m* [1], **~сный** [14] complex; **∠т** *m* [1] (complete) set; **∠тный** [14], **~това́ть** [7], ‹у-› complete.
комплимéнт *m* [1] compliment.

компо|зи́тор *m* [1] composer; **~стиро́вать** [7], ⟨про-⟩ punch; **~т** *m* [1] sauce, *Brt.* stewed fruit.
компре́сс *m* [1] compress.
компром|ети́ровать [7], ⟨с-⟩, **~и́сс** *m* [1] compromise (*v/i. a.* идти́ на ~и́сс).
комсомо́л *m* [1] Komsomol, *cf.* ВЛКСМ; **~ец** *m* [1; -льца], **~ка** *f* [5; *g/pl.*: -лок], **~ьский** [16] Young Communist.
комфо́рт *m* [1] comfort, convenience; **~а́бельный** [14; -лен, -льна] comfortable, convenient.
конве́йер *m* [1] (belt) conveyor; assembly line.
конве́нция *f* [7] convention.
конве́рт *m* [1] envelope.
конв|ои́р *m* [1], **~ои́ровать** [7], **~о́й** *m* [3], **~о́йный** [14] convoy.
конгре́сс *m* [1] congress.
конденс|а́тор (-dɛ-) *m* [1] condenser; **~и́ровать** [7] (*im*)*pf.* condense; evaporate (*milk*).
конди́тер *m* [1] confectioner; **~ская** *f* [16] confectioner's shop; **~ские** изде́лия *pl.* confectionery.
Кондра́т|ий *m* [3], ~ P [1] Conrad.
конду́ктор *m* [1; *pl. a.* -á, *etc. e.*] conductor (🚂 *Brt.* guard).
конево́дство *n* [9] horse breeding.
конёк *m* [1; -нька́] skate; F hobby.
кон|е́ц *m* [1; -нца́] end; close; point; ⚓ rope; F distance; part; case; без ~ца́ endless(ly); в ~е́ц (до ~ца́) completely; в ~це́ (P) at the end of; в ~це́ ~цо́в at long last; в оди́н ~е́ц one way; в о́ба ~ца́ there & back; на худо́й ~е́ц at (the) worst; под ~е́ц in the end; тре́тий с ~ца́ last but two.
коне́чно (-ʃnə) of course, certainly.
коне́чности *f/pl.* [8] extremities.
коне́чн|ый [14; -чен, -чна] *philos.*, ⅌ finite; final, terminal; ultimate.
конкре́тный [14; -тен, -тна] concrete.
конкур|е́нт *m* [1] competitor; **~е́нция** ✝ *f* [7] competition; **~и́ровать** [7] compete; **'~с** *m* [1] competition; ✝ bankruptcy.
ко́нн|ица *f* [5] cavalry; **~ый** [14] horse...; (of) cavalry.
конопа́тить [15], ⟨за-⟩ calk.
конопля́ *f* [6] hemp; **~ный** [14] hempen.
коносаме́нт *m* [1] bill of lading.
консерв|ати́вный [14; -вен, -вна] conservative; **~ато́рия** *f* [7] conservatory, *Brt.* school of music, conservatoire; **~и́ровать** [7] (*im*)*pf.*, *a.* ⟨за-⟩ conserve, preserve; can, *Brt.* tin; **~ный** [14]: ~ная фа́брика *f* cannery; **~ы** *m/pl.* [1] canned (*Brt.* tinned) goods; safety goggles.
ко́нский [16] horse(*hair, etc.*).
конспе́кт *m* [1] summary, abstract; sketch; **~и́вный** [14; -вен, -вна] concise, sketchy; **~и́ровать** [7], ⟨за-⟩ outline, epitomize.
конспир|ати́вный [14; -вен, -вна] secret; **~а́ция** *f* [7] conspiracy.
конст|ати́ровать [7] (*im*)*pf.* state; find; **~иту́ция** *f* [7] constitution.
констр|уи́ровать [7] (*im*)*pf.*, *a.* ⟨с-⟩ design; **~у́ктор** *m* [1] designer; **~у́кция** *f* [7] design; construction.
ко́нсул *m* [1] consul; **~ьский** [16] consular; **~ьство** *n* [9] consulate; **~ьта́ция** *f* [7] consultation; advice; advisory board; **~ьти́ровать** [7], ⟨про-⟩ advise; **-ся** consult (with с Т).
конта́кт *m* [1] contact.
континге́нт *m* [1] contingent, quota.
контине́нт *m* [1] continent.
конто́р|а *f* [5] office; **~ский** [16] office...; ~ский слу́жащий *m*, **~щик** *m* [1] clerk.
контраба́нд|а *f* [5] contraband; занима́ться ~ой smuggle; **~и́ст** *m* [1] smuggler.
контр|аге́нт *m* [1] contractor; **~-адмира́л** *m* [1] rear admiral.
контра́кт *m* [1] contract.
контра́ст *m* [1], **~и́ровать** [7] contrast.
контрата́ка *f* [5] counterattack.
контрибу́ция ⚔ *f* [7] contribution.
контрол|ёр *m* [1] (ticket) inspector (🚂 *a.* ticket collector); **~и́ровать** [7], ⟨про-⟩ control, check; **~ь** *m* [4] control, checkup; **~ьный** [14] control..., check...; **~ьная** рабо́та *f* test (paper).
контр|разве́дка *f* [5] counterespionage, secret service; **~револю́ция** *f* [7] counterrevolution.
конту́з|ить [15] *pf.* bruise, contuse; **~ия** *f* [7] contusion, bruise.
ко́нтур *m* [1] contour, outline.
конура́ *f* [5] kennel.
ко́нус *m* [1] cone; **~ообра́зный** [14; -зен, -зна] conic(al).
конфере́нция *f* [7] conference (at на П).
конфе́та *f* [5] candy, *Brt.* sweet(s).
конфи|денциа́льный [14; -лен, -льна] confidential; **~скова́ть** [7] (*im*)*pf.* confiscate.
конфли́кт *m* [1] conflict.
конфу́з|ить [15], ⟨с-⟩ (**-ся** be [-come]) embarrass(ed), confuse(d); **~ливый** F [14 *sh.*] bashful, shy.
конц|ентрацио́нный [14] *s.* ~ла́герь; **~ентри́ровать** [7], ⟨с-⟩ concentrate (**-ся** *v/i.*); **~е́рт** *m* [1] concert (at на П); ♪ concerto; **~ла́герь** *m* [4] concentration camp.
конч|а́ть [1], ⟨~ить⟩ [16] finish, end (**-ся** *v/i.*); graduate from; P stop; ~ено! F enough!; **~чик** *m* [1] tip; end; **~и́на** *f* [5] decease.
конь *m* [4 *e.*; *nom/pl. st.*] horse; *poet.* steed; *chess*: knight; **~ки́** *m/pl.* [1] (ро́ликовые roller) skates; **~кобе́-**

жец *m* [1; -жца] skater; **~кобе́жный** [14] skating.
конья́к *m* [1 *e.*; *part. g.*: -у́] cognac.
ко́н|юх *m* [1] groom, (h)ostler; **~ю́шня** *f* [6; *g/pl.*: -шен] stable.
коопер|ати́в *m* [1] coöperative (store); **~а́ция** *f* [7] coöperation.
координи́ровать [7] (*im*)*pf.* coördinate.
копа́ть [1], ⟨вы-⟩ dig (up); **-ся** dig, root; rummage (about); dawdle.
копе́йка *f* [5; *g/pl.*: -еек] kopeck.
ко́пи *f/pl.* [8] mine, pit.
копи́лка *f* [5; *g/pl.*: -лок] money box.
копир|ова́льный [14]: ~ова́льная бума́га *f* carbon paper; **∠овать** [7], ⟨с-⟩ copy; **~о́вщик** *m* [1] copyist.
копи́ть [14], ⟨на-⟩ save; store up.
ко́п|ия *f* [7] copy (*vb.* снять ~ию с Р); **~на́** *f* [5; *pl.*: ко́пны, -пён, -пна́м] stack.
ко́поть *f* [8] soot, lampblack.
копоши́ться [16 *e.*; -шу́сь, -ши́шься], ⟨за-⟩ swarm; F stir; mess around.
копти́ть [15 *e.*; -пчу́, -пти́шь; -пчённый], ⟨за-⟩ smoke; soot.
копы́то *n* [9] hoof.
копьё *n* [10; *pl. st.*] spear.
кора́ *f* [5] bark; crust.
кораб|лекруше́ние *n* [12] shipwreck; **~лестрое́ние** *n* [12] shipbuilding; **∠ль** *m* [4 *e.*] ship; nave (*church*).
кора́лл *m* [1] coral; **~овый** [14] coral..., coralline.
Кордилье́ры *f/pl.* [5] Cordilleras.
коре́|ец *m* [1; -ейца], **~йский** [16] Korean.
корен|а́стый [14 *sh.*] thickset, stocky; **~и́ться** [13] root; **~но́й** [14] native, aboriginal; fundamental, radical; molar (*tooth*); **'~ь** *m* [4; -рня; *from g/pl. e.*] root; в ко́рне totally; пусти́ть ко́рни take root; вы́рвать с ко́рнем pull up by the roots; **∠нья** *n/pl.* [*gen.*: -ьев] roots.
корешо́к *m* [1; -шка́] rootlet; stalk (*mushroom*); back (*book*); stub, *Brt.* counterfoil.
Коре́|я *f* [6] Korea; **♀я́нка** *f* [5; *g/pl.*: -нок] Korean.
корзи́н(к)а *f* [5 (*g/pl.*: -нок)] basket.
коридо́р *m* [1] corridor, passage.
кори́нка *f* [5; *g/pl.*: -нок] currant.
корифе́й *m* [3] *fig.* luminary, coryphеus, leader.
кори́ца *f* [5] cinnamon.
кори́чневый [14] brown.
ко́рка *f* [5; *g/pl.*: -рок] crust; rind, peel.
корм *m* [1; *pl.*: -ма́, *etc. e.*] fodder; seed; **~а́** *f* [5] stern.
корм|и́лец *m* [1; -льца] breadwinner; **~и́лица** *f* [5] wet nurse; **~и́ть** [14], ⟨на-, по-⟩ feed; ~и́ть гру́дью nurse; F board; ⟨про-⟩ *fig.* maintain, support; **-ся** live on (T); **~ле́ние** *n* [12] feeding; nursing; **~ово́й** [14] feed(ing), fodder...; ⚓ stern...
корнепло́ды *m/pl.* [1] edible roots.
ко́роб *m* [1; *pl.*: -ба́, *etc. e.*] basket; **~е́йник** *m* [1] hawker; **∠ить** [14], ⟨по-⟩ warp; *fig.* offend, sicken: **∠ка** *f* [5; *g/pl.*: -бок] box, case.
коро́в|а *f* [5] cow; до́йная ~а milch cow; **~ий** [18] cow...; **~ка** *f* [5; *g/pl.*: -вок]: бо́жья ~ка ladybird; **~ник** *m* [1] cowshed.
короле́в|а *f* [5] queen; **~ский** [16] royal, regal; **~ство** *n* [9] kingdom.
корол|ёк *m* [1; -лька́] wren: **∠ь** *m* [4 *e.*] king.
коромы́сло *n* [9; *g/pl.*: -сел] yoke; (*a. scale*) beam; dragonfly.
коро́н|а *f* [5] crown; **~а́ция** coronation; **~ка** *f* [5; *g/pl.*: -нок] (*tooth*) crown; **~ова́ние** *n* [12] coronation; **~ова́ть** [7] (*im*)*pf.* crown.
коро́ста *f* [5] scab, scabies.
корот|а́ть F [1], ⟨с-⟩ while away, beguile; **∠кий** [16; ко́роток, -тка́, ко́ротко́, ко́ротки́; *comp.*; коро́че] short, brief; *fig.* intimate, в ∠ких слова́х in a few words; коро́че (говоря́) in a word, in short (brief); **'~ко** и я́сно (quite) plainly; до́лго ли, ∠ко ли sooner or later.
ко́рпус *m* [1] body; [*pl.*: -са́, *etc. e.*] frame, case; building; (*a.* ⚔) corps.
коррект|и́в *m* [1] correction; **~и́ровать** [7], ⟨про-⟩ correct; *typ.* proofread; **∠ный** [14; -тен, -тна] correct, proper; **∠ор** *m* [1] proofreader; **~у́ра** *f* [5] proof(reading); держа́ть ~у́ру *s.* ~и́ровать (*typ.*).
корреспонд|е́нт *m* [1] correspondent; **~е́нция** *f* [7] correspondence.
корсе́т *m* [1] corset, *Brt. a.* stays *pl.*
ко́ртик *m* [1] cutlass, hanger.
ко́рточк|и *f/pl.* [5; *gen.*: -чек]: сесть (сиде́ть) на ~и (~ах) squat.
корчева́|ние *n* [12] rooting out; **~ть** [7], ⟨вы́-, рас-⟩ root out.
ко́рчить [16], ⟨с-⟩ *impers.* (& **-ся**) writhe (with pain от бо́ли); convulse; (*no pf.*) F make (*faces*); (*a.* ~ из себя́) play, pose, put on airs, set up for.
ко́ршун *m* [1] vulture.
коры́ст|ный [14; -тен, -тна] selfish, self-interested; *a.* = **~олюби́вый** [14 *sh.*] greedy (of gain), mercenary; **~олю́бие** *n* [12] self-interest, greed; **~ь** *f* [8] gain, profit; use; greed.
коры́то *n* [9] trough.
корь *f* [8] measles.
коря́вый [14 *sh.*] knotty, gnarled; rugged, rough; crooked; clumsy.
коса́ *f* [5; *ac/sg.*: ко́су; *pl. st.*] **1.** plait, braid; **2.** [*ac/sg. a.* косу́] scythe; spit (of land); **~рь** *m* [4 *e.*] mower.
ко́свенный [14] oblique, indirect (*a. gr.*); ⚖ circumstantial (*evidence*).
коси́|лка *f* [5; *g/pl.*: -лок] mowing machine; **~ть**, ⟨с-⟩ **1.** [15; кошу́,

ко́сишь] mow; **2.** *a.* ⟨по-⟩ [15 *e.*; -кошу́, коси́шь] squint; twist (*mouth*), be(come) (a)wry; **-ся**, ⟨по-⟩ *v/i.*; *a.* look askance (at на В); **~чка** *f* [5; *g/pl.*: -чек] *dim.* of коса́ 1.
косма́тый [14 *sh.*] shaggy.
косм|е́тика *f* [5] cosmetics *pl.*; **~ети́ческий** [16] cosmetic; **~и́ческий** [16] cosmic; **~она́вт** *m* [1] astronaut.
косн|е́ть [8], ⟨за-⟩ persist, sink, fossilize (*fig.*); **∠ость** *f* [8] sluggishness, indolence; stagnation; **~у́ться** *s.* каса́ться; **∠ый** [14; -сен, -сна] sluggish, dull; stagnant, fossil.
косо|гла́зый [14 *sh.*] squint-eyed; **~го́р** *m* [1] slope; **∠й** [14; кос, -а́, -о] slanting, oblique; squint -(-eyed); F wry; **~ла́пый** [14 *sh.*] bandy-legged; F *s.* неуклю́жий.
костене́ть [8], ⟨о-⟩ ossify; stiffen, grow numb; be(come) transfixed.
костёр *m* [1; -тра́] (camp)fire, bonfire; pile, stake; meeting.
кост|и́стый [14 *sh.*] bony; **~ля́вый** [14 *sh.*] scrawny, raw-boned; **∠очка** *f* [5; *g/pl.*: -чек] bone; ♀ stone; stay.
косты́ль *m* [4 *e.*] crutch; ⊕ spike.
кост|ь *f* [8; в -ти́; *from g/pl. e.*] bone; die; F бе́лая **~ь** blue blood; игра́ть в **∠и** (play at) dice.
костю́м *m* [1] suit; costume; **~иро́ванный** [14]: **~иро́ванный** бал *m* fancy(-dress) ball.
костя́|к *m* [1 *e.*] skeleton; framework; **~но́й** [14] bone...
косу́ля *f* [6] roe (deer).
косы́нка *f* [5; *g/pl.*: -нок] kerchief.
косьба́ *f* [5] mowing.
кося́к *m* [1 *e.*] lintel; slant; felloe; herd; flock; shoal.
кот *m* [1 *e.*] tomcat; *s. a.* ко́тик; купи́ть **~а́** в мешке́ buy a pig in a poke; **~** напла́кал F very little.
кот|ёл *m* [1; -тла́] boiler, caldron; kitchen; **~ело́к** *m* [1; -лка́] kettle, pot; ⚔ mess kit; derby, *Brt.* bowler.
котёнок *m* [2] kitten.
ко́тик *m* [1] *dim. of* кот; fur seal; seal(skin; *adj.*: **~овый** [14]).
котле́та *f* [5] rissole (*without paste*); cutlet, chop.
котлови́на *f* [5] hollow, basin.
кото́мка *f* [5; *g/pl.*: -мок] knapsack; bag.
кото́р|ый [14] which; who; that; what; many a; P some; one; **~ый** раз how many times; **~ый** час? what time is it?; в **~ом** часу́? (at) what time?; **~ый** ему́ год? how old is he?
ко́фе *m* [*indecl.*] coffee; **∠йник** *m* [1] coffee pot; **∠йница** *f* [5] coffee mill; coffee box; **∠йный** [14] coffee...; **∠йная** *f* = **∠йня** *f* [6; *g/pl.*: -е́ен] coffee house, café.
ко́фт|а *f* [5] (woman's) jacket; blouse; (вя́заная **~а**) jersey, cardigan; **~очка** *f* [5; *g/pl.*: -чек] blouse.
коча́н *m* [1 *e.*] head (of cabbage).
кочев|а́ть [7] wander, roam; F move; travel; **∠ник** *m* [1] nomad; **~о́й** [14] nomadic.
кочега́р *m* [1] fireman, stoker.
кочене́ть [8], ⟨за-, о-⟩ grow numb, stiffen.
кочерга́ *f* [5; *g/pl.*: -рёг] poker.
ко́чка *f* [5; *g/pl.*: -чек] mound, hillock.
коша́чий [18] cat('s); feline.
кошелёк *m* [1; -лька́] purse.
ко́шка *f* [5; *g/pl.*: -шек] cat.
кошма́р *m* [1] nightmare; **~ный** [14; -рен, -рна] dreadful, horrible; F awful.
кощу́нств|енный [14 *sh.*] blasphemous; **~о** *n* [9] blasphemy; **~овать** [7] blaspheme (*v/t.* над Т).
коэффицие́нт *m* [1] coefficient.
КПСС (Коммунисти́ческая па́ртия Сове́тского Сою́за) Communist Party of the Soviet Union.
кра́деный [14] stolen (goods *n su.*).
краеуго́льный [14] *fig.* corner (*stone*); fundamental.
кра́жа *f* [5] theft; **~** со взло́мом burglary.
край *m* [3; с кра́ю; в -аю́; *pl.*: -ая́, -аёв, *etc. e.*] edge; (b)rim; brink (*a. fig.* =) edge; end; fringe, border, outskirt; region, land, country; **∠ний** [15] outermost, (*a. fig.*) utmost, extreme(ly, utterly, most, very, badly **∠не**); в **∠нем** слу́чае as a last resort; in case of emergency; **∠ность** *f* [8] extreme; extremity; до **∠ности** = **∠не**, *s.*; впада́ть в (доходи́ть до) **∠йности** go *or* run to extremes.
крамо́ла † *f* [5] sedition, revolt.
кран *m* [1] tap; ⊕ crane.
кра́пать [1 *or* 2 *st.*] drop, drip.
крапи́в|а *f* [5] nettle; **~ник** *m* [1] wren; **~ный** [14] nettle (*a.*, ⚕, *rash*).
кра́пинка *f* [5; *g/pl.*: -нок] speckle, spot.
крас|а́ *f* [5] † *s.* **~ота́**; **~а́вец** *m* [1; -вца] handsome man; **~а́вица** *f* [5] beauty, beautiful woman; **~и́вый** [14 *sh.*] beautiful; handsome; *a. iron.* fine.
крас|и́льный [14] dye...; **~и́льня** *f* [6; *g/pl.*: -лен] dye shop; **~и́льщик** *m* [1] dyer; **~и́тель** *m* [4] dye(stuff); **∠ить** [15], ⟨(п)о-, вы́-, рас-⟩ paint, colo(u)r, dye; F ⟨на-⟩ paint, make up; rouge; **∠ка** *f* [5; *g/pl.*: -сок] colo(u)r, paint, dye.
красне́ть [8], ⟨по-⟩ redden, grow *or* turn red; blush; *impf.* be ashamed; (*a.* **-ся**) appear, show red.
красно|арме́ец *m* [1; -ме́йца] Red Army man; **~ба́й** *m* [3] glib talker; **~ва́тый** [14 *sh.*] reddish; **~знамённый** [14] decorated with the Order of the Red Banner; **~ко́жий** [17] redskin(ned); **~речи́вый** [14 *sh.*] eloquent; **~ре́чие** *n* [12] eloquence;

~тá *f* [5] redness; ruddiness; **~флóтец** *m* [1; -тца] Red Navy man; **~щёкий** [16 *sh.*] ruddy.
краснýха *f* [5] German measles.
крáс|ный [14; -сен, -снá, -о] red (*a. fig.*); † *s.* **~ивый**; ♀ coniferous; **~ный зверь** *m* deer; **~ная строкá** *f typ.* paragraph, new line; **~ная ценá** *f* ✝ F outside price; **~ное словцó** *n* F witticism; **проходи́ть ~ной ни́тью** stand out.
красовáться [7] shine, show (off).
красотá *f* [5; *pl. st.*: -сóты] beauty.
крастъ [25 *pt. st.*; крáденный], ⟨у-⟩ steal (**-ся** *v/i., impf.*; *a.* prowl slink).
крáтк|ий [16; -ток, -ткá, -о; *comp.*: крáтче] short, brief, concise; й **~ое** *or* й с **~ой** *the letter* й; *cf. a.* корóткий; **~ovрéменный** [14; -енен, -енна] short; passing; **~осрóчный** [14; -чен, -чна] short; short-dated; short-term; **~ость** *f* [8] brevity.
крáтный [14; -тен, -тна] divisible; *n su.* multiple; ...~ ...fold.
крах *m* [1] failure, crash, ruin.
крахмáл *m* [1], **~ить** [13], ⟨на-⟩ starch; **~ьный** [14] starch(ed).
крáшеный [14] painted; dyed.
креди́т *m* [1] credit; в ~ on credit; **~ный** [14], **~овáть** [7] (*im*)*pf.* credit; **~óр** *m* [1] creditor; **~оспосóбный** [14; -бен, -бна] solvent.
крéйс|ер *m* [1] cruiser; **~ерство** *n* [9] cruise; **~и́ровать** [7] cruise; ply.
крем *m* [1] cream.
кремéнь *m* [4; -мня́] flint.
кремл|ёвский [16], **ℒь** *m* [4 *e.*] Kremlin.
крéмн|ий [3] silicon; **~и́стый** [14 *sh.*] gravelly, stony; siliceous.
крен ⚓, ✈ *m* [1] list, careen.
крéндель *m* [4] cracknel.
крен|и́ть [13], ⟨на-⟩ list (**-ся** *v/i.*).
креп *m* [1] crepe, crape.
креп|и́ть [14 *e.*; -плю́, -пи́шь] fix, secure; reinforce; ⚓ belay; furl; *fig.* strengthen; **-ся** take courage; F persevere; **ℒкий** [16; -пок, -пкá, -о; *comp.*: крéпче] strong; firm, solid, sound; robust; hard; affectionate; **ℒко** *a.* fast; deep(ly); **ℒнуть** [21], ⟨о-⟩ grow strong(er).
крепост|ни́чество *n* [9] serfdom; **~нóй** [14] (of, in) bond(age); *su.* serf; **~нóе прáво** *s.* **~ни́чество**; (of a) fortress; **′~ь** *f* [8; *from g/pl. e.*] fortress; strength; firmness; ⚖ deed.
крéсло *n* [9; *g/pl.*: -сел] armchair; *pl. thea.* † stall.
крест *m* [1 *e.*] cross (*a. fig.*); **~-нá~** crosswise; **~и́ны** *f/pl.* [5] baptism, christening; **~и́ть** [15; -щённый] (*im*)*pf.*, ⟨о-⟩ baptize, christen; godfather, godmother, sponsor; ⟨пере-⟩ cross (o.s. **-ся**); **ℒник** *m* [1] godson; **ℒница** *f* [5] goddaughter; **ℒный** [14] **1.** (of the) cross; **2.** ('krɔs-) **~ный** (отéц) *m* godfather; **~ная** (мать) *f* godmother.
крестья́н|ин *m* [1; *pl.*: -я́не, -я́н] peasant, farmer; **~ка** *f* [5; *g/pl.*: -нок] countrywoman, country girl; farmer's wife; **~ский** [16] farm (-er['s]), peasant...; country...; **~ство** *n* [9] peasantry.
крещéние *n* [12] baptism (⚔ боевóе ~ baptism of fire), christening; ℒ Epiphany.
крив|áя ℞ *f* [14] curve; **~изнá** *f* [5] crookedness, curvature; **~и́ть** [14 *e.*; -влю́, -ви́шь; -влённый], ⟨по-, с-⟩ (**-ся** be[come]) crook(ed); twist(ed); **~и́ть душóй** (сóвестью) palter; **~ля́ние** *n* [12] grimacing, twisting; **~ля́ться** [28] (make) grimace(s); mince; **~óй** [14; крив, -á, -о] crooked (*a. fig.*), wry; curve(d); F one-eyed; **~онóгий** [16 *sh.*] bandy-legged; **~отóлки** *m/pl.* [1] rumo(u)rs, gossip; **~оши́п** ⊕ *m* [1] crank.
кри́зис *m* [1] crisis.
крик *m* [1] cry, shout; bawl, outcry; (*fashion*) cri; **~ли́вый** [14 *sh.*] shrill; clamorous; (*a. dress, etc.*) loud; **ℒнуть** *s.* кричáть; **~ýн** F *m* [1 *e.*], **~ýнья** F *f* [6] bawler, clamo(u)rer; tattler.
кри|минáльный [14] criminal; **~стáлл** *m* [1] crystal; **~стáльный** [14; -лен, -льна] crystalline.
критéрий *m* [3] criterion.
кри́ти|к *m* [1] critic; **~ка** *f* [5] criticism; critique, review; **~ковáть** [7] criticize; **ℒческий** [16], **ℒчный** [14; -чен, -чна] critical.
кричáть [4 *e.*; -чý, -чи́шь], ⟨за-⟩, *once* ⟨кри́кнуть⟩ [20] cry (out), shout (at на В); scream.
кров *m* [1] shelter; home; † roof.
кровá|вый [14 *sh.*] bloody, sanguinary; **~ть** *f* [8] bed; bedstead.
крóвельщик *m* [1] tiler; slater.
кровенóсный [14] blood (*vessel*).
крóвля *f* [6; *g/pl.*: -вель] roof(ing).
крóвный [14] (*adv.* by) blood; full-blooded, pure-, thoroughbred; vital; arch...
крово|жáдный [14; -ден, -дна] bloodthirsty; **~излия́ние** ⚕ *n* [12] extravasation, hemorrhage; **~обращéние** *n* [12] circulation of the blood; **~пи́йца** *m/f* [5] bloodsucker; **~подтёк** *m* [1] bruise; **~проли́тие** *n* [12] bloodshed; **~проли́тный** [14; -тен, -тна] *s.* кровáвый; **~пускáние** *n* [12] bloodletting; **~смешéние** *n* [12] incest; **~течéние** *n* [12] bleeding; *s.* **~излия́ние**; **~точи́ть** [16 *e.*; -чи́т] bleed.
кров|ь *f* [8; в -ви́; *from g/pl. e.*] blood (*a. fig.*); **~янóй** [14] blood...
кро|и́ть [13; крóенный], ⟨вы́-, с-⟩ cut (out); **ℒйка** *f* [5] cutting (out).
крокоди́л *m* [1] crocodile.
крóлик *m* [1] rabbit.
крóме (Р) except, besides (*a.* ~ тогó), apart (*or* aside) from; but.

кромса́ть [1], ⟨ис-⟩ hack, mangle.
кро́на *f* [5] crown.
кропи́ть [14 *e.*; -плю́, -пи́шь; -плённый], ⟨о-⟩ sprinkle.
кропотли́вый [14 *sh.*] laborious, toilsome; painstaking, assiduous.
кроссво́рд *m* [1] crossword puzzle.
крот *m* [1 *e.*] *zo.* mole.
кро́ткий [16; -ток, -тка́, -о; *comp.*: кро́тче] gentle, meek.
кро|ха́ *f* [5; *ac/sg.*: кро́ху; *from dat/pl. e.*] crumb; bit; **́хотный** F [14; -тен, -тна], **́шечный** F [14] tiny; **~ши́ть** [16], ⟨на-, по-, ис-⟩ crumb(le); P crush; **́шка** *f* [5; *g/pl.*: -шек] crumb; bit; F baby, little one.
круг 1. *m* [1; в, на -у́; *pl. e.*] circle (*a. fig.*); sphere, range; orbit; F average; slice; **~лова́тый** [14 *sh.*] roundish; **~лоли́цый** [14 *sh.*] chubby-faced; **́лый** [14; кругл, -а́, -о] round; F perfect, complete; **~ово́й** [14] circular; mutual (*responsibility*); **~оворо́т** *m* [1] circulation; succession; **~озо́р** *m* [1] horizon, scope; **~о́м** round; around, round about; **~о́м!** ⚔ about face (*Brt.* turn)!; F entirely; **~ооборо́т** *m* [1] circulation; **~ообра́зный** [14; -зен, -зна] circular; **~осве́тный** [14] round the world; ⚓ circum…
кру́ж|ево *n* [9; *pl. e.*; *g/pl.*: кру́жев] lace **~и́ть** [16 & 16 *e.*; кружу́, кру́жи́шь], ⟨за-, вс-⟩ turn (round), whirl; circle; rotate, revolve, spin; stray about; (**-ся** *v/i.*); голова́ **~ится** (у P) feel giddy, **~ка** *f* [5; *g/pl.*: -жек] mug; box.
кру́жный F [14] roundabout.
кружо́к *m* [1; -жка́] (small) circle, disk; *fig.* circle; slice.
круп *m* [1] (⚕ & *horse*) croup.
круп|а́ *f* [5] grits, groats *pl.*; sleet; **~и́нка** *f* [5; *g/pl.*: -нок] grain (*a. fig.* = **~и́ца** *f* [5]).
кру́пный [14; -пен, -пна́, -о] coarse(-grained), gross; big, large(-scale), great; outstanding; † wholesale; (*film*) close(*up*); F ~ разгово́р *m* high words.
крутизна́ *f* [5] steep(ness).
крути́ть [15], ⟨за-, с-⟩ twist; twirl; roll (up); turn; whirl; P *impf.* trick.
круто́|й [14; крут, -а́, -о; *comp.*: кру́че] steep, sharp, abrupt, sudden; hard (*a.*-boiled); harsh; **'~сть** *f* [8] steepness; harshness.
кру́ча *f* [5] *s.* крутизна́.
кручи́на P *f* [5] grief, affliction.
круше́ние *n* [12] 🚂 accident; ⚓ wreck; ruin, breakdown.
крыжо́вник *m* [1] gooseberry, -ries *pl.*
крыл|а́тый [14 *sh.*] winged (*a. fig.*); **~о́** *n* [9; *pl.*: кры́лья, -льев] wing (*a.* ✈, △, ⚔, *pol.*); sail (*windmill*); splashboard; **~ьцо́** *n* [9; *pl.*: кры́льца, -ле́ц, -льца́м] steps *pl.*, (outside) staircase, porch.
Крым *m* [1; в -у́] Crimea; **'♀ский** [16] Crimean.
кры́с|а *f* [5] rat; **~ий** [18] rat('s).
крыть [22], ⟨по-⟩ cover; coat; trump; **-ся** *impf.* lie *or* consist in (в П); be at the bottom of.
кры́ш|а *f* [5] roof; **~ка** *f* [5; *g/pl.*: -шек] lid, cover; P (Д р.'s) end, ruin.
крюк *m* [1 *e.*; *pl. a.* крю́чья, -ьев] hook; F detour.
крюч|кова́тый [14 *sh.*] hooked; **~котво́рство** *n* [9] pettifoggery; **~о́к** *m* [1; -чка́] hook; crochet needle; flourish; F hitch.
кряж *m* [1] range; chain of hills.
кря́к|ать [1], *once* ⟨**~нуть**⟩ [20] quack.
кряхте́ть [11] groan, moan.
кста́ти to the point (*or* purpose); opportune(ly), in the nick of time; apropos; besides, too, as well; incidentally, by the way.
кто [23] who; ~ …, ~ … some …, others …; ~ бы ни whoever; ~ бы то ни́ был who(so)ever it may be; ~ F = **́-либо, ́-нибудь, ́-то** [23] any-, somebody (*or* -one).
куб *m* [1] 𝔄 cube; boiler.
ку́барем F head over heels.
ку́би|к *m* [1] (small) cube; block (*toy*); **́ческий** [16] cubic(al).
ку́бок *m* [1; -бка] goblet; *prize*: cup.
кубоме́тр *m* [1] cubic meter (-tre).
куве́рт † *m* [1] cover; envelope.
кувши́н *m* [1] jug; pitcher.
кувырк|а́ться [1], *once* ⟨**~ну́ться**⟩ [20] somersault, tumble; **~о́м** *s.* ку́барем.
куда́ where (… to); what … for; F (*a.* ~ как[о́й], *etc.*) very, awfully, how; at all; by far, much; (*a.* + Д [& *inf.*]) how can …; (*a.* ~ тут, там) (that's) impossible!, certainly not!, what an idea!, (*esp.* ~ тебе́!) rats!; ~ …, ~ … to some places …, to others …; ~ вы (*i. e.* идёте)? where are you going?; хоть ~ P tiptop, smart; *cf.* ни; ~ F = **~-либо, ~-нибудь, ~-то** any-, somewhere.
куда́хтать [3] cackle, cluck.
куде́сник *m* [1] wizard.
ку́др|и *f/pl.* [-е́й, *etc. e.*] curls; **~я́вый** [14 *sh.*] curly(-headed); tufty; ornate.
Кузба́сс ⚒ *m* [1] Kuznetsk Basin.
кузн|е́ц *m* [1 *e.*] (black)smith; **~е́чик** *m* [1] *zo.* grasshopper; **́ица** *f* [5] smithy.
ку́зов *m* [1; *pl.*: -ва́, *etc. e.*] body; box.
кукаре́кать [1] crow.
ку́киш P *m* [1] fig, fico.
ку́к|ла *f* [5; *g/pl.*: -кол] doll; **~олка** *f* [5; *g/pl.*: -лок] **1.** *dim. of* ~ла; **2.** *zo.* chrysalis; **~ольный** [14] doll('s); dollish; ~ольный теа́тр *m* puppet show.

кукуру́за *f* [5] corn, *Brt.* maize.
куку́шка *f* [5; *g/pl.*: -шек] cuckoo.
кула́|к *m* [1 *e.*] fist; ⊕ cam; kulak; **~цкий** [16] kulak...; **~чество** *n* [9] kulaks *pl.*; **~чный** [14] boxing (*match*); club (*law*); ⊕ cam...
кулёк *m* [1; -лька́] (paper) bag.
кули́к *m* [1 *e.*] curlew; snipe.
кули́са *f* [5] wing, side scene; за ~ми behind the scenes.
кули́ч *m* [1 *e.*] Easter cake.
кулуа́ры *m/pl.* [1] lobbies.
куль *m* [4 *e.*] sack, bag.
культ *m* [1] cult; **~иви́ровать** [7] cultivate; **~рабо́та** *f* [5] cultural & educational work (*Sov.*); **~у́ра** *f* [5] culture; **~у́рный** [14 *sh.*] cultural; cultured, civilized; polite, well-bred.
кум *m* [1; *pl.*: -мовья́, -овьёв] godfather; **~а́** *f* [5] godmother; gossip.
кума́ч *m* [1 *e.*] red bunting.
куми́р *m* [1] idol.
кумовство́ *n* [9] sponsorship, friendship; *fig.* nepotism.
кумы́с *m* [1] k(o)umiss.
куни́ца *f* [5] marten.
купа́|льный [14] bathing (**~льный костю́м** *m* bathing suit, *Brt.* bathing costume); **~льня** *f* [6; *g/pl.*: -лен] (swimming) bath, bathhouse; **~льщик** *m* [1] bather; **~ть(ся)** [1], ⟨вы́-, F ис-⟩ (take a) bath; bathe.
купе́ (-ˈpɛ) [*ind.*] 🚃 *n* compartment.
купе́|ц *m* [1; -пца́] merchant; **~ческий** [16] merchant('s); **~чество** *n* [9] merchants *pl.*
купи́ть *s.* покупа́ть.
купле́т *m* [1] couplet, stanza; song.
ку́пля *f* [6] purchase.
ку́пол *m* [1; *pl.*: -ла́] cupola, dome.
купоро́с *m* [1] vitriol.
ку́пчая *f* [14] purchase deed.
курга́н *m* [1] burial mound, barrow.
ку́р|ево P *n* [9] tobacco, smoke; *a.* = **~е́ние** *n* [12] smoking; **~и́льщик** *m* [1] smoker.
кури́|ный [14] chicken...; hen's; F short (*memory*); night... (*blindness*).
кури́|тельный [14] smoking; **~ть** [13; курю́, ку́ришь], ⟨по-, вы́-⟩ smoke (**-ся** *v/i.*); distil(l).
ку́рица *f* [5; *pl.*: ку́ры, *etc. st.*] hen; chicken, fowl.
курно́сый F [14 *sh.*] snub-nosed.
куро́к *m* [1; -рка́] cock (*gun*).
куропа́тка *f* [5; *g/pl.*: -ток] partridge.
куро́рт *m* [1] health resort.
курс *m* [1] course (⚓, ✈; ⚕; *educ.*; держа́ть ~ на [В] head for; *univ. a.* year); ✝ rate of exchange; *fig.* line, policy; держа́ть (быть) в ~е (Р) keep (be) (well) posted on; **~а́нт** *m* [1] student; ⚔ cadet; **~и́в** *m* [1] *typ.* italics; **~и́ровать** [7] ply.
ку́ртка *f* [5; *g/pl.*: -ток] jacket.
курча́вый [14 *sh.*] curly(-headed).
курь|ёз *m* [1] fun(ny thing); curiosity; **~е́р** *m* [1] messenger; courier; **~е́рский** [16]: ~е́рский по́езд *m* express (train).
куря́тник *m* [1] hen house.
куря́щий *m* [18] smoker.
кус|а́ть [1], ⟨укуси́ть⟩ [15] bite (**-ся** *v/i., impf.*), sting; **~ково́й** [14] lump (*sugar*); **~о́к** *m* [1; -ска́] piece, bit, morsel; scrap; lump (*sugar*); cake (*soap*); slice; ~ка́ми by the piece; на ~ки́ to pieces; ~о́к хле́ба F living; **~о́чек** *m* [1; -чка] *dim. of* ~о́к.
куст *m* [1 *e.*] bush, shrub; **~а́рник** *m* [1] bush(es), shrub(s); *pl. a.* underwood.
куста́р|ный [14] handicraft...; home (-made); *fig.* homespun; **~ь** *m* [4 *e.*] (handi)craftsman.
ку́тать(ся) [1], ⟨за-⟩ muffle, wrap.
кут|ёж *m* [1 *e.*], **~и́ть** [15] carouse.
кух|а́рка *f* [5; *g/pl.*: -рок] cook; **~ня** *f* [6; *g/pl.*: ку́хонь] kitchen; cuisine, cookery; **~онный** [14] kitchen...
ку́цый [14 *sh.*] dock-tailed; short.
ку́ч|а *f* [5] heap, pile; a lot of; ~ами in heaps *or* in crowds; класть в ~у pile up; **~ер** *m* [1; *pl.*: -ра́, *etc. e.*] coachman; **~ка** *f* [5; *g/pl.*: -чек] *dim. of* ~а; group.
куш *m* [1] stake; F lot, sum.
куша́к *m* [1 *e.*] belt, girdle.
ку́ша|нье *n* [10] dish; meal; food; **~ть** [1], ⟨по-⟩ eat (up ⟨с-⟩); drink.
куше́тка *f* [5; *g/pl.*: -ток] lounge.

Л

лабири́нт *m* [1] labyrinth.
лаборато́рия *f* [7] laboratory.
ла́ва *f* [5] lava.
лави́на *f* [5] avalanche.
лави́ровать [7] tack (⚓ & *fig.*).
ла́в|ка *f* [5; *g/pl.*: -вок] bench; (small) store, *Brt.* shop; **~очник** *m* [1] store-, shopkeeper; **~р** *m* [1] laurel; **~ро́вый** [14] (of) laurel(s).
ла́гер|ь 1. [4; *pl.*: -ря́, *etc. e.*] camp (*a., pl.*: -ри, *etc. st., fig.*); располага́ться (стоя́ть) ~ем camp (out); **~ный** [14] camp...
лад *m* [1; в -у́; *pl. e.*] F harmony, concord; order; way; tune; (не) в ~у́ (~а́х) *s.* (не) ~ить; идти́ на ~ work (well), get on *or* along; **~ан** *m* [1] incense; **~ить** F [15], ⟨по-, с-⟩ get along *or* on (well), *pf. a.* make it up; manage; fix; tune; не ~ить *a.* be at odds *or* variance; out of keeping; **-ся** F *impf. s.* идти́ на ~ & ~ить;

∠но F well, all right, O. K.; **∠ный** F [14; -ден, -дна́, -о] harmonious; fine, good(-looking).
ла́дожск|ий [16]: ♀ое о́зеро *n* Lake Ladoga.
ладо́|нь *f* [8], **~ша** P *f* [5] palm; как на ~ни (*lie*) spread before the eyes; бить в ~ши clap (one's hands).
ладья́ *f* [6] boat; *chess*: rook.
лазаре́т ⚔ *m* [1] hospital.
лаз|е́йка *f* [5; *g/pl.*: -е́ек] loophole; **∠ить** [15] climb (*v/t.* на В); creep.
лазу́|рный [14; -рен, -рна], **~рь** *f* [8] azure; **~тчик** *m* [1] scout, spy.
лай *m* [3] bark(ing), yelp; **∠ка** *f* [5; *g/pl.*: ла́ек] **1.** Eskimo dog; **2.** kid (*leather*); **∠ковый** [14] kid...
лак *m* [1] varnish, laquer; **∠овый** [14] varnish(ed), laquer(ed); patent leather...; **~а́ть** [1], ⟨вы́-⟩ lap.
лаке́й *m* [3] footman, lackey; flunk(e)y; **~ский** [16] lackey('s); *fig.* servile.
лакирова́ть [7], ⟨от-⟩ laquer; varnish.
ла́ком|иться [14], ⟨по-⟩ (Т) enjoy, relish (*a. fig.*). eat with delight; be fond of dainties; **~ка** F *m/f* [5] lover of dainties; быть ~кой *a.* have a sweet tooth; **~ство** *n* [9] dainty, delicacy; *pl.* sweetmeats, *Brt.* sweets; **~ый** [14 *sh.*] dainty; † (*a.* ~ый до Р) fond of (dainties); ~ый кусо́(че)к *m* tidbit, *Brt.* titbit.
лакони́ч|еский [16], **~ный** [14; -чен, -чна] laconic(al).
Ла-Ма́нш *m* [1] English Channel.
ла́мп|а *f* [5] lamp; *rad.* tube, *Brt.* valve; **~а́д(к)а** *f* [5 (*g/pl.*: -док)] (*icon*) lamp; **~овый** [14] lamp...; **~очка** *f* [5; *g/pl.*: -чек] bulb.
ландша́фт *m* [1] landscape.
ла́ндыш *m* [1] lily of the valley.
лань *f* [8] fallow deer; hind, doe.
ла́п|а *f* [5] paw; *fig.* clutch; **~оть** *m* [4; -птя; *from g/pl. e.*] bast shoe.
лапша́ *f* [5] noodles *pl.*; noodle soup.
ларёк *m* [1; -рька́] stand, *Brt.* stall.
ларе́ц [1; -рца́] box, chest, casket.
ла́ск|а *f* **1.** [5] caress; F affection; **2.** [5; *g/pl.:* -сок] weasel; **~а́тельный** [14] endearing, pet; † flattering; *s. a.* ~овый; **~а́ть** [1], ⟨при-⟩ caress; pet, fondle; *impf.* cherish; flatter (o.s. with себя́ Т); **-ся** endear o.s. (to к Д); fawn (*dog*); † (Т) cherish; **~овый** [14 *sh.*] affectionate, tender; caressing.
ла́сточка *f* [5; *g/pl.*: -чек] swallow.
лата́ть P [1], ⟨за-⟩ patch, mend.
латви́йский [16] Latvian.
лати́нский [16] Latin.
ла́тка P *f* [5; *g/pl.:* -ток] patch.
лату́к *m* [1] lettuce.
лату́нь *f* [8] brass.
ла́ты *f/pl.* [5] armo(u)r.
латы́нь *f* [13] Latin.
латы́ш *m* [1 *e.*], **~ка** *f* [5; *g/pl.*: -шек] Lett; **~ский** [16] Lettish.
лауреа́т *m* [1] prize winner.
лафе́т *m* [1] gun carriage.
лачу́га *f* [5] hovel, hut.
ла́ять [27], ⟨за-⟩ bark.
лгать [лгу, лжёшь, лгут; лгал, -а́, -о] **1.** ⟨со-⟩ lie; tell a p. (Д, пе́ред Т) a lie; **2.** ⟨на-⟩ (на В) defame.
лгун *m* [1 *e.*], **∠ья** *f* [6] liar.
лебёдка *f* [5; *g/pl.*: -док] windlass.
лебе|ди́ный [14] swan...; **′~дь** *m* [4; *from g/pl. e.*] (*poet. a. f*) swan; **~зи́ть** F [15 *e.*; -бежу́, -бези́шь] fawn (upon пе́ред Т).
лев *m* [1; льва] lion; ♀ Leo.
лев|ша́ *m/f* [5; *g/pl.*: -ше́й] left-handed person; **∠ый** [14] left (*a. fig.*), left-hand; wrong (*side*; on с Р).
лега́льный [14; -лен, -льна] legal.
леге́нд|а *f* [5] legend; **~а́рный** [14; -рен, -рна] legendary.
легио́н *m* [1] legion.
лёгкий (-xk-) [16; лёгок, легка́; *a.* лёгки] light (*a. fig.*); easy; slight; F lucky; (Д) легко́ + *inf.* it is very well for ... + *inf.*; лёгок на поми́не F talk of the devil!
легко|ве́рный (-xk-) [14; -рен, -рна] credulous; **~ве́сный** [14; -сен, -сна] light; *fig.* shallow; **~во́й** [14]: ~во́й автомоби́ль *m* (*a.* ~ва́я [авто]маши́на *f*) auto(mobile), car.
лёгкое (-xk-) *n* [16] lung.
легкомы́сл|енный (-xk-) [14 *sh.*] light-minded, frivolous; thoughtless; **~ие** *n* [12] levity; frivolity; flippancy.
лёгкость (-xk-) *f* [8] lightness; easiness; ease.
лёд *m* [1; льда; на льду́] ice.
лед|ене́ть [8], ⟨за-, о-⟩ freeze, ice; grow numb (with cold); chill; **~ене́ц** *m* [1; -нца́] (sugar) candy; **~ени́ть** [13], ⟨о(б)-⟩ freeze, ice; chill; **∠ник**[1] *m* [1] ice cellar; refrigerator, icebox; **~ни́к**[2] *m* [1 *e.*] glacier; **~нико́вый** [14] glacial; ice...; **~око́л** *m* [1] icebreaker; **~охо́д** *m* [1] ice drift; **~яно́й** [14] ice...; icy (*a. fig.*); chilly.
лежа́лый [14] stale, old, spoiled.
лежа́|ть [4 *e.*; лёжа] lie; be (situated); rest, be incumbent; form (*the basis* в П); **~чий** [17] lying; (*a.* ⚕) prostrate; turndown (*collar*).
ле́звие *n* [12] edge.
лезть [24 *st.*: ле́зу; лезь!; лез, -ла], ⟨по-⟩ (be) climb(ing, *etc.*; *v/t.* на В); creep; penetrate; F reach into; (к Д [с Т]) importune, press; fall out (*hair*); (на В) fit (*v/t.*); P meddle.
лейбори́ст *m* [1] Labo(u)rite.
ле́й|ка *f* [5; *g/pl.*: ле́ек] watering pot, can; **~тена́нт** *m* [1] (second) lieutenant.

лека́р|ственный [14] medicinal, curative; **~ство** *n* [9] medicine, remedy (against, for от, про́тив Р); **'~ь** † & P *m* [4; *from g/pl. e.*] doctor.
ле́ксика *f* [5] vocabulary.
ле́к|тор *m* [1] lecturer; **~ция** *f* [7] lecture (at на П; *vb.*: слу́шать [чита́ть] attend [give, deliver]).
леле́ять [27] cherish, fondle.
ле́ме́х *m* [1 & 1 *e*; *pl.*: -ха́, *etc. e.*] plowshare (*Brt.* plough-share).
лён *m* [1; льна] flax.
лени́в|ец *m* [1; -вца] *s.* лентя́й; **~ица** *f* [5] *s.* лентя́йка; **~ый** [14 *sh.*] lazy, idle; sluggish.
Ленингра́д *m* [1] Leningrad; **♀ец** *m* [1; -дца] Leningrader.
ле́нин|ец *m* [1; -нца], **~ский** [16] Leninist.
лени́ться [13; леню́сь, ле́нишься], be lazy.
ле́нта *f* [5] ribbon; band; ⊕ tape.
лентя́й F *m* [3], **~ка** *f* [5; *g/pl.*: -я́ек] lazybones; **~ничать** F [1] idle.
лень *f* [8] laziness, idleness; listlessness; F (мне) ~ I hate, don't want, won't.
лепе|сто́к *m* [1; -тка́] petal; **'~т** *m* [1], **~та́ть** [4], ‹про-› babble, prattle.
лепёшка *f* [5; *g/pl.*: -шек] scone; lozenge.
леп|и́ть [14], ‹вы́-, с-› sculpture, model, mo(u)ld; F ‹на-› stick (to на В); **∠ка** model(l)ing, mo(u)lding; F sculpture; **~но́й** [14] plastic.
ле́пта *f* [5] mite.
лес *m* [1; и́з лесу & из ле́са; в лесу́; *pl.*: леса́, *etc. e.*] wood, forest; lumber, *Brt.* timber; *pl.* scaffold(ing); **∠ом** through a (the) wood; как в **~у́** F *fig.* at sea; **∠а́** *f* [5; *pl.*: лёсы, *etc. st.*] (fishing) line; **~и́стый** [14 *sh.*] woody, wooded; **∠ка** *f* [5; *g/pl.*: -сок] *s.* **∠а́**; **~ни́к** *m* [1 *e.*] ranger; **~ни́чество** *n* [9] forest district; **~ни́чий** *m* [17] forester; **~но́й** [14] forest...; wood(y); lumber...; *Brt.* timber...
лесо|во́дство *n* [9] forestry; **~насажде́ние** *n* [12] afforestation; (af)forested tract; wood; **~пи́лка** F *f* [5; *g/pl.*: -лок], **~пи́льный** [14]: **~пи́льный заво́д** *m* = **~пи́льня** *f* [6; *g/pl.*: -лен] sawmill; **~ру́б** *m* [1] lumberman, woodcutter.
ле́стница *f* [5] (-şn-) (flight of) stairs *pl.*, staircase; ladder; *fig.* scale.
ле́ст|ный [14; -тен, -тна] flattering; **~ь** *f* [8] flattery.
лёт *m* [1] flight; на лету́ in the air, on the wing; F *fig.* in haste; instantly, quickly.
лета́, лет *s.* ле́то; *cf. a.* год.
лета́тельный [14] flying.
лета́ть [1] fly.
лете́ть [11], ‹по-› (be) fly(ing).
ле́тний [15] summer...
лётный [14] flying; run...
ле́т|о *n* [9; *pl. e.*] summer (in [the] Т; for the на В); *pl.* years, age (at в В); ско́лько вам ~? how old are you? (*cf.* быть); в **~а́х** elderly, advanced in years; **~опи́сец** *m* [1; -сца] chronicler; **~опись** *f* [8] chronicle; **~осчисле́ние** *n* [12] chronology; era.
лету́ч|ий [17 *sh.*] flying; fleeting; offhand, short; ⚗ volatile; **~ая мышь** *f zo.* bat; **~ий листо́к** = **~ка** F *f* [5; *g/pl.*: -чек] leaflet.
лётчи|к *m* [1], **~ца** *f* [5] aviator, flier, pilot, air(wo)man.
лече́бн|ица *f* [5] clinic, hospital; **~ый** [14] medic(in)al.
леч|е́ние ⚕ *n* [12] treatment; **~и́ть** [16] treat; **-ся** undergo treatment, be treated; treat (one's ... от Р).
лечь *s.* ложи́ться; *cf. a.* лежа́ть.
ле́ший *m* [17] satyr; P Old Nick.
лещ *m* [1 *e.*] *zo.* bream.
лж|е... false; pseudo...; **~ец** *m* [1 *e.*] liar; **~и́вость** *f* [8] mendacity; **~и́вый** [14 *sh.*] false, lying; mendacious.
ли, (*short, after vowels, a.*) **ль 1.** (*interr. part.*:) зна́ет ~ он ...? (= он зна́ет ...?) does he know ...?; **2.** (*cj.*:) whether, if; ... ~, ... ~ whether ..., or ...
либера́л *m* [1], **~ьный** [14; -лен, -льна] liberal.
ли́бо or; ~ ..., ~ ... either ... or ...
Лива́н *m* [1] Lebanon.
ли́вень *m* [4; -вня] downpour.
ливре́я *f* [6; *g/pl.*: -ре́й] livery.
ли́га *f* [5] league.
ли́дер *m* [1] (*pol., sport*) leader.
Ли́з(очк)а *f* [5] Liz(zy), Lise.
лиз|а́ть [3], *once* ‹**~ну́ть**› lick.
лик *m* [1] face; countenance; image.
ликвиди́ровать [7] (*im*)*pf.* liquidate.
ликова́ть [7], ‹воз-› exult.
ли́лия *f* [7] lily.
лило́вый [14] lilac(-colo[u]red).
лими́т *m* [1], **~и́ровать** [7] (*im*)*pf.* limit.
лимо́н *m* [1] lemon; **~а́д** *m* [1] lemonade.
ли́мфа *f* [5] lymph.
лингви́стика *f* [5] *s.* языкозна́ние.
лине́й|ка *f* [5; *g/pl.*: -е́ек] line; ruler; slide rule; † carriage; **~ный** [14] linear; ⚔ (of the) line; ⚓ battle...
ли́н|за *f* [5] lens; **~ия** *f* [7] line (*a. fig.*; in по Д); **~ко́р** *m* [1] battleship; **~ова́ть** [7], ‹на-› rule.
Линч: зако́н (*or* суд) **∠а** lynch law; **♀ева́ть** [7] (*im*)*pf.* lynch.
линь *m* [4 *e.*] *zo.* tench; ⚓ line.
ли́н|ька *f* [5] mo(u)lt(ing); **~ю́чий** F [17 *sh.*] fading, faded; mo(u)lting;

~ялый F [14] faded; mo(u)lted; **~ять** [28], ⟨вы́-, по-⟩ fade; mo(u)lt.
ли́па *f* [5] linden, lime tree.
ли́п|кий [16; -пок, -пка́, -о] sticky; sticking (*plaster*); **~нуть** [21], ⟨при-⟩ stick.
ли́р|а *f* [5] lyre; **~ик** *m* [1] lyric poet; **~ика** *f* [5] lyric poetry; **~и́ческий** [16], **~и́чный** [14; -чен, -чна] lyric(al).
лис|(и́ц)а́ *f* [5; *pl. st.*] fox (silver... серебри́стая, черно-бу́рая); **∠ий** [18] fox...; foxy.
лист *m* **1.** [1 *e.*] sheet; certificate; ⚖ deed; *typ.* leaf (= 16 pp.); **2.** [1 *e.*; *pl. st* : ли́стья, -ьев] ⚘ leaf; *a.* = **~ва́**; **~а́ть** F [1] leaf, thumb (through); **~ва́** *f* [5] foliage, leaves *pl.*; **∠венница** *f* [5] larch; **∠венный** [14] foliose, leafy; deciduous; **∠ик** *m* [1] *dim. of* ~; **~о́вка** *f* [5; *g/pl.*: -вок] *pol.* leaflet; **~о́к** *m* [1; -тка́] *dim. of* ~; slip; (news)paper; **~ово́й** [14] leaf(y); sheet...; folio...
Литва́ *f* [5] Lithuania.
лите́й|ная *f* [14], **~ный** [14]: ~ный заво́д *m* foundry; **~щик** *m* [1] founder.
ли́тер|а *f* [5] letter, type; **~а́тор** *m* [1] man of letters; writer; **~ату́ра** *f* [5] literature; **~ату́рный** [14; -рен, -рна] literary.
лито́в|ец *m* [1; -вца], **~ка** *f* [5; *g/pl.*: -вок], **~ский** [16] Lithuanian.
лито́й [14] cast.
литр *m* [1] liter (*Brt.* -tre; = *approx.* 1qt.).
лить [лью, льёшь; лил, -а́, -о; ле́й(-те)! ли́тый (лит, -а́, -о)] pour; shed; ⊕ cast; дождь льёт как из ведра́ it's raining cats and dogs; **-ся** flow, pour; spread; sound; **~ё** *n* [10] founding, cast(ing).
лифт *m* [1] elevator, *Brt.* lift; **~ёр** *m* [1] elevator boy, *Brt.* lift man.
ли́фчик *m* [1] waist, bodice; bra(ssière).
лих|ои́мец † *m* [1; -мца] usurer; bribe taker; **~о́й** [14; лих, -а́, -о] bold, daring; dashing; nimble; smart; **~ора́дка** *f* [5] fever; **~ора́дочный** [14; -чен, -чна] feverish; **∠ость** *f* [8] bravery; smartness.
лицев|а́ть [7], ⟨пере-⟩ face; turn; **~о́й** [14] face...; front...; right (*side*).
лицеме́р *m* [1] hypocrite; **~ие** *n* [12] hypocricy; **~ный** [14; -рен, -рна] hypocritical; **~ить** [13] dissemble.
лице́нзия *f* [7] license (for на B).
лиц|о́ *n* [9; *pl. st.*] face; countenance (*change v/t.* в П); front; person, individual(ity); в ~о́ by sight; to s. b.'s face; от ~а́ (P) in the name of; ~о́м к ~у́ face to face; быть (Д) к ~у́ suit *or* become a p.; нет ~а́ (на П) be bewildered; *s. a.* де́йствующий.
личи́н|а *f* [5] mask, guise; **~ка** *f* [5; *g/pl.*: -нок] larva; maggot.
ли́чн|ый [14] personal; **~ость** *f* [8] personality; identity (*card*).
лиша́й *m* [3 *e.*] ⚘ lichen (*a.* ~ник); ⚕ herpes.
лиш|а́ть [1], ⟨~и́ть⟩ [16 *e.*; -шу́, -ши́шь; -шённый] deprive, bereave, strip (of P); ~а́ть (себя́) жи́зни commit murder (upon B) (suicide); ~ённый *a.* devoid of, lack(-ing); **-ся** (P) lose; ~и́ться чувств faint; **~е́ние** *n* [12] (de)privation; loss; *pl.* privations, hardships; ~е́ние прав disfranchisement; ~е́ние свобо́ды imprisonment; **~и́ть(ся)** *s.* ~а́ть(ся).
ли́шн|ий [15] superfluous, odd, excessive, over..., sur...; spare; extra; needless, unnecessary; outsider; ~ее *n* undue (things, *etc.*), (*a.* a glass) too much; ... с ~им over ...; ~ий раз *m* once again; (Д) не ~е *inf.* (p.) had better.
лишь (*a.* + то́лько) only; merely, just; as soon as, no sooner ... than, hardly; ~ бы if only.
лоб *m* [1; лба; во, на лбу́] forehead.
ло́бзик *m* [1] fret saw.
ло́б|ный *anat.*, **~ово́й** [14] ⚔ frontal.
лови́ть [14], ⟨пойма́ть⟩ [1] catch; (en)trap; grasp, seize; ~ на сло́ве take at one's word.
ло́вк|ий [16; ло́вок, ловка́, -о] dexterous, adroit, deft; **~ость** *f* [8] adroitness, dexterity.
ло́в|ля *f* [6] catching; fishing; **~у́шка** *f* [5; *g/pl.*: -шек] trap; snare.
логари́фм *m* [1] logarithm.
ло́ги|ка *f* [5] logic; **∠ческий** [16], **∠чный** [14; -чен, -чна] logical.
ло́гов|ище *n* [11], **~о** *n* [9] lair, den.
ло́д|ка *f* [5; *g/pl.*: -док] boat; **~очник** *m* [1] boatman.
лоды́жка *f* [5; *g/pl.*: -жек] ankle.
ло́дырь F *m* [4] idler, loafer.
ло́жа *f* [5] *thea.* box; lodge; stock.
ложби́на *f* [5] hollow.
ло́же *n* [11] couch, bed; stock.
ложи́ться [16 *e.*; -жу́сь, -жи́шься], ⟨лечь⟩ [26 г/ж: ля́гу, ля́жешь, ля́гут; ля́г(те)!; лёг, легла́] lie down; ~ в (B) go to (*bed*, *a.* ~ [спать]); fall.
ло́жка *f* [5; *g/pl.*: -жек] spoon.
ло́ж|ный [14; -жен, -жна] false; ~ный путь *m* wrong tack; **~ь** *f* [8; лжи; ло́жью] lie, falsehood.
лоза́ *f* [5; *pl. st.*] vine; switch ⚘.
ло́зунг *m* [1] slogan, watchword.
локализова́ть [7] (*im*)*pf.* localize.
локо|моти́в *m* [1] locomotive, engine; **′~н** *m* [1] curl, lock; **′~ть** *m* [4; -ктя; *from g/pl. e.*] elbow.
лом *m* [1; *from g/pl. e.*] crowbar, pry; scrap (metal); **∠аный** [14] broken; **~а́ть** [1], ⟨с-⟩ break (*a.* up); pull (down), tear; ~а́ть го́лову rack one's brains (over над T); **-ся** break; P clown, jest; mince, be prim.

ломба́рд *m* [1] pawnshop.
лом|и́ть [14] F = **~а́ть**; *impers.* ache, feel a pain in; **-ся** bend, burst; F force (*v/t.* в В), break (into); **~ка** *f* [5] breaking (up); **~кий** [16; ло́мок, ломка́, -о] brittle, fragile; **~ово́й** [14] breaking; scrap...; cart(er)...; **~о́та** *f* [5] acute pains *pl.*; **~о́ть** *m* [4; -мтя́] slice; **~тик** *m* [1] *dim. of* **~о́ть**.
ло́но *n* [9] lap; bosom (in на П).
ло́па|сть *f* [8; *from g/pl. e.*] blade; vane, fan; **~та** *f* [8] shovel, spade; **~тка** *f* [5; *g/pl.*: -ток] **1.** *dim. of* **~та**; **2.** shoulder blade.
ло́п|аться [1], ⟨**~нуть**⟩ [20] burst; crack, break; tear; F be exhausted.
лопу́х *m* [1 *e.*] burdock.
лоск *m* [1] luster, gloss, polish.
лоску́т *m* [1 *e.*; *pl. a.*: -ку́тья, -ьев] rag, shred, scrap, frazzle.
лос|ни́ться [13] be glossy *or* sleek, shine; **~о́сь** *m* [4] salmon.
лось *m* [4; *from g/pl. e.*] elk.
лот *m* [1] plummet, lead.
лотере́я *f* [6] lottery.
лото́к *m* [1; -тка́] hawker's stand, tray.
лоха́н|ка *f* [5], **~ь** *f* [8] tub.
лохм|а́тый [14 *sh.*] shaggy, dishevel(l)ed; **~о́тья** *n/pl.* [*gen.*: -ьев] rags.
ло́цман ⚓ *m* [1] pilot.
лошад|и́ный [14] horse...; **~и́ная си́ла** *f* horsepower; **'~ь** *f* [8; *from g/pl. e., instr.*: -дьми́ & -дя́ми] horse.
лоша́к *m* [1 *e.*] hinny.
лощи́|на *f* [5] hollow, valley; **~ть** [16 *e.*; -щу́, -щи́шь; -щённый] ⟨на-, вы́-⟩ gloss, polish.
лоя́льн|ость *f* [8] loyalty; **~ый** [14; -лен, -льна] loyal.
лу|бо́к *m* [1; -бка́] ⚕ splint; cheap popular print (*or* literature).; **~г** *m* [1; на -у́; *pl.* -а́, *etc. e.*] meadow.
луди́ть [15] tin.
лу́ж|а *f* [5] puddle, pool; сесть в **~у** F be in a pretty pickle (*or* fix).
лужа́йка *f* [5; *g/pl.*: -а́ек] (small) glade.
лук *m* [1] **1.** onion(s); **2.** bow.
лука́в|ить [14], ⟨с-⟩ dissemble, dodge; **~ство** *n* [9] cunning, slyness, ruse; **~ый** [14 *sh.*] crafty, wily.
лу́ковица *f* [5] bulb; onion.
лун|а́ *f* [5] moon; **~а́тик** *m* [1] sleepwalker; **~ный** [14] moon(lit); *astr.* lunar.
лу́па *f* [5] magnifier, magnifying glass.
лупи́ть [14], ⟨об-⟩ peel (*v/i.* **-ся**).
луч *m* [1 *e.*] ray, beam; **~ево́й** [14] radial; **~еза́рный** [14; -рен, -рна] radiant; **~еиспуска́ние** *n* [12] radiation; **~и́на** *f* [5] (burning) chip, spill; **~и́стый** [14 *sh.*] radiant.
лу́чш|е *adv., comp. of* хорошо́; **~ий** [17] better; best (at ... в **~ем** слу́чае).
лущи́ть [16 *e.*; -щу́, -щи́шь], ⟨вы́-⟩ shell, husk.
лы́ж|а *f* [5] ski (*vb.*: ходи́ть, *etc.*, на **~ах**); **~ник** *m* [1], **~ница** *f* [5] skier; **~ный** [14] ski...
лы́ко *n* [9; *nom/pl.*: лы́ки] bast.
лы́с|ый [14] bald; **~ина** *f* [5] bald head; blaze.
ль *s.* ли.
льви́|ный [14] lion's; **~ный зев** ⚘ *m* snapdragon; **~ца** *f* [5] lioness.
льго́т|а *f* [5] privilege; **~ный** [14; -тен, -тна] privileged; reduced; favo(u)rable.
льди́на *f* [5] ice floe.
льну́ть [20], ⟨при-⟩ cling, nestle.
льняно́й [14] flax(en); linen...
льст|е́ц *m* [1 *e.*] flatterer; **~и́вый** [14 *sh.*] flattering; **~ить** [15], ⟨по-⟩ (Д) flatter (o.s. with себя́ Т).
любе́зн|ичать F [1] (с Т) court, flirt, spoon; **~ость** *f* [8] amiability, kindness; favo(u)r; *pl.* compliments; **~ый** [14; -зен, -зна] amiable, kind; dear; *su.* sweetheart; F lovely.
люби́м|ец *m* [1; -мца], **~ица** *f* [5] favo(u)rite, pet; **~ый** [14] beloved, darling; favo(u)rite, pet.
люби́тель *m* [4], **~ница** *f* [5] lover, fan; amateur; **~ский** [16] amateur (-ish).
люби́ть [14] love; like, be (⟨по-⟩ grow) fond of; *pf.* fall in love with.
любов|а́ться [7], ⟨по-⟩ (Т *or* на В) admire, (be) delight(ed) (in); **~ник** *m* [1] lover; **~ница** *f* [5] mistress; **~ный** [14] love...; loving, affectionate; **~ная связь** *f* amour; **~ь** *f* **1.** [8; -бви́; -бо́вью] love (of, for к Д); **2.** ♀ [8] *fem. name* (*cf.* Amanda).
любо|зна́тельный [14; -лен, -льна] inquisitive, curious; inquiring; **~й** [14] any(one *su.*); **~пы́тный** [14; -тен, -тна] curious, inquisitive; interesting; мне **~пы́тно** ... I wonder ...; **~пы́тство** *n* [9] curiosity; interest.
лю́бящий [17] loving, affectionate.
люд *m* [1] *coll.* F, **~и** *pl.* [-е́й, -ям, -ьми́, -ях] people; † servants; вы́йти в **~и** arrive, make one's way in life (*or* fortune); на **~ях** in public; **~ный** [14; -ден, -дна] populous; crowded; **~ое́д** *m* [1] cannibal; ogre; **~ско́й** [16] man...; man's; human(e); servants' (room *su. f*).
люк *m* [1] hatch(way).
лю́лька *f* [5; *g/pl.*: -лек] cradle.
лю́стра *f* [5] chandelier, luster.
лю́тик *m* [1] buttercup.
лю́тый [14; лют, -а́, -о; *comp.*: -те́е] fierce, cruel, grim.
люце́рна *f* [5] alfalfa, *Brt.* lucerne.
ляг|а́ть(ся) [1], ⟨**~ну́ть**⟩ [20] kick.
лягу́шка *f* [5; *g/pl.*: -шек] frog.
ля́жка *f* [5; *g/pl.*: -жек] thigh; haunch.
лязг *m* [1], **~ать** [1] clank, clang, chatter.
ля́мк|а *f* [5; *g/pl.*: -мок] strap; тяну́ть **~у** F drudge, toil.

М

мавзоле́й *m* [3] mausoleum.
магази́н *m* [1] store, *Brt.* shop.
магистра́ль *f* [8] main (✈ air) line 🚂 (✈ *a.* route) *or* waterway; thoroughfare; trunk (line); main.
маг|и́ческий [16] magic(al); **~нети́ческий** [16] magnetic(al).
ма́гний *m* [3] magnesium.
магни́т *m* [1] magnet.
магомета́н|ин *m* [1; *pl.*: -áне, -áн], **~ка** *f* [5; *g/pl.*: -нок] Mohammedan.
мадья́р *m* [1], **~ский** [16] Magyar.
маёвка *f* [5; *g/pl.*: -вок] May Day meeting, outing *or* picnic.
ма́з|анка *f* [5; *g/pl.*: -нок] mud hut; **~ать** [3] **1.** ⟨по-, на-⟩ smear; rub (in); anoint; spread, butter; whitewash; **2.** ⟨с-⟩ oil, lubricate; **3.** F ⟨за-⟩ soil; *impf.* daub; **~ня́** F *f* [6] daub(ing); **~о́к** *m* [1; -зкá] touch, stroke; ⚕ swab; **~ь** *f* [8] ointment; grease.
май *m* [3] May; **~ка** *f* [5; *g/pl.*: мáек] sleeveless sports shirt; **~о́р** *m* [1] major; **~ский** [16] May(-Day)...
мак *m* [1] poppy.
мак|а́ть [1], *once* ⟨**~ну́ть**⟩ [20] dip.
маке́т *m* [1] model; dummy.
ма́клер *m* [1] broker.
макну́ть *s.* макáть.
макре́ль *f* [8] mackerel.
максима́льный [14; -лен, -льна] maximum.
маку́шка *f* [5; *g/pl.*: -шек] top; crown.
мала́|ец *m* [1; -лáйца], **~йка** *f* [5; *g/pl.*: лáек], **~йский** [16] Malay(an).
малева́ть F [6], ⟨на-⟩ paint, daub.
мале́йший [17] least, slightest.
ма́ленький [16] little, small; short; trifling, petty.
мали́н|а *f* [5] raspberry, -ries *pl.*; **~овка** *f* [5; *g/pl.*: -вок] robin (redbreast); **~овый** [14] raspberry-...; crimson; soft, sonorous.
ма́ло little (*a.* ~ что); few (*a.* ~ кто); a little; not enough; less; ~ где in few places; ~ когдá seldom; F ~ ли что much, many things, anything; (*a.* ~ что) yes, but ...; that doesn't matter, even though; ~ тогó besides, and what is more; ~ тогó, что not only (that).
мало|ва́жный [14; -жен, -жна] insignificant, trifling; **~ва́то** F little, not (quite) enough; **~вероя́тный** [14; -тен, -тна] unlikely; **~во́дный** [14; -ден, -дна] shallow; **~говоря́щий** [17] insignificant; **~гра́мотный** [14; -тен, -тна] uneducated, ignorant; faulty; **~ду́шный** [14; -шен, -шна] pusillanimous; **~зна́чащий** [17 *sh.*], **~значи́тельный** [14; -лен, -льна] *s.* **~ва́жный**; **~иму́щий** [17 *sh.*] poor; **~кро́вие** *n* [12] an(a)emia; **~кро́вный** [14; -вен, -вна] an(a)emic; **~ле́тний** [15] minor, underage; little (one); **~лю́дный** [14; -ден, -дна] poorly populated (*or* attended); **~-ма́льски** F a little bit; somewhat; **~общи́тельный** [14; -лен, -льна] unsociable; **~о́пытный** [14; -тен, -тна] inexperienced; **~-пома́лу** F gradually, little by little; **~ро́слый** [14 *sh.*] undersized; **~содержа́тельный** [14; -лен, -льна] vapid.
ма́л|ость *f* [8] smallness; F trifle; a bit; **~оце́нный** [14; -éнен, -éнна] inferior; **~очи́сленный** [14 *sh.*] small (in number), few; **~ый** [14; мал, -á; *comp.*: мéньше] small, little; short; *cf.* **~енький**; *su.* fellow, guy; lad; без **~ого** almost, just shtor of; ~ и стар young & old; с **~ых** лет from (one's) childhood; **~ы́ш** F *m* [1 *e.*] kid(dy).
ма́льч|ик *m* [1] boy; lad; **~и́шеский** [16] boyish; mischievous; **~и́шка** F *m* [5; *g/pl.*: -шек] urchin; greenhorn; **~уга́н** F *m* [1] *s.* малы́ш; *a.* = **~и́шка**.
малю́тка *m/f* [5; *g/pl.*: -ток] baby, infant; *fig.* pygmy..., miniature...
маля́р *m* [1 *e.*] (house) painter.
маляри́я *f* [7] malaria.
ма́м|а *f* [5] ma(mma), mum, mother; **~а́ша** F *f* [5], F **~енька** *f* [5; *g/pl.*: -нек] mammy, mummy.
мандари́н *m* [1] mandarin.
манда́т *m* [1] mandate.
ман|ёвр *m* [1], **~еври́ровать** [7] maneuver, manoeuvre; 🚂 shunt, switch; **~еке́н** *m* [1] mannequin.
мане́р|а *f* [5] manner; **~ка** *f* [5; *g/pl.*: -рок] canteen, *Brt.* water bottle; **~ный** [14; -рен, -рна] affected.
манже́т(к)а *f* [5 (*g/pl.*: -ток)] cuff.
манипули́ровать [7] manipulate.
мани́ть [13; маню́, мáнишь], ⟨по-⟩ (Т) beckon; (al)lure, entice, tempt.
ман|и́шка *f* [5; *g/pl.*: -шек] dick(e)y; **~ия** *f* [7] (вели́чия megalo)mania; **~ки́ровать** [7] (*im*)*pf.* (Т) neglect.
ма́нная [14]: ~ крупá *f* semolina.
мануфакту́ра *f* [5] textiles *pl.*
мара́ть F [1], ⟨за-⟩ soil, stain; ⟨на-⟩ scribble, daub; ⟨вы-⟩ delete.
ма́рганец *m* [1; -нца] manganese.
маргари́тка *f* [5; *g/pl.*: -ток] daisy.
маринова́ть [7], ⟨за-⟩ pickle.
ма́рк|а *f* [5; *g/pl.*: -рок] stamp; mark; counter; make; brand, trademark; **~и́за** *f* [5] awning; **~си́стский** [16] Marxist, Marxian.
ма́рля *f* [6] gauze.
мармела́д *m* [1] fruit candy (*or* drops).
март *m* [1], **~овский** [16] March.

мар|ты́шка *f* [5; *g/pl.*: -шек] marmoset; '♀фа Martha.
марш *m* [1], **~ирова́ть** [7] march; **~ру́т** *m* [1] route.
ма́ск|а *f* [5; *g/pl.*: -сок] mask; **~ара́д** *m* [1] (*a.* бал-~ара́д) masked ball, masquerade; **~ирова́ть** [7], ⟨за-⟩, **~иро́вка** *f* [5; *g/pl.*: -вок] mask; disguise, camouflage.
ма́сл|еница *f* [5] (last week of) carnival; F feast; **~ёнка** *f* [5; *g/pl.*: -нок] butter dish; lubricator; **~еный** [14] *s.* ~яный; **~и́на** *f* [5] olive; **~ичный** [14] olive....; oil ...; **~о** *n* [9; *pl.*: -сла́, -сел, -сла́м] (*a.* коро́вье, сли́вочное ~о) butter; (*a.* расти́тельное ~о) oil; как по ~у *fig.* (*go*) on wheels; **~обо́йка** *f* [5; *g/pl.*: -о́ек] churn; oil mill; **~яный** [14] oil(y); butter(y); greasy, unctuous.
ма́сс|а *f* [5] mass; bulk; multitude; **~а́ж** *m* [1], **~и́ровать** [7] (*pt. a. pf.*) massage; **~и́в** *m* [1] massif; **~и́вный** [14; -вен, -вна] massive; **~овый** [14] mass...
ма́стер *m* [1; *pl.*: -pá, *etc. e.*] master; foreman; craftsman; expert; ~ на все ру́ки jack-of-all-trades; **~и́ть** F [13], ⟨с-⟩ work; make; **~ска́я** *f* [16] workshop; atelier, studio; **~ско́й** [16] masterly (*adv.* ~ски́); **~ство́** *n* [9] mastery, skill; trade, handicraft.
масти́тый [14 *sh.*] venerable.
масть *f* [8; *from g/pl. e.*] colo(u)r; suit.
масшта́б *m* [1] scale (on в П); *fig.* scope; caliber (*Brt.* -bre); repute; standard.
мат *m* [1] mat; (check)mate.
Матве́й *m* [6] Matthew.
матема́ти|к *m* [1] mathematician; **~ка** *f* [5] mathematics; **∠ческий** [16] mathematical.
материа́л *m* [1] material; **~и́зм** *m* [1] materialism; **~и́ст** *m* [1] materialist; **~исти́ческий** [16] materialistic; **~ьный** [14; -лен, -льна] material; economic; financial.
матери́к *m* [1 *e.*] continent.
матери́|нский [16] mother('s), motherly, maternal; **~нство** *n* [9] maternity; **'~я** *f* [7] matter; fabric, material; stuff.
ма́тка *f* [5; *g/pl.*: -ток] *zo.* female; queen (*bee*); *anat.* uterus.
ма́товый [14] dull, dim, mat.
матра́|с, ~ц *m* [1] mattress.
ма́трица *f* [5] *typ.* matrix; stencil.
матро́с *m* [1] sailor.
матч *m* [1] match (*sport*).
мать *f* [ма́тери, *etc.* = 8; *pl.*: ма́тери, -ре́й, *etc. e.*] mother.
мах *m* [1] stroke, flap; с (одного́) ∠у at one stroke *or* stretch; at once; дать ∠у miss one's mark, make a blunder; **~а́ть** [3, F 1], *once* ⟨~ну́ть⟩ [20] (T) wave; wag; strike, flap; *pf.* F jump, go; ~ну́ть руко́й на (B) give up; **~ови́к** *m* [1 *e.*], **~ово́й** [14]: ~ово́е колесо́ *n* flywheel.
махо́рка *f* [5] (poor) tobacco.
ма́чеха *f* [5] stepmother.
ма́чта *f* [5] mast.
Ма́ш([ень]к)а [5] *dim. of* Мари́я.
маши́н|а *f* [5] machine; engine; F car, bike, *etc.*; **~а́льный** [14; -лен, -льна] mechanical, perfunctory; **~и́ст** *m* [1] machinist; 🚂 engineer, *Brt.* engine driver; **~и́стка** *f* [5; *g/pl.*: -ток] (girl) typist; **~ка** *f* [5; *g/pl.*: -нок] (small) machine; typewriter; clipper (под ~ку cropped); **~ный** [14] machine..., engine...; *cf.* МТС; **~опись** *f* [8] typewriting; **~острое́ние** *n* [7] mechanical engineering.
мая́к *m* [1 *e.*] lighthouse.
ма́я|тник *m* [1] pendulum; **~ться** P [27] drudge; **∠чить** F [16] loom.
МВД *abbr.*: Министе́рство вну́тренних дел (*s.* министе́рство).
мгл|а *f* [5] darkness; mist, haze; **~и́стый** [14 *sh.*] hazy, misty.
мгнове́н|ие *n* [12] moment; instant, twinkling; **~ный** [14; -е́нен, -е́нна] momentary, instantaneous.
ме́б|ель *f* [8] furniture; **~лирова́ть** [7] (*im*)*pf.*, об-› furnish (with T); **~лиро́вка** *f* [5] furnishing(s).
мёд *m* [1; *part. g.*: мёду; в меду́; *pl. e.*] honey; mead.
меда́ль *f* [8] medal; **~о́н** *m* [1] locket.
медве́|дица *f* [5] she-bear; *astr.* ♀дица Bear; **~дь** *m* [4] bear (F *a. fig.*); **~жий** [18] bear('s, -skin); bad (*service*); **~жо́нок** *m* [2] bear cub.
ме́ди|к *m* [1] medical man (F student); **~ка́менты** *m/pl.* [1] medicaments, medical supplies; **~ци́на** *f* [5] medicine; **~ци́нский** [16] medical; medicinal.
ме́дл|енный [14 *sh.*] slow; **~и́тельный** [14; -лен, -льна] sluggish, slow, indolent; **~ить** [14], ⟨про-⟩ delay, linger, be slow *or* tardy, hesitate.
ме́дный [14] copper(y); brazen.
медо́вый [14] honey(ed).
мед|осмо́тр *m* [1] medical examination; **~пу́нкт** *m* [1] first-aid post; **~сестра́** *f* [5; *pl. st.*: -сёстры, -сестёр, -сёстрам] nurse.
медь *f* [8] copper; жёлтая ~ brass.
меж *s.* ∠ду; **~а́** *f* [5; *pl.*: ме́жи, меж, межа́м] border; balk; **~доме́тие** *n* [12] *gr.* interjection; **~доусо́бный** [14] internal, civil (*war, etc.*).
ме́жду (T; *a.* P *pl.* †) between; among(st); ~ тем meanwhile, (in the) meantime; ~ тем как whereas, while; **~горо́дный** [14] *teleph.* long-distance..., *Brt.* trunk... (*e. g. exchange, su. f*); interurban; **~наро́дный** [14] international; **~ца́рствие** *n* [12] interregnum.
межплане́тный [14] interplanetary.

Ме́ксик|а *f* [5] Mexico; **♀а́нец** *m* [1; -нца], **♀а́нка** *f* [5; *g/pl.*: -нок], **♀а́нский** [16] Mexican.
мел *m* [1; в -у́] chalk; whitewash.
меланхо́л|ик *m* [1] melancholiac; **~и́ческий** [16], **~и́чный** [14; -чен, -чна] melancholy, melancholic; **~ия** *f* [7] melancholy.
меле́ть [8], ‹об-› (grow) shallow.
ме́лк|ий [16; -лок, -лка́, -о; *comp.*: ме́льче] small, little; petty; fine, shallow; flat (*plate*); ~ий дождь *m* drizzle; **~ово́дный** [14; -ден, -дна] shallow; **~ость** *f* [8], F **~ота́** *f* [8] shallowness; ~ота́ *a.* = ме́лочь *coll.*
мелоди́|ческий [16] melodic; melodious; **~чный** [14; -чен, -чна] melodious; **'~я** *f* [7] melody.
ме́лоч|ность *f* [8] pettiness, paltriness; **~ный** & **~но́й** [14; -чен, -чна] petty, paltry; **~ь** *f* [8; *from g/pl. e.*] trifle; trinket; *coll.*small fry; (small) change; *pl.* details, particulars.
мел|ь *f* [8] shoal, sandbank; на **~и́** aground; F in a fix.
мельк|а́ть [1], ‹~ну́ть› [20] flash; gleam; flit; fly (past); loom; turn up; **∠ом** in passing.
ме́льни|к *m* [1] miller; **~ца** *f* [5] mill.
мельч|а́ть [1], ‹из-› become (**~и́ть** [16 *e.*; -чу́, чи́шь] make) small(er) *or* shallow(er).
мелюзга́ F *f* [5] *s.* ме́лочь *coll.*
мемуа́ры *m/pl.* [1] memoirs.
ме́на *f* [5] exchange; barter.
ме́нее less; ~ всего́ least of all; тем не ~ nevertheless.
менов́ой [14] exchange...; *cf.* ме́на.
ме́ньш|е less; smaller; *s. a.* ме́нее; **~еви́к** *m* [1 *e.*] Menshevik; **~ий** [17] smaller, lesser; smallest, least; F (= † **~о́й**) youngest; **~инство́** *n* [9] minority.
меню́ *n* [*indecl.*] menu, bill of fare.
меня́ть [28], ‹по-, об-› exchange, barter (for на В); change (*cf.* пере~); **-ся** *v/i.* (s. th. with Т/сТ).
ме́р|а *f* [5] measure; degree; way; по ~е (Р) *or* того́ как according as, to (*a.* в ~у Р); as far as; while the ..., the ... (+ *comp.*); по кра́йней (ме́ньшей) ~е at least.
мере́щиться F [16], ‹по-› (Д) seem (*to hear, etc.*); appear; loom.
мерз|а́вец F *m* [1; -вца] rascal; **∠кий** [16; -зок, -зка́, -о] vile, odious.
мёрз|лый [14] frozen; **~нуть** [21], ‹за-› freeze; be cold, numb.
ме́рзость *f* [8] meanness; nasty thing.
мери́ло *n* [9] standard; criterion.
ме́рин *m* [1] gelding.
ме́р|ить [13], ‹с-› measure; ‹при-, по-› F try on; **~иться**, ‹по-› cope, try conclusions with (с Т); **~ка** *f* [5; *g/pl.*: -рок] measure(s) (to по Д).
ме́ркнуть [21], ‹по-› fade, darken.
мерлу́шка *f* [5; *g/pl.*: -шек] astrakhan.
ме́р|ный [14; -рен, -рна] measured; **~оприя́тие** *n* [12] measure, action.
ме́ртв|енный [14 *sh.*] deadly (pale); **~е́ть** [8], ‹о-› deaden; grow *or* turn numb (pale, desolate); **~е́ц** *m* [1 *e.*] corpse; **~е́цкая** F *f* [14] mortuary.
мёртв|ый [14; мёртв, мертва́, мёртво; *fig.*: мертво́, мертвы́] dead; **~ый** час *m* after-dinner rest; **~ая** то́чка *f* ⊕ dead center; *fig.* deadlock (at на П).
мерца́|ние *n* [12], **~ть** [1] twinkle.
меси́ть [15], ‹за-, с-› knead.
мести́ [25 -т-: мету́, метёшь; мётший], ‹под-› sweep.
ме́стн|ость *f* [8] region, district, locality, place; **~ый** [14] local; ~ый жи́тель *m* native.
ме́ст|о *n* [9; *pl. e.*] place, spot; seat; F job, post; passage; package; *pl. a.* = ~ность; о́бщее (*or* изби́тое) ~о commonplace; (заде́ть за) больно́е ~о tender spot (touch on the raw); (не) к ~у in (out of) place; не на ~е in the wrong place; ~а́ми in (some) places, here & there; **~ожи́тельство** *n* [9] residence; **~оиме́ние** *n* [12] *gr.* pronoun; **~онахожде́ние**, **~оположе́ние** *n* [12] location, position; **~опребыва́ние** *n* [12] whereabouts; residence; **~орожде́ние** *n* [12] deposit, field.
месть *f* [8] revenge.
ме́ся|ц *m* [1] month; moon; в ~ц a month, per month; **~чный** [14] month's; monthly; moon...
мета́лл *m* [1] metal; **~и́ст** *m* [1] metalworker; **~и́ческий** [16] metal(lic); **~у́ргия** *f* [7] metallurgy.
мет|а́тельный [14] missile; **~а́ть** [3], *once* ‹~ну́ть› [20] throw; bring forth; keep (*bank*); baste; ~а́ть икру́ spawn; **-ся** toss, jerk; rush about.
мете́л|ица *f* [5], **~ь** [8] snowstorm.
метеоро́лог *m* [1] meteorologist; **~и́ческий** [16] meteorological; **∠ия** *f* [7] meteorology.
ме́т|ить [15], ‹по-› mark; (в, на В) aim, drive at, mean; **~ка** [5; *g/pl.*: -ток] mark(ing); **~кий** [16; -ток, -тка́, -о] well-aimed; good (*shot*); keen, accurate, steady; pointed; neat; ready(-witted).
мет|ла́ *f* [5; *pl. st.*: мётлы, мётел; мётлам] broom; **~ну́ть** *s.* мета́ть.
ме́тод *m* [1] method; **~и́ческий** [16] methodic(al), systematic(al).
метр *m* [1] meter, *Brt.* metre.
ме́трика *f* [5] certificate of birth; metrics.
метро́ *n* [*ind.*], **~полите́н** (-'tɛn) *m* [1] subway, *Brt.* tube, underground.
мех *m* [1] **1.** [*pl. e.*] (*often pl.*) bellows *pl.*; **2.** [*pl.*: -ха́, *etc.*, *e.*] fur; (wine)skin; на ~у́ fur-lined.
механ|изи́ровать [7] (*im*)*pf.* mechanize; **~и́зм** *m* [1] mechanism; **∠ик**

m [1] mechanic(ian); ⁓ика *f* [5] mechanics; ⁓и́ческий [16] mechanical propelling (*pencil*).
мехов|о́й [14] fur...; **⁓щи́к** *m* [1 *e.*] furrier.
меч *m* [1 *e.*] sword.
мече́ть *f* [8] mosque.
мечта́ *f* [5] dream, daydream, reverie; **⁓ние** *n* [12] **1.** = ⁓; **2.** dreaming; **⁓тель** *m* [4] (day)dreamer; **⁓тельный** [14; -лен, -льна] dreamy; **⁓ть** [1] dream (of о П).
меша́|ть [1], ⟨раз-⟩ stir; ⟨с-, пере-⟩ mix, mingle; † confuse; ⟨по-⟩ (Д) disturb; hinder, impede, prevent; вам не ⁓ет (⁓ло бы) you'd better; **-ся** meddle, interfere (with в В); не ⁓йтесь не в своё де́ло! mind your own business!
ме́шк|ать F [1], ⟨про-⟩ = ме́длить; **⁓ова́тый** [14 *sh.*] baggy; clumry.
мешо́к *m* [1; -шка́] sack, bag.
мещан|и́н *m* [1; *pl.*: -а́не, -а́н], **⁓ский** [16] (petty) bourgeois, Philistine; **⁓ство** *n* [9] petty bourgeoisie, lower-middle class; Philistinism, Babbittry.
миг *m* [1] moment, instant; **⁓ом** F in a trice (flash); **⁓а́ть** [1], *once* ⟨⁓ну́ть⟩ [20] blink, wink; twinkle.
мигре́нь *f* [8] sick headache.
мизе́рный [14; -рен, -рна] paltry.
мизи́нец *m* [1; -нца] little finger.
ми́ленький F [16] lovely; dear; darling.
милици|оне́р *m* [1] militiaman; policeman (*Sov.*); **'⁓я** *f* [7] militia; police (*Sov.*).
милли|а́рд *m* [1] billion, *Brt.* milliard; **⁓ме́тр** *m* [1] millimeter (*Brt.* -tre); **⁓о́н** *m* [1] million.
ми́ловать [7] pardon; spare.
мило|ви́дный [14; -ден, -дна] lovely, sweet; **⁓се́рдие** *n* [12] charity, mercy; **⁓се́рдный** [14; -ден, -дна] charitable, merciful; **'⁓стивый** [14 *sh.*] gracious, kind; **'⁓стыня** *f* [6] alms; **'⁓сть** *f* [8] mercy; favo(u)r; pardon, ⚔ quarter; kindness; '⁓сти про́сим! welcome!; *iron.* скажи́(те) на '⁓сть just imagine.
ми́л|ый [14; мил, -а́, -о] nice, lovely, sweet; (my) dear, darling.
ми́ля *f* [6] mile.
ми́мо (Р) past, by; beside (*mark*); бить ⁓ miss; **⁓лётный** [14; -тен, -тна] fleeting, passing; **⁓хо́дом** in passing; incidentally.
ми́на *f* [5] ⚔, ⚒ mine; look, air.
минда́|лина *f* [5] almond; *anat.* tonsil; **⁓ль** *m* [4 *e.*] almond(s); **⁓льничать** F [1] spoon; trifle.
минерало́гия *f* [7] mineralogy.
миниатю́рный [14; -рен, -рна] miniature...; *fig.* tiny, diminutive.
минист|е́рство *n* [9] ministry; ⁓е́рство иностра́нных (вну́тренних) дел Ministry of Foreign (Internal) Affairs (*U.S.S.R.*), State Department (Dept. of the Interior) (*U.S.*), Foreign (Home) Office (*Brt.*); **⁓р** *m* [1] minister, secretary.
мин|ова́ть [7] (*im*)*pf.*, ⟨⁓у́ть⟩ [20] pass; leave out *or* aside, not enter into; (Р) escape; (Д) ⁓уло *s.* испо́лниться; ⁓у́вший, ⁓у́вшее *su.* past.
миноно́сец *m* [1; -сца] torpedo boat; эска́дренный ⁓ destroyer.
ми́нус *m* [1] minus; defect.
мину́т|а *f* [5] minute; moment, instant (at в В; for на В); сию ⁓у at once, immediately; at this moment; с ⁓ы на ⁓у (at) any moment; *cf.* пя́тый & пять; **⁓ный** [14] minute('s); moment('s), momentary; **⁓ь** *s.* минова́ть.
мир *m* [1] **1.** peace; **2.** [*pl. e.*] world, universe; planet; † (peasants') community (meeting); ⁓ во всём ⁓е world peace; ходи́ть (пусти́ть) по́ ⁓у go begging (bring to beggary).
мир|и́ть [13], ⟨по-, при-⟩ reconcile (to с Т); **-ся** make it up, be(come) reconciled; ⟨при-⟩ resign o.s. to; put up with; **⁓ный** [14; -рен, -рна] peace... peaceful.
мировоззре́ние *n* [12] Weltanschauung, world view; ideology.
мирово́й [14] world('s), world-wide, universal; peaceful, peaceable, of peace; F *su. f* arrangement.
миро|люби́вый [14 *sh.*] peaceful; peace loving; **⁓созерца́ние** *n* [12] world view, outlook.
мирско́й [16] worldly; common.
ми́ска *f* [5; *g*/*pl.*: -сок] dish, tureen; bowl.
мисси|оне́р *m* [1] missionary; **'⁓я** *f* [7] mission; legation.
ми́стика *f* [5] mysticism.
Ми́тя *m* [6] *dim. of* Дми́трий.
миф *m* [1] myth; **⁓и́ческий** [16] mythic(al); **⁓оло́гия** *f* [7] mythology.
Ми|ха́ил *m* [1] Michael; **⁓ша** *m* [5] (*dim. of* ⁓хаил) Mike.
мише́нь *f* [8] target.
мишура́ *f* [5] tinsel, spangle.
младе́н|ец *m* [1; -нца] infant, baby; **⁓чество** *n* [9] infancy.
мла́дший [17] younger, youngest; junior.
млекопита́ющее *n* [17] mammal.
млеть [8] die, faint, sink, droop.
мле́чный [14] milky (*a.* ♀, *ast.*).
мне́ние *n* [12] opinion (in по Д).
мни́|мый [14 *sh.*, *no m*] imaginary; supposed, pretended, would-be, sham; **⁓тельный** [14; -лен, -льна] suspicious; hypochondriac(al).
мно́гие *pl.* [16] many (people, *su.*).
мно́го (Р) much, many; a lot (*or* plenty) of; more; ⁓-⁓ at (the) most; **⁓ва́то** F rather much (many); **⁓во́дный** [14; -ден, -дна] abounding in water, deep; **⁓гра́нный** [14; -а́нен, -а́нна] many-sided;

~жёнство *n* [9] polygamy; **~значи́тельный** [14; -лен, -льна] significant; **~зна́чный** [14; -чен, -чна] of many places (♧) *or* meanings; **~кра́тный** [14; -тен, -тна] repeated, frequent(ative *gr.*); ♧ multiple; **~ле́тний** [15] longstanding, of many years; long-lived; long-term ...; ⚘ perennial; **~лю́дный** [14; -ден, -дна] crowded; populous; mass ...; **~обеща́ющий** [17] (very) promising; **~обра́зный** [14; -зен, -зна] varied, manifold; **~речи́вый** [14 *sh.*], **~сло́вный** [14; -вен, -вна] talkative; wordy; **~сторо́нний** [15; -о́нен, -о́ння] many-sided; **~страда́льный** [14; -лен, -льна] long-suffering; **~то́чие** *n* [12] dots *pl.*; **~уважа́емый** [14] dear (*address*); **~цве́тный** [14; -тен, -тна] multicolo(u)red; **~чи́сленный** [14 *sh.*] numerous; **~эта́жный** [14] many-storied (*Brt.*-reyed); **~язы́чный** [14; -чен, -чна] polyglot.
мно́ж|ественный [14 *sh.*] plural; **~ество** *n* [9] multitude; **~имое** *n* [14] multiplicand; **~итель** *m* [4] multiplier; **~ить**, ⟨по-⟩ *s.* умножа́ть.
мобилизова́ть [7] (*im*)*pf.* mobilize.
моги́л|а *f* [5] grave; **~ьный** [14] tomb...; **~ьщик** *m* [1] grave digger.
могу́|чий [17 *sh.*], **~щественный** [14 *sh.*] mighty, powerful; **~щество** *n* [9] might.
мо́д|а *f* [5] fashion, vogue; **~е́ль** (-ˈdɛl) *f* [8] model; ⊕ mo(u)ld; **~ернизи́ровать** (-dɛr-) [7] (*im*)*pf.* modernize; **~и́стка** *f* [5; *g*/*pl.*: -ток] milliner; **~ифици́ровать** [7] (*im*-)*pf.* modify; **~ный** [14; -ден, -дна́, -о] fashionable, stylish; [*no sh.*] fashion...
мо́ж|ет быть perhaps, maybe; **~но** (мне, *etc.*) one (I, *etc.*) can *or* may; it is possible; *cf.* как.
моза́ика *f* [5] mosaic.
мозг *m* [1; -а (-у); в -у́; *pl. e.*] brain; marrow; (*spinal*) cord; **~ово́й** [14] cerebral.
мозо́|листый [14 *sh.*] horny, callous; **~лить** [13]: ~лить глаза́ (Д) F be an eyesore to; **~ль** *f* [8] callosity; corn.
мо|й *m*, **~я́** *f*, **~ё** *n*, **~и́** *pl.* [24] my; mine; *pl. su.* F my folks; *s.* ваш.
мо́кко *m* [*ind.*] mocha.
мо́к|нуть [21], ⟨про-⟩ become wet; soak; **~ро́та**[1] *f* [5] phlegm; **~рота́**[2] F *f* [5] wet(ness), humidity; **~рый** [14; мокр, -а́, -о] wet; moist.
мол *m* [1] jetty, mole.
молв|а́ *f* [5] rumo(u)r; talk; **∠ить** † ⁝ [14] (*im*)*pf.*, ⟨про-⟩ say, utter.
молдава́н|ин *m* [1; *pl.*: -ва́не, -а́н], **~ка** *f* [5; *g*/*pl.*: -нок] Moldavian.
моле́бен *m* [1; -бна] thanksgiving (service), Te Deum.
моле́кул|а *f* [5] molecule; **~я́рный** [14] molecular.
моли́т|ва *f* [5] prayer; **~венник** *m* [1] prayer book; **~ь** [13; молю́, мо́лишь] (о П) implore (s. th.), entreat, beseech (for); **~ься**, ⟨по-⟩ pray (to Д; for о П).
молни|ено́сный [14; -сен, -сна] flash-like; blazing; thunder (*cloud*); violent; ⚔ blitz...; **ˈ~я** *f* [7] lightning; flash; zipper, zip fastener.
молод|ёжь *f* [8] youth, young people *pl.*; **~е́ть** [8], ⟨по-⟩ grow (look) younger; **~е́ц** F *m* [1; -дца́] fine fellow, brick; well done!; **~е́цкий** F [16] brave, valiant; smart; **~и́ть** [15 *e.*; -ложу́, -лоди́шь] rejuvenate; **~ня́к** *m* [1 *e.*] offspring; underwood; saplings *pl.*; **~ожёны** *m*/*pl.* [1] newly wedded couple; **~о́й** [14; мо́лод, -а́, -о; *comp.*: моло́же] young; new; *pl. a.* = ~ожёны; **ˈ~ость** *f* [8] youth, adolescence; **~цева́тый** [14 *sh.*] smart.
моложа́вый [14 *sh.*] youthful, young-looking.
моло́к|и *f*/*pl.* [5] milt; **~о́** *n* [9] milk; **~осо́с** F *m* [1] greenhorn.
мо́лот *m* [1] (large) hammer; **~и́лка** *f* [5; *g*/*pl.*: -лок] threshing machine; **~и́ть** [15], ⟨с-⟩ thresh; **~о́к** *m* [1; -тка́] hammer; с ~ка́ by auction; **∠ь** [17; мелю́, ме́лешь; меля́], ⟨пере-, с-⟩ grind; P *impf.* talk; **~ьба́** *f* [5] threshing (time).
моло́чн|ая *f* [14] dairy, creamery; **~ик** *m* [1] milk jug; F milkman; **~ый** [14] milk...; dairy...
мо́лча silently, tacitly; **~ли́вый** [14 *sh.*] taciturn; **∠ние** *n* [12] silence; **∠ть** [4 *e.*; мо́лча], be (*or* keep) silent; (за)молчи́! shut up!
моль *f* [8] moth; [*ind. adj.*] ♪ minor.
мольба́ *f* [5] entreaty; prayer.
моме́нт *m* [1] moment, instant (at в В); **~а́льный** [14] momentary, instantaneous; snap (*shot*).
мона́рхия *f* [7] monarchy.
мона|сты́рь *m* [4 *e.*] monastery, convent; **∠х** *m* [1] monk; **∠хиня** *f* [6] nun (*a.*, F, **∠шенка** *f* [5; *g*/*pl.*: -нок]); **∠шеский** [16] monastic; monk's.
монго́льский [16] Mongolian.
моне́т|а *f* [5] coin; money, cash; той же ~ой in a p.'s own coin; за чи́стую ~у in good faith; **~ный** [14] monetary; ~ный двор *m* mint.
моно|ло́г *m* [1] monologue; **~полизи́ровать** [7] (*im*)*pf.* monopolize; **~по́лия** *f* [7] monopoly; **~то́нный** [14; -то́нен, -то́нна] monotonous.
монт|а́ж *m* [1] assembling, assemblage; cutting (*film*); montage; **~ёр** *m* [1] assembler, mechanic(ian); electrician; **~и́ровать** [7], ⟨с-⟩ assemble, install; cut (*film*).
мора́ль *f* [8] morals *pl.*; morality; moral; F lecture, lecturing; **~ный**

[14; -лен, -льна] moral; ~ное состояние *n* morale.
морг|áть [1], ⟨~нýть⟩ [20] blink [(T).
мóрда *f* [5] muzzle, snout.
мóре *n* [10; *pl. e.*] sea; seaside (at на П); ~м by sea; зá ~м overseas; **~плáвание** *n* [12] navigation; **~плáватель** *m* [4] seafarer.
морж *m* [1 *e.*], **~óвый** [14] walrus.
мори́ть [13], ⟨за-, у-⟩ exterminate; ~ гóлодом starve; torment, exhaust.
моркóвь *f* [8] carrot(s).
морóженое *n* [14] ice cream.
морóз *m* [1] frost; **~ить** [15], ⟨за-⟩ freeze; **~ный** [14; -зен, -зна] frosty.
мороси́ть [15; -си́т] drizzle.
морóчить F [16] fool, beguile.
морск|óй [14] sea..., maritime; naval; nautical; seaside...; **~óй волк** *m* old salt; ~óй флот *m* navy.
мóрфий *m* [3] morphine, morphia.
морфолóгия *f* [7] morphology.
морщи́|на *f* [5] wrinkle; **~нистый** [14 *sh.*] wrinkled; **′~ть** [16], ⟨на-, с-⟩ wrinkle, frown (*v/i.* **-ся**); distort.
моря́к *m* [1 *e.*] seaman, sailor.
москатéльный [14] drug(gist's).
Моск|вá *f* [5] Moscow; **♀ви́ч** *m* [1 *e.*] **♀ви́чка** *f* [5; *g/pl.*: -чек] Moscower; **♀óвский** [16] Moscow...
моски́т *m* [1] mosquito.
мост *m* [1 & 1 *e.*; на -ý; *pl. e.*] bridge; **~и́ть** [15 *e.*; мощý, мости́шь; мощённый], ⟨вы́-⟩ pave; **~ки́** *m/pl.* [1 *e.*] planked footway, footbridge; **~овáя** *f* [14] pavement; **~овóй** [14] bridge...; **~овщи́к** *m* [1 *e.*] pavio(u)r.
мот *m* [1] spendthrift, prodigal.
мот|áть [1], ⟨на-, с-⟩ reel, wind; F ⟨по-⟩, *once* ⟨~нýть⟩ shake, wag; beckon, point; jerk; F ⟨про-⟩ squander, waste; **-ся** F *impf* dangle; P knock about.
моти́в *m* [1] motiv, motif; **~и́ровать** [7] (*im*)*pf.* motivate.
мотовствó *n* [9] extravagance.
мотóк *m* [1; -ткá] skein.
мотóр *m* [1] motor, engine; **~изовáть** [7] (*im*)*pf.* motorize.
мотоци́кл, ~éт *m* [1], motorcycle; **~и́ст** *m* [1] motorcyclist.
моты́га *f* [8] hoe, mattock.
мотылёк [1; -лькá] butterfly.
мох *m* [1; мха & мóха, во (на) мхý; *pl.*: мхи, мхов] moss.
мохнáтый [14 *sh.*] shaggy, hairy.
моховóй [14] mossy.
моч|á *f* [5] urine; **~áлка** *f* [5; *g/pl.*: -лок] bast whisp; **~евóй** [14]: ~евóй пузы́рь *m* (urinary) bladder; **~и́ть** [16], ⟨на-, за-⟩ wet, moisten; soak, steep (*v/i.* **-ся**; *a.* urinate); **∠ка** *f* [5; *g/pl.*: -чек] lobe (*of the ear*).
мочь[1] [26 г/ж: могý, мóжешь, мóгут; мог, -лá; могýщий], ⟨с-⟩ can, be able; may; я не могý не + *inf.* I can't help ...ing; не могý знать ... I don't know (,sir); не мóжет быть! that's impossible!
моч|ь[2] P *f* [8]: во всю ~ь, изо всей ∠и, что есть ∠и with all one's might; ∠и нет impossible, I, *etc.*, can't; awfully.
мошéнни|к *m* [1] swindler, cheat (-er); **~чать** [1], ⟨с-⟩ swindle; **~ческий** [16] fraudulent; **~чество** *n* [9] swindle. fraud.
мóшка *f* [5; *g/pl.*: -шек] midge.
мощёный [14] paved.
мóщи *f/pl.* [*gen.*: -щéй, *etc. e.*] relics.
мóщ|ность *f* [8] power; **~ный** [14; мóщен, -щнá, -о] powerful, mighty; **~ь** *f* [8] power, might; strength.
м. пр. *abbr.*: мéжду прóчим.
мрак *m* [1] dark(ness); gloom.
мракобéс *m* [1] obscurant; **~ие** *n* [12] obscurantism.
мрáмор *m* [1] marble.
мрачн|éть [8], ⟨по-⟩ darken; **∠ый** [14; -чен, -чнá, -о] dark; obscure; gloomy, somber (*Brt.*-bre).
мсти́|тель *m* [4] avenger; **~тельный** [14; -лен, -льна] revengeful; **~ть** [15], ⟨ото-⟩ revenge o.s., take revenge (on Д); (за В) avenge a p.
МТС (маши́нно-трáкторная стáнция) machine and tractor station.
мудр|ёный F [14; -ён, -енá; -енée] difficult, hard, intricate; fanciful; queer; ~ёного нет (it's) no wonder; **~éц** *m* [1 *e.*] sage; **~и́ть** F [13], ⟨на-, с-⟩ subtilize; quibble; trick; (над Т) bully; **∠ость** *f* [8] wisdom; зуб ∠ости wisdom tooth; F trick; **∠ствовать** F [7] *s.* ~и́ть; **∠ый** [14; мудр, -á, -о] wise, sage.
муж *m* **1.** [1; *pl.*: -жья́, -жéй, -жья́м] husband; **2.** † [1; *pl.*: -жи́, -жéй, -жáм] man; **~áть** [1], ⟨воз-⟩ mature, grow; **-ся** *impf.* take courage; **∠ественный** [14 *sh.*] courageous; manly; **∠ество** *n* [9] courage, spirit; **~и́к** † *m* [1 *e.*] peasant; P boor; man; **~и́цкий** [16], P **~и́чий** [18] peasant's, rustic; **~скóй** [16] male, (*a. gr.*) masculine; (gentle-) man('s); **~чи́на** *m* [5] man.
музéй *m* [3] museum.
мýзык|а *f* [5] music; P business; **~áльный** [14; -лен, -льна] musical; **~áнт** *m* [1] musician.
мýка[1] *f* [5] pain, torment, suffering, torture(s); F harassment.
мукá[2] *f* [5] flour; meal.
мул *m* [1] mule.
мýмия *f* [7] mummy.
мунди́р *m* [1] uniform; картóшка в ~е F potatoes in their jackets *or* skin.
мундштýк (-nʃ-) *m* [1 *e.*] cigarette holder; tip; mouthpiece.
муравá *f* [5] (young) grass; glaze.
мурав|éй *m* [3; -вья́; *pl.*: -вьи́, -вьёв] ant; **~éйник** *m* [1] ant hill; **~ьи́ный** [14] ant...
мурáшки: (от Р) ~ бéгают по спинé (у Р) F (s. th.) gives (a p.) the shivers.
мурлы́кать [3 & 1] purr; F hum.
мускáт *m* [1], **~ный** [14] nutmeg.

му́скул *m* [1] muscle; **~истый** [14 *sh.*], **~ьный** [14] muscular.
му́скус *m* [1] musk.
му́сор *m* [1] rubbish, refuse; **~ный** [14]: **~ный я́щик** *m* ash can, *Brt.* dust bin; **~щик** *m* [1] ashman.
муссо́н *m* [1] monsoon.
мусульма́н|ин *m* [1; *pl.*: -а́не, -а́н], **~ка** *f* [5; *g/pl.*: -нок] Moslem.
мут|и́ть [15; мучу́, му́ти́шь], ⟨вз-, по-⟩ trouble, muddle; fog; меня́ **~и́т** F I feel sick; **-ся** = **~не́ть** [8], ⟨по-⟩ grow turbid; blur; **∠ный** [14; -тен, -тна́, -o] muddy, (*a. fig.*) troubled (*waters*); dull; blurred; foggy; uneasy; **~о́вка** *f* [5; *g/pl.*: -вок] twirling stick; **~ь** *f* [8] dregs *pl.*; mud; blur; haze; dazzle.
му́фта *f* [5] muff; ⊕ socket, sleeve.
му́х|а *f* [5] fly; **~оло́вка** *f* [5; *g/pl.*: -вок] flycatcher; **~омо́р** *m* [1] toadstool.
муч|е́ние *n* [12] *s.* му́ка; **∠еник** *m* [1] martyr; **~и́тель** *m* [4] tormentor; **~и́тельный** [14; -лен, -льна] painful, agonizing; **∠ить** [16], P **∠ать** [1], ⟨за-, из-⟩ torment, torture; vex, worry; **-ся** agonize, suffer torments; toil; **~но́й** [14] flour(y), mealy.
му́шка *f* [5; *g/pl.*: -шек] midge; beauty spot; speck; (Spanish) fly; (fore)sight (*gun*).
муштр(о́вк)а́ ⚔ *f* [5] drill.
мча́ть(ся) [4], ⟨по-⟩ rush, whirl *or* speed (along).
мши́стый [14 *sh.*] mossy.
мще́ние *n* [12] vengeance.
мы [20] we; ~ с ним he and I.
мы́л|ить [13], ⟨на-⟩ soap; **~ить** го́лову (Д) F blow up, scold; **~о** *n* [9; *pl. e.*] soap; lather; **~оваре́ние** *n* [12] soap boiling; **~ьница** *f* [5] soap dish; **~ьный** [14] soap(y).
мыс *m* [1] cape.
мы́сл|енный [14] mental; **~имый** [14 *sh.*] conceivable; **~и́тель** *m* [4] thinker; **~ить** [13] think (of, about о П); imagine; **~ь** *f* [8] thought, idea (of о П); intention.
мыта́рство *n* [9] toil, drudgery.
мы́ть(ся) [22], ⟨по-, у-, вы́-⟩ wash.
мыча́ть [4 *e.*; -чу́, -чи́шь] moo, low; F mumble.
мышело́вка *f* [5; *g/pl.*: -вок] mouse trap.
мы́шечный [14] muscular.
мы́шка *f* [5; *g/pl.*: -шек] **1.** armpit; arm; **2.** *dim. of* мышь.
мышле́ние *n* [12] thougt, thinking
мы́шца *f* [5] muscle.
мышь *f* [8; *from g/pl. e.*] mouse.
мышья́к *m* [1 *e.*] arsenic.
мя́гк|ий (-xk-) [16; -гок, -гка́, -o; *comp.*: мя́гче] soft; smooth, sleek; tender; mild, gentle; lenient; easy (*chair*); **~ий ваго́н** 🚃 first-class coach *or* car(riage); **~осерде́чный** [14; -чен, -чна] soft-hearted; **~ость** *f* [8] softness; **~оте́лый** [14] chubby; *fig.* fladdy, spineless.
мягчи́|тельный (-xtʃ-) [14] lenitive; **~ть** [16; -чи́т] soften.
мяк|и́на *f* [5] chaff; **∠иш** *m* [1] crumb; **∠нуть** [21], ⟨на-, раз-⟩ become soft; **∠оть** *f* [8] flesh, pulp.
мя́млить P [13] mumble; dawdle.
мяс|и́стый [14 *sh.*] fleshy, pulpy; F fat, chubby; **~ни́к** *m* [1 *e.*] butcher; **~но́й** [14] meat...; butcher's; **∠о** *n* [9] meat; flesh, pulp; (*cannon*) fodder; **~oру́бка** *f* [5; *g/pl.*: -бок] mincing machine; *fig.* slaughter.
мя́та *f* [8] mint.
мяте́ж *m* [1 *e.*] rebellion, mutiny; **~ник** *m* [1] rebel; **~ный** [14] rebellious.
мять [мну, мнёшь; мя́тый], ⟨с-, по-, из-⟩ [сомну́; изомну́] (c)rumple, press; knead, wrinkle; trample; **-ся** F waver.
мяу́к|ать [1], *once* ⟨**~нуть**⟩ mew.
мяч *m* [1 *e.*] ball; **∠ик** [1] *dim. of* ~.

Н

на[1] **1.** (В): (*direction*) on, onto; to, toward(s); into, in; (*duration, value, purpose, etc.*) for; till; 𝔄 by; ~ что? what for?; **2.** (П): (*position*) on, upon; in, at; with; for; ~ ней ... she has ... on.
на́[2] F there, here (you are, *a.* ∠ тебе).
наба́в|ка F = надба́вка; **~ля́ть** [28], ⟨**~ить**⟩ [14] raise; add.
наба́т *m* [1] alarm bell, tocsin.
набе́|г *m* [1] incursion, raid; **~га́ть** [1], ⟨**~жа́ть**⟩ [4; -егу́, -ежи́шь, -егу́т; -еги́(те)!] run (against *or* on на В); cover; gather.
набекре́нь F aslant, cocked.
на́бело (*make*) a fair copy.
на́бережная *f* [14] quay, wharf.
наби|ва́ть [1], ⟨**∠ть**⟩ [-бью́, -бьёшь; *cf.* бить] stuff, fill; fix on (*a.* many, much); shoot; print (*calico*); **∠вка** *f* [5; *g/pl.*: -вок] stuffing, padding.
набира́ть [1], ⟨набра́ть⟩ [-беру́, -рёшь; *cf.* брать] gather; enlist, recruit; *teleph.* dial; *typ.* set; take (too many, much); gain (*speed, height*); be, have; **-ся** *a.*, (P), pluck *or* screw up; F catch; acquire.
наби́|тый [14 *sh.*] (Т) packed; P arrant (*fool*); битко́м **~тый** F crammed full; **~ть** *s.* **~ва́ть**.
наблюд|а́тель *m* [4] observer; **~а́тельный** [14; -лен, -льна] observant, alert; observation (*post*); **~а́ть** [1] (*v/t.* & за Т) observe; watch;

see after *or* to (it that); **~éние** *n* [12] observation; supervision.
нáбожный [14; -жен, -жна] pious, devout.
нáбок to *or* on one side.
наболéвший [16] sore; burning.
набóр *m* [1] enlistment, levy; enrol(l)ment; set; typesetting; taking; **~щик** *m* [1] typesetter, compositor.
набр|áсывать [1] **1.** ⟨~осáть⟩ [1] sketch, design, draft; throw (up); **2.** ⟨~óсить⟩ [15] throw over, on (на В); **-ся** fall (up)on.
набрáть *s.* набирáть.
набрести́ F [25] *pf.* come across (на В).
набрóсок *m* [1; -ска] sketch, draft.
набух|áть [1], ⟨ˊнуть⟩ [21] swell.
навáл|ивать [1], ⟨~и́ть⟩ [13; -алю́, -áлишь; -áленный] heap; load; **-ся** press; fall (up)on, go at.
навéд|ываться, ⟨~аться⟩ F [1] call on (к Д); inquire after, about (о П).
навéк, ~и forever, for good.
навéрн|о(е) probably; for certain, definitely; (*a.*, F, **~якá**) without fail.
навёрстывать, ⟨наверстáть⟩ [1] make up for.
навéрх up(ward[s]); upstairs; **~ý** above, on high; upstairs.
навéс *m* [1] awning; shed.
навеселé F tipsy, drunk.
навести́ *s.* наводи́ть.
навести́ть *s.* навещáть.
навéтренный [14] windward.
навéчно forever, for good.
наве|щáть[1], ⟨~сти́ть⟩[15*e.*; -ещý, -ести́шь; -ещённый] call on.
нáвзничь on one's back.
навзры́д: плáкать ~ sob.
навис|áть [1], ⟨ˊнуть⟩ [21] hang (over); impend; **ˊший** beetle (*brow*).
навле|кáть [1], ⟨ˊчь⟩ [26] incur.
наводи́ть [15], ⟨навести́⟩ [25] (на В) direct (to); point (at), turn (to); lead (to), bring on *or* about, cause, raise (*cf.* нагоня́ть); apply (*paint, etc.*); make; construct; ~ спрáвки inquire (after о П).
наводн|éние *n* [12] flood, inundation; **~я́ть** [28], ⟨~и́ть⟩ [13] flood, inundate.
наводя́щий [17] leading.
навóз *m* [1], **~ить** [15], ⟨у-⟩ dung, manure; **~ный** [14] dung...; **~ная** жи́жа *f* liquid manure.
нáволочка *f* [5; *g/pl.*: -чек] pillowcase.
навостри́ть [13] *pf.* prick up (*one's ears*).
навря́д (ли) F hardly, scarcely.
навсегдá forever; (*once*) for all.
навстрéчу toward(s); идти́ ~ (Д) go to meet; *fig.* meet halfway.
навы́ворот P topsy-turvy, inside out, wrongly; дéлать ши́ворот-~ put the cart before the horse.
нáвык *m* [1] experience, skill (in к Д, на В, в П); habit.
навы́кат(е) goggle (*eye[d]*).
навы́лет (*shot*) through.
навы́тяжку at attention.
навя́з|ывать [1], ⟨~áть⟩ [3] tie (to, on на В), fasten; knit; impose, obtrude ([up]on Д; *v/i.* **-ся**); **~чивый** [14 *sh.*] obtrusive; fixed.
нагáйка *f* [5; *g/pl.*: -гáек] whip.
нагáр *m* [1] snuff (*candle*).
наг|ибáть [1], ⟨~нýть⟩ [20] bend, bow, stoop (*v/i.* **-ся**).
нагишóм F naked, nude.
наглáзник *m* [1] blinder.
нагл|éц *m* [1 *e.*] impudent fellow; **ˊость** *f* [8] impudence, insolence; **ˊухо** tightly; **ˊый** [14; нагл, -á, -о] impudent, insolent, F cheeky.
нагляд|éться [11] *pf.* (на В) feast one's eyes (upon); не **~éться** never get tired of looking (at); **ˊный** [14; -ден, -дна] vivid, graphic; obvious; direct; object (*lesson*); visual (*aid*).
нагнáть *s.* нагоня́ть.
нагнетá|тельный [14] force; (*pump*); **~ть** [1], ⟨нагнести́⟩ [25 -т-] pump.
нагноéние *n* [12] suppuration.
нагнýть *s.* нагибáть.
нагов|áривать [1], ⟨~ори́ть⟩ [13] say, tell, talk ([too] much *or* many ...); F slander (a p. на В, о П); conjure; record; **~ори́ться** *pf.* talk one's fill; не **~ори́ться** never ge tired of talking.
нагóй [14; наг, -á, -о] nude, naked, bare.
нáгол|о clean(-*shaven*); **~ó** naked.
нáголову (*defeat*) totally.
нагон|я́й F *m* [3] blowup; **~я́ть** [28], ⟨нагнáть⟩ [-гоню́, -гóнишь; *cf.* гнать] overtake, catch up (with); make up (for); drive (together); F **~я́ть** страх, скýку, *etc.* (на В) frighten, bore, *etc.*
наготá *f* [5] nudity; bareness.
нагот|áвливать [1] [28], ⟨~óвить⟩ [14] prepare; lay in; **~óве** (at the) ready.
нагрáбить [14] *pf.* rob, plunder (a lot of).
награ́|да *f* [5] reward (as a в В), recompense; decoration; **~ждáть** [1], ⟨~ди́ть⟩ [15 *e.*; -ажý, -ади́шь; -аждённый] (Т) reward; decorate; *fig.* endow.
нагревáт|ельный [14] heating; **~ь** [1], *s.* греть.
нагромо|ждáть [1], ⟨~зди́ть⟩ [15 *e.*; -зжý, -зди́шь; -ождённый] pile up.
нагрýдник *m* [1] bib; plastron.
нагру|жáть [1], ⟨~зи́ть⟩ [15 & 15 *e.*; -ужý, -ýзишь; -ужённый] load (with Т); F *a.* burden, busy, assign (*work to*); **ˊзка** *f* [5; *g/pl.*: -зок] load(ing); F *a.* burden, job, assignment.
нагря́нуть [20] *pf.* appear, come (upon) suddenly, unawares; break out (*war*); take by surprise (на В).

над, ~о (Т) over, above; at; about; with.
нада́в|ливать [1], ⟨~и́ть⟩ [14] (*a.* на В) press; push; press out (much).
надба́в|ка *f* [5; *g/pl.:* -вок] raise, increase; extra charge; **~ля́ть** [28], ⟨~ить⟩ [14] F, *s.* набавля́ть.
надви|га́ть [1], ⟨∠нуть⟩ [20] push; pull; **-ся** approach, draw near; cover.
на́двое in two (parts *or* halves).
надгро́бный [14] tomb..., grave...
наде|ва́ть [1], ⟨∠ть⟩ [-е́ну, -е́нешь; -е́тый] put on.
наде́жд|а *f* [5] hope (of на В); подава́ть ~ы show promise; ²а *fem. name, cf.* Hope.
надёжный [14; -жен, -жна] reliable, dependable; firm; safe; sure.
наде́л ⚘ *m* [1] lot, plot, allotment.
наде́л|ать [1] *pf.* make; do, cause, inflict; **~я́ть** [28], ⟨~и́ть⟩ [13] allot (s. th. to Т/В); give; endow.
наде́ть *s.* надева́ть.
наде́яться [27] (на В) hope (for); [rely (on).]
надзе́мный [14] overground; 🚂 elevated, *Brt.* high-level...
надз|ира́тель *m* [4] supervisor; inspector; jailer; **~о́р** *m* [1] supervision; surveillance.
надл|а́мывать, ⟨~ома́ть⟩ [1] F, ⟨~оми́ть⟩ [14] crack, break; shatter.
надлежа́|ть [4; *impers.*] (Д) have to, be to be + *p. pt.*; **~щий** [17] appropriate, suitable: ~щим о́бразом properly, duly.
надло́м *m* [1] crack, fissure; *fig.* crisis; **~а́ть, ~и́ть** *s.* надла́мывать.
надме́нный [14; -е́нен, -е́нна] haughty.
на́до it is necessary (for Д); (Д) (one) must (*go, etc.*); need; want; так ему́ и ~ it serves him right; **~бность** *f* [8] need (of, for в П), necessity; affair, matter (in по Д).
надо|еда́ть [1], ⟨~е́сть⟩ [-е́м, -е́шь, *etc., s.* есть[1]] (Д/Т) tire; bother, molest; мне ~е́л ... I'm tired (of), fed up (with); **~е́дливый** [14 *sh.*] tiresome; troublesome, annoying.
надо́лго for (a) long (time).
надорва́ть *s.* надрыва́ть.
надпи́|сывать [1], ⟨~са́ть⟩ [3] superscribe; ✝ endorse; **′~сь** *f* [8] inscription; ✝ endorsement.
надре́з *m* [1] cut, incision; **~а́ть** & **~ывать** [1], ⟨~ать⟩ [3] cut, incise.
надруга́тельство *n* [9] outrage.
надры́в *m* [1] rent, tear; strain, burst; **~а́ть** [1], ⟨надорва́ть⟩ [-ву́, -вёшь; надорва́л, -а́, -о; -о́рванный] tear; shatter, break, undermine; injure; (over)strain (o. s. себя́, **-ся**; be[come] worn out, exhausted; labo[u]r); ~а́ть живо́тики, ~а́ться (со́ смеху) split one's sides (with laughing).
надсмо́тр *m* [1] supervision (of над, за Т); **~щик** *m* [1] supervisor.
надстр|а́ивать [1], ⟨~о́ить⟩ [13] overbuild; raise; **~о́йка** *f* [5; *g/pl.:* -ро́ек] superstructure.
наду|ва́ть [1], ⟨∠ть⟩ [18] inflate, swell; drift, blow; F dupe; ∠ть гу́бы pout; **-ся** *v/i.*; **~вно́й** [14] inflatable, air...; ∠ть *s.* ~ва́ть.
наду́м|анный [14] far-fetched, strained; **~ать** F [1] *pf.* think (of, out), devise; make up one's mind.
наду́тый [14] swollen; sulky.
На́дя *f* [6] *dim. of* Наде́жда.
наеда́ться [1], ⟨нае́сться⟩ [-е́мся, -е́шься, *etc., s.* есть[1]] eat one's fill.
наедине́ alone, in private; tête-à-tête.
нае́зд *m* [1] (~ом on) short *or* flying visit(s), run; **~ник** *m* [1] horseman, equestrian; (*horse*) trainer.
нае|зжа́ть [1], ⟨∠хать⟩ [5] (на В) run into, knock against; come across; F come (occasionally), call on (к Д); run (up, down to в В).
наём *m* [1; на́йма] hire; rent; **~ник** *m* [1] hireling, mercenary; **~ный** [14] hired, rent(ed); hackney, mercenary.
нае́|сться *s.* ~да́ться; **~хать** *s.* ~зжа́ть.
нажа́ть *s.* ~има́ть.
нажда́|к *m* [1 *e.*], **~чный** [14] emery.
нажи́|ва *f* [5] profit(s), gain(s); *a.* = ~вка; **~ва́ть** [1], ⟨~ть⟩ [-живу́, -вёшь; на́жил, -а́, -о; нажи́вший; на́житый (на́жит, -а́, -о)] earn, gain, profit(eer), amass; make (*a fortune*; *enemies*); get, catch; **~вка** *f* [5; *g/pl.:* -вок] bait.
нажи́м *m* [1] pressure; stress, strain; **~а́ть** [1], ⟨нажа́ть⟩ [-жму́, -жмёшь; -жа́тый] (*a.* на В) press, push (*a.,* F, *fig.* = urge, impel; influence); stress.
нажи́ть *s.* нажива́ть.
наза́втра F the next day; tomorrow.
наза́д back(ward[s]); ~! get back!; тому́ ~ ago; **~и́** F behind.
назва́|ние *n* [12] name; title; **~ть** *s.* называ́ть.
назе́мный [14] land..., ground...
на́земь F to the ground (*or* floor).
назида́|ние *n* [12] edification (for p.'s в В/Д); instruction; **~тельный** [14; -лен, -льна] edifying, instructive.
на́зло́ (Д) to (*or* for) spite (s. b.).
назнач|а́ть [1], ⟨∠ить⟩ [16] appoint (p. s. th. В/Т), designate; fix, settle; prescribe; destine; F assign; **~е́ние** *n* [12] appointment; assignment; prescription; destination.
назо́йливый [14 *sh.*] importunate.
назре|ва́ть [1], ⟨∠ть⟩ [8] ripen; swell; ⚕ gather; *fig.* mature; be imminent *or* impending.
назубо́к F by heart, thoroughly.
называ́|ть [1], ⟨назва́ть⟩ [-зову́, -зовёшь; -зва́л, -а́, -о; на́зван-

ный (на́зван, -а́, -о)] call, name; mention; ~ть себя́ introduce o. s.; F invite; ~ть ве́щи свои́ми имена́ми call a spade a spade; -ся call o. s., be called; как ~ется ...? what is (*or* do you call) ...?

наи... *in compds.* ... of all, very; ~бо́лее most, ...est of all.

наи́вн|ость *f* [12] naïveté; ~ый [14; -вен, -вна] naïve, ingenuous; unsophisticated.

наизна́нку inside out.

наизу́сть by heart.

наиме́нее least... of all.

наименова́ние *n* [12] name; title.

на́искос|ь, F ~о́к obliquely, aslant.

наи́тие *n* [12] inspiration; intuition.

найдёныш *m* [1] foundling.

наймит *m* [1] hireling, mercenary.

найти́ *s.* находи́ть.

нака́з *m* [1] order; mandate.

наказ|а́ние *n* [12] punishment (as a в В); penalty; F nuisance; ~у́емый [14 *sh.*] punishable; ~ы-ва́ть [1], ‹~а́ть› [3] punish; † order.

нака́л *m* [1] incandescence; ~ивать [1], ‹~и́ть› [13] incandesce; ~ённый incandescent, red-hot.

нак|а́лывать [1], ‹~оло́ть› [17] pin, fix; chop, break; prick; kill.

накану́не the day before; ~ (P) on the eve (of).

нак|а́пливать [1] & ~опля́ть [28], ‹~опи́ть› [14] accumulate, amass; collect, gather.

наки́|дка *f* [5; *g/pl.:* -док] cape, cloak; ~дывать [1] **1.** ‹~да́ть› [1] throw (up); **2.** ‹~нуть› [20] throw upon; F add; raise; -ся (на В) F fall (up)on.

на́кипь *f* [8] scum; scale, deposit.

наклад|на́я *f* [14] waybill; ~но́й [14] laid on; plated; false; † overhead; ~ывать & **налага́ть** [1], ‹наложи́ть› [16] (на В) lay (on), apply (to); put (on), set (to); impose; leave (*trace*); fill; pack, load.

накле́|ивать [1], ‹~ить› [13; -е́ю] glue *or* paste on; stick on, affix; ~йка *f* [5; *g/pl.:* -е́ек] label.

накло́н *m* [1] inclination; slope; ~е́ние *n* [12] *s.* ~; *gr.* mode, mood; ~и́ть *s.* ~я́ть; ~ный [14] inclined, slanting; ~я́ть [28], ‹~и́ть› [13; -оню́, -о́нишь; -онённый] bend, tilt; bow, stoop; † incline; -ся *v/i.*

накова́льня *f* [6; *g/pl.:* -лен] anvil.

нако́жный [14] skin..., cutaneous.

наколо́ть *s.* нака́лывать.

наконе́|ц (~ц-то oh) at last, finally; at length; ~чник *m* [1] ferrule; tip, point.

накоп|ле́ние *n* [12] accumulation; ⚔ concentration; ~ля́ть, ~и́ть *s.* нака́пливать.

накра|хма́ленный [14] starched; ~шенный [14] painted, rouged.

на́крепко fast, tightly, firmly.

на́крест crosswise.

накры|ва́ть [1], ‹~ть› [22] cover; (*a.* на) lay (*the table*); serve (*meal*); ⚔ hit; P catch, trap; dupe.

накуп|а́ть [1], ‹~и́ть› [14] (P) buy.

наку́р|ивать [1], ‹~и́ть› [13; -урю́, -у́ришь; -у́ренный] (fill with) smoke *or* perfume, scent.

налага́ть *s.* накла́дывать.

нала́|живать [1], ‹~дить› [15] put right *or* in order, get straight, fix; set going; establish; tune.

нале́во to *or* on the left; *s.* напра́во.

нале|га́ть [1], ‹~чь› [26 г/ж: -ля́гу, -ля́жешь, -ля́гут; -лёг, -легла́; -ля́г(те)!] (на В) press (against, down), *fig.* opress; apply o. s. (to); lie; sink, cover; F stress.

налегке́ F (-хк-) with light *or* no baggage (luggage); lightly dressed.

налёт *m* [1] flight; blast; ⚔, ✈ raid, attack; ⚕ fur; (*a. fig.*) touch; с ~а on the wing, with a swoop; *cf.* лёт; ~а́ть [1], ‹~е́ть› [11] (на В) fly (at, [*a.* knock, strike] against); swoop down; raid, attack; fall ([up]on); rush, squall; ~чик *m* [1] bandit.

нале́чь *s.* налега́ть.

нали|ва́ть [1], ‹~ть› [-лью́, -льёшь; -ле́й(те)!; на́ли́л, -а́, -о; -ли́вший; на́ли́тый (на́ли́т, -а́, -о)] pour (out); fill; ripen; *p. pt. p.* (*a.* ~то́й) ripe; plump; sappy; (-ся *v/i.*; *a.* swell; ~ться кро́вью become bloodshot); ~вка *f* [5; *g/pl.:* -вок] (fruit) liqueur; ~вно́й [14] *s.* ~ва́ть *p. pt. p.*; ~вно́е су́дно *n* tanker; ~м *m* [1] burbot.

налито́й, нали́ть *s.* налива́ть.

налицо́ present, on hand.

нали́ч|ие *n* [12] presence; ~ность *f* [8] stock; cash; *a.* = ~ие; в ~ности = налицо́; ~ный [14] (*a. pl., su.*) cash (*a.* down T), ready (*money*); present, on hand; за ~ные (against) cash (down).

нало́г *m* [1] tax, duty, levy; ~оплате́льщик *m* [1] taxpayer.

нало́ж|енный [14]: ~енным платежо́м cash (*or* collect) on delivery; ~и́ть *s.* накла́дывать.

налюбова́ться [7] *pf.* (T) admire to one's heart's content; не ~ never get tired of admiring (o. s. собо́й).

нама́|зывать [1] *s.* ма́зать; ~тывать [1] *s* мота́ть.

наме́дни P recently, the other day.

нам|ёк *m* [1] (на В) allusion (to), hint (at); ~ека́ть [1], ‹~екну́ть› [20] (на В) allude (to), hint (at).

намер|ева́ться [1] intend = (я I, *etc.*) ~ен(а); ~ение *n* [12] intention, design, purpose (on с T); ~енный [14] intentional, deliberate.

наме́стник *m* [1] governor.

намета́ть *s.* намётывать.

наме́тить *s.* намеча́ть.

нам|ётка *f* [5; *g/pl.:* -ток], ~ёты-

вать [1], ⟨~етáть⟩ [3] draft, plan; tack; *s. a.* метáть.
наме|чáть [1], ⟨~тить⟩ [15] mark, trace; design, plan; select; nominate.
намнóго much, (by) far.
намок|áть [1], ⟨~нуть⟩ [21] get wet.
намóрдник *m* [1] muzzle.
нанести́ *s.* наноси́ть.
нани́з|ывать [1], ⟨~áть⟩ [3] string.
нан|имáть [1], ⟨~я́ть⟩ [наймý, -мёшь; нáнял, -á, -о; -я́вший; нáнятый (нáнят, -á, -о)] hire, engage, rent; F lodge; **-ся** *a.* hire out (as в И*pl. or* Т).
нáново anew, (over) again.
нанóс *m* [1] alluvium; **~и́ть** [15], ⟨нанести́⟩ [24 -с-: -несý, -сёшь; -нёс, -неслá] bring (much, many); carry, waft, deposit, wash ashore; heap; enter, mark; lay on, apply; inflict (on Д), cause; pay (*visit*); deal (*blow*); **~ный** [14] alluvial; *fig.* casual, assumed.
наня́ть(ся) *s.* нанимáть(ся).
наоборóт the other way round, vice versa, conversely; on the contrary.
наобýм F at random, haphazardly.
наотрéз bluntly, categorically.
напа|дáть [1], ⟨~сть⟩ [25; *pt. st.:* -пáл, -а; -пáвший] (на В) attack, fall (up)on; come across *or* upon; hit on; overcome; **~дáющий** *m* [17] assailant; (*sport*) forward; **~дéние** *n* [12] attack; aggression; forwards *pl.*; **~дки** *f/pl.* [5; *gen.:* -док] accusations, cavils; carping, faultfinding *sg*.
нап|áивать [1], ⟨~ои́ть⟩ [13] give to drink; make drunk; imbue.
напá|сть 1. F *f* [8] misfortune, bad luck; **2.** *s.* ~дáть.
напé|в *m* [1] melody, tune; **~вáть** [1] **1.** hum, sing; **2.** ⟨~ть⟩ [-пою́, -поёшь; -пéтый] record.
напере|бóй F vying with each other; **~вéс** atilt; **~гóнки́** F: бежáть ~гóнки́ (run a) race; chase each other; **~д** (-ˈŗɔt) F *s.* вперёд; **~ди́** P *s.* спéреди; **~кóр** (Д) in spite *or* defiance (of), contrary (to); **~рéз** (in a) short cut, cutting (across *or* s.b.'s way Д, Р); **~ры́в** F = ~бóй; **~чёт** each and all; few.
напéрсник *m* [1] favo(u)rite; pet.
напёрсток *m* [1; -тка] thimble.
напи|вáться [1], ⟨~ться⟩ [-пью́сь, -пьёшься; -пи́лся, -пилáсь; -пéйся, -пéйтесь!] drink, quench one's thirst, have enough (P); get drunk.
напи́льник *m* [1] file.
напи́|ток *m* [1; -тка] drink, beverage; **~ться** *s.* ~вáться.
напи́т|ывать, ⟨~áть⟩ [1] (Т) (**-ся** become) saturate(d), soak(ed), imbue(d).
напи́х|ивать, ⟨~áть⟩ F [1] cram.
наплы́|в *m* [1] rush; deposit; excrescence; **~вáть** [1], ⟨~ть⟩ [23] swim (against на В), run (on); flow; deposit; approach, cover; waft, reach; gather; **~внóй** [14] *s.* нанóсный.
наповáл (*kill, etc.*) outright.
наподóбие (Р) like, resembling.
напои́ть *s.* напáивать.
напокáз for show; *cf.* выставля́ть.
наполн|я́ть [28], ⟨~ить⟩ [13] (Т) fill; crowd; imbue; *p.pt.p.* a. full.
наполови́ну half; (*do*) by halves.
напом|инáние *n* [12] reminder; dun(ning); **~инáть** [1],⟨~нить⟩ [13] remind (a p. of Д/о П), dun.
напóр *m* [1] pressure; charge; F rush, push, vigo(u)r.
напослéдок F ultimately.
напр. *abbr.*: напримéр.
напрáв|ить(ся) *s* ~ля́ть(ся); **~лéние** *n* [12] direction (in в П, по Д); trend; *fig.* current, school; assignment; **~ля́ть** [28], ⟨~ить⟩ [14] direct; refer; send; assign, detach; **-ся** go, head for; turn (to на В).
напрáво (от Р) to *or* on the (s.b.'s) right; ~! ⚔ right face!
напрáсн|ый [14; -сен, -сна] vain; groundless, idle; ~о in vain, wrongly.
напр|áшиваться [1], ⟨~оси́ться⟩ [15] (на В) (pr)offer (o.s. for), solicit; provoke; fish (for); suggest o.s.
напримéр for example *or* instance.
напро|кáт for hire; **~лёт** F (all) ... through[out]; on end; **~лóм** F: идти́ ~лóм force one's way.
напроси́ться *s.* напрáшиваться.
напрóтив (Р) opposite; on the contrary; *s. a.* наперекóр & наоборóт.
напря|гáть [1], ⟨~чь⟩ (-ˈpŗe-) [26 г/ж: ягý, -яжёшь; -пря́г (-ˈpŗɔk), -яглá; -яжённый] strain (*a. fig.*); exert; stretch; bend (*bow*); **~жéние** *n* [12] tension (*a.* ⚡; voltage), strain, exertion; effort; close attention; **~жённый** [14 *sh.*] strained; (in-) tense; keen, close.
напрями́к F straight on; outright.
напря́чь *s.* напрягáть.
напýганный [14] scared, frightened.
напус|кáть [1], ⟨~ти́ть⟩ [15] let in, fill; set at (на В); fall; F (~кáть на себя́) put on (*airs*); P cause; **-ся** F fall (up)on (на В); **~кнóй** [14] affected.
напýтств|енный [14] farewell..., parting; **~ие** *n* [12] parting words.
напы́щенный [14 *sh.*] pompous.
наравнé (с Т) on a level with; equally; together (*or* along) with.
нараспáшку F unbuttoned; (душá) ~ frank, candid; in grand style.
нараспéв with a singing accent.
нараст|áть [1], ⟨~и́⟩ [24; -стёт; *cf.* расти́] grow; accrue.
нарасхвáт F greedily; like hot cakes.
нарез|áть [1], ⟨~ать⟩ [3] cut; carve; ⊕ thread; **~ка** *f* [5; *g/pl.:* -зок] ⊕ thread; **~ывать** = ~áть.
нарекáние *n* [12] blame, censure.

наре́чие *n* [12] dialect; *gr.* adverb.
нар|ица́тельный [14] *gr.* common; † nominal; **~ко́з** *m* [1] narcosis.
наро́д *m* [1] people, nation; **~ность** *f* [8] nationality; **~ный** [14] people's, popular, folk...; national; public; **~онаселе́ние** *n* [12] population.
наро|жда́ться [1], ⟨**~ди́ться**⟩ [15] arise, spring up; F be born; grow.
наро́ст *m* [1] (out)growth.
нароч|и́тый [14 *sh.*] deliberate, intentional; *adv.* = **∠но** (-ʃn-) *a.* on purpose; specially, expressly; F in fun; F*a.* = на́зло́; **'~ный** [14] courier.
на́рты *f/pl.* [5] sledge.
нару́ж|ность *f* [8] appearance; exterior; **~ный** [14] external, outward; outdoor, outside; **~у** out (-side), outward(s), (*get*) abroad *fig.*
наруш|а́ть [1], ⟨**∠ить**⟩ [16] disturb; infringe, violate; break (*oath*; *silence*); **~е́ние** *n* [12] violation, transgression, breach; disturbance; **~и́тель** *m* [4] trespasser; disturber; **∠ить** *s.* **~а́ть**.
на́ры *f/pl.* [5] plank bed.
нары́в *m* [1] abcess; *cf.* гнои́ть.
наря́|д *m* [1] attire, dress; assignment, commission, order; ⚔ fatigue (on в П); detachment; **~ди́ть** *s.* **~жа́ть**; **~дный** [14; -ден, -дна] smart, trim, elegant; order...
наряду́ (с Т) together *or* along with, beside(s); side by side; *s. a.* наравне́.
наря|жа́ть [1], ⟨**~ди́ть**⟩ [15 & 15 *e.*; -яжу́, -я́ди́шь; -я́женный & -яжённый] dress (up) (*v/i.* **-ся**); disguise; ⚔ detach; assign; † set up.
наса|жда́ть [1], ⟨**~ди́ть**⟩ [15] (im)plant (*a. fig.*); *cf. a.* **∠живать**; **~жде́ние** *n* [12] planting; (im-) plantation; trees, plants *pl.*; **∠живать**, ⟨**~жа́ть**⟩ [1], ⟨**~ди́ть**⟩ [15] plant (many); F set, put, place.
насви́стывать [1] whistle.
насе|да́ть [1], ⟨**∠сть**⟩ [25; -ся́ду, -ся́дешь; *cf.* сесть] set; sit down; cover; press; **∠дка** *f* [5; *g/pl.*: -док] brood hen.
насеко́мое *n* [14] insect.
насел|е́ние *n* [12] population; **~я́ть** [28], ⟨**~и́ть**⟩ [13] people, populate; *impf.* inhabit, live in.
насе́|ст *m* [1] roost; **~сть** *s.* **~да́ть**; **~чка** *f* [5; *g/pl.*: -чек] notch, cut.
наси́|живать [1], ⟨**~де́ть**⟩ [11] brood, hatch; **~женный** *a.* snug, habitual, long-inhabited.
наси́|лие *n* [12] violence, force, coercion; rape; **~ловать** [7], ⟨из-⟩ violate, force; rape; **~лу** F *s.* е́ле; **~льно** by force; forcedly; **~льственный** [14] forcible, forced; violent.
наск|а́кивать [1], ⟨**~очи́ть**⟩ [16] (на В); fall (up)on; run *or* strike against, come across.
насквозь through(out); F through and through.
наско́лько as (far as); how (much).
на́скоро F hastily, in a hurry.
наскочи́ть *s.* наска́кивать.
наску́чить F [16] *pf.*, *s.* надоеда́ть.
насла|жда́ться [1], ⟨**~ди́ться**⟩ [15 *e.*; -ажу́сь, -ади́шься] (T) enjoy (o.s.), (be) delight(ed); **~жде́ние** *n* [12] enjoyment; delight; pleasure.
насле́д|ие *n* [12] heritage, legacy; *s. a.* **~ство**; **~ник** *m* [1] heir; **~ница** *f* [5] heiress; **~ный** [14] crown...; *s. a.* **~ственный**; **~овать** [7] (*im*)*pf.*, ⟨у-⟩ inherit; (Д) succed; **~ственность** *f* [8] heredity; **~ственный** [14] hereditary, inherited; **~ство** *n* [9] inheritance; *s. a.* **~ие**; *vb.* + в **~ство** (*or* по **~ству**) inherit.
наслое́ние *n* [12] stratification.
насл|у́шаться [1] *pf.* (P) listen to one's heart's content; не мочь **~у́шаться** never get tired of listening to; *a.* = **~ы́шаться** F [4] (P) hear a lot (of), much; *cf.* понаслы́шке.
на́смерть to death; mortal(ly *fig.* P).
насме|ха́ться [1] mock, jeer; sneer (at над T); **∠шка** *f* [5; *g/pl.*: -шек] mockery, sneer; **∠шливый** [14 *sh.*] (fond of) mocking; **∠шник** *m* [1], **∠шница** *f* [5] scoffer, mocker.
на́сморк *m* [1] cold (in the head).
насмотре́ться [9; -отрю́сь, -о́тришься] *pf.* = нагляде́ться, *cf.*
насо́с *m* [1] pump.
на́спех hurriedly, in a hurry.
наста|ва́ть [5], ⟨**∠ть**⟩ [-ста́нет] come; **~ви́тельный** [14; -лен, -льна] instructive; preceptive; **∠вить** *s.* **~вля́ть**; **~вле́ние** *n* [12] instruction; admonition; lecture, lesson *fig.*; **~вля́ть** [28], ⟨**∠вить**⟩ [14] put, place, set (many P); piece (on), add; aim, level (at на B); instruct; teach (s. th. Д, в П); **∠вник** *m* [1] tutor, mentor, preceptor; **∠ивать** [1], ⟨настоя́ть⟩ [-стою́, -стои́шь] insist (on на П); draw, extract; настоя́ть на своём have one's will; **∠ть** *s.* **~ва́ть**.
на́стежь wide (open).
насти|га́ть [1], ⟨**∠гнуть**⟩ & ⟨**∠чь**⟩ [21 -г-: -и́гну] overtake; find, catch.
наст|ила́ть [1], ⟨**~ла́ть**⟩ [-телю́, -те́лешь; на́стланный] lay, spread; plank, pave.
насто́й *m* [3] infusion, extract; **~ка** *f* [5; *g/pl.*: -о́ек] liqueur; *a.* = **~**.
насто́йчивый [14 *sh.*] persevering, pertinacious; persistent; obstinate.
насто́ль|ко so (*or* as [much]); **~ный** [14] table...; reference...
настор|а́живаться [1], ⟨**~ожи́ться**⟩ [16 *e.*; -жу́сь, -жи́шься] prick up one's ears; **~оже́** on the alert, on one's guard.
настоя́|ние *n* [12] insistence, urgent request (at по Д); **~тельный**

[14; -лен, -льна] urgent, pressing, instant; ~ть s. настáивать.
настоящ|ий [17] present (*a. gr.*; at ... *time* в В); true, real, genuine; по- ~ему properly.
настр|áивать [1], ‹~óить› [13] build (many P); tune (up, in); set against; *s. a.* налáживать; ∠ого F most strictly; **~оéние** *n* [12] mood, spirits *pl.*, frame (of mind); disposition; **~óить** *s.* ~áивать; **~óйка** *f* [5; *g/pl.*: -óек] superstructure; tuning.
наступ|áтельный [14] offensive; **~áть** [1], ‹~ить› [14] tread *or* step (on на В); come, set in; *impf.* attack, advance; press (hard); approach; **~лéние** *n* [12] offensive, attack, advance; beginning, ...break, ...fall (at с T).
насýпить(ся) [14] *pf.* frown.
нáсухо *adv.* dry.
насýщный [14; -щен, -щна] vital; daily.
насчёт (P) F concerning, about.
насчи́т|ывать, ‹~áть› [1] count, number; **-ся** *impf.* there is/are.
насып|áть [1], ‹∠ать› [2] pour; strew, scatter; fill; throw up, raise; ′~ь *f* [8] embankment, mound.
насы|щáть [1], ‹∠тить› [15] satisfy; saturate; **~щéние** *n* [12] saturation.
нат|áлкивать [1], ‹~олкнýть› [20] (на В) push (against, on); F prompt, suggest; **-ся** strike against; come across.
натвори́ть F [13] *pf.* do, cause.
натéльный [14] under(*clothes*).
нат|ирáть [1], ‹~ерéть› [12] (T) rub (*a.* sore); get (*corn*); wax, polish.
нáт|иск *m* [1] press(ure), rush; onslaught, charge; urge.
наткнýться *s.* натыкáться.
натолкнýть(ся) *s.* натáлкиваться.
натощáк on an empty stomach.
натрáв|ливать [1], ‹~и́ть› [14] set (on, at на В), incite.
нáтрий *m* [3] natrium.
натý|га F *f* [5] strain, effort; ′~го F tight(ly); **~живать** F [1], ‹~жить› [16] strain, exert (o.s. **-ся**).
натýр|а *f* [5] nature; model (= **~щик** *m* [1], **~щица** *f* [5]); ~ой, в ~е in kind; с ~ы from nature *or* life; **~áльный** [14; -лен, -льна] natural.
нат|ыкáться [1], ‹~кнýться› [20] (на В) run against, (*a.* come) across.
натя́|гивать [1], ‹~нýть› [19] stretch, (*a. fig.*) strain; pull (on на В); draw in (*reins*); **~жка** *f* [5; *g/pl.*: -жек] strain(ing); affectation, forced *or* strained argument(ation), detail, trait, *etc.*; с ~жкой *a.* with great reserve; **~нутый** [14] strained, forced, affected, far-fetched; tense, bad; **~нýть** *s.* ~гивать.
нау|гáд, **~дáчу** at random.
наýка *f* [5] science; lesson.
наутёк F (*take*) to one's heels.
наýтро the next morning.
науч|и́ть [1], ‹~и́ть› [16] teach (a p. s.th. В/Д); **-ся** learn (s.th. Д).
наýчный [14; -чен, -чна] scientific.
наýшник F *m* [1] informer; **~и** *m/pl.* [1] earflaps; headphones.
нахáл *m* [1] impudent fellow; **~ьный** [14; -лен, -льна] impudent, insolent; **~ьство** *n* [12] impudence, insolence.
нахвáт|ывать, ‹~áть› F [1] (P) snatch (up), pick up (a lot of, a smattering of; hoard; *a.* **-ся**).
нахлы́нуть [20] *pf.* rush (up [to]).
нахмýривать [1] = хмýрить, *cf.*
наход|и́ть [15], ‹найти́› [найдý, -дёшь; нашёл, -шлá; -шéдший; нáйденный; *g. pt.*: найдя́] find (*a. fig.* = think, consider); come (across на В); cover; be seized (F wrong) with; *impf.* take (*pleasure*); (**-ся**, ‹найти́сь›) be (found, there, [*impf.*] situated, located); happen to have; not to be at a loss; ∠**ка** *f* [5; *g/pl.*: -док] find; F discovery; бюрó ∠ок lost-property office; ∠**чивый** [14 *sh.*] resourceful; ready-witted, smart.
национал|из(и́р)овáть [7] (*im*)*pf.* nationalize (*Brt.* -ise); ∠**ьность** *f* [8] nationality; **~ьный** [14; -лен, -льна] national.
начá|ло *n* [9] beginning (at в П); source, origin; basis; principle; *pl.* rudiments; **~льник** *m* [1] chief, superior; ⚔ commander; 🚂 (*station*) master, agent; **~льный** [14] initial, first; opening; elementary, primary; **~льство** *n* [9] command(er[s], chief[s], superior[s]); authority, -ties *pl.*; **~льствовать** [7] (над T) command; manage; **~тки** *m/pl.* [1] *s.* ~ло *pl.*; **~ть(ся)** *s.* начинáть(ся).
начекý on the alert, on one's guard.
нáчерно roughly, (in) a draft.
начертá|ние *n* [12] tracing; pattern; outline; **~тельный** [14] descriptive; **~ть** [1] *pf.* trace, design.
начинá|ние *n* [12] undertaking; † beginning; **~ть** [1], ‹начáть› [-чнý, -чнёшь; нáчал, -á, -o; начáвший; нáчатый (нáчат, -á, -o)] begin, start (with с Р, Т); **-ся** *v/i.*; **~ющий** [17] beginner.
начи́н|ка *f* [5; *g/pl.*: -нок] filling; **~я́ть** [28], ‹~и́ть› [13] fill (with T).
начислéние *n* [12] extra fee.
нáчисто clean; *s.* нáбело; outright.
начи́т|анный [14 *sh.*] well-read; **~áться** [1] (P) read (a lot of); have enough (of); не мочь ~áться never get tired of reading.
наш *m*, ∠а *f*, ∠е *n*, ∠и *pl.* [25] our; ours; по-∠ему in our way *or* opinion *or* language; ∠а взялá! we've won!
нашаты́р|ный [14]: ~ный спирт *m* aqueous ammonia; **~ь** *m* [4 *e.*] sal ammoniac, ammonium chloride.
нашéствие *n* [12] invasion, inroad.

нашu|вáть [1], ⟨**ꭥть**⟩ [-шью́, -шьёшь; *cf.* шить] sew on (на В *or* П) *or* many ...; **ꭥвка** *f* [5; *g/pl.*: -вок] galloon, braid; ⚔ stripe.
нащу́п|ывать, ⟨**~ать**⟩ [1] grope, fumble; *fig.* sound; detect, find.
наяву́ in reality; waking.
не not; no; ~ то F (or) else.
неаккура́тный [14; -тен, -тна] careless; inaccurate; unpunctual.
небез... rather ..., not without ...
небе́сный [14] celestial, heavenly; of heaven; divine; *cf.* небосво́д.
неблаго|ви́дный [14; -ден, -дна] unseemly; **~ да́рность** *f* [8] ingratitude; **~да́рный** [14; -рен, -рна] ungrateful; **~нада́ёжный** [14; -жен, -жна] unreliable; **~полу́чный** [14; -чен, -чна] unfortunate, adverse, bad; *adv.* not well, wrong; **~прия́тный** [14; -тен, -тна] unfavo(u)rable, negative; **~разу́мный** [14; -мен, -мна] imprudent; unreasonable; **~ро́дный** [14; -ден, -дна] ignoble; indelicate; **~скло́нный** [14; -о́нен, -о́нна] unkindly; unfavo(u)rable.
не́бо[1] *n* [9; *pl.*: небеса́, -е́с] sky (in на П); heaven(s); air (in the *open* под Т).
нёбо[2] *n* [9] palate.
небога́тый [14 *sh.*] (of) modest (means); poor.
небольш|о́й [17] small; short; ... с **~и́м** ... odd.
небо|сво́д *m* [1] firmament; *a.* **~скло́н** *m* [1]; horizon; **~скрёб** *m* [1] skyscraper.
небо́сь F I suppose; sure.
небре́жный [14; -жен, -жна] careless, negligent.
небы|ва́лый [14] unheard-of, unprecedented; **~ли́ца** *f* [5] tale, fable, invention.
небью́щийся [17] unbreakable.
Нева́ *f* [5] Neva.
нева́жный [14; -жен, -жна́, -о] unimportant, trifling; F poor, bad.
невдалеке́ not far off, *or* from (от Р).
неве́|дение *n* [12] ignorance; **~до́мый** [14 *sh.*] unknown; **~жа** *m/f* [5] boor; **~жда** *m/f* [5] ignoramus; **~жество** *n* [9] ignorance; **~жливость** *f* [8] incivility; **~жливый** [14 *sh.*] impolite, uncivil.
неве́р|ие *n* [12] unbelief; **~ный** [14; -рен, -рна́, -о] incorrect; false; unfaithful; unsteady; *su.* infidel; **~оя́тный** [14; -тен, -тна] incredible; **~ующий** [17] unbelieving.
невесо́мый [14 *sh.*] imponderable.
неве́ст|а *f* [5] fiancée, bride; F marriageable girl; **~ка** *f* [5; *g/pl.*: -ток] daughter-in-law; sister-in-law (*brother's wife*).
невз|го́да *f* [5] adversity, misfortune; affliction; **~ира́я** (на В) in spite of, despite; without respect (of p.'s); **~нача́й** F unexpectedly, by chance; **~ра́чный** [14; -чен, -чна] plain, homely, mean; **~ыска́тельный** [14; -лен, -льна] unpretentious.
неви́д|анный [14] singular, unprecedented; **~имый** [14 *sh.*] invisible.
неви́нный [14; -и́нен, -и́нна] innocent; virgin.
невку́сный [14; -сен, -сна́, -о] insipid.
невме|ня́емый [14 *sh.*] irresponsible; **~ша́тельство** *n* [9] nonintervention.
невнима́тельный [14; -лен, -льна] inattentive.
невня́тный [14; -тен, -тна] indistinct, inarticulate; unintelligible.
не́вод *m* [1] seine.
невоз|врати́мый [14 *sh.*], **~вра́тный** [14; -тен, -тна] irretrievable, irreparable; **~вращéнец** *m* [1; -нца] non-returnee; **~де́ржанный** [14 *sh.*] intemperate; unbridled, uncontrolled; **~мо́жный** [14; -жен, -жна] impossible; **~мути́мый** [14 *sh.*] imperturbable.
нево́л|ить [13] force, compel; **~ьник** *m* [1] slave; captive; **~ьный** [14; -лен, -льна] involuntary; forced; **~я** *f* [6] captivity; bondage; need, necessity.
невоо|брази́мый [14 *sh.*] unimaginable; **~ружённый** [14] unarmed.
невоспи́танный [14 *sh.*] ill-bred.
невпопа́д F *s.* некста́ти.
невреди́мый [14 *sh.*] sound, unhurt.
невы́|годный [14; -ден, -дна] unprofitable; disadvantageous; **~де́ржанный** [14 *sh.*] unbalanced, uneven; unseasoned; **~носи́мый** [14 *sh.*] unbearable, intolerable; **~полне́ние** *n* [12] nonfulfillment; **~полни́мый** *s.* неисполни́мый; **~рази́мый** [14 *sh.*] inexpressible, ineffable; **~рази́тельный** [14; -лен, -льна] inexpressive; **~со́кий** [16; -со́к, -а́, -со́ко́] low, small; short; inferior, slight.
не́га *f* [5] luxury, comfort; bliss, delight; affection.
не́где there is no(where *or* room *or* place to [... from] *inf.*; Д for).
негла́сный [14; -сен, -сна] secret, private.
него́д|ный [14; -ден, -дна́, -о] useless; unfit; F nasty; **~ова́ние** *n* [12] indignation; **~ова́ть** [7] be indignant (with на В); **~я́й** *m* [3] scoundrel, rascal.
негр *m* [1] Negro; **~а́мотность** *s.* безгра́мотность; **~а́мотный** *s.* безгра́мотный; **~итя́нка** *f* [5; *g/pl.*: -нок] Negress; **~итя́нский** [16] Negro...
неда́|вний [15] recent; с **~вних** (**~вней**) пор(ы́) of late; **~вно**

recently; **~лёкий** [16; -ёк, -ека́, -еко́ & -ёко] near(by), close; short; not far (off); recent; dull, stupid; **~льнови́дный** [14; -ден, -дна] short-sighted; **~ром** not in vain, not without reason; justly.
недви́жи́мый [14 *sh.*] immovable.
неде|йстви́тельный [14; -лен, -льна] invalid, void; ineffective, ineffectual; **~ли́мый** [14] indivisible.
неде́л|ьный [14] a week's, weekly; **~я** *f* [6] week; в ~ю a *or* per week; на э́той (про́шлой, бу́дущей) ~е this (last, next) week.
недобро|жела́тельный [14; -лен, -льна] unkindly, ill-natured; **~ка́чественный** [14 *sh.*] inferior, off--grade; **~со́вестный** [14; -тен, -тна] unfair; unprincipled; careless.
недо́брый [14; -до́бр, -а́, -о] unkind(ly), hostile; evil, bad, ill(-boding).
недове́р|ие *n* [12] distrust; **~чи́вый** [14 *sh.*] distrustful (of к Д).
недово́ль|ный [14; -лен, -льна] (Т) dissatisfied, discontented; **~ство** *n* [9] discontent, dissatisfaction.
недога́дливый [14 *sh.*] slow-witted.
недоеда́|ние *n* [12] malnutrition; **~ть** [1] not eat enough (*or* one's fill).
недои́мки *f/pl.* [5; *gen.*: -мок] arrears.
недо́лго not long, short; F easily.
недомога́ть [1] be unwell, sick.
недомо́лвка *f* [5; *g/pl.*: -вок] omission.
недоно́сок *m* [1; -ска] abortion.
недооце́н|ивать [1], ⟨~и́ть⟩ [13] underestimate, undervalue.
недо|пусти́мый [14 *sh.*] inadmissible; intolerable, impossible; **~ра́звитый** [14 *sh.*] underdeveloped; **~разуме́ние** *n* [12] misunderstanding (through по Д); **~рого́й** [16; -до́рог, -а́, -о] inexpensive.
не́до|росль *m* [4] greenhorn; ignoramus; **~слы́шать** [1] *pf.* fail to hear.
недосмо́тр *m* [1] oversight, inadvertence (through по Д); **~е́ть** [9; -отрю́, -о́тришь; -о́тренный] *pf.* overlook (*s. th.*).
недост|ава́ть [5], ⟨~а́ть⟩ [-ста́нет] *impers.*: (Д) (be) lack(ing), want(-ing), be short *or* in want of (Р); miss; э́того ещё ~ава́ло! and that too!; **~а́ток** *m* [1; -тка] want (for за Т, по Д), lack, shortage (of Р, в П); deficiency; defect, shortcoming; privation; **~а́точный** [14; -чен, -чна] insufficient, deficient, inadequate; *gr.* defective; **~а́ть** *s.* ~ава́ть.
недо|стижи́мый [14 *sh.*] unattainable; **~сто́йный** [14; -о́ин, -о́йна] unworthy; **~сту́пный** [14; -пен, -пна] inaccessible.
недосу́г F *m* [1] lack of time (for за Т, по Д); мне ~ I have no time.
недо|сяга́емый [14 *sh.*] unattainable; **~у́здок** *m* [1; -дка] halter.
недоум|ева́ть [1] (be) puzzle(d, perplexed); **~е́ние** *n* [12] bewilderment; в ~е́нии at a loss.
недочёт *m* [1] deficit; defect.
не́дра *n/pl.* [9] bosom, entrails.
недружелю́бный [14; -бен, -бна] unfriendly.
неду́г *m* [1] ailment, infirmity.
недурно́й [14; -ду́рен & -рён, -рна́, -о] not bad, pretty, nice, handsome.
недю́жинный [14] remarkable.
неесте́ственный [14 *sh.*] unnatural; affected, forced.
нежела́|ние *n* [12] unwillingness; **~тельный** [14; -лен, -льна] undesirable.
не́жели † = чем than.
нежена́тый [14] single, unmarried.
нежи́зненный [14 *sh.*] impracticable; unreal.
нежило́й [14] uninhabited; deserted, desolate; store...
не́ж|ить [16] coddle, pamper, fondle; -ся loll, lounge; **~ничать** F [1] indulge in caresses; **~ность** *f* [8] tenderness; fondness; civility; **~ный** [14; -жен, -жна́, -о] tender, fond; delicate; soft; sentimental.
незаб|ве́нный [14 *sh.*], **~ыва́емый** [14 *sh.*] unforgettable; **~у́дка** *f* [5; *g/pl.*: -док] forget-me-not.
незави́сим|ость *f* [8] independence; **~ый** [14 *sh.*] independent.
незада́чливый F [14 *sh.*] unlucky.
незадо́лго shortly (before до Р).
незако́нный [14; -о́нен, -о́нна] illegal, unlawful, illegitimate; illicit.
незаме|ни́мый [14 *sh.*] irreplaceable; **~́тный** [14; -тен, -тна] imperceptible, unnoticeable; plain, ordinary, humdrum; **~́ченный** [14] unnoticed.
неза|мыслова́тый F [14 *sh.*] simple, plain; dull; **~па́мятный** [14] immemorial; **~те́йливый** [14 *sh.*] plain, simple; **~уря́дный** [14; -ден, -дна] remarkable.
не́зачем there is no need *or* point.
незва́ный [14] uninvited.
нездоро́в|иться [14]: мне ~ится I feel (am) sick *or* ill, unwell; **~ый** [14 *sh.*] sick; morbid.
незло́бивый [14 *sh.*] gentle, placid.
незнако́м|ец *m* [1; -мца], **~ка** *f* [5; *g/pl.*: -мок] stranger; *a.*, F, **~ый** [14], unknown, strange; unacquainted.
незна́|ние *n* [12] ignorance; **~чи́тельный** [14; -лен, -льна] insignificant.
незр|е́лый [14 *sh.*] unripe; immature; **~и́мый** [14 *sh.*] invisible.
незы́блемый [14 *sh.*] firm; unshakable.
неиз|бе́жный [14; -жен, -жна] inevitable; **~ве́данный** [14 *sh.*] *s.*

~вéстный [14; -тен, -тна] unknown; *su. a.* stranger; **~гладúмый** [14 *sh.*] indelible; **~лечúмый** [14 *sh.*] incurable; **~мéнный** [14; -éнен, -éнна] invariable; permanent; true; **~мерúмый** [14 *sh.*] immense; **~ъяснúмый** [14 *sh.*] inexplicable.

неим|éние *n* [12]: за ~éнием (P) for want of; **~óверный** [14; -рен, -рна] incredible; **~ýщий** [17] poor.

неúс|кренний [15; -енен, -енна] insincere; **~кýсный** [14; -сен, -сна] unskillful; **~полнéние** *n* [12] nonfulfillment; **~полнúмый** [14 *sh.*] impracticable.

неиспр|авúмый [14 *sh.*] incorrigible; **~áвность** *f* [8] ⊕ disrepair; **~áвный** [14; -вен, -вна] out of repair *or* order, broken, defective; careless, faulty; inaccurate; unpunctual.

неиссякáемый [14 *sh.*] inexhaustible.

неúстов|ство *n* [9] rage, frenzy; atrocity; **~ствовать** [7] rage; **~ый** [14 *sh.*] frantic, furious.

неис|тощúмый [14 *sh.*] inexhaustible; **~требúмый** [14 *sh.*] ineradicable; **~целúмый** [14 *sh.*] incurable; **~черпáемый** [14 *sh.*] *s.* ~тощúмый; **~числúмый** [14 *sh.*] innumerable.

нейтрал|итéт *m* [1] neutrality; **~ьный** [14; -лен, -льна] neutral.

неказúстый F [14 *sh.*] = невзрáчный.

нé|кий [24 *st.*] a certain, some; **~когда** there is (мне ~когда I have) no time; once; **~кого** [23] there is (мне ~кого I have) nobody *or* no one (to *inf.*); **~который** [14] some (*pl.* of из P); **~красúвый** [14 *sh.*] homely, ugly; mean.

некролóг *m* [1] obituary.

некстáти inopportunely; inappropriately, malapropos, off the point.

нéкто somebody, -one; a certain.

нéкуда there is no(where *or* room *or* place to *inf.*; Д for); *s. a.* нéзачем; F could not be (*better, etc.*).

неку|льтýрный [14; -рен, -рна] uncultured; ill-mannered; **~рящий** [17] nonsmoker, nonsmoking.

нел|áдный F [14; -ден, -дна] wrong, bad; **~егáльный** [14; -лен, -льна] illegal; **~éпый** [14 *sh.*] absurd; F awkward.

нелóвкий [16; -вок, -вкá, -о] awkward, clumsy; inconvenient, embarrassing.

нельзя́ (it is) impossible, one (мне I) cannot, must not; ~! no!; как ~ лýчше in the best way possible, excellently; ~ не *s.* (не) мочь.

нелюдúмый [14 *sh.*] unsociable.

немáло (P) a lot, a great deal (of).

немéдленный [14] immediate.

немéть [8], ⟨о-⟩ grow dumb, numb.

нéм|ец *m* [1; -мца], **~éцкий** [16], **~ка** *f* [5; *g/pl.*: -мок] German.

немилосéрдный [14; -ден, -дна] unmerciful, ruthless.

немúлост|ивый [14 *sh.*] ungracious; **~ь** *f* [8] disgrace.

неминýемый [14 *sh.*] inevitable.

немнó|гие *pl.* [16] (a) few, some; **~го** a little; slightly, somewhat; *s. a.* ~гие; **~гое** *n* [16] little; **~гим** a little; **~ж(еч)ко** F a (little) bit.

немóй [14; нем, -á, -о] dumb, mute.

немо|лодóй [14; -мóлод, -á, -о] elderly; **~тá** *f* [5] muteness.

нéмощный [14; -щен, -щна] infirm.

немы́слимый [14 *sh.*] inconceivable.

ненавú|деть [11], ⟨воз-⟩ hate; **~стный** [14; -тен, -тна] hateful, odious; **~сть** ('ne-) *f* [8] hatred (against к Д).

нена|гля́дный [14] dear, beloved; **~дёжный** [14; -жен, -жна] unreliable; unsafe, insecure; **~дóлго** for a short while; **~мéренный** [14] unintentional; **~падéние** *n* [12] nonagression; **~рушúмый** [14 *sh.*] inviolable; **~́стный** [14; -тен, -тна] rainy, foul; **~́стье** *n* [10] foul weather; **~сы́тный** [14; -тен, -тна] insatiable.

нен|ормáльный [14; -лен, -льна] abnormal; F (mentally) deranged; **~ýжный** [14; -жен, -жнá, -о] unnecessary.

необ|дýманный [14 *sh.*] rash, hasty; **~итáемый** [14 *sh.*] uninhabited; desert; **~озрúмый** [14 *sh.*] immense, vast; **~оснóванный** [14 *sh.*] unfounded; **~рабóтанный** [14] uncultivated; crude, unpolished; **~ýзданный** [14 *sh.*] unbridled, unruly.

необходúм|ость *f* [8] necessity (of по Д), need (of, for P, в П); **~ый** [14 *sh.*] necessary (for Д; для P), essential; *cf.* нýжный.

необ|щúтельный [14; -лен, -льна] unsociable, reserved; **~ъяснúмый** [14 *sh.*] inexplicable; **~ъя́тный** [14; -тен, -тна] immense, vast, huge; **~ыкновéнный** [14; -éнен, -éнна], **~ы́ч(áй)ный** [14; -ч(á)ен, ч(áй)на] unusual, uncommon; **~язáтельный** [14; -лен, -льна] optional.

неограничéнный [14 *sh.*] unrestricted.

неод|нокрáтный [14] repeated; **~обрéние** *n* [12] disapproval; **~обрúтельный** [14; -лен, -льна] disapproving; **~олúмый** *s.* непреодолúмый; **~ушевлённый** [14] inanimate.

неожúданн|ость *f* [8] surprise; **~ый** [14 *sh.*] unexpected, sudden.

неóн *m* [1] neon; **~овый** [14] neon-...

неоп|ису́емый [14 *sh.*] indescribable; **~ла́ченный** [14 *sh.*] unpaid, unsettled; **~ра́вданный** [14] unjustified; **~ределённый** [14; -ёнен, -ённа] indefinite (*a. gr.*), uncertain, vague; *gr.* (*vb.*) infinitive; **~ровержи́мый** [14 *sh.*] irrefutable; **~ытный** [14; -тен, -тна] inexperienced.

неос|ла́бный [14; -бен, -бна] unremitting, unabated; **~мотри́тельный** [14; -лен, -льна] imprudent; **~нова́тельный** [14; -лен, -льна] unfounded, baseless; **~пори́мый** [14 *sh.*] incontestable; **~торо́жный** [14; -жен, -жна] careless, incautious; imprudent; **~уществи́мый** [14 *sh.*] impracticable; **~яза́емый** [14 *sh.*] intangible.

неот|врати́мый [14 *sh.*] unavoidable; fatal; **~вя́зный** [14; -зен, -зна], **~вя́зчивый** [14 *sh.*] obtrusive, importunate; **~ёсанный** [14 *sh.*] unhewn; F rude; **'~куда** *s.* не́где; **~ло́жный** [14; -жен, -жна] pressing, urgent; **~лу́чный** *s.* неразлу́чный & постоя́нный; **~рази́мый** [14 *sh.*] irresistible; **~сту́пный** [14; -пен, -пна] persistent; importunate; **~чётливый** [14 *sh.*] indistinct; **~ъе́млемый** [14 *sh.*] integral; inalienable.

неохо́т|а *f* [5] listlessness; reluctance; (мне) **~а** F I (*etc.*) am not in the mood; **~но** unwillingly.

не|оцени́мый [14 *sh.*] invaluable; **~перехо́дный** [14] intransitive; **~платёж** *m* [1 *e.*] nonpayment; **~платёжеспосо́бный** [14; -бен, -бна] insolvent.

непо|беди́мый [14 *sh.*] invincible; **~воро́тливый** [14 *sh.*] clumsy, slow; **~го́да** *f* [5] foul weather; **~греши́мый** [14 *sh.*] infallible; **~далёку** not far (away *or* off); **~да́тливый** [14 *sh.*] unyielding, refractory.

непод|ви́жный [14; -жен, -жна] motionless, (*a. ast.*) fixed; sluggish; **~де́льный** [14; -лен, -льна] genuine, true; sincere; **~ку́пный** [14; -пен, -пна] incorruptible; **~обаю́щий** [17] improper, unbecoming; undue; **~ража́емый** [14 *sh.*] inimitable; **~ходя́щий** [17] unsuitable; **~чине́ние** *n* [12] insubordination.

непо|зволи́тельный [14; -лен, -льна] improper, unbecoming; **~колеби́мый** [14 *sh.*] firm, steadfast; unflinching; imperturbable; **~ко́рный** [14; -рен, -рна] intractable; **~ла́дка** F *f* [5; *g/pl.*: -док] defect, trouble; strife; **~лный** [14; -лон, -лна́, -о] incomplete; short; **~ме́рный** [14; -рен, -рна] excessive, exorbitant.

непоня́т|ливый [14 *sh.*] slow-witted; **~ный** [14; -тен, -тна] unintelligible, incomprehensible; strange, odd.

непо|прави́мый [14 *sh.*] irreparable; **~ро́чный** [14; -чен, -чна] chaste, immaculate; virgin...; **~ря́дочный** [14; -чен, -чна] dishono(u)rable, disreputable; **~се́дливый** [14 *sh.*] fidgety; **~си́льный** [14; -лен, -льна] beyond one's strength; **~сле́довательный** [14; -лен, -льна] inconsistent; **~слу́шный** [14; -шен, -шна] disobedient.

непо|сре́дственный [14 *sh.*] immediate, direct; spontaneous; **~стижи́мый** [14 *sh.*] inconceivable; **~стоя́нный** [14; -я́нен, -я́нна] inconstant, unsteady, fickle; **~хо́жий** [17 *sh.*] unlike, different (from на B).

непра́в|да *f* [5] untruth, lie; (it is) not true; ... и **~дами** (*by hook*) or by crook; **~доподо́бный** [14; -бен, -бна] improbable; **~едный** [14; -ден, -дна] unjust; sinful; **~ильный** [14; -лен, -льна] incorrect, wrong; irregular (*a. gr.*); improper (*a.* ⚕); **~ота́** *f* [5] wrong(fulness); **~ый** [14; непра́в, -а́, -о] wrong; unjust.

непре|взойдённый [14 *sh.*] unsurpassed; **~дви́денный** [14] unforeseen; **~дубеждённый** [14] unbias(s)ed; **~кло́нный** [14; -о́нен, -о́нна] uncompromising; steadfast; **~ло́жный** [14; -жен, -жна] inviolable, invariable; incontestable; **~ме́нный** [14; -е́нен, -е́нна] indispensable; permanent; **~ме́нно** *s.* обяза́тельно; **~одоли́мый** [14 *sh.*] insuperable; irresistible; **~река́емый** [14 *sh.*] indisputable; **~ры́вный** [14; -вен, -вна] continuous; **~ста́нный** [14; -а́нен, -а́нна] incessant.

непри|вы́чный [14; -чен, -чна] unaccustomed; unusual; **~гля́дный** [14; -ден, -дна] homely, mean; **~го́дный** [14; -ден, -дна] unfit; useless; **~е́млемый** [14 *sh.*] unacceptable; **~коснове́нный** [14; -е́нен, -е́нна] inviolable; untouched, untouchable; **~кра́шенный** [14] unvarnished; **~ли́чный** [14; -чен, -чна] indecent, unseemly; **~ме́тный** [14; -тен, -тна] imperceptible, unnoticeable; plain; **~мири́мый** [14 *sh.*] irreconcilable, implacable; **~нуждённый** [14 *sh.*] (free and) easy, at ease; **~сто́йный** [14; -оен, -о́йна] obscene, indecent; **~сту́пный** [14; -пен, -пна] inaccessible; impregnable; unapproachable, haughty; **~тво́рный** [14; -рен, -рна] sincere, unfeigned; **~тяза́тельный** [14; -лен, -льна] unpretentious, modest, plain.

неприя́|зненный [14 *sh.*] hostile, unkind(ly); **~знь** *f* [8] dislike; **~тель** *m* [4] enemy; **~тельский**

[16] enemy('s); **~тность** *f* [8] trouble; **~тный** [14; -тен, -тна] disagreeable, unpleasant.

непро|гля́дный [14; -ден, -дна] pitch-dark; **~должи́тельный** [14; -лен, -льна] short, brief; **~е́зжий** [17] impassable; **~зра́чный** [14; -чен, -чна] opaque; **~изводи́тельный** [14; -лен, -льна] unproductive; **~изво́льный** [14; -лен, -льна] involuntary; **~мока́емый** [14 *sh.*] waterproof; **~ница́емый** [14 *sh.*] impenetrable, impermeable, impervious; **~сти́тельный** [14; -лен, -льна] unpardonable; **~ходи́мый** [14 *sh.*] impassable; F complete; **∠чный** [14; -чен, -чна́, -o] flimsy, unstable.

нера́бочий [17] free, off (*day*).

нера́в|енство *n* [9] inequality; **~номе́рный** [14; -рен, -рна] uneven; **~ный** [14; -вен, -вна́, -o] unequal.

небреди́вый [14 *sh.*] careless, listless.

нераз|бери́ха F *f* [5] mess; **~бо́рчивый** [14 *sh.*] illegible; unscrupulous; **~вито́й** [14; -ра́звит, -а́, -o] undeveloped; **~де́льный** [14; -лен, -льна] indivisible, integral; undivided; **~личи́мый** [14 *sh.*] indistinguishable; **~лу́чный** [14; -чен, -чна] inseparable; **~реши́мый** [14 *sh.*] insoluble; **~ры́вный** [14; -вен, -вна] indissoluble; **~у́мный** [14; -мен, -мна] injudicious.

нерас|положе́ние *n* [12] dislike; **~суди́тельный** [14; -лен, -льна] imprudent.

нерв *m* [1] nerve; **~и́ровать** [7] make nervous; **∠ничать** [1] be nervous; **~нобольно́й** [14] neurotic; **∠(о́з)ный** [14; -вен, -вна́, -o (-зен, -зна)] nervous; high-strung.

нереши́тельн|ость *f* [8] indecision; в **~ости** at a loss; **~ый** [14; лен, -льна] irresolute.

неро́|бкий [16; -бок, -бка́, -o] brave; **~вный** [14; -вен, -вна́, -o] uneven.

неруши́мый [14 *sh.*] inviolable.

неря́|ха *m/f* [5] sloven; **~шливый** [14 *sh.*] slovenly; careless.

несамостоя́тельный [14; -лен, -льна] dependent (on, *or* influenced by, others).

несбы́точный [14; -чен, -чна] unrealizable.

не|све́дущий [17 *sh.*] ignorant (of в П); **~своевре́менный** [14; -енен, -енна] untimely; tardy; **~свя́зный** [14; -зен, -зна] incoherent; **~сгора́емый** [14] fireproof; **~сде́ржанный** [14 *sh.*] unrestrained; **~серьёзный** [14; -зен, -зна] frivolous; **~сказа́нный** [14 *sh.*, *no m*] indescribable; **~скла́дный** [14; -ден, -дна] ungainly, unwieldy; incoherent; **~склоня́емый** [14 *sh.*] indeclinable.

не́сколько [32] a few, some, several; somewhat.

не|скро́мный [14; -мен, -мна́, -o] immodest; **~слы́ханный** [14 *sh.*] unheard-of; awful; **~слы́шный** [14; -шен, -шна] inaudible, noiseless; **~сме́тный** [14; -тен, -тна] innumerable.

несмотря́ (на В) in spite of, despite, notwithstanding; (al)though.

несно́сный [14; -сен, -сна] intolerable.

несо|блюде́ние *n* [12] nonobservance; **~вершеннолéтие** *n* [12] minority; **~верше́нный** [14; -е́нен, -е́нна] imperfect(ive *gr.*); **~верше́нство** *n* [8] imperfection; **~вмести́мый** [14 *sh.*] incompatible; **~гла́сие** *n* [12] disagreement; **~гла́сный** [14; -сен, -сна] discordant; inconsistent; **~измери́мый** [14 *sh.*] incommensurable; **~круши́мый** [14 *sh.*] indestructible; **~мне́нный** [14; -е́нен, -е́нна] doubtless; ~мне́нно *a.* undoubtedly, without doubt; **~обра́зный** [14; -зен, -зна] incompatible; absurd, foolish; **~отве́тствие** *n* [12] discrepancy; **~разме́рный** [14; -рен, -рна] disproportionate; **~стоя́тельный** [14; -лен, -льна] needy; insolvent; unsound, baseless.

несп|око́йный [14; -о́ен, -о́йна] restless, uneasy; **~осо́бный** [14; -бен, -бна] incapable (of к Д, на В), unfit (for); **~раведли́вость** *f* [8] injustice; wrong; **~раведли́вый** [14 *sh.*] unjust, wrong; **~роста́** F *s.* нeда́ром.

несравне́нный [14; -е́нен, -е́нна] incomparable.

нестерпи́мый [14 *sh.*] intolerable.

нести́ [24 -с-: -су́], ⟨по-⟩ (be) carry(ing, *etc.*); bear; bring; suffer (*loss*); do (*duty*); drift, waft, speed (along) (**-сь** *v/i.*; *a.* be heard; spread); ⟨с-⟩ lay (eggs **-сь**); F talk (*nonsense*); smell (of T); несёт there's a draught.

не|строево́й [14] noncombatant; **~стро́йный** [14; -о́ен, -ойна́, -o] ungainly; discordant; disorderly; **~сура́зный** F [14; -зен, -зна] foolish, absurd; ungainly; **~схо́дный** [14; -ден, -дна] unlike, different (from с T).

несча́ст|ный [14; -тен, -тна] unhappy, unlucky; F paltry; **~ье** *n* [12] misfortune; disaster; accident; к ~ью *or* на ~ье unfortunately.

несчётный [14; -тен, -тна] innumerable.

нет 1. *part.*: no; ~ ещё not yet; **2.** *impers. vb.* [*pt.* не́ было, *ft.* не бу́дет] (P): there is (are) no; у меня́ (*etc.*) ~ I (*etc.*) have no(ne); его́ (её) ~ (s)he is not (t)here *or* in.

нетерп|ели́вый [14 *sh.*] impatient;

~éние *n* [12] impatience; **~и́мый** [14 *sh.*] intolerant; intolerable.
не|тле́нный [14; -éнен, -éнна] imperishable; **~тре́звый** [14; -трéзв, -á, -o] drunk (*a.* в ~трéзвом ви́де); **~тро́нутый** [14 *sh.*] untouched; **~трудоспосо́бный** [14; -бен, -бна] disabled.
нет|то ('nɛ-) [*ind.*] net; **∠у** F = нет 2.
неу|важе́ние *n* [12] disrespect (for к Д); **~ве́ренный** [14 *sh.*] uncertain; **~вяда́емый** [14 *sh.*] unfading; **~гаси́мый** [14 *sh.*] inextinguishable; **~гомо́нный** [14; -óнен, -óнна] restless, unquiet; untiring.
неуда́ч|а *f* [5] misfortune; failure; **~ливый** [14 *sh.*] unlucky; **~ник** *m* [1] unlucky fellow; **~ный** [14; -чен, -чна] unsuccessful, unfortunate.
неуд|ержи́мый [14 *sh.*] irrepressible; **~иви́тельно** (it is) no wonder.
неудо́б|ный [14; -бен, -бна] inconvenient; uncomfortable; improper; **~ство** *n* [9] inconvenience.
неудов|летвори́тельный [14; -лен, -льна] unsatisfactory; **~о́льствие** *n* [12] displeasure.
неужéли really?, is it possible?
неу|жи́вчивый [14 *sh.*] unsociable, unaccomodating; **~кло́нный** [14; -óнен, -óнна] unswerving, firm; **~клю́жий** [17 *sh.*] clumsy, awkward; **~кроти́мый** [14 *sh.*] indomitable; **~лови́мый** [14 *sh.*] elusive; imperceptible; **~ме́лый** [14 *sh.*] unskillful, awkward; **~ме́ние** *n* [12] inability; **~ме́ренный** [14 *sh.*] intemperate, immoderate; **~ме́стный** [14; -тен, -тна] inappropriate; **~моли́мый** [14 *sh.*] inexorable; **~мы́шленный** [14 *sh.*] unintentional; **~потреби́тельный** [14; -лен, -льна] not in use; **~рожа́й** *m* [3] bad harvest; **~ро́чный** [14] unseasonable; **~спе́х** *m* [1] failure; **~ста́нный** [14; -áнен, -áнна] incessant; constant; *s. a.* ~томи́мый; **~сто́йка** *f* [5; *g/pl.*: -óек] forfeit; **~сто́йчивый** [14 *sh.*] unstable; unsteady; **~страши́мый** [14 *sh.*] intrepid, dauntless; **~сту́пчивый** [14 *sh.*] uncomplying, tenacious; **~сы́пный** [14; -пен, -пна] incessant, unremitting; *s. a.* ~томи́мый; **~те́шный** [14; -шен, -шна] disconsolate, inconsolable; **~толи́мый** [14 *sh.*] unquenchable; insatiable; **~томи́мый** [14 *sh.*] tireless, indefatigable, untiring.
не́уч F *m* [1] ignoramus; **~ёный** [14] illiterate; **~е́нье** *n* [10] ignorance.
неу|чти́вый [14 *sh.*] uncivil; **~ю́тный** [14; -тен, -тна] uncomfortable; **~язви́мый** [14 *sh.*] invulnerable.
нефт|еналивно́й *s.* наливнóй; **~епрово́д** *m* [1] pipe line; **~ь** *f* [8] (mineral) oil; **~яно́й** [14] oil...
не|хва́тка F *f* [5; *g/pl.*: -ток] shortage; **~хоро́ший** [17; -рóш, -á] bad; **∠хотя** unwillingly; **~цензу́рный** [14; -рен, -рна] *s.* ~пристóйный; **~ча́янный** [14] unexpected; accidental, casual.
не́чего [23]: (мне, *etc.*) ~ + *inf.* (there is *or* one can) (I have) nothing to ...; (one) need not, (there is) no need; (it is) no use; stop ...ing.
не|челове́ческий [16] inhuman; superhuman; **~чести́вый** [14 *sh.*] ungodly; **~че́стность** *f* [8] dishonesty; **~че́стный** [14; -тен, -тнá, -o] dishonest; **∠чет** F *m* [1] *s.* нечётный; **~чётный** [14] odd (*number*).
нечист|опло́тный [14; -тен, -тна] uncleanly, dirty; **~ота́** *f* [5; *pl. st.*: -óты] unclean(li)ness; *pl.* sewage; **∠ый** [14; -чи́ст, -á, -o] unclean, dirty; impure; evil, vile, bad, foul.
не́что something.
не|чувстви́тельный [14; -лен, -льна] insensitive; insensible; **~щáдный** [14; -ден, -дна] unmerciful; **~я́вка** *f* [5] nonappearance; **~я́ркий** [16; -я́рок, -яркá, -o] dull, dim; mediocre; **~я́сный** [14; -сен, -снá, -o] not clear; *fig.* vague.
ни not a (single оди́н); ~ ..., ~ neither ... nor; ... ever (*e. g.* кто [бы] ~ whoever); кто (что, когдá, где, кудá) бы то ∠ был(о) whosoever (what-, when-, wheresoever); как ~ + *vb. a.* in spite *or* for all + *su.*; как бы (то) ∠ было be that as it may; ~ за что ~ про что for nothing.
ни́ва *f* [5] field (*a. fig.*; in на П).
нигдé nowhere.
Нидерла́нды *pl.* [1] The Netherlands.
ни́ж|е below, beneath, under; lower; shorter; **~еподписа́вшийся** *m* [17] the undersigned; **~ний** [15] lower; under...; ground *or* first (*floor*).
низ *m* [1; *pl. e.*] bottom, lower part; *pl. a.* masses; **~áть** [3], ⟨на-⟩ string.
низвер|гáть [1], ⟨∠гнуть⟩ [21]; **~жéние** *n* [12] (over)throw.
низи́на *f* [5] hollow, lowland.
ни́зк|ий [16; -зок, -зкá, -o; *comp.*: ни́же] low; mean, base; short; **~опокло́нник** *m* [1] groveler; **~опокло́нничать** [1] grovel, fawn, cringe.
ни́зменн|ость *f* [8] lowland, plain; **~ый** [14 *sh.*] low(er).
низо|во́й [14] lower; local; **∠вье** *n* [10; *g/pl.*: -ьев] lower (course); **~йти́** *s.* нисходи́ть; **'~сть** *f* [8] meanness.
никáк by no means, not at all; **~óй** [16] no (at all F); ни в какóм слу́чае on no account; *s. a.* ~.
ни́кел|евый [14], **~ь** *m* [4] nickel.
никогдá never.
Никола́й [3] Nicholas.

ни|ко́й *s.* никак(ой); **~кто́** [23] nobody, no one, none; **~куда́** nowhere; *cf. a.* годиться, годный; **~кчёмный** F [14] good-for-nothing; **~ма́ло** *s.* ~сколько; **~отку́да** from nowhere; **~почём** F very cheap, easy, *etc.*; **~ско́лько** not in the least, not at all.
нисходя́щий [17] descending.
ни́т|ка *f* [5; *g/pl.*: -ток], **~ь** [8] thread; string; cotton; **~ь** *a.* filament; до (последней) ~ки F to the skin; (как) по ~ке straight; шито белыми ~ками be transparent, на живую ~ку carelessly, superficially.
ниц: падать ~ prostrate o. s.
ничего́ (-'vɔ) nothing; ~ (себе) not bad; so-so; no(t) matter; ~! never mind!, that's all right!
нич|е́й *m*, **~ья́** *f*, **~ьё** *n*, **~ьи́** *pl.* [26] nobody's; *su. f* draw (*games*).
ничко́м prone; *s. a.* ниц.
ничто́ [23] nothing; *s.* ничего; **~жество** *n* [9], **~жность** *f* [8] nothingness, vanity, nonentity; **~жный** [14; -жен, -жна] insignificant, tiny; vain.
нич|у́ть F *s.* нисколько; **~ья́** *s.* **~е́й.**
ни́ша *f* [5] niche.
ни́щ|ая *f* [17], **~енка** F [5; *g/pl.*: -нок] beggar woman; **~енский** [16] beggarly; **~енство** *n* [9] begging; beggary; **~енствовать** [7] beg; **~ета́** *f* [5] poverty, destitution; **~ий** **1.** [17; нищ, -á, -e] beggarly; **2.** *m* [17] beggar.
НКВД (Народный комиссариат внутренних дел) People's Commissariat of Internal Affairs (*1935 to 1946*; *since 1946* МВД, *cf.*).
но but, yet.
нова́тор *m* [1] innovator.
нове́лла *f* [5] short story.
но́в|енький [16; -нек] (brand-) new; **~изна́** *f* [5], **~и́нка** [5; *g/pl.*: -нок] novelty; news; **~ичо́к** *m* [1; -чка] novice, tyro; newcomer.
ново|бра́нец *m* [1; -нца] recruit; **~бра́чный** [14] newly married; **~введе́ние** *n* [12] innovation; **~го́дний** [15] New Year's (Eve ~годний вечер *m*); **~лу́ние** *n* [12] new moon; **~прибы́вший** [17] newly arrived; newcomer; **~рождённый** [14] newborn (child); **~се́лье** *n* [10] new home; house-warming; **~стро́йка** *f* [5; *g/pl.*: -оек] new building (project).
но́в|ость *f* [8] (piece of) news; novelty; **~шество** *n* [9] innovation, novelty; **~ый** [14; нов, -á, -o] new; novel; recent; modern; **Ⴈый год** *m* New Year's Day; с Ⴈым годом! a happy New Year!; ~ый месяц *m* crescent; что ~ого? what's (the) new(s *Brt.*)?; **~ь** *f* [8] virgin soil.
ног|а́ *f* [5; *ac/sg.*: ногу; *pl.*: ноги, ног, ногам, *etc. e.*] foot, leg; идти в ⁓у march in (*or* keep) step; со всех ~ with all one's might, at full speed; стать на ~и recover; become independent; положить ⁓у на ~у cross one's legs; на ... ~е *or* ⁓у on ... terms *or* a ... footing; in (*grand*) style; ни ~ой (к Д) not visit (a p.); (еле) ⁓и унести (have a narrow) escape; в ~ах at the foot (*cf.* голова); под ~ами underfoot.
но́готь *m* [4; -гтя; *from g/pl. e.*] nail.
нож *m* [1 *e.*] knife; на ~ах at daggers drawn; **⁓ик** *m* [1] F = нож; **⁓ка** *f* [5; *g/pl.*: -жек] *dim. of* нога, *s.*; leg (*chair, etc.*); **⁓ницы** *f/pl.* [5] (pair of) scissors; disproportion; **~но́й** [14] foot...; **⁓ны́** *f/pl.* [5; *g/pl.*; -жен & -жон] sheath.
ноздря́ [6; *pl.*: ноздри, ноздрей, *etc. e.*] nostril.
ноль & нуль *m* [4 *e.*] naught; zero.
но́мер *m* [1; *pl.*: -рá, *etc. e.*] number ([with] за T); size; (*hotel*) room; item, turn, trick; (*a.*, *dim.*, **~о́к** *m* [1; -рка]) tag, plate.
номина́льный [14; -лен, -льна] nominal.
нора́ *f* [5; *ac/sg.*: -ру; *pl.st.*] hole, burrow.
Норве́|гия *f* [7] Norway; **Ⴈжец** *m* [1; -жца], **Ⴈжка** *f* [5; *g/pl.*: -жек], **Ⴈжский** [16] Norwegian.
но́рка *f* [5; *g/pl.*: -рок] **1.** *dim. of* нора; **2.** *zo.* mink.
но́рм|а *f* [5] norm, standard; rate; **~а́льный** [14; -лен, -льна] normal; **~ирова́ть** [7] (*im*)*pf.* standardize.
нос *m* [1; в, на носу; *pl. e.*] nose; beak; prow; F spout; в ~ (*speak*) through one's nose; за ~ (*lead*) by the nose; на ~у́ (*time*) at hand; у меня идёт кровь ⁓ом my nose is bleeding; **⁓ик** *m* [1] *dim. of* ~; spout.
носи́|лки *f/pl.* [5; *gen.*: -лок] stretcher, litter; **~льщик** *m* [1] porter; **~тель** *m* [4] bearer; carrier; **~ть** [15] carry, bear, *etc.*, *s.* нести; wear (*v/i.* **-ся**); F **-ся** (с T) *a.* have one's mind occupied with.
носово́й [14] nasal; prow ...; ~ платок *m* handkerchief.
носо́к *m* [1; -ска] sock; toe; *a.* = носик.
носоро́г *m* [1] rhinoceros.
но́та *f* [5] note; *pl. a.* music.
нота́риус *m* [1] notary (public).
нота́ция *f* [7] reprimand, lecture.
ноч|ева́ть [7], ⟨пере-⟩ pass (*or* spend) the night; **~ёвка** *f* [5; *g/pl.*: -вок] overnight stop (*or* stay *or* rest); *a.* = ~лег; **~ле́г** *m* [1] night's lodging, night quarters; *a.* = ~ёвка; **~но́й** [14] night(ly), (*a.* ♀, *zo.*) nocturnal; ~ная бабочка *f* moth; **~ь** *f* [8; в ночи; *from g/pl. e.*] night; **⁓ью** at (*or* by) night (= *a.* в ~ь, по ~ам); ~ь под ... (B) ... night.
но́ша *f* [5] load, burden.
ноя́брь *m* [4 *e.*] November.

нрав *m* [1] disposition, temper; *pl.* customs; (не) по **∠**у (Д) (not) to one's liking; **∠иться** [14], ⟨по-⟩ please (a p. Д); он мне ∠ится I like him; **~оучение** *n* [12] moral(ity), moral teaching; **~оучительный** [14] moral(izing); **∠ственность** *f* [8] morals *pl.*, morality; **~ственный** [14 *sh.*] moral.
ну (*a.* ∠-ка) well *or* now (then же)!, come (on)!, why!, what!; the deuce (take him *or* it ~ его́)!; (*a.* да ~?) indeed?, really?, you don't say!; ha?; ~ да of course, sure; ~ + *inf.* begin to; ~ так что́ же? what about it?
ну́дный F [14; ну́ден, -дна́, -о] tedious, humdrum.
нужд|а́ *f* [5; *pl. st.*] need, want (of в П); necessity (of из Р, по Д); F request; concern; **~ы́** нет it doesn't matter; **~а́ться** [1] (в П) (be in) need (of), be hard up, needy.
ну́жн|ый [14; ну́жен, -жна́, -о, ну́жны́] necessary (for Д); (Д) **~о** + *inf.* must (*cf.* на́до).
нуль = ноль.
ну́мер = но́мер; **~а́ция** *f* [7] numeration; **~ова́ть** [7], ⟨за-, про-⟩ number.
ны́н|е now(adays), today; **~ешний** F [15] present, this; actual, today's; **~че** F = ~е.
ныр|я́ть [28], *once* ⟨~ну́ть⟩ [20] dive.
ныть [22] ache; whimper; F lament.
Нью-Йо́рк *m* [1] New York.
н. э. (на́шей э́ры) A. D.
нэп (но́вая экономи́ческая поли́тика) NEP (New Economic Policy. *Sov., from 1922 to 1928*).
нюх *m* [1] flair, scent; **∠ательный** [14]: ∠ательный таба́к *m* snuff; **∠ать** [1], ⟨по-⟩ smell; scent; snuff.
ня́н|чить [16] nurse, tend (*a.* **-ся**; F fuss over, busy o. s. with [с Т]); **~я** *f* [6] (F **~ька** [5; *g/pl.*: -нек]) nurse, *Brt. a.* nanny.

О

о, об, обо 1. (П) about, of; on; with; **2.** (В) against, (up)on; by, in.
о! oh!, o!
о́б|а *m & n*, **~е** *f* [37] both.
обагр|я́ть [28], ⟨~и́ть⟩ [13] redden, purple; stain (with Т); steep.
обанкро́титься *s.* банкро́титься.
обая́|ние *n* [12] spell, charm; **~тельный** [14; -лен, -льна] fascinating.
обва́л *m* [1] collapse; landslide; avalanche; **~иваться** [1], ⟨~и́ться⟩ [13; обва́лится] fall in *or* off; **~я́ть** [1] *pf.* roll.
обвари́ть [13; -арю́, -а́ришь] scald.
обвёр|тывать [1], ⟨~ну́ть⟩ [20] wrap (up), envelop.
обве́|сить [15] F = ~шать.
обвести́ *s.* обводи́ть.
обве́тренный [14 *sh.*] weather-beaten.
обветша́лый [14] decayed.
обве́ш|ивать, ⟨~ать⟩ [1] hang (with Т).
обви|ва́ть [1], ⟨∠ть⟩ [обовью́, -вьёшь; *cf.* вить] wind round; embrace (with Т).
обвин|е́ние *n* [12] accusation, charge; indictment; prosecution; **~и́тель** *m* [4] accuser; prosecutor; **~и́тельный** [14] accusatory; of 'guilty'; ~и́тельный акт *m* indictment; **~я́ть** [28], ⟨~и́ть⟩ [13] (в П) accuse (of), charge (with); find guilty; ~я́емый accused; defendant.
обви́слый F [14] flabby.
обви́|ть *s.* ~ва́ть.
обводи́ть [13], ⟨обвести́⟩ [25] lead, see *or* look (round, about); enclose, encircle *or* border (with Т); draw out; F turn (*a p. round one's finger*).
обвор|а́живать [1], ⟨~ожи́ть⟩ [16 *e.*; -жу́, -жи́шь; -жённый] charm, fascinate; **~ожи́тельный** [14; -лен, -льна] charming, fascinating; **~ожи́ть** *s.* ~а́живать.
обвя́з|ывать [1], ⟨~а́ть⟩ [3] tie up *or* round; dress; hang.
обгоня́ть [28], ⟨обогна́ть⟩ [обгоню́, -о́нишь; обогна́л, -а́, -о; обо́гнанный] (out)distance, outstrip.
обгор|а́ть [1], ⟨~е́ть⟩ [9] scorch.
обгрыз|а́ть [1], ⟨∠ть⟩ [24; *pt. st.*] gnaw (at, round, away).
обда|ва́ть [5], ⟨∠ть⟩ [-а́м, -а́шь; *cf.* дать; о́бдал, -а́, -о; о́бданный (о́бдан, -а́, -о)] pour over; scald; bespatter; wrap up; seize.
обде́л|ать *s.* ~ывать; **~и́ть** *s.* ~я́ть; **~ывать**, ⟨~ать⟩ [1] work; lay out; cut (*gem*); F manage, wangle; **~я́ть** [28], ⟨~и́ть⟩ [13; -елю́, -е́лишь] deprive of one's due share (of Т).
обдира́ть [1], ⟨ободра́ть⟩ [обдеру́, -рёшь; ободра́л, -а́, -о; обо́дранный] bark, peel; tear (off).
обду́м|ать *s.* ~ывать; **~анный** [14 *sh.*] deliberate; **~ывать**, ⟨~ать⟩ [1] consider, think over.
обе́д *m* [1] dinner (at за Т; for на В, к Д), lunch; F noon; до (по́сле) **~а** in the morning (afternoon); **~ать** [1], ⟨по-⟩ have dinner (lunch), dine; **~енный** [14] dinner..., lunch...
обедне́вший [17] impoverished.
обе́дня *f* [6; *g/pl.*: -ден] mass.
обез|бо́ливание *n* [12] an(a)esthetization; **~вре́живать** [1], ⟨~вре́дить⟩ [15] neutralize; **~гла́вли-**

вать [1], ⟨**~гла́вить**⟩ [14] behead; **~до́ленный** [14] wretched, miserable; **~зара́живание** *n* [12] disinfection; **~ли́чивать** [1], ⟨**~ли́чить**⟩ [16] deprive of personal character, assignment *or* responsibility; **~лю́деть** [8] *pf.* become deserted; **~надёживать** [1], ⟨**~надёжить**⟩ [16] bereave of hope; **~обра́живать** [1], ⟨**~обра́зить**⟩ [15] disfigure; **~опа́сить** [15] *pf.* secure (against от P); **~ору́живать** [1], ⟨**~ору́жить**⟩ [16] disarm; **~у́меть** [8] *pf.* lose one's senses, go mad.

обезья́н|а *f* [5] monkey; ape; **~ий** [18] monkey('s); apish, apelike; **~ничать** F [1] ape.

обер|ега́ть [1], ⟨**~е́чь**⟩ [26 г/ж: -гу́, -жёшь] guard (*v/i.* **-ся**), protect (o. s.; against, from от P).

оберну́ть(ся) *s.* обёртывать(ся).

обёрт|ка *f* [5; *g/pl.*: -ток] cover; (book) jacket; **~очный** [14] wrapping (*or* brown *paper*); **~ывать** [1], ⟨оберну́ть⟩ [20] wrap (up); wind; turn (*a.* F, *cf.* обводи́ть F); **-ся** turn (round, F back); F wangle.

обескура́ж|ивать [1], ⟨**~ить**⟩ [16] discourage, dishearten.

обеспе́ч|ение *n* [12] securing; security (on под B), guarantee; maintenance; (*social*) security; **~енность** *f* [8] (adequate) provision; prosperity; **~енный** [14] well-to-do; **~ивать** [1], ⟨**~ить**⟩ [16] provide (for; with T); secure, guarantee; protect.

обесси́л|еть [8] *pf.* become enervated; **~ивать** [1], ⟨**~ить**⟩ [13] enervate.

обессме́ртить [13] *pf.* immortalize.

обесцве́|чивать [1], ⟨**~тить**⟩ [15] discolo(u)r, make colo(u)rless.

обесце́н|ивать [1], ⟨**~ить**⟩ [13] depreciate.

обесче́стить [15] *pf.* dishono(u)r.

обе́т *m* [1] vow, promise; **~ова́нный** [14] Promised (*Land*).

обеща́|ние *n* [12], **~ть** [1] (*im*)*pf.*, F *a.* ⟨по-⟩ promise.

обжа́лование ⚖ *n* [12] appeal.

обж|ига́ть [1], ⟨**~е́чь**⟩ [26 г/ж: обожгу́, -жжёшь, обожгу́т; обжёг, обожгла́; обожжённый] burn; scorch; ⊕ bake, calcine (*cf.* **~ига́тельная печь** *f* kiln); **-ся** burn o. s. (F one's fingers).

обжо́р|а F *m/f* [5] glutton; **~ливый** F [14 *sh.*] gluttonous; **~ство** F *n* [9] gluttony.

обзав|оди́ться [15], ⟨**~ести́сь**⟩ [25] provide o. s. (with T), acquire, get.

обзо́р *m* [1] survey; review.

обзыва́ть [1], ⟨обозва́ть⟩ [обзову́, -ёшь; обозва́л, -а́, -о; обо́званный] call (*names* T).

оби|ва́ть [1], ⟨**~ть**⟩ [обобью́, обобьёшь; *cf.* бить] upholster; strike off; F wear out; **~ва́ть поро́ги** (у P) importune; **~вка** *f* [5] upholstery.

оби́|да *f* [5] insult; не в **~ду** будь ска́зано no offence meant; не дать в **~ду** let not be offended; **~деть (-ся)** *s.* **~жа́ть(ся)**; **~дный** [14; -ден, -дна] offensive, insulting; (мне) **~дно** it is a shame *or* vexing (it offends *or* vexes me; I am sorry [for за B]); **~дчивый** [14 *sh.*] touchy; **~дчик** F *m* [1] offender; **~жа́ть** [1], ⟨**~деть**⟩ [11] (**-ся** be) offend(ed), hurt (*a.* be angry with *or* at на B); wrong; overreach (*cf. a.* обделя́ть); **~женный** [14 *sh.*] offended (*s. a.* **~жа́ть[ся]**).

оби́л|ие *n* [12] abundance, wealth; **~ьный** [14; -лен, -льна] abundant (in T), plentiful, rich.

обиня́к *m* [1 *e.*]: говори́ть **~а́ми** speak in a roundabout way.

обира́ть F [1], ⟨обобра́ть⟩ [оберу́, -ёшь; обобра́л, -а́, -о; обо́бранный] rob; P gather.

обита́|емый [14 *sh.*] inhabited; **~тель** *m* [4] inhabitant; **~ть** [1] live, dwell, reside.

оби́ть *s.* обива́ть.

обихо́д *m* [1] use, custom, way; дома́шний ~ household; **~ный** [14; -ден, -дна] everyday; colloquial.

обкла́д|ка *f* [5] facing; **~ывать** [1], ⟨обложи́ть⟩ [16] lay round; face, cover; ✂ fur; *pf.* besiege; *s.* облага́ть.

обко́м *m* [1] (областно́й комите́т) regional committee *Sov.*).

обкра́дывать [1], ⟨обокра́сть⟩ [25; обкраду́, -дёшь; *pt. st.* обкра́денный] rob.

обла́ва *f* [5] battue; raid.

облага́ть [1], ⟨обложи́ть⟩ [16] impose (*tax, fine* T); tax; fine.

облагор|а́живать [1], ⟨**~о́дить**⟩ [15] ennoble, refine; finish.

облада́|ние *n* [12] possession (of T); **~ть** [1] (T) possess; command; (*health*) be in; **~ть собо́й** control o. s.

о́блако *n* [9; *pl.*: -ка́, -ко́в] cloud.

обл|а́мывать [1], ⟨**~ома́ть**⟩ [1] & ⟨**~оми́ть**⟩ [14] break off.

обласка́ть [1] *pf.* treat kindly.

област|но́й [14] regional; **'~ь** *f* [8; *from g/pl. e.*] region; province, sphere, field (*fig.*).

obла́тка *f* [5; *g/pl.*: -ток] wafer; capsule.

обла|че́ние *n* [12] *eccl.* vestments [*pl.*]

о́блачный [14; -чен, -чна] cloudy.

обле|га́ть [1], ⟨**~чь**⟩ [26 г/ж; *cf.* лечь] cover; fit (*close*).

облегч|а́ть (-xtʃ-) [1], ⟨**~и́ть**⟩ [16 *e.*; -чу́, -чи́шь; -чённый] lighten; facilitate; ease, relieve.

обледене́лый [14] ice-covered.

облёзлый F [14] mangy, shabby.

обле|ка́ть [1], ⟨**~чь**⟩ [26] dress; invest (with T); put, express; **-ся** put on (в B); be(come) invested.

облеп|ля́ть [28], ⟨~и́ть⟩ [14] stick all over (*or* round); besiege.
облет|а́ть [1], ⟨~е́ть⟩ [11] fly round (*or: all over*, past, in); fall.
облéчь [1], *s.* облегáть & облекáть.
обли|ва́ть [1], ⟨~ть⟩ [оболью́, -льёшь; облéй!; óбли́л, -á, -о; óбли́тый (óбли́т, -á, -о)] pour (s. th. T) over, wet; flood; soak; **-ся** [*pf.*: -и́лся, -илáсь, -и́лóсь] (T) pour over o. s.; shed (*tears*); be dripping (*with sweat*) *or* covered (*with blood*); bleed (*heart*).
облигáция *f* [7] bond.
обли́з|ывать [1], ⟨~áть⟩ [3] lick (off); **-ся** lick one's lips (*or* o. s.).
óблик *m* [1] face, look; figure.
обли́|ть(ся) *s.* ~вáть(ся); **~цóвывать** [1], ⟨~цевáть⟩ [7] face.
облич|áть [1], ⟨~и́ть⟩ [16 *e.*; -чý, -чи́шь; -чённый] unmask; reveal; convict (of в П); **~éние** *n* [12] exposure; conviction; **~и́тельный** [14; -лен, -льна] accusatory, incriminating; **~и́ть** *s.* ~áть.
облож|éние *n* [12] taxation; ⚔ siege; **~и́ть** *s.* обклáдывать & облагáть; **~ка** [5; *g/pl.*: -жек] cover, (book) jacket.
облок|áчиваться [1], ⟨~оти́ться⟩ [15 & 15 *e.*; -кочýсь, -кóти́шься] lean one's elbows (on на В).
облом|áть, ~и́ть *s.* облáмывать; **~ок** *m* [1; -мка] fragment; *pl.* debris, wreckage.
облуч|áть [1], ⟨~и́ть⟩ [16 *e.*; -чý, -чи́шь; -чённый] ray.
облучóк *m* [1; -чкá] (coach) box.
облюбовáть [7] *pf.* take a fancy to.
обмáз|ывать [1], ⟨~ать⟩ [3] besmear; plaster, coat, cement.
обмáк|ивать [1], ⟨~нýть⟩ [20] dip.
обмáн *m* [1] deception; deceit, fraud; ~ зрéния optical illusion; **~ный** [14] deceitful, fraudulent; **~ýть(ся)** *s.* ~ывать(ся); **~чивый** [14 *sh.*] deceptive; **~щик** *m* [1], **~щица** *f* [5] cheat, deceiver; **~ывать** [1], ⟨~ýть⟩ [20] (**-ся** be) deceive(d), cheat; (be mistaken in в П).
обм|áтывать, ⟨~отáть⟩ [1] wind (round); **~áхивать** [1], ⟨~ахнýть⟩ [19] wipe, dust; fan.
обмéн *m* [1] exchange (in/for в В/на В); interchange (of T, P); **~ивать** [1], ⟨~я́ть⟩ [28] & F ⟨~и́ть⟩ [13; -еню́, -éнишь; ~енённый] exchange (for на В; **-ся** s. th. T).
обм|ерéть *s.* ~ирáть; **~етáть** [1], ⟨~ести́⟩ [25 -т-: обметý] sweep (off), dust; **~ирáть** F [1], ⟨~ерéть⟩ [12; обомрý, -рёшь; óбмер, -рлá, -о; обмéрший] be struck *or* stunned (with *fear* от P).
обмóлв|иться [14] *pf.* make a slip (in speaking); (T) mention, say; **~ка** *f* [5; *g/pl.*: -вок] slip of the tongue.
обмолóт *m* [1] thresh(ing).
обморóзить [15] *pf.* frostbite.
óбморок *m* [1] faint, swoon (*vb.*: пáдать, *pf.* упáсть в ~).
обмот|áть *s.* обмáтывать; **~ка** *f* [5; *g/pl.*: -ток] ⚡ winding; *pl.* puttees.
обмундировá|ние *n* [12], **~ть** [7] *pf.* uniform, outfit.
обмы|вáть [1], ⟨~ть⟩ [22] wash (off); **~вáние** *n* [12] *a.* ablution.
обнадёж|ивать [1], ⟨~ить⟩ [16] (re)assure, encourage, raise hopes.
обнаж|áть [1], ⟨~и́ть⟩ [16 *e.*; -жý, -жи́шь; -жённый] bare, strip; lay bare; uncover; unsheathe.
обнарóдовать [7] *pf.* promulgate.
обнарýж|ивать [1], ⟨~ить⟩ [16] disclose, show, reveal; discover, detect; **-ся** appear, show; come to light; be found, discovered.
обнести́ *s.* обноси́ть.
обн|имáть [1], ⟨~я́ть⟩ [обнимý, обни́мешь; óбнял, -á, -о; óбнятый (óбнят, -á, -о)] embrace, hug, clasp.
обнищáлый [14] impoverished.
обнóв|(к)а F *f* [5; (*g/pl.*: -вок)] new thing, novelty; **~и́ть** *s.* ~ля́ть; **~лéние** *n* [12] renewal; renovation; **~ля́ть** [28], ⟨~и́ть⟩ [14 *e.*; -влю́, -ви́шь; -влённый] renew; renovate.
обн|оси́ть [15], ⟨~ести́⟩ [24 -с-: -сý] carry (round); serve; pass by; (T) fence in, enclose; **-ся** F *impf.* wear out one's clothes.
обню́х|ивать, ⟨~ать⟩ [1] smell at.
обня́ть *s.* обнимáть.
обобрáть *s.* обирáть.
обобщ|áть [1], ⟨~и́ть⟩ [16 *e.*; -щý, -щи́шь; -щённый] generalize; **~ествля́ть** [28], ⟨~естви́ть⟩ [14 *e.*; -влю́, -ви́шь; -влённый] socialize; **~и́ть** *s.* ~áть.
обога|щáть [1], ⟨~ти́ть⟩ [15 *e.*; -ащý, -ти́шь; -ащённый] enrich.
обогнáть *s.* обгоня́ть.
обогнýть *s.* огибáть.
обоготворя́ть [28] *s.* боготвори́ть.
обогревáть [1] *s.* греть.
óбод *m* [1; *pl.*: обóдья, -дьев] rim, felloe; **~óк** *m* [1; -дкá] rim.
обóдр|анный F [14 *sh.*] ragged, shabby; **~áть** *s.* обдирáть; **~éние** *n* [12] encouragement; **~я́ть** [28], ⟨~и́ть⟩ [13] encourage; **-ся** take courage.
обожáть [1] adore, worship.
обождáть F = подождáть.
обожеств|ля́ть [28], ⟨~и́ть⟩ [14 *e.*; -влю́, -ви́шь; -влённый] deify.
обожжённый [14; -ён, -енá] burnt.
обóз *m* [1] train (*a.* ⚔), carts *pl.*
обозвáть *s.* обзывáть.
обознач|áть [1], ⟨~ить⟩ [16] denote, designate, mark; **-ся** appear; **~éние** *n* [12] designation.
обозр|евáть [1], ⟨~éть⟩ [9], **~éние** *n* [12] survey; review.
обó|и *m/pl.* [3] wallpaper; **~йти́(сь)**

s. обходи́ть(ся); **~йщик** *m* [1] upholsterer; **~кра́сть** *s.* обкра́дывать.

оболо́чка *f* [5; *g/pl.*: -чек] cover(-ing), envelope; *anat.* membrane; ⊕ jacket, casing; ра́дужная ~ iris.

оболь|сти́тель *m* [4] seducer; **~сти́тельный** [14; -лен, -льна] seductive; **~щать** [1], ‹**~сти́ть**› [15 *e.*; -льщу́, -льсти́шь; -льщённый] seduce; (**-ся** be) delude(d; flatter o. s.); **~ще́ние** *n* [12] seduction; delusion.

обомле́ть F [8] *pf.* be stupefied.

обоня́ние *n* [12] (sense of) smell.

обора́чивать(ся) *s.* обёртывать(-ся).

оборв|а́нец F *m* [1; -нца] ragamuffin; **∠анный** [14 *sh.*] ragged; **~а́ть** *s.* обрыва́ть.

обо́рка *f* [5; *g/pl.*: -рок] frill, ruffle.

оборо́н|а *f* [5] defense (*Brt.* defence); **~и́тельный** [14] defensive, defense...; **~ный** [14] defense..., armament...; **~оспосо́бность** *f* [8] defensive capacity; **~я́ть** [28] defend.

оборо́т *m* [1] revolution; rotation; circulation; turn; turnover; transaction; back, reverse; (см.) на ~е p. t. o.; в ~ F (*take*) to task; **~и́ть(ся)** P [15] *pf.* *s.* оберну́ть(ся); **~ливый** F [14 *sh.*] sharp, smart; **~ный** [14] back, reverse, seamy (*side*); ✝ circulating.

обору́дова|ние [12] equipment; **~ть** [7] (*im*)*pf.* equip; fit out.

обосн|ова́ние *n* [12] substantiation; ground(s); **~о́вывать** [1], ‹**~ова́ть**› [7] prove, substantiate; **-ся** settle down.

обос|обля́ть [28], ‹**~о́бить**› [14] segregate, isolate, detach.

обостр|я́ть [28], ‹**~и́ть**› [13] (**-ся** become) aggravate(d), strain(ed); refine(d).

обою́д|ный [14; -ден, -дна] mutual; **~оо́стрый** [14 *sh.*] double-edged.

обраб|а́тывать, ‹**~о́тать**› [1] work, process; ⚒ till; elaborate, finish, polish; treat; adapt; F work; *p. pr. a.* ⊕ manufacturing; **~о́тка** *f* [5; *g/pl.*: -ток] processing; ⚒ cultivation; elaboration; adaptation.

о́браз *m* [1] manner, way (in T), mode; form; figure, character; image; [*pl.*: ~а́, *etc. e.*] icon; каки́м (таки́м) ~ом how (thus); нико́им ~ом by no means; **~е́ц** *m* [1; -зца́] specimen, sample; model, example; pattern; fashion, way (in на В); **~ный** [14; -зен, -зна] graphic, vivid; **~ова́ние** *n* [12] formation; constitution; education; **~о́ванный** [14 *sh.*] educated; **~ова́тельный** [14; -лен, -льна] (in)formative; **~о́вывать** [1], ‹**~ова́ть**› [7] form (*v/i.* **-ся**; arise); constitute; educate; cultivate; **~у́мить(ся)** F [14] *pf.* bring (come) to one's senses; **~цо́вый** [14] exemplary, model...; **∠чик** *m* [1] *s.* ~е́ц.

обрам|ля́ть [28], ‹**∠ить**› [14 *st.*], *fig.* ‹**~и́ть**› [14 *e.*; -млю́, -ми́шь; -млённый] frame.

обраст|а́ть [1], ‹**~и́**› [24 -ст-: -сту́; обро́с, -ла́] overgrow; be overgrown.

обра|ти́ть *s.* ~ща́ть; **∠тный** [14] back, return...; reverse, (*a.* ⚗) inverse; ⚖ retroactive; ∠тно back; conversely; **~ща́ть** [1], ‹**~ти́ть**› [15 *e.*; -ащу́, -ати́шь; -ащённый] turn; direct; convert; employ; draw *or* pay *or* (на себя́) attract (*attention*; to на В); не ~ща́ть внима́ния (на В) disregard; **-ся** turn (to в В); address o. s. (to к Д), apply (to; for за Т); appeal; take (to *flight* в В); *impf.* (с Т) treat, handle; circulate; **~ще́ние** *n* [12] conversion; transformation; circulation; (с Т) treatment (of), management; manners *pl.*; address; appeal.

обре́з *m* [1] edge; **~а́ть** [1], ‹**~ать**› [3] cut off; cut short; **~ок** *m* [1; -зка] scrap; **~ывать** [1] *s.* ~а́ть.

обре|ка́ть [1], ‹**∠чь**› [26] doom (to на В, Д).

обремен|и́тельный [14; -лен, -льна] burdensome; **~я́ть** [28], ‹**~и́ть**› [13] burden.

обре|чённый [14] doomed (to на В); **∠чь** *s.* ~ка́ть.

обрисо́в|ывать [1], ‹**~а́ть**› [7] outline, sketch; **-ся** loom, appear.

обро́к *m* [1] (quit)rent, tribute.

обро́сший [17] overgrown.

обруб|а́ть [1], ‹**~и́ть**› [14] hew (off), lop; **∠ок** *m* [1; -бка] stump, block.

о́бруч *m* [1; *from g/pl. e.*] hoop; **~а́льный** [14] engagement...; **~а́ть** [1], ‹**~и́ть**› [16 *e.*; -чу́, -чи́шь; -чённый] affiance, betroth; **-ся** be(come) engaged (to с Т); **~е́ние** *n* [12] betrothal; **~ённый** [14] fiancé(e ~ённая *f*).

обру́ш|ивать [1], ‹**~ить**› [16] demolish; cast; **-ся** fall in, collapse; fall (up)on (на В).

обры́в *m* [1] precipice, steep; **~а́ть** [1], ‹оборва́ть› [-ву́, -вёшь; -ва́л, -вала́, -о; обо́рванный] tear *or* pluck (off, round); break off, cut short; **-ся** *a.* fall (from с Р); **~истый** [14 *sh.*] steep; abrupt; **~ок** *m* [1; -вка] scrap, shred; **~очный** [14; -чен, -чна] scrappy.

обры́зг|ивать, ‹**~ать**› [1] sprinkle.

обрю́зглый [14] flabby, bloated.

обря́д *m* [1] ceremony, rite.

об|са́живать [1], ‹**~сади́ть**› [15] plant (with Т); **~сева́ть** [1], ‹**~се́ять**› [27] sow; stud (with Т).

обсервато́рия *f* [7] observatory.

обсле́дова|ние *n* [12] (P) inspection (of), inquiry (into), investiga-

tion (of); ~ть [7] (*im*)*pf.* inspect, examine, investigate.
обслу́ж|ивание *n* [12] service; operation; **~ивать** [1], ⟨**~и́ть**⟩ [16] serve, attend; operate; supply (В/Т).
обсо́хнуть *s.* обсыха́ть.
обста|вля́ть [28], ⟨**~́вить**⟩ [14] surround; furnish, fit out (with Т); F arrange, settle; **~но́вка** *f* [5; *g/pl.*: -вок] furniture; *thea.* scenery; situation, conditions *pl.*
обстоя́тель|ный [14; -лен, -льна] detailed, circumstantial; F solid, thorough; **~ственный** [14] adverbial; **~ство** *n* [9] circumstance (under, in при П, в П; for по Д); *gr.* adverb.
обстоя́ть [-ойт] be, stand; как обсто́ит де́ло с (Т)? what about ...?
обстре́л *m* [1] bombardment, fire; **~ивать** [1], ⟨**~я́ть**⟩ [28] fire on, shell; *p. pt. p.* F tried.
обступ|а́ть [1], ⟨**~и́ть**⟩ [14] surround.
об|сужда́ть [1], ⟨**~суди́ть**⟩ [15; -ждённый] discuss; **~сужде́ние** *n* [12] discussion; **~суши́ть** [16] *pf.* dry; **~счита́ть** [1] *pf.* cheat; **-ся** miscalculate.
обсып|а́ть [1], ⟨**~́ать**⟩ [2] strew.
обс|ыха́ть [1], ⟨**~о́хнуть**⟩ [21] dry.
обт|а́чивать [1], ⟨**~очи́ть**⟩ [16] turn; **~ека́емый** [14] streamline...; **~ере́ть** *s.* **~ира́ть**; **~ёсывать** [1], ⟨**~еса́ть**⟩ [3] hew; **~ира́ть** [1], ⟨**~ере́ть**⟩ [12; оботру́; обтёр; *ger. pt. a.*: -тёрши & -терёв] rub off *or* down, wipe (off), dry; F fray.
обточи́ть *s.* обта́чивать.
обтрёпанный [14] shabby, frayed.
обтя́|гивать [1], ⟨**~ну́ть**⟩ [19] cover (with Т); *impf.* fit close; **~жка** *f* [5]: в ~жку close-fitting.
обу|ва́ть [1], ⟨**~́ть**⟩ [18] put (**-ся** one's) shoes on; F shoe; **'~вь** *f* [8] footwear, shoes *pl.*
обу́гл|ивать [1], ⟨**~ить**⟩ [13] char.
обу́за *f* [5] burden, load.
обу́зд|ывать [1], ⟨**~ать**⟩ [1] bridle.
обусло́в|ливать [1], ⟨**~ить**⟩ [14] condition (on Т); cause.
обу́ть(ся) *s.* обува́ть(ся).
о́бух *m* [1] butt; F thunder(*struck*).
обуч|а́ть [1], ⟨**~и́ть**⟩ [16] teach (s. th. Д), train; **-ся** (Д) learn, be taught; **~е́ние** *n* [12] instruction, training; education.
обхва́т *m* [1] arm's span; circumference; **~ывать** [1], ⟨**~и́ть**⟩ [15] clasp (in Т), embrace, infold.
обхо́|д *m* [1] round, beat (be on де́лать); detour; *vb.* + в ~д *s.* **~ди́ть**; evasion; **~ди́тельный** [14; -лен, -льна] affable, amiable; **~ди́ть** [15], ⟨обойти́⟩ [обойду́, -дёшь; *cf.* идти́] go *or* pass round; travel through (many) *or* over; visit (all [one's]); ⚔ outflank; avoid; pass over (in Т); (**-ся**, ⟨-сь⟩) cost (me мне); manage; do without (без Р); there is (*no* ... *without*); treat (s.b. с Т); **~дный** [14] roundabout; **~жде́ние** *n* [12] treatment, manners *pl.*
обш|а́ривать [1], ⟨**~а́рить**⟩ [13] rummage (around); **~ива́ть** [1], ⟨**~и́ть**⟩ [обошью́, -шьёшь; *cf.* шить] sew round, border (with Т); plank, face, sheath; F clothe; **~и́вка** *f* [5] trimming, *etc.* (*s. vb.*).
обши́|рный [14; -рен, -рна] vast, extensive; numerous; **~ть** *s.* **~ва́ть**.
обща́ться [1] associate (with с Т).
обще|досту́пный [14; -пен, -пна] popular; *s. a.* досту́пный; **~жи́тие** *n* [12] hostel, home; social intercourse *or* (way of) life; **~изве́стный** [14; -тен, -тна] well-known.
обще́ние *n* [12] intercourse.
общепри́нятый [14 *sh.*] generally accepted, common.
обще́ств|енность *f* [8] community, public (opinion); **~енный** [14] social, public; common; **'~о** *n* [9] society; company; association; community; **~ове́дение** *n* [12] social science.
общеупотреби́тельный [14; -лен, -льна] current, common, widespread.
о́бщ|ий [17; общ, -а́, -е] general; common (in ~его); public; total, (в ~ем on the) whole; (*table*) d'hôte; **~ина** *f* [5] community; † *a.* = **~ество**; **~и́тельный** [14; -лен, -льна] sociable, affable; **~ность** *f* [8] community; commonness.
объе|да́ть [1], ⟨**~́сть**⟩ [-е́м, -е́шь, *etc. s.* есть[1]] eat *or* gnaw round, away; **-ся** overeat o.s.
объедин|е́ние *n* [12] association, union; unification; **~я́ть** [28], ⟨**~и́ть**⟩ [13] unite (*cf. a.* ООН), join (**-ся** *v/i.*); rally.
объе́дки F *m/pl.* [1] leavings.
объе́|зд *m* [1] detour, by-pass; *vb.* + в ~зд = **~зжа́ть** [1] **1.** ⟨**~хать**⟩ [-е́ду, -е́дешь] go, drive round; travel through *or* over; visit (all [one's]); **2.** ⟨**~здить**⟩ [15] break in; F *s.* 1.; **~кт** *m* [1] object; **~кти́вный** [14; -вен, -вна] objective.
объём *m* [1] volume; size; extent, range; **~истый** [14 *sh.*] voluminous.
объе́сть(ся) *s.* объеда́ть(ся).
объе́хать *s.* объезжа́ть 1.
объяв|и́ть *s.* **~ля́ть**; **~ле́ние** *n* [12] announcement, notice; advertisement; declaration; **~ля́ть** [28], ⟨**~и́ть**⟩ [14] declare (s. th. *a.* о П; s.b. [to be] s.th. В/Т), tell; announce, proclaim; advertise; express.
объясн|е́ние *n* [12] explanation; declaration (of *love* в П); **~и́мый** [14 *sh.*] explicable, accountable; **~и́тельный** [14] explanatory; **~я́ть** [28], ⟨**~и́ть**⟩ [13] explain, illustrate; account for; **-ся** explain o.s.; be

accounted for; declare o.s.; *impf.* make o.s. understood (by T).
объя́тия *n/pl.* [12] embrace (*vb.*: заключи́ть в ~); (*with open*) arms.
обыва́тель *m* [4], inhabitant; Philistine; **~ский** [16] Philistine...
обы́гр|ывать, ⟨~а́ть⟩ [1] beat; win.
обы́денный [14] everyday, ordinary.
обыкнове́н|ие *n* [12] habit; по ~ию as usual; **~ный** [14; -е́нен, -е́нна] ordinary, usual, habitual.
о́быск *m* [1], **∠ивать** [1], ⟨~а́ть⟩ [3] search.
обы́ч|ай *m* [3] custom; F habit; **~ный** [14; -чен, -чна] customary, usual, habitual.
обя́занн|ость *f* [8] duty; ⚔ service; исполня́ющий ~ости (P) acting; **~ый** [14 *sh.*] obliged; indebted, owe; responsible.
обяза́тель|ный [14; -лен, -льна] obligatory, compulsory; ~но without fail, certainly; **~ство** *n* [9] obligation; liability; engagement.
обя́з|ывать [1], ⟨~а́ть⟩ [3] oblige; bind, commit; **-ся** engage, undertake, pledge o.s.
овдове́вший [17] widowed.
овёс *m* [1; овса́] oats *pl.*
ове́чий [18] sheep('s).
овлад|ева́ть [1], ⟨~е́ть⟩ [8] (T) seize, take possession of; get control over; master.
о́вощ|и *m/pl.* [1; *gen.*: -ще́й, *etc. e.*] vegetables; **~но́й** [14]: ~но́й магази́н *m* greengrocery.
овра́г *m* [1] ravine.
овся́нка *f* [5; *g/pl.*: -нок] oatmeal.
овц|а́ *f* [5; *pl. st.*; *g/pl.*: ове́ц] sheep; **~ево́дство** *n* [9] sheep breeding.
овча́рка *f* [5; *g/pl.*: -рок] sheep dog.
овчи́на *f* [5] sheepskin.
ога́рок *m* [1; -рка] candle end.
огиба́ть [1], ⟨обогну́ть⟩ [20] turn *or* bend (round); ⚓ double.
оглавле́ние *n* [12] table of contents.
огла́|ска *f* [5] publicity; **~ша́ть** [1], ⟨~си́ть⟩ [15 *e.*; -ашу́, -аси́шь -ашённый] announce; divulge; publish (the banns of); fill, resound; **-ся** ring; **~ше́ние** [12] announcement; publication; banns *pl.*
огло́бля *f* [6; *g/pl.*: -бель] shaft.
оглуш|а́ть [1], ⟨~и́ть⟩ [16 *e.*; -шу́, -ши́шь; -шённый] deafen, stun; **~и́тельный** [14; -лен, -льна] deafening, stunning.
огля́|дка F *f* [5]: без ~дки headlong, hastily; **~дывать** [1], ⟨~де́ть⟩ [11] examine, take a view of; **-ся 1.** look round; **2.** *pf.*: ⟨~ну́ться⟩ [20] look back (at на B).
огне|во́й [14] fire...; fiery; **~ды́шащий** [17] volcanic; **~мёт** *m* [1] flame thrower; **ʹ~нный** [14] fiery; **~опа́сный** [14; -сен, -сна] inflammable; **~сто́йкий** [16; -о́ек, -о́йка] *s.* ~упо́рный; **~стре́льный** [14] fire(*arm*); **~туши́тель** *m* [4] fire extinguisher; **~упо́рный** [14; -рен, -рна] fireproof; fire (*clay, etc.*).
огни́во *n* [9] (fire) steel, stone.
огов|а́ривать [1], ⟨~ори́ть⟩ [13] slander; stipulate; *a.* = **-ся** make a reservation; *s. a.* обмо́лвиться; **~о́р** F *m* [1] slander; **~о́рка** *f* [5; *g/pl.*: -рок] reservation, reserve, proviso; *a.* = обмо́лвка, *cf.*
огол|я́ть [28], ⟨~и́ть⟩ [13] bare.
огонёк *m* [1; -нька́] light; spark.
ого́нь *m* [4; огня́] fire (*a. fig.*); light; из огня́ да в по́лымя out of the frying pan into the fire; сквозь ~ и во́ду through thick & thin.
огор|а́живать [1], ⟨~оди́ть⟩ [15 & 15 *e.*; -ожу́, -о́ди́шь; -о́женный] enclose, fence (in); **~о́д** *m* [1] kitchen garden; **~о́дник** *m* [1] trucker, market *or* kitchen gardener; **~о́дничество** *n* [9] trucking, market gardening.
огорч|а́ть [1], ⟨~и́ть⟩ [16 *e.*; -чу́, -чи́шь; -чённый] grieve (**-ся** *v/i.*), (be) afflict(ed), vex(ed), distress(ed with T); **~е́ние** *n* [9] grief, affliction, trouble; **~и́тельный** [14; -лен, -льна] grievous; vexatious.
огра|бле́ние *n* [12] robbing, robbery; **∠да** *f* [5] fence; wall; **~жда́ть** [1], ⟨~ди́ть⟩ [15 *e.*; -ажу́, -ади́шь; -аждённый] enclose; guard, protect; **~жде́ние** *n* [12] enclosure; protection.
огранич|е́ние *n* [12] limitation; restriction; **∠енный** [14 *sh.*] confined; limited; narrow(-minded); **∠ивать** [1], ⟨∠ить⟩ [16] confine, limit, restrict (o.s. **-ся**; to T; content o.s. with; not go beyond); **~и́тельный** [14]; -лен, -льна] restrictive.
огро́мный [14; -мен, -мна] huge, vast; enormous, tremendous.
огрубе́лый [14] coarse, hardened.
огрыз|а́ться F [1], *once* ⟨~ну́ться⟩ [20] snap; **∠ок** *m* [1; -зка] bit, end; stump, stub.
огу́льный F [14; -лен, -льна] wholesale, indiscriminate; unfounded; *adv. a.* in the lump.
огуре́ц *m* [1; -рца́] cucumber.
ода́лживать [1], ⟨одолжи́ть⟩ [16 *e.*; -жу́, -жи́шь] lend (a. p. s. th. Д/В); borrow; oblige (a p. by В/Т).
одар|ённый [14 *sh.*] gifted; **∠ивать** [1], ⟨~и́ть⟩ [13] present, gift; (with T); *fig.* (*impf.* **~я́ть** [28]) endow (with T).
оде|ва́ть [1], ⟨∠ть⟩ [-е́ну, -е́нешь; -е́тый) dress (**-ся** *v/i.*); **∠жда** *f* [5] clothes *pl.*, clothing.
одеколо́н *m* [1] cologne.
одел|я́ть [28], ⟨~и́ть⟩ [13] *s.* одари́вать.
одеревене́лый [14] numb.
оде́рж|ивать [1], ⟨~а́ть⟩ [4] gain,

win; **~и́мый** [14 *sh.*] (T) obsessed (by), afflicted (with).
оде́ть(ся) *s.* одева́ть(ся).
одея́ло *n* [9] blanket, cover(let).
оди́н *m*, одна́ *f*, одно́ *n*, одни́ *pl.* [33] one; alone; only; a, a certain, some; одно́ *su.* one thing, thought, *etc.*; ~ на ~ face to face; tête-à-tête; hand to hand; все до одного́ (*or* все как ~) all to a (*or* the last) man; *cf.* пять & пя́тый.
один|а́ковый [14 *sh.*] equal, identical, the same; **~ёшенек** [-нька] F quite alone; **~надцатый** [14] eleventh; *cf.* пя́тый; **~надцать** [35] eleven; *cf.* пять; **~о́кий** [16 *sh.*] lonely; single; lonesome; **~о́чество** *n* [9] solitude, loneliness; **~о́чка** *m/f* [5; *g/pl.*: -чек] lone person; individualist; one-man boat (*or* F cell); **~о́чкой**, в **~о́чку** alone; **~о́чный** [14] single, solitary; individual; one-man...
одича́лый [14] (run) wild.
одна́жды once, one day.
одна́ко, (*a.* ~ ж[е]) however, yet, still.
одно́... : **~бо́ртный** [14] single-breasted; **~вре́ме́нный** [14] simultaneous; **~гла́зый** [14] one-eyed; **~дне́вный** [14] one-day; **~зву́чный** [14; -чен, -чна] monotonous; **~зна́чный** [14; -чен, -чна] synonymous (*a.* **~зна́чащий** [17]); & simple, of one place; **~имённый** [14; -ёнен, -ённа] of the same name; **~кла́ссник** *m* [1] classmate; **~коле́йный** [14] single-track; **~кра́тный** [14; -тен, -тна] occuring once, single; *gr.* momentary; **~ле́тний** [15] one-year(-old); ♀ annual; **~ле́ток** *m* [1; -тка] coeval; **~ме́стный** [14] single-seated; **~обра́зный** [14; -зен, -зна] monotonous; **~ро́дный** [14; -ден, -дна] homogeneous; **~ру́кий** [16] one-armed; **~сло́жный** [14; -жен, -жна] monosyllabic; **~сторо́нний** [15; -о́нен, -о́ння] one-sided (*a. fig.*); unilateral; **~фами́лец** *m* [1; -льца] namesake; **~цве́тный** [14; -тен, -тна] monochromatic; plain; **~эта́жный** [14] one-storied (*Brt.* -reyed).
одобр|е́ние *n* [12] approval, approbation; **~и́тельный** [14; -лен, -льна] approving; **~я́ть** [28], ⟨**~ить**⟩ [13] approve (of).
одол|ева́ть [1], ⟨**~е́ть**⟩ [8] overcome, defeat; F exhaust; master.
одолж|е́ние *n* [12] favo(u)r; **~и́ть** *s.* ода́лживать.
одр † *m* [1 *e.*] bed, couch; bier.
одува́нчик *m* [1] dandelion.
оду́м|ываться, ⟨**~аться**⟩ [1] change one's mind.
одур|ма́нивать [1], ⟨**~ма́нить**⟩ [13] stupefy; **'~ь** F [8] stupor; **~я́ть** F [28] stupefy.
одутлова́тый [14 *sh.*] puffed up.
одухотвор|я́ть [28], ⟨**~и́ть**⟩ [13] inspire.
одушев|лённый [14] *gr.* animate; **~ля́ть** [28], ⟨**~и́ть**⟩ [14 *e.*; -влю́, -ви́шь; -влённый] animate, inspire.
оды́шка *f* [5] short wind.
ожере́лье *n* [10] necklace.
ожесточ|а́ть [1], ⟨**~и́ть**⟩ [16 *e.*; -чу́, чи́шь; чённый] harden; exasperate; **~е́ние** *n* [12] exasperation; bitterness; **~ённый** [14 *sh.*] *a.* violent, fierce, bitter.
ожи|ва́ть [1], ⟨**~ть**⟩ [-иву́, -ивёшь; о́жил, -а́, -о] revive; **~ви́ть(ся)** *s.* **~вля́ть(ся)**; **~вле́ние** *n* [12] animation; **~влённый** [14 *sh.*] animated, lively; bright; **~вля́ть** [28], ⟨**~ви́ть**⟩ [14 *e.*; -влю́, -ви́шь, -влённый] enliven, animate, resuscitate; **-ся** quicken, revive; brighten.
ожида́|ние *n* [12] expectation; зал **~ния** waiting room; **~ть** [1] wait (for P); expect, await.
ожи́ть *s.* ожива́ть.
ожо́г *m* [1] burn; scald.
озабо́|чивать [1], ⟨**~тить**⟩ [15] disquiet, alarm; **-ся** attend to (T); **~ченный** [14 *sh.*] anxious, solicitous (about T); preoccupied.
озагла́в|ливать [1], ⟨**~ить**⟩ [14] entitle, supply with a title.
озада́ч|ивать [1], ⟨**~ить**⟩ [16] puzzle, perplex.
озар|я́ть [28], ⟨**~и́ть**⟩ [13] (**-ся** be[come]) illuminate(d), light (lit) up; brighten, lighten.
озвере́ть [8] *pf.* become brutal.
оздоров|ля́ть [1], ⟨**~и́ть**⟩ [14] reorganize, reform, improve (the health of).
о́зеро *n* [9; *pl.*: озёра, -ёр] lake.
ози́мый [14] winter (*crops*).
озира́ться [1] look (round *or* back).
озлоб|ля́ть [28], ⟨**~ить**⟩ [14] (**-ся** become) exasperate(d), embitter(ed); **~ле́ние** *n* [12] exasperation.
ознак|омля́ть [28], ⟨**~о́мить**⟩ [14] familiarize (o.s. **-ся**, с T with).
ознамен|ова́ние *n* [12] commemoration (in в B); **~о́вывать** [1], ⟨**~ова́ть**⟩ [7] mark, commemorate, celebrate.
означа́ть [1] signify, mean.
озно́б *m* [1] chill.
озор|ни́к *m* [1 *e.*], **~ни́ца** *f* [5] F *s.* шалу́н(ья); P ruffian; **~ннча́ть** [1] F *s.* шали́ть; P behave outrageously; **~но́й** F [14] mischievous, naughty; **~ство́** F *n* [9] mischief; outrage, excess.
ой oh! o dear!; ~ како́й F awful.
ока́з|ывать [1], ⟨**~а́ть**⟩ [3] show; render, do; exert (*influence*); give (*preference*); **-ся** (T) turn out (to be), be found; find o.s.; be (shown, rendered, given).
окайм|ля́ть [1], ⟨**~и́ть**⟩ [14 *e.*; -млю́, -ми́шь, -млённый] border.
окамене́лый [14] petrified.

ока́нчивать [1], ⟨око́нчить⟩ [16] finish, end (**-ся** *v/i.*).
ока́пывать [1], ⟨окопа́ть⟩ [1] dig round; entrench (o.s. **-ся**).
окая́нный [14] damned, cursed.
океа́н *m* [1], **~ский** [16] ocean.
оки́|дывать [1], ⟨~нуть⟩ [20] (взгля́дом) take a view of, look at.
окис|ля́ть [28], ⟨~ли́ть⟩ [13] oxidize; **'~ь** *f* [8] oxide.
оккуп|ацио́нный [14] occupation-...; **~и́ровать** [7] (*im*)*pf.* occupy.
окла́д *m* [1] salary; tax rate.
окла́дистый [14 *sh.*] full (*beard*).
окле́и|вать [1], ⟨~ть⟩ [13] paste; paper.
о́клик *m* [1], **~а́ть** [1], ⟨**́**нуть⟩ [20] call, hail.
окно́ *n* [9; *pl. st.:* о́кна, о́кон, о́кнам] window (*look* through в В).
о́ко ✎ [9; *pl.*: о́чи, оче́й, *etc. e.*] eye.
оков|а́ть *s.* **́ывать**; **́ы** *f/pl.* [5] fetters; **́ывать** [1], ⟨~а́ть⟩ [7 *e.*; окую́, окуёшь; око́ванный] bind; fetter.
околдова́ть [7] *pf.* bewitch.
окол|ева́ть [1], ⟨~е́ть⟩ [8] die.
око́лица *f* [5] *s.* окра́ина & обиня́к.
о́кол|о (Р) about, around; by, at, near(ly); nearby; **́ыш** *m* [1] cap-band; **́ьный** [14] roundabout.
око́нный [14] window...
оконч|а́ние *n* [12] end(ing *gr.*), close, termination, completion ([up]on по П), conclusion; **~а́тельный** [14; -лен, -льна] final, definitive; **́ить** *s.* ока́нчивать.
око́п *m* [1] trench; **~а́ть(ся)** *s.* ока́пывать(ся).
о́корок *m* [1; *pl.:* -ка́, *etc. e.*] ham.
око|стене́лый [14] ossified; hardened; *a.* = **~чене́лый** [14] numb (with cold).
око́ш|ечко *n* [9; *g/pl.*: -чек], **~ко** *n* [9; *g/pl.:* -шек] *dim. of* окно́.
окра́ина *f* [5] outskirts *pl.*
окра́|ска *f* [5] painting; dyeing; tinge; **~шивать** [1], ⟨~сить⟩ [15] paint; dye; tinge.
окре́стн|ость (*often pl.*) *f* [8] environs *pl.*, neighbo(u)rhood; **~ый** [14] surrounding; in the vicinity.
окрова́вленный [14] bloodstained.
о́круг *m* [1; *pl.*: -га́, *etc. e.*] district; избира́тельный ~ constituency.
округл|я́ть [28], ⟨~и́ть⟩ [13] round (off); **́ый** [14 *sh.*] roundish.
окруж|а́ть [1], ⟨~и́ть⟩ [16 *e.*; -жу́, -жи́шь; -жённый] surround; **~а́ющий** [17] surrounding; **~е́ние** *n* [12] environment; environs *pl.*, neighbo(u)rhood; encirclement; circle, company; **~и́ть** *s.* **~а́ть**; **~но́й** [14] district...; circular; **́ность** *f* [8] circumference; circle; † vicinity.
окрыл|я́ть [28], ⟨~и́ть⟩ [13] *fig.* wing, encourage.
октя́брь *m* [4 *e.*], **~ский** [16] October.
окули́ровать [7] (*im*)*pf.* graft.
окун|а́ть [1], ⟨~у́ть⟩ [20] dip, plunge (*v/i.* **-ся**; dive, *a. fig.*).
о́кунь *m* [4; *from g/pl. e.*] perch.
окуп|а́ть [1], ⟨~и́ть⟩ [14] (**-ся** be) offset, recompense(d), compensate(d).
оку́рок *m* [1; -рка] cigarette end, cigar stub.
оку́т|ывать, ⟨~ать⟩ [1] wrap (up).
ола́дья *f* [6; *g/pl.:* -дий] fritter.
оледене́лый [14] frozen, iced.
оле́нь *m* [4] deer; се́верный ~ reindeer.
оли́в|а *f* [5], **~ка** *f* [5; *g/pl.*: -вок], **~ковый** [14] olive.
олимп|иа́да *f* [5] Olympiad; **~и́йский** [16] Olympic.
олицетвор|е́ние *n* [12] personification, embodiment; **~я́ть** [28], ⟨~и́ть⟩ personify, embody.
о́лов|о *n* [8], **~я́нный** [14] tin.
о́лух Р *m* [1] blockhead, dolt.
ольх|а́ *f* [5], **~о́вый** [14] alder.
ома́р *m* [1] lobster.
оме́ла *f* [5] mistletoe.
омерз|е́ние *n* [12] abhorrence, loathing; **~и́тельный** [14; -лен, -льна] abominable, detestable, loathsome; F lousy.
омертве́лый [14] numb; dead.
омле́т *m* [1] omelet(te).
омоложе́ние *n* [12] rejuvenation.
омо́ним *m* [1] *ling.* homonym.
омрач|а́ть [1], ⟨~и́ть⟩ [16 *e.*; -чу́, -чи́шь; -чённый] darken, sadden (*v/i.* **-ся**).
о́мут *m* [1] whirlpool, vortex; deep.
омы|ва́ть [1], ⟨**́**ть⟩ [22] wash.
он *m*, **~а́** *f*, **~о́** *n*, **~и́** *pl.* [22] he, she, it, they.
онеме́лый [14] numb; F dumb.
оне́жск|ий [16]: **Ꙭ**ое о́зеро *n* Lake Onega.
ону́ча *f* [5] *s.* портя́нка.
ООН (Организа́ция Объединённых На́ций) U.N.O. (United Nations Organization).
опа|да́ть [1], ⟨**́**сть⟩ [25; *pt. st.*] fall (off); diminish, decrease.
опа́|здывать, ⟨опозда́ть⟩ [1] be late (for на В, к Д), arrive (5 min.) late (на пять мину́т); miss (*train* на В); **~ла** *f* [5] disgrace, ban; **~льный** [14] disgraced.
опал|я́ть [28], ⟨~и́ть⟩ [13] singe.
опас|а́ться [1] (Р) fear, apprehend; beware (of); **~е́ние** *n* [12] fear, apprehension, anxiety; **́ливый** [14 *sh.*] wary; anxious; **́ность** *f* [8] danger, peril, jeopardy; risk (at/of с Т/для Р); **́ный** [14; -сен, -сна] dangerous (to для Р); **́ть** *s.* опада́ть.
опе́к|а *f* [5] guardianship, (*a. fig.*) tutelage; trusteeship; **~а́ть** [1] be guardian (trustee) to; patronize; **~а́емый** [14] ward; **~у́н** *m* [1 *e.*], **~у́нша** *f* [5] guardian; trustee.
опер|ати́вный [14] operative; surgical; executive; ⚔ front..., war...;

~áтор *m* [1] operator (*a.* ⚕ = surgeon); **~ациóнный** [14] operating.
опере|жáть [1], ⟨**~дить**⟩ [15] outstrip (*a. fig.* = outdo, surpass); **∠ние** *n* [12] plumage; **∠ться** *s.* опирáться.
оперúровать [7] (*im*)*pf.* operate.
óперный [14] opera(tic).
опер|я́ться [28], ⟨**~и́ться**⟩ [13] fledge.
опечáт|ка *f* [5; *g*/*pl.*: -ток] misprint, erratum; **~ывать**, ⟨**~ать**⟩ [1] seal (up).
опи́лки *f*/*pl.* [5; *gen.*: -лок] sawdust.
опирáться [1], ⟨опере́ться⟩ [12; обопру́сь, -рёшься; опёрся, оперлáсь] lean (against, on на B), *a. fig.* = rest, rely ([up]on).
опис|áние *n* [12] description; **~áтельный** [14] descriptive; **~áть** *s.* ∠ывать; **∠ка** *f* [5; *g*/*pl.*: -сок] slip of the pen; **∠ывать** [1], ⟨**~áть**⟩ [3] describe (*a.* ⚘); make (*an inventory* [of]); distrain (upon); **-ся** make a slip of the pen; **'~сь** *f* [8] list, inventory; distraint.
оплáк|ивать [1], ⟨**~ать**⟩ [3] bewail, deplore, mourn (over).
оплá|та *f* [5] pay(ment); settlement; **~чивать** [1], ⟨**~ти́ть**⟩ [15] pay (for); remunerate; settle.
оплеу́ха F *f* [5] box on the ear.
оплодотвор|éние *n* [12] fertilization; **~я́ть** [28], ⟨**~и́ть**⟩ [13] fertilize, fecundate.
оплóт *m* [1] bulwark, stronghold.
оплóшность *f* [8] blunder.
опове|щáть [1], ⟨**~сти́ть**⟩ [15 *e.*; -ещу́, -ести́шь; -ещённый] notify; inform, ✝ *a.* advise (of о П).
опоздá|ние *n* [12] delay; *vb.* + с **~нием** = **~ть**, *s.* опáздывать.
опозн|авáтельный [14] distinctive; **~авáть** [5], ⟨**~áть**⟩ [1] identify.
óползень *m* [4; -зня] landslide.
ополч|áться [1], ⟨**~и́ться**⟩ [16 *e.*; -чу́сь, -чи́шься; -чённый] rise in arms; **~éние** *n* [12] militia; Territorial Army; **~éнец** *m* [1; -нца] militiaman.
опóмниться [13] *pf.* come to *or* recover one's senses, come round.
опóр *m* [1]: во весь ~ at full speed, at a gallop; **~а** *f* [5] support, prop, rest; **~ный** [14] strong, of support.
опорó|жнить [13] *pf.* empty; **~чивать** [1], ⟨**~чить**⟩ [16] defile.
опошл|я́ть [28], ⟨**∠ить**⟩ [13] vulgarize.
опоя́с|ывать [1], ⟨**~ать**⟩ [3] gird.
оппозициóнный [14] opposition...
оппони́ровать [7] (Д) oppose.
опрáва *f* [5] setting; rim, frame.
оправд|áние *n* [12] justification, excuse; ⚖ acquittal; **~áтельный** [14] justificatory; of 'not guilty'; **~áтельный** докумéнт *m* voucher; **∠ывать** [1], ⟨**~áть**⟩ [1] justify, excuse; acquit; **-ся** *a.* prove (*or* come) true.
оправ|ля́ть [28], ⟨**∠ить**⟩ [14] put in order; set; **-ся** recover (*a.* o.s.); put one's dress, hair in order.
опрáшивать [1], ⟨опроси́ть⟩ [15] interrogate, question.
определ|éние *n* [12] determination; definition; designation (to, for на B); ⚖ decision; *gr.* attribute; **~ённый** [14; -ёнен, -ённа] definite; fixed; certain, positive; **~я́ть** [28], ⟨**~и́ть**⟩ [13] determine; define; designate (to, for на B, к Д); appoint, fix; **-ся** take shape; enter, enlist (in[to] на B).
опров|ергáть [1], ⟨**~éргнуть**⟩ [21] refute; deny; **~ержéние** *n* [12] refutation; denial.
опроки́|дывать [1], ⟨**~нуть**⟩ [20; overturn, upset, capsize (-ся *v*/*i.*)] overthrow, throw (down, over).
опро|мéтчивый [14 *sh.*] rash, precipitate; **'~метью** headlong, at top speed.
опрóс *m* [1] interrogation, inquiry; **~и́ть** *s.* опрáшивать; **~ный** [14]: **~ный** лист *m* questionnaire.
опры́ск|ивать, ⟨**~ать**⟩ [1] sprinkle.
опря́тный [14; -тен, -тна] tidy.
óптик *m* [1] optician; **~а** *f* [5] optics.
оптó|вый [14], **'~м** *adv.* wholesale.
опубликов|áние *n* [12] publication; **∠ывать** [1] *s.* публиковáть.
опус|кáть [1], ⟨**~ти́ть**⟩ [15] lower; cast down; hang; drop; draw (down); **~ти́ть** ру́ки lose heart; **-ся** sink; fall; go down; *fig.* come down (in the world); *p.pt. a.* down & out.
опуст|éлый [14] deserted; **~и́ть** (-ся) *s.* опускáть(ся); **~ошáть** [1], ⟨**~оши́ть**⟩ [16 *e.*; -шу́, -ши́шь; -шённый] devastate; **~ошéние** *n* [12] devastation; **~оши́тельный** [14; -лен, -льна] devastating.
опу́т|ывать, ⟨**~ать**⟩ [1] wrap (up), muffle (in); *fig.* entangle.
опух|áть [1], ⟨**∠нуть**⟩ [21] swell; **'~оль** *f* [8] swelling, tumo(u)r.
опу́|шка *f* [5; *g*/*pl.*: -шек] edge, border; **~щéние** *n* [12] ommission.
опыл|я́ть [28], ⟨**~и́ть**⟩ [13] pollinate.
óпыт *m* [1] experiment; attempt; essay; [*sg.*, *pl.* †] experience; **~ный** [14] experiment(al); empirical; [-тен, -тна] experienced.
опьянéние *n* [12] intoxication.
опя́ть again (*a.*, F, ~-таки; and ..., too).
орáва P *f* [5] gang, horde, mob.
орáкул *m* [1] oracle.
орáнже|вый [14] orange...; **~ре́я** *f* [6] greenhouse.
орáть F [ору́, орёшь] yell, bawl.
орби́та *f* [5] orbit.
óрган[1] *m* [1] organ.
оргáн[2] ♪ *m* [1] organ.
организ|áтор *m* [1] organizer; **∠м** *m* [1] organism; constitution; **~овáть** [7] (*im*)*pf.* (*impf. a.* **~óвывать** [1]) organize (*v*/*i.* **-ся**).

органи́ческий [16] organic.
о́ргия *f* [7] orgy.
орда́ *f* [5; *pl. st.*] horde.
о́рден *m* [1; *pl.*: -на́, *etc. e.*] order, decoration.
о́рдер *m* [1; *pl.*: -pá, *etc. e.*] warrant.
ордина́р|ец ⚔ *m* [1; -рца] orderly.
орёл *m* [1; орла́] eagle; ~ и́ли ре́шка? heads or tails?
орео́л *m* [1] halo, aureole.
оре́х *m* [1] nut; лесно́й ~ hazel (-nut); **~овый** [14] (wal)nut...
оригина́льный [14; -лен, -льна] original.
ориенти́р|оваться [7] (*im*)*pf.* orient o. s. (to на В), take one's bearings; familiarize o. s.; **~о́вка** *f* [5; *g/pl.*: -вок] orientation, bearings *pl.*; **~о́вочный** [14; -чен, -чна] approximate, tentative.
орке́стр *m* [1] orchestra; band.
орли́ный [14] aquiline.
оро|ша́ть [1], ⟨**~си́ть**⟩ [15 *e.*; -ошу́, -оси́шь; -ошённый] irrigate; **~ше́ние** *n* [12] irrigation.
ору́д|ие *n* [12] tool, instrument, implement; ⚔ gun; **~и́йный** [14] gun...; **~овать** F [7] (T) handle, operate.
оруж|е́йный [14] arms...; **∠ие** *n* [12] weapon(s), arm(s); (*cold*) steel.
орфогра́ф|ия *f* [7] spelling; **~и́ческий** [16] orthographic(al).
орхиде́я *f* [6] orchid.
оса́ *f* [5; *pl. st.*] wasp.
оса́|да *f* [5] siege; **~ди́ть** *s.* **~жда́ть** & **~живать**; **~дный** [14] of siege *or* martial law; **~док** *m* [1; -дка] sediment; *fig.* aftertaste; **~дки** *pl.* precipitations; **~жда́ть** [1], ⟨**~ди́ть**⟩ [15 & 15 *e.*; -ажу́, -а́ди́шь; -аждённый] besiege; ⚗ precipitate; F importune; **~живать** [1], ⟨**~ди́ть**⟩ [15] check, snub.
оса́н|истый [14 *sh.*] dignified, stately; **~ка** *f* [5] bearing.
осв|а́ивать [1], ⟨**~о́ить**⟩ [13] master; open up; ⚘ acclimate (*Brt.* -tize); **-ся** accustom o. s. (to в П); familiarize o. s. (with с T).
осведом|ля́ть [28], ⟨**'~ить**⟩ [14] inform (of о П); **-ся** inquire (after, for; about о П); **~лённый** [14] informed; versed.
освеж|а́ть [1], ⟨**~и́ть**⟩ [16 *e.*; -жу́, -жи́шь; -жённый] refresh; freshen *or* touch up; brush up; **~и́тельный** [14; -лен, -льна] refreshing.
осве|щать [1], ⟨**~ти́ть**⟩ [15 *e.*; -ещу́, -ети́шь; -ещённый] light (up), illuminate; *fig.* elucidate, illustrate.
освиде́тельствова|ние *n* [12] examination; **~ть** [7] *pf.* examine.
осви́ст|ывать [1], ⟨**~а́ть**⟩ [3] hiss.
освобо|ди́тель *m* [4] liberator; **~ди́тельный** [14] emancipatory; **~жда́ть** [1], ⟨**~ди́ть**⟩ [15*e.*; -ожу́, -оди́шь; -ождённый] (set) free, release; liberate, deliver; emancipate; exempt, excuse; clear; vacate, quit; **~жде́ние** *n* [12] liberation; release; emancipation; exemption.
осво|е́ние *n* [12] mastering; opening up; **∠ить(ся)** *s.* осва́ивать(ся).
освя|ща́ть [1], ⟨**~ти́ть**⟩ [15 *e.*; -ящу́, -яти́шь; -ящённый] consecrate.
осе|да́ть [1], ⟨**∠сть**⟩ [25; ося́дет; осе́л; *cf.* сесть] subside, settle; **∠длый** [14] settled.
осёл *m* [1; осла́] donkey, (*a. fig.*) ass.
осени́ть *s.* осеня́ть.
осе́н|ний [15] autumnal, fall...; **'~ь** *f* [8] fall, *Brt.* autumn (in [the] T).
осен|я́ть [28], ⟨**~и́ть**⟩ [13] shade; invest; bless, make (*cross*); flash on.
осе́сть *s.* оседа́ть.
осётр *m* [1 *e.*] sturgeon.
осе́чка *f* [5; *g/pl.*: -чек] misfire.
оси́ли|вать [1], ⟨**~ть**⟩ [13] *s.* одолева́ть.
оси́н|а *f* [5] asp; **~овый** [14] asp(en).
оси́пнуть [21] *pf.* grow hoarse.
осироте́лый [14] orphan(ed).
оска́ли|вать [1], ⟨**~ть**⟩ [13] show.
оскверн|я́ть [28], ⟨**~и́ть**⟩ [13] profane, desecrate, defile.
оско́лок *m* [1; -лка] splinter.
оскорб|и́тельный [14; -лен, -льна] offensive, insulting; **~ле́ние** *n* [12] insult, offence; **~ля́ть** [28], ⟨**~и́ть**⟩ [14 *e.*; -блю́, -би́шь; -блённый] (**-ся** feel) offend(ed), insult.
оскуд|ева́ть [1], ⟨**~е́ть**⟩ [8] become poor *or* scanty.
ослаб|ева́ть [1], ⟨**~е́ть**⟩ [8] grow weak *or* feeble, languish; slacken; abate; **∠ить** *s.* **~ля́ть**; **~ле́ние** *n* [12] weakening; relaxation; **~ля́ть** [28], ⟨**∠ить**⟩ [14] weaken, enfeeble; relax, slacken, loosen.
ослеп|и́тельный [14; -лен. -льна] dazzling; **~ля́ть** [28], ⟨**~и́ть**⟩ [14 *e.*; -плю́, -пи́шь; -плённый] blind; dazzle.
осложн|е́ние *n* [12 complication; **~я́ть** [28],⟨**~и́ть**⟩[13](**-ся** be[come]) complicate(d).
ослу́ш|иваться, ⟨**~аться**⟩ [1] disobey; **~ник** *m* [1] disobedient p.
ослы́шаться [4] *pf.* hear amiss.
осм|а́тривать [1], ⟨**~отре́ть**⟩ [9; -отрю́, -о́тришь; -о́тренный] view, examine; inspect; see (*sights*); **-ся** look round; take a view of (в П).
осме́|ивать [1], ⟨**~я́ть**⟩ [27 *e.*; -ею́, -еёшь; -е́янный] laugh at, ridicule, deride.
осме́ли|ваться [1], ⟨**~ться**⟩ [13] dare, venture; beg *to*.
осмея́|ние *n* [12] ridicule, derision; **~ть** *s.* осме́ивать.
осмо́тр *m* [1] examination, inspection; (*sight*)seeing; visit (to P); **~е́ть(ся)** *s.* осма́тривать(ся); **~и́тельность** *f* [8] circumspection, prudence; **~и́тельный** [14; -лен, -льна] circumspect, prudent.

осмы́сл|енный [14 *sh.*] sensible; intelligent; **~ивать** [1] & **~я́ть** [28], ‹**~ить**› [13] comprehend, conceive; grasp, make sense of.
осна́|стка *f* [5] rigging (out, up); **~ща́ть** [1], ‹**~сти́ть**› [15 *e.*; -ащу́, -асти́шь; -ащённый] rig (out, up); **~ще́ние** *n* [12] equipment.
осно́в|а *f* [5] basis, foundation; fundamental, essential, principle; *gr.* stem; *text.* warp; **~а́ние** *n* [12] foundation, basis; ⚗, ⛺, ⚒ base; fundamental; ground(s), reason; argument; **~а́тель** *m* [4] founder; **~а́тельный** [14; -лен, -льна] valid; sound, solid; thorough; **~а́ть** *s.* **~ывать**; **~но́й** [14] fundamental, basic, principal, primary; ✝ original (*stock*); **~ополо́жник** *m* [1] founder; **~ывать** [1], ‹**~а́ть**› [7] found; establish; **-ся** be based, rest; settle.
осо́ба *f* [5] person; personage.
осо́бенн|ость *f* [8] peculiarity; **~ый** [14] (e)special, particular, peculiar.
особня́к *m* [1 *e.*] villa, private residence; **~о́м** apart; aloof; separate (-ly).
осо́б|ый [14] *s.* **~енный**; separate.
осозн|ава́ть [5], ‹**~а́ть**› [1] realize.
осо́ка *f* [5] sedge.
о́сп|а *f* [5] smallpox; **~опрививáние** *n* [12] vaccination.
осп|а́ривать [1], ‹**~о́рить**› [13] contest, dispute; contend (for).
остава́ться [5], ‹оста́ться› [-а́нусь, -а́нешься] (Т) remain, stay; be left; keep; stick (to); be(come); have to; go, get off; ~ (за Т) get, win; reserve, take; owe; ~ без (Р) lose, have no (left); ~ с но́сом F get nothing.
остав|ля́ть [28], ‹**~ить**› [14] leave; give up; drop, stop; let (*alone*); keep; ~ля́ть за собо́й reserve to o.s.
остально́|й [14] remaining; *pl. a.* the others; *n* & *pl. a. su.* the rest (в ~м as for the rest).
останав|ливать [1], ‹**~ови́ть**› [14] stop, bring to a stop; fix; **-ся** stop; put up (at в П); dwell (on на П); **~ки** *m/pl.* [1] remains; **~ови́ть(ся)** *s.* **~а́вливать(ся)**; **~о́вка** *f* [5; *g/pl.*: -вок] stop(page); break; ~о́вка за ... (Т) (*only*) ... is wanting.
оста́|ток *m* [1; -тка] remainder (*a.* ⚗), rest; remnant; *pl.* remains; **~ться** *s.* **~ва́ться**.
остекл|я́ть [28], ‹**~и́ть**› [13] glaze.
остервене́лый [14] furious.
остер|ега́ться [1], ‹**~е́чься**› [26 г/ж: -егу́сь, -ежёшься, -егу́тся] (Р) beware of, be careful of.
о́стов *m* [1] skeleton, framework.
остолбене́лый F [14] stunned.
остоло́п F *contp. m* [1] dolt, dunce.
осторо́жн|ость *f* [8] caution, heed; **~ый** [14; -жен, -жна] cautious, careful, wary; prudent; ~о! look out!; with care!
остри|га́ть [1], ‹**~чь**› [26 г/ж: -игу́, -ижёшь, -игу́т] (-ся have one's hair) cut; crop; shear; pare; **~ё** *n* [12; *g/pl.*: -иёв] point; edge; **~ть** [13], ‹за-› sharpen; ‹с-› joke, be witty; **~чь(ся)** *s.* **~га́ть(ся)**.
о́стров *m* [1; *pl.*: -ва́, *etc. e.*] island; isle; **~итя́нин** *m* [1; *pl.*: -я́не, -я́н] islander; **~о́к** *m* [1; -вка́] islet.
остро́г *m* [1] prison; *hist.* burg.
остро|гла́зый F [14 *sh.*] sharp-sighted; **~коне́чный** [14; -чен, -чна] pointed; **~та́** *f* [5; *pl. st.*: -о́ты] sharpness, keenness, acuteness; witticism; joke; **~у́мие** *n* [12] wit; sagacity; **~у́мный** [14; -мен, -мна] witty; ingenious.
о́стр|ый [14; остр (F *a.* остёр), -а́, -о] sharp, pointed; keen; acute; critical; **~я́к** *m* [1 *e.*] wit(ty fellow).
оступ|а́ться [1], ‹**~и́ться**› [14] stumble.
остыва́ть [1] *s.* сты́нуть.
осу|жда́ть [1], ‹**~ди́ть**› [15; -уждённый] condemn; doom (to на В); **~жде́ние** *n* [12] condemnation; conviction.
осу́нуться [20] *pf.* grow lean.
осуш|а́ть [1], ‹**~и́ть**› [16] drain; dry (up); empty.
осуществ|и́мый [14 *sh.*] practicable; **~ля́ть** [28], ‹**~и́ть**› [14 *e.*; -влю́, -ви́шь; -влённый] realize; **-ся** be carried out; come true; **~ле́ние** *n* [12] realization.
осчастли́вить [14] *pf.* make happy.
осып|а́ть [1], ‹**~ать**› [2] strew (over); stud; *fig.* heap; **-ся** crumble; fall.
ось *f* [8; *from g/pl. e.*] axis; axle.
осяза́|емый [14 *sh.*] tangible; **~ние** *n* [12] sense of touch; **~тельный** [14] of touch; [-лен, -льна] palpable; **~ть** [1] touch, feel.
от, ото (Р) from; of; off; against; for, with; in; on behalf
ота́пливать [1], ‹отопи́ть› [14] heat.
отбав|ля́ть [28], ‹**~ить**› [14] take away *or* off; diminish.
отбе|га́ть [1], ‹**~жа́ть**› [4; -бегу́, -бежи́шь, -бегу́т] run off.
отби|ва́ть [1], ‹**~ть**› [отобью́, -бьёшь; *cf.* бить] beat, strike (*or* kick) off; ⚔ repel; deliver; snatch away (from у Р); break off; **-ся** ward off (от Р); get lost, drop behind; break off; F get rid.
отбира́ть [1], ‹отобра́ть› [отберу́, -рёшь; отобра́л, -а́, -о; ото́бранный] take away *or* off; select, pick out; collect.
отби́ть(ся) *s.* отбива́ть(ся).
о́тблеск *m* [1] reflection; vestige.
отбо́й *m* [3] ⚔ retreat; all clear (*signal*); *teleph.* ring off.
отбо́р *m* [1] selection, choice; **~ный** [14] select, choice, picked.
отбр|а́сывать [1], ‹**~о́сить**› [15] throw off *or* away; ⚔ throw back; reject; **~о́сы** *m/pl.* [1] refuse, waste.
отбы|ва́ть [1], ‹**~ть**› [-бу́ду, -бу́-

дешь; о́тбыл, -а́, -о] **1.** *v/i.* leave, depart (for в В); **2.** *v/t.* serve; do; **∠тие** *n* [12] departure.

отва́|га *f* [5] bravery, valo(u)r; **~живаться** [1], ⟨**~житься**⟩ [16] venture, dare; **~жный** [14; -жен, -жна] valiant, brave.

отва́л: до ~а F one's fill; **~иваться** [1], ⟨**~и́ться**⟩ [13; -а́лится] fall off.

отварно́й [14] boiled.

отве́|дывать, ⟨**~дать**⟩ [1] (*a.* Р) taste; **~зти́** *s.* отвози́ть.

отверг|а́ть [1], ⟨**∠нуть**⟩ [21] reject, repudiate.

отвердева́ть [1] *s.* тверде́ть.

отве́рженный [14] outcast.

отверну́ть(ся) *s.* отвёртывать & отвора́чивать(ся).

отвёр|тка [5; *g/pl.*: -ток] screwdriver; **~тывать** [1], ⟨отверну́ть⟩ [20; отвёрнутый], ⟨отверте́ть⟩ F [10] turn off.

отве́с *m* [1] plummet; **~ить** *s.* отве́шивать; **~ный** [14; -сен, -сна] plumb; sheer; **~ти́** *s.* отводи́ть.

отве́т *m* [1] answer, reply (в ~ на В in reply to); responsibility.

ответвл|е́ние *n* [12] branch, offshoot; **~я́ться** [28] branch off.

отве́|тить *s.* ~ча́ть; **~тственность** *f* [8] responsibility; **~тственный** [14 *sh.*] responsible (to пе́ред Т); **~тчик** *m* [1] defendant; **~ча́ть** [1], ⟨**~тить**⟩ [15] (на В) answer, reply (to); (за В) answer, account (for); (Д) answer, suit.

отве́|шивать [1], ⟨**~сить**⟩ [15] weigh out; make (*a bow*).

отви́н|чивать [1], ⟨**~ти́ть**⟩ [15 *e.*; -нчу́, -нти́шь; -и́нченный] unscrew, unfasten.

отвис|а́ть [1], ⟨**∠нуть**⟩ [21] hang down, lop; **∠лый** [14] loppy.

отвле|ка́ть [1], ⟨**∠чь**⟩ [26] divert, distract; abstract; **~чённый** [14 *sh.*] abstract.

отво́д *m* [1] allotment; rejection; **~и́ть** [15], ⟨отвести́⟩ [25] lead, get, take (off); turn off, avert; parry; reject; allot; ~и́ть ду́шу F unburden one's heart; **~ный** [14] drain ...

отво|ёвывать [1], ⟨**~ева́ть**⟩ [6] (re)conquer, win; **~зи́ть** [15], ⟨отвезти́⟩ [24] take, get, drive (off).

отвора́чивать [1], ⟨отверну́ть⟩ [20] turn off; **-ся** turn away.

отвори́ть(ся) *s.* отворя́ть(ся).

отворо́т *m* [1] lapel; (*boot*) top.

отвор|я́ть [28], ⟨**~и́ть**⟩ [13; -орю́, -о́ришь; -о́ренный] open (*v/i.* **-ся**).

отвра|ти́тельный [14; -лен, -льна] disgusting, abominable; **~ща́ть** [1], ⟨**~ти́ть**⟩ [15 *e.*; -ащу́, -ати́шь; -ащённый] avert; **~ще́ние** *n* [12] aversion, disgust (for, at к Д).

отвык|а́ть [1], ⟨**∠нуть**⟩ [21] (от Р) wean (from), leave off, become disaccustomed (to).

отвя́з|ывать [1], ⟨**~а́ть**⟩ [3] (**-ся** [be]come) untie(d), undo(ne); F get rid of (от Р); let a person alone.

отга́д|ывать, ⟨**~а́ть**⟩ [1] guess; **~ка** *f* [5; *g/pl.*: -док] solution.

отгиба́ть [1], ⟨отогну́ть⟩ [20] unbend; turn up (*or* back).

отгов|а́ривать [1], ⟨**~ори́ть**⟩ [13] dissuade (from от Р); **-ся** pretend (s. th. Т), extricate o. s.; **~о́рка** *f* [5; *g/pl.*: -рок] excuse, pretext.

отголо́сок *m* [1; -ска] *s.* о́тзвук.

отгоня́ть [28], ⟨отогна́ть⟩ [отгоню́, -о́нишь; ото́гнанный; *cf.* гнать] drive (*or* frighten) away; *fig.* banish.

отгор|а́живать [1], ⟨**~оди́ть**⟩ [15 & 15 *e.*; -ожу́, -о́ди́шь; -о́женный] fence in; partition off.

отгру|жа́ть [1], ⟨**~зи́ть**⟩ [15 & 15 *e.*; -ужу́, -у́зи́шь; -у́женный & -ужённый] load, ship.

отгрыз|а́ть [1], ⟨**∠ть**⟩ [24; *pt. st.*] gnaw (off), pick.

отда|ва́ть [5], ⟨**∠ть**⟩ [-да́м, -да́шь, *etc.*, *cf.* дать; о́тдал, -а́, -о] give back, return; give (away); send (to в В); devote; deliver, (*baggage*) check, *Brt.* book; put; pay; marry; make (*bow*); cast (*anchor*); recoil (*gun*); ~ва́ть честь (Д) ⚔ salute; F sell; *impf.* smell *or* taste (of Т); **-ся** devote o. s.; surrender, give o. s. up; resound; be reflected.

отда́в|ливать [1], ⟨**~и́ть**⟩ [14] crush.

отдал|е́ние *n* [12] removal; estrangement; distance; **~ённый** [14 *sh.*] remote; **~я́ть** [28], ⟨**~и́ть**⟩ [13] move away, remove; put off, postpone; alienate; **-ся** move away (from от Р); become estranged.

отда́|ть(ся) *s.* ~ва́ть(ся); **~ча** *f* [5] delivery; recoil; return.

отде́л *m* [1] department; office; section; **~ать(ся)** *s.* ~ывать(ся); **~е́ние** *n* [12] separation; secretion; department, division; branch (office); ⚔ squad; compartment; (police) station; **~и́мый** [14 *sh.*] separable; **~и́ть(ся)** *s.* ~я́ть(ся); **~ка** *f* [5; *g/pl.*: -лок] finishing; trimming; **~ывать,** ⟨**~ать**⟩ [1] finish, put the final touches on; trim; **-ся** get rid of (от Р); get off, escape (with Т); **~ьность** *f* [8]: в ~ьности individually; **~ьный** [14] separate; individual, single; **~я́ть** [28], ⟨**~и́ть**⟩ [13; -елю́, -е́лишь] separate (*v/i.* **-ся** from от Р; come off); secrete.

отдёр|гивать [1], ⟨**~нуть**⟩ [20] draw back; draw open.

отдира́ть [1], ⟨отодра́ть⟩ [отдеру́, -рёшь; отодра́л, -а́, -о; ото́дранный] tear (off); *pf.* F thrash; pull.

отдохну́ть *s.* отдыха́ть.

отду́шина *f* [5] vent (*a. fig.*).

о́тдых *m* [1] rest, relaxation; дом ~а rest home, sanatorium; **~а́ть** [1], ⟨отдохну́ть⟩ [20] rest, relax.

отдыша́ться [4] *pf.* recover breath.

отёк *m* [1] edema.
оте|ка́ть [1], ⟨**∠чь**⟩ [26] swell; become dropsical.
оте́ц *m* [1; отца́] father.
оте́че|ский [16] fatherly; paternal; **~ственный** [14] native, home...; patriotic (*war*); **~ство** *n* [9] motherland, fatherland, one's (native) country.
оте́чь *s.* отека́ть.
отжи|ва́ть [1], ⟨**∠ть**⟩ [-живу́, -вёшь; о́тжил, -а́, -о; о́тжи́тый (о́тжи́т, -а́, -о)] (have) live(d, had) (one's time *or* day); become obsolete, die out.
о́тзвук *m* [1] echo, repercussion; response; reminiscence.
о́тзыв *m* [1] response; opinion (in по Д *pl.*), reference; comment, review; recall; password; **~а́ть** [1], ⟨отозва́ть⟩ [отзову́, -вёшь; отозва́л, -а́, -о; ото́званный] take aside; recall; **-ся** respond, answer; speak (of о П); (re)sound; call forth (s. th. Т); affect (s. th. на П); *impf.* smack (of Т); **∠чивый** [14 *sh.*] responsive, sympathetic.
отка́з *m* [1] refusal, denial, rejection (of в П, Р); renunciation (of от Р); ⊕ breakdown; ♪ natural; без **~а** smoothly; до **~а** to the full; получи́ть **~** be refused; **~ывать** [1], ⟨**~а́ть**⟩ [3] refuse, deny (a p. s. th. Д/в П); (от Р) dismiss; ⊕ break; **-ся** (от Р) refuse, decline, reject; renounce, give up; would(*n't*) mind.
отка́|лывать [1], ⟨отколо́ть⟩ [17] cut *or* chop off; unfasten; **-ся** come off; secede; **~пывать**, ⟨откопа́ть⟩ [1] dig up, unearth; **~рмливать** [1], ⟨откорми́ть⟩ [14] feed, fatten; **~тывать** [1], ⟨**~ти́ть**⟩ [15] roll (aside, away) (**-ся** *v/i.*); **~чивать**, ⟨**~ча́ть**⟩ [1] pump out; **~шливаться** [1], ⟨**~шляться**⟩ [28] clear one's throat.
отки|дно́й [14] folding, tip-up; **∠дывать** [1], ⟨**∠нуть**⟩ [20] throw (off; back); turn down; drop, leave; **-ся** recline.
откла́|дывать [1], ⟨отложи́ть⟩ [16] lay aside; save; put off, defer, postpone; **~няться** [28] *pf.* take one's leave.
откле́|ивать [1], ⟨**~ить**⟩ [13] unstick; **-ся** come unstuck.
о́тклик *m* [1] response; comment; suggestion; *s. a.* о́тзвук; **~а́ться** [1], ⟨**∠нуться**⟩ [20] (на В) respond (to), answer; comment (on).
отклон|е́ние *n* [12] deviation, defection; digression; rejection; **~я́ть** [28], ⟨**~и́ть**⟩ [13; -оню́, -о́нишь] deflect; decline, reject; divert, dissuade; **-ся** deviate, deflect; digress.
отк|оло́ть *s.* **~а́лывать**; **~опа́ть** *s.* **~а́пывать**; **~орми́ть** *s.* **~а́рмливать**.
отко́с *m* [1] slope, slant, (e)scarp.
открове́н|ие *n* [12] revelation; **~ный** [14; -е́нен, -е́нна] frank, candid, open(-hearted), outspoken.
откры|ва́ть [1], ⟨**∠ть**⟩ [22] open; turn on; discover; disclose; reveal; unveil; inaugurate; **-ся** open; declare *or* unbosom o. s.; **∠тие** *n* [12] opening; discovery; revelation; inauguration; unveiling; **∠тка** *f* [5; *g/pl.*: -ток] (с ви́дом picture) post card; **∠тый** [14] open; public; **∠ть(ся)** *s.* **~ва́ть(ся)**.
отку́да where from?; wherefrom; P why; *a.*, F, = **~-нибудь**, **~-то** (from) somewhere *or* anywhere.
о́ткуп *m* [1; *pl.*: -па́, *etc. e.*] *hist.* lease; **~а́ть** [1], ⟨**~и́ть**⟩ [14] buy (up); take on lease; **-ся** ransom o. s.
отку́пори|вать [1], ⟨**~ть**⟩ [13] uncork; open.
отку́с|ывать [1], ⟨**~и́ть**⟩ [15] bite off; pinch off.
отлага́тельство *n* [9] delay.
отлага́ться [1], ⟨отложи́ться⟩ [16] be deposited; secede, fall away.
отла́мывать, ⟨отлома́ть⟩ [1], ⟨отломи́ть⟩ [14] break off (*v/i.* -ся).
отл|епи́ть(ся) [14] *pf.*, *s.* откле́ить (-ся); **~ёт** *m* [1] ✈ start; **~ета́ть** [1], ⟨**~ете́ть**⟩ [11] fly away *or* off; F come off.
отли́|в *m* [1] ebb (tide); shimmer; **~ва́ть** [1], ⟨**~ть**⟩ [отолью́, -льёшь; о́тли́л, -а́, -о; *cf.* лить] pour off, in, out (some ... Р); ⊕ found, cast; *impf.* (Т) shimmer, play.
отлич|а́ть [1], ⟨**~и́ть**⟩ [16 *e.*; -чу́, -чи́шь; -чённый] distinguish (from от Р); decorate; **-ся** *a.*, *impf.*, differ; be noted (for Т); **∠ие** *n* [12] distinction, difference; в **∠ие** от (Р) as against; зна́ки **∠ия** decorations; **~и́тельный** [14] distinctive; **∠ник** *m* [1], **∠ница** *f* [5] excellent pupil, *etc.*; **∠ный** [14; -чен, -чна] excellent, perfect; different; *adv. a.* very good, A (*mark*, *cf.* пятёрка).
отло́гий [16 *sh.*] sloping.
отлож|е́ние *n* [12] deposit; **~и́ть** (-ся) *s.* откла́дывать отлага́ться; **~но́й** [14] turndown (*collar*).
отлом|а́ть, **~и́ть** *s.* отла́мывать.
отлуч|а́ть [1], ⟨**~и́ть**⟩ [16 *e.*; -чу́, -чи́шь; -чённый] separate; wean; **~и́ть** от це́ркви excommunicate; **-ся** (из Р) leave, absent o. s. (from); **∠ка** *f* [5] absence.
отма́лчиваться [1] keep silence.
отма́|тывать [1], ⟨отмота́ть⟩ [1] wind *or* reel off, unwind; **~хивать** [1], ⟨**~хну́ть**⟩ [20] drive (*or* brush) away (aside) (*a.* **-ся** от Р; F disregard, dismiss).
о́тмель *f* [8] shoal, sandbank.
отме́н|а *f* [5] abolition; cancellation; countermand; **~ный** [14; -е́нен, -е́нна] *s.* отли́чный; **~я́ть** [28], ⟨**~и́ть**⟩ [13; -еню́, -е́нишь] abolish; cancel; countermand.
отмер|е́ть *s.* отмира́ть; **~за́ть** [1], ⟨отмёрзнуть⟩ [21] be frostbitten.

отме́р|ивать [1] *&* **~я́ть** [28], ⟨~ить⟩ [13] measure (off).
отме́стк|а F *f* [5]: в ~у in revenge.
отме́|тка *f* [5; *g/pl.*: -ток] mark, grade; **~ча́ть** [1], ⟨~тить⟩ [15] mark, note.
отмира́ть [1], ⟨отмере́ть⟩ [12; отомрёт; о́тмер,- рла́, -о; отме́рший] die away *or* out; fade; mortify.
отмор|а́живать [1], ⟨~о́зить⟩ [15] frostbite.
отмота́ть *s.* отма́тывать.
отмы|ва́ть [1], ⟨∠ть⟩ [22] wash (off); **~ка́ть** [1], ⟨отомкну́ть⟩ [20] unlock, open; **∠чка** *f* [5; *g/pl.*: -чек] picklock.
отне́киваться F [1] deny, disavow.
отнести́(сь) *s.* относи́ть(ся).
отнима́ть [1], ⟨отня́ть⟩ [-ниму́, -ни́мешь; о́тнял, -а́, -о; о́тнятый (о́тнят, -а́, -о)] take away (from у Р); take (*time, etc.*); F amputate; ~ от груди wean; **-ся** grow numb.
относи́тельн|ый [14; -лен, -льна] relative; ~о (Р) concerning, about.
отно|си́ть [15], ⟨отнести́⟩ [24 -с-: -есу́; -ёс, -есла́] take (to Д, в В); carry (off, away); put; refer to; ascribe; **-ся**, ⟨отнести́сь⟩ (к Д) treat, be; show; speak (of о П); *impf.* concern; refer; belong; date from; be relevant; **~ше́ние** *n* [12] attitude (toward[s] к Д); treatment; relation; ratio; (official) letter; respect (in, with в П, по Д); по ~ше́нию (к Д) as regards, to (-ward[s]); име́ть ~ше́ние concern.
отны́не henceforth, henceforward.
отню́дь: ~ не by no means.
отня́|тие *n* [12] taking (away); amputation; weaning; **~ть(ся)** *s.* отнима́ть(ся).
отобра|жа́ть [1], ⟨~зи́ть⟩ [15 *e.*; -ажу́, -ази́шь] (**-ся** be) reflect(ed); **~же́ние** *n* [12] reflection.
ото|бра́ть *s.* отбира́ть; **~всю́ду** from everywhere; **~гна́ть** *s.* отгоня́ть; **~гну́ть** *s.* отгиба́ть; **~грева́ть** [1], ⟨~гре́ть⟩ [8; -гре́тый] warm (up); **~двига́ть** [1], ⟨~дви́нуть⟩ [20 *st.*] move aside, away (*v/i.* **-ся**); F put off.
отодра́ть *s.* отдира́ть.
отож(д)еств|ля́ть [28], ⟨~и́ть⟩ [14 *e.*; -влю́, -ви́шь; -влённый] identify.
ото|зва́ть(ся) *s.* отзыва́ть(ся); **~йти́** *s.* отходи́ть; **~мкну́ть** *s.* отмыка́ть; **~мсти́ть** *s.* мстить.
отоп|и́ть [28] *s.* ота́пливать; **~ле́ние** *n* [12] heating.
оторва́ть(ся) *s.* отрыва́ть(ся).
оторопе́ть F [8] *pf.* be struck dumb.
отосла́ть *s.* отсыла́ть.
отпа|да́ть [1], ⟨∠сть⟩ [25; *pt. st.*] (от Р) fall off; fall away, secede, desert; be dropped; pass.
отпе|ва́ние *n* [12] burial service; **∠тый** F [14] inveterate, incorrigible; **~ре́ть(ся)** *s.* отпира́ть(ся).
отпеча́т|ок *m* [1; -тка] (im)print; mark; stamp; **~ывать**, ⟨~ать⟩ [1] print; type; imprint, impress.
отпи|ва́ть [1], ⟨∠ть⟩ [отопью́, -пьёшь; о́тпил, -а́, -о; -пе́й(те)!] drink (some ... Р); **∠ливать** [1], ⟨~ли́ть⟩ [13] saw off.
отпира́т|ельство *n* [9] disavowel; **~ь** [1], ⟨отпере́ть⟩ [12; отопру́, -прёшь; о́тпер, -рла́, -о; отпёрший; о́тпертый (-ерт, -а́, -о)] unlock, unbar, open; **-ся** open; (от Р) disavow.
отпи́ть *s.* отпива́ть.
отпи́х|ивать F [1], *once* ⟨~ну́ть⟩ [20] push off, away, aside, back.
отпла́|та *f* [5] repayment, requital; **~чивать** [1], ⟨~ти́ть⟩ [15] (re)pay, requite.
отплы|ва́ть [1], ⟨∠ть⟩ [23] sail, leave; swim (off); **∠тие** *n* [12] sailing off, departure.
о́тповедь *f* [8] rebuff, snub.
отпо́р *m* [1] repulse, rebuff.
отноро́ть [17] *pf.* rip (off).
отправ|и́тель *m* [4] sender; **∠ить (-ся)** *s.* ~ля́ть(ся); **∠ка** F *f* [5] dispatch; **~ле́ние** *n* [12] dispatch; departure; exercise, practice; function; **~ля́ть** [28], ⟨∠ить⟩ [14] send, dispatch, forward; mail, *Brt.* post; exercise, perform; **-ся** go; leave, set off (for в, на В); *impf.* (от Р) start from (*fig.*); **~но́й** [14] starting.
отпра́шиваться [1], ⟨отпроси́ться⟩ [15] ask (and get) leave (*to go ...*).
отпры́г|ивать [1], *once* ⟨~нуть⟩ [20] jump back (*or* aside); rebound.
о́тпрыск *m* [1] offshoot.
отпря|га́ть [1], ⟨∠чь⟩ [26 г/ж: -ягу́, -яжёшь] unharness; **∠нуть** [20 *st.*] *pf.* recoil.
отпу́г|ивать [1], ⟨~ну́ть⟩ [20] scare.
о́тпуск *m* [1; *pl.* -ка́, *etc. e.*] leave, vacation (on: *go* в В; *be* в П: *a.*, F, в ~у́); sale; supply; allotment; **~а́ть** [1], ⟨отпусти́ть⟩ [15] let go; release, set free; dismiss; sell; provide; allot; slacken; remit; grow; F crack; **~ни́к** *m* [1 *e.*] vacationist; **~но́й** [14] vacation..., holiday...; selling (*price*).
отпуще́н|ие *n* [12] remission; козёл ~ия scapegoat.
отраб|а́тывать, ⟨~о́тать⟩ [1] work off; finish work; *p. pt. p. a.* waste.
отра́в|а *f* [5] poison; *fig.* bane; **~ле́ние** *n* [12] poisoning; **~ля́ть** [28], ⟨~и́ть⟩ [14] poison; spoil.
отра́д|а *f* [5] comfort, joy, pleasure; **~ный** [14; -ден, -дна] pleasant, gratifying, comforting.
отра|жа́ть [1], ⟨~зи́ть⟩ [15 *e.*; -ажу́, -ази́шь; -ажённый] repel, ward off; refute; reflect, mirror (*v/i.* **-ся**; на П affect; show).
о́трасль *f* [8] branch.
отра|ста́ть [1], ⟨~сти́⟩ [24 **-ст-**:

-сту́; *cf.* расти́] grow; grow again; **∠щивать** [1], ⟨**~сти́ть**⟩ [15 *e.*; -ащу́, -асти́шь; -ащённый] grow.
отре́бье *n* [10] rubbish; rabble.
отре́з *m* [1] pattern, length (*of material*); **~а́ть** & **~ывать** [1], ⟨**~ать**⟩ [3] cut off; F cut short.
отрезв|ля́ть [28], ⟨**~и́ть**⟩ [14 *e.*; -влю́, -ви́шь; -влённый] sober; *fig.* disillusion.
отре́з|ок *m* [1; -зка] piece; stretch; ⚲ segment; **~ывать** *s.* **~а́ть**.
отре|ка́ться [1], ⟨**∠чься**⟩ [26] (от P) disown, disavow; renounce; **∠чься** от престо́ла abdicate.
отре́пье *n* [10] *coll.* rags *pl.*
отре|че́ние *n* [12] (от P) disavowal; renunciation; abdication; **∠чься** *s.* **~ка́ться**; **~ша́ть** [1], ⟨**~ши́ть**⟩ [16 *e.*; -шу́, -ши́шь; -шённый] dismiss; release; -ся relinquish; **~ше́ние** *n* [12] dismissal, removal; renunciation (of от P).
отрица́|ние *n* [12] negation, denial; **~тельный** [14; -лен, -льна] negative; **~ть** [1] deny.
отро́|г *m* [1] spur; **'~ду** F from birth; in one's life; **~дье** F *n* [10] spawn; **'~к** † *m* [1] boy; **~сток** *m* [1; -тка] ⚘ shoot; *anat.* appendix; **'~чество** *n* [9] boyhood; adolescence.
отруб|а́ть [1], ⟨**~и́ть**⟩ [14] cut off.
о́труби *f/pl.* [8; *from g/pl. e.*] bran.
отры́в *m* [1] separation; disengagement (*a.* ⚔); alienation; interruption; **~а́ть** [1] **1.** ⟨оторва́ть⟩ [-ву́, -вёшь; -ва́л, -а́, -о; ото́рванный] tear (*or* pull, turn) off, away; separate; -ся (от P) come off; turn (tear o. s.) away; lose contact (with); ⚔ disengage; не **~а́ясь** without rest; **2.** ⟨отры́ть⟩ [22] dig up, out, away; F disinter; **~истый** [14 *sh.*] abrupt; **~но́й** [14] sheet *or* block (*calendar*); **~ок** *m* [1; -вка] fragment; extract, passage; **~очный** [14; -чен, -чна] fragmentary; scrappy.
отры́жка *f* [5; *g/pl.*: -жек] belch (-ing); F survival.
отры́ть *s.* отрыва́ть.
отря́|д *m* [1] detachment; squadron; troop; ⚘, *zo.* class; **~жа́ть** [1], ⟨**~ди́ть**⟩ [15 *e.*; -яжу́, -яди́шь; -яжённый] detach; **~хивать** [1], *once* ⟨**~хну́ть**⟩ [20] shake off.
отсве́чивать [1] shimmer (with T).
отсе́|ивать [1], ⟨**~ять**⟩ [27] sift; *fig.* eliminate; **~ка́ть** [1], ⟨**~чь**⟩ [26; *pt.*: -се́к, -секла́; -сечённый] cut off; **~че́ние** *n* [12] cutting off.
отск|а́кивать [1], ⟨**~очи́ть**⟩ [16] jump off, back; rebound; F fall off.
отслу́ж|ивать [1], ⟨**~и́ть**⟩ [16] serve (one's time); be worn out; hold.
отсове́т|овать [1] *pf.* dissuade (from).

отсохну́ть *s.* отсыха́ть.
отсро́ч|ивать [1], ⟨**~ить**⟩ [16] postpone; respite; **~ка** *f* [5; *g/pl.*: -чек] delay; respite; prolongation.
отста|ва́ть [5], ⟨**∠ть**⟩ [-а́ну, -а́нешь] (от P) lag, fall *or* remain behind; *clock*: be slow (5 min. на пять мину́т); desert; leave off; come (*or* fall) off; F *pf.* leave alone.
отста́в|ка *f* [5] resignation, retirement; dismissal; в **~ке** = **ной**; **~ля́ть** [28], ⟨**~ить**⟩ [14] remove, set aside; dismiss; F countermand; **~но́й** [14] retired.
отст|а́ивать [1], ⟨**~оя́ть**⟩ [-ою́, -ои́шь] defend, save; maintain, assert; push; F stand; tire; *pf.* be away; -ся settle.
отста́|лость *f* [8] backwardness; **~лый** [14] backward; **~ть** *s.* **~ва́ть**.
отстёгивать [1], ⟨отстегну́ть⟩ [20; -ёгнутый] unbutton, unfasten.
отстоя́ть(ся) *s.* отста́ивать(ся).
отстр|а́ивать [1], ⟨**~о́ить**⟩ [13] build (up); **~аня́ть** [28], ⟨**~ани́ть**⟩ [13] push aside, remove; dismiss; debar; -ся (от P) dodge; shirk; **~о́ить** *s.* **~а́ивать**.
отступ|а́ть [1], ⟨**~и́ть**⟩ [14] step back; retreat, fall back; recoil; *fig.* recede; deviate; indent; -ся renounce (s. th. от P); **~ле́ние** *n* [12] retreat; deviation; digression; **∠ник** *m* [1] apostate; **~но́е** *n* [14] smart money.
отсу́тств|ие *n* [12] absence (in в B; in the/of за T/P); lack; в **~ии** absent; **~овать** [7] be absent; be lacking.
отсчи́т|ывать, ⟨**~а́ть**⟩ [1] count.
отсыл|а́ть [1], ⟨отосла́ть⟩ [-ошлю́, -шлёшь; ото́сланный] send (off, back); refer (to к Д); **∠ка** *f* [5; *g/pl.*: -лок] dispatch; reference.
отсып|а́ть [1], ⟨**∠ать**⟩ [2] pour (out).
отсы|ре́лый [14] damp; **~ха́ть** [1], ⟨отсо́хнуть⟩ [21] wither (off).
отсю́да from here; hence.
отта́|ивать [1], ⟨**~ять**⟩ [27] thaw; **~лкивать** [1], ⟨оттолкну́ть⟩ [20] push off, away, aside; repel; **~лкивающий** [17] repellent; **~скивать** [1], ⟨**~щи́ть**⟩ [16] pull off, away, aside; **~чивать** [1], ⟨отточи́ть⟩ [16] sharpen; **~ять** *s.* **~ивать**.
отте́н|ок *m* [1; -нка] shade, nuance, tinge; **~я́ть** [28], ⟨**~и́ть**⟩ [13] shade; set off, emphasize.
о́ттепель *f* [8] thaw.
оттесн|я́ть [28], ⟨**~и́ть**⟩ [13] push off, aside; ⚔ drive back; F oust.
о́ттис|к *m* [1] impression, reprint; **∠кивать** [1], ⟨**∠нуть**⟩ [20] print (off).
отто|го́ therefore, (*a.* **~го́** и) that's why; **~го́** что because; **~лкну́ть** *s.* отта́лкивать; **~пы́рить** F [13] *pf.* bulge, protrude (*v/i.* -ся); **~чи́ть** *s.* отта́чивать.
отту́да from there.

оття́|гивать [1], ⟨~ну́ть⟩ [20; -я́нутый] draw off (back); delay.
отуч|а́ть [1], ⟨~и́ть⟩ [16] disaccustom (to от P), cure (of); **-ся** leave off.
отхлы́нуть [20] *pf.* rush away, back.
отхо́д *m* [1] departure; ⚔ withdrawal; deviation; rupture; **~и́ть** [15], ⟨отойти́⟩ [-ойду́, -дёшь; отошёл, -шла́; отоше́дший; отойдя́] go (away, aside); leave; deviate; ⚔ withdraw; turn away; come (*or* fall) off; thaw; recover; expire; *impers.* be relieved; **~ы** *m/pl.* [1] waste.
отцве|та́ть [1], ⟨~сти́⟩ [25 -т-: -ету́] fade, wither.
отцеп|ля́ть [28], ⟨~и́ть⟩ [14] unhook; uncouple; F remove.
отцо́в|ский [16] paternal; fatherly; **~ство** *n* [9] paternity.
отча́|иваться [1], ⟨~яться⟩ [27] despair (of в П), despond.
отча́ли|вать [1], ⟨~ть⟩ [13] unmoor; push off; sail away.
отча́сти partly, in part.
отча́я|ние *n* [12] despair; **~нный** [14 *sh.*] desperate; **~ться** *s.* отча́иваться.
о́тче: ~ наш Our Father; Lord's Prayer.
отчего́ why; ~-то for some reason.
отчека́н|ивать [1], ⟨~ить⟩ [13] coin; say distinctly.
о́тчество *n* [9] patronymic.
отчёт *m* [1] account (of о, в П), report (on); return; (от)дава́ть себе́ ~ в П realize *v/t.*; **~ливый** [14 *sh.*] distinct, clear; precise; **~ность** *f* [8] accounting; F accounts *pl.*; **~ный** [14] of account.
отчи́|зна *f* [5] fatherland; **'~й** [17] paternal; **'~м** *m* [1] stepfather.
отчисл|е́ние *n* [12] deduction; subscription; dismissal; **~я́ть** [28], ⟨~ить⟩ [13] deduct; allot; dismiss.
отчи́т|ывать F, ⟨~а́ть⟩ [1] blow up, rebuke; **-ся** give *or* render an account (to пе́ред Т).
от|чужда́ть [1] alienate, expropriate; **~шатну́ться** [20] *pf.* start *or* shrink back; **~швырну́ть** F [20] *pf.* hurl (away); **~ше́льник** *m* [1] hermit.
отшиб|а́ть F [1], ⟨~и́ть⟩ [-бу́, -бёшь; -ши́б(ла); -ши́бленный] strike (off).
отщепе́нец *m* [1; -нца] renegade.
отъе́|зд *m* [1] departure; **~зжа́ть** [1], ⟨~хать⟩ [-е́ду, -е́дешь] drive (off), depart.
отъя́вленный [14] notorious, arch.
оты́гр|ывать, ⟨~а́ть⟩ [1] win back, regain (one's [lost] money **-ся**).
оты́ск|ивать [1], ⟨~а́ть⟩ [3] find.
отяго|ща́ть [1], ⟨~ти́ть⟩ [15 *e.*; -щу́, -оти́шь; -ощённый] (over-) burden.
офиц|е́р *m* [1] officer; **~е́рский** [16] office(r's, -s'); **~иа́льный** [14; -лен, -льна] official; **~иа́нт** *m* [1] waiter; **~ио́зный** [14; -зен, -зна] semiofficial.
оформ|ля́ть [28], ⟨~ить⟩ [14] form, shape; get up (*book*); mount (*play*); legalize; adjust.
ох oh!, ah!; **~анье** *n* [10] groan(s).
оха́пка *f* [5; *g/pl.*: -пок] armful; fagot.
о́х|ать [1], *once* ⟨~нуть⟩ [20] groan.
охва́т|ывать [1], ⟨~и́ть⟩ [15] seize, grasp; embrace; envelop.
охла|дева́ть, ⟨~де́ть⟩ [8] cool down; **~жда́ть** [1], ⟨~ди́ть⟩ [15 *e.*; -ажу́, -ади́шь; -аждённый] cool; **~жде́ние** *n* [12] cooling.
охмел|я́ть [28], ⟨~и́ть⟩ [13] (**~еть** F [8] become) intoxicate(d).
о́хнуть *s.* о́хать.
охо́т|а *f* [5] (на В, за Т) hunt(ing) (of, for); chase (after); (к Д) F desire (for), mind (to); ~а Д + *inf.*! what do(es) ... want + *inf.* for?; **~иться** [15] (на В, за Т) hunt; chase (after); **~ник** *m* [1] hunter; volunteer; lover (of до P); **~ничий** [18] hunting, shooting; hunter's (-s'); **~но** willingly, gladly, with pleasure; **~нее** rather; ~нее всего́ best of all.
охра́н|а *f* [5] guard(s); protection; **~е́ние** *n* [12] protection; ⚔ outpost (-s); **~я́ть** [28], ⟨~и́ть⟩ [13] guard, protect (from, against от P).
охри́п|лый F [14], **~ший** [17] hoarse.
оце́н|ивать [1], ⟨~и́ть⟩ [13; -еню́, -е́нишь] value (at в В), appraise, estimate; appreciate; **~ка** *f* [5; *g/pl.*: -нок] valuation, appraisal; estimation, appreciation; mark.
оцепене́|лый [14] benumbed; stupefied; **~ние** *n* [12] numbness.
оцеп|ля́ть [28] ⟨~и́ть⟩ [14] encircle.
оча́г *m* [1 *e.*] fireplace, (*a. fig.* = home) hearth; *fig.* center (-tre), seat.
очаров|а́ние *n* [12] charm, fascination; **~а́тельный** [14; -лен, -льна] charming; **~ывать** [1], ⟨~а́ть⟩ [7] charm, fascinate, enchant.
очеви́д|ец *m* [1; -дца] eyewitness; **~ный** [14; -ден, -дна] evident.
о́чень very, (very) much.
очередно́й [14] next (in turn); regular; foremost; latest.
о́черед|ь *f* [8; *from g/pl. e.*] turn (in; by turns по ~ди); order, succession; line (*Brt.* queue); ⚔ volley; ва́ша ~ь *or* ~ь за ва́ми it is your turn; на ~и next; в свою́ ~ь in (for) my, *etc.*, turn (part).
о́черк *m* [1] sketch; outline; essay.
очерня́ть [28] *s.* черни́ть.
очерстве́лый [14] hardened.
очер|та́ние *n* [12] outline, contour; **~чивать** [1], ⟨~ти́ть⟩ [15] outline, sketch; ~тя́ го́лову F headlong.
очи́|стка *f* [5; *g/pl.*: -ток] clean(s)-

ing; clearance; *pl.* peelings; **~щáть** [1], ⟨~стить⟩ [15] clean(se); clear; peel; purify; evacuate, quit; empty.
очк|и́ *n/pl.* [1] spectacles, glasses; **~ó** *n* [9; *pl.*: -кú, -кóв] *sport*: point; *cards*: spot, *Brt.* pip; ⚘, ⊕ eye; **~овтирáтельство** F *n* [9] eyewash, humbug.
очну́ться [20] *pf.*, *s.* опóмниться.
очумéлый P [14] crazy, mad.
очути́ться [15; *1st. p. sg. not used*] get, find o. s.
ошалéлый F [14] crazy, mad.
ошéйник *m* [1] collar (*on a dog only*).
ошелом|ля́ть [28], ⟨~и́ть⟩ [14 *e.*; -млю́, -ми́шь; -млённый] stun, stupefy.
ошиб|áться [1], ⟨~и́ться⟩ [-бу́сь, -бёшься; -и́бся, -и́блась] be mistaken, make a mistake (-s), err; miss; **∠ка** *f* [5; *g/pl.*: -бок] mistake (by по Д), error, fault; **∠очный** [14; -чен, -чна] erroneous, mistaken.
ошпáр|ивать [1], ⟨~ить⟩ [13] scald.
ощу́п|ывать, ⟨~ать⟩ [1] feel, touch; **'~ь** *f* [8]: на '~ь to the touch; **'~ью** *adv.* gropingly.
ощу|ти́мый [14 *sh.*], **~ти́тельный** [14; -лен, -льна] palpable, tangible; felt; not(ice)able; **~щáть** [1], ⟨~ти́ть⟩ [15 *e.*; -ущу́, -ути́шь; -ущённый] feel, sense; **-ся** be felt; **~щéние** *n* [12] sensation; feeling.

П

Пáвел *m* [1; -вла] Paul.
павиáн *m* [1] baboon.
павильóн *m* [1] pavilion; (*fair*) hall; (*film*) studio.
павли́н *m* [1], **~ий** [18] peacock.
пáводок *m* [1; -дка] flood.
пá|губный [14; -бен, -бна] pernicious; **~даль** *f* [8] carrion.
пáда|ть [1] **1.** ⟨упáсть⟩ [25; *pt. st.*] fall; **2.** ⟨пасть⟩ *fig.* fall; die; **~ть** ду́хом lose courage (*or* heart).
пад|éж[1] *m* [1 *e.*] *gr.* case; **~ёж**[2] *m* [1 *e.*] (*cattle*) plague, rinderpest; **~éние** *n* [12] fall; downfall, overthrow; ☨ slump; **∠кий** [16; -док, -дка] (на В) greedy (of, for), mad (after); **~у́чая** *f* [17] epilepsy.
пáдчерица *f* [5] stepdaughter.
паёк *m* [1; пайкá] ration.
пáзуха *f* [5] bosom (in за В); cavity.
пай *m* [3; *pl. e.*: пай, паёв] share; **∠щик** *m* [1] shareholder.
пакéт *m* [1] parcel, package, packet; dispatch; paper bag.
пáкля *f* [6] tow, oakum.
паковáть [7], ⟨у-, за-⟩ pack.
пáк|ость *f* [8] filth, smut, dirt(y trick); **~т** *m* [1] pact, treaty.
палáт|а *f* [5] chamber; *parl.* house; board; ward; оружéйная ~а armo(u)ry; **~ка** *f* [5; *g/pl.*: -ток] tent; booth.
палáч *m* [1 *e.*] hangman, executioner.
Палести́на *f* [5] Palestine.
пáл|ец *m* [1; -льца] finger; toe; смотрéть сквозь ~ьцы wink (at на В); знать как свой пять ~ьцев have at one's fingertips; **~исáдник** *m* [1] (small) front garden
пали́тра *f* [5] palette.
пали́ть [13] **1.** ⟨с-⟩ burn, scorch; **2.** ⟨о-⟩ singe; **3.** ⟨вы-⟩ fire, shoot.
пáл|ка *f* [5; *g/pl.*: -лок] stick; cane; club; из-под ~ки F under *or* in constraint; **~очка** *f* [5; *g/pl.*: -чек] (small) stick; ♪ baton; wand; ⚕ bacillus.
палóмни|к *m* [1] pilgrim; **~чество** *n* [9] pilgrimage.
пáлуба *f* [5] deck.
пальбá *f* [5] firing, fire.
пáльма *f* [5] palm (tree).
пальтó *n* [*indecl.*] (over)coat.
пáмят|ник *m* [1] monument; memorial; **~ный** [14; -тен, -тна] memorable; unforgettable; **~ь** *f* [8] memory (in/of на В/о П); remembrance; recollection (of о П); на ~ь *a.* by heart; без ~и unconscious; F mad (about от P).
Панáмский [16]: ~ проли́в *m* Panama Canal.
панéль *f* [8] pavement; wainscot.
пáника *f* [5] panic.
панихи́да *f* [5] requiem, dirge.
пансиóн *m* [1] boarding house; boarding school.
панталóны *m/pl.* [5] drawers, pants.
пантéра *f* [5] panther.
пáнцирь *m* [4] coat of mail.
пáпа[1] F *m* [5] papa; dad(dy).
пáпа[2] *m* [5] pope.
пáперть *f* [8] porch (*of a church*).
папильóтка *f* [5; *g/pl.*: -ток] hair curler.
папирóса *f* [5] cigarette.
пáпка *f* [5; *g/pl.*: -пок] folder; cardboard.
пáпоротник *m* [1] fern.
пар *m* [1; в -у́; *pl. e.*] **1.** steam; **2.** fallow; **∠а** *f* [5] pair; couple.
Парагвáй *m* [4] Paraguay.
парáграф *m* [1] paragraph.
парáд *m* [1] parade; **~ный** [14] full (dress); front (door).
парашю́т (-'ʃut) *m* [1] parachute; **~и́ст** *m* [1] parachutist; ⚔ paratrooper.
парéние *n* [12] soar(ing), hover.
пáрень *m* [4; -рня; *from g/pl. e.*] lad, guy.

пари́ *n* [*indecl.*] bet, wager (*vb.*: держа́ть ~); (идёт) ~? what do you bet?

Пари́ж *m* [1] Paris; **2а́нин** *m* [1; *pl.*: -а́не, -а́н], **2а́нка** *f* [5; *g/pl.*: -нок] Parisian.

пари́к *m* [1 *e.*] wig; **~ма́хер** *m* [1] hairdresser, barber; **~ма́херская** *f* [16] hairdressing saloon, barber's (shop).

пари́|ровать [7] (*im*)*pf.*, *a.* ⟨от-⟩ parry; **~ть**[1] [13] soar, hover.

па́рить[2] [13] steam (*in a bath*: **-ся**).

парла́мент *m* [1] parliament; **~а́рий** *m* [3] parliamentarian; **~ский** [16] parliamentary.

парни́к *m* [1 *e.*], **~о́вый** [14] hotbed.

парни́шка F *m* [5; *g/pl.*: -шек] guy, lad, youngster.

парно́й [14] fresh (*milk, meat*).

па́рный [14] paired; twin...

паро|во́з *m* [1] 🚂 engine; **~во́й** [14] steam...; **~ди́ровать** [7] (*im*)*pf.*, **∠дия** *f* [7] parody.

паро́ль *m* [4] password, parole.

паро́м *m* [1] ferry(boat); **~щик** *m* [1] ferryman.

парохо́д *m* [1] steamer; **~ный** [14] steamship...; **~ство** *n* [9] (steamship) line.

па́рт|а *f* [5] (*school*) bench, *Brt. a.* form; **~акти́в** *m* [1] = **~и́йный** акти́в; **~би́лет** *m* [1] = **~и́йный** биле́т; **~е́р** (-ˈtɛr) *m* [1] parterre, *Brt.* pit; **~и́ец** F *m* [1; -и́йца] Party man *or* member (*Sov.*); **~иза́н** *m* [1] guerilla, partisan; **~и́йность** *f* [8] Party membership; partisanship; Party discipline (*Sov.*); **~и́йный** [14] party...; *su.* = **~и́ец**; **~иту́ра** *f* [5] ♪ score; **~ия** *f* [7] party; ✝ parcel, lot, consignment; ⚔ detachment; batch; game, set; match; ♪ part; ✝ **~иями** in lots; **~нёр** *m* [1], **~нёрша** *f* [5] partner; **~о́рг** *m* [1] Party organizer (*Sov.*).

па́рус *m* [1; *pl.*: -са́, *etc. e.*] sail; на всех ~а́х under full sail; **~и́на** *f* [5] sailcloth, canvas, duck; **~и́новый** [14] canvas...; **~ник** *m* [1] = **~ное** су́дно *n* [14/9] sailing ship.

парфюме́рия *f* [7] perfumery.

парч|а́ *f* [5] brocade; **~о́вый** [14] brocade(d).

парши́вый [14 *sh.*] mangy.

пас *m* [1] pass (*sport, cards*).

па́сквиль *m* [4] lampoon.

паску́дный P [14; -ден, -дна] foul, filthy.

па́смурный [14; -рен, -рна] dull; gloomy.

пасова́ть [7] pass (*sport*; *cards*, ⟨с-⟩); F yield (to пе́ред T).

па́спорт *m* [1; *pl.*: -та́, *etc. e.*], **~ный** [14] passport.

пассажи́р *m* [1], **~ка** *f* [5; *g/pl.*: -рок], **~ский** [16] passenger.

пасси́в *m* [1] ✝ liabilities *pl.*; **~ный** [14; -вен, -вна] passive.

па́ста *f* [5] paste.

па́ст|бище *n* [11] pasture; **~ва** *f* [5] *eccl.* flock; **~и́** [24 -с-] graze (*v/i.* **-сь**), pasture; **~у́х** *m* [1 *e.*] herder (*Brt.* herdsman), shepherd; **~у́шка** *f* [5; *g/pl.*: -шек] shepherdess; **~у́ший** [18] shepherd's; **~ырь** *m* [4] pastor; **~ь 1.** *s.* па́дать; **2.** *f* [8] jaws *pl.*, mouth.

па́сха *f* [5] Easter (for на B; on на П); Easter cake; Passover; **∠льный** [14] Easter...

па́сынок *m* [1; -нка] stepson.

пате́нт *m* [1], **~ова́ть** [7] (*im*)*pf.*, *a.* ⟨за-⟩ patent.

патефо́н *m* [1] record player.

па́тока *f* [5] molasses, *Brt. a.* treacle.

патр|ио́т *m* [1]; patriot; **~иоти́ческий** [16] patriotic; **~о́н** *m* [1] **1.** cartridge, shell; (lamp) socket; **2.** patron; **3.** pattern; **~онта́ш** *m* [1] cartridge belt, pouch; **~ули́ровать** [7], **~у́ль** *m* [4 *e.*] patrol.

па́уза *f* [5] pause.

пау́к *m* [1 *e.*] spider.

паути́на *f* [5] cobweb.

па́фос *m* [1] pathos; verve, vim.

пах *m* [1; в -у́] *anat.* groin; **∠арь** *m* [4] plowman, *Brt.* ploughman; **~а́ть** [3], ⟨вс-⟩ plow (*Brt.* plough), till.

па́хн|уть[1] [20] smell (of T); **~у́ть**[2] F [20] *pf.* puff.

па́хот|а *f* [5] tillage; **~ный** [14] arable.

паху́чий [17 *sh.*] fragrant.

пацие́нт *m* [1], **~ка** *f* [5; *g/pl.*: -ток] patient.

па́че F: тем ~ all the more.

па́чка *f* [5; *g/pl.*: -чек] pack(et), package; batch.

па́чкать [1], ⟨за-, ис-, вы́-⟩ soil.

па́шня *f* [6; *g/pl.*: -шен] tillage, field.

паште́т *m* [1] pie.

пая́льник *m* [1] soldering iron.

пая́сничать F [1] play the fool.

пая́ть [28], ⟨за-⟩ solder.

пая́ц *m* [1] buffoon, merry-andrew.

ПВО = противовозду́шная оборо́на.

пев|е́ц *m* [1; -вца́], **~и́ца** *f* [5] singer; **~у́чий** [17 *sh.*] melodious; **∠чий** [17] singing (*bird*); *su.* chorister, choirboy.

пе́гий [16 *sh.*] piebald.

педаго́г *m* [1] pedagogue, teacher; **~ика** *f* [5] pedagogics; **~и́ческий** [16], **~и́чный** [14; -чен, -чна] pedagogic(al).

педа́ль *f* [8] treadle, pedal.

педа́нт *m* [1] pedant, **~и́чный** [14; -чен, -чна] pedantic(al).

пейза́ж *m* [1] landscape.

пека́р|ня *f* [6; *g/pl.*: -рен] bakery; **ʼь** *m* [4; *pl. a.* -ря́, *etc. e.*] baker.

пелен|а́ *f* [5] shroud; **~а́ть** [1], ⟨за-, с-⟩ swaddle; **~ка** (-ˈlɔn-) *f* [5; *g/pl.*: -нок] swaddling band (*pl.* clothes), diaper, *Brt. a.* napkin.

пельме́ни *m/pl.* [*gen.*: -ней] ravioli.
пе́на *f* [5] foam, froth; lather.
пена́л *m* [1] pen case.
пе́ние *n* [12] singing; crow.
пе́н|истый [14 *sh.*] foamy, frothy; **~иться** [13], ⟨вс-⟩ foam, froth; sparkle, mantle; **~ка** *f* [5; *g/pl.*: -нок] scum; froth.
пе́нсия *f* [7] pension.
пенсне́ (-'nɛ) *n* [*indecl.*] pince-nez, eyeglasses *pl.*
пе́нь *m* [4; пня] stump; blockhead.
пеньк|а́ *f* [5] hemp; **~о́вый** [14] hemp(en).
пе́ня *f* [6; *g/pl.*: -ней] fine.
пеня́ть F [28], ⟨по-⟩ blame (a p. for Д *or* на В/за В).
пе́пел *m* [1; -пла] ashes *pl.*; **~и́ще** *n* [11] the ashes; *s. a.* пожа́рище; **~ьница** *f* [5] ash tray; **~ьный** [14] ashy.
пе́рвен|ец *m* [1; -нца] first-born; **~ство** *n* [9] primogeniture; superiority; championship.
перви́чный [14; -чен, -чна] primary.
перво|бы́тный [14; -тен, -тна] primitive, primeval; **~исто́чник** *m* [1] (first) source, origin; **~кла́ссный** [14] first-rate *or* -class; **~ку́рсник** *m* [1] freshman; **~-на́перво** P first of all; **~нача́льный** [14; -лен, -льна] original; primary; **~о́браз** *m* [1] prototype; **~осно́вы** *f/pl.* [5] elements; **~очередно́й** [14] top-priority; **~со́ртный** = ~кла́ссный; **~степе́нный** [14; -е́нен, -е́нна] paramount, supreme.
пе́рв|ый [14] first; chief, main; *Brt.* ground (*floor*); *thea.* dress (*circle*); ~ое *n* first course (*meal*; for на В); ~ым де́лом (до́лгом) *or* в ~ую о́чередь first of all, first thing; ~е́йший the very first; first-rate; *cf.* пя́тый.
перга́мент *m* [1] parchment.
переб|ега́ть [1], ⟨~ежа́ть⟩ [4; -егу́, -ежи́шь, -егу́т] run over (*or* across); desert; **~е́жчик** *m* [1] deserter; turncoat; **~ива́ть** [1], ⟨~и́ть⟩ [-бью́, -бьёшь, *cf.* бить] interrupt; break; kill; **-ся** break; F rough it.
переб|ира́ть [1], ⟨~ра́ть⟩ [-беру́, -рёшь; -бра́л, -а́, -о; -е́бранный] look a th. over; sort (out); *impf.* ♪ finger; tell (one's beads); **-ся** move (into на, в В); cross (*v/t.* че́рез В).
переб|и́ть *s.* ~ива́ть; **~о́й** *m* [3] stoppage, break; irregularity; **~оро́ть** [17] *pf.* overcome, master.
перебр|а́нка F *f* [5; *g/pl.*: -нок] wrangle; **~а́сывать** [1], ⟨~о́сить⟩ [15] throw over; ⚔, ✝ transfer, shift; lay (*bridge*); **-ся** exchange (*v/t.* Т); **~а́ть(ся)** *s.* перебира́ть (-ся); **~о́ска** *f* [5; *g/pl.*: -сок] transference.
перева́л *m* [1] pass; **~ивать** [1], ⟨~и́ть⟩ [13; -алю́, -а́лишь; -а́ленный] tumble, turn (over; *v/i.* **-ся**; *impf.* waddle); F pass; *impers.* (Д) ~и́ло за (В) (р.) is past ...
перева́р|ивать [1], ⟨~и́ть⟩ [13; -арю́, -а́ришь; -а́ренный] digest.
пере|везти́ *s.* ~вози́ть; **~вёртывать** [1], ⟨~верну́ть⟩ [20; -вёрнутый] turn over (*v/i.* -ся); overturn; turn; **~ве́с** *m* [1] preponderance; **~вести́(сь)** *s.* переводи́ть(ся); **~ве́шивать** [1], ⟨~ве́сить⟩ [15] hang (elsewhere); reweigh; outweigh; **-ся** hang *or* bend over; **~вира́ть** F [1], ⟨~вра́ть⟩ [-вру́, -врёшь; -е́вранный] misquote, distort.
перево́д *m* [1] transfer(ence); translation (from/into с Р/на В); remittance; (*money*) order; **~и́ть** [15], ⟨перевести́⟩ [25] lead; transfer; translate (from/into с Р/на В), turn; interpret; remit; set (*watch, clock*; *usu.* стре́лку); ~и́ть дух take breath; (-ся, ⟨-сь⟩) transfer; die out; (у Р/И) run out/of; **~ный** [14] translated; (*a.* ✝) transfer...; ~ный ве́ксель *m* draft; **~чик** *m* [1], **~чица** *f* [5] translator; interpreter.
перево́з *m* [1] ferriage, ferry; *a.* = ~ка; **~и́ть** [15], ⟨перевезти́⟩ [24] transport, convey; remove; ferry (over); **~ка** *f* [5; *g/pl.*: -зок] transport(ation), conveyance; **~чик** *m* [1] ferryman.
пере|вооруже́ние *n* [12] rearmament; **~вора́чивать** [1] = ~вёртывать; **~воро́т** *m* [1] revolution; **~воспита́ние** *n* [12] reëducation; **~вра́ть** *s.* ~вира́ть; **~вы́боры** *m/pl.* [1] reëlection.
перевыполн|е́ние *n* [12] overfulfil(l)ment (*Sov.*); **~я́ть** [28], ⟨'~ить⟩ [13] exceed, surpass.
перевя́з|ка *f* [5; *g/pl.*: -зок] dressing, bandage; **~очный** [14] dressing; **~ывать** [1], ⟨~а́ть⟩ [3] tie up; dress, bandage.
переги́б *m* [1] bend, fold; dog-ear; **~а́ть** [1], ⟨перегну́ть⟩ [20] bend; **-ся** lean over.
перегля́|дываться [1], *once* ⟨~ну́ться⟩ [19] exchange glances.
пере|гна́ть *s.* ~гоня́ть; **~гно́й** *m* [3] humus; **~гну́ть(ся)** *s.* ~гиба́ть(ся).
перегов|а́ривать [1], ⟨~ори́ть⟩ [13] talk (s. th.) over (о Т), discuss; **~о́ры** *m/pl.* [1] negotiations; ⚔ parley.
перег|о́нка *f* [5] distillation; **~оня́ть** [28], ⟨~на́ть⟩ [-гоню́, -го́нишь; -гна́л, -а́, -о; -е́гнанный] (out)distance, outstrip; surpass, outdo; ⚗ distil.
перегор|а́живать [1], ⟨~оди́ть⟩ [15 & 15 *e.*; -рожу́, -ро́дишь] partition (off); **~а́ть** [1], ⟨~е́ть⟩ [9] (*lamp*) burn out; (*fuse, etc.*) blow

(out); **~óдка** *f* [5; *g/pl.:* -док] partition.
перегр|евáть [1], ⟨**~éть**⟩ [8; -éтый] overheat; **~ужáть** [1], ⟨**~узи́ть**⟩ [15 & 15 *e.*; -ужу́, -у́зи́шь], **~у́зка** *f* [5; *g/pl.:* -зок] overload; overwork; **~уппировáть** [7] *pf.* regroup; **~уппиро́вка** *f* [5; *g/pl.:* -вок] regrouping; **~ызáть** [1], ⟨**~ы́зть**⟩ [24; *pt. st.*; -ы́зенный] gnaw through.
пéред[1], **~о** (T) before, in front of.
перёд[2] *m* [1; пéреда; *pl.:* -дá, *etc. e.*] front.
перед|авáть [5], ⟨**~áть**⟩ [-да́м, -да́шь, *etc., cf.* дать; *pt.* пéредал, -á, -o] pass, hand (over), deliver; give (*a.* regards); broadcast; transmit; reproduce; render; tell; take a message (for Д, *on the phone*); ✝ endorse; -ся ⚕ be communicated; **~áточный** [14] transmissive; **~áтчик** *m* [1] transmitter; **~áть(ся)** *s.* **~авáть(ся)**; **~áча** *f* [5] delivery, handing over; transfer; broadcast, (*a.* ⊕) transmission; gear; ⚕ communication; reproduction; package.
передв|игáть [1], ⟨**~и́нуть**⟩ [20] move, shift; **~ижéние** *n* [12] movement; transportation; **~и́жка** *f* [5; *g/pl.:* -жек], **~ижно́й** [14] travel(l)ing, mobile, itinerant.
передéл *m* [1] repartition; **~ка** *f* [5; *g/pl.:* -лок] alteration; recast; F mess; **~ывать**, ⟨**~ать**⟩ [1] recast; make over, alter.
перéдн|ий [15] front..., fore...; **~ик** *m* [1] apron; **~яя** *f* [15] hall, antechamber.
передов|и́к *m* [1 *e.*] best worker *or* farmer (*Sov.*); **~и́ца** *f* [5] leading article, editorial; **~о́й** [14] progressive; leading, foremost; front (*line*); **~óй** отря́д *m* vanguard.
пере|до́к *m* [1; -дкá] front; ⚔ limber; **~дохну́ть** [20] *pf.* take breath *or* rest; **~дрáзнивать** [1], ⟨**~дразни́ть**⟩ [13; -азню́, -áзнишь] mimic; **~дря́га** F *f* [5] fix, scrape; **~ду́мывать**, ⟨**~ду́мать**⟩ [1] change one's mind; F *s.* обду́мать; **~ды́шка** *f* [5; *g/pl.:* -шек] respite.
переé|зд *m* [1] passage; crossing; move, removal (в, на В [in]to); **~зжáть** [1], ⟨**~хать**⟩ [-éду, -éдешь; -езжáй] **1.** *v/i.* cross (*v/t.* чéрез В); (re)move (в, на В [in]to); **2.** *v/t.* run over.
пережд|áть *s.* **~идáть**; **~ёвывать** [1], ⟨**~евáть**⟩ [7 *e.*; -жую́, -жуёшь] chew (well); F repeat over and over again; **~ивáние** *n* [12] experience; **~ивáть** [1], ⟨**~и́ть**⟩ [-живу́, -вёшь; пéрежил, -á, -o; пéрежи́тый (пéрежит, -á, -o)] experience; go through, endure; survive, outlive; **~идáть** [1], ⟨**~дáть**⟩ [-жду́, -ждёшь; -ждáл, -á, -o] wait (till *s. th.* is over); **~и́ток** *m* [1; -тка] survival.
перезрéлый [14] overripe.
переиз|бирáть [1], ⟨**~брáть**⟩ [-беру́, -рёшь; -брáл, -á, -o; -и́збранный] reëlect; **~брáние** *n* [12] reëlection; **~давáть** [5], ⟨**~дáть**⟩ [-да́м, -да́шь, *etc. cf.* дать; -дáл, -á, -o] republish; **~дáние** *n* [12] reëdition; **~дáть** *s.* **~давáть**.
переименовáть [7] *pf.* rename.
перeинáчи|вать F [1], ⟨**~ть**⟩ [16] alter, modify; distort.
перейти́ *s.* переходи́ть.
переки́|дывать [1], ⟨**~нуть**⟩ [20] throw over (чéрез В); upset; -ся exchange (*v/t.* T).
переки|пáть [1], ⟨**~пéть**⟩ [10 *e.*; *3rd. p. only*] boil over; **~сь** ('pe-) *f* [8] peroxide.
переклáд|ина *f* [5] crossbar, crossbeam; **~ывать** [1], ⟨переложи́ть⟩ [16] put, lay *or* pack (elsewhere), shift; interlay (with T); *cf.* перелагáть.
перекл|икáться [1], ⟨**~и́кнуться**⟩ [20] shout to o.a.; reëcho (*v/t.* с T); **~и́чка** *f* [5; *g/pl.:* -чек] roll call.
переключ|áть [1], ⟨**~и́ть**⟩ [16 *e.*; -чу́, -чи́шь; -чённый] switch over (*v/i.* -ся); **~éние** *n* [12] switching over; **~и́ть** *s.* **~áть**.
перековáть [7 *e.*; -кую́, -куёшь] *pf.* shoe over again; *fig.* reëducate, remake.
перекóшенный [14] wry.
перекр|áивать [1], ⟨**~ои́ть**⟩ [13; -óенный] cut again; remake.
перекрёст|ный [14] cross (*fire, -examination*); **~ок** *m* [1; -тка] crossroad(s).
перекрои́ть *s.* перекрáивать.
перекр|ывáть [1], ⟨**~ы́ть**⟩ [22] (re-)cover; exceed, surpass; **~ы́тие** *n* [12] covering.
переку́с|ывать [1], ⟨**~и́ть**⟩ [15] bite through; F take a bite.
перел|агáть [1], ⟨**~ожи́ть**⟩ [16] transpose; arrange.
перел|áмывать [1] **1.** ⟨**~оми́ть**⟩ [14] break in two; overcome; **2.** ⟨**~омáть**⟩ [1] break to pieces.
перел|езáть [1], ⟨**~éзть**⟩ [24 *st.*; -лéз] climb over (чéрез В).
перел|ёт *m* [1] passage (*birds*); ✈ flight; **~етáть** [1], ⟨**~етéть**⟩ [11] fly (across); pass, migrate; flit; **~ётный** [14] (*bird*) of passage.
перели́|в *m* [1] ♪ run, roulade; play (*colo[u]rs*); **~вáние** ⚕ *n* [12] transfusion; **~вáть** [1], ⟨**~ть**⟩ [-лью́, -льёшь, *etc., cf.* лить] decant, pour; ⚕ transfuse; **~вáть** из пустóго в порóжнее mill the wind; -ся overflow; *impf.* ♪ warble, roll; (*colo[u]rs*) play, shimmer.
перели́ст|ывать, ⟨**~áть**⟩ [1] turn over (*pages*); look through.
перели́ть *s.* переливáть.

перелицева́ть [7] *pf.* turn (*clothes*).

перелож|е́ние *n* [12] transposition; arrangement; setting to music; **~и́ть** *s.* перекла́дывать & перелага́ть.

перело́м *m* [1] fracture; crisis, turning point; **~а́ть, ~и́ть** *s.* перела́мывать.

перем|а́лывать [1], ⟨~оло́ть⟩ [17; -мелю́, -ме́лешь; -меля́] grind, mill; **~ежа́ть(ся)** [1] alternate; intermit.

переме́н|а *f* [5] change; recess, break (*school*); **~и́ть(ся)** *s.* **~я́ться**; **~ный** [14] variable; ⚡ alternating; **~чивый** F [14] changeable, variable; **~я́ть** [28], ⟨~и́ть⟩ [13; -еню́, -е́нишь] change (*v/i.* **-ся**); exchange.

переме|сти́ть(ся) *s.* **~ща́ть(ся)**; **~́шивать**, ⟨~ша́ть⟩ [1] mix (up); confuse; **~ща́ть** [1], ⟨~сти́ть⟩ [15 *e.*; -ещу́, -ести́шь; -ещённый] move, shift (*v/i.* **-ся**); **~щённый** [14]: **~щённые ли́ца** *pl.* displaced persons.

переми́рие *n* [12] armistice, truce.

перемоло́ть *s.* перема́лывать.

перенаселе́ние *n* [12] overpopulation.

перенести́ *s.* переноси́ть.

перен|има́ть [1], ⟨~я́ть⟩ [-ейму́, -мёшь; пе́ренял, -а́, -о; пе́ренятый (пе́ренят, -а́, -о)] adopt, take over.

перено́с *m* [1] transfer, carrying over; sum carried over; syllabification; **~и́ть** [15], ⟨перенести́⟩ [24 -с-] transfer, carry over; bear, endure, stand; postpone, put off (till на В); **~ица** *f* [5] bridge (*of nose*).

перено́с|ка *f* [5; *g/pl.:* -сок] carrying, transport(ation); **~ный** [14] portable; figurative.

переня́ть *s.* перенима́ть.

переобору́дова|ть [7] (*im*)*pf.* reëquip; **~ние** *n* [12] reëquipment.

переод|ева́ться [1], ⟨~е́ться⟩ [-е́нусь, -нешься] change (one's clothes); **~е́тый** [14 *sh.*] *a.* disguised.

переоце́н|ивать [1], ⟨~и́ть⟩ [13; -еню́, -е́нишь] overestimate, overrate; revalue; **~ка** *f* [5; *g/pl.:* -нок] overestimation; revaluation.

пе́репел *m* [1; *pl.*: -ла́, *etc. e.*] quail.

перепеча́т|ка *f* [5; *g/pl.:* -ток] reprint; **~ывать**, ⟨~ать⟩ [1] reprint; type.

перепи́с|ка *f* [5; *g/pl.:* -сок] copying; typing; correspondence; **~чик** *m* [1] copyist; **~ывать** [1], ⟨~а́ть⟩ [3] copy; type; list; enumerate; **-ся** *impf.* correspond (with с Т); **~ь** ('р̦е-) *f* [8] census.

перепла́|чивать [1], ⟨~ти́ть⟩ [15] overpay.

перепл|ета́ть [1], ⟨~ести́⟩ [25 -т-] bind (*book*); interlace, intertwine (*v/i.* **-ся**, ⟨-сь⟩); **~ёт** *m* [1] binding, book cover; **~ётчик** *m* [1] bookbinder; **~ыва́ть** [1], ⟨~ы́ть⟩ [23] swim *or* sail (across че́рез В).

перепол|за́ть [1], ⟨~ти́⟩ [24] creep, crawl (over).

перепо́лн|енный [14 *sh.*] overcrowded; overflowing; **~я́ть** [28], ⟨~ить⟩ [13] overfill (*v/i.* **-ся**), cram; overcrowd.

переполо́|х *m* [1] tumult, turmoil; dismay, fright; **~ши́ть** F [16 *e.*; -шу́, -ши́шь; -шённый] *pf.* (**-ся** get) alarm(ed), perturb(ed).

перепо́нка *f* [5; *g/pl.:* -нок] membrane; web.

перепра́в|а *f* [5] crossing, passage; ford; temporary bridge; **~ля́ть** [28], ⟨~ить⟩ [14] carry (over), convey; **-ся** cross, pass.

перепрод|ава́ть [5], ⟨~а́ть⟩ [-да́м, -да́шь, *etc.*, *cf.* дать; *pt.:* -о́да́л, -ла́, -о] resell; **~а́жа** *f* [5] resale.

перепры́г|ивать [1], ⟨~нуть⟩ [20] jump (over).

перепу́г F *m* [1] fright (for с ~у); **~а́ть** [1] *pf.* (**-ся** get) frighten(ed).

перепу́тывать [1] *s.* пу́тать.

перепу́тье *n* [10] crossroad(s).

перераб|а́тывать, ⟨~о́тать⟩ [1] work (up), process; remake; **~о́тка** *f* [5; *g/pl.:* -ток] working (up), processing; remaking.

перерас|та́ть [1], ⟨~ти́⟩ [24 -ст-; -ро́с, -сла́] grow, develop; overgrow; **~хо́д** *m* [1] excess expenditure.

перерез|а́ть & **~́ывать** [1], ⟨~́ать⟩ [3] cut (through); cut off; kill.

переро|жда́ться [1], ⟨~ди́ться⟩ [15 *e.*; -ожу́сь, -оди́шься; -ождённый] regenerate; degenerate.

переруб|а́ть [1], ⟨~и́ть⟩ [14] hew *or* cut through.

переры́в *m* [1] interruption; stop, break, interval; (*lunch*) time.

переса́|дка *f* [5; *g/pl.:* -док] transplanting; grafting; 🚂 change; **~живать** [1], ⟨~ди́ть⟩ [15] transplant; graft; make change seats; **-ся**, ⟨пересе́сть⟩ [25; -ся́ду, -дешь; се́л] take another seat, change seats; change (*trains*).

пересд|ава́ть [5], ⟨~а́ть⟩ [-да́м, -да́шь, *etc.*, *cf.* дать] repeat (*exam.*).

пересе|ка́ть [1], ⟨~́чь⟩ [26; *pt.* -се́к, -секла́] cut (through, off); intersect, cross (*v/i.* **-ся**).

пересел|е́нец *m* [1; -нца] (re-) settler; **~е́ние** *n* [12] (e)migration; removal, move; **~я́ть** [28], ⟨~и́ть⟩ [13] (re)move (*v/i.* **-ся**; [e]migrate).

пересе́сть *s.* переса́живаться.

пересе|че́ние *n* [12] intersection; **~́чь** *s.* **~ка́ть**.

переси́ли|вать [1], ⟨~ть⟩ [13] overpower, master, subdue.

переска́з *m* [1] retelling; **~ывать** [1], ⟨~а́ть⟩ [3] retell.

переск|а́кивать [1], ⟨~очи́ть⟩ [16] jump (over че́рез В); skip.

пересла́ть *s.* пересыла́ть.
пересм|а́тривать [1], ⟨~отре́ть⟩ [9; -отрю́, -о́тришь; -о́тренный] reconsider, revise; ⚖ review; **~о́тр** *m* [1] reconsideration, revision; ⚖ review.
пересо|ли́ть [13; -солю́, -о́ли́шь] *pf.* oversalt; **~́хнуть** *s.* пересыха́ть.
переспр|а́шивать [1], ⟨~оси́ть⟩ [15] repeat one's question.
перессо́риться [13] *pf.* quarrel.
перест|ава́ть [5], ⟨~а́ть⟩ [-а́ну, -а́нешь] stop, cease, quit; **~авля́ть** [28], ⟨~а́вить⟩ [14] put (elsewhere), (*a. clock*) set, move; rearrange; transpose; convert (into на В); ⅍ permute; **~ано́вка** *f* [5; *g/pl.:* -вок] shift, move; rearrangement; transposition; conversion (into на В); ⅍ permutation; **~а́ть** *s.* ~ава́ть.
перестр|а́ивать [1], ⟨~о́ить⟩ [13] rebuild, reconstruct; reorganize; regroup (*v/i.* -ся; adapt o. s., change one's views); **~е́ливаться** [1], **~е́лка** *f* [5; *g/pl.:* -лок] skirmish; **~о́ить** *s.* ~а́ивать; **~о́йка** *f* [5; *g/pl.:* -о́ек] rebuilding, reconstruction; reorganization.
переступ|а́ть [1], ⟨~и́ть⟩ [14] step over, cross; *fig.* transgress.
пересу́ды F *m/pl.* [1] gossip.
пересчи́т|ывать, ⟨~а́ть⟩ [1] re--count; (*a.* ⟨перече́сть⟩ [-чту́, -чтёшь; -чёл, -чла́]) count (down).
перес|ыла́ть [1], ⟨~ла́ть⟩ [-ешлю́, -шлёшь; -е́сланный] send (over), transmit; forward; **~ы́лка** *f* [5; *g/pl.:* -лок] consignment, conveyance; carriage; **~ыха́ть** [1], ⟨~о́хнуть⟩ [21] dry up; parch.
перета́|скивать [1], ⟨~щи́ть⟩ [16] drag *or* carry (over, across че́рез В).
пере́т|ь F [12] press, push; **~я́гивать** [1], ⟨~яну́ть⟩ [19] draw (*fig.* win) over; outweigh; cord.
переубе|жда́ть [1], ⟨~ди́ть⟩ [15 *e.*; *no 1st p. sg.*; -ди́шь; -еждённый] make s. o. change his mind.
переу́лок *m* [1; -лка] lane, alleyway, side street.
переутомл|е́ние *n* [12] overfatigue; **~ённый** [14 *sh.*] overtired.
переучёт *m* [1] inventory; stock--taking.
перехва́т|ывать [1], ⟨~и́ть⟩ [15] intercept; embrace; F borrow.
перехитри́ть [13] *pf.* outwit.
перехо́д *m* [1] passage; crossing; ⚔ march; *fig.* transition; conversion; **~и́ть** [15], ⟨перейти́⟩ [-йду́, -дёшь; -шёл, -шла́; *cf.* идти́] cross, go over; pass (on), proceed (to); turn ([in]to); exceed, transgress; **~ный** [14] transitional; *gr.* transitive; **~я́щий** [17] challenge (*cup, etc.*).
пе́рец *m* [1; -рца] pepper; paprika.
пе́речень *m* [4; -чня] list; index.
пере|чёркивать [1], ⟨~черкну́ть⟩ [20] cross out; **~че́сть** *s.* ~счи́тывать & ~чи́тывать; **~числя́ть** [28], ⟨~чи́слить⟩ [13] enumerate; **~чи́тывать**, ⟨~чита́ть⟩ [1] & ⟨~че́сть⟩ [-чту́, чтёшь; -чёл, -чла́] reread; read (many, all ...); **~́чить** F [16] contradict, oppose; **~шагну́ть** [20] *pf.* step over, cross; transgress; **~ше́ек** *m* [1; -ше́йка] isthmus; **~шёптываться** [1] whisper (to one another); **~шива́ть** [1], ⟨~ши́ть⟩ [-шью́, -шьёшь, *etc.*, *cf.* шить] make over, alter; **~щеголя́ть** F [28] *pf.* outdo.
пери́ла *n/pl.* [9] railing; banisters.
пери́на *f* [5] feather bed.
пери́од *m* [1] period; epoch, age; **~и́ческий** [16] periodic(al); ⅍ circulating.
перифери́я *f* [7] circumference, periphery; outskirts *pl.* (in на П).
перламу́тр *m* [1] mother-of-pearl.
перло́вый [14] pearl (*barley*).
перманéнт *m* [1] permanent wave.
перна́тый [14 *sh.*] feathered, feathery.
перо́ *n* [9; *pl.:* пе́рья, -ьев] feather, plume; pen; ве́чное ~ fountain pen; **~чи́нный** [14]: ~чи́нный но́ж(ик) *m* penknife.
перро́н *m* [1] 🚂 platform.
перс *m* [1], **~и́дский** [16] Persian; **~́ик** *m* [1] peach; **~ия́нин** *m* [1; *pl.:* -я́не, -я́н], **~ия́нка** *f* [5; *g/pl.:* -нок] Persian; **~о́на** *f* [5] person; **~она́л** *m* [1] personnel; **~пекти́ва** *f* [5] perspective; *fig.* prospect, outlook.
пе́рстень *m* [4; -тня] (*finger*) ring.
пе́рхоть *f* [8] dandruff.
перча́тка *f* [5; *g/pl.:* -ток] glove.
пёс *m* [1; пса] dog; F cur.
пе́сенка *f* [5; *g/pl.:* -нок] ditty.
песе́ц *m* [1; песца́] Arctic fox.
песка́рь *m* [4 *e.*] gudgeon.
песн|ь *f* [8] (*poet., eccl.*), **~́я** *f* [6; *g/pl.:* -сен] song; F story.
песо́|к *m* [1; -ска́] sand; granulated sugar; **~чный** [14] sand(y).
пессимисти́ч|еский [16], **~ный** [14; -чен, -чна] pessimistic.
пестр|е́ть [8] grow (*or* appear, *a.* **~и́ть** [13]) variegated; gleam, glisten; **~ота́** *f* [5] motley; gayness; **~ый** ('pɔ-) [14; пёстр, пестра́, пёстро & пестро́] variegated, parti--colo(u)red, motley (*a. fig.*); gay.
песч|а́ный [14] sand(y); **~и́нка** *f* [5; *g/pl.:* -нок] grain (of sand).
петли́ца *f* [5] buttonhole; tab.
пе́тля *f* [6; *g/pl.:* -тель] loop (*a.*, ✈, мёртвая ~); eye; mesh; stitch; hinge.
Пётр *m* [1; Петра́] Peter.
Петру́шка [5; *g/pl.:* -шек] **1.** *m* Punch (and Judy); **2.** ♀ *f* parsley.
петý|х *m* [1 *e.*] rooster, cock; **~ши́ный** [14] cock(s)...
петь [пою́, поёшь; пе́тый] **1.** ⟨с-, про-⟩ sing; **2.** ⟨про-⟩ crow.

пехо́т|а *f* [5], **~ный** [14] infantry; **~и́нец** *m* [1; -нца] infantryman.
печа́л|ить [13], ⟨о-⟩ grieve (*v/i.* **-ся**); **~ь** *f* [8] grief, sorrow; F business, concern; **~ьный** [14; -лен, -льна] sad, grieved, sorrowful.
печа́т|ать [1], ⟨на-⟩ print; type; **-ся** *impf.* be in the press; write for, appear in (в П); **~ник** *m* [1] printer; **~ный** [14] printed; printing; **~ь** *f* [8] seal, stamp (*a. fig.*); press; print, type.
печён|ка *f* [5; *g/pl.:* -нок] liver (*food*); **~ый** [14] baked.
пе́чень *f* [8] liver (*anat.*); **∠е** *n* [10] pastry; cookie, biscuit.
пе́чка *f* [5; *g/pl.:* -чек] *s.* печь[1].
печь[1] *f* [8; в -чи́; *from g/pl. e.*] stove; oven; furnace; kiln.
печь[2] [26], ⟨ис-⟩ bake; scorch (*sun*).
пе́чься [26] care (for о П).
пеш|ехо́д *m* [1] pedestrian; **∠ий** [17] unmounted; **∠ка** *f* [5; *g/pl.:* -шек] pawn (*a. fig.*); **~ко́м** on foot.
пеще́ра *f* [5] cave.
пиани́но *n* [*indecl.*] piano.
пивна́я *f* [14] alehouse, bar, saloon.
пи́во *n* [9] beer; ale; **~ва́р** *m* [1] brewer; **~ва́ренный** [14]: **~ва́ренный заво́д** *m* brewery.
пиджа́к *m* [1 *e.*] coat, jacket.
пижа́ма *f* [5] pajamas (*Brt.* py-) *pl.*
пик *m* [1] peak.
пи́ка *f* [5] pike, lance; **∠нтный** [14; -тен, -тна] piquant, spicy (*a. fig.*).
пи́ки *f/pl.* [5] spades (*cards*).
пики́ровать ✈ [7] (*im*)*pf.* dive.
пи́кнуть [20] *pf.* peep; F stir.
пил|а́ *f* [5; *pl. st.*], **~и́ть** [13; пилю́, пи́лишь] saw; **~о́т** *m* [1] pilot.
пилю́ля *f* [6] pill.
пингви́н *m* [1] penguin.
пино́к *m* [1; -нка́] kick.
пинце́т *m* [1] tweezers *pl.*
пионе́р *m* [1] pioneer (*a. member of Communist youth organization in the U.S.S.R.*); **~ский** [16] pioneer...
пир *m* [1; в -у́; *pl. e.*] feast.
пирами́да *f* [5] pyramid.
пирова́ть [7] feast, banquet.
пиро́|г *m* [1 *e.*] pie; **~жник** *m* [1] pastry cook; **~жное** *n* [14] pastry; fancy cake; **~жо́к** *m* [1; -жка́] patty.
пир|у́шка *f* [5; *g/pl.:* -шек] carousal, revel(ry); **∠шество** *n* [9] feast, banquet.
писа́|ние *n* [12] writing; (*Holy*) Scripture; **′~рь** *m* [4; *pl.:* -ря́, *etc. e.*] clerk; **~тель** *m* [4] writer, author; **~тельница** *f* [5] authoress; **~ть** [3], ⟨на-⟩ write; type(write); paint.
писк *m* [1] squeak; **~ли́вый** [14 *sh.*] squeaky; **∠нуть** *s.* пища́ть.
пистоле́т *m* [1] pistol.
писч|ебума́жный [14] stationery (*store, Brt. shop*); **∠ий** [17] note (*paper*).
пи́сьмен|ность *f* [8] literature; **~ный** [14] written; in writing; writing (*a. table*).
письмо́ *n* [9; *pl. st., gen.:* пи́сем] letter; writin- (in н- П); **~но́сец** *m* [1; -сца] postman, mailman.
пита́|ние *n* [12] nutrition; nourishment, food; board; ⊕ feeding; **~тельный** [14; -лен, -льна] nutritious, nourishing; **~ть** [1] nourish (*a. fig.*), feed (*a.* ⊕); cherish (*hope, etc.*), bear (*hatred, etc.,* against к Д); **-ся** feed *or* live (on Т).
пито́м|ец *m* [1; -мца], **~ица** *f* [5] pupil; nursling; **~ник** *m* [1] nursery.
пить [пью, пьёшь; пил, -á, -о; пе́й(-те)!; пи́тый (пит, -á, -о)], ⟨вы́-⟩ drink (*pf. a.* up; to за В); have, take; **~ё** *n* [10] drink(ing); **~ево́й** [14] drinking (*water*), drinkable.
пих|а́ть F [1], ⟨~ну́ть⟩ [20] shove.
пи́хта *f* [5] fir.
пи́чкать F [1], ⟨на-⟩ stuff (with Т).
пи́шущ|ий [17] writing; **~ая маши́нка** *f* typewriter.
пи́ща *f* [5] food; fare, board.
пища́ть [4 *e.*; -щу́, -щи́шь], ⟨за-⟩, *once* ⟨пи́скнуть⟩ [20] peep, squeak, cheep.
пище|варе́ние *n* [12] digestion; **~во́д** *m* [1] *anat.* gullet; **~во́й** [14] food(*stuffs*).
пия́вка *f* [5; *g/pl.:* -вок] leech.
пла́ва|ние *n* [12] swimming; navigation; voyage, trip; **~ть** [1] swim; float; sail, navigate.
плав|и́льный [14] melting; **~и́льня** *f* [6; *g/pl.:* -лен] foundry; **∠ить** [14], ⟨рас-⟩ smelt, fuse; **∠ка** *f* [5] fusion; **~ни́к** *m* [1 *e.*] fin.
пла́вный [14; -вен, -вна] fluent, smooth; *gr.* liquid.
плагиа́т *m* [1] plagiarism.
плака́т *m* [1] poster, placard, bill.
пла́к|ать [3] weep (for от Р; о П), cry; **-ся** F complain (of на В); **~са** F *m/f* [5] crybaby; **~си́вый** F [14 *sh.*] whining.
плам|ене́ть [8] flame; **∠енный** [14] flaming, fiery; *fig. a.* ardent; **∠я** *n* [13] flame; blaze.
план *m* [1] plan; draft; plane; пе́рвый, пере́дний (за́дний) ~ fore(back)ground (in на П).
планёр ✈ *m* [1] glider.
плане́та *f* [5] planet.
плани́ров|ать[1] [7] **1.** ⟨за-⟩ plan; **2.** ⟨с-⟩ ✈ glide; **~а́ть**[2], ⟨рас-⟩ level; **∠ка** *f* [5; *g/pl.:* -вок] planning; level(l)ing.
пла́нка *f* [5; *g/pl.:* -нок] lath.
пла́но|вый [14] planned; plan(-ning); **~ме́рный** [14; -рен, -рна] systematic, planned.
планта́тор *m* [1] planter.
пласт *m* [1 *e.*] layer, stratum; **∠ика** *f* [5] plastic arts *pl.*; plastic figure; **~и́нка** *f* [5; *g/pl.:* -нок] plate; (*gramophone*) record; **~ма́сса** *f* [5] plastic; **∠ырь** *m* [4] plaster.

пла́т|а *f* [5] pay(ment); fee; wages *pl.*; fare; rent; **~ёж** *m* [1 *e.*] payment; **~ёжеспосо́бный** [14; -бен, -бна] solvent; **~ёжный** [14] of payment; **~е́льщик** *m* [1] payer; **~ина** *f* [5] platinum; **~и́ть** [15], ⟨за-, у-⟩ pay (in T; for за B); settle (*account* по Д); **-ся**, ⟨по-⟩ *fig.* pay (with T); **~ный** [14] paid; to be paid for.

плато́к *m* [1; -тка́] (hand)kerchief.

платфо́рма *f* [5] platform.

пла́т|ье *n* [10; *g/pl.*: -ьев] dress, gown; **~яно́й** [14] clothes...

пла́ха *f* [5] block.

плац|да́рм *m* [1] base; bridgehead; **~ка́рта** *f* [5] reserved seat (ticket).

пла|ч *m* [1] weeping; **~че́вный** [14; -вен, -вна] deplorable, pitiable, lamentable; plaintive; **~шмя́** flat.

плащ *m* [1 *e.*] raincoat; cloak.

плебисци́т *m* [1] plebiscite.

плева́ *f* [5] membrane; pleura.

плева́т|ельница *f* [5] cuspidor, spittoon; **~ь** [6 *e.*; плюю́, плюёшь], *once* ⟨плю́нуть⟩ [20] spit (out); F not care (for на B).

пле́вел *m* [1] weed.

плево́к *m* [1; -вка́] spit(tle).

плеври́т *m* [1] pleurisy.

плед *m* [1] plaid, travel(l)ing rug.

плем|енно́й [14] tribal; brood..., stud...; **∠я** *n* [13] tribe; race; family; generation; breed; F brood.

племя́нни|к *m* [1] nephew; **~ца** *f* [5] niece.

плен *m* [1; в -у́] captivity; взять (попа́сть) в ~ (be) take(n) prisoner; **~а́рный** [14] plenary; **~и́тельный** [14; -лен, -льна] captivating, fascinating; **~и́ть(ся)** *s.* **~я́ть(ся)**.

плён|ка *f* [5; *g/pl.*: -нок] film; pellicle.

пле́н|ник *m* [1], **~ный** *m* [14] captive, prisoner; **~я́ть** [28], ⟨**~и́ть**⟩ [13] (**-ся** be) captivate(d).

пле́нум *m* [1] plenary session.

пле́сень *f* [8] mo(u)ld.

плеск *m* [1], **~а́ть** [3], *once* ⟨плесну́ть⟩ [20], **-ся** *impf.* splash.

пле́сневеть [8], ⟨за-⟩ get mo(u)ldy.

пле|сти́ [25 -т-: плету́], ⟨с-, за-⟩ braid, plait; weave; spin; F twaddle; lie; **-сь** F drag, lag; **~тёный** [14] wicker...; **~те́нь** *m* [4; -тня́] wicker fence.

плётка *f* [5; *g/pl.*: -ток], **плеть** *f* [8; *from g/pl. e.*] lash, scourge.

плеч|о́ *n* [9; *pl.*: пле́чи, плеч, -ча́м] shoulder; back; ⊕ arm; с ~ доло́й F be rid of s.th.; с(о всего́) **~а́** with all one's might; straight from the shoulder; (И) не по **~у́** (Д) not be equal to a th.; на **~о́!** shoulder arms!; пра́вое **~о́** вперёд! ⚔ left turn (*Brt.* wheel)!; *cf. a.* гора́ F.

плеш|и́вый [14 *sh.*] bald; **~ь** *f* [8] bald patch.

плит|а́ *f* [5; *pl.st.*] slab, (flag-, *grave*-) stone; plate; (*kitchen*) range; (*gas*) stove; **∠ка** *f* [5; *g/pl.*: -ток] tablet, cake, bar; hot plate.

плов|е́ц *m* [1; -вца́] swimmer; **~у́чий** [17] floating (*dock*); **~у́чий мая́к** *m* lightship; *s. a.* льди́на.

плод *m* [1 *e.*] fruit; **~и́ть** [15 *e.*; пложу́, -ди́шь], ⟨рас-⟩ propagate, multiply (*v/i.* **-ся**); **~ови́тый** [14 *sh.*] fruitful, prolific; **~ово́дство** *n* [9] fruit growing; **~о́вый** [14] fruit...; **~оно́сный** [14; -сен, -сна] fructiferous; **~оро́дие** *n* [12] fertility; **~оро́дный** [14; -ден, -дна] fertile, fruitful, fecund; **~отво́рный** [14; -рен, -рна] fruitful, productive; profitable; favo(u)rable.

пло́мб|а *f* [5] (lead) seal; (*tooth*) filling; **~ирова́ть** [7], ⟨о-⟩ seal; ⟨за-⟩ fill, stop.

пло́ск|ий [16; -сок, -ска́, -о; *comp.*: пло́ще] flat (*a. fig.* = stale, trite), plain, level; **~ого́рье** *n* [10] plateau, tableland; **~огу́бцы** *pl.* [1] pliers; **~ость** *f* [8; *from g/pl. e.*] flatness; plane; level (on в П); angle (under в П); platitude.

плот *m* [1 *e.*] raft; **~и́на** *f* [5] dam, dike; **∠ник** *m* [1] carpenter.

пло́тн|ость *f* [8] density; solidity; **~ый** [14; -тен, -тна́, -о] compact, solid; dense; close, thick; thickset.

плот|оя́дный [14; -ден, -дна] carnivorous; **∠ский** [16] carnal, fleshly; **~ь** *f* [8] flesh.

плох|о́й [16; плох, -а́, -о] bad; **∠о** bad(ly); bad, F (*mark*; *cf.* дво́йка & едини́ца).

плоша́ть F [1], ⟨с-⟩ blunder.

площа́д|ка *f* [5; *g/pl.*: -док] ground; playground; (*tennis*) court; platform; landing; **~но́й** [14] vulgar; **'~ь** *f* [8; *from g/pl. e.*] square; area (*a.* ⚘); (*living*) space, *s.* жилпло́щадь.

плуг *m* [1; *pl. e.*] plow, *Brt.* plough.

плут *m* [1 *e.*] rogue; trickster, cheat; **~а́ть** F [1] stray; **~ова́ть** [7], ⟨с-⟩ trick, cheat; **~овско́й** [16] roguish; rogue...; **~овство́** *n* [9] roguery.

плыть [23] (be) swim(ming); float (-ing), sail(ing); *cf.* пла́вать.

плюга́вый F [14 *sh.*] shabby.

плю́нуть *s.* плева́ть.

плюс (*su. m* [1]) plus; F advantage.

плюш *m* [1] plush.

плющ *m* [1 *e.*] ivy.

пляж *m* [1] beach.

пляс|а́ть [3], ⟨с-⟩ dance; **∠ка** *f* [5; *g/pl.*: -сок] (folk) dance; dancing; **~ово́й** [14] dance..., dancing.

пневмати́ческий [16] pneumatic.

по 1. (Д) on, along; through; all over; in; by; according to, after; through; owing to; for; over; across; upon; each, at a time (*2, 3, 4 with* B: по́ два); 2. (B) to, up to; till, through; for; 3. (П) (up)on; ~ мне

for all I care; ~ часу в день an hour a day.
по- (in *compds.*): *cf.* русский; ваш.
побаиваться [1] be (a little) afraid of (P).
побе́г *m* [1] escape, flight; ♀ shoot, sprout; **~у́шки**: быть на ~у́шках F run errands (for у P).
побе́|да *f* [5] victory; **~ди́тель** *m* [4] victor; winner; **~ди́ть** *s.* ~ждать; **~дный** [14], **~доно́сный** [14; -сен, -сна] victorious; **~жда́ть** [1], ⟨~ди́ть⟩ [15 *e.*; *1st p. sg. not used*; -ди́шь; -еждённый] be victorious (over B), win (a victory), conquer, vanquish, defeat; overcome; beat.
побере́жье *n* [10] shore, coast.
побла́жка F *f* [5; *g/pl.*: -жек] indulgence.
поблизости close by; (от P) near.
побо́и *m/pl.* [3] beating; **~ще** *n* [11] (great) battle.
побо́р|ник *m* [1] advocate; **~о́ть** [17] *pf.* conquer; overcome; beat.
побо́чный [14] accessory, incidental, casual; secondary; subsidiary; by-(*product*); illegitimate.
побу|ди́тельный [14]: ~ди́тельная причи́на *f* motive; **~жда́ть** [1], ⟨~ди́ть⟩ [15 *e.*; -ужу́, -уди́шь; -уждённый] induce, prompt, impel; **~жде́ние** *n* [12] motive, impulse, incentive.
побы́вка F *f* [5; *g/pl.*: -вок] stay, visit (for, on на B [*or* П]).
пова́д|иться F [15] *pf.* fall into the habit (of [visiting] *inf.*); **~ка** *f* [5; *g/pl.*: -док] F habit; P encouragement.
пова́льный [14] epidemic; general.
по́вар *m* [1; *pl.*: -pá, *etc. e.*] cook; **∠енный** [14] culinary; cook(*book*, *Brt.* cookery book); kitchen (*salt*); **~и́ха** *f* [5] cook.
пове|де́ние *n* [12] behavio(u)r, conduct; **~лева́ть** [1] (T) rule; ⟨~ле́ть⟩ [9] (Д) order; command; **~ли́тельный** [14; -лен, -льна] imperative (*a. gr.*).
поверг|а́ть [1], ⟨∠нуть⟩ [21] throw *or* cast (down); put into (в B).
пове́р|енный [14] confidant; plenipotentiary; chargé (d'affaires в дела́х); **~ить** *s.* ~я́ть & ве́рить; **~ка** *f* [5; *g/pl.*: -рок] check(up); roll call; **~ну́ть(ся)** *s.* повора́чивать (-ся).
пове́рх (P) over, above; **~ностный** [14; -тен, -тна] superficial; surface...; **~ность** *f* [8] surface.
пове́р|ье *n* [10] legend, popular belief; **~я́ть** [28], ⟨~ить⟩ [13] entrust, confide (to Д); check (up).
пове́с|а F *m* [5] scapegrace; **~ить** (-ся) *s.* ве́шать(ся); **~ничать** F [1] romp, play pranks.
повествова́|ние *n* [12] narration, narrative; **~тель** *m* [4] narrator; **~тельный** [14] narrative; ~тельное предложе́ние *n gr.* statement; **~ть** [7] narrate (*v/t.* о П).
пове́ст|ка *f* [5; *g/pl.*: -ток] summons; notice; ~ка дня agenda; **′~ь** *f* [8; *from g/pl. e.*] story, tale; narrative.
повеше́ние *n* [12] hanging.
по-ви́димому apparently.
пови́дло *n* [9] jam, fruit butter.
пови́н|ность *f* [8] duty; **~ный** [14; -и́нен, -и́нна] guilty; owing; **~ная** *f* confession; **~ова́ться** [7] (*pt. a. pf.*) (Д) obey; submit (to); **~ове́ние** *n* [12] obedience.
по́вод *m* **1.** [1] cause; occasion (on по Д); по ~у (P) *a.* concerning; **2.** [1; в -ду́; *pl.*: -о́дья, -о́дьев] rein; на ~у́ (у P) in (s.b.'s) leading strings.
пово́зка *f* [5; *g/pl.*: -зок] cart; wag(g)on.
Пово́лжье *n* [10] Volga region.
повор|а́чивать [1], ⟨поверну́ть⟩ [20], F ⟨~оти́ть⟩ [15] turn (*v/i.* -ся; ~а́чивайся! come on!); **~о́т** *m* [1] turn; **~о́тливый** [14 *sh.*] nimble, agile; **~о́тный** [14] turning.
повре|жда́ть [1], ⟨~ди́ть⟩ [15 *e.*; -ежу́, -еди́шь; -еждённый] damage; injure, hurt; spoil; **~жде́ние** *n* [12] damage; injury.
поврем|ени́ть F [13] *pf.* wait a little; **~е́нный** [14] periodical; time...
повсе|дне́вный [14; -вен, -вна] everyday, daily; **~ме́стный** [14; -тен, -тна] general, universal; **~ме́стно** everywhere.
повста́н|ец *m* [1; -нца] rebel, insurgent; **~ческий** [16] rebel(lious).
повсю́ду everywhere.
повтор|е́ние *n* [12] repetition; review; **~и́тельный** [14] repetitive; **∠ный** [14] repeated, second; **~я́ть** [28], ⟨~и́ть⟩ [13] repeat (o.s. -ся); review (*lessons, etc.*).
повы|ша́ть [1], ⟨∠сить⟩ [15] raise; promote; -ся rise; advance; **~ше́ние** *n* [12] rise; promotion; **∠шенный** [14] increased, higher.
повя́з|ка *f* [5; *g/pl.*: -зок] bandage; band, armlet; **~ывать** [1], ⟨~а́ть⟩ [3] bind (up); put on.
пога|ша́ть [1], ⟨~си́ть⟩ [15] put out, extinguish; discharge (*debt*).
погиб|а́ть [1], ⟨∠нуть⟩ [21] perish; **∠ель** † *s.* ги́бель; **∠ший** [17] lost.
погло|ща́ть [1], ⟨~ти́ть⟩ [15; -ощу́; -ощённый] swallow up, devour; absorb; **~ще́ние** *n* [12] absorption.
погля́дывать [1] look (F *a.* after).
погов|а́ривать [1] speak; say; **~о́рка** [5; *g/pl.*: -рок] saying, proverb.
пого́|да *f* [5] weather (in в B, при П); **~ди́ть** F [15 *e.*; -гожу́, -годи́шь] *pf.* wait; **~дя́** later; **~ло́вный** [14] general, universal; ~ло́в-

но without exception; **~ло́вье** *n* [10] livestock.
пого́н *m* [1] epaulet, shoulder strap; **~щик** *m* [1] drover; **~я** *f* [6] pursuit (of за T); pursuers *pl.*; **~я́ть** [28] drive *or* urge (on), hurry (up).
пого|ре́лец *m* [1; -льца] burnt down p.; **∠ст** [1] churchyard.
пограни́чн|ый [14] frontier...; **~ик** *m* [1] frontier guard.
по́гре|б *m* [1; *pl.*: -ба́, *etc. e.*] cellar; (*powder*) magazine; **~ба́льный** [14] funeral; **~ба́ть** [1], ⟨~сти́⟩ [24 -б-: -бу́] bury, inter; **~бе́ние** *n* [12] burial; funeral; **~му́шка** *f* [5; *g/pl.*: -шек] rattle; **∠шность** *f* [8] error, fault.
погру|жа́ть [1], ⟨~зи́ть⟩ [15 & 15 *e.*; -ужу́, -у́зишь; -у́женный & -ужённый] immerse; sink, plunge, submerge (*v/i.* **-ся**); ~жённый *a.* absorbed, lost (in в B); load, ship; **~же́ние** *n* [12] immersion; **∠зка** [5; *g/pl.*: -зок] loading, shipment.
погряз|а́ть [1], ⟨∠нуть⟩ [21] sink.
под[1], ~о **1.** (B): (*direction*) under; toward(s), to; (*age, time*) about; on the eve of; à la, in imitation of; for, suitable as; **2.** (T): (*position*) under, below, beneath; near, by, (*battle*) of; (used) for, with; по́ле ~ ро́жью rye field; **~**[2] *m* [1; на -у́] hearth, floor.
подава́льщица *f* [5] waitress.
пода|ва́ть [5], ⟨∠ть⟩ [-да́м, -да́шь, *etc., cf.* дать] give; serve (*a. sport*); drive up, get ready; move (in); hand (*or* send) in; lodge (*complaint*), bring (*action*); set (*example*); render; raise (*voice*); не ~ва́ть ви́ду *s.* пока́зывать; **-ся** move; yield.
подав|и́ть *s.* ~ля́ть; **~и́ться** *pf.* choke, suffocate; **~ле́ние** *n* [12] suppression; **~ля́ть** [28], ⟨~и́ть⟩ [14] suppress; repress; depress; crush; ~ля́ющий *a.* overwhelming.
пода́вно F so much *or* all the more.
пода́гра *f* [5] gout; podagra.
пода́льше F rather far off.
пода́|рок *m* [1; -рка] present, gift; **~тель** *m* [4] bearer; petitioner; **~тливый** [14 *sh.*] (com)pliant; **'~ть** *f* [8; *from g/pl. e.*] tax; **~ть(ся)** *s.* ~ва́ть(ся); **~ча** *f* [5] giving; serving; serve; presentation; rendering; supply; ~ча го́лоса voting; **~чка** *f* [5; *g/pl.*: -чек] charity, gift; **~я́ние** *n* [12] alms.
подбе|га́ть [1], ⟨~жа́ть⟩ [4; -бегу́, -бежи́шь, -бегу́т] run up (to к Д).
подби|ва́ть [1], ⟨∠ть⟩ [подобью́, -бьёшь, *etc., cf.* бить] line, fur; (re)sole; hit, injure; F instigate, incite; ∠тый F black (*eye*).
под|бира́ть [1], ⟨~обра́ть⟩ [подберу́, -рёшь; подобра́л, -а́, -о; подо́бранный] pick up; tuck up; draw in; pick out, select; **-ся** sneak up (to к Д); **~би́ть** *s.* ~бива́ть; **~бо́р** *m* [1] picking up *or* out; selection; assortment; на ~бо́р chosen, select.
подборо́док *m* [1; -дка] chin.
подбр|а́сывать [1], ⟨~о́сить⟩ [15] throw (up); jolt; add; foist, palm (on Д).
подва́л *m* [1] basement; cellar.
подвезти́ *s.* подвози́ть.
подвер|га́ть [1], ⟨∠гнуть⟩ [21] subject, expose; **-ся** undergo; be exposed; run (*risk*); **∠женный** [14 *sh.*] subject; **~же́ние** *n* [12] subjection.
подве́с|ить *s.* подве́шивать; **~но́й** [14] hanging (*lamp*); ⊕ suspension.
подвести́ *s.* подводи́ть.
подве́тренный [14] leeward.
подве́|шивать [1], ⟨~сить⟩ [15] hang (under; on); fix.
по́двиг *m* [1] feat, exploit, deed.
подви|га́ть [1], ⟨∠нуть⟩ [20] move (*v/i.* **-ся**; advance, get on); push (on, ahead); **~жно́й** [14] mobile; movable; nimble; 🚂 rolling (*stock*); **∠жность** *f* [8] mobility; agility; **~за́ться** [1] be active; **∠нуть(ся)** *s.* ~га́ть(ся).
подв|ла́стный [14; -тен, -тна] subject; **~о́да** *f* [5] cart; wag(g)on.
подводи́ть [15], ⟨подвести́⟩ [25] lead ([up] to); bring, get; lay; build; make (up); F let a p. down.
подво́дн|ый [14] submarine ~ая ло́дка *f* submarine; ~ый ка́мень *m* reef.
подво́з *m* [1] supplies *pl.*; **~и́ть** [15], ⟨подвезти́⟩ [24] bring, get; give a p. a lift.
подвы́пивший F [17] tipsy, drunk.
подвя́з|ка *f* [5; *g/pl.*: -зок] garter; **~ывать** [1], ⟨~а́ть⟩ [3] tie (up).
под|гиба́ть [1], ⟨~огну́ть⟩ [20] tuck (under); bend; **-ся** fail.
подгля́д|ывать [1], ⟨~е́ть⟩ [11] peep, spy.
подгов|а́ривать [1], ⟨~ори́ть⟩ [13] instigate, talk a p. into.
под|гоня́ть [28], ⟨~огна́ть⟩ [подгоню́, -го́нишь; *cf.* гнать] drive *or* urge on, hurry (up); fit, adapt.
подгор|а́ть [1], ⟨~е́ть⟩ [9] burn.
подготов|и́тельный [14] preparatory; **∠ка** *f* [5; *g/pl.*: -вок] preparation (for к Д); training; ⚔ drill; **~ля́ть** [28], ⟨∠ить⟩[14] prepare.
подда|ва́ться [5], ⟨∠ться⟩ [-да́мся, -да́шься, *etc., cf.* дать] yield; не ~ва́ться (Д) defy (*description*).
подда́к|ивать F [1], ⟨~нуть⟩ [20] say yes (to everything), consent.
по́дда|нный *m* [14] subject; **~нство** *n* [9] nationality, citizenship; **∠ться** *s.* ~ва́ться.
подде́л|ка *f* [5; *g/pl.*: -лок] forgery, counterfeit; **~ывать**, ⟨~ать⟩ [1] forge; **~ьный** [14] counterfeit...; sham...
подде́рж|ивать [1], ⟨~а́ть⟩ [4] support; back up; uphold; maintain;

~ка *f* [5; *g/pl.*: -жек] support; approval.
поде́л|ать F [1] *pf.* do; ничего́ не ~аешь there's nothing to be done; *cf. a.* де́лать F; **~о́м** F rightly; ~о́м ему́ it serves him right; **~ывать** F [1]: что (вы) ~ываете? what are you doing (now)?
поде́ржанный [14] second-hand; worn, used.
поджа́р|ивать [1], ⟨~ить⟩ [13] roast, brown; toast; **~ый** [14 *sh.*] lean.
поджа́ть *s.* поджима́ть.
под|же́чь *s.* ~жига́ть; **~жига́тель** *m* [4] incendiary; **~жига́ть** [1], ⟨~же́чь⟩ [26; подожгу́, -жжёшь; поджёг, подожгла́; подожжённый] set on fire (*or* fire to).
под|жида́ть [1], ⟨~ожда́ть⟩ [-ду́, -дёшь; -а́л, -а́, -о] wait (for P, B).
под|жима́ть [1], ⟨~жа́ть⟩ [подожму́, -мёшь; поджа́тый] cross (*legs* under под B); purse (*lips*); draw in (*tail*).
поджо́г *m* [1] arson; burning.
подзаголо́вок *m* [1; -вка] subtitle.
подзадо́р|ивать F [1], ⟨~ить⟩ [13] instigate, incite (to на B).
подза|ты́льник *m* [1] cuff on the nape; **~щи́тный** *m* [14] ⚖ client.
подзем|е́лье *n* [10] (underground) vault, cave; dungeon; **∠ный** [14] underground, subterranean; *cf.* метро́.
подзо́рная [14]: ~ труба́ *f* spyglass.
под|зыва́ть [1], ⟨~озва́ть⟩ [подзову́, -ёшь; подозва́л, -а́, -о; подо́званный] call, beckon; **~ь́** P come (,now); go; try; I suppose.
под|ка́пываться [1], ⟨~копа́ться⟩ undermine (*v/t.* под B); **~карау́ливать** F [1], ⟨~карау́лить⟩ [13] *s.* подстерега́ть; **~ка́рмливать** [1], ⟨~корми́ть⟩ [14] feed, fatten; **~ка́тывать** [1], ⟨~кати́ть⟩ [15] roll *or* drive up (under); **~ка́шиваться** [1], ⟨~коси́ться⟩ [15] fail.
подки́|дывать [1], ⟨~нуть⟩ [20] *s.* подбра́сывать; **~дыш** *m* [1] foundling.
подкла́д|ка *f* [5; *g/pl.*: -док] lining; ⊕ support; **~ывать** [1], ⟨подложи́ть⟩ [16] lay (under); add; enclose; foist (on Д).
подкле́|ивать [1], ⟨~ить⟩ [13] glue, paste (under).
подко́в|а *f* [5] horseshoe; **~ывать** [1], ⟨~а́ть⟩ [7 *e.*; -кую́, -куёшь] shoe; ~анный *a.* versed.
подко́жный [14] hypodermic.
подко́п *m* [1] sap, mine; **~а́ться** *s.* подка́пываться.
подкоси́ться *s.* подка́шиваться.
подкра́|дываться [1], ⟨~сться⟩ [25] steal *or* sneak up (to к Д); **~шивать** [1], ⟨~сить⟩ [15] touch up; make up.
подкреп|ля́ть [28], ⟨~и́ть⟩ [14 *e.*; -плю́, -пи́шь; -плённый] reinforce, fortify; corroborate; refresh; **~ле́ние** *n* [12] reinforcement; corroboration; refreshment.
по́дкуп *m* [1] bribery; **~а́ть** [1], ⟨~и́ть⟩ [14] bribe; win, prepossess; **~но́й** [14] corrupt.
подла́|живаться F [1], ⟨~диться⟩ [15] adapt o. s.; make up to.
по́дле (P) beside, by (the side of); nearby.
подлеж|а́ть [4 *e.*; -жу́, -жи́шь] be subject to; be to be; (И) не ~и́т (Д) there can be no (*doubt* about); **~а́щий** [17] subject (to Д); ...able; ~а́щее *n gr.* subject.
подле|за́ть [1], ⟨∠зть⟩ [24 *st.*] creep (under; up); **~та́ть** [1], ⟨~те́ть⟩ [11] fly (up).
подле́ц *m* [1 *e.*] scoundrel, rascal.
подли|ва́ть [1], ⟨∠ть⟩ [подолью́, -льёшь; подле́й!; по́дли́л, -а́, -о; по́дли́тый (-ли́т, -а́, -о)] pour, add; **∠вка** *f* [5; *g/pl.*: -вок] gravy; sauce.
подли́з|а *m/f* [5] toady; **~ываться** F [1], ⟨~а́ться⟩ [3] flatter, insinuate o. s. (with к Д).
по́длинн|ик *m* [1] original; **~ый** [14; -инен, -инна] original; authentic, genuine; true; pure.
подли́ть *s.* подлива́ть.
по́дличать F [1], ⟨с-⟩ act meanly.
подло́|г *m* [1] forgery; **~жи́ть** *s.* подкла́дывать; **~жный** [14; -жен, -жна] spurious, false.
по́дл|ость *f* [8] meanness; low act; **~ый** [14; подл, -а́, -о] mean, base, low.
подма́з|ывать [1], ⟨~ать⟩ [3] grease (*a.*, F, *fig.*), smear; F make up; -ся F insinuate o. s. (with к Д).
подма́н|ивать [1], ⟨~и́ть⟩ [13; -аню́, -а́нишь] beckon.
подмасте́рье *m* [10; *g/pl.*: -ьев] journeyman.
подме́н|а *f* [5] substitution, exchange; **~ивать** [1], ⟨~и́ть⟩ [13; -еню́, -е́нишь] substitute (s.th./for T/B) (ex)change.
подме|та́ть [1], ⟨~сти́⟩ [25 -т-: -мету́] sweep; **∠тить** *s.* подмеча́ть.
подмётка *f* [5; *g/pl.*: -ток] sole.
подме|ча́ть [1], ⟨∠тить⟩ [15] notice, observe, perceive.
подме́ш|ивать, ⟨~а́ть⟩ [1] mix (s. th. with s. th. P/в B), adulterate.
подми́г|ивать [1], ⟨~ну́ть⟩ [20] wink (at Д).
подмо́га F *f* [5] help, assistance.
подмок|а́ть [1], ⟨∠нуть⟩ get wet.
подмо́стки *m/pl.* [1] scaffold; stage.
подмо́ченный [14] wet; F stained.
подмы|ва́ть [1], ⟨∠ть⟩ [22] wash (*a.* out, away); F press.
подне|бе́сье *n* [10] firmament; **~во́льный** [14; -лен, -льна] dependent; forced; **~сти́** *s.* подноси́ть.
поднима́ть [1], ⟨подня́ть⟩ [-ниму́, -ни́мешь; по́днял, -а́, -о; по́дня-

тый (-нят, -á, -о)] lift; pick up (from с P); elevate; set (up; off); take up (*arms*); hoist (*flag*); weigh (*anchor*); set (*sail*); give (*alarm*); make (*noise*); scare (*game*); plow (*Brt.* plough) up; ~ нос assume airs; ~ нá ноги alarm; ~ нá смех ridicule; -ся [*pt.*: -нялcя́, -лáсь] (с P from) rise; arise; go up(*stairs* по Д); climb (*hill* на В); set out; get agitated.

подногóтная F *f* [14] ins & outs *pl.*

поднóж|ие *n* [12] foot, bottom (at у P); pedestal; **~ка** *f* [5; *g/pl.*: -жек] footboard; *mot.* running board; trip; **~ный** [14] green (*fodder*).

поднó|с *m* [1] tray; **~сить** [15], ⟨поднести́⟩ [24 -с-] bring, carry; offer, present (Д); **~шéние** *n* [12] gift.

подня́т|ие *n* [12] raise, raising; rise; elevation, *etc.*, *cf.* поднимáть(ся); **~ь(ся)** *s.* поднимáть(ся).

подоб|áть: ~áет it becomes; ought; **∠ие** *n* [12] resemblance; image (*a. eccl.*); ⚔ similarity; **∠ный** [14; -бен, -бна] similar (to Д); such; и тому́ ∠ное and the like; ничегó ∠ного nothing of the kind; **~острáстный** [14; -тен, -тна] servile.

подо|брáть(ся) *s.* подбирáть(ся); **~гнáть** *s.* подгоня́ть; **~гнýть(ся)** *s.* подгибáть(ся); **~гревáть** [1], ⟨~грéть⟩ [8; -éтый] warm up; **~двигáть** [1], ⟨~дви́нуть⟩ [20] move ([up] to к Д) (*v/i.* -ся; draw near); **~ждáть** *s.* поджидáть & ждать; **~звáть** *s.* подзывáть.

подозр|евáть [1], ⟨заподóзрить⟩ [13] suspect (of в П); **~éние** *n* [12] suspicion; **~и́тельный** [14; -лен, -льна] suspicious.

подойти́ *s.* подходи́ть.

подокóнник *m* [1] window sill.

подóл *m* [1] lap, hem.

подóлгу (for a) long (time).

подóнки *m/pl.* [1] dregs (*a. fig.*).

подóпытный [14] test...

подорвáть *s.* подрывáть.

подорóжн|ая *f* [14] *hist.* post-horse order; **~ик** *m* [1] plantain, ribwort.

подо|слáть *s.* подсылáть; **~спéть** [8] *pf.* come (in time); **~стлáть** *s.* подстилáть.

подотдéл *m* [1] sub-division.

подотчётный [14; -тен, -тна] accountable.

подохóдный [14] income (*tax*).

подóшва *f* [5] sole; foot, bottom.

подпа|дáть [1], ⟨∠сть⟩ [25; *pt. st.*] fall (under); **∠ивать** F [1], ⟨подпои́ть⟩ [13] make drunk; **~ли́ть** [13] *pf.* F = поджéчь; singe; **∠сок** *m* [1; -ска] shepherd boy; **∠сть** *s.* ~дáть.

подпевáть [1] *s.* втóрить.

подпирáть [1], ⟨подперéть⟩ [12; подопрý, -прёшь] support, prop.

подпис|áть(ся) *s.* ∠ывать(ся); **∠ка** *f* [5; *g/pl.*: -сок] subscription (to; for на В); pledge (take дать); **~нóй** [14] subscription...; **∠чик** *m* [1] subscriber; **∠ывать(ся)** [1], ⟨~áть (-ся)⟩ [3] sign; subscribe (to; for на В); **'~ь** *f* [8] signature (for на В); за '~ью (P) signed by.

подплы|вáть [1], ⟨∠ть⟩ [23] swim (under *or* up [to к Д]).

подпо|и́ть *s.* подпáивать; **~лзáть** [1], ⟨~лзти́⟩ [24] creep *or* crawl (under *or* up [to к Д]); **~лкóвник** *m* [1] lieutenant colonel; **∠лье** *n* [10; *g/pl.*: -ьев], **∠льный** [14] underground; **∠р(к)а** *f* [5 (*g/pl.*: -рок)] prop; **∠чва** *f* [5] subsoil; **~я́сывать** [1], ⟨~я́сать⟩ [3] gird.

подпр|ýга *f* [5] girth; **~ы́гивать** [1], *once* ⟨~ы́гнуть⟩ [20] jump up.

подпус|кáть [1], ⟨~ти́ть⟩ [15] allow to approach; admit; F add.

подр|áвнивать [1], ⟨~овня́ть⟩ [28] straighten; level; clip.

подражá|ние *n* [12] imitation (in /of в В/Д); **~тель** *m* [4] imitator (of Д); **~ть** [1] imitate, copy (*v/t.* Д); counterfeit.

подраздел|éние *n* [12] subdivision; ⚔ unit; **~я́ть** [28], ⟨~и́ть⟩ [13] (-ся be) subdivide(d) (into на В).

подра|зумевáть [1] mean (by под Т), imply; -ся be implied; † be understood; **~стáть** [1], ⟨~сти́⟩ [24 -ст-; -рóс, -лá] grow (up); rise.

подрез|áть & **∠ывать** [1], ⟨∠ать⟩ [3] cut; crop, clip.

подрóбн|ость *f* [8] detail; **~ый** [14; -бен, -бна] detailed, full-length; **~о** in detail, in full.

подровня́ть *s.* подрáвнивать.

подрóсток *m* [1; -стка] teenager; youth, juvenile.

подруб|áть [1], ⟨~и́ть⟩ [14] cut; hem.

подрýга [5] (girl) friend; playmate.

по-дрýжески (in a) friendly (way).

подружи́ться [16 *e.*; -жýсь, -жи́шься] *pf.* make friends (with с Т).

подрумя́нить [13] *pf.* redden.

подрýчный [14] assistant; helper.

подры́|в *m* [1] undermining; blowing up; **~вáть** [1] 1. ⟨~ть⟩ [22] sap, undermine; 2. ⟨подорвáть⟩ [-рвý, -рвёшь; -рвáл, -á, -о; подóрванный] blow up, blast, spring; *fig.* undermine; **~внóй** [14] blasting, explosive; subversive.

подря́д 1. *adv.* successive(ly), running; one after another; 2. *m* [1] contract; **~чик** *m* [1] contractor.

подс|áживать [1], ⟨~адить⟩ [15] help; plant; -ся, ⟨~éсть⟩ [25; -ся́ду, -ся́дешь; -сéл] sit down (by к Д).

подсвéчник *m* [1] candlestick.

подсéсть *s.* подсáживаться.

подскáз|ывать [1], ⟨~áть⟩ [3] prompt; **~ка** F *f* [5] prompting.

подскак|áть [3] *pf.* gallop (up to к Д); **∠ивать** [1], ⟨подскочи́ть⟩ [16] run ([up] to к Д); jump up.

под|сла́щивать [1], 〈~сласти́ть〉 [15 *e.*; -ащу́, -асти́шь; -ащённый] sweeten; **~сле́дственный** *m* [14] (prisoner) on trial; **~слепова́тый** [14 *sh.*] weak-sighted; **~слу́шивать**, 〈~слу́шать〉 [1] eavesdrop, overhear; **~сма́тривать** [1], 〈~смотре́ть〉 [9; -отрю́, -о́тришь] spy, peep; **~сме́иваться** [1] laugh (at над Т); **~смотре́ть** *s.* ~сма́тривать.

подсне́жник *m* [1] snowdrop.

подсо́|бный [14] subsidiary, by-..., side..., subordinate; **~вывать** [1], 〈подсу́нуть〉 [20] push, shove; present; F palm ([off] on Д); **~зна́тельный** [14; -лен, -льна] subconscious; **~лнечник** *m* [1] sunflower; **~хнуть** *s.* подсыха́ть.

подспо́рье F *n* [10] help, support.

подста́в|ить *s.* ~ля́ть; **~ка** *f* [5; *g/pl.*: -вок] support, prop, stay; stand; saucer; **~ля́ть** [28], 〈~ить〉 [14] put, place, set (under под В); move up (to [к] Д); expose; ⚒ substitute; ~ля́ть но́гу *or* но́жку (Д) trip (a p.) up; **~но́й** [14] false, straw...; ~но́е лицо́ *n* dummy.

подстан|о́вка ⚒ *f* [5; *g/pl.*: -вок] substitution; **∠ция** *f* [7] substation.

подстер|ега́ть [1], 〈~е́чь〉 [26 г/ж: -регу́, -режёшь; -рёг, -регла́] lie in wait of; *pf.* trap.

подстил|а́ть [1], 〈подостла́ть〉 [подстелю́, -е́лешь; подо́стланный & подсте́ленный] spread (under под В); **∠ка** *f* [5; *g/pl.*: -лок] bedding; spreading.

подстр|а́ивать [1], 〈~о́ить〉 [13] ⚠ build, add; F ♪ tune (to под В); plot.

подстрек|а́тель *m* [4] instigator, monger; **~а́тельство** *n* [9] instigation; **~а́ть** [1], 〈~ну́ть〉 [20] incite (to на В); stir up, provoke.

подстр|е́ливать [1], 〈~ели́ть〉 [13; -елю́, -е́лишь] hit, wound; **~ига́ть** [1], 〈~и́чь〉 [26 г/ж: -игу́, -ижёшь; -и́г, -и́гла; -и́женный] cut, crop, clip; trim, lop; **~о́ить** *s.* подстра́ивать; **~о́чный** [14] interlinear; foot(*note*).

по́дступ *m* [1] approach (*a.* ⚔); **~а́ть** [1], 〈~и́ть〉 [14] approach (*v/t.* к Д); rise; press.

подсуд|и́мый *m* [14] defendant; **∠ность** *f* [8] jurisdiction.

подсу́нуть *s.* подсо́вывать.

подсч|ёт *m* [1] calculation, computation, cast; **~и́тывать**, 〈~ита́ть〉 [1] count (up), compute.

подсы|ла́ть [1], 〈подосла́ть〉 [-шлю́, -шлёшь; -о́сланный] send (secretely); **~па́ть** [1], 〈∠пать〉 [2] add, pour; **~ха́ть** [1], 〈подсо́хнуть〉 [21] dry (up).

подта́|лкивать [1], 〈подтолкну́ть〉 [20] push; nudge; **~со́вывать** [1], 〈~сова́ть〉 [7] shuffle (trickily); garble; **~чивать** [1], 〈подточи́ть〉 [16] eat (away); wash (out); sharpen; *fig.* undermine.

подтвер|жда́ть [1], 〈~ди́ть〉 [15 *e.*; -ржу́, -рди́шь; -рждённый] confirm, corroborate; acknowledge; **-ся** prove (to be) true; **~жде́ние** *n* [12] confirmation; acknowledg(e)ment.

под|тере́ть *s.* ~тира́ть; **~тёк** *m* [1] bloodshot spot; **~тира́ть** [1], 〈~тере́ть〉 [12; подотру́; подтёр] wipe (up); **~толкну́ть** *s.* ~та́лкивать; **~точи́ть** *s.* ~та́чивать.

подтру́н|ивать [1], 〈~и́ть〉 [13] tease, banter, chaff (*v/t.* над Т).

подтя́|гивать [1], 〈~ну́ть〉 [19] pull (up); draw (in *reins*); tighten; raise (*wages*); wind *or* key up, egg on; join in (*song*); **-ся** chin; brace up; improve, pick up; **~жки** *f/pl.* [5; *gen.*: -жек] suspenders, *Brt.* braces.

поду́мывать [1] think (about о П).

подуч|а́ть [1], 〈~и́ть〉 [16] *s.* учи́ть.

поду́шка *f* [5; *g/pl.*: -шек] pillow; cushion, pad.

подхали́м *m* [1] toady, lickspittle.

подхва́т|ывать [1], 〈~и́ть〉 [15] catch; pick up; take up; join in.

подхо́д *m* [1] approach (*a. fig.*); **~и́ть** [15], 〈подойти́〉 [-ойду́, -дёшь; -ошёл; -шла́; *g. pt.* -ойдя́] (к Д) approach, go (up to); arrive, come; (Д) suit, fit; **~я́щий** [17] suitable, fit(ting), appropriate; convenient.

подцеп|ля́ть [28], 〈~и́ть〉 [14] hook (*a. fig.*); pick up, catch.

подча́с at times, sometimes.

подч|ёркивать [1], 〈~еркну́ть〉 [20; -ёркнутый] underline; stress.

подчин|е́ние *n* [12] submission; subjection; *gr.* hypotaxis; **~ённый** [14] subordinate; **~я́ть** [28], 〈~и́ть〉 [13] subject, subdue; subordinate; put under (s.b.'s Д) supervision; **-ся** (Д) submit (to); obey.

под|ше́фный [14] sponsored; **~шива́ть** [1], 〈~ши́ть〉 [подошью́, -шьёшь; *cf.* шить] sew on (to к Д); hem; file; **~ши́пник** ⊕ *m* [1] bearing; **~ши́ть** *s.* ~шива́ть; **~шу́чивать** [1], 〈~шути́ть〉 [15] play a trick (on над Т).

подъе́|зд *m* [1] entrance, porch; drive; approach; **~здно́й** [14] 🚂 branch (*line*); **~зжа́ть** [1], 〈~хать〉 [-е́ду, -е́дешь] (к Д) drive *or* ride up (to), approach; F drop in (on); make up to.

подъём *m* [1] lift(ing); ascent, rise (*a. fig.*); enthusiasm; instep; лёгок (тяжёл) на ~ nimble (slow); **~ник** *m* [1] elevator, lift, hoist; **~ный** [14]: ~ный мост *m* drawbridge; ~ная си́ла *f* carrying capacity; ~ные (де́ньги) *pl.* travel(l)ing expenses.

подъе́|хать *s.* ~зжа́ть.

под|ыма́ть(ся) *s.* ~нима́ть(ся).

поды́ск|ивать [1], 〈~а́ть〉 [3] *impf.* look for; *pf.* find; choose.

подытóж|ивать [1], ⟨**~ить**⟩ [16] sum up.
поедáть [1], ⟨поéсть⟩ *cf.* есть[1].
поеди́нок *m* [1; -нка] duel (with *arms* на П).
пóезд *m* [1; *pl.:* -дá, *etc. e.*] train; **∠ка** *f* [5; *g/pl.:* -док] trip, journey; voyage; tour; **~нóй** 🚂 [14] train...
поéние *n* [12] watering.
пожáлуй maybe, perhaps; I suppose; **~ста** (pa'ʒałustə) please; *cf. a.* (нé за) что; скажи́(те) ~ста! I say!; **~те** come in(to в В), please; ~те сюдá! this way, please; *cf.* жáловать & добрó[2].
пожáр *m* [1] fire (to/at на В/П); conflagration; **~ище** *n* [11] scene of conflagration; **~ник** *m* [1] fireman; **~ный** [14] fire...; *su.* = ~ник; *cf.* комáнда.
пожáт|ие *n* [12] shake (*of hand*); **~ь** *s.* пожимáть & пожинáть.
пожелáние *n* [12] wish; request.
пожелтéлый [14] yellow, faded.
пожéртвование *n* [12] donation.
пожи́|ва *f* [5] F = нажи́ва, *s.*; **~вáть** [1] F live; как (вы) ~вáете? how are you (getting on)?; **~ви́ться** [14*e.*; -влю́сь, -ви́шься] *pf.* F (Т) = нажи́ть; **~зненный** [14] life...; **~лóй** [14] elderly.
пожи|мáть [1], ⟨пожáть⟩ [-жмý, -жмёшь; -áтый] *s.* жать[1]; **~мáть** плечáми shrug one's shoulders; **~нáть** [1], ⟨пожáть⟩ [-жнý, -жнёшь; -жáтый] *s.* жать[2]; **~рáть** P [1], ⟨пожрáть⟩ [-жрý, -рёшь; -áл, -á, -о] eat up; devour; **∠тки** F *m/pl.* [1] belongings, things; со всéми ∠тками with bag & baggage.
пóза *f* [5] pose, posture, attitude.
поза|вчерá the day before yesterday; **~ди́** (P) behind; past; **~прóшлый** [14] the ... before last.
позвол|éние *n* [12] permission (with с Р), leave (by); **~и́тельный** [14; -лен, -льна] permissible; ~и́тельно one may; **~я́ть** [28], ⟨**∠ить**⟩ [13] allow (*a.* of), permit (Д); ~я́ть себé venture, presume; ✝ beg *to*; afford; **∠ь(те)** may I; let; I say.
позвонó|к *m* [1; -нкá] *anat.* vertebra; **~чник** *m* [1] spinal (*or* vertebral) column, spine, backbone; **~чный** [14] vertebral; vertebrate.
пóздн|ий [15] (-ʒŋ-) (~о *a.* it is) late.
поздорóвит|ься F *pf.*: емý не ~ся he will (have to) pay for it.
поздрав|и́тель *m* [4] congratulator; **~и́тельный** [14] congratulatory; **∠ить** *s.* ~ля́ть; **~лéние** *n* [12] congratulation; *pl.* compliments (of the season с Т); **~ля́ть** [28], ⟨∠ить⟩ [14] (с Т) congratulate (on), wish (many happy returns [of the day]); send (*or* give) one's compliments (of the season).
поземéльный [14] land..., ground...
пóзже later; не ~ (P) ... at the latest.
позити́вный [14; -вен, -вна] positive.
позици|óнный [14] trench..., position...; **ʹ~я** *f* [7] position; *pl.* ⚔ line; *fig.* attitude (on по Д).
позна|вáть [5], ⟨**∠ть**⟩ [1] perceive; (come to) know; **∠ние** *n* [12] perception; *pl.* knowledge.
позолóта *f* [5] gilding.
позóр *m* [1] shame, disgrace, infamy; **~ить** [13], ⟨о-⟩ dishono(u)r, disgrace; **~ный** [14; -рен, -рна] shameful, disgraceful, infamous, ignominious; ~ный столб *m* pillory.
пози́в *m* [1] desire; impulse.
поим|ённый [14] of names; by (roll) call; **~еновáть** [7] *pf.* name; **~ýщественный** [14] property...
пóис|ки *m/pl.* [1] search (in в П), quest; **∠тине** truly, really.
по|и́ть [13], ⟨на-⟩ water; give to drink (s. th. T); **∠йло** *n* [9] swill.
пой|мáть *s.* лови́ть; **~ти́** *s.* идти́.
покá for the time being (*a.* ~ что); meanwhile; while; ~ (не) until; ~! F so long!, (I'll) see you later.
покáз *m* [1] demonstration; showing; **~áние** (*usu. pl.*) *n* [12] evidence; ⊕ indication; **~áтель** *m* [4] 𝔄 exponent; index; figure; **~áтельный** [14; -лен, -льна] significant; demonstrative; model; show (*trial*); **~áть(ся)** *s.* ~ывать(ся); **~нóй** [14] ostentatious; sham...; **~ывать** [1], ⟨~áть⟩ [3] show; demonstrate; point (at на В); ⚖ testify, depose (against на В); ⊕ read; ~áть себя́ (Т) prove; и ви́ду не ~ывать seem to know nothing; look unconcerned; **-ся** appear (*a.* = seem, T), turn up.
покáмест P, *s.* покá.
покáт|ость *f* [8] declivity; slope, slant; **~ый** [14 *sh.*] slanting, sloping; retreating (*forehead*).
покая́н|ие *n* [12] penance (do быть на П); penitence; repentance.
поквитáться F [1] *pf.* settle accounts.
поки|дáть [1], ⟨∠нуть⟩ [20] leave, quit; abandon, desert.
покла|дáя: не ~дáя рук unremittingly; **∠дистый** [14 *sh.*] accommodating; **∠жа** *f* [5] load, lading.
поклóн *m* [1] bow; regards *pl.*; **~éние** *n* [12] (Д) worship; deference; **~и́ться** *s.* кля́няться; **~ник** *m* [1] worship(p)er; admirer; **~я́ться** [28] (Д) worship; bow (to).
покóиться [13] rest, lie; be based.
покóй *m* [3] rest; repose, peace; calm; † apartment; (остáвить в П let) alone; **~ник** *m* [1], **~ница** *f* [5] the deceased; ⚖ decedent; **~ницкая** *f* [14] mortuary; **~ный** [14; -óен, -óйна] quiet; calm; easy; the late; *su.* = ~ник, ~ница; *cf.* спокóйный.
поколéние *n* [12] generation.
покóнчить [16] *pf.* ([с] Т) finish;

(с Т) do away with; commit (suicide с собой).

покор|éние *n* [12] conquest; subjugation; **~и́тель** *m* [4] conqueror; **~и́ть(ся)** *s.* ~я́ть(ся); **∠ность** *f* [8] submission, obedience; **∠ный** [14; -рен, -рна] obedient; humble, submissive; ∠но *a.* (*thank*) very much; **~я́ть** [28], ⟨~и́ть⟩ [13] conquer, subdue; -ся submit; resign o. s.

покóс *m* [1] (hay)mowing; meadow.

покри́кивать F [1] shout (at на В).

покрóв *m* [1] cover; hearse cloth.

покрови́тель *m* [4] patron, protector; **~ница** *f* [5] patroness, protectress; **~ственный** [14] patronizing; ✝ protective; **~ство** *n* [9] protection (of Д); patronage; **~ствовать** [7] (Д) patronize; protect.

покрóй *m* [3] cut; kind, breed.

покры|вáло *n* [9] coverlet; veil; **~вáть** [1], ⟨∠ть⟩ [22] (Т) cover (*a.* = defray); coat; beat, trump; P call *or* run down; -ся cover o. s.; be(come) covered; **∠тие** *n* [12] cover(ing); coat(ing); defrayal; **∠шка** *f* [5; *g/pl.*: -шек] (tire) cover; F lid.

покуп|áтель *m* [4], **~áтельница** *f* [5] buyer; customer; **~áтельный** [14] purchasing; **~áть** [1], ⟨купи́ть⟩ [14] buy, purchase (from у Р); **∠ка** *f* [5; *g/pl.*: -пок] purchase; package; за ∠ками (*go*) shopping; **~нóй** [14] purchasing; purchase(d).

поку|шáться [1], ⟨~си́ться⟩ [15 *e.*; -ушу́сь, -уси́шься] attempt (*v/t.* на В); encroach ([up]on); **~шéние** *n* [12] attempt ([up]on на В).

пол[1] *m* [1; нá ~; на -у́; *pl. e.*] floor.

пол[2] *m* [1; *from g/pl. e.*] sex.

пол[3](...) [*g/sg., etc.*: ~(у)...] half (...).

полá *f* [5; *pl. st.*] skirt, tail.

полагá|ть [1], ⟨положи́ть⟩ [16] put; decide; ♪ set (to на В); *impf.* think, suppose, guess; fancy; нáдо ~ть probably; полóжим, что ... suppose, let's assume that; -ся rely (on на В); (Д) ~ется must; be due *or* proper; как ~ется properly.

пóл|день *m* [*gen.*: -(у́)дня; *g/pl.*: -дён] noon (at в В); *cf.* обéд; **~днéвный** [14] midday...; **~дорóги** *s.* ~пути́; **~дю́жины** [*gen.*: -удю́жины] half (a) dozen.

пóле *n* [10; *pl. e.*] field (*a. fig.*; in на, в П; across пó Д; Т); ground; *mst. pl.* margin; **~вóй** [14] field...; **∠зный** [14; -зен, -зна] useful, of use; helpful; wholesome; ⊕ effective; net.

полем|изи́ровать [7] polemize; **∠ика** *f* [5], **~и́ческий** [16] polemic.

полéно *n* [9; -нья, -ньев] log.

полёт *m* [1] flight; брéющий ~ low-level flight; слепóй ~ blind flying.

пóлз|ать [1], **~ти́** [24] creep, crawl; **~кóм** on all fours; **~у́чий** [17]: ~у́чее растéние *n* creeper, climber.

поли|вáть [1], ⟨∠ть⟩ [-лью, -лёшь; *cf.* лить] water; *pf.* start raining (*or* pouring); **∠вка** *f* [5] watering; flushing.

полигóн *m* [1] (target) range.

полиня́лый [14] faded.

поли|ровáть [7], ⟨от-⟩ polish, burnish; **~рóвка** *f* [5; *g/pl.*: -вок] polish(ing); **'~с** *m* [1] (*insurance*) policy.

Полит|бюрó *n* [*indecl.*] Politburo (*Sov.*), Political Bureau; **♀грáмота** *f* [5] political primer (*Sov.*); **♀éхникум** *m* [1] polytechnic; **♀заключённый** *m* [14] political prisoner.

поли́т|ик *m* [1] politician; **~ика** *f* [5] policy; politics *pl.*; **~и́ческий** [16] political; **~ру́к** *m* [1] political instructor (*or* commissar[y]) (*Sov.*); **~у́ра** *f* [5] polish; **~учёба** *f* [5] political instruction (*Sov.*); **~ь** *s.* поливáть; **~экономия** *f* [7] political economy, economics.

полиц|éйский [16] police(man *su.*); **∠ия** *f* [7] police.

поли́чн|ое *n* [14] corpus delicti; с **~ым** (*catch*) red-handed.

полк *m* [1 *e.*; в -у́] regiment; **∠а** *f* [5; *g/pl.*: -лок] shelf; pan (*gun*).

полкóв|ник *m* [1] colonel; **~óдец** *m* [1; -дца] commander, general; **~óй** [14] regimental.

полнéть [8], ⟨по-⟩ grow stout.

пóлно 1. full, to the brim; **2.** F (*a.* ~те) okay, all right; never mind; enough *or* no more (of this); (*a.* ~ Д + *inf.*) stop, quit (that) (...ing)!; **~вéсный** [14; -сен, -сна] weighty; **~влáстный** [14; -тен, -тна] absolute; **~вóдный** [14; -ден, -дна] deep; **~крóвный** [14; -вен, -вна] full-blooded; ⚕ plethoric; **~лу́ние** *n* [12] full moon; **~мóчие** *n* [12] (full) power; **~мóчный** [14; -чен, -чна] plenipotentiary; *cf.* полпрéд (-ство); **~прáвный** [14; -вен, -вна]: ~прáвный член *m* full member; **~стью** completely, entirely; **~тá** *f* [5] fullness, plenitude; completeness; corpulence; **~цéнный** [14; -éнен, -éнна] full (value)...; *fig.* full-fledged.

пóлночь *f* [8; -(у́)ночи] midnight.

пóлн|ый [14; пóлон, полнá, пóлнó; полнéе] full (of Р *or* Т); complete, absolute; perfect (*a. right*); stout; chubby; **~ы́м-~ы́й** F full up, packed (with Р).

полови́к *m* [1 *e.*] mat.

полови́н|а *f* [5] half (by на В); ~а (в ~е) пя́того (at) half past four; два с ~ой two & a half; **~ка** *f* [5; *g/pl.*: -нок] half; leaf (*door*); **~чатый** [14] *fig.* vague, evasive.

полови́ца *f* [5] deal, board.

половóдье *n* [10] high water (*in spring*).

полов|óй[1] [14] floor...; ~áя тря́пка *f* mop; **~óй**[2] [14] sexual; ~áя зрéлость *f* puberty; ~ы́е óрганы *m/pl.* genitals.

пóлог *m* [1] bed curtain.
пологий [16; *comp.*: полóже] slightly sloping, flat.
полож|éние *n* [12] position, location; situation; state, condition; standing; regulations *pl.*; thesis; в (интерéсном) ~éнии F in the family way; **~ительный** [14; -лен, -льна] positive; affirmative; **~ить** (**-ся**) *s.* класть 1. & полагáть(ся).
пóлоз *m* [1; *pl.*: -лóзья, -лóзьев] runner.
полóмка *f* [5; *g/pl.*: -мок] breakage.
полосá *f* [5; *ac/sg.*: пóлосу; *pl.*: пóлосы, полóс, -сáм] stripe, streak; strip; belt, zone; bar; field; period; **~тый** [14 *sh.*] striped.
полоскáть [3], ⟨про-⟩ rinse; gargle; **-ся** paddle; flap (*flag, etc.*).
пóлость *f* [8; *from g/pl. e.*] cavity.
полотéнце *n* [11; *g/pl.*: -нец] towel (on T); мохнáтое ~ Turkish towel.
полóтн|ище *n* [11] width; **~ó** *n* [9; *pl.*: -óтна, -óтен, -óтнам] linen; bunting; 🚂 roadbed; embankment; (*saw*) blade; **~яный** [14] linen...
полóть [17], ⟨вы́-, про-⟩ weed.
пол|прéд *m* [1] ambassador; **~прéдство** *n* [9] embassy (*Sov., till 1941*); **~пути́** halfway (*a.* на ~пути́); **~слóва** [9; *gen.*: -(у)слóва] half a word; (a few) word(s); на ~(у)слóве (*stop*) short; **~сóтни** [6; *g/sg.*: -(у)сóтни; *g/pl.*: -лусóтен] fifty; **~ти́нник** F *m* [1], P **~ти́на** *f* [5] half (a) ruble, 50 kopecks.
полтор|á *m & n*, ~ы́ *f* [*gen.*: -ýтора; -ры (*f*)] one and a half; **~áста** [*obl. cases*; -ýтораста] a hundred and fifty.
полу|боти́нки *m/pl.* [1; *g/pl.*: -нок] (low) shoes; **~глáсный** [14] semivowel; **~гóдие** *n* [12] half year, six months; **~годи́чный, ~годовóй** [14] semiannual, half-yearly; **~грáмотный** [14; -тен, -тна] semiliterate; **∠денный** [14] midday...; meridional; **~живóй** [14; -жив, -á, -о] half dead; **~защи́тник** *m* [1] halfback; **~крýг** *m* [1] semicircle; **~мéсяц** *m* [1] half moon, crescent; **~мрáк** *m* [1] twilight, semi-darkness; **∠ночный** [14] midnight...; **~оборóт** *m* [1] half-turn; **~óстров** *m* [1; *pl.*: -вá, *etc. e.*] peninsula; **~свéт** *m* [1] twilight; demimonde; **~спýщенный** [14] half-mast; **~стáнок** *m* [1; -нка] 🚂 stop, substation; **~тьмá** *f* [5] = ~мрáк.
получ|áтель *m* [4] addressee, recipient; **~áть** [1], ⟨~и́ть⟩ [16] receive, get; obtain; catch; have; **-ся** come in, arrive; result; prove, turn out; **~чéние** *n* [12] receipt; getting; **∠чка** F *f* [5; *g/pl.*: -чек] pay (day).
полу|шáрие *n* [12] hemisphere; **~шýбок** *m* [1; -бка] short fur coat.
пол|фýнта [*g/sg.*: -уфýнта] half pound; **~цены́**: за ~цены́ at half price; **~чacá** *m* [1; *g/sg.*: -учáса] half (an) hour.
пóлчище *n* [11] horde; mass.
пóлый [14] hollow; high; iceless.
полы́нь *f* [8] wormwood.
полыньá *f* [6] ice-hole (*on frozen river etc.*).
пóльз|а *f* [5] use; benefit (for на, в В, для Р); profit; advantage; utility; в ~у (Р) in favo(u)r of; **~овать** [7] treat; **-ся**, ⟨вос~оваться⟩ (Т) use, make use of; avail o. s. of; enjoy, have; take (*opportunity*).
пóль|ка *f* [5; *g/pl.*: -лек] **1.** Pole; **2.** polka; **~ский** [16] Polish; **~ша** *f* [5] Poland.
полюбóвный [14] amicable.
пóлюс *m* [1] pole; ⚡ *a.* terminal.
поля́|к *m* [1] Pole; **~на** *f* [5] glade; meadow; **~рный** [14] polar.
помáда *f* [5] pomade; (*lip*)stick.
помáз|ание *n* [12] unction; **~ывать** [1], ⟨~ать⟩ [3] anoint; *s.* мáзать.
помалéньку F so-so; little by little.
помáлкивать F [1] keep silent.
помá|рка *f* [5; *g/pl.*: -рок] blot, erasure; **~хивать** [1] wag; flourish.
поместú́т|ельный [14; -лен, -льна] spacious; **~ь(ся)** *s.* помещáть[(-ся).]
помéстье *n* [10] estate.
пóмесь *f* [8] cross breed, mongrel.
помéсячный [14] monthly.
помёт *m* [1] dung; litter, brood.
помé|тить *s.* ~чáть; **~тка** *f* [5; *g/pl.*: -ток] mark, note; **~ха** *f* [5] hindrance; trouble, disturbance (*a.* ⊕); **~чáть** [1], ⟨∠тить⟩ [15] mark, note.
помéш|анный [14 *sh.*] crazy; mad (about на П); **~áтельство** *n* [9] insanity; **~áть** *s.* мешáть; **-ся** *pf.* go mad (*a.* ~áться в умé); F be mad (about на П).
поме|щáть [1], ⟨~сти́ть⟩ [15 *e.*; -ещý, -ести́шь; -ещённый] place; lodge, accommodate; settle; invest; insert, publish; **-ся** settle (o. s.), locate; lodge; find room; hold; be placed *or* invested; *impf.* be (located); **~щéние** *n* [12] lodg(e)ment, premise(s), room; investment; **∠щик** *m* [1] landowner, landlord.
помидóр *m* [1] tomato.
поми́л|ование *n* [12], **~овать** [7] *pf.* pardon; **~уй(те)**! for goodness' sake; good gracious; ~уй бог! God forbid!; гóсподи ~уй! God, have mercy upon us.
поми́мо (Р) besides; in spite of; ~ негó without his knowledge.
поми́н *m* [1] mention (of о П); **~áть** [1], ⟨помянýть⟩ [19] recollect, remember; speak about, mention; pray for (*a.* о П); commemorate; ~áй, как звáли (be) off and away; не ~áть ли́хом bear no ill will (toward[s] a p. В); **~ки** *f/pl.* [5; *gen.*: -нок] commemoration (for the dead); **~ýтно** every minute; constantly.

по́мнит|ь [13], ⟨вс-⟩ remember, recollect, think of (*a.* о П); мне **~ся** (as far as) I remember.
помо|га́ть [1], ⟨**∠чь**⟩ [26 г/ж: -огу́, -о́жешь, -о́гут; -о́г, -огла́] (Д) help; aid, assist; avail.
помо́|и *m/pl.* [3] slops; **~йный** [14] slop, garbage, dust (*hole* =, F, **~йка** *f* [5; *g/pl.*: -оек]).
помо́л *m* [1] grind(ing); **~вить** [14] *pf.* affiance (to с Т); **~вка** *f* [5; *g/pl.*: -вок] betrothal, engagement.
помо́ст *m* [1] dais; rostrum; scaffold.
по́моч|и F *f/pl.* [8; *from gen. e.*] leading strings (in на П); = подтя́жки; **∠ь** *s.* помога́ть.
помо́щ|ник *m* [1], **~ница** *f* [5] assistant; deputy (s. th. P); helper, aid; **'~ь** *f* [8] help, aid, assistance (with с Т *or* при П; to one's на В/Д; *call* for на В, о П); ⚕ treatment; relief; каре́та ско́рой **'~и** ambulance.
по́мпа *f* [5] pomp; ⊕ pump.
помрача́ть *s.* омрача́ть.
помутне́ние *n* [12] turbidity.
по́мы|сел *m* [1; -сла] thought; design; **~шля́ть** [28] think (of о П).
помяну́ть *s.* помина́ть.
помя́тый [14] (c)rumpled; trodden.
пона́|добиться [14] *pf.* (Д) need, want; **~пра́сну** F = напра́сно; **~слы́шке** F by hearsay.
поне|во́ле F willy-nilly; against one's will; **~де́льник** *m* [1] Monday (on: в В, *pl.*: по Д).
понемно́|гу, F **~жку** (a) little; little by little, gradually; F *a.* so-so.
пони|жа́ть [1], ⟨**∠зить**⟩ [15] lower, reduce (*v/i.* -ся; fall, sink); **~же́ние** *n* [12] fall; reduction; decrease; degradation.
поник|а́ть [1], ⟨**∠нуть**⟩ [21] hang (one's head голово́й); droop; wilt.
понима́|ние *n* [12] comprehension, understanding; conception; **~ть** [1], ⟨поня́ть⟩ [пойму́, -ёшь; по́нял, -а́, -о; по́нятый (по́нят, -а́, -о)] understand, comprehend, see; realize; appreciate; **~ю** (**~ешь**, **~ете** [ли]) I (you) see.
пономáрь *m* [4 *e.*] sexton.
поно́|с *m* [1] diarrhea; **~си́ть** [15], **~ше́ние** *n* [12] abuse.
поно́шенный [14 *sh.*[worn, shabby.
понто́н *m* [1], **~ный** [14] pontoon.
пону|жда́ть [1], ⟨**∠дить**⟩ [15; -ужде́нный] force, compel; **~жде́ние** *n* [12] compulsion.
понука́ть [1] urge on, spur.
пону́р|ить [13] hang; **~ый** [14 *sh.*] downcast.
по́нчик *m* [1] doughnut.
поны́не until now.
поня́т|ие *n* [12] idea, notion; concept(ion); comprehension; **~ливый** [14 *sh.*] quick-witted, bright; **~ный** [14; -тен, -тна] intelligible, understandable; clear, plain; **~но** *a.*, F, = коне́чно; **~ь** *s.* понима́ть.
поо́б|даль at some distance; **~ди-но́чке** one by one; **~чере́дный** [14] alternate.
поощр|е́ние *n* [12] encouragement; **~я́ть** [28], ⟨**~и́ть**⟩ [13] encourage.
поп F *m* [1 *e.*] priest.
попа|да́ние *n* [12] hit; **~да́ть** [1], ⟨**∠сть**⟩ [25; *pt. st.*] (в *or* на В) get, come (*a.* across), fall, find o. s.; hit; catch (*train*); become (в И *pl.*); F (Д *impers.*) get it; не **∠сть** miss; как **∠ло** anyhow, at random, haphazard; кому́ **∠ло** to the first comer (= пе́рвому **∠вшемуся**); **-ся** (в В) be caught; fall (into a trap на у́дочку); F (Д + *vb.* + И) come across, chance (up)on, meet; occur, there is (are); strike (a p.'s eye Д на глаза́; не **~да́ться** be out of a p.'s sight).
попадья́ *f* [6] priest's wife.
попа́рно by pairs, in couples.
попа́сть(ся) *s.* попада́ть(ся).
попер|ёк (P) across, crosswise; in (*a p.'s way*); **~ме́нно** by turns; **~е́чный** [14] transverse, transversal; cross...
попеч|е́ние *n* [12] care, charge (in на П); **~и́тель** *m* [4] curator, trustee.
попира́ть [1] trample (on) (*fig.*).
по́пка F *m* [5; *g/pl.*: -пок] parrot.
поплаво́к *m* [1; -вка́] float (*a.* ⊕).
попо́йка F *f* [5; *g/pl.*: -оек] booze.
попол|а́м in half; half & half; fifty-fifty; **~знове́ние** *n* [12] mind; pretension (to на В); **~ня́ть** [28], ⟨**∠нить**⟩ [13] replenish, supplement; enrich; reman, reinforce.
пополу́дни in the afternoon, p. m.
попо́на *f* [5] horsecloth.
попра́в|ить(ся) *s.* **~ля́ть(ся)**; **~ка** *f* [5; *g/pl.*: -вок], **~ле́ние** *n* [12] correction; amendment; improvement; recovery; repair; **~ля́ть** [28], ⟨**~ить**⟩ [14] repair; adjust; correct, (a)mend; improve; recover (*v/i.* **-ся**; put on weight, look better).
по-пре́жнему (now) as before.
попрек|а́ть [1], ⟨**~ну́ть**⟩ [20] reproach (with Т).
по́прище *n* [11] field (in на П).
по́про|сту plainly, unceremoniously; downright; **~ша́йка** F *m/f* [5; *g/pl.*: -а́ек] beggar.
попуга́й *m* [3] parrot.
популя́рн|ость *f* [8] popularity; **~ый** [14; -рен, -рна] popular.
попус|ти́тельство *n* [9] connivance; **'~т(о́м)у** F in vain, to no purpose.
попу́т|ный [14] fair, favo(u)rable (*wind*); (**~но** in) passing, incidental(ly); **~чик** *m* [1] fellow travel(l)er.
попыт|а́ть F [1] *pf.* try (one's luck сча́стья); **∠ка** *f* [5; *g/pl.*: -ток] attempt.

пор|á[1] *f* [5; *ac/sg.*: пóру; *pl. st.*] time; season; weather (in в В); period; F prime; (давнó) ~á it's (high) time (for Д); в (сáмую) ~у in the nick of time; до ~ы́, до врéмени not last forever; *wait* for one's opportunity; до (с) какѝх ~? how long (since when)?; до сих ~ hitherto, so far, up to now (here); до тех ~ (, покá) so (*or* as) long (as); с тех ~ (как) since then (since); на пéрвых ~áх at first, in the beginning; ~óй at times; вечéрней ~óй = вéчером.

пóра[2] *f* [5] pore.

порабо|щáть [1], ‹~тѝть› [15 *e.*; -ощу́, -отѝшь; -ощённый] enslave, subjugate.

поравня́ться [28] *pf.* overtake (с Т).

пора|жáть [1], ‹~зѝть› [15 *e.*; -ажу́, -азѝшь; -ажённый] strike (*a. fig.* = amaze, & ⚕ = affect); defeat; **~жéнец** *m* [1; -нца] defeatist; **~жéние** *n* [12] defeat; ⚕ affection; ⚖ deprivation; striking; **~жéнчество** *n* [9] defeatism; **~зѝтельный** [14; -лен, -льна] striking; **~зѝть** *s.* ~жáть; **~нить** [13] *pf.* wound, cut.

порвáть(ся) *s.* порывáть(ся).

порéз *m* [1], **~ать** [3] *pf.* cut.

порéй *m* [3] leek.

пóристый [14 *sh.*] porous.

порицá|ние *n* [12], **~ть** [1] censure.

пóровну (in) equal parts.

порóг *m* [1] threshold; *pl.* rapids.

порó|да *f* [5] breed, species, race; stock; ⚒ rock; layer; **~дистый** [14 *sh.*] thoroughbred; racy; **~ждáть** [1], ‹~дѝть› [15 *e.*; -ожу́, -одѝшь; -ождённый] cause, give rise to, entail; **~ждéние** *n* [12] brood; production.

порóжний F [15] empty.

пóрознь F separately; one by one.

порóк *m* [1] vice; defect; disease.

поросёнок *m* [2] young pig.

порó|ть [17] **1.** ‹рас-› undo, unpick; *impf.* F talk (*nonsense*); **2.** F ‹вы́-› whip, flog; **'~х** *m* [1] gunpowder; **~ховóй** [14] (gun)powder...

порóч|ить [16], ‹о-› discredit; defile; **~ный** [14; -чен, -чна] vicious.

порошóк *m* [1; -шкá] powder.

порт *m* [1; в -у́; *from g/pl. e.*] port; harbo(u)r; **~атѝвный** [14; -вен, -вна] portable; **~ить** [15], ‹ис-› spoil (*v/i.* **-ся**; break down).

портн|и́ха *f* [5] dressmaker; **~óй** *m* [14] tailor.

портов|и́к *m* [1 *e.*] longshoreman, *Brt. a.* docker; **~ый** [14] port..., dock...; **~ый** гóрод *m* seaport.

портсигáр *m* [1] cigar(ette) case.

португáл|ец *m* [1; -льца] Portuguese; **2ия** *f* [7] Portugal; **~ка** *f* [5; *g/pl.*: -лок], **~ьский** [16] Portuguese.

порт|упéя *f* [6] sword knot; **~фéль** *m* [4] brief case; portfolio; **~я́нка** *f* [5; *g/pl.*: -нок] foot wrap (rag).

поругáние *n* [12] abuse, affront.

пору́|ка *f* [5] bail (on на В *pl.*), security; guarantee; responsibility; **~чáть** [1], ‹~чѝть› [16] charge (a p. with Д/В); commission, bid, tell (+ *inf.*); entrust; **~чéние** *n* [12] commission; instruction; message; mission; (*a.* ✝) order (by по Д; *a.* on behalf); **~чик** † *m* [1] (first) lieutenant; **~чѝтель** *m* [4] bail, surety; **~чѝть** *s.* ~чáть.

порх|áть [1], *once* ‹~ну́ть› [20] flit.

пóрция *f* [7] portion, helping.

пóр|ча *f* [5] spoiling, spoilage; damage; **~шень** *m* [4; -шня] piston.

поры́в *m* [1] gust, squall; fit, outburst; impulse; **~áть** [1], ‹порвáть› [-ву́, -вёшь; -áл, -á, -о; пóрванный] tear; break (off; with с Т); **-ся** *v/i.*; *impf.* jerk; strive; *s. a.* рвáть(ся); **~истый** [14 *sh.*] gusty; jerky; impulsive.

поря́дко|вый [14] current; *gr.* ordinal; **~м** F rather; properly.

поря́д|ок *m* [1; -дка] order; way (by в П; in Т), form; course; *pl.* conditions; kind; ~ок дня agenda; по ~ку one after another; current (*no.*); **~очный** [14; -чен, -чна] orderly, decent; fair(ly large *or* great).

посáд|ить *s.* сажáть & садѝть; **~ка** *f* [5; *g/pl.*: -док] planting; embarkation, (*a.* 🚂) boarding; ✈ landing, alighting; **~очный** [14] landing...

по-своéму in one's own way.

посвя|щáть [1], ‹~тѝть› [15 *e.*; -ящу́, -ятѝшь; -ящённый] devote ([o.s.] to [себя́] Д); dedicate; initiate (into в В); (в И *pl.*) ordain; knight; **~щéние** *n* [12] dedication; initiation.

посéв *m* [1] sowing; crop; **~нóй** [14] sowing (campaign *su. f*).

поседéлый [14] (turned) gray, *Brt.* grey.

посел|éнец *m* [1; -нца] settler; **~éние** *n* [12] colony (*a.* **посёлок** *m* [1; -лка]); **~я́ть** [28], ‹~ѝть› [13] settle (*v/i.* **-ся**; put up [at в П]); inspire.

посередѝне in the middle *or* midst.

посе|тѝтель *m* [4], **~тѝтельница** *f* [5] visitor, caller; **~тѝть** *s.* ~щáть; **~щáемость** *f* [8] attendance; **~щáть** [1], ‹~тѝть› [15 *e.*; -ещу́, -етѝшь; -ещённый] visit, call on; *impf.* attend; **~щéние** *n* [12] visit (to Р), call.

посѝльный [14; -лен, -льна] according to one's strength *or* possibilities, adequate, equal to.

поскользну́ться [20] *pf.* slip.

поскóльку inasmuch as, as.

послаблéние *n* [12] indulgence.

послá|ние *n* [12] message; epistle; **~нник** *m* [1] envoy; messenger; **~ть** *s.* посылáть.

по́сле 1. (P) after (*a.* ~ того́ как + *vb.*); ~ чего́ whereupon; **2.** *adv.* after(ward[s]), later (on); **~вое́нный** [14] postwar.
после́дний [15] last; latest; ultimate, final; latter; worst; highest.
после́д|ователь *m* [4] follower; **~овательный** [14; -лен, -льна] consistent; successive; **~ствие** *n* [12] consequence; **~ующий** [17] following.
после|за́втра the day after tomorrow; **~сло́вие** *n* [12] epilogue.
посло́вица *f* [5] proverb.
послуш|а́ние *n* [12] obedience; **∠ник** *m* [1] novice; **∠ный** [14; -шен, -шна] obedient; docile.
посм|а́тривать [1] (keep) look(-ing); **~е́иваться** [1] chuckle; laugh (in one's sleeve в кула́к; at над T); **~е́ртный** [14] posthumous; **~е́шище** *n* [11] laughing-stock; **~ея́ние** *n* [12] ridicule.
посо́б|ие *n* [12] grant; relief, dole, benefit; aid, means; textbook, manual; **~ля́ть** P [28], ⟨**~и́ть**⟩ [14 *e.*; -блю́, -би́шь] (Д) help, remedy.
посо́л *m* [1; -сла́] ambassador; **~ьство** *n* [9] embassy.
по́сох *m* [1] staff, stick.
поспа́ть [-сплю́, -спи́шь; -спа́л, -а́, -о] *pf.* (have a) nap.
поспе|ва́ть [1], ⟨**∠ть**⟩ [8] ripen; F = успева́ть; be done; get ready.
поспе́шн|ость *f* [8] haste; **~ый** [14; -шен, -шна] hasty, hurried; rash.
посред|и́(не) (P) amid(st), in the middle; **∠ник** *m* [1] mediator, intermediary, middleman; **∠ничество** *n* [9] mediation; **∠ственность** *f* [8] mediocrity; **∠ственный** [14 *sh.*] middling; mediocre; **∠ственно** *a.* fair, satisfactory, C (*mark*; *cf.* тро́йка); **∠ство** *n* [9]: при **∠стве**, че́рез **∠ство** = **~ством** (P) by means of.
пост *m* [1 *e.*] **1.** post; на **~у́** ⚔ *stand* sentinel; **2.** fast; вели́кий ~ Lent.
поста́в|ить *s.* **~ля́ть** & ста́вить; **~ка** *f* [5; *g/pl.*: -вок] delivery (on при П); supply; **~ля́ть** [28], ⟨**~ить**⟩ [14] deliver (*v/t.*; p. Д); supply, furnish; **~щи́к** *m* [1 *e.*] supplier.
постан|ови́ть *s.* **~овля́ть**; **~о́вка** *f* [5; *g/pl.*: -вок] erection; staging, production; performance; position; organization; **~овле́ние** *n* [12] resolution, decision; decree; **~овля́ть** [28], ⟨**~ови́ть**⟩ [14] decide; decree; **~о́вщик** *m* [1] stage manager, director.
посте|ли́ть *s.* стлать; **∠ль** *f* [8] bed; **~пе́нный** [14; -е́нен, -е́нна] gradual.
пости|га́ть [1], ⟨**∠гнуть**⟩ & ⟨**∠чь**⟩ [21] comprehend, grasp; overtake; **~жи́мый** [14 *sh.*] conceivable.
пост|ила́ть [1] *s.* стлать; **~и́ться** [15 *e.*; пощу́сь, пости́шься] fast; **~и́чь** *s.* **~ига́ть**; **∠ный** [14; -тен, -тна́, -о] fast...; vegetable (*oil*); F lean (*meat*); *fig.* sour; sanctimonious; **~ово́й** *m* [14] sentry; **~о́й** *m* [3] quarters, billets *pl.*
посто́льку insomuch.
посторо́нний [15] strange(r *su.*), outside(r), foreign (*a. body*); unauthorized; accessory, secondary.
постоя́лый [14]: ~ двор *m* inn.
постоя́н|ный [14; -я́нен, -я́нна] constant, permanent; continual, continuous; steady; ⚔ standing; ⚡ direct; **~ство** *n* [9] constancy.
пострада́вший [17] injured.
постре́л F *m* [1] scapegrace, rogue.
постри|га́ть [1] ⟨**∠чь**⟩ [26 г/ж: -игу́, -ижёшь, -игу́т] (**-ся** have one's hair) cut; make (become) a monk *or* nun.
постро|е́ние [12], **∠йка** *f* [5; *g/pl.*: -о́ек] construction; building.
поступ|а́тельный [14] progressive; **~а́ть** [1], ⟨**~и́ть**⟩ [14] act; (с T) treat, deal (with), handle; (в, на В) enter, join, matriculate; become; come in, be received (for на В); **-ся** (T) renounce; **~ле́ние** *n* [12] entrance, entry; matriculation; receipt; **∠ок** *m* [1; -пка] act; behavio(u)r, conduct; **'~ь** *f* [8] gait, step.
посты́|дный [14; -ден, -дна] shameful; **~лый** [14 *sh.*] odious.
посу́д|а *f* [5] crockery; (*tea*) service, F things *pl.*; F vessel; **~ный** [14] cup(*board*); dish (*towel*).
посу́точный [14] daily; 24 hours'.
посчастли́ви|ться [14; *impers.*] *pf.*: ему́ **~лось** he succeeded (in *inf.*) *or* was lucky (enough).
посыл|а́ть [1], ⟨посла́ть⟩ [пошлю́, -шлёшь; по́сланный] send (for за T); dispatch; **∠ка** *f* [5; *g/pl.*: -лок] dispatch, sending; package, parcel; premise; *cf. a.* побегу́шки; **∠ьный** *m* [14] messenger.
посып|а́ть [1], ⟨**∠ать**⟩ [2] (be)strew (over; with T); sprinkle; **∠аться** *pf.* fall down; F shower (down).
посяг|а́тельство *n* [9] encroachment; **~а́ть** [1], ⟨**~нуть**⟩ [20] encroach (on на В), attempt.
пот *m* [1] sweat; весь в **~у́** sweating all over.
пота|йно́й [14] secret; **~ка́ть** F [1] connive (at Д); **~со́вка** F *f* [5; *g/pl.*: -вок] scuffle; thrashing; **∠ш** *m* [1] potash.
потво́рство *n* [9] indulgence, connivance; **~вать** [7] indulge, connive (at Д).
пот|ёмки *f/pl.* [5; *gen.*: -мок] darkness; **~енциа́л** (-tɛ-) *m* [1] potential.
потерпе́вший [17] (*ship*)wrecked.
потёртый [14 *sh.*] shabby, worn.

потéря *f* [6] loss; waste.
потéть [8], ‹вс-› sweat (*a.* F = toil; *pane:* ‹за-›), perspire.
потé|ха *f* [5] fun, F lark; **~шáть** [1], ‹~шить› [16] entertain, amuse; **~шный** [14; -шен, -шна] funny, amusing.
поти|рáть F [1] rub; **~хóньку** F slowly; silently; secretly, on the sly.
пóтный [14; -тен, -тнá; -о] sweaty.
потóк *m* [1] stream; torrent; flow.
потолóк *m* [1; -лкá] ceiling (*a.* ✈).
потóм afterward(s); then; **~ок** *m* [1; -мка] descendant, offspring; **~ственный** [14] hereditary; **~ство** *n* [9] posterity, descendants *pl.*
потомý therefore; ~ что because.
потóп *m* [1] flood, deluge.
потреб|ѝтель *m* [4] consumer; buyer; **~ѝть** *s.* ~лять; **~лéние** *n* [12] consumption; use; **~лять** [28], ‹~ѝть› [14 *e.*; -блю, -бѝшь; -блённый] consume; use; **∠ность** *f* [8] need, want (of в П), requirement; **∠бный** [14; -бен, -бна] necessary.
потрёпанный F [14] shabby, worn.
потро|хá *m/pl.* [1 *e.*] giblets; bowels; **~шѝть** [16 *e.*; -шý, -шѝшь; -шённый], ‹вы́-› draw, disembowel.
потряс|áть [1], ‹~тѝ› [24 -с-] shake (*a. fig.*); **~áющий** [17] tremendous; **~éние** *n* [12] shock, shake; **~тѝ** *s.* ~áть.
потý|ги *f/pl.* [5] travail, labo(u)r; **~плять** [28], ‹~пить› [14] cast down (*eyes*); hang (*head*); **~хáние** *n* [12] extinction; **~хáть** [1] *s.* тýхнуть.
пóтчевать [7], ‹по-› F = угощáть.
потягивать(ся) *s.* тянýть(ся).
поутрý F early in the morning.
поуч|áть [1] teach (s. th. Д); **~ѝтельный** [14; -лен, -льна] instructive; edifying.
похáбный P [14; -бен, -бна] obscene, smutty.
похвал|á *f* [5] praise; commendation; **∠ьный** [14; -лен, -льна] laudable, commendable, praiseworthy; laudatory.
похи|щáть [1], ‹∠тить› [15; -ѝщу; -ѝщенный] purloin; kidnap; **~щéние** *n* [12] kidnap(p)ing, abduction.
пох|лёбка *f* [5; *g/pl.*: -бок] soup; skilly; **~мéлье** *n* [10] hang-over.
похóд *m* [1] campaign; march; cruise; крестóвый ~ crusade; **~ѝть** [15] (на В) be like, resemble; **~ка** *f* [5] gait; **~ный** [14] marching; camp-...; battle...
похождéние *n* [12] adventure.
похóж|ий [17 *sh.*] (на В) like, resembling; similar (to); быть ~им look like; ни на что не ~е F shocking.
похо|рóнный [14] funeral...; dead (*march*); undertaker's (*office*); **′~ роны** *f/pl.* [5; -óн, -онáм] funeral, burial (at на П); **~тлѝвый** [14 *sh.*] lustful, lewd; **′~ть** *f* [8] lust.
поцелýй *m* [3] kiss (on в В).
почáсно hourly.
пóчва *f* [5] soil, (*a. fig.*) ground.
почём F how much (is); how should.
почемý why; ~-то for some reason.
пóчерк *m* [1] handwriting.
почерп|áть [1], ‹~нýть› [20; -ёрпнутый] gather, derive; obtain.
пóчесть¹ *f* [8] hono(u)r.
почéсть² *s.* почитáть 2.
почёт *m* [1] hono(u)r, esteem; **~ный** [14; -тен, -тна] honorary; hono(u)rable; (*e. g. guard*) of hono(u)r.
почи|вáть [1], ‹∠ть› [-ѝю, -ѝешь] rest, repose; F sleep.
почѝн *m* [1] initiative; F ✝ start.
почѝн|ка *f* [5; *g/pl.*: -нок] repair (for в В); **~ять** [28] *s.* чинѝть 1 a.
поч|итáть¹ [1] **1.** ‹~тѝть› [-чтý, -тѝшь; -чтённый] esteem, respect, hono(u)r; worship; ✝ favo(u)r (with Т); **2.** ‹~éсть› [25; -чтý, -тёшь; -члá; -чтённый] (Т, за В) esteem, consider; **-ся** be held *or* reputed (to be Т); **~итáть²** [1] *pf.* read (a while); **~ѝть** *s.* почивáть; **∠ка** *f* [5; *g/pl.*: -чек] ⚘ bud; *anat.* kidney.
пóчт|а *f* [5] mail, *Brt.* post (by по Д, Т); post; *a.* = ~áмт; **~альóн** *m* [1] mailman, postman; **~áмт** *m* [1] post office (at на П).
почтéн|ие *n* [12] respect (for к Д), esteem, obeisance; F compliments; с совершéнным ~ием respectfully yours, yours faithfully; **~ный** [14; -éнен, -éнна] respectable; venerable.
почтѝ almost, nearly, all but; **~тельность** *f* [8] respect; **~тельный** [14; -лен, -льна] respectful; respectable; **~ть** *s.* почитáть.
почтóв|ый [14] post(al), mail...; post-office; note (*paper*); ~ый ящик *m* mail (*Brt.* letter) box; (*abbr.*: п/я) Post Office Box (POB); ~ая мáрка *f* (postage) stamp.
пóшл|ина *f* [5] custom, duty; **~ость** *f* [8] platitude; **~ый** [14; пошл, -á, -о] common(place), trite, stale.
поштýчный [14] (by the) piece.
пощáда *f* [5] mercy; ⚔ quarter.
пощёчина *f* [5] slap in the face.
поэ́|зия *f* [7] poetry; **~тѝческий** [16] poetic(al); **~тому** therefore.
появ|ѝться *s.* ~ляться; **~лéние** *n* [12] appearance; **~ляться** [28], ‹~ѝться› [14] appear; emerge.
пóяс *m* [1; *pl.*: -cá, *etc. e.*] belt; zone.
поясн|éние *n* [12] explanation; **~ѝтельный** [14] explanatory; **~ѝть** *s.* ~ять; **~ѝца** *f* [5] small of the back; **~óй** [14] belt...; zone...; half-length; **~ять** [28], ‹~ѝть› [13] explain.
прабáбушка *f* [5; *g/pl.*: -шек] great-grandmother.

пра́вд|а *f* [5] truth; (э́то) ~а it is true; ва́ша ~а you are right; не ~а ли? isn't it, (s)he?, aren't you, they?, do(es)n't ... (*etc.*)?; **~и́вый** [14 *sh.*] truthful; **~оподо́бный** [14; -бен, -бна] likely, probable, verisimilar.
пра́ведн|ик *m* [1] (*pl.* the) righteous (man); **~ый** [14; -ден, -дна] just, righteous, godly.
пра́вил|о *n* [9] rule; principle; *pl.* regulations; **~ьный** [14; -лен, -льна] correct, right; regular.
прави́тель *m* [4] ruler; regent; **~ственный** [14] governmental; **~ство** *n* [9] government.
пра́в|ить [14] (T) govern, rule; drive; ⚓ steer; (B) (proof)read; strop; perform; **~ка** *f* [5] proofreading; stropping; **~ле́ние** *n* [12] government; board of directors, managing *or* executive committee; † administration.
пра́внук *m* [1] great-grandson.
пра́во 1. *n* [9; *pl. e.*] right (to на B; of, by по Д); law; justice; *pl.* F license; 2. *adv.* F indeed, really; **~ве́д** *m* [1] jurist; **~ве́дение** *n* [12] jurisprudence; **~ве́рный** [14; -рен, -рна] orthodox; **~во́й** [14] legal; **~мо́чный** [14; -чен, -чна] authorized; **~писа́ние** *n* [12] orthography, spelling; **~сла́вие** *n* [12] Orthodoxy; **~сла́вный** [14] Orthodox; **~су́дие** *n* [12] (administration of) justice; **~та́** *f* [5] right(fulness), rectitude.
пра́вый [14; *fig.* прав, -á, -o] right (*a. fig.*; *a. side*, on *a.* с P), right-hand.
пра́вящий [17] ruling.
Пра́га *f* [5] Prague.
пра́дед *m* [1] (great-)grandfather.
пра́здн|ик *m* [1] holiday; festival; с ~иком! compliments *pl.* (of the season)!; **~ичный** [14] festive, holiday...; **~ование** *n* [12] celebration; **~овать** [7], ⟨от-⟩ celebrate; **~осло́вие** *n* [12] idle talk; **~ость** *f* [8] idleness; **~ый** [14; -ден, -дна] idle.
пра́кти|к *m* [1] practical man; expert; **~ка** *f* [5] practice (in на П); **~кова́ть** [7] practice, -ise (*v/i.* **-ся**; *a.* be practiced); **´ческий** [16], **´чный** [14; -чен, -чна] practical.
пра́порщик † *m* [1] ensign.
прах *m* [1] dust; ashes *pl.* (*fig.*).
пра́ч|ечная (-ʃn-) *f* [14] laundry; **~ка** *f* [5; *g/pl.:* -чек] laundress.
праща́ *f* [5; *g/pl.:* -ще́й] sling.
пребыва́|ние *n* [12], **~ть** [1] stay.
превзойти́ *s.* превосходи́ть.
превоз|мога́ть [1], ⟨**~мо́чь**⟩ [26 г/ж: -огу́, -о́жешь, -о́гут; -о́г, -гла́] overcome, subdue; **~носи́ть** [15], ⟨**~нести́**⟩ [24 -с-] extol, exalt.
превосх|оди́тельство *n* [9] Excellency; **~оди́ть** [15], ⟨превзойти́⟩ [-йду́, -йдёшь, *etc.*, *cf.* идти́; -йдённый] excel, surpass; **~о́дный** [14; -ден, -дна] excellent, splendid; superior; *gr.* superlative; **~о́дство** *n* [9] superiority.
превра|ти́ть(ся) *s.* **~ща́ть(ся)**; **´тность** *f* [8] vicissitude; wrongness; **´тный** [14; -тен, -тна] wrong, mis-...; adverse, changeful; **~ща́ть** [1], ⟨**~ти́ть**⟩ [15 *e.*; -ащу́, -ати́шь; -ащённый] change, turn, transform (into в B) (*v/i.* **-ся**); **~ще́ние** *n* [12] change; transformation; conversion.
превы|ша́ть [1], ⟨**´сить**⟩ [15] exceed; **~ше́ние** *n* [12] excess.
прегра́|да *f* [5] barrier; obstacle; **~жда́ть** [1], ⟨**~ди́ть**⟩ [15 *e.*; -ажу́, -ади́шь; -аждённый] bar, block (up).
прегреш|а́ть [1], ⟨**~и́ть**⟩ [16] sin.
пред = пе́ред.
преда|ва́ть [5], ⟨**´ть**⟩ [-да́м, -да́шь, *etc.*, *cf.* -дать; пре́дал, -á, -o; -да́й (-те)!; пре́данный (-ан, -á, -o)] betray; subject, expose; **´ть** забве́нию bury in oblivion; **-ся** (Д) indulge (in); devote o. s., give o. s. up (to); **´ние** *n* [12] legend; tradition; **ʹ~нный** [14*sh.*] devoted, faithful, true; *cf.* и́скренний; **´тель** *m* [4] traitor; **´тельский** [16] treacherous; **´тельство** *n* [9] treason, treachery; **´ть(ся)** *s.* **~ва́ть(ся)**.
предвар|и́тельно previously, before(hand); **~и́тельный** [14] preliminary; ⚖ *a.* on remand; **~я́ть** [28], ⟨**~и́ть**⟩ [13] (B) forestall; advise (of о П).
предве́|стие = предзнаменова́ние; **~стник** *m* [1] harbinger; **~ща́ть** [1] forebode, presage.
предвзя́тый [14 *sh.*] preconceived.
предви́деть [11] foresee.
предвку|ша́ть [1], ⟨**~си́ть**⟩ [15] foretaste; **~ше́ние** *n* [12] foretaste.
предводи́тель *m* [4] (ring)leader; † marshal; **~ство** *n* [9] leadership.
предвосх|ища́ть [1], ⟨**~и́тить**⟩ [15; -и́щу] anticipate, forestall.
предвы́борный [14] election...
преде́л *m* [1] limit, bound(ary) (within в П); border; *pl.* precincts; **~ьный** [14] limit..., maximum...; utmost, extreme.
предзнаменова́|ние *n* [12] omen, presage, portent; **~ть** [7] *pf.* portend, presage.
предисло́вие *n* [12] preface.
предл|ага́ть [1], ⟨**~ожи́ть**⟩ [16] offer (a p. s. th. Д/B); propose; suggest; order.
предло́|г *m* [1] pretext (on, under под T), pretense (under); *gr.* preposition; **~же́ние** *n* [12] offer; proposal, proposition, suggestion; *parl.* motion; † supply; *gr.* sentence, clause (*cf.* пя́тый); **~жи́ть** *s.* предлага́ть; **~жный** [14] *gr.* prepositional (*case*).
предме́стье *n* [10] suburb.

предме́т *m* [1] object; subject (matter); ✝ article; на ~ (P) for the purpose of; **~ный** [14] subject...; [-тен, -тна] objective.

предназн|ача́ть [1], ‹**~а́чить**› [16] (-ся be) destine(d).

предна|ме́ренный [14 *sh.*] premeditated, deliberate; **~черта́ть** [1] *pf.* predetermine.

пре́док *m* [1; -дка] ancestor.

предопредел|е́ние *n* [12] predestination; **~я́ть** [28], ‹**~и́ть**› [13] predetermine.

предост|авля́ть [28], ‹**~а́вить**› [14] (Д) let (a p.) have; leave (to); give, render; grant; place (at a p.'s disposal).

предостер|ега́ть [1], ‹**~е́чь**› [26 г/ж] warn (of от P); **~еже́ние** *n* [12] warning.

предосторо́жност|ь *f* [8] precaution(ary measure ме́ра ~и).

предосуди́тельный [14; -лен, -льна] reprehensible, scandalous.

предотвра|ща́ть [1], ‹**~ти́ть**› [15 *e.*; -ащу́, -ати́шь; -ащённый] avert, prevent; **~ще́ние** *n* [12] prevention.

предохран|е́ние *n* [12] protection (from, against от P); **~и́тельный** [14] precautionary; ⚕ preventive; ⊕ safety...; **~я́ть** [28], ‹**~и́ть**› [13] guard, preserve (from от P).

предпис|а́ние *n* [12] order, instruction, direction; **~ывать** [1], ‹**~а́ть**› [3] order, prescribe.

предпол|ага́ть [1], ‹**~ожи́ть**› [16] suppose, assume; *impf.* intend, plan; presuppose; **~ожи́тельный** [14; -лен, -льна] presumable; **~ожи́ть** *s.* **~ага́ть**.

предпо|сла́ть *s.* **~сыла́ть**; **~сле́дний** [15] last but one; **~сыла́ть** [1], ‹**~сла́ть**› [-шлю, -шлёшь; *cf.* слать] premise; **~сы́лка** *f* [5; *g/pl.*: -лок] (pre)supposition; (pre-)condition, prerequisite.

предпоч|ита́ть [1], ‹**~е́сть**› [25 -т-: -чту́, -чтёшь; -чёл, -чла́; -чтённый] prefer; *pt.* + бы would rather; **~те́ние** *n* [12] preference; favo(u)r; отда́ть ~те́ние (Д) prefer; **~ти́тельный** [14; -лен, -льна] preferable.

предпри|и́мчивость *f* [8] enterprise; **~и́мчивый** [14 *sh.*] enterprising; **~нима́тель** *m* [4] employer; industrialist, businessman; **~нима́ть** [1], ‹**~ня́ть**› [-иму́, -и́мешь; -и́нял, -а́, -о; -и́нятый (-и́нят, -а́, -о)] undertake; **~я́тие** *n* [12] undertaking, enterprise; business; plant, works, factory (at на П).

предраспол|ага́ть [1], ‹**~ожи́ть**› [16] predispose; **~оже́ние** *n* [12] predisposition.

предрассу́док *m* [1; -дка] prejudice.

председа́тель *m* [4] chairman, president; **~ство** *n* [9] presidency; **~ствовать** [7] preside (over на П), be in the chair.

предсказ|а́ние *n* [12] prediction; forecast; prophecy; **~ывать** [1], ‹**~а́ть**› [3] foretell, predict; forecast; prophesy.

предсме́ртный [14] death..., dying.

представи́тель *m* [4] representative; *cf. a.* полпре́д; advocate; **~ный** [14; -лен, -льна] representative; stately, imposing; **~ство** *n* [9] representation; *cf. a.* полпре́дство.

предста́в|ить(ся) *s.* **~ля́ть(ся)**; **~ле́ние** *n* [12] presentation; performance; introduction; idea, notion; application (for на В); **~ля́ть** [28], ‹**~ить**› [14] present (o.s., occur, offer **-ся**); produce; introduce (o.s.); (*a.* собо́й) represent, be; act (*a.* = feign -ся [T]); (*esp.* ~ля́ть себе́) imagine; propose (for к Д); *refl. a.* appear; seem.

предст|ава́ть [5], ‹**~а́ть**› [-а́ну, -а́нешь] appear; **~оя́ть** [-ои́т] be in store (of Д), expect; (will) have to; **~оя́щий** [17] (forth)coming.

преду|бежде́ние *n* [12] prejudice, bias; **~ведомля́ть** [28], ‹**~ве́домить**› [14] advise (of о П); **~га́дывать** [1], ‹**~гада́ть**› [1] guess (beforehand), foresee; **~мы́шленный** [14] *s.* преднаме́ренный.

предупре|ди́тельный [14; -лен, -льна] preventive; obliging; **~жда́ть** [1], ‹**~ди́ть**› [15 *e.*; -ежу́, -еди́шь; -еждённый] forestall, anticipate (*p.*), prevent (*th.*); warn (of о П); give notice (of); **~жде́ние** *n* [12] warning; notice; notification; prevention.

предусм|а́тривать [1], ‹**~отре́ть**› [9; -отрю́, -о́тришь] foresee; provide (for), stipulate; **~отри́тельный** [14; -лен, -льна] prudent.

предчу́вств|ие *n* [12] presentiment; **~овать** [7] have a presentiment (of).

предше́ств|енник *m* [1] predecessor; **~овать** [7] (Д) precede.

предъяв|и́тель *m* [4] bearer; **~ля́ть** [28], ‹**~и́ть**› [14] present, produce, show; ⚖ bring (*action* against к Д); assert (*claim*).

пре|дыду́щий [17] preceding, previous; **~е́мник** *m* [1] successor.

пре́ж|де formerly; (at) first; (P) before (*a.* ~де чем); **~девре́менный** [14; -енен, -енна] premature, early; **~ний** [15] former, previous.

презид|е́нт *m* [1] president; **~иум** *m* [1] presidium (*Sov.*).

през|ира́ть [1] despise; ‹**~ре́ть**› [9] scorn, disdain; **~ре́ние** *n* [12] contempt (for к Д); **~ре́нный** [14 *sh.*] contemptible, despicable; **~ре́ть** *s.* **~ира́ть**; **~ри́тельный** [14; -лен, -льна] contemptuous, scornful.

преиму́committee

ly, mainly; **~о** *n* [9] advantage; preference; privilege; по ~у = ~енно.

прейскура́нт *m* [1] price list.

преклон|е́ние *n* [12] inclination; admiration (of пе́ред Т); **~и́ться** *s.* ~я́ться; **~ный** [14] old, advanced; senile; **~я́ться** [28], ‹~и́ться› [13] bow (to, before пе́ред Т); admire.

прекосло́вить [14] contradict.

прекра́сный [14; -сен, -сна] beautiful; fine, splendid, excellent; *a.* very well.

прекра|ща́ть [1], ‹~ти́ть› [15 *e.*; -ащу́, -ати́шь; -ащённый] stop, cease, end (*v/i.* **-ся**); break off; **~ще́ние** *n* [12] cessation, stoppage.

преле́ст|ный [14; -тен, -тна] lovely, charming, delightful; **'~ь** *f* [8] charm; F *s.* ~ный.

прелом|ле́ние *n* [12] refraction; **~ля́ть** [28], ‹~и́ть [14; -млённый] (**-ся** be) refract(ed).

пре́лый [14 *sh.*] rotten, putrid.

прель|ща́ть [1], ‹~сти́ть› [15 *e.*; -льщу́, -льсти́шь; -льщённый] (**-ся** be) charm(ed), tempt(ed), entice(d), seduce(d).

прелю́дия *f* [7] prelude.

преми́|нуть [19] *pf.* fail; **~рова́ть** [7] (*im*)*pf.* award a prize (to В); **'~я** *f* [7] prize; bonus; premium; rate.

премье́р *m* [1] premier, (*usu.* ~-мини́стр) prime minister; **~а** *f* [5] première, first night.

пренебр|ега́ть [1], ‹~е́чь› [26 г/ж], **~еже́ние** *n* [12] (Т) neglect, disregard, disdain, scorn, slight; **~ежи́тельный** [14; -лен, -льна] slighting, scornful, disparaging; ~е́чь *s.* ~ега́ть.

пре́ния *n/pl.* [12] debate, discussion.

преоблада́|ние *n* [12] predominance; **~ть** [1] prevail, predominate.

преобра|жа́ть [1], ‹~зи́ть› [15 *e.*; -ажу́, -ази́шь; -ажённый] change, transform (*v/i.* **-ся**); **~же́ние** *n* [12] transformation; *eccl.* Transfiguration; **~зи́ть(ся)** *s.* ~жа́ть(ся); **~зова́ние** *n* [12] transformation; reorganization; reform; **~зова́тель** *m* [4] reformer; **~зо́вывать** [1], ‹~зова́ть› [7] reform, reorganize; transform.

преодол|ева́ть [1], ‹~е́ть› [8] overcome, subdue; surmount.

препара́т *m* [1] preparation.

препира́тельство *n* [9] wrangle.

преподава́|ние *n* [12] teaching, instruction; **~тель** *m* [4], **~тельница** *f* [5] teacher, instructor; **~ть** [5] teach.

преподн|оси́ть [15], ‹~ести́› [24 -с-] present, offer.

препрово|жда́ть [1], ‹~ди́ть› [15 *e.*; -ожу́, -оди́шь; -ождённый] forward, send; spend, pass.

препя́тств|ие *n* [12] obstacle, hindrance; бег (*or* ска́чки) с ~иями steeplechase; **~овать** [7], ‹вос-› hinder, prevent (a p. from Д/в П).

прер|ва́ть(ся) *s.* ~ыва́ть(ся); **~ека́ние** *n* [12] squabble; **~ыва́ть** [1], ‹~ва́ть› [-ву́, -вёшь; -а́л, -а́, -о; пре́рванный (-ан, -а́, -о)] interrupt; break (off), *v/i.* **-ся**; **~ы́вистый** [14 *sh.*] broken, faltering.

пресе|ка́ть [1], ‹~чь› [26] cut short; suppress; **-ся** break; stop.

пресле́дов|ание *n* [12] pursuit; persecution; ⚖ prosecution; **~ать** [7] pursue; persecute; haunt; ⚖ prosecute.

пресловý тый [14] notorious.

пресмыка́|ться [1] creep, crawl; *fig.* cringe (to пе́ред Т); **~ющиеся** *n/pl.* [17] reptiles.

пре́сный [14; -сен, -сна́, -о] fresh (*water*); unleavened (*bread*); stale.

пресс *m* [1] ⊕ press; **~а** *f* [5] press; **~-конфере́нция** *f* [7] press conference; **~-папье́** *n* [*ind.*] paperweight.

престаре́лый [14] aged.

престо́л *m* [1] throne; altar.

преступ|а́ть [1], ‹~и́ть› [14] break, infringe; **~ле́ние** *n* [12] crime; на ме́сте ~ле́ния red-handed; **~ник** *m* [1] criminal, delinquent; **~ность** *f* [8] criminality, delinquency.

пресы|ща́ть [1], ‹~тить› [15] surfeit (*v/i.* **-ся**), satiate; **~ще́ние** *n* [12] satiety.

претвор|я́ть [28], ‹~и́ть› [13] change, transform; ~я́ть в жизнь put into practice, realize.

претен|дова́ть [7] (на В) (lay) claim (to); **~зия** *f* [7] claim, pretension, title (to на В, к Д); быть в ~зии (на В [за В]) take (a p.'s [th.]) amiss *or* ill.

преувел|иче́ние *n* [12] exaggeration; **~и́чивать** [1], ‹~и́чить› [16] exaggerate.

преусп|ева́ть [1], ‹~е́ть› [8] succeed; thrive, prosper.

при (П) by, at, near; (*battle*) of; under, in the time of; in a p.'s presence; about (one ~ себе́), with; in (*health*, *weather*, *etc.*); for (all that ~ всём том); when, on (*-ing*); быть ~ have; be attached to; ~ э́том at that; ✝ ~ сём herewith; быть ни ~ чём F have nothing to do with (it тут), not be p.'s fault.

приба́в|ить(ся) *s.* ~ля́ть(ся); **~ка** *f* [5; *g/pl.*: -вок], **~ле́ние** *n* [12] increase, raise; addition; addendum; **~ля́ть** [28], ‹~ить› [14] (В *or* Р) add; increase; put on (*weight* в П); mend (one's pace ~ля́ть шáгу) **-ся** increase; be added; (a)rise; grow longer; **~очный** [14] additional; surplus...

прибалти́йский [16] Baltic.

прибау́тка F *f* [5; *g/pl.:* -ток] byword, saying.

прибе|га́ть [1] **1.** ⟨~жа́ть⟩ [4; -егу́, -ежи́шь, -егу́т] come running; **2.** ⟨∠гнуть⟩ [20] resort, have recourse (to к Д); **~рега́ть** [1], ⟨~ре́чь⟩ [26 г/ж] save, reserve.

прибн|ва́ть [1], ⟨∠ть⟩ [-бью́, -бьёшь, *etc.*, *cf.* бить] fasten, nail; beat (down); throw (*ashore*); **~ра́ть** [1], ⟨прибра́ть⟩ [-беру́, -рёшь; -бра́л, -а́, -о; при́бранный] tidy *or* clean (up); прибра́ть к рука́м appropriate; **-ся** F make o.s. up; **∠ть** *s.* ~ва́ть.

прибли|жа́ть [1], ⟨∠зить⟩ [15] approach, draw near (к Д; *v/i.* **-ся**); approximate; **~же́ние** *n* [12] approach(ing); approximation; **~жённый** [14] confidant; *a.* = **~зи́тельный** [14; -лен, -льна] approximate; **∠зить(ся)** *s.* ~жа́ть(ся).

прибо́й *m* [3] surf.

прибо́р *m* [1] apparatus, instrument; set; cover; service; (*table*)ware; utensils *pl.*, (*shaving*) things *pl.*

прибра́ть *s.* прибира́ть.

прибре́жный [14] littoral.

прибы|ва́ть [1], ⟨∠ть⟩ [-бу́ду, -дешь; при́был, -а́, -о] arrive (in, at в В); increase, rise; **′~ль** *f* [8] profit, gains *pl.*; rise; **′~льный** [14; -лен, -льна] profitable; **∠тие** *n* [12] arrival (in, at в В; upon по П); **∠ть** *s.* ~ва́ть.

прива́л *m* [1] halt, rest.

приве|де́ние *n* [12] putting (*in order* в В); ⚔ reduction; **~сти́** *s.* привози́ть; **~ре́дливый** [14 *sh.*] fastidious.

приве́ржен|ец *m* [1; -нца] adherent; **~ный** [14 *sh.*] attached.

привести́ *s.* приводи́ть.

приве́т *m* [1] greeting(s); *esp.* ⚔ salute; regards, compliments *pl.*; F hello!, hi!; **~ливый** [14 *sh.*] affable; **~ственный** [14] of welcome; **~ствие** *n* [12] greeting, welcome; **~ствовать** [7; *pt. a. pf.*] greet, salute; welcome.

приви|ва́ть [1], ⟨∠ть⟩ [-вью́, -вьёшь, *etc.*, *cf.* вить] inoculate, vaccinate; ⚘ (en)graft; **-ся** take; **∠вка** *f* [5; *g/pl.:* -вок] inoculation, vaccination; grafting; **~де́ние** *n* [12] ghost, specter (*Brt.*-tre), apparition; **~легиро́ванный** [14] privileged; **~ле́гия** *f* [7] privilege; **∠нчивать** [1], ⟨~нти́ть⟩ [15 *e.*; -нчу́, -нти́шь] screw on; **∠ть(ся)** *s.* ~ва́ть(ся).

при́вкус *m* [1] smack (*a. fig.*).

привле|ка́тельный [14; -лен, -льна] attractive; **~ка́ть** [1], ⟨∠чь⟩ [26] draw, attract; engage (in к Д); call (*to account*); bring (*to trial*); **~че́ние** *n* [12] attraction; calling.

приво́д *m* [1] bringing; ⊕ drive; **~и́ть** [15], ⟨привести́⟩ [25] bring; lead; result (in к Д); quote, cite; ⚔ reduce; put, set; drive, throw; **-ся**, ⟨-сь⟩ Д + *vb.* F happen; have to; **~но́й** [14] driving (*belt, etc.*).

привоз|и́ть [15], ⟨привезти́⟩ [24] bring; import; **~но́й** & **∠ный** [14] imported.

приво́лье *n* [10] open (space), expanse; freedom; ease, comfort; в ~ *a.* in clover.

привы|ка́ть [1], ⟨∠кнуть⟩ [21] get *or* be(come) accustomed *or* used (to к Д); **∠чка** *f* [5; *g/pl.:* -чек] habit; custom; **∠чный** [14; -чен, -чна] habitual.

привя́з|анность *f* [8] attachment; **~а́ть(ся)** *s.* ~ывать(ся); **~чивый** F [14 *sh.*] affectionate; captious; obtrusive; **~ывать** [1], ⟨~а́ть⟩ [3] (к Д) tie, attach (to); **-ся** become attached; F run after; intrude (upon); cavil; **′~ь** *f* [8] leash.

пригла|си́тельный [14] invitation...; **~ша́ть** [1], ⟨~си́ть⟩ [15 *e.*; -ашу́, -аси́шь; -ашённый] invite (to *mst* на В), ask; call (*doctor*); **~ше́ние** *n* [12] invitation.

пригна́ть *s.* пригоня́ть.

пригов|а́ривать [1], ⟨~ори́ть⟩ [13] sentence; condemn; *impf.* F say (at the same time); **~о́р** *m* [1] sentence; verdict (*a. fig.*); **~ори́ть** *s.* ~а́ривать.

приго́дный [14; -ден, -дна] *s.* го́дный.

пригоня́ть [28], ⟨пригна́ть⟩ [-гоню́, -го́нишь; -гна́л, -а́, -о; при́гнанный] drive; fit, adjust.

пригор|а́ть [1], ⟨~е́ть⟩ [9] burn; **′~од** *m* [1] suburb; **′~одный** [14] suburban; **′∠шня** *f* [6; *g/pl.:* -ней & -шен] hand(ful).

пригот|а́вливать(ся) [1] *s.* ~овля́ть(ся); **~ови́тельный** [14] preparatory; **~о́вить(ся)** *s.* ~овля́ть (-ся); **~овле́ние** *n* [12] preparation (for к Д); **~овля́ть** [28], ⟨~о́вить⟩ [14] prepare (*v/i.*, o.s. **-ся**) (for к Д).

прида|ва́ть [5], ⟨∠ть⟩ [-да́м, -да́шь, *etc.*, *cf.* дать; при́дал, -а́, -о; при́данный (-ан, -а́, -о)] add; give; attach; **∠ное** *n* [14] dowry; **∠ток** *m* [1; -тка] appendage; *anat.* appendix; **∠точный** [14] *gr.* subordinate (*clause*); **∠ть** *s.* ~ва́ть; **∠ча** *f* [5]: в ∠чу to boot.

придви|га́ть [1], ⟨∠нуть⟩ [20] move up (*v/i.* **-ся**; draw near).

придво́рный [14] court(ier *su. m*).

приде́л|ывать, ⟨~ать⟩ [1] fasten, fix (to к Д).

приде́рж|ивать [1], ⟨~а́ть⟩ [4] hold (back); **-ся** *impf.* (P) adhere to; F hold (on [to]).

приди́р|аться [1], ⟨придра́ться⟩ [-деру́сь, -рёшься; -дра́лся, -ала́сь, -а́лось] (к Д) find fault (with), carp *or* cavil (at); seize; **~ка** *f* [5; *g/pl.:* -рок] cavil; **~чивый** [14 *sh.*] captious.

придра́ться *s.* придира́ться.
приду́м|ывать, ‹~ать› [1] think out, devise, contrive.
придыха́ние *n* [12] aspiration.
прие́з|д *m* [1] arrival (in в В; upon по П); **~жа́ть** [1], ‹прие́хать› [-е́ду, -е́дешь] arrive (in, at в В); **~жий** [17] visitant..., guest...
приём *m* [1] reception; acceptance, admission; consultation; engagement, ⚔ enlistment; taking; dose; movement (with в В); draught; sitting (at в В); device, trick; method, way; **~ник** *m* [1] receiver, receiving set; *s.* радиоприёмник; **~ный** [14] reception (*day*; *room: a.* waiting, *usu. su. f* ~ная), receiving, consultation..., office (*hours*); entrance (*examination*); foster (*father, etc.*; foster child *a.* **~ыш** *m* [1]).
при|е́хать *s.* ~езжа́ть; **~жа́ть(ся)** *s.* ~жима́ть(ся); **~жига́ть** [1], ‹~же́чь› [26 г/ж: -жгу́, -жжёшь; *cf.* жечь] cauterize; **~жима́ть** [1], ‹~жа́ть› [-жму́, -жмёшь; -а́тый] press (to, on к Д); **-ся** press; nestle; **~з** *m* [1] prize; **~заду́м(ыв)аться** *s.* заду́м(ыв)аться.
призва́|ние *n* [12] vocation, calling; **~ть** *s.* призыва́ть.
приземл|я́ться ✈ [28], ‹~и́ться› [13] land; **~е́ние** *n* [12] landing.
при́зма *f* [5] prism.
призна|ва́ть [5], ‹~́ть› [1] (Т; *a.* за В) recognize, acknowledge (as); see, admit, own; find, consider, declare; **-ся** confess (s. th. в П), avow, admit; ~́ться *or* ~ю́сь to tell the truth, frankly speaking; **'~к** *m* [1] sign; feature, characteristic; **~́ние** *n* [12] acknowledg(e)ment, recognition; confession; declaration (of love в любви); **~́тельность** *f* [8] gratitude; **~́тельный** [14; -лен, -льна] grateful, thankful (for за В); **~́ть(ся)** *s.* ~ва́ть(ся).
при́зра|к *m* [1] phantom, specter (*Brt.* -tre); **~чный** [14; -чен, -чна] ghostly; illusive.
призы́в *m* [1] appeal, call (for на В), summons; ⚔ draft, conscription; **~а́ть** [1], ‹призва́ть› [-зову́, -вёшь; -зва́л, -а́, -о; при́званный] call (for на В; to witness в свиде́тели), appeal; ⚔ draft, call out *or* up (for на В); призванный *a.* qualified; **~ни́к** *m* [1 *e.*] draftee, conscript; **~но́й** [14] ⚔ draft(ee)...
при́иск *m* [1] mine, field.
прийти́(сь) *s.* приходи́ть(ся).
прика́з *m* [1] order, command; *hist.* office, board; **~а́ть** *s.* ~ывать; **~чик** *m* [1] † *s.* продаве́ц; steward; **~ывать** [1], ‹~а́ть› [3] order, command; tell; F should, ought; *s. a.* уго́дно.
при|ка́лывать [1], ‹~коло́ть› [17] pin, fasten; stab; **~каса́ться** [1], ‹~косну́ться› [20] (к Д, † Р) touch; **~ки́дывать** [1], ‹~ки́нуть› [20] weigh; calculate; estimate; **-ся** F pretend *or* feign to be, act (the Т).
прикла́д *m* [1] (*rifle*) butt; **~но́й** [14] applied; **~ывать** [1], ‹приложи́ть› [16] (к Д) apply (to), put (on); enclose (with); affix (*seal*); **-ся** kiss; F level; apply (s. th. to Т/к Д).
прикле́и|вать [1], ‹~ть› [13] paste.
приключ|а́ться F [1], ‹~и́ться› [16 *e.*; *3rd p. only*] happen, occur; **~е́ние** *n* [12] (**~е́нческий** [16] of) adventure.
прико́|вывать [1], ‹~ва́ть› [7 *e.*; -кую́, -куёшь] chain, fetter; arrest, captivate; **~ла́чивать** [1], ‹~лоти́ть› [15] nail (on, to к Д), fasten; **~ло́ть** *s.* прика́лывать; **~мандирова́ть** [7] *pf.* attach; **~снове́ние** *n* [12] touch, contact; **~сну́ться** *s.* прикаса́ться.
прикра́|са F *f* [5] embellishment; **~шивать** [1], ‹~сить› [15] embellish.
прикреп|и́ть(ся) *s.* ~ля́ть(ся); **~ле́ние** *n* [12] fastening; attaching; **~ля́ть** [28], ‹~и́ть› [14 *e.*; -плю́, -пи́шь; плённый] fasten; attach; **-ся** register (with к Д).
прикри́к|ивать [1], ‹~нуть› [20] shout (at на В).
прикры|ва́ть [1], ‹~́ть› [22] cover; protect; **~́тие** *n* [12] cover (*a.* ⚔); convoy; *fig.* cloak.
прила́вок *m* [1; -вка] counter.
прилага́|тельное *n* [14] adjective (*a.* и́мя ~тельное); **~ть** [1], ‹приложи́ть› [16] (к Д) enclose (with); apply (to); take (*pains*), make (*efforts*); ~емый enclosed.
прила́|живать [1], ‹~дить› [15] fit.
приле|га́ть [1] **1.** (к Д) (ad)join, border; **2.** ‹~́чь› [26 г/ж: -ля́гу, -ля́жешь, -ля́гут; -лёг, -легла́; -ля́г(те)!] lie down (for a while); fit (closely); **~жа́ние** *n* [12] diligence; **~́жный** [14; -жен, -жна] diligent, industrious; **~пля́ть** [28], ‹~пи́ть› [14] stick; **~та́ть** [1], ‹~те́ть› [11] arrive, fly; **~́чь** *s.* ~га́ть 2.
прили́|в *m* [1] flood, flow; *fig.* rush; **~ва́ть** [1], ‹~ть› [-лью́, -льёшь; *cf.* лить] rush; add; **~па́ть** [1], ‹~пнуть› [21] stick; **~ть** *s.* ~ва́ть.
прили́ч|ие *n* [12] decency (for d.'s sake из *or* для Р), decorum; **~ный** [14; -чен, -чна] decent, proper; F respectable.
прилож|е́ние *n* [12] enclosure; supplement; application; *gr.* apposition; *seal*: affixture; **~и́ть** *s.* прикла́дывать & прилага́ть.
прима́нка *f* [5; *g/pl.*: -нок] bait, lure.
примен|е́ние *n* [12] application; use; adaptation; **~и́мый** [14 *sh.*] applicable; **~я́ть** [28], ‹~и́ть› [13;

-еню́, -е́нишь; -енённый] apply (to к Д); use, employ; **-ся** adapt o.s.
приме́р *m* [1] example (в ~ *cite* as an example); не в ~ F far + *comp.*; к ~у F = наприме́р; **~ивать** [1], ⟨~ить⟩ [13] try *or* fit on; **~ка** *f* [5; *g/pl.*: -рок] trying *or* fitting on; **~ный** [14; -рен, -рна] exemplary; approximate; **~я́ть** [28] = ~ивать.
при́месь *f* [8] admixture.
приме́|та *f* [5] mark, sign, token; omen; *pl.* signalment, description; на ~те in view; **~тить** *s.* ~ча́ть; **~тный** *s.* заме́тный; **~ча́ние** *n* [12] (foot)note; notice; **~ча́тельный** [14; -лен, -льна] notable, remarkable; **~ча́ть** F [1], ⟨~ти́ть⟩ [15] notice; **~шивать** [1], ⟨~ша́ть⟩ [1] add, (ad)mix.
примир|е́ние *n* [12] reconciliation; **~и́тельный** [14; -лен, -льна] (re-)conciliatory; arbitration...; **~и́ть** (**-ся**) [28] *s.* мири́ть(ся).
примити́вный [14; -вен, -вна] primitive.
прим|кну́ть *s.* ~ыка́ть; **~о́рский** [16] coastal, seaside...; **~о́чка** *f* [5; *g/pl.*: -чек] lotion; **∠ула** *f* [5] primrose; **∠ус** *m* [1] kerosene stove; **~ча́ться** [4 *e.*; -мчу́сь, -чи́шься] *pf.* come in a great hurry; **~ыка́ть** [1], ⟨~кну́ть⟩ [20] join (*v/t.* к Д); *impf.* adjoin.
принадл|ежа́ть [4 *e.*; -жу́, -жи́шь] belong (to [к] Д), pertain; **~е́жность** *f* [8] accessory; material, implement; *pl.* *a.* equipment; membership.
принести́ *s.* приноси́ть.
принима́ть [1], ⟨приня́ть⟩ [приму́, -и́мешь; при́нял, -а́, -о; при́нятый (-ят, -а́, -о)] take (*a.* over; for за В; *measures*); accept; receive; admit ([in]to в, на В); pass (*law, etc.*); adopt; assume; ~ на себя́ take (up)on o.s., undertake; ~ на свой счёт feel hurt; ~ пара́д review troops; **-ся** [-нялся́, -ла́сь] (за В) set about *or* to, start; F take to task; ♀, ⚕ take.
приноровить F [14 *e.*; -влю́, -ви́шь] *pf.* adapt; fit.
прин|оси́ть [15], ⟨~ести́⟩ [24 -с-: -есу́; -ёс, -есла́] bring (*a.* forth, in); yield (*a. profit, thanks*); make (*sacrifice* в В); ~оси́ть в дар *s.* дари́ть.
прину|ди́тельный [14; -лен, -льна] forced, compulsory, coercive; **~жда́ть** [1], ⟨∠дить⟩ [15] force, compel, constrain, oblige; **~жде́ние** *n* [12] compulsion, coercion, constraint (under по Д); **~ждённый** [14] forced, constrained, obliged.
при́нцип *m* [1] principle; (on в П, ~иа́льно); **~иа́льный** [14; -лен, -льна] of principle(s) (*a.* из ~а).
приня́|тие *n* [12] taking (over); acceptance; admission ([in]to в, на В); passing (*law, etc.*); adoption; assumption; **'~тый** [14] customary; *cf. a.* **~ть(ся)** → принима́ть(ся).
приобре|та́ть [1], ⟨~сти́⟩ [25 -т-] acquire, obtain, get; buy; **~те́ние** *n* [12] acquisition.
приобщ|а́ть [1], ⟨~и́ть⟩ [16 *e.*; -щу́, -щи́шь; -щённый] (к Д) join, add; **-ся** join.
приостан|а́вливать [1], ⟨~ови́ть⟩ [14] stop (*v/i.* **-ся**); ⚖ suspend.
припа́док *m* [1; -дка] fit, attack.
припа́сы *m/pl.* [1] supplies, stores.
припая́ть [28] *pf.* solder (on to к Д).
припе́|в *m* [1] refrain; **~ва́ть** F [1] sing; ~ва́ючи F in clover; **~ка́ть** [1], ⟨~чь⟩ [26] burn, be hot.
припи́с|ка *f* [5; *g/pl.*: -сок] postscript; addition; **~ывать** [1], ⟨~а́ть⟩ [3] ascribe, attribute (to к Д); add.
припла́та *f* [5] extra payment.
припло́д *m* [1] increase, offspring.
приплы|ва́ть [1], ⟨∠ть⟩ [23] come, arrive, swim *or* sail (up to к Д).
приплю́снутый [14] flat (*nose*).
приподн|има́ть [1], ⟨~я́ть⟩ [-ниму́, -ни́мешь; -по́днял, -а́, -о; -по́днятый (-ят, -а́, -о)] lift *or* raise (**-ся** rise) (a little); **∠ятый** [14] high (*spirits*); elevated (*style*).
приполз|а́ть [1], ⟨~ти́⟩ [24] creep.
припом|ина́ть [1], ⟨∠нить⟩ [13] remember (*a. impers.* Д **-ся** И).
припра́в|а *f* [5] seasoning; **~ля́ть** [28], ⟨~ить⟩ [14] season, dress.
припух|а́ть [1], ⟨∠нуть⟩ [21] swell.
прира́вн|ивать [1], ⟨~я́ть⟩ [28] compare (to к Д); level.
прира|ста́ть [1], ⟨~сти́⟩ [24 -ст-: -стёт; -ро́с, -сла́] take; grow (to к Д); increase (by на В); **~ще́ние** *n* [12] increase; taking.
приро́|да *f* [5] nature (by, *a.* birth от Р [*a.* in]; по Д); **~дный** [14] natural; *a.* = **~ждённый** [14] (in)born; **~ст** *m* [1] increase.
прируч|а́ть [1], ⟨~и́ть⟩ [16 *e.*; -чу́, -чи́шь; -чённый] tame.
при|са́живаться [1], ⟨~се́сть⟩ [25; -ся́ду; -се́л] sit down (a while).
присв|а́ивать [1], ⟨~о́ить⟩ [13] appropriate; adopt; confer ([up]on Д); **~о́ение** *n* [12] appropriation; adoption; conferment.
присе|да́ть [1], ⟨∠сть⟩ [25; -ся́ду; -се́л] squat; curts(e)y; **∠ст** *m* [1] sitting (at, in в В); **∠сть** *s.* ~да́ть & приса́живаться.
приска́к|ивать [1], ⟨~а́ть⟩ [3] come, arrive (at full gallop; leaping).
приско́рб|ие *n* [12] regret; **~ный** [14; -бен, -бна] deplorable, pitiable.
присла́ть *s.* присыла́ть.
прислон|я́ть [28], ⟨~и́ть⟩ [13] lean (*v/i.* **-ся**; against к Д).
прислу́|га *f* [5] servant(s); ⚔ crew, gunners *pl.*; **~живать** [1] wait

(up)on (Д), serve; **-ся** (Д) be subservient (to), ingratiate o. s. (with); **~шиваться, ⟨~шаться⟩** [1] listen (to к Д).
присм|áтривать [1], ⟨**~отрéть**⟩ [9; -отрю́, -óтришь; -óтренный] look after (за Т); F find; **-ся** (к Д) peer, look narrowly (at); examine (closely); familiarize o.s., get acquainted (with, *or* accustomed to); **~óтр** *m* [1] care, supervision; **~отрéть(ся)** *s.* **~áтривать(ся)**.
присовокуп|ля́ть [28], ⟨**~и́ть**⟩ [14 *e.*; -плю́, -пи́шь; -плённый] add; enclose (with к Д).
присоедин|éние *n* [12] joining; connection; annexation; **~я́ть** [28], ⟨**~и́ть**⟩ [13] (к Д) join (*a.* **-ся**); connect, attach (to); annex, incorporate.
приспéшник *m* [1] accomplice.
приспосóб|ить(ся) *s.* **~ля́ть(ся)**; **~лéние** *n* [12] adaptation; device; **~ля́ть** [28], ⟨**~ить**⟩ [14] fit, adapt (o.s. **-ся**; to, for к Д, под В).
при́став *m* [1] (*form.*) police officer.
приста|вáть [5], ⟨**́~ть**⟩ [-áну, -áнешь] (к Д) stick (to); importune, pester; join; ⚓ land; F become; befit; ⚕ be taken (with); **́~вить** *s.* **~вля́ть**; **́~вка** *f* [5; *g/pl.*: -вок] prefix; **~вля́ть** [28], ⟨**́~вить**⟩ [14] (к Д) set, put (to), lean (against); add, piece on; appoint (to look after); **'~льный** [14; -лен, -льна] steadfast; **'~нь** *f* [8; *from g/pl. e.*] quay, wharf, pier; **́~ть** *s.* **~вáть**.
пристёгивать [1], ⟨**пристегну́ть**⟩ [20] button *or* fasten (to).
пристр|áивать [1], ⟨**~óить**⟩ [13] (к Д) add *or* attach (to); settle; place; provide; **-ся** F = устрáиваться; join.
пристрáст|ие *n* [12] predilection (for к Д); bias; **~ный** [14; -тен, -тна] bias(s)ed, partial (to к Д).
пристрéли|вать [1], ⟨**́~ть**⟩ [13; -стрелю́, -éлишь] shoot.
пристр|óить(ся) *s.* **~áивать(ся)**; **~óйка** *f* [5; *g/pl.*: -óек] addition; annex.
при́ступ *m* [1] assault, onset, onslaught, storm (by Т); ⚕ & *fig.* fit, attack; F access; **~áть** [1], ⟨**~и́ть**⟩ [14] set about, start, begin; proceed (to); approach (*a.*, F, **-ся**).
прису|ждáть [1], ⟨**~ди́ть**⟩ [15; -уждённый] (к Д) sentence, condemn (to); award; **~ждéние** *n* [12] awarding.
прису́тств|ие *n* [12] presence (in в П; of mind ду́ха); † office (hours); **~овать** [7] be present (at на, в, при П); **~ующий** [17] present.
прису́щий [17 *sh.*] peculiar (to Д).
прис|ылáть [1], ⟨**~лáть**⟩ [-шлю́, -шлёшь; при́сланный] send (for за Т); **~ыпáть** [1], ⟨**~ы́пать**⟩ [2] (be)strew.
прися́|га *f* [5] oath (upon под Т); **~гáть** [1], ⟨**~гну́ть**⟩ [20] swear; **~жный** [14] juror; суд **~жных** jury.
прита|и́ть [13] *pf.* F *s.* затаи́ть; **-ся** hold (*breath*); hide; keep quiet; **́~скивать** [1], ⟨**~щи́ть**⟩ [16] drag (o.s. **-ся** F; [up] to к Д); F bring (come).
притвор|я́ть(ся) *s.* **~я́ть(ся)**; **́~ный** [14; -рен, -рна] feigned, pretended, sham; **́~ство** *n* [9] pretense, dissimulation; **~я́ть** [28], ⟨**~и́ть**⟩ [13; -орю́, -óришь; -óренный] close; leave ajar; **-ся** [13] feign, pretend (to be Т).
притесн|éние *n* [12] oppression; **~и́тель** *m* [4] oppressor; **~я́ть** [28], ⟨**~и́ть**⟩ [13] oppress; † press.
притих|áть [1], ⟨**́~нуть**⟩ [21] become silent, stop; abate (*wind*).
притóк *m* [1] tributary; afflux.
притóм besides; to that *or* it.
притóн *m* [1] den, nest.
при́торный [14; -рен, -рна] sugary, luscious.
притр|áгиваться [1], ⟨**~óнуться**⟩ [20] touch (slightly; *v/t.* к Д).
притуп|ля́ть [28], ⟨**~и́ть**⟩ [14] (**-ся** become) blunt, dull.
при́тча *f* [5] parable.
притя́|гивать [1], ⟨**~ну́ть**⟩ [19] draw, pull; attract; F *s.* привлекáть; **~жáтельный** [14] possessive; **~жéние** *n* [12] attraction; **~зáние** *n* [12] claim, pretension (to на В); **~ну́ть** *s.* **~гивать**.
приу|рóчить [16] *pf.* time, date (for к Д); **~чáть** [1], ⟨**~чи́ть**⟩ [16] accustom, habituate; train.
при|хвáрывать F [1], ⟨**~хворну́ть**⟩ [20] be(come *pf.*) unwell *or* sickly.
прихóд *m* [1] arrival, coming; † receipt(s), credit; parish; **~и́ть** [15], ⟨**прийти́**⟩ [приду́, -дёшь; пришёл, -шлá; -шéдший; *g. pt.*: придя́] come (to), arrive (in, at в, на В; for за Т); *fig.* fall, get, fly (into в В); (Д) **~и́ть** в гóлову, на ум, *etc.* think of, hit on (the idea), take into one's head; *not: a.* dream; **~и́ть** в себя́ (*or* чу́вство) come to (o.s.); **-ся**, ⟨**~сь**⟩ suit, fit ([p.'s] s. th. [Д] по Д), be (to; Т p.'s *aunt, etc.*); fall (on в В; to на В); мне **~ится** I have to, must; придётся *a.* = попáло, *s.* попáсть; **~ный** [14] receipt...; **~o-~расхóдный** [14] cash(*book*); **~ский** [16] parish...; **~я́щий** [17] day (*servant*); ⚕ ambulatory.
прихож|áнин *m* [1; *pl.* -áне, -áн] parishioner; **́~ая** *f* [17] *s.* перéдняя.
прихот|ли́вый [14 *sh.*] freakish; fastidious; **'~ь** *f* [8] whim, freak.
прихрáмывать [1] limp slightly.
прицéл *m* [1] sight; *a.* = **~ивание** *n* [12] (taking) aim; **~иваться** [1], ⟨**~иться**⟩ [13] (take) aim (at в В).
прицéп *m* [1] trailer; **~ка** *f* [5; *g/pl.*:

-пок] coupling; **~ля́ть** [28], ⟨~и́ть⟩ [14] hook (on; to к Д); couple; **-ся** stick, cling; *s. a.* приста́(ва́)ть; **~но́й** [14]: ~но́й ваго́н *m* = ~.

прича́л *m* [1] mooring(s); **~ивать** [1], ⟨~ить⟩ [13] moor; land.

прича́|стие *n* [12] *gr.* participle; *eccl.* Eucharist; F = ~щение; **~стный** [14; -тен, -тна] participating *or* involved (in к Д); **~ща́ть** [1], ⟨~сти́ть⟩ [15 *e.*; -ащу́, -asти́шь; -ащённый] administer (**-ся** receive) the Lord's Supper *or* Sacraments; **~ще́ние** *n* [12] administration of the Lord's Supper.

причём: … ~ изве́стно, что … = … it being known that …

причёс|ка *f* [5; *g/pl.*: -сок] hairdo (*Brt.* -dress), coiffure; **~ывать** [1], ⟨причеса́ть⟩ [3] do, brush, comb (one's hair **-ся**).

причи́н|а *f* [5] cause; reason (for по Д); по ~е because of; **~ность** *f* [8] causality; **~ный** [14] causal; **~я́ть** [28], ⟨~и́ть⟩ [13] cause, do.

причи|сля́ть [28], ⟨~сли́ть⟩ [13] rank, number (among к Д); ⚔ assign; F add; **~та́ние** *n* [12] lamentation; **~та́ть** [1] lament; **~та́ться** [1] be due, (p.: с Р) have to pay.

причу́д|а *f* [5] whim, freak; **~ливый** [14 *sh.*] freakish; cranky.

при|ше́лец *m* [1; -льца] newcomer, arrival; **~ши́бленный** F [14] dejected; **~шива́ть** [1], ⟨~ши́ть⟩ [-шью́, -шьёшь, *etc.*, *cf.* шить] (к Д) sew ([on] to); F involve (in), impose ([up]on); **~шпо́рить** [13] *pf.* spur on; **~щемля́ть** [28], ⟨~щеми́ть⟩ [14 *e.*; -млю́, -ми́шь; -млённый] pinch, squeeze in; **~щу́ривать** [1], ⟨~щу́рить⟩ [13] *s.* жму́рить.

прию́т *m* [1] refuge, shelter; asylum, orphanage; **~и́ть** [15 *e.*; -ючу́, -юти́шь] *pf.* shelter (*v/i.* **-ся**).

прия́|тель *m* [4], **~тельница** *f* [5] friend; **~тельский** [16] friendly; **~тный** [14; -тен, -тна] pleasant, pleasing, agreeable.

про F (В) about, of; ~ **себя́** to o.s., (*read*) silently.

про́ба *f* [5] trial (on [= probation] на В), test; ⊕ assay, sample; standard, hallmark.

пробе́|г *m* [1] run, race; **~га́ть** [1], ⟨~жа́ть⟩ [4 *e.*; -егу́, -ежи́шь, -гу́т] run (through, over), pass (by); cover; skim.

пробе́л *m* [1] blank, gap; defect.

проби|ва́ть [1], ⟨~ть⟩ [-бью́, -бьёшь; -бе́й(те)!; проби́л, -а, -о] break through; pierce, punch; *s. a.* бить 2.; **-ся** fight (*or* make) one's way (through сквозь В); *fig.* F rough it; ⚘ come up; shine through; *pf.* toil (at над Т); **~ра́ть** [1], ⟨пробра́ть⟩ [-беру́, -рёшь; *cf.* брать] F scold; blow up, upbraid; **-ся** [-бра́лся, -ла́сь, -ло́сь] make one's way (through сквозь В); steal *or* slip; **~рка** *f* [5; *g/pl.*: -рок] test tube; **~ть(ся)** *s.* ~ва́ть(ся).

про́бк|а *f* [5; *g/pl.*: -бок] cork; stopper, plug; ⚡ fuse; *traffic*: jam; **~овый** [14] cork…

пробле́ма *f* [5] problem; **~ти́ческий** [16], **~ти́чный** [14; -чен, -чна] problematic(al).

про́блеск *m* [1] gleam; flash.

про́б|ный [14] trial…, test…; specimen…, sample…; touch(*stone*); pilot (*balloon*); **~овать** [7], ⟨по-⟩ try; taste.

пробо́ина *f* [5] hole; ⚓ leak.

пробо́р *m* [1] (hair) parting.

про́бочник *m* [1] corkscrew.

пробра́ться *s.* пробира́ть(ся).

пробу|жда́ть [1], ⟨~ди́ть⟩ [15; -уждённый] waken, rouse; **-ся** awake, wake up; **~жде́ние** *n* [12] awakening.

пробы́ть [-бу́ду, -бу́дешь; про́бы́л, -а́, -о] *pf.* stay.

прова́л *m* [1] collapse; *fig.* failure; **~ивать** [1], ⟨~и́ть⟩ [13; -алю́, -а́лишь; -а́ленный] wreck; fail; reject; *thea.* damn; ~ивай(те)! F decamp; **-ся** break *or* fall in; fail, flunk; *thea.* be damned; disappear; ~и́сь! F the deuce take you!

прова́нский [16] olive (*oil*).

прове́|дать F [1] *pf.* visit; find out; **~де́ние** *n* [12] carrying out, realization; construction, installation; **~зти́** *s.* провози́ть; **~рить** *s.* ~ря́ть; **~рка** *f* [5; *g/pl.*: -рок] check(up), examination, control; **~ря́ть** [28], ⟨~рить⟩ [13] examine, check (up), control; **~сти́** *s.* проводи́ть; **~трива́ть** [1], ⟨~трить⟩ [13] air, ventilate.

прови|а́нт *m* [1] *s.* ~зия; **~зия** *f* [7] provisions, foodstuffs, victuals *pl.*; **~ни́ться** [13] *pf.* commit offence, be guilty (of в П), offend (p. пе́ред Т; with в П); **~нциа́льный** [14; -лен, -льна] provincial; **~нция** *f* [7] province.

про́во|д *m* [1; *pl.*: -да́, *etc. e.*] wire, line; cable; lead; **~ди́мость** *f* [8] conductivity; **~ди́ть** [15] **1.** ⟨провести́⟩ [25] lead, *a.* ⚡, *impf.* conduct, guide; carry out (*or* through), realize, put (*into practice*); put *or* get through; pass; spend (*time*; at за Т); draw (*line, etc.*); lay, construct; develop (*idea*); pursue (*policy*); hold (*meeting*); ✝ enter, book; *pf.* F trick, cheat; **2.** *s.* ~жа́ть; **~дка** *f* [5; *g/pl.*: -док] construction, installation; ⚡ lead; *tel.* line, wire(s); **~дни́к** *m* [1 *e.*] guide; 🚂, ⚡ conductor (*Brt.* 🚂 guard); **~жа́ть** [1], ⟨~ди́ть⟩ [15] see (off), accompany; follow; **~з** *m* [1] transport(ation).

провозгла|ша́ть [1], ⟨~си́ть⟩ [15 *e.*; -ашу́, -аси́шь; -ашённый] proclaim; propose (*toast*).

провози́ть [15], ⟨провезти́⟩ [24] drive, convey; take, get, carry.
провока́|тор *m* [1] agent provocateur; **~ция** *f* [7] provocation.
прово́л|ока *f* [5] wire; **~о́чка** F *f* [5; *g/pl.*: -чек] delay (in с T), protraction.
прово́р|ный [14; -рен, -рна] quick, nimble, deft; **~ство** *n* [9] quickness, nimbleness, deftness.
провоци́ровать [7] (*im*)*pf*., *a*. ⟨с-⟩ provoke (to на B).
прогада́ть F [1] *pf*. lose (by на П).
прога́лина *f* [5] glade; patch, spot.
прогл|а́тывать [1], ⟨**~оти́ть**⟩ [15] swallow, gulp; F lose (*tongue*); **~я́дывать** [1] **1.** ⟨**~яде́ть**⟩ [11] overlook; look over (*or* through); **2.** ⟨**~яну́ть**⟩ [19] peep out, appear.
прогн|а́ть *s*. прогоня́ть; **~о́з** *m* [1] forecast; ⚕ prognosis.
прого|ва́ривать [1], ⟨**~вори́ть**⟩ [13] say; talk; **-ся** blab (*v/t*. о П); **~лода́ться** [1] *pf*. get *or* feel hungry; **~ня́ть** [28], ⟨прогна́ть⟩ [-гоню́, -го́нишь; -гна́л, -а́, -о; про́гнанный] drive (away); F *fig*. banish; F fire; run (the gantlet сквозь строй); **~ра́ть** [1], ⟨**~ре́ть**⟩ [9] burn through; F smash (up).
програ́мма *f* [5] program(me *Brt*.).
прогре́сс *m* [1] progress; **~и́вный** [14; -вен, -вна] progressive; **~и́ровать** [7] (make) progress.
прогрыз|а́ть [1], ⟨**~ть**⟩ [24; *pt. st*.] gnaw *or* bite through.
прогу́л *m* [1] truancy; **~ивать** [1], ⟨**~я́ть**⟩ [28] shirk (work), play truant; **-ся** take (*or* go for a) walk; **~ка** *f* [5; *g/pl*.: -лок] walk (for на B), stroll, ride; **~ьщик** *m* [1] shirker, truant; **~я́ть(ся)** *s*. **~ивать(ся)**.
прода|ва́ть [5], ⟨**~ть**⟩ [-да́м, -да́шь, *etc*., *cf*. дать; про́дал, -а́, -о; про́данный (про́дан, -а́, -о)] sell (*v/i*. **-ся**; *a*. = be for *or* on sale); **~ве́ц** *m* [1; -вца́], **~вщи́ца** *f* [5] seller, sales(wo)man, (store) clerk, *Brt*. shop assistant; **~жа** *f* [5] sale (on в П; for в B); **~жный** [14] for sale; [-жен, -жна] venal, corrupt; **~ть** (**-ся**) *s*. **~ва́ть(ся)**.
продви|га́ть [1], ⟨**~нуть**⟩ [20] move, push (ahead); **-ся** advance; **~же́ние** *n* [12] advance(ment).
проде́л|ать *s*. **~ывать**; **~ка** *f* [5; *g/pl*.: -лок] trick, prank; **~ывать**, ⟨**~ать**⟩ [1] break through, make; carry through *or* out, do; F play (*trick*).
проде́ть [-де́ну, -де́нешь; -де́нь (-те)!; -де́тый] *pf*. pass through, thread.
продл|ева́ть [1], ⟨**~и́ть**⟩ [13] prolong; **~е́ние** *n* [12] prolongation.
продово́льств|енный [14] food...; grocery...; **~ие** *n* [12] food(stuffs), provisions *pl*.
продол|гова́тый [14 *sh*.] oblong; **~жа́тель** *m* [4] continuator; **~жа́ть** [1], ⟨**~жить**⟩ [16] continue, go on; lengthen; prolong; **-ся** last; **~же́ние** *n* [12] continuation; sequel; course (in в B); **~же́ние сле́дует** to be continued; **~жи́тельность** *f* [8] duration; **~жи́тельный** [14; -лен, -льна] long; **~жить** (**-ся**) *s*. **~жа́ть(ся)**; **~ьный** [14] longitudinal.
продро́гнуть [21] *pf*. be chilled (to the marrow).
проду́к|т *m* [1] product; material; *pl*. *a*. (food)stuffs; **~ти́вный** [14; -вен, -вна] productive; **~то́вый** [14] grocery (*store*); **~ция** *f* [7] production (= product[s]), output.
проду́м|ывать, ⟨**~ать**⟩ [1] think over.
про|еда́ть [1], ⟨**~е́сть**⟩ [-е́м, -е́шь, *etc*., *cf*. есть[1]] eat away *or* through; F spend (on eating); eat.
прое́з|д *m* [1] passage, thoroughfare (no t.! **~а** нет!); **~ом** on the way, in passing; transient(ly); **~дить** *s*. **~жа́ть**; **~дно́й** [14]: **~дно́й** биле́т *m* ticket; **~дна́я** пла́та *f* fare; **~жа́ть** [1] **1.** ⟨прое́хать⟩ [-е́ду, -е́дешь; -езжа́й(те)!] pass, drive *or* ride through (*or* past, by); travel; **-ся** F take a drive *or* ride; **2.** ⟨**~дить**⟩ [15] break in (*horse*); F spend (on fare *or* in driving, riding); **~жий** [17] (through) traveller, transient; **~жая** доро́га *f* highway.
прое́к|т *m* [1] project, plan, scheme; draft; **~ти́ровать** [7], ⟨с-⟩ project, plan: **~цио́нный** [14]: **~цио́нный** аппара́т *m* projector.
прое́|сть *s*. **~да́ть**; **~хать** *s*. **~зжа́ть**.
проже́ктор *m* [1] searchlight.
прожи|ва́ть [1], ⟨**~ть**⟩ [-иву́, -ивёшь; про́жил, -а́, -о; про́житый (про́жит, -а́, -о)] live; F spend; **~га́ть** [1], ⟨проже́чь⟩ [26 г/ж: -жгу́, -жжёшь] burn (through); **~га́ть** жизнь F live fast; **~точный** [14]: **~точный** ми́нимум *m* living wage; **~ть** *s*. **~ва́ть**.
прожо́рлив|ость *f* [8] gluttony, voracity; **~ый** [14 *sh*.] gluttonous.
про́за *f* [5] prose; **~ик** *m* [1] prose writer; **~и́ческий** [16] prosaic.
про́|звище *n* [11] nickname; по **~звищу** nicknamed; **~зва́ть** *s*. **~зыва́ть**; **~зева́ть** F [1] *pf*. miss; let slip; **~зорли́вый** [14 *sh*.] perspicacious; **~зра́чный** [14; -чен, -чна] transparent; **~зре́ть** [9] *pf*. recover one's sight: see, perceive; **~зыва́ть** [1], ⟨**~зва́ть**⟩ [-зову́, -вёшь; -зва́л, -а́, -о; про́званный] (T) nickname; **~зяба́ть** [1] vegetate; **~зя́бнуть** F [21] *s*. продро́гнуть.
проигр|ывать [1], ⟨**~а́ть**⟩ [1] lose (at play); F play; **-ся** lose all one's money; **'~ыш** *m* [1] loss (в П lose).

произв|еде́ние *n* [12] work, product(ion); **~ести́** *s.* ~оди́ть; **~оди́тель** *m* [4] producer; **~оди́тельность** *f* [8] productivity; output; **~оди́тельный** [14; -лен, -льна] productive; **~оди́ть** [15], ⟨~ести́⟩ [25] (**-ся** *impf.* be) make (made), carry (-ried) out, execute(d), effect (-ed); (⊕ *usu. impf.*) produce(d); bring forth; promote(d [to the rank of] [в И *pl.*]); *impf.* derive(d; from от P); **~о́дный** [14] derivative (*a. su. f* ⅍); **~о́дственный** [14] production...; manufacturing; works...; industrial; **~о́дство** *n* [9] production, manufacture; plant, works, factory (at на П); execution; promotion.

произ|во́л *m* [1] arbitrariness; mercy; despotism, tyranny; **~во́льный** [14; -лен, -льна] arbitrary; **~носи́ть** [15], ⟨~нести́⟩ [24 -с-] pronounce; deliver, make (*speech*); utter; **~ноше́ние** *n* [12] pronunciation; **~ойти́** *s.* происходи́ть.

про́нс|ки *m/pl.* [1] intrigues; **~ходи́ть** [15], ⟨произойти́⟩ [-зойдёт; -зошёл, -шла́; *g. pt.*: произойдя́] take place, happen; arise, originate (from от P); descend (from от, из P); **~хожде́ние** *n* [12] origin (by [= birth] по Д), descent; **~ше́ствие** *n* [12] incident, occurrence, event.

про|йти́(сь) *s.* ~ходи́ть & ~ха́живаться).

прок F *m* [1] *s.* по́льза & впрок.

прока́з|а *f* [5] prank, mischief; ⚕ leprosy; **~ник** *m* [1], **~ница** *f* [5] F *s.* шалу́н(ья); **~ничать** [1] F *s.* шали́ть.

прока́|лывать [1], ⟨проколо́ть⟩ [17] pierce, stick, stab; **~пывать** [1], ⟨прокопа́ть⟩ [1] dig (through); **~рмливать** [1], ⟨прокорми́ть⟩ [14] support, nourish; feed; **-ся** F subsist (on, by T).

прока́т *m* [1] hire (for на B), lease; (*film, etc.*) distribution; отда́ть в ~ hire out; **~а́ть(ся)** [15] *pf.* give (take) a drive *or* ride; **~ный** [14] rolled (*iron*); rolling (*mill*); for hire; lending; **~ывать**, ⟨~а́ть⟩ [1] mangle; ⊕ roll; ride; **-ся** F *s.* ~и́ться.

прокла́д|ка *f* [5; *g/pl.*: -док] laying; construction; packing; lining; **~ывать** [1], ⟨проложи́ть⟩ [16] lay (*a.* = build); *fig.* pave; force (one's *way* себе́), interlay; draw.

проклама́ция *f* [7] leaflet.

прокл|ина́ть [1], ⟨~я́сть⟩ [-яну́, -янёшь; про́клял, -а́, -о; про́клятый (про́клят, -а́, -о)] curse, damn; **~я́тие** *n* [12] damnation; **~я́тый** [14] cursed, damned.

проко́|л *m* [1] perforation; **~ло́ть** *s.* прока́лывать; **~па́ть** *s.* прока́пывать; **~рми́ть(ся)** *s.* прока́рмливать(ся); **~рмле́ние** *n* [12] support.

прокра́|дываться [1], ⟨~сться⟩ [25; *pt. st.*] steal; go stealthily.

прокуро́р *m* [1] public prosecutor.

про|лага́ть *s.* ~кла́дывать; **~ла́мывать**, ⟨~лома́ть⟩ [1] & ⟨~ломи́ть⟩ [14] break (through; *v/i.* **-ся**); fracture; **~лега́ть** [1] run; **~леза́ть** [1], ⟨~ле́зть⟩ [24 *st.*] creep *or* get (in[to]); **~лёт** *m* [1] passage; flight; ⚠ span; well; **~летариа́т** *m* [1] proletariat; **~лета́рий** *m* [3], **~лета́рский** [16] proletarian; **~лета́ть** [1], ⟨~лете́ть⟩ [11] fly (past, by, over), pass (by, quickly); **~лётка** *f* [5; *g/pl.*: -ток] droshky.

проли́|в *m* [1] strait (*e.g.* Strait of Dover ~в Па-де-Кале́); **~ва́ть** [1], ⟨~ть⟩ [-лью́, -льёшь; -ле́й(те)!; про́ли́л, -а́, -о; про́ли́тый (про́ли́т, -а́, -о)] spill (*v/i.* **-ся**); shed; **~вно́й** [14]: ~вно́й дождь *m* downpour, cloudburst; **~ть** *s.* ~ва́ть.

проло́|г *m* [1] prologue; **~жи́ть** *s.* прокла́дывать; **~м** *m* [1] breach; fracture; **~ма́ть**, **~ми́ть** *s.* прола́мывать.

про́мах *m* [1] miss; blunder (make дать *or* сде́лать; *a.* miss, fail; F fool); **~́иваться** [1], ⟨~ну́ться⟩ [20] miss; blunder.

промедле́ние *n* [12] delay.

промежу́то|к *m* [1; -тка] interval (at в П; ... of в B); period; **~чный** [14] intermediate.

проме|лькну́ть *s.* мелька́ть; **~́нивать** [1], ⟨~ня́ть⟩ [28] exchange (for на B); **~рза́ть** [1], ⟨промёрзнуть⟩ [21] freeze (through); F *s.* продро́гнуть.

промо|ка́тельный [14]: ~ка́тельная бума́га *f* blotting paper; **~ка́ть** [1], ⟨~́кнуть⟩ [21] get wet *or* drenched; **~лча́ть** [4 *e.*; -чу́, -чи́шь] *pf.* keep silent; **~чи́ть** [16] *pf.* wet, drench.

промтова́ры *m/pl.* [1] *s.* ширпотре́б.

промча́ться [4] *pf.* dash *or* fly (past, by).

промы|ва́ть [1], ⟨~́ть⟩ [22] wash (out, away); ⚕ irrigate.

про́мыс|ел *m* [1; -сла] trade, (line of) business; (*oil, gold*) field; (*salt, etc.*) works; **~ло́вый** [14] trade(s) ...; **~́ть** *s.* ~ва́ть.

промы́шлен|ник *m* [1] industrialist; **~ность** *f* [8] industry; **~ный** [14] industrial.

пронести́(сь) *s.* проноси́ть(ся).

прон|за́ть [1], ⟨~зи́ть⟩ [15*e.*; -нжу́, -нзи́шь; -нзённый] pierce, stab; **~зи́тельный** [14; -лен, -льна] shrill, piercing, penetrating; **~и́зывать** [1], ⟨~иза́ть⟩ [3] penetrate, pierce.

прони|ка́ть [1], ⟨~́кнуть⟩ [21] penetrate; permeate; get (in); spread; **-ся** be imbued *or* inspired (with T); **~кнове́ние** *n* [12] penetration; fervo(u)r; **~кнове́нный** [14; -е́нен, -е́нна] feeling, heartfelt, pathetic; **~ца́емый** [14 *sh.*] permeable; **~ца́тельный** [14; -лен, -льна] penetrating, searching; acute, shrewd; **~ца́ть** *s.* **~ка́ть.**

про|носи́ть [15] **1.** ⟨**~нести́**⟩ [24 -с-: -есу́; -ёс, -есла́] carry (through, by, away); speed; **-ся,** ⟨**-сь**⟩ fly (past, by), pass *or* spread (swiftly); **2.** *pf.* F wear out; **~ны́рливый** [14 *sh.*] crafty; **~ню́хать** P [1] smell out.

прообраз *m* [1] prototype.

пропага́нд|и́ровать [7] propagandize; **~и́стский** [16] propagandist...; propaganda...

пропа|да́ть [1], ⟨**~сть**⟩ [25; *pt. st.*] get *or* be lost, be gone (wasted); be (missing; *a.* **~сть** бе́з вести); lose, fail; vanish; perish, die; **~жа** *f* [5] loss; **~сть¹** *s.* **~да́ть**; **'~сть²** *f* [8] precipice, abyss; chasm, gap; disaster; F lots *or* a lot (of).

пропи|ва́ть [1], ⟨**~ть**⟩ [-пью́, -пьёшь; -пе́й(те)!; про́пи́л, -а́, -о; про́питый (про́пит, -а́, -о)] spend (on drinking); drink.

прописа|ть(ся) *s.* **~ывать(ся)**; **~ска** *f* [5; *g/pl.*: -сок] registration; **~но́й** [14] capital, *cf.* бу́ква; common; registration...; **~ывать** [1], ⟨**~а́ть**⟩ [3] prescribe (for Д), order; register (*v/i.* **-ся**); **'~ью** (*write*) in full.

пропи|та́ние *n* [12] livelihood, living (*earn* one's себе́ на В); **~тывать,** ⟨**~та́ть**⟩ [1] (**-ся** be[come]) impregnate(d), imbue(d; with Т); **~ть** *s.* **~ва́ть.**

проплы|ва́ть [1], ⟨**~ть**⟩ [23] swim *or* sail (by, under); pass; strut.

пропове́д|ник *m* [1] preacher; **~овать** [1] preach; **~ь** ('prɔ-) *f* [8] *eccl.* sermon; propagation.

пропол|за́ть [1], ⟨**~зти́**⟩ [24] creep (by, through, under); **~ка** *f* [5] weeding.

пропорциона́льный [14; -лен, -льна] proportional, proportionate.

про́пус|к *m* [1] **1.** ommission, blank; absence; **2.** [*pl.*: -ка́, *etc. e.*] pass(-age); ⚔ password; **~ка́ть** [1], ⟨**~ти́ть**⟩ [15] let pass (*or* through); pass; omit; miss; let slip; *impf.* leak; **~кно́й** [14] blotting (*paper*).

прора|ба́тывать, ⟨**~бо́тать**⟩ F, [1] study; **~ста́ть** [1], ⟨**~сти́**⟩ [24 -ст-: -стёт; -рос, -росла́] grow (through); come up.

прорва́ть(ся) *s.* прорыва́ть(ся).

прорез|а́ть [1], ⟨**~ать**⟩ [3] cut (through); **-ся** cut (*teeth*); **~и́ненный** [14] gummed.

проре́ха *f* [5] slit, hole, tear.

проро́|к *m* [1] prophet; **~ни́ть** [13; -оню́, -о́нишь; -о́ненный] *pf.* utter; **~ческий** [16] prophetic(al); **~чество** *n* [9] prophecy; **~чить** [16] prophesy.

проруб|а́ть [1], ⟨**~и́ть**⟩ [14] cut (through); **'~ь** *f* [8] ice-hole.

прор|ы́в *m* [1] break; breach; gap, arrear(s), hitch; **~ыва́ть** [1] **1.** ⟨**~ва́ть**⟩ [-ву́, -вёшь; -ва́л, -а́, -о; про́рванный (-ан, -а́, -о)] tear; break through (*v/i.* **-ся**; burst open; force one's way); **2.** ⟨**~ы́ть**⟩ [22] dig (through).

про|са́чиваться [1], ⟨**~сочи́ться**⟩ [16 *e.*; *3rd p. only*] ooze (out), percolate; **~сверли́ть** [13] *pf.* bore (through).

просве́|т *m* [1] gleam, glimpse; chink; ⚓ bay, opening; *fig.* hope; **~ти́тельный** [14] of enlightenment; educational; **~ти́ть** *s.* **~ща́ть** *&* **~чивать 2.**; **~тле́ть** [8] *pf.* clear up, brighten; **~чивать** [1] **1.** shine through, be seen; **2.** ⟨**~ти́ть**⟩ [15] radiograph, X-ray; test (*egg*); **~ща́ть** [1], ⟨**~ти́ть**⟩ [15 *e.*; -ещу́, -ети́шь; -ещённый] enlighten, educate, instruct; **~ще́ние** *n* [12] enlightenment, education, instruction.

про́|седь *f* [8] grayish (*Brt.* greyish), grizzly (hair); **~се́ивать** [1], ⟨**~се́ять**⟩ [27] sift; **~сека** *f* [5] glade; **~сёлок** *m* [1; -лка] = **~сёлочная** доро́га; **~сёлочный** [14]: **~сёлочная** доро́га *f* by-road, field path; **~се́ять** *s.* **~се́ивать.**

проси́|живать [1], ⟨**~де́ть**⟩ [11] sit (up); stay, remain; spend; F wear out; **~тель** *m* [4], **~тельница** *f* [5] petitioner, applicant; **~ть** [15], ⟨по-⟩ ask (p. for В/о П; у Р/Р, *a.* beg p.'s), request; entreat; invite; intercede (for за В); прошу́, про́сят *a.* please; **-ся** (в, на В) ask (for; leave [to enter, go]; F suggest o. s.; **~я́ть** [28] *pf.* shine forth, brighten.

проск|ользну́ть [20] *pf.* slip (into в В); **~очи́ть** [16] *pf.* jump *or* slip (by, through, in[to]).

просл|авля́ть [28], ⟨**~а́вить**⟩ [14] glorify, make (**-ся** become) famous; **~еди́ть** [15 *e.*; -ежу́, -еди́шь; -е́женный] *pf.* follow up; **~ези́ться** [15 *e.*; -ежу́сь, -ези́шься] *pf.* shed tears.

просло́йка *f* [5; *g/pl.*: -о́ек] streak, layer.

про|слу́шать [1] *pf.* hear; ⚕ auscultate; F miss; **~сма́тривать** [1], ⟨**~смотре́ть**⟩ [9; -отрю́, -о́тришь; -о́тренный] look through *or* over; overlook; **~смо́тр** *m* [1] examination, review, revision; oversight; **~сну́ться** *s.* **~сыпа́ться**; **~со** *n* [9] millet; **~со́вывать** [1], ⟨**~су́нуть**⟩ [20] pass *or* push (through); **~со́хнуть** *s.* **~сыха́ть**; **~сочи́ться** *s.* **~са́чиваться**; **~спа́ть** *s.* **~сыпа́ть.**

проспе́кт *m* [1] avenue; prospectus.

просро́ч|ивать [1], ⟨**~ить**⟩ [16] let lapse, expire; exceed; **~ка** *f* [5; *g/pl.*: -чек] expiration; exceeding.

прост|а́ивать [1], ⟨**~оя́ть**⟩ [-ою́,

-ойшь] stand; stay; **~áк** *m* [1 *e.*] simpleton; **~ёнок** *m* [1; -нка] pier.

прост|ирáть [1], ‹~ерéть› [12] stretch (out; *v/i.* **-ся**), extend.

простúтельный [14; -лен, -льна] pardonable, excusable, venial.

проститýтка *f* [5; *g/pl.*: -ток] prostitute.

простúть(ся) *s.* прощáть(ся).

простодýш|ие *n* [12] naïveté; **~ный** [14; -шен, -шна] simple-minded, ingenuous, artless.

простóй 1. [14; прост, -á, -о; *comp.*: прóще] simple, plain; easy; artless, unsophisticated; ordinary, common; prime (*number*); **2.** *m* [3] stoppage, standstill.

простоквáша *f* [5] curdled milk.

простó|р *m* [1] open (space); freedom (in на П); scope; **~рéчие** *n* [12] language of the (uneducated) people; vernacular; **~рный** [14; -рен, -рна] spacious, roomy; **~сердéчный** [14; -чен, -чна] *s.* ~дýшный; **~тá** *f* [5] simplicity; naïveté; silliness; **~фúля** *m/f* F [6] ninny; **~ять** *s.* простáивать.

прострáн|ный [14; -áнен, -áнна] vast; diffuse; **~ство** *n* [9] space; room; area.

прострéл *m* [1] lumbago; **~ивать** [1], ‹~úть› [13; -елю́, -éлишь; -éленный] shoot (through).

простý|да *f* [5] cold; **~живать** [1], ‹~дúть› [15] chill; **-ся** catch a cold.

простýпок *m* [1; -пка] offence.

простынá *f* [6; *pl.*: прóстыни, -ы́нь, *etc. e.*] (*bed*) sheet.

просý|нуть *s.* просóвывать; **~шивать** [1], ‹~шúть› [16] dry (up).

просфорá *f* [5; *pl.*: прóсфоры, -фóр, *etc. e.*] *eccl.* Host.

просчитáться [1] *pf.* miscalculate.

просыпáть [1], ‹проспáть› [-плю́, -пúшь; -спáл, -á, -о] oversleep; sleep; F miss (by sleeping); **~ся**, ‹проснýться› [20] awake, wake up.

прос|ыхáть [1], ‹~óхнуть› [21] dry.

прóсьба *f* [5] request (at по П; for о П); entreaty; † petition; please (don't не + *inf.*); (у Р/к Д) ~ (may p.) ask (p.) a favo(u)r.

про|тáлкивать [1], *once* ‹~толкнýть› [20], F ‹~толкáть› [1] push (through); **-ся** force one's way (through); **~тáптывать** [1], ‹~топтáть› [3] tread (out); F wear out *or* down; **~тáскивать** [1], ‹~тащúть› [16] carry *or* drag (past, by); F smuggle in.

протéз (-'tes) *m* [1] artificial limb.

проте|кáть [1], ‹∠чь› [26] flow (by); leak; pass, elapse; take a ... course; **∠кция** *f* [7] patronage; **~рéть** *s.* протирáть; **∠ст** *m* [1], **~стовáть** [7], *v/t.* (*im*)*pf.* & ‹о-› protest; **∠чь** *s.* ~кáть.

прóтив (P) against (*a.* as against); opposite; быть *or* имéть ~ (have) object(ion; to), mind; **∠иться** [14], ‹вос-› (Д) oppose, object; **∠ник** *m* [1] opponent, adversary; enemy; **∠ный** [14; -вен, -вна] repugnant, disgusting, offensive, nasty; opposite, contrary; мне ∠но *a.* I hate; в ∠ном слýчае otherwise, failing which.

противо|вéс *m* [1] counterbalance; **~воздýшный** [14] anti-aircraft (*defense*), air-raid (*precautions, protection*); **~гáз** *m* [1] gas mask; **~дéйствие** *n* [12] counteraction; resistance; **~дéйствовать** [7] counteract; resist; **~естéственный** [14 *sh.*] unnatural; **~закóнный** [14; -óнен, -óнна] unlawful, illegal; **~общéственный** [14] antisocial; **~положность** *f* [8] contrast, opposition (in в В); antithesis; **~полóжный** [14; -жен, -жна] opposite; contrary, opposed; **~поставля́ть** [28], ‹~постáвить› [14] oppose; **~поставлéние** *n* [12] opposition; **~рéчие** *n* [12] contradiction; **~речúвый** [14 *sh.*] contradictory; **~рéчить** [16] (Д) contradict; **~стоя́ть** [-ою́, -оúшь] (Д) withstand; stand against; **~тáнковый** [14] antitank...; **~химúческий** [16] (anti)gas...; **~я́дие** *n* [12] antidote.

про|тирáть [1], ‹~терéть› [12] rub (through); wipe; **~ткнýть** *s.* ~тыкáть; **~тóкол** *m* [1] (**~токолúровать** [7] [*im*]*pf.*, *a.* ‹за-› take down the) minutes *pl.*, record; *su. a.* protocol; **~толкáть**, **~толкнýть** *s.* ~тáлкивать; **~топтáть** *s.* ~тáптывать; **~торённый** [14] beaten (*path*), trodden; **~тотúп** *m* [1] prototype; **~тóчный** [14] flowing, running; **~трезвля́ться** [28], ‹~трезвúться› [14 *e.*; -влю́сь, -вúшься; -влённый] (become) sober; **~тыкáть** [1], *once* ‹~ткнýть› [20] pierce.

протя́|гивать [1], ‹~нýть› [19] stretch (out), extend, hold out; pass; drawl; P turn up (one's toes нóги); **~жéние** *n* [12] extent, stretch (at на П); course (in на П); **~жный** [14; -жен, -жна] drawling, lingering; **~нýть** *s.* ~гивать.

проучúть F [16] *pf.* teach a lesson.

професс|ионáльный [14] professional; trade (*union, cf.* профсою́з); **∠ия** *f* [7] profession (by по Д), calling, trade; **∠ор** *m* [1; *pl.*: -рá, *etc. e.*] professor; **~ýра** *f* [5] professorship; professorate.

прóфиль *m* [4] profile.

профóрма F *f* [5] formality.

профсою́з *m* [1], **~ный** [14] trade union.

про|хáживаться [1], ‹~йтúсь› [-йдýсь, -йдёшься; -шёлся, -шлáсь] (go for a) walk, stroll; F pass; mock (at насчёт P); **~хвáты-**

вать F [1], ⟨**~хвати́ть**⟩ [15] pierce; blow up; **~хво́ст** F *m* [1] scoundrel.
прохла́д|а *f* [5] cool(ness); **~и́тельный** [14; -лен, -льна] refreshing, cooling; **~ный** [14; -ден, -дна] cool (*a. fig.*), fresh.
прохо́|д *m* [1] passage, pass; *anat.* duct (за́дний ~д anus); **~ди́мец** *m* [1; -мца] impostor, villain; **~ди́мость** *f* [8] passableness; maneuverability; **~ди́ть** [15], ⟨**пройти́**⟩ [пройду́, -дёшь; прошёл, -шла́; -ше́дший; про́йденный; *g. pt.*: пройдя́] pass, go (by, through, over, along); take a ... course, be; spread; **~дно́й** [14] (with a) through passage; **~жде́ние** *n* [12] passing *or* going (through, over); **~жий** *m* [17] passer-by; traveller.
процвета́ть [1] prosper, thrive.
проце|ду́ра *f* [5] procedure; **~жи́вать** [1], ⟨**~ди́ть**⟩ [15] filter; **~нт** *m* [1] percent(age) (by на В); (*usu. pl.*) interest; **~сс** *m* [1] process; ⚖ trial (at на П); **~ссия** *f* [7] procession.
проче́сть *s.* прочи́тывать.
про́чи|ий [17] other; *n & pl. a. su.* the rest; и ~ее and so on *or* forth, etc.; ме́жду ~им by the way, incidentally; among other things.
прочи́|стить *s.* ~ща́ть; **~тывать**, ⟨**~та́ть**⟩ [1] & ⟨**проче́сть**⟩ [25 -т-: -чту́, -тёшь; -чёл, -чла́; *g. pt.*: -чтя́; -чтённый] read (through); recite; '**~ть** [16] designate (to в В); **~ща́ть** [1], ⟨**~стить**⟩ [15] clean.
про́чн|ость *f* [8] durability; **~ый** [14; -чен, -чна́, -о] firm, solid, strong; lasting.
прочте́ние *n* [12] reading, perusal.
прочь away, off (with you поди́[те] ~); *cf.* доло́й; я не ~ + *inf.* F I wouldn't mind ...ing.
прош|е́дший [17] past (*a. su. n* ~е́дшее), *a. gr.*, last; **~е́ние** *n* [12] petition, application (for о П; on по Д); **~е́ствие** *n* [12] *s.* истече́ние; **~ло**-**го́дний** [15] last year's; **~лый** [14] past (*a. su. n* ~лое), last; **~мыгну́ть** F [20] *pf.* slip, whisk.
прощ|а́й(те)! farewell!, goodby(e)!, adieu!; **~а́льный** [14] farewell...; parting; **~а́ние** *n* [12] parting (when, at при П; на В), leave-taking, farewell; **~а́ть** [1], ⟨**прости́ть**⟩ [15 *e.*; -ощу́, ости́шь; -ощённый] forgive (р. Д), excuse, pardon; прости́(те) *a.* = ~а́й(те), *s.*; **-ся** (с Т) take leave (of), say goodby (to); **~е́ние** *n* [12] forgiveness; pardon.
проявл|и́тель *m* [4] *phot.* developer; **~и́ть(ся)** *s.* ~ля́ть(ся); **~ле́ние** *n* [12] manifestation, display, demonstration; *phot.* development; **~ля́ть** [28], ⟨**~и́ть**⟩ [14] show, display, evince, manifest; *phot.* develop.
проясн|я́ться [28], ⟨**~и́ться**⟩ [13] clear up, brighten.

пруд *m* [1 *e.*; в -у́] pond.
пружи́на *f* [5] spring; motive.
прусс|а́к *m* [1*e.*], **~кий** [16] Prussian.
прут *m* [1; *a. e.*; *pl.*: -ья, -ьев] rod, switch.
пры́|гать [1], *once* ⟨**~гнуть**⟩ [20] jump, spring, leap; **~гу́н** *m* [1 *e.*] jumper; **~жо́к** *m* [1; -жка́] jump, leap, bound; dive; **~ткий** [16; -ток, -тка́, -о] nimble, quick; **~ть** F *f* [8] agility; speed (at full во всю); **~щ** *m* [1 *e.*], **~щик** *m* [1] pimple.
пряди́ль|ный [14] spinning; **~щик** *m* [1], **~щица** *f* [5] spinner.
пря|дь *f* [8] lock, tress, strand; **~жа** *f* [5] yarn; **~жка** *f* [5; *g/pl.*: -жек] buckle **~лка** *f* [*g/pl.*: -лок] spinning wheel.
прям|изна́ *f* [5] straightness; **~оду́шие** *n* [12] *s.* ~ота́; **~оду́шный** [14; -шен, -шна] *s.* ~о́й *fig.*; **~о́й** [14; прям, -а́, -о] straight (*a.* [= bee] line ~а́я *su. f*); direct (*a. gr.*); 🚂 through...; ⚡ right; *fig.* straight (-forward), downright, outspoken, frank; ~а́я кишка́ *f* rectum; **~олине́йный** [14; -е́ен, -е́йна] rectilinear; *fig. s.* ~о́й *fig.*; **~ота́** *f* [5] straightforwardness, frankness; **~оуго́льник** *m* [1] rectangle; **~оуго́льный** [14] rectangular.
пря́н|ик *m* [1] gingerbread; **~ость** *f* [8] spice, *pl.* spicery; spiciness; **~ый** [14 *sh.*] spicy, piquant.
прясть [25; -ял, -а́, -о], ⟨с-⟩ spin.
пря́т|ать [3], ⟨с-⟩ hide (*v/i.* **-ся**), conceal; **~ки** *f/pl.* [5; gen.: -ток] hide-and-seek.
пря́ха *f* [5] spinner.
псал|о́м *m* [1; -лма́] psalm; **~о́мщик** *m* [1] *s.* дьяк; **~ты́рь** *f* [8] Psalter.
пса́рня *f* [6; *g/pl.*: -рен] kennel(s).
псевдони́м *m* [1] pseudonym.
псих|иа́тр *m* [1] psychiatrist; **~ика** *f* [5] mind, psyche; mentality; **~и́ческий** [16] mental, psychic(al); **~о́лог** *m* [1] psychologist; **~оло́гия** *f* [7] psychology.
птене́ц [1; -нца́] nestling.
пти́|ца *f* [5] bird; дома́шняя ~ца poultry; **~чий** [18] bird('s); poultry...; вид с ~чьего полёта bird's-eye view; **~чка** *f* [5; *g/pl.*: -чек] birdie.
пу́бли|ка *f* [5] audience; public; **~ка́ция** *f* [7] publication; advertisement; **~кова́ть** [7], ⟨о-⟩ publish; **~ци́ст** *m* [1] publicist; **~чность** *f* [8] publicity; **~чный** [14] public; ~чная же́нщина *f* prostitute.
пу́г|ало *n* [9] scarecrow; **~а́ть** [1], ⟨ис-, на-⟩, *once* ⟨**~ну́ть**⟩ [20] (**-ся** be) frighten(ed; of Р), scare(d); **~ли́вый** [14 *sh.*] timid, fearful.
пу́говица *f* [5] button.
пуд *m* [1; *pl. e.*] pood (= *36 lbs.*); **~ель** *m* [4; *pl. a.* -ля́, *etc. e.*] poodle.

пу́др|а *f* [5] powder; са́харная **~а** powdered sugar; **~еница** *f* [5] powder box; **~ить** [13], ‹на-› powder.
пуз|а́тый P [14 *sh.*] paunchy; **~о** P *n* [9] paunch.
пузыр|ёк [1; -рька́] vial; *a. dim. of* **~ь** *m* [4 *e.*] bubble; *anat.* bladder; F blister; kid.
пук *m* [1; *pl. e.*] wisp; bunch, bundle.
пулемёт *m* [1] machine gun; **~ный** [14] machine-gun; cartridge (*belt*); **~чик** *m* [1] machine gunner.
пуль|веризáтор *m* [1] spray(er); **~с** *m* [1] pulse; **~си́ровать** [7] puls(at)e; **~т** *m* [1] desk, stand.
пу́ля *f* [6] bullet.
пункт *m* [1] point (at *all* по Д); station; place, spot; item, clause, article; **~и́р** *m* [1] dotted line; **~и́рный** [14] dotted; **~уа́льность** *f* [8] punctuality; accuracy; **~уа́льный** [14; -лен, -льна] punctual; accurate.
пунцо́вый [14] crimson.
пунш *m* [1] punch (*drink*).
пуп|о́к *m* [1; -пка́], F **~** *m* [1 *e.*] navel.
пурга́ *f* [5] blizzard, snowstorm.
пу́рпур *m* [1], **~ный**, **~овый** [14] purple.
пуск *m* [1] (*a.* **~** в ход) start(ing), setting in operation; **~а́й** F *s.* пусть; **~а́ть** [1], ‹пусти́ть› [15] let (go; in[to]), set (free; going, in motion *or* operation [*a.* **~а́ть** в ход]); start; launch, throw; release; allow; put (forth); send; force; take (*root*); **~а́ть** под отко́с derail; **-ся** (+ *inf.*) start (...ing; *v/t.* в В), set out (on в В); enter *or* engage (into), begin, undertake.
пуст|е́ть [8], ‹о-, за-› become empty *or* deserted; **~и́ть** *s.* пуска́ть.
пуст|о́й [14; пуст, -á, -о] empty; void; vain, idle (talk **~о́е** *n su.*; *s. a.* **~я́к**); vacant; blank; dead (*rock*); F hollow; **~ота́** *f* [5; *pl. st.*: -о́ты] emptiness; void; *phys.* vacuum; vacancy.
пусты́|нный [14; -ы́нен, -ы́нна] desert, desolate; **~ня** *f* [6] desert, waste, wilderness; **~рь** *m* [4 *e.*] waste ground; **~шка** F *f* [5; *g/pl.*: -шек] blank; nonentity.
пусть let (him, *etc.*, + *vb.*; **~** [он] + *vb. 3rd. p.*), may; even (if).
пустя́|к F *m* [1 *e.*] trifle; *pl.* nonsense; (it's) nothing; **~ко́вый**, **~чный** (-ʃn-) F [14] trifling.
пу́та|ница *f* [5] confusion, muddle, mess; **~ть** [1], ‹за-, с-, пере-› (**-ся** get) confuse(d), muddle(d), mix(ed) up, entangle(d; interfere in в В).
путёвка *f* [5; *g/pl.*: -вок] pass (*Sov.*), permit.
путе|води́тель *m* [4] guide(book) (to по Д); **~во́дный** [14] lode..., pole(*star*); **~во́й** [14] travelling; traveller's; road...
путеше́ств|енник *m* [1] travel(l)er; **~ие** *n* [12] journey, trawel, tour (on в В *or* П); voyage; **~овать** [7] travel (through по Д).
пу́т|ник *m* [1] travel(l)er; **~ный** F [14] *s.* де́льный; **~ы** *pl.* [9] shackles.
пут|ь *m* [8 *e.*; *instr/sg.*: -тём] way (*a. fig.*: [in] *that* way **~ём**, *a.* by means of P), road, path; 🚂 track (*a. fig.*), line; means; trip, journey (on в В *or* П); route; в *or* по **~и́** on the way; in passing; нам по **~и́** I (we) have the same way (as с Т); F *s.* толк.
пух *m* [1; в -хý] down; в **~** (и прах) (*smash*) to pieces; (*defeat*) utterly, totally; F over(*dress*); **~ленький** F [16], **~лый** [14; пухл, -á, -о] chubby, plump; **~нуть** [21], ‹рас-› swell; **~о́вка** *f* [5; *g/pl.*: -вок] powder puff; **~о́вый** [14] down...
пучи́на *f* [5] gulf, abyss; eddy.
пучо́к *m* [1; -чка́] *dim. of* пук, *s.*
пу́ш|ечный [14] gun..., cannon...; **~и́нка** *f* [5; *g/pl.*: -нок] down, fluff; **~и́стый** [14 *sh.*] downy, fluffy; **~ка** *f* [5; *g/pl.*: -шек] gun, cannon; F hoax; **~ни́на** *f* [5] furs *pl.*; **~но́й** [14] fur...; **~о́к** F *m* [1; -шка́] down.
пу́ще P more (than P).
пчел|á *f* [5; *pl. st.*: пчёлы] bee; **~ово́д** *m* [1] beekeeper; **~ово́дство** *n* [9] beekeeping; **~ьник** *m* [1] apiary.
пшен|и́ца *f* [5] wheat; **~и́чный** [14] wheaten; **~ный** ('pʃɔ-) [14] millet...; **~о́** *n* [9] millet.
пыл *m* [1] ardo(u)r, zeal, blaze; в **~ý** in the thick (*of the fight*); **~а́ть** [1], ‹вос-, за-› blaze, flare (up), (in-) flame; glow, burn; (en)rage (with Т); **~есо́с** *m* [1] vacuum cleaner; **~и́нка** *f* [5; *g/pl.*: -нок] mote; **~и́ть** [13], ‹за-› dust; **-ся** be(come) dusty; **~кий** [16; -лок, -лка́, -о] ardent, fiery.
пыль *f* [8; в -ли́] dust; **~ный** [14; -лен, -льна́, -о] dusty (*a.* = в -ли́); **~ца́** *f* [5] pollen.
пыт|а́ть [1] torture; **~а́ться** [1], ‹по-› try, attempt; **~ка** *f* [5; *g/pl.*: -ток] torture; **~ли́вый** [14 *sh.*] inquisitive, searching.
пыхте́ть [11] puff, pant; F sweat.
пы́шн|ость *f* [8] splendo(u)r, pomp; **~ый** [14; -шен, -шна́, -о] magnificent, splendid, sumptuous; luxuriant, rich.
пьедеста́л *m* [1] pedestal.
пье́са *f* [5] *thea.* play; ♪ piece.
пьян|е́ть [8], ‹о-› get drunk (*a. fig.*; with от Р); **~ица** *m/f* [5] drunkard; **~ство** *n* [9] drunkenness; **~ствовать** [7] drink, F booze; **~ый** [14; пьян, -á, -о] drunk(en), *a. fig.* (with от Р).
пюре́ (-'rɛ) *n* [*ind.*] mashed potatoes *pl.*
пядь *f* [8; *from g/pl. e.*] span; *fig.* inch.
пята́ *f* [5; *nom/pl. st.*] heel (on по Д).
пят|а́к F *m* [1 *e.*], **~ачо́к** F *m* [1; -чка́]

five-kopeck coin; **~ёрка** *f* [5; *g/pl.*: -рок] five (*cf.* двойка); F (*mark*) = отлично, *cf.*; five-ruble note; **~еро** [37] five (*cf.* двое).
пяти|десятый [14] fiftieth; **~десятые** годы *pl.* the fifties; *cf.* пятый; **~конечный** [14] five-pointed (*star*); **~летка** *f* [5; *g/pl.*: -ток] five-year plan (*Sov.*); **~летний** [15] five-year (old), of five; **~сотый** [14] five hundredth.
пятиться [15], ⟨по-⟩ (move) back.
пятка *f* [5; *g/pl.*: -ток] heel (take to one's heels показать ~и).
пятнадцат|ый [14] fifteenth; *cf.* пятый; **~ь** [35] fifteen; *cf.* пять.
пятнистый [14 *sh.*] spotty, spotted.
пятн|ица *f* [5] Friday (on: в В, *pl.*: по Д); **~о** *n* [9; *pl. st.*; *g/pl.*: -тен] spot, stain, blot(ch) (with *pl.* в П); родимое ~о birthmark, mole.
пят|ый [14] fifth; (*page, chapter, year, etc., sentence or lesson no.*) five; **~ая** *f su.* ♧ fifth (*part*); **~ое** *n su.* fifth (*date*; on P: ~ого; *cf.* число); **~ь** (минут) ~ого five (minutes) past four; **~ь** [35] five; без **~и** (минут) час (два, *etc.*, [часа], ~ь, *etc.* [часов]) five (minutes) to one (two, *etc.* [o'clock]); **~ьдесят** [35] fifty; **~ьсот** [36] five hundred; **~ью** five times.

Р

р. *abbr.*: **1.** рубль, -ля, -лей; **2.** река.
раб *m* [1 *e.*], **~а** *f* [5] slave; **~овладелец** *m* [1; -льца] slaveholder; **~олепство** *n* [9] servility, **~олепствовать** [7] cringe (to перед Т).
работ|а *f* [5] work (at за Т; на П); labo(u)r, toil; assignment, task; **~ать** [1] work (on th. над Т; for p. на В; as Т), function; labo(u)r, toil; be open; **~ник** *m* [1], **~ница** *f* [5] worker, working (wo)man; (day) labo(u)rer, (farm)hand; (*house*)maid; official, functionary; employee; member; clerk; **~одатель** *m* [4] employer, F boss; **~оспособный** [14; -бен, -бна] able to work, able-bodied; hard-working, efficient.
рабоч|ий *m* [17] (*esp. industrial*) worker; *adj.*: working, work (*a. day*); workers', labo(u)r...; **~ая сила** *f* man power; labo(u)r.
раб|ский [16] slave...; slavish, servile; **~ство** *n* [9] slavery; **~ыня** *f* [6] *s.* ~а.
рав|енство *n* [9] equality; **~нение** *n* [12] ⚔ eyes (*right!*); **~нина** *f* [5] plain; **~но** equal(ly); as well (as); всё ~но it's all the same, it doesn't matter; anyway, in any case.
равно|весие *n* [12] balance (*a. fig.*), equilibrium; **~душие** *n* [12] indifference (to к Д) **~душный** [14; -шен, -шна] indifferent (to к Д); **~значный** [14; -чен, -чна] equivalent; **~мерный** [14; -рен, -рна] uniform, even, equal; **~правие** *n* [12] equality (of rights); **~правный** [14; -вен, -вна] (enjoying) equal (rights); **~сильный** [14; -лен, -льна] equivalent; **~ценный** [14; -енен, -енна] equal (in value).
равн|ый [14; равен, -вна] equal; (*a. su.*); ~ым образом *s.* ~о; ему нет ~ого he has no match; **~ять** [28], ⟨с-⟩ equalize; ⚔ dress (*ranks*); F compare; (*v/i.* **-ся**; *a.* be [equal to Д]).
рад [14; рада] (be) glad (at, of Д; *a.* to see p.), pleased, delighted; would like; (be) willing; не ~ (be) sorry; ~ не ~ willy-nilly; **~ар** *m* [1] radar; **~и** (Р) for the sake of (*or*... ['s] sake); for.
радиатор *m* [1] radiator.
радий *m* [3] radium.
радикал *m* [1], **~ьный** [14; -лен, льна] radical.
радио *n* [*ind.*] radio, *Brt. a.* wireless (on по Д); **~активность** *f* [8] radioactivity; **~активный** [14; -вен, -вна] radioactive; **~аппарат** *m* [1] *s.* ~приёмник; **~вещание** *n* [12] broadcasting (system); **~ла** *f* [5] radio-gramophone; **~любитель** *m* [4] radiofan; **~передача** *f* [5] (radio)broadcast, transmission; **~приёмник** *m* [1] receiving set, radio, *Brt.* wireless (set); **~слушатель** *m* [4] listener; **~станция** *f* [7] radio station; **~узел** [1; -зла] radio center (*Brt.*: -tre); **~установка** *f* [5; *g/pl.*: -вок] radio plant.
ради|ст *m* [1] radio (wireless) operator; **'~ус** *m* [1] radius.
радо|вать [7], ⟨об-, по-⟩ (В) gladden, please, rejoice; **-ся** (Д) rejoice (at), be glad *or* pleased (of, at); look forward (to); **~стный** [14; -тен, -тна] joyful, glad; merry; **~сть** *f* [8] joy, gladness; pleasure.
раду|га *f* [5] rainbow; **~жный** [14] iridescent, rainbow...; *fig.* rosy.
радуш|ие *n* [12] kindliness; hospitality; **~ный** [14; -шен, -шна] kindly, hearty; hospitable.
раз *m* [1; *pl. e., gen.* раз] time (*this, etc.* [в] В); one; (один) ~ once; два ~а twice; ни ~у not once, never; не ~ repeatedly; как ~ just (in time F в самый ~; *s. a.* впору), the very; вот тебе ~ F *s.* на[2].
разба|влять [28], ⟨~вить⟩ [14] dilute; **~лтывать** F, ⟨разболтать⟩ [1] let out.

разбе́|г *m* [1] start, run (with, at с P); **~га́ться** [1], ⟨**~жа́ться**⟩ [4; -егу́сь, -ежи́шься, -егу́тся] take a run; scatter; disperse.

разби|ва́ть [1], ⟨**∠ть**⟩ [разобью́, -бьёшь; разбе́й(те)!; -и́тый] break (to pieces), crash, crush; defeat; divide (into на B); lay out (*park*); pitch (*tent*); knock; **-ся** break; crash; split; come to nothing; **~ра́тельство** *n* [9] trial; **~ра́ть** [1], ⟨разобра́ть⟩ [разберу́, -рёшь; разобра́л, -а́, -о; -о́бранный] take to pieces, dismantle, pull down; investigate, inquire into; review; analyze (*Brt.* -se), parse; make out, decipher, understand; sort out; ⚖ try; buy up; F take; *impf.* be particular; **-ся** F (в П) grasp, understand; unpack; **∠тие** *n* [12] crash, defeat (*cf.* ~ва́ть); **∠тый** [14 *sh.*] broken; F jaded; **∠ть(ся)** *s.* ~ва́ть(ся).

разбо́й *m* [3] robbery; **~ник** *m* [1] robber; **~ничать** [1] rob; pirate; **~нический** [16], **~ничий** [18] predatory; of robbers *or* brigands.

разболта́ть *s.* разба́лтывать.

разбо́р *m* [1] analysis; review, critique; investigation, inquiry (into); ⚖ trial; без ~а, ~у F indiscriminately; **~ка** *f* [5] taking to pieces, dismantling; sorting (out); **~ный** [14] folding, collapsible; **~чивость** *f* [8] legibility; scrupulousness; **~чивый** [14 *sh.*] legible; discerning; scrupulous, fastidious.

разбр|а́сывать, ⟨**~оса́ть**⟩ [1] scatter, throw about, strew; F squander; **~еда́ться** [1], ⟨**~ести́сь**⟩ [25] disperse; **~о́д** *m* [1] disorder, mess; **~о́санный** [14] scattered; **~оса́ть** *s.* ~а́сывать.

разбух|а́ть [1], ⟨**∠нуть**⟩ [21] swell.

разва́л *m* [1] collapse, breakdown; chaos; **~ивать** [1], ⟨**~и́ть**⟩ [13; -алю́, -а́лишь] pull (*or* break) down; disorganize; **-ся** fall to pieces, collapse; F sprawl; **~ины** *f/pl.* ruins (F *a. sg* = *p.*).

ра́зве really; perhaps; only; F unless.

развева́ться [1] flutter; stream.

разве́д|ать *s.* ~ывать; **~е́ние** *n* [12] breeding; cultivation; **~ённый** [14] divorced, divorcé(e) *su.*; **~ка** *f* [5; *g/pl.*: -док] reconnaissance; intelligence service; **~очный** [14] reconnaissance...; **~чик** *m* [1] scout; intelligence officer; reconnaissance plane; **~ывательный** [14] *s.* ~очный; **~ывать**, ⟨**~ать**⟩ [1] reconnoiter (*Brt.* -tre); F find out.

разве|сти́ *s.* разводи́ть; **~нча́ть** [1] *pf.* uncrown, dethrone; unmask.

развёр|нутый [14] large-scale; **~тывать** [1], ⟨разверну́ть⟩ [20] unfold, unroll, unwrap; open; ⚔ deploy; *fig.* develop; (**-ся** *v/i.*; *a.* turn).

разве|сно́й [14] weighed out; **∠сить** *s.* ∠шивать; **~сти́(сь)** *s.* разводи́ть(ся); **~твле́ние** *n* [12] ramification, branching; **~твля́ться** [28], ⟨**~тви́ться**⟩ [14 *e.*; *3rd p. only*] ramify, branch; **∠шивать** [1], ⟨**∠сить**⟩ [15] weigh (out); hang (out); **∠ять** [27] *pf.* disperse, dispel.

разви|ва́ть [1], ⟨**∠ть**⟩ [разовью́, -вьёшь; разве́й(те)!; разви́л, -а́, -о; -ви́тый (ра́зви́т, -а́, -о)] develop (*v/i.* **-ся**); evolve; untwist; **∠нчивать** [1], ⟨**~нти́ть**⟩ [15 *e.*; -нчу́, -нти́шь; -и́нченный] unscrew; **∠тие** *n* [12] development; evolution; **~то́й** [14; ра́звит, -а́, -о] developed; intelligent; advanced; **∠ть(ся)** *s.* ~ва́ть(ся).

развле|ка́ть [1], ⟨**∠чь**⟩ [26] entertain, amuse (o.s. **-ся**); divert; **~че́ние** *n* [12] entertainment, amusement, diversion.

разво́д *m* [1] divorce; ⚔ relief, mounting; **~и́ть** [15], ⟨развести́⟩ [25] take (along), bring; divorce (from с T); separate; dilute; mix; rear, breed; plant, cultivate; light, make; ⚔ mount, relieve; **-ся**, ⟨**-сь**⟩ get divorced (from с T); F multiply, grow *or* increase in number.

раз|вози́ть [15], ⟨**~везти́**⟩ [24] deliver, carry; **~вора́чивать** F *s.* ~вёртывать.

развра́|т *m* [1] debauch; depravity; **~ти́ть(ся)** *s.* ~ща́ть(ся); **~тник** *m* [1] libertine, debauchee, rake; **~тничать** F [1] (indulge in) debauch; **~тный** [14; -тен, -тна] dissolute, licentious; **~ща́ть** [1], ⟨**~ти́ть**⟩ [15 *e.*; -ащу́; -ати́шь; -щённый] (**-ся** become) deprave(d), debauch(ed), corrupt; **~ще́ние** *n* [12], **~щённость** *f* [8] depravity.

развяз|а́ть *s.* ∠ывать; **∠ка** *f* [5; *g/pl.*: -зок] denouement; outcome, conclusion, head; **∠ный** [14; -зен, -зна] forward, (free &) easy; **∠ывать** [1], ⟨**~а́ть**⟩ [3] untie, undo; *fig.* unleash; F loosen; **-ся** come untied; F get rid (of с T).

разгад|а́ть *s.* ∠ывать; **∠ка** *f* [5; *g/pl.*: -док] solution; **∠ывать**, ⟨**~а́ть**⟩ [1] solve, unriddle.

разга́р *m* [1] (в П *or* B) heat, thick (in), height (at), (in full) swing.

раз|гиба́ть [1], ⟨**~огну́ть**⟩ [20] unbend, straighten (o.s. **-ся**).

разгла́|живать [1], ⟨**~дить**⟩ [15] smooth; iron, press; **~ша́ть** [1], ⟨**~си́ть**⟩ [15 *e.*; -ашу́, -аси́шь; -ашённый] divulge; trumpet.

разгляд|е́ть [11] *pf.* make out; **∠ывать** [1] examine, view.

разгне́ванный [14] angry.

разгов|а́ривать [1] talk (to, with с T; about, of о П), converse, speak; **~о́р** *m* [1] talk, conversation; *cf.* речь; **~о́рный** [14] colloquial; **~о́рчивый** [14 *sh.*] talkative.

разгóн *m* [1] dispersal; *a.* = разбéг; в ~е out; **~я́ть** [28], ⟨разогнáть⟩ [разгоню́, -óнишь; разогнáл, -á, -o; разóгнанный] disperse, scatter; dispel; F drive away; **-ся** take a run.
разгор|áться [1], ⟨**~éться**⟩ [9] kindle (*a. fig.*), (in)flame, blaze up.
разгра|бля́ть [28], ⟨**~́бить**⟩ [14], **~блéние** *n* [12] plunder, pillage, loot; **~ничéние** *n* [12] delimitation; **~ни́чивать** [1], ⟨**~ни́чить**⟩ [16] demarcate, delimit.
разгрóм *m* [1] rout; debacle, destruction, ruin, chaos.
разгру|жáть [1], ⟨**~зи́ть**⟩ [15 & 15 *e.*; -ужу́, -у́зи́шь; -у́женный & -ужённый] (**-ся** be) unload(ed); F relieve(d); **~́зка** *f* [5; *g/pl.*: -зок] unloading.
разгу́л *m* [1] revelry, carouse; debauch(ery), licentiousness; **~ивать** F [1] stroll, saunter; **-ся**, ⟨**~я́ться**⟩ [28] clear up; F have a good walk *or* run, move without restraint; **~ьный** F [14; -лен, -льна] dissolute; loose, easy.
разда|вáть [5], ⟨**~́ть**⟩ [-дáм, -дáшь, *etc.*, *s.* дать; рóздал, раздалá, рóздало; рóзданный (-ан, разданá, рóздано)] distribute; play (*cards:* deal) out; **-ся** (re)sound, be heard; give way; split, separate; F expand; **~́вливать** [1] *s.* дави́ть 2.; **~́ть(ся)** *s.* **~вáть(ся)**; **~́ча** *f* [5] distribution.
раздвáиваться *s.* двои́ться.
раздви|гáть [1], ⟨**~́нуть**⟩ [20] part, separate, move apart; pull out; **~жнóй** [14] sash...; telescope, -pic.
раздвоéние *n* [12] bifurcation.
раздевá|лка F *f* [5; *g/pl.*: -лок], F **~льня** *f* [6; *g/pl.*: -лен] checkroom, cloakroom; **~ть** [1], ⟨раздéть⟩ [-дéну, -дéнешь; -дéтый] undress (*v/i.* **-ся**), take off; F strip (of).
раздéл *m* [1] division; section; **~аться** F [1] *pf.* get rid *or* be quit (of с T); **~éние** *n* [12] division (into на B); *eccl.* schism; **~и́тельный** [14] dividing; *gr.* disjunctive; **~и́ть(ся)** *s.* **~я́ть(ся)** & дели́ть(ся); **~ьный** [14] separate; distinct; **~я́ть** [28], ⟨**~и́ть**⟩ [13; елю́, -éлишь; -елённый] divide (into на B; *a.* [-ed] by); separate; share; **-ся** (be) divide(d), fall.
раздéть(ся) *s.* раздевáть(ся).
раз|дирáть F [1], ⟨**~одрáть**⟩ [раздеру́, -рёшь; разодрáл, -á, -o; -óдранный] *impf.* rend; *pf.* F tear; **~добы́ть** F [-бу́ду, -бу́дешь] *pf.* get, procure.
раздóлье *n* [10] *s.* привóлье.
раздóр *m* [1] discord, contention.
раздосáдованный F [14] angry.
раздраж|áть [1], ⟨**~и́ть**⟩ [16 *e.*; -жу́, -жи́шь; -жённый] irritate, provoke; vex, annoy; **-ся** lose one's temper; **~éние** *n* [12] irritation; temper; **~и́тельный** [14; -лен, -льна] irritable, touchy; **~и́ть(ся)** *s.* **~áть(ся)**.
раздробл|éние *n* [12] breaking; smashing; **~я́ть** [28] *s.* дроби́ть.
разду|вáть [1], ⟨**~́ть**⟩ [18] fan; blow (away); swell; puff up, exaggerate; **-ся** swell, inflate.
разду́м|ывать, ⟨**~ать**⟩ [1] change one's mind; *impf.* deliberate, consider; **~ье** *n* [10] thought(s), meditation; doubt(s).
разду́ть(ся) *s.* раздувáть(ся).
раз|евáть F [1], ⟨**~и́нуть**⟩ [20] open wide; **~евáть** рот gape; **~жáлобить** [14] *pf.* move to pity; **~жáловать** [7] *pf.* degrade (to в И *pl.*); **~жáть** *s.* **~жимáть**; **~жёвывать** [1], ⟨**~жевáть**⟩ [7 *e.*; -жую́, -жуёшь] chew; **~жигáть** [1], ⟨**~жéчь**⟩ [г/ж: -зожгу́, -жжёшь, -жгу́т; разжёг, -зожглá; разожжённый] kindle (*a. fig.*); heat; rouse; unleash; **~жимáть** [1], ⟨**~жáть**⟩ [разожму́, -мёшь; разжáтый] unclench, open; **~и́нуть** *s.* **~евáть**; **~и́ня** F *m/f* [6] gawk, gaper; **~и́тельный** [14; -лен, -льна] striking.
раз|лагáть [1], ⟨**~ложи́ть**⟩ [16] analyze (*Brt.* -yse); decompose; (*v/i.* **-ся**); (become) demoralize(d), corrupt(ed; decay); **~лáд** *m* [1] dissension, discord, dissonance; disturbance; **~лáмывать** [1], ⟨**~ломáть**⟩ [1], ⟨**~ломи́ть**⟩ [14] break; pull down; **~летáться** [1], ⟨**~летéться**⟩ [11] fly (away, asunder); F break (to pieces); come to naught; take a sweep.
разли́|в *m* [1] flood; **~вáть** [1], ⟨**~ть**⟩ [разолью́, -льёшь; *cf.* лить; -лéй(те)!; -и́л, -á, -o; -и́тый (-и́т, -á, -o)] spill; pour out; bottle; ladle; flood, overflow; spread; bestow; (*v/i.* **-ся**).
различ|áть [1], ⟨**~и́ть**⟩ [16 *e.*; -чу́, -чи́шь; -чённый] distinguish; **-ся** *impf.* differ (in T, по Д); **~́ие** *n* [12] distinction, difference; **~и́тельный** [14] distinctive; **~и́ть** *s.* **~áть**; **~́ный** [14; -чен, -чна] different (from от P); different, various, diverse.
разлож|éние *n* [12] analysis; decomposition, decay; corruption, degeneration; **~и́ть(ся)** *s.* разлагáть(ся) & раскла́дывать.
разлом|áть, **~и́ть** *s.* разлáмывать.
разлу́|ка *f* [5] separation (from с T), parting; **~чáть** [1], ⟨**~чи́ть**⟩ [16 *e.*; -чу́, -чи́шь; -чённый] separate (*v/i.* **-ся**; from с T), part.
размá|зывать [1], ⟨**~зать**⟩ [3] smear, spread; **~тывать** [1], ⟨размотáть⟩ unwind, wind off; **~х** *m* [1] swing, brandish (with [*a.* might] с **~ху**); span (✈ & *fig.*), sweep; amplitude; *fig.* vim, verve, élan; scope; **~хивать** [1], *once* ⟨**~хну́ть**⟩ [20] (T) swing, sway,

dangle; brandish; gesticulate; **-ся** lift (one's hand T); **~шистый** F [14 *sh.*] wide; diffuse.
разме|жевать [7] *pf.* mark off, demarcate; **~льчать** [1], ⟨**~льчить**⟩ [16 *e.*; чу́, -чи́шь; -чённый] pound, crush.
размен *m* [1], **~ивать** [1], ⟨**~ять**⟩ [28] (ex)change (for на В); **~ный** [14]: **~ная** монета *f* change.
размер *m* [1] size; dimension(s), measure(ment); rate (at в П), amount; scale; *poetic.*, ♪ meter (*Brt.* -tre; in T), ♪ *a.* time, measure (of в В); **~енный** [14 *sh.*] measured; **~ять** [28], ⟨**~ить**⟩ [13] measure (off).
разме|стить *s.* **~щать**; **~чать** [1], ⟨**~тить**⟩ [15] mark; **~шивать** [1], ⟨**~шать**⟩ [1] stir (up); knead; **~щать** [1], ⟨**~стить**⟩ [15 *e.*; -ещу́, -ести́шь; -ещённый] place; lodge, accommodate (in, at, with в П, по Д); distribute; **~щение** *n* [12] distribution; accomodation; arrangement, order.
размин|ать [1], ⟨размять⟩ [разомну́, -нёшь; размя́тый] knead; F stretch (*limbs*); **~уться** F *pf.* [20] cross; miss o. a.
размнож|ать [1], ⟨**~ить**⟩ [16] multiply (*v/i.* **-ся**); mimeograph; **~ение** *n* [12] multiplication; propagation, reproduction; **~ить(ся)** *s.* **~ать(ся)**.
размо|зжить [16 *e.*; -жу́, -жи́шь; -жённый] *pf.* smash, crush; **~кать** [1], ⟨**~кнуть**⟩ [21] soak, swell; **~лвка** *f* [5; *g/pl.*: -вок] tiff, quarrel; **~лоть** [17; -мелю́, -ме́лешь] *pf.* grind, crush; **~тать** *s.* разматывать; **~чить** [16] *pf.* soak.
размы|вать [1], ⟨**~ть**⟩ [22] wash out *or* away; **~кать** [1], ⟨разомкнуть⟩ [20] open (⚡, ⊕); **~ть** *s.* **~вать**.
размышл|ение *n* [12] reflection (for на В), thought; **~ять** [28] reflect, meditate (on о П).
размягч|ать (-xt∫-) [1], ⟨**~ить**⟩ [16 *e.*; -чу́, -чи́шь; -чённый] soften, mollify.
раз|мять *s.* **~минать**; **~нашивать**, ⟨**~носить**⟩ [15] tread out, wear to shape; **~нести** *s.* **~носить 1.**; **~нимать** [1], ⟨**~нять**⟩ [-ниму́, -ни́мешь; -нял & ро́знял, -а́, -о; -ня́тый (-ня́т, -а́, -о)] part; take to pieces.
разница *f* [5] difference.
разно|видность *f* [8] variety, sort; **~гласие** *n* [12] discord, disagreement, difference, variance; discrepancy; **~калиберный** F [14], **~мастный** [14; -тен, -тна] *s.* **~**шёрстный; **~образие** *n* [12] variety, diversity, multiplicity; **~образный** [14; -зен, -зна] manifold, multifarious, various; **~реч...** *s.* противореч...; **~родный** [14; -ден, -дна] heterogeneous.
разнос *m* [1] delivery; peddl(e)ry; **~ить** [15] **1.** ⟨разнести⟩ [25 -с-] deliver (to, at по Д), carry; hawk, peddle; F spread; smash, destroy; blow up; scatter; swell; **2.** *s.* разнашивать; **~ка** *f* [5] *s.* **~**; **~ный** [14] peddling.
разно|сторонний [15; -о́нен, -о́ння] many-sided; **'~сть** *f* [8] difference; **~счик** *m* [1] peddler, hawker; (*news*)boy, man; messenger; **~цветный** [14; -тен, -тна] multicolo(u)red; **~шёрстный** [14; -тен, -тна] variegated; F motley, mixed.
разнузданный [14 *sh.*] unbridled.
разн|ый [14] various, different, diverse; **~ять** *s.* **~имать**.
разо|блачать [1], ⟨**~блачить**⟩ [16 *e.*; -чу́, -чи́шь; -чённый] expose, disclose, unmask; **~блачение** *n* [12] exposure, disclosure, unmasking; **~брать(ся)** *s.* разбирать(ся); **~гнать(ся)** *s.* разгонять(ся); **~гнуть(ся)** *s.* разгибать(ся); **~гревать** [1], ⟨**~греть**⟩ [8; -етый] warm (up); **~детый** F [14 *sh.*] dressed up; **~драть** *s.* раздирать; **~йтись** *s.* расходиться; **~мкнуть** *s.* размыкать; **~рвать(ся)** *s.* разрывать (-ся).
разор|ение *n* [12] ruin, destruction, devastation; **~ительный** [14; -лен, -льна] ruinous; **~ить(ся)** *s.* **~ять(ся)**; **~ужать** [1], ⟨**~ужить**⟩ [16 *e.*; -жу́, -жи́шь; -жённый] disarm (*v/i.* **-ся**); **~ужение** *n* [12] disarmament; **~ять** [28], ⟨**~ить**⟩ [13] (**-ся** be[come]) ruin(ed), destroy(ed), ravage(d).
разослать *s.* рассылать.
разостлать *s.* расстилать.
разочар|ование *n* [12] disappointment; **~овывать** [1], ⟨**~овать**⟩ [7] (**-ся** be) disappoint(ed) (in в П).
разра|батывать, ⟨**~ботать**⟩ [1] work up (into на В), process; work out, elaborate; ⚒ till; ⚒ exploit; **~ботка** *f* [5; *g/pl.*: -ток] working (out); elaboration; ⚒ tillage; ⚒ exploitation; **~жаться** [1], ⟨**~зиться**⟩ [15 *e.*; -ажу́сь, -ази́шься] burst out (into T); **~статься** [1], ⟨**~стись**⟩ [24; *3rd p. only*: -тётся; -ро́сся, -сла́сь] grow; enlarge, expand.
разрежённый [14] rarefied.
разрез *m* [1] cut; section; angle (from в П); **~ать** [1], ⟨**~ать**⟩ [3] cut (up), slit; **~ной** [14]: **~ной** нож *m* paper knife; **~ывать** [1] *s.* **~ать**.
разреш|ать [1], ⟨**~ить**⟩ [16 *e.*; -шу́, -ши́шь; -шённый] permit, allow; (re)solve; release (for к Д); absolve; settle; **-ся** be (re)solved; end, burst (in[to] T); be delivered (of T); **~ение** *n* [12] permission (with с Р); licence (for на В); (re)solution; settlement; absolution; delivery; **~ить(ся)** *s.* **~ать(ся)**.
раз|рисовать [7] *pf.* ornament;

~ро́зненный [14] odd; isolated; **~руба́ть** [1], ‹~руби́ть› [14] split.

разру́|ха *f* [5] ruin; **~ша́ть** [1], ‹~шить› [16] destroy, demolish; ruin; frustrate; **-ся** (fall *or* come to) ruin; **~ше́ние** *n* [12] destruction, demolition, devastation; **~шить** (**-ся**) *s.* ~ша́ть(ся).

разры́|в *m* [1] breach, break, rupture; explosion; gap; ⊕ на ~в tensile; **~ва́ть** [1] **1.** ‹разорва́ть› [-ву́, -вёшь; -ва́л, -а́, -о; -о́рванный] tear (to *pieces* на В); break (off); *impers.* burst, explode; (**-ся** *v/i.*); **2.** ‹~ть› [22] dig up; **~вно́й** [14] explosive; **~да́ться** [1] *pf.* break into sobs; **~ть** *s.* ~ва́ть 2.; **~хля́ть** [28] *s.* рыхли́ть.

разря́|д *m* [1] category, class; discharge; unloading; **~ди́ть** *s.* ~жа́ть; **~дка** *f* [5; *g/pl.*: -док] spacing, space; slackening; disengagement; **~жа́ть** [1], ‹~ди́ть› [15 *e.* & 15; -яжу́, -я́ди́шь; -яжённый & -я́женный] unload; discharge; reduce, disengage (*tension*); *typ.* space; [15] F dress up.

разу|бежда́ть [1], ‹~беди́ть› [15 *e.*; -ежу́, -еди́шь; -еждённый] (в П) dissuade (from); **-ся** change one's mind (about); **~ва́ться** [1], ‹∠ться› [18] take off one's shoes; **~веря́ть** [28], ‹~ве́рить› [13] (в П) (**-ся** be) undeceive(d), disabuse(d) (of); disappoint(ed); **~знава́ть** F [5], ‹~зна́ть› [1] find out (about о П, В); **~кра́шивать** [1], ‹~кра́сить› [15] decorate; embellish; **~крупня́ть** [28], ‹~крупни́ть› [14] diminish; decentralize.

ра́зум *m* [1] reason; sense(s); **~е́ть** [8] understand; know; mean, imply (by под Т); **-ся** be meant *or* understood; ~е́ется of course; **∠ный** [14; -мен, -мна] rational; reasonable, sensible; clever, wise.

разу́|ться *s.* ~ва́ться; **~чивать** [1], ‹~чи́ть› [16] study, learn; **-ся** forget, unlearn.

разъе|да́ть [1] *s.* есть[1] 2; **~диня́ть** [28], ‹~дини́ть› [13] separate; ⚡ disconnect; **∠зд** *m* [1] trip, journey (on в П); setting out, departure; ⚔ horse patrol; 🚂 siding; **~зжа́ть** [1] drive, ride, go about; be on a journey *or* trip; **-ся**, ‹∠хаться› [-е́дусь, -е́дешься; -езжа́йтесь!] leave (for по Д); separate; pass o. a. (с Т).

разъярённый [14] enraged, furious.

разъясн|е́ние *n* [12] explanation; clarification; **~я́ть** [28], ‹~и́ть› [13] explain, elucidate.

разы́|грывать, ‹~гра́ть› [1] play; raffle (off); **-ся** break out; run high; happen; **~скивать** [1], ‹~ска́ть› [3] seek, search (for; *pf.* out = find).

рай *m* [3; в раю́] paradise.

рай|ко́м *m* [1] (райо́нный комите́т) district committee (*Sov.*); **~о́н** *m* [1] district; region, area; **~о́нный** [14] district...; regional; **~сове́т** *m* [1] (райо́нный сове́т) district soviet (*or* council).

рак *m* [1] crawfish, *Brt.* crayfish; морско́й ~ lobster; ⚕, *ast.* (♋) cancer.

раке́т|а *f* [5] (*a.* sky) rocket; **~ка** *f* [5; *g/pl.*: -ток] racket (*sport*); **~ный** [14] rocket...

ра́ковина *f* [5] shell; sink; bowl.

ра́м|(к)а *f* [5; (*g/pl.*: -мок)] frame (-work, *a. fig.* = limits; within в П); **~па** *f* [5] footlights *pl.*; stage.

ра́н|а *f* [5] wound; **~г** *m* [1] rank; **~е́ние** *n* [12] wound(ing); **~еный** [14] wounded (*a. su.*); **~ец** *m* [1; -нца] satchel; ⚔ knapsack; **~ить** [13] (*im*)*pf.* wound, injure (in в В).

ра́н|ний [15] early (*adv.* ~о); morning...; spring...; ~о и́ли по́здно sooner or later; **~ова́то** F rather early; **~ьше** earlier; formerly; first; (P) before.

рап|и́ра *f* [5] rapier; **∠орт** *m* [1], **~ортова́ть** [7] (*im*)*pf.* report; **~с** *m* [1] ⚘ rape; **~со́дия** *f* [7] rhapsody.

ра́са *f* [5] race.

раска́|иваться [1], ‹~яться› [27] repent (*v/t.*, of в П); **~лённый** [14], **~ли́ть(ся)** *s.* ~ля́ть(ся); **~лывать** [1], ‹расколо́ть› [17] split, cleave; crack; (*v/i.* **-ся**); **~ля́ть** [28], ‹~ли́ть› [13] make (**-ся** become) red-hot, white-hot; **~пывать** [1], ‹раскопа́ть› [1] dig out *or* up; **~т** *m* [1] roll, peal; **~тистый** [14 *sh.*] rolling; **~тывать**, ‹~та́ть› [1] (un-) roll; *v/i.* **-ся**; ‹~ти́ться› [15] gain speed; roll (off); **~чивать**, ‹~ча́ть› [1] swing; shake; F bestir; **~яние** *n* [12] repentance (of в П); **~яться** *s.* ~иваться.

расквартирова́ть [7] *pf.* quarter.

раски́|дывать [1], ‹~нуть› [20] spread (out); throw out; pitch (*tent*), set up.

раскла|дно́й [14] folding, collapsible; **∠дывать** [1], ‹разложи́ть› [16] lay *or* spread out, display; lay; set up; make, light; apportion, repartition; **∠ниваться** [1], ‹∠няться› [28] (с Т) bow (to), greet; take leave (of).

раско́|л *m* [1] split, schism; **~ло́ть** (**-ся**) *s.* раска́лывать(ся); **~па́ть** *s.* раска́пывать; **~пка** *f* [5; *g/pl.*: -пок] excavation.

раскр|а́шивать [1] *s.* кра́сить; **~епоща́ть** [1], ‹~епости́ть› [15 *e.*; -ощу́, -ости́шь; -ощённый] emancipate, liberate; **~епоще́ние** *n* [12] emancipation, liberation; **~итикова́ть** [7] *pf.* scarify; **~ича́ться** [4*e.*; -чу́сь, -чи́шься] *pf.* shout, bawl (at на В); **~ыва́ть** [1], ‹~ы́ть› [22] open (*v/i.* **-ся**); uncover; disclose, reveal; put *one's cards* on the table.

раску|ла́чить [16] *pf.* dispossess *or* oust (the kulak[s]) **~па́ть** [1],

⟨~пи́ть⟩ [14] buy up; **∠поривать** [1], ⟨∠порить⟩ [13] uncork; open; **∠сывать** [1], ⟨~си́ть⟩ [15] crack; F see through, get (the hang of); **∠тывать**, ⟨∠тать⟩ [1] unwind, unwrap.
ра́совый [14] racial.
распа́д *m* [1] disintegration; decay.
распа|да́ться [1], ⟨∠сться⟩ [25; -па́лся, -лась; -па́вшийся] fall to pieces; decay; disintegrate; break up (into на В), split; **~ко́вывать** [1], ⟨~кова́ть⟩ [7] unpack; **∠рывать** [1] *s.* поро́ть; **∠сться** *s.* ~да́ться; **∠хивать** [1] **1.** ⟨~ха́ть⟩ [3] plow (*Brt.* plough) up; **2.** ⟨~хну́ть⟩ [20] throw *or* fling open (*v/i.* **-ся**); **~я́ть** [24] *pf.* (**-ся** come) unsolder(ed).
распе|ва́ть [1] sing; **~ка́ть** F [1], ⟨∠чь⟩ [26] dress down, scold, call down, blow up; **~ча́тывать**, ⟨~ча́тать⟩ [1] unseal; open.
распи́|ливать [1], ⟨~ли́ть⟩ [13; -илю́, -и́лишь; -и́ленный] saw; **~на́ть** [1], ⟨распя́ть⟩ [-пну, -пнёшь; -пя́тый] crucify.
распис|а́ние *n* [12] timetable (🚂 ~а́ние поездо́в; *school:* ~а́ние уро́ков), schedule (on по Д); **~а́ть(ся)** *s.* ∠ывать(ся); **∠ка** *f* [5; *g/pl.*: -сок] receipt (against под В); **∠ывать** [1], ⟨~а́ть⟩ [3] write, enter; paint; ornament; **-ся** sign (one's name); (acknowledge) receipt (в П); F register one's marriage.
распл|авля́ть [28] *s.* пла́вить; **~а́каться** [3] *pf.* burst into tears; **~а́та** *f* [5] payment; requital; **~а́чиваться** [1], ⟨~ати́ться⟩ [15] (с Т) pay off, settle accounts (with); pay (for за В); **~еска́ть** [3] *pf.* spill.
распле|та́ть [1], ⟨~сти́⟩ [25 -т-] (**-ся**, ⟨-сь⟩ get) unbraid(ed); untwist.
расплы|ва́ться [1], ⟨∠ться⟩ [23] spread; run; swim about; blur; swell; F grow fat; **∠вчатый** [14 *sh.*] blurred, diffuse, vague.
расплю́щить [16] *pf.* flatten.
распозн|ава́ть [5], ⟨~а́ть⟩ [1] perceive, discern; find out.
распол|ага́ть [1], ⟨~ожи́ть⟩ [16] dispose (*a. fig.* = incline), arrange; place, lodge; *impf.* (Т) dispose (of), have (at one's disposal); **-ся** settle; encamp; *pf.* be situated; **~ага́ющий** [17] engaging; **~за́ться** [1], ⟨~зти́сь⟩ [24] creep *or* crawl (away); **~оже́ние** *n* [12] arrangement, order, (dis)position (toward[s] к Д); situation; inclination, favo(u)r; mind; ~оже́ние ду́ха mood; **~о́женный** [14 *sh.*] *a.* situated; (well-) disposed (toward[s] к Д); inclined; **~ожи́ть(ся)** *s.* ~ага́ть(ся).
распор|яди́тельность *f* [8] administrative ability, management; **~яди́тельный** [14; -лен, -льна] circumspect, efficient; **~яди́ться** *s.* ~яжа́ться; **~я́док** *m* [1; -дка] order, rule, (*office, etc.*) regulations *pl.*; **~яжа́ться** [1], ⟨~яди́ться⟩ [15 *e.*; -яжу́сь, -яди́шься] give orders; (Т) dispose (of); take charge *or* care (of); *impf.* manage, direct; **~яже́ние** *n* [12] order(s), instruction(s); decree; disposal (at в В; в П); charge, command (to в В).
распра́в|а *f* [5] punishment (of с Т); massacre; *short* work (of с Т); **~ля́ть** [28], ⟨~ить⟩ [14] straighten; smooth; spread, stretch; **-ся** (с Т) punish, avenge o.s. (on).
распредел|е́ние *n* [12] distribution; **~и́тельный** [14] distributing; ⊕ control...; ⚡ switch...; **~я́ть** [28], ⟨~и́ть⟩ [13] distribute; allot; assign (to по Д); arrange, classify.
распрод|ава́ть [5], ⟨~а́ть⟩ [-да́м, -да́шь, *etc.*, *s.* дать; -про́дал, -а́, -о; -про́данный] sell out (*or* off); **~а́жа** *f* [5] (clearance) sale.
распрост|ира́ть [1], ⟨~ере́ть⟩ [12] spread, stretch; extend; (*v/i.* **-ся**); **~ёртый** *a.* open (arms объя́тия *pl.*); **~и́ться** [15 *e.*; -ощу́сь, -ости́шься] (с Т) bid farewell (to); give up, abandon.
распростран|е́ние *n* [12] spread (-ing), expansion; dissemination, propagation; circulation; **~ённый** [14] widespread; **~я́ть** [28], ⟨~и́ть⟩ [13] spread, extend (*v/i.* **-ся**); propagate, disseminate; diffuse; **-ся** F enlarge upon.
распро|ща́ться [1] F = ~сти́ться.
ра́спря *f* [6; *g/pl.*: -рей] strife, contention, conflict; **~га́ть** [1], ⟨∠чь⟩ [26 г/ж: -ягу́, -яжёшь] unharness.
распу|ска́ть [1], ⟨~сти́ть⟩ [15] dismiss, disband, dissolve, break up; unfurl; undo; loosen; spread; melt; *fig.* spoil; **-ся** open; expand; loosen, untie; dissolve; F become spoiled; **∠тать** *s.* ∠тывать; **∠тица** *f* [5] impassability of roads; **∠тник** *s.* развра́тник; **∠тывать**, ⟨∠тать⟩ [1] untangle; **∠тье** *n* [10] crossroad(s); **~ха́ть** [1], ⟨∠хнуть⟩ [21] swell; **∠хший** [17] swollen; **∠щенный** [14 *sh.*] spoiled, undisciplined; dissolute.
распыл|и́тель *m* [4] spray(er), atomizer; **~я́ть** [28], ⟨~и́ть⟩ [13] spray, atomize; scatter.
распя́|тие *n* [12] crucifixion; **~ть** *s.* распина́ть.
расса́|да *f* [5] sprout(s); **~ди́ть** *s.* ~живать; **~дник** *m* [1] nursery; *fig.* hotbed; **~живать** [1], ⟨~ди́ть⟩ [15] transplant; seat; **-ся**, ⟨рассе́сться⟩ [рассядусь, -дешься; -се́лся, -се́лась] sit down, take seats; F sit at ease.
рассве́|т *m* [1] dawn (at на П), daybreak; **~та́ть** [1], ⟨~сти́⟩ [25 -т-: -светёт; -свело́] dawn.
рассе|дла́ть [1] *pf.* unsaddle; **∠ивать** [1], ⟨∠ять⟩ [27] disseminate;

scatter, disperse (*v/i.* **-ся**); dissipate, dispel; divert (*usu.* **-ся** o.s.); **~кáть** [1], ‹**∠**чь› [26] cut (up), dissect, hew, cleave; swish; **~лять** [28], ‹**~**лить› [13] settle (*v/i.* **-ся**); separate; **∠ться** *s.* рассáживаться; **∠янность** *f* [8] absent-mindedness; **∠янный** [14 *sh.*] absent-minded; dissipated; scattered; *phys.* diffused; **∠ять(ся)** *s.* **∠**ивать(ся).

расскáз *m* [1] story, tale, narrative; short novel (*or* story); **~áть** *s.* **~**ывать; **~чик** *m* [1] narrator; storyteller; **~ывать** [1], ‹**~**áть› [3] tell; relate, narrate.

расслаб|лять [28], ‹**∠**ить› [14] weaken, enervate (*v/i.* **~éть** [8] *pf.*).

рассл|éдование *n* [12] investigation, inquiry into; **~éдовать** [7] (*im*)*pf.* investigate, inquire into; **~оéние** *n* [12] stratification; **~ы́шать** [16] *pf.* hear distinctly; **не ~**ы́шать not (quite) catch.

рассм|áтривать [1], ‹**~**отрéть› [-отрю́, -óтришь; -óтренный] examine, view; consider; discern, distinguish; **~еяться** [27 *e.*; -ею́сь, -еёшься] *pf.* burst out laughing; **~отрéние** *n* [12] examination (at при П); consideration; **~отрéть** *s.* **~**áтривать.

рассóл *m* [1] brine, pickle.

расспр|áшивать [1], ‹**~**оси́ть› [15] inquire, ask; **~óсы** *pl.* [1] inquiries.

рассрóчка *f* [5] (payment by) instal(l)ments (by в В *sg.*).

расста|вáние *s.* прощáние; **~вáться** [5], ‹**∠**ться› [-áнусь, -áнешься] part, separate (from с Т); leave; **~влять** [28], ‹**∠**вить› [14] place; arrange; set (up); move apart; **~нóвка** *f* [5; *g/pl.*: -вок] arrangement; distribution; order; punctuation; drawing up; pause; **∠ться** *s.* **~**вáться.

расст|ёгивать [1], ‹**~**егнýть› [20] unbutton; unfasten (*v/i.* **-ся**); **~илáть** [1], ‹разостлáть› [расстелю́, -éлешь; разóстланный] spread (*v/i.* **-ся**); **~ояние** *n* [12] distance (at на П).

расстр|áивать [1], ‹**~**óить› [13] upset, derange; disorganize; disturb, spoil; shatter; frustrate; ♪ put out of tune (*or* humo[u]r, *fig.*); **-ся** be(come) upset, *etc.*; fail.

расстрéл *m* [1] (death by) shooting, execution; **~ивать** [1], ‹**~**ять› [28] shoot, execute.

расстрó|ить(ся) *s.* расстрáивать (-ся); **~йство** *n* [9] disorder, confusion; disturbance, derangement; frustration.

расступ|áться [1], ‹**~**и́ться› [14] give way, part; open, split.

рассу|ди́тельность *f* [8] judiciousness; **~ди́тельный** [14; -лен, -льна] judicious, wise; **~ди́ть** [15] *pf.* judge; decide (*a. issue*); consider; **∠док** *m* [1; -дка] reason, sense(s); judg(e)ment, mind (of в П); **∠дочный** [14; -чен, -чна] rational; **~ждáть** [1] argue, reason; talk; **~ждéние** *n* [12] reasoning, argument(ation); objection; treatise, essay (on о П).

рассчи́т|ывать [1], ‹**~**áть› [1] & ‹расчéсть› [25; разочтý, -тёшь; расчёл, разочлá; разочтённый; *g. pt.*: разочтя́]; (не mis)calculate, estimate; judge; dismiss, pay off; *impf.* count *or* reckon (on на В); expect; intend; **-ся** settle accounts, get even (with с Т), pay off; count off.

рассыл|áть [1], ‹разослáть› [-ошлю́, -ошлёшь; -óсланный] send out (*or* round); **∠ка** *f* [5] distribution, dispatch.

рассып|áть [1], ‹**∠**ать› [2] scatter, spill; spread; (*v/i.* **-ся**; crumble, fall to pieces; break up; fail; shower [s. th. on в П/Д]; resound; burst out).

растá|лкивать, ‹растолкáть› [1] push aside; push; **~пливать** [1], ‹растопи́ть› [14] light, kindle; melt; (*v/i.* **-ся**); **~птывать** [1], ‹растоптáть› [3] tread down; **~скивать** [1], ‹**~**щи́ть› [16], F ‹**~**скáть› [1] pilfer; take to pieces; F separate.

раствóр *m* [1] solution; mortar; **~и́мый** [14 *sh.*] soluble; **~я́ть** [28], ‹**~**и́ть› **1.** [13] dissolve; **2.** [13; -орю́, -óришь; -óренный] open.

растé|ние *n* [12] plant; **~рéть** *s.* растирáть; **~рзáть** [1] *pf.* tear to pieces; lacerate; **~рянный** [14 *sh.*] confused, perplexed, bewildered; **~ря́ть** [28] *pf.* lose (one's head **-ся**; be[come] perplexed *or* puzzled).

расти́ [24 -ст-: -стý, -стёшь; рос, -слá; рóсший], ‹вы́-› grow, increase.

раст|ирáть [1], ‹**~**ерéть› [12; разотрý, -трёшь] pound, pulverize; rub; smear.

расти́тельн|ость *f* [8] vegetation, flora; hair; **~ый** [14] vegetable; vegetative.

расти́ть [15 *e.*; ращý, расти́шь] rear; F grow:

расто|лкáть *s.* растáлкивать; **~лковáть** [7] *pf.* expound, explain; **~пи́ть** *s.* растáпливать; **~птáть** *s.* растáптывать; **~пы́рить** F [13] *pf.* spread; **~ргáть** [1], ‹**∠**ргнуть› [21] break (off), annul; dissolve, sever; **~ржéние** *n* [12] breaking off; annulment; dissolution; **~рóпный** [14; -пен, -пна] deft, quick; **~чáть** [1], ‹**~**чи́ть› [16 *e.*; -чý, -чи́шь; -чённый] squander, waste, dissipate; lavish (on Д); **~чи́тель** *m* [4], **~чи́тельный** [14; -лен, -льна] prodigal, spendthrift, extravagant.

растра|влять [28], ‹**~**ви́ть› [14] irritate; fret, stir (up); **∠та** *f* [5]

waste; embezzlement; **⁓тчик** *m* [1] embezzler; **⁓чивать** [1], ⟨**⁓тить**⟩ [15] spend, waste; embezzle.
растр|епать [2] *pf.* (-**ся** be[come]) tousle(d, **⁓ёпанный** [14]), dishevel(-[1]ed); tear (torn), thumb(ed).
растрогать [1] *pf.* move, touch.
растя|гивать [1], ⟨**⁓нуть**⟩ [19] stretch (*v/i.* -**ся**; F fall flat); ⚕ strain; drawl; extend, prolong; **⁓жение** *n* [12] stretching; strain(ing); **⁓жимый** [14 *sh.*] extensible, elastic; *fig.* vague; **⁓нутый** [14] long-drawn; **⁓нуть(ся)** *s.* **⁓гивать(ся)**.
рас|формировать [8] *pf.* disband; **⁓хаживать** [1] walk about *or* up & down, pace; **⁓хваливать** [1], ⟨**⁓хвалить**⟩ [13; -алю, -алишь; -аленный] extol(l *Brt.*), praise (highly); **⁓хватывать** F, ⟨**⁓хватать**⟩ [1] snatch away; buy up (quickly).
расхи|щать [1], ⟨**⁓тить**⟩ [15] plunder; **⁓щение** *n* [12] plunder.
расхо|д *m* [1] expenditure (for на В), expense(s); ⚓ *a.* debit; consumption; sale; **⁓диться** [15], ⟨**разойтись**⟩ [-ойдусь, -ойдёшься; -ошёлся, -ошлась; -ошедшийся; *g. pt.*: -ойдясь] disperse; break up; differ (from с Т); diverge; part, separate, get divorced (from с Т); pass *or* miss o.a., (*letters*) cross; be sold out, sell; be spent, (у Р) run out of; melt, dissolve; ramify; radiate; F spread; become enraged; get excited *or* animated; **⁓довать** [7], ⟨из-⟩ spend, expend; *pf. a.* use up; **⁓ждение** *n* [12] divergence, difference (of в П); radiation.
расцарап|ывать, ⟨**⁓ать**⟩ [1] scratch.
расцве|т *m* [1] blossom, (*a. fig.*) bloom; prime; prosperity; **⁓тать** [1], ⟨**⁓сти**⟩ [25 -т-] blo(ss)om; flourish, thrive; **⁓тка** *f* [5; *g/pl.*: -ток] colo(u)ring.
расце|нивать [1], ⟨**⁓нить**⟩ [13; -еню, -енишь; -енённый] estimate, value, rate; **⁓нка** *f* [5; *g/pl.*: -нок] valuation; rate, tariff; **⁓плять** [28], ⟨**⁓пить**⟩ [14] uncouple, unhook.
рас|чесать *s.* **⁓чёсывать**; **⁓чёска** *f* [5; *g/pl.*: -сок] comb; **⁓честь** *s.* рассчитать; **⁓чёсывать** [1], ⟨**⁓чесать**⟩ [3] comb (one's hair -**ся** F).
расчёт *m* [1] calculation; estimation; settlement (of accounts); payment; dismissal, *Brt.* F *a.* sack; account, consideration; intention; providence; F use; ⚔ gunners *pl.*; из **⁓а** on the basis (of); в **⁓е** quits; **⁓ливый** [14 *sh.*] provident, thrifty; circumspect.
рас|чищать [1], ⟨**⁓чистить**⟩ [15] clear (away); **⁓членять** [28], ⟨**⁓членить**⟩ [13] dismember; **⁓шатывать**, ⟨**⁓шатать**⟩ [1] loosen (*v/i.* -**ся**); (be[come]) shatter(ed); **⁓шевелить** F [13] *pf.* stir (up).
расши|бать F *s.* ушибать; **⁓вать** [1], ⟨**⁓ть**⟩ [разошью, -шьёшь; *cf.* шить] embroider; undo, rip; **⁓рение** *n* [12] widening, enlargement; expansion; **⁓рять** [28], ⟨**⁓рить**⟩ [13] widen, enlarge; extend, expand; ⚕ dilate; **⁓ть** *s.* **⁓вать**; **⁓фровывать** [1], ⟨**⁓фровать**⟩ [7] decipher, decode.
рас|шнуровать [7] *pf.* untie; **⁓щелина** *f* [5] crevice, cleft, crack; **⁓щепление** *n* [12] splitting; fission; **⁓щеплять** [28], ⟨**⁓щепить**⟩ [14 *e.*; -плю, -пишь; -плённый] split.
ратифи|кация *f* [7] ratification; **⁓цировать** [7] (*im*)*pf.* ratify.
ратовать [7] fight, struggle.
рафинад *m* [1] lump sugar.
рахит *m* [1] rickets.
рацион|ализировать [7] (*im*)*pf.* rationalize; **⁓альный** [14; -лен, -льна] rational (*a.* ⅍, *no sh.*).
рвануть [20] *pf.* jerk; -**ся** dart.
рвать [рву, рвёшь; рвал, -á, -o] **1.** ⟨разо-, изо-⟩ [-орванный] tear (to, in *pieces* на, в В), *v/i.* -**ся**; **2.** ⟨со-⟩ pluck; **3.** ⟨вы-⟩ pull out; *impers.* (В) vomit, spew; **4.** ⟨пре-⟩ break off; **5.** ⟨взо-⟩ blow up; ⁓ и метать F be in a rage; -**ся** break; strive *or* long (eagerly).
рвение *n* [12] zeal; eagerness.
рвот|а *f* [5] vomit(ing); **⁓ный** [14] emetic (*a. n, su.*).
рдеть [8] redden, flush.
реа|билитировать [7] (*im*)*pf.* rehabilitate; **⁓гировать** [7] (на В) react (upon); respond (to); **⁓ктивный** [14] reactive; jet (*plane*); **⁓кционер** *m* [1], **⁓кционный** [14] reactionary.
реал|изм *m* [1] realism; **⁓изовать** [7] (*im*)*pf.* realize; ⚓ *a.* sell; **⁓истический** [16] realistic; **⁓ьность** *f* [8] reality; **⁓ьный** [14; -лен, -льна] real; realistic.
ребёнок *m* [2; *pl. a.* дети, *s.*] child; baby, F kid; грудной ⁓ suckling.
ребро *n* [9; *pl.*: рёбра, рёбер, рёбрам] rib; edge (on **⁓м**); **⁓м** *fig.* point-blank.
ребя|та *pl. of* ребёнок; F boys; **⁓ческий** [16], **⁓чий** F [18] childish; **⁓чество** F [9] childishness; **⁓читься** F [16] behave childishly.
рёв *m* [1] roar; bellow; howl.
рев|анш *m* [1] revenge; return match; **⁓ень** *m* [4 *e.*] rhubarb; **⁓еть** [-ву, -вёшь] roar; bellow; howl; F cry.
ревиз|ия *f* [7] inspection; auditing; revision; **⁓ор** *m* [1] inspector; auditor.
ревмати|зм *m* [1] rheumatism; **⁓ческий** [16] rheumatic.
ревн|ивый [14 *sh.*] jealous; **⁓овать** [7], ⟨при-⟩ be jealous (of [p.'s] к Д [В]); **⁓ость** *f* [8] jealousy; zeal, eagerness; **⁓остный** [14; -тен, -тна] zealous, eager.

револ|ьве́р *m* [1] revolver; **~юционе́р** *m* [1], **~юцио́нный** [14] revolutionary; **~ю́ция** *f* [7] revolution.

реги́стр *m* [1], **~и́ровать** [7], ⟨за-⟩ register (*v/i.* **-ся**; *a.* get married *in a civil ceremony*); index.

рег|ла́мент *m* [1] order, regulations *pl.*; **~ре́сс** *m* [1] retrogression.

регул|и́ровать [7], ⟨у-⟩ regulate; (*esp. pf.*) settle; **~я́рный** [14; -рен, -рна] regular; **~я́тор** *m* [1] regulator.

редак|ти́ровать [7], ⟨от-⟩ edit, redact; **∠тор** *m* [1] editor; **∠ция** *f* [7] editorial staff; editorship; editor's office; wording, text, version; redaction; (*radio*) desk.

ред|е́ть [8], ⟨по-⟩ (grow) thin; **~и́ска** *f* [5; *g/pl.*: -сок] (*red*) radish.

ре́дк|ий [16; -док, -дка́, -о; *comp.*: ре́же] rare; thin, sparse; scarce; *adv. a.* seldom; **~ость** *f* [8] rarity, curiosity; sparsity, thinness; uncommon(thing); на **~ость** F extremely, awfully.

ре́дька *f* [5; *g/pl.*: -дек] radish.

режи́м *m* [1] regime(n); conditions *pl.*; regulations *pl.*, order.

режисс|ёр *m* [1] stage manager; director, producer; **~и́ровать** [7] stage.

ре́зать [3] **1.** ⟨раз-⟩ cut (up, open); carve (*meat*); **2.** ⟨за-⟩ slaughter, kill; **3.** ⟨вы́-⟩ carve, cut (in *wood* по Д, на П); **4.** ⟨с-⟩ cut off; F fail; *impf.* hurt; F say; P talk; **5. -ся** F cut (one's teeth); gamble.

резв|и́ться [14 *e.*; -влю́сь, -ви́шься] frolic, frisk, gambol; **∠ый** [14; резв, -á, -о] frisky, sportive, frolicsome; quick; lively.

резе́рв *m* [1], reserve(s); **~и́ст** *m* [1] reservist; **~ный** [14] reserve...

резе́ц *m* [1; -зца́] incisor.

рези́н|а *f* [5] rubber; **~овый** [14] rubber...; **~ка** *f* [5; *g/pl.*: -нок] eraser, (india) rubber; elastic.

ре́з|кий [16; -зок, -зка́, -о; *comp.*: ре́зче] sharp, keen; biting, piercing; acute; harsh, shrill; glaring; rough, abrupt; **~кость** *f* [8] sharpness, *etc.*, *s.* **~кий**; harsh word; **~но́й** [14] carved; **~ня́** *f* [6] slaughter; **~олю́ция** *f* [7] resolution; decision; **~о́н** *m* [1] reason; **~они́нс** *m* [1] resonance; **~о́нный** F [14; -о́нен, -о́нна] reasonable; **~ульта́т** *m* [1] result (as a в П); **~ьба́** *f* [5] carving.

резюм|е́ *n* [*ind.*] summary; **~и́ровать** [7] (*im*)*pf.* summarize.

рейд *m* [1] ⚓ road(stead); ⚔ raid.

Рейн *m* [1] Rhine.

рейс *m* [1] trip; voyage; flight.

река́ *f* [5; *ac/sg. a. st.*; *pl. st.*; *from dat/pl. a. e.*] river, stream.

рекла́м|а *f* [5] advertising; advertisement; publicity; **~и́ровать** [7] (*im*)*pf.* advertise; boost; (re-)claim, complain; **~ный** [14] advertising.

реко|менда́тельный [14] of recommendation; **~мента́ция** *f* [7] recommendation; reference; **~мендова́ть** [7] (*im*)*pf.*, *a.* ⟨по-⟩ recommend, advise; † introduce; **~нструи́ровать** [7] (*im*)*pf.* reconstruct; **∠рд** *m* [1] record; **∠рдный** [14] record...; **~рдсме́н** *m* [1], **~рдсме́нка** *f* [5; *g/pl.*: -нок] champion.

ре́ктор *m* [1] president, (*Brt.* vice-)-chancellor, rector (*univ.*).

рели|гио́зный [14; -зен, -зна] religious; **∠гия** *f* [7] religion; **∠квия** *f* [7] relic.

рельс *m* [1], **∠овый** [14] rail; track.

реме́нь *m* [4; -мня́] strap; belt.

реме́сл|енник *m* [1] (handi)craftsman, artisan; *fig.* bungler; **~енный** [14] trade...; handicraft...; home-made; bungling; **~о́** *n* [9; *pl.*: -мёсла, -мёсел, -мёслам] trade, (handi)craft; occupation.

ремо́нт *m* [1] repair(s); remount (-ing); **~и́ровать** [7] (*im*)*pf.*, **~ный** [14] repair.

ре́нта *f* [5] rent; revenue; (*life*) annuity; **∠бельный** [14; -лен, -льна] profitable.

рентге́новск|ий [16]: **~ий** сни́мок *m* roentgenogram; **~ие** лучи́ *m/pl.* X-rays.

реорганизова́ть [7] (*im*)*pf.* reorganize (*Brt.* -se).

ре́па *f* [5] turnip.

репа|рацио́нный [14] reparation...; **~три́ровать** [7] (*im*)*pf.* repatriate.

репе́йник *m* [1] bur(dock); agrimony.

репертуа́р *m* [1] repertoire, repertory.

репети́|ровать [7], ⟨про-⟩ rehearse; **~ция** *f* [7] rehearsal.

ре́плика *f* [5] retort; *thea.* cue.

репорта́ж *m* [1] report(ing).

репортёр *m* [1] reporter.

репре́сс(а́л)ия *f* [7] reprisal.

репроду́ктор *m* [1] loud-speaker.

ресни́ца *f* [5] eyelash.

респу́блик|а *f* [5] republic; **~а́нец** *m* [1; -нца], **~а́нский** [16] republican.

рессо́ра *f* [5] spring.

рестора́н *m* [1] restaurant (at в П).

ресу́рсы *m/pl.* [1] resources.

рети́вый [14] zealous; mettlesome.

ре|туши́ровать [7] (*im*)*pf.*, ⟨от-⟩ retouch; **~фера́т** *m* [1] report, paper.

рефо́рм|а *f* [5], **~и́ровать** [7] (*im*)*pf.* reform; **~а́тор** *m* [1] reformer.

реценз|е́нт *m* [1] reviewer; **~и́ровать** [7], ⟨про-⟩, **∠ия** *f* [7] review.

реце́пт *m* [1] recipe.

рециди́в *m* [1] relapse.

речево́й [14] speech...

ре́ч|ка *f* [5; *g/pl.*: -чек] (small) river; **~но́й** [14] river...

реч|ь *f* [8; *from g/pl. e.*] speech;

discourse, talk, conversation; word; об этом не может быть и ~и that is out of the question; *cf.* идти.

реш|ать [1], ⟨~ить⟩ [*e.*; -шу, -шишь; -шённый] solve; decide, resolve (*a.* **-ся** [on, to на B]; make up one's mind); dare, risk; не ~**аться** hesitate; ~**ающий** [17] decisive; ~**ение** *n* [12] decision; (re)solution; ~**ётка** *f* [5; *g/pl.*: -ток] grating; lattice; trellis; grate; ~**ето** *n* [9; *pl. st.*: -шёта] sieve; ~**ётчатый** [14] trellis(ed); ~**имость** *f* [8] determination; ~**ительный** [14; -лен, -льна] resolute, firm; decisive; definite; absolute; ~**ить(ся)** *s.* ~**ать(ся)**.

реять [27] soar, fly.

ржа|веть [8], ⟨за-⟩, ~**вчина** *f* [5] rust; ~**вый** [14] rusty; ~**ной** [14] rye...; ~**ть** [ржёт], ⟨за-⟩ neigh.

риза *f* [5] chasuble; robe.

Рим *m* [1] Rome; '~**лянин** *m* [1; *pl.*: -яне, -ян], '~**лянка** *f* [5; *g/pl.*: -нок], '~**ский** [14] Roman.

ринуться [20] *pf.* rush; plunge.

рис *m* [1] rice.

риск *m* [1] risk (at на B); ~**ованный** [14 *sh.*] risky; ~**овать** [7], ⟨~**нуть**⟩ [20] (*usu.* T) risk, venture.

рисова|ние *n* [12] drawing; designing; ~**ть** [7], ⟨на-⟩ draw; design; **-ся** appear, loom; pose, mince.

рисовый [14] rice...

рисунок *m* [1; -нка] drawing, design; picture, illustration (in на П).

ритм *m* [1] rhythm; ~**ичный** [14; -чен, -чна] rhythmical.

риф *m* [1] reef; ~**ма** *f* [5] rhyme.

роб|еть [8], ⟨о-⟩ be timid, quail; не ~**ей!** courage!; ~**кий** [16; -бок, -бка, -о; *comp.*: робче] shy, timid; ~**ость** *f* [8] shyness, timitidy.

ров *m* [1; рва; во рву] ditch.

ровесник *m* [1] coeval, of the same age.

ровн|ый [14; -вен, -вна, -о] even, level, flat; straight; equal; equable; ~**о** precisely, exactly, *time a.* sharp; F absolutely; ~**я** F *f* [5] equal.

рог *m* [1; *pl. e.*: -га] horn; antler; bugle; ~**атый** [14 *sh.*] horned; ~**овица** *f* [5] cornea; ~**овой** [14] horn ...

рогожа *f* [5] (bast) mat.

род *m* [1; в, на -у; *pl. e.*] genus; race; generation; kind; way; *gr.* gender; birth (by T); F class; ~**ом** из, с P come *or* be from; от ~**у** (Д) *be* ... old; с ~**у** in one's life.

роди|льный [14] maternity (hospital дом *m*); ~**мый** [14] *s.* родной & '~**нка**; '~**на** *f* [5] native land, home(land) (in на П); '~**нка** *f* [5; *g/pl.*: -нок] birthmark, mole; ~**тели** *m/pl.* [4] parents; ~**тельный** [14] genitive (*case*); ~**тельский** [16] parental.

родить [15 *e.*; рожу, родишь; -ил, -а (*pf.*: -а), -о; рождённый] (*im-*) *pf.*, (*impf. a.* **рождать**, F **рожать** [1]) bear, give birth to; beget; *fig.* bring forth, produce; **-ся** [*pf.* -ился] be born; arise; come up, grow.

родн|ик *m* [1 *e.*] spring; ~**ой** [14] own; native; (my) dear; *pl.* = ~**я** *f* [6] relative(s), relation(s).

родо|вой [14] patrimonial; generic; ~**начальник** *m* [1] ancestor, (*a. fig.*) father; ~**словный** [14] genealogical; ~словная *f* family tree.

родствен|ник *m* [1], ~**ница** *f* [5] relative, relation; ~**ный** [14 *sh.*] related, kindred, cognate; of blood.

родств|о *n* [9] relationship; cognation; F relatives; в ~е related (to c T).

роды *pl.* [1] (child)birth.

рожа *f* [5] ⚕ erysipelas; P mug.

рожд|аемость *f* [8] birth rate; ~**ать(ся)** *s.* родить(ся); ~**ение** *n* [12] birth (by от P); день ~ения birthday (on в B); ~**ественский** [16] Christmas...; ~**ество** *n* [9] (*a.* ~ество [Христово]) Christmas (at на B); поздравить с ~еством Христовым wish a Merry Xmas; до (после) Р. Хр. В. С. (A. D.).

рож|ок *m* [1; -жка] *dim. of* рог; ear trumpet; feeding bottle; (*gas*) burner; shoehorn; ~**ь** *f* [8; **ржи**; *instr/sg.*: рожью] rye.

роза *f* [5] rose.

розга *f* [5; *g/pl.*: -зог] rod.

розетка *f* [5; *g/pl.*: -ток] rosette; ⚡ (*plug*) socket.

розн|ица *f* [5]: в ~ицу by retail; ~**ичный** [14] retail...; ~**ь** F *f* [8] discord; И/Д ~ь th. *or* p. & th/p. are not the same *or* different.

розовый [14 *sh.*] pink, rosy.

розыгрыш *m* [1] draw; drawn game; drawing of a lottery; ~ первенства play(s) for championship.

розыск *m* [1] search (in/of в П *pl.*/P); ⚖ preliminary trial; уголовный ~ criminal investigation department.

ро|иться [13], ~**й** *m* [3; в рою; *pl. e.*: рои, роёв] swarm.

рок *m* [1] fate; ~**овой** [14] fatal; ~**от** *m* [1], ~**отать** [3] roll.

ролик *m* [1] roller (skates *pl.*).

роль *f* [8; *from g/pl. e.*] part, role.

ром *m* [1] rum.

роман *m* [1] novel; F (love) affair, romance; ~**ист** *m* [1] novelist; ~**тизм** *m* [1] romanticism; ~**тический** [16], ~**тичный** [14; -чен, -чна] romantic.

ром|ашка *f* [5; *g/pl.*: -шек] camomile; ~**б** *m* [1] rhombus.

ронять [28], ⟨уронить⟩ [13; -оню, -онишь; -оненный] drop; droop; lose; shed; *fig.* disparage, discredit.

ропт|от *m* [1], ~**тать** [3; -пщу, ропщешь] murmur, grumble, growl (at на B).

роса *f* [5; *pl. st.*] dew.

роскош|ный [14; -шен, -шна] luxurious; magnificent, splendid,

sumptuous; F luxuriant, exuberant; **'~ь** *f* [8] luxury; magnificence, sumptuousness; luxuriance.
рóслый [14] big, tall.
рóспись *f* [8] list; fresco.
рóспуск *m* [1] dissolution; dismissal; disbandment; breaking up.
Россú|я *f* [7] Russia; **2йский** [16] Russian; *cf.* РСФСР.
рост *m* [1] growth; increase; stature, size; ... высóкого **∠а** tall ...
ростовщúк *m* [1 *e.*] usurer.
рос|тóк *m* [1; -ткá] sprout, shoot; **∠черк** *m* [1] flourish; stroke.
рот *m* [1; рта; во ртý] mouth; **∠а** *f* [5] company; **∠ный** [14] company (commander); **~озéй** F [3] gaper.
рóща *f* [5] grove.
роя́ль *m* [4] (grand) piano.
РСФСР (Росси́йская Совéтская Федерати́вная Социалисти́ческая Респýблика) Russian Soviet Federative Socialist Republic.
ртýть *f* [8] mercury.
рубá|нок *m* [1; -нка] plane; **~шка** *f* [5; *g/pl.*: -шек] shirt; chemise.
рубéж *m* [1 *e.*] boundary; border (line), frontier; за **~óм** abroad.
рубéц *m* [1; -бцá] hem; scar, wake.
руби́ть [14] **1.** ⟨на-⟩ chop, cut, hew, hack; mince; **2.** ⟨с-⟩ fell; F *impf.* speak bluntly; **-ся** fight (hand to hand).
рýбка *f* [5] felling; ⚓ cabin.
рýбленый [14] chopped, minced.
рубль *m* [*e.*] r(o)uble.
рýб|рика *f* [5] heading; column; **~чатый** [14] ribbed.
рýга|нь *f* [8] abuse; **∠тельный** [14] abusive; **∠тельство** *n* [9] curse, oath; **∠ть** [1], ⟨вы́-⟩ abuse, scold; **-ся** swear, curse; abuse o. a.
руд|á *f* [5; *pl. st.*] ore; **~ни́к** *m* [1 *e.*] mine, pit; **~ни́чный** [14] mine(r's); fire(*damp*); **~окóп** *m* [1] miner.
руж|éйный [14] gun...; **~ьё** *n* [10; *pl. st.*; *g/pl.*: -жей] gun, rifle.
рук|á *f* [5; *ac/sg.*: рýку; *pl.*: рýки, рук, -кáм] hand; arm; **~á** в **∠у** (*or* óб **~у**) hand in hand (arm in arm; *a.* пóд **~у**); из **~** вон (плóхо) F quite wretched(ly); быть нá **~у** (Д) suit a p. (well); нá **~у** нечи́ст light-fingered; от **~и́** in handwriting; по **~áм**! it's bargain!; под **~óй** at hand, within reach; **~óй** подáть it's no distance (a stone's throw); (у Р) **∠и** кóротки́ F it's not in (p.'s) power; из пéрвых **~** at first hand; приложи́ть **∠у** sign.
рукáв *m* [1 *e.*; *pl.*: -вá, -вóв] sleeve; branch; hose; **~и́ца** *f* [5] mitten; gauntlet; **~чик** *m* [1] cuff.
руковод|и́тель *m* [4] leader; chief; manager; teacher; **~и́ть** [15] (Т) lead; direct, manage; **-ся** follow, conform (to); **∠ство** *n* [9] leadership; guidance; instruction; textbook, guide; **∠ствовать(ся)** [7] *s.* **~и́ть(ся)**; **~я́щий** [17] leading.
руко|дéлие *n* [12] needlework; **~мóйник** *m* [1] washstand; **~пáшный** [14] hand-to-hand; **'~пись** *f* [8] manuscript; **~плескáние** *n* [12] (*mst pl.*) applause; **~пожáтие** *n* [12] hand shake; **~я́тка** *f* [5; *g/pl.*: -ток] handle, gripe; hilt.
рул|евóй [14] steering; control...; *su.* steersman, helmsman; **~ь** *m* [4 *e.*] rudder; helm; steering wheel; handle bar; **~ь** высоты́ ✈ elevator.
румы́н *m* [1], **~ка** *f* [5; *g/pl.*: -нок]; **~ский** [16] R(o)umanian.
румя́н|а *n/pl.* [9] rouge; **~ец** *m* [1; -нца] ruddiness; blush; **~ить** [13] **1.** ⟨за-⟩ redden; **2.** ⟨на-⟩ rouge; **~ый** [14 *sh.*] ruddy, rosy; red, scarlet.
ру|нó *n* [9; *pl. st.*] fleece; **∠пор** *m* [1] megaphone; mouthpiece.
русáлка *f* [5; *g/pl.*: -лок] mermaid.
рýсло *n* [9] bed, (*a. fig.*) channel.
рýсский [16] Russian (*a. su.*); *adv.* по-рýсски (in) Russian.
рýсый [14 *sh.*] fair(-haired), blond(e).
Русь *f* [8; -си́] *hist.*, *poet.* Russia.
рути́н|а *f* [5], **~ный** [14] routine.
рýхлядь F *f* [8] lumber, stuff.
рýхнуть [20] *pf.* crash down; fail.
ручá|тельство *n* [9] guarantee; **~ться** [1], ⟨поручи́ться⟩ [16] (за В) warrant, guarantee, vouch for.
ручéй *m* [3 *e.*; -чья́] brook, stream.
рýчка *f* [5; *g/pl.*: -чек] (small) hand; handle, knob; *chair* arm; lever; pen(holder).
ручнóй [14] hand...; manual; handmade; small; ⚔ *a.* light; tame; wrist (*watch*).
рýшить(ся) [16] (*im*)*pf.* collapse, break down.
ры́б|а *f* [5] fish; **~áк** *m* [1 *e.*] fisherman; **~ий** [18] fish...; cod-liver (*oil*); **~ный** [14] fish(y); **~ный** прóмысел *m* fishery.
рыболóв *m* [1] angler; **~ный** [14] fishing; fish...; **~ство** *n* [9] fishery.
рывóк *m* [1; -вкá] jerk.
рыг|áть [1], ⟨**~нýть**⟩ [20] belch.
рыдá|ние *n* [12] sob(bing); **~ть** [1] sob.
ры́жий [17; рыж, -á, -е] red; sorrel.
ры́ло *n* [9] snout; P mug.
ры́но|к *m* [1]; -нка] market (in на П); **~чный** [14] market...
рыс|áк *m* [1 *e.*] trotter; **∠кать** [3] rove, run about; **~ь** *f* [8] trot (at, in в В, на **~и́**, Т); *zo.* lynx.
ры́твина *f* [5] rut, groove, hole.
рыть [22], ⟨вы́-⟩ dig; burrow, mine; **~ся** rummage.
рыхл|и́ть [13], ⟨вз-, раз-⟩ loosen (*soil*); **∠ый** [14; рыхл, -á, -о] friable, crumbly, loose.

ры́цар|ский [16] knightly, chivalrous; knight's; **~ь** *m* [4] knight.
рыча́г *m* [1 *e.*] lever.
рыча́ть [4 *e.*; -чу́, -чи́шь] growl.
рья́ный [14 *sh.*] zealous; mettlesome.
рю́мка *f* [5; *g/pl.*: -мок] (wine-) glass.
ряби́на *f* [5] mountain ash; F pit.
ряби́ть [14 *e.*; -и́т] ripple; mottle; *impers.* flicker (before p.'s *eyes* в П/у Р).
рябо́й [14; ряб, -á, -о] pockmarked; piebald, spotted; freckled.
ря́б|чик *m* [1] hazel grouse; **~ь** *f* ripples *pl.*; flicker.
ря́вк|ать F [1], *once* ⟨~нуть⟩ [20] bellow, bawl; snap (at на В).
ряд *m* [1; в -у́; *pl. e.*; *after* 2,3,4, ряда́] row; line; file; series; [в -е] number, several; *pl.* ranks; *thea. a.* tier; **~а́ми** in rows; из **~а** вон выходя́щий remarkable, outstanding; **~ово́й** [14] ordinary; *su.* ⚔ private; **~ом** side by side; (с Т) beside, next to; next door; close by.
ря́женый [14] disguised, masked; [masker.]
ря́са *f* [5] cassock.

С

с. *abbr.*: село́.
с, со: 1. (Р) from; since; with; for; **2.** (В) about; **3.** (Т) with; of; to.
са́бля *f* [6; *g/pl.*: -бель] saber (*Brt.* -bre).
сабот|а́ж *m* [1], sabotage; **~а́жник** *m* [1] saboteur; **~и́ровать** [7] (*im*)*pf.* sabotage.
са́ван *m* [1] shroud.
савра́сый [14] roan.
сад *m* [1; в -у́; *pl. e.*] garden.
сади́ть [15], ⟨по-⟩ *s.* сажа́ть; **~ся**, ⟨сесть⟩ [25; ся́ду, -дешь; сел, -а; се́вший] (на, в В) sit down; get in(to) *or* on, board; ⚓ embark, 🚂 entrain; mount (*horse*); alight (*bird*); ✈ land; set (*sun*); settle; sink; shrink (*fabric*); set (to *work* за В); run (aground на мель).
садо́в|ник *m* [1] gardener; **~о́дство** *n* [9] gardening, horticulture.
са́ж|а *f* [5] soot; в **~е** sooty.
сажа́ть [1] (*iter. of* сади́ть) seat; put; plant; ⚓ embark, 🚂 entrain.
са́же́нь *f* [8] *Russ.* fathom (= 7*ft.*).
саквоя́ж *m* [1] travel(l)ing bag.
сала́зки *f/pl.* [5; *gen.*: -зок] sled.
сала́т *m* [1] salad; lettuce.
са́ло *n* [9] bacon; suet, tallow.
салфе́тка *f* [5; *g/pl.*: -ток] napkin.
са́льдо *n* [*ind.*] ☤ balance.
са́льный [14; -лен, -льна] greasy; obscene.
салю́т *m* [1], **~ова́ть** [7] (*im*)*pf.* salute.
сам *m*, **~а́** *f*, **~о́** *n*, **~и** *pl.* [30] -self: я **~**(á) I ... myself; мы **~и** we ... ourselves; **~е́ц** *m* [1; -мца́] *zo.* male; **~ка** *f* [5; *g/pl.*: -мок] *zo.* female.
само|бы́тный [14; -тен, тна] original; **~ва́р** *m* [1] samovar; **~вла́стный** [14; -тен, -тна] autocratic; **~во́льный** [14; -лен, льна] arbitrary; **~го́н** *m* [1] home-brew; **~де́льный** [14] homemad, self-made.
самодержа́в|ие *n* [12] autocracy; **~ный** [14; -вен, -вна] autocratic.
само|де́ятельность *f* [8] amateur performance(s); **~дово́льный** [14; -лен, -льна] self-satisfied, self-complacent; **~ду́р** *m* [1] despot; **~защи́та** *f* [5] self-defense; **~зва́нец** *m* [1; -нца] impostor, usurper; pseudo...; **~ка́т** *m* [1] scooter; **~кри́тика** *f* [5] self-criticism.
самолёт *m* [1] airplane (*Brt.* aeroplane), aircraft; пассажи́рский **~** air liner; **~**-снаря́д *m* guided missile.
само|люби́вый [14 *sh.*] ambitious; vain, conceited; **~лю́бие** *n* [12] ambition; vanity; **~мне́ние** *n* [12] self-conceit; **~наде́янный** [14 *sh.*] self-confident, self-assertive; **~облада́ние** *n* [12] self-control; **~обма́н** *m* [1] self-deception; **~оборо́на** *f* [5] self-defense; **~обслу́живание** *n* [12] self-service; **~определе́ние** *n* [12] self-determination; **~отве́рженный** [14 *sh.*] self-denying, self-sacrificing; **~пи́шущий** [17] fountain (*pen*); **~поже́ртвование** *n* [12] self-sacrifice; **~ро́дный** [14; -ден, -дна] native, pure; original; **~сохране́ние** *n* [12] self-preservation.
самостоя́тельн|ость *f* [8] independence; **~ый** [14; -лен, -льна] independent.
само|су́д *m* [1] lynch law; **~убийство** *n* [9], **~уби́йца** *m/f* [5] suicide; **~уве́ренный** [14 *sh.*] self-confident; **~управле́ние** *n* [12] self-government; **~у́чка** *m/f* [5; *g/pl.*: -чек] self-taught p.; **~хва́льство** F *n* [9] boasting; **~хо́дный** [14] self-propelled; **~це́ль** *f* [8] end in itself; **~чу́вствие** *n* [12] (state of) health.
са́м|ый [14] the most, **~**est; the very; the (self)same; just, right; early *or* late; **~ое** бо́льшее (ма́лое) F at (the) most (least).
сан *m* [1] dignity.
санато́рий *m* [3] sanatorium.
санда́лии *f/pl.* [7] sandals.
са́ни *f/pl.* [8; *from g/pl. e.*] sled(ge).
санита́р *m* [1], **~ка** *f* [5; *g/pl.*:

-рок] nurse; *m a.* hospital attendant, orderly; **~ный** [14] sanitary.
сан|кциони́ровать [7] *(im)pf.* sanction; **~о́вник** *m* [1] dignitary.
сантиме́тр *m* [1] centimeter.
сапёр *m* [1] engineer, *Brt.* sapper.
сапо́г *m* [1 *e.*; *g/pl.:* сапо́г] boot.
сапо́жник *m* [1] shoemaker.
сара́й *m* [3] shed; barn.
саранча́ *f* [5; *g/pl.:* -че́й] locust.
сарафа́н *m* [1] sarafan (*long sleeveless gown of countrywomen*).
сард|е́лька *f* [5; *g/pl.:* -лек] wiener (thick variety); **~и́на** *f* [5] sardine.
сатана́ *m* [8] Satan.
сателли́т *m* [1] satellite.
сати́н *m* [1] sateen, glazed cotton.
сати́р|а *f* [5] satire; **~ик** *m* [1] satirist; **~и́ческий** [16] satirical.
сафья́н *m* [1] morocco.
са́хар *m* [1; *part. g.:* -у] sugar; **~истый** [14 *sh.*] sugary; **~ница** *f* [5] sugar bowl; **~ный** [14] sugar...; **~ная** боле́знь *f* diabetes.
сачо́к *m* [1; -чка́] butterfly net.
Са́ш([ень]к)а *m/f* [5] *dim. of* Алекса́ндр, -а.
сба́в|ить *s.* **~ля́ть**; **~ка** *f* [5; *g/pl.:* -вок] reduction; **~ля́ть** [28], ⟨**~ить**⟩ [14] reduce.
сбе|га́ть[1] [1], ⟨**~жа́ть**⟩ [4; -гу́, -жи́шь, -гу́т] run down; *pf.* run away, escape, flee; **-ся** come running; **∠гать**[2] [1] *pf.* run (for за T).
сбере|га́тельный [14] savings (*bank*)...; **~га́ть** [1], ⟨**∠чь**⟩ [26 г/ж: -регу́, -режёшь, -регу́т] save; preserve; **~же́ние** *n* [12] saving; preservation.
сберка́сса *f* [5] savings bank.
сби|ва́ть [1], ⟨**~ть**⟩ [собью́, -бьёшь; сбей!; сби́тый] knock down (*or* off); overthrow (*a.* с ног); shoot down; whip (*cream*), beat up (*eggs*), churn (*butter*); mix; lead (astray с пути́; **-ся** lose one's way); (**-ся** be[come] confus(ed) *or* puzzl(ed) (с то́лку); *refl. a.* run o.s. off (one's legs с ног); flock; **∠вчивый** [14 *sh.*] confused; uneven; **∠ть(ся)** *s.* **~ва́ть(ся)**.
сбли|жа́ть [1], ⟨**∠зить**⟩ [15] bring *or* draw together; **-ся** become friends (with с T); **~же́ние** *n* [12] (*a. pol.*) rapprochement; approach (-es).
сбо́ку sideways; next to it.
сбор *m* [1] collection; gathering; harvest; levy; tax; duty; receipts *pl.*; ⚔ muster; *pl.* preparations; в **∠е** assembled; **∠ище** *n* [11] concourse, crowd; **∠ка** *f* [5; *g/pl.:* -рок] pleat, tuck; ⊕ assemblage; **∠ник** *m* [1] collection; symposium; **∠ный** [14] ⚔ assembly (*point*); *sport:* select (*team*); **∠очный** [14] assembling.
сбр|а́сывать [1], ⟨**~о́сить**⟩ [15] throw off, drop, shed; discard; **~од** *m* [1] rabble, riff-raff; **~о́сить** *s.* **~а́сывать**; **~у́я** *f* [6] harness.

сбы|ва́ть [1], ⟨**~ть**⟩ [сбу́ду, -дешь; сбыл, -а́, -о] sell, market; get rid of (*a.* с рук); fall; **-ся** come true; **~т** *m* [1] sale; **~ть(ся)** *s.* **~ва́ть(ся)**.
сва́д|ебный [14], **~ьба** *f* [5; *g/pl.:* -деб] wedding.
сва́л|ивать [1], ⟨**~и́ть**⟩ [13; -алю́, -а́лишь] knock down, overthrow; fell; dump; heap up; shift (off) (to на B); **-ся** fall down; **~ка** *f* [5; *g/pl.:* -лок] dump; brawl.
сва́р|ивать [1], ⟨**~и́ть**⟩ [13; сварю́, сва́ришь; сва́ренный] weld; **~ка** *f* [5], **~очный** [14] welding.
сварли́вый [14 *sh.*] quarrelsome.
сва|т *m* [1] matchmaker; **∠тать** [1], ⟨по-⟩ seek (**-ся** ask) in marriage (for за B); **∠ха** *f* [5] matchmaker.
сва́я *f* [6; *g/pl.:* свай] pile.
све́д|ение *n* [12] information; приня́ть к **~ению** take notice (of B); **~ущий** [17 *sh.*] expert, versed.
све́ж|есть *f* [8] freshness; **~е́ть** [8], ⟨по-⟩ freshen, become fresh; **~ий** [15; свеж, -а́, -о́, све́жи́] fresh; cool; latest; new.
свезти́ *s.* свози́ть.
свёкла *f* [5; *g/pl.:* -кол] beet.
свёкор *m* [1; -кра] (**свекро́вь** *f* [8]) father-(mother-)in-law (*husband's father or mother resp.*).
свер|га́ть [1], ⟨**∠гнуть**⟩ [21] overthrow; dethrone (с тро́на); shake off (*yoke*); **~же́ние** *n* [12] overthrow; **∠ить** *s.* **~я́ть**.
сверк|а́ть [1], *once* ⟨**~ну́ть**⟩ [20] sparkle, glitter; flash; мо́лния **~а́ет** it lightens.
сверл|е́ние *n* [12], **~и́льный** [14] drilling; **~и́ть** [13], ⟨про-⟩, **~о́** *n* [9; *pl. st.:* свёрла] drill.
свер|ну́ть(ся) *s.* свёртывать(ся) & свора́чивать; **∠стник** *s.* рове́сник.
свёрт|ок *m* [1; -тка] roll; parcel; **~ывать** [1], ⟨сверну́ть⟩ [20] roll (up); turn; curtail; break up (*camp*); twist; **-ся** coil up; curdle; coagulate.
сверх (P) above, beyond; over; besides; **~** того́ moreover; **~звуково́й** [14] supersonic; **~при́быль** *f* [8] surplus profit; **∠у** from above; **~уро́чный** [14] overtime; **~шта́тный** [14] supernumerary; **~ъесте́ственный** [14 *sh.*] supernatural.
сверчо́к *m* [1; -чка́] *zo.* cricket.
свер|я́ть [28], ⟨**∠ить**⟩ [13] compare, collate.
све́сить *s.* све́шивать.
свести́(сь) *s.* своди́ть(ся).
свет *m* [1] light; world (in на П); day(light); (high) society; P dear, darling; чуть **~** at dawn; **~а́ть** [1] dawn; **~и́ло** *n* [9] star; (*celestial*) body; **~и́ть(ся)** [15] shine.
светл|е́ть [8], ⟨по-⟩ brighten; grow light(er); **~о...** light...; **∠ый** [14; -тел, -тла́, -о] light, bright; serene; **~я́к** *m* [1 *e.*], **~ячо́к** [1 *e.*; -чка́] glowworm.

свето|во́й [14] light...; **~маскиро́вка** *f* [5; *g/pl.*: -вок] blackout; **~фо́р** *m* [1] traffic light.

све́тский [16] secular, worldly; of high society.

светя́щийся [17] luminous.

свеча́ *f* [5; *pl.*: све́чи, -е́й, -а́м] candle; ⚡ plug.

све́|шивать [1], ⟨**~сить**⟩ [15] hang down; dangle; **-ся** hang over.

сви|ва́ть [1], ⟨**~ть**⟩ [совью́, -вьёшь; *cf.* вить] braid, plait; build (*nest*).

свида́ни|е *n* [12] appointment, meeting (at на П); до **~я** good-by(e).

свиде́тель *m* [4], **~ница** *f* [5] witness; **~ство** *n* [9] evidence; certificate; licence; **~ствовать** [7], ⟨за-⟩ testify; *impf.* (о П) show.

свина́рник *m* [1] pigsty.

свине́ц *m* [1; -нца́] lead.

свин|и́на *f* [5] pork; **~ка** *f* [5; *g/pl.*: -нок] mumps; морска́я **~ка** guinea pig; **~о́й** [14] pig...; pork...; **~ство** *n* [9] dirty *or* rotten act, smut; **~цо́вый** [14] lead(en).

сви́н|чивать [1], ⟨**~ти́ть**⟩ [15 *e.*; -нчу́, -нти́шь; сви́нченный] screw together, fasten with screws.

свинья́ *f* [6; *pl. st.*, *gen.*: -не́й; *a.* -нья́м] pig, hog, swine.

свире́ль *f* [8] pipe, reed.

свире́п|ствовать [7] rage; **~ый** [14 *sh.*] fierce, furious, grim.

свиса́ть [1] hang down; slouch.

свист *m* [1] whistle; hiss; **~а́ть** [3] & **~е́ть** [11], *once* ⟨**~нуть**⟩ [20] whistle; *pf.* P pilfer; **~о́к** *m* [1; -тка́] whistle.

сви́т|а *f* [5] retinue, suite; **~ер** (-ter) *m* [1] sweater; **~ок** *m* [1; -тка] roll; **~ь** *s.* свива́ть.

свихну́ть F [20] *pf.* sprain; **-ся** go mad.

свищ *m* [1 *e.*] fistula; crack.

свобо́д|а *f* [5] freedom, liberty; на **~у** (*set*) free; **~ный** [14; -ден, -дна] free (from, of от Р); vacant (*seat, etc.*); spare (*time, etc.*); ready (*money*); easy; loose; fluent; exempt (from от Р); **~омы́слящий** [17] freethinking; *su.* freethinker, liberal.

свод *m* [1] △ vault; ⚖ code.

своди́ть [15], ⟨свести́⟩ [25] lead, take (down); bring (together); close (*vault*); reduce (to в В); square (*accounts*); contract; remove; drive (mad с ума́); **~** на нет bring to nought; **-ся**, ⟨-сь⟩ (к Д) come *or* amount (to), result (in); turn (into на В).

сво́д|ка *f* [5; *g/pl.*: -док] summary; report, communiqué; *typ.* revise; **~ный** [14] summary; step...; **~ча́тый** [14] vaulted.

свое|во́льный [14; -лен, -льна] self-willed, wil(l)ful; **~вре́менный** [14; -менен, -менна]] timely; **~нра́вный** [14; -вен, -вна] capricious; **~обра́зный** [14; -зен, -зна] original; peculiar.

свози́ть [15], ⟨свезти́⟩ [24] take.

сво|й *m*, **~я́** *f*, **~ё** *n*, **~и́** *pl.* [24] my, his, her, its, our, your, their (*refl.*); one's own; peculiar; *su. pl.* one's people, folks, relations; не **~й** frantic (*voice* in Т); **~йственный** [14 *sh.*] peculiar (to Д); (p.'s Д) usual; **~йство** *n* [9] property, quality; F kind.

сво́|лочь *f* [8] rabble, riff-raff; rascal; **~ра** *f* [5] pack; **~ра́чивать** [1], ⟨сверну́ть⟩ [20] &, P, ⟨**~роти́ть**⟩ [15] turn (off с Р); **~я́ченица** *f* [5] sister-in-law (*wife's sister*).

сшы|ка́ться [1], ⟨**~кнуться**⟩ [21] get used (to с Т); **~сока́** haughtily; **~ше** from above; (Р) over; beyond.

связ|а́ть(ся) *s.* **~ывать(ся)**; **~и́ст** *m* [1] signalman; **~ка** *f* [5; *g/pl.*: -зок] bunch; *anat.* ligament; (*vocal*) cord; *gr.* copula; **~ный** [16; -зен, -зна] coherent; **~ывать** [1], ⟨**~а́ть**⟩ [3] tie (together), bind; connect, join; unite; associate; *teleph.* put through, connect; **-ся** get into touch, contact; associate (with с Т); **~ь** *f* [8; в -зи́] tie, bond; connection (*Brt.* connexion); relation; contact; liaison; ⚔ signal (*service, etc.*); communication; post(al system).

свят|и́ть [15 *e.*; -ячу́, -яти́шь], ⟨о-⟩ consecrate, hallow; **~ки** *f/pl.* [5; *gen.*: -ток] Christmastide (at на П); **~о́й** [14; свят, -á, -о] holy; sacred; godly; solemn; Easter (week *su. f*); *su.* saint; **~ость** *f* [8] holiness, sanctity; **~ота́тство** *n* [9] sacrilege; **~о́ша** *m/f* [5] hypocrite; **~ы́ня** *f* [6] relic; sanctuary.

свяще́нн|ик *m* [1] priest; **~ый** [14 *sh.*] holy; sacred.

с. г. *abbr.*: сего́ го́да; *cf.* сей.

сгиб *m* [1], **~а́ть** [1], ⟨согну́ть⟩ [20] bend, curve, fold; *v/i.* **-ся**.

сгла́|живать [1], ⟨**~дить**⟩ [15] smooth; **-ся** be smoothed (out).

сгнива́ть [1] *s.* гнить.

сго́вор *m* [1] F *s.* угово́р; **~и́ться** [13] *pf.* agree; come to terms; **~чивый** [14 *sh.*] compliant, amenable.

сго|ня́ть [28], ⟨согна́ть⟩ [сгоню́, сго́нишь; согна́л, -á, -о; со́гнанный] drive (off); **~ра́ние** *n* [12] combustion; **~ра́ть** [1], ⟨**~ре́ть**⟩ [9] burn down; perish; die (of от, с Р); **~ряча́** in a temper.

сгр|еба́ть [1], ⟨**~ести́**⟩ [24-б-: сгребу́; сгрёб, сгребла́] rake up; shovel (down); **~ужа́ть** [1], ⟨**~узи́ть**⟩ [15 & 15 *e.*; -ужу́, -у́зи́шь; -у́женный & -ужённый] unload.

сгу|сти́ть *s.* **~ща́ть**; **~сток** *m* [1; -тка] clot; **~ща́ть** [1], ⟨**~сти́ть**⟩ [15 *e.*; -ущу́, -усти́шь; -ущённый] thicken; condense; **~ща́ть** кра́ски exaggerate.

сда|ва́ть [5], ⟨**~ть**⟩ [сдам, сдашь, *etc. s.* дать] deliver, hand in (*or* over); surrender; check, register; rent, let (out); deal (*cards*); return

(*change*); pass (*examination*); yield; P seem; **-ся** surrender; **~ётся ... ...** for rent (*Brt.* to let); **∠вливать** [1], ⟨**~вить**⟩ [14] squeeze; **~ть(ся)** *s.* **~вáть(ся)**; **∠ча** *f* [5] surrender; delivery; deal; change; check, register.
сдвиг *m* [1] shift; (land)slide; **~áть** [1], ⟨**сдви́нуть**⟩ [20] move (*v/i.* **-ся**); join; knit (*brow*).
сдéл|ка *f* [5; *g/pl.*: **-лок**] bargain, transaction, deal; arrangement, settlement; **~ьный** [14] piece(*-work*).
сдéрж|анный [14 *sh.*] reserved, (self-)restrained; **~ивать** [1], ⟨**~áть**⟩ [4] check, restrain; suppress; keep (*word, etc.*); **-ся** control o.s.
сдирáть [1], ⟨**содрáть**⟩ [**сдерý, -рёшь; содрáл, -á, -о; сóдранный**] tear off (*or* down), strip; flay (*a. fig*).
сдóбн|ый [14]: **~ая бýл(оч)ка** *f* bun.
сдружи́ться *s.* **подружи́ться**.
сду|вáть [1], ⟨**~ть**⟩ [16], *once* ⟨**∠нуть**⟩ [20] blow off (*or* away); **∠ру** F foolishly.
сеáнс *m* [1] sitting; *cinema:* show.
себестóимость *f* [8] prime cost.
себ|я́ [21] myself, yourself, himself, herself, itself, ourselves, yourselves, themselves (*refl.*); oneself; **к ~é** home; into one's room; **от ~я́** on p.'s behalf; **тáк ~é** so-so; **~ялюби́вый** [14 *sh.*] selfish, self-loving.
сев *m* [1] sowing.
Севастóполь *m* [4] Sevastopol.
сéвер *m* [1] north; *cf.* **востóк**; **~ный** [14] north(ern); northerly; arctic; **Ⓢный Ледови́тый океáн** *m* Arctic Ocean; **~о-востóк** *m* [1] northeast; **~о-востóчный** [14] northeast...; **~о-зáпад** *m* [1] northwest; **~о-зáпадный** [14] northwest...
сегóдня today; **~ ýтром** this morning; **~шний** [15] today's; this (*day*).
сед|éть [8], ⟨**по-**⟩ turn gray (*Brt.* grey); **~инá** *f* [5] gray hair; *pl. a. fig.* great age.
седл|áть [1], ⟨**о-**⟩, **~ó** *n* [9; *pl. st.*: **сёдла, сёдел, сёдлам**] saddle.
седо|волóсый [14 *sh.*], **∠й** [14; **сед, -á, -о**] gray(-haired, -headed), *Brt.* grey.
седóк *m* [1 *e.*] horseman; passenger.
седьмóй [14] seventh; *cf.* **пя́тый**.
сезóн *m* [1] season; **~ный** [14] seasonal.
сей *m*, **сия́** *f*, **сиé** *n*, **сии́** *pl.* † [29] this; **сим** herewith, hereby; **при сём** enclosed; **сегó гóда (мéсяца)** of this year (month); *cf.* **порá**.
сейчáс now, at present; presently, (*a.* **~ же**) immediately, at once; just (now).
секрéт *m* [1] secret (in **по** Д, **под** T); **~ариáт** *m* [1] secretariat; **~áрь** *m* [4 *e.*] secretary; **~ничать** F [1] be secretive, act secretely; whisper; **~ный** [14; **-тен, -тна**] secret; confidential.
сек|суáльный [14; **-лен, -льна**] sexual; **∠та** *f* [5] sect; **∠тор** *m* [1] sector; sphere, branch.
секýнд|а *f* [5] second; **~ный** [14] second...; **~омéр** *m* [1] stop watch.
селёдка *f* [5; *g/pl.*: **-док**] herring.
селез|ёнка *f* [5; *g/pl.*: **-нок**] *anat.* spleen; **'~ень** *m* [4; **-зня**] drake.
селéние *n* [12] settlement, colony.
сели́т|ра *f* [5] saltpeter, niter, *Brt.* nitre; **~ь(ся)** [13] *s.* **поселя́ть(ся)**.
сел|ó *n* [9; *pl. st.*: **сёла**] village (in **в** *or* **на** П); **на ~é** *a.* in the country; **ни к ~ý ни к гóроду** F without rhyme or reason.
сельд|ерéй *m* [3] celery; **~ь** *f* [8; *from g/pl. e.*] herring.
сéль|ский [16] rural, country..., village...; **~ское хозя́йство** *n* agriculture; **~скохозя́йственный** [14] agricultural; farming; **~совéт** *m* [1] village soviet.
сéльтерская *f* [16] Seltzer.
сёмга *f* [5] salmon.
семéй|ный [14] family...; married; **~ство** *n* [9] family.
Семён *m* [1] Simeon.
семен|и́ть F [13] trip, mince; **~нóй** [14] seed...; seminal.
семёрка *f* [5; *g/pl.*: **-рок**] seven; *cf.* **двóйка**.
сéмеро [37] seven; *cf.* **двóе**.
семé|стр *m* [1] term, semester; **'~чко** *n* [9; *pl.*: **-чки, -чек, -чкам**] seed.
семи|деся́тый [14] seventieth; *cf.* **пя́(тидеся́)тый**; **~лéтка** *f* [5; *g/pl.*: **-ток**] seven-year school (*or* plan); **~лéтний** [15] seven-year (old), of seven.
семинáр *m* [1], **~ий** *m* [3] seminar; **~ия** *f* [7] seminary.
семисóтый [14] seven hundredth.
семнáдцат|ый [14] seventeenth; *cf.* **пя́тый**; **~ь** [35] seventeen; *cf.* **пять**.
семь [35] seven; *cf.* **пять** & **пя́тый**; **∠десят** [35] seventy; **~сóт** [36] seven hundred; **∠ю** seven times.
семья́ *f* [6; *pl.*: **сéмьи, семéй, сéмьям**] family; **~ни́н** *m* [1] family man.
сéмя *n* [13; *pl.*: **-менá, -мя́н, -менáм**] seed (*a. fig.*).
сенáт *m* [1] senate; **~ор** *m* [1] senator.
сéни *f/pl.* [8; *from gen. e.*] hall(way).
сéно *n* [9] hay; **~вáл** *m* [1] hayloft; **~кóс** *m* [1] haymaking; *cf.* **коси́лка**.
сен|сациóнный [14; **-óнен, -óнна**] sensational; **~тиментáльный** [14; **-лен, -льна**] sentimental.
сентя́брь *m* [4 *e.*] September.
сень † *f* [8; **в -ни́**] shade; shelter.
сепарáтный [14] separate.
сéра *f* [5] sulfur; F earwax.
серб *m* [1], **∠(ия́н)ка** *f* [5; *g/pl.*: **-б(ия́н)ок**] Serb(ian); **∠ский** [16] Serbian.
серви́|з *m* [1] service, set; **~ровáть** [7] (*im*)*pf.* serve.
Сергéй *m* [3] Sergius, Serge.

серде́чный [14; -чен, -чна] heart('s); hearty, cordial; intimate; dear; best.
серди́|тый [14 *sh.*] angry, mad (with, at на В), wrathful; irascible, fretful; spiteful, vicious; **~ть** [15], ⟨рас-⟩ annoy, vex, fret, anger; **-ся** be(come) angry (with на В).
се́рдц|е *n* [11; *pl. e.*: -дца́, -де́ц, -дца́м] heart; temper; anger; darling, love, sweetheart (*address*); от всего́ ~а whole-heartedly; по́ ~у (Д) to one's liking; положа́ ру́ку на́ ~е F (quite) frankly; **~ебие́ние** *n* [12] palpitation; **~еви́на** *f* [5] core, heart.
серебр|и́стый [14 *sh.*] silvery; **~и́ть** [13], ⟨по-, вы́-⟩ silver; **-ся** glisten like silver; **~о́** *n* [9] silver; **∠яный** [14] silver(y).
середи́на *f* [5] middle; center (*Brt.* -tre); mean.
Сер|ёж([ень]к)а *m* [5] *dim. of* Серге́й; **2е́ть** [8], ⟨по-⟩ turn (*impf.* show) gray (*Brt.* grey).
сержа́нт *m* [1] sergeant; мла́дший ~ corporal.
сери́|йный [14] serial; multiple; **'~я** *f* [7] series.
се́рна *f* [5] chamois.
се́р|ный [14] sulfuric; sulfur...; **~ова́тый** [14 *sh.*] grayish, Brt. greyish.
серп *m* [1 *e.*] sickle; crescent.
се́рый [14; сер, -а́, -о] gray, *Brt.* grey; dull (*a. fig.* = humdrum).
се́рьги *f/pl.* [5; серёг, серьга́м; *sg. e.*] earrings.
серьёзн|ый [14; -зен, -зна] serious, grave; earnest (in ~o); **~o** *a.* indeed, really.
се́ссия *f* [7] session (in на П).
сестра́ *f* [5; *pl.*: сёстры, сестёр, сёстрам] sister; nurse; на́ша ~ F (such as) we.
сесть *s.* сади́ться.
се́т|ка *f* [5; *g/pl.*: -ток] net; ⚡ grid; scale; **~овать** [1] complain (about на В); **~ча́тка** *f* [5; *g/pl.*: -ток] retina; **~ь** *f* [8; в се́ти́; *from g/pl. e.*] net; network.
сече́ние *n* [12] section.
сечь[1] [26; *pt. e.*; сек, секла́] cut (up), chop, hew; cleave; **-ся** split; ravel; **~**[2] [26: *pt. st.*; сек, се́кла], ⟨вы́-⟩ whip, flog.
се́ялка *f* [5; *g/pl.*: -лок] seeder.
се́ять [27], ⟨по-⟩ sow (*a. fig.*).
сжа́литься [13] *pf.* (над Т) have *or* take pity (on), pity.
сжа́т|ие *n* [12] pressure; compression; **~ый** [14] compressed; compact, concise, terse; **~ь(ся)** *s.* сжима́ть(ся) & жать[1], жать[2].
сжига́ть [1], ⟨сжечь⟩ *cf.* жечь.
сжима́ть [1], ⟨сжать⟩ [сожму́, -мёшь; сжа́тый] (com)press, squeeze; clench; **-ся** contract; shrink; become clenched.
сза́ди (from) behind (*as prp.*: Р).
сзыва́ть *s.* созыва́ть.
Сиби́р|ь *f* [8] Siberia; **2ский** [16], **2я́к** *m* [1 *e.*], **2я́чка** *f* [5; *g/pl.*: -чек] Siberian.
си́вый [14; сив, -а́, -о] (ash) gray (grey).
сига́р(е́т)а *f* [5] cigar(ette).
сигна́л *m* [1], **~изи́ровать** [7] (*im*)*pf.*, **~ьный** [14] signal; alarm.
сиде́лка *f* [5; *g/pl.*: -лок] nurse.
сиде́|нье *n* [10] seat; **~ть** [11; си́дя] sit (at, over за Т); be, stay; fit (a p. на П); **-ся**: ему́ не сиди́тся he can't sit still.
сидр *m* [1] cider.
сидя́чий [17] sedentary; sitting.
си́зый [14; сиз, -а́, -о] (bluish) gray, *Brt.* grey; dove-colo(u)red.
си́л|а *f* [5] strength; force; power, might; vigo(u)r; intensity; efficacy; energy; volume; свои́ми ~ами by o. s.; в ~у (Р) by virtue (of); не в ~ах unable; не по ~ам above one's strength; ~ нет F awfully; изо всех ~ F with all one's might; **~а́ч** *m* [1 *e.*] athlete; **~иться** [13] try, endeavo(u)r; **~ово́й** [14] power...
сило́к *m* [1; -лка́] snare, noose.
си́льн|ый [14; си́лен & силён, -льна́, -о, си́льны́] strong; powerful, mighty; intense; heavy (*rain*); bad (*cold*); great; ⚡ power...; **~о** *a.* very much; hard.
си́мвол *m* [1] symbol; **~и́ческий** [16], **~и́чный** [14; -чен, -чна] symbolic(al).
симметри́|чный [14; -чен, -чна] symmetrical; **~я** *f* [7] symmetry.
симпат|изи́ровать [7] sympathize (with Д); **~и́чный** [14; -чен, -чна] nice, sympathetic; он мне ~и́чен I like him; **∠тия** *f* [7] sympathy.
симул|и́ровать [7] (*im*)*pf.* feign, sham; malinger; **~я́нт** *m* [1], **~я́нтка** *f* [5; *g/pl.*: -ток] simulator.
симфони́|ческий [16] symphonic, symphony...; **'~я** *f* [7] symphony.
синдика́т *m* [1] syndicate.
син|ева́ *f* [5] blue; **~ева́тый** [14 *sh.*] bluish; **~е́ть** [8], ⟨по-⟩ turn (*impf.* show) blue; **∠ий** [15; синь, синя́, си́не] blue; **~и́льный** [14] hydrocyanic, prussic (*acid*); **~и́ть** [13], ⟨под-⟩ blue; **~и́ца** *f* [5] titmouse.
син|о́д *m* [1] synod; **~о́ним** *m* [1] synonym; **∠таксис** *m* [1] syntax; **∠тез** *m* [1] synthesis; **~тети́ческий** [16] synthetic(al); **~хронизи́ровать** [7] (*im*)*pf.* synchronize.
синь *f* [8], **∠ка** *f* [5; *g/pl.*: -нек] blue.
синя́к *m* [1 *e.*] livid spot, bruise.
си́плый [14; сипл, -а́, -о] hoarse.
сире́на *f* [5] siren.
сире́н|евый [14], **~ь** *f* [8] lilac.
сиро́п *m* [1] syrup.
сирота́ *m/f* [5; *pl. st.*: сиро́ты] orphan.
систе́ма *f* [5] system; **~ти́ческий**

[16], **~ти́чный** [14; -чен, -чна] systematic(al).
си́тец *m* [1; -тца] chintz, cotton.
си́то *n* [9] sieve.
Сици́лия *f* [7] Sicily.
сия́|ние *n* [12] radiance; light, shine; halo; **~ть** [28] shine, beam; radiate.
сказ|а́ние *n* [12] legend; saga; story; **~а́ть** *s.* говори́ть; **∠ка** *f* [5; *g/pl.*: -зок] fairy tale; tale, fib; **∠очный** [14; -чен, -чна] fabulous, fantastic; fairy (tale)...
сказу́емое *n* [14] *gr.* predicate.
скак|а́ть [3] skip, hop, leap; gallop; race; **~ово́й** [14] race...; racing.
скал|а́ *f* [5; *pl. st.*] rock, cliff, crag; **~и́стый** [14 *sh.*] rocky, cliffy; **∠ить** [13], ⟨о-⟩ show, bare (*one's teeth*); F *impf.* grin; jeer; **∠ка** *f* [5; *g/pl.*: -лок] rolling pin; **∠ывать** [1], ⟨сколо́ть⟩ [17] pin together; split (off); prick.
скам|е́ечка *f* [5; *g/pl.*: -чек] footstool; *a. dim. of* **~е́йка** *f* [5; *g/pl.*: -е́ек], **~ья́** *f* [6; *nom/pl. a. st.*] bench; **~ья́** подсуди́мых dock.
сканда́л *m* [1] scandal; row; F shame; **~ить** [13], ⟨на-⟩ row; **~ьный** [14; -лен, -льна] scandalous; F wretched.
скандина́вский [16] Scandinavian.
ска́пливать(ся) [1] *s.* **скопля́ть** (-ся).
скар|б F [1] belongings, things *pl.*; **∠едный** F [14; -ден, -дна] stingy; **~лати́на** *f* [5] scarlet fever.
скат *m* [1] slope, pitch.
скат|а́ть *s.* ска́тывать 2; **∠ерть** *f* [8; *from g/pl. e.*] tablecloth.
ска́т|ывать [1] **1.** ⟨**~и́ть**⟩ [15] roll (*or* slide) down (*v/i.* **-ся**); **2.** ⟨**~а́ть**⟩ [1] roll (up); P copy.
ска́ч|ка *f* [5; *g/pl.*: -чек] gallop; *pl.* horse race(s); **~о́к** *s.* **прыжо́к.**
ска́шивать [1], ⟨скоси́ть⟩ [15] mow off *or* down; slope; bevel.
сква́жина *f* [5] chink, crack; pore; ⊕ hole; замо́чная ~ keyhole.
сквер *m* [1] square, park; **~nосло́вить** [14] talk smut; **∠ный** [14; -рен, -рна́, -o] nasty, foul.
сквоз|и́ть [15; -и́т] shine through, appear; **~и́т** there is a draft, *Brt.* draught; **~но́й** [14] through...; thorough...; transparent; **~ня́к** *m* [1 *e.*] draft, *Brt.* draught; **~ь** (B) through.
скворе́|ц *m* [1; -рца́] starling; **~чница** (-ʃn-) *f* [5] nestling box.
скеле́т *m* [1] skeleton.
скепти́ческий [16] skeptic(al).
ски́|дка *f* [5; *g/pl.*: -док] discount, rebate; **~дывать** [1], ⟨**~нуть**⟩ [20] throw off *or* down; take *or* put off; discount, reduce; **~петр** *m* [1] scepter, *Brt.* -tre; **~пида́р** *m* [1] turpentine; **~рд** *m* [1 *e.*] haystack.
скис|а́ть [1], ⟨**∠нуть**⟩ [21] turn sour.
скита́|лец *m* [1; -льца] wanderer; **~ться** [1] wander, rove.
склад *m* [1] warehouse, storehouse (in на П); ⚔ depot; constitution, disposition, turn; breed; way (*of life*); F harmony; sense; **∠ка** *f* [5; *g/pl.*: -док] pleat, fold; crease; wrinkle; **~но́й** [14] fold(ing), collapsible; camp...; falt(*boat*); **∠ный** [14; -ден, -дна́, -o] harmonious; coherent; fluent, smooth; P well-made (*or* -built); accommodating; **∠чина** *f* [5]: в ~чину by clubbing (together); **∠ывать** [1], ⟨сложи́ть⟩ [16] lay *or* put (together, up, down); pile up; pack (up); fold; add; compose; lay down (*arms; one's life*); сложа́ ру́ки idle; **-ся** (be) form (-ed), develop; F club (together).
скле́и|вать [1], ⟨**~ть**⟩ [13; **-е́ю**] stick together (*v/i.* **-ся**).
склеп *m* [1] crypt, vault.
скло́ка *f* [5] squabble.
склон *m* [1] slope; **~е́ние** *n* [12] inclination; *gr.* declension; *ast.* declination; **~и́ть(ся)** *s.* **~я́ть(ся)**; **∠ность** *f* [8] inclination (*fig.*; to, for к Д), disposition; **∠ный** [14; -о́нен, -онна́, -o] inclined (to к Д), disposed; **~я́ть** [28] **1.** ⟨**~и́ть**⟩ [13; -оню́, -о́нишь; -онённый] bend, incline (*a. fig.*; *v/i.* **-ся**; sink); persuade; **2.** ⟨просклоня́ть⟩ *gr.* (**-ся** be) decline(d).
скоб|а́ *f* [5; *pl.*: ско́бы, скоб, скоба́м] cramp (iron); **∠ка** *f* [5; *g/pl.*: -бок] cramp; *gr.*, *typ.* bracket, parenthesis; **~ли́ть** [13; -облю́, -о́бли́шь; -о́бленный] scrape; **~яно́й** [14] hard(*ware*).
скова́ть *s.* ско́вывать.
сковорода́ *f* [5; *pl.*: ско́вороды, -ро́д, -да́м] frying pan.
ско́в|ывать [1], ⟨**~а́ть**⟩ [7 *e.*; скую́, скуёшь] forge (together); weld; fetter, chain; bind; arrest.
сколо́ть *s.* ска́лывать.
скольз|и́ть [15 *e.*; -льжу́, -льзи́шь], *once* ⟨**~ну́ть**⟩ [20] slide, glide, slip; **∠кий** [16; -зок, -зка́, -o] slippery.
ско́лько [32] how (*or* as) much, many; ~ лет, ~ зим *s.* ве́чность F.
сконча́ться [1] *pf.* die, expire.
скоп|ля́ть [28], ⟨**~и́ть**⟩ [14] accumulate, gather (*v/i.* **-ся**), amass; save; **~ле́ние** *n* [12] accumulation; gathering, crowd.
скорб|е́ть [10 *e.*; -блю́, -би́шь] grieve (over о П); **∠ный** [14; -бен, -бна] mournful, sorrowful; **~ь** *f* [8] grief, sorrow.
скорлупа́ *f* [5; *pl. st.*: -лу́пы] shell.
скорня́к *m* [1 *e.*] furrier.
скоро|гово́рка *f* [5; *g/pl.*: -рок] tongue twister; rapid speech, sputter; **∠мный** [14; -мен, -мна] meat, milk (*food, forbidden in Lent*); **~пости́жный** [14; -жен, -жна] sudden; **~спе́лый** [14 *sh.*] early; pre-

cocious; **\~стно́й** [14] (high-)speed-...; **'\~сть** *f* [8; *from g/pl. e.*] speed; rate; *mot.* gear; груз большо́й (ма́лой) '\~сти express (ordinary) freight; **\~те́чный** [14; -чен, -чна] transient; ♞ galloping.

ско́р|ый [14; скор, -а́, -о] quick, fast, rapid, swift; speedy, prompt; first (*aid*); near (*future*); early (*reply*); \~о *a.* soon; \~ée всего́ F most probably; на \~ую ру́ку F in haste, offhand, anyhow.

скоси́ть *s.* ска́шивать.

скот *m* [1 *e.*] cattle, livestock; **\~и́на** *f* [5] F cattle; P brute; dolt, boor; **\~ный** [14]: \~ный двор cattle yard; **\~обо́йня** *f* [6; *g/pl.*: -óен] slaughterhouse; **\~ово́дство** *n* [9] cattle breeding; **\~ский** [16] brutish, bestial, swinish.

скребо́к *m* [1; -бка́] scraper.

скре́жет *m* [1], **\~а́ть** [3] (T) gnash.

скре́п|а *f* [5] cramp, clamp; **\~и́ть** *s.* \~ля́ть; **\~ка** *f* [5; *g/pl.*: -пок] (paper) clip; **\~ле́ние** *n* [12] fastening; **\~ля́ть** [28], ‹\~и́ть› [14 *e.*; -плю́, -пи́шь; -плённый] fasten; tighten; corroborate; validate; countersign; \~я́ се́рдце reluctantly.

скрести́ [24 -б-: скребу́; скрёб] scrape; scratch.

скре́щива|ть [1], ‹скрести́ть› [15 *e.*; -ещу́, -ести́шь; -ещённый] cross (*v/i.* **-ся**); **\~ние** *n* [12] crossing.

скрип *m* [1] creak; scratch; **\~а́ч** *m* [1 *e.*] violinist; **\~е́ть** [10 *e.*; -плю́, -пи́шь], ‹про-›, *once* ‹\~нуть› [20] creak; scratch; grit, gnash; **\~ка** *f* [5; *g/pl.*: -пок] violin.

скро́мн|ость *f* [8] modesty; **\~ый** [14; -мен, -мна́, -о] modest; frugal.

скру́|чивать [1], ‹\~ти́ть› [15] braid; roll; bind; P bend.

скры|ва́ть [1], ‹\~ть› [22] hide, conceal (from от P); **-ся** disappear; hide; **\~тность** *f* [8] reserve; **\~тный** [14; -тен, -тна] reserved, reticent; **\~тый** [14] concealed; latent; secret; **\~ть(ся)** *s.* \~ва́ть(ся).

скря́га *m/f* [5] miser.

ску́дный [14; -ден, -дна́, -о] scanty, poor.

ску́ка *f* [5] boredom, ennui.

скула́ *f* [5; *pl. st.*] cheekbone; **\~стый** [14 *sh.*] with high cheekbones.

скули́ть [13] whimper.

скульпту́ра *f* [5] sculpture.

ску́мбрия *f* [7] mackerel.

скуп|а́ть [1], ‹\~и́ть› [14] buy up.

скуп|и́ться [14], ‹по-› be stingy (*or* sparing), stint (in, of на В); **\~о́й** [14; скуп, -а́, -о] avaricious, stingy; sparing (in на В); scanty, poor; taciturn (на слова́); *su.* miser; **\~ость** *f* [8] avarice.

скуч|а́ть [1] be bored; (по П *or* Д) long (for), miss; **\~ный** (-ʃn-) [14; -чен, -чна́, -о] boring, tedious, dull; sad; (Д) \~но feel bored.

слаб|е́ть [8], ‹о-› weaken, slacken; **\~и́тельный** [14] laxative (*n a. su.*); **\~ово́льный** [14; -лен, -льна] weak-willed (*or* -minded); **\~оси́льный** [14; -лен, -льна] *s.* \~ый; **\~ость** *f* [8] weakness (*a. fig.* = foible; for к Д); infirmity; **\~оу́мный** [14; -мен, -мна] feeble-minded; **\~охара́ктерный** [14; -рен, -рна] flabby; **\~ый** [14; слаб, -а́, -о] weak (*a.* ⚡), feeble; faint; infirm; delicate; flabby; poor.

сла́в|а *f* [5] glory; fame, renown; reputation, repute; (Д) hail; long live; \~а бо́гу! God be praised!, thank goodness!; на \~у F first-rate, A-one; **\~ить** [14], ‹про-› glorify; praise, extol; **-ся** be famous (for T) **\~ный** [14; -вен, -вна́, -о] famous; glorious; F nice; capital, dandy.

славян|и́н *m* [1; *pl.*: -я́не, -я́н], **\~ка** *f* [5; *g/pl.*: -нок] Slav; **\~ский** [16] Slavic, *Brt.* Slavonic.

слага́ть [1], ‹сложи́ть› [16] compose; lay down; resign (from); exonerate; relieve o.s. (of); *cf.* скла́дывать(ся); **-ся** *a.* be composed.

сла́д|кий [16; -док, -дка́, -о; *comp.*: сла́ще] sweet; sugary; \~ое *su.* dessert (for на В); **\~остный** [14; -тен, -тна] sweet, delightful; **\~остра́стие** *n* [12] voluptuousness; **\~остра́стный** [14; -тен, -тна] voluptuous; **\~ость** *f* [8] sweetness; delight; *cf.* сла́сти.

сла́женный [14 *sh.*] harmonious.

сла́нец *m* [1; -нца] slate.

сла́сти *f/pl.* [8; *from gen. e.*] candy *sg.*, *Brt. a.* sweets.

слать [шлю, шлёшь], ‹по-› send.

слаща́вый [14 *sh.*] sugary.

сле́ва on, to (*or* from) the left.

слегка́ (-xk-) slightly; in passing.

след *m* [1; *g/sg. e.* & -ду; на -ду́; *pl. e.*] trace (*a. fig.*), track; footprint, footstep; print; scent; \~ом (right) behind; его́ и \~ простыл F he was off and away; **\~и́ть** [15 *e.*; -ежу́, -еди́шь] (за T, † В) watch, follow; look after; shadow; trace.

сле́доват|ель *m* [4] examining magistrate; **\~ельно** consequently, therefore; so; **\~ь** [7] (за T; Д) follow; ensue (from из Р); go, move; (Д) *impers.* should, ought to; be to be; как сле́дует properly, duly; F downright, thoroughly; as it should be; кому́ *or* куда́ сле́дует to the proper p. *or* quarter; ско́лько с меня́ сле́дует? how much do I have to pay?

сле́дствие *n* [12] consequence; inquest, trial.

сле́дующий [17] following, next.

сле́жка *f* [5; *g/pl.*: -жек] shadowing.

слез|а́ *f* [5; *pl.*: слёзы, слёз, слеза́м] tear; **\~а́ть** [1], ‹\~ть› [24 *st.*] climb *or* get down; dismount, alight;

get out; F come off; ~и́ться [15; -и́тся] water; ~ли́вый [14 *h.*] tearful, lachrymose; ~оточи́вый [14] tear (*gas*); watering; ~ть *s.* ~а́ть.
слеп|е́нь *m* [4; -пня́] gadfly; **~е́ц** *m* [1; -пца́] blind man; **~и́ть 1.** [14 *e.*; -плю́, -пи́шь], ⟨о-⟩ [ослеплённый] blind; dazzle; **2.** [14] *pf.*; *impf.*: ~ля́ть [28] stick together (*v/i.* -ся); *s. a.* лепи́ть; **∠нуть** [21], ⟨о-⟩ grow (*or* become) blind; **~о́й** [14; слеп, -а́, -о] blind (in, *Brt.* of *one eye* на В); dull (*glass*); indistinct; *su.* blind man; **∠ок** *m* [1; -пка] mould, cast; **~ота́** *f* [5] blindness.
сле́сар|ь *m* [4; *pl.*: -ря́, *etc. e.*, & -ри] locksmith; fitter, mechanic.
слёт *m* [1] flight; rally, meeting (at на П).
слет|а́ть [1], ⟨~е́ть⟩ [11] fly (down, off); F fall (down, off); **-ся** fly together; F gather.
слечь F [26 г/ж: сля́гу, сля́жешь; сля́г(те)!] *pf.* fall ill.
сли́ва *f* [5] plum.
сли|ва́ть [1], ⟨~ть⟩ [солью́, -льёшь; *cf.* лить] pour (off, out, together); fuse, merge, amalgamate (*v/i.* **-ся**).
сли́в|ки *f/pl.* [5; *gen.*: -вок] cream (*a. fig.* = elite); **~очный** [14] creamy; (*ice*) cream.
слиз|истый [14 *sh.*] mucous; slimy; **~ь** *f* [8] slime; mucus, phlegm.
слипа́ться [1] stick together; close.
сли́т|ный [14] conjoint; continuous; ~но *a.* together; in one word; **~ок** *m* [1; -тка] ingot; **~ь(ся)** *s.* слива́ть(ся).
слич|а́ть [1], ⟨~и́ть⟩ [16 *e.*; -чу́, -чи́шь; -чённый] compare, collate.
сли́шком too, too much; э́то (уж) ~ F that beats everything.
слия́ние *n* [12] confluence; fusion, amalgamation; blending.
слова́к *m* [1] Slovak.
слова́р|ный [14]: ~ный соста́в *m* stock of words; **~ь** *m* [4 *e.*] dictionary; vocabulary, glossary; lexicon.
слов|а́цкий [16], **~а́чка** *f* [5; *g/pl.*: -чек] Slovak; **~е́нец** *m* [1; -нца], **~е́нка** *f* [5; *g/pl.*: -нок], **~е́нский** [16] Slovene.
слове́сн|ость *f* [8] literature; (*folk*-) lore; philology; **~ый** [14] verbal, oral; literary; philologic(al).
сло́вно as if; like; F as it were.
сло́во *n* [9; *pl. e.*] word (in a Т; ... for ... И/в В); term; speech; к сло́ву сказа́ть by the way; на слова́х by word of mouth, orally; по слова́м according to; проси́ть (предоста́вить Д) ~ ask (give p.) permission to speak; **~измене́ние** *n* [12] inflection (*Brt.* -xion); **~охо́тливый** [14 *sh.*] talkative.
слог *m* [1; *from g/pl. e.*] syllable; [style.
слоёный [14] puff (*paste*).
слож|е́ние *n* [12] addition; composition; constitution, build; laying down; resignation; **~и́ть(ся)** *s.* скла́дывать(ся), слага́ть(ся) & класть 2.; **∠ность** *f* [8] complexity, complicacy, complication; **∠ный** [14; -жен, -жна́, -о] complicated, complex, intricate; compound.
сло|и́стый [14 *sh.*] stratiform; flaky; **~й** *m* [3; *pl. e.*: слои́, слоёв] layer, stratum (in Т *pl.*); coat(ing).
слом *m* [1] demolition, destruction; **~и́ть** [14] *pf.* break, overcome; overpower; ~я́ го́лову F headlong.
слон *m* [1 *e.*] elephant; bishop (*chess*); **~о́вый** [14]: ~о́вая кость *f* ivory.
слоня́ться F [28] linger, loaf.
слу|га́ *m* [5; *pl. st.*] servant; **∠жащий** *m* [17] employee; **∠жба** *f* [5] (на П) service (in); employment, job; office, work (at); duty (on); **~же́бный** [14] office...; official; secondary, subordinate, subservient; *gr.* relational; **~же́ние** *n* [12] service; **~жи́ть** [16], ⟨по-⟩ serve (a p./th. Д); work (as Т); be.
слух *m* [1] hearing; ear (by на В; по Д); rumo(u)r, hearsay; news, sign; **~ово́й** [14] of hearing; acoustic(al); ear...; dormer (*window*).
слу́ча|й *m* [3] case; occurrence, event; occasion (on по Д; при П), opportunity, chance, (*a.* несча́стный ~й) accident; на вся́кий (пожа́рный F) ~й to be on the safe side; по ~ю second hand; (Р) on account of; **∠йность** *f* [8] chance, fortuity; **∠йный** [14; -а́ен, -а́йна] accidental, casual, chance (by ∠йно); **∠ться** [1], ⟨случи́ться⟩ [16 *e.*; *3rd p. or impers.*] happen (to с Т); come; take place; F be.
слу́ша|тель *m* [4] listener, hearer; student; *pl.* audience; **~ть** [1], ⟨по-⟩ listen (to В), hear; attend; ⚕ auscultate; ~й! *a.*, ⚔, attention!; ~ю! *teleph.*: hullo!; ~ю(сь)! yes (, sir); **-ся** obey (p. Р); take (*advice*).
слыть [23], ⟨про-⟩ (Т, за В) pass for, have the reputation of.
слыха́ть, ⟨у-⟩ *s.* слы́шать.
слы́|шать [4] (F ~ха́ть [*no pr.*]), ⟨у-⟩ hear (of, about о П); F feel, notice; **~шаться** [4] be heard; **~шимость** *f* [8] audibility; **~шно** it can be heard (of о П); it is said; (мне) ~шно one (I) can hear; что ~шно? what is the news?; **~шный** [14; -шен, -шна́, -о] audible.
слюда́ *f* [5] mica.
слюн|а́ *f* [5], **∠и** F *pl.* [8; *from gen. e.*] saliva, spittle; **∠ки** F *f/pl.*: ∠ки теку́т mouth waters; **~я́вый** F [14 *sh.*] slobbery.
сля́коть *f* [8] slush.
см. *abbr.*: смотри́ see, v(ide).
с. м. *abbr.*: сего́ ме́сяца; *cf.* сей.
сма́з|ать *s.* ~ывать; **~ка** *f* [5 *g/pl.*: -зок] greasing, oiling, lubrication; **~очный** [14] lubricant; **~ывать**

[1], ⟨~ать⟩ [3] grease, oil, lubricate; F blur.
сма́|нивать [1], ⟨~ни́ть⟩ [13; сманю́, -а́нишь; -а́ненный & -анённый] lure away, entice; **~тывать**, ⟨смота́ть⟩ [1] reel on *or* off; **~хивать** [1], ⟨~хну́ть⟩ [20] brush off (*or* aside); *impf.* F have a likeness (with на В); **~чивать** [1], ⟨смочи́ть⟩ [16] moisten.
сме́жный [14; -жен, -жна] adjacent.
сме́л|ость *f* [8] boldness; courage; **~ый** [14; смел, -а́, -о] courageous, bold; ~о *a.* F easily; offhand.
сме́н|а *f* [5] shift (in в В); ⚔ relief; change; supersession; successors *pl.*; прийти́ на ~у *s.* ~и́ться; **~я́ть** [28], ⟨~и́ть⟩ [13; -ню́, -е́нишь; -енённый] (**-ся** be) supersede(d; o. a.), ⚔ relieve(d), replace(d; by T), substitute(d; for); change.
смерк|а́ться [1], ⟨ʌнуться⟩ [20] grow dusky *or* dark.
смерт|е́льный [14; -лен, -льна] mortal, fatal, (*a. adv.*) deadly; **ʌность** *f* [8] mortality, death rate; **ʌный** [14; -тен, -тна] mortal (*a. su.*), deadly, fatal; (a. ⚖) death ...; ⚖ capital; **~ь** *f* [8; *from g/pl. e.*] death; F (*a.* ~ь как, до́ ~и, на́ ~ь) deadly, utterly; при́ ~и at death's door.
смерч *m* [1] waterspout; tornado.
смести́ *s.* смета́ть; **~ть** *s.* смеща́ть.
сме|сь *f* [8] mixture; blend; alloy; miscellanies *pl.*; **ʌта** *f* [5] estimate.
смета́на *f* [5] sour cream.
сме|та́ть [1], ⟨~сти́⟩ [25 -т-] sweep away; sweep together; wipe off.
сме́тливый [14 *sh.*] sharp(-witted).
сметь [8], ⟨по-⟩ dare, venture; beg.
смех *m* [1] laughter (with со́ ~у); joke, fun (for ра́ди Р, в *or* на В); *cf.* шу́тка.
сме́ш|анный [14] mixed; **~а́ть(ся)** *s.* ~ивать(ся); **~е́ние** *n* [12] mixture; confusion; **~ивать**, ⟨~а́ть⟩ [1] mix (up), mingle, blend (*v/i.* **-ся**; get *or* be[come]) confuse(d).
смеш|и́ть [16 *e.*; -шу́, -ши́шь], ⟨рас-⟩ [-шённый] make laugh; **~но́й** [14; -шо́н, -шна́] laughable, ludicrous, ridiculous; funny; (Д) ~но́ amuse (p.).
сме|ща́ть [1], ⟨~сти́ть⟩ [15 *e.*; -ещу́, -ести́шь; -ещённый] displace, shift, dislocate; **~ще́ние** *n* [12] displacement.
смея́ться [27 *e.*; -ею́сь, -еёшься], ⟨за-⟩ laugh (at *impf.* над T); mock (at); deride; F joke.
смир|е́ние *n* [12], **~е́нность** *f* [8] humility; meekness; **~е́нный** [14 *sh.*] humble; meek; **~и́ть(ся)** *s.* ~я́ть(ся); **ʌный** [14; -рен (F -рён), -рна́, -о] quiet, still; meek, gentle; **ʌно!** ⚔ (at) attention!; **~я́ть** [28], ⟨~и́ть⟩ [13] subdue; restrain, check; **-ся** humble o.s.
смо́кинг *m* [1] tuxedo, dinner jacket.
смол|а́ *f* [5; *pl. st.*] resin; pitch; tar; **~и́стый** [14 *sh.*] resinous; **~и́ть** [13], ⟨вы́-, за-⟩ pitch, tar; **~ка́ть** [1], ⟨ʌкнуть⟩ [21] grow silent; cease; **ʌоду** F from one's youth; **~яно́й** [14 pitch..., tar...
сморка́ться [1], ⟨вы́-⟩ blow one's nose.
сморо́дина *f* [5] currant(s *pl.*).
смота́ть *s.* сма́тывать.
смотр *m* [1; ⚔ на -у́ & *pl. e.*] review; parade, show; inspection; **~е́ть** [9; -отрю́, -о́тришь; -о́тренный], ⟨по-⟩ look (at на В; after за Т), gaze; (re)view, see, watch; examine, inspect; mind (*v/t.* на В); look out; ~я́ it depends (on по Д), according (to); ~е́ть в о́ба be all eyes; **~и́тель** *m* [4] inspector; (*post*)master.
смочи́ть *s.* сма́чивать.
смрад *m* [1] stench; **ʌный** [14; -ден, -дна] stinking.
сму́глый [14; смугл, -а́, -о] swarthy.
смут|и́ть(ся) *s.* смуща́ть(ся); **ʌный** [14; -тен, -тна́, -о] vague, dim; restless, uneasy; of unrest.
смущ|а́ть [1], ⟨смути́ть⟩ [15 *e.*; -ущу́, -ути́шь; -ущённый] (**-ся** be[come]) embarrass(ed), confuse(d), perplex(ed); **~е́ние** *n* [12] embarrassment, confusion; **~ённый** [14] embarrassed.
смы|ва́ть [1], ⟨~ть⟩ (22) wash off (*or* away); **~ка́ть** [1], ⟨сомкну́ть⟩ [20] close (*v/i.* **-ся**); **~сл** *m* [1] sense, meaning; respect; F use; **ʌслить** F [13] understand; **~ть** *s.* ~ва́ть; **~чко́вый** [14] ♪ stringed; **~чо́к** *m* [1; -чка́] ♪ bow; **~шлёный** F [14 *sh.*] clever, bright.
смягч|а́ть (-xtʃ-) [1], ⟨~и́ть⟩ [16 *e.*; -чу́, -чи́шь; -чённый] soften (*v/i.* **-ся**); mitigate, alleviate; extenuate; *phon.* palatalize; **-ся** *a.* relent; ~а́ющий ⚖ extenuating; **~е́ние** *n* [12] mitigation; extenuation; palatalization; **~и́ть(ся)** *s.* ~а́ть(ся).
смяте́ние *n* [12] confusion.
снаб|жа́ть [1], ⟨~ди́ть⟩ [15 *e.*; -бжу́, -бди́шь; -бжённый] supply, furnish, provide (with T); **~же́ние** *n* [12] supply, provision; purchasing (*dept.*).
сна́йпер *m* [1] sharpshooter.
снару́жи from (the) outside.
снаря́|д shell; missile, projectile; apparatus; tool, equipment; tackle; **~жа́ть** [1], ⟨~ди́ть⟩ [15 *e.*; -яжу́, -яди́шь; -яжённый] equip, fit out (with T); **~же́ние** *n* [12] equipment; munitions *pl.*
снасть *f* [8; *from g/pl. e.*] tackle; rigging.
сначала at first; first; over again.
снег *m* [1; в -у́; *pl. e.*: -а́] snow; ~ идёт it is snowing; **~и́рь** *m* [4 *e.*] bullfinch; **~опа́д** *m* [1] snowfall.

снеж|и́нка *f* [5; *g/pl.*: -нок] snowflake; **∠ный** [14; -жен, -жна] snow(y); **~óк** *m* [1; -жкá] *dim. of* снег; snowball.
снести́(сь) *s.* сноси́ть(ся).
сни|жáть [1], ⟨∠зить⟩ [15] lower; reduce, decrease; (-ся *v/i.*; *a.* fall; ✈ land); **~жéние** *n* [12] lowering; reduction, decrease; fall; landing; **~зойти́** *s.* ~сходи́ть; ∠зу from below.
сним|áть [1], ⟨снять⟩ [сниму́, сни́мешь; снял, -á, -о; сня́тый (снят, -á, -о)] take (off, away *or* down); remove, discard, dismiss; withdraw; cut (off); rent; (take a) photograph (of); reap, gather cancel, strike off; deprive (of); release (from с Р); raise (*siege*); strike (*camp*); make (*copy, etc.*); ~áть сли́вки skim; -ся take off; weigh (*anchor* с Р); have a picture of o.s. taken; be struck off (*a list*); ∠ок *m* [1; -мка] photograph, picture (in на П).
сни́ск|ивать [1], ⟨~áть⟩ [3] get, win.
снисхо|ди́тельный [14; -лен, -льна] indulgent; condescending; **~ди́ть** [15], ⟨снизойти́⟩ [-ойду́, -ойдёшь; *cf.* идти́] condescend; **~ждéние** *n* [12] indulgence, leniency; condescension.
сни́ться [13], ⟨при-⟩ *impers.*: (Д) dream (of И).
снóва (over) again, anew.
сно|вáть [7 *e.*] scurry, whisk; **~ви дéние** *n* [12] vision, dream.
сноп *m* [1 *e.*] sheaf.
сноровка *f* [5] knack, skill.
снос|и́ть [15], ⟨снести́⟩ [24 -с-: снесу́; снёс] carry (down, away *or* off, together), take; pull down, demolish; endure, bear, tolerate; *cf. a.* нести́; -ся, ⟨-сь⟩ communicate (with с Т); get in touch, contact; **∠ка** *f* [5; *g/pl.*: -сок] footnote; **∠ный** [14; -сен, -сна] tolerable.
снохá [5; *pl. st.*] daughter-in-law.
сношéние *n* [12] (*usu. pl.*) intercourse; relations.
сня́т|ие *n* [12] taking down; raising; removal; dismissal; **~óй** [14] skim (*milk*); **~ь(ся)** *s.* снимáть(ся).
собá|ка *f* [5] dog; hound; **~чий** [18] dog('s).
собесéдник *m* [1] interlocutor.
собирáт|ель *m* [4] collector; **~ельный** [14] *gr.* collective; **~ь** [1], ⟨собрáть⟩ [-беру́, -рёшь; -áл, -á, -о; сóбранный (-ан, -á, -о)] gather, collect; ⊕ assemble; prepare; -ся gather, assemble; prepare, make o.s. *or* be ready to start (*or* set out *or* go; on a journey в путь); be going, intend, collect (*one's thoughts* с Т); brace up (с си́лами).
соблáзн *m* [1] temptation; **~и́тель** *m* [4] seducer, temper; **~и́тельный** [14; -лен, -льна] tempting, seductive; **~я́ть** [28], ⟨~и́ть⟩ [13] (-ся be) tempt(ed); seduce(d).
соблю|дáть [1], ⟨~сти́⟩ [25] observe, obey, adhere (to); maintain (*order*); **~дéние** *n* [12] observance; maintenance; **~сти́** *s.* ~дáть.
соболéзнова|ние *n* [12] condolence; **~ть** [7] condole (with Д).
сóбо|ль *m* [4; *pl. a.* -ля́, *etc. e.*] sable; **∠р** *m* [1] cathedral; council; diet; **∠ровать(ся)** [7] administer (receive) extreme unction.
собрá|ние *n* [12] meeting (at, in на П), assembly; collection; **~ть(ся)** *s.* собирáть(ся).
сóбственн|ик *m* [1] owner, proprietor; **~ость** *f* [8] property; **~ый** [14] own; proper; personal; dead (*weight*).
собы́тие *n* [12] event, occurrence.
совá *f* [5; *pl. st.*] owl.
совáть [7 *e.*; сую́, суёшь], ⟨су́нуть⟩ [20] put; F slip, give; poke (one's nose -ся; *a.* butt in).
соверш|áть [1], ⟨~и́ть⟩ [16 *e.*; -шу́, -ши́шь; -шённый] accomplish; commit; make (*a. trip*); strike (*bargain*), effect; celebrate, do; -ся happen, take place; be effected, *etc.*; **~еннолéтие** *n* [12] majority, full age; **~еннолéтний** [15] (стать Т come) of age; **~éнный** [14; -éнен, -éнна] perfect(ive *gr.*); absolute, complete; *adv. a.* quite; **~éнство** *n* [9] perfection; в ~éнстве *a.* perfectly; **~éнствовать** [7], ⟨у-⟩ perfect (o.s. -ся), improve, polish up; **~и́ть(ся)** *s.* совершáть(ся).
сóвест|ливый [14 *sh.*] conscientious; **~но** (р. Д) ashamed; **~ь** *f* [8] conscience; по ~и honestly.
совéт *m* [1] advice, counsel; council, board; *USSR a.* soviet; Верхóвный ♀ Supreme Soviet; **~ник** *m* [1] council(l)or; **~овать** [7], ⟨по-⟩ advise (р. Д); -ся consult, deliberate (on о П); **~ский** [16] Soviet; **~чик** *m* [1] adviser.
совещá|ние *n* [12] conference (at на П), meeting (*a.* in); deliberation, consultation (for на В); **~тельный** [14] advisory, consultative; **~ться** [1] confer, consult, deliberate.
совладáть F [1] *pf.* (с Т) master.
совме|сти́мый [14 *sh.*] compatible; **~сти́ть** *s.* ~щáть; **∠стный** [14] joint, combined; co(*education*); ∠стно together, conjointly; **~щáть** [1], ⟨~сти́ть⟩ [15 *e.*; -ещу́, ести́шь; -ещённый] combine; unite; reconcile.
совóк *m* [1; -вкá] scoop.
совоку́пн|ость *f* [8] total(ity), aggregate, whole; **~ый** [14] joint.
совпа|дáть [1], ⟨∠сть⟩ [25; *pt. st.*] coincide; agree; ⩓ be congruent; **~дéние** *n* [12] coincidence, *etc. s. vb.*
совремéнн|ик *m* [1] contemporary; **~ый** [14; -éнен, -éнна] modern; present-day, up-to-date; *s. a.* ~ик.

совсе́м quite, entirely; at all.
совхо́з *m* [1] (сове́тское хозя́йство) state farm; *cf.* колхо́з.
согла́|сие *n* [12] consent (to на В; with с Р); agreement (by по Д); harmony, concord; accordance; **~си́ться** *s.* ~ша́ться; **~сно** (Д) according to, in accordance with; **~сный** [14; -сен, -сна] agreeable, accordant; harmonious; я ~сен (*f* ~сна) I agree (with с Т; to на В); (*a. su.*) consonant; **~сова́ние** *n* [12] coördination; *gr.* agreement, concord; **~сова́ть** *s.* ~со́вывать; **~сова́ться** [7] (*im*)*pf.* (с Т) conform (to); agree (with); **~со́вывать** [1], ⟨~сова́ть⟩ [7] coördinate; adjust; (*a. gr.*) make agree; **~ша́тельский** [16] conciliatory; **~ша́ться** [1], ⟨~си́ться⟩ [15 *e.*; -ашу́сь, -аси́шься] agree (with с Т; to на В), consent (to), assent; F admit; **~ше́ние** *n* [12] agreement, understanding; [consent.
согна́ть *s.* сгоня́ть.
согну́ть(ся) *s.* сгиба́ть(ся).
согре|ва́ть [1], ⟨**~**ть⟩ [8] warm, heat.
соде́йств|ие *n* [12] assistance, help; **~овать** [7] (*im*)*pf.*, *a.* ⟨по-⟩ (Д) assist, help, coöperate; contribute (to), further, promote.
содерж|а́ние *n* [12] content(s); maintenance, support, upkeep; cost (at на П); salary; **~а́тель** *m* [4] holder, owner; **~а́тельный** [14; -лен, -льна] pithy, substantial; **~а́ть** [4] contain, hold; maintain, support; keep; **-ся** be contained, *etc.*; **~и́мое** *n* [14] contents *pl.*
содра́ть *s.* сдира́ть.
содрог|а́ние *n* [12], **~а́ться** [1], *once* ⟨~ну́ться⟩ [20] shudder.
содру́жество *n* [9] community.
соедин|е́ние *n* [12] union, junction, (at *a.* на П), connection; combination; ⚗ compound; ⚔ formation; **~и́тельный** [14] connective; *gr. a.* copulative; **~я́ть** [28], ⟨**~и́ть**⟩ [13] unite, join; (*a. teleph.*) connect; (*a.* ⚗) combine; (*v/i.* **-ся**); *cf.* США.
сожал|е́ние *n* [12] regret (for о П); pity (on к Д); к ~е́нию unfortunately, to (*p.*'s) regret; **~е́ть** [8] (о П) regret.
сожже́ние *n* [12] burning.
сожи́тельство *n* [9] cohabitation.
созв|а́ть *s.* созыва́ть; **~е́здие** *n* [12] constellation; **~они́ться** F [13] *pf.* (с Т) phone; **~у́чный** [14; -чен, -чна] conformable, accordant; concordant.
созда|ва́ть [5], ⟨**~**ть⟩ [-да́м, -да́шь *etc.*, *cf.* дать; со́здал, -а́, -о; со́зданный (-ан, -а́, -о)] create; produce; build up; prepare; **-ся** arise, form; **~ние** *n* [12] creation; creature; **~тель** *m* [4] creator; founder; **~ть (-ся)** *s.* ~ва́ть(ся).
созерца́т|ельный [14; -лен, -льна] contemplative; **~ь** [1] contemplate.
созида́тельный [14; -лен, -льна] creative.
созна|ва́ть [5], ⟨**~**ть⟩ [1] realize (*Brt.* realise), see; **-ся** (в П) confess, avow, own; **~ние** *n* [12] consciousness; realization, perception, awareness; confession (of в П); без ~ния unconscious; **~тельный** [14; -лен, -льна] conscious; class conscious; conscientious; **~ть(ся)** *s.* ~ва́ть(ся).
созы́в *m* [1] convocation; **~а́ть** [1], ⟨созва́ть⟩ [созову́, -вёшь; -зва́л, -а́, -о; со́званный] call, invite; convoke, convene, summon.
соизмери́мый [14 *sh.*] commensurable.
сойти́(сь) *s.* сходи́ть(ся).
сок *m* [1; в -у́] juice; sap.
со́кол *m* [1] falcon.
сокра|ща́ть [1], ⟨~ти́ть⟩ [15 *e.*; -ащу́, -ати́шь; -ащённый] shorten; abbreviate; abridge; reduce, curtail; *p. pt. p. a.* short, brief; **-ся** decrease, shorten; contract; **~ще́ние** *n* [12] abbreviation; reduction, curtailment; abridg(e)ment; contraction.
сокров|е́нный [14 *sh.*] secret; **~ище** *n* [11] treasure; F darling; **~ищница** *f* [5] treasury, thesaurus.
сокруш|а́ть [1], ⟨~и́ть⟩ [16 *e.*; -шу́, -ши́шь; -шённый] smash, break; distress, afflict; **-ся** *impf.* grieve, be distressed; **~е́ние** *n* [12] destruction; distress, contrition; **~и́тельный** [14; -лен, -льна] shattering; **~и́ть** *s.* ~а́ть.
солда́т *m* [1; *g/pl.*: солда́т] soldier; **~ский** [16] soldier's.
сол|е́ние *n* [12] salting; **~ёный** [14; со́лон, -а́, -о] salt(y); saline; pickled; corned; *fig.* spicy.
солида́рн|ость *f* [8] solidarity; **~ый** [14; -рен, -рна] solidary; in sympathy with.
соли́дн|ость *f* [8] solidity; **~ый** [14; -ден, -дна] solid, firm, sound; respectable.
соли́ст *m* [1], **~ка** *f* [5; *g/pl.*: -ток] soloist.
солитёр *m* [1] tapeworm.
соли́ть [13; солю́, со́ли́шь; со́ленный] **1.** ⟨по-⟩ salt; **2.** ⟨за-⟩ pickle.
со́лн|ечный [14; -чен, -чна] sun (-ny); solar; **~це** ('sɔn-) *n* [11] sun (*lie* in на П).
со́лод *m* [1], **~о́вый** [14] malt.
солове́й *m* [3; -вья́] nightingale.
соло́м|а *f* [5] straw; thatch; **~енный** [14] straw...; thatched; grass (*widow*[*er*]); **~инка** *f* [5; *g/pl.*: -нок] straw.
солони́на *f* [5] corned beef.
соло́нка *f* [5; *g/pl.*: -нок] saltcellar.
сол|ь *f* [8; *from g/pl. e.*] salt (*a. fig.*); F point; **~яно́й** [14] salt...; hydrochloric (*acid*).
сом *m* [1 *e.*] catfish, sheatfish.

сомкну́ть(ся) *s.* смыка́ть(ся).
сомн|ева́ться [1], ⟨усомни́ться⟩ [13] (в П) doubt; **~е́ние** *n* [12] doubt (about в П); question (in под Т); **~и́тельный** [14; -лен, -льна] doubtful; dubious.
сон *m* [1; сна] sleep; dream (in во П); **~ли́вый** [14 *sh.*] sleepy; **~ный** [14] sleeping (*a.* ⚕); sleepy, drowsy; soporific; **~я** F *m/f* [6; *g/pl.*: -ней] sleepyhead; '**♀я** *f* [6] *dim. of* Со́фья.
сообра|жа́ть [1], ⟨**~зи́ть**⟩ [15 *e.*; -ажу́, -ази́шь; -ажённый] consider, weigh, think (over); grasp, understand; **~же́ние** *n* [12] consideration; reason; grasp, understanding; **~зи́тельный** [14; -лен, -льна] sharp, quick-witted; **~зи́ть** *s.* **~жа́ть**; **~зный** [14; -зен, -зна] conformable (to с Т); *adv. a.* according (to); **~зова́ть** [7] (*im*)*pf.* (make) conform, adapt (to с Т), coördinate (with); **-ся** conform (to с Т).
сообща́ together, conjointly.
сообщ|а́ть [1], ⟨**~и́ть**⟩ [16 *e.*; -щу́, -щи́шь; -щённый] communicate (*v/i.* **-ся** *impf.*), report; inform (p. of Д/о П); impart; **~е́ние** *n* [12] communication; report, statement, announcement, information; **~ество** *n* [9] community; company; **~и́ть** *s.* **~а́ть**; **~ник** *m* [1], **~ница** *f* [5] accomplice.
сооруж|а́ть [1], ⟨**~ди́ть**⟩ [15 *e.*; -ужу́, -уди́шь; -ужённый] build, construct, erect, raise; **~же́ние** *n* [12] construction, building, structure.
соотве́тств|енный [14 *sh.*] corresponding; *adv. a.* according(ly) (to Д), in accordance (with); **~ие** *n* [12] conformity. accordance; **~овать** [7] (Д) correspond, conform (to), agree, comply (with); **~ующий** [17] corresponding, respective; suitable.
соотéчественни|к *m* [1], **~ца** *f* [5] compatriot,fellow country(wo)man.
соотноше́ние *n* [12] correlation.
сопе́рни|к *m* [1] rival; **~чать** [1] compete, rival, vie; be a match (for с Т); **~чество** *n* [9] rivalry.
соп|е́ть [10 *e.*; соплю́, сопи́шь] wheeze; **~ли** P *pl.* [6; *gen.*: -ле́й, *etc. e.*] snot; **~ля́к** P *m* [1 *e.*] snot nose.
сопостав|ле́ние *n* [12] comparison; **~ля́ть** [28], ⟨**~вить**⟩ [14] compare.
сопри|каса́ться [1], ⟨**~косну́ться**⟩ [20] (с Т) adjoin; (get in) touch (with); **~коснове́ние** *n* [12] contact, touch.
сопрово|ди́тельный [14] covering (*letter*); **~жда́ть** [1] **1.** accompany; escort; **2.** ⟨**~ди́ть**⟩ [15 *e.*; -ожу́, -оди́шь; -ождённый] provide (with Т); **-ся** *impf.* be accompanied (by Т); entail; **~жде́ние** *n* [12] accompaniment; в **~жде́нии** (Р) accompanied (by).
сопротивл|е́ние *n* [12] resistance; **~я́ться** [28] (Д) resist, oppose.
сопряжённый [14; -жён, -жена́] connected.
сопу́тствовать [7] (Д) accompany.
сор *m* [1] rubbish, litter.
соразме́рно in proportion (to Д).
сора́тник *m* [1] brother-in-arms.
сорв|ане́ц F *m* [1; -нца́] madcap (fellow); **~а́ть(ся)** *s.* срыва́ть(ся); **~иголова́** F *m/f* [5; *ac/sg.*: сорвиголову́; *pl. s.* голова́] daredevil.
соревнова́|ние *n* [12] competition; contest; emulation; **~ться** [7] (с Т) compete (with); emulate.
сор|и́ть [13], ⟨на-⟩ litter; make dirty; **~ный** [14]: **~ная трава́** *f* = **~ня́к** *m* [1 *e.*] weed.
со́рок [35] forty; **~а** *f* [5] magpie.
сороко|во́й [14] fortieth; *cf.* пят(и-деся́т)ый; **~но́жка** *f* [5; *g/pl.*: -жек] centipede.
соро́чка *f* [5; *g/pl.*: -чек] (under-) shirt.
сорт *m* [1; *pl.*: -та́, *etc. e.*] sort; quality; **~ирова́ть** [7], ⟨рас-⟩ (as-) sort; **~иро́вка** *f* [5] (as)sorting; **~иро́вочный** [14] 🚂 switching.
соса́ть [-су́, -сёшь; со́санный] suck.
сосе́д *m* [*sg.*: 1; *pl.*: 4], **~ка** *f* [5; *g/pl.*: -док] neighbo(u)r; **~ний** [15] neighbo(u)ring, adjoining; **~ский** [16] neighbo(u)r's; **~ство** *n* [9] neighbo(u)rhood.
соси́ска *f* [5; *g/pl.*: -сок] sausage.
со́ска *f* [5; *g/pl.*: -сок] (baby's) dummy.
соск|а́кивать [1], ⟨**~очи́ть**⟩ [16] jump *or* spring (off, down); **~а́льзывать** [1], ⟨**~ользну́ть**⟩ [20] slide (down, off); slip (off); **~у́читься** [16] *pf.* become bored; *s.* скуча́ть.
сосл|ага́тельный [14] *gr.* subjunctive; **~а́ть(ся)** *s.* ссыла́ть(ся); **~о́вие** *n* [12] estate, class; **~ужи́вец** *m* [1; -вца] colleague.
сосна́ *f* [5; *pl. st.*: со́сны, со́сен, со́снам] pine.
сосо́к *m* [1; -ска́] nipple, teat.
сосредото́ч|ение *n* [12] concentration; **~ивать** [1], ⟨**~ить**⟩ [16] concentrate (*v/i.* **-ся**); *p. pt. p. a.* intent.
соста́в *m* [1] composition, structure; body; (ли́чный **~**) staff; рядово́й **~** rank & file; strength (of в П); *thea.* cast; 🚂 stock; ⚖ facts *pl.*; ⚗ solution, mixture; в **~е** (Р) *a.* consisting of; **~и́тель** *m* [4] compiler, author; **~ить** *s.* **~ля́ть**; **~ле́ние** *n* [12] composition; compilation; drawing up; **~ля́ть** [28], ⟨**~ить**⟩ [14] compose, make (up); put together, arrange; draw up, work out; compile; form, constitute; amount (*or* come) to; **~но́й** [14] composite, compound; component, constituent (*part*; **~на́я** часть *f a.* ingredient).
состоя́|ние *n* [12] state, condition; status, station; position; fortune;

быть в ~нии ... *a.* be able to ...; **~тельный** [14; -лен, -льна] well-to-do, well-off; solvent; valid, sound, well-founded; **~ть** [-ою́, -ои́шь] consist (of из P; in в П); be (*a.* T); occupy (*position* в П), work (with при П); **-ся** *pf.* take place; come about.

сострада́ние *n* [12] compassion.

состяза́|ние *n* [12] contest, competition; match; **~ться** [1] compete, vie, contend.

сосу́д *m* [1] vessel.

сосу́лька *f* [5; *g/pl.*: -лек] icicle.

сосуществова́|ние *n* [12] coexistence; **~ть** [7] coexist.

сотворе́ние *n* [12] creation.

со́тня *f* [6; *g/pl.*: -тен] a hundred.

сотру́дни|к *m* [1] collaborator; employee, member; *pl.* staff; contributor; colleague; **~чать** [1] collaborate, coöperate; **~чество** *n* [9] collaboration, coöperation.

сотрясе́ние *n* [12] concussion.

со́ты *m/pl.* [1] honeycomb(s); **~й** [14] hundredth; *cf.* пя́тый; две це́лых и два́дцать пять ~х 2.25.

со́ус *m* [1] sauce; gravy.

соуча́ст|ие *n* [12] complicity; **~ник** *m* [1] accomplice.

соучени́к *m* [1 *e.*] schoolmate.

Со́фья *f* [6] Sophia.

соха́ *f* [5; *pl. st.*] (wooden) plow, plough.

со́хнуть [21] **1.** ⟨вы́-⟩ dry; **2.** ⟨за-⟩ fade, wither; **3.** F *impf.* pine away.

сохран|е́ние *n* [12] preservation, conservation; charge (*give* into, *take* ... of на В); **~и́ть(ся)** *s.* **~я́ть** (-ся); **~́ность** *f* [8] safety; integrity; в ~́ности *a.* safe; **~я́ть** [28], ⟨~и́ть⟩ [13] keep; preserve; retain; maintain; reserve (to o.s. за собо́й); (*God*) forbid!; **-ся** be preserved; keep (safe, *etc.*).

социа́л|-демокра́т *m* [1] Social Democrat; **~-демократи́ческий** [16] Social Democrat(ic); **~и́зм** *m* [1] socialism; **~и́ст** *m* [1] socialist; **~исти́ческий** [16] socialist(ic); **~ьный** [14] social.

соц|соревнова́ние *n* [12] socialist competition (*Sov.*); **~стра́х** *m* [1] social insurance (*Sov.*).

соче́льник *m* [1] (Xmas) Eve.

сочета́|ние *n* [12] combination; union; **~ть** [1] combine (*v/i.* **-ся**); unite (in T).

сочин|е́ние *n* [12] composition; writing, work; thesis; *gr.* parataxis, coördination; **~и́тель** *m* [4] author; **~я́ть** [28], ⟨~и́ть⟩ [13] compose, write; invent; *gr.* coördinate.

соч|и́ться [16 *e.*; *3rd. p. only*] ooze (out); ~и́ться кро́вью bleed; **~́ный** [14; -чен, -чна́, -о] juicy; rich.

сочу́вств|енный [14 *sh.*] sympathetic, sympathizing; **~ие** *n* [12] sympathy (with, for к Д); **~овать** [7] (Д) sympathyze, feel with; approve (of); **~ующий** *m* [17] sympathizer.

сою́з *m* [1] union; alliance; confederacy; league; *gr.* conjunction; Сове́тский ♀ Soviet Union; *cf.* СССР; **~ник** *m* [1] ally; **~ный** [14] allied; (of the) Union (*Sov.*).

со́я *f* [6] soy(bean).

спа|да́ть [1], ⟨~сть⟩ [25; *pt. st.*] fall (down); **~́ивать 1.** ⟨~я́ть⟩ [28] solder; **2.** F ⟨спои́ть⟩ [13] make drunk; **~́йка** *f* [5] solder(ing); **~́лзывать** *s.* сполза́ть.

спа́льн|ый [14] sleeping; bed...; **~я** *f* [6; *g/pl.*: -лен] bedroom.

спа́ржа *f* [5] asparagus.

спас|а́тельный [14] life...; **~а́ть** [1], ⟨~ти́⟩ [24 -с-] save, rescue; redeem; **-ся**, ⟨-сь⟩ *a.* escape (*v/t.* от P); **~е́ние** *n* [12] rescue; redemption.

спаси́бо (вам) thank you (very much большо́е ~), thanks (for за В, на П).

спаси́тель *m* [4] savio(u)r, rescuer; **~ный** [14] saving.

спас|ти́ *s.* ~а́ть; **~ть** *s.* спада́ть.

спать [сплю, спишь; спал, -á, -о] sleep; (*a.* идти́, ложи́ться ~) go to bed; мне не спи́тся F I can't sleep.

спая́ть *s.* спа́ивать 1.

спека́ться [1] F *s.* запека́ться; ⊕ conglomerate.

спекта́кль *m* [4] performance.

спекул|и́ровать [7] speculate (with T); **~я́нт** *m* [1] speculator.

спе́лый [14; спел, -á, -о] ripe.

сперва́ F (at) first.

спе́реди in (from) front (*as prp.*: P).

спёртый F [14 *sh.*] stuffy, close.

спеси́вый [14 *sh.*] haughty.

спеть [8], ⟨по-⟩ ripen; *s. a.* петь.

спех F *m* [1] haste, hurry.

специ|ализи́роваться [7] (*im*)*pf.* specialize (in в П, по Д) **~али́ст** *m* [1] specialist, expert (in по Д); **~а́льность** *f* [8] special(i)ty, line, profession (by по Д); **~а́льный** [14; -лен, -льна] special; express; **~фи́ческий** [16] specific.

спецоде́жда *f* [5] overalls *pl.*

спеш|и́ть [16 *e.*; -шу́, -ши́шь] hurry (up), hasten; *clock*: be fast (5 min. на 5 мину́т); **~́иться** [16] *pf.* dismount; **~́ка** F *f* [5] haste, hurry; **~́ный** [14; -шен, -шна] urgent, pressing; special, express.

спин|а́ *f* [5; *ac/sg.*: спи́ну; *pl. st.*] back; **~́ка** *f* [5; *g/pl.*: -нок] back (*of chair, etc.*); **~но́й** [14] spinal (cord мозг *m*); vertebral (column хребе́т *m*), back(*bone*).

спира́ль *f* [8], **~ный** [14] spiral.

спирт *m* [1; *a.* в -у́; *pl. e.*] spirit(s *pl.*), alcohol; **~но́й** [14] alcoholic, strong (*drink*).

спис|а́ть *s.* ~́ывать; **~́ок** *m* [1; -ска] list, register; copy; **~́ывать** [1],

⟨~áть⟩ [3] copy; write (off); plagiarize, crib; ⚓ pay off.
спи́х|ивать [1], *once* ⟨~ну́ть⟩ F [20] push (down, aside).
спи́ца *f* [5] spoke; knitting needle.
спи́чка *f* [5; *g/pl.*: -чек] match.
сплав *m* [1] alloy; float(ing); **~ля́ть** [28], ⟨*~*ить⟩ [14] float; alloy.
спла́чивать [1], ⟨сплоти́ть⟩ [15 *e.*; -очу́, -оти́шь; -очённый] rally (*v/i.* **-ся**); fasten.
сплет|а́ть [1], ⟨сплести́⟩ [25 -т-] plait, braid; (inter)lace; F invent; **~е́ние** *n* [12] interlacement, texture; **∠ник** *m* [1], **∠ница** *f* [5] scandalmonger; **∠ничать** [1], ⟨на-⟩ gossip; **∠ня** *f* [6; *g/pl.*: -тен] gossip; *pl.* scandal.
сплo|ти́ть(ся) *s.* спла́чивать(ся); **~хова́ть** F [7] *pf.* blunder; **~че́ние** *n* [12] rallying; **~шно́й** [14] solid, compact; sheer, complete; continuous; **~шь** throughout, entirely, everywhere; quite often.
сплю́щить [16] *pf.* flatten.
сподви́жник *s.* сора́тник.
спои́ть *s.* спа́ивать 2.
споко́й|ный [14; -óен, -óйна] calm, quiet, tranquil; composed; **~но** F *s.* сме́ло F; **~ной** но́чи! good night!; бу́дьте **~ны**! don't worry!; **~ствие** *n* [12] calm(ness), tranquility; composure; peace, order.
сполз|а́ть [1], ⟨~ти́⟩ [24] climb *or* slip (down, off).
сполна́ ... wholly, whole ..., total ...
сполосну́ть [20] *pf.* rinse.
спор *m* [1] dispute, controversy, argument; wrangle, quarrel; **∠у** нет no doubt; **∠ить** [13], ⟨по-⟩ dispute, argue, debate; quarrel; F bet; *poet.* fight; **∠иться** F [13] succeed, get along; **∠ный** [14; -рен, -рна] disputable, questionable.
спорт *m* [1] sport; лы́жный ~ skiing; **~и́вный** [14] sporting, athletic; sport(s)...; **~сме́н** *m* [1] sportsman; **~сме́нка** *f* [5; *g/pl.*: -нок] sportswoman.
спо́соб *m* [1] method, means; manner, way (in T); directions *pl.* (for *use* P); **∠ность** *f* [8] (cap)ability (for к Д), talent; faculty; capacity; power; quality; **∠ный** [14; -бен, -бна] (к Д) able, talented, clever (at); capable (of; *a.* на B); **∠ствовать** [7], ⟨по-⟩ (Д) promote, further, contribute to.
спот|ыка́ться [1], ⟨~кну́ться⟩ [20] stumble (over о B).
спохва́т|ываться [1], ⟨~и́ться⟩ [15] bethink o.s.
спра́ва on, to (*or* from) the right.
справедли́в|ость *f* [8] justice; truth; по **~ости** by rights; **~ый** [14 *sh.*] just, fair; true, right.
спра́в|ить(ся) *s.* **~ля́ть(ся)**; **~ка** *f* [5; *g/pl.*: -вок] inquiry (make наводи́ть); information; certificate; **~ля́ть** [28], ⟨~ить⟩ [14] F celebrate; make (*holiday*); **-ся** inquire (after, about о П); consult (*v/t.* в П); (с T) manage, cope with; **~очник** *m* [1] reference book, vade mecum; directory; guide; **~очный** [14] (of) information, inquiry; reference...
спра́шива|ть [1], ⟨спроси́ть⟩ [15] ask (p. *a.* у P; for, s.th. *a.* P), inquire; demand; (с P) be taken to account; **-ся** *s.* проси́ться; **~ется** one may ask.
спрос *m* [1] demand (for на B); без **∠а** *or* **∠у** F without permission; **~и́ть(ся)** *s.* спра́шивать(ся).
спросо́нок F half asleep.
проста́ F unintentionally, innocently.
спры́|гивать [1], *once* ⟨~гнуть⟩ [20] jump down (*or* off); **~скивать** [1], ⟨~снуть⟩ [20] sprinkle; F wet.
спря|га́ть [1], ⟨про-⟩ *gr.* (**-ся** *impf.* be) conjugate(d); **~же́ние** *n* [12] *gr.* conjugation.
спус|к *m* [1] lowering; descent; slope; launch(ing); drain(ing); *fig.* F quarter; **~ка́ть** [1], ⟨~ти́ть⟩ [15] lower, let down; launch; drain; unchain, set free; pull (*trigger*); slacken; F pardon; lose, gamble away; **-ся** go (*or* come) down(*stairs* по Д), descend; slip down, sink; **~тя́** (B) later, after.
спу́тни|к *m* [1], **~ца** *f* [5] fellow travel(l)er; (*life's*) companion; **~к** *ast.* satellite.
спя́чка *f* [5] hibernation; sleep.
ср. *abbr.*: сравни́ compare, cf.
сравн|е́ние *n* [12] comparison (in/with по Д/с T); compare; simile; **∠ивать** [1] **1.** ⟨~и́ть⟩ [13] compare (to, with с T; *v/i.* **-ся**); **2.** ⟨~я́ть⟩ [28] level; equalize; **~и́тельный** [14] comparative; **~и́ть(ся)** *s.* **∠ивать(ся)**; **~я́ть** *s.* **∠ивать** 2.
сра|жа́ть [1], ⟨~зи́ть⟩ [15 *e.*; -ажу́, -ази́шь; -ажённый] smite; overwhelm; overtake; **-ся** fight, battle; F contend, play; **~же́ние** *n* [12] battle; **~зи́ть(ся)** *s.* **~жа́ть(ся)**.
сра́зу at once; at one stroke.
срам *m* [1] shame, disgrace; **~и́ть** [14 *e.*; -млю́, -ми́шь], ⟨о-⟩ [осрамлённый] disgrace, shame, compromise; **-ся** bring shame upon o.s.
сраст|а́ться [1], ⟨~и́сь⟩ [24 -ст-; сро́сся, сросла́сь] grow together, knit.
сред|а́ *f* **1.** [5; *ac/sg.*: сре́ду; *nom/pl. st.*] Wednesday (on: в B, *pl.*: по Д); **2.** [5; *ac/sg.*: -ду́; *pl. st.*] environment, surroundings *pl.*, sphere; medium; midst; **~и́** (P) among; in the middle (of), amid(st); **~иземный** [14], **~иземномо́рский** [16] Mediterranean; **~невеко́вый** [14] medieval; **∠ний** [15] middle; medium...; central; middling; average... (on в П); ♠ mean; *gr.* neuter; secondary (*school*).

средото́чие *n* [12] center (*Brt.* -tre).
сре́дство *n* [9] means (within [beyond] one's [не] по Д *pl.*); remedy; ⚗ agent; *pl. a.* facilities.
срез|а́ть & **∠ывать** [1], ⟨**∠ать**⟩ [3] cut off; F cut short; fail (*v/i.* **-ся**).
сровня́ть *s.* сра́внивать 2.
сро́д|ный [14; -ден, -дна] related, cognate; **~ство́** *n* [9] affinity.
сро|к *m* [1] term (for/of Т/на В), date, deadline; time (in, on в В, к Д), period; **∠чный** [14; -чен, -чна́, -о] urgent, pressing; timed.
сруб|а́ть [1], ⟨**~и́ть**⟩ [14] cut down, fell; carpenter, build.
сры|в *m* [1] frustration; failure, breakdown; breaking up; **~ва́ть** [1] **1.** ⟨сорва́ть⟩ [-ву́, -вёшь; сорва́л, -а́, -о; со́рванный] tear off; pluck, pick; F break up, disrupt, frustrate; vent; **-ся** (с Р) come off; break away (*or* loose); fall down; F dart off; escape; fail, go wrong; **2.** ⟨**~ть**⟩ [22] level, raze to the ground.
сса́дин|на *f* [5] graze, abrasion; **∠ть** [15] *pf.* graze; make alight; drop.
ссо́р|а *f* [5] quarrel; altercation; variance (at в П); **~иться** [13], ⟨по-⟩ quarrel, fall out.
СССР (Сою́з Сове́тских Социалисти́ческих Респу́блик) U.S.S.R. (Union of Soviet Socialist Republics).
ссу́д|а *f* [5] loan; **~и́ть** [15] *pf.* lend; **~ный** [14] loan...
ссыл|а́ть [1], ⟨сосла́ть⟩ [сошлю́, -лёшь; со́сланный] exile, banish; **-ся** (на В) refer to, cite; **∠ка** *f* [5; *g/pl.*: -лок] exile; deportation; reference (to на В); **∠ьный** [14] exiled (p.).
ссыпа́|ть [1], ⟨**'~ть**⟩ [2] pour, sack.
ст. *abbr.*: **1.** столе́тие; **2.** ста́нция; **3.** ста́рший.
стабил|из(и́р)ова́ть [7] (*im*)*pf.* stabilize; **∠ьный** [14; -лен, -льна] stable.
ста́вень *m* [4; -вня] shutter.
ста́в|ить [14], ⟨по-⟩ put, place, set, stand; (*clock, etc.*) set; put (*or* set) up; stake, (на В) back; *thea.* stage; ⚔ billet; make (*conditions, etc.*); drive; cite; impute (в В); bring (to p.'s *notice* В/в В); give; organize; value, esteem; F appoint, engage; **~ка** *f* [5; *g/pl.*: -вок] rate; wage, salary; stake; (head)quarters *pl.*; *fig.* hope; о́чная **~ка** confrontation; **~ленник** *m* [1] protegé; **~ня** *f* [6; *g/pl.*: -вен] *s.* **~ень**.
стадио́н *m* [1] stadium (in на П).
ста́дия *f* [7] stage.
ста́до *n* [9; *pl. e.*] herd; flock.
стаж *m* [1] length of service.
стака́н *m* [1] glass.
сталелите́йный [14] steel (*mill.*).
ста́лкивать [1], ⟨столкну́ть⟩ [20] push (off, down, together); **-ся** (с Т) collide, run into; come across.
сталь *f* [8] steel; **~но́й** [14] steel...
стаме́ска *f* [5; *g/pl.*: -сок] chisel.
стан *m* [1] figure; camp; ⊕ mill.
станда́рт *m* [1] standard; **~ный** [14; -тен, -тна] standard...; prefabricated.
стани́ца *f* [5] Cossack village.
станови́ться [14], ⟨стать⟩ [ста́ну, -нешь] stand; (Т) become, grow, get; step, place o.s., get, stop; **~** в о́чередь line, *Brt.* queue up; *pf.* begin; will; feel (*better*); во что́ бы то ни ста́ло at all costs, at any cost.
стано́к *m* [1; -нка́] machine; lathe; press; bench; тка́цкий **~** loom.
станци|о́нный [14] station...; waiting; post(*master*); **'~я** *f* [7] station (at на П); *teleph.* office, exchange; 🚂 *a.* yard; узлова́я **'~я** junction.
ста́птывать [1], ⟨стопта́ть⟩ [3] tread down; wear out.
стара́|ние *n* [12] pains *pl.*, care(ful effort); endeavo(u)r, trouble; **~тельный** [14; -лен, -льна] assiduous, diligent; careful; **~ться** [1], ⟨по-⟩ endeavo(u)r, try (hard); strive (for о П).
стар|е́ть [21] **1.** ⟨по-⟩ grow old, age; **2.** ⟨у-⟩ grow obsolete; **∠ец** *m* [1; -рца] (old) monk; *a.* = **~и́к** *m* [1 *e.*] old man; **~ина́** *f* [5] olden time *or* days (of yore) (in в В); F old man; **~и́нный** [14] ancient, antique; old; longstanding; **∠ить** [13], ⟨со-⟩ make (**-ся** grow) old.
старо|мо́дный [14; -ден, -дна] old-fashioned, out-of-date; **'~ста** *m* [5] (*village*) elder; (*church*) warden; (*class*) monitor; **'~сть** *f* [8] old age (in one's на П лет).
стартова́ть [7] (*im*)*pf.* start.
стар|у́ха *f* [5] old woman; **∠ческий** [16] senile; **∠ший** [17] elder, older, senior; eldest, oldest; higher, highest; fore(*man*); first (*lieutenant*); **~шина́** *m* [5] foreman; chairman, manager; ⚔ first sergeant (*or*, ⚓, mate); **~шинство́** *n* [9] seniority.
ста́р|ый [14; стар, -а́, -о] old; ancient, antique; olden; **~ьё** *n* [10] second-hand articles *pl.*; junk, *Brt.* lumber.
ста́|скивать [1], ⟨**~щи́ть**⟩ [16] pull (off, down); take, bring.
стати́ст *m* [1], **~ка** *f* [5; *g/pl.*: -ток] *thea.* supernumerary; *film*: extra; **~ика** *f* [5] statistics; **~и́ческий** [16] statistical.
ста́т|ный [14; -тен, -тна́, -о] stately, portly; **~уя** [6; *g/pl.*: -у́й] statue; **~ь**[1] *f* [8] build; trait; F need, seemly; с како́й **~и**? F why (should I, *etc.*).
стать[2] *s.* станови́ться; **~ся** F (*impers.*) happen (to с Т); (*may*)be.
статья́ *f* [6; *g/pl.*: -те́й] article; item, entry; F matter, business (another осо́бая).
стаха́новец *m* [1; -вца] Stakhanovite.

стационáрный [14] stationary.
стáчка *f* [5; *g/pl.*: -чек] strike.
стащúть *s.* стáскивать.
стáя *f* [6; *g/pl.*: стай] flight, flock; shoal; pack, troop.
стáять [27] *pf.* thaw off, melt.
ствол *m* [1 *e.*] trunk; barrel.
ствóрчатый [14] folding (*doors*).
стéбель *m* [4; -бля; *from g/pl. e.*] stalk, stem.
стёганый [14] quilted.
стегáть [1] **1.** ⟨вы́-, про-⟩ quilt; **2.** *once* ⟨стегну́ть⟩ [20] whip.
сте|кáть [1], ⟨**~**чь⟩ [26] flow (down); **-ся** join; flock, gather.
стек|лó *n* [9; *pl.*: стёкла, стёкол, стёклам] glass; pane; (*lamp*) chimney; **~ля́нный** [14] glass...; glassy; **~óльщик** *m* [1] glazier.
стел|úть(ся) F *s.* стлать(ся); **~лáж** *m* [1 *e.*] shelf; **∠ька** *f* [5; *g/pl.*: -лек] inner sole; **∠ьный** [14]: **~**ьная корóва cow with calf.
стен|á *f* [5; *ac/sg.*: стéну; *pl.*: стéны, стен, стенáм] wall; **~газéта** *f* [5] (стеннáя газéта) wall newspaper; **∠**ка *f* [5; *g/pl.*: -нок] wall; **~нóй** [14] wall...
стеногрá|мма *f* [5] shorthand (verbatim) report *or* notes *pl.*; **~фи́ст** *m* [1], **~фи́стка** *f* [5; *g/pl.*: -ток] stenographer; **~фия** *f* [7] shorthand.
Степáн *m* [1] Stephen.
степéнный [14; -éнен, -éнна] sedate, staid, grave, dignified; mature.
стéпень *f* [8; *from g/pl. e.*] degree (to до P), extent; ⅍ power.
степ|нóй [14] steppe...; **~ь** *f* [8; в -пи́; *from g/pl. e.*] steppe.
стéрва P *contp. f* [5] damned wretch.
стере|оти́пный [14; -пен, -пна] stereotyped; **∠ть** *s.* стирáть
стерéчь [26 г/ж: -егу́, -ежёшь; -ёг, -еглá] guard, watch (over).
стéржень *m* [4; -жня] core (*a. fig.*); pivot.
стерил|изовáть [7] (*im*)*pf.* sterilize; **∠ьный** [14; -лен, -льна] sterile.
стерпéть [10] *pf.* endure, bear.
стесн|éние *n* [12] constraint, restraint; **~и́тельный** [14; -лен, -льна] constraining, embarrassing; **~я́ть** [28], ⟨**~**и́ть⟩ [13] constrain, restrain; embarrass, hamper; cramp; trouble, press; **~я́ться**, ⟨по-⟩ feel (*or* be) shy, self-conscious *or* embarrassed; (P) be ashamed of; hesitate.
стеч|éние *n* [12] confluence; coincidence; **~ь(ся)** *s.* стекáть(ся).
стиль *m* [4] style; (*Old, New*) Style.
стипéндия *f* [7] scholarship.
стир|áльный [14] washing; **~áть** [1] **1.** ⟨стерéть⟩ [12; сотру́, -трёшь; стёр(ла); стёрши & стерéв] wipe *or* rub off, out; erase, efface, blot out; clean; pulverize; **2.** ⟨вы́-⟩ wash, launder; **∠ка** *f* [5] wash(ing), laundry; отдáть в **∠**ку send to the wash.
сти́с|кивать [1], ⟨**~**нуть⟩ [20] clench; grasp, press.
стих (*a.* **~**и́ *pl.*) *m* [1 *e.*] verse; *pl. a.* poem(s); **~áть** [1], ⟨**∠**нуть⟩ [21] abate; fall; cease; calm down, (become) quiet; **~и́йный** [14; -и́ен, -и́йна] elemental; spontaneous; natural; **~и́я** *f* [7] element(s); **∠нуть** *s.* **~**áть.
стихотворéние *n* [12] poem.
стлать & F **стели́ть** [стелю́, -стéлешь], ⟨по-⟩ [пóстланный] spread, lay; make (*bed*); **-ся** *impf.* (be) spread; drift; ⚘ creep.
сто [35] hundred.
стог *m* [1; в стóге & в стогу́; *pl.*: -á, *etc. e.*] stack, rick.
стóи|мость *f* [8] cost; value, worth (... Т/в В); **~ть** [13] cost; be worth; pay; take, require; (Д) need, if (*only*); matter; не **~**т F = нé за что.
стой! stop!, halt!; **∠ка** *f* [5; *g/pl.*: стóек] stand(ard); support; counter; **∠кий** [16; стóек, стойкá, -о; *comp.*: стóйче] firm, steadfast, steady; **∠кость** *f* [8] firmness; **∠ло** *n* [9] box (stall); **~мя́** upright.
сток *m* [1] flowing (off); drain.
Стокгóльм *m* [1] Stockholm.
стокрáтный [14] hundredfold.
стол *m* [1 *e.*] table (at за Т); board, fare; meal; office, bureau; *hist.* throne.
столб *m* [1 *e.*] post, pole; column; pillar; **~енéть** [8], ⟨о-⟩ petrify; **~éц** *m* [1; -бцá], **∠ик** *m* [1] column; **~ня́к** *m* [1 *e.*] stupor; tetanus; **~овóй** [14]: **~**овáя дорóга *f* highway.
столéтие *n* [12] century; centenary.
стóлик *m* [1] *dim. of* стол; F table.
столи́|ца *f* [5] capital; **~чный** [14] metropolitan.
столкн|овéние *n* [12] collision, clash; **~у́ть(ся)** *s.* стáлкивать(ся).
столóв|ая *f* [14] dining room; restaurant; **~ый** [14] table(*spoon*); dinner (*service*).
столп *m* [1 *e.*] pillar; column.
столь so; **∠ко** [32] so much, so many; **∠**ко же as much *or* many.
столя́р *m* [1 *e.*] joiner; cabinetmaker; **~ный** [14] joiner's (*shop, etc.*).
стон *m* [1], **~áть** [-ну́, стóнешь; стонáя], ⟨про-⟩ groan, moan.
стоп! stop!; **~á** *f* **1.** [5 *e.*] foot; footstep (with Т; in по Д); **2.** [5; *pl. st.*] foot (*verse*); pile; **∠ка** *f* [5; *g/pl.*: -пок] cup; roll, rouleau; **∠орить** [13], ⟨за-⟩ stop; **~тáть** *s.* стáптывать.
стóрож *m* [1; *pl.*: -á, *etc. e.*] guard, watchman; **~евóй** [14] watch...; on duty; sentry (*box*); observation (*post*); ⚓ patrol...; **~и́ть** [16 *e.*; -жу́, -жи́шь] guard, watch (over).
сторон|á *f* [5; *ac/sg.*: стóрону; *pl.*: стóроны, сторóн, -нáм] side (on *a.* по Д; с Р); direction; part (on с[о]

P); place, region, country; party; distance (at в П; from с P); в '~у aside, apart (*a.* joking шýтки); в ~é aloof, apart; нá ~у abroad; с однóй ~ы́ on the one hand; ... с вáшей ~ы́ *a.* ... of you; **~и́ться** [13; -онюсь, -óнишься], ⟨по-⟩ make way, step aside; (P) avoid, shun; **~и́сь!** look out!; **∠ник** *m* [1] adherent, follower, supporter; partisan.

стóчный [14] waste..., soil...

стоя́|лый [14] stale; **~нка** *f* [5; *g/pl.*: -нок] stop (at на П); stand, station, (fixed) quarters *pl.*; parking place *or* lot; ⚓ anchorage.

стоя́|ть [стою, стоúшь; стóя] stand; be; stop; lodge, quarter; stand up (for за В), defend; insist (on на П); стóй(те)! stop!; F wait!; **~чий** [17] standing; stagnant; stand-up (*collar*); standard (*lamp*).

стр. *abbr.*: страни́ца page, p.

страдá|лец *m* [1; -льца] martyr; **~ние** *n* [12] suffering; **~тельный** [14] *gr.* passive; **~ть** [1], ⟨по-⟩ suffer (from от P, T; for за B); F be poor.

страж *m* [1] guard; **∠а** *f* [5] guard(s); watch; custody (in[to] под T [B]).

стран|á *f* [5; *pl. st.*] country; **~и́ца** *f* [5] page (*cf.* пя́тый); column (in на П); **∠ник** *m* [1] wanderer, travel(l)er; pilgrim; **∠ность** *f* [8] strangeness, oddity; **∠ный** [14; -áнен, -аннá, -o] strange, odd; **∠ств(ован)ие** *n* [12] wandering, travel; **∠ствовать** [7] wander, travel; **∠ствующий** *a.* (*knight-*)errant.

страст|нóй (-sn-) [14] Holy; Good (*Friday*); **∠ный** (-sn-) [14; -тен, -тнá, -o] passionate, fervent; **~ь** *f* [8; *from g/pl. e.*] passion (for к Д); P awfully.

стратег|и́ческий [16] strategic(al); **∠ия** *f* [7] strategy.

стратосфéра *f* [5] stratosphere.

стрáус *m* [1] ostrich.

страх *m* [1] fear (for от, со P); risk, peril (at на B); F awfully; **~кáсса** *f* [5] insurance office; **~овáние** *n* [12] insurance (*fire* ... от P); **~овáть** [7], ⟨за-⟩ insure (against от P); **~óвка** *f* [5; *g/pl.*: -вок] insurance (rate); **~овóй** [14] insurance...

страш|и́ть [16 *e.*; -шý, -ши́шь], ⟨у-⟩ [-шённый] (**-ся** be) frighten (-ed; at P; fear, dread, be afraid of); **∠ный** [14; -шен, -шнá, -o] terrible, frightful, dreadful; Last (*Judg[e]ment*); F awful; мне ∠но I'm afraid, I fear.

стрекозá *f* [5; *pl. st.*: -óзы, -óз, -óзам] dragonfly.

стрел|á *f* [5; *pl. st.*] arrow(like T); ⚘ shaft; **∠ка** *f* [5; *g/pl.*: -лок] hand, pointer, indicator; needle; arrow (*drawing, etc.*); clock (*stocking*); tongue (*land*); 🚂 switch, *Brt.* point; **~кóвый** [14] shooting...; (of) rifles *pl.*; **~óк** *m* [1; -лкá] marksman, shot; ⚔ rifleman; **∠очник** 🚂 *m* [1] switchman, *Brt.* pointsman; **~ьбá** *f* [5; *pl. st.*] shooting, fire; **~я́ть** [28], ⟨вы́стрелить⟩ [13] shoot, fire (at в B, по Д; *gun* из P); F *impers.* feel acute pains *pl.*; **-ся** *impf.* (fight a) duel.

стрем|глáв headlong, headfirst; **~и́тельный** [14; -лен, -льна] impetuous, violent, rash; **~и́ться** [14 *e.*; -млюсь, -ми́шься] (к Д) aspire (to, after), strive (for, after); rush; **~лéние** *n* [12] aspiration, striving, urge; tendency.

стрéмя *n* [13; *pl.*: -менá, -мя́н, -менáм] stirrup.

стриж *m* [1 *e.*] sand martin.

стри́|женый [14] bobbed, short-haired; shorn; trimmed; **~жка** *f* [5] haircut(ting); shearing; trimming; **~чь** [26 г/ж: -игý, -ижёшь; *pt. st.*], ⟨по-, о(б)-⟩ cut; shear; clip, trim; **-ся** have one's hair cut.

строгáть [1], ⟨вы́-⟩ plane.

стрóг|ий [16; строг, -á, -o; *comp.*: стрóже] severe; strict; austere; stern; **~ость** *f* [8] severity, austerity, strictness.

строе|вóй [14] fighting, front(line); ~вóй лес *m* timber; **∠ние** *n* [12] construction, building; structure.

строи́тель *m* [4] builder, constructor; **~ный** [14] building...; **~ство** *n* [9] construction.

стрóить [13] **1.** ⟨по-⟩ build (up), construct; make, scheme; play *fig.* (из P); **2.** ⟨вы́-⟩ ⚔ draw up, form; **-ся,** ⟨вы́-, по-⟩ be built; build a house; ⚔ fall in.

строй *m* **1.** [3; в строю; *pl. e.*: строи́, строёв] order, array; line; **2.** [3] system, order, regime; ♪ tune; **∠ка** *f* [5; *g/pl.*: -óек] construction; **∠ность** *f* [8] harmony; slenderness; **∠ный** [14; -óен, -ойнá, -o] slender, slim; harmonious; symmetrical, well-shaped, well-disposed.

строкá *f* [5; *ac/sg.*: стрóкý; *pl.*: стрóки, строк, строкáм] line.

стропи́ло *n* [9] rafter.

строптúвый [14 *sh.*] obstinate, refractory.

строфá *f* [5; *nom/pl. st.*] stanza.

строч|и́ть [16 & 16 *e.*; -очý, -óчи́шь; -óченный & -очённый] stitch, sew; F scribble, write; crackle; **∠ка** *f* [5; *g/pl.*: -чек] line; seam.

стрý|жка *f* [5; *g/pl.*: -жек] shaving; **~и́ться** [13] stream, flow, run; purl; **~йка** *f* [5; *g/pl.*: -ýек] *dim. of* ~я́.

структýра *f* [5] structure.

струн|á ♪ *f* [5; *pl. st.*], **∠ный** [14] string.

струч|кóвый *s.* бобóвый; **~óк** *m* [1; -чкá] pod, husk.

струя́ *f* [6; *pl. st.*: -ýи] stream (in T); jet; current; flood.

стря́|пать F [1], ⟨со-⟩ cook; **~хивать** [1], ⟨~хнýть⟩ [20] shake off.

студе́н|т *m* [1], **~тка** *f* [5; *g/pl.*: -ток] student, undergraduate; **~ческий** [16] students'.
студёный F [14 *sh.*] (icy) cold.
сту́день *m* [4; -дня] jellied meat.
сту́дия *f* [7] studio, atelier.
стук *m* [1] knock; rattle, clatter, noise; **∠нуть** *s.* стуча́ть.
стул *m* [1; *pl.*: сту́лья, -льев] chair; seat; ⚕ stool.
сту́па *f* [5] mortar (*vessel*).
ступ|а́ть [1], ⟨**~и́ть**⟩ [14] step, tread, go; **~е́нчатый** [14 *sh.*] (multi)graded; **~е́нь** *f* **1.** [8; *pl.*: ступе́ни, ступе́ней] step; **2.** [8; *pl.*: ступе́ни, -не́й, *etc. e.*] stage, grade; **~е́нька** *f* [5; *g/pl.*: -нек] step; rung; **~и́ть** *s.* **~а́ть**; **∠ка** *f* [5; *g/pl.*: -пок] (small) mortar; **~ня́** *f* [6; *g/pl.*: -не́й] foot; sole.
сту|ча́ть [4 *e.*; -чу́, -чи́шь] ⟨по-⟩, *once* ⟨**∠кнуть**⟩ [20] knock (at *door* в В; *a.* **-ся**); rap, tap; throb; chatter; clatter, rattle; **~ча́т** there's a knock at the door; **∠кнуть** F *s.* испо́лниться.
стыд *m* [1 *e.*] shame; **~и́ть** [15 *e.*; -ыжу́, -ыди́шь], ⟨при-⟩ [пристыжённый] shame, make ashamed; **-ся**, ⟨по-⟩ be ashamed (of P); **~ли́вый** [14 *sh.*] shy, bashful; **∠ный** F [14; -ден, -дна́, -о] shameful; **∠но!** (for) shame!; мне **∠но** I am ashamed (for p. за В).
стык *m* [1] joint, juncture (at на П).
сты́(ну)ть [21], ⟨о-⟩ (become) cool.
сты́чка *f* [5; *g/pl.*: -чек] skirmish.
стя́|гивать [1], ⟨**~ну́ть**⟩ [19] draw *or* pull together (off, down); tie up; ⚔ concentrate; F pilfer; **~жа́ть** [1] gain, acquire; **~ну́ть** *s.* **~гивать**.
суб|бо́та *f* [5] Saturday (on: в В, *pl.*: по Д); **~си́дия** *f* [7] subsidy.
субтропи́ческий [16] subtropical.
субъе́кт *m* [1] subject; F fellow; **~и́вный** [14; -вен, -вна] subjective.
суверен|ите́т *m* [1] sovereignty; **∠ный** [14; -е́нен, -е́нна] sovereign.
суг|ро́б *m* [1] snowdrift, bank; **~у́бый** [14 *sh.*] especial, exceptional.
суд *m* [1 *e.*] judg(e)ment (to на В); court (of justice); tribunal; trial (put on отда́ть под В; bring to преда́ть Д); justice; полево́й ~ court martial; **~а́к** *m* [1 *e.*] pike perch.
суда́р|ыня *f* [6] madam; **'~ь** *m* [4] sir.
суд|е́бный [14] judicial, legal; law-...; (of the) court; **~е́йский** [16] judicial; referee's; **~и́ть** [15; суждённый] **1.** ⟨по-⟩ judge *fig.* (of о П; by по Д); **2.** (*im*)*pf.* try, judge; destine; **∠я** по (Д) judging by; **-ся** be at law (with с Т).
су́д|но *n* **1.** [9; *pl.*: суда́, -о́в] ⚓ ship, vessel; **2.** [9; *pl.*: су́дна, -ден] vessel; **~омо́йка** *f* [5; *g/pl.*: -о́ек] scullery *or* kitchen maid.

су́доро|га *f* [5] cramp, spasm; **~жный** [14; -жен, -жна] convulsive.
судо|строе́ние *n* [12] shipbuilding; **~строи́тельный** [14] shipbuilding...; ship(*yard*); **~хо́дный** [14; -ден, -дна] navigable; **~хо́дство** *n* [9] navigation.
судьба́ *f* [5; *pl.*: су́дьбы, су́деб, су́дьбам] fate.
судья́ *m* [6; *pl.*: су́дьи, суде́й, су́дьям] judge; arbitrator, referee, umpire.
суеве́р|ие *n* [12] superstition; **~ный** [14; -рен, -рна] superstitious.
сует|а́ *f* [5] vanity; fuss; **~и́ться** [15 *e.*; суечу́сь, суети́шься] fuss; **~ли́вый** [14 *sh.*] fussy.
суж|де́ние *n* [12] judg(e)ment; **~е́ние** *n* [12] narrowing; ⚕ constriction; **∠ивать** [1], ⟨су́зить⟩ [15] narrow (*v/i.* **-ся**; taper).
сук *m* [1 *e.*; на -у́; *pl.*: су́чья, -ьев & -и́, -о́в] bough, branch; knot; **∠а** *f* [5] bitch; **∠ин** [19] of a bitch.
сукно́ *n* [9; *pl. st.*; су́кна, су́кон, су́кнам] cloth.
суко́нный [14] cloth...
сули́ть [13], ⟨по-⟩ promise.
султа́н *m* [1] sultan; plume.
сумасбро́д *m* [1] madman; crank; **~ный** [14; -ден, -дна] crazy, cranky, foolish; **~ство** *n* [9] folly, madness.
сумасше́|дший [17] mad, insane; *su.* madman; lunatic (asylum дом *m*); **~ствие** *n* [12] madness, insanity.
сумато́ха *f* [5] turmoil, fuss.
сум|бу́р *m* [1] *s.* пу́таница; **∠ерки** *f/pl.* [5; *gen.*: -рек] dusk, twilight; **∠ка** *f* [5; *g/pl.*: -мок] (hand)bag; pouch; satchel; wallet; **∠ма** *f* [5] sum (for/of на В/в В), amount; **~ма́рный** [14; -рен. -рна] summary; **~ми́ровать** [7] (*im*)*pf.* sum up.
су́мочка *f* [5; *g/pl.*: -чек] handbag.
су́мра|к *m* [1] twilight, dusk; gloom; **~чный** [14; -чен, -чна] gloomy.
сунду́к *m* [1 *e.*] trunk, chest.
су́нуть(ся) *s.* сова́ть(ся).
суп *m* [1; *pl. e.*], **~ово́й** [14] soup.
супру́|г *m* [1] husband; **~га** *f* [5] wife; **~жеский** [16] matrimonial, conjugal; married; **~жество** *n* [9] matrimony, wedlock.
сургу́ч *m* [1 *e.*] sealing wax.
суро́в|ость *f* [8] severity; **~ый** [14 *sh.*] harsh, rough; severe, austere; stern; rigorous.
суррога́т *m* [1] substitute.
сурьма́ *f* [5] antimony.
суста́в *m* [1] joint.
су́тки *f/pl.* [5; *gen.*: -ток] 24 hours, day (and night); кру́глые ~ round the clock.
су́толока *f* [5] turmoil.
су́точный [14] day's, daily, 24 hours'; *pl. su.* daily allowance.

суту́лый [14 *sh.*] round-shouldered.
сут|ь *f* [8] essence, core, main point; по ⁓и (де́ла) at bottom.
суфл|ёр *m* [1] prompter; **⁓и́ровать** [7] prompt (p. Д).
сух|а́рь *m* [4 *e.*] cracker, zwieback, *Brt.* biscuit; **⁓ожи́лие** *n* [12] sinew; **⁓о́й** [14; сух, -а́, -о; *comp.*: су́ше] dry; arid; lean; land...; *fig.* cool, cold; boring, dull; **⁓опу́тный** [14] land...; **⁓ость** *f* [8] dryness, *etc.*, *s.* ⁓о́й; **⁓ощáвый** [14 *sh.*] lean, meager.
сучи́ть [16] twist; roll.
сучо́к *m* [1; -чка́] *dim. of* сук, *cf.*
су́ш|а *f* [5] (main)land; **⁓е́ние** *n* [12] drying; **⁓ёный** [14] dried; **⁓и́лка** *f* [5; *g/pl.*: -лок] drying apparatus; *a.* = **⁓и́льня** *f* [6; *g/pl.*: -лен] drying room; **⁓и́ть** [16] **1.** ⟨вы́-⟩ dry; air; **2.** ⟨ис-⟩ wear out, emaciate; **⁓ка** *f* [5; *g/pl.*: -шек] drying; ring-shaped cracknel.
суще́ств|енный [14 *sh.*] essential, substantial; **⁓и́тельное** *n* [14] noun, substantive (*a.* и́мя ⁓и́тельное); **⁓о́** *n* [9] creature, being; essence; по ⁓у́ at bottom; to the point; **⁓ова́ние** *n* [12] existence, being; subsistence; **⁓ова́ть** [7] exist, be; live.
су́щ|ий [17] existing; F plain (*truth*), quite (*true* or *right*), sheer, downright; **⁓ность** *f* [8] essence, substance; в ⁓ности at bottom, properly.
суэ́цкий [16]: ♀ кана́л Suez Canal.
сфе́ра *f* [5] sphere; field, realm.
с.-х. *abbr.*: сельскохозя́йственный.
схват|и́ть(ся) *s.* ⁓ывать(ся); **⁓ка** *f* [5; *g/pl.*: -ток] skirmish, fight, combat; scuffle; *pl. a.* (*childbirth*) labo(u)r; **⁓ывать** [1], ⟨⁓и́ть⟩ [15] seize (by за В), grasp (*a. fig.*), grab; snatch; catch; **-ся** seize, lay hold of; F grapple.
схе́ма *f* [5] diagram, scheme (in на П); **⁓ти́ческий** [16] schematic.
сход|и́ть [15], ⟨сойти́⟩ [сойду́, -дёшь; сошёл, -шла́; с(о)ше́дший; *g. pt.*: сойдя́] go (*or* come) down, descend (from с Р); get off (out); come off (out); run off; leave; disappear; F pass (for за В); P do; pass off; **⁓и́ть** *pf.* go (& get, fetch за Т); *cf.* ум; **-ся**, ⟨-сь⟩ meet; gather; become friends; agree (upon в П); harmonize (in Т); coincide; approximate; F click; **⁓ка** *f* [5; *g/pl.*: -док] meeting (at на П); **⁓ни** *f/pl.* [6; *gen.*: -ней] gangplank, gangway; **⁓ный** [14; -ден, -дна́, -о] similar (to с Т), like; F reasonable; **⁓ство** *n* [9] similarity (to с Т), likeness.
сцеди́ть [15] *pf.* draw off.
сце́н|а *f* [5] stage; scene (*a. fig.*); **⁓а́рий** *m* [3] scenario, script; **⁓и́ческий** [16] stage..., scenic.
сцеп|и́ть(ся) *s.* ⁓ля́ть(ся); **⁓ка** *f* [5; *g/pl.*: -пок] coupling; **⁓ле́ние** *n* [12] *phys.* cohesion; ⊕ coupling; *fig.* concatenation; **⁓ля́ть** [28], ⟨⁓и́ть⟩ [14] link; ⊕ couple (*v/i.* **-ся**; concatenate; F grapple).
счаст|ли́вец *m* [1; -вца] lucky man; **⁓ли́вый** [14; сча́стли́в, -а, -о] happy; fortunate, lucky; ⁓ли́вого пути́ bon voyage!; ⁓ли́во F bye-bye, so long: ⁓ли́во отде́латься have a narrow escape; **⁓ье** *n* [10] happiness; good luck; fortune; к, по ⁓ью fortunately.
счесть(ся) *s.* счита́ть(ся).
счёт *m* [1; на -е & счету́; *pl.*: счета́, *etc. e.*] count, calculation; account (on в В; на В); bill; invoice; *sport* score; в коне́чном ⁓е ultimately; за ⁓ (Р) at the expense (of); на э́тот ⁓ in this respect, as for this; ска́зано на мой ⁓ aimed at me; быть на хоро́шем ⁓у́ (у Р) stand high (in p.'s) favo(u)r; у него́ ⁓у нет (Д) he has lots (of); **⁓ный** [14] calculating (*machine*, calculator); slide (*rule*).
счетово́д *m* [1] accountant.
счёт|чик *m* [1] meter; counter; **⁓ы** *pl.* [1] abacus *sg.*; accounts *fig.*
счисле́ние *n* [12] calculation.
счита́|ть [1], ⟨со-⟩ & ⟨счесть⟩ [25; сочту́, -тёшь; счёл, сочла́; сочтённый; *g. pt.*: сочтя́] count; (*pf.* счесть) (Т, за В) consider, regard (*a.* as), hold, think; **⁓я** *a.* including; '⁓нные *pl.* very few; **-ся** count; settle accounts; (Т) be considered (*or* reputed) to be, pass for; (с Т) consider, regard.
США (Соединённые Шта́ты Аме́рики) U.S.A. (United States of America).
сши|ба́ть [1], ⟨⁓би́ть⟩ [-бу́, -бёшь; *cf.* ушиби́ть] F *s.* сби(ва́)ть; **⁓ва́ть** [1], ⟨⁓ть⟩ [сошью́, -шьёшь; сшей(-те)!; сши́тый] sew (together).
съед|а́ть [1], ⟨съесть⟩ *s.* есть[1]; **⁓о́бный** [14; -бен, -бна] edible.
съез|д *m* [1] congress (at на П); **⁓дить** [15] *pf.* go; (за Т) fetch; (к Д) visit; **⁓жа́ть** [1], ⟨съе́хать⟩ [съе́ду, -дешь] go, drive (*or* slide) down; move; **-ся** meet; gather.
съёмка *f* [5; *g/pl.*: -мок] survey; shooting.
съестно́й [14] food...
съе́хать(ся) *s.* съезжа́ть(ся).
сы́|воротка *f* [5; *g/pl.*: -ток] whey; serum; **⁓гра́ть** *s.* игра́ть.
сы́знова F anew, (once) again.
сын *m* [1; *pl.*: сыновья́, -ве́й, -вья́м; *fig. pl.*: сыны́] son; *fig. a.* child; **⁓о́вний** [15] filial; **⁓о́к** F *m* [1; -нка́] sonny.
сы́п|ать [2], ⟨по-⟩ strew, scatter; pour; F (Т, В) sputter, pelt, (*jokes*) crack, (*money*) squander; **-ся** pour; F spatter, hail, pelt; **⁓но́й** [14]: ⁓но́й тиф spotted fever; **⁓у́чий** [17 *sh.*] dry; quick(*sand*); **⁓ь** *f* [8] rash.

сыр *m* [1; *pl. e.*] cheese; как ~ в масле (*live*) in clover; **~éть** [8], ⟨от-⟩ dampen; **~éц** *m* [1; -рца́]: шёлк-~éц raw silk; **∠ник** *m* [1] cheese cake; **∠ный** [14] cheese...; caseous; **~ова́тый** [14 *sh.*] dampish; rare, *Brt.* underdone; **~о́й** [14; сыр, -á, -o] damp; moist; raw; crude; unbaked; **∠ость** *f* [8] dampness; moisture; **~ьё** *n* [10] *coll.* raw material.

сыск|а́ть F [3] *pf.* find; **-ся** be found; **~но́й** [14] detective.

сы́т|ный [14; сы́тен, -тна́, -o] substantial, rich; F fat; **~ый** [14; сыт, -á, -o] satisfied; fat.

сыч *m* [1 *e.*] horned owl.

сы́щик *m* [1] detective, policeman.

сюда́ here, hither; this way.

сюже́т *m* [1] subject; plot.

сюрпри́з *m* [1] surprise.

сюрту́к *m* [1 *e.*] frock coat.

Т

т. *abbr.*: **1.** това́рищ; **2.** том; **3.** то́нна; **4.** ты́сяча.

таба́|к *m* [1 *e.*; *part. g.*: -у́] tobacco; **~ке́рка** *f* [5; *g/pl.*: -рок] snuffbox; **~чный** [14] tobacco...

та́б|ель *m* [4] time sheet; **~ле́тка** *f* [5; *g/pl.*: -ток] tablet; **~ли́ца** *f* [5] table, schedule, list; scale; *gr.* paradigm; **~ор** *m* [1] (*gipsy's*) camp; ⚔ [party.]

табу́н *m* [1 *e.*] herd, drove.

табуре́тка *f* [5; *g/pl.*: -ток] stool.

таджи́к *m* [1], **~ский** [16] Tajik.

таз *m* [1; в -у́; *pl. e.*] basin; *anat.* pelvis.

таи́нств|енный [14 *sh.*] mysterious; secret(ive); **'~о** *n* [9] sacrament.

таи́ть [13] conceal; **-ся** hide.

тайга́ *f* [5] taiga.

тай|ко́м secretly; behind (one's) back (от P); **∠на** *f* [5] secret; mystery; **~ни́к** *m* [1 *e.*] hiding (place); (inmost) recess; **∠ный** [14] secret; stealthy; vague; privy.

так so, thus; like that; (~ же just) as; so much; just so; then; well; yes; one way ...; *s. a.* пра́вда; F properly; не ~ wrong(ly); ~ и (*both*...) and; F downright; ∠ как as, since; и ~ without that; ∠же also, too; ∠же не neither, nor; а ∠же as well as; **~и́** F all the same; indeed; **~ наз.** *abbr.*: ~ называ́емый so-called; alleged; **~ово́й** [14; -ко́в, -кова́] such; (a)like; same; был(á) ~о́в(á) disappeared, vanished; **~о́й** [16] such; so; ~о́е *su.* such things; ~о́й же the same; as ...; ~о́й-то such-and-such; so-and-so; что (э́то) ~о́е? F what's the matter?, what's on?; кто вы ~о́й (~а́я)? = кто́ вы?

та́кса *f* [5] (fixed) rate.

такси́ *n* [*ind.*] taxi(cab).

такси́ровать [7] (*im*)*pf.* rate.

такт *m* [1] ♪ time, measure, bar; *fig.* tact; **∠ика** *f* [5] tactics *pl.* & *sg.*; **~и́ческий** [16] tactical; **~и́чность** *f* [8] tactfulness; **~и́чный** [14; -чен, -чна] tactful.

тала́нт *m* [1] talent, gift (for к Д); **~ливый** [14 *sh.*] talented, gifted.

та́лия *f* [7] waist.

тало́н *m* [1] coupon.

та́лый [14] thawed; slushy.

там there; F then; ~ же in the same place; ibidem; ~ и сям F here and there.

тамо́ж|енный [14] custom(s)...; **~ня** *f* [6; *g/pl.*: -жен] custom house.

та́мошний [15] of that place, there.

та́н|ец *m* [1; -нца] dance (*go* dancing на В *pl.*); **~к** *m* [1] tank; **~ковый** [14] armo(u)red...; tank...

танц|ева́льный [14] dancing...; **~ева́ть** [7], ⟨с-⟩ dance; **~о́вщик** *m* [1], **~о́вщица** *f* [5] (ballet) dancer; **~о́р** *m* [1], **~о́рка** *f* [5; *g/pl.*: -рок] dancer.

Та́ня *f* [6] *dim. of* Татья́на.

та́почка *f* [5; *g/pl.*: -чек] sport slipper.

та́ра *f* [5] tare; packing.

тарака́н *m* [1] cockroach.

тара́нить [13], ⟨про-⟩ ram.

тарахте́ть F [11] rumble.

тара́щить [16], ⟨вы́-⟩: ~ глаза́ stare (at на В; with *surprise* от Р).

таре́лка *f* [5; *g/pl.*: -лок] plate.

тари́ф *m* [1] tariff; **~ный** [14] tariff...; standard (*wages*).

таска́ть [1] carry; drag, pull; F steal; P wear; **-ся** F roam; go; frequent; gad about.

тасова́ть [7], ⟨с-⟩ shuffle.

ТАСС (Телегра́фное Аге́нтство Сове́тского Сою́за) TASS (Telegraph Agency of the U.S.S.R.).

тата́р|ин *m* [1; *pl.*: -ры, -р, -рам], **~ка** *f* [5; *g/pl.*: -рок], **~ский** [16] Tartar.

Татья́на *f* [5] Tatyana.

тафта́ *f* [5] taffeta.

тача́ть [1], ⟨с-, вы́-⟩ seam, sew.

тащи́ть [16] **1.** ⟨по-⟩ drag, pull; carry, bring; **2.** F ⟨с-⟩ steal, pilfer; **~ся** F trudge, drag (o.s.) along.

та́ять [27], ⟨рас-⟩ thaw, melt; fade, die (away); languish, pine.

тварь *f* [8] creature; F wretch.

тверде́ть [8], ⟨за-, о-⟩ harden.

тверди́ть F [15 *e.*; -ржу́, -рди́шь] reiterate, repeat (over & over again); talk; practice; ⟨за-, вы́-⟩ learn.

твёрд|ость *f* [8] firmness; hardness; **~ый** [14; твёрд, тверда́, -o] hard;

solid; firm (*a. fig.*); (stead)fast, steady; fixed (*a. prices*); sound, good; F sure; ~o *a.* well, for sure.
тверды́ня *f* [6] stronghold.
тво|й *m*, ~я́ *f*, ~ё *n*, ~и́ *pl.* [24] your; yours; *pl. su.* F your folks; *cf.* ваш.
твор|е́ние *n* [12] work; creature; ~е́ц *m* [1; -рца́] creator; author; ~и́тельный [14] *gr.* instrumental (*case*); ~и́ть [13], ⟨со-⟩ create, do; perform; -ся F be (going) on; ~о́г *m* [1 *e.*] curd(s).
тво́рче|ский [16] creative; ~ство *n* [9] work(s), creation.
т. е. *abbr.*: то́ есть, *cf.*
теа́тр *m* [1] theater (*Brt.* -tre; at в П); house; stage; ~а́льный [14; -лен, -льна] theatrical; theater...
тёзка *m/f* [5; *g/pl.*: -зок] namesake.
тексти́ль *m* [4] *coll.* textiles *pl.*; ~ный [14] textile; cotton (*mill*).
теку́|чий [17 *sh.*] fluid; fluctuating; ~щий [17] current; instant; present; miscellaneous.
телеви́|дение *n* [12] television (on по Д); ~зио́нный [14] TV; ~зор *m* [1] TV set.
теле́га *f* [5] cart, telega.
телегра́мма *f* [5] telegram, wire.
телегра́ф *m* [1] telegraph (office); wire (by по Д); ~и́ровать [7] (*im*)*pf.* telegraph, wire, cable; ~ный [14] telegraph(ic); telegram..., by wire.
теле́жка *f* [5; *g/pl.*: -жек] handcart.
телёнок *m* [2] calf.
телепереда́ча *f* [5] telecast.
телеско́п *m* [1] telescope.
теле́сный [14] corporal; corporeal; flesh-colo(u)red.
телефо́н *m* [1] telephone (by по Д); ~и́ровать [7] (*im*)*pf.* (Д) telephone, F phone; ~и́ст *m* [1], ~и́стка *f* [5; *g/pl.*: -ток] operator; ~ный [14] tele(phone)...; call (*box*).
тели́ться [13; те́лится], ⟨о-⟩ calve.
тёлка *f* [5; *g/pl.*: -лок] heifer.
те́ло *n* [9; *pl. e.*] body; *phys.* solid; иноро́дное ~ foreign matter; всем ~м all over; ~сложе́ние *n* [12] build; constitution; ~храни́тель *m* [4] bodyguard.
теля́|тина *f* [5], ~чий [18] veal.
тем *s.* тот.
те́м(а́тик)а *f* [5] subject, theme(s).
тембр (tɛ-) *m* [1] timbre.
Те́мза *f* [5] Thames.
темн|е́ть [8] **1.** ⟨по-⟩ darken; **2.** ⟨с-⟩ grow *or* get dark; **3.** (*a.* -ся) appear *or* show dark; loom; ~и́ца *f* [5] prison, dungeon.
тёмно... (*in compds.*) dark...
темнота́ *f* [5] darkness; obscurity.
тёмн|ый [14; тёмен, темна́] dark; *fig.* obscure; gloomy; shady, dubious; evil, malicious; ignorant, slow, backward.
темп (tɛ-) *m* [1] tempo; rate, pace.
темпера́мент *m* [1] temperament; spirits *pl.*; ~ный [14; -тен, -тна] temperamental.
температу́ра *f* [5] temperature.
те́мя *n* [13] crown.
тенденци|о́зный (tɛndɛ-) [14; -зен, -зна] tendentious; '~я (tɛn'dɛ-) *f* [7] tendency.
те́ндер 🚂, ⚓ ('tɛndɛr) *m* [1] tender.
тени́стый [14 *sh.*] shady.
те́ннис ('tɛ-) *m* [1] tennis.
те́нор ♪ *m* [1; *pl.*: -pá, *etc. e.*] tenor.
тень *f* [8; в тени́; *pl.*: те́ни, тене́й, *etc. e.*] shade; shadow.
теор|е́тик *m* [1] theorist; ~ети́ческий [16] theoretical; ∠ия *f* [7] theory; ∠ия позна́ния epistemology.
тепе́р|ешний [15] present, actual; ~ь now, at present.
тепл|е́ть [8; *3rd p. only*], ⟨по-⟩ grow warm; ~и́ться [13] burn; glimmer; ~и́ца *f* [5], ~и́чный [14] hothouse; ~о́ **1.** *n* [9] warmth; *phys.* heat; warm weather; **2.** *adv.*, *s.* тёплый; ~ово́й [14] (of) heat, thermal; ~ота́ *f* [5] warmth; *phys.* heat; ~охо́д *m* [1] motor ship; ~у́шка *f* [5; *g/pl.*: -шек] heatable boxcar.
тёплый [14; тёпел, тепла́, -о́ & тёпло] warm (*a. fig.*); hot (*sun*); (мне) тепло́ it is (I am) warm.
терапи́я *f* [7] therapy.
тере|би́ть [14 *e.*; -блю, -би́шь] pull; tousle; twitch; F pester; '~м *m* [1; *pl.*: -á, *etc. e.*] attic; (tower-)chamber; ∠ть [12] rub; grate; -ся F hang about.
терза́|ние *n* [12] torment, agony; ~ть [1] **1.** ⟨ис-⟩ torment, torture; **2.** ⟨рас-⟩ tear to pieces.
тёрка *f* [5; *g/pl.*: -рок] grater.
те́рмин *m* [1] term; ~оло́гия *f* [7] terminology.
термо́|метр *m* [1] thermometer; '~с ('tɛ-) *m* [1] vacuum *or* thermos bottle.
терни́стый [14 *sh.*] thorny.
терп|ели́вый [14 *sh.*] patient; ~е́ние *n* [12] patience; ~е́ть [10], ⟨по-⟩ suffer, endure; tolerate, bear, stand; not press, permit of delay; (Д) не -ся *impf.* be impatient *or* eager; ~и́мость *f* [8] tolerance (toward[s] к Д); ~и́мый [14 *sh.*] tolerant; bearable.
те́рпкий [16; -пок, -пка́, -о; *comp.*: те́рпче] tart.
терра́са *f* [5] terrace.
террит|ориа́льный [14] territorial; ~о́рия *f* [7] territory.
терро́р *m* [1] terror; ~изи́ровать & ~изова́ть [7] *im*(*pf.*) terrorize.
тёртый F [14] cunning, sly.
теря́ть [28], ⟨по-⟩ lose; waste; shed (*leaves*); give up (*hope*); -ся be lost; disappear, vanish; become embarrassed, be at a loss.
теса́ть [3], ⟨об-⟩ hew, cut.
тесн|и́ть [13], ⟨с-⟩ press; oppress; -ся crowd, throng; jostle; ~ота́ *f* [5] narrowness; throng; ∠ый [14;

те́сен, тесна́, -о] narrow; tight; clore; intimate.
те́ст|о *n* [9] dough, paste; **~ь** *m* [4] father-in-law (*wife's father*).
тесьма́ *f* [5; *g/pl.*: -сём] tape.
те́тер|ев *m* [1; *pl.*: -á, *etc. e.*] black grouse, blackcock; **∠я** P *f* [6]: глуха́я ∠я deaf fellow; со́нная ∠я sleepyhead.
тетива́ *f* [5] bowstring.
тётка *f* [5; *g/pl.*: -ток] aunt.
тетра́д|ь *f* [8], **~ка** *f* [5; *g/pl.*: -док] exercise book, notebook, copybook.
тётя F *f* [6; *g/pl.*: -тей] aunt.
те́хн|ик *m* [1] technician; **~ика** *f* [5] technics; technique; equipment; F skill; **~икум** *m* [1] technical school; **~и́ческий** [16] technical; **~ологи́ческий** [16] technological; **~оло́гия** *f* [7] technology.
теч|е́ние *n* [12] current; stream (up- [down-] вверх [вниз] по Д); course (in в В; in/of *time* с Т/Р); *fig.* trend; movement; **~ь** [26] 1. flow, run; stream; move; leak; 2. *f* [8] leak (spring дать).
те́шить [16], ⟨по-⟩ amuse; please; **-ся** amuse o. s.; take comfort; banter.
тёща *f* [5] mother-in-law (*wife's mother*).
тибе́тец *m* [1; -тца] Tibetan.
тигр *m* [1] tiger; **~и́ца** *f* [5] tigress.
ти́ка|нье *n* [10], **~ть** [1] tick.
Тимофе́й *m* [3] Timothy.
ти́н|а *f* [5] ooze; **~истый** [14 *sh.*] oozy.
тип *m* [1] type; F character; **~и́чный** [14; -чен, -чна] typical; **~огра́фия** *f* [7] printing plant *or* office; **~огра́фский** [16] printing (*press*); printer's (ink кра́ска *f*).
тир *m* [1] shooting gallery, rifle range.
тира́да *f* [5] tirade.
тира́ж *m* [1 *e.*] circulation; drawing (*of a lottery*).
тира́н *m* [1] tyrant; **~ить** [13] tyrannize; **~и́я** *f* [7], **~ство** *n* [9] tyranny.
тире́ *n* [*ind.*] dash.
ти́с|кать [1], ⟨~нуть⟩ [20] squeeze, press; print; **~ки́** *m/pl.* [1 *e.*] vice, grip; F fix; **~нёный** [14] (im-) printed.
ти́тул *m* [1], **~ьный** [14] title.
тиф *m* [1] typhus.
ти́|хий [16; тих, -á, -о; *comp.*: ти́ше] quiet, still; calm; soft, gentle; slow; ✝ dull, flat; *cap.* Pacific; **~хомо́лком** F on the quiet; **~ше**! silence!; **~шина́** *f* [5] silence, stillness, calm (-ness); **~шь** *f* [8; в тиши́] calm; silence.
т. к. *abbr.*: та́к как, *cf.* так.
тка|нь *f* [8] fabric, cloth; *biol.* tissue; **~ть** [тку, ткёшь; ткал, ткалá, -о], ⟨со-⟩ [со́тканный] weave; **∠цкий** [16] weaver's; weaving; **~ч** *m* [1 *e.*], **~чи́ха** *f* [5] weaver.
ткнуть(ся) *s.* ты́кать(ся).
тле́|ние *n* [12] decay, putrefaction; smo(u)ldering; **~ть** [8], ⟨ис-⟩ (s)mo(u)lder, decay, rot, putrefy; glimmer.
то 1. [28] that; ~ же the same; к ~му́ (же) in addition (to that), moreover; add to this; ни ~ ни сё F neither fish nor flesh; ни с ~го́ ни с сего́ F all of a sudden, without any visible reason; до ~го́ so much; **2.** (*cj.*) then; ~ ... ~ now ... now; не ~ ... не ~ *or* ~ ли ... ~ ли either ... or, half ... half; не ~, что́бы not that; а не ~ (or) else; **3.** ∠ -~ just, exactly; although; oh ...
тов. *abbr.*: това́рищ.
това́р *m* [1] commodity, article (of trade); *pl.* goods, wares.
това́рищ *m* [1] comrade, friend; mate, companion (in *arms* по Д); colleague; assistant; ~ по шко́ле schoolmate; ~ по университе́ту fellow student; **~еский** [16] friendly; companionable; **~ество** *n* [9] comradeship, fellowship; partnership; association, company.
това́р|ный [14] ware(*house*); goods-...; 🚂 freight..., *Brt.* goods...; **~ообме́н** *m* [1] barter; **~ооборо́т** *m* [1] commodity circulation.
тогда́ then, at that time; ~ как whereas, while; **~шний** [15] of that (*or* the) time, then.
то́ есть that is (to say), i. e.
тожде́ств|енный [14 *sh.*] identical; **'~о** *n* [9] identity.
то́же also, too, as well; *cf.* та́кже.
ток *m* **1.** [1] current; **2.** [1; на -у́; *from g/pl. e.*] (threshing) floor.
тока́р|ный [14] turner's; turning (*lathe*); **'~ь** *m* [4] turner.
толк *m* [1; бе́з-у] sense; use; judg(e)ment; F talk, rumo(u)r; † doctrine; sect; знать ~ в (П) be a judge of; **~а́ть** [1], *once* ⟨~ну́ть⟩ [20] push, shove, thrust; *fig.* induce, prompt; F urge on, spur; **-ся** push (o. a.); F knock (at в В; about); **~ова́ть** [7] **1.** ⟨ис-⟩ interpret, expound, explain; comment; take (in ... part в ... сто́рону); **2.** ⟨по-⟩ F talk (to с Т); speak, tell, say; **~о́вый** [14] explanatory, commenting; F [*sh.*] sensible, smart, wise; **∠ом** = **~о́во**; *a.* in earnest; **~отня́** F *f* [6] crush, crowd; **~у́чка** P *f* [5; *g/pl.*: -чек] second-hand market.
толо|кно́ *n* [9] oat flour; **∠чь** [26; -лку́, -лчёшь, -лку́т; -ло́к, -лкла́; -лчённый], ⟨рас-, ис-⟩ pound; **∠чься** P hang about.
толп|á *f* [5; *pl. st.*], **~и́ться** [14 *e.*; *no 1st. & 2nd p. sg.*], ⟨с-⟩ crowd, throng; mob; swarm.
толст|е́ть [8], ⟨по-, рас-⟩ grow stout; **~око́жий** [17 *sh.*] thick-skinned; **∠ый** [14; толст, -á, -о; *comp.*: то́лще] thick; large, big; stout, fat; **~я́к** F *m* [1 *e.*] fat man.
толч|ёный [14] pounded; **~ея́** F *f*

[6] crush, crowd; **~óк** *m* [1; -чкá] push; shock; jolt; *fig.* impulse.

толщин|á *f* [5] thickness; stoutness; ~óй в (В), ... в ~ý ... thick.

толь *m* [4] roofing felt.

тóлько only, but; как ~ as soon as; лишь (*or* едвá) ~ no sooner ... than; ~ бы if only; ~ что just (now); ~-~ F barely.

том *m* [1; *pl.*: -á, *etc. e.*] volume.

том|и́тельный [14; -лен, -льна] painful, tormenting; oppressive; **~и́ть** [14 *e.*; томлю́, томи́шь, томлённый], ⟨ис-⟩ torment, plague, harass, pester; pinch, oppress; **-ся** pine (for T), languish (with; be tormented, *etc.*, *s.* ~и́ть); **~лéние** *n* [12], **∠ность** *f* [8] languor; **∠ный** [14; -мен, -мнá, -о] languishing.

тон *m* [1; *pl.*: -á, *etc. e.*] tone.

тóнк|ий [16; -нок, -нкá, -о; *comp.*: тóньше] thin; slim, slender; small; fine; delicate, subtle; keen; light (*sleep*); high (*voice*); F cunning; **~ость** *f* [8] thinness, *etc. s.* ~ий; delicacy, subtlety; *pl.* details (go into вдавáться в В; F split hairs).

тóнна *f* [5] ton; **∠ж** *m* [1] tonnage.

тонýть [19] *v/i.* **1.** ⟨по-, за-⟩ sink; submerge; **2.** ⟨у-⟩ drown.

Тóня *f* [6] *dim. of* Антони́на.

тóп|ать [1], *once* ⟨~нуть⟩ [20] stamp; **~и́ть** [14] *v/t.* **1.** ⟨за-, по-⟩ sink; flood; **2.** ⟨за-, ис-, на-⟩ heat; light a fire; **3.** ⟨рас-⟩ melt; **4.** ⟨у-⟩ drown; **~ка** *f* [5; *g/pl.*: -пок] heating; furnace; **~кий** [16; -пок, -пкá, -о] boggy, marshy; **~лёный** [14] melted; molten; **~ливо** *n* [9] fuel; **~нуть** *s.* ~ать.

топогрáфия *f* [7] topography.

тóполь *m* [4; *pl.*: -ля́, *etc. e.*] poplar.

топóр *m* [1 *e.*] ax(e); **~ный** [14; -рен, -рна] coarse.

тóпот *m* [1] stamp(ing), tramp(ing).

топтáть [3], ⟨по-, за-⟩ trample, tread; ⟨вы́-⟩ press; ⟨с-⟩ wear out; **~ся** tramp(le); F hang about; mark time (на мéсте).

топь *f* [8] marsh, mire, bog, fen.

торг *m* [1; на -ý; *pl.*: -и́, *etc. e.*] bargaining, chaffer; *pl.* auction (by с Р; at на П); **~áш** *contp. m* [1 *e.*] dealer; **~овáть** [8] trade, deal (in T); sell; be open; **-ся**, ⟨с-⟩ (strike a) bargain (for о П); **~óвец** *m* [1; -вца] dealer, trader, merchant; **~óвка** *f* [5; *g/pl.*: -вок] market woman; **~óвля** *f* [6] trade, commerce; traffic; business; **~óвый** [14] trade..., trading, commercial, of commerce; ⚓ mercantile, merchant...; **~прéд** *m* [1] Soviet trade representative; **~прéдство** *n* [9] trade agency of the U.S.S.R.

торжéств|енность *f* [8] solemnity; **~енный** [14 *sh.*] solemn; festive; triumphant; **~ó** *n* [9] triumph; festivity, celebration; **~овáть** [7], ⟨вос-⟩ triumph (over над T); *impf.* celebrate.

тóрмо|з *m* **1.** [1; *pl.*: -á, *etc. e.*] brake; **2.** [1] *fig.* drag; **~зи́ть** [15 *e.*; -ожý, -ози́шь; -ожённый], ⟨за-⟩ (put the) brake(s on); *fig.* hamper; *psych.* curb, restrain; **~ши́ть** F [16 *e.*; -шý, -ши́шь] *s.* теребить.

тóрный [14] beaten (*road*, *a. fig.*).

тороп|и́ть [14], ⟨по-⟩ hasten, hurry up (*v/i.* **-ся**; *a.* be in a hurry); **~ли́вый** [14 *sh.*] hasty, hurried.

торпéд|а *f* [5], **~и́ровать** [7] (*im*)*pf.* torpedo; **~ный** [14] torpedo...

торт *m* [1] pie; fancy cake.

торф *m* [1] peat; **~янóй** [14] peat...

торчáть [4 *e.*; -чý, чи́шь] stick out; F hang about.

тоск|á *f* [5] melancholy; anxiety, grief; yearning; boredom, ennui; ~á по рóдине homesickness; **~ли́вый** [14 *sh.*] melancholy; sad, dreary; **~овáть** [7] grieve, feel sad (*or* lonely); feel bored; yearn *or* long (for по П *or* Д); be homesick (по рóдине).

тот *m*, та *f*, то *n*, те *pl.* [28] that, *pl.* those; the one; the other; не ~ wrong; (н)и тот (н)и другóй both (neither); тот же (сáмый) the same; тем бóлее the more so; тем лýчше so much the better; тем сáмым thereby; *cf. a.* то.

тóтчас (же) immediately, at once.

точи́|льный [14] grinding; **~льщик** *m* [1] grinder; **~ть** [16] **1.** ⟨на-⟩ whet, grind; sharpen; **2.** ⟨вы́-⟩ turn; **3.** ⟨ис-⟩ eat (*or* gnaw) away; gnaw at; perforate; wear; weather.

тóчк|а *f* [5; *g/pl.*: -чек] point; dot; *typ.*, *gr.* period, full stop; вы́сшая ~а zenith, climax (at на П); ~а с запятóй *gr.* semicolon; ~а! F enough!; *s. a.* точь.

тóчн|о *adv. of* ~ый; *a.* = слóвно; indeed; так ~о! ⚔ yes, sir!; **~ость** *f* [8] accuracy, exactness, precision; в ~ости *s.* ~о; **~ый** [14; -чен, -чнá, -о] exact, precise, accurate; punctual; (of) precision.

точь: ~ в ~ F exactly.

тошн|и́ть [13]; меня́ ~и́т I feel sick; I loathe; **~отá** *f* [5] nausea; F loathing; **∠ый** [14; -шен, -шнá, -о] loathsome, nauseous; мне ∠о *s.* ~и́ть.

тóщий [17; тощ, -á, -е] lean, lank, gaunt; F empty; scanty, poor.

травá *f* [5; *pl. st.*] grass; herb; weed.

трав|и́ть [14] **1.** ⟨за-⟩ bait, chase, course; *fig.* attack; **2.** ⟨с-, вы́-⟩ corrode, stain; exterminate; **3.** ⚓ ⟨вы́-⟩ loosen; **∠ля** *f* [6; *g/pl.*: -лей] baiting; *fig.* defamation.

травян|и́стый [14 *sh.*], **~óй** [14] grass(y).

траг|éдия *f* [7] tragedy; **∠ик** *m* [1] tragedian; **~и́ческий** [16], **~и́чный** [14; -чен, -чна] tragic(al).

традицио́нный [14; -óнен, -óнна] traditional.
тракт *m* [1] highway; *anat.* tract; **~áт** *m* [1] treatise; **~и́р** *m* [1] inn, tavern, *Brt.* public house, F pub; **~и́рщик** *m* [1] innkeeper; **~ова́ть** [7] treat; **~о́вка** *f* [5; *g/pl.*: -вок] treatment; **~ори́ст** *m* [1] tractor operator; **~орный** [14] tractor...
тра́льщик *m* [1] trawler; ⚔ mine sweeper.
трамбова́ть [7], ⟨у-⟩ ram.
трамва́й *m* [3] streetcar, *Brt.* tramway, tram(car) (by Т, на П).
трампли́н *m* [1] springboard.
транзи́т *m* [1], **~ный** [14] transit.
транс|криби́ровать [7] (*im*)*pf.* transcribe; **~ли́ровать** [7] (*im*)*pf.* transmit; relay; **~ля́ция** *f* [7] transmission; **~пара́нт** *m* [1] transparency.
тра́нспорт *m* [1] transport(ation; *a.* system [of]); **~и́ровать** [7] (*im*)*pf.* transport, convey; **~ный** [14] (of) transport(ation).
трансформа́тор *m* [1] transformer.
транше́я *f* [6; *g/pl.*: -е́й] trench.
трап *m* [1] gangway; **~е́ция** *f* [7] trapeze; ⩕ trapezium.
тра́сса *f* [5] route, line.
тра́т|а *f* [5] expenditure; expense; waste; **~ить** [15], ⟨ис-, по-⟩ spend; waste; **~та** ✝ *f* [5] draft.
тра́ур *m* [1] mourning; **~ный** [14] mourning...; funeral...
трафаре́т *m* [1] cliché (*a. fig.*).
трах! crack!
тре́бова|ние *n* [12] demand (on по Д); requirement; claim; order; **~тельный** [14; -лен, -льна] exacting; particular; pretentious; **~ть** [7], ⟨по-⟩ (Р) demand; require; claim; cite, summon; call; **-ся** be required (*or* wanted); be necessary.
трево́|га *f* [5] alarm; warning, alert; anxiety; **~жить** [16] **1.** ⟨вс-, рас-⟩ alarm, disquiet; **2.** ⟨по-⟩ disturb, trouble; **-ся** be anxious; worry; **~жный** [14; -жен, -жна] restless, uneasy; alarm(ing), disturbing.
тре́зв|ость *f* [8] sobriety; **~ый** [14; трезв, -á, -o] sober (*a. fig.*).
трель *f* [8] trill, shake; warble.
тре́нер *m* [1] trainer, coach.
тре́ние *n* [12] friction (*a. fig.*).
тренир|ова́ть [7], ⟨на-⟩ train, coach; *v/i.* **-ся**; **~о́вка** *f* [5] training.
трепа́ть [2] **1.** ⟨по-⟩ tousle; twitch; flutter; F tap (on по Д); wear out, fray; harass; prate; **2.** ⟨вы-⟩ scutch.
тре́пет *m* [1] tremor; quiver; **~а́ть** [3], ⟨за-⟩ tremble (with от Р); quiver, shiver; flicker; palpitate; **~ный** [14; -тен, -тна] quivering; flickering.
треск *m* [1] crack, crash; **~а́** *f* [5] cod; **~аться** [1], ⟨по-, тре́снуть⟩ [20] burst; crack, split; chap; **~отня́** *f* [6] crackle; rattle; chirp; gabble; **~у́чий** [17 *sh.*] hard, ringing (*frost*); *fig.* bombastic.
тре́снуть *s.* тре́скаться & треща́ть.
трест *m* [1] trust.
трет|е́йский [16] of arbitration; **~ий** [18] third; **~ьего дня** = позавчера́; *cf.* пя́тый; **~и́ровать** [7] (mal)treat; **~ь** *f* [8; *from g/pl. e.*] (one) third.
треуго́льн|ик *m* [1] triangle; **~ый** [14] triangular; three-cornered (*hat*).
тре́фы *f/pl.* [5] clubs (*cards*).
трёх|годи́чный [14] three years'; triennial; **~дне́вный** [14] three days'; **~колёсный** [14] three-wheeled; **~ле́тний** [15] three-years(-old)'; **~со́тый** [14] three hundredth; **~цве́тный** [14] three-colo(u)r; tricolor(ed); **~эта́жный** [14] three-storied (*Brt.* -reyed).
трещ|а́ть [4 *e.*; -щу́, -щи́шь] **1.** ⟨за-⟩ crack; **2.** ⟨про-⟩ crackle; rattle; chirp; F prattle; **3.** ⟨тре́снуть⟩ [20] burst; **~ина** *f* [5] split (*a. fig.*), crack, cleft, crevice, fissure; chap; **~о́тка** *f* [5; *g/pl.*: -ток] rattle; F chatterbox.
три [34] three; *cf.* пять.
трибу́н|а *f* [5] tribune, platform; stand; **~а́л** *m* [1] tribunal.
тригономе́трия *f* [7] trigonometry.
тридца́|тый [14] thirtieth; *cf.* пятидеся́тый; **'~ть** [35 *e.*] thirty.
три́жды three times, thrice.
трико́ *n* [*ind.*] tights *pl.*; **~та́ж** *m* [1] hosiery; jersey.
трило́гия *f* [7] trilogy.
трина́дца|тый [14] thirteenth; *cf.* пя́тый; **~ть** [35] thirteen; *cf.* пять.
три́ста [36] three hundred.
триу́мф *m* [1] triumph; **~а́льный** [14] triumphal; triumphant.
тро́га|тельный [14; -лен, -льна] touching, moving; **~ть** [1], *once* ⟨тро́нуть⟩ [20] touch (*a. fig.* = move); F pester; **~й**! go!; **-ся** start; set out (on a journey в путь); move; be touched.
тро́е [37] three (*cf.* дво́е); **~кра́тный** [14; -тен, -тна] repeated three times.
тро́иц|а *f* [5] Trinity; Whitsunday.
тро́й|ка *f* [5; *g/pl.*: тро́ек] three (*cf.* дво́йка); troika (*team of 3 horses abreast* [+ *vehicle*]); triumvirate; F (*mark* =) посре́дственно, *cf.*; **~но́й** [14] threefold, triple, treble; **~ня** *f* [6; *g/pl.*: тро́ен] triplets *pl.*
тролле́йбус *m* [1] trolley bus.
трон *m* [1] throne; **~ный** [14] *Brt.* King's (Queen's) (*speech*).
тро́нуть(ся) *s.* тро́гать(ся).
троп|а́ *f* [5; *pl.*: тро́пы, троп, -па́м] path, track; **~и́нка** [5; *g/pl.*: -нок] (small) path.
тропи́ческий [16] tropic(al).
трос *m* [1] hawser, cable.
трост|ни́к *m* [1 *e.*] reed; cane; **~ни-**

ко́вый [14] reed...; cane...; **∠очка** *f* [5; *g/pl.*: -чек], **~ь** *f* [8; *from g/pl. e.*] cane, *Brt. a.* walking stick.
тротуа́р *m* [1] sidewalk, *Brt.* pavement, footpath, footway.
трофе́й *m* [3], **~ный** [14] trophy.
тро|ю́родный [14] second (cousin брат *m*, сестра́ *f*); **~я́кий** [16 *sh.*] threefold, triple.
труб|а́ *f* [5; *pl. st.*] pipe, (*a. anat.*) tube; chimney; 🚂, ⚓ smokestack, funnel; (*fire*) engine; ♪ trumpet; **~а́ч** *m* [1 *e.*] trumpeter; **~и́ть** [14 *e.*; -блю́, -би́шь], ⟨про-⟩ blow (the в В); **∠ка** *f* [5; *g/pl.*: -бок] tube; pipe (*to smoke*); *teleph.* receiver; roll; **~опрово́д** *m* [1] pipe line; **~очи́ст** *m* [1] chimney sweep; **∠чатый** [14] tubular.
труд *m* [1 *e.*] labo(u)r, work; pains *pl.*, trouble; difficulty (with с Т; *a.* hard[ly]); *pl. a.* transactions; F service; **~и́ться** [15], ⟨по-⟩ work; toil, exert o.s.; trouble; **∠ность** *f* [8] difficulty; **∠ный** [14; -ден, -дна́, -о] difficult, hard; F heavy; **~ово́й** [14] labo(u)r...; working; workman's; earned; service...; **~олюби́вый** [14 *sh.*] industrious; **~оспосо́бный** [14; -бен, -бна] able-bodied, able to work; **~я́щийся** [17] working; *su.* worker.
тру́женик *m* [1] toiler, worker.
труни́ть [13] make fun (of над Т).
труп *m* [1] corpse, body.
тру́ппа *f* [5] company, troupe.
трус *m* [1] coward; **∠ики** *m/pl.* [1] trunks, shorts; **∠ить** [15], ⟨с-⟩ be afraid (of Р); **~и́ха** F *f* [5] *f of* ~; **~ли́вый** [14 *sh.*] cowardly; **∠ость** *f* [8] cowardice; **~ы́** *s.* **∠ики**.
трут *m* [1] tinder.
тру́тень *m* [4; -тня] drone.
трущо́ба *f* [5] slum, den, nest.
трюк *m* [1] trick, F stunt.
трюм ⚓ *m* [1] hold.
трюмо́ *n* [*ind.*] pier glass.
тряп|и́чник *m* [1] ragpicker; **∠ка**; [5; *g/pl.*: -пок] rag; duster; patch; F milksop; **~ьё** *n* [10] rag(s).
тряси́на *f* [5] bog, fen, quagmire.
тря́с|ка *f* [5] jolting; **~кий** [16; -сок, -ска] shaky; jolty; **~ти́** [24 -с-], *once* ⟨тряхну́ть⟩ [20] shake (a p.'s Д *hand*; *head, etc.* Т; *a. fig.*); F (*impers.*) jolt; **~ти́сь** shake; shiver (with от Р).
тряхну́ть *s.* трясти́.
тсс! hush!
тт. *abbr.*: **1.** това́рищи; **2.** тома́.
туале́т *m* [1] toilet.
туберкулёз *m* [1] tuberculosis; **~ный** [14] tubercular; tuberculous (patient).
туго́|й [14; туг, -а́, -о; *comp.*: ту́же] tight, taut; stiff; crammed; F stingy; slow, hard (*a.* of hearing на́ ухо); *adv. a.* hard put to it; hard up; hard, with difficulty.
туда́ there, thither; that way.
тужи́ть F [16] grieve; long for (о П).
тужу́рка *f* [5; *g/pl.*: -рок] jacket.
туз *m* [1 *e.*] ace; F boss.
тузе́м|ец *m* [1; -мца] native; **~ный** [14] native.
ту́ловище *n* [11] trunk.
тулу́п *m* [1] sheepskin coat.
тума́н *m* [1] fog, mist; haze; smog; **~ный** [14; -а́нен, -а́нна] foggy, misty; *fig.* hazy, vague.
ту́мб|а *f* [5] curbstone (*Brt.* kerb-); pedestal; **~очка** *f* [5; *g/pl.*: -чек] bedside table.
тунея́дец *m* [1; -дца] parasite.
Туни́с *m* [1] Tunisia; Tunis.
тунне́ль (-'nɛ-) *m* [4] tunnel.
туп|е́ть [8], ⟨(п)о-⟩ grow blunt; **~и́к** *m* [1 *e.*] blind alley, dead end, (*a. fig.*) impasse; nonplus, tight corner; ста́вить в **~и́к** baffle; стать в **~и́к** be at one's wit's end; **~о́й** [14; туп, -а́, -о] blunt; ⚔ obtuse; *fig.* dull, stupid; apathetic; **∠ость** *f* [8] bluntness; dullness; **~оу́мный** [14; -мен, -мна] stupid.
тур *m* [1] round; tour; *zo.* aurochs.
тура́ *f* [5] rook, castle (*chess*).
турби́на *f* [5] turbine.
туре́цкий [16] Turkish.
тури́|зм *m* [1] tourism; **~ст** *m* [1] tourist.
туркме́н *m* [1] Turk(o)man; **~ский** [16] Turkmen(ian).
турне́ (-'nɛ) *n* [*ind.*] tour.
турни́к *m* [1 *e.*] horizontal bar.
турни́р *m* [1] tournament (in на П).
ту́р|ок *m* [1; -рка; *g/pl.*: ту́рок], **~ча́нка** *f* [5; *g/pl.*: -нок] Turk; **♀ция** *f* [7] Turkey.
ту́ск|лый [14; тускл, -а́, -о] dim; dull; dead (*gold, etc.*); **~не́ть** [8], ⟨по-⟩ & **~нуть** [20] grow dim *or* dull.
тут F here; there; then; ~! present!; ~ же there & then, on the spot; ~ как ~ already there.
ту́тов|ый [14]: **~ое** де́рево *n* mulberry.
ту́фля *f* [6; *g/pl.*: -фель] shoe; slipper.
ту́х|лый [14; тухл, -а́, -о] bad (*egg*), rotten; **~нуть** [21] **1.** ⟨по-⟩ go *or* die out, expire; **2.** ⟨про-⟩ go bad.
ту́ч|а *f* [5] cloud; *dim.* **~ка** *f* [5; *g/pl.*: -чек]; **~ный** [14; -чен, -чна́, -о] corpulent, obese, stout, fat; fertile (*soil*).
туш ♪ *m* [1] flourish.
ту́ша *f* [5] carcass.
туш|ёный [14] stewed; **~и́ть** [16] ⟨по-, F за-⟩ put out, extinguish; *impf.* stew; *fig.* subdue.
тушь *f* [8] Indian ink.
тща́тельн|ость *f* [8] care(fulness); **~ый** [14; -лен, -льна] careful.
тще|ду́шный [14; -шен, -шна] sickly; **~сла́вие** *n* [12] vanity; **~сла́вный** [14; -вен, -вна] vain

(-glorious); ∠тный [14; -тен, -тна] vain, futile; ∠тно in vain.
ты [21] you, † thou; быть на ~ (с Т) thou (p.), be familiar (with).
тыкать [3], ⟨ткнуть⟩ [20] poke, jab, thrust (*v/i.* -ся); F (thee &) thou.
тыква *f* [5] pumpkin.
тыл *m* [1; в -у́; *pl. e.*] rear, base; глубо́кий ~ hinterland.
тысяч|а *f* [5] thousand; **~еле́тие** *n* [12] millenium; **~ный** [14] thousandth; of thousand(s).
тьма *f* [5] dark(ness); F lots of.
тьфу! F fie!, for shame!
тюбик *m* [1] tube.
тюк *m* [1 *e.*] bale, pack.
тюле́нь *m* [4] seal; F lout.
тюль *m* [4] tulle.
тюльпа́н *m* [1] tulip.
тюр|е́мный [14] prison ...; **~е́мщик** *m* [1] jailer, *Brt.* gaoler, warder; **~ьма́** *f* [5; *pl.*: тю́рьмы, -рем, -рьмам] prison, jail, *Brt.* gaol.
тюфя́к *m* [1 *e.*] mattress.
тя́вкать F [1] yap, yelp.
тя́г|а *f* [5] draft, *Brt.* draught; traction; *fig.* bent (for к Д), desire (of); **~а́ться** F [1] (с Т) be a match (for), cope, vie (with); be at law (with); **~остный** [14; -тен, -тна] burdensome; painful; **~ость** *f* [8] burden (*be* ... to в В/Д); **~оте́ние** *n* [12] gravitation; *a.* = ∠а *fig.*; **~оте́ть** [8] gravitate (toward[s] к Д); weigh (upon над Т); **~оти́ть** [15 *e.*; -ощу́, -оти́шь] weigh upon, be a burden to; -ся feel the burden (of Т); **~у́чий** [17 *sh.*] viscous; ductile; drawling, lingering.
тя́ж|ба *f* [5] action, lawsuit; **~елове́с** *m* [1] heavyweight; **~елове́сный** [14; -сен -сна] heavy, ponderous; **~ёлый** [14; -жёл, -жела́] heavy; difficult, hard; laborious; serious (*wound, etc.*); (*a.* ⚕) severe, grave; grievous, sad, oppressive, painful; close (*air*); (Д) **~ело́** feel sad; **~есть** *f* [8] heaviness; weight; load; burden; gravity; seriousness; painfulness; **~кий** [16; тя́жек, тяжка́, -о] heavy (*fig.*), *etc.*, *cf.* **~ёлый**.
тян|у́ть [19] pull, draw; ⚓ tow; draw in (out = delay); protract; drawl (out); attract; gravitate; drive at; long; have a mind to; would like; waft; ∠ет there is a draft (*Brt.* draught) (of Т); F drag (on); steal; take (from с Р); -ся stretch (*a.* = extend); last; drag, draw on; reach out (for к Д).

У

у (Р) at, by, near; with; (at) ...'s; at p.'s place; у меня́ (был, -а́ ...) I have (had); my; (*borrow, learn, etc.*) from; of; off (*coast*); in; у себя́ in (at) one's home *or* room, office.
убав|ля́ть [28], ⟨∠ить⟩ [14] lower, reduce, diminish, decrease; *v/i.* -ся.
убе|га́ть [1], ⟨~жа́ть⟩ [4; -егу́, -жи́шь, -гу́т] run away; escape.
убе|ди́тельный [14; -лен, -льна] convincing; urgent (*request*); **~жда́ть** [1], ⟨~ди́ть⟩ [15 *e.*; *no 1st p. sg.*; -еди́шь; -еждённый] convince (of в П), persuade (*impf. a.* try to ...); **~жде́ние** *n* [12] persuasion; conviction.
убеж|а́ть *s.* убега́ть; **∠ище** *n* [11] shelter, refuge; asylum.
убер|ега́ть [1], ⟨~е́чь⟩ [26 г/ж] save, safeguard.
уби|ва́ть [1], ⟨∠ть⟩ [убью́, -ьёшь; уби́тый] kill; murder; beat (*card*); drive into despair; blight; F waste.
уби́й|ственный [14 *sh.*] killing; murderous; F deadly, terrible; **~ство** *n* [9] murder; покуше́ние на ~ство murderous assault; **~ца** *m/f* [5] murderer; assassin.
убира́|ть [1], ⟨убра́ть⟩ [уберу́, -рёшь; убра́л, -а́, -о; у́бранный] take (*or* put, clear) away (in); gather, harvest; tidy up; decorate, adorn, trim; dress up; -ся F clear off, away; **~йся** (вон)! get out of here!
уби́ть *s.* убива́ть.
убо́|гий [16 *sh.*] needy, poor; wretched, miserable; scanty; crippled; **~жество** *n* [9] poverty.
убо́й *m* [3] slaughter (for на В).
убо́р *m* [1] attire; (*head*)gear; **~истый** [14 *sh.*] close: **~ка** *f* [5; *g/pl.*: -рок] harvest, gathering; tidying up; **~ная** *f* [14] lavatory, toilet, water closet; dressing room; **~очный** [14] harvest(ing); **~щица** *f* [5] charwoman.
убра́|нство *n* [9] attire; furniture; **~ть(ся)** *s.* убира́ть(ся).
убы|ва́ть [1], ⟨∠ть⟩ [убу́ду, убу́дешь; у́был, -а́, -о] subside, fall; decrease; leave; fall out; **′~ль** *f* [8] decrease, fall; loss; **∠ток** *m* [1; -тка] loss, damage; disadvantage (*be* at в П); **∠точный** [14; -чен, -чна] unprofitable; **∠ть** *s.* **~ва́ть**.
уваж|а́емый [14] dear (*address*); **~а́ть** [1], **~е́ние** *n* [12] respect, esteem (*su.* for к Д); **~и́тельный** [14; -лен, -льна] valid.
уведом|ля́ть [28], ⟨′~ить⟩ [14] inform, notify, advise (of о П); **~ле́ние** *n* [12] notification, † advice.
увезти́ *s.* увози́ть.
увекове́чи|вать [1], ⟨~ть⟩ [16] immortalize.
увелич|е́ние *n* [12] increase; en-

largement; **∠ивать** [1], ⟨∠ить⟩ [16] increase; enlarge; magnify; *v/i.* **-ся**; **~ительный** [14] *opt.* magnifying; *gr.* augmentative.
увенча́ться [1] *pf.* (T) be crowned.
увер|е́ние *n* [12] assurance (of в П); **∠енность** *f* [8] firmness, assurance; certainty; confidence (in в П); **∠енный** [14 *sh.*] firm, steady; confident (of в П); positive, sure, certain; бу́дьте ∠ены I assure you, you may depend on it; **∠ить** *s.* **~я́ть**.
увёрт|ка F *f* [5; *g/pl.*: -ток] subterfuge, dodge; **~ливый** [14 *sh.*] evasive.
увертю́ра *f* [5] overture.
увер|я́ть [28], ⟨∠ить⟩ [13] assure (of в П); make believe (sure **-ся**), persuade.
увесел|е́ние *n* [12] amusement; **~и́тельный** [14] pleasure...; **~я́ть** [28] amuse.
увести́ *s.* уводи́ть.
уве́ч|ить [16], ⟨из-⟩ mutilate; **~ный** [14] crippled; **~ье** *n* [10] mutilation.
увещ(ев)а́|ние *n* [12] admonition; **~ть** [1] admonish.
уви́л|ивать [1], ⟨~ьну́ть⟩ [20] shirk.
увлажн|я́ть [28], ⟨~и́ть⟩ [13] wet, dampen.
увле|ка́тельный [14; -лен, -льна] fascinating; **~ка́ть** [1], ⟨∠чь⟩ [26] carry (away; *a. fig.* = transport, captivate); **-ся** (T) be carried away (by), be(come) enthusiastic (about); be(come) absorbed (in); take to; fall (*or* be) in love (with); **~че́ние** *n* [12] enthusiasm, passion (for T).
уво́|д *m* [1] ⚔ withdrawal; theft; **~ди́ть** [15], ⟨увести́⟩ [25] take, lead (away, off); steal; ⚔ withdraw; **~зи́ть** [15], ⟨увезти́⟩ [24] take, carry, drive (away, off); F steal, kidnap.
уво́л|ить *s.* **~ьня́ть**; **~ьне́ние** *n* [12] dismissal (from с Р); granting (of *leave* в В); **~ьня́ть** [28], ⟨~ить⟩ [13] dismiss (from с Р); give (leave of absence в о́тпуск); (от Р) dispense (with), spare.
увы́! alas!
увя|да́ние *n* [12] withering; **~да́ть** [1], ⟨∠нуть⟩ [20] wither, fade; **∠дший** [17] withered.
увяз|а́ть [1] **1.** ⟨∠нуть⟩ [21] stick, sink; **2.** *s.* ∠ывать(ся); **∠ка** *f* [5] coördination; **∠ывать** [1], ⟨~а́ть⟩ [3] tie up; coördinate (*v/i.* **-ся**).
уга́д|ывать [1], ⟨~а́ть⟩ [1] guess.
уга́р *m* [1] coal gas; poisoning by coalgas; *fig.* frenzy, intoxication; **~ный** [14] full of coal gas; charcoal...
угас|а́ть [1], ⟨∠нуть⟩ [21] die (*or* fade) out, away, expire, become extinct.
угле|кислота́ *f* [5] carbonic acid; **~ки́слый** [14] carbon(ic); chokedamp...; **~ко́п** *m* [1] *s.* шахтёр; **~ро́д** *m* [1] carbon.
углово́й [14] corner...; angle...
углуб|и́ть(ся) *s.* ~ля́ть(ся); **~ле́ние** *n* [12] deepening; hollow, cavity; absorption; extension; **~лённый** [14 *sh.*] profound; *a. p.pt.p. of* ~и́ть(ся); **~ля́ть** [28], ⟨~и́ть⟩ [14 *e.*; -блю́, -би́шь; блённый] deepen (*v/i.* **-ся**); make (become) more profound, extend; -ся *a.* go deep (into в В), be(come) absorbed (in).
угна́ть *s.* угоня́ть.
угнет|а́тель *m* [4] oppressor; **~а́ть** [1] oppress; depress; **~е́ние** *n* [12] oppression; (*a.* **~ённость** *f* [8]) depression; **~ённый** [14; -тён, -тена́] oppressed; depressed.
угов|а́ривать [1], ⟨~ори́ть⟩ [13] (В) (*impf.* try to) persuade; **-ся** arrange, agree; **~о́р** *m* [1] agreement, arrangement (by по Д); condition (on с Т); *pl.* persuasion(s); **~ори́ть(ся)** *s.* ~а́ривать(ся).
уго́д|а *f* [5]: в ~у (Д) for p.'s sake, to please s. o.; **~и́ть** *s.* угожда́ть; **~ливый** [14 *sh.*] complaisant; obliging; ingratiating, toadyish; **~ник** *m* [1] saint; **~но** please; как (что) вам ~но just as (whatever) you like; что вам ~но? what can I do for you?; не ~но ли вам ...? wouldn't you like ...; ско́лько (душе́) ~но *s.* вдо́воль & вдоволь.
уго|жда́ть [1], ⟨~ди́ть⟩ [15 *e.*; -ожу́, -оди́шь] (Д, на В) please; *pf.* F get, come; (в В) hit.
у́гол *m* [1; угла́; в, на углу́] corner (at на П); ⊿ angle; nook; home; **~о́вный** [14] criminal.
уголо́к *m* [1; -лка́] nook, corner.
у́голь *m* [4; у́гля] coal; как на ∠ях F on tenterhooks; **~ный**[1] [14] coal...; carbonic; **∠ный**[2] F [14] corner...
угомони́ть(ся) [13] *pf.* calm (down).
угоня́ть [28], ⟨угна́ть⟩ [угоню́, уго́нишь; угна́л, -а́, -о; у́гнанный] drive (away, off); steal; **-ся** F catch up (with за Т).
угор|а́ть [1], ⟨~е́ть⟩ [9] be poisoned by coal gas; F go mad.
у́горь *m* [4 *e.*; угря́] eel; blackhead.
уго|ща́ть [1], ⟨~сти́ть⟩ [15 *e.*; -ощу́, -ости́шь; -ощённый] treat (with T), entertain; **~ще́ние** *n* [12] entertainment; food, drinks *pl.*
угро|жа́ть [1] threaten (p. with Д/Т); **∠за** *f* [5] threat, menace.
угрызе́ни|е *n* [12]; ~я *pl.* со́вести remorse.
угрю́мый [14 *sh.*] morose, gloomy.
уда́в *m* [1] boa.
уда|ва́ться [5], ⟨∠ться⟩ [уда́стся, -аду́тся; уда́лся, -ла́сь] succeed; мне ∠ётся (~ло́сь) (+ *inf.*) I succeed (-ed) (in ...ing).
удал|е́ние *n* [12] removal; extraction; **~и́ть(ся)** *s.* **~я́ть(ся)**; **~о́й**, **∠ый** [14; уда́л, -а́, -о] bold, daring; **'~ь** *f* [8], F **~ьство́** *n* [9] boldness, daring; **~я́ть** [28], ⟨~и́ть⟩

[13] remove; extract (*tooth*); **-ся** retire, withdraw; move away.
удáр *m* [1] blow (*a. fig.*); (*a.* ⚕) stroke; ⚡, *fig.* shock; impact; slash; (*thunder*)clap; F form; **~éние** *n* [12] stress, accent; **~ить(ся)** *s.* **~я́ть(ся)**; **~ник** *m* [1] shock worker, Stakhanovite (*Sov.*); **~ный** [14] shock...; impact...; foremost; **~я́ть** [28], ⟨**~ить**⟩ [13] strike (on по Д), hit; knock; beat, sound; punch (кулакóм); butt (головóй); kick (ногóй); set about, start (...ing в В *pl.*); attack (*v/t.* на В; with в В *pl.*); go (to *head* в В); F set in; stir; **-ся** strike *or* knock (with/against Т/о В); hit (в В); F fall into; throw o.s., plunge.
удáться *s.* удавáться.
удáч|а *f* [5] (good) luck; **~ник** F *m* [1] lucky man; **~ный** [14; -чен, -чна] successful; good.
удв|áивать [1], ⟨**~óить**⟩ [13] double (*v/i.* **-ся**).
удéл *m* [1] lot, destiny; appanage; **~и́ть** *s.* **~я́ть**; **~ьный** [14] specific (*gravity, a. fig.*); **~я́ть** [28], ⟨**~и́ть**⟩ [13] devote; spare; allot.
удéрж|ивать [1], ⟨**~áть**⟩ [4] withhold, restrain; keep, retain; suppress; deduct; **-ся** hold (on; to за В; *a.* out); refrain (from от Р).
удешев|ля́ть [28], ⟨**~и́ть**⟩ [14 *e.*; -влю́, -ви́шь; -влённый] cheapen.
удив|и́тельный [14; -лен, -льна] wonderful, marvel(l)ous; miraculous; amazing, strange; (не) **~и́тельно** it is a (no) wonder **~и́ть(ся)** *s.* **~ля́ть(ся)**; **~лéние** *n* [12] astonishment, surprise; **~ля́ть** [28], ⟨**~и́ть**⟩ [14 *e.*; -влю́, -ви́шь; -влённый] (**-ся** be) astonish(ed at Д), surprise(d, wonder).
удилá *n/pl.* [9; -и́л, -илáм] bit.
удирáть F [1], ⟨удрáть⟩ [удеру́, -рёшь; удрáл, -á, -о] run away.
уди́ть [15] angle (for *v/t.*), fish (ры́бу).
удлин|éние *n* [12] lengthening; **~я́ть** [28], ⟨**~и́ть**⟩ [13] lengthen.
удóб|ный [14; -бен, -бна] convenient; comfortable; **~о...** easily ...; **~овари́мый** [14 *sh.*] digestible; **~рéние** *n* [12] manure, fertilizer; fertilization; **~ря́ть** [28], ⟨**~рить**⟩ [13] fertilize, manure, dung; **~ство** *n* [9] convenience; comfort; *pl.* facilities.
удовлетвор|éние *n* [12] satisfaction; **~и́тельный** [14; -лен, -льна] satisfactory; *adv. a.* D (*mark*); **~я́ть** [28], ⟨**~и́ть**⟩ [13] satisfy; grant; (Д) meet; **-ся** content o.s. (with Т).
удо|вóльствие *n* [12] pleasure; **~рожáть** [1], ⟨**~рожи́ть**⟩ [16] raise the price of.
удост|áивать [1], ⟨**~óить**⟩ [13] (**-ся** be) hono(u)r(ed), (*a.* ✝) favo(u)r(ed) (with Р, Т); bestow, confer (on); award; deign (to look at р. взгля́да, -ом В); **~оверéние** *n* [12] certificate, certification; (*identity*) card; corroboration (in в В); **~оверя́ть** [28], ⟨**~овéрить**⟩ [13] certify, attest; prove (*one's identity*); convince (of в П; o.s. **-ся**; *a.* make sure); **~óить(ся)** *s.* **~áивать(ся)**.
удосу́житься F [16] find time.
у́дочк|а *f* [5; *g/pl.*: -чек] fishing tackle; *fig.* trap; заки́нуть **~у** F *fig.* drop a hint.
удрáть *s.* удирáть.
удружи́ть [16 *e.*; -жу́, -жи́шь] F *s.* услужи́ть.
удруч|áть [1], ⟨**~и́ть**⟩ [16 *e.*; -чу́, -чи́шь; -чённый] deject, depress.
удуш|éние *n* [12] suffocation; poisoning; **∠ливый** [14 *sh.*] stifling, suffocating; oppressive (*heat*); poison (*gas*); **∠ье** *n* [10] asthma.
уедин|éние *n* [12] solitude; **~ённый** [14 *sh.*] retired, secluded, lonely, solitary; **~я́ться** [28], ⟨**~и́ться**⟩ [13] retire, seclude o.s.
уéзд † *m* [1], **~ный** [14] district.
уезжáть [1], ⟨уéхать⟩ [уéду, -дешь] (в В) leave (for), go (away; to).
уж 1. *m* [1 *e.*] grass snake; **2.** = ужé; F indeed, well; *do, be* (+ *vb.*).
у́жас *m* [1] horror; terror, fright; F = **∠ный**, **∠но**; **~áть** [1], ⟨**~ну́ть**⟩ [20] horrify; **-ся** be horrified *or* terrified (at Р, Д); **~áющий** [17] horrifying; **∠ный** [14; -сен, -сна] terrible, horrible, dreadful; F awful.
ужé already; as early as; **~** не not ... any more; (вóт) **~** for (*time*).
ужéние *n* [12] angling, fishing.
ужи|вáться [1], ⟨**∠ться**⟩ [-иву́сь, -вёшься; -и́лся, -илáсь] get accustomed (to в П); live in harmony (with с Т); **∠вчивый** [14 *sh.*] sociable, accomodating; **∠мка** *f* [5; *g/pl.*: -мок] grimace; gesture.
у́жин *m* [1] supper (at за Т; for на В, к Д); **~ать** [1], ⟨по-⟩ have supper.
ужи́ться *s.* уживáться.
узакон|éние *n* [12] legalization; statute; **∠ивать** & **~я́ть** [28], ⟨**∠ить**⟩ [13] legalize.
узбéк *m* [1], **~ский** [16] Uzbek.
узд|á *f* [5; *pl. st.*], **~éчка** *f* [5; *g/pl.*: -чек] bridle.
у́зел *m* [1; узлá] knot; 🚂 junction; center, *Brt.* centre; *anat.* ganglion; bundle; **~óк** *m* [1; -лкá] knot; packet.
у́зк|ий [16; у́зок, узкá, -о; *comp.*: у́же] narrow (*a. fig.*); tight; **~ое** мéсто *n* bottleneck; weak point; **~околéйный** [14] narrow-gauge.
узлов|áтый [14 *sh.*] knotty; **~óй** [14] knot(ty); central, chief; 🚂 *s.* у́зел.
узна|вáть [5], ⟨**∠ть**⟩ [1] recognize (by по Д); learn (from: p. от Р; th. из Р), find out, (get to) know, hear; позвóльте **∠ть** tell me, please.

у́зник *m* [1] prisoner.
узо́р *m* [1] pattern, design; с **~ами** = **~чатый** [14 *sh.*] figured; pattern.
у́зость *f* [8] narrow(-minded)ness.
у́зы *f/pl.* [5] bonds, ties.
у́йма F *f* [5] a great lot.
уйти́ *s.* уходи́ть.
ука́з *m* [1] decree, edict, ukase; **~а́ние** *n* [12] instruction (by по Д), direction; indication (of P, на B); **~а́тель** *m* [4] index; indicator; guide; **~а́тельный** [14] indicatory; fore(*finger*), index; *gr.* demonstrative; **~а́ть** *s.* **~ывать**; **~ка** *f* [5] pointer; F order (by по Д); **~ывать** [1], ⟨**~а́ть**⟩ [3] point out; point (to на B); show; indicate.
ука́ч|ивать, ⟨**~а́ть**⟩ [1] rock to sleep, lull; *impers.* make (sea)sick.
укла́д *m* [1] mode, way (*of life*); form; **~ка** *f* [5] packing; laying; **~ывать** [1], ⟨уложи́ть⟩ [16] put (to bed); lay; pack (up F **-ся**); place; cover; **-ся** *a.* find room; F manage.
укло́н *m* [1] slope, incline; slant (*a. fig.* = bias, bent, tendency); *pol.* deviation; **~е́ние** *n* [12] swerve, deviation; evasion; **~и́ться** *s.* **~я́ться**; **~чивый** [14 *sh.*] evasive; **~я́ться** [28], ⟨**~и́ться**⟩ [13; -оню́сь, -о́нишься] deviate; evade (*v/t.* от P); swerve; digress.
уклю́чина *f* [5] oarlock (*Brt.* row-).
уко́л *m* [1] prick; ⚕ injection.
укомплекто́в|ывать [1], ⟨**~а́ть**⟩ [7] complete, fill; supply (fully; with T).
уко́р *m* [1] reproach; **~а́чивать** [1], ⟨**~оти́ть**⟩ [15 *e.*; -очу́, -оти́шь; -о́ченный] shorten; **~еня́ть** [28], ⟨**~ени́ть**⟩ [13] implant; **-ся** take root; **~и́зна** *f* [5] *s.* **~**; **~и́зненный** [14] reproachful; **~и́ть** *s.* **~я́ть**; **~оти́ть** *s.* **~а́чивать**; **~я́ть** [28], ⟨**~и́ть**⟩ [13] reproach, blame (of в П, за B).
укра́дкой furtively.
Украи́н|а *f* [5] Ukraine (in на П); **2ец** *m* [1; -нца], **2ка** *f* [5; *g/pl.:* -нок], **2ский** [16] Ukrainian.
укра|ша́ть [1], ⟨**~сить**⟩ [15] adorn; (**-ся** be) decorate(d); trim; embellish; **~ше́ние** *n* [12] adornment; decoration; ornament; embellishment.
укреп|и́ть(ся) *s.* **~ля́ть(ся)**; **~ле́ние** *n* [12] strengthening; consolidation; ⚔ fortification; **~ля́ть** [28], ⟨**~и́ть**⟩ [14 *e.*; -плю́, -пи́шь; -плённый] strengthen; fasten; consolidate; ⚔ fortify; **~ля́ющий** *a.* ⚕ restorative; **-ся** strengthen, become stronger; ⚔ entrench.
укро́|мный [14; -мен, -мна] secluded; **~п** *m* [1] fennel.
укро|ти́тель *m* [4], **~ти́тельница**; [5] tamer; **~ща́ть** [1], ⟨**~ти́ть**⟩ [15 *e.*; -ощу́, -оти́шь; -ощённый] tame; break (*horse*); subdue, restrain; **~ще́ние** *n* [12] taming; subdual.
укрупн|я́ть [28], ⟨**~и́ть**⟩ [13] enlarge, extend; centralize.
укры|ва́тель *m* [4] receiver; **~ва́ть** [1], ⟨**~ть**⟩ [22] cover; shelter; conceal, harbo(u)r; **-ся** cover o.s.; hide; take shelter *or* cover; **~тие** *n* [12] cover, shelter.
у́ксус *m* [1] vinegar.
уку́с *m* [1] bite; **~и́ть** *s.* куса́ть.
уку́т|ывать, ⟨**~ать**⟩ [1] wrap up.
ул. *abbr.*: у́лица.
ула́|вливать [1], ⟨улови́ть⟩ [14] catch, seize; grasp; **~живать** [1], ⟨**~дить**⟩ [15] settle, arrange; reconcile.
у́лей *m* [3; у́лья] beehive.
улет|а́ть [1], ⟨**~е́ть**⟩ [11] fly (away).
улету́чи|ваться [1], ⟨**~ться**] [16] volatilize; F disappear, vanish.
уле́чься [26 г/ж: уля́гусь, уля́жешься, уля́гутся] lie down, go (to bed); settle; calm down, abate.
ули́ка *f* [5] corpus delicti, proof.
ули́тка *f* [5; *g/pl.*: -ток] snail; *anat.* cochlea.
у́лиц|а *f* [5] street (in, on на П); на **~е** *a.* outside, outdoors.
улич|а́ть [1], ⟨**~и́ть**⟩ [16 *e.*; -чу́, -чи́шь; -чённый] (в П) detect, catch (in the act [of]); convict (of); give (a p. *the lie*).
у́личный [14] street...
уло́в *m* [1] catch; **~и́мый** [14 *sh.*] perceptible; **~и́ть** *s.* ула́вливать; **~ка** *f* [5; *g/pl.*: -вок] trick, ruse.
уложи́ть(ся) *s.* укла́дывать(ся).
улуч|а́ть F [1], ⟨**~и́ть**⟩ [16 *e.*; -чу́, -чи́шь; -чённый] find.
улучш|а́ть [1], ⟨**~ить**⟩ [16] improve; *v/i.* **-ся**; **~е́ние** *n* [12] improvement; **~ить(ся)** *s.* **~а́ть(ся)**.
улыб|а́ться [1], ⟨**~ну́ться**⟩ [20], **~ка** *f* [5; *g/pl.*: -бок] smile (at Д).
ультракоро́ткий [16] very-high-frequency (*radio*).
ум *m* [1 *e.*] intellect; mind; sense(s); head (off не в П); без **~а́** mad (about от P); за́дним **~о́м** кре́пок *be* wise after the event; быть на **~е́** (у P) have in mind; не его́ **~а́** де́ло beyond his reach; сойти́ (F спя́тить) с **~а́** go mad; сходи́ть с **~а́** F *a.* be mad (about по П); (у P) **~** за ра́зум захо́дит F *be* crazy; (у P) **~** коро́ток F *be* dull *or* dense.
умал|е́ние *n* [12] belittling; **~и́ть (-ся)** *s.* **~я́ть(ся)**; **~ишённый** [14] *s.* сумасше́дший; **~чивать** [1], ⟨умолча́ть⟩ [4 *e.*; -чу́, -чи́шь] (о П) pass (th.) over in silence; **~я́ть** [28], ⟨**~и́ть**⟩ [13] belittle, derogate, disparage; curtail; **-ся** decrease, lessen.
уме́|лый [14] skil(l)ful, skilled; **~ние** *n* [12] skill, faculty, knowhow.
уменьш|а́ть [1], ⟨**~и́ть**⟩ [16 & 16 *e.*; -е́ньшу́, -е́ньши́шь; -е́ньшенный & -шённый] reduce, diminish,

decrease (*v/i.* **-ся**); **~éние** *n* [12] decrease, reduction; **~ительный** [14] diminutive; **∠ить(ся)** *s.* **~áть** (-ся).

умéренн|ость *f* [8] moderation, moderateness; **~ый** [14 *sh.*] moderate, (*a. geogr.* [*no sh.*]) temperate.

умер|éть *s.* умирáть; **∠ить** *s.* **~ять**; **~твить** *s.* ~щвлять; **∠ший** [17] dead; **~щвлять** [28], ⟨**~твить**⟩ [14 *e.*; -рщвлю, -ртвишь; -рщвлённый] kill, destroy; mortify; **~ять** [28], ⟨**∠ить**⟩ [13] moderate.

уме|стить(ся) *s.* ~щáть(ся); **∠стный** (-ˈmesn-) [14; -тен, -тна] appropriate; **∠ть** [8], ⟨с-⟩ can; know how; **~щáть** [1], ⟨**~стить**⟩ [15 *e.*; -ещý, -естишь; -ещённый] get (into в В); **-ся** find room; sit down.

умил|éние *n* [12] deep emotion, affection; **~ённый** [14] affected; affectionate; **~ять** [28], ⟨**~ить**⟩ [13] (**-ся** be) move(d), touch(ed).

умирáть [1], ⟨умерéть⟩ [12; *pt.*: ýмер, умерлá, -о; умéрший] die (of, from от, с Р).

умн|éть [8], ⟨по-⟩ grow wiser; **∠ик** F *m* [1], **∠ица** *m/f* [5] clever (*or* good) boy, girl, (wo)man; **∠ичать** F [1] *s.* мудрить.

умнож|áть [1], ⟨**∠ить**⟩ [16] multiply (by на В); *v/i.* **-ся**; **~éние** *n* [12] multiplication.

ýм|ный [14; умён, умнá, ýмнó] clever, smart, wise; **~озаключéние** *n* [12] conclusion; **~озрительный** [14; -лен, -льна] speculative.

умол|ить *s* ~ять; **ˈ~к**: без ˈ~ку incessantly; **~кáть** [1], ⟨**∠кнуть**⟩ [21] stop, become silent; subside; **~чáть** *s.* умáлчивать; **~ять** [28], ⟨**~ить**⟩ [13; -олю, -óлишь] implore (*v/t.*), beseech, entreat (for о П).

умопо|мешáтельство *n* [9], **~мрачéние** *n* [12] (mental) derangement.

умóр|а F *f* [5], **~ительный** F [14; -лен, -льна] side-splitting, awfully funny; **~ить** F [13] *pf.* kill; exhaust, fatigue (*a.* with laughing có смеху).

ýмственный [14] intellectual, mental; brain (*work[er]*).

умудр|ять [28], ⟨**~ить**⟩ [13] make wise; **-ся** F contrive, manage.

умывá|льная *f* [14] washroom; **~льник** *m* [1] wash(ing) stand; washbowl, *Brt.* wash-basin; **~ние** *n* [12] washing; wash; **~ть** [1], ⟨умыть⟩ [22] (**-ся**) wash (*a.* o.s.).

ýмы|сел *m* [1; -сла] design, intent(ion); с ~слом (без ~ла) (un-) intentionally; **∠ть(ся)** *s.* ~вáть(ся); **∠шленный** [14] deliberate; intentional.

унавóживать [1], *s.* навóзить.

унести(сь) *s.* уносить(ся).

универ|мáг *m* [1] (~сáльный магазин) department store, *Brt.* stores *pl.*; **~сáльный** [14; -лен, -льна] universal; *cf. a.* универмáг; **~ситéт** *m* [1] university (at, in в П).

уни|жáть [1], ⟨**∠зить**⟩ [15] humble, humiliate, abase; **~жéние** *n* [12] humiliation; **~жённый** [14 *sh.*] humble; **~зительный** [14; -лен, -льна] humiliating; **∠зить** *s.* **~жáть**.

унимáть [1], ⟨унять⟩ [уймý, уймёшь; унял, -á, -о; -ятый (-ят, -á, -о)] appease, soothe; still (*pain*); stanch (*blood*); **-ся** calm *or* quiet down; subside.

уничижительный [14] *ling.* pejorative.

уничт|ожáть [1], ⟨**~óжить**⟩ [16] annihilate; destroy; abolish, annul; **~ожéние** *n* [12] annihilation; **~óжить** *s.* ~ожáть.

уносить [15], ⟨унести⟩ [24 -с-] carry, take (away, off); **-ся**, ⟨**-сь**⟩ speed away.

ýнтер-офицéр *m* [1] corporal.

уны|вáть [1] despond; **∠лый** [14 *sh.*] sad, dejected; **∠ние** *n* [12] despondency; ennui.

унять(ся) *s.* унимáть(ся).

упáдо|к *m* [1; -дка] decay, decadence; ~к дýха dejection; ~к сил collapse; **~чный** [14; -чен, -чна] decadent; depressive.

упаков|áть *s.* **∠ывать**; **∠ка** *f* [5; *g/pl.*: -вок] packing; wrappings *pl.*; **∠щик** *m* [1] packer; **∠ывать** [1], ⟨**~áть**⟩ [7] pack (up).

упáсть *s.* пáдать.

упирáть [1], ⟨уперéть⟩ [12] prop, stay (against в В); rest (*a.*, F, *eyes* on в В); P steal; **-ся** lean, prop (s.th. Т; against в В); F rest (on в В); insist on; be obstinate.

упитанный [14 *sh.*] well-fed, fat.

уплá|та *f* [5] payment (in в В); **~чивать** [1], ⟨**~тить**⟩ [15] pay; meet (*bill*).

уплотн|ять [28], ⟨**~ить**⟩ [13] condense, compact; fill up (with work).

уплы|вáть [1], ⟨**∠ть**⟩ [23] swim *or* sail (away, off); pass (away), vanish.

уповáть [1] (на В) trust (in), hope (for).

упод|облять [28], ⟨**~óбить**⟩ [14] liken; assimilate (*v/i.* **-ся**).

упо|éние *n* [12] rapture, ecstasy; **~ённый** [14; -ён, -енá] enraptured; **~ительный** [14; -лен, -льна] rapturous, delightful; intoxicating.

уползти [24] *pf.* creep away.

уполномóч|енный *m* [14] plenipotentiary; **~ивать** [1], ⟨**~ить**⟩ [16] authorize, empower (to на В).

упоминá|ние *n* [12] mention (of о П); **~ть** [1], ⟨упомянýть⟩ [19] mention (*v/t.* В, о П).

упо́р *m* [1] rest; support, prop; 🚂 buffer stop; ⊕ stop, catch; де́лать ~ lay stress *or* emphasis (on на В); в ~ point-blank, straightforward (*a. look* at на В); **~ный** [14; -рен, -рна] pertinacious, persistent, persevering; stubborn, obstinate; **~ство** *n* [9] persistence, perseverance; obstinacy; **~ствовать** [7] persevere, persist (in в П).

употреб|и́тельный [14; -лен, -льна] common, customary; current; **~и́ть** *s.* ~ля́ть; **~ле́ние** *n* [12] use; usage; **~ля́ть** [28], ⟨~и́ть⟩ [14 *e.*; -блю́, -би́шь; -блённый] (*impf.* **-ся** be) use(d), employ(ed); take (*medicine*); make (*efforts*); ~и́ть во зло abuse.

управ|до́м *m* [1] (управля́ющий до́мом) manager of the house; **∠иться** *s.* ~ля́ться; **~ле́ние** *n* [12] administration (of P; T), management; direction; board; ⊕ control; *gr.* government; **~ля́ть** [28] (T) manage, operate; rule; govern (*a. gr.*); drive; ⚓ steer; ⊕ control; guide; ♪ conduct; **-ся**, ⟨∠иться⟩ F [14] (с T) manage; finish; **~ля́ющий** *m* [17] manager; steward.

упражн|е́ние *n* [12] exercise; practice; **~я́ть** [28] exercise (*v/t.*, *v/refl.* **-ся**; в П: practise s.th.).

упраздн|е́ние *n* [12] abolition; **~я́ть** [28], ⟨~и́ть⟩ [13] abolish.

упра́шивать [1], ⟨упроси́ть⟩ [15] (*impf.* try to) persuade.

упрёк *m* [1] reproach, blame.

упрек|а́ть [1], ⟨~ну́ть⟩ [20] reproach, blame (with в П).

упро|си́ть *s.* упра́шивать; **~сти́ть** *s.* ~ща́ть; **∠чение** *n* [12] consolidation; **∠чивать** [1], ⟨∠чить⟩ [16] consolidate (*v/i.* **-ся**), stabilize; **~ща́ть** [1], ⟨~сти́ть⟩ [15 *e.*; -ощу́, -ости́шь; -ощённый] simplify; **~ще́ние** *n* [12] simplification.

упру́г|ий [16 *sh.*] elastic, resilient; **~ость** *f* [8] elasticity.

у́пряжь *f* [8] harness.

упря́м|иться [14] be obstinate; persist; **~ство** *n* [9] obstinacy, stubbornness; **~ый** [14 *sh.*] obstinate, stubborn.

упря́т|ывать [1], ⟨~ать⟩ [3] hide.

упу|ска́ть [1], ⟨~сти́ть⟩ [15] let go; let escape; miss; *cf.* вид); **~ще́ние** *n* [12] neglect, ommission.

ура́! hurrah!

уравн|е́ние *n* [12] equation; **∠ивать** [1] **1.** ⟨уровня́ть⟩ [28] level; **2.** ⟨~я́ть⟩ [28] equalize, level *fig.*; **~и́тельный** [14] level(l)ing; **~ове́шивать** [1], ⟨~ове́сить⟩ [15] balance; *p.pt.p. a.* well-balanced, composed, calm; **~я́ть** *s.* ∠ивать **2.**

урага́н *m* [1] hurricane.

Ура́л *m* [1], **☉ьский** [16] Ural.

ура́н *m* [1], **~овый** [14] uranium.

урегули́рование *n* [12] settlement; regulation; *vb. cf.* регули́ровать.

урез|а́ть & **∠ывать** F [1], ⟨∠ать⟩ [3] cut (down), curtail; **~о́нить** F [13] *pf.* bring to reason.

у́рна *f* [5] urn; (*voting*) box.

у́ров|ень *m* [4; -вня] level (at, on на П; в В); standard; gauge; rate; **~ня́ть** *s.* ура́внивать 1.

уро́д *m* [1] monster; F ugly creature; **~и́ться** [15 *e.*; -и́тся; -ождённый] *pf.* grow, be born; F be like (p. в В); **~ливый** [14 *sh.*] deformed; ugly; abnormal; **~овать** [7], ⟨из-⟩ deform, disfigure; mutilate; spoil; **~ство** *n* [9] deformity; ugliness; abnormity.

урож|а́й *m* [3] harvest, (abundant) crop; **~а́йность** *f* [8] yield (heavy высо́кая), productivity; **~а́йный** [14] fruitful; **~дённая** [14] nee; **~е́нец** *m* [1; -нца], **~е́нка** *f* [5; *g/pl.*: -нок] native.

уро́|к *m* [1] lesson (in на П); task; **~н** *m* [1] loss(es); injury; **~ни́ть** *s.* роня́ть; **~чный** [14] set, fixed.

Уругва́й *m* [4] Uruguay.

урча́ть [4 *e.*; -чу́, -чи́шь] (g)rumble; murmur.

уры́вками F by fits (& starts).

ус *m* [1; *pl. e.*] (*mst pl.*) m(o)ustache; кито́вый ~ whalebone.

уса|ди́ть *s.* ∠живать; **∠дьба** *f* [5; *g/pl.*: -деб] farm (land); manor; **∠живать** [1], ⟨~ди́ть⟩ [15] seat; set; plant (with T); **-ся**, ⟨усе́сться⟩ [25; уся́дусь, -дешься; уся́дься, -дьтесь!; усе́лся, -лась] sit down, take a seat; settle down.

уса́тый [14] with a m(o)ustache.

усв|а́ивать [1], ⟨~о́ить⟩ [13] adopt; acquire, assimilate; master, learn; **~ое́ние** *n* [12] adoption; acquirement, assimilation; mastering, learning.

усе́|ивать [1], ⟨~ять⟩ [27] stud.

усе́рд|ие *n* [12] zeal, eagerness (for к Д); assiduity; **~ный** [14; -ден, -дна] eager, zealous; assiduous.

усе́сться *s.* уса́живаться.

усе́ять *s.* усе́ивать.

усид|е́ть [11] *pf.* remain seated, sit still, (can) sit; hold out; **∠чивый** [14 *sh.*] assiduous, persevering.

у́сик *m* [1] *dim. of* ус; *zo.* feeler.

усил|е́ние *n* [12] strengthening, reinforcement; intensification; amplification; **∠енный** [14] intens(iv)e; substantial; pressing; **∠ивать** [1], ⟨∠ить⟩ [13] strengthen, reinforce; intensify; (*sound*) amplify; aggravate; **-ся** increase; **∠ие** *n* [12] effort, strain, exertion; **~и́тель** *m* [4] amplifier (*radio*); **∠ить(ся)** *s.* ∠ивать(ся).

ускака́ть [3] *pf.* leap *or* gallop (away).

ускольз|а́ть [1], ⟨~ну́ть⟩ [20] slip (off, away), escape (from от Р).
ускор|е́ние *n* [12] acceleration; **~я́ть** [28], ⟨~ить⟩ [13] speed up, accelerate; *v/i.* **-ся.**
усла́|вливаться F *s.* усло́вливаться; **~жда́ть** [1], ⟨~ди́ть⟩ [15 *e.*; -ажу́, -адишь; -аждённый] sweeten, soften; delight, **~ть** *s.* усыла́ть.
усло́в|ие *n* [12] condition (on с Т, при П; under на П), term; stipulation; proviso; agreement, contract; **~иться** *s.* ~ливаться; **~ленный** [14 *sh.*] agreed upon, fixed; **~ливаться** [1], ⟨~иться⟩ [14] arrange, fix, agree (upon о П); **~ность** *f* [8] convention; **~ный** [14; -вен, -вна] conditional; conventional; relative; ⚖ probational; ~ные зна́ки *pl.* conditional signes.
усложн|я́ть [28], ⟨~и́ть⟩ [13] (**-ся** become) complicate(d).
услу́|га *f* [5] service (at к Д *pl.*), favo(u)r; **~живать** [1], ⟨~жи́ть⟩ [16] do (p. Д) a service *or* favo(u)r; **~жливый** [14 *sh.*] obliging.
усм|а́тривать [1], ⟨~отре́ть⟩ [9; -отрю́, -о́тришь; -о́тренный] see (after за Т); **~еха́ться** [1], ⟨~ехну́ться⟩ [20], **~е́шка** *f* [5; *g/pl.:* -шек] smile, grin; **~ире́ние** *n* [12] suppression; **~иря́ть** [28], ⟨~ири́ть⟩ [13] pacify; suppress; **~отре́ние** *n* [12] discretion (at по Д; to на В), judg(e)ment; **~отре́ть** *s.* ~а́тривать.
усну́ть [20] *pf.* fall asleep; sleep.
усоверше́нствован|ие *n* [12] improvement, perfection; **~ный** [14] improved, perfected.
усомни́ться *s.* сомнева́ться.
усо́пший [17] deceased.
успе|ва́емость *f* [8] progress; **~ва́ть** [1], ⟨~ть⟩ [8] have (*or* find) time, manage, succeed; arrive, be in time (for к Д, на В); catch (*train* на В); *impf.* get on, make progress, learn; не ~л(а) (+ *inf.*), как no sooner + *pt.* than; **~ва́ющий** [17] advanced; **~х** *m* [1] success; result; *pl. a.* progress; **~шный** [14; -шен, -шна] successful; ~шно *a.* with success.
успок|а́ивать [1], ⟨~о́ить⟩ [13] calm, soothe; reassure; satisfy; **-ся** calm down; subside; become quiet; content o.s. (with на П); **~ое́ние** *n* [12] peace; calm; **~ои́тельный** [14; -лен, -льна] soothing, reassuring; **~о́ить(ся)** *s.* ~а́ивать(ся).
УССР (Украи́нская Сове́тская Социалисти́ческая Респу́блика) Ukrainian Soviet Socialist Republic.
уста́ † *n/pl.* [9] mouth, lips *pl.*
уста́в *m* [1] statute(s); regulations *pl.*; charter (*a. UNO*).
уста|ва́ть [5], ⟨~ть⟩ [-а́ну, -а́нешь] get tired; **~вля́ть** [28], ⟨~вить⟩ [14] place; cover (with Т), fill; fix (*eyes* on на В); **-ся** stare (at, на *or* в В); **~лость** *f* [8] weariness, fatigue; **~лый** [14] tired, weary; **~на́вливать** [1], ⟨~нови́ть⟩ [14] set *or* put up; mount; arrange; fix; establish; find out, ascertain; adjust (to на В); **-ся** be established; form; set in; **~но́вка** *f* [5; *g/pl.:* -вок] mounting, installation; ⊕ plant; *fig.* orientation (toward[s] на В); **~новле́ние** *n* [12] establishment; **~ре́лый** [14] obsolete, out-of-date; **~ть** *s.* ~ва́ть.
устила́ть [1], ⟨устла́ть⟩ [-телю́, -те́лешь; у́стланный] cover, lay out (with Т).
у́стный [14] oral, verbal.
усто́|и *m/pl.* [3] foundations; **~йчивость** *f* [8] stability; **~йчивый** [14 *sh.*] stable; **~я́ть** [-ою́, -ои́шь] keep one's balance; hold one's ground; resist (*v/t.* про́тив Р, пе́ред Т).
устр|а́ивать [1], ⟨~о́ить⟩ [13] arrange; organize, set up; furnish; construct; make (*scene, etc.*); provide (*job* на В, place in в В); F suit; **-ся** be settled; settle; get a job (*a.* на В); **~ане́ние** *n* [12] removal; elimination; **~аня́ть** [28], ⟨~ани́ть⟩ [13] remove; eliminate; **~аша́ть** (**-ся**) [1], *s.* страши́ть(ся); **~емля́ть** [28], ⟨~еми́ть⟩ [14 *e.*; -млю́, -ми́шь; -млённый] (на В) direct (to, at), fix (on); **-ся** rush; be directed; **~ица** *f* [5] oyster; **~о́ить** (**-ся**) *s.* ~а́ивать(ся); **~о́йство** *n* [9] arrangement; establishment; equipment; installation; organization; system; mechanism.
усту́п *m* [1] ledge; projection; step; terrace; **~а́ть** [1], ⟨~и́ть⟩ [14] cede, let (p. Д) have; yield; be inferior to (Д); sell; abate (*v/t.* с Р, в П); ~а́ть доро́гу (Д) let p. pass, give way; **~и́тельный** [14] *gr.* concessive; **~ка** *f* [5; *g/pl.:* -пок] concession; cession; † abatement, reduction; **~чивый** [14 *sh.*] compliant, pliant.
усты|жа́ть [1], ⟨~ди́ть⟩ [15 *e.*; -ыжу́, -ыди́шь; -ыжённый] (**-ся** be) ashame(d; of Р).
у́стье *n* [10; *g/pl.:* -ьев] mouth (at в П).
усугуб|ля́ть [28], ⟨~и́ть⟩ [14 & 14 *e.*; -гу́блю, -гу́би́шь; -гу́бленный & -гублённый] increase, redouble.
усы́ *s.* ус; **~ла́ть** [1], ⟨усла́ть⟩ [ушлю́, ушлёшь; у́сланный] send (away); **~новля́ть** [28], ⟨~нови́ть⟩ [14 *e.*; -влю́, -ви́шь; -влённый] adopt; **~па́ть** [1], ⟨~пать⟩ [2] (be)strew (with Т); **~пи́тельный** [14; -лен, -льна] soporific; drowsy;

\~плять [28], ⟨\~пить⟩ [14 *e.*; -плю, -пишь; -плённый] lull (to sleep); ⚕ narcotize.
ута́|ивать [1], ⟨\~и́ть⟩ [13] conceal, hide; embezzle; **\~йка** F: без \~йки frankly; **\~птывать** [1], ⟨утопта́ть⟩ [3] tread *or* trample (down); **\~скивать** [1], ⟨\~щи́ть⟩ [16] carry, drag *or* take (off, away); F pilfer.
у́тварь *f* [8] implements, utensils *pl.*
утвер|ди́тельный [14; -лен, -льна] affirmative (in the -но); **\~жда́ть** [1], ⟨\~ди́ть⟩ [15 *e.*; -ржу́, -рди́шь; -рждённый] confirm; consolidate (*v/i.* -ся); *impf.* affirm, assert, maintain; **\~жде́ние** *n* [12] confirmation; affirmation, assertion; consolidation.
уте|ка́ть [1], ⟨\~́чь⟩ [26] flow (away); F escape; **\~ре́ть** *s.* утира́ть; **\~рпе́ть** [10] *pf.:* не \~рпе́л, что́бы не (+ *inf. pf.*) could not help ...ing.
утёс *m* [1] cliff, rock.
уте́|чка *f* [5] leakage, escape; **\~чь** *s.* \~ка́ть; **\~ша́ть** [1], ⟨\~шить⟩ [16] console, comfort; -ся *a.* take comfort (in T); **\~ше́ние** *n* [12] comfort, consolation; **\~ши́тельный** [14; -лен, -льна] comforting, consolatory.
ути́|ль *m* [4], **\~льсырьё** *n* [10] scrap(s); **\~ра́ть** [1], ⟨утере́ть⟩ [12] wipe; **\~ха́ть** [1], ⟨\~хнуть⟩ [21] subside, abate; cease; calm down.
у́тка *f* [5; *g/pl.:* у́ток] duck; canard.
уткну́ть(ся) F [20] *pf.* thrust; hide; put; be(come) engrossed.
утол|и́ть *s.* \~я́ть; **\~ща́ть** [1], ⟨\~сти́ть⟩ [15 *e.*; -лщу́, -лсти́шь; -лщённый] thicken; **\~ще́ние** *n* [12] thickening; **\~я́ть** [28], ⟨\~и́ть⟩ [13] quench; appease; allay, still.
утом|и́тельный [14; -лен, -льна] wearisome, tiresome; **\~и́ть(ся)** *s.* \~ля́ть(ся); **\~ле́ние** *n* [12] fatigue, exhaustion; **\~лённый** [14; -лён, -ена́] tired, weary; **\~ля́ть** [28], ⟨\~и́ть⟩ [14 *e.*; -млю́, -ми́шь; -млённый] tire, weary (*v/i.* -ся; *a.* get tired).
утонч|а́ть [1], ⟨\~и́ть⟩ [16 *e.*; -чу́, -чи́шь; -чённый] thin; *fig.* refine; (*v/i.* -ся).
утоп|а́ть [1] **1.** ⟨утону́ть⟩ *s.* тону́ть **2.**; **2.** overflow (with в П); wallow, revel; **\~́ленник** *m* [1] drowned man; **\~́ленница** *f* [5] drowned woman; **\~та́ть** *s.* ута́птывать.
уточн|е́ние *n* [12] specification; **\~и́ть** [28], ⟨\~и́ть⟩ [13] specify.
утра́|ивать [1], ⟨утро́ить [13] treble; *v/i.* -ся; **\~мбова́ть** [7] *pf.* ram; stamp; **\~та** *f* [5] loss; **\~чивать** [1], ⟨\~тить⟩ [15] lose.
у́тренн|ий [15] morning; **\~ик** *m* [1] matinee; morning frost.
у́тр|о *n* [9; с, до -а́; к -у́] morning (in the \~ом; по \~́ам);... \~а́ *a.* ... a.m. (*cf.* день); **\~о́ба** *f* [5] womb; **\~о́бить (-ся)** *s.* \~́аивать(ся); **\~ужда́ть** [1], ⟨\~уди́ть⟩ [15 *e.*; -ужу́, -уди́шь; -уждённый] trouble, bother.
утю|г *m* [1 *e.*] (flat)iron; **\~жить** [16], ⟨вы́-, от-⟩ iron; stroke.
уха́ *f* [5] fish soup; **\~б** *m* [1] hole; **\~бистый** [14 *sh.*] bumpy.
уха́живать [1] (за T) nurse, look after; (pay) court (to), woo.
у́харский F [16] dashing.
у́хать [1], *once* ⟨у́хнуть⟩ [20] boom.
ухва́т|ывать [1], ⟨\~и́ть⟩ [15] (за В) seize, grasp; -ся snatch; cling to.
ухи|тря́ться [28], ⟨\~три́ться⟩ [13] contrive, manage; **\~щре́ние** *n* [12], **\~щря́ться** [28] shift.
ухмыл|я́ться F [28], ⟨\~ьну́ться⟩ [20] grin, smile (contentedly).
у́хнуть *s.* у́хать.
у́хо *n* [9; *pl.:* у́ши, уше́й, *etc. e.*] ear (in на́ В); по́ уши over head and ears; пропуска́ть ми́мо уше́й turn a deaf ear (to В); держа́ть \~ востро́ *s.* насторо́же.
ухо́д *m* [1] departure; (за T) care, tendance; nursing; **\~и́ть** [15], ⟨уйти́⟩ [уйду́, уйдёшь; ушёл, ушла́; уше́дший; *g.pt.:* уйдя́] leave (*v/t.* из, от Р), depart (from), go (away); pass; escape; evade; resign; retire; be lost; fail; take; sink; plunge; F be spent (for на В).
ухудш|а́ть [1], ⟨\~́ить⟩ [16] deteriorate (*v/i.* -ся); **\~е́ние** *n* [12] deterioration; change for the worse.
уцеле́ть [8] *pf.* escape; be spared.
уцепи́ться [14] F *s.* ухвати́ться.
уча́ст|вовать [7] participate, take part (in в П); **\~вующий** [17] *s.* \~ник; **\~ие** *n* [12] (в П) participation (in); interest (in), sympathy (with); **\~и́ть(ся)** *s.* учаща́ть(ся); **\~ливый** [14 *sh.*] sympathizing, sympathetic; **\~ник** *m* [1], **\~ница** *f* [5] participant, participator; competitor (*sports*); member; **\~ок** *m* [1; -тка] (p)lot; section; region; district; site; *fig.* field, branch; † (police) station; **'\~ь** *f* [8] fate, lot.
уча|ща́ть [1], ⟨\~сти́ть⟩ [15 *e.*; -ащу́, -асти́шь; -ащённый] make (-ся become) more frequent; speed up.
уч|а́щийся *m* [17] schoolboy, pupil, student; **\~ёба** *f* [5] studies *pl.*, study; training; drill; **\~е́бник** *m* [1] textbook; **\~е́бный** [14] school...; educational; text(*book*), exercise...; training; ⚔ drill...; \~е́бный план *m* curriculum.
уче́н|ие *n* [12] learning; instruction; apprenticeship; ⚔ drill; teaching, doctrine; **\~и́к** *m* [1 *e.*] schoolboy (**\~и́ца** *f* [5] schoolgirl), pupil;

student; apprentice; disciple; **~и́ческий** [16] pupils', students'.
учён|ость *f* [8] learning; **~ый** [14 *sh.*] learned; *su.* scholar.
уч|е́сть *s.* учитывать; **~ёт** *m* [1] calculation; registration; inventory; discount; list(s); *fig.* consideration, regard; вести́ ~ёт keep books *pl.*; взять на ~ёт register.
учи́лище *n* [11] school (at в П).
учиня́ть [28] *s.* чини́ть 2.
учи́тель *m* [4; *pl.*: -ля́, *etc. e.*; *fig. st.*], **~ница** *f* [5] teacher, instructor; **~ский** [16] (of) teachers(').
учи́тывать [1], ⟨уче́сть⟩ [25; учту́, -тёшь; учёл, учла́; *g. pt.*: учтя́; учтённый] take into account, consider; calculate; register; ✝ take late; stock; discount.
учи́ть [16] **1.** ⟨на-, об-, вы́-⟩ teach (p. s.th. В/Д), instruct; ⚔ drill; train; (*a.* **-ся** Д); **2.** ⟨вы́-⟩ learn, study.
учреди́тель *m* [4] founder; **~ный** [14] constituent.
учре|жда́ть [1], ⟨**~ди́ть**⟩ [15 *e.*; -ежу́, -еди́шь; -еждённый] found, constitute; establish, introduce; **~жде́ние** *n* [12] foundation, constitution; institution; institute, office (at в П).
учти́вый [14 *sh.*] polite; obliging.
уша́т *m* [1] tub, bucket.
ушиб *m* [1] bruise; injury; **~а́ть** [1], ⟨**~и́ть**⟩ [-бу́, -бёшь; -и́б(ла); ушибленный] hurt, bruise (o.s. **-ся**).
ушко́ *n* [9; *pl.*: **-ки́, -ко́в**] eye.
ушно́й [14] ear...
уще́лье *n* [10] gorge, ravine.
ущем|ля́ть [28], ⟨**~и́ть**⟩ [14 *e.*; -млю́, -ми́шь; -млённый] pinch, jam; *fig.* restrain; F wound, impair.
уще́рб *m* [1] damage; wane.
ущи́пнуть [20] *s.* щипа́ть.
Уэ́льс *m* [1] Wales.
ую́т *m* [1] coziness; **~ный** [14; **-тен, -тна**] snug, cozy, comfortable.
уязв|и́мый [14 *sh.*] vulnerable; **~ля́ть** [28], ⟨**~и́ть**⟩ [14 *e.*; -влю́, -ви́шь; -влённый] wound, sting; *fig.* hurt.
уясн|я́ть [28], ⟨**~и́ть**⟩ [13] comprehend; make clear, clear up.

Ф

фабзавко́м *m* [1] *s.* завко́м.
фа́бри|ка *f* [5] factory (in на П); mill; **~ка́нт** *m* [1] manufacturer; **~ка́т** *m* [1] product; **~чный** [14] factory (*a.* worker); trade(*mark*).
фа́була *f* [5] plot.
фа́з|а *f* [5], **~ис** *m* [1] phase.
фаза́н *m* [1] pheasant.
фа́кел *m* [1] torch.
факт *m* [1] fact; ~ тот the matter is; **~и́ческий** [16] (f)actual, real; *adv. a.* in fact; **~у́ра** *f* [5] invoice.
факульте́т *m* [1] faculty (in на П).
фаль|сифици́ровать [7] (*im*)*pf.* falsify, forge; adulterate; **~ши́вить** [14], ⟨с-⟩ sing out of tune, play falsely; F cheat, be false; **~ши́вка** F *f* [5; *g/pl.*: -вок] forgery; **~ши́вый** [14 *sh.*] false; forged, counterfeit; base (*coin*); **~шь** *f* [8] falseness; hypocrisy; deceit(fulness).
фами́л|ия *f* [7] surname, family name; как ва́ша ~ия? what is your name?; **~ья́рный** [14; -рен, -рна] familiar.
фанати́|зм *m* [1] fanaticism; **~ческий** [16], **~чный** [14; -чен, -чна] fanatical.
фане́ра *f* [5] plywood; veneer.
фанта|зёр *m* [1] visionary; **~зи́ровать** [7] indulge in fancies, dream; ⟨с-⟩ invent; **~зия** *f* [7] imagination; fancy; invention, fib; ♪ fantasia; F whim, freak; **~сти́ческий** [16], **~сти́чный** [14; -чен, -чна] fantastic.
фа́р|а *f* [5] headlight; **~ва́тер** *m* [1] waterway, fairway; *fig.* track; **~маце́вт** *m* [1] pharmac(eut)ist; **~тук** *m* [1] apron; **~фо́р** *m* [1], **~фо́ровый** [14] china, porcelain; **~ш** *m* [1] stuffing; forcemeat; **~широва́ть** [7] stuff.
фасо́|ль *f* [8] string (*Brt.* runner) bean(s); **~н** *m* [1] cut, style.
фат *m* [1] dandy, fop, dude.
фата́льный [14; -лен, -льна] fatal.
фаши́|зм *m* [1] fascism; **~ст** *m* [1] fascist; **~стский** [16] fascist...
фая́нс *m* [1], **~овый** [14] faïence.
февра́ль *m* [4 *e.*] February.
федера́|льный [14] federal; **~ти́вный** [14] federative, federal.
Фёдор *m* [1] Theodore; *dim.* **Фе́дя** [*m* [6].
феери́ческий [16] fairylike.
фейерве́рк *m* [1] firework.
фельд|ма́ршал *m* [1] field marshal; **~фе́бель** *m* [4] sergeant; **~шер** *m* [1] medical assistant.
фельето́н *m* [1] feuilleton.
фено́мен *m* [1] phenomenon.
феода́льный [14] feudal.
ферзь *m* [4 *e.*] queen (*chess*).
фе́рм|а *f* [5] farm; **~ер** *m* [1] farmer.
фестива́ль *m* [4] festival.
фетр *m* [1] felt; **~овый** [14] felt...
фехтова́|льщик *m* [1] fencer; **~ние** *n* [12] fencing; **~ть** [7] fence.
фиа́лка *f* [5; *g/pl.*: -лок] violet.
фи́бра *f* [5] fiber, *Brt.* fibre.
фи́г|а *f* [5], **~овый** [14] fig.
фигу́р|а *f* [5] figure; (*chess*)man;

~áльный [14; -лен, -льна] figurative; **~и́ровать** [7] figure, appear; **~ный** [14] figured; trick..., stunt...
фи́зи|к *m* [1] physicist; **~ка** *f* [5] physics; **~оло́гия** *f* [7] physiology; **~оно́мия** *f* [7] physiognomy; **∠ческий** [16] physical; manual.
физкульту́р|а *f* [5] physical culture; gymnastics; **~ник** *m* [1], **~ница** *f* [5] sports(wo)man, gymnast.
фик|са́ж *m* [1] fixative; **~си́ровать** [7], ⟨за-⟩ fix; **~ти́вный** [14; -вен, -вна] fictitious.
фила|нтро́п *m* [1] philanthropist; **~рмони́ческий** [16] philharmonic.
филе́ *n* [*ind.*] tenderloin, fillet.
филиа́л *m* [1] branch (office); **~ьный** [14] branch...
фи́лин *m* [1] eagle owl.
Филиппи́ны *f/pl.* [5] Philippines.
фило́л|ог *m* [1] philologist; **~оги́ческий** [16] philological; **~о́гия** *f* [7] philology.
фило́с|оф *m* [1] philosopher; **~о́фия** *f* [7] philosophy; **~о́фский** [16] philosophical; **~о́фствовать** [7] philosophize.
фильм *m* [1] film (*vb.*: снима́ть ~).
фильтр *m* [1], **~ова́ть** [7] filter.
фимиа́м *m* [1] incense.
фина́л *m* [1] final; ♪ finale.
финанс|и́ровать [7] (*im*)*pf.* finance; **∠овый** [14] financial; **∠ы** *m/pl.* [1] finance(s).
фи́ник *m* [1] date; **~овый** [14] date...
фин|ля́ндец *m* [1; -дца], **~н** *m* [1], **∠(ля́нд)ка** *f* [5; *g/pl.*: -н(ля́нд)ок] Finn; **♀ля́ндия** *f* [7] Finland; **∠(ля́нд)ский** [16] Finnish.
фиоле́товый [14] violet.
фи́рма *f* [5] firm.
фити́ль *m* [4 *e.*] wick; match.
флаг *m* [1] flag, colo(u)rs *pl.*; banner.
фланг *m* [1], **∠овый** [14] flank.
Фла́ндрия *f* [7] Flanders.
флане́л|евый [14], **~ь** *f* [8] flannel.
фле́гма *f* [5] phlegm; **~ти́чный** [14; -чен, -чна] phlegmatic(al).
фле́йта *f* [5] flute.
фли́|гель ⚠ *m* [4; *pl.*: -ля́, *etc. e.*] wing; **~рт** *m* [1] flirtation; **~ртова́ть** [7] flirt.
флот *m* [1] fleet; marine; navy; (*air*) force; **∠ский** [16] naval; *su.* F sailor.
флю|гер *m* [1] weathercock, weather vane; **~с** *m* [1] gumboil.
фля́|га, ~жка *f* [5; *g/pl.*: -жек] flask; canteen, *Brt.* water bottle.
фойе́ *n* [*ind.*] *thea.* lobby, foyer.
фокстро́т *m* [1] fox trot.
фо́кус *m* [1] hocus-pocus, (juggler's) trick, sleight of hand; F trick; freak, whim; **~ник** *m* [1] juggler, conjurer; **~ничать** F [1] trick.
фо́льга *f* [5] foil.
фолькло́р *m* [1], **~ный** [14] folklore.
Фо|ма́ *m* [5] Thomas; **♀н** *m* [1] background (against на П).
фона́р|ик *m* [1] flashlight, *Brt.* (electric) torch; **~ь** *m* [4 *e.*] lantern; (street) lamp; (head)light; F *s.* синя́к.
фонд *m* [1] fund.
фоне́т|ика *f* [5] phonetics; **~и́ческий** [16] phonetic(al).
фонта́н *m* [1] fountain.
форе́ль *f* [8] trout.
фо́рм|а *f* [5] form, shape; model; ⊕ mo(u)ld; ⚔ uniform; dress (*sports*); **~а́льность** *f* [8] formality; **~а́льный** [14; -лен, -льна] formal; **~а́т** *m* [1] size; form; **~енный** [14] formal; F downright; **~енная оде́жда** *f* uniform; **~ирова́ть** [7], ⟨с-⟩ (**-ся** be) form(ed); **~ова́ть** [7], ⟨с-, от-⟩ mo(u)ld, model; **~ули́ровать** [7] (*im*)*pf.* & ⟨с-⟩ formulate; **~ули-ро́вка** *f* [5; *g/pl.*: -вок] formulation; **~уля́р** *m* [1] form.
форпо́ст *m* [1] advanced post.
форси́ровать [7] (*im*)*pf.* force.
фо́|рточка *f* [5; *g/pl.*: -чек] window leaf; **~сфор** *m* [1] phosphorus.
фото|аппара́т *m* [1] camera; **∠граф** *m* [1] photographer; **~графи́ровать** [7], ⟨с-⟩ photograph; **~графи́ческий** [16] photographic; *cf.* ~аппара́т; **~гра́фия** *f* [7] photograph; photography; photographer's.
фра́за *f* [5] phrase; empty talk.
фрак *m* [1] dress coat.
фра́кция *f* [7] faction.
франки́ровать [7] (*im*)*pf.* stamp.
франт *m* [1] dandy, fop; **~и́ть** F [15 *e.*; -нчу́, -нти́шь] overdress; **~овско́й** [16] dandyish, dudish.
Фра́нц|ия *f* [7] France; **♀у́женка** *f* [5; *g/pl.*: -нок] Frenchwoman; **♀у́з** *m* [1] Frenchman; **♀у́зский** [16] French.
фрахт *m* [1], **~ова́ть** [7] freight.
ФРГ *cf.* Герма́ния.
фре́зер *m* [1] milling cutter.
френч *m* [1] (army-type) jacket.
фре́ска *f* [5] fresco.
фронт *m* [1] front; **~ово́й** [14] front...
фрукт *m* [1] (*mst pl.*) fruit; **~о́вый** [14] fruit...; ~о́вый сад *m* orchard.
фу! fie!, ugh!
фуга́сный [14] demolition (*bomb*).
фунда́мент *m* [1] foundation; basis; **~а́льный** [14; -лен, -льна] fundamental.
функциони́ровать [7] function.
фунт *m* [1] pound (= *409.5 g*).
фур|а́ж *m* [1 *e.*] fodder; **~а́жка** *f* [5; *g/pl.*: -жек] (service) cap; **~го́н** *m* [1] van; **∠ия** *f* [7] fury; **~о́р** *m* [1] furor; **~у́нкул** *m* [1] furuncle, boil.
футбо́л *m* [1] soccer, *Brt. a.* association football; **~и́ст** *m* [1] soccer player; **~ьный** [14] soccer..., football...
футля́р *m* [1] case; sheath; box.
фуфа́йка *f* [5; *g/pl.*: -а́ек] jersey.
фы́рк|ать [1], ⟨**~нуть**⟩ [20] snort.

Х

хáки [*ind.*] khaki.
халáт *m* [1] dressing gown, bathrobe; smock; **~ный** F [14; -тен, -тна] careless, negligent; sluggish.
халтýра F *f* [5] botch, bungle.
хам F *m* [1] cad, boor, churl.
хандр|á *f* [5] melancholy, blues *pl.*; **~и́ть** [13] be in the dumps.
ханж|á F *m/f* [5; *g/pl.*: -жéй] hypocrite; **~ествó** *n* [9] hypocrisy, bigotry.
хаó|с *m* [1] chaos; **~ти́ческий** [16], **~ти́чный** [14; -чен, -чна] chaotic.
харáктер *m* [1] character, nature; temper, disposition; principles *pl.*; **~изовáть** [7] (*im*)*pf.* & ⟨о-⟩ characterize, mark; **~и́стика** *f* [5] character(istic); characterization; **~ный** [14; -рен, -рна] characteristic (of для Р).
хáрк|ать F [1], ⟨**~**нуть⟩ [20] spit.
харч|éвня *f* [6; *g/pl.*: -вен] tavern; **~и́** P *m/pl.* [1 *e.*] food, grub; board.
хáря P *f* [6] mug, phiz.
хáта *f* [5] (peasant's) hut.
хвал|á *f* [5] praise; **~éбный** [14; -бен, -бна] laudatory; **~и́ть** [13; хвалю́, хвáлишь] praise; **-ся** boast (of T).
хвáст|аться &, F, **~ать** [1], ⟨по-⟩ boast, brag (of T); **~ли́вый** [14 *sh.*] boastful; **~овствó** *n* [9] boasting; **~ýн** *m* [1 *e.*] boaster, braggart.
хват|áть [1] **1.** ⟨(с)хвати́ть⟩ [15] (за В) snatch (at); grasp, seize (by); *a.*, F, (**-ся** за В; lay hold of); **2.** ⟨**~и́ть**⟩ (*impers.*) (P) suffice, be sufficient; (р. Д, у Р) have enough; last (*v/t.* на В); (э́того мне) **~**ит (that's) enough (for me); F hit, knock, strike; drink, eat; take; go.
хвóйный [14] coniferous.
хворáть F [1] be sick *or* ill.
хвóрост *m* [1] brushwood.
хвост *m* [1 *e.*] tail; brush (*fox*); F train; line, *Brt.* queue; в **~**тé (*lag*) behind; поджáть **~** F come down a peg (or two).
хвóя *f* [6] (pine) needle(s *or* branches *pl.*).
хи́жина *f* [5] hut, cabin.
хи́лый [14; хил, -á, -о] sickly.
хи́ми|к *m* [1] (*Brt.* analytical) chemist; **~ческий** [16] chemical; indelible *or* copying-ink (*pencil*); **~я** *f* [7] chemistry.
хини́н *m* [1] quinine.
хирéть [8] weaken, grow sickly.
хирýрг *m* [1] surgeon; **~и́ческий** [16] surgical; **~и́я** *f* [7] surgery.
хитр|éц *m* [1 *e.*] cunning fellow, dodger; **~и́ть** [13], ⟨с-⟩ dodge; fox; quibble; *cf.* мудри́ть; **~ость** *f* [8] craft(iness), cunning; artifice, ruse, trick; stratagem; **~ый** [14; -тёр, -трá, хи́тро] cunning, crafty, sly, artful; ingenious.
хихи́кать [1] chuckle, giggle, titter.
хищéние *n* [12] embezzlement.
хи́щн|ик *m* [1] beast (*or* bird) of prey; **~ый** [14; -щен, -щна] rapacious, predatory; of prey.
хладнокрóв|ие *n* [12] composure; **~ный** [14; -вен, -вна] cool(-headed), calm.
хлам *m* [1] trash, stuff, lumber.
хлеб *m* **1.** [1] bread; loaf; **2.** [1; *pl.*: -бá, *etc. e.*] grain, *Brt.* corn; livelihood; *pl.* cereals; **~áть** [1], *once* ⟨**~**нýть⟩ [20] drink, sip; P eat; **~ный** [14] grain..., corn..., cereal; bread...; baker's; F profitable; **~опекáрня** *f* [6; *g/pl.*: -рен] bakery; **~осóльный** [14; -лен, -льна] hospitable; **~осóльство** *n* [9], F **~-сóль** *f* [1/8] hospitality.
хлев *m* [1; в -е & -ý; *pl.*: -á, *etc. e.*] shed; cote; sty.
хлест|áть [3], *once* ⟨**~**нýть⟩ [20] lash, whip, beat; splash; gush, spurt; pour.
хли́пать F [1] sob.
хлоп! crack!, plop!; *cf. a.* **~ать** [1], ⟨по-⟩, *once* ⟨**~**нуть⟩ [20] slap; clap; bang, slam (*v/t.* T); crack; pop (*cork*); detonate; resound; blink.
хлóпок *m* [1; -пка] cotton.
хлопот|áть [3], ⟨по-⟩ (о П) strive (for), endeavo(u)r; exert o. s. (on behalf of о П, за В); apply (for); *impf.* bustle (about); **~ли́вый** [14 *sh.*] troublesome; busy, fussy; **'~ы** *f/pl.* [5; *gen.*: -пóт] trouble(s), cares; business, commissions.
хлопýшка *f* [5; *g/pl.*: -шек] fly flap; cracker.
хлопчатобумáжный [14] cotton...
хлóпья *n/pl.* [10; *gen.*: -ьев] flakes.
хлор *m* [1] chlorine; **~истый** [14] ... chloride; **~ный** [14] chloric; **~офóрм** *m* [1], **~оформи́ровать** [7] (*im*)*pf.* chloroform.
хлы́нуть [20] *pf.* gush (forth); rush; (begin to) pour in torrents.
хлыст *m* [1 *e.*] horsewhip; switch.
хлю́пать F [1] squelch.
хмел|ь *m* [4] hop; intoxication; во **~**ю drunk; **~ьнóй** F [14; -лён, -льнá] intoxicated; intoxicating.
хмýр|ить [13], ⟨на-⟩ knit (*the brow*); **-ся** frown, scowl; be(come) overcast; **~ый** [14; хмур, -á, -о] gloomy, sullen; cloudy.
хны́кать F [3] whine, snivel.
хóбот *m* [1] *zo.* trunk.
ход *m* [1; в (на) -ý & -е; *pl.*: хóды́] motion; speed (at на П), pace; course; passage; walk; ⊕ *a.* action, movement; stroke (*piston*); entrance; access; lead (*cards*); move (*chess, etc.*); turn; vogue, currency;

в ~ý *a.* = ∠кий; на ~ý *a.* while walking, *etc.*; F in progress; пусти́ть в ~ start, set going *or* on foot, circulate; все ~ы́ и вы́ходы the ins and outs.

хода́тай *m* [3] intercessor, advocate; **~ство** *n* [9] intercession; petition; **~ствовать** [7], ⟨по-⟩ intercede (with/for у Р/за В); petition (for о П).

ход|и́ть [15] go (to в, на В); walk; sail; run, ply; move; visit, attend (*v/t.* в, на В; р. к Д); circulate; (в П) wear; (за Т) look after, take care of, nurse; tend; (на В) hunt; lead (*cards*); F be current; ease o. s.; **∠кий** [16; хо́док, -дка́, -о; *comp.*: хо́дче] marketable, sal(e)able; current; F quick, easygoing; **~кая кни́га** *f* best seller; **~у́льный** [14; -лен, -льна] stilted; **~ьба́** *f* [5] walking; walk; **~я́чий** [17] current; trivial; F walking. circulation.

хожде́ние *n* [12] going, walking;

хозя́|ин *m* [1; *pl.*: хозя́ева, хозя́ев] master, owner; boss, principal; landlord; host; innkeeper; manager; farmer; **~ева** = **~ин** & **~йка**; **~йка** *f* [5; *g/pl.*: -я́ек] mistress; landlady; hostess; housewife; **~йничать** [1] keep house; manage (at will); make o. s. at home; **~йственный** [14 *sh.*] economic(al); thrifty; **~йство** *n* [9] economy; household; farm.

хокке́й *m* [3] hockey.

холе́ра *f* [5] cholera.

хо́лить [13] groom, care for, fondle.

хо́л|ка *f* [5; *g/pl.*: -лок] withers; **~м** *m* [1 *e.*] hill; **~ми́стый** [14 *sh.*] hilly.

хо́лод *m* [1] cold (in на П); chill (*a. fig.*); *pl.* [-а́, *etc. e.*] cold (weather) (in в В); **~е́ть** [8], ⟨по-⟩ grow cold, chill; **~е́ц** *m* [1; -дца́] = сту́день; **~и́льник** *m* [1] refrigerator; **∠ность** *f* [8] coldness; **∠ный** [14; хо́лоден, -дна́, -о] cold (*a. fig.*); *geogr.* & *fig.* frigid; (мне) ~но it is (I am) cold.

холо́п *m* [1] bondman; F toady.

холост|о́й [14; хо́лост] single, unmarried; bachelor('s); blank (*cartridge*); ⊕ idle (*motion*); **~я́к** *m* [1 *e.*] bachelor.

холст *m* [1 *e.*] linen; canvas.

холу́й P *m* [3] cad; toady.

хому́т *m* [1 *e.*] (horse) collar.

хомя́к *m* [1 *e.*] hamster.

хор *m* [1] chorus; choir.

хорва́т *m* [1], **~ка** *f* [5; *g/pl.*: -ток] Croat; **~ский** [16] Croatian.

хорёк *m* [1; -рька́] polecat, fitch.

хорово́д *m* [1] round dance.

хорони́ть [13; -оню́, -о́нишь], ⟨по-⟩ bury.

хоро́ш|енький [16] pretty; **~е́нько** F properly; **~е́ть** [8], ⟨по-⟩ grow prettier; **~ий** [17; хоро́ш, -а́; *comp.*: лу́чше] good; fine, nice; (*a.* собо́й) pretty, good-looking, handsome; **~о́** well; *mark*: good, В (*cf.* четвёрка); all right!, O.K.!, good!; мне ~о́ I am well off; ~о́ вам (+ *inf.*) it is very well for you to ...

хоте́|ть [хочу́, хо́чешь, хо́чет, хоти́м, хоти́те, хотя́т], ⟨за-⟩ (P) want, wish; я ~л(а) бы I would (*Brt.* should) like; я хочу́, что́бы вы + *pt.* I want you to ...; хо́чешь не хо́чешь willy-nilly; **-ся** (*impers.*): мне хо́чется I'd like; *a.* = ~ть.

хоть (*a.* ~ бы) at least; even (if *or* though); if only; ~ ... ~ whether ... whether, (either ...) or; if you please; so much, *etc.*, that; any ...; I wish I could (*or* you'd); ~ бы и так even if it be so; ~ убей for the life of me; *s. a.* хотя́.

хотя́ although, though (*a.* ~ и); ~ бы even though; if; *s. a.* хоть.

хохо́л *m* [1; хохла́] tuft; crest; forelock; *contp.* Ukrainian (*man*).

хо́хот *m* [1] (loud) laughter, roar; **~а́ть** [3], ⟨за-⟩ roar (with laughter).

храбр|е́ц *m* [1 *e.*] brave; **∠ость** *f* [8] valo(u)r, bravery; **∠ый** [14; храбр, -а́, -о] brave, valient.

храм *m* [1] *eccl.* temple.

хран|е́ние *n* [12] keeping; storage; ка́мера ~е́ния ручно́го багажа́ 🚂 cloackroom, *Brt.* left-luggage office; **~и́лище** *n* [11] storehouse; archives *pl.*; **~и́тель** *m* [4] keeper, guardian; custodian; **~и́ть** [13], ⟨со-⟩ keep; store; preserve; observe; guard.

храп *m* [1], **~е́ть** [10 *e.*; -плю́, -пи́шь] snore; snort.

хребе́т *m* [1; -бта́] *anat.* spine; range.

хрен *m* [1] horseradish.

хрип *m* [1], **~е́ние** *n* [12] rattle; **~е́ть** [10 *e.*; -плю, -пи́шь] rattle; be hoarse; F speak hoarsely; **∠лый** [14; хрипл, -а́, -о] hoarse, husky; **∠нуть** [21], ⟨о-⟩ become hoarse; **~ота́** *f* [5] hoarseness; husky voice.

христ|иани́н *m* [1; *pl.*: -а́не, -а́н], **~иа́нка** *f* [5; *g/pl.*: -нок], **~иа́нский** [16] Christian; **~иа́нство** *n* [9] Christianity; **2о́в** [19] Christ's; **2о́с** *m* [Христа́] Christ.

хром *m* [1] chromium; chrome.

хром|а́ть [1] limp; be lame; **~о́й** [14; хром, -а́, -о] lame; **~ота́** *f* [5] lameness.

хро́н|ика *f* [5] chronicle; current events; newsreel; **~и́ческий** [16] chronic(al); **~ологи́ческий** [16] chronological; **~оло́гия** *f* [7] chronology.

хру́|пкий [16; -пок, -пка́, -о; *comp.*: хру́пче] brittle, fragile; frail, infirm; **~ста́ль** *m* [4 *e.*] crystal; **~ста́льный** [14] crystal...; **~сте́ть** [11] crunch; **~щ** *m* [1 *e.*] cockchafer.

хрюк|ать [1], *once* ⟨~нуть⟩ [20] grunt.

хрящ *m* [1 *e.*] cartilage.

худе́ть [8], ⟨по-⟩ grow thin.

ху́до *n* [9] evil; *s. a.* худо́й.
худо́ж|ественный [14 *sh.*] artistic; art(s)...; of art; belles(-*lettres*); applied (*arts*); **~ество** *n* [9] (applied) art; **~ник** *m* [1] artist; painter.
худ|о́й [14; худ, -á, -о; *comp.*: худе́е] thin, lean, scrawny (*a.* **~ощáвый** [14 *sh.*]); [*comp.*: ху́же] bad, evil; **ʼ~ший** [16] worse, worst; *cf.* лу́чший.
ху́же worse; *cf.* лу́чше & тот.
хулигáн *m* [1] rowdy, hooligan.
ху́тор *m* [1] farm(stead); hamlet.

Ц

цáп|ать F [1], *once* ⟨**~нуть**⟩ [20] snatch.
цáпля *f* [6; *g/pl.*: -пель] heron.
царáп|ать [1], ⟨(п)о-⟩, *once* ⟨**~нуть**⟩ [20], **~ина** *f* [5] scratch.
цар|е́вич *m* [1] czarevitch; prince; **~е́вна** *f* [5; *g/pl.*: -вен] princess; **~и́ть** [13] reign; prevail; **~и́ца** *f* [5] czarina; empress; *fig.* queen; **ʼ~ский** [16] of the czar(s), czarist; imperial; **ʼ~ство** *n* [9] empire; kingdom (*a. fig.*); rule; *a.* = **ʼ~ствование** *n* [12] reign (in в В); **ʼ~ствовать** [7] reign, rule; prevail; **~ь** *m* [4 *e.*] czar, (Russian) emperor; king.
цвести́ [25 -т-] bloom, blossom.
цвет *m* [1] **1.** [*pl.*: -á, *etc. e.*] colo(u)r; ~ лицá complexion; защи́тного **ʼ~а** khaki; **2.** [*only pl.*: -ы́, *etc. e.*] flowers; **3.** [*no pl.*; в -у́; *fig.* в(о) цвете] blossom, bloom; *fig. a.* prime; **~е́ние** *n* [12] flowering; **~и́стый** [14 *sh.*] florid; **~ни́к** *m* [1 *e.*] flower bed; **~но́й** [14] colo(u)red; variegated; nonferrous (*metals*); technicolor (*film*); **~нáя** капу́ста *f* cauliflower; **~о́к** *m* [1; -ткá; *pl. usu.* = ~ 2] flower (*a. fig.*); **~о́чник** *m* [1] florist; **~о́чница** *f* [5] florist, *Brt.* flower girl; **~о́чный** [14] flower...; **~у́щий** [17 *sh.*] flowering; flourishing; prime (*of life*).
цеди́ть [15] **1.** ⟨про-⟩ strain, pass, filter; F murmur, utter (between one's teeth); **2.** ⟨вы́-⟩ draw (off).
Цейло́н *m* [1] Ceylon.
цейхгáуз (cɛjˈxa-) *m* [1] arsenal.
целе́|бный [14; -бен, -бна] curative, medicinal; **~во́й** [14] special, for a specified purpose, purposeful; principal; **~сообрáзный** [14; -зен, -зна] expedient; **~устремлённый** [14 *sh.*] purposeful.
цели|ко́м entirely, wholly; **~нá** *f* [5] virgin soil; **ʼ~тельный** [14; -лен, -льна] salutary, curative; **ʼ~ть** (-ся) [13], ⟨при-⟩ aim (at в В).
целлюло́за *f* [5] cellulose.
целовáть(ся) [7], ⟨по-⟩ kiss.
це́л|ое *n* [14] whole (on the в П; ✝ in the lump); **~ому́дренный** [14 *sh.*] chaste; **~ому́дрие** *n* [12] chastity; **~ость** *f* [8] integrity; в ~ости intact; **~ый** [14; цел, -á, -о] whole; entire; safe, sound; intact; ~ое число́ *n* integer; *cf.* деся́тый & со́тый.
цель *f* [8] aim, end, goal, object; target; purpose (for с Т, в П *pl.*); име́ть **ʼ~ю** aim at; **ʼ~ность** *f* [8] integrity; **ʼ~ный** [14; це́лен, -льнá, -о] entire, whole; righteous; [*no sh.*] rich (*milk*).
цеме́нт *m* [1], **~и́ровать** [7] cement.
цен|á *f* [5; *ac/sg.*: це́ну; *pl. st.*] price (of Р, на В, Д; at/of по Д/в В), cost (at Т); value (of *or* one's Д); **~ы́** нет (Д) be invaluable; любо́й **~о́й** at any price; **~зу́ра** *f* [5] censorship.
цен|и́тель *m* [4] judge, connoisseur; **~и́ть** [13; ценю́, це́нишь], ⟨о-⟩ value, estimate, appreciate; **ʼ~ность** *f* [8] value; *pl.* valuables; **ʼ~ный** [14; -е́нен, -е́нна] valuable; money (*letter*); **ʼ~ные** бумáги *pl.* securities.
це́нтнер *m* [1] centner (= *100 kg*).
центр *m* [1] center, *Brt.* centre; **~ализовáть** [7] (*im*)*pf.* centralize; **~áльный** [14] central; *cf.* ЦИК & ЦК; **~обе́жный** [14] centrifugal.
цеп *m* [1 *e.*] flail.
цеп|ене́ть [8], ⟨о-⟩ grow numb, stiffen; be transfixed; **ʼ~кий** [16; -пок, -пкá, -о] clinging; tenacious; **~ля́ться** [28] cling (to за В); **~но́й** [14] chain(ed); **~о́чка** *f* [5; *g/pl.*: -чек] chain; **~ь** *f* [8; в, на -и́; *from g/pl. e.*] chain (*a. fig.*); ⚔ line; ⚡ circuit.
церемо́н|иться [13], ⟨по-⟩ stand on ceremony, be ceremonious; **~ия** *f* [7] ceremony; **~ный** [14] ceremonious.
церко́в|ный [14] church...; **ʼ~ь** *f* [8; -кви; *instr/sg.*: -ковью; *pl.*: -кви, -ве́й, -вáм] church.
цех *m* [1] shop, section; † guild.
цивилиз|овáть [7] (*im*)*pf.* civilize; **~о́ванный** [14] civilized.
ЦИК (Центрáльный Исполни́тельный Комите́т) Central Executive Committee (*Sov.*); *cf.* ЦК.
цикл *m* [1] cycle; course, set; **~о́н** *m* [1] cyclone.
цико́рий *m* [3] chicory.
цили́ндр *m* [1] cylinder; top (*or* high) hat; **~и́ческий** [16] cylindrical.
цингá *f* [5] scurvy.
цини́|зм *m* [1] cynicism; **ʼ~к** *m* [1] cynic; **~чный** [14; -чен, -чна] cynical.
цинк *m* [1] zinc; **ʼ~овый** [14] zinc ...
цино́вка *f* [5; *g/pl.*: -вок] mat.
цирк *m* [1], **~ово́й** [14] circus.
циркул|и́ровать [7] circulate; **ʼ~ь**

m [4] (оди́н a pair of) compasses *pl.*; **~я́р** *m* [1] circular.
цисте́рна *f* [5] cistern, tank.
цитаде́ль (-ˈdɛ-) *f* [8] citadel; stronghold.
цита́та *f* [5] quotation.
цити́ровать [7], ⟨про-⟩ quote.
циф|ербла́т *m* [1] dial, face (*watch, etc.*); **∠ра** *f* [5] figure.
ЦК (Центра́льный Комите́т) Central Committee (*Sov.*); *cf.* ЦИК.
цо́коль *m* [4] ⚠ socle; ⊕ socket.
цыга́н *m* [1; *nom/pl.*: -е & -ы; *gen.*: цыга́н], **~ка** *f* [5; *g/pl.*: -нок], **~ский** [16] Gypsy, *Brt.* Gipsy.
цыплёнок *m* [2] chicken.
цы́почк|и: на ~ах (*or* ~и) on tiptoe.

Ч

ч. *abbr.*: **1.** час; **2.** часть.
чад *m* [1; в -у́] smoke, fume(s); *fig.* daze; frenzy; **~и́ть** [15 *e.*; чажу́, чади́шь], ⟨на-⟩ smoke.
ча́до † & *iron. n* [9] child.
чаевы́е *pl.* [14] tip.
чай[1] *m* [3; *part. g.*: -ю; в -е & -ю́; *pl. e.*: чаи́, чаёв] tea; tea party; дать на ~ tip; ~[2] P perhaps, I suppose.
ча́йка *f* [5; *g/pl.*: ча́ек] (sea) gull, mew.
ча́йн|ик *m* [1] teapot; teakettle; **~ый** [14] tea(*spoon, etc.*).
чалма́ *f* [5] turban.
чан *m* [1; *pl. e.*] tub, vat.
ча́р|ка *f* [5; *g/pl.*: -рок] (*wine- etc.*) glass; **~ова́ть** [20] charm; **~оде́й** *m* [3] magician.
час *m* [1; в -е & -у́; *after* **2, 3, 4**: -а́; *pl. e.*] hour (by the по ~а́м; for *pl.* ~а́ми); (one) o'clock (at в В); time, moment (at в В); an hour's ...; второ́й ~ (it is) past one; в пя́том ~у́ between four & five; (*cf.* пять & пя́тый); ~ о́т ~у *or* с ∠у на ~ hourly; на ~а́х (*stand*) sentinel; **~о́вня** *f* [6; *g/pl.*: -вен] chapel; **~ово́й** [14] hour's; by the hour; watch..., clock-...; *su.* sentry, sentinel; ~ово́й ма́стер *m* = **~овщи́к** [1 *e.*] watchmaker.
част|и́ца *f* [5] particle; **~и́чный** [14; -чен, -чна] partial; **∠ное** *n* [14] quotient; **∠ность** *f* [8] particular; **∠ный** [14] private; particular; individual; **~око́л** *m* [1] palisade; **~ота́** *f* [5; *pl. st.*: -о́ты] frequency; **~у́шка** *f* [5; *g/pl.*: -шек] couplet; **∠ый** [14; част, -а́, -о; *comp.*: ча́ще] frequent (*adv. a.* often); thick(-set), dense; close; quick, rapid; **~ь** *f* [8; *from g/pl. e.*] part (in Т; *pl. a.* по Д); share; piece; department, section (in *a.* по Д), F line, branch; ⚔ unit; † police station; бо́льшей ∠ью, по бо́льшей ∠и for the most part, mostly.
час|ы́ *m/pl.* [1] watch; clock; (*sun*)dial; на мои́х ~а́х by my watch.
ча́х|лый [14 *sh.*] sickly; stunted; **~нуть** [21], ⟨за-⟩ wither, shrivel; grow stunted; **~о́тка** *f* [5] consumption; **~о́точный** [14; -чен, -чна] consumptive.
ча́ша *f* [5] cup, chalice; bowl.
ча́шка *f* [5; *g/pl.*: -шек] cup; pan; cap; надколе́нная ~ kneecap.
ча́ща *f* [5] thicket.
ча́ще more (~ всего́ most) often.
ча́я|ние *n* [12] expectation (contrary to па́че *or* сверх Р), hope, dream.
чва́н|иться F [13], **~ство** *n* [9] brag, blow, swagger.
чей *m*, **чья** *f*, **чьё** *n*, **чьи** *pl.* [26] whose; ~ э́то дом? whose house is this?
чек *m* [1] check, *Brt.* cheque; **~а́нить** [13], ⟨вы́-⟩ mint, coin; chase; **~а́нка** *f* [5; *g/pl.*: -нок] minting, coinage; chase; **~и́ст** *m* [1] member of ЧК, *cf.*; **∠овый** [14] check...
чёлн *m* [1 *e.*; челна́] boat; canoe.
челно́к *m* [1 *e.*] *dim. of* чёлн; *a.* shuttle.
чело́ † *n* [9; *pl. st.*] forehead, brow.
челове́|к *m* [1; *pl.*: лю́ди, *cf.*; **5, 6,** *etc.* -е́к] man, human being; person, individual; one; † servant; waiter; ру́сский ~к Russian; **~колю́бие** *n* [12] philanthropy; **~ческий** [16] human(e); **~чество** *n* [9] mankind, humanity; **~чный** [14; -чен, -чна] humane.
че́люсть *f* [8] jaw; (full) denture.
че́лядь *f* [8] servants *pl.*
чем than; F instead of; ~ ..., тем ... the ... the ...; **~ода́н** *m* [1] suitcase.
чемпио́н *m* [1] champion; **~а́т** *m* [1] championship.
чепе́ц *m* [1; -пца́] cap.
чепуха́ F *f* [5] nonsense; trifle.
че́пчик *m* [1] cap.
че́рв|и *f/pl.* [4; *from gen. e.*] & **~ы** *f/pl.* [5] hearts (*cards*).
черви́вый [14 *sh.*] worm-eaten.
черво́нец *m* [1; -нца] 10 rubles.
черв|ь *m* [4 *e.*; *nom/pl. st.*: че́рви, черве́й], **~я́к** *m* [1 *e.*] worm.
черда́к *m* [1 *e.*] garret, attic, loft.
черёд F *m* [1 *e.*] turn; course.
чередова́|ние *n* [12] alternation; **~ть(ся)** [7] alternate.
че́рез (В) through; across, over;

time: in, after; *go*: via; with (the help of); because of; ~ день *a.* every other day.
черёмуха *f* [5] bird cherry.
чéреп *m* [1; *pl.*: -á, *etc. e.*] skull.
черепá|ха *f* [5] tortoise; turtle; tortoise shell; **~ховый** [14] tortoise(-shell)...; **~ший** [18] tortoise's, snail's (pace шаг *m*; at T).
череп|и́ца *f* [5] tile (*of roof*); **~и́чный** [14] tiled; **~óк** *m* [1; -пкá] fragment, piece.
чере|счýр too, too much; **∠шня** *f* [6; *g/pl.*: -шен] (sweet) cherry.
черкнýть F [20] *pf.*: ~ пáру (*or* нéсколько) слов drop a line.
черн|éть [8], ⟨по-⟩ blacken, grow black; *impf.* (*a.* **-ся**) show black; **~éц** *m* [1 *e.*] monk; **~и́ка** *f* [5] bilberry, -ries *pl.*; **~и́ла** *n/pl.* [9] ink; **~и́льница** *f* [5] inkwell (*Brt.* inkpot), inkstand; **~и́льный** [14] ink...; **~и́ть** [13] **1.** ⟨на-⟩ blacken; **2.** ⟨о-⟩ blacken (*fig.*), denigrate, slander.
черно|ви́к *m* [1 *e.*] rough copy; draft; **~вóй** [14] draft...; rough; waste (*book*); **~волóсый** [14 *sh.*] black-haired; **~глáзый** [14 *sh.*] black-eyed; **~гóрец** *m* [1; -рца] Montenegrin; **~зём** *m* [1] chernozem, black earth; **~кóжий** [17 *sh.*] Negro; **~мáзый** [14 *sh.*] swarthy; **~мóрский** [16] Black Sea ...; **~рабóчий** *m* [17] unskilled worker; **~сли́в** *m* [1] prune(s); **~тá** *f* [5] blackness.
чёрн|ый [14; чёрен, чернá] black (*a. fig.*); brown (*bread*); ferrous (*metals*); rough (*work*); back(*stairs, etc.*); leafy (*wood*); на **~ый** день for a rainy day; **~ым** по бéлому in black & white.
чернь *f* [8] mob, rabble.
чéрп|ать [1], ⟨**~нýть**⟩ [20] scoop, draw; gather (from из P, в П).
черст|вéть [8], ⟨за-, по-⟩ grow stale; harden; **∠вый** (ˈtʃɔ-) [14; чёрств, -á, -о] stale, hard; callous.
чёрт *m* [1; *pl.* 4 чéрти, -тéй, *etc. e.*] devil; F the deuce (go: *a.* ступáй, убирáйся; take: возьми́, побери́, [по]дери́; *a.* confound; blast, damn it!); к **~у**, на кой ~ F *a.* the deuce; ни чертá F nothing at all; never mind!
черт|á *f* [5] line; trait, feature (*a.* **~ы** лицá); precincts *pl.* (within в П); term.
чертёж *m* [1 *e.*] (mechanical) drawing, draft (*Brt.* draught), design; **~ни́к** *m* [1] draftsman, *Brt.* draughtsman; **~ный** [14] drawing (*board, etc.*).
черт|и́ть [15], ⟨на-⟩ draw, design; **~óвский** [16] devilish.
чёрточка *f* [5; *g/pl.*: -чек] hyphen.
черчéние *n* [12] drawing.
чесáть [3] **1.** ⟨по-⟩ scratch; **2.** ⟨при⟩ F comb; **3.** *impf.* hackle, card; **-ся** *a.*, F, itch (му у меня́).
чеснóк *m* [1 *e.*] garlic.
чесóтка *f* [5] itch.
чéст|вование *n* [12] celebration; **~вовать** [7] celebrate, hono(u)r; **~ность** *f* [8] honesty; **~ный** [14; чéстен, -тнá, -о] honest, of hono(u)r; fair; **~олюби́вый** [14 *sh.*] ambitious; **~олю́бие** *n* [12] ambition; **~ь** *f* [8] hono(u)r (in в B); credit; по **~и** F honestly; **~ь ~ю** F properly, well.
четá *f* [5] couple, pair; F match.
четвéр|г *m* [1 *e.*] Thursday (on: в B, *pl.*: по Д); **~еньки** F *f/pl.* [5] all fours (on на B, П); **~ка** (-ˈvɔr-) *f* [5; *g/pl.*: -рок] four (*cf.* трóйка); F (*mark*) = хорошó, *cf.*; **ʹ~о** [37] four (*cf.* двóе); **~онóгий** [16] four-footed; **~тый** (-ˈvɔr-) [14] fourth; *cf.* пя́тый; **ʹ~ть** *f* [8; *from g/pl. e.*] (one) fourth; quarter (to без P; past one вторóго).
чёткий [16; чёток, четкá, -о] distinct, clear; legible; exact, accurate.
чётный [14] even.
четы́ре [34] four; *cf.* пять; **~жды** four times; **~ста** [36] four hundred.
четырёх|лéтний [15] four-years(-old)'; **~мéстный** [14] four-seated; **~сóтый** [14] four hundredth; **~угóльник** *m* [1] quadrangle; **~угóльный** [14] quadrangular; **~этáжный** [14] four-storied (*Brt.* -storeyed).
четы́рнадца|тый [14] fourteenth; *cf.* пя́тый; **~ть** [35] fourteen; *cf.* пять.
чех *m* [1] Czech.
чехардá *f* [5] leapfrog.
чехóл *m* [1; -хлá] case, cover.
Чехословá|кия *f* [7] Czechoslovakia; **♀цкий** [16] Czechoslovak.
чечеви́ца *f* [5] lentil(s).
чéш|ка *f* [5; *g/pl.*: -шек] Czech (woman); **~ский** [16] Czech(ic).
чешуя́ *f* [6] scales *pl.*
чи́бис *m* [1] lapwing.
чиж *m* [1 *e.*], F **∠ик** *m* [1] siskin.
Чи|кáго *n* [*ind.*] Chicago; **∠ли** *n* [*ind.*] Chile; **♀ли́ец** *m* [1; -и́йца] Chilean.
чин *m* [1; *pl. e.*] rank, grade; station; order, ceremony; official; **~и́ть** **1.** [13; чиню́, чи́нишь] a) ⟨по-⟩ mend, repair; b) ⟨о-⟩ sharpen, point; **2.** [13], ⟨у-⟩ raise, cause; administer; **∠ный** [14; чи́нен, чиннá, чи́нно] proper; sedate; **~óвник** *m* [1] official; bureaucrat.
чири́к|ать [1], ⟨**~нуть**⟩ [20] chirp.
чи́рк|ать [1], ⟨**~нуть**⟩ [20] strike.
чи́сл|енность *f* [8] number; ⚔ strength (of/of T/в B); **~енный** [14] numerical; **~и́тель** ⅍ *m* [4]

numerator; **~и́тельное** *n* [14] *gr.* numeral (*a.* и́мя ~и́тельное); **~иться** [13] be on the ... list (в П *or* по Д/Р); **~о́** *n* [9; *pl. st.*: чи́сла, чи́сел, чи́слам] number; date; day (in в П; on Р); кото́рое (како́е) сего́дня ~о́? what date is today? (*cf.* пя́тый); в ~е́ (Р), в том ~е́ including.
чи́стильщик *m* [1] (*boot*)black.
чи́ст|ить [15] **1.** ⟨по-, вы́-⟩ clean(se); brush; polish; **2.** ⟨о-⟩ peel; *pol.* purge; **~ка** *f* [5; *g/pl.*: -ток] clean(s)ing; polish(ing); *pol.* purge; **~окро́вный** [14; -вен, -вна] thoroughbred; *fig.* genuine; **~опло́тный** [14; -тен, -тна] cleanly; *fig.* clean; **~осерде́чный** [14; -чен, -чна] open-hearted, frank, sincere; **~ота́** *f* [5] clean(li)ness; purity; **~ый** [14; чист, -а́, -о; *comp.*: чи́ще] clean; pure; neat, cleanly; clear; net; blank (*sheet*); fine, faultless; genuine; sheer; plain (*truth*); mere (*chance*); hard (*cash*); free, open (*field*).
чита́|льный [14]: **~льный зал** *m*, **~льня** *f* [6; *g/pl.*: -лен] reading room; **~тель** *m* [4] reader; **~ть** [1], ⟨про-⟩ & ⟨проче́сть⟩ F [25; -чту́, -чтёшь; -чёл, -чла́; -чтённый] read, recite; give (*lecture* on о П), deliver, lecture; teach; **~ть по склада́м** spell.
чи́тка *f* [5; *g/pl.*: -ток] reading.
чих|а́ть [1], *once* ⟨~ну́ть⟩ [20] sneeze.
ЧК (Чрезвыча́йная коми́ссия ...) Cheka (*predecessor, 1917—22, of the* ГПУ, *cf.*).
член *m* [1] member; limb; *gr.* article; part; **~ора́здельный** [14; -лен, -льна] articulate; **~ский** [16] member(-ship)...; **~ство** *n* [9] membership.
чмо́к|ать F [1], *once* ⟨~нуть⟩ [20] smack.
чо́к|аться [1], *once* ⟨~нуться⟩ [20] touch (glasses T) (with с T).
чо́|порный [14; -рен, -рна] prim, prudish; **~рт** *s.* чёрт.
чрев|а́тый [14 *sh.*] pregnant (*a. fig.*); **~о** *n* [9] womb.
чрез *s.* че́рез; **~вычáйный** [14; -а́ен, -а́йна] extraordinary; extreme; special; **~ме́рный** [14; -рен, -рна] excessive.
чте́|ние *n* [12] reading; recital; **~ц** *m* [1 *e.*] reader.
чтить *s.* почита́ть[1].
что [23] **1.** *pron.* what (*a.* ~ за); that, which; how; (*a.* а ~?) why (so?); (*a.* а ~) what about; what's the matter; F а ~? well?; how (*or* as) much, how many; во́т ~ the following; listen; that's it; ~ до меня́ as for me; ~ вы (ты)! you don't say!, what next!; не́ за ~ (you are) welcome, *Brt.* don't mention it; ни за ~ not for the world; ну ~ же? what of that?; (уж) на ~ F however; с чего́? F why?, wherefore?; ~ и говори́ть F sure; *cf.* ни; F *s.* ~-нибудь, ~-то; **2.** *cj.* that; like, as if; ~ (ни) ..., то ... every ... (a)...
что́б(ы) (in order) that *or* to (*a.* с тем, ~); ~ не lest, for fear that; вме́сто того́ ~ + *inf.* instead of ...ing; скажи́ ему́, ~ он + *pt.* tell him to *inf.*
что́|-либо, ~-нибудь, ~-то [23] something; anything; ~-то *a.* F somewhat; somehow, for some reason or other.
чу́вств|енный [14 *sh.*] sensuous; sensual; material; **~и́тельность** *f* [8] sensibility; **~и́тельный** [14; -лен, -льна] sensitive; sentimental; sensible (*a.* = considerable, great, strong); biting (*cold*); grievous (*loss*); **~о** *n* [9] sense; feeling; sensation; F love; без ~ unconscious, senseless; **~овать** [7], ⟨по-⟩ feel (*a.* себя́ [T s. th.]); **-ся** be felt.
чугу́н *m* [1 *e.*] cast iron; **~ный** [14] cast-iron; **~олите́йный** [14]: ~олите́йный заво́д *m* iron foundry.
чуд|а́к *m* [1 *e.*] crank, character; **~а́чество** *n* [9] eccentricity; **~е́сный** [14; -сен, -сна] wonderful, marvel(l)ous; miraculous; **~и́ть** [15 *e.*] F *s.* дури́ть; **~иться** [15] F = мере́щиться; **~но́й** F [14; -дён, -дна́] queer, odd, strange; funny; **~ный** [14; -ден, -дна] wonderful, marvel(l)ous; **~о** *n* [9; *pl.*: чудеса́, -е́с, -еса́м] miracle, marvel; wonder; *a.* = ~но; **~о́вище** *n* [11] monster; **~о́вищный** [14; -щен, -щна] monstrous; **~отво́рец** *m* [1; -рца] wonderworker.
чуж|би́на *f* [5] foreign country (in на П; *a.* abroad); **~да́ться** [1] (Р) shun, avoid; **~дый** [14; чу́жд, -а́, -о] foreign; strange, alien; free (from Р); **~езе́мец** *m* [1; -мца] foreigner; **~о́й** [14] someone else's, alien; strange, foreign; *su. a.* stranger, outsider.
чул|а́н *m* [1] closet; pantry; **~о́к** *m* [1; -лка́; *g/pl.*: -ло́к] stocking.
чума́ *f* [5] plague, pestilence.
чума́зый F [14 *sh.*] dirty.
чурба́н *m* [1] block; blockhead.
чу́тк|ий [16; -ток, -тка́, -о; *comp.*: чу́тче] sensitive (to на В), keen; light (*sleep*); vigilant, watchful; wary; quick (of hearing); responsive; sympathetic; **~ость** *f* [8] keenness; delicacy (of feeling).
чу́точку F a bit.
чуть hardly, scarcely; a little; ~ не nearly, almost; ~ ли не F seem (-ingly); ~ что F on the least occasion; ~-~ *s.* ~; **~ё** *n* [10] instinct (for на В); scent, flair.
чу́чело *n* [9] stuffed animal *or* bird; scarecrow; ~ горо́ховое F dolt.
чушь F *f* [8] bosh, baloney.
чу́ять [27], ⟨по-⟩ scent, feel.

Ш

шаба́ш F **1.** *m* [1] (knocking-)off--time; **2.** *int.* enough!, no more!; **~ить** F [16], ⟨по-⟩ knock off.
шабло́н *m* [1] stencil, pattern, cliché; **~ный** [14] trite, hackneyed.
шаг *m* [1; *after 2, 3, 4*: -а́; в -у́; *pl. e.*] step (by step ~ за T) (*a. fig.*); pace (at T); stride; démarche; ни ˊу (да́льше) no step further; на ка́ждом ~у́ everywhere, on end; **~а́ть** [1], *once* ⟨~ну́ть⟩ [20] step, stride; march; walk; advance; (че́рез) cross; *pf. a.* take a step; далеко́ ~ну́ть *fig.* make great progress; **ˊом** at a slow pace, slowly.
ша́йба *f* [5] disk.
ша́йка *f* [5; *g/pl.*: ша́ек] gang.
шака́л *m* [1] jackal.
шала́ш *m* [1] hut; tent.
шал|и́ть [13] be naughty, frolic, romp; fool (about), play (pranks); be up to mischief; buck; **~и́шь!** P fiddlesticks!, on no account!; **~ов-ли́вый** [14 *sh.*] frolicsome, playful; **~опа́й** F *m* [3] good-for-nothing; **ˊость** *f* [8] prank; **~у́н** *m* [1 *e.*] naughty boy; **~у́нья** *f* [6; *g/pl.*: -ний] tomboy, madcap.
шаль *f* [8] shawl.
шально́й [14] mad, crazy; stray...
ша́мкать [1] mumble.
шампа́нское *n* [16] champagne.
шампу́нь *m* [4] shampoo.
шанс *m* [1] chance, prospect (of на B).
шанта́ж *m* [1], **~и́ровать** [7] blackmail.
ша́пка *f* [5; *g/pl.*: -пок] cap; heading.
шар *m* [1; *after 2, 3, 4*: -а́; *pl. e.*] sphere; ball; возду́шный ~ balloon; земно́й ~ globe.
шара́х|аться F [1], ⟨~нуться⟩ [20] rush (aside), recoil; shy; plop.
шарж *m* [1] cartoon, caricature.
ша́рик *m* [1] *dim. of* шар; corpuscle; **~овый** [14] ball (point *pen*); **~оподши́пник** *m* [1] ball bearing.
ша́рить [13], ⟨по-⟩ rummage.
ша́р|кать [1], *once* ⟨~кнуть⟩ [20] scrape; bow; **~ма́нка** *f* [5; *g/pl.*: -нок] hand organ.
шарни́р *m* [1] hinge, joint.
шаро|ва́ры *f/pl.* [5] baggy trousers; **~ви́дный** [14; -ден, -дна] **~обра́зный** [14; -зен, -зна] spherical, globular.
шарф *m* [1] scarf, neckerchief.
шасси́ *n* [*ind.*] chassis; ✈ undercarriage.
шат|а́ть [1], *once* ⟨(по)шатну́ть⟩ [20] (**-ся** be[come]) shake(n); rock; -ся *a.* stagger, reel, totter; F lounge *or* loaf, gad about.
шатёр *m* [1; -тра́] tent.
ша́т|кий [16; -ток, -тка] shaky, rickety, tottering; *fig.* unsteady, fickle; **~ну́ть(ся)** *s.* ~а́ть(ся).
ша́|фер *m* [1; *pl.*: -а́, *etc. e.*] best man; **~х** *m* [1] shah; check (*chess*).
шахмат|и́ст *m* [1] chess player; **ˈ~ный** [14] chess...; **ˈ~ы** *f/pl.* [5] chess (*play v/t.* в B).
ша́хт|а *f* [5] mine, pit; **~ёр** *m* [1] miner, pitman; **~ёрский** [16] miner's.
ша́шка *f* [5; *g/pl.*: -шек] saber, *Brt.* sabre; checker, draughtsman; *pl.* checkers, *Brt.* draughts.
швед *m* [1], **ˊка** *f* [5; *g/pl.*: -док] Swede; **ˊский** [16] Swedish.
шве́йный [14] sewing (*machine*).
швейца́р *m* [1] doorman, doorkeeper, porter; **~ец** *m* [1; -рца], **~ка** *f* [5; *g/pl.*: -рок] Swiss; **2ия** *f* [7] Switzerland; **~ский** [16] Swiss; doorman's, porter's.
Шве́ция *f* [7] Sweden.
швея́ *f* [6] seamstress.
швыр|я́ть [28], *once* ⟨~ну́ть⟩ [20] hurl, fling (*a.* T); squander.
шеве|ли́ть [13; -елю́, -е́ли́шь], ⟨по-⟩, *once* ⟨(по)~льну́ть⟩ [20] stir, move (*v/i.* **-ся**); turn (*hay*).
шеде́вр (-ˈdɛvr) *m* [1] masterpiece.
ше́йка *f* [5; *g/pl.*: ше́ек] neck.
ше́лест *m* [1], **~е́ть** [11] rustle.
шёлк *m* [1; *g/sg. a.* -у; в шелку́; *pl.*: шелка́, *etc. e.*] silk.
шелкови́|стый [14 *sh.*] silky; **~ца** *f* [5] mulberry (tree); **~чный** [14]: ~чный червь *m* silkworm.
шёлковый [14] silk(en).
шел|охну́ться [20] *pf.* stir; **~уха́** *f* [5], **~уши́ть** [16 *e.*; -шу́, -ши́шь] peel, husk; **ˊьма** F *f* [5] rascal, rogue.
шепеля́в|ить [14] lisp; **~ый** [14 *sh.*] lisping.
шёпот *m* [1] whisper (in a T).
шеп|та́ть [3], ⟨про-⟩, *once* ⟨~ну́ть⟩ [20] whisper (*v/i. a.* **-ся**).
шере́нга *f* [5] file, rank.
шероховáтый [14 *sh.*] rough.
шерст|ь *f* [8; *from g/pl. e.*] wool; coat; fleece; **~яно́й** [14] wool([l]en).
шерша́вый [14 *sh.*] rough; shaggy.
шест *m* [1 *e.*] pole.
ше́ств|ие *n* [12] procession; **~овать** [7] step, stride, go, walk.
шест|ёрка [5; *g/pl.*: -рок] six (*cf.* тро́йка); **~ерня́** ⊕ *f* [6; *g/pl.*: -рён] pinion; cogwheel; **ˊеро** [37] six (*cf.* дво́е); **~идеся́тый** [14] sixtieth; *cf.* пя́т(идеся́т)ый; **~име́сячный** [14] six-months(-old)'; **~исо́тый** [14] six hundredth; **~иуго́льник** *m* [1] hexagon; **~на́дцатый** [14] sixteenth; *cf.* пя́тый; **~на́дцать** [35] sixteen; *cf.* пять;

~óй [14] sixth; *cf.* пя́тый; **~ь** [35 *e.*] six; *cf.* пять; **~десят** [35] sixty; **~сóт** [36] six hundred; **∠ью** six times.
шеф *m* [1] chief, head, F boss; patron, sponsor; **∠ство** *n* [9] patronage, sponsorship.
шéя *f* [6; *g/pl.*: шей] neck; back.
ши́|бко P swiftly; very; **~ворот**: взять за ~ворот collar.
шик|áрный [14; -рен, -рна] chic, smart; **∠ать** F [1], *once* ⟨∠нуть⟩ [20] hiss.
ши́ло *n* [1; *pl.*: -лья, -льев] awl.
ши́на *f* [5] tire, *Brt.* tyre; ⚕ splint.
шинéль *f* [8] greatcoat, overcoat.
шинковáть [7] chop, shred.
шип *m* [1 *e.*] thorn; (dowel) pin.
шипé|ние *n* [12] hiss(ing); **~ть** [10], ⟨про-⟩ hiss; spit; whiz.
шипóвник *m* [1] dogrose.
шип|у́чий [17 *sh.*] sparkling, fizzy; **~я́щий** [17] sibilant.
шири|нá *f* [5] width, breadth; **~нóй** в (B) *or* ... в ~ну́ ... wide; **′~ть** [13], (-ся) widen, spread.
ши́рма *f* [5] (*mst pl.*) screen.
ширóк|ий [16; ширóк, -окá, -óкó; *comp.*: ши́ре] broad; wide; vast; (at) large; great; mass...; large-scale; *phon.* open; на ~ую нóгу in grand style; **~овещáтельный** [14] broadcasting; [-лен, -льна] promising; **~оплéчий** [17 *sh.*] broad-shouldered.
шир|отá *f* [5; *pl. st.*: -óты] breadth; *geogr.* latitude; **~потрéб** F *m* [1] consumers' goods; **~ь** *f* [8] breadth, width; open (space).
шить [шью, шьёшь; шéй(те)!; ши́тый], ⟨с-⟩ [сошью́, -ьёшь; сши́тый] sew (*pf. a.* together); embroider; have made; **~ё** *n* [10] sewing; embroidery.
шифр *m* [1] cipher, code; pressmark; **~овáть** [7], ⟨за-⟩ cipher, code.
шиш F *m* [1 *e.*] fig; **∠ка** *f* [5; *g/pl.*: -шек] bump, lump; ♣ cone; knot; F bigwig.
шка|лá *f* [5; *pl. st.*] scale; **~ту́лка** *f* [5; *g/pl.*: -лок] casket; **~ф** *m* [1; в -у́; *pl. e.*] cupboard; wardrobe; (*book*)case; несгорáемый ~ф safe.
шквал *m* [1] squall, gust.
шкив ⊕ *m* [1] pulley.
шкóл|а *f* [5] school (*go* to в B; *be* at, in в П); вы́сшая ~а academy; university; **~ьник** *m* [1] schoolboy; **~ьница** *f* [5] schoolgirl; **~ьный** [14] school...
шку́р|а *f* [5] skin (*a.* **~ка** *f* [5; *g/pl.*: -рок]), hide; **~ник** F *m* [1] self-seeker.
шлагбáум *m* [1] barrier, turnpike.
шлак *m* [1] slag, scoria; cinder.
шланг *m* [1] hose.
шлем *m* [1] helmet.
шлёп F crack!; **~ать** [1], *once* ⟨~нуть⟩ [20] slap; shuffle; plump (*v/i.* F -ся; plop).
шлифовáть [7], ⟨от-⟩ grind; polish.
шлю|з *m* [1] sluice, lock; **∠пка** *f* [5; *g/pl.*: -пок] boat; launch.
шля́п|а *f* [5] hat; F milksop; **~ка** *f* [5; *g/pl.*: -пок] *dim. of.* ~а; (*lady's*) hat; head (*nail*); **~очник** *m* [1] hatter; **~ный** [14] hat...; hatter's; milliner's.
шля́ться P [1] *s.* шатáться.
шмель *m* [4 *e.*] bumblebee.
шмыг quick!; **∠ать** F [1], *once* ⟨~ну́ть⟩ [20] whisk, scurry, slip.
шни́цель *m* [4] cutlet.
шнур *m* [1 *e.*] cord; **~овáть** [7], ⟨за-⟩ lace (*or* tie) up; **~óк** *m* [1; -ркá] shoestring, (shoe) lace.
шныря́ть F [28] poke about.
шов *m* [1; шва] seam; ⊕ *a.* joint.
шоколáд *m* [1] chocolate.
шóмпол *m* [1; *pl.*: -á, *etc. e.*] ramrod.
шóпот *m* [1] *s.* шёпот.
шóрник *m* [1] saddler.
шóрох *m* [1] rustle.
шоссé (-'sɛ) *n* [*ind.*] high road.
шотлáнд|ец *m* [1; -дца] Scotchman, *pl.* the Scotch; **~ка** *f* [5; *g/pl.*: -док] Scotchwoman; **♀ия** *f* [7] Scotland; **~ский** [16] Scotch, Scottish.
шофёр *m* [1] driver, chauffeur.
шпáга *f* [5] sword.
шпагáт *m* [1] packthread, string.
шпáл|а 🚂 *f* [5] cross tie, *Brt.* sleeper; **~éра** *f* [5] trellis; lane.
шпа|ргáлка F *f* [5; *g/pl.*: -лок] pony, *Brt.* crib; **~т** *m* [1] *min.* spar.
шпиговáть [7], ⟨на-⟩ lard.
шпик *m* [1] slab bacon, fat; F sleuth.
шпи́|лька *f* [5; *g/pl.*: -лек] hairpin; hat pin; tack; *fig.* taunt, twit (*vb.*: пусти́ть B); **~нáт** *m* [1] spinach.
шпиóн *m* [1], **~ка** *f* [5; *g/pl.*: -нок] spy; **~áж** *m* [1] espionage; **~ить** [13] spy.
шпиц *m* [1] Pomeranian (*dog*).
шпóр|а *f* [5], **~ить** [13] spur.
шприц *m* [1] syringe, squirt.
шпрот *m* [1] sprat, brisling.
шпу́лька *f* [5; *g/pl.*: -лек] spool, bobbin.
шрам *m* [1] scar.
шрифт *m* [1] type, print.
штаб ⚔ *m* [1] staff; headquarters.
штáбель *m* [4; *pl.*: -ля́, *etc. e.*] pile.
штабнóй ⚔ [14] staff...
штамп *m* [1], **~овáть** [7], ⟨от-⟩ stamp.
штáнга *f* [5] ⊕ pole; *sport*: weight.
штаны́ F *m/pl.* [1 *e.*] pants, trousers.
штат *m* [1] state; staff; *cf.* США; **~и́в** *m* [1] support; *phot.* tripod; **∠ный** [14] (on the) staff; **∠ский** [16] civil; civilian; plain (*clothes*).
штемпел|евáть (ʃtɛ-) [6], **′~ь** *m* [4; *pl.*: -ля́, *etc. e.*] stamp; postmark.
штéпсель ('ʃtɛ-) *m* [4; *pl.*: -ля́, *etc. e.*] plug; jack.

шти|ль *m* [4] calm; **~фт** *m* [1 *e.*] pin.
што́п|ать [1], ⟨за-⟩ darn; **~ка** *f* [5] darning.
што́пор *m* [1] corkscrew; ✈ spin.
што́|ра *f* [5] blind; curtain; **~рм** *m* [1] storm; **~ф** *m* [1] quart, bottle; damask.
штраф *m* [1] fine, penalty, mulct; **~но́й** [14] fine...; penalty...; convict...; **~ова́ть** [7], ⟨о-⟩ fine.
штрейкбре́хер *m* [1] strikebreaker.
штрих *m* [1 *e.*] stroke; trait; touch; **~ова́ть** [7], ⟨за-⟩ hatch; shade.
штуди́ровать [7], ⟨про-⟩ study.
шту́ка *f* [5] piece; F thing; fish; trick; story; business; point.
штукату́р|ить [13], ⟨о-⟩, **~ка** *f* [5] plaster.
штурва́л *m* [1] steering wheel.
штурм *m* [1] storm, onslaught; **∠ан** *m* [1] navigator; **~ова́ть** [7] storm, assail; **~ови́к** *m* [1 *e.*] battleplane.
шту́чный [14] (by the) piece.
штык *m* [1 *e.*] bayonet.
шу́ба *f* [5] fur (coat).
шу́лер *m* [1; *pl.*: -á, *etc. e.*] sharper.
шум *m* [1] noise; din; rush; bustle; buzz; F hubbub, row, ado; ~ и гам hullabaloo; наде́лать ∠у cause a sensation; **~е́ть** [10 *e.*; шумлю́, шуми́шь] make a noise; rustle; rush; roar; bustle; buzz; **~и́ха** F *f* [5] sensation, clamo(u)r; **~ли́вый** [14 *sh.*] clamorous; **∠ный** [14; -мен, -мна́, -о] noisy, loud; sensational; **~ово́й** [14] noise...; jazz...; **~о́к** *m* [1; -мка́]: под ~о́к F on the sly.
Шу́ра *m/f* [5] *dim. of* Алекса́ндр(а).
шу́р|ин *m* [1] brother-in-law (*wife's brother*); **~ша́ть** [4 *e.*; -шу́, ши́шь], ⟨за-⟩ rustle.
шу́стрый F [14; -тёр, -тра́, -о] nimble.
шут *m* [1 *e.*] fool, jester, clown, buffoon; F deuce; **~и́ть** [15], ⟨по-⟩ joke, jest; make fun (of над Т); **∠ка** *f* [5; *g/pl.*: -ток] joke, jest (in в В); fun (for ра́ди Р); trick (*play:* on с Т); F trifle (it's no ∠ка ли); кро́ме ∠ок joking apart; are you in earnest?; не на ∠ку serious(ly); (Д) не до ∠ок be in no laughing mood; **~ли́вый** F [14 *sh.*] jocose, playful; **~ни́к** *m* [1 *e.*] joker, wag; **∠очный** [14] jocose, sportive, comic; laughing (*matter*); **~я́** jokingly (не in earnest).
шушу́кать(ся) F [1] whisper.
шху́на *f* [5] schooner.
ш-ш hush!

Щ

щаве́ль *m* [4 *e.*] ⚘ sorrel.
щади́ть [15 *e.*; щажу́, щади́шь], ⟨по-⟩ [-щажённый], spare.
ще́бень *m* [4; -бня] road metal.
щебета́ть [3] chirp, twitter.
щего́л *m* [1; -гла́] goldfinch; **~ева́тый** [14 *sh.*] stylish, smart; **'~ь** ('ʃtʃɔ-) *m* [4] dandy, fop; **~ьско́й** [16] foppish; **~я́ть** [28] flaunt, parade.
ще́др|ость *f* [8] liberality; **~ый** [14; щедр, -á, -о] liberal, generous.
щека́ *f* [5; *ac/sg.*: щёку; *pl.*: щёки, щёк, щека́м, *etc. e.*] cheek.
щеко́лда *f* [5] latch.
щекот|а́ть [3], ⟨по-⟩, **∠ка** *f* [5] tickle; **~ли́вый** [14 *sh.*] ticklish.
щёлк|ать [1], *once* ⟨~нуть⟩ [20] **1.** *v/i.* click (*one's tongue* T), snap (*one's fingers* T), crack (*whip* T); chatter (*one's teeth* T); warble, sing (*birds*); **2.** *v/t.* fillip (on по Д); crack (*nuts*).
щёло|к *m* [1] lye; **~чь** *f* [8; *from g/pl. e.*] alkali; **~чно́й** [14] alkaline.
щелчо́к *m* [1; -чка́] fillip; crack.
щель *f* [8; *from g/pl. e.*] chink, crack, crevice; slit; голосова́я ~ glottis.
щеми́ть [14 *e.*; *3rd. p., a. impers.*] press; *fig.* oppress.
щено́к *m* [1; -нка́; *pl.*: -нки́ & (2) -ня́та] puppy, whelp.
щеп|ети́льный [14; -лен, -льна] scrupulous, punctilious, squeamish, fancy...; **∠ка** *f* [5; *g/pl.*: -пок] chip; *fig.* lath
щепо́тка *f* [5; *g/pl.*: -ток] pinch.
щети́н|а *f* [5] bristle(s); **~истый** [14 *sh.*] bristly; **~иться** [13], ⟨о-⟩ bristle up.
щётка *f* [5; *g/pl.*: -ток] brush.
щи *f/pl.* [5; *gen.*: щей] cabbage soup.
щи́колотка *f* [5; *g/pl.*: -ток] ankle.
щип|а́ть [2], *once* ⟨(у)~ну́ть⟩ [20] pinch, tweak (*v/t.* за В), (*a. cold*) nip; bite; twitch; pluck; browse; **~цы́** *m/pl.* [1 *e.*] tongs, pliers, pincers, nippers; ⚕ forceps; (nut)crackers; **∠чики** *m/pl.* [1] tweezers.
щит *m* [1 *e.*] shield; buckler; screen, guard, protection; (snow)shed; (⚡ switch)board; sluice gate; (tortoise) shell.
щитови́дный [14] thyroid (*gland*).
щу́ка *f* [5] pike (*fish*).
щу́п|альце *n* [11; *g/pl.*: -лец] feeler, tentacle; **~ать** [1], ⟨по-⟩ feel; touch; *fig.* sound; **~лый** F [14; щупл, -á, -о] puny.
щу́рить [13] screw up (one's eyes -ся).

Э

эвакуи́ровать [7] (*im*)*pf.* evacuate.
эволюцио́нный [14] evolution(ary).
эгои́|зм *m* [1] ego(t)ism, selfishness; **~ст** *m* [1], **~стка** *f* [5; *g/pl.*: -ток] egoist; **~сти́ческий** [16], **~сти́чный** [14; -чен, -чна] selfish.
Эдинбу́рг *m* [1] Edinburgh.
эй! halloo!, hullo!, hey!
эквивале́нт *m* [1], **~ный** [14; -тен, -тна] equivalent.
экза́м|ен *m* [1] examination (in ... на П; ... in по Д); **~ена́тор** *m* [1] examiner; **~енова́ть** [7], ⟨про-⟩ examine; **-ся** be examined (by у Р), have one's examination (with); *p. pr. p.* examinee.
экземпля́р *m* [1] copy; specimen.
экзоти́ческий [16] exotic.
э́кий F [16; *sh.*: *no m*, -а] what (a).
экип|а́ж *m* [1] carriage; ⚓, ✈ crew; **~ирова́ть** [7] (*im*)*pf.* fit out, equip.
эконо́м|ика *f* [5] economy; economics; **~ить** [14], ⟨с-⟩ save; economize; **~и́ческий** [16] economic; **~ия** *f* [7] economy; saving (of P, в П); **~ный** [14; -мен, -мна] economical, thrifty.
экра́н *m* [1] screen.
экскава́тор *m* [1] dredge(r *Brt.*).
экскурс|а́нт *m* [1] excursionist; **~ия** *f* [7] excursion, outing, trip; **~ово́д** *m* [1] guide.
экспеди́|тор *m* [1] forwarding agent(s); **~цио́нный** [14] forwarding...; expedition...; **~ция** *f* [7] dispatch (office); forwarding agency; expedition.
экспер|имента́льный [14] experimental; **~т** *m* [1] expert (in по Д); **~ти́за** *f* [5] examination; (expert) opinion.
эксплуа|та́тор *m* [1] exploiter; **~та́ция** *f* [7] exploitation; ⊕ operation; **~ти́ровать** [7] exploit; sweat; ⊕ operate, run.
экспон|а́т *m* [1] exhibit; **~и́ровать** [7] (*im*)*pf.* exhibit; *phot.* expose.
э́кспорт *m* [1], **~и́ровать** [7] (*im*)*pf.* export; **~ный** [14] export...
экс|про́мт *m* [1] impromptu; **~про́мтом** *a.* extempore; **~та́з** *m* [1] ecstasy; **~тра́кт** *m* [1] extract; **~тренный** [14 *sh.*] special; extra; urgent; **~центри́чный** [14; -чен, -чна] eccentric.
эласти́чн|ость *f* [8] elasticity; **~ый** [14; -чен, -чна] elastic.
элега́нтн|ость *f* [8] elegance; **~ый** [14; -тен, -тна] elegant, stylish.
эле́ктр|ик *m* [1] electrician; **~ифици́ровать** [7] (*im*)*pf.* electrify; **~и́ческий** [16] electric(al); **~и́чество** *n* [9] electricity; **~ово́з** *m* [1] electric locomotive; **~о́д** *m* [1] electrode; **~омонтёр** *s.* **~ик**; **~о́н** *m* [1], electron; **~оста́нция** *f* [7] power station; **~оте́хник** *m* [1] electrical engineer; **~оте́хника** *f* [5] electrical engineering.
элеме́нт *m* [1] element; **~а́рный** [14; -рен, -рна] elementary.
эма́л|евый [14], **~ирова́ть** [7], **~ь** *f* [8] enamel.
эмбле́ма *f* [5] emblem.
эмигр|а́нт *m* [1], **~а́нтка** *f* [5; *g/pl.*: -ток], **~а́нтский** [16] emigrant; emigre; **~и́ровать** [7] (*im*)*pf.* emigrate.
эмоциона́льный [14; -лен, -льна] emotional.
эмпири́зм *m* [1] empiricism.
энерг|и́чный [14; -чен, -чна] energetic; drastic; **~ия** *f* [7] energy.
энтузиа́зм *m* [1] enthusiasm.
энциклопе́д|ия *f* [7] (*a.* **~и́ческий слова́рь** *m*) encyclop(a)edia.
эпи|гра́мма *f* [5] epigram; **~деми́ческий** [16], **~де́мия** *f* [7] epidemic; **~зо́д** *m* [1] episode; **~ле́псия** *f* [7] epilepsy; **~ло́г** *m* [1] epilogue; **~тет** *m* [1] epithet.
э́по|с *m* [1] epic (poem), epos; **~ха** *f* [5] epoch, era, period (in в В).
эроти́ческий [16] erotic.
эска́др|а *f* [5] ⚓ spuadron; **~и́лья** *f* [6; *g/pl.*: -лий] ✈ squadron.
эс|кала́тор *m* [1] escalator; **~ки́з** *m* [1] sketch; **~кимо́с** *m* [1] Eskimo; **~корти́ровать** [7] escort; **~ми́нец** *m* [1; -нца] ⚓ destroyer; **~се́нция** *f* [7] essence; **~тафе́та** *f* [5] relay race; **~тети́ческий** [16] aesthetic.
эсто́н|ец *m* [1; -нца], **~ка** *f* [5; *g/pl.*: -нок], **~ский** [16] Estonian.
эстра́да *f* [5] platform; *s.* варьете́.
эта́ж *m* [1 *e.*] floor, stor(e)y; дом в три **~а́** three-storied (*Brt.* -reyed) house; **~е́рка** *f* [5; *g/pl.*: -рок] whatnot; bookshelf.
э́так(ий) F *s.* так(о́й).
эта́п *m* [1] stage; base; transport(s).
э́тика *f* [5] ethics (*a. pl.*).
этике́тка *f* [5; *g/pl.*: -ток] label.
этимоло́гия *f* [7] etymology.
этногра́фия *f* [7] ethnography.
э́т|от *m*, **~а** *f*, **~о** *n*, **~и** *pl.* [27] this, *pl.* these; *su.* this one; that; it; there (-*in*, *etc.*); **~о** *a.* well, then, as a matter of fact.
этю́д *m* [1] study, étude; sketch.
эф|е́с *m* [1] (*sword*) hilt; **~и́р** *m* [1] ether; **~и́рный** [14; -рен, -рна] ethereal.
эффект|и́вность *f* [8] efficacy; **~и́вный** [14; -вен, -вна] efficacious; **~ный** [14; -тен, -тна] effective.
эх ah!
эшафо́т *m* [1] scaffold.
эшело́н *m* [1] echelon; troop train.

Ю

юбил|е́й *m* [3] jubilee; **~е́йный** [14] jubilee...; **~я́р** *m* [1] p. celebrating his jubilee.
ю́бка *f* [5; *g/pl.*: ю́бок] skirt.
ювели́р *m* [1] jeweller(' **~ный** [14]).
юг *m* [1] south; éхать на ~ travel south; *cf.* восто́к; **~о-восто́к** *m* [1] southeast; **~о-восто́чный** [14] southeast ...; **~о-за́пад** *m* [1] southwest; **~о-за́падный** [14] southwest ...; **2осла́вия** *f* [7] Yugoslavia.
югу́рт *m* [1] yogurt.
Южно-Африка́нский Сою́з *m* [16/1] Union of South Africa.
ю́жный [14] south(ern); southerly.
юла́ *f* [5] humming top; F fidgety p.
ю́мор *m* [1] humo(u)r; **~исти́ческий** [16] humorous; comic.
ю́нга *m* [5] cabin boy.
ю́ность *f* [8] youth (*age*).
ю́нош|а *m* [5; *g/pl.*: -шей] youth (*young man*); **~ество** *n* [9] youth.
ю́ный [14; юн, -á, -o] young, youthful.
юри|ди́ческий [16] juridical; of law; **~ско́нсульт** *m* [1] legal adviser.
'**Ю́рий** *m* [3] George.
юри́ст *m* [1] lawyer; F law student.
ю́рк|ий [16; ю́рок, юрка́, -o] nimble, quick; **~ну́ть** [20] *pf.* vanish (quickly).
юр|о́дивый [14] fool(ish) „in Christ"; **∠та** *f* [5] nomad's tent.
юсти́ция *f* [7] justice.
юти́ться [15 *e.*; ючу́сь, юти́шься] nestle; be cooped.
юфть *f* [8] Russia leather.

Я

я [20] I; э́то я it's me.
я́бед|а F *f* [5] slander, talebearing; **~ник** *m* [1] slanderer, informer; **~ничать** [1] slander (*v/t.* на В).
я́бло|ко *n* [9; *pl.*: -ки, -к] apple; (*eye*)ball; **~ня** *f* [6] apple tree.
яв|и́ть(ся) *s.* **~ля́ть(ся)**; **∠ка** *f* [5] appearance; presence, attendance; submission, presentation; place of secret meeting; **~ле́ние** *n* [12] phenomenon; occurrence, event; *thea.* scene; appearance, apparition; **~ля́ть** [28], ⟨**~и́ть**⟩ [14] present, submit; do; show; **-ся** appear, turn up; come; (T) be; **∠ный** [14; я́вен, я́вна] open; obvious, evident; avowed; **∠ствовать** [7] follow.
ягнёнок *m* [2] lamb.
я́год|а *f* [5], **~ный** [14] berry.
я́годица *f* [5] buttock.
яд *m* [1] poison; *fig. a.* venom.
я́дерный [14] nuclear.
ядови́тый [14 *sh.*] poisonous; venomous.
ядр|ёный F [14 *sh.*] strong, stalwart, solid; pithy; fresh; **~о́** *n* [9; *pl. st.*; *g/pl.*: я́дер] kernel; *phys.*, ⚘ nucleus; cannon ball; *fig.* core, pith.
я́зв|а *f* [5] ulcer; plague; wound; **~и́тельный** [14; -лен, -льна] venomous; caustic.
язы́к *m* [1 *e.*] tongue; language (in на П); speech; на ру́сском **~е́** *speak* (*text, etc.* in) Russian; держа́ть ~ за зуба́ми hold one's tongue; **~ове́д** *m* [1] linguist; **~ово́й** [14] language...; **~о́вый** [14] tongue...; **~озна́ние** *n* [12] linguistics.
язы́ч|еский [16] pagan; **~ество** *n* [9] paganism; **~ник** *m* [1] pagan.
язычо́к *m* [1; -чка́] uvula; tongue.
яи́чн|ица (-ʃn-) *f* [5] (scrambled *or* fried) eggs *pl.*; **~ый** [14] egg...
яйцо́ *n* [9; *pl.*: я́йца, яи́ц, я́йцам] egg.
я́кобы allegedly; as it were.
'**Я́ков** *m* [1] Jakob.
я́кор|ь *m* [4; *pl.*: -ря́, *etc. e.*] anchor (at на П); стоя́ть на **~е** anchor.
я́лик *m* [1] jolly boat.
я́м|а *f* [5] hole, pit; F dungeon; **~(оч)ка** *f* [5; *g/pl.*: я́мо(че)к] dimple.
ямщи́к *m* [1 *e.*] coachman, driver.
янва́рь *m* [4 *e.*] January.
янта́рь *m* [4 *e.*] amber.
япо́н|ец *m* [1; -нца], **~ка** *f* [5; *g/pl.*: -нок], **~ский** [16] Japanese; **2ия** *f* [7] Japan.
я́ркий [16; я́рок, ярка́, -o; *comp.*: я́рче] bright; glaring; vivid, rich (*colo*[*u*]*r*); blazing; *fig.* striking, outstanding.
яр|лы́к *m* [1 *e.*] label; **∠марка** *f* [5; *g/pl.*: -рок] fair (at на П).
ярмо́ *n* [9; *pl.*: я́рма, *etc. st.*] yoke.
яров́ой [14] summer, spring (*crops*).
я́рост|ный [14; -тен, -тна] furious, fierce; **~ь** *f* [8] fury, rage.
я́рус *m* [1] circle (*thea.*); layer.
я́рый [14 *sh.*] fierce, violent; ardent.
я́сень *m* [4] ash (*tree*).
я́сли *m/pl.* [4; *gen.*: я́слей] crib, manger; day nursery, *Brt.* crèche.
ясн|ови́дец *m* [1; -дца] clairvoyant; **∠ость** *f* [8] clarity; **∠ый** [14; я́сен, ясна́, -o] clear; bright; fine; limpid; distinct; evident; plain (*answer*).
я́стреб *m* [1; *pl.*: -бá & -бы] hawk.
я́хта *f* [5] yacht.
яче́|йка *f* [5; *g/pl.*: -éек], **~я́** *f* [6; *g/pl.*: ячéй] cell; mesh.
ячме́нь *m* [4 *e.*] barley; ⚕ sty.
'**Я́ш(к)а** *m* [5] *dim.* of 'Я́ков.
я́щерица *f* [5] lizard.
я́щик *m* [1] box, case, chest; drawer; откла́дывать в до́лгий ~ shelve; *cf.* для.

PART TWO

ENGLISH-RUSSIAN VOCABULARY

A

a [ei, ə] неопределённый артикль; как правило, не переводится; ~ table стол; 10 roubles a dozen десять рублей дюжина.
A 1 [ei'wʌn] **1.** F первоклассный; **2.** прекрасно.
aback [ə'bæk] *adv.* назад.
abandon [ə'bændən] отказываться [-заться] от (P); оставлять [-авить], покидать [-инуть]; **~ed** покинутый; распутный; **~ment** [-mənt] оставление.
abase [ə'beis] унижать [унизить]; **~ment** [-mənt] унижение.
abash [ə'bæʃ] смущать [смутить]; **~ment** [-mənt] смущение.
abate [ə'beit] *v/t.* уменьшать [-еньшить]; *v/i.* утихать [утихнуть] (о буре и т. п.); **~ment** [-mənt] уменьшение; скидка.
abattoir ['æbətwa:] скотобойня.
abb|ess ['æbis] настоятельница монастыря; **~ey** ['æbi] монастырь *m*; **~ot** ['æbət] аббат, настоятель *m*.
abbreviat|e [ə'bri:vieit] сокращать [-ратить]; **~ion** [əbri:vi'eiʃən] сокращение.
abdicat|e ['æbdikeit] отрекаться от престола; отказываться [-заться] от (P); **~ion** [æbdi'keiʃən] отречение от престола.
abdomen [æb'doumen] живот; брюшная полость *f.*
abduct [æb'dʌkt] похищать [-итить] (женщину).
aberration [æbə'reiʃən] заблуждение; *ast.* аберрация.
abet [ə'bet] *v/t.* подстрекать [-кнуть]; [по]содействовать (дурному); **~tor** [-ə] подстрекатель (-ница *f*) *m*.
abeyance [ə'beiəns] состояние неизвестности; in ~ без владельца; временно отменённый (закон).
abhor [əb'hɔ:] ненавидеть; **~rence** [əb'hɔrəns] отвращение; **~rent** [-ənt] □ отвратительный.
abide [ə'baid] [*irr.*] *v/i.* пребывать; ~ by твёрдо держаться (P); *v/t.* not ~ не терпеть.
ability [ə'biliti] способность *f.*
abject ['æbdʒekt] □ презренный, жалкий.
abjure [əb'dʒuə] отрекаться [-ечься] от (P).
able ['eibl] □ способный; be ~ мочь, быть в состоянии; **~-bodied** ['bɔdid] здоровый; годный.
abnegat|e ['æbnigeit] отказывать [-зать] себе в (П); отрицать; **~ion** [æbni'geiʃən] отрицание; (само-) отречение.
abnormal [æb'nɔ:məl] □ ненормальный.
aboard [ə'bɔ:d] ⚓ на корабль, на корабле.
abode [ə'boud] **1.** *pt.* от abide; **2.** местопребывание; жилище.
aboli|sh [ə'bɔliʃ] отменять [-нить]; упразднять [-нить]; **~tion** [æbo'liʃən] отмена.
abomina|ble [ə'bɔminəbl] □ отвратительный; **~te** [-neit] *v/t.* питать отвращение к (Д); **~tion** [əbɔmi'neiʃən] отвращение.
aboriginal [æbə'ridʒənəl] **1.** туземный; **2.** туземец.
abortion [ə'bɔ:ʃən] выкидыш, аборт.
abound [ə'baund] изобиловать (in (T).)
about [ə'baut] **1.** *prp.* вокруг (P); около (P); о (П), об (П), обо (П), насчёт (P); у (P); про (B); I had no money ~ me у меня не было с собой денег; **2.** *adv.* вокруг, везде; приблизительно; be ~ to do собираться делать.
above [ə'bʌv] **1.** *prp.* над (T); выше (P); свыше (P); ~ all главным образом; **2.** *adv.* наверху, наверх; выше; **3.** *adj.* вышесказанный.
abreast [ə'brest] в ряд.
abridg|e [ə'bridʒ] сокращать [-ратить]; **~(e)ment** [-mənt] сокращение.
abroad [ə'brɔ:d] за границей, за границу; there is a report ~ ходит слух.
abrogate ['æbrogeit] *v/t.* отменять [-нить]; аннулировать (*im*)*pf.*
abrupt [ə'brʌpt] □ обрывистый; внезапный; резкий.
abscond [əb'skɔnd] *v/i.* скры(ва)ться.
absence ['æbsns] отсутствие; отлучка; ~ of mind рассеянность *f.*
absent **1.** ['æbsnt] □ отсутствующий; **2.** [æb'sent] ~ o. s. отлучаться [-читься]; **~-minded** □ рассеянный.
absolut|e ['æbsəlu:t] □ абсолютный; беспримерный; **~ion** [æbsə'lu:ʃən] отпущение грехов.
absolve [əb'zɔlv] прощать [простить]; освобождать [-бодить] (from от P).
absorb [əb'sɔ:b] впитывать [впитать]; абсорбировать (*im*)*pf.*
absorption [əb'sɔ:pʃən] всасывание, впитывание; *fig.* погружённость *f* (в думы).
abstain [əbs'tein] воздерживаться [-жаться] (from от P).

abstemious [əbs'ti:miəs] □ возде́ржанный, уме́ренный.
abstention [æbs'tenʃən] воздержа́ние.
abstinen|ce ['æbstinəns] уме́ренность *f*; тре́звость *f*; **~t** [-nənt] □ уме́ренный, возде́ржанный; непью́щий.
abstract 1. ['æbstrækt] □ отвлечённый, абстра́ктный; **2.** конспе́кт; извлече́ние; *gr.* отвлечённое и́мя существи́тельное **3.** [æbs'trækt] отвлека́ть [-е́чь]; резюми́ровать (*im*)*pf.*; **~ed** [-id] □ отвлечённый; **~ion** [-kʃən] абстра́кция.
abstruse [æbs'tru:s] □ *fig.* непоня́тный, тёмный.
abundan|ce [ə'bʌndəns] избы́ток, изоби́лие; **~t** [-dənt] □ оби́льный, бога́тый.
abus|e 1. [ə'bju:s] злоупотребле́ние; оскорбле́ние; брань *f*; **2.** [ə'bju:z] злоупотребля́ть [-би́ть] (Т); [вы́]руга́ть; **~ive** [ə'bju:siv] □ оскорби́тельный.
abut [ə'bʌt] грани́чить (upon с Т).
abyss [ə'bis] бе́здна.
academic|(al □) [ækə'demik(əl)] академи́ческий; **~ian** [əkædə'miʃən] акаде́мик.
accede [æk'si:d]: **~** to вступа́ть [-пи́ть] в (В).
accelerat|e [æk'seləreit] ускоря́ть [-о́рить]; **~or** [æk'seləreitə] ускори́тель *m.*
accent 1. ['æksənt] ударе́ние; произноше́ние, акце́нт; **2.** [æk'sent] *v/t.* де́лать и́ли ста́вить ударе́ние на (П); **~uate** [æk'sentjueit] де́лать и́ли ста́вить ударе́ние на (П); *fig.* подчёркивать [-черкну́ть].
accept [ək'sept] принима́ть [-ня́ть]; соглаша́ться [-гласи́ться] с (Т); **~able** [ək'septəbl] □ прие́млемый; прия́тный; **~ance** [ək'septəns] приём, приня́тие; † акце́пт.
access ['ækses] до́ступ; прохо́д; ⚕ при́ступ; easy of **~** досту́пный; **~ary** [æk'sesəri] соуча́стник (-ица); **~ible** [æk'sesəbl] □ досту́пный, достижи́мый; **~ion** [æk'seʃən] вступле́ние (to в В); до́ступ (to к Д); **~** to the throne вступле́ние на престо́л.
accessory [æk'sesəri] □ **1.** доба́вочный, второстепе́нный; **2.** *pl.* принадле́жности *f/pl.*
accident ['æksidənt] случа́йность *f*; катастро́фа, ава́рия; **~al** [æksi'dentl] □ случа́йный.
acclaim [ə'kleim] шу́мно приве́тствовать (В); аплоди́ровать (Д).
acclamation [æklə'meiʃən] шу́мное одобре́ние.
acclimatize [ə'klaimətaiz] акклиматизи́ровать(ся) (*im*)*pf*.
acclivity [ə'kliviti] подъём (доро́ги).
accommodat|e [ə'kɔmədeit] приспособля́ть [-посо́бить]; дава́ть жильё (Д); **~ion** [əkɔmə'deiʃən] прию́т; помеще́ние.
accompan|iment [ə'kʌmpənimənt] аккомпанеме́нт; сопровожде́ние; **~y** [-pəni] *v/t.* аккомпани́ровать (Д); сопровожда́ть [-води́ть].
accomplice [ə'kɔmplis] соуча́стник (-ица).
accomplish [-pliʃ] выполня́ть [вы́полнить]; достига́ть [-и́гнуть] (Р); **~ment** [-mənt] выполне́ние; достиже́ние; **~s** *pl.* образо́ванность *f.*
accord [ə'kɔ:d] **1.** соглаше́ние; гармо́ния; with one **~** единоду́шно; **2.** *v/i.* согласо́вываться [-сова́ться] (с Т); гармони́ровать (с Т); *v/t.* предоставля́ть [-ста́вить]; **~ance** [-əns] согла́сие; **~ant** [-ənt] □ согла́сный (с Т); **~ing** [-iŋ]: **~** to согла́сно (Д); **~ingly** [-iŋli] *adv.* соотве́тственно; таки́м о́бразом.
accost [ə'kɔst] загова́ривать [-вори́ть] с (Т).
account [ə'kaunt] **1.** счёт; отчёт; of no **~** незначи́тельный; on no **~** ни в ко́ем слу́чае; on **~** of из-за (Р); take into **~**, take **~** of принима́ть во внима́ние; turn to **~** испо́льзовать (*im*)*pf.*; call to **~** призыва́ть к отве́ту; make **~** of придава́ть значе́ние (Д); **2.** *v/i.* **~** for отвеча́ть [-е́тить] за (В); объясня́ть [-ни́ть]; be much **~ed** of име́ть хоро́шую репута́цию; *v/t.* счита́ть [счесть] (В/Т); **~able** [ə'kauntəbl] □ объясни́мый; **~ant** [-ənt] счетово́д; (chartered, *Am.* certified public **~** прися́жный) бухга́лтер; **~ing** [-iŋ] отчётность *f*; учёт.
accredit [ə'kredit] аккредитова́ть (*im*)*pf.*; припи́сывать [-са́ть].
accrue [ə'kru:] накопля́ться [-пи́ться]; происходи́ть [произойти́] (from из Р).
accumulat|e [ə'kju:mjuleit] нака́пливать(ся) [-копи́ть(ся)]; скопля́ть(ся) [-пи́ть(ся)]; **~ion** [əkju:mju'leiʃən] накопле́ние; скопле́ние.
accura|cy ['ækjurəsi] то́чность *f*; тща́тельность *f*; **~te** [-rit] □ то́чный; тща́тельный.
accurs|ed [ə'kə:sid], **~t** [-st] прокля́тый.
accus|ation [ækju'zeiʃən] обвине́ние; **~e** [ə'kju:z] *v/t.* обвиня́ть [-ни́ть]; **~er** [-ə] обвини́тель(ница *f*) *m.*
accustom [ə'kʌstəm] приуча́ть [-чи́ть] (to к Д); get **~ed** привыка́ть [-вы́кнуть] [to к Д); **~ed** [-d] привы́чный; приу́ченный.
ace [eis] туз; *fig.* первокла́ссный лётчик.
acerbity [ə'sə:biti] те́рпкость *f.*
acet|ic [ə'si:tik] у́ксусный; **~ify** [ə'setifai] окисля́ть(ся) [-ли́ть(ся)].

ache [eik] **1.** боль *f*; **2.** *v/i.* болéть (о чáсти тéла).
achieve [ə'tʃi:v] достигáть [-и́гнуть] (Р); **~ment** [-mənt] достижéние.
acid ['æsid] ки́слый; éдкий; **~ity** [ə'siditi] кислотá; éдкость *f*.
acknowledg|e [ək'nɔlidʒ] *v/t.* подтверждáть [-ерди́ть]; признá(вá)ть; **~(e)ment** [-mənt] признáние; распи́ска.
acme ['ækmi] вы́сшая тóчка (Р); кри́зис.
acorn ['eikɔ:n] ♀ жёлудь *m*.
acoustics [ə'kaustiks] акýстика.
acquaint [ə'kweint] *v/t.* [по]знакóмить; be **~ed** with быть знакóмым с (Т); **~ance** [-əns] знакóмство; знакóмый.
acquiesce [ækwi'es] мóлча и́ли неохóтно соглашáться (in на В); **~ment** [-mənt] молчали́вое и́ли неохóтное соглáсие.
acquire [ə'kwaiə] *v/t.* приобретáть [-ести́]; достигáть [-и́гнуть] (Р); **~ment** [-mənt] приобретéние.
acquisition [ækwi'ziʃən] приобретéние.
acquit [ə'kwit] *v/t.* опрáвдывать [-дáть]; ~ of освобождáть [-боди́ть] от (Р); выполня́ть [вы́полнить] (обя́занности); ~ o. s. well хорошó справля́ться с рабóтой; **~tal** [-l] оправдáние; **~tance** уплáта (дóлга и т. п.).
acre ['eikə] акр (0,4 га).
acrid ['ækrid] óстрый, éдкий.
across [ə'krɔs] **1.** *adv.* поперёк; на ту стóрону; крестóм; **2.** *prp.* сквозь (В), чéрез (В).
act [ækt] **1.** *v/i.* дéйствовать; поступáть [-пи́ть]; *v/t. thea.* игрáть [сыгрáть] **2.** дéло; постановлéние; акт; **~ing** [-iŋ] **1.** исполня́ющий обя́занности; **2.** дéйствия *n/pl.*; *thea.* игрá.
action ['ækʃən] постýпок; дéйствие (*a. thea.*); дéятельность *f*; ⚔ бой; иск; take ~ принимáть мéры.
activ|e ['æktiv] □ акти́вный; энерги́чный; дéятельный; **~ity** [æk'tiviti] дéятельность *f*; акти́вность *f*; энéргия.
act|or ['æktə] актёр; **~ress** [-tris] актри́са.
actual ['æktjuəl] □ действи́тельный.
actuate ['æktjueit] приводи́ть в дéйствие.
acute [ə'kju:t] □ óстрый; проницáтельный.
adamant ['ædəmənt] *fig.* несокруши́мый.
adapt [ə'dæpt] приспособля́ть [-пособить] (to, for к Д); **~ation** [ædæp'teiʃən] приспособлéние; передéлка; аранжирóвка.
add [æd] *v/t.* прибавля́ть [-áвить]; ⅍ склáдывать [сложи́ть]; *v/i.* увели́чи(ва)ть (to В).

addict ['ædikt] наркомáн; **~ed** [ə'diktid] склóнный (to к Д).
addition [ə'diʃən] ⅍ сложéние; прибавлéние; in ~ крóме тогó, к томý же; in ~ to вдобáвок к (Д); **~al** [-l] □ добáвочный, дополни́тельный.
address [ə'dres] *v/t.* **1.** адресовáть (*im*)*pf.*; обращáться [обрати́ться] к (Д); **2.** áдрес; обращéние; речь *f*; **~ee** [ædre'si] адресáт.
adept ['ædept] адéпт.
adequa|cy ['ædikwəsi] соразмéрность *f*; **~te** [-kwit] □ достáточный; адеквáтный.
adhere [əd'hiə] прилипáть [-ли́пнуть] (to к Д); *fig.* придéрживаться (to Р); **~nce** [-rəns] привéрженность *f*; **~nt** [-rənt] привéрженец (-нка).
adhesive [əd'hi:siv] □ ли́пкий, клéйкий; ~ plaster, ~ tape ли́пкий плáстырь *m*.
adjacent [ə'dʒeisənt] □ смéжный (to с Т), сосéдний.
adjoin [ə'dʒɔin] примыкáть [-мкнýть] к (Д); грани́чить с (Т).
adjourn [ə'dʒə:n] *v/t.* отклáдывать [отложи́ть]; отсрóчи(ва)ть; *parl.* дéлать переры́в; **~ment** [-mənt] отсрóчка; переры́в.
adjudge [ə'dʒʌdʒ] выноси́ть пригово́р (Д).
administ|er [əd'ministə] управля́ть (Т); ~ justice отправля́ть правосýдие; **~ration** [ədminis'treiʃən] администрáция; **~rative** [əd'ministrətiv] администрати́вный; исполни́тельный; **~rator** [əd'ministreitə] администрáтор.
admir|able ['ædmərəbl] □ превосхóдный; восхити́тельный; **~ation** [ædmi'reiʃən] восхищéние; **~e** [əd'maiə] восхищáться [-ити́ться] (Т); [по]любовáться (Т *or* на В).
admiss|ible [əd'misəbl] □ допусти́мый, приéмлемый; **~ion** [əd'miʃən] вход; допущéние; признáние.
admit [əd'mit] *v/t.* допускáть [-сти́ть]; **~tance** [-əns] дóступ, вход.
admixture [əd'mikstʃə] при́месь *f*.
admon|ish [əd'mɔniʃ] увещ(ев)áть *impf.*; предостерегáть [-рéчь] (of от Р); **~ition** [ædmo'niʃən] увещáние; предостережéние.
ado [ə'du:] суетá; хлóпоты *f/pl.*
adolescen|ce [ædo'lesns] ю́ность *f*; **~nt** [-snt] ю́ный, ю́ношеский.
adopt [ə'dɔpt] *v/t.* усыновля́ть [-ви́ть]; усвáивать [усвóить]; **~ion** [ə'dɔpʃən] усыновлéние; усвáивание.
ador|ation [ædo'reiʃən] обожáние; **~e** [ə'dɔ:] *v/t.* обожáть.
adorn [ə'dɔ:n] украшáть [укрáсить]; **~ment** [-mənt] украшéние.
adroit [ə'drɔit] □ лóвкий; нахóдчивый.

adult ['ædʌlt] взрóслый, совершеннолéтний.
adulter|ate [ə'dʌltəreit] фальсифицúровать (*im*)*pf*.; **~er** [ə'dʌltərə] нарушáющий супрýжескую вéрность; **~ess** [-ris] нарушáющая супрýжескую вéрность; **~y** [-ri] нарушéние супрýжеской вéрности.
advance [əd'vɑ:ns] **1.** *v/i.* подвигáться вперёд; ⚔ наступáть [-пúть]; продвигáтся [-úнуться]; дéлать успéхи; *v/t.* продвигáть [-úнуть]; выдвигáть [вы́двинуть]; платúть авáнсом; **2.** ⚔ наступлéние; успéх (в учéнии); прогрéсс; **~d** [-t] передовóй; **~ment** [-mənt] успéх; продвижéние.
advantage [əd'vɑ:ntidʒ] преимýщество; вы́года; take **~** of [вос-]пóльзоваться (Т); **~ous** [ædvən'teidʒəs] □ вы́годный.
adventur|e [əd'ventʃə] приключéние; **~er** [-rə] искáтель приключéний; авантюрúст; **~ous** [-rəs] □ предприúмчивый; авантю́рный.
advers|ary ['ædvəsəri] протúвник (-ица); сопéрник (-ица); **~e** ['ædvə:s] □ враждéбный; **~ity** [əd'və:siti] бéдствие, несчáстье.
advertis|e ['ædvətaiz] рекламúровать (*im*)*pf*.; объявлять [-вúть]; **~ement** [əd'və:tismənt] объявлéние; реклáма; **~ing** ['ædvətaiziŋ] реклáмный.
advice [əd'vais] совéт.
advis|able □ [əd'vaizəbl] желáтельный; **~e** [əd'vaiz] *v/t.* [по]совéтовать (Д); *v/i.* [по]совéтоваться (with с Т; on, about о П); **~er** [-ə] совéтник (-ица), совéтчик (-ица).
advocate **1.** ['ædvəkit] защúтник (-ица); сторóнник (-ица); адвокáт; **2.** [-keit] отстáивать [отстоять].
aerial ['ɛəriəl] **1.** □ воздýшный; **2.** антéнна; outdoor **~** нарýжная антéнна.
aero... ['ɛərou] аэро...; **~drome** ['ɛərədroum] аэродрóм; **~naut** [-nɔ:t] аэронáвт; **~nautics** [-'nɔ:tiks] аэронáвтика; **~plane** [-plein] самолёт, аэроплáн; **~stat** [-stæt] аэростáт.
aesthetic [i:s'θetik] эстетúчный; **~s** [-s] эстéтика.
afar [ə'fɑ:] *adv.* вдалекé, вдалú; from **~** издалекá.
affable ['æfəbl] привéтливый.
affair [ə'fɛə] дéло.
affect [ə'fekt] *v/t.* [по]дéйствовать на (В); задé(вá)ть; ⚕ поражáть [-разúть]; **~ation** [æfek'teiʃən] жемáнство; **~ed** [ə'fektid] □ жемáнный; **~ion** [ə'fekʃən] привязанность *f*; заболевáние; **~ionate** □ нéжный.
affidavit [æfi'deivit] пúсьменное показáние под присягóй.
affiliate [ə'filieit] *v/t.* присоединять [-нúть] (как филиáл).
affinity [ə'finiti] сродствó.
affirm [ə'fə:m] утверждáть [-рдúть]; **~ation** [æfə:'meiʃən] утверждéние; **~ative** [ə'fə:mətiv] □ утвердúтельный.
affix [ə'fiks] прикреплять [-пúть] (to к Д).
afflict [ə'flikt] *v/t.* огорчáть [-чúть]; be **~**ed страдáть (with от Р); **~ion** [ə'flikʃən] гóре; болéзнь *f*.
affluen|ce ['æfluəns] изобúлие, богáтство; **~t** [-ənt] **1.** □ обúльный, богáтый; **2.** притóк.
afford [ə'fɔ:d] позволять [-вóлить] себé; I can **~** it я могý себé это позвóлить; предоставлять [-áвить].
affront [ə'frʌnt] **1.** оскорблять [-бúть]; **2.** оскорблéние.
afield [ə'fi:ld] *adv.* вдалекé; в пóле; на войнé.
afloat [ə'flout] ⚓ на водé; в мóре; в ходý.
afraid [ə'freid] испýганный; be **~** of боя́ться (Р).
afresh [ə'freʃ] *adv.* снóва, сы́знова.
African ['æfrikən] **1.** африкáнец (-нка); **2.** африкáнский.
after ['ɑ:ftə] **1.** *adv.* потóм, пóсле, затéм; позадú; **2.** *prp.* за (Т), позадú (Р); чéрез (В); пóсле (Р); **3.** *cj.* с тех пор, как; пóсле тогó, как; **4.** *adj.* послéдующий; **~crop** вторóй урожáй; **~math** [-mæθ] отáва; *fig.* послéдствия *n/pl.*; **~noon** [-'nu:n] врéмя пóсле полýдня; **~-taste** (остаю́щийся) прúвкус; **~-thought** мысль, пришéдшая пóздно; **~wards** [-wədz] *adv.* потóм.
again [ə'gein *Am.* ə'gen] *adv.* снóва, опять; **~** and **~**, time and **~** то и дéло; as much **~** ещё стóлько же.
against [ə'geinst] *prp.* прóтив (Р); о, об (В); на (В); as **~** прóтив (Р); **~** the wall у стены́; к стенé.
age [eidʒ] вóзраст; годá *m/pl.*; эпóха; of **~** совершеннолéтний; under **~** несовершеннолéтний; **~d** ['eidʒid] стáрый, постарéвший; **~** twenty двадцатú лет.
agency ['eidʒənsi] дéйствие; агéнтство.
agent ['eidʒənt] фáктор; агéнт; довéренное лицó.
agglomerate [ə'glɔməreit] *v/t.* соб(и)рáть; *v/i.* скопляться [-пúться].
agglutinate [ə'glu:tineit] склéи(ва)ть.
aggrandize ['ægrəndaiz) увелúчи(ва)ть; возвелúчи(ва)ть.
aggravate ['ægrəveit] усугублять [-бúть]; ухудшáть [ухýдшить]; раздражáть [-жúть].
aggregate **1.** ['ægrigeit] собирáть (-ся) в однó цéлое; **2.** □ [-git] совокýпный; **3.** [-git] совокýпность *f*; агрегáт.

aggress|ion [ə'greʃən] нападе́ние; агре́ссия; **~or** [ə'gresə] агре́ссор.
aghast [ə'gɑ:st] ошеломлённый, поражённый у́жасом.
agil|e ['ædʒail] □ прово́рный, живо́й; **~ity** [ə'dʒiliti] прово́рство, жи́вость *f*.
agitat|e ['ædʒiteit] *v/t*. [вз]волнова́ть, возбужда́ть [-уди́ть]; *v/i*. агити́ровать (for за В); **~ion** [ædʒi'teiʃən] волне́ние; агита́ция.
agnail ['ægneil] ⚕ заусе́ница.
ago [ə'gou]: a year ~ год тому́ наза́д.
agonize ['ægənaiz] быть в аго́нии; си́льно му́чить(ся).
agony ['ægəni] аго́ния; боль *f*.
agree [ə'gri:] *v/i*. соглаша́ться [-ласи́ться] (to с Т, на В); ~ [up]on усла́вливаться [усло́виться] о (П); **~able** [-əbl] согла́сный (to с Т, на В); прия́тный; **~ment** [-mənt] согла́сие; соглаше́ние, догово́р.
agricultur|al [ægri'kʌltʃərəl] сельскохозя́йственный; **~e** ['ægrikʌltʃə] се́льское хозя́йство; земледе́лие; агроно́мия; **~ist** [ægri'kʌltʃərist] агроно́м; земледе́лец.
ague ['eigju:] лихора́дочный озно́б.
ahead [ə'hed] вперёд, впереди́; straight ~ пря́мо, вперёд.
aid [eid] **1.** по́мощь *f*; помо́щник (-ица); **2.** помога́ть [помо́чь] (Д).
ail [eil]: what ~s him? что его́ беспоко́ит?; **~ing** ['eiliŋ] больно́й, нездоро́вый; **~ment** ['eilmənt] нездоро́вье.
aim [eim] **1.** *v/i*. прице́ли(ва)ться (at в В); *fig*. ~ at име́ть в виду́; *v/t*. направля́ть [-ра́вить] (at на В); **2.** цель *f*, наме́рение; **~less** [eimlis] □ бесце́льный.
air[1] [ɛə] **1.** во́здух; by ~ самолётом; возду́шной по́чтой; *Am*. be on the ~ рабо́тать (о радиоста́нции); *Am*. put on the ~ передава́ть по ра́дио; *Am*. be off the ~ не рабо́тать (о радиоста́нции); **2.** прове́три(ва)ть.
air[2] [~] *mst pl*. аффекта́ция, ва́жничанье; give o.s. ~s ва́жничать.
air[3] [~] ♪ мело́дия; пе́сня; а́рия.
air|-base авиаба́за; **~-brake** возду́шный то́рмоз; **~conditioned** ⚙ с кондициони́рованным во́здухом; **~craft** самолёт; **~field** аэродро́м; **~force** вое́нно-возду́шный флот; **~-jacket** надувно́й спаса́тельный нагру́дник; **~-lift** «возду́шный мост», возду́шная перево́зка; **~-liner** ре́йсовый самолёт; **~-mail** возду́шная по́чта; **~man** лётчик, авиа́тор; **~plane** *Am*. самолёт; **~-port** аэропо́рт; **~-raid** возду́шный налёт; ~ precautions *pl*. противовозду́шная оборо́на; **~-route** возду́шная тра́сса; **~shelter** бомбоубе́жище; **~ship** дирижа́бль *m*; **~-tight** гермети́ческий; **~-tube** ка́мера ши́ны; *anat*. трахе́я; **~way** возду́шная тра́сса.
airy ['ɛəri] □ возду́шный; легкомы́сленный.
aisle [ail] ⛪ приде́л (хра́ма); прохо́д.
ajar [ə'dʒɑ:] приотво́ренный.
akin [ə'kin] ро́дственный, бли́зкий (to Д).
alarm [ə'lɑ:m] **1.** трево́га; страх; **2.** [вс]трево́жить], [вз]волнова́ть; **~-clock** буди́льник.
albuminous [æl'bju:minəs] содержа́щий бело́к; альбуми́нный.
alcohol ['ælkəhɔl] алкого́ль *m*; спирт; **~ic** [ælkə'hɔlik] **1.** алкого́льный; **2.** алкого́лик; **~ism** ['ælkəhɔlizm] алкоголи́зм.
alcove ['ælkouv] алько́в, ни́ша.
ale [eil] пи́во, эль *m*.
alert [ə'lə:t] **1.** □ живо́й, прово́рный; **2.** (возду́шная) трево́га; on the ~ настороже́.
alien ['eiliən] **1.** иностра́нный; чу́ждый; **2.** иностра́нец, чужестра́нец; **~able** [-əbl] отчужда́емый; **~ate** [-eit] отчужда́ть [-уди́ть]; **~ist** ['eiliənist] психиа́тр.
alight [ə'lait] **1.** сходи́ть [сойти́] (с Р); приземля́ться [-ли́ться]; **2.** *adj. predic*. зажжённый, в огне́; освещённый.
align [ə'lain] выра́внивать(ся) [вы́ровнять(ся)].
alike [ə'laik] **1.** *adj. pred*. одина́ковый; похо́жий; **2.** *adv*. то́чно так же; подо́бно.
aliment ['ælimənt] пита́ние; **~ary** [æli'mentəri] пищево́й; пита́тельный; ~ canal пищево́д.
alimony ['æliməni] алиме́нты *m/pl*.
alive [e'laiv] живо́й, бо́дрый; чу́ткий (to к Д); кипя́щий (with Т); be ~ to я́сно понима́ть.
all [ɔ:l] **1.** *adj*. весь *m*, вся *f*, всё *n*, все *pl*; вся́кий; всевозмо́жный; for ~ that несмотря́ на то; **2.** всё, все; at ~ вообще́; not at ~ во́все не; for ~ (that) I care мне безразли́чно; for ~ I know поско́льку я зна́ю; **3.** *adv*. вполне́, всеце́ло, соверше́нно; ~ at once сра́зу; ~ the better тем лу́чше; ~ but почти́; ~ right хорошо́, ла́дно.
allay [ə'lei] успока́ивать [-ко́ить].
alleg|ation [æle'geiʃən] заявле́ние; голосло́вное утвержде́ние; **~e** [ə'ledʒ] ссыла́ться [сосла́ться] на (В); утвержда́ть (без основа́ния).
allegiance [ə'li:dʒəns] ве́рность *f*, пре́данность *f*.
alleviate [ə'li:vieit] облегча́ть [-чи́ть].
alley ['æli] алле́я; переу́лок.
alliance [ə'laiəns] сою́з.
allocat|e ['ælokeit] размеща́ть [-мести́ть]; распределя́ть [-ли́ть]; **~ion** [ælo'keiʃən] распределе́ние.

allot [ə'lɔt] *v/t.* распределя́ть [-ли́ть]; разда́(ва́)ть.
allow [ə'lau] позволя́ть [-о́лить]; допуска́ть [-сти́ть]; *Am.* утвержда́ть; **~able** [-əbl] □ позволи́тельный; **~ance** [-əns] (материа́льное) содержа́ние; ски́дка; разреше́ние; make ~ for принима́ть во внима́ние.
alloy [ə'lɔi] **1.** при́месь *f*; сплав; **2.** сплавля́ть [-а́вить].
all-round всесторо́нний.
allude [ə'lu:d] ссыла́ться [сосла́ться] (to на В); намека́ть [-кну́ть] (to на В).
allure [ə'ljuə] завлека́ть [-е́чь]; **~ment** [-mənt] обольще́ние.
allusion [ə'luʒən] намёк; ссы́лка.
ally **1.** [ə'lai] соединя́ть [-ни́ть] (to, with с Т); **2.** ['ælɑi] сою́зник.
almanac ['ɔ:lmənæk] календа́рь *m*, альмана́х.
almighty [ɔ:l'maiti] всемогу́щий.
almond ['ɑ:mənd] **1.** минда́ль *m*; минда́лина (*a.* ⚕); **2.** минда́льный.
almost ['ɔ:lmoust] почти́, едва́ не.
alms [ɑ:mz] *sg. a. pl.* ми́лостыня; **~-house** богаде́льня.
aloft [ə'lɔft] наверху́, наве́рх.
alone ['loun] оди́н *m*, одна́ *f*, одно́ *n*, одни́ *pl.*; одино́кий (-кая); let (или leave) ~ оста́вить в поко́е; let ~ ... не говоря́ уже́ о ... (П).
along [ə'lɔŋ] **1.** *adv.* вперёд; all ~ всё вре́мя; ~ with вме́сте с (Т); F get ~ with you! убира́йтесь!; **2.** *prp.* вдоль (Р), по (Д); **~side** [-said] бок-о́-бок, ря́дом.
aloof [ə'lu:f] по́одаль, в стороне́; stand ~ держа́ться в стороне́.
aloud [ə'laud] гро́мко, вслух.
alp [ælp] го́рное па́стбище; **2s** 'Альпы *f/pl.*
already [ɔ:l'redi] уже́.
also ['ɔ:lsou] та́кже, то́же.
alter ['ɔ:ltə] изменя́ть(ся) [-ни́ть (-ся)]; **~ation** [ɔ:ltə'reiʃən] переме́на, измене́ние, переде́лка (to Р).
alternat|e **1.** ['ɔ:ltə:neit] чередова́ть(ся); **2.** □ [ɔ:l'tə:nit] переме́нный; ⚡ alternating current переме́нный ток; **~ion** [ɔ:ltə:'neiʃən] чередова́ние; **~ive** [ɔ:l'tə:nətiv] **1.** □ взаимоисключа́ющий, альтернати́вный; переме́нно де́йствующий; **2.** альтернати́ва; вы́бор, возмо́жность *f*.
although [ɔ:l'ðou] хотя́.
altitude ['æltitju:d] высота́; возвы́шенность *f*.
altogether [ɔ:ltə'geðə] вполне́, всеце́ло; в о́бщем.
alumin(i)um [ælju'minjəm] алюми́ний.
always ['ɔ:lwəz] всегда́.
am [æm; в предложе́нии: əm] [*irr.*] *1. pers. sg. prs.* от be.
amalgamate [ə'mælgəmeit] амальгами́ровать (*im*)*pf*.
amass [ə'mæs] соб(и)ра́ть; накопля́ть [-пи́ть].
amateur ['æmətə:, -tjuə] люби́тель(ница *f*) *m*; дилета́нт(ка).
amaz|e [ə'meiz] изумля́ть [-ми́ть], поража́ть [порази́ть]; **~ement** [-mənt] изумле́ние; **~ing** [ə'meiziŋ] удиви́тельный, изуми́тельный.
ambassador [æm'bæsədə] посо́л; посла́нец.
amber ['æmbə] янта́рь *m*.
ambigu|ity [æmbi'gjuiti] двусмы́сленность *f*; **~ous** [-'bigjuəs] □ двусмы́сленный; сомни́тельный.
ambitio|n [æm'biʃən] честолю́бие; **~us** [-ʃəs] □ честолюби́вый.
amble ['æmbl] **1.** и́ноходь *f*; **2.** идти́ и́ноходью.
ambulance ['æmbjuləns] каре́та ско́рой по́мощи.
ambuscade [æmbəs'keid], **ambush** ['æmbuʃ] заса́да.
ameliorate [ə'mi:liəreit] улучша́ть(ся) [улу́чшить(ся)].
amend [ə'mend] исправля́ть(ся) [-а́вить(ся)]; *parl.* вноси́ть попра́вки в (В); **~ment** [-mənt] исправле́ние; *parl.* попра́вка (к резолю́ции, законопрое́кту); **~s** [ə'mendz] компенса́ция.
amenity [ə'mi:niti] прия́тность *f*.
American [ə'merikən] **1.** америка́нец (-нка); **2.** америка́нский; **~ism** [-izm] американи́зм; **~ize** [-aiz] американизи́ровать (*im*)*pf*.
amiable ['eimjəbl] □ дружелю́бный; доброду́шный.
amicable ['æmikəbl] □ дру́жеский, дру́жественный.
amid(st) [ə'mid(st)] среди́ (Р), посреди́ (Р), ме́жду (Т *sometimes* Р).
amiss [ə'mis] *adv.* пло́хо, непра́вильно; некста́ти; несвоевре́менно; take ~ обижа́ться [оби́деться].
amity ['æmiti] дру́жба.
ammonia [ə'mounjə] ⚗ аммиа́к.
ammunition [æmju'niʃən] боеприпа́сы *m/pl.*
amnesty ['æmnesti] **1.** амни́стия; **2.** амнисти́ровать (*im*)*pf*.
among(st) [ə'mʌŋ(st)] среди́ (Р), ме́жду (Т *sometimes* Р).
amorous ['æmərəs] □ влюблённый (of в В); влю́бчивый.
amount [ə'maunt] **1.** ~ to равня́ться (Д); **2.** су́мма; коли́чество.
ample ['æmpl] □ доста́точный, оби́льный; просто́рный.
ampli|fication [æmplifi'keiʃən] расшире́ние; увеличе́ние; усиле́ние; **~fier** ['æmplifaiə] *phys.* усили́тель *m*; **~fy** ['æmplifai] уси́ли(ва)ть; распространя́ть(ся) [-ни́ть(ся)]; **~tude** [-tju:d] широта́, разма́х (мы́сли); *phys.*, *astr.* амплиту́да.
amputate ['æmpjuteit] ампути́ровать (*im*)*pf*., отнима́ть [-ня́ть].

amuse [ə'mju:z] забавля́ть, позаба́вить *pf.*, развлека́ть [-е́чь]; **~ment** [-mənt] развлече́ние, заба́ва.
an [æn, ən] неопределённый член.
an(a)esthetic [æni:s'θetik] нарко́тик.
analog|ous [ə'næləgəs] □ аналоги́чный, схо́дный; **~y** [ə'nælədʒi] анало́гия, схо́дство.
analys|e ['ænəlaiz] анализи́ровать (*im*)*pf.*, *pf. a.* [про-]; **~is** [ə'næləsis] ана́лиз.
anarchy ['ænəki] ана́рхия.
anatom|ize [ə'nætəmaiz] анатоми́ровать (*im*)*pf.*; [про]анализи́ровать (*im*)*pf.*; **~y** анато́мия.
ancest|or ['ænsistə] пре́док; **~ral** [æn'sestrəl] насле́дственный, родово́й; **~ress** ['ænsistris] прароди́тельница; **~ry** ['ænsistri] происхожде́ние; пре́дки *m/pl.*
anchor ['æŋkə] **1.** я́корь *m*; at ~ на я́коре; **2.** ста́вить (стать) на я́корь.
anchovy [æn'tʃouvi] анчо́ус.
ancient ['einʃənt] **1.** дре́вний; анти́чный; **2.** the **~s** *pl. hist.* дре́вние наро́ды *m/pl.*
and [ænd, ənd, F ən] и; а.
anew [ə'nju:] *adv.* сно́ва, сы́знова; по-но́вому.
angel ['eindʒəl] а́нгел; **~ic(al** □) [æn'dʒelik(əl)] а́нгельский.
anger ['æŋgə] **1.** гнев; **2.** [рас]серди́ть.
angle ['æŋgl] **1.** у́гол; то́чка зре́ния; **2.** уди́ть (for В); уди́ть ры́бу; *fig.* заки́дывать у́дочку.
Anglican ['æŋglikən] **1.** член англика́нской це́ркви; **2.** англика́нский.
Anglo-Saxon ['æŋglou'sæksn] **1.** англоса́кс; **2.** англосаксо́нский.
angry ['æŋgri] серди́тый (with на В).
anguish ['æŋgwiʃ] му́ка.
angular ['æŋgjulə] углово́й, уго́льный; *fig.* углова́тый; нело́вкий.
animal ['ænimәl] **1.** живо́тное; **2.** живо́тный; ско́тский.
animat|e ['ænimeit] оживля́ть [-ви́ть]; воодушевля́ть [-ви́ть]; **~ion** [æni'meiʃən] жи́вость *f*; оживле́ние.
animosity [æni'mɔsiti] вражде́бность *f*.
ankle ['æŋkl] лоды́жка.
annals ['ænlz] *pl.* ле́топись *f*.
annex **1.** [ə'neks] аннекси́ровать (*im*)*pf.*; присоединя́ть [-ни́ть]; **2.** ['æneks] пристро́йка; приложе́ние; **~ation** [ænek'seiʃən] анне́ксия.
annihilate [ə'naiəleit] уничтожа́ть [-о́жить], истребля́ть [-би́ть].
anniversary [æni'və:səri] годовщи́на.
annotat|e ['ænouteit] анноти́ровать (*im*)*pf.*; снабжа́ть примеча́ниями; **~ion** [ænou'teiʃən] примеча́ние.
announce [ə'nauns] объявля́ть [-ви́ть]; дава́ть знать; заявля́ть [-ви́ть]; **~ment** [-mənt] объявле́ние; **~r** [-ə] *radio* ди́ктор.
annoy [ə'nɔi] надоеда́ть [-е́сть] (Д); досажда́ть [досади́ть] (Д); **~ance** [-əns] доса́да; раздраже́ние; неприя́тность *f*.
annual ['ænjuəl] **1.** □ ежего́дный; годово́й; **2.** ежего́дник; одноле́тнее расте́ние.
annuity [ə'njuiti] годова́я ре́нта.
annul [ə'nʌl] аннули́ровать (*im*)*pf.*; отменя́ть [-ни́ть]; **~ment** [-mənt] аннули́рование.
anoint [ə'nɔint] нама́з(ыв)ать; *eccl.* пома́з(ыв)ать.
anomalous [ə'nɔmələs] □ анома́льный, непра́вильный.
anonymous [ə'nɔniməs] □ анони́мный.
another [ə'nʌðə] друго́й; ещё оди́н.
answer ['ɑ:nsə] **1.** *v/t.* отвеча́ть [-е́тить] (Д); удовлетворя́ть [-ри́ть]; ~ the bell *or* door открыва́ть дверь на звоно́к; *v/i.* отвеча́ть [-е́тить] (to a p. Д, to a question на вопро́с); ~ for отвеча́ть [-е́тить] за (В); **2.** отве́т (to на В); **~able** ['ɑ:nsərəbl] □ отве́тственный.
ant [ænt] мураве́й.
antagonis|m [æn'tægənizm] антагони́зм, вражда́; **~t** [-ist] антагони́ст, проти́вник.
antecedent [ænti'si:dənt] **1.** □ предше́ствующий, предыду́щий (to Д); **2.** **~s** *pl.* про́шлое (челове́ка).
anterior [æn'tiriə] предше́ствующий (to Д); пере́дний.
ante-room ['æntirum] пере́дняя.
anthem ['ænθəm] гимн.
anti... [ænti...] противо..., анти...; **~-aircraft** [ænti'εəkra:ft] противовозду́шный; ~ alarm возду́шная трево́га; ~ defence противовозду́шная оборо́на (ПВО).
antic ['æntik] **1.** □ шутовско́й; **2.** гроте́ск; **~s** *pl.* ужи́мки *f/pl.*; ша́лости *f/pl.*
anticipat|e [æn'tisipeit] предвкуша́ть [-уси́ть]; предчу́вствовать; предупрежда́ть [-реди́ть]; **~ion** [æntisi'peiʃən] ожида́ние; предчу́вствие; in ~ зара́нее.
antidote ['æntidout] противоя́дие.
antipathy [æn'tipəθi] антипа́тия.
antiqua|ry ['æntikwəri] антиква́р; **~ted** [-kweitid] устаре́лый; старомо́дный.
antiqu|e [æn'ti:k] **1.** □ анти́чный; стари́нный; **2.** анти́чное произведе́ние иску́сства; антиква́рная вещь *f*; **~ity** [æn'tikwiti] дре́вность *f*; старина́; анти́чность *f*.

antlers ['æntləz] *pl.* оле́ньи рога́ *m/pl.*
anvil ['ænvil] накова́льня.
anxiety [æŋ'zaiəti] беспоко́йство; стра́стное жела́ние; опасе́ние.
anxious ['æŋkʃəs] □ озабо́ченный; беспоко́ящийся (about, for о П).
any ['əni] **1.** *pron.* како́й-нибудь; вся́кий, любо́й; not ~ никако́й; **2.** *adv.* ско́лько-нибудь; не́сколько; **~body, ~one** кто́-нибудь; вся́кий; **~how** ка́к-нибудь; так и́ли ина́че, во вся́ком слу́чае; **~thing** что́-нибудь; ~ but далеко́ не ..., совсе́м не ...; **~where** где́-нибудь, куда́-нибудь.
apart [ə'pɑ:t] отде́льно; по́рознь; ~ from кро́ме (Р); **~ment** [-mənt] ко́мната (меблиро́ванная); ~s *pl.* кварти́ра; *Am.* ~ house многокварти́рный дом.
ape [eip] **1.** обезья́на; **2.** подража́ть (Д), [с]обезья́нничать.
aperient [ə'piəriənt] слаби́тельное сре́дство.
aperture ['æpətjuə] отве́рстие; проём.
apiculture ['eipikʌltʃə] пчелово́дство.
apiece [ə'pi:s] за шту́ку; за ка́ждого, с челове́ка.
apish ['eipiʃ] □ обезья́ний; глу́пый.
apolog|etic [əpɔlə'dʒetik] (**~ally**) извини́тельный; извиня́ющийся; защити́тельный; **~ize** [ə'pɔlədʒaiz] извиня́ться [-ни́ться] (for за В; to пе́ред Т); **~y** [-dʒi] извине́ние.
apoplexy ['æpopleksi] уда́р, парали́ч.
apostate [ə'pɔstit] отсту́пник.
apostle [ə'pɔsl] апо́стол.
apostroph|e [ə'pɔstrefi] апостро́фа; апостро́ф; **~ize** [-faiz] обраща́ться [обрати́ться] к (Д).
appal [ə'pɔ:l] [ис]пуга́ть; устраша́ть [-ши́ть].
apparatus [æpə'reitəs] прибо́р; аппарату́ра, аппара́т.
apparel [ə'pærəl] оде́жда, пла́тье.
appar|ent [ə'pærənt] □ очеви́дный, несомне́нный; **~ition** [æpə'riʃən] появле́ние; при́зрак.
appeal [ə'pi:l] **1.** апелли́ровать (*im*)*pf.*; подава́ть жа́лобу; обраща́ться [обрати́ться] (to к Д); привлека́ть [-е́чь] (to В); **2.** воззва́ние, призы́в; апелля́ция; привлека́телность *f*; **~ing** [-iŋ] тро́гательный; привлека́тельный.
appear [ə'piə] появля́ться [-ви́ться]; пока́зываться [-за́ться]; выступа́ть [вы́ступить] (на конце́рте и т. п.); **~ance** [ə'piərəns] появле́ние; вне́шний вид, нару́жность *f*; ~s *pl.* прили́чия *n/pl.*
appease [ə'pi:z] умиротворя́ть [-ри́ть]; успока́ивать [-ко́ить].
appellant [ə'pelənt] апелля́нт.
append [ə'pend] прилага́ть [-ложи́ть] (к Д), прибавля́ть [-а́вить] (к Д); **~age** [-idʒ] прида́ток; **~ix** [ə'pendiks] приложе́ние.
appertain [æpə'tein] принадлежа́ть; относи́ться (to к Д).
appetite ['æpitait] аппети́т (for на В); *fig.* влече́ние, скло́нность *f* (for к Д).
appetizing ['æpitaiziŋ] аппети́тный.
applaud [ə'plɔ:d] *v/t.* аплоди́ровать (Д); одобря́ть [одо́брить].
applause [ə'plɔ:z] аплодисме́нты *m/pl.*; одобре́ние.
apple [æpl] я́блоко; **~sauce** я́блочный мусс; *sl.* лесть *f*; ерунда́.
appliance [ə'plaiəns] приспособле́ние, прибо́р.
applica|ble ['æplikəbl] примени́мый, подходя́щий (to к Д); **~nt** [-kənt] проси́тель(ница *f*) *m*; кандида́т (for на В); **~tion** [æpli'keiʃən] примене́ние; заявле́ние; про́сьба (for о П).
apply [ə'plai] *v/t.* прилага́ть [-ложи́ть] (to к Д); применя́ть [-ни́ть] (to к Д); ~ o. s. to занима́ться [заня́ться] (Т); *v/i.* обраща́ться [обрати́ться] (for за Т; to к Д); относи́ться.
appoint [ə'pɔint] назнача́ть [-на́чить]; определя́ть [-ли́ть]; снаряжа́ть [-яди́ть]; well ~ed хорошо́ обору́дованный; **~ment** [-mənt] назначе́ние; свида́ние; ~s *pl.* обору́дование; обстано́вка.
apportion [ə'pɔ:ʃən] [по]дели́ть, разделя́ть [-ли́ть]; **~ment** [-mənt] пропорциона́льное распределе́ние.
apprais|al [ə'preizəl] оце́нка; **~e** [ə'preiz] оце́нивать [-ни́ть], расце́нивать [-ни́ть].
apprecia|ble [ə'pri:ʃəbl] □ заме́тный, ощути́мый; **~te** [-ieit] *v/t.* оце́нивать [-ни́ть]; [о]цени́ть; понима́ть [-ня́ть]; *v/i.* повыша́ться в це́нности; **~tion** [əpri:ʃi'eiʃən] оце́нка; понима́ние.
apprehen|d [æpri'hend] предчу́вствовать; боя́ться; заде́рживать [-жа́ть], аресто́вывать [-ова́ть]; **~sion** [-'henʃən] опасе́ние, предчу́вствие; аре́ст; **~sive** [-'hensiv] □ озабо́ченный; поня́тливый.
apprentice [ə'prentis] **1.** подмасте́рье, учени́к; **2.** отдава́ть в уче́ние; **~ship** [-ʃip] уче́ние, учени́чество.
approach [ə'proutʃ] **1.** приближа́ться [-бли́зиться] к (Д); обраща́ться [обрати́ться] к (Д); **2.** приближе́ние; по́дступ; *fig.* подхо́д.
approbation [æpro'beiʃən] одобре́ние; са́нкция.
appropriat|e 1. [ə'prouprieit] присва́ивать [-сво́ить]; *parl.* пред-

назнача́ть [-зна́чить]; 2. [-it] □ подходя́щий; соотве́тствующий; ~ion [əproupri'eiʃən] присвое́ние; *parl.* ассигнова́ние.
approv|al [ə'pru:vəl] одобре́ние; утвержде́ние; ~e [ə'pru:v] одобря́ть [одо́брить]; утвержда́ть [-рди́ть]; санкциони́ровать (*im*)*pf*.
approximate 1. [ə'prɔksimeit] приближа́ть(ся) [-бли́зить(ся)] к (Д); 2. [-mit] □ приблизи́тельный.
apricot ['eiprikɔt] абрико́с.
April ['eiprəl] апре́ль *m*.
apron ['eiprən] пере́дник, фа́ртук.
apt [æpt] □ подходя́щий; спосо́бный; ~ to скло́нный к (Д); ~itude ['æptitju:d], ~ness [-nis] спосо́бность *f*; скло́нность *f* (for, to к Д); уме́стность *f*.
aquatic [ə'kwætik] 1. водяно́й; во́дный; 2. ~s *pl*. во́дный спорт.
aque|duct ['ækwidʌkt] акведу́к; ~ous ['eikwiəs] водяни́стый.
Arab ['ærəb] ара́б(ка); ~ic ['ærəbik] 1. ара́бский язы́к; 2. ара́бский.
arable ['ærəbl] па́хотный.
arbit|er ['ɑbitə] арби́тр, трете́йский судья́ *m*; *fig*. верши́тель су́деб; ~rariness ['ɑ:bitrərinis] произво́л; ~rary [-trəri] □ произво́льный; ~rate ['ɑ:bitreit] реша́ть трете́йским судо́м; ~ration [ɑ:bi'treiʃən] трете́йское реше́ние; ~rator ['ɑ:bitreitə] ⚖ арби́тр, трете́йский судья́ *m*.
arbo(u)r ['ɑ:bə] бесе́дка.
arc [ɑ:k] *ast*., ⚔, ⚡ дуга́; ~ade [ɑ:'keid] пасса́ж; сво́дчатая галере́я.
arch[1] [ɑ:tʃ] 1. а́рка; свод; дуга́; 2. придава́ть фо́рму а́рки; изгиба́ть(ся) дуго́й.
arch[2] [~] 1. хи́трый, лука́вый; 2. *pref*. архи... (выраже́ние превосхо́дной сте́пени).
archaic [ɑ:'keiik] (~ally) устаре́лый.
archbishop ['ɑ:tʃbiʃəp] архиепи́скоп.
archery ['ɑ:tʃəri] стрельба́ из лу́ка.
architect ['ɑ:kitekt] архите́ктор; ~onic [-'ɔnik] (~ally) архитекту́рный, конструкти́вный; ~ure ['ɑ:kitektʃə] архитекту́ра.
archway ['ɑ:tʃwei] сво́дчатый прохо́д.
arc-lamp ['ɑ:klæmp] ⚡ дугова́я ла́мпа.
arctic ['ɑ:ktik] поля́рный, аркти́ческий.
arden|cy ['ɑ:dənsi] жар, пыл; рве́ние; ~t ['ɑ:dənt] □ *mst fig*. горя́чий, пы́лкий; ре́вностный.
ardo(u)r ['ɑ:də] рве́ние; пыл.
arduous ['ɑ:djuəs] □ тру́дный.
are [ɑ:; в предложе́нии: ɑ] *s*. be.
area ['ɛəriə] пло́щадь *f*; о́бласть *f*, райо́н.
Argentine ['ɑ:dʒəntain] 1. аргенти́нский; 2. аргенти́нец (-и́нка).
argue ['ɑ:gju:] *v/t*. обсужда́ть [-уди́ть]; дока́зывать [-за́ть]; ~ a p. into убежда́ть [убеди́ть] в (П); *v/i*. [по]спо́рить (с Т).
argument ['ɑ:gjumənt] до́вод, аргуме́нт; спор; ~ation [ɑ:gjumen'teiʃən] аргумента́ция.
arid ['ærid] сухо́й (*a. fig*.), безво́дный.
arise [ə'raiz] [*irr*.] *fig*. возника́ть [-ни́кнуть] (from из Р); восст(ав)а́ть; ~n [ə'rizn] *p. pt*. от arise.
aristocra|cy [æris'tɔkrəsi] аристокра́тия; ~t ['æristəkræt] аристокра́т; ~tic(al □) [æristə'krætik, -ikəl] аристократи́ческий.
arithmetic [ə'riθmətik] арифме́тика.
ark [ɑ:k] ковче́г.
arm[1] [ɑ:m] рука́; рука́в (реки́).
arm[2] [~] 1. ору́жие; род войск; 2. вооружа́ть(ся) [-жи́ть(ся)].
arma|ment ['ɑ:məmənt] вооруже́ние; ~ture ['ɑ:mətjuə] броня́; ⊕ армату́ра.
armchair кре́сло.
armistice ['ɑ:mistis] переми́рие.
armo(u)r ['ɑ:mə] 1. доспе́хи *m/pl*.; броня́, па́нцирная обши́вка; 2. покрыва́ть броне́й; ~y [-ri] арсена́л.
armpit [ɑ:mpit] подмы́шка.
army ['ɑ:mi] а́рмия; *fig*. мно́жество.
arose [ə'rouz] *pt*. от *arise*.
around [ə'raund] 1. *adv*. всю́ду, круго́м; 2. *prp*. вокру́г (Р).
arouse [ə'rauz] [раз]буди́ть; возбужда́ть [-уди́ть]; вызыва́ть [вы́звать].
arraign [ə'rein] привлека́ть к суду́; *fig*. находи́ть недоста́тки в (П).
arrange [ə'reindʒ] приводи́ть в поря́док; устра́ивать [-ро́ить]; классифици́ровать (*im*)*pf*.; усла́вливаться [усло́виться]; ♪ аранжи́ровать (*im*)*pf*.; ~ment [-mənt] устро́йство; расположе́ние; соглаше́ние; мероприя́тие; ♪ аранжиро́вка.
array [ə'rei] 1. боево́й поря́док; *fig*. мно́жество, це́лый ряд; 2. оде́(ва́)ть; украша́ть [укра́сить]; выстра́ивать в ряд.
arrear [ə'riə] *mst. pl*. задо́лженность *f*, недои́мка.
arrest [ə'rest] 1. аре́ст, задержа́ние; 2. аресто́вывать [-ова́ть], заде́рживать [-жа́ть].
arriv|al [ə'raivəl] прибы́тие, прие́зд; ~s *pl*. прибы́вшие *pl*.; ~e [ə'raiv] прибы́(ва́)ть; приезжа́ть [-е́хать] (at в, на В).
arroga|nce ['ærəgəns] надме́н-

ность *f*, высокомéрие; **~nt** □ надмéнный, высокомéрный; **~te** [-geit] дéрзко трéбовать (Р).
arrow ['ærou] стрелá.
arsenal ['ɑ:sinl] арсенáл.
arsenic ['ɑ:snik] мышья́к.
arson ['ɑ:sn] ⚖ поджóг.
art [ɑ:t] искýсство; *fig.* хи́трость *f.*
arter|ial [ɑ'tiəriəl]: ~ road магистрáль *f*; **~y** ['ɑ:təri] артéрия; глáвная дорóга.
artful ['ɑ:tful] лóвкий; хи́трый.
article ['ɑ:tikl] статья́; парáграф; *gr.* арти́кль *m*, член; **~d** to óтданный (в учéние) к (Д).
articulat|e 1. [ɑ:'tikjuleit] отчётливо, я́сно произноси́ть; 2. [-lit] отчётливый; членораздéльный; колéнчатый; **~ion** [ɑ:tikju'leiʃən] артикуля́ция; членораздéльное произношéние; *anat.* сочленéние.
artific|e ['ɑ:tifis] лóвкость *f*; изобретéние, вы́думка; **~ial** [ɑ:ti'fiʃəl] □ искýсственный.
artillery [ɑ:'tiləri] артиллéрия; **~man** [-mən] артиллери́ст.
artisan [ɑ:ti'zæn] ремéсленник.
artist ['ɑ:tist] худóжник (-ица); актёр, актри́са; **~e** [ɑ:'tist] эстрáдный (-ная) арти́ст(ка); **~ic(al** □) [ɑ:'tistik, -tikəl] артисти́ческий, худóжественный.
as [æz] *cj. a. adv.* когдá; в то врéмя как; тáк как; хотя́; ~ it were кáк бы; ~ well тáк же; в такóй же мéре; such ~ такóй как; как напри́мéр; ~ well ~ и ... и ...; *prp.* ~ for, ~ to что касáется (Р); ~ from с (Р).
ascend [ə'send] поднимáться [-ня́ться]; всходи́ть [взойти́] на (В); восходи́ть (to к Д); ✈ наб(и)рáть высотý.
ascension [ə'senʃən] восхождéние; ♀ (Day) вознесéние.
ascent [ə'sent] подъём; крутизнá.
ascertain [æsə'tein] удостоверя́ться [-вéриться] в (П).
ascribe [ə'skraib] припи́сывать [-сáть] (Д/В).
aseptic [ei'septik] ⚕ стери́льный.
ash¹ [æʃ] ♀ я́сень *m*; mountain ~ряби́на.
ash² [~], *mst pl.* **~es** [æʃiz] золá, пéпел.
ashamed [ə'ʃeimd] пристыжённый.
ash-can *Am.* ведрó для мýсора.
ashen [æʃn] пéпельный (цвет).
ashore [ə'ʃɔ:] нá берег, на берегý; run ~, be driven ~ наскочи́ть на мель.
ash-tray пéпельница.
ashy ['æʃi] пéпельный; блéдный.
Asiatic [eiʃi'ætik] 1. азиáтский; 2. азиáт(ка).
aside [ə'said] в стóрону, в сторонé; отдéльно.
ask [ɑ:sk] *v/t.* [по]проси́ть (a th. of, from a p. что-нибудь у когó-нибудь); ~ that проси́ть, чтóбы ...; спрáшивать [спроси́ть]; ~ (a p.) a question задавáть вопрóс (Д); *v/i.* ~ for [по]проси́ть (В *or* Р *or* о П).
askance [əs'kæns], **askew** [əs'kju:] и́скоса, кóсо; кри́во.
asleep [ə'sli:p] спя́щий; be ~ спать.
aslope [ə'sloup] *adv.* покáто; на склóне, на скáте.
asparagus [əs'pærəgəs] ♀ спáржа.
aspect ['æspekt] вид (*a. gr.*); аспéкт; сторонá.
asperity [æs'periti] стрóгость *f*; сурóвость *f.*
asphalt ['æsfælt] 1. асфáльт; 2. покрывáть асфáльтом.
aspir|ant [əs'paiərənt] кандидáт; **~ate** ['æspəreit] произноси́ть с придыхáнием; **~ation** [æspə'reiʃən] стремлéние; *phon.* придыхáние; **~e** [əs'paiə] стреми́ться (to, after, at к Д); домогáться (Р).
ass [æs] осёл.
assail [ə'seil] нападáть [-пáсть] на (В), атаковáть (В) (*im*)*pf.*; *fig.* энерги́чно брáться за (дéло); **~ant** [-ənt] проти́вник; нападáющий.
assassin [ə'sæsin] уби́йца *m/f*; **~ate** [-ineit] уби́(вá)ть; **~ation** [əsæsi'neiʃən] уби́йство.
assault [ə'sɔ:lt] 1. нападéние, атáка; ⚖ словéсное оскорблéние; физи́ческое наси́лие; 2. нападáть [напáсть], набрáсываться [-рóситься] на (В).
assay [ə'sei] 1. испытáние, опрóбование (метáллов); 2. [ис]прóбовать, испы́тывать [испытáть].
assembl|age [ə'semblidʒ] собрáние; скоплéние; сбор; ⊕ монтáж, сбóрка; **~e** [ə'sembl] соз(ы)вáть; ⊕ [с]монти́ровать; **~y** [-i] собрáние; ассамблéя; ⊕ сбóрка частéй.
assent [ə'sent] 1. соглáсие; 2. соглашáться [-ласи́ться] (to на В; с Т).
assert [ə'sə:t] утверждáть [-рди́ть]; **~ion** [ə'sə:ʃən] утверждéние.
assess [ə'ses] облагáть налóгом; оцéнивать имýщество (Р); **~able** [-əbl] □ подлежáщий обложéнию; **~ment** [-mənt] обложéние; оцéнка.
asset ['æset] цéнное кáчество; ✝ статья́ дохóда; **~s** *pl.* ✝ акти́в.
assiduous [ə'sidjuəs] □ прилéжный.
assign [ə'sain] определя́ть [-ли́ть]; назначáть [-нáчить]; ассигнóвывать, ассигновáть (*im*)*pf*; поручáть [-чи́ть]; **~ment** [ə'sainmənt] назначéние; ⚖ передáча; задáние.
assimilat|e [ə'simileit] ассимили́ровать(ся) (*im*)*pf.*; осваивать [освóить]; прирáвнивать [-ня́ть];

~ion [əsimi'leiʃən] уподобле́ние; ассимиля́ция; усвое́ние.
assist [ə'sist] помога́ть [-мо́чь] (Д), [по]соде́йствовать (*im*)*pf.* (Д); **~ance** [-əns] по́мощь *f*; **~ant** [-ənt] ассисте́нт(ка); помо́щник (-ица).
associa|te 1. [ə'souʃieit] обща́ться (with с Т); ассоции́ровать(ся) (*im*)*pf.*; присоединя́ть(ся) [-ни́ть (-ся)] (with к Д); 2. [-ʃiit] a) свя́занный; объединённый; b) това́рищ, колле́га; соуча́стник; **~tion** [əsousi'eiʃən] ассоциа́ция; соедине́ние; о́бщество.
assort [ə'sɔ:t] [рас]сортирова́ть; подбира́ть [подобра́ть]; снабжа́ть ассортиме́нтом; **~ment** [-mənt] сортиро́вка.
assum|e [ə'sju:m] принима́ть [-ня́ть] (на себя́); предполага́ть [-ложи́ть]; **~ption** [ə'sʌmpʃən] предположе́ние; присвое́ние; *eccl.* ♀ успе́ние.
assur|ance [ə'ʃuərəns] увере́ние; уве́ренность *f*; страхо́вка; **~e** [ə'ʃuə] уверя́ть [уве́рить]; обеспе́чи(ва)ть; [за]страхова́ть; **~edly** [-ridli] *adv.* коне́чно, несомне́нно.
astir [əs'tə:] в движе́нии; на нога́х.
astonish [əs'tɔniʃ] удивля́ть [-ви́ть], изумля́ть [-ми́ть]; be **~ed** удивля́ться [-ви́ться] (at Д); **~ing** [-iʃiŋ] □ удиви́телный, изуми́тельный; **~ment** [əs'tɔniʃmənt] удивле́ние, изумле́ние.
astound [əs'taund] поража́ть [порази́ть].
astray [əs'trei]: go ~ заблуди́ться, сби́ться с пути́.
astride [əs'traid] верхо́м (of на П).
astringent [əs'trindʒənt] □ ⚕ вя́жущий (о сре́дстве).
astro|logy [əs'trɔlədʒi] астроло́гия; **~nomer** [əs'trɔnəmə] астроно́м; **~nomy** [əs'trɔnəmi] астроно́мия.
astute [əs'tju:t] □ хи́трый; проница́тельный; **~ness** [-nis] хи́трость *f*; проница́тельность *f*.
asunder [ə'sʌndə] по́рознь, отде́льно; в куски́, на ча́сти.
asylum [ə'sailəm] прию́т; убе́жище.
at [æt] *prp.* в (П, В); у (Р); при (П); на (П, В); о́коло (Р); за (Т); ~ school в шко́ле; ~ the age of в во́зрасте (Р).
ate [et, eit] *pt.* от eat.
atheism ['eiθiizm] атеи́зм.
athlet|e ['æθli:t] атле́т; **~ic(al** □) [æθ'letik(əl)] атлети́ческий; **~ics** *pl.* [æθ'letiks] атле́тика.
Atlantic [ət'læntik] 1. атланти́ческий; 2. (*a.* ~ Ocean) Атланти́ческий океа́н.
atmospher|e ['ætməsfiə] атмосфе́ра; **~ic(al** □) [ætməs'ferik(əl)] атмосфе́рный, атмосфери́ческий.
atom ['ætəm] ⚛ а́том; ~ (*a.* **~ic**) bomb а́томная бо́мба; **~ic** [ə'tɔmik] а́томный; ~ pile а́томный реа́ктор; ~ smashing расщепле́ние а́тома; **~izer** ['ætəmaizə] распыли́тель *m.*
atone [ə'toun]: ~ for загла́живать [-ла́дить], искупа́ть [-пи́ть]; **~ment** [-mənt] искупле́ние.
atroci|ous [ə'trouʃəs] □ зве́рский, ужа́сный; **~ty** [ə'trɔsiti] зве́рство.
attach [ə'tætʃ] *v/t.* *com.* прикрепля́ть [-пи́ть]; прикомандиро́вывать [-рова́ть] (к Д); прид(ав)а́ть; ⚖ налага́ть аре́ст на (В); аресто́вывать [-ова́ть]; ~ o. s. to привя́зываться [-за́ться] к (Д); **~ment** [-mənt] привя́занность *f*; прикрепле́ние; наложе́ние аре́ста.
attack [ə'tæk] 1. ата́ка, наступле́ние; припа́док; 2. *v/t.* атакова́ть (*im*)*pf.*; напада́ть [напа́сть] на (В); набра́сываться [-ро́ситься] на (В); ⚕ поража́ть [порази́ть] (о боле́зни).
attain [ə'tein] *v/t.* достига́ть [-и́гнуть] (Р), доби́(ва́)ться (Р); **~ment** [-mənt] приобрете́ние; достиже́ние; **~s** *pl.* зна́ния *n/pl.*; на́выки *m/pl.*
attempt [ə'tempt] 1. попы́тка; покуше́ние; 2. [по]пыта́ться; покуша́ться [-уси́ться] на (В).
attend [ə'tend] обслу́живать [-жи́ть]; посеща́ть [-ети́ть]; ⚕ ходи́ть, уха́живать за (Т); прислу́живать (to Д); прису́тствовать (at на П); быть внима́тельным; **~ance** [ə'tendəns] прису́тствие (at на П); обслу́живание; пу́блика; посеща́емость *f*; ⚕ ухо́д (за Т); **~ant** [-ənt] 1. сопровожда́ющий (on В); прису́тствующий (at на П); 2. посети́тель(ница *f*) *m*; спу́тник (-ица); ⚕ санита́р; служи́тель *m.*
attent|ion [ə'tenʃən] внима́ние; **~ive** [-tiv] □ внима́тельный.
attest [ə'test] [за]свиде́тельствовать; удостоверя́ть [-ве́рить]; *part.* ⚔ приводи́ть к прися́ге.
attic ['ætik] черда́к; манса́рда.
attire [ə'taiə] 1. наря́д; 2. оде́(ва́)ть, наряжа́ть [-яди́ть].
attitude ['ætitju:d] отноше́ние; пози́ция; по́за, оса́нка; *fig.* то́чка зре́ния.
attorney [ə'tə:ni] пове́ренный; power of ~ полномо́чие; ♀ General *Am.* мини́стр юсти́ции.
attract [ə'trækt] *v/t.* привлека́ть [-вле́чь] (*a.* *fig.*); притя́гивать [-яну́ть]; *fig.* прельща́ть [-льсти́ть]; **~ion** [ə'trækʃən] притяже́ние, тяготе́ние; *fig.* привлека́тельность *f*; *thea.* аттракцио́н; **~ive** [-tiv] привлека́тельный; зама́нчивый; **~iveness** [-tivnis] привлека́тельность *f*.
attribute 1. [ə'tribju:t] припи́сывать [-са́ть] (Д/В); относи́ть [от-

нести́] (к Д); **2.** ['ætribju:t] сво́йство, при́знак; *gr.* определе́ние.
attune [ə'tju:n] приводи́ть в созву́чие.
auction ['ɔ:kʃən] **1.** аукцио́н, торги́ *m/pl.*; sell by ~, put up for ~ продава́ть с аукцио́на; **2.** продава́ть с аукцио́на (*mst* ~ off); **~eer** [ɔ:kʃə'niə] аукциони́ст.
audaci|ous [ɔ:'deiʃəs] □ сме́лый; де́рзкий; *b.s.* на́глый; **~ty** [ɔ:'dæsiti] сме́лость *f*; де́рзость *f*; *b.s.* на́глость *f*.
audible ['ɔ:debl] □ вня́тный, слы́шный.
audience ['ɔ:djəns] слу́шатели *m/pl.*, зри́тели *m/pl.*, пу́блика; аудие́нция (of, with у Р).
audit ['ɔ:dit] **1.** прове́рка, реви́зия (бухга́лтерских книг); **2.** проверя́ть [-е́рить] (отчётность); **~or** ['ɔ:ditə] слу́шатель *m*; ревизо́р, (фина́нсовый) контролёр.
auger ['ɔ:gə] ⊕ сверло́, бура́в.
augment [ɔ:g'ment] увели́чи(ва)ть; **~ation** [ɔ:gmen'teiʃən] увеличе́ние, приро́ст, прираще́ние.
augur ['ɔ:gə] **1.** авгу́р, прорица́тель *m*; **2.** предска́зывать [-за́ть] (well хоро́шее, ill плохо́е); **~y** предзнамнова́ние.
August ['ɔ:gəst] а́вгуст.
aunt [ɑ:nt] тётя, тётка.
auspic|e ['ɔ:spis] до́брое предзнамнова́ние; **~s** *pl.* покрови́тельство; **~ious** [ɔ:s'piʃəs] □ благоприя́тный.
auster|e [ɔ:s'tiə] □ стро́гий, суро́вый; **~ity** [ɔ:s'teriti] стро́гость *f*, суро́вость *f*.
Australian [ɔ:s'treiljən] **1.** австрали́ец (-и́йка); **2.** австрали́йский.
Austrian ['ɔ:striən] **1.** австри́ец (-и́йка); **2.** австри́йский.
authentic [ɔ:'θentik] (**~ally**) по́длинный, достове́рный.
author ['ɔ:θə] а́втор; **~itative** [ɔ:'θɔriteitiv] □ авторите́тный; **~ity** [ɔ:'θɔriti] авторите́т; полномо́чие; власть *f* (over над Т); on the ~ of на основа́нии (Р); по утвержде́нию (Р); **~ize** ['ɔ:θəraiz] уполномо́чи(ва)ть; санкциони́ровать (*im*)*pf.*
autocar ['ɔ:təkɑ:] автомоби́ль *m*.
autocra|cy [ɔ:'tɔkrəsi] самодержа́вие, автокра́тия; **~tic(al** □) [ɔ:tə'krætik(əl)] самодержа́вный; деспоти́ческий.
autogyro ['ɔ:tou'dʒaiərou] ✈ автожи́р.
autograph ['ɔ:təgrɑ:f] авто́граф.
automat|ic [ɔ:tə'mætik] (**~ally**) автомати́ческий; ~ machine автома́т; **~on** [ɔ:'tɔmətən] автома́т.
automobile ['ɔtəməbi:l] *part. Am.* автомоби́ль *m*.
autonomy [ɔ:'tɔnəmi] автоно́мия, самоуправле́ние.
autumn ['ɔ:təm] о́сень *f*; **~al** [ɔ:'tʌmnəl] осе́нний.
auxiliary [ɔ:g'ziljəri] вспомога́тельный; доба́вочный.
avail [ə'veil] **1.** помога́ть [помо́чь] (Д); ~ o. s. of [вос]по́льзоваться (Т); **2.** по́льза, вы́года; of no ~ бесполе́зный; **~able** [ə'veiləbl] □ досту́пный; нали́чный.
avalanche ['ævəlɑ:nʃ] лави́на.
avaric|e ['ævəris] ску́пость *f*; жа́дность *f*; **~ious** [ævə'riʃəs] □ скупо́й; жа́дный.
aveng|e [ə'vendʒ] [ото]мсти́ть (Д за В); **~er** [-ə] мсти́тель(ница *f*) *m*.
avenue ['ævinju:] алле́я; *Am.* широ́кая у́лица, проспе́кт; *fig.* путь *m*.
aver [ə'və:] утвержда́ть.
average ['ævəridʒ] **1.** сре́днее число́; at an ~ в сре́днем; **2.** сре́дний; **3.** выводи́ть сре́днее число́.
avers|e [ə'və:s] □ нерасполо́женный (to, from к Д); неохо́тный; **~ion** отвраще́ние, антипа́тия.
avert [ə'və:t] отвраща́ть [-рати́ть].
aviat|ion [eivi'eiʃən] авиа́ция; **~or** ['eivietə] лётчик, авиа́тор.
avoid [ə'vɔid] избега́ть [-ежа́ть] (Р); **~ance** [-əns] избежа́ние.
avow [ə'vau] призн(ав)а́ть; ~ oneself призн(ав)а́ться; **~al** [-əl] призна́ние.
await [ə'weit] ожида́ть (Р).
awake [ə'weik] **1.** бо́дрствующий; be ~ to я́сно понима́ть; **2.** [*irr.*] *v/t.* (*mst* **~n** [ə'weikən]) [раз]буди́ть; пробужда́ть [-уди́ть] (созна́ние, интере́с) (к Д); *v/i.* просыпа́ться [просну́ться]; ~ to a th. осозн(ав)а́ть (В).
aware [ə'wɛə]: be ~ of знать (В *or* о П), созн(ав)а́ть (В); become ~ of отдава́ть себе́ отчёт в (П).
away [ə'wei] прочь; далеко́.
awe [ɔ:] **1.** благогове́ние, тре́пет (of пе́ред Т); **2.** внуша́ть благогове́ние, страх (Д).
awful [ɔ:ful] □ внуша́ющий благогове́ние; стра́шный; F ужа́сный; чрезвыча́йный.
awhile [ə'wail] на не́которое вре́мя, ненадо́лго.
awkward ['ɔ:kwəd] неуклю́жий, нело́вкий; неудо́бный.
awl [ɔ:l] ши́ло.
awning ['ɔ:niŋ] наве́с, тент.
awoke [ə'wouk] *pt.* и *p. pt.* от awake.
awry [ə'rai] ко́со, на́бок; *fig.* непра́вильно.
ax(e) [æks] топо́р, колу́н.
axis ['æksis], *pl.* axes [-si:z] ось *f*.
axle ['æksl] ⊕ ось *f*; **~-tree** колёсный вал.
ay(e) [ai] да; *parl.* утверди́тельный го́лос (при голосова́нии).
azure ['æʒə] **1.** лазу́рь *f*; **2.** лазу́рный.

B

babble ['bæbl] **1.** ле́пет; болтовня́; **2.** [по]болта́ть; [за]лепета́ть.
baboon [bə'bu:n] *zo.* бабуи́н.
baby ['beibi] **1.** младе́нец, ребёнок, дитя́ *n*; **2.** небольшо́й, ма́лый; **~hood** ['beibihud] младе́нчество.
bachelor ['bætʃələ] холостя́к; *univ.* бакала́вр.
back [bæk] **1.** спина́; спи́нка (сту́ла, пла́тья и т. п.); изна́нка (мате́рии); *football* защи́тник; **2.** *adj.* за́дний; обра́тный; отдалённый; **3.** *adv.* наза́д, обра́тно; тому́ наза́д; **4.** *v/t.* подде́рживать [-жа́ть]; подкрепля́ть [-епи́ть]; [по]пя́тить; держа́ть пари́ на (В), [по]ста́вить на (ло́шадь); ✝ индосси́ровать; *v/i.* отступа́ть [-пи́ть]; [по]пя́титься; **~bone** позвоно́чник, спинно́й хребе́т; *fig.* опо́ра; **~er** ['bækə] ✝ индосса́нт; **~ground** за́дний план, фон; **~ing** подде́ржка; ✝ индоссаме́нт; **~side** за́дняя, ты́льная сторона́; зад; **~slide** [*irr.* (slide)] отпада́ть [отпа́сть] (от ве́ры); **~stairs** чёрная ле́стница; **~stroke** пла́вание на спине́; **~-talk** *Am.* де́рзкий отве́т; **~ward** ['bækwəd] **1.** *adj.* обра́тный; *fig.* отста́лый; **2.** *adv.* (*a.* **~wards** [-z]) наза́д; за́дом; наоборо́т; обра́тно; **~water** за́водь *f*; **~wheel** за́днее колесо́.
bacon ['beikən] беко́н, копчёная груди́нка.
bacteri|ologist [bæktiəri'ɔlədʒist] бактерио́лог; **~um** [bæk'tiəriəm], *pl.* **~a** [-riə] бакте́рия.
bad [bæd] □ плохо́й, дурно́й, скве́рный; he is **~ly** off его́ дела́ пло́хи; **~ly** wounded тяжелора́неный; F want **~ly** о́чень хоте́ть.
bade [beid, bæd] *pt.* от **bid.**
badge [bædʒ] значо́к.
badger ['bædʒə] **1.** *zo.* барсу́к; **2.** [за]трави́ть; изводи́ть [извести́].
badness ['bædnis] него́дность *f*; вре́дность *f*.
baffle ['bæfl] расстра́ивать [-ро́ить]; сбива́ть с то́лку.
bag [bæg] **1.** мешо́к; су́мка; **2.** класть в мешо́к; *hunt.* уби́(ва́)ть.
baggage ['bægidʒ] бага́ж; **~-check** *Am.* бага́жная квита́нция.
bagpipe ['bægpaip] волы́нка.
bail [beil] **1.** поручи́тельство; admit to **~** ⚖ выпуска́ть на пору́ки; **2. ~** out ⚖ брать на пору́ки.
bailiff ['beilif] суде́бный при́став; управля́ющий (име́нием).
bait [beit] **1.** прима́нка, нажи́вка; *fig.* искуше́ние; **2.** прима́нивать [-ни́ть]; *hunt.* трави́ть соба́ками; *fig.* пресле́довать насме́шками, изводи́ть [-вести́].
bak|e [beik] [ис]пе́чь(ся); обжига́ть [обже́чь] (кирпичи́); **~er** ['beikə] пе́карь *m*, бу́лочник; **~ery** [-ri] пека́рня; **~ing-powder** пека́рный порошо́к.
balance ['bæləns] **1.** весы́ *m/pl.*; равнове́сие; противове́с; баланси́р; ✝ бала́нс; са́льдо *n indecl.*; *sl.* оста́ток; **~** of power полити́ческое равнове́сие; **~** of trade акти́вный бала́нс; **2.** [с]баланси́ровать (В); сохраня́ть равнове́сие; ✝ подводи́ть бала́нс; взве́шивать [-е́сить] (в уме́); быть в равнове́сии.
balcony ['bælkəni] балко́н.
bald [bɔ:ld] лы́сый, плеши́вый; *fig.* просто́й; бесцве́тный (стиль).
bale [beil] ✝ ки́па, тюк.
balk [bɔ:k] **1.** межа́; брус; ба́лка; **2.** *v/t.* [вос]препя́тствовать (Д), [по]меша́ть (Д); [за]арта́читься (*a. fig.*).
ball¹ [bɔ:l] **1.** мяч; шар; клубо́к (ше́рсти); keep the **~** rolling подде́рживать разгово́р; **2.** собира́ть(ся) в клубо́к; сви́(ва́)ть(ся).
ball² [~] бал, танцева́льный ве́чер.
ballad ['bæləd] балла́да.
ballast ['bæləst] **1.** ще́бень *m*; 🚂, ⚓ балла́ст; **2.** грузи́ть балла́стом.
ball-bearing(s *pl.*) шарикоподши́пник.
ballet ['bælei] бале́т.
balloon [bə'lu:n] возду́шный шар, аэроста́т; **~ist** [-ist] аэрона́вт, пило́т аэроста́та.
ballot ['bælət] **1.** баллотиро́вка, голосова́ние; **2.** [про]голосова́ть; **~-box** избира́тельная у́рна.
ball-point (*a.* **~ pen**) ша́риковая ру́чка.
ball-room ба́льный зал.
balm [bɑ:m] бальза́м; *fig.* утеше́ние.
balmy [bɑ:mi] □ арома́тный.
baloney [bə'louni] *Am. sl.* вздор.
balsam ['bɔ:lsəm] бальза́м; ⚘ бальзами́н.
balustrade ['bæləstreid] балюстра́да.
bamboo [bæm'bu:] бамбу́к.
bamboozle F [-zl] наду́(ва́)ть, обма́нывать [-ну́ть].
ban [bæn] **1.** запреще́ние, запре́т; **2.** налага́ть запреще́ние на (В).
banana [bə'nɑ:nə] бана́н.
band [bænd] **1.** ле́нта, тесьма́; о́бод; ба́нда; отря́д; ♪ орке́стр; **2.** свя́зывать [-за́ть]; **~ o. s.** объединя́ться [-ни́ться].
bandage ['bændidʒ] **1.** бинт, банда́ж; **2.** [за]бинтова́ть, перевя́зывать [-за́ть].
bandbox ['bændbɔks] карто́нка (для шляп).

bandit ['bændit] банди́т.
band-master ['bændmɑːstə] капельме́йстер.
bandy ['bændi] обме́ниваться [-ня́ться] (слова́ми, мячо́м и т. п.).
bane [bein] *fig.* отра́ва.
bang [bæŋ] **1.** уда́р, стук; **2.** ударя́ть(ся) [уда́рить(ся)]; сту́кать(ся) [-кнуть(ся)].
banish ['bæniʃ] изгоня́ть [изгна́ть]; высыла́ть [вы́слать]; **~ment** [-mənt] изгна́ние.
banisters ['bænistəz] *pl.* пери́ла *n/pl.*
bank [bæŋk] **1.** бе́рег; на́сыпь *f*; банк; ~ of issue эмиссио́нный банк; **2.** *v/t.* окружа́ть ва́лом; запру́живать [-уди́ть]; ✝ класть (де́ньги) в банк; *v/i.* быть банки́ром; ✈ де́лать вира́ж, накреня́ться [-ни́ться]; ~ on полага́ться [-ложи́ться] на (В); **~er** ['bæŋkə] банки́р; **~ing** ['bæŋkiŋ] ба́нковое де́ло; **~rupt** ['bæŋkrʌpt] **1.** банкро́т; **2.** обанкро́тившийся; **3.** де́лать банкро́том; **~ruptcy** ['bæŋkrʌptsi] банкро́тство.
banner ['bænə] зна́мя *n*, стяг.
banns [bænz] *pl.* оглаше́ние (вступа́ющих в брак).
banquet ['bæŋkwit] **1.** банке́т, пир; **2.** дава́ть банке́т; пирова́ть.
banter ['bæntə] подшу́чивать [-у-ти́ть], поддра́знивать [-ни́ть].
baptism [bæp'tizm] креще́ние.
baptize [bæp'taiz] [о]крести́ть.
bar [bɑː] **1.** бру́со́к; засо́в; о́тмель *f*; бар; сто́йка; ♪ такт; *fig.* прегра́да, препя́тствие; ⚖ адвокату́ра; **2.** запира́ть на засо́в; прегражда́ть [-ради́ть]; исключа́ть [-чи́ть].
barb [bɑːb] колю́чка; зубе́ц; **~ed** wire колю́чая про́волока.
barbar|ian [bɑː'bɛəriən] **1.** ва́рвар; **2.** ва́рварский; **~ous** ['bɑːbərəs] □ ди́кий; гру́бый, жесто́кий.
barbecue ['bɑːbikjuː] **1.** целико́м жа́рить (ту́шу); **2.** целико́м зажа́ренная ту́ша.
barber ['bɑːbə] парикма́хер.
bare [bɛə] **1.** го́лый, обнажённый; пусто́й; **2.** обнажа́ть [-жи́ть], откры́(ва́)ть; **~faced** ['bɛəfeist] □ бессты́дный; **~-foot** босико́м; **~-footed** бо́со́й; **~-headed** с непокры́той голово́й; **~ly** ['bɛəli] едва́.
bargain ['bɑːgin] **1.** сде́лка, вы́годная поку́пка; **2.** [по]торгова́ться (о П, с Т).
barge [bɑːdʒ] ба́ржа; **~man** ['bɑːdʒmən] ло́дочник с ба́ржи.
bark[1] [bɑːk] **1.** кора́; **2.** сдира́ть кору́ с (Р).
bark[2] [~] **1.** лай; **2.** [за]ла́ять.
bar-keeper буфе́тчик.
barley ['bɑːli] ячме́нь *m*.
barn [bɑːn] амба́р.

baron ['bærən] баро́н; **~ess** [-is] бароне́сса.
barrack(s *pl.*) ['bærək(s)] бара́к; [каза́рма.]
barrage ['bærɑːʒ] загражде́ние; ⚔ загради́тельный ого́нь *m*.
barrel ['bærəl] **1.** бо́чка, бочо́нок; ствол (ружья́); ⊕ цили́ндр; бараба́н; вал; **2.** разлива́ть по бо́чкам.
barren ['bærən] □ неплодоро́дный, беспло́дный.
barricade [bæri'keid] **1.** баррика́да; **2.** [за]баррикади́ровать.
barrier ['bæriə] барье́р, заста́ва; препя́тствие, поме́ха.
barrister ['bæristə] адвока́т.
barrow ['bærou] та́чка.
barter ['bɑːtə] **1.** товарообме́н, менова́я торго́вля; **2.** [по]меня́ть, обме́нивать [-ня́ть] (for на В).
base[1] [beis] □ по́длый, ни́зкий.
base[2] [~] **1.** осно́ва, ба́зис, фунда́мент; ⚗ основа́ние; **2.** осно́вывать [-ова́ть] (В на П), бази́ровать.
base|-ball *Am.* бейсбо́л; **~less** ['beislis] без основа́ний; **~ment** [-mənt] подва́л, подва́льный эта́ж.
baseness ['beisnis] ни́зость *f*.
bashful ['bæʃful] □ засте́нчивый, ро́бкий.
basic ['beisik] (**~ally**) основно́й; ⚗ осно́вный.
basin [beisn] таз, ми́ска; бассе́йн.
bas|is ['beisis], *pl.* **~es** [-iːz] основа́ние, исхо́дный пункт; ⚔, ⚓ ба́за.
bask [bɑːsk] гре́ться (на со́лнце).
basket ['bɑːskit] корзи́на; **~-ball** баскетбо́л.
bass [beis] ♪ **1.** бас; **2.** басо́вый.
basso ['bæsou] ♪ бас.
bastard ['bæstəd] **1.** □ внебра́чный; подде́льный; ло́маный (о языке́); **2.** внебра́чный ребёнок.
baste[1] [beist] полива́ть жарко́е со́ком (во вре́мя жа́рения).
baste[2] [~] намётывать [намета́ть].
bat[1] [bæt] лету́чая мышь *f*.
bat[2] [~] **1.** бита́ (в крике́те); **2.** бить, ударя́ть в мяч.
bath [bɑːθ] **1.** ва́нна; купа́льня; **2.** [вы́-, по]мы́ть, [вы́]купа́ть.
bathe [beið] [вы́]купа́ться.
bathing ['beiðiŋ] купа́ние; **~-hut** каби́на; **~-suit** купа́льный костю́м.
bath|-room ва́нная ко́мната; **~-sheet** купа́льная простыня́; **~-towel** купа́льное полоте́нце.
batiste [bæ'tiːst] ✝ бати́ст.
baton ['bætən] жезл; дирижёрская па́лочка; полице́йская дуби́нка.
battalion [bə'tæljən] баталь́он.
batter ['bætə] **1.** взби́тое те́сто; **2.** си́льно бить, [по]колоти́ть, [от-]дуба́сить; ~ down и́ли in взла́мывать [взлома́ть]; **~y** [-ri] батаре́я; assault and ~ оскорбле́ние де́йствием.
battle ['bætl] **1.** би́тва, сраже́ние

(of под T); 2. сража́ться [срази́ться]; боро́ться; ~-ax(e) *hist.* боево́й топо́р; *Am. fig.* бой-ба́ба.
battle|-field по́ле би́твы; **~-plane** ⚔ штурмови́к; **~-ship** ⚔ лине́йный кора́бль *m.*
bawdy ['bɔ:di] непристо́йный.
bawl [bɔ:l] крича́ть [кри́кнуть], [за]ора́ть; ~ out выкри́кивать [вы́крикнуть].
bay[1] [bei] 1. гнедо́й; 2. гнеда́я ло́шадь *f.*
bay[2] [~] зали́в, бу́хта.
bay[3] [~] ла́вровое де́рево.
bay[4] [~] 1. лай; 2. [за]ла́ять; bring to ~ *fig.* припере́ть к стене́; загоня́ть [загна́ть] (зве́ря).
bayonet ['beiənit] ⚔ 1. штык; 2. коло́ть штыко́м.
bay-window ['bei'windou] ▲ э́ркер; *Am.* брюшко́.
baza(a)r [bə'zɑ:] база́р.
be [bi:, bi] [*irr.*]: a) быть, быва́ть; жить; находи́ться; пожива́ть, чу́вствовать себя́; there is, are есть; ~ about соб(и)ра́ться (+ *inf.*); ~ at s. th. быть за́нятым (T); ~ off отправля́ться [-а́виться]; ~ on быть в де́йствии; b) *v/aux.* (для образова́ния дли́тельной фо́рмы): ~ reading чита́ть; c) *v/aux.* (для образова́ния пасси́ва): ~ read чита́ться, быть чи́танным (чита́емым).
beach [bi:tʃ] 1. пляж, взмо́рье; 2. ⚓ вы́тащить на бе́рег; посади́ть на мель.
beacon ['bi:kən] сигна́льный ого́нь *m*; ба́кен; буй.
bead [bi:d] бу́сина, би́серина; ка́пля; **~s** *pl. a.* чётки *f/pl.;* бу́сы *f/pl.;* би́сер.
beak [bi:k] клюв; но́сик (сосу́да).
beam [bi:m] 1. ба́лка, брус; луч; 2. сия́ть; излуча́ть [-чи́ть].
bean [bi:n] боб.
bear[1] [bɛə] медве́дь *m* (-ве́дица *f*); † *sl.* спекуля́нт, игра́ющий на пониже́ние.
bear[2] [~] [*irr.*] *v/t.* носи́ть [нести́]; [вы́]терпе́ть, выде́рживать [вы́держать]; рожда́ть [роди́ть]; ~ down преодоле́(ва́)ть; ~ out подтвержда́ть [-рди́ть]; ~ o. s. держа́ться, вести́ себя́; ~ up подде́рживать [-жа́ть]; ~ (up)on каса́ться [косну́ться] (P); име́ть отноше́ние к (Д); bring to ~ употребля́ть [-би́ть].
beard [biəd] 1. борода́; зубе́ц; ⚘ ость *f* (ко́лоса); 2. *v/t.* сме́ло выступа́ть про́тив (P).
bearer ['bɛərə] носи́льщик; пода́тель(ница *f*) *m*, предъяви́тель (-ница *f*) *m.*
bearing ['bɛəriŋ] ноше́ние; терпе́ние; мане́ра держа́ть себя́; деторожде́ние.
beast [bi:st] зверь *m*; скоти́на; **~ly** [-li] гру́бый, ужа́сный.
beat [bi:t] 1. [*irr.*] *v/t.* [по]би́ть; ударя́ть [уда́рить]; [по]колоти́ть; ~ a retreat отступа́ть [-пи́ть]; ~ up изби́(ва́)ть; взби(ва́)ть; ~ about the bush подходи́ть к де́лу издалека́; *v/i.* бить; би́ться; [по]стуча́ться; 2. уда́р; бой; бие́ние; ритм; **~en** [bi:tn] 1. *p. pt.* от beat; 2. би́тый, побеждённый; проторённый (путь).
beatitude [bi'ætitju:d] блаже́нство.
beau [bou] щёголь *m*; кавале́р.
beautiful ['bju:tiful] □ прекра́сный, краси́вый.
beautify ['bju:tifai] украша́ть [укра́сить].
beauty ['bju:ti] красота́; краса́вица.
beaver ['bi:və] бобр.
became [bi'keim *pt.* от become.
because [bi'kɔz] потому́ что, та́к как; ~ of из-за (P).
beckon ['bekən] [по]мани́ть.
becom|e [bi'kʌm] [*irr.* (come)] *v/i.* [с]де́латься; станови́ться [стать]; *v/t.* быть к лицу́, идти́ (об оде́жде) (Д); подоба́ть (Д); **~ing** [-iŋ] □ к лицу́ (оде́жда).
bed bed] 1. посте́ль *f*; крова́ть *f*; ⚘ гря́дка, клу́мба; 2. класть и́ли ложи́ться в посте́ль; выса́живать [вы́садить] (цветы́).
bed-clothes *pl.* посте́льное бельё.
bedding ['bediŋ] посте́льные принадле́жности *f/pl.*
bedevil [bi'devl] [ис]терза́ть, [из-]му́чить; околдо́вывать [-дова́ть].
bed|rid(den) прико́ванный к посте́ли (боле́знью); **~room** спа́льня; **~spread** покрыва́ло (на крова́ть); **~stead** крова́ть *f*; **~time** вре́мя ложи́ться спать.
bee [bi:] пчела́; have a ~ in one's bonnet F быть с причу́дой.
beech [bi:tʃ] ⚘ бук, бу́ковое де́рево; **~nut** бу́ковый оре́шек.
beef [bi:f] говя́дина; **~-tea** кре́пкий бульо́н; **~y** [bi:fi] му́скулистый; мяси́стый.
bee|hive у́лей; **~-line** пряма́я ли́ния.
been [bi:n, bin] *p. pt.* от be.
beer [biə] пи́во; small ~ сла́бое пи́во.
beet [bit] ⚘ свёкла.
beetle [bi:tl] жук.
befall [bi'fɔ:l] [*irr.* (fall)] *v/t.* постига́ть [-и́гнуть, -и́чь] (о судьбе́) (B); *v/i.* случа́ться [-чи́ться].
befit [bi'fit] прили́чествовать (Д), подходи́ть [подойти́] (Д).
before [bi'fɔ:] 1. *adv.* впереди́, вперёд; ра́ньше; long ~ задо́лго; 2. *cj.* пре́жде чем; скоре́е чем; 3. *prp.* пе́ред (T); впереди́ (P); до (P); **~hand** зара́нее, заблаговре́менно.
befriend [bi'frend] относи́ться по-дру́жески к (Д).
beg [beg] *v/t.* [по]проси́ть (P);

умоля́ть [-ли́ть] (for о П); выпра́шивать [вы́просить] (of у Р); *v/i.* ни́щенствовать.
began [bi'gæn] *pt.* от begin.
beget [bi'get] [*irr.* (get)] рожда́ть [роди́ть], производи́ть [-вести́].
beggar ['begə] **1.** ни́щий, ни́щенка; **2.** разоря́ть [-ри́ть], доводи́ть до нищеты́; *fig.* превосходи́ть [-взойти́]; it ~s all description не поддаётся описа́нию.
begin [bi'gin] [*irr.*] нач(ин)а́ть (with с Р); **~ner** [-ə] начина́ющий, новичо́к; **~ning** [-iŋ] нача́ло.
begot(ten) [bi'gɔt(n)] *pt.* от beget.
begrudge [bi'grʌdʒ] [по]зави́довать (Д в П).
beguile [bi'gail] обма́нывать [-ну́ть]; [с]корота́ть (вре́мя).
begun [bi'gʌn] *pt.* от begin.
behalf [bi'hɑ:f] : on *or* in ~ of для (Р), ра́ди (Р); от и́мени (Р).
behav|e [bi'heiv] вести́ себя́; поступа́ть [-пи́ть]; **~iour** [-jə] поведе́ние.
behead [bi'hed] обезгла́вливать [-гла́вить].
behind [bi'haind] **1.** *adv.* по́сле; позади́, сза́ди; **2.** *prp.* за (Т); позади́ (Р), сза́ди (Р); по́сле (Р).
behold [bi'hould] [*irr.* (hold)] **1.** замеча́ть [-е́тить], [у]ви́деть; **2.** смотри́!, вот!
behoof [bi'hu:f]: to (for, on) (the) ~ of в по́льзу (Р), за (В).
being ['bi:iŋ] бытие́, существова́ние.
belated [bi'leitid] запозда́лый.
belch [beltʃ] **1.** отры́жка; столб (огня́, ды́ма); **2.** рыга́ть [рыгну́ть]; изверга́ть [-е́ргнуть].
belfry ['belfri] колоко́льня.
Belgian ['beldʒən] **1.** бельги́ец (-и́йка); **2.** бельги́йский.
belief [bi'li:f] ве́ра (in в В); убежде́ние.
believable [bi'li:vəbl] правдоподо́бный.
believe [bi'li:v] [по]ве́рить (in в В); **~r** [-ə] ве́рующий.
belittle [bi'litl] *fig.* умаля́ть [-ли́ть]; принижа́ть [-ни́зить].
bell [bel] ко́локол; звоно́к.
belle [bel] краса́вица.
belles-lettres ['be'letr] *pl.* худо́жественная литерату́ра, беллетри́стика.
belligerent [bi'lidʒərənt] **1.** вою́ющая сторона́; **2.** вою́ющий.
bellow ['belou] **1.** мыча́ние; рёв (бу́ри); **2.** [за]мыча́ть; [за]реве́ть, [за]бушева́ть; **~s** [-z] *pl.* кузне́чные мехи́ *m/pl.*
belly ['beli] **1.** живо́т, брю́хо; **2.** наду́(ва́)ть(ся).
belong [bi'lɔŋ] принадлежа́ть (Д); относи́ться (к Д); **~ings** [-iŋz] *pl.* принадле́жности *f/pl.*; пожи́тки *m/pl.*
beloved [bi'lʌvid, *pred.* bi'lʌvd] возлю́бленный, люби́мый.
below [bi'lou] **1.** *adv.* внизу́; ни́же; **2.** *prp.* ни́же (Р); под (В, Т).
belt [belt] **1.** по́яс; зо́на; ⊕ приводно́й реме́нь *m*; ⚔ портупе́я; **2.** подпоя́с(ыв)ать; поро́ть ремнём.
bemoan [bi'moun] опла́к(ив)ать.
bench [bentʃ] скамья́; ⊕ верста́к.
bend [bend] **1.** сгиб; изги́б (доро́ги); излу́чина (реки́); ⚓ у́зел, шпанго́ут; **2.** [*irr.*] сгиба́ть(ся) [согну́ть(ся)]; направля́ть [-ра́вить]; покоря́ть [-ри́ть].
beneath [bi'ni:θ] *s.* below.
benediction [beni'dikʃən] благослове́ние.
benefact|ion [-'fækʃən] благодея́ние; **~or** ['benifæktə] благоде́тель *m.*
benefice|nce [bi'nefisns] благотвори́тельность *f*; **~nt** □ благоде́тельный.
beneficial [beni'fiʃə] □ благотво́рный, поле́зный.
benefit ['benifit] **1.** вы́года, по́льза; посо́бие; *thea.* бенефи́с; **2.** приноси́ть по́льзу; извлека́ть по́льзу.
benevolen|ce [bi'nevələns] благожела́тельность *f*; **~t** [-ənt] □ благожела́тельный.
benign [bi'nain] □ до́брый, милости́вый; ⚕ доброка́чественный.
bent [bent] **1.** *pt.* и *p. pt.* от bend; ~ on поме́шанный на (П); **2.** скло́нность *f.*
benz|ene [ben'zi:n] ⚗ бензо́л; **~ine** [~] бензи́н.
bequeath [bi'kwi:ð] завеща́ть (*im*)*pf*.
bequest [bi'kwest] насле́дство.
bereave [bi'ri:v] [*irr.*] лиша́ть [-ши́ть] (Р); отнима́ть [-ня́ть].
berry ['beri] я́года.
berth [bə:θ] ⚓ яко́рная стоя́нка; ко́йка; *fig.* (вы́годная) до́лжность *f.*
beseech [bi'si:tʃ] [*irr.*] умоля́ть [-ли́ть], упра́шивать [упроси́ть] (+ *inf.*).
beset [bi'set] [*irr.* (set)] окружа́ть [-жи́ть]; осажда́ть [осади́ть].
beside [bi'said] *prp.* ря́дом с (Т), о́коло (Р), близ (Р); ми́мо (Р); ~ o. s. вне себя́ (with от Р); ~ the question некста́ти, не по существу́; **~s** [-z] **1.** *adv.* кро́ме того́, сверх того́; **2.** *prp.* кро́ме (Р).
besiege [bi'si:dʒ] осажда́ть [осади́ть].
besmear [bi'smiə] [за]па́чкать, [за-] мара́ть.
besom ['bi:zəm] метла́, ве́ник.
besought [bi'sɔ:t] *pt.* от beseech.
bespatter [bi'spætə] забры́зг(ив)ать.
bespeak [bi'spi:k] [*irr.* (speak)] зака́зывать [-за́ть]; bespoke tailor портно́й, рабо́тающий по зака́зу.

best [best] **1.** *adj.* лу́чший; ~ man ша́фер; **2.** *adv.* лу́чше всего́, всех; **3.** са́мое лу́чшее; to the ~ of ... на-ско́лько ...; по ме́ре ...; make the ~ of испо́льзовать наилу́чшим о́б-разом; at ~ в лу́чшем слу́чае.
bestial ['bestjəl] □ ско́тский, жи-во́тный.
bestow [bi'stou] дарова́ть ([up]on Д/В *or* В/Т), награжда́ть [-ра-ди́ть].
bet [bet] **1.** пари́ *n indecl.*; **2.** [*irr.*] держа́ть пари́; би́ться об закла́д.
betake [bi'teik] [*irr.* (take)]: ~ o. s. to отправля́ться [-а́виться] в (В); *fig.* прибега́ть [-е́гнуть] к (Д).
bethink [bi'θiŋk] [*irr.* (think)]: ~ o. s. вспомина́ть [вспо́мнить]; ду́-мать (of о П); ~ o. s. to *inf.* заду́-м(ыв)ать.
betray [bi'trei] преда́(ва́)ть; вы́-да(ва́)ть; **~er** [-ə] преда́тель(ница *f*) *m*.
betrothal [bi'trouðəl] помо́лвка, обруче́ние.
better ['betə] **1.** *adj.* лу́чший; he is ~ ему́ лу́чше; **2.** преиму́щество; **~s** *pl.* ли́ца стоя́щие вы́ше; get the ~ of взять верх над (Т); **3.** *adv.* лу́чше; бо́льше; so much the ~ тем лу́чше; you had ~ go вам бы лу́чше пойти́; **4.** *v/t.* улучша́ть [улу́чшить]; поправля́ть [-а́вить]; *v/i.* поправля́ться [-а́виться]; **~ment** [-mənt] улучше́ние.
between [bi'twi:n] **1.** *adv.* ме́жду ни́ми; **2.** *prp.* ме́жду (Т).
beverage ['bevəridʒ] напи́ток.
bevy ['bevi] ста́я (птиц); ста́до; гру́ппа, толпа́ (де́вушек).
bewail [bi'weil] скорбе́ть о (П), опла́к(ив)ать.
beware [bi'wɛə] оберега́ться [-ре́чься] (Р).
bewilder [bi'wildə] смуща́ть [сму-ти́ть]; ста́вить в тупи́к; сбива́ть с то́лку; **~ment** [-mənt] смуще́-ние, замеша́тельство; пу́таница.
bewitch [bi'witʃ] околдо́вывать [-дова́ть]; очаро́вывать [-рова́ть].
beyond [bi'jɔnd] **1.** *adv.* вдали́, на расстоя́нии; **2.** *prp.* за (В, Т); вне (Р); сверх (Р); по ту сто́рону (Р).
bias ['baiəs] предубежде́ние (про́-тив Р); склон, укло́н; **2.** склоня́ть [-ни́ть]; **3.** ко́со.
bib [bib] де́тский нагру́дник.
Bible [baibl] би́блия.
biblical ['biblikəl] □ библе́йский.
bicarbonate [bai'kɑ:bənit] ⚗: ~ of soda двууглеки́слый на́трий.
bicker ['bikə] пререка́ться (с Т).
bicycle ['baisikl] **1.** велосипе́д; **2.** е́здить на велосипе́де.
bid [bid] **1.** [*irr.*] прика́зывать [-за́ть]; предлага́ть [-ложи́ть] (це́ну); ~ fair [по]сули́ть, [по]обе-ща́ть; ~ farewell [по]проща́ться [прости́ться]; **2.** предложе́ние (цены́), зая́вка (на торга́х); *Am.* F приглаше́ние; **~den** [bidn] *p. pt.* от bid.
bide [baid] : ~ one's time ожида́ть благоприя́тного слу́чая.
biennial [bai'enjəl] двухле́тний.
bier [biə] похоро́нные дро́ги *f/pl.*
big [big] большо́й, кру́пный; взро́слый; F *fig.* ва́жный, ва́ж-ничающий; F *fig.* ~ shot ва́жная «ши́шка»; talk ~ [по]хва́статься.
bigamy ['bigəmi] бига́мия, двое-бра́чие.
bigot ['bigət] слепо́й приве́рже-нец; **~ry** [-ri] слепа́я приве́ржен-ность *f*.
bigwig ['bigwig] F ва́жная «ши́шка».
bike [baik] F велосипе́д.
bile [bail] жёлчь *f*; *fig.* раздражи́-тельность *f*.
bilious ['biljəs] □ жёлчный.
bill[1] [bil] клюв; носо́к я́коря.
bill[2] [~] **1.** законопрое́кт, билль *m*; счёт; афи́ша; † ве́ксель *m*; ~ of fare меню́; ~ of lading коносаме́нт; ~ of sale ⚖ закладна́я; **2.** объ-явля́ть [-ви́ть] (афи́шей).
billfold бума́жник.
billiards ['biljədz] *pl.* билья́рд.
billion ['biljən] биллио́н; *Am.* мил-лиа́рд.
billow ['bilou] больша́я волна́; **2.** вздыма́ться (во́лна́ми), [вз]вол-нова́ться (о мо́ре); **~y** ['biloui] вздыма́ющийся (о во́лна́х).
bin [bin] за́кром; ларь *m*; му́сор-ное ведро́.
bind [baind] [*irr.*] **1.** *v/t.* [с]вяза́ть; свя́зывать [-за́ть]; обя́зывать [-за́ть]; переплета́ть [-плести́]; **2.** *v/i.* затверде́(ва́)ть; **~er** ['baində] переплётчик; **~ing** [-iŋ] **1.** пере-плёт; **2.** связу́ющий.
binocular [bai'nɔkjulə] бино́кль *m*.
biography [bai'ɔgrəfi] биогра́фия.
biology [bai'ɔlədʒi] биоло́гия.
birch [bə:tʃ] **1.** ♀ (и́ли **~-tree**) бе-рёза, берёзовое де́рево; ро́зга; **2.** сечь ро́згой.
bird [bə:d] пти́ца; **~'s-eye** ['bə:d-zai]: ~ view вид с пти́чьего полёта.
birth [bə:θ] рожде́ние; происхож-де́ние; bring to ~ порожда́ть [-ро-ди́ть]; **~day** день рожде́ния; **~-place** ме́сто рожде́ния.
biscuit ['biskit] пече́нье.
bishop ['biʃəp] епи́скоп; *chess* слон; **~ric** [-rik] епа́рхия.
bison ['baisn] *zo.* бизо́н, зубр.
bit [bit] **1.** кусо́чек, части́ца; не-мно́го; удила́ *n/pl.*; боро́дка (клю-ча́); **2.** *pt.* от **~e**.
bitch [bitʃ] су́ка.
bite [bait] **1.** уку́с; клёв (ры́бы); кусо́к; острота́; **2.** [*irr.*] куса́ть [укуси́ть]; клева́ть [клю́нуть] (о ры́бе); жечь (о пе́рце); щипа́ть (о моро́зе); ⊕ брать [взять]; *fig.* [съ]язви́ть.

bitten ['bitn] *pt.* от bite.
bitter ['bitə] □ го́рький; ре́зкий; *fig.* го́рький, мучи́тельный; **~s** *pl.* [-z] го́рький лека́рственный напи́ток.
blab [blæb] F разба́лтывать [-болта́ть].
black [blæk] 1. □ чёрный; тёмный, мра́чный; 2. [по]черни́ть; *fig.* [о]позо́рить; ~ out затемня́ть [-ни́ть]; 3. чернота́; чёрный цвет; чернокóжий (негр); **~berry** ежеви́ка; **~bird** чёрный дрозд; **~board** кла́ссная доска́; **~en** ['blækn] *v/t.* [на]черни́ть; *fig.* [о]черни́ть; *v/i.* [по]черне́ть; **~guard** ['blægɑ:d] 1. негодя́й, подле́ц; 2. □ по́длый; **~head** ⚕ угри́ *m/pl.*; **~ing** [blækiŋ] ва́кса; **~ish** ['blækiʃ] □ чернова́тый; **~leg** моше́нник; штрейкбре́хер; **~letter** *typ.* стари́нный готи́ческий шрифт; **~mail** 1. вымога́тельство, шанта́ж; 2. вымога́ть де́ньги у (Р); **~ness** [-nis] чернота́; **~out** затемне́ние; **~smith** кузне́ц.
bladder ['blædə] *anat.* пузы́рь *m.*
blade [bleid] ло́пасть *f; anat.* лопа́тка; ле́звие; клино́к; ⚘ лист; сте́бель *m*, былúнка.
blame [bleim] 1. упрёк; вина́; порица́ние; 2. порица́ть; обвиня́ть [-ни́ть]; be to ~ for быть винова́тым в (П); **~ful** ['bleimful] заслу́живающий порица́ния; **~less** ['bleimlis] □ безупре́чный.
blanch [blɑ:ntʃ] [вы́]бели́ть; [вы́-] чи́стить (мета́лл); ~ over обеля́ть [-ли́ть], опра́вдывать [-да́ть].
bland [blænd] □ ве́жливый; мя́гкий.
blank [blæŋk] 1. □ пусто́й; бессодержа́тельный; невырази́тельный; † незапо́лненный; ~ cartridge ⚔ холосто́й патро́н; 2. бланк; пробе́л; пустота́ (душе́вная).
blanket [blæŋkit] 1. шерстяно́е одея́ло; 2. покрыва́ть одея́лом.
blare [blɛə] [за]труби́ть.
blasphem|e [blæs'fi:m] богоху́льствовать; поноси́ть (against В); **~y** ['blæsfimi] богоху́льство.
blast [blɑ:st] 1. си́льный поры́в ве́тра; звук (духово́го инструме́нта); взрывна́я волна́; подрывно́й заря́д; ⚘ головня́; ⊕ дутьё; *fig.* па́губное влия́ние; 2. взрыва́ть [взорва́ть]; проклина́ть [-кля́сть]; **~-furnace** ⊕ до́мна, до́менная печь *f.*
blaze [bleiz] 1. я́ркое пла́мя *n*; вспы́шка (огня́, стра́сти); 2. *v/i.* горе́ть; пыла́ть; сверка́ть [-кну́ть]; *v/t.* разглаша́ть [-гласи́ть]; **~r** ['bleizə] спорти́вная ку́ртка.
blazon ['bleizn] герб.
bleach [bli:tʃ] [вы́]бели́ть.
bleak [bli:k] □ го́лый, пусты́нный; суро́вый (по кли́мату).
blear [bliə] 1. затума́ненный, нея́сный; 2. затума́ни(ва)ть; **~-eyed** ['bliəraid] с затума́ненными глаза́ми.
bleat [bli:t] 1. бле́яние; 2. [за-] бле́ять.
bleb [bleb] волды́рь *m*; пузырёк во́здуха (в воде́).
bled [bled] *pt.* и *p. pt.* от bleed.
bleed [bli:d] [*irr.*] 1. *v/i.* кровоточи́ть; истека́ть кро́вью; 2. *v/t.* пуска́ть кровь (Д); **~ing** ['bli:diŋ] кровотече́ние; кровопуска́ние.
blemish ['blemiʃ] 1. недоста́ток; пятно́; позо́р; 2. [за]пятна́ть; [ис]по́ртить; [о]позо́рить.
blench [blentʃ] отступа́ть [-пи́ть] (пе́ред Т).
blend [blend] 1. сме́шивать(ся) [-ша́ть(ся)]; разбавля́ть [-ба́вить]; сочета́ть(ся) (*im*)*pf.*; 2. сме́шивание; смесь *f.*
bless [bles] благословля́ть [-ви́ть]; осчастли́вливать [-тли́вить]; **~ed** (*pt.* blest; *adj.* 'blesid) □ счастли́вый, блаже́нный; **~ing** ['blesiŋ] благослове́ние.
blew [blu:] *pt.* от blow², ³.
blight [blait] 1. ⚘ ми́лдью *n indecl.* (и други́е боле́зни расте́ний); *fig.* ги́бель *f*; 2. приноси́ть вред (расте́ниям); разби́(ва́)ть (наде́жды и т. п.).
blind [blaind] □ 1. слепо́й (*fig.* ~ to к Д); нечёткий, нея́сный; ~ alley тупи́к; **~ly** *fig.* науга́д, наобу́м; 2. што́ра; марки́за; жалюзи́ *n indecl.*; 3. ослепля́ть [-пи́ть]; **~fold** ['blaindfould] завя́зывать глаза́ (Д).
blink [bliŋk] 1. мерца́ние; морга́ние; миг; 2. *v/i.* мига́ть [мигну́ть]; морга́ть [-гну́ть]; прищу́ри(ва)ться; *v/t.* закрыва́ть глаза́ на (В).
bliss [blis] блаже́нство.
blister ['blistə] 1. волды́рь *m*; 2. покрыва́ться пузыря́ми.
blizzard ['blizəd] бура́н, си́льная мете́ль *f.*
bloat [blout] распуха́ть [-пу́хнуть]; разду́(ва́)ться; **~er** ['bloutə] копчёная сельдь *f.*
block [blɔk] 1. коло́да, чурба́н; пла́ха; глы́ба; кварта́л (го́рода); 2. ~ in набра́сывать вчерне́; (*mst* ~ up) блоки́ровать (*im*)*pf.*
blockade [blɔ'keid] 1. блока́да; 2. блоки́ровать (*im*)*pf.*
blockhead ['blɔkhed] болва́н.
blond [blɔnd] 1. белоку́рый; **~e** блонди́нка.
blood [blʌd] кровь *f*; in cold ~ хладнокро́вно; **~-hörse** чистокро́вная ло́шадь *f*; **~shed** кровопроли́тие; **~shot** нали́тый кро́вью (о глаза́х); **~thirsty** кровожа́дный; **~-vessel** кровено́сный сосу́д; **~y** ['blʌdi] □ окрова́вленный; крова́вый.

bloom [blu:m] **1.** цвето́к; цвете́ние; расцве́т (*a. fig.*); **2.** цвести́, быть в цвету́.
blossom ['blɔsəm] **1.** цвето́к (фрукто́вого де́рева); расцве́т; **2.** цвести́, расцвета́ть [-есть́].
blot [blɔt] **1.** пятно́, кля́кса; *fig.* пятно́; **2.** [за]па́чкать; промока́ть [-кну́ть]; вычёркивать [вы́черкнуть].
blotch [blɔtʃ] прыщ; пятно́; кля́кса.
blotter ['blɔtə] пресс-папье́ *n indecl.*
blotting-paper промока́тельная бума́га.
blouse [blauz] блу́за; блу́зка.
blow[1] [blou] уда́р.
blow[2] [~] [*irr.*] **1.** цвести́; **2.** цвете́ние.
blow[3] [~] [*irr.*] **1.** [по]ду́ть; ве́ять; [за]пыхте́ть; игра́ть на (духово́м инструме́нте); ~ up взрыва́ть (-ся) [взорва́ть(ся)]; разду́(ва́)ть (ого́нь); гна́ть (ту́чи); ~ one's nose [вы́]сморка́ться; **2.** дунове́ние; **~er** ['blouə] труба́ч; **~n** [-n] *p. pt.* от blow[2],[3]; **~-out** *mot.* разры́в ши́ны; **~-pipe** пая́льная тру́бка.
bludgeon ['blʌdʒən] дуби́на.
blue [blu:] **1.** □ голубо́й; лазу́рный; си́ний; F уны́лый, пода́вленный; **2.** си́няя кра́ска; си́ний цвет; голуба́я кра́ска; си́нька; **~s** *pl.* меланхо́лия, хандра́; **3.** окра́шивать в си́ний, голубо́й цвет; [по]сини́ть (бельё).
bluff [blʌf] **1.** □ ре́зкий; грубова́тый; обры́вистый; **2.** обма́н, блеф; **3.** запу́гивать [-га́ть]; обма́нывать [-ну́ть].
bluish ['blu:iʃ] синева́тый, голубова́тый.
blunder ['blʌndə] **1.** гру́бая оши́бка; **2.** де́лать гру́бую оши́бку.
blunt [blʌnt] **1.** □ тупо́й; ре́зкий; **2.** притупля́ть [-пи́ть].
blur [blə:] **1.** нея́сное очерта́ние; кля́кса, пятно́; **2.** *v/t.* [за]мара́ть, [за]па́чкать, [за]пятна́ть (*a. fig.*); *fig.* затемня́ть [-ни́ть] (созна́ние).
blush [blʌʃ] **1.** кра́ска стыда́; **2.** [по]красне́ть.
bluster ['blʌstə] **1.** хвастовство́, самохва́льство; пусты́е угро́зы *f/pl.*; **2.** грози́ться; [по]хва́статься.
boar [bɔ:] бо́ров; *hunt.* каба́н.
board [bɔ:d] **1.** доска́; стол (пита́ние); ⚓ борт; сце́на, подмо́стки *m/pl.*; правле́ние; ♀ of Trade министе́рство торго́вли; *Am.* торго́вая пала́та; **2.** *v/t.* наст(и)ла́ть (пол); ⚓ брать на аборда́ж; *v/i.* столова́ться; сади́ться [сесть] на (по́езд, кора́бль); **~er** [ˌbɔ:də] пансионе́р(ка); **~ing-house** меблиро́ванные ко́мнаты со столо́м.
boast [boust] **1.** хвастовство́; **2.** (of, about) горди́ться (Т); [по]хва́статься (Т); **~ful** ['boustful] □ хвастли́вый.
boat [bout] ло́дка; су́дно; **~ing** ['boutiŋ] ката́ние на ло́дке.
bob [bɔb] **1.** ги́ря (ма́ятника); рыво́к; ко́ротко подстри́женные во́лосы *m/pl.*; **2.** *v/t.* стри́чь ко́ротко; *v/i.* подпры́гивать [-гнуть].
bobbin ['bɔbin] кату́шка; шпу́лька.
bode [boud] предвеща́ть [-сти́ть], предска́зывать [-за́ть].
bodice ['bɔdis] лиф, ли́фчик.
bodily ['bɔdili] теле́сный.
body ['bɔdi] те́ло; труп; *mot.* ку́зов; ⚔ войскова́я часть *f.*
bog [bɔg] **1.** боло́то, тряси́на; **2.** be **~ed** увяза́ть [увя́знуть] (в тряси́не).
boggle ['bɔgl] [ис]пуга́ться (at P); неуме́ло рабо́тать.
bogus ['bougəs] подде́льный.
boil [bɔil] **1.** кипе́ние; фуру́нкул, нары́в; **2.** [с]вари́ть(ся); [вс]кипяти́ть(ся); кипе́ть; **~er** ['bɔilə] котёл; куб, бак (для кипяче́ния).
boisterous ['bɔistərəs] □ бу́рный, шу́мный.
bold [bould] □ сме́лый; самоуве́ренный; на́глый; *typ.* жи́рный, отчётливый (шрифт); **~ness** ['bouldnis] сме́лость *f*; на́глость *f.*
bolster ['boulstə] **1.** (дива́нный) ва́лик; поду́шка; **2.** подде́рживать [-жа́ть].
bolt [boult] **1.** болт; засо́в, задви́жка; мо́лния; **2.** *v/t.* запира́ть на засо́в; *v/i.* нести́сь стрело́й; убега́ть [убежа́ть]; понести́ *pf.* (о лошадя́х).
bomb [bɔm] **1.** бо́мба; **2.** бомби́ть.
bombard [bɔm'bɑ:d] бомбардирова́ть.
bombastic [bɔm'bæstik] напы́щенный.
bomb-proof непробива́емый бо́мбами.
bond [bɔnd] *pl.*: **~s** у́зы *f/pl.*; око́вы *f/pl.*; ✝ долгово́е обяза́тельство; **~age** ['bɔndidʒ] ра́бство; зави́симость *f*; **~(s)man** ['bɔnd(z)mən] раб.
bone [boun] **1.** кость *f*; ~ of contention я́блоко раздо́ра; make no **~s** about F не церемо́ниться с (Т); **2.** вынима́ть, выреза́ть ко́сти.
bonfire ['bɔnfaiə] костёр.
bonnet ['bɔnit] че́пчик; ка́пор; шля́пка; *mot.* капо́т.
bonus ['bounəs] ✝ пре́мия; тантье́ма.
bony ['bouni] костля́вый; кости́стый.
booby ['bu:bi] болва́н, дура́к.
book [buk] **1.** кни́га; **2.** заноси́ть в кни́гу; регистри́ровать (*im*)*pf.*, *pf. a.* [за-]; зака́зывать и́ли брать (биле́т в теа́тр, на по́езд и т. п.); приглаша́ть [-ласи́ть] (арти́стов); **~-case** кни́жный шкаф; **~ing-clerk** ['bukiŋklɑ:k] касси́р; **~ing-office** биле́тная ка́сса; **~-keeping**

счетово́дство; ~**let** ['buklit] брошю́ра; ~**seller** книгопрода́вец; букини́ст.
boom[1] [bu:m] 1. ⚓ бум; 2. производи́ть сенса́цию, шум вокруг (Р).
boom[2] [~] 1. гул; гуде́ние; 2. [за-] гуде́ть; [за]жужжа́ть.
boon[1] [bu:n] благодея́ние.
boon[2] [~] благотво́рный; прия́тный.
boor [buə] гру́бый, невоспи́танный челове́к; ~**ish** ['buəriʃ] □ гру́бый, невоспи́танный.
boost [bu:st] поднима́ть [-ня́ть] (торго́влю).
boot[1] [bu:t]: to ~ в прида́чу, вдоба́вок *adv.*
boot[2] [~] сапо́г.
booth [bu:ð] пала́тка; кио́ск.
bootlegger ['bu:tlegə] *Am.* торго́вец контраба́ндными напи́тками.
booty ['bu:ti] добы́ча; награ́бленное добро́.
border ['bɔ:də] 1. грани́ца; край; кайма́ (на ска́терти и т. п.); 2. грани́чить (upon с Т); окаймля́ть [-ми́ть].
bore[1] [bɔ:] 1. вы́сверленное отве́рстие; кали́бр; *fig.* ску́чный челове́к; 2. [про]сверли́ть; [про-] бура́вить; надоеда́ть [-е́сть] (Д).
bore[2] [~] 1. *pt.* от bear[2].
born [bɔ:n] рождённый; прирождённый; ~**e** [~] *p. pt.* от bear[2].
borough ['bʌrə] небольшо́й го́род; municipal ~ го́род, име́ющий самоуправле́ние.
borrow ['bɔrou] занима́ть [-ня́ть] (from, of у Р).
bosom ['buzəm] грудь *f*; па́зуха; *fig.* ло́но; не́дра *n/pl.*
boss F [bɔs] 1. хозя́ин; предпринима́тель(ница *f*) *m*; *pol. Am.* руководи́тель полити́ческой па́ртии; 2. распоряжа́ться [-яди́ться] (Т), быть хозя́ином (Р); ~**y** *Am.* ['bɔsi] лю́бящий распоряжа́ться.
botany ['bɔtəni] бота́ника.
botch [bɔtʃ] 1. гру́бая запла́та; плоха́я почи́нка; 2. дела́ть гру́бые запла́ты на (П); пло́хо чини́ть.
both [bouθ] о́ба, о́бе; и тот и друго́й; ~ ... and ... как ... так и ...; и ... и ...
bother ['bɔðə] F 1. беспоко́йство; oh ~! кака́я доса́да!; 2. надоеда́ть [-е́сть] (Д); [по]беспоко́ить.
bottle [bɔtl] 1. буты́лка; 2. разлива́ть по буты́лкам.
bottom ['bɔtəm] 1. дно, дни́ще; ни́жняя часть *f*; грунт, по́чва; F зад; *fig.* осно́ва, суть *f*; at the ~ внизу́; *fig.* в су́щности; на дне (о́бщества); 2. са́мый ни́жний.
bough [bau] ве́тка, ветвь *f*.
bought [bɔ:t] *pt.* и *p. pt.* от buy.
boulder ['bouldə] валу́н.
bounce [bauns] 1. прыжо́к, скачо́к; 2. подпры́гивать [-гнуть]; отска́кивать [отскочи́ть] (о мяче́); F преувеличе́ние.
bound[1] [baund] 1. преде́л; ограниче́ние; 2. ограни́чи(ва)ть; сде́рживать [-жа́ть].
bound[2] [~] ⚔ гото́вый к отправле́нию, направля́ющийся (for в В).
bound[3] [~] 1. прыжо́к, скачо́к; 2. пры́гать [-гнуть], [по]скака́ть; отска́кивать [отскочи́ть].
bound[4] [~] 1. *pt.* и *p. pt.* от bind; 2. свя́занный; обя́занный; переплетённый.
boundary ['baundəri] грани́ца.
boundless [-lis] □ безграни́чный.
bounteous ['bauntiəs] □, **bountiful** ['bauntiful] □ ще́дрый (челове́к); оби́льный.
bounty ['baunti] ще́дрость *f*; ⚓ прави́тельственная пре́мия.
bouquet ['bukei] буке́т; арома́т (вина́).
bout [baut] черёд; раз; ⚕ припа́док; *sport*: схва́тка.
bow[1] [bau] 1. покло́н; ⚓ нос; 2. *v/i.* [со]гну́ться; кла́няться [поклони́ться]; подчиня́ться [-ни́ться] (Д); *v/t.* [со]гну́ть.
bow[2] [bou] 1. лук; дуга́; бант; ♪ смычо́к; rain~ ра́дуга; 2. ♪ владе́ть смычко́м.
bowels ['bauəlz] *pl.* кишки́ *f/pl.*; вну́тренности *f/pl.*; не́дра *n/pl.* (земли́); *fig.* сострада́ние.
bower ['bauə] бесе́дка.
bowl[1] [boul] ку́бок, ча́ша; ва́за.
bowl[2] [~] 1. шар; 2. *v/t.* [по]кати́ть; *v/i.* игра́ть в шары́; ~ along кати́ться бы́стро.
box[1] [bɔks] 1. коро́бка; я́щик; сунду́к; ⊕ бу́кса; вту́лка; ⚘ букс; *thea.* ло́жа; 2. вкла́дывать в я́щик.
box[2] [~] 1. *sport* бокс; ~ on the ear пощёчина.
box|-keeper капельди́нер; ~**-office** театра́льная ка́сса.
boy [bɔi] ма́льчик; молодо́й челове́к; ~**hood** ['bɔihud] о́трочество; ~**ish** ['bɔiiʃ] □ мальчи́шеский, о́троческий.
brace [breis] 1. ⊕ связь *f*; ско́бка; па́ра (о ди́чи); ~**s** *pl.* подтя́жки *f/pl.*; 2. свя́зывать [-за́ть]; подпира́ть [-пере́ть]; ~ up подба́дривать [-бодри́ть].
bracelet ['breislit] брасле́т.
bracket ['brækit] 1. ⚠ кронште́йн, консо́ль *f*; га́зовый рожо́к; *typ.* ско́бка; 2. заключа́ть в ско́бки; *fig.* ста́вить на одну́ до́ску с (Т).
brag [bræg] 1. [по]хва́статься; 2. хвастовство́.
braggart ['brægət] 1. хвасту́н; 2. □ хвастли́вый.
braid [breid] 1. коса́ (воло́с); тесьма́; галу́н; 2. заплета́ть [-ести́]; обшива́ть тесьмо́й.
brain [brein] 1. мозг; голова́; (*fig.*

mst ~s) рассу́док, ум; у́мственные спосо́бности *f/pl.*; **2.** размозжи́ть го́лову (Д).
brake [breik] **1.** ⊕ то́рмоз; **2.** [за-] тормози́ть.
bramble ['bræmbl] ♀ ежеви́ка.
bran [bræn] о́труби *f/pl.*
branch [brɑ:ntʃ] **1.** ветвь *f*, ве́тка, сук (*pl.*: су́чья); о́трасль *f* (нау́ки); филиа́л; **2.** разветвля́ть(ся) [-етви́ть(ся)]; расширя́ться [-ши́риться].
brand [brænd] **1.** вы́жженное клеймо́, тавро́; ⊕ фабри́чное клеймо́; сорт; **2.** выжига́ть клеймо́; *fig.* [за]клейми́ть, [о]позо́рить.
brandish ['brændiʃ] разма́хивать [-хну́ть] (Т).
bran(d)new ['brænd'nju:] F соверше́нно но́вый, «с иго́лочки».
brandy ['brændi] конья́к.
brass [brɑ:s] лату́нь *f*, жёлтая медь *f*; F бессты́дство; ~ band духово́й орке́стр.
brassiere ['bræsiɛə] бюстга́льтер.
brave [breiv] **1.** хра́брый, сме́лый; **2.** брави́ровать; хра́бро встреча́ть (опа́сность и т. п.); ~**ry** ['breivəri] хра́брость *f*, сме́лость *f*.
brawl [brɔ:l] **1.** шу́мная ссо́ра, у́личный сканда́л; **2.** [по]ссо́риться (с Т).
brawny ['brɔ:ni] си́льный; му́скулистый.
bray[1] [brei] **1.** крик осла́; **2.** [за-] крича́ть (об осле́).
bray[2] [~] [ис]толо́чь.
brazen ['breizn] □ ме́дный, бро́нзовый; бессты́дный, на́глый (*a.* ~-**faced**).
Brazilian [brə'ziljən] **1.** брази́льский; **2.** брази́лец, бразилья́нка.
breach [bri:tʃ] **1.** проло́м; *fig.* разры́в (отноше́ний); наруше́ние; ⚔ брешь *f*; **2.** пробива́ть брешь в (П).
bread [bred] хлеб.
breadth [bredθ] ширина́; широта́ (кругозо́ра); широ́кий разма́х.
break [breik] **1.** переры́в; па́уза; рассве́т; тре́щина; F a bad ~ неуда́ча; **2.** [*irr.*] *v/t.* [с]лома́ть; разби́(ва́)ть; разруша́ть [-ру́шить]; прер(ы)ва́ть; взла́мывать [взлома́ть]; ~ up разла́мывать [-лома́ть]; разби́(ва́)ть; *v/i.* пор(ы)ва́ть (с Т); [по]лома́ться, разби́(ва́)ться; ~ away отделя́ться [-ли́ться] (от Р); ~ down потерпе́ть ава́рию, неуда́чу; ~**able** ['breikəbl] ло́мкий, хру́пкий; ~**age** ['breikidʒ] поло́мка; ~-**down** разва́л, расстро́йство; *mot.* ава́рия; ~**fast** ['breikfəst] **1.** за́втрак; **2.** [по]за́втракать; ~-**up** распа́д, разва́л; ~**water** мол; волноре́з.
breast [brest] грудь *f*; make a clean ~ of a th. чистосерде́чно сознава́ться в чём-либо; ~-**stroke** брасс.
breath [breθ] дыха́ние; вздох; ~**e** [bri:ð] *v/i.* дыша́ть [дохну́ть]; перевести́ дух; ~**less** ['breθlis] □ запыха́вшийся; безве́тренный.
bred [bred] **1.** вско́рмленный; воспи́танный; **2.** *pt.* и *p. pt.* от breed.
breeches ['bretʃiz] *pl.* бри́джи *pl.*, штаны́ *m/pl.*
breed [bri:d] **1.** поро́да; **2.** [*irr.*] *v/t.* выводи́ть [вы́вести]; разводи́ть [-вести́]; выси́живать [вы́сидеть]; вска́рмливать [вскорми́ть]; *v/i.* размножа́ться [-о́житься]; [вы́]расти́; ~**er** ['bri:də] производи́тель *m*; скотово́д; ~**ing** [-diŋ] разведе́ние (живо́тных); хоро́шие мане́ры *f/pl.*; воспита́ние.
breez|e [bri:z] лёгкий ветеро́к, бриз; ~**y** ['bri:zi] све́жий, живо́й, весёлый.
brethren ['breðrin] собра́тья *m/pl.*, бра́тия.
brevity ['breviti] кра́ткость *f*.
brew [bru:] *v/t.* [с]вари́ть (пи́во); зава́ривать [-ри́ть] (чай); приготовля́ть [-то́вить]; *fig.* затева́ть [зате́ять]; ~**ery** ['bruəri] пивова́ренный заво́д.
brib|e [braib] **1.** взя́тка; по́дкуп; **2.** подкупа́ть [-пи́ть]; дава́ть взя́тку (Д); ~**ery** ['braibəri] взя́точничество.
brick [brik] **1.** кирпи́ч; *fig.* сла́вный па́рень *m*; **2.** класть кирпичи́; облицо́вывать кирпича́ми; ~**layer** ка́менщик.
bridal ['braidl] □ сва́дебный; ~ procession сва́дебная проце́ссия.
bride [braid] неве́ста; новобра́чная; ~**groom** жени́х; новобра́чный; ~**smaid** подру́жка неве́сты.
bridge [bridʒ] **1.** мост; **2.** соединя́ть мосто́м; наводи́ть мост че́рез (В); *fig.* преодоле́(ва́)ть (препя́тствия).
bridle ['braidl] **1.** узда́; по́вод; **2.** *v/t.* взну́здывать [-да́ть]; *v/i.* [за]арта́читься; задира́ть нос (*a.* ~ up); ~-**path** верхова́я тропа́.
brief [bri:f] **1.** □ коро́ткий, кра́ткий, сжа́тый; **2.** ⚖ резюме́ де́ла для защи́тника; hold a ~ for принима́ть на себя́ веде́ние де́ла (Р); ~-**case** портфе́ль *m*.
brigade [bri'geid] ⚔ бряга́да.
bright [brait] □ я́ркий; све́тлый, я́сный; ~**en** ['braitn] *v/t.* [на]полирова́ть; придава́ть блеск (Д); *v/i.* проясня́ться [-ни́ться]; ~**ness** [-nis] я́ркость *f*; блеск.
brillian|ce, ~cy ['briljəns, -si] я́ркость *f*; блеск; великоле́пие; ~**t** [-jənt] **1.** □ блестя́щий (*a. fig.*); сверка́ющий; **2.** бриллиа́нт.
brim [brim] **1.** край; поля́ *n/pl.* (шля́пы); **2.** наполня́ть(ся) до краёв.
brine [brain] рассо́л; морска́я вода́.
bring [briŋ] [*irr.*] приноси́ть [-нести́]; доставля́ть [-а́вить];

привози́ть [-везти́]; приводи́ть [-вести́]; ~ about осуществля́ть [-ви́ть]; ~ down снижа́ть [сни́зить] (це́ны); ~ forth производи́ть [-вести́]; ~ home to дава́ть поня́ть (Д); ~ round приводи́ть [-вести́] в себя́ (по́сле о́бморока); ~ up воспи́тывать [-та́ть].
brink [briŋk] край (обры́ва); (круто́й) бе́рег.
brisk [brisk] □ живо́й, оживлённый.
bristl|e ['brisl] 1. щети́на; 2. [о]щети́ниться; [рас]серди́ться; ~ with изоби́ловать (Т); **~ed** [-d], **~y** [-i] щети́нистый, колю́чий.
British ['britiʃ] брита́нский; **the ~** англича́не *m/pl.*
brittle ['britl] хру́пкий, ло́мкий.
broach [broutʃ] поч(ин)а́ть; поднима́ть [-ня́ть] (вопро́с); нач(ин)а́ть (разгово́р).
broad [brɔ:d] □ широ́кий; обши́рный; грубова́тый; **~cast 1.** разбра́сывать [-роса́ть] (семена́); распространя́ть [-ни́ть]; передава́ть по ра́дио, веща́ть; **2.** радиопереда́ча; радиовеща́ние; **~cloth** то́нкое сукно́; бума́жная ткань *f.*
brocade [bro'keid] парча́.
broil [brɔil] **1.** жа́реное мя́со; **2.** жа́рить(ся) на огне́; F жа́риться на со́лнце.
broke [brouk] *pt.* от break.
broken ['broukən] **1.** *p. pt.* от **break**; **2.** разби́тый, раско́лотый; **~ health** надло́мленное здоро́вье.
broker ['broukə] ма́клер.
bronc(h)o ['brɔŋkou] *Am.* полуди́кая ло́шадь *f.*
bronze [brɔnz] **1.** бро́нза; **2.** бро́нзовый; **3.** бронзирова́ть *(im)pf.*; загора́ть на со́лнце.
brooch [broutʃ] бро́шка.
brood [bru:d] **1.** вы́водок; ста́я; **2.** сиде́ть на я́йцах; *fig.* гру́стно размышля́ть.
brook [bruk] руче́й.
broom [bru:m, brum] метла́, ве́ник; **~stick** метлови́ще.
broth [brɔ:θ, brɔθ] бульо́н.
brothel ['brɔθl] публи́чный дом.
brother [brʌðə] брат; собра́т; **~hood** [-hud] бра́тство; **~-in-law** [-rinlɔ] шу́рин; зять *m*; де́верь *m*; своя́к; **~ly** [-li] бра́тский.
brought [brɔ:t] *pt.* и *pt.* от **bring.**
brow [brau] бровь *f*; вы́ступ (скалы́); **~beat** ['braubi:t] [*irr.* (beat)] запу́гивать [-га́ть].
brown [braun] **1.** кори́чневый цвет; **2.** кори́чневый; сму́глый; загоре́лый; **3.** загора́ть [-ре́ть].
browse [brauz] **1.** ощи́пывать, объеда́ть ли́стья; *fig.* чита́ть беспоря́дочно; **2.** молоды́е побе́ги *m/pl.*
bruise [bru:z] **1.** синя́к, кровоподтёк; **2.** ушиба́ть [-би́ть]; подставля́ть синяки́.
brunt [brʌnt] гла́вный уда́р; вся тя́жесть *f.*
brush [brʌʃ] **1.** щётка; кисть *f*; чи́стка щёткой; *Am.* ~wood; за́росль *f*; **2.** *v/t.* чи́стить щёткой; причёсывать щёткой (во́лосы); ~ up приводи́ть в поря́док; *fig.* освежа́ть в па́мяти; *v/i.* ~ by прошмы́гивать [-гну́ть]; ~ against a p. слегка́ заде́ть кого́-либо (проходя́ ми́мо); **~wood** [brʌʃwud] хво́рост, валёжник.
brusque [brusk] □ гру́бый; ре́зкий.
brut|al ['bru:tl] □ гру́бый; жесто́кий; **~ality** [bru:'tæliti] гру́бость *f*; жесто́кость *f*; **~e** [bru:t] **1.** жесто́кий; бессозна́тельный; **2.** живо́тное; F скоти́на (руга́тельство).
bubble ['bʌbl] **1.** пузы́рь *m*; **2.** пузы́риться; кипе́ть; бить ключо́м.
buccaneer [bʌkə'niə] пира́т.
buck [bʌk] **1.** *zo.* саме́ц (оле́нь, за́яц и др.); **2.** станови́ться на дыбы́; брыка́ться [-кну́ться]; ~ up F встряхну́ться *pf.*; оживля́ться, [-ви́ться].
bucket ['bʌkit] ведро́; бадья́.
buckle ['bʌkl] **1.** пря́жка; **2.** *v/t.* застёгивать [-тегну́ть] (пря́жкой); *v/i.* ⊕ сгиба́ться [согну́ться] (от давле́ния); ~ to *fig.* подтя́гиваться [-тяну́ться]; принима́ться энерги́чно за де́ло.
buckshot ['bʌkʃɔt] *hunt.* кру́пная дробь *f.*
bud [bʌd] **1.** по́чка, буто́н; *fig.* заро́дыш; **2.** *v/i.* ✓ дава́ть по́чки; пуска́ть ростки́; *fig.* разви́(ва́)ться.
budge ['bʌdʒ] шевели́ть(ся) [-льну́ть(ся)]; сдвига́ть с ме́ста.
budget ['bʌdʒit] бюдже́т; фина́нсовая сме́та; draft ~ прое́кт госуда́рственного бюдже́та.
buff [bʌf] **1.** бу́йволовая ко́жа; **2.** тёмно-жёлтый.
buffalo ['bʌfəlou] *zo.* бу́йвол.
buffer ['bʌfə] 🚂 бу́фер; амортиза́тор, де́мпфер.
buffet[1] ['bʌfit] **1.** уда́р (руко́й), толчо́к; **2.** наноси́ть уда́р (Д).
buffet[2] **1.** [~] буфе́т; **2.** ['bufei] буфе́тная сто́йка.
buffoon [bʌ'fu:n] шут, фигля́р.
bug [bʌg] клоп; *Am.* насеко́мое.
bugle ['bju:gl] рожо́к, горн.
build [bild] **1.** [*irr.*] [по]стро́ить; сооружа́ть [-руди́ть]; [с]вить (гнездо́); ~ on полага́ться [положи́ться] на (В); **2.** констру́кция; стиль *m*; телосложе́ние; **~er** ['bildə] строи́тель *m*; подря́дчик; пло́тник; **~ing** [-iŋ] зда́ние; постро́йка; строи́тельство.
built [bilt] *pt.* и *p. pt.* от build.
bulb [bʌlb] ⚘ лу́ковица; ла́мпочка

bulge [bʌldʒ] **1.** вы́пуклость *f*; **2.** выпя́чиваться [вы́пятиться], выдава́ться [вы́даться].
bulk [bʌlk] объём; ⚓ вмести́мость *f*; in ~ в нава́лку; in the ~ в це́лом; **~y** [bʌlki] громо́здкий.
bull[1] [bul] бык; † *sl.* спекуля́нт, игра́ющий на повыше́ние; *Am. sl.* неле́пость *f*; противоре́чие.
bull[2] [~] па́пская бу́лла.
bulldog ['buldɔg] бульдо́г.
bullet ['bulit] пу́ля; ядро́.
bulletin ['bulitin] бюллете́нь *m*.
bullion ['buljən] сли́ток зо́лота или серебра́.
bully ['buli] **1.** задира *m*, забия́ка *m*; **2.** задира́ть; запу́гивать [-га́ть]; **3.** *Am.* F первокла́ссный, великоле́пный; хвастли́вый.
bulwark ['bulwək] ⚔ вал; *mst fig.* оплот, защи́та.
bum [bam] *Am.* F **1.** за́д(ница); ло́дырь *m*, безде́льник, лентя́й; **2.** ло́дырничать.
bumble-bee ['bʌmblbi] шмель *m*.
bump [bʌmp] **1.** столкнове́ние; глухо́й уда́р; ши́шка; *fig.* спосо́бность *f* (of к Д); **2.** ударя́ть(ся) [уда́рить(ся)].
bumper ['bʌmpə] **1.** бока́л, по́лный до краёв; ~ crop F *sl.* небыва́лый урожа́й; **2.** *Am. mot.* амортиза́тор.
bun [bʌn] бу́лочка (с изю́мом).
bunch [bʌntʃ] **1.** свя́зка; пучо́к; па́чка; **2.** свя́зывать в пучо́к.
bundle ['bʌndl] **1.** у́зел; вяза́нка; **2.** *v/t.* собира́ть вме́сте (ве́щи); свя́зывать в у́зел (*a.* ~ up).
bungalow ['bʌŋgəlou] одноэта́жная да́ча, бу́нгало *n indecl.*
bungle ['bʌŋgl] **1.** (плоха́я) небре́жная рабо́та; оши́бка; пу́таница; **2.** неуме́ло, небре́жно рабо́тать; по́ртить рабо́ту.
bunk[1] [bʌŋk] *Am.* вздор.
bunk[2] [~] ложи́ться спать.
bunny ['bʌni] кро́лик.
buoy [bɔi] ⚓ **1.** ба́кен, буй; **2.** ста́вить ба́кены; подде́рживать на пове́рхности; (*mst* ~ up) *fig.* подде́рживать [-жа́ть]; **~ant** ['bɔiənt] □ плаву́чий; жизнера́достный; бо́дрый.
burden ['bə:dn] **1.** но́ша; тя́жесть *f*; бре́мя *n*; груз; **2.** нагружа́ть [-рузи́ть]; обременя́ть [-ни́ть]; **~some** [-səm] обремени́тельный.
bureau [bjuə'rou, 'bjuərou] конто́рка; конто́ра; бюро́ *n indecl.*; отде́л; **~cracy** [bjuə'rɔkrəsi] бюрокра́тия.
burglar ['bə:glə] вор-взло́мщик; **~y** [-ri] кра́жа со взло́мом.
burial ['beriəl] по́хороны *f/pl.*
burlesque [bə:'lesk] **1.** коми́чный; **2.** карикату́ра, паро́дия; **3.** пароди́ровать (*im*)*pf.*
burly ['bə:li] доро́дный.
burn [bə:n] **1.** ожо́г; клеймо́; **2.** [*irr.*] *v/i.* горе́ть; подгора́ть [-ре́ть] (о пи́ще); же́чь; *v/t.* [с]жечь; сжига́ть [сжечь]; **~er** ['bə:nə] горе́лка.
burnish ['bə:niʃ] **1.** полиро́вка; блеск (мета́лла); **2.** [от]полирова́ть (мета́лл); блесте́ть.
burnt [bə:nt] *pt.* и *p. pt.* от burn.
burrow ['bʌrou] **1.** нора́; **2.** рыть нору́; [по]ры́ться в (кни́гах и т. п.).
burst [bə:st] **1.** разры́в (снаря́да); взрыв *a. fig.*; вспы́шка (гне́ва, пла́мени); **2.** [*irr.*] *v/i.* взрыва́ться [взорва́ться] (о котле́, бо́мбе); прор(ы)ва́ться (о плоти́не); ло́паться [ло́пнуть] (with от Р); ~ forth или out вспы́хивать [-хнуть] (о вражде́, войне́); ~ into tears залива́ться слеза́ми; *v/t.* взрыва́ть [взорва́ть]; разруша́ть [-ру́шить].
bury ['beri] [по]хорони́ть; зары́(ва́)ть.
bus [bʌs] F авто́бус.
bush ['buʃ] куст, куста́рник.
bushel ['buʃl] бу́шель *m* (ме́ра ёмкости сыпу́чих тел в 'Англии [= 36,3 л] и в США [=35,2 л]).
bushy ['buʃi] густо́й.
business ['biznis] де́ло, заня́тие; профе́ссия; † фи́рма; торго́вое предприя́тие; ~ of the day пове́стка дня; ~ (*or* professional) discretion служе́бная обя́занность храни́ть молча́ние; have no ~ to *inf.* не име́ть пра́ва (+ *inf.*); **~-like** [-laik] делово́й; практи́чный.
bust [bʌst] бюст; же́нская грудь *f.*
bustle ['bʌsl] **1.** сумато́ха; суета́; **2.** *v/i.* [по]торопи́ться, [за]суети́ться; *v/t.* [по]торопи́ть.
busy ['bizi] **1.** □ де́ятельный; занято́й (at T); за́нятый; *Am. teleph.* за́нятая (ли́ния); **2.** (*mst* ~ o. s.) занима́ться [заня́ться] (with T).
but [bʌt] **1.** *cj.* но, а; одна́ко; тем не ме́нее; е́сли бы не (*a.* ~ that) **2.** *prp.* кроме (Р), за исключе́нием (Р); the last ~ one предпосле́дний; ~ for без (Р); **3.** *adv.* то́лько, лишь; ~ just то́лько что; ~ now лишь тепе́рь; all ~ едва́ не ...; nothing ~ ничего́ кро́ме, то́лько; I cannot ~ *inf.* не могу́ не (+ *inf.*).
butcher ['butʃə] **1.** мясни́к; *fig.* уби́йца *m*; **2.** бить (скот); уби́(ва́)ть; **~y** [-ri] скотобо́йня; резня́.
butler ['bʌtlə] дворе́цкий.
butt [bʌt] **1.** уда́р; прикла́д (ружья́); (*a.* ~ end) то́лстый коне́ц; **~s** *pl.* стре́льбище, полиго́н; *fig.* посме́шище; **2.** ударя́ть голово́й; бода́ть(ся) [бодну́ть]; натыка́ться [наткну́ться].
butter ['bʌtə] **1.** ма́сло; **2.** нама́зывать ма́слом; **~cup** ⚘ лю́тик; **~fly** ба́бочка; **~y** ['bʌtəri] **1.** кладова́я; **2.** ма́сляный.
buttocks ['bʌtəks] *pl.* я́годицы *f/pl.*

button ['bʌtn] **1.** пу́говица; кно́пка; буто́н (цветка́); **2.** застёгивать [-тегну́ть] (на пу́говицу).
buttress ['bʌtris] **1.** подпо́ра, усто́й; бык (моста́); *fig.* опо́ра, подде́ржка; **2.** подде́рживать [-жа́ть]; служи́ть опо́рой (Д).
buxom ['bʌksəm] здоро́вый; миловидный.
buy [bai] [*irr.*] *v/t.* покупа́ть [купи́ть] (from у Р); **~er** ['baiə] покупа́тель(ница *f*) *m*.
buzz [bʌz] **1.** жужжа́ние; гул; **2.** *v/i.* [за]жужжа́ть; [за]гуде́ть.
buzzard ['bʌzəd] сары́ч.
by [bai] **1.** *prp.* у (Р), при (П), о́коло (Р); вдоль (Р); ~ **the dozen** дю́жинами; ~ o. s. оди́н *m*, одна́ *f*; ~ land сухи́м путём; ~ rail по желе́зной доро́ге; day ~ day изо дня́ в де́нь; **2.** *adv.* бли́зко, ря́дом; ми́мо; ~ and ~ вско́ре; ~ the ~ ме́жду про́чим; ~ and large *Am.* вообще́ говоря́; **~-election** ['baii'lekʃən] дополни́тельные вы́боры *m/pl.*; **~-gone** про́шлый; **~-law** постановле́ние ме́стной вла́сти; **~-path** обхо́д, обхо́дная доро́га; **~-product** побо́чный проду́кт; **~-stander** свиде́тель(ница *f*) *m*; зри́тель(ница *f*) *m*; **~-street** глуха́я у́лица; переу́лок; **~-way** малопрое́зжая доро́га; **~-word** погово́рка.

C

cab [kæb] экипа́ж; такси́ *n indecl.*; 🚂 бу́дка (на парово́зе).
cabbage ['kæbidʒ] капу́ста.
cabin ['kæbin] **1.** хи́жина; бу́дка; ⚓ каю́та; **2.** помеща́ть в те́сную ко́мнату и т. п.
cabinet ['kæbinit] кабине́т; го́рка; я́щик; ♀ Council сове́т мини́стров; **~-maker** столя́р.
cable ['keibl] **1.** ка́бель *m*; кана́т; **2.** *tel.* телеграфи́ровать *(im)pf.*; **~gram** [-græm] телегра́мма.
cabman ['kæbmən] изво́зчик.
cacao [kə'kɑːou] кака́овое де́рево; кака́о *n indecl.*
cackle ['kækl] **1.** куда́хтанье; гогота́нье; **2.** [за]куда́хтать; [за]гогота́ть.
cad [kæd] F невоспи́танный, гру́бый челове́к.
cadaverous [kə'dævərəs] □ исхуда́лый как труп; тру́пный.
cadence ['keidəns] ♪ каде́нция; модуля́ция.
cadet [kə'det] каде́т.
café ['kæfei] кафе́ *n indecl.*, кафе́-рестора́н.
cafeteria [kæfi'tiəriə] кафете́рий, кафе́-заку́сочная.
age [keidʒ] **1.** кле́тка; лифт; ⚒ склеть *f* (в ша́хтах); **2.** сажа́ть в кле́тку.
cajole [kə'dʒoul] [по]льсти́ть (Д).
cake [keik] **1.** торт; кекс; пиро́жное; **2.** спека́ться [спе́чься].
calami|tous [kə'læmitəs] □ па́губный; бе́дственный; **~ty** [-ti] бе́дствие.
calcify ['kælsifai] превраща́ться в и́звесть.
calculat|e ['kælkjuleit] *v/t.* вычисля́ть [вы́числить]; подсчи́тывать [-ита́ть]; [с]калькули́ровать; *v/i.* рассчи́тывать (on на В); **~ion** [kælkju'leiʃən] вычисле́ние; калькуля́ция; расчёт.
caldron ['kɔːldrən] котёл.
calendar ['kælində] **1.** календа́рь *m*; рее́стр; **2.** составля́ть и́ндекс (Р); [за]регистри́ровать.
calf¹ [kɑːf], *pl.* calves [kɑːvz] телёнок (*pl.*: теля́та); (и́ли **~-skin**) теля́чья ко́жа, опо́ек.
calf² [~], *pl.* calves [~] икра́ (ноги́).
calibre ['kælibə] кали́бр.
calico ['kælikou] ✝ коленко́р; *Am.* си́тец.
call [kɔːl] **1.** зов, о́клик; *teleph.* вы́зов; *fig.* предложе́ние (ме́ста, ка́федры и т. п.); призы́в; сигна́л; тре́бование; спрос (for на В); визи́т, посеще́ние; on ~ по тре́бованию; **2.** *v/t.* [по]зва́ть; соз(ы)ва́ть; вызыва́ть [вы́звать]; [раз]буди́ть; приз(ы)ва́ть; ~ in тре́бовать наза́д (долг); ~ over де́лать перекли́чку (Р); ~ up призыва́ть на вое́нную слу́жбу; *teleph.* вызыва́ть [вы́звать]; *v/i.* крича́ть [кри́кнуть]; *teleph.* [по]звони́ть; заходи́ть [зайти́] (at в В; on a p. к Д); ~ for [по-] тре́бова́ть; [по]зва́ть на (В); ~ for a p. заходи́ть [зайти́] за (Т); ~ in F забега́ть [-ежа́ть] (к Д); ~ on навеща́ть [-ести́ть] (В); взыва́ть [воззва́ть] к (Д) (for о П); приз(ы)ва́ть (to do *etc.* сде́лать и т. д.); **~-box** ['kɔːlbɔks] телефо́нная бу́дка; **~er** ['kɔːlə] го́сть(я *f*) *m*.
calling ['kɔːliŋ] призва́ние; профе́ссия.
call-office ['kɔːlɔfis] телефо́нная ста́нция.
callous ['kæləs] □ огрубе́лый, мозо́листый; *fig.* бессерде́чный.
calm [kɑːm] **1.** □ споко́йный; безве́тренный; **2.** тишина́; штиль *m*; споко́йствие; **3.** ~ down успока́ивать(ся) [-ко́ить(ся)].
calori|c [kə'lɔrik] **1.** *phys.* теплота́ **2.** теплово́й; **~e** ['kæləri] *phys.* кало́рия.

calumn|iate [kəˈlʌmnieit] [о]клеветать; **~iation** [kəlʌmniˈeiʃən], **~y** [ˈkæləmni] клевета́.
calve [kɑːv] [о]тели́ться; **~s** *pl.* от calf.
cambric [ˈkeimbrik] † батист.
came [keim] *pt.* от come.
camera [ˈkæmərə] фотографи́ческий аппара́т; in ~ ⚖ в кабине́те судьи́.
camomile [ˈkæməmail] ♀ рома́шка.
camouflage [ˈkæmuːflɑːʃ] ⚔ маскиро́вка; **2.** [за]маскирова́ть(ся).
camp [kæmp] **1.** ла́герь *m*; ~ bed похо́дная крова́ть *f*; **2.** располага́ться ла́герем; ~ out ночева́ть на откры́том во́здухе.
campaign [kæmˈpein] **1.** ⚔ похо́д; кампа́ния; **2** уча́ствовать в похо́де; проводи́ть кампа́нию.
camphor [ˈkæmfə] камфара́.
can¹ [kæn] [*irr.*] могу́ и т. д.; *inf.*: be able = [с]мочь, быть в состоя́нии; [с]уме́ть.
can² [~] **1.** бидо́н; ба́нка; **2.** *Am.* консерви́ровать (*im*)*pf.*, *pf. a.* [за-].
canal [kəˈnæl] кана́л.
canard [kəˈnɑː] «у́тка», ло́жный слух.
canary [kəˈnɛəri] канаре́йка.
cancel [ˈkænsəl] вычёркивать [вы́черкнуть]; аннули́ровать (*im*)*pf.*; погаша́ть [погаси́ть] (ма́рки); ✠ (*a.* ~ out) сокраща́ть [-рати́ть].
cancer [ˈkænsə] *ast.* созве́здие Ра́ка; ⚕ рак; **~ous** [-rəs] ра́ковый.
candid [ˈkændid] □ и́скренний, прямо́й.
candidate [ˈkændidit] кандида́т(ка) (for на В).
candied [ˈkændid] заса́харенный.
candle [ˈkændl] свеча́; **~stick** [-stik] подсве́чник.
cando(u)r [ˈkændə] и́скренность *f*.
candy [ˈkændi] **1.** ледене́ц; *Am.* конфе́ты *f/pl.*, сла́сти *f/pl.*; **2.** *v/t.* заса́хари(ва)ть.
cane [kein] **1.** ♀ камы́ш; тростни́к; трость *f*; **2.** бить па́лкой.
canker [ˈkæŋkə] ⚕ гангрено́зный стомати́т; ♀ рак.
canned [kænd] *Am.* консерви́рованный (проду́кт).
cannibal [ˈkænibəl] канниба́л.
cannon [ˈkænən] пу́шка; ору́дие.
cannot [ˈkænɔt] не в состоя́нии, *s.* can.
canoe [kəˈnuː] челно́к; байда́рка.
canon [ˈkænən] ♪ кано́н; пра́вило; крите́рий.
canopy [ˈkænəpi] по́лог; *fig.* небе́сный свод; △ наве́с.
cant¹ [kænt] **1.** craft, накло́н; **2.** ска́шивать [скоси́ть]; наклоня́ть [-ни́ть].
cant² [~] **1.** плакси́вый тон; ханжество́; **2.** говори́ть на распе́в; ханжи́ть.
can't [kɑːnt] F не в состоя́нии.
canteen [kænˈtiːn] ⚔ ла́вка; столо́вая; похо́дная ку́хня.
canton 1. [ˈkæntɔn] канто́н; **2.** [kənˈtuːn] ⚔ расквартиро́вывать [-ова́ть] (войска́).
canvas [ˈkænvəs] холст; канва́; *paint.* карти́на.
canvass [~] **1.** обсужде́ние; **2.** *v/t.* обсужда́ть [-уди́ть]; *v/i.* собира́ть голоса́; иска́ть зака́зов.
caoutchouc [ˈkautʃuk] каучу́к.
cap [kæp] **1.** ке́пка, фура́жка, ша́пка; ⊕ колпачо́к, голо́вка; шля́пка (гриба́); писто́н; set one's ~ at a p. заи́грывать с ке́м-либо (о же́нщине); **2.** присужда́ть учёную сте́пень (Д); *fig.* заверша́ть [-ши́ть]; F перещеголя́ть.
capab|ility [keipəˈbiliti] спосо́бность *f*; **~le** [ˈkeipəbl] □ спосо́бный (of на В), одарённый.
capaci|ous [kəˈpeiʃəs] □ просто́рный; объёмистый; **~ty** [kəˈpæsiti] объём, вмести́тельность *f*; спосо́бность *f*; in the ~ of в ка́честве (Р).
cape¹ [keip] плащ; пелери́на.
cape² [~] мыс.
caper [ˈkeipə] скачо́к; ша́лость *f*, прока́за; cut ~s дура́читься.
capital [ˈkæpitl] **1.** □ основно́й, капита́льный; (*crime*) уголо́вный; (*sentence, punishment*) сме́ртный; **2.** столи́ца; капита́л; (и́ли ~ letter) прописна́я бу́ква; **~ism** [ˈkæpitəlizm] капитали́зм; **~ize** [kəˈpitəlaiz] капитализи́ровать (*im*)*pf.*
capitulate [kəˈpitjuleit] сд(ав)а́ться (to Д).
capric|e [kəˈpriːs] капри́з, причу́да; **~ious** [kəˈpriʃəs] □ капри́зный.
capsize [kæpˈsaiz] *v/i.* ⚓ опроки́дываться [-ки́нуться]; *v/t.* опроки́дывать [-ки́нуть] (ло́дку и т.п.).
capsule [ˈkæpsjuːl] ка́псюль *m*; ⚕ ка́псула.
captain [ˈkæptin] ⚔ капита́н; руководи́тель(ница *f*) *m*; ⚓ капита́н, команди́р.
caption [ˈkæpʃən] *part. Am.* заголо́вок (статьи́, главы́); (кино́) на́дпись на экра́не.
captious [ˈkæpʃəs] □ приди́рчивый.
captiv|ate [ˈkæptiveit] пленя́ть [-ни́ть]; очаро́вывать [-ова́ть]; **~e** [ˈkæptiv] **1.** пле́нник; пле́нный; **2.** взя́тый в плен; **~ity** [kæpˈtiviti] плен.
capture [ˈkæptʃə] **1.** захва́тывать си́лой; брать в плен; **2.** пои́мка; захва́т; добы́ча; ⚓ приз.
car [kɑː] ваго́н; автомоби́ль *m*.
caramel [ˈkærəmel] караме́ль *f*.
caravan [kærəˈvæn] карава́н; дом-автоприце́п.
caraway [ˈkærəwei] ♀ тмин.
carbine [ˈkɑːbain] караби́н.
carbohydrate [ˈkɑːbouˈhaidreit] ⚗ углево́д.

carbon ['kɑ:bən] ⚗ углеро́д; (и́ли ~ paper) копи́рка.
carburet(t)or ['kɑ:bjuretə] *mot.* карбюра́тор.
carcas|e, *mst* **~s** ['kɑ:kəs] труп; ту́ша.
card ['kɑ:d] ка́рта; ка́рточка; **~board** [kɑ:dbɔ:d] карто́н.
cardigan ['kɑ:digən] шерстяно́й дже́мпер.
cardinal ['kɑ:dinl] **1.** □ гла́вный, основно́й; кардина́льный; ~ number коли́чественное числи́тельное; **2.** кардина́л.
card-index ['kɑ:dindeks] картоте́ка.
card-sharp(er) [kɑ:dʃɑ:pə] шу́лер.
care [kɛə] **1.** забо́та; попече́ние; внима́ние; ~ of (*abbr.* c/o) по а́дресу (Р); take ~ of [с]бере́чь (В); [по-]смотре́ть за (Т); with ~! осторо́жно!; **2.** име́ть жела́ние, [за-]хоте́ть (to: + *inf.*); ~ for: a) [по]забо́титься о (П); b) люби́ть (В); пита́ть интере́с к (Д); F I don't ~! мне всё равно́!; well ~d-for вы́холенный; хорошо́ обеспе́ченный.
career [kə'riə] **1.** карье́р; *fig.* карье́ра, успе́х; **2.** бы́стро продвига́ться.
carefree ['kɛəfri:] беззабо́тный.
careful ['kɛəful] □ забо́тливый (for о П); аккура́тный; внима́тельный (к Д); **~ness** [-nis] забо́тливость *f.*
careless [-lis] □ легкомы́сленный; небре́жный; **~ness** [-nis] небре́жность *f.*
caress [kə'res] **1.** ла́ска; **2.** ласка́ть; [по]гла́дить.
caretaker ['kɛəteikə] дво́рник; сто́рож.
carfare ['kɑ:fɛə] *Am.* проездны́е (де́ньги).
cargo ['kɑ:gou] ⚓ груз.
caricature ['kærikə'tjuə] **1.** карикату́ра; **2.** изобража́ть в карикату́рном ви́де.
carn|al ['kɑ:nl] □ чу́вственный, пло́тский; **~ation** [kɑ:'neiʃən] ⚘ гвозди́ка.
carnival ['kɑ:nivəl] карнава́л.
carnivorous [kɑ:'nivərəs] плотоя́дный.
carol ['kærəl] **1.** рожде́ственский гимн; **2.** воспе́(ва́)ть, сла́вить.
carous|e [kə'rauz] **1.** *a.* **~al** [-əl] пиру́шка, попо́йка; **2.** пирова́ть.
carp[1] [kɑ:p] *zo.* карп.
carp[2] [~] прид(и)ра́ться (at к Д).
carpent|er ['kɑ:pintə] пло́тник; **~ry** [-tri] пло́тничное де́ло.
carpet [kɑ:pit] **1.** ковёр; **2.** устила́ть ковро́м.
carriage ['kæridʒ] экипа́ж; перево́зка; тра́нспорт; **~-drive** подъе́зд; ~ **free,** ~ **paid** пересы́лка беспла́тно.
carrier ['kæriə] посы́льный; носи́льщик; ⚔ транспортёр.
carrot ['kærət] морко́вь *f.*
carry ['kæri] **1.** *v/t.* носи́ть, [по-]нести́; вози́ть, [по]везти́; ~ o. s. держа́ться, вести́ себя́; be carried быть при́нятым; ✝ ~ forward и́ли over переноси́ть на другу́ю страни́цу; ~ on продолжа́ть [-до́лжить]; вести́ (де́ло, борьбу́ и т. п.); ~ out и́ли through доводи́ть до конца́; выполня́ть [вы́полнить]; *v/i.* доноси́ться [донести́сь]; ⚔ долета́ть [долете́ть] (о снаря́де); **2.** ⚔ дальнобо́йность *f*; да́льность полёта (снаря́да).
cart [kɑ:t] **1.** теле́га, пово́зка; **2.** везти́ в теле́ге; **~age** ['kɑ:tidʒ] перево́зка, сто́имость перево́зки.
carter ['kɑ:tə] во́зчик.
cartilage ['kɑ:tilidʒ] хрящ.
carton ['kɑ:tən] карто́н.
cartoon [kɑ:'tu:n] карикату́ра; ⊕ карто́н.
cartridge ['kɑ:tridʒ] патро́н; заря́д.
carve [kɑ:v] ре́зать (по де́реву); [вы́]гравирова́ть; нареза́ть [наре́зать] (мя́со); **~r** ['kɑ:və] ре́зчик (по де́реву); гравёр; нож для разде́лки мя́са.
carving ['kɑ:viŋ] резьба́ (по де́реву).
case[1] [keis] **1.** я́щик; футля́р; су́мка; витри́на; *typ.* набо́рная ка́сса; **2.** класть в я́щик.
case[2] [~] слу́чай; положе́ние; обстоя́тельство; ⚖ суде́бное де́ло.
case-harden ['keishɑ:dn] ⊕ цементи́ровать (сталь) (*im*)*pf.*; *fig.* де́лать нечувстви́тельным.
casement ['keismənt] ство́рный око́нный переплёт.
cash [kæʃ] **1.** де́ньги; нали́чные де́ньги *f/pl.*; ~ down, for ~ за нали́чный расчёт; ~ on delivery нало́женным платежо́м; ~ register ка́ссовый аппара́т; **2.** получа́ть де́ньги по (Д); **~-book** ка́ссовая кни́га; **~ier** [kæ'ʃiə] касси́р(ша).
casing ['keisiŋ] опра́ва; ра́ма; обши́вка, оби́вка.
cask [kɑ:sk] бо́чка, бочо́нок.
casket ['kɑ:skit] шкату́лка; *Am.* гроб.
casserole ['kæsəroul] кастрю́ля.
cassock ['kæsək] ря́са, сута́на.
cast [kɑ:st] **1.** бросо́к, мета́ние; ги́псовый сле́пок; ⚓ броса́ние (я́коря); *thea.* распределе́ние роле́й; соста́в исполни́телей; **2.** [*irr.*] *v/t.* броса́ть [бро́сить]; кида́ть [ки́нуть]; мета́ть [-тну́ть]; ⊕ отли́(ва́)ть (мета́ллы); *thea.* распределя́ть [-ли́ть] (ро́ли); ~ iron чугу́н; ~ lots броса́ть жре́бий; be ~ down быть в уны́нии; *v/i.* ~ about for обду́м(ыв)ать (В).
castaway ['kɑ:stəwei] **1.** па́рия, отве́рженец; ⚓ потерпе́вший кораблекруше́ние; **2.** отве́рженный.
caste [kɑ:st] ка́ста.

castigate ['kæstigeit] нака́зывать [-за́ть]; *fig.* жесто́ко критикова́ть.
cast-iron чугу́нный.
castle ['kɑ:sl] за́мок; *chess* ладья́.
castor[1] ['kɑ:stə]: ~ oil касто́ровое ма́сло.
castor[2] [~] колёсико (на но́жке ме́бели).
castrate [kæs'treit] кастри́ровать (*im*)*pf.*
casual ['kæʒjuəl] □ случа́йный; небре́жный; **~ty** [-ti] несча́стный слу́чай; *pl.* ⚔ поте́ри (на войне́) *f/pl.*
cat [kæt] ко́шка.
catalog, *Brt.* **~ue** ['kætəlɔg] **1.** катало́г; прейскура́нт; **2.** каталогизи́ровать (*im*)*pf.*, вноси́ть в катало́г.
cataract ['kætərækt] водопа́д; ⚕ катара́кта.
catarrh [kə'tɑ:] ката́р.
catastrophe [kə'tæstrəfi] катастро́фа.
catch [kætʃ] **1.** по́имка; захва́т; уло́в; добы́ча; лову́шка; ⊕ задви́жка; шпингале́т; **2.** [*irr.*] *v/t.* лови́ть [пойма́ть]; схва́тывать [схвати́ть]; заража́ться [зарази́ться] (Т); поспе́(ва́)ть к (по́езду и т. п.); ~ cold простужа́ться [-уди́ться]; ~ a p.'s eye ула́вливать взгляд (Р); ~ up догоня́ть [догна́ть]; F поднима́ть [-ня́ть]; **3.** *v/i.* зацепля́ться [-пи́ться]; F ~ on станови́ться мо́дным; ~ up with догоня́ть [догна́ть] (В); **~er** ['kætʃə] лове́ц; **~ing** ['kætʃiŋ] *fig.* зарази́тельный (смех); привлека́тельный; ⚕ зарази́тельный; **~word** мо́дное слове́чко; загла́вное сло́во.
catechism ['kætikizm] катехи́зис.
categor|ical [kæti'gɔrikəl] □ категори́ческий; реши́тельный; **~y** ['kætigəri] катего́рия, разря́д.
cater ['keitə]: ~ for поставля́ть прови́зию (Д); *fig.* [по]забо́титься о (П).
caterpillar *zo.*, ⊕ ['kætəpilə] гу́сеница.
catgut ['kætgʌt] кише́чная струна́.
cathedral [kɔ'θi:drəl] собо́р.
Catholic ['kæθəlik] **1.** като́лик; **2.** католи́ческий.
cattle [kætl] кру́пный рога́тый скот; **~-breeding** скотово́дство; **~-plague** чума́.
caught [kɔ:t] *pt.* и *pt.* от **catch.**
cauldron ['kɔ:ldrən] котёл.
cauliflower ['kɔliflauə] ⚘ цветна́я капу́ста.
caulk [kɔ:k] ⚓ [про]конопа́тить.
caus|al ['kɔ:zəl] □ причи́нный; **~e** [kɔ:z] **1.** причи́на, основа́ние; по́вод; ⚖ де́ло, проце́сс; **2.** причини́ть [-ни́ть]; вызыва́ть [вы́звать]; **~eless** ['kɔ:zlis] □ беспричи́нный, необосно́ванный.
caution ['kɔ:ʃən] **1.** (пред)осторо́жность *f*; предостереже́ние; ~ money зало́г; **2.** предостерега́ть [-ре́чь] (against от Р).
cautious ['kɔ:ʃəs] □ осторо́жный; предусмотри́тельный; **~ness** [-nis] осторо́жность *f*; предусмотри́тельность *f.*
cavalry ['kævəlri] ⚔ ко́нница.
cave ['keiv] **1.** пеще́ра; **2.** ~ in: *v/i.* оседа́ть [осе́сть], опуска́ться [-сти́ться].
cavil ['kævil] **1.** приди́рка; **2.** прид(и)ра́ться (at, about к Д, за В).
cavity ['kæviti] впа́дина; по́лость *f.*
caw [kɔ:] **1.** ка́рканье; **2.** [за]ка́ркать.
cease [si:s] *v/i.* перест(ав)а́ть; *v/t.* прекраща́ть [-крати́ть]; приостана́вливать [-нови́ть]; **~less** ['si:slis] □ непреры́вный, непреста́нный.
cede [si:d] уступа́ть [-пи́ть] (В).
ceiling ['si:liŋ] потоло́к; *attr.* максима́льный; ~ price преде́льная цена́.
celebrat|e ['selibreit] [от]пра́здновать; **~ed** [-id] знамени́тый; **~ion** [seli'breiʃən] торжества́ *n/pl.*; пра́зднование.
celebrity [si'lebriti] знамени́тость *f.*
celerity [-riti] быстрота́.
celery ['seləri] ⚘ сельдере́й.
celestial [si'lestjəl] □ небе́сный.
celibacy ['selibəsi] целиба́т; обе́т безбра́чия.
cell [sel] яче́йка; тюре́мная ка́мера; ке́лья; ⚡ элеме́нт.
cellar ['selə] подва́л; ви́нный по́греб.
cement [si'ment] **1.** цеме́нт; **2.** цементи́ровать (*im*)*pf.*
cemetery ['semitri] кла́дбище.
censor ['sensə) **1.** це́нзор; **2.** подверга́ть цензу́ре; **~ious** [sen'sɔ:riəs] □ стро́гий, критику́ющий; **~ship** ['sensəʃip] цензу́ра.
censure [senʃə] **1.** осужде́ние, порица́ние; **2.** осужда́ть [осуди́ть], порица́ть.
census ['sensəs] пе́репись *f.*
cent [sent] со́тня *f*; *Am.* цент (0,01 до́ллара); per ~ проце́нт.
centennial [sen'tenjəl] столе́тний; происходя́щий раз в сто лет.
center *s.* centre.
centi|grade ['sentigreid] стогра́дусный; **~metre** [-mi:tə] сантиме́тр; **~pede** [-pi:d] *zo.* сороконо́жка.
central ['sentrəl] □ центра́льный; гла́вный; ~ office центра́льная конто́ра; ~ station гла́вный вокза́л; **~ize** [-laiz] централизова́ть (*im*)*pf.*
centre ['sentə] **1.** центр; средото́чие; **2.** [с]концентри́ровать(ся); сосредото́чи(ва)ть(ся).
century ['sentʃəri] столе́тие, век.
cereal ['siəriəl] хле́бный злак; *Am.* ка́ша.
ceremon|ial [seri'mounjəl] □ фор-

ма́льный; церемониа́льный; **~ious** [-njəs] церемо́нный; жема́нный; **~y** ['seriməni] церемо́ния.
certain ['sə:tn] □ определённый; уве́ренный; не́кий; не́который; **~ty** [-ti] уве́ренность *f*; определённость *f*.
certi|ficate 1. [sə'tifikit] свиде́тельство; сертифика́т; ~ of birth свиде́тельство о рожде́нии, ме́трика; 2. [-keit] вы́дать пи́сьменное удостовере́ние (Д); **~fication** [sə:tifi'keiʃən] удостовере́ние; **~fy** ['sə:tifai] удостоверя́ть [-е́рить]; **~tude** [-tju:d] уве́ренность *f*.
cessation [se'seiʃən] прекраще́ние.
cession ['seʃən] усту́пка, переда́ча.
cesspool ['sespu:l] выгребна́я я́ма; сто́чный коло́дец.
chafe [tʃeif] *v/t.* натира́ть [натере́ть]; нагре́(ва́)ть; *v/i.* раздража́ться [-жи́ться], не́рвничать.
chaff [tʃɑ:f] 1. мяки́на; отбро́сы *m/pl.*; F подшу́чивание, поддра́знивание; 2. ме́лко наре́зать (соло́му и т. п.); F подшу́чивать [-шути́ть] над (Т), поддра́знивать [-зни́ть].
chagrin ['ʃægrin] 1. доса́да, огорче́ние; 2. досажда́ть [досади́ть] (Д); огорча́ть [-чи́ть].
chain [tʃein] 1. цепь *f*; **~s** *pl. fig.* око́вы *f/pl.*; у́зы *f/pl.*; 2. ско́вывать [скова́ть]; держа́ть в цепя́х; *fig.* прико́вывать [-ова́ть].
chair [tʃɛə] стул; ка́федра; председа́тельское ме́сто; be in the ~ председа́тельствовать; **~man** ['tʃɛəmən] председа́тель *m*.
chalk [tʃɔ:k] 1. мел; 2. писа́ть, рисова́ть ме́лом; (*mst* ~ up) запи́сывать [-иса́ть] (долг) ~ out набра́сывать [-броса́ть]; намеча́ть [-е́тить].
challenge ['tʃælindʒ] 1. вы́зов; ⚔ о́клик (часово́го); *part.* ⚖ отво́д (прися́жных); 2. вызыва́ть [вы́звать]; оспа́ривать [оспо́рить]; [по]тре́бовать (внима́ния).
chamber ['tʃeimbə] ко́мната; пала́та; **~s** *pl.* конто́ра адвока́та; ка́мера судьи́; **~maid** го́рничная.
chamois ['ʃæmwɑ:] 1. се́рна; ['ʃæmi] за́мша; 2. жёлто-кори́чневый.
champion ['tʃæmpjən] 1. чемпио́н (-ка); победи́тель(ница) *f*) *m*; защи́тник (-ница); 2. защища́ть [-ити́ть]; боро́ться за (В).
chance [tʃɑ:ns] 1. случа́йность *f*; риск (в игре́); уда́ча; удо́бный слу́чай; шанс (of на В); by ~ случа́йно; take a ~ рискова́ть [-кну́ть]; 2. случа́йный; 3. *v/i.* случа́ться [-чи́ться]; ~ upon случа́йно найти́ *pf.*; *v/t.* F про́бовать наудачу.
chancellor ['tʃɑ:nsələ] ка́нцлер.
chandelier [ʃændi'liə] лю́стра.
chandler ['tʃɑ:ndlə] ла́вочник.
change ['tʃeindʒ] 1. переме́на, измене́ние; сме́на (белья́); ме́лочь *f*, сда́ча (о де́ньга́х); 2. *v/t.* [по-]меня́ть; изменя́ть [-ни́ть], переменя́ть [-ни́ть]; обме́нивать [-ня́ть]; разме́нивать [-ня́ть] (де́ньги); *v/i.* [по]меня́ться; изменя́ться [-ни́ться]; переменя́ться [-ни́ться]; переоде́(ва́)ться; обме́ниваться [-ня́ться]; 🚂 переса́живаться [-се́сть]; **~able** ['tʃeindʒəbl] □ непостоя́нный, переме́нчивый; **~less** [-lis] □ неизме́нный, постоя́нный.
channel ['tʃænl] ру́сло; фарва́тер; проли́в; *fig.* путь *m*; исто́чник.
chant [tʃɑ:nt] 1. песнь *f*; песнопе́ние; 2. петь моното́нно; *fig.* вос-[пе́(ва́)ть.
chaos ['keiɔs] хао́с.
chap[1] [tʃæp] 1. щель *f*; тре́щина; 2. [по]тре́скаться.
chap[2] [~] F ма́лый, па́рень *m*.
chapel ['tʃæpəl] часо́вня; капе́лла.
chaplain ['tʃæplin] свяще́нник.
chapter ['tʃæptə] глава́.
char [tʃɑ:] обжига́ть [обже́чь]; обу́гли(ва)ть(ся).
character ['kæriktə] хара́ктер; ли́чность *f*; *thea.* де́йствующее лицо́; бу́ква; **~istic** [kæriktə'ristik] 1. (**~ally**) характе́рный; типи́чный (of для Р); 2. характе́рная осо́бенность *f*; **~ize** ['kæriktəraiz] характеризова́ть (*im*)*pf.*; изобража́ть [-рази́ть].
charcoal ['tʃɑ:koul] древе́сный у́голь *m*.
charge [tʃɑ:dʒ] 1. заря́д; нагру́зка; поруче́ние; цена́; обвине́ние; ата́ка; *fig.* попече́ние, забо́та; **~s** *pl.* ✝ расхо́ды *m/pl.*; изде́ржки *f/pl.*; be in ~ of заве́довать (Т); 2. *v/t.* заряжа́ть [-яди́ть]; нагружа́ть [-узи́ть]; поруча́ть [-чи́ть] (Д); обвиня́ть [-ни́ть] (with в П); назнача́ть [-на́чить] (це́ну) (to на В); *Am.* утвержда́ть [-рди́ть].
charitable ['tʃæritəbl] □ благотвори́тельный; милосе́рдный.
charity ['tʃæriti] милосе́рдие; благотвори́тельность *f*.
charlatan ['ʃɑ:lətən] шарлата́н.
charm [tʃɑ:m] 1. амуле́т; *fig.* ча́ры *f/pl.*; обая́ние, очарова́ние; 2. заколдо́вывать [-дова́ть]; *fig.* очаро́вывать [-ова́ть]; **~ing** ['tʃɑ:miŋ] □ очарова́тельный, обая́тельный.
chart [tʃɑ:t] 1. ⚓ морска́я ка́рта; 2. наноси́ть на ка́рту; черти́ть ка́рту.
charter ['tʃɑ:tə] 1. ха́ртия; пра́во; привиле́гия; 2. дарова́ть привиле́гию (Д); ⚓ [за]фрахтова́ть (су́дно).
charwoman ['tʃɑ:wumən] подённщица.
chary ['tʃɛəri] □ осторо́жный; скупо́й (на слова́ и т. п.).
chase [tʃeis] 1. пого́ня *f*; охо́та; 2. охо́титься за (Т); пресле́довать; прогоня́ть [-гна́ть].

chasm [kæzm] бе́здна, про́пасть *f*.
chaste [tʃeist] □ целому́дренный.
chastity ['tʃæstiti] целому́дрие; де́вственность *f*.
chat [tʃæt] **1.** бесе́да; **2.** [по]болта́ть, [по]бесе́довать.
chattels ['tʃætlz] *pl*. (*mst* goods and ~) иму́щество, ве́щи *f/pl*.
chatter [tʃætə] **1.** болтовня́ *f*; щебета́ние) **2.** [по]болта́ть; **~er** [-rə] болту́н(ья).
chatty ['tʃæti] болтли́вый.
chauffeur ['ʃoufə] води́тель *m*, шофёр.
cheap [tʃi:p] □ дешёвый; *fig*. плохо́й; **~en** ['tʃi:pən] [по]дешеве́ть; снижа́ть це́ну (В); *fig*. унижа́ть [уни́зить].
cheat [tʃi:t] **1.** обма́нщик, плут; обма́н; **2.** обма́нывать [-ну́ть].
check [tʃek] **1.** *chess* шах; препя́тствие; остано́вка; контро́ль *m* (on над Т), прове́рка (on Р); *Am*. бага́жная квита́нция; *Am*. ✝ чек; клётчатая ткань *f*; **2.** проверя́ть [-ве́рить]; [про]контроли́ровать; остана́вливать [-нови́ть]; препя́тствовать; **~er** ['tʃekə] контролёр; **~s** *pl*. *Am*. ша́шки *f/pl*.; **~ing-room** *Am*. ка́мера хране́ния (багажа́); **~mate 1.** шах и мат; **2.** де́лать мат; **~-up** *Am*. стро́гая прове́рка.
cheek [tʃi:k] щека́ (*pl*.: щёки); F на́глость *f*, де́рзость *f*.
cheer [tʃiə] **1.** весе́лье; одобри́тельные во́згласы *m/pl*.; **2.** *v/t*. ободря́ть [-ри́ть]; поощря́ть [-ри́ть]; приве́тстсвовать гро́мкими во́згласами; *v/i*. ликова́ть; **~ful** ['tʃiəful] □ бо́дрый, весёлый; **~less** [-lis] □ уны́лый, мра́чный; **~y** [-ri] □ живо́й, весёлый, ра́достный.
cheese [tʃi:z] сыр.
chemical ['kemikəl] **1.** □ хими́ческий; **2.** **~s** [-s] *pl*. хими́ческие препара́ты *m/pl*., химика́лии *f/pl*.
chemist ['kemist] хи́мик; апте́карь *m*; **~ry** ['kemistri] хи́мия.
cheque [tʃek] ✝ ба́нковый чек.
chequer ['tʃekə] **1.** *mst* **~s** *pl*. клётчатый узо́р; **2.** графи́ть в клётку.
cherish ['tʃeriʃ] леле́ять (наде́жду); храни́ть (в па́мяти); не́жно [люби́ть.]
cherry ['tʃeri] ви́шня.
chess [tʃes] ша́хматы *f/pl*.; **~board** ша́хматная доска́; **~man** ша́хматная фигу́ра.
chest [tʃest] я́щик, сунду́к; грудна́я клётка; ~ of drawers комо́д.
chestnut ['tʃesnʌt] **1.** кашта́н; F изби́тый анекдо́т; **2.** кашта́новый; гнедо́й (о ло́шади).
chevy ['tʃevi] *Brit*. F **1.** охо́та; пого́ня; **2.** гна́ться за (Т); уд(и)ра́ть.
chew [tʃu:] жева́ть; размышля́ть; **~ing-gum** ['tʃu:iŋgʌm] жева́тельная рези́нка.
chicane [ʃi'kein] **1.** приди́рка; **2.** прид(и)ра́ться к (Д).
chick [tʃik], **~en** ['tʃikin] цыплёнок; птене́ц; **~en-pox** ⚕ ве́тряная о́спа.
chief [tʃi:f] **1.** □ гла́вный; руководя́щий; ~ clerk нача́льник отде́ла; **2.** глава́, руководи́тель (-ница *f*) *m*; ...-in-~ гла́вный ...; **~tain** ['tʃi:ftən] вождь *m* (кла́на); атама́н.
chilblain ['tʃilblein] отморо́женное ме́сто.
child [tʃaild] ребёнок, дитя́ *n* (*pl*.: де́ти); from a ~ с де́тства; with ~ бере́менная; **~birth** ро́ды *m/pl*.; **~hood** [-hud] де́тство; **~ish** ['tʃaildiʃ] □ де́тский; **~like** [-laik] как ребёнок; неви́нный; **~ren** ['tʃildrən] *pl*. от child.
chill [tʃil] **1.** хо́лод; хо́лодность *f*; ⚕ просту́да; **2.** холо́дный; расхола́живающий; **3.** *v/t*. охлажда́ть [-лади́ть]; [о]студи́ть; *v/i*. охлажда́ться [-лади́ться]; **~y** ['tʃili] зя́бкий; холо́дный.
chime [tʃaim] **1.** звон колоколо́в; бой часо́в; *fig*. гармони́чное сочета́ние; **2.** [по]звони́ть (о колокола́х); [про]би́ть (о часа́х); *fig*. соотве́тствовать; гармони́ровать.
chimney ['tʃimni] дымова́я труба́; ла́мповое стекло́.
chin [tʃin] подборо́док.
china ['tʃainə] фарфо́р.
Chinese ['tʃai'ni:z] **1.** кита́ец (-аянка); **2.** кита́йский.
chink [tʃiŋk] щель *f*, сква́жина.
chip [tʃip] **1.** ще́пка, лучи́на; стру́жка; оско́лок (стекла́); **2.** *v/t*. отбива́ть края́ (посу́ды и т. п.); *v/i*. отла́мываться [отлома́ться].
chirp [tʃə:p] **1.** чири́канье; щебета́ние; **2.** чири́кать [-кнуть]; [за-] щебета́ть.
chisel ['tʃizl] **1.** долото́, stаме́ска; **2.** [из]вая́ть; *sl*. наду́(ва́)ть, обма́нывать [-ну́ть].
chit-chat ['tʃit-tʃæt] болтовня́.
chivalr|ous ['ʃivəlrəs] □ ры́царский; **~y** [-ri] ры́царство.
chlor|ine ['klɔ:ri:n] ⚗ хлор; **~oform** ['klɔrəfɔ:m] **1.** хлорофо́рм; **2.** хлороформи́ровать (*im*)*pf*.
chocolate ['tʃɔkəlit] шокола́д.
choice [tʃɔis] **1.** вы́бор; отбо́р; альтернати́ва; **2.** □ отбо́рный.
choir ['kwaiə] хор.
choke [tʃouk] **1.** *v/t*. [за]души́ть; засоря́ть [-ри́ть]; ⚡ дроссели́ровать; (*mst* ~ down) глота́ть с трудо́м; дави́ться (with от Р); задыха́ться [-дохну́ться]; **2.** припа́док уду́шья; ⊕ засло́нка.
choose [tʃu:z] [*irr*.] выбира́ть [вы́брать]; предпочита́ть [-че́сть]; ~ to *inf*. хоте́ть (+ *inf*.).
chop [tʃɔp] **1.** отбивна́я котлёта; **~s** *pl*. че́люсть *f*; **2.** *v/t*. ⊕ стёсывать [стеса́ть]; долби́ть; [на]руби́ть; [на]кроши́ть; *v/i*. колеба́ть-

ся; меня́ться, перемени́ться *pf.* (о ве́тре); **~per** ['tʃɔpə] коса́рь (нож) *m*; лесору́б; колу́н; **~py** ['tʃɔpi] неспоко́йный (о мо́ре).
choral ['kɔrəl] □ хорово́й; **~(e)** [kɔ'rɑ:l] ♪ хора́л.
chord [kɔ:d] струна́; ♪ акко́рд; созву́чие.
chore [tʃɔ:] *Am.* подённая рабо́та; рути́нная дома́шняя рабо́та.
chorus ['kɔ:rəs] **1.** хор; му́зыка для хо́ра; **2.** петь хо́ром.
chose [tʃouz] *pt.* от choose; **~n** (~n) **1.** *p. pt.* от choose; **2.** и́збранный.
Christ [kraist] Христо́с.
christen ['krisn] [о]крести́ть; **~ing** [-iŋ] крести́ны *f/pl.*; креще́ние.
Christian ['kristjən] **1.** христиа́нский; ~ name и́мя (в отли́чие от фами́лии); **2.** христиани́н (-а́нка); **~ity** [kristi'æniti] христиа́нство.
Christmas ['krisməs] рождество́.
chromium ['kroumiəm] ⚗ хром; **~-plated** покры́тый хро́мом.
chronic ['krɔnik] (**~ally**) хрони́ческий; ⚕ застаре́лый; P отврати́тельный; **~le** [~l] **1.** хро́ника, ле́топись *f*; **2.** вести́ хро́нику (P).
chronolog|ical [krɔnə'lɔdʒikəl] □ хронологи́ческий; **~y** [krə'nɔlədʒi] хроноло́гия.
chubby ['tʃʌbi] F по́лный, то́лстый.
chuck[1] [tʃʌk] **1.** куда́хтанье; цыплёнок; my ~! голу́бчик !; **2.** [за-] куда́хтать.
chuck[2] [~] **1.** броса́ть [бро́сить]; F швыря́ть [-рну́ть]; **2.** F увольне́ние.
chuckle ['tʃʌkl] посме́иваться.
chum [tʃʌm] F **1.** това́рищ; закады́чный друг; **2.** быть в дру́жбе.
chump [tʃʌmp] коло́да, чурба́н; F «башка́».
chunk [tʃʌŋk] F ломо́ть *m*; болва́н.
church [tʃə:tʃ] це́рковь *f*; ~ service богослуже́ние; **~yard** кла́дбище.
churl [tʃə:l] гру́бый челове́к; **~ish** ['tʃə:liʃ] □ скупо́й; гру́бый.
churn [tʃə:n] **1.** маслобо́йка; **2.** сбива́ть ма́сло; *fig.* взба́лтывать [взболта́ть]; вспе́ни(ва)ть.
cider ['saidə] сидр.
cigar [si'gɑ:] сига́ра.
cigarette [sigə'ret] папиро́са, сигаре́та; **~-case** портсига́р.
cigar-holder мундшту́к.
cinch [sintʃ] *Am. sl.* не́что надёжное, ве́рное.
cincture ['siŋktʃə] по́яс; опо́ясывание.
cinder ['sində] шлак; ока́лина; **~s** *pl.* зола́; **~-path** *sport*: гарева́я доро́жка.
cinema ['sinimə] кинемато́граф, кино́ *n indecl.*
cinnamon ['sinəmən] кори́ца.
cipher ['saifə] **1.** шифр; ци́фра; нуль *m or* ноль *m*; **2.** зашифро́вывать [-ова́ть]; вычисля́ть [вы́числить]; высчи́тывать [вы́считать].
circle ['sə:kl] **1.** круг; окру́жность *f*; орби́та; кружо́к; сфе́ра; *thea.* я́рус; **2.** враща́ться вокру́г (P); соверша́ть круги́, кружи́ть(ся).
circuit ['sə:kit] кругооборо́т; объе́зд; о́круг (суде́бный); ⚡ цепь *f*, ко́нтур; ⚡ short ~ коро́ткое замыка́ние; ✈ кругово́й полёт.
circular ['sə:kjulə] **1.** □ кру́глый, кругово́й; ~ letter циркуля́р, циркуля́рное письмо́; ~ note † ба́нковый аккредити́в; **2.** циркуля́р; проспе́кт.
circulat|e ['sə:kjuleit] *v/i.* распространя́ться [-ни́ться]; име́ть кругово́е движе́ние; циркули́ровать; **~ing** [-iŋ]: ~ library библиоте́ка с вы́дачей книг на́ дом; **~ion** [sə:kju'leiʃən] кровообраще́ние; циркуля́ция; тира́ж (газе́т и т. п.); *fig.* распростране́ние (слу́хов и т. п.).
circum... ['sə:kəm] *pref.* (в сло́жных слова́х) вокру́г, круго́м; **~ference** [sə'kʌmfərəns] окру́жность *f*; перифери́я; **~jacent** [sə:kəm'dʒeisnt] окружа́ющий; **~locution** [-lə'kju:ʃən] многоречи́вость *f*; **~navigate** [-'nævigeit] соверша́ть пла́вание вокру́г (P); **~scribe** ['sə:kəmskraib] & опи́сывать [описа́ть] (круг); *fig.* ограни́чи(ва)ть (права́ и т. п.); **~spect** [-spekt] □ осмотри́тельный, осторо́жный; **~stance** ['sə:kəmstəns] обстоя́тельство; **~stantial** [sə:kəm'stænʃəl] □ обстоя́тельный, подро́бный; **~vent** [-'vent] обходи́ть [обойти́] (зако́н и т. п.).
cistern ['sistən] бак; водоём; цисте́рна.
cit|ation [sai'teiʃən] цита́та, ссы́лка; цити́рование; **~e** [sait] ссыла́ться [сосла́ться] на (B).
citizen ['sitizn] граждани́н (-да́нка); **~ship** [-ʃip] гражда́нство.
citron ['sitrən] цитро́н.
city ['siti] го́род; *attr.* городско́й; **2.** the ♀ делово́й кварта́л в Ло́ндоне; ♀ article биржево́й бюллете́нь *m*; статья́ в газе́те по фина́нсовым и комме́рческим вопро́сам.
civic ['sivik] гражда́нский; **~s** [-s] *pl.* ⚖ гражда́нские дела́ *n/pl.*; осно́вы гражда́нственности.
civil ['sivil] □ гражда́нский; шта́тский; ве́жливый; ⚖ гражда́нский (противополо́жный уголо́вному); ~ servant чино́вник; ~ service госуда́рственная слу́жба; **~ian** [si'viljən] ⚔ шта́тский; **~ity** [si'viliti] ве́жливость *f*; **~ization** [sivilai'zeiʃən] цивилиза́ция; **~ize** ['sivilaiz] цивилизова́ть (*im*)*pf.*
clad [klæd] *pt.* и *p. pt.* от clothe.
claim [kleim] **1.** предъявля́ть прете́нзию на (B); [по]тре́бовать; заявля́ть права́; утвержда́ть [-рди́ть]; заявля́ть права́ на (B); **2.** тре́бование; иск; прете́нзия; ~ to be

выдава́ть себя́ за (B); **~ant** ['kleimənt] претенде́нт; ⚖ исте́ц.

clairvoyant [klɛə'vɔiənt] ясновидец.

clamber ['klæmbə] [вс]кара́бкаться.

clammy ['klæmi] □ кле́йкий, ли́пкий; холо́дный и вла́жный.

clamo(u)r ['klæmə] 1. шум, кри́ки *m/pl.*; проте́сты *m/pl.* (шу́мные); 2. шу́мно тре́бовать (P).

clamp [klæmp] ⊕ скоба́; скре́па; зажи́м; 2. скрепля́ть [-пи́ть]; зажи(им)а́ть; смыка́ть [сомкну́ть].

clandestine [klæn'destin] □ та́йный.

clang [klæŋ] 1. лязг, звон (ору́жия, колоколо́в, мо́лота); 2. ля́згать [-гнуть].

clank [klæŋk] 1. звон, лязг (цепе́й, желе́за и т. п.), бряца́ние; 2. бряца́ть, [за]греме́ть.

clap [klæp] 1. хлопо́к; хло́панье; уда́р (гро́ма); 2. хло́пать (в ладо́ши); **~trap** пого́ня за эффе́ктом.

clarify ['klærifai] *v/t.* очища́ть [очи́стить]; де́лать прозра́чным; *fig.* выясня́ть [вы́яснить]; *v/i.* де́латься прозра́чным, я́сным.

clarity ['klæriti] я́сность *f.*

clash [klæʃ] 1. столкнове́ние; противоре́чие; конфли́кт; 2. ста́лкиваться [столкну́ться]; расходи́ться [разойти́сь] (о взгля́дах).

clasp [klɑ:sp] 1. пря́жка, застёжка; *fig.* объя́тия *n/pl.*; 2. *v/t.* застёгивать [застегну́ть]; сж(им)а́ть; *fig.* заключа́ть в объя́тия; *v/i.* обви́(ва́)ться (о расте́нии).

class [klɑ:s] 1. класс (шко́лы); обще́ственный класс; 2. классифици́ровать (*im*)*pf.*

classic ['klæsik] 1. кла́ссик; 2. **~(al** □) [~, -ikəl] класси́ческий.

classi|fication [klæsifi'keiʃən] классифика́ция; **~fy** [klæ'sifai] классифици́ровать (*im*)*pf.*

clatter ['klætə] 1. звон (посу́ды); гро́хот (маши́н); болтовня́; то́пот; 2. [за]греме́ть; [за]то́пать; *fig.* [по]болта́ть.

clause [klɔ:z] пункт; статья́; клау́зула (в догово́ре).

claw [klɔ:] 1. ко́готь *m*; клешня́ (ра́ка); 2. разрыва́ть, терза́ть когтя́ми.

clay [klei] гли́на; *fig.* прах.

clean [kli:n] 1. *adj.* □ чи́стый; опря́тный; чистопло́тный; 2. *adv.* на́чисто; соверше́нно, по́лностью; 3. [вы́]чистить; прочища́ть [-чи́стить]; счища́ть [счи́стить]; ~ up уб(и)ра́ть; приводи́ть в поря́док; **~ing** ['kli:niŋ] чи́стка; убо́рка; очи́стка; **~liness** ['klenlinis] чистопло́тность *f*; **~ly** 1. *adv.* ['kli:nli] чи́сто; целому́дренно; 2. *adj.* ['klenli] чистопло́тный; **~se** [klenz] очища́ть [очи́стить]; дезинфици́ровать (*im*)*pf.*

clear [kliə] 1. □ я́сный, све́тлый; прозра́чный; *fig.* свобо́дный (from, of от P); ✝ чи́стый (вес, дохо́д и т. п.); 2. *v/t.* очища́ть [очи́стить] (from, of от P); расчища́ть [-и́стить]; распрод(ав)а́ть (това́р); ⚖ опра́вдывать [-да́ть] (обвиня́емого); *v/i.* (*a.* ~ up) рассе́иваться [-е́яться] (о тума́не); проясня́ться [-ни́ться]; **~ance** ['kliərəns] очи́стка; устране́ние препя́тствий; очи́стка от тамо́женных по́шлин; расчи́стка (под па́шню); **~ing** ['kliəriŋ] проясне́ние; про́сека; кли́ринг (ме́жду ба́нками); ♀ House расчётная пала́та.

cleave[1] [kli:v] [*irr.*] раска́лывать (-ся) [-коло́ть(ся)]; рассека́ть [-е́чь] (во́лны, во́здух).

cleave[2] [~] *fig.* остава́ться ве́рным (to Д).

cleaver ['kli:və] большо́й нож мясника́.

clef [klef] ♪ ключ.

cleft [kleft] 1. рассе́лина; 2. расколо́тый.

clemen|cy ['klemənsi] милосе́рдие; снисходи́тельность *f*; **~t** ['klemənt] □ милосе́рдный, ми́лостивый.

clench [klentʃ] зажи(им)а́ть; сж(имм)а́ть (кулаки́); сти́скивать [сти́снуть] (зу́бы); *s.* clinch.

clergy ['klə:dʒi] духове́нство; **~man** [-mən] свяще́нник.

clerical ['klerikəl] 1. □ клерика́льный; канцеля́рский; 2. клерика́л.

clerk [klə:k] чино́вник; конто́рский слу́жащий; *Am.* прика́зчик.

clever ['klevə] □ у́мный; дарови́тый, одарённый; ло́вкий.

clew [klu:] 1. клубо́к; 2. сма́тывать в клубо́к.

click [klik] 1. щёлканье; ⊕ защёлка, соба́чка; 2. щёлкать [-кнуть] (замко́м); прищёлкивать [-кнуть] (языко́м); *Am.* име́ть успе́х.

client ['klaiənt] клие́нт(ка); постоя́нный (-ная) покупа́тель(ница *f*) *m*; **~èle** [kli:ɑn'teil] клиенту́ра.

cliff [klif] утёс, скала́.

climate ['klaimit] кли́мат.

climax ['klaimæks] 1. кульминацио́нный пункт; 2. достига́ть кульминацио́нного пу́нкта.

climb [klaim] [*irr.*] влез(а́)ть на (B); поднима́ться [-ня́ться] (на́ гору); **~er** ['klaimə] альпини́ст; *fig.* честолю́бец; ♀ выо́щееся расте́ние.

clinch [klintʃ] 1. ⊕ зажи́м; скоба́; 2. *v/t.* заклёпывать [-лепа́ть]; ~ a bargain заключа́ть сде́лку; *s.* clench.

cling [kliŋ] [*irr.*] (to) [при]льну́ть к (Д); ~ together держа́ться вме́сте.

clinic ['klinik] 1. кли́ника; 2. = **~al** [-ikəl] клини́ческий.

clink [kliŋk] 1. звон (мета́лла, стекла́); 2. [за]звене́ть; [за]звуча́ть.
clip[1] [klip] 1. стри́жка; 2. обреза́ть [обре́зать]; [о]стри́чь.
clip[2] [~] скре́пка.
clipp|er ['klipə]: (a pair of) **~s** *pl.* но́жницы *f/pl.*; сека́тор; ⚓ кли́ппер (па́русное су́дно); (flying ~) самолёт гражда́нской авиа́ции; **~ings** [-iŋz] *pl.* газе́тные вы́резки *f/pl.*; обре́зки *m/pl.*
cloak [klouk] 1. плащ; ма́нтия; покро́в; *fig.* предло́г; 2. покры́(ва́)ть (плащо́м и т. п.); *fig.* прикры́(ва́)ть; **~-room** раздева́льня; 🚂 ка́мера хране́ния.
clock [klɔk] часы́ *m/pl.* (стенны́е, насто́льные, ба́шенные).
clod [klɔd] ком (гря́зи); ду́рень *m*, о́лух.
clog [klɔg] 1. препя́тствие; пу́ты *f/pl.*; деревя́нный башма́к; 2. [вос]препя́тствовать (Д); засоря́ть(ся) [-ри́ть(ся)].
cloister ['klɔistə] монасты́рь *m*; кры́тая арка́да.
close 1. [klous] □ закры́тый; бли́зкий; те́сный; ду́шный, спёртый (во́здух); скупо́й; ~ by *adv.* ря́дом, поблизости; ~ to о́коло (Р); ~ fight, ~ quarters *pl.* рукопа́шный бой; *hunt.* ~ season, ~ time запре́тное вре́мя охо́ты; 2. a) [klouz] коне́ц; заключе́ние; b) [klous] огоро́женное ме́сто; 3. [klouz] *v/t.* закры́(ва́)ть; зака́нчивать [-ко́нчить]; конча́ть [ко́нчить]; заключа́ть [-чи́ть] (речь); *v/i.* закры́(ва́)ться; конча́ться [ко́нчиться]; ~ in приближа́ться [-ли́зиться]; наступа́ть [-пи́ть]; ~ on (*prp.*) замыка́ться вокру́г (Р); **~ness** ['klousnis] бли́зость *f*; ску́пость *f*.
closet ['klɔzit] 1. чула́н; убо́рная; стенно́й шкаф; 2. be **~ed** with совеща́ться наедине́ с (Т).
closure ['klouʒə] закры́тие; *parl.* прекраще́ние пре́ний.
clot [klɔt] 1. сгу́сток (кро́ви); комо́к; 2. сгуща́ться [сгусти́ться], свёртываться [сверну́ться].
cloth [klɔ:θ, klɔθ], *pl.* **~s** [klɔ:ðz, klɔθs] ска́терть *f*; ткань *f*; сукно́; F the ~ духове́нство; ~ binding тка́невый переплёт.
clothe [klouð] [*a. irr.*] оде́(ва́)ть; *fig.* облека́ть [-е́чь].
clothes [klouðz] *pl.* оде́жда, пла́тье; бельё; **~-basket** бельева́я корзи́на; **~-line** верёвка для су́шки белья́; **~-peg** зажи́мка для разве́шенного белья́.
clothier ['klouðiə] фабрика́нт суко́н.
clothing ['klouðiŋ] оде́жда, пла́тье.
cloud [klaud] 1. о́блако, ту́ча; 2. покрыва́ть(ся) ту́чами, облака́ми; омрача́ть(ся) [-чи́ть(ся)]; **~-burst** ли́вень *m*; **~less** ['klaudlis] □ безо́блачный; **~y** [-i] □ о́блачный; му́тный (о жи́дкости); тума́нный (о мы́сли).
clove[1] [klouv] гвозди́ка (пря́ность).
clove[2] [~] *pt.* от cleave; **~n** ['klouvn] *p. pt.* от cleave.
clover ['klouvə] ⚘ кле́вер.
clown [klaun] кло́ун.
cloy [klɔi] пресыща́ть [-сы́тить].
club [klʌb] 1. клуб; дуби́на; *Am.* па́лка полице́йского; **~s** *pl.* тре́фы *f/pl.* (ка́рточная масть); 2. *v/t.* [по]би́ть (па́лкой и т.п.); *v/i.* собира́ться вме́сте; устра́ивать скла́дчину.
clue [klu:] ключ к разга́дке; путево́дная нить *f*.
clump [klʌmp] 1. комо́к; гру́ппа (дере́вьев); 2. тяжело́ ступа́ть.
clumsy ['klʌmzi] □ неуклю́жий; нело́вкий; беста́ктный.
clung [klʌŋ] *pt.* и *p. pt.* от cling.
cluster ['klʌstə] 1. кисть *f*; пучо́к; гроздь *f*; 2. расти́ гро́здьями, пучка́ми.
clutch [klʌtʃ] 1. сжа́тие; захва́т; ⊕ зажи́м; защёлка; му́фта сцепле́ния; 2. схва́тывать [-ти́ть]; заж(им)а́ть.
clutter ['klʌtə] 1. сумато́ха; хао́с; 2. приводи́ть в беспоря́док.
coach [koutʃ] 1. экипа́ж; тре́нер; инстру́ктор; 🚂 пассажи́рский ваго́н; 2. е́хать в каре́те; [на]тренирова́ть;ната́скивать к экза́мену; **~man** ку́чер.
coagulate [kou'ægjuleit] сгуща́ться [сгусти́ться].
coal [koul] 1. у́голь *m* (ка́менный); 2. ⚓ грузи́ть(ся) у́глем.
coalesce [kouə'les] сраста́ться [срасти́сь].
coalition [kouə'liʃən] коали́ция; сою́з.
coal-pit у́гольная ша́хта, копь *f*.
coarse [kɔ:s] □ гру́бый; кру́пный; неотёсанный.
coast [koust] 1. морско́й бе́рег, побере́жье; 2. плыть вдоль побере́жья; **~er** ['koustə] ⚓ кабота́жное су́дно.
coat [kout] 1. пиджа́к; пальто́ *n indecl.*; мех, шерсть *f* (у живо́тных); слой; ~ of arms ге́рбовый щит; 2. покры́(ва́)ть (кра́ской, пы́лью и т. п.); облицо́вывать [-цева́ть]; **~-hanger** ве́шалка; **~ing** ['koutiŋ] слой (кра́ски и т. п.).
coax [kouks] угова́ривать [уговори́ть].
cob [kɔb] ком; *Am.* поча́ток кукуру́зы.
cobbler ['kɔblə] сапо́жник; *fig.* халту́рщик, плохо́й ма́стер.
cobweb ['kɔbweb] паути́на.
cock [kɔk] 1. пету́х; кран; флю́гер; куро́к; 2. (*a.* ~ up) настора́живать [-рожи́ть] (у́ши).
cockade [kɔ'keid] кока́рда.

cockatoo [kɔkə'tu:] какаду́ *m indecl.*
cockboat ['kɔkbout] ⚓ судова́я шлю́пка.
cockchafer ['kɔktʃeifə] ма́йский жук.
cock-eyed ['kɔkaid] *sl.* косогла́зый; косо́й; *Am.* пья́ный.
cockpit ['kɔkpit] ме́сто петуши́ных боёв; ⚓ ку́брик; ✈ каби́на.
cockroach ['kɔkroutʃ] *zo.* тарака́н.
cock|sure F самоуве́ренный; **~tail** кокте́йль *m*; *fig.* вы́скочка; **~y** ['kɔki] □ F наха́льный; де́рзкий.
coco ['koukou] коко́совая па́льма.
cocoa ['koukou] кака́о (порошо́к, напи́ток) *n indecl.*
coco-nut ['koukənʌt] коко́совый оре́х.
cocoon [kɔ'ku:n] ко́кон.
cod [kɔd] треска́.
coddle ['kɔdl] изне́жи(ва)ть; [из-] балова́ть.
code [koud] **1.** ко́декс; *telegr.* код; **2.** коди́ровать *(im)pf.*
codger ['kɔdʒə] F чуда́к.
cod-liver: ~ oil ры́бий жир.
coerc|e [kou'ə:s] принужда́ть [-ну́дить]; **~ion** [-ʃən] принужде́ние.
coeval [kou'i:vəl] □ совреме́нный.
coexist ['kouig'zist] сосуществова́ть (с Т).
coffee ['kɔfi] ко́фе *m indecl.*; **~-pot** кофе́йник; **~-room** столо́вая в гости́нице; **~-set** кофе́йный серви́з.
coffer ['kɔfə] металли́ческий сунду́к.
coffin ['kɔfin] гроб.
cogent ['koudʒənt] □ неоспори́мый; убеди́тельный.
cogitate ['kɔdʒiteit] *v/i.* размышля́ть; *v/t.* обду́м(ыв)ать.
cognate ['kɔgneit] ро́дственный; схо́дный.
cognition [kɔg'niʃən] зна́ние; позна́ние.
coheir ['kou'ɛə] сонасле́дник.
coheren|ce [kou'hiərəns] связь *f*; свя́зность *f*; согласо́ванность *f*; **~t** [-rənt] □ свя́зный; согласо́ванный.
cohesi|on [kou'hi:ʒən] связь *f*; сплочённость *f*; **~ve** [-siv] связу́ющий; спосо́бный к сцепле́нию.
coiff|eur [kwɑ:'fə:] парикма́хер; **~ure** [-'fjuə] причёска.
coil [kɔil] **1.** кольцо́ (верёвки, змей и т. п.); ⚡ кату́шка; ⊕ змееви́к; **2.** (*a.* ~ up) свёртываться кольцо́м (спира́лью).
coin [kɔin] **1.** моне́та; **2.** [вы́]чека́нить (моне́ты); вы́би(ва́)ть (меда́ли); **~age** ['kɔinidʒ] чека́нка (моне́т).
coincide [kouin'said] совпада́ть [-па́сть]; **~nce** [kou'insidəns] совпаде́ние; *fig.* случа́йное стече́ние обстоя́тельств.
coke [kouk] **1.** кокс; **2.** коксова́ть.
cold [kould] **1.** □ холо́дный; неприве́тливый; **2.** хо́лод; просту́да; **~ness** ['kouldnis] хо́лодность *f*; равноду́шие.
colic ['kɔlik] ⚕ ко́лики *f/pl.*
collaborat|e [kə'læbəreit] сотру́дничать; **~ion** [kəlæbə'reiʃən] сотру́дничество; in ~ в сотру́дничестве (с Т).
collapse [kə'læps] **1.** обва́л; разруше́ние; упа́док сил; **2.** обру́ши(ва)ться; обва́ливаться [-ли́ться]; си́льно слабе́ть.
collar ['kɔlə] **1.** воротни́к; оше́йник; хому́т; ⊕ вту́лка; о́бруч; ша́йба; **2.** схвати́ть за во́рот; *sl.* завладе́(ва́)ть (Т); захва́тывать [-ти́ть] (си́лой).
collate [kɔ'leit] слича́ть [-чи́ть]; сопоставля́ть [-ста́вить].
collateral [kɔ'lætərəl] **1.** □ побо́чный; ко́свенный; **2.** родство́ по боково́й ли́нии.
colleague ['kɔli:g] колле́га *f/m*, сослужи́вец (-вица).
collect **1.** ['kɔlekt] *eccl.* кра́ткая моли́тва; **2.** [kə'lekt] *v/t.* соб(и-)ра́ть; коллекциони́ровать; заходи́ть [зайти́] за (Т); *v/i.* соб(и)ра́ться; овладева́ть собо́й; **~ed** [kə'lektid] □ *fig.* хладнокро́вный; споко́йный; **~ion** [kə'lekʃən] колле́кция; собра́ние; **~ive** [-tiv] □ коллекти́вный; совоку́пный; **~or** [-tə] коллекционе́р; сбо́рщик.
college ['kɔlidʒ] колле́дж; сре́дняя шко́ла.
collide [kə'laid] ста́лкиваться [столкну́ться].
collie ['kɔli] ко́лли *m/f indecl.* (шотла́ндская овча́рка).
collier [kɔliə] шахтёр; ⚓ у́гольщик (су́дно); **~y** [kɔ'ljəri] каменноуго́льный рудни́к.
collision ['kəliʒən] столкнове́ние.
colloquial [kə'loukwiəl] □ разгово́рный.
colloquy ['kɔləkwi] разгово́р, собесе́дование.
colon ['koulən] *typ.* двоето́чие.
colonel ['kə:nl] ⚔ полко́вник.
coloni|al [kə'lounjəl] **1.** колониа́льный; **2.** жи́тель(ница *f*) *m* коло́ний; **~ze** ['kɔlənaiz] колонизи́ровать *(im)pf.*; заселя́ть [-ли́ть].
colony ['kɔləni] коло́ния.
colo(u)r ['kʌlə] **1.** цвет; кра́ска; румя́нец (на лице́); *fig.* колори́т; **~s** *pl.* зна́мя *n*; **2.** *v/t.* [по]кра́сить; окра́шивать [окра́сить]; *fig.* прикра́шивать [-кра́сить]; *v/i.* [по-] красне́ть; [за]рде́ться (о лице́, плоде́ и т. п.); **~ed** [-d] окра́шенный; цветно́й; **~ful** [-ful] я́ркий; **~ing** [-riŋ] окра́ска, раскра́ска; *fig.* прикра́шивание; **~less** [-lis] □ бесцве́тный.
colt [koult] жеребёнок (*pl.* жеребя́та); *fig.* нови́чо́к.

column ['kɔləm] ⚠, ⚔ коло́нна; столб; *typ.* столбе́ц.

comb [koum] **1.** гре́бень *m*, гребёнка; со́ты *m/pl.*; ⊕ бёрдо, чеса́лка; **2.** *v/t.* расчёсывать [-чеса́ть]; чеса́ть (*a.* ⊕); трепа́ть (лён и т. п.).

combat ['kɔmbət, 'kʌm-] **1.** бой, сраже́ние; **2.** сража́ться [срази́ться]; **~ant** [-ənt] бое́ц.

combin|ation [kɔmbi'neiʃən] соедине́ние; сочета́ние; *mst* **~s** *pl.* комбина́ция (бельё); **~e** [kəm'bain] объединя́ть(ся) [-ни́ть(ся)]; сочета́ть(ся) (*im*)*pf.*

combusti|ble [kəm'bʌstəbl] **1.** горю́чий, воспламеня́емый; **2.** **~s** *pl.* то́пливо; *mot.* горю́чее; **~on** [-tʃən] горе́ние, сгора́ние.

come [kʌm] [*irr.*] приходи́ть [прийти́]; приезжа́ть [прие́хать]; to ~ бу́дущий; ~ about случа́ться [-чи́ться], происходи́ть [произойти́]; ~ across a p. встреча́ться [-ре́титься] с (Т),ната́лкиваться [натолкну́ться] на (В); ~ at доб(и)ра́ться до (Р); ~ by дост(ав)а́ть (случа́йно); ~ off отде́л(ыв)аться; сходи́ть [сойти́]; ~ round приходи́ть в себя́; F заходи́ть [зайти́] (к Д); *fig.* идти́ на усту́пки; ~ to доходи́ть [дойти́] до (Р); ⚓ останови́ть су́дно; равня́ться (Д), сто́ить (В *or* Р); ~ up to соотве́тствовать (Д).

comedian [kə'mi:diən] актёр-ко́мик; а́втор коме́дии.

comedy ['kɔmidi] коме́дия.

comeliness ['kʌmlinis] милови́дность *f.*

comfort ['kʌmfət] **1.** комфо́рт, удо́бство; *fig.* утеше́ние; подде́ржка; **2.** утеша́ть [уте́шить]; успока́ивать [-ко́ить]; **~able** [-əbl] □ удо́бный, комфорта́бельный; *Am.* F доста́точный; **~er** [-ə] утеши́тель *m*; *Am.* стёганое одея́ло; **~less** [-lis] □ неую́тный.

comic(al □) ['kɔmik(əl)] коми́ческий, смешно́й; юмористи́ческий.

coming ['kʌmiŋ] **1.** прие́зд, прибы́тие; **2.** бу́дущий; ожида́емый.

command [kə'mɑ:nd] **1.** кома́нда, прика́з; кома́ндование; have at ~ име́ть в своём распоряже́нии; **2.** прика́зывать [-за́ть] (Д); владе́ть (Т); ⚔ кома́ндовать; **~er** [kə'mɑ:ndə] ⚔ команди́р; ⚓ капита́н; **℞er-in-Chief** [-rin'tʃi:f] главнокома́ндующий; **~ment** [-mənt] прика́з; *eccl.* за́поведь *f.*

commemora|te [kə'meməreit] [от]пра́здновать (годовщи́ну); отмеча́ть [отме́тить] (собы́тие); **~tion** [kəmemə'reʃən] пра́зднование (годовщи́ны).

commence [kə'mens] нач(ин)а́ть (-ся); **~ment** [-mənt] нача́ло.

commend [kə'mend] рекомендова́ть (*im*)*pf.*

comment ['kɔment] **1.** толкова́ние; коммента́рий; **2.** (upon) комменти́ровать (*im*)*pf.*; объясня́ть [-ни́ть]; **~ary** ['kɔməntəri] коммента́рий; **~ator** ['kɔmenteitə] коммента́тор.

commerc|e ['kɔməs, -ə:s] торго́вля; обще́ние; **~ial** [kə'mə:ʃəl] □ торго́вый, комме́рческий.

commiseration [kəmizə'reiʃən] сочу́вствие, соболе́знование.

commissary ['kɔmisəri] комисса́р; уполномо́ченный; ⚔ интенда́нт.

commission [kə'miʃən] **1.** коми́ссия; полномо́чие; поруче́ние; ⚔ пате́нт на офице́рский чин; **2.** назнача́ть на до́лжность; уполномо́чи(ва)ть; ⚓ гото́вить (кора́бль) к пла́ванию; **~er** [kə'miʃənə] уполномо́ченный; комисса́р.

commit [kə'mit] поруча́ть [-чи́ть], вверя́ть [вве́рить]; преда́(ва́)ть (огню́, земле́, суду́ и т.п.); соверша́ть [-ши́ть] (преступле́ние); ~ (o. s.) [с]компромети́ровать (себя́); обя́зывать(ся) [-за́ть(ся)]; ~ (to prison) заключа́ть [-чи́ть] (в тюрьму́); **~ment** [-mənt], **~tal** [-l] переда́ча; обяза́тельство; **~tee** [-i] коми́ссия; комите́т.

commodity [kə'mɔditi] това́р, предме́т потребле́ния.

common ['kɔmən] **1.** □ о́бщий; просто́й; гру́бый; обыкнове́нный; зауря́дный; ℞ Council муниципа́льный сове́т; ~ law обы́чное пра́во; ~ sense здра́вый смысл; in ~ совме́стно, сообща́; **2.** общи́нная земля́; вы́гон; **~place** **1.** бана́льность *f*; **2.** бана́льный, F изби́тый; **~s** [-z] *pl.* о́бщий стол; (*mst* House of) ℞ пала́та о́бщин; **~wealth** [-welθ] содру́жество; федера́ция; the British ℞ of Nations Брита́нское Содру́жество На́ций.

commotion [kə'mouʃən] волне́ние; смяте́ние.

communal ['kɔmjunl] □ коммуна́льный; общи́нный; коллекти́вный.

communicat|e [kə'mju:nikeit] *v/t.* сообща́ть [-щи́ть]; перед(ав)а́ть; *v/i.* сообща́ться; **~ion** [kəmju:ni'keiʃən] сообще́ние; коммуника́ция; связь *f*; **~ive** [kə'mju:nikeitiv] □ общи́тельный, разгово́рчивый.

communion [kə'mju:njən] обще́ние; *eccl.* прича́стие.

communis|m ['kɔmjunizm] коммуни́зм; **~t** **1.** коммуни́ст(ка); **2.** коммунисти́ческий.

community [kə'mju:niti] общи́на; о́бщество.

commutation [kɔmju'teiʃən] заме́на; ⚖ смягче́ние наказа́ния; ⚡ коммута́ция; переключе́ние.

compact **1.** ['kɔmpækt] догово́р; **2.**

[kəm'pækt] *adj.* компа́ктный; пло́тный; сжа́тый (о сти́ле); **3.** *v/t.* сж(им)а́ть; уплотня́ть [-ни́ть].
companion [kəm'pænjən] това́рищ; спу́тник; собесе́дник; **~ship** [-ʃip] компа́ния; това́рищеские отноше́ния *n/pl.*
company ['kʌmpəni] о́бщество; компа́ния, това́рищество; го́сти *pl.*; ⚓ экипа́ж (су́дна); *thea.* тру́ппа; have ~ име́ть госте́й; keep ~ with подде́рживать знако́мство с (Т).
compar|able ['kɔmpərəbl] □ сравни́мый; **~ative** [kəm'pærətiv] □ сравни́тельный; **~e** [kəm'pɛə] **1.** beyond ~, without ~, past ~ вне вся́кого сравне́ния; **2.** *v/t.* сра́внивать [-ни́ть], сличáть [-чи́ть], (to с Т); уподобля́ть [-до́бить] (В/Д); *v/i.* сра́вниваться [-ни́ться]; **~ison** [kəm'pærisn] сравне́ние.
compartment [kəm'pɑ:tmənt] отделе́ние; перегоро́дка; 🚂 купе́ *n indecl.*
compass ['kʌmpəs] **1.** ко́мпас; объём; окру́жность *f*; ♪ диапазо́н; (a pair of) ~es *pl.* ци́ркуль *m*; **2.** достига́ть [дости́гнуть] (Р); замышля́ть [-ы́слить] (дурно́е).
compassion [kəm'pæʃən] сострада́ние, жа́лость *f*; **~ate** [-it] □ сострада́тельный, жа́лостливый.
compatible [kəm'pætəbl] □ совмести́мый.
compatriot [-triət] сооте́чественник (-ица).
compel [kəm'pel] заставля́ть [-а́вить]; принужда́ть [-ну́дить].
compensat|e ['kɔmpenseit] *v/t.* вознагражда́ть [-ади́ть]; возмеща́ть [-ести́ть] (убытки); **~ion** [kɔmpen'seiʃən] вознагражде́ние; компенса́ция.
compete [kəm'pi:t] состяза́ться; конкури́ровать (with с Т, for ра́ди Р).
competen|ce, ~cy ['kɔmpitəns, -i] спосо́бность *f*; компете́нтность *f*; **~t** [-tənt] □ компете́нтный.
competit|ion [kɔmpi'tiʃən] состяза́ние; соревнова́ние; ✝ конкуре́нция; **~or** [kəm'petitə] конкуре́нт(ка); сопе́рник (-ица).
compile [kəm'pail] [с]компили́ровать; составля́ть [-а́вить] (from из Р).
complacen|ce, ~cy [kəm'pleisns, -snsi] самодово́льство.
complain [kəm'plein] [по]жа́ловаться (of на В); подава́ть жа́лобу; **~t** жа́лоба; ⚕ боле́знь *f*; **~ant** [-ənt] исте́ц.
complement ['kɔmplimənt] **1.** дополне́ние; компле́кт; **2.** дополня́ть [допо́лнить]; [у]комплектова́ть.
complet|e [kəm'pli:t] **1.** □ по́лный; зако́нченный; **2.** зака́нчивать [зако́нчить]; дополня́ть [-о́лнить]; **~ion** [-ʃən] оконча́ние.
complex ['kɔmpleks] **1.** □ сло́жный; ко́мплексный, составно́й; *fig.* сло́жный, запу́танный; **2.** ко́мплекс; **~ion** [kəm'plekʃən] цвет лица́; **~ity** [-siti] сло́жность *f*.
compliance [kəm'plaiəns] согла́сие; in ~ with в соотве́тствии с (Т).
complicate ['kɔmplikeit] усложня́ть(ся) [-ни́ть(ся)].
compliment 1. ['kɔmplimənt] комплиме́нт; приве́т; **2.** [-'ment] *v/t.* говори́ть комплиме́нты (Д); поздравля́ть [-а́вить] (on с Т).
comply [kəm'plai] соглаша́ться [-ласи́ться] (with с Т); подчиня́ться [-ни́ться] (with Д).
component [kəm'pounənt] **1.** компоне́нт; составна́я часть *f*; **2.** составно́й.
compos|e [kəm'pouz] составля́ть [-а́вить]; сочиня́ть [-ни́ть]; писа́ть му́зыку; успока́иваться [-ко́иться]; *typ.* наб(и)ра́ть; **~ed** [-d] □ споко́йный, сде́ржанный; **~er** [-ə] компози́тор; **~ition** [kɔmpə'ziʃən] компози́ция; соста́в; сочине́ние; ✝ полюбо́вная сде́лка; **~ure** [kəm'pouʒə] самооблада́ние.
compound 1. ['kɔmpaund] соста́в, соедине́ние; **2.** составно́й; сло́жный; ~ interest сло́жные проце́нты *m/pl.*; **3.** [kəm'paund] *v/t.* сме́шивать [-ша́ть]; соединя́ть [-ни́ть]; ула́живать [ула́дить]; *v/i.* приходи́ть к компроми́ссу.
comprehend [kɔmpri'hend] постига́ть [пости́гнуть]; охва́тывать [охвати́ть].
comprehen|sible [kɔmpri'hensəbl] □ поня́тный, постижи́мый; **~sion** [-ʃən] понима́ние; поня́тливость *f*; **~sive** [-siv] □ объе́млющий; исче́рпывающий.
compress [kəm'pres] сж(им)а́ть; сда́вливать [сдави́ть]; ~ed air сжа́тый во́здух; **~ion** [kəm'preʃən] *phys.* сжа́тие; ⊕ компре́ссия; наби́вка; прокла́дка.
comprise [kəm'praiz] содержа́ть; заключа́ть в себе́.
compromise ['kɔmprəmaiz] **1.** компроми́сс; **2.** *v/t.* [с]компромети́ровать; подверга́ть ри́ску; *v/i.* пойти́ на компроми́сс.
compuls|ion [kəm'pʌlʃən] принужде́ние; **~ory** [-səri] принуди́тельный; обяза́тельный.
comput|ation [kɔmpju'teiʃən] вычисле́ние; вы́кладка; расчёт; **~e** [kəm'pju:t] вычисля́ть [вы́числить]; де́лать вы́кладки.
comrade ['kɔmrid] това́рищ.
con [kɔn] = contra про́тив.
conceal [kən'si:l] скры(ва́)ть; утáивать [-и́ть], ума́лчивать [умолча́ть].
concede [kən'si:d] уступа́ть [-пи́ть]; допуска́ть [-сти́ть].
conceit [kən'si:t] самомне́ние; тще-

сла́вие; **~ed** [-id] □ самодово́льный; тщесла́вный.
conceiv|able [kən'si:vəbl] мы́слимый; постижи́мый; **~e** [kən'si:v] *v/i.* представля́ть себе́; *v/t.* постига́ть [пости́гнуть]; понима́ть [-ня́ть]; заду́м(ыв)ать.
concentrate ['kɔnsentreit] сосредото́чи(ва)ть(ся).
conception [kən'sepʃən] поня́тие; конце́пция; за́мысел; *biol.* зача́тие; оплодотворе́ние.
concern [kən'sə:n] **1.** де́ло; уча́стие; интере́с; забо́та; ✝ предприя́тие; **2.** каса́ться [косну́ться] (Р); име́ть отноше́ние к (Д); ~ o. s. about, for [за]интересова́ться, занима́ться [заня́ться] (Т); **~ed** [-d] □ заинтересо́ванный; име́ющий отноше́ние; озабо́ченный; **~ing** [-iŋ] *prp.* относи́тельно (Р), каса́тельно (Р).
concert 1. ['kɔnsət] конце́рт; согла́сие, соглаше́ние; **2.** [kən'sə:t] сгова́риваться [сговори́ться]; **~ed** согласо́ванный.
concession [kən'seʃən] усту́пка; конце́ссия.
conciliat|e [kən'silieit] примиря́ть [-ри́ть]; **~or** [-ə] посре́дник.
concise [kən'sais] □ сжа́тый, кра́ткий; **~ness** [-nis] сжа́тость *f*, кра́ткость *f*.
conclude [kən'klu:d] заключа́ть [-чи́ть]; зака́нчивать [зако́нчить]; to be ~d оконча́ние сле́дует.
conclusi|on [kən'klu:ʒən] оконча́ние; заключе́ние; вы́вод; **~ve** [-siv] □ заключи́тельный; реша́ющий; убеди́тельный.
concoct [kən'kɔkt] [со]стря́пать (*a. fig.*); *fig.* приду́м(ыв)ать; **~ion** [kən'kɔkʃən] стряпня́; *fig.* небыли́ца.
concord ['kɔŋkɔ:d] согла́сие; соглаше́ние; догово́р, конве́нция; ♪ гармо́ния; **~ant** [kən'kɔ:dənt] □ согла́сный; согласу́ющийся; ♪ гармони́чный.
concrete ['kɔnkri:t] **1.** □ конкре́тный; **2.** бето́н; **3.** [за]бетони́ровать; [kən'kri:t] сгуща́ть(ся) [сгусти́ть(ся)]; [за]тверде́ть.
concur [kən'kə:] соглаша́ться [-ласи́ться]; совпада́ть [-па́сть]; [по]соде́йствовать; **~rence** [kən'kʌrəns] совпаде́ние; согла́сие.
condemn [kən'dem] осужда́ть [осуди́ть]; пригова́ривать [-вори́ть] (к Д); [за]бракова́ть; **~ation** ['kɔndem'neiʃən] осужде́ние.
condens|ation ['kɔnden''seiʃən] конденса́ция, уплотне́ние, сгуще́ние; **~e** [kən'dens] сгуща́ть(ся); ⊕ конденси́ровать *(im)pf.*; *fig.* сокраща́ть [-рати́ть].
condescen|d [kɔndi'send] снисходи́ть [снизойти́]; удоста́ивать [-сто́ить]; **~sion** [-'senʃən] снисхожде́ние; снисходи́тельность *f*.
condiment ['kɔndimənt] припра́ва.
condition [kən'diʃən] **1.** усло́вие; состоя́ние; ~s *pl.* обстоя́тельства *n/pl.*; усло́вия *n/pl.*; **2.** ста́вить усло́вия; обусло́вливать [-о́вить]; **~al** [-l] □ усло́вный.
condol|e [kən'doul] соболе́зновать (with Д); **~ence** [-əns] соболе́знование.
conduc|e [kən'dju:s] спосо́бствовать (to Д); **~ive** [-iv] спосо́бствующий.
conduct 1. ['kɔndəkt] поведе́ние; **2.** [kən'dʌkt] вести́ себя́; руководи́ть (де́лом); ♪ дирижи́ровать; **~ion** [-kʃən] ⊕ проводи́мость *f*; **~or** [kəndʌktə] конду́ктор (трамва́я и т. п.); *Am.* 🚃 вагонovoжа́тый; ♪ дирижёр.
conduit ['kɔndjuit, 'kɔndit] трубопрово́д.
cone [koun] ко́нус; ⚘ ши́шка.
confabulation [kənfæbju'leiʃən] болтовня́.
confection [kən'fekʃən] сла́сти *f/pl.*; **~er** [-ə] конди́тер; **~ery** [-əri] конди́терская; конди́терские изде́лия *n/pl.*
confedera|cy [kən'fedərəsi] конфедера́ция; сою́з; **~te 1.** [-rit] федерати́вный, сою́зный; **2.** [-rit] член конфедера́ции, сою́зник; **3.** [-reit] объединя́ться в сою́з; **~tion** [kənfedə'reiʃən] конфедера́ция; сою́з.
confer [kənfə:] *v/t.* дарова́ть; присужда́ть [-уди́ть]; *v/i.* совеща́ться; **~ence** ['kɔnfərəns] конфере́нция; съезд; совеща́ние.
confess [kən'fes] призн(ав)а́ться, созн(ав)а́ться в (П); испове́д(ов)ать(ся); **~ion** [-ʃən] призна́ние; и́споведь *f*; вероиспове́дание; **~ional** [-ʃənl] исповеда́льня *f*; **~or** [-sə] испове́дник.
confide [kən'faid] доверя́ть (in Д); вверя́ть [вве́рить]; полага́ться [положи́ться] (in на В); **~nce** ['kɔnfidəns] дове́рие; уве́ренность *f*; **~nt** ['kɔnfidənt] □ уве́ренный; **~ntial** [kɔnfi'denʃəl] □ конфиденциа́льный; секре́тный.
confine [kən'fain] ограни́чи(ва)ть; заключа́ть [-чи́ть] (в тюрьму́); be ~d рожа́ть [роди́ть] (of В); **~ment** [-mənt] ограниче́ние; заключе́ние; ро́ды *m/pl.*
confirm [kən'fə:m] подтвержда́ть [-рди́ть]; подде́рживать [-жа́ть]; **~ation** [kɔnfə'meiʃən] подтвержде́ние; *eccl.* конфирма́ция.
confiscat|e ['kɔnfiskeit] конфискова́ть *(im)pf.*; **~ion** [kɔnfis'keiʃən] конфиска́ция.
conflagration [kɔnflə'greiʃən] сожже́ние; бушу́ющий пожа́р.
conflict 1. ['kɔnflikt] конфли́кт; столкнове́ние; **2.** [kən'flikt] быть в конфли́кте.

conflu|ence ['kɔnfluəns] слия́ние (рек); стече́ние наро́да; **~ent** [-fluənt] 1. слива́ющийся; 2. прито́к (реки́).
conform [kən'fɔ:m] согласо́вываться [-сова́ться] (to с T); подчиня́ться [-ни́ться] (to Д); **~able** [-əbl] □ (to) соотве́тствующий (Д); подчиня́ющийся (Д); **~ity** [-iti] соотве́тствие; подчине́ние.
confound [kən'faund] [с]пута́ть; поража́ть [порази́ть], приводи́ть в смуще́ние.
confront [kən'frʌnt] стоя́ть лицо́м к лицу́ с (T); слича́ть [-чи́ть] (with с T).
confus|e [kən'fju:z] сме́шивать [-ша́ть]; смуща́ть [-ути́ть]; **~ion** [kən'fju:ʒən] смуще́ние; беспоря́док.
confut|ation [kɔnfju:teiʃən] опроверже́ние; **~e** [kən'fju:t] опроверга́ть [-ве́ргнуть].
congeal [kən'dʒi:l] засты́(ва́)ть.
congenial [kən'dʒi:niəl] □ бли́зкий по ду́ху; благоприя́тный.
congestion [kən'dʒestʃən] перегру́женность *f*; перенаселённость *f*.
conglomeration [kɔn'glɔmə''reiʃən]накопле́ние, скопле́ние.
congratulat|e [kən'grætjuleit] поздравля́ть [-а́вить] (on с T); **~ion** [kəngrætju'leiʃən] поздравле́ние.
congregat|e ['kɔŋgrigeit] соб(и)ра́ть(ся); **~ion** [kɔŋgri'geiʃən] собра́ние; *eccl.* прихожа́не *m/pl.*.
congress ['kɔŋgres] конгре́сс; съезд.
congruous ['kɔŋgruəs] □ соотве́тствующий; гармони́рующий (to с T).
conifer ['kounifə] хво́йное де́рево.
conjecture [kən'dʒektʃə] 1. дога́дка, предположе́ние; 2. предполага́ть [-ложи́ть].
conjoin [kən'dʒɔin] соединя́ть(ся) [-ни́ть(ся)]; сочета́ть(ся) *(im)pf.*; **~t** [-t] о́бщий; объединённый.
conjugal ['kɔndʒugəl] □ супру́жеский, бра́чный.
conjunction [kən'dʒʌŋkʃən] соедине́ние, связь *f*.
conjur|e 1. ['kʌndʒə] *v/t.* вызыва́ть [вы́звать], заклина́ть [-ля́сть] (ду́хов); изгоня́ть ду́хов; ~ **up** *fig.* вызыва́ть в воображе́нии; *v/i.* занима́ться ма́гией; пока́зывать фо́кусы; 2. [kən'dʒuə] умоля́ть [-ли́ть], заклина́ть; **~er, ~or** [-rə] волше́бник; фо́кусник.
connect [kə'nekt] соединя́ть(ся) [-ни́ть(ся)]; свя́зывать(ся) [-за́ть (-ся)]; ⚡ соединя́ть [-ни́ть]; **~ed** [-id] □ свя́занный; свя́зный (о ре́чи); **be ~ with** име́ть свя́зи (с T); **~ion** *s.* connexion.
connexion [kə'nekʃən] связь *f*; соедине́ние; родство́.
connive [kə'naiv]: ~ **at** потво́рствовать (Д), смотре́ть сквозь па́льцы на (B).
connoisseur [kɔni'sə:] знато́к.
connubial [kə'nju:biəl] □ бра́чный.
conquer ['kɔŋkə] завоёвывать [-оева́ть]; побежда́ть [победи́ть]; **~able** [-rəbl] победи́мый; **~or** [-rə] победи́тель(ница *f*) *m*; завоева́тель(ница *f*) *m*.
conquest ['kɔŋkwest] завоева́ние; побе́да.
conscience ['kɔnʃəns] со́весть *f*.
conscientious [kɔnʃi'enʃəs] □ добросо́вестный; **~ness** [-nis] добросо́вестность *f*.
conscious ['kɔnʃəs] □ созна́тельный; сознаю́щий; **~ness** [-nis] созна́ние; созна́тельность *f*.
conscript ['kɔnskript] ⚔ призывни́к; **~ion** [kən'skripʃən] ⚔ во́инская пови́нность *f*.
consecrat|e ['kɔnsikreit] освяща́ть [-яти́ть]; посвящать [-яти́ть]; **~ion** [kɔnsi'kreiʃən] освяще́ние; посвяще́ние.
consecutive [kən'sekjutiv] □ после́довательный.
consent [kən'sent] 1. согла́сие; 2. соглаша́ться [-ласи́ться].
consequen|ce ['kɔnsikwəns] (по-) сле́дствие; вы́вод, заключе́ние; **~t** [-kwənt] 1. после́довательный; 2. (по)сле́дствие; **~tial** [kɔnsi'kwenʃəl] □ логи́чески вытека́ющий; ва́жный; **~tly** ['kɔnsikwəntli] сле́довательно; поэ́тому.
conserv|ation [kɔnsə'veiʃən] сохране́ние; **~ative** [kən'sə:vətiv] 1. □ консервати́вный; охрани́тельный; 2. *pol.* консерва́тор; **~atory** [-tri] оранжере́я; ♪ консервато́рия; **~e** [kən'sə:v] сохраня́ть [-ни́ть].
consider [kən'sidə] *v/t.* обсужда́ть [-уди́ть]; обду́м(ыв)ать; полага́ть, счита́ть; счита́ться с (T); *v/i.* сообража́ть [-рази́ть]; **~able** [-rəbl] □ значи́тельный; ва́жный; большо́й; **~ate** [-rit] □ внима́тельный (к Д); **~ation** [kənsidə'reiʃən] обсужде́ние; соображе́ние; внима́ние; **on no ~** ни под каки́м ви́дом; **~ing** [kən'sidəriŋ] *prp.* учи́тывая (B), принима́я во внима́ние (B).
consign [kən'sain] перед(ав)а́ть; поруча́ть [-чи́ть]; ✝ посыла́ть (груз) на консигна́цию; **~ment** [-ment] па́ртия това́ров; коносаме́нт.
consist [kən'sist] состоя́ть (of из P); заключа́ться (in в П); **~ence, ~ency** [-əns, -ənsi] логи́чность *f*; пло́тность *f*; **~ent** [-ənt] □ пло́тный; после́довательный; согласу́ющийся (with с T).
consol|ation [kɔnsə'leiʃən] утеше́ние; **~e** [kən'soul] утеша́ть [уте́шить].
consolidate [kən'sɔlideit] под-

тверждать [-рдить]; объединять (-ся) [-нить(ся)]; консолидировать (займы) (*im*)*pf*.
consonan|ce ['kɔnsənəns] созвучие; согласие; **~t** [-nənt] □ согласный (*a.* noun); совместимый.
consort ['kɔnsɔ:t] супруг(а).
conspicuous [kən'spikjuəs] □ заметный, бросающийся в глаза.
conspir|acy [kən'spirəsi] заговор; **~ator** [-tə] заговорщик (-ица); **~e** [kən'spaiə] устраивать заговор; сговариваться [-вориться].
constab|le ['kʌnstəbl] констебль *m*, полицейский; **~ulary** [kən'stæbjuləri] полиция.
constan|cy ['kɔnstənsi] постоянство; верность *f*; **~t** ['kɔnstənt] □ постоянный; верный.
consternation [kɔnstə'neiʃən] оцепенение (от страха).
constipation [kɔnsti'peiʃən] ⚕ запор.
constituen|cy [kən'stitjuənsi] избирательный округ; избиратели *m*/*pl*.; **~t** [-ənt] существенный; учредительный; 2. избиратель *m*; составная часть *f*.
constitut|e ['kɔnstitju:t] составлять [-авить]; основывать [-новать]; **~ion** [kɔnsti'tju:ʃn] конституция; учреждение; телосложение; состав; **~ional** [-l] □ конституционный; органический.
constrain [kən'strein] принуждать [-нудить]; сдерживать [-жать]; **~t** [-t] принуждение; принуждённость *f*.
constrict [kən'strikt] стягивать [стянуть]; сж(им)ать; **~ion** [kən'strikʃən] сжатие; стягивание.
construct [kən'strʌkt] [по]строить; сооружать [-удить]; *fig.* созд(ав)ать; **~ion** [-kʃən] строительство, стройка; строение; **~ive** [-tiv] конструктивный; строительный; творческий; **~or** [-tə] строитель *m*.
construe [kən'stru:] истолковывать [-ковать]; *gr.* делать синтаксический разбор.
consul ['kɔnsəl] консул; **~ general** генеральный консул; **~ate** ['kɔnsjulit] консульство.
consult [kən'sʌlt] *v*/*t*. спрашивать совета у (Р); *v*/*i*. [по]советоваться, совещаться; **~ation** [kɔnsəl'teiʃən] консультация; консилиум (врачей); **~ative** [kən'sʌltətiv] совещательный.
consum|e [kən'sju:m] *v*/*t*. потреблять [-бить]; [из]расходовать; **~er** [-ə] потребитель *m*.
consummate 1. [kən'sʌmit] □ совершенный, законченный; 2. ['kɔnsʌmeit] доводить до конца; завершать [-шить].
consumpti|on [kən'sʌmpʃən] потребление, расход; ⚕ туберкулёз лёгких; **~ve** [-tiv] □ туберкулёзный, чахоточный.
contact ['kɔntækt] контакт; соприкосновение.
contagi|on [kən'teidʒən] ⚕ зараза, инфекция; **~ous** [-dʒəs] □ заразительный, инфекционный.
contain [kən'tein] содержать (в себе), вмещать [-естить]; **~ o. s.** сдерживаться [-жаться]; **~er** [-ə] вместилище; контейнер.
contaminate [kən'tæmineit] загрязнять [-нить]; *fig.* заражать [заразить]; осквернять [-нить].
contemplat|e ['kɔntempleit] созерцать; обдум(ыв)ать; **~ion** [kɔntem'pleiʃən] созерцание; размышление; **~ive** [kən'templətiv] □ созерцательный.
contempora|neous [kəntempə'reinjəs] □ современный; одновременный; **~ry** [kən'tempərəri] 1. современный; одновременный; 2. современник (-ица).
contempt [kən'tempt] презрение (for к Д); **~ible** [-əbl] □ презренный; **~uous** [-juəs] □ презрительный.
contend [kən'tend] *v*/*i*. бороться; соперничать; *v*/*t*. утверждать.
content [kən'tent] 1. довольный; 2. удовлетворять [-рить]; 3. довольство; 4. ['kɔntent] содержание; объём; **~ed** [kən'tentid] □ довольный, удовлетворённый.
contention [kən'tenʃən] спор, ссора.
contentment [kən'tentmənt] довольство.
contest 1. ['kɔntest] соревнование; 2. [kən'test] оспаривать [оспорить]; доби(ва)ться (места); отстаивать [отстоять] (территорию).
context ['kɔntekst] контекст.
contiguous [kən'tiguəs] □ смежный, соприкасающийся (to с Т).
continent ['kɔntinənt] 1. □ сдержанный; целомудренный; 2. материк, континент.
contingen|cy [kən'tindʒənsi] случайность *f*; непредвиденное обстоятельство; **~t** [-dʒənt] 1. □ случайный, непредвиденный; 2. ⚔, † контингент.
continu|al [kən'tinjuəl] □ беспрерывный, беспрестанный; **~ance** [-juəns] продолжительность *f*; **~ation** [kəntinju'eiʃən] продолжение; **~e** [kən'tinju:] *v*/*t*. продолжать [-должить]; to be **~d** продолжение следует; *v*/*i*. продолжаться [-должиться]; простираться; **~ity** [kɔntin'juiti] непрерывность *f*; **~ous** [kən'tinjuəs] □ непрерывный; сплошной.
contort [kən'tɔ:t] искажать [исказить] **~ion** [kən'tɔ:ʃən] искажение; искривление.
contour ['kɔntuə] контур, очертание.

contraband ['kɔntrəbænd] контрабáнда.

contract 1. [kən'trækt] *v/t.* сокращáть [-ратить]; сж(им)áть; заключáть [-чить] (сдéлку, дрýжбу); заводить [-вести](знакомство); вступáть [-пить] в (брак); *v/i.* сокращáться [-ратиться]; сж(им)áть (-ся); **2.** ['kɔntrækt] контрáкт, договóр; **~ion** [kən'trækʃən] сжáтие; сокращéние; **~or** [-tə] подрядчик.

contradict [kɔntrə'dikt] противорéчить (Д); **~ion** [kɔntrə'dikʃən] противорéчие; **~ory** [-təri] □ противоречивый.

contrar|iety [kɔntrə'raiəti] разноглáсие, противорéчие; **~y** ['kɔntrəri] **1.** противоположный; ~ to *prp.* вопреки (Д), прóтив (Р); **2.** обрáтное; on the ~ наоборóт.

contrast 1. ['kɔntræst] противоположность *f*, контрáст; **2.** [kən'træst] сопоставлять [-áвить], противополагáть [-ложить]; составлять контрáст.

contribut|e [kən'tribju:t] содéйствовать, способствовать; [по]жéртвовать; сотрýдничать (to в П); **~ion** [kɔntri'bju:ʃən] вклад; взнос; статья; сотрýдничество; **~or** [kən'tribjutə] сотрýдник (-ица); **~ory** [-təri] содéйствующий; сотрýдничающий.

contrit|e ['kɔntrait] □ сокрушáющийся, кáющийся; **~ion** [kən'triʃən] раскáяние.

contriv|ance [kən'traivəns] выдумка; изобретéние; **~e** [kən'traiv] *v/t.* придýм(ыв)ать; изобретáть [-ести]; затевáть [-éять]; *v/i.* ухитряться [-риться]; умудряться [-риться]; **~er** [-ə] изобретáтель (ница *f*) *m*.

control [kən'troul] **1.** руковóдство; надзóр; контрóль *m*; **2.** управлять (Т); [про]контролировать, регулировать (*im*)*pf*.; сдéрживать [-жáть] (чýвства, слёзы); **~ler** [-ə] контролёр, инспéктор.

controver|sial [kɔntrə'və:ʃəl] □ спóрный; **~sy** ['kɔntrəvə:si] спор, дискýссия, полéмика; **~t** ['kɔntrəvə:t] оспáривать [оспóрить].

contumacious [kɔntju'meiʃes] □ упóрный; непокóрный; ⚖ неподчиняющийся распоряжéнию судá.

contumely ['kɔntjum(i)li] оскорблéние; дéрзость *f*; бесчéстье.

convalesce [kɔnvə'les] выздорáвливать [выздороветь]; **~nce** [-ns] выздоровлéние; **~nt** [-nt] □ выздорáвливающий.

convene [kən'vi:n] соз(ы)вáть; соб(и)рáть(ся); ⚖ вызывáть [вызвать] (в суд).

convenien|ce [kən'vi:njəns] удóбство; at your earliest как мóжно скорée; **~t** [-jənt] □ удóбный.

convent ['kɔnvənt] монастырь *m*; **~ion** [kən'venʃən] собрáние; съезд; соглашéние; обычай.

converge [kən'və:dʒ] сходиться [сойтись]; сводить в однý тóчку.

convers|ant ['kɔnvəsnt] свéдущий; **~ation** [kɔnvə'seiʃn] разговóр, бесéда; **~ational** [-l] разговóрный; **~e** [kən'və:s] разговáривать, бесéдовать; **~ion** [kən'və:ʃən] превращéние; изменéние; ⊕ перерабóтка, превращéние; ⚡ трансформирование; *eccl.* обращéние в другýю вéру; ✝ конвéрсия.

convert 1. ['kɔnvə:t] новообращённый; **2.** [kən'və:t] превращáть [-атить]; ⊕ перерабáтывать [-бóтать]; ⚡ трансформировать (*im*)*pf*.; *eccl.* обращáть [-ратить] (в другýю вéру); ✝ конвертировать (*im*)*pf*.; **~er** [-ə] ⚡ конвéртер; **~ible** [-əbl] □ изменяемый; обратимый; ✝ подлежáщий конвéрсии.

convey [kən'vei] перевозить [-везти], переправлять [-прáвить]; перед(ав)áть; **~ance** [-əns] перевóзка; достáвка; **~or** [-ə] ⊕ (или ~ belt) конвéйер; транспортёр.

convict 1. ['kɔnvikt] осуждённый; кáторжник; **2.** [kən'vikt] признавáть винóвным; изобличáть [-чить]; **~ion** [kən'vikʃən] ⚖ осуждéние; убеждéние.

convince [kən'vins] убеждáть [убедить] (of в П).

convocation [kɔnvo'keiʃən] созыв; собрáние.

convoke [kən'vouk] соз(ы)вáть.

convoy 1. ['kɔnvɔi] конвóй; сопровождéние; **2.** [kən'vɔi] сопровождáть; конвоировать.

convuls|ion [kən'vʌlʃən] колебáние (пóчвы); сýдорога; **~ive** [-siv] □ сýдорожный.

coo [ku:] ворковáть.

cook [kuk] **1.** кухáрка, пóвар; **2.** [со]стряпать, [при]готóвить; **~ery** ['kukəri] кулинáрия; стряпня; **~ie**, **~y** ['kuki] *Am.* печéнье.

cool [ku:l] **1.** прохлáдный; *fig.* хладнокрóвный; невозмутимый; *b. s.* дéрзкий, нахáльный; **2.** прохлáда; хладнокрóвие; **3.** охлаждáть(ся) [охладить(ся)]; осты(вá)ть.

coolness ['ku:lnis] холодóк; прохлáда; хладнокрóвие.

coop [ku:p] **1.** курятник; **2.** ~ up или in держáть взаперти.

cooper ['ku:pə] бóндáрь *m*.

co-operat|e [kou'ɔpəreit] сотрýдничать; **~ion** [kouɔpə'reiʃən] кооперáция; сотрýдничество; **~ive** [kou'ɔpərətiv] совмéстный, объединённый; ~ society кооперативное óбщество; **~or** [-eitə] сотрýдник; кооперáтор.

co-ordinat|e 1. [kou'ɔ:dnit] □ неподчинённый; рáвный; **2.** [-neit]

координи́ровать (*im*)*pf.*; согласо́вывать [-ова́ть]; **~ion** [kou'ɔːdi''neiʃən] координа́ция.
cope [koup]: ~ with справля́ться [-а́виться] с (Т).
copious ['koupjəs] □ оби́льный; **~ness** [-nis] оби́лие.
copper ['kɔpə] **1.** медь *f*; ме́дная моне́та; **2.** ме́дный; **~y** [-ri] цве́та ме́ди.
coppice, copse ['kɔpis, kɔps] ро́ща.
copy ['kɔpi] **1.** ко́пия; ру́копись *f*; экземпля́р; **2.** переписывать [-са́ть]; снима́ть ко́пию с (Р); **~-book** тетра́дь *f*; **~ing** ['kɔpiiŋ] перепи́сывание; **~ist** ['kɔpiist] перепи́счик; подража́тель *m*; **~right** [-rait] а́вторское пра́во.
coral ['kɔrəl] кора́лл.
cord [kɔːd] **1.** верёвка, шнуро́к; *anat.* свя́зка; **2.** свя́зывать [-за́ть]; **~ed** ['kɔːdid] ру́бчатый (о мате́рии).
cordial ['kɔːdiəl] **1.** □ серде́чный, и́скренний; **2.** стимули́рующее (серде́чное) сре́дство; **~ity** [kɔːdi'æliti] серде́чность *f*, раду́шие.
cordon ['kɔːdən] **1.** кордо́н; **2.** ~ off отгора́живать [-роди́ть].
corduroy ['kɔːdərɔi, -dju] ру́бчатый плис, вельве́т; **~s** *pl.* плисо́вые (*or* вельве́товые) штаны́ *m/pl.*
core [kɔː] **1.** сердцеви́на; вну́тренность *f*; ядро́; *fig.* суть *f*; **2.** выре́зывать сердцеви́ну из (Р).
cork [kɔːk] **1.** про́бка; **2.** затыка́ть про́бкой; **~-jacket** спаса́тельный жиле́т; **~-screw** што́пор.
corn [kɔːn] зерно́; хлеба́ *m/pl.*; *Am.* кукуру́за, маи́с; ⚕ мозо́ль *f*.
corner ['kɔːnə] **1.** у́гол; **2.** ✝ ску́пка това́ра; **3.** *fig.* загна́ть в тупи́к; припере́ть к стене́; ✝ скупа́ть това́р.
cornet ['kɔːnit] ♪ корне́т, корне́т-а-писто́н.
cornice ['kɔːnis] △ карни́з.
coron|ation [kɔrə'neiʃən] корона́ция; **~et** ['kɔrənit] коро́на, диаде́ма.
corpor|al ['kɔːpərəl] **1.** □ теле́сный; **2.** ⚔ капра́л; **~ation** [kɔːpə'reiʃən] корпора́ция; муниципалите́т; *Am.* акционе́рное о́бщество.
corpse [kɔːps] труп.
corpulen|ce, ~cy ['kɔːpjuləns] доро́дность *f*, ту́чность *f*; **~t** [-lənt] доро́дный, ту́чный.
corral *Am.* [kɔ'rɑːl] **1.** заго́н (для скота́); **2.** загоня́ть [загна́ть].
correct [kə'rekt] **1.** □ пра́вильный, ве́рный, то́чный; **2.** *v/t.* исправля́ть [-а́вить], [про]корректи́ровать; **~ion** [kə'rekʃən] исправле́ние, попра́вка; house of ~ исправи́тельный дом.
correlate ['kɔrileit] устана́вливать соотноше́ние.
correspond [kɔris'pɔnd] соотве́тствовать (with, to Д); согласо́вываться [-сова́ться] (с Т); перепи́сываться (с Т); **~ence** [-əns] соотве́тствие, соотноше́ние; перепи́ска; **~ent** [-ənt] **1.** □ соотве́тствующий; **2.** корреспонде́нт(ка).
corridor ['kɔridɔː] коридо́р; ~ train по́езд, состоя́щий из ваго́нов, соединённых та́мбурами.
corroborate [kə'rɔbəreit] подде́рживать [-жа́ть]; подтвержда́ть [-рди́ть].
corro|de [kə'roud] разъеда́ть [-е́сть]; [за]ржаве́ть; **~sion** [kə'rouʒən] корро́зия; ржа́вчина; окисле́ние; **~sive** [-siv] **1.** □ е́дкий; **2.** е́дкое вещество́.
corrugate ['kɔrugeit] смо́рщи(ва)ть(ся); ⊕ де́лать рифлёным, волни́стым; **~d** iron рифлёное желе́зо.
corrupt [kə'rʌpt] **1.** □ испо́рченный; искажённый; развращённый; **2.** *v/t.* искажа́ть [-зи́ть]; развраща́ть [-рати́ть]; подкупа́ть [-пи́ть]; *v/i.* [ис]по́ртиться; искажа́ться [-зи́ться]; **~ible** [kə'rʌptəbl] □ подкупно́й; **~ion** [-ʃən] по́рча; искаже́ние; прода́жность *f*.
corsage [kɔː'sɑːʒ] корса́ж.
corset ['kɔːsit] корсе́т.
co-signatory ['kou'signətəri] **1.** лицо́, подписа́вшее соглаше́ние совме́стно с други́ми; **2.** подпи́сывающий соглаше́ние совме́стно с други́ми.
cosmetic [kɔz'metik] **1.** космети́ческий; **2.** косме́тика.
cosmopolit|an [kɔzmo'pɔlitən] космополити́ческий; **~e** [kɔz'mɔpəlait] **1.** космополи́т(ка); **2.** космополити́ческий.
cost [kɔst] **1.** цена́, сто́имость *f*; first или prime ~ фабри́чная себесто́имость *f*; **2.** [*irr.*] сто́ить.
costl|iness ['kɔstlinis] дорогови́зна; **~y** [-li] дорого́й, це́нный.
costume ['kɔstjuːm] (национа́льный или маскара́дный) костю́м.
cosy ['kouzi] **1.** □ ую́тный; **2.** стёганный чехо́л (для ча́йника).
cot [kɔt] де́тская крова́ть *f*; ⚓ ко́йка.
cottage ['kɔtidʒ] котте́дж; изба́; *Am.* ле́тняя да́ча; ~ piano небольшо́е пиани́но *n indecl.*
cotton ['kɔtn] **1.** хло́пок; хлопча́тая бума́га; ✝ си́тец; ни́тка; **2.** хлопчатобума́жный; ~ wool ва́та; **3.** F сдружи́ться (to с Т) *pf.*
couch [kautʃ] **1.** куше́тка; ло́говище; **2.** *v/t.* излага́ть [изложи́ть]; [с]формули́ровать; *v/i.* лежа́ть, притаи́ться *pf.* (о звеpя́х).
cough [kɔːf, kɔf] **1.** ка́шель *m*; **2.** ка́шлять [кашляну́ть].
could [kud] *pt.* от can.

council ['kaunsl] совéт; **~(l)or** [-silə] член совéта; совéтник.
counsel ['kaunsəl] 1. обсуждéние, совещáние; ⚖ адвокáт; ~ for the prosecution обвини́тель *m*; 2. давáть совéт (Д); **~(l)or** [-ə] совéтник; *Am.* адвокáт.
count¹ [kaunt] 1. счёт, подсчёт; итóг; ⚖ статья́ в обвини́тельном áкте; 2. *v/t.* [со]считáть; подсчи́тывать [-итáть]; зачисля́ть [-и́слить]; *v/i.* считáться; имéть значéние.
count² [~] граф (не англи́йский).
countenance ['kauntinəns] 1. лицó; самообладáние; поддéржка; 2. поддéрживать [-жáть], поощря́ть [-ри́ть].
counter¹ ['kauntə] прилáвок; стóйка; таксóметр; счётчик; фи́шка.
counter² [~] 1. противополóжный (to Д); встрéчный; 2. *adv.* обрáтно; напрóтив; 3. [вос]проти́виться (Д); (в бóксе) наноси́ть встрéчный удáр.
counteract [kauntə'rækt] противодéйствовать (Д); нейтрализовáть (*im*)*pf*.
counterbalance 1. ['kauntəbæləns] противовéс; 2. [kauntə'bæləns] уравновéшивать [-вéсить]; служи́ть противовéсом (Д).
counter-espionage ['kauntər'espiə'nɑːʒ] контрразвéдка.
counterfeit ['kauntəfit] 1. поддéльный, подлóжный; 2. поддéлка; 3. поддéл(ыв)ать; обмáнывать [-нýть].
countermand 1. ['kauntə'mɑːnd] контрприкáз; 2. [kauntə'mɑːnd] отменя́ть [-ни́ть] (закáз, прикáз); отзывáть [отозвáть] (лицó, вóинскую часть).
counter-move ['kauntəmuːv] *fig.* отвéтная мéра.
counterpane [-pein] покрывáло; стёганое одея́ло.
counterpart [-pɑːt] кóпия; двойни́к; **~s** ли́ца и́ли вéщи, взаи́мно дополня́ющие друг дрýга.
counterpoise [-pɔiz] 1. противовéс; равновéсие; 2. держáть равновéсие; (*a. fig.*) уравновéшивать [-éсить].
countersign [-sain] 1. контрасси́гнóвка; ⚔ парóль *m*; 2. скрепля́ть [-пи́ть] (пóдписью).
countervail [-veil] противостоя́ть (Д); уравновéшивать [-éсить].
countess ['kauntis] графи́ня.
counting-house ['kauntiŋhaus] контóра.
countless ['kauntlis] бесчи́сленный, несчётный.
country ['kʌntri] 1. странá; мéстность *f*; дерéвня; 2. деревéнский; **~man** [-mən] крестья́нин; земля́к; **~side** [-'said] сéльская мéстность *f*; сёльское населéние.
county ['kaunti] грáфство; *Am.* óкруг.
coup [kuː] удáчный ход (удáр и т. п.).
couple [kʌpl] 1. пáра; свóра; 2. соединя́ть [-ни́ть]; ассоции́ровать (*im*)*pf*.; ⊕ сцепля́ть [-пи́ть]; **~r** [-ə] *radio* устрóйство связи.
coupling ['kʌpliŋ] совокуплéние; ⊕ мýфта; сцеплéние; *radio* связь *f*.
coupon ['kuːpɔn] купóн, талóн.
courage ['kʌridʒ] мýжество, смéлость *f*, хрáбрость *f*, отвáга; **~ous** [kə'reidʒəs] □ мýжественный, смéлый, хрáбрый.
courier ['kuriə] курьéр, нарóчный.
course ['kɔːs] 1. направлéние, курс; ход; течéние; блю́до (за обéдом); of ~ конéчно; 2. *v/t.* гнáться за (Т); охóтиться (с гóнчими) на (В) *or* за (Т); *v/i.* бéгать, [по]бежáть.
court [kɔːt] 1. двор (*a. fig.*); суд; pay (one's) ~ ухáживать (to за Т); 2. ухáживать за (Т); искáть расположéния (Р); **~eous** ['kəːtiəs] □ вéжливый, учти́вый; **~esy** ['kəːtisi] учти́вость *f*, вéжливость *f*; **~ier** ['kɔːtjə] придвóрный; **~ly** [-ly] вéжливый; **~-martial** ⚔ 1. воéнный трибунáл; 2. суди́ть воéнным судóм; **~ship** [-ʃip] ухáживание; **~yard** двор.
cousin ['kʌzn] двою́родный брат, двою́родная сестрá.
cove [kouv] (мáленькая) бýхта; *fig.* убéжище.
covenant ['kʌvinənt] 1. ⚖ договóр; завéт; 2. соглашáться [-ласи́ться].
cover ['kʌvə] 1. кры́шка; обёртка; покрывáло; переплёт; конвéрт; ⚔ укры́тие; *fig.* покрóв; ⊕ кожýх; *mot.* покры́шка; 2. покры́(вá)ть (*a.* ✝); прикры́(вá)ть; скры(вá)ть; **~ing** [-riŋ] (по)кры́шка; обши́вка; облицóвка.
covert ['kʌvət] 1. □ прикры́тый, тáйный; 2. убéжище для ди́чи.
covet ['kʌvit] жáждать (Р); **~ous** [-əs] □ жáдный, áлчный; скупóй.
cow¹ [kau] корóва.
cow² [~] запýгивать [-гáть]; терроризовáть (*im*)*pf*.
coward ['kauəd] 1. □ трусли́вый; малодýшный, рóбкий; 2. трус (-и́ха); **~ice** [-is] трýсость *f*; малодýшие; **~ly** [-li] трусли́вый.
cowboy ['kaubɔi] пастýх; *Am.* ковбóй.
cower ['kauə] съёжи(ва)ться.
cowl [kaul] капюшóн.
coxcomb ['kɔkskoum] ♀ петýший гребешóк; фат.
coxswain ['kɔkswein, *mst* 'kɔksn] рулевóй.
coy [kɔi] □ застéнчивый, скрóмный.
crab [kræb] *zo.* краб; ⊕ лебёдка, вóрот; F ворчли́вый человéк.
crab-louse ['kræblaus] площа́ца.

crack ['kræk] **1.** треск; тре́щина; щель *f*; рассе́лина; F уда́р; *Am.* саркасти́ческое замеча́ние; *Am.* **at ~ of day** на заре́; **2.** F первокла́ссный; **3.** *v/t.* раска́лывать [-коло́ть], коло́ть; **~ a joke** отпусти́ть шу́тку; *v/i.* производи́ть треск, шум; тре́скаться [тре́снуть], раска́лываться [-коло́ться]; лома́ться (о го́лосе); **~ed** [krækt] тре́снувший; F вы́живший из ума́; **~er** ['krækə] хлопу́шка-конфе́та; *Am.* то́нкое сухо́е пече́нье; **~le** ['krækl] потре́скивание; треск.

cradle ['kreidl] **1.** колыбе́ль *f*; *fig.* нача́ло; младе́нчество; **2.** убаю́к(ив)ать.

craft [krɑ:ft] ло́вкость; сноро́вка; ремесло́; су́дно (*pl.* суда́); **~sman** ['krɑ:ftsmən] ма́стер; реме́сленник; **~y** ['krɑ:fti] □ ло́вкий, иску́сный; хи́трый.

crag [kræg] скала́, утёс.

cram [kræm] впи́хивать [-хну́ть]; переполня́ть [-о́лнить]; [на]пи́чкать; F [за]зубри́ть.

cramp [kræmp] **1.** су́дорога, спа́змы *f/pl.*; ⊕ зажи́м, скоба́; **2.** вызыва́ть су́дорогу у (Р); стесня́ть [-ни́ть] (разви́тие); су́живать [су́зить] (по́ле де́йствия).

cranberry ['krænbəri] клю́ква.

crane [krein] **1.** жура́вль *m*; ⊕ подъёмный кран; **2.** поднима́ть кра́ном; вытя́гивать ше́ю.

crank [kræŋk] **1.** рукоя́тка; причу́да; челове́к с причу́дами; **2.** заводи́ть рукоя́тью (автомоби́ль и т. п.); **~-shaft** ⊕ коле́нчатый вал; **~y** [kræŋki] неиспра́вный (механи́зм); капри́зный; эксцентри́чный.

cranny ['kræni] щель *f*, тре́щина.

crape [kreip] креп; тра́ур.

crash [kræʃ] **1.** гро́хот, треск; ✈ ава́рия; 🚂 круше́ние; ✝ крах; **2.** па́дать, ру́шиться с тре́ском; разби́(ва́)ть(ся); ✈ потерпе́ть ава́рию.

crater ['kreitə] кра́тер; ⚔ воро́нка.

crave [kreiv] *v/t.* настоя́тельно проси́ть; *v/i.* стра́стно жела́ть, жа́ждать (for P).

crawfish ['krɔ:fiʃ] речно́й рак.

crawl [krɔ:l] **1.** по́лзание; *fig.* пресмыка́тельство; **2.** пресмыка́ться; по́лзать, [по]ползти́.

crayfish ['kreifiʃ] речно́й рак.

crayon ['kreiən] цветно́й каранда́ш; пасте́ль *f* (каранда́ш); пасте́льный рису́нок.

craz|e [kreiz] **1.** ма́ния; F мо́да, пова́льное увлече́ние; **be the ~** быть в мо́де; **2.** своди́ть с ума́; сходи́ть с ума́; **~y** ['kreizi] □ поме́шанный; ша́ткий.

creak [kri:k] **1.** скрип; **2.** [за]скрипе́ть.

cream [kri:m] **1.** сли́вки *f/pl.*; крем; са́мое лу́чшее; **2.** снима́ть сли́вки с (Р); **~ery** ['kri:məri] маслобо́йня; моло́чная; **~y** ['kri:mi] □ сли́вочный; кре́мовый.

crease [kri:s] **1.** скла́дка; сгиб; **2.** [с]мя́ть(ся); загиба́ть [загну́ть].

creat|e [kri'eit] [со]твори́ть; созд(ав)а́ть; **~ion** [-ʃən] созда́ние, (со)творе́ние; **~ive** [-tiv] тво́рческий; **~or** [-tə] созда́тель *m*, творе́ц; **~ure** ['kri:tʃə] созда́ние; существо́; тварь *f*.

creden|ce ['kri:dəns] ве́ра, дове́рие; **~tials** [kri:'denʃəlz] *pl.* вери́тельные гра́моты *f/pl.*, докуме́нты *m/pl.*

credible ['kredəbl] □ заслу́живающий дове́рие; вероя́тный.

credit ['kredit] **1.** дове́рие; хоро́шая репута́ция; ✝ креди́т; **2.** ве́рить, доверя́ть (Д); ✝ кредитова́ть (*im*)*pf.*; **~ a p. with a th.** припи́сывать кому́-либо что-либо; **~able** ['kreditəbl] □ похва́льный; **~or** [-tə] кредито́р.

credulous ['kredjuləs] □ легкове́рный, дове́рчивый.

creed [kri:d] вероуче́ние; кре́до *indecl. n.*

creek [kri:k] бу́хта; зали́в; рука́в реки́; *Am.* прито́к; руче́й.

creep [kri:p] [*irr.*] по́лзать, [по-] ползти́; ви́ться (о расте́ниях); кра́сться; *fig.* **~ in** вкра́дываться [вкра́сться]; **~er** ['kri:pə] вью́щееся расте́ние.

crept [krept] *pt.* и *p. pt.* от creep.

crescent ['kresnt] **1.** расту́щий; ['kreznt] серпови́дный; **2.** полуме́сяц.

crest [krest] гребешо́к (петуха́); хохоло́к (пти́цы); гре́бень *m* (волны́, горы́, шле́ма); **~-fallen** ['krestfɔ:lən] упа́вший ду́хом; уны́лый.

crevasse [kri'væs] рассе́лина (в леднике́); *Am.* проры́в плоти́ны.

crevice ['krevis] щель *f*, расще́лина, тре́щина.

crew[1] [kru:] брига́да, арте́ль рабо́чих; ⚓ судова́я кома́нда.

crew[2] [~] *pt.* от crow.

crib [krib] **1.** я́сли *m/pl.*, корму́шка; де́тская крова́тка; *school*: шпарга́лка; **2.** помеща́ть в те́сное помеще́ние; F спи́сывать тайко́м.

cricket ['krikit] *zo.* сверчо́к; крике́т (игра́); F **not ~** не по пра́вилам, нече́стно.

crime [kraim] преступле́ние.

crimina|l ['kriminəl] **1.** престу́пник; **2.** престу́пный; кримина́льный, уголо́вный; **~lity** [krimi'næliti] престу́пность *f*; вино́вность *f*.

crimp [krimp] гофрирова́ть (*im*)*pf.*

crimson ['krimzn] **1.** багро́вый, мали́новый **2.** [по]красне́ть.

cringe [krindʒ] раболе́пствовать.

crinkle ['kriŋkl] **1.** скла́дка; морщи́на; 2. [с]мо́рщиться; зави́(ва́)ться; [по]мя́ться.

cripple ['kripl] 1. кале́ка *m/f*, инвали́д; 2. [ис]кале́чить, [из]уро́довать; *fig.* парализова́ть (*im*)*pf*.

crisp [krisp] 1. кудря́вый; хрустя́щий; све́жий (о во́здухе); 2. зави́(ва́)ть(ся); хрусте́ть [хру́стнуть]; покрыва́ться ря́бью (о реке́ и т. п.).

criss-cross ['kriskrɔs] 1. *adv.* крест-на́крест; вкось; 2. перекре́щивать [-крести́ть].

criteri|on [krai'tiəriən], *pl.* **~a** [-riə] крите́рий, мери́ло.

criti|c ['kritik] кри́тик; **~cal** ['kritikəl] □ крити́ческий; разбо́рчивый; **~cism** [-sizm], **~que** ['kriti:k] кри́тика; реце́нзия; **~cize** [k'ritisaiz] [рас]критикова́ть; осужда́ть [осуди́ть].

croak [krouk] [за]ка́ркать; [за-]ква́кать.

crochet ['krouʃei] 1. вяза́ние (крючко́м); 2. вяза́ть (крючко́м).

crock [krɔk] гли́няный кувши́н; **~ery** ['krɔkəri] посу́да.

crone [kroun] F стару́ха; ста́рая карга́.

crony ['krouni] F закады́чный [друг.]

crook [kruk] 1. по́сох; крюк; поворо́т; заги́б; *sl.* обма́нщик, плут; 2. сгиба́ть(ся) [согну́ть(ся)]; искривля́ть(ся) [-ви́ть(ся)]; **~ed** ['krukid] изо́гнутый; криво́й; нече́стный.

croon [kru:n] 1. моното́нное пе́ние; 2. напева́ть.

crop [krɔp] 1. урожа́й; хлеба́ на корню́; кнутови́ще; зоб; 2. засева́ть [засе́ять]; собира́ть урожа́й; подстрига́ть [-ри́чь]; ~ up (внеза́пно) появля́ться [-ви́ться].

cross [krɔs, krɔ:s] 1. крест; распя́тие; 2. □ попере́чный; серди́тый; 3. *v/t.* [о]крести́ть; скре́щивать [-ести́ть] (ру́ки и т. п.); переходи́ть [перейти́], переезжа́ть [перее́хать]; *fig.* противоде́йствовать (Д); противоре́чить (Д); ~ o. s. [пере]крести́ться; *v/i.* ✆ разминýться *pf.*; **~-bar** попере́чина; **~-breed** по́месь *f*; гибри́д; **~-examination** перекрёстный допро́с; **~-eyed** косо́й, косогла́зый; **~ing** ['krɔsiŋ] перекрёсток; перепра́ва; перее́зд, перехо́д; **~-road** попере́чная доро́га; **~s** *pl.* или *sg.* перекрёсток; **~-section** попере́чное сече́ние; **~wise** крестообра́зно; кресто́м.

crotchet ['krɔtʃit] крючо́к; причу́да; ♪ четвертна́я но́та.

crouch [krautʃ] раболе́пствовать; притаи́ться *pf.*

crow [krou] 1. воро́на; пе́ние петуха́; ра́достный крик (младе́нца); 2. [*irr.*] [про]пе́ть (о петухе́); ликова́ть; **~-bar** лом, ва́га.

crowd [kraud] 1. толпа́; мно́жество, ма́сса; толкотня́, да́вка; F компа́ния; 2. собира́ться толпо́й, толпи́ться; набива́ться битко́м.

crown [kraun] 1. вене́ц, коро́на; *fig.* заверше́ние; кро́на (де́рева); маку́шка (головы́); коро́нка (зу́ба); 2. [у]венча́ть; коронова́ть (*im*)*pf.*; *fig.* заверша́ть [-ши́ть]; поста́вить коро́нку (на зуб).

cruci|al ['kru:ʃiəl] □ крити́ческий; реша́ющий; **~ble** [-sibl] ти́гель *m*; **~fixion** [kru:si'fikʃən] распя́тие; **~fy** ['kru:sifai] распина́ть [-пя́ть].

crude [kru:d] □ сыро́й; необрабо́танный; незре́лый; гру́бый.

cruel ['kru:əl] □ жесто́кий; *fig.* мучи́тельный; **~ty** [-ti] жесто́кость *f*.

cruet-stand ['kruitstænd] судо́к.

cruise [kru:z] ⚓ 1. морско́е путеше́ствие; 2. крейси́ровать; соверша́ть ре́йсы; **~r** ['kru:zə] ⚓ кре́йсер.

crumb [krʌm] 1. кро́шка; 2. (= **~le** ['krʌmbl]) [рас-, ис]кроши́ть(ся).

crumple ['krʌmpl] [с]мя́ть(ся); [с]ко́мкать(ся).

crunch [krʌntʃ] разжёвывать [-жева́ть]; хрусте́ть [хру́стнуть].

crusade [kru:'seid] кресто́вый похо́д; кампа́ния; **~r** [-ə] крестоно́сец.

crush [krʌʃ] 1. да́вка; толкотня́; 2. *v/t.* [раз]дави́ть; выжима́ть [вы́жать]; уничтожа́ть [-о́жить].

crust [krʌst] 1. ко́рка; кора́; 2. покрыва́ть(ся) ко́ркой, коро́й; **~y** ['krʌsti] □ покры́тый ко́ркой, коро́й.

crutch [krʌtʃ] косты́ль *m*.

cry [krai] 1. крик; вопль *m*; плач; 2. [за]пла́кать; восклица́ть [-и́кнуть]; крича́ть [кри́кнуть]; ~ for [по]тре́бовать (Р).

crypt [kript] склеп; **~ic** ['kriptik] таи́нственный; сокрове́нный.

crystal ['kristl] хруста́ль *m*; криста́лл; *Am.* стекло́ для часо́в; **~line** [-təlain] хруста́льный; **~lize** [-təlaiz] кристаллизова́ть(ся) (*im*)*pf*.

cub [kʌb] 1. детёныш (зве́ря); *Am.* нович́ок; 2. [о]щени́ться.

cub|e [kju:b] ⅍ 1. куб; ~ root куби́ческий ко́рень *m*; 2. возводи́ть в куб; **~ic**(**al** □) ['kju:bik, -ikəl] куби́ческий.

cuckoo ['kuku:] куку́шка.

cucumber ['kju:kəmbə] огуре́ц.

cud [kʌd] жва́чка; chew the ~ жева́ть жва́чку.

cuddle ['kʌdl] *v/t.* прижима́ть к себе́; *v/i.* приж(им)а́ться (друг к дру́гу).

cudgel ['kʌdʒəl] 1. дуби́на; 2. дубаси́ть дуби́ной.

cue [kju:] (билья́рдный) кий; намёк; *thea.* ре́плика.

cuff [kʌf] 1. манже́та, обшла́г; 2. [по]би́ть (руко́й), [по]колоти́ть.

culminate ['kʌlmineit] достигáть вы́сшей тóчки (и́ли стéпени).
culpable ['kʌlpəbl] □ винóвный; престу́пный.
culprit ['kʌlprit] престу́пник; винóвный.
cultivat|e ['kʌltiveit] обрабáтывать [-бóтать]; воздéл(ыв)ать; культиви́ровать; **~ion** [kʌlti'veiʃən] воздéлывание (земли́); разведéние, культу́ра (растéний); **~or** ['kʌltiveitə] культивáтор (орýдие); землеДéлец.
cultural ['kʌltʃərəl] □ культу́рный.
culture ['kʌltʃə] культу́ра; разведéние, воздéлывание; **~d** [-d] культу́рный; культиви́рованный.
cumber ['kʌmbə] затрудня́ть [-ни́ть]; стесня́ть [-ни́ть]; **~some** [-səm], **cumbrous** ['kʌmbrəs] громóздкий; обремени́тельный.
cumulative ['kju:mjulətiv] □ совоку́пный; кумуляти́вный; накóпленный.
cunning ['kʌniŋ] 1. лóвкий; хи́трый; ковáрный; *Am.* изя́щный; прелéстный; 2. лóвкость *f*; хи́трость *f*; ковáрство.
cup [kʌp] чáшка; чáша; ку́бок; **~board** ['kʌbəd] шкаф.
cupidity [kju'piditi] áлчность *f*, жáдность *f*, скáредность *f*.
cupola ['kju:pələ] ку́пол.
cur [kə:] дворня́жка (собáка).
curate ['kjuərit] помóщник прихóдского свящéнника.
curb [kə:b] 1. мундшту́чная уздéчка; уздá (*a. fig.*); (*a.* ~-stone) обóчина тротуáра; 2. обу́здывать [-дáть] (*a. fig.*).
curd [kə:d] 1. творóг; 2. (*mst* **~le**, [kə:dl]) свёртываться [сверну́ться] (о молокé, крóви).
cure [kjuə] 1. лечéние; срéдство; 2. [вы́]лечи́ть, исцеля́ть [-ли́ть]; заготовля́ть [-тóвить], консерви́ровать (*im*)*pf*.
curio ['kjuəriou] рéдкая антиквáрная вещь *f*; **~sity** [kjuəri'ɔsiti] любопы́тство; рéдкость *f*; **~us** ['kjuəriəs] □ любопы́тный; пытли́вый; стрáнный.
curl [kə:l] 1. лóкон; завитóк; спирáль *f*; 2. ви́ться; клуби́ться; **~y** ['kə:li] кудря́вый; курчáвый; вью́щийся.
currant ['kʌrənt] сморóдина; (*a.* dried ~) кори́нка.
curren|cy ['kʌrənsi] † дéньги *f*/*pl.*, валю́та; дéнежное обращéние; **~t** [-ənt] 1. □ теку́щий; ходя́чий; † находя́щийся в обращéнии; 2. потóк; течéние; ⚡ ток.
curse [kə:s] 1. прокля́тие; ругáтельство; бич, бéдствие; 2. проклинáть [-кля́сть]; ругáться; **~d** ['kə:sid] □ прокля́тый.
curt [kə:t] □ крáткий.
curtail [kə:'teil] укорáчивать [-ро-ти́ть]; урéз(ыв)ать; *fig.* сокращáть [сократи́ть].
curtain ['kə:tn] 1. занавéска; зáнавес; 2. занавéшивать [-вéсить].
curts(e)y ['kə:tsi] 1. реверáнс; поклóн; 2. дéлать реверáнс (to Д).
curv|ature ['kə:vətʃə] искривлéние; **~e** [kə:v] 1. ⅄ кривáя; изги́б; кривизнá; 2. [со]гну́ть; изгибáть (-ся) [изогну́ть(ся)].
cushion ['kuʃin] 1. поду́шка; борт (бильярдного столá); 2. подклáдывать поду́шку под (В).
custody ['kʌstədi] опéка, попечéние; заточéние.
custom ['kʌstəm] обы́чай; привы́чка; клиенту́ра; **~s** *pl.* тамóженные пóшлины *f*/*pl.*; **~ary** [-əri] □ обы́чный; **~er** [-ə] постоя́нный (-ная) покупáтель(ница *f*) *m*; клиéнт(ка); **~-house** тамóжня; **~-made** *Am.* изготóвленный на закáз.
cut [kʌt] 1. разрéз, порéз; зару́бка, засéчка; отрéз (матéрии); покрóй (плáтья); (*mst* short-~) сокращённый путь *m*; 2. [*irr.*] *v*/*t.* рéзать; разрезáть [-рéзать]; [по]стри́чь; [от]шлифовáть; [с]коси́ть (травý); прорéз(ыв)аться (о зубáх); ~ short прер(ы)вáть; ~ down сокращáть [-рати́ть] (расхóды); ~ out вырезáть [вы́резать]; [с]крои́ть; выключáть [вы́ключить]; *fig.* вытесня́ть [вы́теснить]; be ~ out for быть слóвно сóзданным для (Р); *v*/*i.* рéзать; ~ in вмéшиваться [-шáться].
cute [kju:t] □ F хи́трый; *Am.* ми́лый, привлекáтельный.
cutlery ['kʌtləri] ножевы́е издéлия *n*/*pl.*
cutlet ['kʌtlit] котлéта.
cut|-out ⚡ автомати́ческий выключáтель *m*, предохрани́тель *m*; **~ter** ['kʌtə] рéзчик (по дéреву); закрóйщик; ⊕ рéжущий инструмéнт; ⚓ кáтер; **~-throat** головорéз; уби́йца *m*; **~ting** ['kʌtiŋ] 1. □ óстрый, рéзкий; язви́тельный; 2. рéзание; закрóйка; ⊕ фрезеровáние; гранéние; ⚘ побéг, черенóк; **~s** *pl.* обрéзки *m*/*pl.*; (газéтные) вы́резки *f*/*pl.*; ⊕ стру́жки *f*/*pl.*
cycl|e ['saikl] 1. цикл; круг; велосипéд; ⊕ кругов́ой процéсс; 2. éздить на велосипéде; **~ist** [-ist] велосипеди́ст(ка).
cyclone ['saikloun] циклóн.
cylinder ['silində] цили́ндр (*geom.*); ⊕ барабáн; вáлик.
cymbal ['simbəl] ♪ тарéлки *f*/*pl.*
cynic ['sinik] 1. (*a.* ~al □, -ikəl) цини́чный; 2. ци́ник.
cypress ['saipris] ⚘ кипари́с.
Czech [tʃek] 1. чех, чéшка; 2. чéшский.
Czecho-Slovak ['tʃekou'slouvæk] 1. жи́тель(ница) Чехословáкии; 2. чехословáцкий.

D

dab [dæb] **1.** шлепо́к; мазо́к; пятно́ (кра́ски); **2.** слегка́ тро́гать (В); де́лать лёгкие мазки́ на (П).

dabble ['dæbl] плеска́ть(ся); бара́хтаться (в воде́ и т. п.); халту́рить, занима́ться че́м-либо пове́рхностно.

dad [dæd] F, **~dy** ['dædi] F па́па.

daffodil ['dæfədil] жёлтый нарци́сс.

dagger ['dægə] кинжа́л; **be at ~s drawn** быть на ножа́х (с T).

daily ['deili] **1.** *adv.* ежедне́вно; **2.** ежедне́вный; **3.** ежедне́вная газе́та.

dainty ['deinti] **1.** □ ла́комый; изя́щный; изы́сканный; **2.** ла́комство, деликате́с.

dairy ['dɛəri] моло́чная; маслоде́льня.

daisy ['deizi] маргари́тка.

dale [deil] доли́на, дол.

dall|iance ['dæliəns] несерьёзное заня́тие; флирт; **~y** ['dæli] зря теря́ть вре́мя; флиртова́ть.

dam [dæm] **1.** ма́тка (живо́тных); да́мба, плоти́на; **2.** запру́живать [-уди́ть].

damage ['dæmidʒ] **1.** вред; повреждéние; убы́ток; **~s** *pl.* ⚖ убы́тки *m/pl.*; компенса́ция за убы́тки; **2.** поврежда́ть [-еди́ть], [ис]по́ртить.

damask ['dæməsk] камка́.

damn [dæm] **1.** проклина́ть [-ля́сть]; осужда́ть [осуди́ть]; руга́ться; **2.** прокля́тие; руга́тельство; **~ation** [dæm'neiʃən] прокля́тие; осужде́ние.

damp [dæmp] **1.** сы́рость *f*, вла́жность *f*; **2.** вла́жный, за́тхлый; **3.** *a.* **~en** ['dæmpən] [на]мочи́ть; [от-]сыре́ть; *fig.* обескура́жи(ва)ть.

danc|e [dɑ:ns] **1.** та́нец; бал; **2.** танцева́ть; **~er** ['dɑ:nsə] танцо́р, танцо́вщик (-ица); **~ing** [-iŋ] та́нцы *m/pl.*; пля́ска; *attr.* танцева́льный.

dandelion ['dændilaiən] ♀ одува́нчик.

dandle ['dændl] [по]кача́ть (на рука́х).

dandruff ['dændrəf] пе́рхоть *f*.

dandy ['dændi] **1.** щёголь *m*; *sl.* первокла́ссная вещь *f*; **2.** *Am. sl.* первокла́ссный.

Dane [dein] датча́нин (-ча́нка).

danger ['deindʒə] опа́сность *f*; **~ous** ['deindʒrəs] □ опа́сный.

dangle ['dæŋgl] висе́ть, свиса́ть [сви́снуть]; болта́ть (T).

Danish ['deiniʃ] да́тский.

dapple ['dæpl] испещря́ть [-ри́ть]; **~d** [-d] испещрённый, пёстрый; **~-grey** се́рый в я́блоках (конь).

dar|e [dɛə] *v/i.* [по]сме́ть; отва́жи(ва)ться; *v/t.* вызыва́ть [вы́звать]; **~e-devil** смельча́к, сорвиголова́ *m*; **~ing** [dɛəriŋ] **1.** □ сме́лый, отва́жный; де́рзкий; **2.** сме́лость *f*, отва́жность *f*.

dark [dɑ:k] **1.** тёмный; сму́глый; та́йный; мра́чный; **~ horse** „тёмная лоша́дка"; **~ lantern** потайно́й фона́рь *m*; **2.** темнота́, тьма; неве́дение; **~en** ['dɑ:kən] затемня́ть(ся) [-ни́ть(ся)]; **~ness** ['dɑ:knis] темнота́, тьма; **~y** ['dɑ:ki] F черноко́жий, чёрный (о не́гре).

darling ['dɑ:liŋ] **1.** люби́мец (-ми́ца); ба́ловень *m*; **2.** люби́мый.

darn [dɑ:n] [за]што́пать.

dart [dɑ:t] **1.** стрела́; дро́тик; прыжо́к; **2.** *v/t.* мета́ть [метну́ть] (стре́лы, взгля́ды и т. п.); *v/i. fig.* мча́ться стрело́й.

dash [dæʃ] **1.** поры́в; уда́р; взмах; плеск (воды́); *fig.* при́месь *f*, чу́точка; набро́сок; штрих; тире́ *n indecl.* **2.** *v/t.* броса́ть [бро́сить]; разби́(ва́)ть; разбавля́ть [-а́вить]; *v/i.* ри́нуться; броса́ться [бро́ситься]; **~-board** *mot.*, ✈ прибо́рная доска́; **~ing** ['dæʃiŋ] □ лихо́й.

data ['deitə] *pl.*, *Am. a. sg.* да́нные *n/pl.*; но́вости *f/pl.*; фа́кты *m/pl.*

date [deit] **1.** да́та, число́; F свида́ние; **out of ~** устаре́лый; **up to ~** нове́йший; совреме́нный; **2.** дати́ровать (*im*)*pf.*; *Am.* F усло́вливаться [-о́виться] с (T) (о встре́че); име́ть свида́ние.

daub [dɔ:b] [по]ма́зать; [на]малева́ть.

daughter ['dɔ:tə] дочь *f*; **~-in-law** [-rinlɔ:] неве́стка, сноха́.

daunt [dɔ:nt] устраша́ть [-ши́ть], запу́гивать [-га́ть]; **~less** ['dɔ:ntlis] неустраши́мый, бесстра́шный.

dawdle ['dɔ:dl] F безде́льничать.

dawn [dɔ:n] **1.** рассве́т, у́тренняя заря́; *fig.* зача́тки *m/pl.*; про́блески *m/pl.*; **2.** света́ть.

day [dei] день *m*; (*mst* **~s** *pl.*) жизнь *f*; **~ off** выходно́й день *m*; **the other ~** на днях; неда́вно; **~break** рассве́т; **~-labo(u)rer** подёнщик (-ица); **~-star** у́треняя звезда́.

daze [deiz] ошеломля́ть [-ми́ть]; ослепля́ть [-пи́ть].

dazzle ['dæzl] ослепля́ть [-пи́ть]; ⚓ маскирова́ть окра́ской.

dead [ded] **1.** мёртвый; увя́дший (о цвета́х); онеме́вший (о па́льцах); неподви́жный; безразли́чный; **~ bargain** дешёвка; **~ letter** письмо́, недоста́вленное по а́дресу; **a ~ shot** стрело́к, не даю́щий про́маха; **~ wall** глуха́я стена́; **2.** *adv.* по́лно, соверше́нно; **~ against** реши́тельно про́тив; **3. the ~** по-

ко́йники *m/pl.*; **~en** [dedn] лиша́ть (-ся) си́лы; заглуша́ть [-ши́ть]; **~-lock** *fig.* мёртвая то́чка; застой; **~ly** [-li] смерте́льный; смертоно́сный.
deaf [def] □ глухо́й; **~en** [defn] оглуша́ть [-ши́ть].
deal [di:l] **1.** коли́чество; соглаше́ние; обхожде́ние; F сде́лка; a good ~ весьма́ мно́го; a great ~ о́чень мно́го; **2.** [*irr.*] *v/t.* разд(ав)а́ть; распределя́ть [-ли́ть]; *v/i.* торгова́ть; ~ with обходи́ться [обойти́сь] *or* поступа́ть [-пи́ть] с (Т); име́ть де́ло с (Т); **~er** ['di:lə] торго́вец; **~ing** ['di:liŋ] (*mst* ~s *pl.*) торго́вые дела́ *n/pl.*; **~t** [delt] *pt.* и *p. pt.* от ~.
dean [di:n] настоя́тель собо́ра; дека́н (факульте́та).
dear [diə] **1.** □ дорого́й, ми́лый; **2.** прекра́сный челове́к; **3.** F o(h) ~!, ~ me! го́споди!
death [deθ] смерть *f*; **~-bed** сме́ртное ло́же; **~-duty** нало́г на насле́дство; **~less** ['deθlis] бессме́ртный; **~ly** [-li] смерте́льный; **~-rate** проце́нт сме́ртности; **~-warrant** сме́ртный пригово́р.
debar [di'bɑ:] исключа́ть [-чи́ть]; лиша́ть пра́ва.
debase [di'beis] унижа́ть [уни́зить]; понижа́ть ка́чество (Р).
debat|able [di'beitəbl] □ спо́рный, дискуссио́нный; **~e** [di'beit] **1.** диску́ссия; пре́ния *n/pl.*, деба́ты *m/pl.*; **2.** обсужда́ть [-уди́ть]; [по-] спо́рить; обду́м(ыв)ать.
debauch [di'bɔtʃ] **1.** распу́тство; попо́йка; **2.** развраща́ть [-рати́ть]; обольща́ть [-льсти́ть].
debilitate [di'biliteit] ослабля́ть [-а́бить]; расслабля́ть [-а́бить].
debit ['debit] ✝ **1.** де́бет; **2.** дебетова́ть (*im*)*pf.*, вноси́ть в де́бет.
debris ['debri:] разва́лины *f/pl.*; обло́мки *m/pl.*
debt [det] долг; **~or** ['dətə] должни́к (-и́ца).
decade ['dekəd] дека́да; десятиле́тие.
decadence ['dekədəns] упа́док; декаде́нтство.
decamp [di'kæmp] снима́ться с ла́геря; уд(и)ра́ть; **~ment** [-mənt] выступле́ние из ла́геря; бы́стрый ухо́д.
decant [di'kænt] [про]фильтрова́ть; сце́живать [сцеди́ть]; **~er** [-ə] графи́н.
decapitate [di'kæpiteit] обезгла́вливать [-ла́вить].
decay [di'kei] **1.** гние́ние; разложе́ние; **2.** [с]гнить; разлага́ться [-ложи́ться].
decease [di'si:s] *part.* ⚖ **1.** смерть *f*, кончи́на; **2.** умира́ть [умере́ть], сконча́ться *pf.*
deceit [di'si:t] обма́н; **~ful** [-ful] □ обма́нчивый.
deceiv|e [di'si:v] обма́нывать [-ну́ть]; **~er** [-ə] обма́нщик (-ица).
December [di'sembə] дека́брь *m.*
decen|cy ['di:snsi] прили́чие; благопристо́йность *f*; **~t** [-t] □ прили́чный; сла́вный.
deception [di'sepʃən] обма́н; ложь *f.*
decide [di'said] реша́ть(ся) [реши́ть(ся)]; принима́ть реше́ние; **~d** [-id] □ реши́тельный; определённый; бесспо́рный.
decimal ['desiməl] **1.** десяти́чный; **2.** десяти́чная дробь *f.*
decipher [di'saifə] расшифро́вывать [-ова́ть]; разбира́ть [разобра́ть].
decisi|on [di'siʒən] реше́ние; реши́тельность *f*; ⚖ пригово́р; **~ve** [di'saisiv] реша́ющий.
deck [dek] **1.** ⚓ па́луба; *Am.* коло́да (карт); **2.** украша́ть [укра́сить]; уб(и)ра́ть (цвета́ми и т. п.); **~-chair** складно́й стул.
declaim [di'kleim] произноси́ть [-нести́] (речь); [про]деклами́ровать.
declar|able [di'kleərəbl] подлежа́щий деклара́ции; **~ation** [deklə'reiʃən] заявле́ние; деклара́ция (*a.* ✝); **~e** [di'klɛə] объявля́ть [-ви́ть]; заявля́ть [-ви́ть]; выска́зываться [вы́сказаться] (for за В, against про́тив Р); предъявля́ть [-ви́ть] (ве́щи в тамо́жне).
declin|ation [dekli'neiʃən] отклоне́ние; накло́н; **~e** [di'klain] **1.** склон, укло́н; паде́ние; упа́док (сил); сниже́ние (цен); ухудше́ние (здоро́вья); зака́т (жи́зни); **2.** *v/t.* отклоня́ть [-ни́ть] (предложе́ние); *gr.* [про]склоня́ть; *v/i.* приходи́ть в упа́док; ухудша́ться [уху́дшиться] (о здоро́вье и т. п.).
declivity [di'kliviti] пока́тость *f*; отло́гий спуск.
decode [di:'koud] *tel.* расшифро́вывать [-рова́ть].
decompose [di:kəm'pouz] разлага́ть(ся) [-ложи́ть(ся)]; [с]гнить.
decontrol ['di:kən'troul] освобожда́ть от контро́ля (торго́влю и т. п.).
decorat|e ['dekəreit] украша́ть [укра́сить]; награжда́ть зна́ком отли́чия; **~ion** [dekə'reiʃən] украше́ние; о́рден, знак отли́чия; **~ive** ['dekərətiv] декорати́вный.
decor|ous ['dekərəs] □ присто́йный; **~um** [di'kɔ:rəm] этике́т.
decoy [di'kɔi] **1.** прима́нка, мано́к; **2.** прима́нивать [-ни́ть]; завлека́ть [-е́чь].
decrease 1. ['di:kri:s] уменьше́ние, убыва́ние, пониже́ние; **2.** [di:'kri:s] уменьша́ть(ся) [уме́ньшить (-ся)], убы́(ва́)ть.
decree [di'kri:] **1.** ука́з, декре́т, прика́з; ⚖ постановле́ние **2.** издава́ть декре́т.

decrepit [di'krepit] дряхлый; ветхий.
dedicat|e ['dedikeit] посвящать [-ятить]; **~ion** [dedi'keiʃən] посвящение.
deduce [di'dju:s] выводить [вывести] (заключение, формулу и т. п.).
deduct [di'dʌkt] вычитать [вычесть]; **~ion** [di'dʌkʃən] вычет; вывод, заключение; ✝ скидка.
deed [di:d] **1.** действие; поступок; подвиг; ⚖ документ; **2.** *Am.* передавать по акту.
deem [di:m] *v/t.* считать [счесть]; *v/i.* полагать; [по]думать (of о П).
deep [di:p] **1.** □ глубокий; хитрый; густой (о краске); **2.** бездна; *poet.* море, океан; **~en** ['di:pən] углублять(ся) [-бить(ся)]; сгущать(ся) [сгустить(ся)] (о красках, тенях); **~ness** [-nis] глубина.
deer [diə] *coll.* красный зверь *m*; олень *m*; лань *f*.
deface [di'feis] искажать [исказить]; стирать [стереть].
defam|ation [defə'meiʃən] диффамация; клевета; **~e** [di'feim] поносить; [о]клеветать.
default [di'fɔ:lt] **1.** невыполнение обязательств; неявка в суд; in ~ of за неимением (Р); **2.** не выполнять обязательств; прекращать платежи; не являться по вызову суда.
defeat [di'fi:t] **1.** поражение; расстройство (планов); **2.** ⚔ побеждать [-едить]; расстраивать [-роить] (планы).
defect [di'fekt] недостаток; неисправность *f*, дефект; изъян; **~ive** [-tiv] □ недостаточный; дефектный, повреждённый.
defence, *Am.* **defense** [di'fens] оборона, защита; **~less** [-lis] беззащитный.
defend [di'fend] оборонять(ся), [-нить(ся)], защищать(ся) [-итить(ся)]; ⚖ защищать на суде; **~ant** [-ənt] ⚖ подсудимый; **~er** [-ə] защитник.
defensive [di'fensiv] **1.** оборона; **2.** оборонный, оборонительный.
defer [di'fə] откладывать [отложить]; отсрочи(ва)ть; *Am.* ⚔ давать отсрочку от призыва.
defian|ce [di'faiəns] вызов; неповиновение; пренебрежение; **~t** [-ənt] □ вызывающий.
deficien|cy [di'fiʃənsi] недостаток; дефицит; **~t** [-ənt] недостаточный; несовершенный.
deficit ['defisit] недочёт, дефицит.
defile [di'fail] [про]дефилировать.
defin|e [di'fain] определять [-лить]; давать характеристику (Р); устанавливать значение (Р); **~ite** ['definit] □ определённый; точный; **~ition** [defi'niʃən] определение; **~itive** [di'finitiv] □ определительный.
deflect [di'flekt] отклонять(ся) [-нить(ся)].
deform [di'fɔ:m] [из]уродовать; искажать [исказить] (мысль); **~ed** изуродованный; искажённый (о мысли); **~ity** [di'fɔmiti] уродство.
defraud [di'frɔ:d] обманывать [-нуть]; выманивать [выманить] (of В).
defray [di'frei] оплачивать [оплатить].
deft [deft] □ ловкий, искусный.
defy [di'fai] вызывать [вызвать] (на спор, борьбу); пренебрегать [-бречь] (Т).
degenerate **1.** [di'dʒenəreit] вырождаться [выродиться]; **2.** [-rit] □ вырождающийся.
degrad|ation [degrə'deiʃən] понижение, деградация; **~e** [di'greid] *v/t.* понижать [понизить]; разжаловать *pf.*; унижать [унизить].
degree [di'gri:] градус; ступень *f*; уровень *m*; степень *f*; звание; by ~s *adv.* постепенно; in no ~ *adv.* ничуть, нисколько.
deify ['di:ifai] боготворить.
deign [dein] соизволять [-олить]; удостаивать [-стоить].
deity ['di:iti] божество.
deject [di'dʒekt] удручать [-чить]; угнетать [-ести]; **~ed** [-id] □ удручённый; угнетённый; **~ion** [di'dʒekʃən] уныние.
delay [di'lei] **1.** задержка; отсрочка; замедление; **2.** *v/t.* задерживать [-жать]; откладывать [отложить]; медлить с (Т); *v/i.* медлить, мешкать.
delega|te **1.** ['deligit] делегат, представитель(ница *f*) *m*; **2.** [-geit] делегировать (*im*)*pf.*, поручать [-чить]; **~tion** [deli'geiʃən] делегация, депутация.
deliberat|e **1.** [di'libəreit] *v/t.* обдум(ыв)ать; взвешивать [-есить]; обсуждать [обсудить]; *v/i.* совещаться; **2.** [-rit] □ преднамеренный, умышленный; **~ion** [dilibə'reiʃən] размышление; обсуждение; осмотрительность *f*.
delica|cy ['delikəsi] деликатность *f*; лакомство; утончённость *f*; нежность *f*; чувствительность *f*; **~te** [-kit] □ деликатный; хрупкий; изящный; искусный (о работе); чувствительный; щепетильный; **~tessen** *Am.* [delikə'tesn] гастрономический магазин.
delicious [di'liʃəs] восхитительный; очень вкусный.
delight [di'lait] **1.** удовольствие; восторг; наслаждение; **2.** восхищать [-итить]; доставлять наслаждение (Д); наслаждаться (in Т); ~ to *inf.* иметь удовольствие (+*inf.*); **~ful** [-ful] □ очаровательный; восхитительный.

delineate [di'linieit] обрисóвывать [-ова́ть]; опи́сывать [-са́ть].
delinquent [di'liŋkwənt] **1.** правонаруши́тель(ница *f*) *m*; престу́пник (-ица); **2.** престу́пный.
deliri|ous [di'liriəs] находя́щийся в бреду́, вне себя́, в исступле́нии; **~um** [-əm] бред; исступле́ние.
deliver [di'livə] освобожда́ть [-боди́ть]; доставля́ть [-а́вить]; разноси́ть [-нести́] (газе́ты и т. п.); произноси́ть [-нести́] (речь); сда(ва́)ть (зака́з); наноси́ть [нанести́] (уда́р); **be ~ed** ⚕ разреши́ться от бре́мени, роди́ть; **~ance** [-rəns] освобожде́ние; **~er** [-rə] освободи́тель *m*; поставщи́к; **~y** [-ri] ⚕ ро́ды *m/pl.*; ✉ разно́ска; ✝ доста́вка.
dell [del] лéси́стая доли́на.
delude [di'lu:d] вводи́ть в заблужде́ние; обма́нывать [-ну́ть].
deluge ['delju:dʒ] **1.** наводне́ние; пото́п; **2.** затопля́ть [-пи́ть]; наводня́ть [-ни́ть] (*a. fig.*).
delus|ion [di'lu:ʒən] заблужде́ние; иллю́зия; **~ive** [-siv] □ обма́нчивый; иллюзо́рный.
demand [di'mɑ:nd] **1.** тре́бование (*a.* ⚖); запро́с; потре́бность *f*; ✝ спрос (на това́р); **2.** [по]тре́бовать (Р).
demean [di'mi:n] вести́ себя́; **~ o. s.** роня́ть своё досто́инство; **~o(u)r** [-ə] поведе́ние.
demented [di'mentid] сумасше́дший.
demilitarize [di:'militəraiz] демилитаризова́ть (*im*)*pf*.
demobilize [di:'moubilaiz] демобилизова́ть (*im*)*pf*.
democra|cy [di'mɔkrəsi] демокра́тия; **~tic(al** □) [demə'krætik(əl)] демократи́ческий.
demolish [di'mɔliʃ] разруша́ть [-ру́шить]; сноси́ть [снести́].
demon ['di:mən] де́мон, дья́вол.
demonstrat|e ['demənstreit] [про-] демонстри́ровать; дока́зывать [-за́ть]; **~ion** [deməns'treiʃən] демонстра́ция; демонстри́рование; доказа́тельство; **~ive** [di'mɔnstrətiv] □ убеди́тельный; демонстрати́вный; экспанси́вный; *gr.* указа́тельный.
demote [di:'mout] снижа́ть в до́лжности.
demur [di'mə:] **1.** [по]колеба́ться; возража́ть [-рази́ть]; **2.** колеба́ние; возраже́ние.
demure [di'mjuə] □ серьёзный; чо́порный.
den [den] ло́говище; берло́га; *sl.* прито́н.
denial [di'naiəl] отрица́ние; опроверже́ние; отка́з.
denominat|e [di'nɔmineit] наз(ы)ва́ть; дава́ть и́мя (Д); **~ion** [dinɔmi'neiʃn] наименова́ние; се́кта.
denote [di'nout] означа́ть [-на́чить], обознача́ть [-на́чить].
denounce [di'nauns] обвиня́ть [-ни́ть]; поноси́ть; денонси́ровать (догово́р) (*im*)*pf*.
dens|e [dens] □ густо́й; пло́тный; *fig.* глу́пый, тупо́й; **~ity** ['densiti] густота́; пло́тность *f*.
dent [dent] **1.** вы́боина, вда́вленное ме́сто; **2.** вда́вливать [вдави́ть].
dentist ['dentist] зубно́й врач.
denunciat|ion [dinʌnsi'eiʃən] доно́с; обличе́ние, обвине́ние; **~or** [di'nʌnsieitə] обвини́тель *m*; доно́счик (-ица).
deny [di'nai] отрица́ть; отка́зываться [-за́ться] от (Р); отка́зывать [-за́ть] в (П).
depart [di'pɑ:t] *v/i.* уходи́ть [уйти́], уезжа́ть [уе́хать]; отбы́(ва́)ть, отправля́ться [-а́виться]; отступа́ть [-пи́ть] (from от Р); **~ment** [-mənt] ве́домство; департа́мент; о́трасль *f* (нау́ки); отде́л, отделе́ние; о́бласть *f*; *Am.* министе́рство; State **♀** министе́рство иностра́нных дел; **~ store** универма́г; **~ure** [di'pɑ:tʃə] отхо́д, отбы́тие, отъезд; ухо́д; отправле́ние; отклоне́ние.
depend [di'pend]: **~ (up)on** зави́сеть от (Р); F it **~s** смотря́ по обстоя́тельствам; **~able** [-əbl] надёжный; **~ant** [-ənt] подчинённый; иждиве́нец; **~ence** [-əns] зави́симость *f*; дове́рие; **~ency** [-ənsi] зави́симость *f*; коло́ния; **~ent** [-ənt] □ (on) зави́сящий (от Р); подчинённый (*a. gr.*).
depict [di'pikt] изобража́ть [-рази́ть]; *fig.* опи́сывать [-са́ть].
deplete [di'pli:t] опорожня́ть [-ни́ть]; *fig.* истоща́ть [-щи́ть].
deplor|able [di'plɔ:rəbl] □ плаче́вный; заслу́живающий сожале́ния; **~e** [di'plɔ:] опла́к(ив)ать; сожале́ть о (П).
deport [di'pɔ:t] высыла́ть [вы́слать]; ссыла́ть [сосла́ть]; **~ o. s.** вести́ себя́; **~ment** [-mənt] мане́ры *f/pl.*, уме́ние держа́ть себя́.
depose [di'pouz] смеща́ть [смести́ть]; сверга́ть [све́ргнуть] (с престо́ла); ⚖ дать показа́ния под прися́гой.
deposit [di'pɔzit] **1.** отложе́ние; за́лежь *f*; ✝ вклад (в банк); депози́т; зало́г; **2.** класть [положи́ть]; депони́ровать (*im*)*pf.*; дава́ть оса́док; **~ion** [depə'ziʃən] сверже́ние (с престо́ла); показа́ние под прися́гой; оса́док; **~or** [di'pɔzitə] вкла́дчик (-ица).
depot 1. ['depou] 🚂 депо́ *n indecl.*; склад; сара́й; **2.** ['di:po] *Am.* 🚂 ста́нция.
deprave [di'preiv] развраща́ть [-рати́ть].
depreciate [di'pri:ʃieit] обесце́ни(ва)ть; недооце́нивать [-и́ть].

depress [di'pres] угнетáть [-ести́]; подавля́ть [-ви́ть]; унижáть [-и́зить]; **~ed** [-t] *fig.* уны́лый; **~ion** [di'preʃən] сниже́ние; впа́дина; тоска́; ✝ депре́ссия.
deprive [di'praiv] лишáть [лиши́ть] (of P).
depth [depθ] глубина́.
deput|ation [depju'teiʃən] депутáция, делегáция; **~e** [di'pju:t] делеги́ровать (*im*)*pf*.; **~y** ['depjuti] делегáт(ка); депутáт(ка); замести́тель(ница *f*) *m*.
derail [di'reil] 🚂 *v/i.* сходи́ть с ре́льсов; *v/t.* устрóить круше́ние (пóезда).
derange [di'reindʒ] расстрáивать [-рóить] (мы́сли, плáны); приводи́ть в беспоря́док.
derelict ['derilikt] поки́нутый (кора́бль, дом), (за)брóшенный; **~ion** [deri'likʃən] забрóшенность *f*.
deri|de [di'raid] осме́ивать [-ея́ть], высме́ивать [вы́смеять]; **~sion** [di'riʒən] высме́ивание; **~sive** [di'raisiv] □ насме́шливый.
deriv|ation [deri'veiʃən] истóчник; происхожде́ние; **~e** [di'raiv] происходи́ть [-изойти́]; извлекáть [-влéчь] (пóльзу) (from от P); устанáвливать происхожде́ние (P).
derogat|e ['derogeit] умаля́ть [-ли́ть] (from B); **~ion** [dero'geiʃən] умале́ние.
derrick ['derik] ⊕ дéррик-кран; ⚒ буровáя вы́шка; ⚓ подъёмная стрелá.
descend [di'send] спускáться [спусти́ться]; сходи́ть [сойти́]; ✈ снижáться [сни́зиться]; ~ (up)on обру́ши(ва)ться на (B); происходи́ть [-изойти́] (*from* из P); **~ant** [-ənt] потóмок.
descent [di'sent] спуск; сниже́ние; склон; скат; происхожде́ние.
describe [dis'kraib] опи́сывать [-сáть].
description [dis'kripʃən] описáние; изображе́ние.
desert 1. ['dezət] a) пусты́нный; забрóшенный; b) пусты́ня; **2.** [di'zə:t] a) *v/t.* бросáть [брóсить]; покидáть [-ки́нуть]; *v/i.* дезерти́ровать (*im*)*pf*.; b) заслу́га; **~er** [-ə] дезерти́р; **~ion** [-ʃən] дезерти́рство; оставле́ние.
deserv|e [di'zə:v] заслу́живать [-жи́ть]; имéть заслу́ги (of пéред T); **~ing** [-iŋ] заслу́живающий; достóйный (of P).
design [di'zain] **1.** зáмысел; проéкт; план; рису́нок; узóр; намéрение; **2.** предназначáть [-знáчить]; заду́м(ыв)ать; составля́ть план (P); [на]рисовáть.
designat|e ['dezigneit] определя́ть [-ли́ть]; обозначáть [-знáчить]; предназначáть [-знáчить]; **~ion** [dezig'neiʃən] указáние; назначе́ние.
designer [di'zainə] констру́ктор; чертёжник; *fig.* интригáн.
desir|able [di'zaiərəbl] □ желáтельный; **~e** [di'zaiə] **1.** желáние; трéбование; **2.** [по]желáть (P); [по]трéбовать (P); **~ous** [-rəs] □ желáющий, жáждущий (of P).
desist [di'zist] откáзываться [-зáться] (from от P).
desk [desk] контóрка; пи́сьменный стол.
desolat|e 1. ['desoleit] опустошáть [-ши́ть]; разоря́ть [-ри́ть]; **2.** [-lit] □ опустошённый; несчáстный; одинóкий; **~ion** [deso'leiʃən] опустоше́ние; одинóчество.
despair [dis'pɛə] **1.** отчáяние; безнадёжность *f*; **2.** отчáиваться [-чáяться]; теря́ть надéжду (of на B); **~ing** [-riŋ] □ отчáивающийся.
despatch *s.* dispatch.
desperat|e ['despərit] □ отчáянный; безнадёжный; отъя́вленный; *adv.* отчáянно; стрáшно; **~ion** [despə'reiʃən] отчáяние; безрассу́дство.
despise [dis'paiz] презирáть.
despite [dis'pait] **1.** злóба; in ~ of вопреки́ (Д); несмотря́ на (B); нáзлó (Д); **2.** *prp.* (*a.* ~ of) несмотря́ на (B).
despoil [dis'pɔil] [о]грáбить; лишáть [лиши́ть] (of P).
despond [dis'pɔnd] уныва́ть; теря́ть надéжду; пáдать ду́хом; **~ency** [-ənsi] уны́ние; упáдок ду́ха; **~ent** [-ənt] □ подáвленный; уны́лый.
dessert [di:'zə:t] десéрт.
destin|ation [desti'neiʃən] назначéние; мéсто назначéния, цель *f* (путешéствия); **~e** ['destin] предназначáть [-знáчить]; предопределя́ть [-ли́ть]; **~y** [-tini] судьбá; удéл.
destitute ['destitju:t] □ нуждáющийся; лишённый (of P).
destroy [dis'trɔi] уничтожáть [-óжить]; истребля́ть [-би́ть]; разрушáть [-у́шить].
destruct|ion [dis'trʌkʃən] разрушéние; уничтожéние; разорéние; **~ive** [-tiv] □ разруши́тельный; пáгубный; врéдный.
detach [di'tætʃ] отделя́ть [-ли́ть]; отвя́зывать [-зáть]; разъединя́ть [-ни́ть]; ⚔, ⚓ отряжáть [-яди́ть], пос(ы)лáть; **~ed** [-t] отдéльный; беспристрáстный; **~ment** [-mənt] разъединéние; ⚔ командировáние; ⚔ отря́д.
detail 1. ['di:teil] подрóбность *f*, детáль *f*; ⚔ наря́д, комáнда; in ~ в подрóбностях, подрóбно; **2.** [di'teil] входи́ть в подрóбности; ⚔ откомандирóвывать [-ровáть].
detain [di'tein] задéрживать [-жáть]; содержáть под стрáжей.

detect [di'tekt] обнару́жи(ва)ть; ⚡ детекти́ровать; **~ion** [di'tekʃən] обнару́жение; ⚡ детекти́рование; **~ive** [-tiv] **1.** сы́щик, аге́нт сыскно́й поли́ции; **2.** сыскно́й, детекти́вный.

detention [di'tənʃən] задержа́ние, содержа́ние под аре́стом.

deter [di'tə:] отпу́гивать [-гну́ть] (from от Р).

deteriorat|e [di'tiəriəreit] ухудша́ть(ся) [уху́дшить(ся)]; [ис]по́ртить(ся); **~ion** [ditiəriə'reiʃən] ухудше́ние; по́рча.

determin|ation [ditə:mi'neiʃən] определе́ние; установле́ние (грани́ц); калькуля́ция (цен); реши́тельность *f*; **~e** [di'tə:min] *v/t.* устана́вливать [-нови́ть]; определя́ть [-ли́ть]; реша́ть [реши́ть]; *v/i.* реша́ться [реши́ться]; **~ed** [-d] реши́тельный; твёрдый (хара́ктер).

detest [di'test] ненави́деть; пита́ть отвраще́ние к (Д); **~able** [-əbl] □ отврати́тельный; **~ation** [dites'teiʃən] отвраще́ние.

dethrone [di'θroun] сверга́ть с престо́ла.

detonate ['di:touneit] детони́ровать; взрыва́ть(ся) [взорва́ть(ся)].

detour [di'tuə] **1.** око́льный путь *m*; *Am.* объе́зд; make a ~ де́лать крюк.

detract [di'trækt] умаля́ть [-ли́ть], уменьша́ть [уме́ньшить]; **~ion** [di'trækʃən] умале́ние (досто́инства); клевета́.

detriment ['detrimənt] уще́рб, вред.

devaluate [di:'væljueit] обесце́ни(ва)ть.

devastat|e ['devəsteit] опустоша́ть [-ши́ть]; разоря́ть [-ри́ть]; **~ion** [devəs'teiʃən] опустоше́ние.

develop [di'veləp] разви́(ва́)ть(ся); излага́ть [изложи́ть] (пробле́му); *phot.* проявля́ть [-ви́ть]; *Am.* обнару́жи(ва)ть; **~ment** [-mənt] разви́тие; эволю́ция; рост; расшире́ние; собы́тие.

deviat|e ['di:vieit] отклоня́ться [-ни́ться]; уклоня́ться [-ни́ться]; **~ion** [di:vi'eiʃən] отклоне́ние; девиа́ция (ко́мпаса); *pol.* укло́н.

device [di'vais] приспособле́ние, изобрете́ние; деви́з, эмбле́ма; leave a p. to his own ~s предоставля́ть челове́ка самому́ себе́.

devil [devl] **1.** дья́вол, чёрт, бес; **2.** *v/i.* исполня́ть черново́ю рабо́ту для како́го-либо литера́тора; **~ish** [-iʃ] □ дья́вольский; а́дский; **~(t)ry** чёрная ма́гия; чертовщи́на.

devious ['di:viəs] □ блужда́ющий.

devise [di'vaiz] **1.** ⚖ завеща́ние; **2.** приду́м(ыв)ать; изобрета́ть [-рести́]; ⚖ завеща́ть (*im*)*pf.*

devoid [di'vɔid] (of) лишённый (Р).

devot|e [di'vout] посвяща́ть [-яти́ть] (В/Д); отд(ав)а́ть; **~ed** [-id] □ пре́данный; привя́занный; **~ion** [di'vouʃən] пре́данность *f*, привя́занность *f*; ~s *pl.* религио́зные обря́ды *m/pl.*, моли́твы *f/pl.*

devour [di'vauə] пож(и)ра́ть.

devout [di'vaut] □ благогове́йный; на́божный, благочести́вый.

dew [dju:] **1.** роса́; *poet.* све́жесть *f*; **2.** ороша́ть [ороси́ть]; **~y** покры́тый росо́й; вла́жный.

dexter|ity [deks'teriti] прово́рство; ло́вкость *f*; **~ous** ['dekstərəs] □ ло́вкий; прово́рный.

diabolic(al □) [daiə'bɔlik(əl)] дья́вольский; *fig.* жесто́кий; злой.

diagram ['daiəgræm] диагра́мма; схе́ма.

dial ['daiəl] **1.** цифербла́т; со́лнечные часы́ *m/pl.*; *teleph.* диск; **2.** *teleph.* набира́ть но́мер.

dialect ['daiəlekt] диале́кт, наре́чие.

dialogue ['daiəlɔg] диало́г; разгово́р.

diameter [dai'æmitə] диа́метр.

diamond ['daiəmənd] алма́з; бриллиа́нт; ромб; ~s *pl. cards*: бу́бны *f/pl.*

diaper ['daiəpə] пелёнка.

diaphragm ['daiəfræm] диафра́гма *a. opt.*; *teleph.* мембра́на.

diary ['daiəri] дневни́к.

dice [dais] **1.** (*pl.* от die²) ко́сти *f/pl.*; **2.** игра́ть в ко́сти; **~-box** стака́нчик для игра́льных косте́й.

dicker ['dikə] *Am.* торгова́ться по мелоча́м.

dictat|e 1. ['dikteit] предписа́ние; веле́ние; *pol.* дикта́т; **2.** [dik'teit] [про]диктова́ть (*a. fig.*); предпи́сывать [-са́ть]; **~ion** [dik'teiʃən] дикто́вка, дикта́нт; предписа́ние; **~orship** [dik'teitəʃip] диктату́ра.

diction ['dikʃən] ди́кция; **~ary** [-ri] слова́рь *m.*

did [did] *pt.* от do.

die¹ [dai] умира́ть [умере́ть]; сконча́ться *pf.*; F томи́ться жела́нием; ~ away, ~ down замира́ть [-мере́ть] (о зву́ке); затиха́ть [-и́хнуть] (о ве́тре); увяда́ть [-я́нуть]; угаса́ть [уга́снуть].

die² [~] (*pl.* dice) игра́льная кость *f*; (*pl.* dies [daiz]) ⊕ штамп; чека́н; lower ~ ма́трица.

diet ['daiət] **1.** пи́ща, стол; дие́та; **2.** *v/t.* держа́ть на дие́те; *v/i.* быть на дие́те.

differ ['difə] различа́ться, отлича́ться; не соглаша́ться [-ласи́ться], расходи́ться [разойти́сь] (*from* с Т, in в П); **~ence** ['difrəns] ра́зница; разли́чие; разногла́сие; ⅍ ра́зность *f*; **~ent** [-t] □ ра́зный; друго́й, не тако́й (from как), ино́й; **~entiate** [difə'renʃieit] различа́ть (-ся) [-чи́ть(ся)], отлича́ть(ся) [-чи́ть(ся)].

difficult ['difikəlt] □ тру́дный; тре́бовательный; **~y** тру́дность *f*; затрудне́ние.
diffiden|ce ['difidəns] неуве́ренность *f*; засте́нчивость *f*; **~t** [-dənt] □ неуве́ренный; засте́нчивый.
diffus|e 1. [di'fju:z] *fig.* распространя́ть [-ни́ть]; разглаша́ть [-ласи́ть]; 2. [di'fju:s] □ распространённый; рассе́янный (о све́те); **~ion** [di'fju:ʒən] распростране́ние; рассе́ивание.
dig [dig] 1. [*irr.*] копа́ться; [вы́]копа́ть; ры́ться; [вы́]рыть; 2. F толчо́к, тычо́к.
digest 1. [di'dʒest] перева́ривать [-ри́ть] (пи́щу); усва́ивать [усво́ить]; *v/i.* перева́риваться [-ри́ться]; усва́иваться [усво́иться]; 2. ['daidʒest] о́черк, резюме́ *n indecl.*; ⚖ сво́д зако́нов; **~ible** [di'dʒestəbl] удобовари́мый; *fig.* легко́ усва́иваемый; **~ion** [-tʃən] пищеваре́ние.
dignif|ied ['dignifaid] досто́йный; вели́чественный; **~y** [-fai] возводи́ть в сан; *fig.* облагора́живать [-ро́дить].
dignit|ary ['dignitəri] сано́вник; **~y** [-ti] досто́инство; сан.
digress [dai'gres] отступа́ть [-пи́ть]; отклоня́ться [-ни́ться] (от те́мы).
dike [daik] 1. да́мба; плоти́на; гать *f*; 2. ока́пывать рвом; защища́ть да́мбой; осуша́ть кана́вами.
dilapidate [di'læpideit] приходи́ть в упа́док; приводи́ть в упа́док.
dilat|e [dai'leit] расширя́ть(ся) [-ши́рить(ся)]; **~ory** ['dilətəri] □ ме́дленный; запозда́лый.
diligen|ce ['dilidʒəns] прилежа́ние, усе́рдие; **~t** □ приле́жный, усе́рдный.
dilute [dai'lju:t] разбавля́ть [-ба́вить]; разводи́ть [-вести́].
dim [dim] 1. □ ту́склый, нея́сный (свет); сла́бый (о зре́нии); сму́тный (о воспомина́ниях); 2. [по-] тускне́ть; [за]тума́нить(ся).
dime [daim] *Am.* моне́та в 10 це́нтов (= 0,1 до́ллара).
dimin|ish [di'miniʃ] уменьша́ть(ся) [уме́ньши́ть(ся)]; убы́(ва́)ть; **~ution** [dimi'nju:ʃən] уменьше́ние; убавле́ние; **~utive** [di'minjutiv] □ миниатю́рный.
dimple ['dimpl] я́мочка (на щеке́).
din [din] шум; гро́хот.
dine [dain] [по]обе́дать; угоща́ть обе́дом; **~r** ['dainə] обе́дающий; 🚃 (*part. Am.*) ваго́н-рестора́н.
dingle ['diŋgl] глубо́кая лощи́на.
dingy ['dindʒi] □ гря́зный; ту́склый.
dining|-car 🚃 ваго́н-рестора́н; **~-room** столо́вая.
dinner ['dinə] обе́д; **~-party** го́сти на зва́ном обе́де.
dint [dint]: by ~ of посре́дством (Р).
dip [dip] 1. *v/t.* погружа́ть [-узи́ть]; окуна́ть [-ну́ть]; обма́кивать [-кну́ть]; *v/i.* погружа́ться [-узи́ться], окуна́ться [-ну́ться]; салютова́ть (фла́гом) (*im*)*pf.*; спуска́ться [-сти́ться]; 2. погруже́ние; отко́с; F карма́нник.
diploma [di'ploumə] дипло́м; свиде́тельство; **~cy** [-si] диплома́тия; **~t** *s.* **~tist**; **tic(al** □) [diplo'mætik, -ikəl] дипломати́ческий; **~tist** [di'ploumətist] диплома́т.
dipper ['dipə] ковш; черпа́к.
dire ['daiə] ужа́сный.
direct [di'rekt] 1. □ прямо́й; непосре́дственный; диаметра́льный; я́сный; откры́тый; ~ current ⚡ постоя́нный ток; ~ train беспереса́дочный по́езд; 2. *adv.* = **~ly**: непосре́дственно; пря́мо, неме́дленно; 3. руководи́ть (Т); управля́ть (Т); направля́ть [-а́вить]; ука́зывать доро́гу (Д); **~ion** [di'rekʃən] руково́дство; указа́ние; инстру́кция; направле́ние; **~ion-finder** радиопеленга́тор; **~ive** [di'rektiv] директи́вный; направля́ющий; **~ly** [-li] 1. *adv.* пря́мо, непосре́дственно; неме́дленно; 2. *cj.* как то́лько.
director [di'rektə] руководи́тель *m*, дире́ктор; *films* режиссёр; board of **~s** наблюда́тельный сове́т; **~ate** [-rit] дире́кция; правле́ние; дире́кторство; **~y** [-ri] а́дресная (и́ли телефо́нная) кни́га.
dirge [də:dʒ] погреба́льная песнь *f*.
dirigible ['diridʒəbl] дирижа́бль *m*.
dirt [də:t] грязь *f*; нечисто́ты *f/pl.*; **~-cheap** F дешёвле па́реной ре́пы; **~y** ['də:ti] 1. □ гря́зный; неприли́чный, скабрёзный; нена́стный (о пого́де); 2. загрязня́ть [-ни́ть].
disability [disə'biliti] неспосо́бность *f*, бесси́лие.
disable [dis'eibl] де́лать неприго́дным; [ис]кале́чить; **~d** [-d] искале́ченный; ~ veteran инвали́д войны́.
disadvantage [disəd'vɑ:ntidʒ] невы́года; уще́рб; неудо́бство.
disagree [disə'gri:] расходи́ться во взгля́дах; противоре́чить друг дру́гу; быть вре́дным (with для Р); **~able** [-əbl] □ неприя́тный; **~ment** [-mənt] разла́д, разногла́сие.
disappear [disə'piə] исчеза́ть [-е́знуть]; скры́(ва́)ться; **~ance** [-rəns] исчезнове́ние.
disappoint [disə'pɔint] разочаро́вывать [-рова́ть]; обма́нывать [-ну́ть]; **~ment** разочарова́ние.
disapprov|al [disə'pru:vəl] неодобре́ние; **~e** ['disəpru:v] не одобря́ть [одо́брить] (Р); неодобри́тельно относи́ться (of к Д).
disarm [dis'ɑ:m] *v/t.* обезору́жи(ва)ть; разоружа́ть [-жи́ть];

v/i. разоружáться [-жи́ться]; **~ament** [dis'ɑːməmənt] разоружéние.
disarrange ['dise'reindʒ] расстрáивать [-рóить]; приводи́ть в беспоря́док.
disast|er [di'zɑːstə] бéдствие; катастрóфа; **~rous** [-rəs] □ бéдственный; катастрофи́ческий.
disband [dis'bænd] распускáть [-усти́ть].
disbelieve [disbi'liːv] не [по]вéрить; не доверя́ть (Д).
disburse [dis'bəːs] расплáчиваться [-лати́ться].
disc [disk] *s.* disk.
discard [dis'kɑːd] отбрáсывать [-рóсить] (за ненáдобностью); отвергáть [-éргнуть].
discern [di'səːn] различáть [-чи́ть]; распозн(ав)áть; разглядéть *pf.*; отличáть [-чи́ть]; **~ing** [-iŋ] □ проницáтельный; **~ment** [-mənt] распознавáние; проницáтельность *f.*
discharge [dis'tʃɑːdʒ] **1.** *v/t.* разгружáть [-узи́ть]; освобождáть [-боди́ть]; увольня́ть [увóлить]; уплáчивать [уплати́ть] (долги́); выполня́ть [вы́полнить] (обязáтельства); *v/i.* разряжáться [-яди́ться]; гнои́ться; **2.** разгру́зка; вы́стрел; освобождéние; увольнéние; разря́д; выполнéние.
disciple [di'saibl] учени́к (-и́ца); послéдователь(ница *f*) *m.*
discipline ['disiplin] **1.** дисципли́на, поря́док; **2.** дисциплини́ровать (*im*)*pf.*
disclose [dis'klouz] обнару́живать(ва)ть; разоблачáть [-чи́ть]; раскры́(вá)ть.
discolo(u)r [dis'kʌlə] обесцвéчивать(ся) [-éтить(ся)].
discomfort [dis'kʌmfət] **1.** неудóбство; беспокóйство; **2.** причиня́ть неудóбство (Д).
discompose [diskəm'pouz] расстрáивать [-рóить]; [вз]волновáть, [вс]тревóжить.
disconcert [diskən'səːt] смущáть [смути́ть]; приводи́ть в замешáтельство.
disconnect [diskə'nekt] разъединя́ть [-ни́ть] (*a.* ⚡); разобщáть [-щи́ть]; расцепля́ть [-пи́ть]; **~ed** [-id] □ бессвя́зный; отры́вистый.
disconsolate [dis'kɔnsəlit] □ неутéшный.
discontent ['diskən'tent] недовóльство; неудовлетворённость *f*; **~ed** [-id] □ недовóльный; неудовлетворённый.
discontinue ['diskən'tinjuː] прер(ы)вáть; прекращáть [-рати́ть].
discord ['diskɔːd], **~ance** [dis'kɔːdəns] разноглáсие; разлáд; ♪ диссонáнс.
discount 1. ['diskaunt] ✝ дискóнт, учёт векселéй; ски́дка; **2.** [dis'kaunt] ✝ дисконти́ровать (*im*)*pf.*, учи́тывать [учéсть] (векселя́); дéлать ски́дку.
discourage [dis'kʌridʒ] обескурáживать(ва)ть; отбивáть охóту (Д; from к Д); **~ment** [-mənt] обескурáженность *f*, упáдок ду́ха.
discourse [dis'kɔːs] **1.** рассуждéние; речь *f*; бесéда, разговóр; **2.** орáторствовать; вести́ бесéду.
discourte|ous [dis'kəːtiəs] □ невéжливый, неучти́вый; **~sy** [-tisi] невéжливость *f*, неучти́вость *f.*
discover [dis'kʌvə] дéлать откры́тие (Р); обнару́жи(ва)ть, раскры́(вá)ть; **~y** [-ri] откры́тие.
discredit [dis'kredit] **1.** дискредитáция; **2.** дискредити́ровать (*im*)*pf.*; [о]позóрить.
discreet [dis'kriːt] □ осторóжный; не болтли́вый.
discrepancy [dis'krepənsi] разноглáсие; рáзница; несхóдство.
discretion [dis'kreʃən] благоразу́мие; осторóжность *f*; усмотрéние.
discriminat|e [dis'krimineit] выделя́ть [вы́делить]; относи́ться по-рáзному; умéть распознавáть, различáть; ~ against стáвить в неблагоприя́тные услóвия (В); **~ing** [-iŋ] □ умéющий различáть, распознавáть; **~ion** [-'neiʃən] проницáтельность *f*; дискриминáция.
discuss [dis'kʌs] обсуждáть [-уди́ть], дискути́ровать; **~ion** [-ʃən] обсуждéние, диску́ссия; прéния *n/pl.*
disdain [dis'dein] **1.** презирáть [-зрéть]; считáть ни́же своегó достóинства; **2.** презрéние; пренебрежéние. [больнóй.]
disease [di'ziːz] болéзнь *f*; **~d** [-d]
disembark ['disim'bɑːk] сходи́ть нá берег (с су́дна); выгружáть [вы́грузить] (товáры).
disengage ['disin'geidʒ] высвобождáть(ся) [вы́свободить(ся)]; разобщáть [-щи́ть]; ⊕ разъединя́ть [-ни́ть].
disentangle ['disin'tæŋgl] распу́т(ыв)ать(ся); *fig.* выпу́тываться [вы́путать(ся)] (из затруднéний).
disfavo(u)r ['dis'feivə] **1.** неми́лость *f*; **2.** не одобря́ть [одóбрить].
disfigure [dis'figə] обезобрáживать [-рáзить]; искажáть [искази́ть].
disgorge [dis'gɔːdʒ] извергáть [-éргнуть] (лáву); изрыгáть [-гну́ть] (пи́щу).
disgrace [dis'greis] **1.** неми́лость *f*; позóр, бесчéстие; **2.** [о]позóрить; подвéргнуть неми́лости; **~ful** [-ful] □ посты́дный, позóрный.
disguise [dis'gaiz] **1.** маскирóвка; переодевáние; мáска; **2.** [за]маскировáть(ся); переодé(вá)ть(ся); скры(вá)ть.

disgust [dis'gʌst] **1.** отвращéние; **2.** внушáть отвращéние (Д); **~ing** [-iŋ] □ отвратúтельный.

dish [diʃ] **1.** блюдо, тарéлка, мúска; **~s** *pl.* посýда; блюдо, кýшанье; **2.** класть на блюдо; (*mst* **~ up**) подавáть на стол.

dishearten [dis'hɑːtn] приводúть в унынúе.

dishevel(l)ed [di'ʃevəld] растрёпанный, взъерóшенный.

dishonest [dis'ɔnist] □ нечéстный; недобросóвестный; **~y** [-i] недобросóвестность *f*; обмáн.

dishono(u)r [dis'ɔnə] **1.** бесчéстие, позóр; **2.** [о]бесчéстить, [о]позóрить; **~able** [-rəbl] □ бесчéстный; нúзкий.

disillusion [disi'luːʒən] **1.** разочаровáние; **2.** (*a.* **~ize** [-aiz]) разрушáть иллюзии (Р); открывáть прáвду (Д).

disinclined ['disin'klaind] нерасполóженный.

disinfect ['disin'fekt] дезинфицúровать (*im*)*pf.*; **~ant** [-ənt] дезинфицúрующее срéдство.

disintegrate [dis'intigreit] распадáться [-пáсться]; разрушáться [-ýшиться].

disinterested [dis'intristid] □ бескорыстный; беспристрáстный.

disk [disk] диск.

dislike [dis'laik] **1.** не любúть; питáть отвращéние к (Д); **2.** нелюбóвь *f* (for к Д); антипáтия.

dislocate ['dislokeit] вывúхивать [вывихнуть]; нарушáть [нарýшить]; расстрáивать [-рóить].

dislodge [dis'lɔdʒ] смещáть [сместúть]; изгонять [изогнáть].

disloyal [dis'lɔiəl] □ нелояльный; верολóмный.

dismal ['dizməl] □ мрáчный; унылый; гнетýщий.

dismantl|e [dis'mæntl] ⚓ расснáщивать [-настúть]; ⊕ демонтúровать (*im*)*pf.*; **~ing** [-iŋ] демонтáж.

dismay [dis'mei] **1.** унынúе; страх; **2.** *v/t.* приводúть в унынúе.

dismiss [dis'mis] *v/t.* отпускáть [-стúть]; увольнять [увóлить]; освобождáть [-бодúть]; ⚖ прекращáть [-ратúть] (дéло); отклонять [-нúть] (иск); **~al** [-əl] рóспуск; увольнéние; освобождéние; ⚖ отклонéние.

dismount ['dis'maunt] *v/t.* разнимáть [-нять]; ⊕ разбирáть [разобрáть]; *v/i.* слезáть с лóшади, спéши(ва)ться.

disobedien|ce [diso'biːdʒəns] непослушáние, неповиновéние; **~t** [-t] □ непослýшный, непокóрный.

disobey ['diso'bei] ослýшаться *pf.* (Р), не повиновáться (*im*)*pf.* (Д).

disorder [dis'ɔːdə] **1.** беспорядок; ⚕ расстрóйство; **~s** *pl.* мáссовые волнéния *n/pl.*; **2.** приводúть в беспорядок; расстрáивать [-рóить] (здорóвье); **~ly** [-li] беспорядочный; беспокóйный; распýщенный.

disorganize [dis'ɔːgənaiz) дезорганизовáть (*im*)*pf.*, расстрáивать [-рóить].

disown [dis'oun] не призн(ав)áть; откáзываться [-зáться] от (Р).

dispassionate [dis'pæʃnit] □ беспристрáстный; бесстрáстный.

dispatch [dis'pætʃ] **1.** отпрáвка; отправлéние; депéша; донесéние; **by ~** с курьéром **2.** пос(ы)лáть; отправлять [-áвить].

dispel [dis'pel] рассéивать [-сéять]; разгонять [разогнáть].

dispensa|ry [dis'pensəri] аптéка; амбулатóрия; **~tion** [dispen'seiʃən] раздáча; разделéние; велéние (судьбы); освобождéние.

dispense [dis'pens] *v/t.* освобождáть [-бодúть]; приготовлять и распределять (лекáрства); отправлять [-áвить] (правосýдие).

disperse [dis'pəːs] разгонять [разогнáть]; рассéивать(ся) [-éять (-ся)]; распространять [-нúть].

dispirit [dis'pirit] удручáть [-чúть]; приводúть в унынúе.

displace [dis'pleis] смещáть [сместúть]; переставлять [-áвить]; перекладывать [переложúть]; вытеснять [вытеснить].

display [dis'plei] **1.** выставлять [выставить] (в витрúне); проявлять [-вúть]; выставлять напокáз; **2.** выставка; проявлéние.

displeas|e [dis'pliːz] не [по]нрáвиться (Д); быть не по вкýсу (Д); **~ed** [-d] □ недовóльный; **~ure** [dis'pleʒə] недовóльство.

dispos|al [dis'pouzəl] расположéние; распоряжéние; употреблéние; удалéние (нечистóт и т. п.); **~e** [dis'pouz] *v/t.* располагáть [-ложúть] (В); склонять [-нúть]; *v/i.* **~ of** распоряжáться [-ядúться] (Т); отдéл(ыв)аться от (Р); **~ed** [-d] □ располóженный; настрóенный; **~ition** [dispə'ziʃən] расположéние; распоряжéние; предрасположéние (к Д), склóнность *f* (к Д).

disproof ['dis'pruːf] опровержéние.

disproportionate [disprə'pɔːʃənit] □ непропорционáльный, несоразмéрный.

disprove ['dis'pruːv] опровергáть [-вéргнуть].

dispute [dis'pjuːt] **1.** оспáривать [оспóрить]; пререкáться; [по]спóрить; **2.** дúспут; дебáты *m/pl.*; полéмика.

disqualify [dis'kwɔlifai] дисквалифицúровать (*im*)*pf.*; лишáть прáва.

disregard ['disri'gɑ:d] **1.** пренебрежéние; игнорúрование; **2.** игнорúровать *(im)pf.*; пренебрегáть [-брéчь] (T).
disreput|able [dis'repjutəbl] □ дискредитúрующий; пóльзующийся дурнóй репутáцией; **~e** ['disri'pju:t] дурнáя слáва.
disrespect ['disris'pekt] неуважéние, непочтúтельность *f*; **~ful** [-ful] □ непочтúтельный.
dissatis|faction ['dissætis'fækʃən] недовóльство; **~factory** [-təri] неудовлетворúтельный; **~fy** ['dis'sætisfai] не удовлетворя́ть [-рúть].
dissect [di'sekt] рассекáть [-éчь]; вскры(вá)ть (труп).
dissemble [di'sembl] *v/t.* скры(вá)ть; *v/i.* притворя́ться [-рúться], лицемéрить.
dissen|sion [di'senʃən] разноглáсие; рáспря, разлáд; **~t** [-t] **1.** несоглáсие; **2.** расходúться во взгля́дах, мнéниях.
dissimilar ['di'similə] □ непохóжий, несхóдный, разнорóдный.
dissimulation [disimju'leiʃən] симуля́ция; притвóрство, обмáн, лицемéрие.
dissipat|e ['disipeit] рассéивать [-éять]; растoчáть [-чúть], растрáчивать [-трáтить]; **~ion** [disi'peiʃən] рассéяние; расточéние; беспýтный óбраз жúзни.
dissoluble [di'sɔljubl] ⚗ растворúмый; расторжúмый (о брáке, договóре).
dissolut|e ['disəlu:t] □ распýщенный; беспýтный; **~ion** [disə'lu:ʃən] расторжéние (брáка, договóра); рóспуск (парлáмента).
dissolve [di'zɔlv] *v/t.* распускáть [-устúть] (парлáмент и т. п.); расторгáть [-óргнуть]; аннулúровать *(im)pf.*; *v/i.* растворя́ться [-рúться]; разлагáться [-ложúться].
dissonant ['disonənt] ♪ нестрóйный, диссонúрующий.
dissuade [di'sweid] отговáривать [-ворúть] (from от P).
distan|ce ['distəns] **1.** расстоя́ние; даль *f*; промежýток, перúод (врéмени); at a ~ на извéстном расстоя́нии; **2.** оставля́ть далекó позадú себя́; размещáть на рáвном расстоя́нии; **~t** [-t] □ дáльний, далёкий; отдалённый; сдéржанный; холóдный.
distaste ['dis'teist] отвращéние; **~ful** [-ful] □ протúвный, неприя́тный (на вкус, вид; to Д).
distemper [dis'tempə] нездорóвье; собáчья чумá.
distend [dis'tend] надý(вá)ть(ся).
distil [dis'til] сочúться, кáпать; гнать (спирт и т. п.); ⚗ перегоня́ть [-гнáть], дистиллúровать *(im)pf.*; **~lery** [-əri] винокýренный завóд.
distinct [dis'tiŋkt] □ осóбый, индивидуáльный; отчётливый; определённый; **~ion** [dis'tiŋkʃən] различéние; отлúчие; отличúтельная осóбенность *f*; знак отлúчия; **~ive** [-tiv] □ отличúтельный, характéрный.
distinguish [dis'tiŋgwiʃ] различáть [-чúть]; разгля́дывать [-дéть]; выделя́ть [вы́делить]; **~ed** [-t] выдаю́щийся, извéстный.
distort [-'tɔ:t] искажáть [искaзúть]; искривля́ть [-вúть]; извращáть [-ратúть].
distract [dis'trækt] отвлекáть [отвлéчь], рассéивать [-éять]; **~ion** [dis'trækʃən] развлечéние; отвлечéние (внимáния).
distress [dis'tres] **1.** гóре; бéдствие; страдáние; нуждá, нищетá; **2.** причиня́ть гóре, страдáние (Д); **~ed** [-t] нуждáющийся; страдáющий.
distribut|e [dis'tribju:t] распределя́ть [-лúть]; разд(ав)áть; распространя́ть [-нúть]; **~ion** [dis-tri'bju:ʃən] распределéние; раздáча; распространéние.
district ['distrikt] рай́он; óкруг; óбласть *f*.
distrust [dis'trʌst] **1.** недовéрие; подозрéние; **2.** не доверя́ть (Д); **~ful** [-ful] □ недовéрчивый; подозрúтельный; ~ (of o. s.) невéренный в себé.
disturb [dis'tə:b] [по]беспокóить; [по]мешáть (Д); нарушáть [-ýшить]; **~ance** [-əns] нарушéние; тревóга, волнéние.
disunite ['disju:'nait] разделя́ть [-лúть]; разъединя́ть(ся) [-нúть (-ся)].
disuse ['dis'ju:z] изъя́ть из употреблéния.
ditch [ditʃ] канáва, ров.
ditto ['ditou] то же; стóлько же.
dive [daiv] **1.** ныря́ть [нырнýть]; погружáться [-узúться]; бросáться в вóду; ✈ пикúровать *(im)pf.*; **2.** ныря́ние; погружéние; пикúрование; *Am.* притóн; **~r** ['daivə] водолáз; ныря́льщик (-ица).
diverge [dai'və:dʒ] расходúться [разойтúсь]; отклоня́ться [-нúться], уклоня́ться [-нúться]; **~nce** [-əns] расхождéние; отклонéние, уклонéние; **~nt** [-ənt] □ расходя́щийся; отклоня́ющийся.
divers|e [dai'və:s] □ различный, разнообрáзный; инóй; **~ion** [dai'və:ʃən] развлечéние; **~ity** [-siti] разнообрáзие; различие.
divert [dai'və:t] отводúть в стóрону (дорóгу и т. п.); отвлекáть [-éчь] (внимáние); развлекáть [-éчь].
divest [dai'vest] раздé(вá)ть; *fig.* лишáть [-шúть] (of P).
divid|e [di'vaid] *v/t.* [раз]делúть;

разделя́ть [-ли́ть]; *v/i.* [раз]дели́ться; разделя́ться [-ли́ться]; ♁ дели́ться без оста́тка; **~end** ['dividend] дивиде́нд; ♁ дели́мое.
divine [di'vain] **1.** □ боже́ственный; ~ service богослуже́ние; **2.** уга́дывать [-да́ть].
diving ['daiviŋ] ныря́ние; *sport* прыжки́ в во́ду.
divinity [di'viniti] богосло́вие; божество́; боже́ственность *f*.
divis|ible [di'vizəbl] □ дели́мый; **~ion** [di'viʒən] деле́ние; разделе́ние; перегоро́дка; ⚔ диви́зия; ♁ деле́ние без оста́тка.
divorce [di'vɔ:s] **1.** разво́д; разры́в; **2.** расторга́ть брак (Р); разводи́ться [-вести́сь] с (Т).
divulge [dai'vʌldʒ] разглаша́ть [-ласи́ть] (та́йну).
dizz|iness ['dizinis] головокруже́ние; **~y** ['dizi] □ чу́вствующий головокруже́ние; головокружи́тельный.
do [du:] [*irr.*] (*s. a.* done) **1.** *v/t.* [с]де́лать; выполня́ть [вы́полнить]; устра́ивать [-ро́ить]; приготовля́ть [-то́вить]; ~ London осма́тривать Ло́ндон; have done reading ко́нчить чита́ть; F ~ in обма́нывать [-ну́ть]; уби́(ва́)ть; ~ into переводи́ть [-вести́]; ~ over переде́л(ыв)ать; покры́(ва́)ть; обма́з(ыв)ать; ~ up завора́чивать [заверну́ть]; приводи́ть в поря́док; уб(и)ра́ть; **2.** *v/i.* [с]де́лать; поступа́ть [-пи́ть], де́йствовать; ~ so as to ... устра́ивать так, что́бы ...; that will ~ доста́точно, дово́льно; сойдёт; how ~ you ~? здра́вствуй(те)!; как вы пожива́ете?; ~ well успева́ть; хорошо́ вести́ де́ло; ~ away with уничтожа́ть [-о́жить]; I could ~ with ... мне мог бы пригоди́ться (И); ~ without обходи́ться [обойти́сь] без (Р); ~ be quick поспеши́те!, скоре́й!; ~ you like London? — I do вам нра́вится Ло́ндон? — Да.
docil|e ['dousail] послу́шный; поня́тливый; **~ity** [dou'siliti] послуша́ние; поня́тливость *f*.
dock[1] [dɔk] обруба́ть [-руби́ть] (хвост); ко́ротко стричь (во́лосы); *fig.* сокраща́ть [сократи́ть].
dock[2] [~] **1.** ⚓ док; ⚖ скамья́ подсуди́мых; **2.** ⚓ ста́вить су́дно в док; входи́ть в док.
dockyard ['dɔkjɑ:d] верфь *f*.
doctor ['dɔktə] **1.** врач; до́ктор (учёная сте́пень); **2.** F лечи́ть.
doctrine ['dɔktrin] уче́ние, доктри́на.
document **1.** ['dɔkjumənt] докуме́нт; свиде́тельство; **2.** [-'mənt] подтвержда́ть докуме́нтами.
dodge [dɔdʒ] **1.** увёртка, уло́вка, хи́трость *f*; **2.** увиливать [-льну́ть]; [с]хитри́ть; избега́ть [-ежа́ть] (Р).
doe [dou] са́мка (оле́ня, за́йца, кры́сы, кро́лика).
dog [dɔg] **1.** соба́ка, пёс; **2.** ходи́ть по пята́м (Р); высле́живать [вы́следить].
dogged ['dɔgid] □ упря́мый, упо́рный, насто́йчивый.
dogma ['dɔgmə] до́гма; до́гмат; **~tic(al** □) [dɔg'mætik, -ikəl] догмати́ческий; **~tism** ['dɔgmətizm] догмати́зм.
dog's-ear F заги́б (за́гнутый у́гол страни́цы).
dog-tired ['dɔg'taiəd] уста́лый как соба́ка.
doings ['du:iŋz] де́йствия *n/pl.*, посту́пки *m/pl.*
dole [doul] **1.** *Brt.* посо́бие (безрабо́тным); **2.** выдава́ть ску́по.
doleful ['doulful] □ ско́рбный, печа́льный.
doll [dɔl] ку́кла.
dollar ['dɔlə] до́ллар.
dolly ['dɔli] ку́колка.
dolt [doult] ду́рень *m*, болва́н.
domain [do'mein] владе́ние; име́ние; террито́рия; *fig.* о́бласть *f*, сфе́ра.
dome [doum] ку́пол; свод.
domestic [do'mestik] **1.** (**~al**) дома́шний; семе́йный; домосе́дливый; **2.** дома́шняя рабо́тница; слуга́ *m*; **~ate** [-tikeit] привя́зывать к семе́йной жи́зни; прируча́ть [-чи́ть] (живо́тное).
domicile ['dɔmisail] постоя́нное местожи́тельство; **~d** [-d] осе́длый; прожива́ющий.
domin|ant ['dɔminənt] господ́ствующий, преоблада́ющий; **~ate** [-neit] госпо́дствовать, преоблада́ть; **~ation** [dɔmi'neiʃən] госпо́дство, преоблада́ние; **~eer** [dɔmi'niə] де́йствовать деспоти́чески; влады́чествовать; **~eering** [-riŋ] □ деспоти́ческий, вла́стный.
dominion [də'minjən] доминио́н; владе́ние.
don [dɔn] наде́(ва́)ть.
donat|e [dou'neit] *Am.* [по]же́ртвовать; **~ion** [-ʃən] поже́ртвование.
done [dʌn] **1.** *p. pt.* от do; **2.** *adj.* гото́вый; уста́лый; обма́нутый; well ~ хорошо́ пригото́вленный; прожа́ренный.
donkey ['dɔŋki] осёл.
donor ['dounɔ:] же́ртвователь(ница *f*) *m*; ⚕ до́нор.
doom [du:m] **1.** рок, судьба́; **2.** осужда́ть [осуди́ть]; обрека́ть [-е́чь] (to на В).
door [dɔ:] дверь *f*; next ~ ря́дом; (with)in **~s** внутри́, в до́ме; **~-handle** ру́чка две́ри; **~-keeper**, *Am.* **~man** швейца́р, привра́тник; **~way** вход; пролёт две́ри.
dope [doup] **1.** нарко́тик; F дурма́н; **2.** дава́ть нарко́тики (Д).
dormant ['dɔ:mənt] *mst fig.* безде́йствующий, спя́щий.

dormer(-window) ['dɔ:mə('win-dou)] слуховое окно.
dormitory ['dɔ:mitəri] дортуар, общая спальня; *Am.* общежитие.
dose [dous] **1.** доза, приём; **2.** дозировать *(im)pf.*; давать дозами.
dot [dɔt] **1.** точка; крошечная вещь *f*; **2.** ставить точки над (Т); отмечать пунктиром.
dot|e [dout]: ~ (up)on любить до безумия; **~ing** ['doutiŋ] безумно любящий.
double ['dʌbl] □ двойной; двоякий; двуличный; **2.** двойник; двойное количество; парная игра; *thea.* дублёр; **3.** *v/t.* удваивать [удвоить]; складывать вдвое; ~d up скрючившийся; *v/i.* удваиваться [удвоиться]; **~-breasted** двубортный (пиджак); **~-dealing** двурушничество; **~-edged** обоюдоострый; ~ **entry** ✝ двойная бухгалтерия.
doubt [daut] **1.** *v/t.* сомневаться [усомниться] в (П); не доверять (Д); подозревать; *v/i.* иметь сомнения; **2.** сомнение; no ~ без сомнения; **~ful** ['dautful] □ сомнительный; **~fulness** [-nis] сомнительность *f*; **~less** ['dautlis] несомненно; вероятно.
douche [du:ʃ] **1.** душ; обливание; **2.** принимать душ; обливать(ся) водой.
dough [dou] тесто; **~nut** ['dounʌt] пончик.
dove [dʌv] голубь *m*; *fig.* голубчик (-бушка).
dowel ['dauəl] ⊕ дюбель *m*, штифт.
down[1] [daun] пух; холм; безлесная возвышенность *f*.
down[2] [~] **1.** *adv.* вниз, внизу; ~ to вплоть до (Р); F be ~ upon нападать [напасть] на (В); **2.** *prp.* вниз по (Д); вдоль по (Д); ~ the river вниз по реке; **3.** *adj.* направленный вниз; ~ platform перрон для поездов, идущих из столицы (или большого города); **4.** *v/t.* опускать [опустить]; сби(ва)ть (самолёт); одоле(ва)ть; **~cast** ['daunkɑ:st] удручённый; **~fall** падение; **~-hearted** павший духом; **~hill** вниз; под гору; **~pour** ливень *m*; **~right 1.** *adv.* совершенно; прямо; **2.** *adj.* прямой; откровенный, честный; **~stairs** ['daun'stɛəz] вниз, внизу; **~stream** вниз по течению; **~town** *part. Am.* в деловую часть города, в деловой части города; **~ward(s)** [-wəd(z)] вниз, книзу.
downy ['dauni] пушистый, мягкий как пух; *sl.* хитрый.
dowry ['dauəri] приданое.
doze [douz] **1.** дремота; **2.** дремать, «клевать носом».
dozen ['dʌzn] дюжина.
drab [dræb] желтовато-серый; однообразный.
draft [drɑ:ft] **1.** = draught; чек; сумма, полученная по чеку; ⚔ пополнение, подкрепление; **2.** набрасывать [-росать].
drag [dræg] **1.** обуза, бремя *n*; драга; борона; **2.** *v/t.* [по]тянуть, [по]волочить; чистить дно (реки и т. п.); *v/i.* [по]волочиться; ~ on тянуться (о времени).
dragon ['drægən] дракон; **~-fly** стрекоза.
drain [drein] **1.** дренаж; канализация; водосток; **2.** *v/t.* дренировать *(im)pf.*; истощать [-щить]; осушать [-шить]; **~age** ['dreinidʒ] дренаж; сток; канализация.
drake [dreik] селезень *m*.
drama|tic [drə'mætik] (~ally) драматический; драматичный; **~tist** ['dræmətist] драматург; **~tize** [-taiz] драматизировать *(im)pf.*
drank [dræŋk] *pt.* от drink.
drape [dreip] [за]драпировать; располагать складками; **~ry** ['dreipəri] драпировка; ткани *f/pl.*
drastic ['dræstik] (~ally) решительный, крутой (о мерах).
draught [drɑ:ft] тяга; сквозняк; глоток; черновик, набросок; ⚓ водоизмещение; ~s *pl.* шашки *f/pl.*; *s.* draft; ~ beer пиво в бочке; **~-horse** ломовая лошадь *f*; **~sman** [-smən] чертёжник.
draw [drɔ:] **1.** [*irr.*] [на]рисовать; [по]тянуть; [по]тащить; вырывать [вырвать]; черпать (воду); привлекать [-ечь] (внимание); выводить [вывести] (заключение); кончать (игру) вничью; ~ near приближаться [-лизиться]; ~ out вытягивать [вытянуть]; ~ up составлять [-авить] (документ) [останавливаться [-новиться]; ~ (up)on ✝ выставить вексель на (В); **2.** тяга; жеребьёвка; F гвоздь *m* (сезона, вечера и т. п.); **~back** ['drɔ:-bæk] помеха; недостаток; ✝ возвратная пошлина; **~er 1.** ['drɔ:ə] чертёжник; ✝ трассант; **2.** [drɔ:] выдвижной ящик; (a pair of) ~s *pl.* кальсоны *f/pl.*
drawing ['drɔ:iŋ] рисунок; рисование; чертёж; черчение; **~-board** чертёжная доска; **~-room** гостиная.
drawn [drɔ:n] *p. pt.* от draw.
dread [dred] **1.** бояться, страшиться (Р); **2.** страх, боязнь *f*; **~ful** ['dredful] □ ужасный, страшный.
dream [dri:m] **1.** сон, сновидение; мечта; грёза; **2.** [*a. irr.*] видеть во сне; мечтать; грезить; воображать [-разить]; **~er** ['dri:mə] мечтатель(ница *f*) *m*, фантазёр(ка); **~y** [-i] □ мечтательный.
dreary ['driəri] □ тоскливый; скучный.
dredge [dredʒ] **1.** землечерпалка,

дра́га, экскава́тор; **2.** драги́ровать (*im*)*pf.*; углубля́ть фарва́тер.
dregs [dregz] *pl.* оса́док; небольшо́й оста́ток; подо́нки *m/pl.*
drench [drentʃ] **1.** промока́ние (под дождём); **2.** прома́чивать насквозь.
dress [dres] **1.** оде́жда, пла́тье; одея́ние; *thea.* ~ rehearsal генера́льная репети́ция; **2.** оде́(ва́)ть (-ся); украша́ть(ся) [укра́сить(ся)]; де́лать причёску; ⚔ равня́ться [вы́ровняться]; выра́внивать [вы́ровнять]; ⚕ перевя́зывать [-за́ть]; **~-circle** *thea.* бельэта́ж; **~er** ['dresə] ку́хонный шкаф; *Am.* туале́тный сто́лик.
dressing ['dresiŋ] перевя́зочный материа́л; перевя́зка; *cook.* припра́ва; ~ down вы́говор, головомо́йка; **~-gown** хала́т; **~table** туале́тный сто́лик.
dress|maker портни́ха; **~-parade** вы́ставка мод.
drew ['dru:] *pt.* от draw.
dribble ['dribl] ка́пать; пуска́ть слю́ни.
dried [draid] сухо́й; вы́сохший.
drift [drift] **1.** дрейф; сугро́б (сне́га); нано́с (песка́); *fig.* стремле́ние; тенде́нция; **2.** *v/t.* относи́ть [отнести́]; наноси́ть [нанести́]; мести́ (сне́г, о ве́тре); *v/i.* дрейфова́ть (*im*)*pf.*; скопля́ться ку́чами (о ли́стьях и т. п.); *fig.* безде́йствовать, быть пасси́вным, не сопротивля́ться.
drill [dril] **1.** сверло́; бура́в; коловоро́т; физи́ческое упражне́ние; ↗ борозда́; ⚔ строево́е обуче́ние; **2.** [на]тренирова́ть; ⚔ проводи́ть строево́е обуче́ние.
drink [driŋk] **1.** питьё; напи́ток; **2.** [*irr.*] [вы́]пить; пья́нствовать.
drip [drip] **1.** ка́пание; **2.** ка́пать.
drive [draiv] **1.** ката́нье, езда́; подъездна́я алле́я (к до́му); ⚔ уда́р, ата́ка; ⊕ переда́ча, приво́д; *fig.* эне́ргия; си́ла; **2.** [*irr.*] *v/t.* [по]гнать; вби(ва́)ть (гвоздь и т. п.); вози́ть, [по]везти́ (в автомоби́ле, экипа́же и т. п.); пра́вить (лошадьми́ и т. п.); управля́ть (маши́ной); *v./i.* е́здить, [по]е́хать; ката́ться; [по]нести́сь; ~ at [на-] ме́тить на (В).
drivel ['drivl] **1.** распуска́ть слю́ни; нести́ вздор; **2.** бессмы́слица, чепуха́.
driven ['drivn] *p. pt.* от drive.
driver ['draivə] пого́нщик (скота́); *mot.* шофёр, води́тель *m*; 🚂 машини́ст; ⊕ веду́щее колесо́.
drizzle ['drizl] **1.** ме́лкий дождь *m*, и́зморось *f*; **2.** мороси́ть.
drone [droun] **1.** *zo.* тру́тень *m*; *fig.* безде́льник, лентя́й; **2.** [за-] жужжа́ть; [за]гуде́ть.
droop [dru:p] *v/t.* склоня́ть [-ни́ть] (го́лову); *v/i.* свиса́ть [сви́снуть], поника́ть [-и́кнуть]; увяда́ть [увя́нуть] (о цвета́х).
drop [drɔp] **1.** ка́пля; леденец; паде́ние, пониже́ние; *thea.* за́навес; **2.** *v/t.* роня́ть [урони́ть]; броса́ть [бро́сить] (привы́чку); ~ a p. a line черкну́ть кому́-либо слове́чко; *v/i.* ка́пать [ка́пнуть]; спада́ть [спасть]; па́дать [упа́сть]; понижа́ться [-и́зиться]; ~ in заходи́ть [зайти́], загля́дывать [загляну́ть].
drought [draut] за́суха.
drove [drouv] **1.** гурт, ста́до; **2.** *pt.* от drive.
drown [draun] *v/t.* затопля́ть [-пи́ть]; *fig.* заглуша́ть [-ши́ть] (звук); *v/i.* [у]тону́ть = be ~ed; ~ o. s. [у]топи́ться.
drows|e [drauz] [за]дрема́ть; **~y** ['drausi] со́нный.
drudge [drʌdʒ] исполня́ть ску́чную, тяжёлую рабо́ту, «тяну́ть ля́мку».
drug [drʌg] **1.** лека́рство, медикаме́нт; нарко́тик; **2.** употребля́ть нарко́тики; дава́ть нарко́тики (Д); **~gist** ['drʌgist] апте́карь *m.*
drum [drʌm] **1.** бараба́н; бараба́нный бой; *anat.* бараба́нная перепо́нка; **2.** бить в бараба́н, бараба́нить.
drunk [drʌŋk] **1.** *p. pt.* от drink; **2.** пья́ный; get ~ напива́ться пья́ным; **~ard** ['drʌŋkəd] пья́ница *m/f*; **~en** ['drʌŋkən] пья́ный.
dry [drai] **1.** □ сухо́й, вы́сохший; F жа́ждущий; F антиалкого́льный; ~ goods *pl. Am.* мануфакту́ра; галантере́я; **2.** [вы́]суши́ть; [вы́]со́хнуть; ~ up высу́шивать [вы́сушить]; высыха́ть [вы́сохнуть], пересыха́ть [-со́хнуть] (о реке́ и т. п.); **~-clean** чи́стить хими́чески; **~-nurse** ня́ня.
dual ['dju:əl] □ двойственный; двойно́й.
dubious ['dju:biəs] □ сомни́тельный, подозри́тельный.
duchess ['dʌtʃis] герцоги́ня.
duck [dʌk] **1.** у́тка; наклоне́ние головы́; ныря́ние; F ду́шка; **2.** ныря́ть [нырну́ть]; окуна́ться [-ну́ться]; увёртываться [уверну́ться].
duckling ['dʌkliŋ] утёнок.
dudgeon ['dʌdʒən] оби́да.
due [dju:] **1.** до́лжный, надлежа́щий; обя́занный; ожида́емый; in ~ time в своё вре́мя; it is his ~ ему́ э́то полага́ется; **2.** *adv.* ⚓ то́чно, пря́мо (о стре́лке ко́мпаса); **3.** до́лжное; то, что причита́ется; *mst* ~s *pl.* сбо́ры *m/pl.*, нало́ги *m/pl.*; по́шлины *f/pl.*; чле́нский взнос.
duel ['dju:əl] **1.** ду́эль *f*; **2.** дра́ться на ду́эли.
dug [dʌg] *pt.* и *p. pt.* от dig.

duke [dju:k] ге́рцог; **~dom** ['dju:kdəm] ге́рцогство.
dull [dʌl] **1.** □ тупо́й (*a. fig.*); скучный; ✝ вя́лый; па́смурный (день); **2.** притупля́ть(ся) [-пи́ть (-ся)]; *fig.* де́лать(ся) тупы́м, ску́чным; **~ness** ['dʌlnis] ску́ка; вя́лость *f*; ту́пость *f*.
duly ['dju:li] до́лжным о́бразом.
dumb [dʌm] [немо́й; глу́пый.
dummy ['dʌmi] манеке́н, ку́кла; ⚔ маке́т; *fig.* фикти́вное лицо́.
dump [dʌmp] **1.** сва́лка; ⚔ полево́й склад; **2.** сбра́сывать [сбро́сить]; нава́ливать [-ли́ть]; сва́ливать [-ли́ть] (му́сор); **~s** *pl.* плохо́е настрое́ние; **~ing** ✝ де́мпинг.
dun [dʌn] насто́йчиво тре́бовать упла́ты до́лга.
dunce [dʌns] тупи́ца *m/f*.
dune [dʒu:n] дю́на.
dung [dʌŋ] **1.** наво́з; **2.** унава́живать [унаво́зить].
dungeon ['dʌndʒən] подзе́мная тюрьма́.
duplic|ate **1.** ['dju:plikit] a) двойно́й; запасно́й; b) дублика́т, ко́пия; **2.** [-keit] снима́ть, де́лать ко́пию с (Р); удва́ивать [удво́ить]; **~ity** [dju:'plisiti] двули́чность *f*.
dura|ble ['djuərəbl] [про́чный; долговре́менный; **~tion** [djuə'reiʃən] продолжи́тельность *f*.
duress(e) [djuə'res] принужде́ние.
during ['djuəriŋ] *prp.* в тече́ние (Р), во вре́мя (Р).
dusk [dʌsk] су́мерки; **~y** ['dʌski] □ су́меречный; сму́глый.
dust [dʌst] **1.** пыль *f*; **2.** [за-, на-] пыли́ть; вытира́ть пыль; **~-bin** му́сорный я́щик; **~er** ['dʌstə] пы́льная тря́пка; **~y** ['dʌsti] □ пы́льный.
Dutch [dʌtʃ] **1.** голла́ндец (-дка); **2.** голла́ндский; the ~ голла́ндцы *pl.*
duty ['dju:ti] долг, обя́занность *f*; дежу́рство; по́шлина; off ~ свобо́дный от дежу́рства; **~-free** *adv.* беспо́шлинно.
dwarf [dwɔ:f] **1.** ка́рлик; **2.** меша́ть ро́сту, остана́вливать разви́тие (Р).
dwell [dwel] [*irr.*] жить, пребыва́ть; ~ (up)on заде́рживаться [-жа́ться] на (П); **~ing** ['dweliŋ] жили́ще, дом.
dwelt [dwelt] *pt.* и *p. pt.* от dwell.
dwindle ['dwindl] уменьша́ться [уме́ньши́ться], сокраща́ться [-рати́ться].
dye [dai] **1.** кра́ска; окра́ска; *fig.* of deepest ~ настоя́щий; **2.** [по-] кра́сить, окра́шивать [окра́сить].
dying ['daiiŋ] (*s.* die[1]) **1.** □ умира́ющий; предсме́ртный; **2.** умира́ние.
dynam|ic [dai'næmik] динами́ческий; акти́вный; энерги́чный; **~ics** [-iks] *mst sg.* дина́мика; **~ite** ['dainəmait] **1.** динами́т; **2.** взрыва́ть динами́том.

E

each [i:tʃ] ка́ждый; ~ other друг дру́га.
eager [i:gə] □ стремя́щийся; усе́рдный; энерги́чный; **~ness** [-nis] пыл, рве́ние.
eagle [i:gl] орёл, орли́ца.
ear [iə] у́хо (*pl.*: у́ши); **~-drum** бараба́нная перепо́нка.
earl [ə:l] граф ((англи́йский).
early ['ə:li] **1.** ра́нний; преждевре́менный; **2.** *adv.* ра́но; заблаговре́ммено; as ~ as уже́.
ear-mark ['iəmɑ:k] отмеча́ть [-е́тить].
earn [ə:n] зараба́тывать [-бо́тать]; заслу́живать [-жи́ть].
earnest ['ə:nist] **1.** □ серьёзный; убеждённый; и́скренний; **2.** серьёзность *f*.
earnings ['ə:niŋz] за́работок.
ear|piece ра́ковина телефо́нной тру́бки; **~-shot** преде́лы слы́шимости.
earth [ə:θ] **1.** земля́, земно́й шар; земля́, по́чва; **2.** *v/t.* зары́(ва́)ть; зака́пывать [закопа́ть]; ⚡ заземля́ть [-ли́ть]; **~en** ['ə:θən] земляно́й; **~enware** [-weə] гли́няная посу́да; **~ing** ['ə:θiŋ] ⚡ заземле́ние; **~ly** ['ə:θli] земно́й; *fig.* су́етный; **~quake** [-kweik] землетрясе́ние; **~worm** земляно́й червь *m*.
ease [i:z] **1.** поко́й; лёгкость *f*; непринуждённость *f*; at ~ свобо́дно, удо́бно; **2.** облегча́ть [-чи́ть]; успока́ивать [-ко́ить].
easel ['i:zl] мольбе́рт.
easiness ['i:zinis] *s.* ease 1.
east [i:st] **1.** восто́к; **2.** восто́чный; **3.** *adv.* на восто́к; к восто́ку (of от Р).
Easter ['i:stə] па́сха.
easter|ly ['i:stəli], **~n** ['i:stən] восто́чный.
eastward(s) ['i:stwəd(z)] на восто́к.
easy [i:zi] лёгкий; споко́йный; непринуждённый; take it~! не торопи́(те)сь!; споко́йнее!; **~-chair** кре́сло; **~-going** *fig.* доброду́шный; беззабо́тный.
eat [i:t] **1.** [*irr.*] [съ]есть; разъеда́ть [-е́сть] **2.** [et] *pt.* от eat 1; **~ables** ['i:təblz] *pl.* съестно́е; **~en** ['i:tn] *p. pt.* от eat 1.

eaves [i:vz] *pl.* карни́з; стреха́; **~drop** подслу́ш(ив)ать.
ebb [eb] **1.** (*a.* **~-tide**) отли́в; *fig.* переме́на к ху́дшему; **2.** отли́-(ва́)ть, убы́(ва́)ть (о воде́); *fig.* ослабе́(ва́)ть.
ebony ['ebəni] чёрное де́рево.
ebullition [ebə'liʃən] кипе́ние; вскипа́ние.
eccentric [ik'sentrik] **1.** эксцентри́чный; ⚙ эксцентри́ческий; **2.** чуда́к.
ecclesiastic [ikli:zi'æstik] **1.** ✝, *mst* **~al** □ [-tikəl] духо́вный, церко́вный; **2.** духо́вное лицо́.
echo ['ekou] **1.** э́хо; *fig.* отголо́сок; **2.** отдава́ться как э́хо.
eclipse [i'klips] **1.** затме́ние; **2.** затмева́ть [-ми́ть]; заслоня́ть [-ни́ть].
econom|ic(al □) [i:kə'nɔmik(əl)] экономи́ческий; эконо́мный, бережли́вый; **~ics** [-iks] *pl.* эконо́мика; наро́дное хозя́йство; **~ist** [i:'kɔnəmist] экономи́ст; **~ize** [-maiz] [с]эконо́мить; **~y** [-mi] хозя́йство; эконо́мия; бережли́вость *f*; political ~ полити́ческая эконо́мия.
ecsta|sy ['ekstəsi] экста́з; **~tic** [eks'tætik] (**~ally**) исступлённый.
eddy ['edi] **1.** водоворо́т; **2.** крути́ться в водоворо́те.
edge [edʒ] **1.** край; ле́звие, остриё; кряж, хребе́т (гор); кро́мка (мате́рии); обре́з (кни́ги); be on ~ быть как на иго́лках; **2.** обреза́ть кра́й; окаймля́ть [-ми́ть]; ната́чивать [наточи́ть]; **~ways, ~wise** [-weiz, -waiz] кра́ем, бо́ком.
edging ['edʒiŋ] край, кайма́, бордю́р.
edible ['edibl] съедо́бный.
edifice ['edifis] зда́ние.
edit ['edit] изд(ав)а́ть; [от]редакти́ровать; **~ion** [i'diʃən] изда́ние; **~or** ['editə] изда́тель *m*; реда́ктор; **~orial** [edi'tɔ:riəl] **1.** реда́кторский; редакцио́нный; **2.** передова́я статья́; **~orship** ['editəʃip] реда́кторство.
educat|e ['edju:keit] дава́ть образова́ние (Д); воспи́тывать [-та́ть]; **~ion** [edju'keiʃən] образова́ние; воспита́ние; Board of ♀ министе́рство просвеще́ния; **~ional** [-ʃnl] □ педагоги́ческий; уче́бный; **~or** ['edjukeitə] педаго́г.
eel [i:l] у́горь *m*.
efface [i'feis] стира́ть [стере́ть]; вычёркивать [вы́черкнуть]; *fig.* ~ o. s. стушёвываться [-шева́ться].
effect [i'fekt] **1.** сле́дствие; результа́т; ⊕ производи́тельность *f*; де́йствие; **~s** *pl.* иму́щество; пожи́тки *m/pl.*; take ~, be of ~ вступа́ть в си́лу; in ~ в действи́тельности; to the ~ сле́дующего содержа́ния; **2.** производи́ть [-вести́]; выполня́ть [вы́полнить]; соверша́ть [-ши́ть]; **~ive** [-iv] □ эффекти́вный, действи́тельный; име́ющий си́лу; ⊕ поле́зный; ~ date да́та вступле́ния в си́лу (Р); **~ual** [juəl] □ действи́тельный; ⚖ име́ющий си́лу.
effeminate [i'feminit] □ женоподо́бный.
effervesce [efə'ves] [вс]пе́ниться; игра́ть (о вине́).
effete [e'fi:t] истощённый; беспло́дный.
efficacy ['efikəsi] действи́тельность *f*, си́ла.
efficien|cy [i'fiʃənsi] эффекти́вность *f*; уме́лость *f*; **~t** [-ənt] □ уме́лый, квалифици́рованный; эффекти́вный.
efflorescence [əflɔ:'resns] расцве́т.
effluence ['efluəns] истече́ние; эмана́ция.
effort ['efət] уси́лие; достиже́ние.
effrontery [e'frʌntəri] бессты́дство.
effulgent [e'fʌldʒənt] □ лучеза́рный.
effus|ion [i'fju:ʒən] излия́ние; **~ive** [i'fju:siv] □ экспанси́вный; несде́ржанный.
egg[1] [eg] подстрека́ть [-кну́ть] (*mst ~ on*).
egg[2] [~] яйцо́; buttered, scrambled **~s** *pl.* я́ичница-болту́нья; fried **~s** *pl.* я́ичница-глазу́нья.
egotism ['egoutizm] эготи́зм; самомне́ние.
egress ['i:gres] вы́ход; исто́к, истече́ние.
Egyptian [i'dʒipʃən] **1.** египтя́нин (-я́нка); **2.** еги́петский.
eight [eit] **1.** во́семь; **2.** восьмёрка; **~een** ['ei'ti:n] восемна́дцать; **~eenth** [-θ] восемна́дцатый; **~h** [eitθ] **1.** восьмо́й; **2.** восьма́я часть *f*; **~ieth** ['eitiiθ] восьмидеся́тый; **~y** ['eiti] во́семьдесят.
either ['aiðə] **1.** *pron.* оди́н из двух; тот и́ли друго́й; и тот и друго́й, о́ба; **2.** *cj.* ~ ... or ... и́ли ... и́ли ...; ли́бо ... ли́бо ...; not (...) ~ та́кже не.
ejaculate [i'dʒækjuleit] восклица́ть [-ли́кнуть]; изверга́ть [-е́ргнуть].
eject [i'dʒekt] изгоня́ть [изгна́ть]; выселя́ть [вы́селить]; изверга́ть [-е́ргнуть]; выпуска́ть [вы́пустить] (дым).
eke [i:k]: ~ out восполня́ть [-по́лнить]; ~ out one's existence перебива́ться кое-ка́к.
elaborat|e 1. [i'læbərit] □ сло́жный; тща́тельно вы́работанный; **2.** [-reit] разраба́тывать [-бо́тать]; разви́(ва́)ть; **~eness** [-ritnis], **~ion** [ilæbə'reiʃən] разрабо́тка; разви́тие; уточне́ние.
elapse [i'læps] проходи́ть [пройти́], пролета́ть [-лете́ть] (о вре́мени).
elastic [i'læstik] **1.** [**~ally**] эласти́ч-

ный; упру́гий; **2.** рези́нка (шнур); **~ity** [elæs'tisiti] эласти́чность *f.*
elate [i'leit] **1.** □ лику́ющий; **2.** поднима́ть настрое́ние (Р).
elbow ['elbou] **1.** ло́коть *m*; ⊕ коле́но; уго́льник; at one's ~ под руко́й, ря́дом; **2.** толка́ть локтя́ми; ~ out выта́лкивать [вы́толкнуть].
elder ['eldə] **1.** ста́рший; **2.** ⚘ бузина́; **~ly** ['eldəli] пожило́й.
eldest ['eldist] (са́мый) ста́рший.
elect [i'lekt] **1.** изб(и)ра́ть; выбира́ть [вы́брать]; назнача́ть [-на́чить]; **2.** и́збранный; **~ion** [i'lekʃən] вы́боры *m/pl.*; **~or** [-tə] избира́тель *m*; **~oral** [-tərəl] избира́тельный; **~orate** [-tərit] континге́нт избира́телей.
electri|c [i'lektrik] электри́ческий; ~ circuit электри́ческая цепь *f*; **~cal** [-trikəl] □ электри́ческий; ~ engineering электроте́хника; **~cian** [ilek'triʃən] электромонтёр.
electri|city [ilek'trisiti] электри́чество; **~fy** [i'lektrifai], **~ze** [i'lektraiz] электрифици́ровать (*im*)*pf.*; [на-] электризова́ть.
electro|cute [i'lektrəkju:t] казни́ть на электри́ческом сту́ле.
electron [i'lektrən] электро́н; **~-ray tube** опти́ческий индика́тор настро́йки, «маги́ческий глаз».
electro|plate гальванизи́ровать (*im*)*pf.*; **~type** гальванопла́стика.
elegan|ce ['eligəns] элега́нтность *f*, изя́щество; **~t** ['eligənt] □ элега́нтный, изя́щный.
element ['elimənt] элеме́нт; стихи́я; **~s** *pl.* осно́вы *f/pl.*; **~al** [eli'mentl] □ основно́й; стихи́йный; **~ary** [-təri] □ элемента́рный; elementaries *pl.* осно́вы *f/pl.* (како́й-либо нау́ки).
elephant ['elifənt] слон.
elevat|e ['eliveit] поднима́ть [-ня́ть], повыша́ть [-вы́сить]; *fig.* возвыша́ть [-высить]; **~ion** [eli'veiʃən] возвыше́ние, возвы́шенность *f*; высота́ (над у́ровнем мо́ря); **~or** ['eliveitə] ⊕ элева́тор, грузоподъёмник; *Am.* лифт; ✈ руль высоты́.
eleven [i'levn] оди́ннадцать; **~th** [-θ] **1.** оди́ннадцатый; **2.** оди́ннадцатая часть *f.*
elf [elf] эльф; прока́зник.
elicit [i'lisit] извлека́ть [-е́чь]; вызыва́ть [вы́звать].
eligible ['elidʒəbl] □ могу́щий быть и́збранным; подходя́щий.
eliminat|e [i'limineit] устраня́ть [-ни́ть]; уничтожа́ть [-то́жить]; **~ion** [ilimi'neiʃən] выключе́ние; уничтоже́ние.
elk [elk] *zo.* лось *m.*
elm [elm] ⚘ вяз.
elocution [elə'kju:ʃən] ора́торское иску́сство.
elope [i'loup] [у]бежа́ть (с возлю́бленным).
eloquen|ce ['elokwəns] красноре́чие; **~t** [-t] □ красноречи́вый.
else [els] ещё; кро́ме; и́наче; ино́й, друго́й; or ~ а то; и́ли же; **~where** ['els'wɛə] где́-нибудь в друго́м ме́сте.
elucidat|e [i'lu:sideit] разъясня́ть [-ни́ть]; **~ion** [ilu:si'deiʃən] разъясне́ние.
elude [i'lu:d] избега́ть [-ежа́ть] (Р), уклоня́ться [-ни́ться] от (Р).
elus|ive [i'lu:siv] неулови́мый; **~ory** [-səri] ускольза́ющий.
emaciate [i'meiʃieit] истоща́ть [-щи́ть], изнуря́ть [-ри́ть].
emanat|e ['eməneit] истека́ть [-е́чь]; происходи́ть [произойти́] (from от Р); **~ion** [emə'neiʃən] emана́ция; испуска́ние; *fig.* излуче́ние.
emancipat|e [i'mænsipeit] освободи́ть от ограниче́ний; **~ion** [imænsi'peiʃən] освобожде́ние.
embalm [im'bɑ:m] [на]бальзами́ровать.
embankment [im'bæŋkmənt] да́мба, на́сыпь *f*; на́бережная.
embargo [em'bɑ:gou] эмба́рго *n indecl.*; запреще́ние.
embark [im'bɑ:k] [по]грузи́ть(ся); сади́ться [сесть] (на кора́бль); *fig.* ~ in, (up)on нач(ин)а́ть (В).
embarras [im'bærəs] затрудня́ть [-ни́ть]; смуща́ть [смути́ть]; стесня́ть [-ни́ть]; **~ing** [-iŋ] □ затрудни́тельный; неудо́бный; стесни́тельный; **~ment** [-mənt] затрудне́ние; смуще́ние; замеша́тельство.
embassy ['embəsi] посо́льство.
embellish [im'beliʃ] украша́ть [укра́сить].
embers ['embəz] *pl.* после́дние тле́ющие уголькй *m/pl.*
embezzle [im'bezl] растра́чивать [-а́тить] (чужи́е де́ньги); **~ment** [-mənt] растра́та.
embitter [im'bitə] озлобля́ть [озло́бить].
emblem ['embləm] эмбле́ма, си́мвол.
embody [im'bɔdi] воплоща́ть [-лоти́ть]; олицетворя́ть [-ри́ть]; включа́ть [-чи́ть] (в соста́в).
embosom [im'buzəm] обнима́ть [обня́ть]; **~ed** with окружённый (Т).
emboss [im'bɔs] выбива́ть вы́пуклый рису́нок на (П), [от-, вы́]чека́нить; лепи́ть релье́ф.
embrace [im'breis] **1.** объя́тие; **2.** обнима́ть(ся) [-ня́ть(ся)]; принима́ть [-ня́ть] (ве́ру и т. п.); обхва́тывать [обхвати́ть].
embroider [im'brɔidə] вы́ши(ва́)ть; **~y** [-ri] вышива́ние; вы́шивка.

embroil [im'brɔil] запу́т(ыв)ать (дела́); впу́т(ыв)ать (в неприя́тности).
emerald ['emərəld] изумру́д.
emerge [i'mə:dʒ] появля́ться [-ви́ться]; всплы(ва́)ть; **~ncy** [-ənsi] непредви́денный слу́чай; *attr.* запасно́й, вспомога́тельный; ~ call *teleph.* сро́чный вы́зов по телефо́ну; **~nt** [-ənt] непредви́денный; сро́чный.
emigra|nt ['emigrənt] **1.** эмигра́нт, переселе́нец; **2.** эмигри́рующий, переселе́нческий; **~te** [-greit] эмигри́ровать (*im*)*pf.*, переселя́ться [-ли́ться]; **~tion** [emi'greiʃən] эмигра́ция, переселе́ние.
eminen|ce ['eminəns] высота́; высо́кое положе́ние; **2ce** высокопреосвяще́нство; **~t** [-ənt] □ *fig.* выдаю́щийся, замеча́тельный; *adv.* замеча́тельно.
emit [i'mit] изд(ав)а́ть, испуска́ть [-усти́ть] (за́пах, звук, крик); выделя́ть [вы́делить].
emoti|on [i'mouʃən] душе́вное волне́ние, возбужде́ние; эмо́ция; **~onal** [-l] □ взволно́ванный; волну́ющий (о му́зыке и т. п.).
emperor ['empərə] импера́тор.
empha|sis ['emfəsis] вырази́тельность *f*; ударе́ние, акце́нт; **~size** [-saiz] подчёркивать [-черкну́ть]; **~tic** [im'fætik] (~ally) вырази́тельный; подчёркнутый; насто́йчивый.
empire ['empaiə] импе́рия.
employ [im'plɔi] **1.** употребля́ть [-би́ть], применя́ть [-ни́ть], испо́льзовать (*im*)*pf.*; дава́ть рабо́ту (Д); **2.** in the ~ of на рабо́те у (Р), рабо́тающий у (Р); **~ee** [emplɔi'i:] слу́жащий (-щая), рабо́тник (-ица); **~er** [im'plɔiə] нанима́тель (-ница *f*) *m*, работода́тель(ница *f*) *m*; ✝ зака́зчик (-ица); **~ment** [-mənt] примене́ние; рабо́та, заня́тие; 2 Exchange би́ржа труда́.
empower [im'pauə] уполномо́чи(ва)ть.
empress ['empris] императри́ца.
empt|iness ['emptinis] пустота́; **~y** [-ti] **1.** □ пусто́й, поро́жний; F голо́дный; **2.** опорожня́ть(ся) [-ни́ть(ся)]; [о]пусте́ть.
emul|ate ['emjuleit] соревнова́ться с (Т); **~ation** [emju'leiʃən] соревнова́ние.
enable [i'neibl] дава́ть возмо́жность и́ли пра́во (Д).
enact [i'nækt] предпи́сывать [-са́ть]; постановля́ть [-ви́ть]; *thea.* игра́ть роль; ста́вить на сце́не.
enamel [i'næml] **1.** эма́ль *f*; **2.** эмалирова́ть (*im*)*pf.*; покрыва́ть эма́лью.
enamo(u)red [i'næməd]: ~ of влюблённый в (В).
encamp [in'kæmp] ⚔ располага́ться ла́герем.
enchain [in'tʃein] зако́вывать [-ова́ть]; прико́вывать [-ова́ть].
enchant [in'tʃɑ:nt] очаро́вывать [-ова́ть]; **~ment** [-ment] очарова́ние; **~ress** [-ris] чароде́йка.
encircle [in'sə:kl] окружа́ть [-жи́ть].
enclos|e [in'klouz] заключа́ть [-чи́ть]; огора́живать [-роди́ть]; прилага́ть [-ложи́ть]; **~ure** [-ʒə] огоро́женное ме́сто; вложе́ние, приложе́ние.
encompass [in'kʌmpəs] окружа́ть [-жи́ть].
encore [ɔŋ'kɔ:] *thea.* **1.** бис!; **2.** крича́ть «бис»; вызыва́ть [вы́звать].
encounter [in'kauntə] **1.** встре́ча; столкнове́ние; **2.** встреча́ть(ся) [-е́тить(ся)]; ната́лкиваться [натолкну́ться] на (тру́дности и т. п.).
encourage [in'kʌridʒ] ободря́ть [-ри́ть]; поощря́ть [-ри́ть]; **~ment** [-mənt] ободре́ние; поощре́ние.
encroach [in'kroutʃ]: ~ (up)on вторга́ться [вто́ргнуться] в (В); **~ment** [-mənt] вторже́ние.
encumb|er [in'kʌmbə] обременя́ть [-ни́ть]; загроможда́ть [-мозди́ть]; затрудня́ть [-ни́ть]; [вос]препя́тствовать (Д); **~rance** [-brəns] бре́мя *n*; обу́за; *fig.* препя́тствие.
encyclop(a)edia [ensaiklo'pi:diə] энциклопе́дия.
end [end] **1.** коне́ц, оконча́ние; цель *f*; результа́т; no ~ of безме́рно, бесконе́чно мно́го (Р); in the ~ в конце́ концо́в; on ~ стоймя́; ды́бом; беспреры́вно, подря́д; **2.** конча́ть(ся) [ко́нчить(ся)].
endanger [in'deindʒə] подверга́ть опа́сности.
endear [in'diə] внуша́ть любо́вь, заставля́ть полюби́ть; **~ment** [-mənt] ла́ска, выраже́ние не́жности.
endeavo(u)r [in'devə] **1.** [по]пыта́ться, прилага́ть уси́лия, [по-] стара́ться; **2.** попы́тка, стара́ние.
end|ing ['endiŋ] оконча́ние; **~less** ['endlis] □ бесконе́чный.
endorse [in'dɔ:s] ✝ индосси́ровать (*im*)*pf.*; одобря́ть [одо́брить]; **~ment** [in'dɔ:smənt] ✝ индосса́ме́нт.
endow [in'dau] одаря́ть [-ри́ть] (умо́м и т. п.); наделя́ть [-ли́ть]; **~ment** [-mənt] наде́л.
endue [in'dju:] облека́ть [-е́чь].
endur|ance [in'djuərəns] выно́сливость *f*; про́чность *f*; **~e** [in'djuə] выноси́ть [вы́нести], терпе́ть.
enema ['enimə] кли́зма.
enemy ['enimi] враг; неприя́тель *m*; проти́вник.
energ|etic [enə'dʒetik] (~ally) энерги́чный; **~y** ['enədʒi] эне́ргия.
enervate ['enə:veit] обесси́ли(ва)ть, ослабля́ть [-а́бить].

enfold [in'fould] обнимáть [обнять], обхвáтывать [обхватить].
enforce [in'fɔ:s] навязывать [-зáть] (upon Д); настáивать [настоять] на (П); добивáться (Р) силой; усили(ва)ть; **~ment** [-mənt] принуждéние.
engage [in'geidʒ] *v/t.* нанимáть [нанять]; закáзывать [-зáть]; занимáть [занять]; привлекáть [-éчь]; завладé(вá)ть; *fig.* привязывать [-зáть]; вовлекáть [-éчь]; ⚔ вводить в бой; be **~d** быть зáнятым; быть помóлвленным; *v/i.* обязываться [-зáться]; занимáться [заняться] (in Т); ⚔ вступáть в бой; **~ment** [-mənt] обязáтельство; свидáние; приглашéние; помóлвка; ⚔ бой.
engaging [-iŋ] □ очаровáтельный.
engender [in'dʒendə] *fig.* порождáть [породить].
engine ['endʒin] машина; ⊕ мотóр; 🚂 паровóз; **~-driver** машинист.
engineer [endʒi'niə] **1.** инженéр; механик; машинист; **2.** сооружáть [-дить]; [за]проектировать; **~ing** [-riŋ] тéхника.
English ['iŋgliʃ] **1.** английский; **2.** английский язык; the **~** англичáне *pl.*; **~man** [-mən] англичáнин; **~woman** [-'wumən] англичáнка.
engrav|e [in'greiv] [вы]гравировáть; *fig.* запечатлé(вá)ть (в пáмяти); **~er** [-ə] гравёр; **~ing** [-iŋ] гравировáние; гравюра.
engross [in'grous] поглощáть [-лотить] (внимáние).
engulf [in'gʌlf] *fig.* поглощáть [-лотить] (о пучине).
enhance [in'hɑ:ns] повышáть [повысить]; усили(ва)ть.
enigma [i'nigmə] загáдка; **~tic(al** □) [enig'mætik, -ikəl] загáдочный.
enjoin [in'dʒɔin] втолкóвывать [-ковáть] (Д).
enjoy [in'dʒɔi] наслаждáться [насладиться] (Т); **~** o. s. забавляться [забáвиться]; **~able** [-əbl] приятный; **~ment** [-mənt] наслаждéние, удовóльствие.
enlarge [in'lɑ:dʒ] увеличи(ва)ть (-ся); распространяться (on o П); **~ment** [-mənt] расширéние; увеличéние.
enlighten [in'laitn] *fig.* озарять [-рить]; просвещáть [-етить]; **~ment** просвéщение; просвещённость *f*.
enlist [in'list] *v/t.* ⚔ вербовáть на воéнную слýжбу; **~ed man** ⚔ рядовóй.
enliven [in'laivn] оживлять [-вить].
enmity ['enmiti] враждá, неприязнь *f*.
ennoble [i'noubl] облагорáживать [[-рóдить].
enorm|ity [i'nɔ:miti] чудóвищность *f*; **~ous** [-əs] □ огрóмный, громáдный; чудóвищный.
enou h [i'nʌf] достáточно, довóльно.
enquire [in'kwaiə] *s.* inquire.
enrage [in'reidʒ] [вз]бесить, приводить в ярость.
enrapture [in'ræptʃə] восхищáть [-итить], очарóвывать [-овáть].
enrich [in'ritʃ] обогащáть [-гатить].
enrol(l) [in'roul] *v/t.* [за]регистрировать; ⚔ [за]вербовáть; *v/i.* поступáть на воéнную слýжбу; **~ment** [-mənt] регистрáция; вербóвка.
ensign ['ensain] значóк, эмблéма; знáмя, флаг; *Am.* ⚓ млáдший лейтенáнт.
enslave [in'sleiv] порабощáть [-ботить]; **~ment** [-mənt] порабощéние.
ensnare [in'snɛə] замáнивать [-нить].
ensue [in'sju:] [по]слéдовать; получáться в результáте.
entail [in'teil] влечь за собóй, вызывáть [вызвать] (чтó-либо).
entangle [in'tæŋgl] запýт(ыв)ать; **~ment** [-mənt] ⚔ (прóволочное) заграждéние.
enter ['entə] *v/t.* вступáть [-пить] в (В); поступáть [-пить] в (В); † вносить [внести] (в книгу); входить [войти] в (В); проникáть [-никнуть] в (В); *v/i.* входить [войти], вступáть [-пить]; **~** (up)on ⚖ вступáть во владéние (Т).
enterpris|e ['entəpraiz] предприятие; предприимчивость *f*; **~ing** [-iŋ] □ предприимчивый.
entertain [entə'tein] угощáть [угостить]; развлекáть [-лéчь], занимáть [занять]; **~ment** [-mənt] развлечéние; приём (гостéй).
enthrone [in'θroun] возводить на престóл.
enthusias|m [in'θju:ziæzm] востóрг; энтузиáзм; **~t** [-æst] энтузиáст(ка); **~tic** [inθju:zi'æstik] (**~ally**) востóрженный; пóлный энтузиáзма.
entic|e [in'tais] замáнивать [-нить]; соблазнять [-нить]; **~ement** [-mənt] соблáзн, примáнка.
entire [in'taiə] □ цéлый, цéльный; сплошнóй; **~ly** [-li] всецéло; совершéнно; **~ty** [-ti] полнотá, цéльность *f*; óбщая сýмма.
entitle [in'taitl] озаглáвливать [-лáвить]; давáть прáво (Д).
entity ['entiti] бытиé; сýщность *f*.
entrails ['entreilz] *pl.* внýтренности *f/pl.*; нéдра *n/pl.* (земли).
entrance ['entrəns] вход, въезд; выход (актёра на сцéну); дóступ.
entrap [in'træp] поймáть в ловýшку; запýт(ыв)ать.
entreat [in'tri:t] умолять; **~y** [-i] мольбá, прóсьба.
entrench [in'trentʃ] ⚔ окружáть окóпами.

entrust [in'trʌst] поручать [-чи́ть], вверя́ть [вве́рить].
entry ['entri] вход, вступле́ние, въезд; *thea.* вы́ход (на сце́ну); ⚖ вступле́ние во владе́ние; *sport*: зая́вка.
enumerate [i'nju:məreit] перечисля́ть [-и́слить].
enunciate [i'nʌnsieit] хорошо́ произноси́ть; [с]формули́ровать.
envelop [in'veləp] заку́т(ыв)ать; завора́чивать [заверну́ть]; ⚔ окружа́ть [-жи́ть]; **~e** ['enviloup] конве́рт; оболо́чка.
envi|able ['enviəbl] □ зави́дный; **~ous** □ зави́стливый.
environ [in'vaiərən] окружа́ть [-жи́ть]; **~ment** [-mənt] окружа́ющая обстано́вка; **~s** ['envirənz] *pl.* окре́стности *f/pl.*
envoy ['envɔi] посла́нник.
envy ['envi] **1.** за́висть *f*; **2.** [по]зави́довать (Д).
epic ['epik] **1.** эпи́ческая поэ́ма; **2.** эпи́ческий.
epicure ['epikjuə] эпикуре́ец.
epidemic [epi'demik] ◫ **1.** (**~ally**) эпидеми́ческий; **2.** эпиде́мия.
epilogue ['epilɔg] эпило́г.
episcopa|cy [i'piskəpəsi] епископа́льная систе́ма церко́вного управле́ния; **~l** [-pəl] епи́скопский.
epist|le [i'pisl] посла́ние; **~olary** [-tələri] эпистоля́рный.
epitaph ['epitɑ:f] эпита́фия.
epitome [i'pitəmi] конспе́кт, о́черк.
epoch ['i:pɔk] эпо́ха.
equable ['ekwəbl] □ равноме́рный, ро́вный; *fig.* уравнове́шенный.
equal ['i:kwəl] **1.** □ ра́вный; одина́ковый; **~ to** *fig.* спосо́бный на (В); **2.** равня́ться (Д); **~ity** [i'kwɔliti] ра́венство; **~ization** [i:kwəlai'zeiʃən] ура́внивание; **~ize** [-aiz] ура́внивать [-ня́ть].
equat|ion [i'kweiʃən] ℞ уравне́ние; **~or** [-tə] эква́тор.
equestrian [i'kwestriən] **1.** ко́нный; **2.** вса́дник.
equilibrium [i:kwi'libriəm] равнове́сие.
equip [i'kwip] снаряжа́ть [-яди́ть]; снабжа́ть [-бди́ть]; **~ment** [-mənt] снаряже́ние; обмундирова́ние; обору́дование.
equipoise ['ekwipɔiz] равнове́сие; противове́с.
equity ['ekwiti] беспристра́стность [*f.*]
equivalent [i'kwivələnt] **1.** эквивале́нт (to Д); **2.** равноце́нный; равнозна́чащий.
equivoca|l [i'kwivəkəl] □ двусмы́сленный; сомни́тельный; **~te** [i'kwivəkeit] говори́ть двусмы́сленно.
era ['iərə] э́ра; эпо́ха.
eradicate [i'rædikeit] искореня́ть [-ни́ть].
eras|e [i'reiz] стира́ть [стере́ть]; подчища́ть [-и́стить]; **~er** [-ə] рези́нка; **~ure** [i'reiʒə] подчи́стка; стёртое рези́нкой.
ere [ɛə] **1.** *cj.* пре́жде чем, скоре́е чем; **2.** *prp.* до (Р); пе́ред (Т).
erect [i'rekt] **1.** □ прямо́й; по́днятый; **2.** сооружа́ть [-уди́ть], воздвига́ть [-и́гнуть]; **~ion** [i'rekʃən] сооруже́ние, строе́ние.
eremite ['erimait] отше́льник.
ermine ['ə:min] *zo.* горноста́й.
erosion [i'rouʒən] эро́зия; разъеда́ние.
erotic [i'rɔtik] эроти́ческий.
err [ə:] ошиба́ться [-би́ться], заблужда́ться.
errand ['erənd] поруче́ние; **~boy** ма́льчик на посы́лках.
errant ['erənt] □ стра́нствующий; блужда́ющий (о мы́слях).
errat|ic [i'rætik] (**~ally**) неусто́йчивый; **~um** [i'reitəm], *pl.* **~a** [-tə] опеча́тка, опи́ска.
erroneous [i'rounjəs] □ оши́бочный.
error ['erə] оши́бка, заблужде́ние; **~s excepted** исключа́я оши́бки.
erudit|e ['erudait] □ учёный; **~ion** [eru'diʃən] эруди́ция, учёность *f.*
eruption [i'rʌpʃən] изверже́ние; ⚕ высыпа́ние (сы́пи, прыще́й).
escalator ['eskəleitə] эскала́тор.
escap|ade [eskə'peid] сме́лая проде́лка; побе́г (из тюрьмы́); **~e** [is'keip] **1.** *v/i.* бежа́ть (из тюрьмы́) (*im*)*pf.*; спаса́ться [спасти́сь]; *v/t.* избега́ть [-ежа́ть] (опа́сности и т. п.); ускольза́ть [-зну́ть] от (Р); **2.** бе́гство; спасе́ние.
escort 1. ['eskɔ:t] эско́рт, конво́й; **2.** [is'kɔ:t] конвои́ровать, сопровожда́ть.
escutcheon [is'kʌtʃən] щит герба́.
especial [is'peʃəl] осо́бенный; специа́льный; **~ly** [-i] осо́бенно.
espionage [espiə'nɑ:ʒ] шпиона́ж.
essay 1. ['esei] о́черк; попы́тка; сочине́ние; **2.** [e'sei] подверга́ть испыта́нию; [по]пыта́ться.
essen|ce ['esns] су́щность *f*; существо́; эссе́нция; **~tial** [i'senʃəl] **1.** □ суще́ственный (to для Р), ва́жный; **2.** су́щность *f.*
establish [is'tæbliʃ] устана́вливать [-нови́ть]; учрежда́ть [-еди́ть], осно́вывать [-ова́ть]; **~ o. s.** поселя́ться [-ли́ться], устра́иваться [-ро́иться] (в П); **2ed Church** госуда́рственная це́рковь *f*; **~ment** [-mənt] учрежде́ние, заведе́ние; хозя́йство.
estate [es'teit] *pol.* сосло́вие; иму́щество; име́ние; **real ~** недви́жимость *f.*
esteem [is'ti:m] **1.** уваже́ние; **2.** уважа́ть.
estimable ['estiməbl] досто́йный уваже́ния.

estimat|e 1. [-meit] оце́нивать [-ни́ть]; 2. [-mit] сме́та, калькуля́ция; оце́нка; **~ion** [esti'meiʃən] оце́нка; мне́ние.
estrange [is'treindʒ] отчужда́ть [-уди́ть].
etch [etʃ] гравирова́ть травле́нием.
etern|al [i'tə:nəl] □ ве́чный; неизме́нный; **~ity** [-niti] ве́чность *f*.
ether ['i:θə] эфи́р; **~eal** [i'θiəriəl] □ эфи́рный; возду́шный.
ethic|al ['eθikəl] □ эти́чный, эти́ческий; **~s** ['eθiks] э́тика.
etiquette [eti'ket] этике́т.
etymology [eti'mɔlədʒi] этимоло́гия.
eucharist ['ju:kərist] евхари́стия.
European [juərə'piən] 1. европе́ец [-пе́йка]; 2. европе́йский.
evacuate [i'vækjueit] эвакуи́ровать (*im*)*pf*.
evade [i'veid] избега́ть [-ежа́ть] (P); ускольза́ть [-зну́ть] от (P); обходи́ть [обойти́] (зако́н и т. п.).
evaluate [i'væljueit] оце́нивать [-ни́ть]; выража́ть в чи́слах.
evangelic, ~al □ [ivæn'dʒelik, -ikəl] евангели́ческий; ева́нгельский.
evaporat|e [i'væpəreit] испаря́ть (-ся) [-ри́ть(ся)]; **~ion** [ivæpə'reiʃən] испаре́ние.
evasi|on [i'veiʒən] уклоне́ние, увёртка; **~ve** [-siv] □ укло́нчивый (of от P).
eve [i:v] кану́н; on the ~ of накану́не (P).
even ['i:vən] 1. *adj*. □ ро́вный, гла́дкий; ра́вный, одина́ковый; моното́нный; беспристра́стный; чётный (о числе́); 2. *adv*. ро́вно; как раз; да́же; not ~ да́же не; ~ though, ~ if хотя́ бы, да́же е́сли; 3. выра́внивать [вы́ровнять]; сгла́живать [сгла́дить]; **~-handed** ['hændid] беспристра́стный.
evening ['i:vniŋ] ве́чер; вечери́нка; ~ dress вече́рний туале́т, фрак.
evenness ['i:vənnis] ро́вность *f*; гла́дкость; равноме́рность *f*.
evensong вече́рня.
event [i'vent] собы́тие, происше́ствие; *fig*. исхо́д; но́мер (в програ́мме); at all **~s** во вся́ком слу́чае; in the ~ of в слу́чае (P); **~ful** [-ful] по́лный собы́тий.
eventual [i'ventjuəl] □ возмо́жный; коне́чный; **~ly** в конце́ концо́в; со вре́менем.
ever ['evə] всегда́; когда́-нибудь, когда́-либо; ~ so о́чень; как бы ни; as soon as ~ I can как то́лько я смогу́; for ~ навсегда́; yours ~ ваш ... (в конце́ письма́); **~green** вечнозелёный; **~lasting** [evə'lɑ:stiŋ] □ про́чный; постоя́нный; **~more** ['evəmɔ:] наве́ки, навсегда́.
every ['evri] ка́ждый; ~ now and then вре́мя от вре́мени; ~ other day че́рез день; **~body** все *pl*.; ка́ждый, вся́кий; **~day** ежедне́вный; **~one** ка́ждый, вся́кий; все *pl*.; **~thing** всё; **~where** везде́, всю́ду.
evict [i'vikt] выселя́ть [вы́селить]; оттяга́ть по суду́.
eviden|ce ['evidəns] 1. очеви́дность *f*; доказа́тельство; ⚖ ули́ка, свиде́тельское показа́ние; in ~ в доказа́тельство; 2. служи́ть доказа́тельством; **~t** [-t] □ очеви́дный.
evil ['i:vl] 1. □ злой; па́губный; дурно́й, плохо́й; the ♀ One дья́вол; 2. зло; бе́дствие.
evince [i'vins] проявля́ть [-ви́ть].
evoke [i'vouk] вызыва́ть [вы́звать] (воспомина́ния и т. п.).
evolution [i:və'lu:ʃən] эволю́ция; разви́тие; передвиже́ние.
evolve [i'vɔlv] разви́(ва́)ться; эволюциони́ровать (*im*)*pf*.
ewe [ju:] овца́.
exact [ig'zækt] 1. □ то́чный, аккура́тный; 2. [по]тре́бовать (P); взы́скивать [-ка́ть]; **~ing** [-iŋ] тре́бовательный, взыска́тельный; **~itude** [-titju:d], **~ness** [-nis] то́чность *f*.
exaggerate [ig'zædʒəreit] преувели́чи(ва)ть.
exalt [ig'zɔ:lt] возвыша́ть [-ы́сить]; превозноси́ть [-нести́]; **~ation** [egzɔ:l'teiʃən] возвыше́ние; восто́рг.
examin|ation [igzæmi'neiʃən] осмо́тр; иссле́дование; освиде́тельствование; эксперти́за; экза́мен; **~e** [ig'zæmin] осма́тривать [-мотре́ть]; иссле́довать (*im*)*pf*.; [про-] экзаменова́ть.
example [ig'zɑ:mpl] приме́р; образе́ц; for ~ наприме́р.
exasperate [ig'zɑ:spəreit] доводи́ть до бе́лого кале́ния; уси́ли(ва)ть.
excavate ['ekskəveit] выка́пывать [вы́копать].
exceed [ik'si:d] превыша́ть [-вы́сить]; переходи́ть грани́цы (P); **~ing** [-iŋ] □ огро́мный; чрезвыча́йный.
excel [ik'sel] *v/t*. превосходи́ть [-взойти́] (in, at T); *v/i*. выделя́ться [вы́делиться]; **~lence** ['eksələns] превосхо́дство; **~lency** [-i] превосходи́тельство; **~lent** ['eksələnt] □ превосхо́дный.
except [ik'sept] 1. исключа́ть [-чи́ть]; 2. *prp*. исключа́я (P); кро́ме (P); ~ for за исключе́нием (P); **~ing** [-iŋ] *prp*. за исключе́нием (P); **~ion** [ik'sepʃən] исключе́ние; take ~ to возража́ть [-рази́ть] про́тив (P); **~ional** [~l] исключи́тельный; **~ionally** [-əli] исключи́тельно.
excess [ik'ses] избы́ток, изли́шек; эксце́сс; ~ fare допла́та, припла́та;

~ luggage бага́ж вы́ше но́рмы; **~ive** [-iv] □ чрезме́рный.
exchange [iks'tʃeindʒ] **1.** обме́ниваться [-ня́ться] (T); обме́нивать [-ня́ть], *by mistake*: [-ни́ть] (for на B); [по]меня́ться (T); **2.** обме́н; разме́н; (*a.* ♀) би́ржа; foreign ~(s *pl.*) иностра́нная валю́та; ~ office меня́льная конто́ра.
exchequer [iks'tʃekə] казначе́йство; казна́; Chancellor of the ♀ мини́стр фина́нсов Великобрита́нии.
excit|able [ik'saitəbl] возбуди́мый; **~e** [ik'sait] возбужда́ть [-уди́ть], [вз]волнова́ть; **~ement** [-mənt] возбужде́ние, волне́ние.
exclaim [iks'kleim] восклица́ть [-и́кнуть].
exclamation [eksklə'meiʃən] восклица́ние.
exclude [iks'klu:d] исключа́ть [-чи́ть].
exclusi|on [iks'klu:ʒən] исключе́ние; **~ve** [-siv] □ исключи́тельный; еди́нственный; ~ of за исключе́нием (P).
excommunicat|e [ekskə'mju:nikeit] отлуча́ть от це́ркви; **~ion** [ekskəmju:ni'keiʃən] отлуче́ние от це́ркви.
excrement ['ekskrimənt] экскреме́нты *m/pl.*, испражне́ния *n/pl.*
excrete [eks'kri:t] выделя́ть [вы́делить], изверга́ть [-е́ргнуть].
excruciate [iks'kru:ʃieit] [из-, за-] му́чить; терза́ть.
exculpate ['ekskʌlpeit] опра́вдывать [-да́ть].
excursion [iks'kə:ʃən] экску́рсия.
excursive [eks'kə:siv] □ отклоня́ющийся (от те́мы).
excus|able [iks'kju:zəbl] □ извини́тельный, прости́тельный; **~e** **1.** [iks'kju:z] извиня́ть [-ни́ть], проща́ть [прости́ть]; **2.** [iks'kju:s] извине́ние; оправда́ние; отгово́рка.
execra|ble ['eksikrəbl] □ отврати́тельный; **~te** ['eksikreit] пита́ть отвраще́ние к (Д); проклина́ть [-кля́сть].
execut|e ['eksikju:t] исполня́ть [-о́лнить]; выполня́ть [вы́полнить]; казни́ть (*im*)*pf.*; **~ion** [eksi'kju:ʃən] исполне́ние; выполне́ние; казнь *f*; **~ioner** [-ə] пала́ч; **~ive** [ig'zekjutiv] **1.** □ исполни́тельный; администрати́вный; ~ committee исполни́тельный комите́т; **2.** исполни́тельная власть *f*; ✝ администра́тор; **~or** [-tə] душеприка́зчик.
exemplary [ig'zempləri] образцо́вый, приме́рный.
exemplify [ig'zemplifai] поясня́ть приме́ром; служи́ть приме́ром (P).
exempt [ig'zempt] **1.** освобожда́ть [-боди́ть] (от вое́нный слу́жбы и т. п.); **2.** освобождённый, свобо́дный (of от P).
exercise ['eksəsaiz] **1.** упражне́ние; трениро́вка; моцио́н; take ~ де́лать моцио́н; **2.** упражня́ть(ся); разви́(ва́)ть; [на]тренирова́ть(ся); ⚔ обуча́ть(ся) [-чи́ть(ся)].
exert [ig'zə:t] напряга́ть [-ря́чь] (си́лы); ока́зывать [-за́ть] (влия́ние и т. п.); ~ o. s. [по]стара́ться; **~ion** [ig'zə:ʃən] напряже́ние и т. д.
exhale [eks'heil] выдыха́ть [вы́дохнуть]; испаря́ть(ся) [-ри́ть(ся)].
exhaust [ig'zɔ:st] **1.** изнуря́ть [-ри́ть], истоща́ть [-щи́ть]; **2.** ⊕ выхлопна́я труба́; вы́хлоп, вы́пуск; **~ion** [-ʃən] истоще́ние, изнуре́ние; **~ive** [-iv] □ истоща́ющий; исче́рпывающий.
exhibit [ig'zibit] **1.** пока́зывать [-за́ть], проявля́ть [-ви́ть]; выставля́ть [вы́ставить]; **2.** экспона́т; ⚖ веще́ственное доказа́тельство; **~ion** [eksi'biʃən] проявле́ние, пока́з; вы́ставка; **~or** [ig'zibitə] экспоне́нт.
exhilarate [ig'ziləreit] оживля́ть [-ви́ть]; развеселя́ть [-ли́ть].
exhort [ig'zɔ:t] увеща́ть, увещева́ть.
exigen|ce, ~cy ['eksidʒəns(i)] о́страя необходи́мость *f*, кра́йность *f*.
exile ['eksail] **1.** изгна́ние, ссы́лка; изгна́нник; **2.** изгоня́ть [изгна́ть], ссыла́ть [сосла́ть].
exist [ig'zist] существова́ть, жить; **~ence** [-əns] существова́ние, жизнь *f*; in ~ = **~ent** [-ənt] существу́ющий.
exit ['eksit] вы́ход; *fig.* смерть *f*; *thea.* ухо́д со сце́ны.
exodus ['eksədəs] ма́ссовый отъе́зд; исхо́д евре́ев из Еги́пта.
exonerate [ig'zɔnəreit] *fig.* реабилити́ровать (*im*)*pf.*; снять бре́мя (вины́ и т. п.) с (P).
exorbitant [ig'zɔ:bitənt] □ непоме́рный, чрезме́рный.
exorci|se, ~ze ['eksɔ:saiz] изгоня́ть [изгна́ть] (ду́хов, нечи́стую си́лу); освобожда́ть [-боди́ть] (of от P).
exotic [eg'zɔtik] экзоти́ческий.
expan|d [iks'pænd] расширя́ть(ся) [-и́рить(ся)], увели́чи(ва)ть(ся); разви́(ва́)ть(ся); **~se** [iks'pæns], **~sion** [-ʃən] простра́нство; протяже́ние; экспа́нсия; расшире́ние; **~sive** [-siv] □ спосо́бный расширя́ться; обши́рный; *fig.* экспанси́вный.
expatriate [eks'pætrieit] изгоня́ть [из оте́чества.]
expect [iks'pekt] ожида́ть (P); рассчи́тывать, наде́яться; F полага́ть, [по]ду́мать; **~ant** [-ənt] **1.** ~ ожида́ющий; ~ mother бере́менная же́нщина; **2.** кандида́т; **~ation** [ekspek'teiʃən] ожида́ние; расчёт; наде́жда.

expectorate [eks'pektəreit] отхаркивать [-кнуть]; плевать [плюнуть].
expedi|ent [iks'pi:diənt] **1.** подходящий, целесообразный, соответствующий (обстоятельствам); **2.** подручное средство; уловка; **~tion** [ekspi'diʃən] экспедиция; быстрота; поспешность *f*.
expel [iks'pel] изгонять [изгнать] (из P), исключать [-чить] (из P).
expen|d [iks'pend] [ис]тратить; [из]расходовать; **~diture** [-itʃə] расход, трата; **~se** [iks'pens] расход, трата; **~s** *pl.* расходы *m/pl.*; **~sive** [-siv] □ дорогой, дорого стоящий.
experience [iks'piərəns] **1.** опыт (жизненный); переживание; **2.** испытывать [испытать]; пережи(ва)ть; **~d** [-t] опытный.
experiment 1. [iks'perimənt] опыт, эксперимент; **2.** [-'ment] производить опыты; **~al** [eksperi'mentl] □ экспериментальный, основанный на опыте; пробный.
expert ['ekspə:t] **1.** □ [*pred.* eks'pə:t] опытный, искусный; **2.** эксперт, знаток, специалист.
expir|ation [ekspai'reiʃən] выдыхание; окончание, истечение (срока); **~e** [iks'paiə] выдыхать [выдохнуть]; умирать [умереть]; ✝ кончаться [кончиться], истекать [-ечь] (о сроке).
explain [iks'plein] объяснять [-нить]; оправдывать [-дать] (поведение).
explanat|ion [eksplə'neiʃən] объяснение; толкование; **~ory** [iks'plænətəri] □ объяснительный.
explicable ['eksplikəbl] объяснимый.
explicit [iks'plisit] □ ясный, недвусмысленный.
explode [iks'ploud] взрывать(ся) [взорвать(ся)]; подрывать [подорвать]; разражаться [-разиться] (with T).
exploit 1. ['eksplɔit] подвиг; **2.** [iks'plɔit] эксплуатировать; ⚒ разрабатывать [-ботать]; **~ation** [eksplɔi'teiʃən] эксплуатация; ⚒ разработка.
explor|ation [eksplɔ:'reiʃən] исследование; **~e** [iks'plɔ:] исследовать (*im*)*pf.*; развед(ыв)ать **~er** [-rə] исследователь(ница *f*) *m*.
explosi|on [iks'plouʒən] взрыв; вспышка (гнева); **~ve** [-siv] **1.** □ взрывчатый; *fig.* вспыльчивый; **2.** взрывчатое вещество.
exponent [eks'pounənt] объяснитель *m*; представитель *m*; образец; ⅍ показатель степени.
export 1. ['ekspɔ:t] экспорт, вывоз; **2.** [eks'pɔ:t] экспортировать (*im*)*pf.*, вывозить [вывезти] (товары); **~ation** [ekspɔ:'teiʃən] вывоз.
expos|e [iks'pouz] подвергать [-ергнуть] (опасности и т. п.); бросать на произвол судьбы; выставлять [выставить]; разоблачать [-чить]; *phot.* экспонировать (*im*)*pf.*; **~ition** [ekspo'ziʃən] выставка; изложение
exposure [iks'pouʒə] подвергание; выставление; разоблачение; *phot.* экспозиция, выдержка.
expound [iks'paund] излагать [изложить]; разъяснять [-нить].
express [iks'pres] **1.** □ определённый, точно выраженный; специальный; срочный; ~ company *Am.* транспортная контора; **2.** курьер, нарочный; (*a.* ~ train) экспресс, курьерский поезд; **3.** *adv.* спешно; с нарочным; **4.** выражать [выразить]; **~ion** [iks'preʃən] выражение; выразительность *f*; **~ive** [iks'presiv] □ выразительный; выражающий.
expropriate [eks'prouprieit] экспроприировать (*im*)*pf.*; лишать собственности.
expulsion [iks'pʌlʃən] изгнание; исключение (из школы и т. п.).
exquisite ['ekskwizit] **1.** □ изысканный, утончённый; прелестный; **2.** фат, щёголь *m*.
extant [eks'tænt] сохранившийся.
extempor|aneous [ekstempə'reinjəs] □, **~ary** [iks'tempərəri] неподготовленный; **~e** [-pəri] *adv.* экспромтом.
extend [iks'tend] *v/t.* протягивать [-тянуть]; распространять [-нить] (влияние); продлевать [-лить] (срок); ⚔ рассыпать в цепь; *v/i.* простираться [простереться].
extensi|on [iks'tenʃən] вытягивание; расширение; распространение; протяжение; продление; University ♀ популярные лекции, организуемые университетом; **~ve** [-siv] □ обширный, пространный.
extent [iks'tent] протяжение; размер, степень *f*, мера; to the ~ of в размере (P); to some ~ до известной степени.
extenuate [eks'tenjueit] уменьшать [уменьшить] (вину); стараться найти извинение; ослаблять [-абить].
exterior [eks'tiəriə] **1.** □ внешний, наружный; **2.** внешность *f*, наружность *f*.
exterminate [eks'tə:mineit] искоренять [-нить], истреблять [-бить].
external [eks'tə:nl] **1.** □ наружный, внешний; **2.** **~s** *pl.* внешность *f*, наружность *f*; *fig.* внешние обстоятельства.
extinct [iks'tiŋkt] угасший; вымерший; потухший.
extinguish [iks'tiŋgwiʃ] [по]гасить; [по]тушить; погашать [погасить] (долг).

extirpate ['ekstə:peit] искореня́ть [-ни́ть], истребля́ть [-би́ть].
extol [iks'tɔl] превозноси́ть [-нести́].
extort [iks'tɔ:t] вымога́ть (де́ньги); выпы́тывать [вы́пытать] (та́йну); **~ion** [iks'tɔ:ʃən] вымога́тельство.
extra ['ekstrə] **1.** доба́вочный, дополни́телный; э́кстренный; **2.** *adv.* осо́бо; осо́бенно; дополни́тельно; **3.** припла́та; *Am.* э́кстренный вы́пуск газе́ты; **~s** *pl.* побо́чные расхо́ды (дохо́ды).
extract **1.** ['ekstrækt] экстра́кт; вы́держка, извлече́ние; **2.** [iks'trækt] удаля́ть [-ли́ть]; извлека́ть [-е́чь]; вырыва́ть [вы́рвать]; **~ion** [-kʃən] извлече́ние; происхожде́ние (челове́ка).
extraordinary [iks'trɔ:dnri] необыча́йный; удиви́тельный, стра́нный.
extravagan|ce [iks'trævigəns] расточи́тельность *f*; неле́пость *f*; изли́шество; **~t** [-gənt] □ расточи́тельный; сумасбро́дный, неле́пый.
extrem|e [iks'tri:m] **1.** □ кра́йний; после́дний; чрезвыча́йный; **2.** кра́йность *f*; **~ity** [iks'tremiti] оконе́чность *f*; кра́йность *f*; кра́йняя нужда́; кра́йняя ме́ра; **~ities** [-z] *pl.* коне́чности *f/pl.*
extricate ['ekstrikeit] выводи́ть [вы́вести] (из затрудни́тельного положе́ния).
exuberan|ce [ig'zju:bərəns] изоби́лие, избы́ток; **~t** [-t] оби́льный; пы́шный; цвети́стый, многосло́вный.
exult [ig'zʌlt] ликова́ть; торжествова́ть.
eye [ai] **1.** глаз, о́ко; взгляд; ушко́; with an ~ to с це́лью (+ *inf.*); **2.** смотре́ть на (В), при́стально разгля́дывать; **~ball** глазно́е я́блоко; **~brow** бровь *f*; **...~d** [aid] ...гла́зый; **~-glass** ли́нза; (a pair of) ~es *pl.* очки́ *n/pl.*; лорне́т; **~lash** ресни́ца; **~lid** ве́ко; **~sight** зре́ние.

F

fable ['feibl] ба́сня.
fabric ['fæbrik] сооруже́ние; структу́ра; вы́делка; фабрика́т; ткань *f*, мате́рия; **~ate** ['fæbrikeit] (*mst fig.*) выду́мывать [вы́думать]; выде́лывать [вы́делать].
fabulous ['fæbjuləs] □ баснослóвный; неправдоподо́бный.
face [feis] **1.** лицо́, физионо́мия; грима́са; лицева́я сторона́ (тка́ни); фаса́д; on the ~ of it с пе́рвого взгля́да; **2.** *v/t.* встреча́ть сме́ло; смотре́ть в лицо́ (Д); стоя́ть лицо́м к (Д); выходи́ть на (В) (об окне́); ⚠ облицо́вывать [-цева́ть]; [на-, от]полирова́ть; *v/i.* ~ about ⚔ повора́чиваться круго́м.
facetious [fə'si:ʃəs] □ шутли́вый.
facil|e ['fæsail] лёгкий; свобо́дный (о ре́чи и т. п.); **~itate** [fə'siliteit] облегча́ть [-чи́ть]; **~ity** [fə'siliti] лёгкость *f*; спосо́бность *f*; пла́вность *f* (ре́чи); облегче́ние.
facing ['feisiŋ] ⊕ облицо́вка; **~s** *pl.* отде́лка мунди́ра.
fact [fækt] факт; де́ло; явле́ние; и́стина; действи́тельность *f*.
faction ['fækʃən] фра́кция; кли́ка.
factitious [fæk'tiʃəs] □ иску́сственный.
factor ['fæktə] фа́ктор; аге́нт; † комиссионе́р; **~y** [-ri] фа́брика, заво́д.
faculty ['fækəlti] спосо́бность *f*; *fig.* дар; *univ.* факульте́т.
fad [fæd] F конёк; при́хоть *f*, при- }чу́да.
fade [feid] увяда́ть [увя́нуть]; постепе́нно исчеза́ть.
fag [fæg] *v/i.* потруди́ться; корпе́ть (над Т); *v/t.* утомля́ть [-ми́ть].
fail [feil] **1.** *v/i.* ослабе́(ва́)ть; недост(ав)а́ть; потерпе́ть неуда́чу; прова́ливаться [-ли́ться] (на экза́мене); he ~ed to do ему́ не удало́сь сде́лать (Р); забы(ва́)ть; *v/t.* изменя́ть [-ни́ть] (Д), покида́ть [-и́нуть]; **2.** *su.*: without ~ наверняка́; непреме́нно; **~ing** ['feiliŋ] недоста́ток; сла́бость *f*; **~ure** ['feiljə] неуда́ча, неуспе́х; прова́л (на экза́мене); банкро́тство; неуда́чник (-ица).
faint [feint] **1.** □ сла́бый; ро́бкий (го́лос); ту́склый; **2.** [о]слабе́ть; потеря́ть созна́ние (with от Р); **3.** о́бморок, поте́ря созна́ния; **~hearted** ['feint'hɑ:tid] малоду́шный.
fair[1] [fɛə] **1.** *adj.* прекра́сный, краси́вый; благоприя́тный; белоку́рый; я́сный; попу́тный; справедли́вый; **2.** *adv.* че́стно; любе́зно; пря́мо, я́сно; ~ copy чистови́к; ~ play игра́ по пра́вилам.
fair[2] [~] я́рмарка.
fair|ly ['fɛəli] справедли́во; дово́льно; сно́сно; **~ness** ['fɛənis] справедли́вость *f*; красота́ (*s.* fair[1]); **~way** ⚓ фарва́тер.
fairy ['fɛəri] фе́я; **~land** ска́зочная страна́; **~-tale** ска́зка.
faith [feiθ] дове́рие, ве́ра; ве́ра (рели́гия); **~ful** ['feiθful] □ ве́рный, пре́данный; правди́вый; yours ~ly уважа́ющий Вас; **~less** ['feiθlis] □ вероло́мный; неве́рующий.

fake [feik] *sl.* **1.** подде́лка, фальши́вка; **2.** подде́л(ыв)ать.
falcon ['fɔ:lkən] со́кол.
fall [fɔ:l] **1.** паде́ние; упа́док; обры́в, склон; напо́р; *Am.* о́сень *f*; (*mst* ~s *pl.*) водопа́д; **2.** [*irr.*] па́дать [упа́сть]; спада́ть [спасть]; убы́(ва́)ть (о воде́); обва́ливаться [-ли́ться] (о земле́); ~ back отступа́ть [-пи́ть]; ~ ill и́ли sick заболе́(ва́)ть; ~ out [по]ссо́риться; ~ short of не оправда́ть (ожида́ний); не достига́ть [-и́чь] *a.* [-и́гнуть] (це́ли); ~ short не хвата́ть [-ти́ть], конча́ться [ко́нчиться]; ~ to принима́ться [-ня́ться] за (В).
fallacious [fə'leiʃəs] □ оши́бочный, ло́жный.
fallacy ['fæləsi] заблужде́ние, оши́бка.
fallen ['fɔ:lən] *p. pt.* от fall.
falling ['fɔ:liŋ] паде́ние; пониже́ние; **~-sickness** эпиле́псия; **~-star** метео́р, па́дающая звезда́.
fallow ['fælou] *adj.* вспа́ханный под па́р.
false [fɔ:ls] □ ло́жный, оши́бочный; фальши́вый; вероло́мный; иску́ственный (о зуба́х); **~hood** ['fɔ:lshud], **~ness** [-nis] ложь *f*; фальши́вость *f*; оши́бочность *f*.
falsi|fication [fɔ:lsifi'keiʃən] подде́лка; **~fy** ['fɔ:lsifai] подде́л(ыв)ать; **~ty** [-ti] ло́жность *f*, оши́бочность *f*; вероло́мство.
falter ['fɔ:ltə] спотыка́ться [-ткну́ться]; запина́ться [запну́ться]; *fig.* колеба́ться.
fame [feim] сла́ва; молва́; **~d** [feimd] изве́стный, знамени́тый.
familiar [fə'miljə] **1.** □ бли́зкий, хорошо́ знако́мый; обы́чный; **2.** бли́зкий друг; **~ity** [fəmili'æriti] бли́зость *f*; фамилья́рность *f*; осведомлённость *f*; **~ize** [fə'miljəraiz] ознакомля́ть [-ко́мить].
family ['fæmili] семья́, семе́йство; in the ~ way в интере́сном положе́нии (бере́менна); ~ tree родосло́вное де́рево.
fami|ne ['fæmin] го́лод; голода́ние; **~sh** голода́ть; мори́ть го́лодом.
famous ['feiməs] □ знамени́тый.
fan [fæn] **1.** ве́ер; вентиля́тор; *sport* боле́льщик (-ица); покло́нник (-ица); **2.** обма́хивать [-хну́ть].
fanatic [fə'nætik] **1.** (*a.* **~al** □ [-ikəl]) фанати́ческий; **2.** фана́тик (-ти́чка).
fanciful ['fænsiful] □ прихотли́вый, капри́зный, причу́дливый.
fancy ['fænsi] **1.** фанта́зия, воображе́ние; при́хоть *f*; пристра́стие; скло́нность *f*; **2.** прихотли́вый; фантасти́ческий; орнамента́льный; ~ ball костюміро́ванный бал; ~ goods *pl.* мо́дные това́ры *m/pl.*; **3.** вообража́ть [-рази́ть]; представля́ть [-а́вить] себе́; [по-]люби́ть; [за]хоте́ть; just ~! предста́вьте себе́!
fang [fæŋ] клык; ядови́тый зуб (зме́й).
fantas|tic [fæn'tæstik] (**~ally**) причу́дливый, фантасти́чный; **~y** ['fæntəsi] фанта́зия, воображе́ние.
far [fɑ:] *adj.* да́льний, далёкий, отдалённый; *adv.* далеко́; гора́здо; as ~ as до (Р); in so ~ as поско́льку; ~ **away** далеко́.
fare [fɛə] **1.** проездны́е де́ньги *f/pl.*; пассажи́р; съестны́е припа́сы *m/pl.*; **2.** быть, пожива́ть; пита́ться; **~well** ['fɛə'wel] **1.** проща́й(те)!; **2.** проща́ние.
far-fetched ['fɑ:'fetʃt] *fig.* притя́нутый за́ волосы.
farm [fɑ:m] **1.** фе́рма; **2.** обраба́тывать зе́млю; **~er** ['fɑ:mə] крестья́нин, фе́рмер; **~house** жило́й дом на фе́рме; **~ing 1.** заня́тие се́льским хозя́йством; **2.** сельскохозя́йственный; **~stead** ['fɑ:msted] уса́дьба.
far-off ['fɑ:rɔf] далёкий.
farthe|r ['fɑ:ðə] **1.** *adv.* да́льше; **2.** *adj.* отдалённый; **~st** [-ðist] **1.** *adj.* са́мый далёкий, са́мый да́льний; **2.** *adv.* да́льше всего́.
fascinat|e ['fæsineit] очаро́вывать [-ова́ть], пленя́ть [-ни́ть]; **~ion** [fæsi'neiʃən] очарова́ние, обая́ние.
fashion ['fæʃn] **1.** мо́да; стиль *m*; фасо́н, покро́й; о́браз, мане́ра; in (out of) ~ (не)мо́дный; **2.** придава́ть фо́рму, вид (Д into Р); **~able** ['fæʃnəbl] □ мо́дный, фешене́бельный.
fast[1] [fɑ:st] про́чный, кре́пкий, твёрдый; бы́стрый; легкомы́сленный.
fast[2] [~] **1.** *eccl.* пост; **2.** пости́ться.
fasten ['fɑ:sn] *v/t.* прикрепля́ть [-пи́ть]; привя́зывать [-за́ть]; сви́нчивать [-нти́ть]; застёгивать [-тегну́ть]; *v/i.* запира́ться [запере́ться]; застёгивать(ся) [-тегну́ть(-ся)]; ~ upon *fig.* ухвати́ться за (В); **~er** [-ə] запо́р, задви́жка; застёжка.
fastidious [fæs'tidiəs] □ приве-ре́дливый.
fat [fæt] **1.** □ жи́рный; са́льный; ту́чный; **2.** жир; са́ло; **3.** отка́рмливать [откорми́ть]; [раз-]жире́ть.
fatal ['feitl] □ рокова́й, фата́льный, неизбе́жный; смерте́льный; **~ity** [fə'tæliti] обречённость *f*; фата́льность *f*; несча́стье; смерть *f* (от несча́стного слу́чая).
fate [feit] рок, судьба́.
father ['fɑ:ðə] оте́ц; **~hood** [-hud] отцо́вство; **~-in-law** ['fɑ:ðərinlɔ:] свёкор; тесть *m*; **~less** [-lis] оста́вшийся без отца́; **~ly** [-li] оте́ческий.

fathom ['fæðəm] **1.** ⚓ морска́я са́жень *f* (= 6 футам = 182 сантиме́трам); **2.** ⚓ измеря́ть глубину́ (Р); *fig.* вника́ть [вни́кнуть] в (В), понима́ть [поня́ть]; **~less** [-lis] неизмери́мый; бездо́нный.
fatigue [fə'ti:g] **1.** утомле́ние, уста́лость *f*; **2.** утомля́ть [-ми́ть], изнуря́ть [-ри́ть].
fat|ness ['fætnis] жи́рность *f*; **~ten** ['fætn] отка́рмливать [откорми́ть] (на убо́й); [раз]жире́ть.
fatuous ['fætjuəs] □ глу́пый, пусто́й.
faucet ['fɔ:sit] *Am.* (водопрово́дный) кран.
fault [fɔ:lt] недоста́ток, дефе́кт; просту́пок, вина́; find ~ with прид(и)ра́ться к (Д); be at ~ потеря́ть след; **~-finder** приди́ра *m/f*; **~less** ['fɔ:ltlis] □ безупре́чный; **~y** ['fɔ:lti] □ име́ющий недоста́ток, дефе́ктный.
favo(u)r ['feivə] **1.** благоскло́нность *f*, расположе́ние; одобре́ние; одолже́ние; your ~ ✝ Ва́ше письмо́; **2.** благоволи́ть к (Д); ока́зывать внима́ние (Д); покрови́тельствовать (Д); **~able** [-rəbl] □ благоприя́тный, удо́бный; **~ite** ['feivərit] **1.** люби́мец (-мица); фаво́рит(ка); **2.** люби́мый.
fawn [fɔ:n] **1.** молодо́й оле́нь *m*; кори́чневый цвет; **2.** подли́зываться [-за́ться] (upon к Д).
fear [fiə] **1.** страх, боя́знь *f*; опасе́ние; **2.** боя́ться (Р); **~ful** ['fiəful] □ стра́шный, ужа́сный; **~less** ['fiəlis] □ бесстра́шный, неустраши́мый.
feasible ['fi:zəbl] возмо́жный, вероя́тный; выполни́мый.
feast [fi:st] **1.** пир, пра́зднество, банке́т; **2.** *v/t.* угоща́ть [угости́ть]; че́ствовать; *v/i.* пирова́ть.
feat [fi:t] по́двиг; трюк.
feather ['feðə] **1.** перо́; опере́ние; show the white ~ F прояви́ть тру́сость; in high ~ в отли́чном настрое́нии; **2.** украша́ть пе́рьями; **~-brained, ~-headed** пусто́й, ве́треный, глу́пый; **~ed** ['feðəd] перна́тый; **~y** [-ri] оперённый; пуши́стый.
feature ['fi:tʃə] **1.** осо́бенность *f*, сво́йство; *Am.* газе́тная статья́; **~s** *pl.* черты́ лица́; **2.** изобража́ть [-рази́ть]; пока́зывать [-за́ть] (на экра́не); выводи́ть в гла́вной ро́ли.
February ['februəri] февра́ль *m.*
fecund ['fekənd] плодоро́дный.
fed [fed] *pt.* и *p. pt.* от feed; I am ~ up with ... мне надое́л (-ла, -ло).
federa|l ['fedərəl] федера́льный; сою́зный; **~tion** [fedə'reiʃən] федера́ция.
fee [fi:] **1.** гонора́р; взнос; пла́та; чаевы́е *pl.* **2.** [за]плати́ть.
feeble ['fi:bl] □ сла́бый, хи́лый.
feed [fi:d] **1.** пита́ние, кормле́ние; пи́ща; ⊕ пода́ча (материа́ла); **2.** [*irr.*] *v/t.* пита́ть, [по]корми́ть; ⊕ снабжа́ть [-бди́ть] (материа́лом); *v/i.* пита́ться, корми́ться; пасти́сь; **~ing-bottle** де́тский рожо́к.
feel [fi:l] **1.** [*irr.*] [по]чу́вствовать (себя́); испы́тывать [-та́ть]; ощуща́ть [ощути́ть], осяза́ть; ~ like doing быть скло́нным сде́лать; **2.** ощуще́ние, осяза́ние; чутьё; **~er** ['fi:lə] щу́пальце; **~ing** ['fi:liŋ] **1.** □ чувстви́тельный; прочу́вствованный; **2.** чу́вство.
feet [fi:t] *pl.* от foot 1.
feign [fein] притворя́ться [-ри́ться], симули́ровать (*im*)*pf.*
feint [feint] притво́рство; манёвр.
felicit|ate [fi'lisiteit] поздравля́ть [-а́вить]; **~ous** [-təs] □ уда́чный; счастли́вый.
fell [fel] **1.** *pt.* от fall; **2.** [с]руби́ть.
felloe ['felou] о́бод (колеса́).
fellow [~] това́рищ, собра́т; челове́к; the ~ of a glove па́рная перча́тка; **~-countryman** сооте́чественник; **~ship** [-ʃip] това́рищество.
felly ['feli] о́бод (колеса́).
felon ['felən] ⚖ уголо́вный престу́пник; **~y** ['feləni] уголо́вное преступле́ние.
felt[1] [felt] *pt.* и *p. pt.* от feel.
felt[2] [~] **1.** во́йлок, фетр; **2.** сбива́ть (*or* сбива́ться в) во́йлок.
female ['fi:meil] **1.** же́нский; **2.** же́нщина.
feminine ['feminin] □ же́нский; же́нственный.
fen [fen] боло́то, топь *f*.
fence [fens] **1.** забо́р, и́згородь *f*, огра́да; sit on the ~ колеба́ться ме́жду двумя́ мне́ниями; занима́ть выжида́тельную пози́цию; **2.** *v/t.* огора́живать [-роди́ть]; защища́ть [-ити́ть]; *v/i.* фехтова́ть; укрыва́ть кра́деное.
fencing ['fensiŋ] **1.** и́згородь *f*, забо́р, огра́да; фехтова́ние; **2.** *attr.* фехтова́льный.
fender ['fendə] ками́нная решётка; *mot. Am.* крыло́.
ferment **1.** ['fə:ment] заква́ска, ферме́нт; ⚗ броже́ние; *fig.* возбужде́ние, волне́ние; **2.** [fə'ment] вызыва́ть броже́ние; броди́ть; *fig.* волнова́ться; **~ation** [fə:men'teiʃən] броже́ние, фермента́ция.
fern [fə:n] ⚘ па́поротник.
feroci|ous [fə'rouʃəs] □ жесто́кий, свире́пый; **~ty** [fə'rɔsiti] жесто́кость *f*, свире́пость *f*.
ferret ['ferit] **1.** *zo.* хорёк; **2.** [по-]ры́ться, [по]ша́рить; ~ out вы́искивать [вы́искать]; разве́д(ыв)ать.
ferry ['feri] **1.** перево́з, перепра́ва; паро́м; **2.** перевози́ть [-везти́]; **~man** перево́зчик.

fertil|e ['fə:tail] □ плодоро́дный; изоби́льный; изоби́лующий (T); **~ity** [fə:'tiliti] плодоро́дие; изоби́лие; **~ize** ['fə:tilaiz] удобря́ть [удо́брить]; оплодотворя́ть [-ри́ть]; **~izer** удобре́ние.
ferven|cy ['fə:vənsi] рве́ние, пыл; **~t** [-t] □ горя́чий, пы́лкий.
fervour ['fə:və] жар, пыл.
festal ['festl] □ пра́здничный.
fester [-tə] гнои́ться.
festiv|al ['festəvəl] пра́зднество; фестива́ль *m*; **~e** ['festiv] □ пра́здничный; **~ity** [fes'tiviti] пра́зднество; весе́лье.
fetch [fetʃ] сходи́ть, съе́здить за (T); приноси́ть [-нести́]; **~ing** F □ привлека́тельный.
fetid ['fetid] □ злово́нный, воню́чий.
fetter ['fetə] **1.** *mst* **~s** *pl.* пу́ты *f/pl.*; кандалы́ *m/pl.*; *fig.* око́вы *f/pl.*, у́зы *f/pl.*; **2.** зако́вывать [-ова́ть].
feud [fju:d] вражда́; феода́льное поме́стье; **~al** ['fju:dəl] □ феода́льный; **~alism** [-delizm] феодали́зм.
fever ['fi:və] лихора́дка, жар; **~ish** [-riʃ] □ лихора́дочный.
few [fju:] немно́гие; немно́го, ма́ло (P); a **~** не́сколько (P).
fiancé(e) [fi'ɑ:ŋsei] жени́х (неве́ста).
fib [fib] **1.** вы́думка, непра́вда; **2.** прив(и)ра́ть.
fibr|e ['faibə] фи́бра, волокно́, нить *f*; **~ous** ['faibrəs] □ волокни́стый.
fickle ['fikl] непостоя́нный; **~ness** [-nis] непостоя́нство.
fiction ['fikʃən] вы́мысел, вы́думка; беллетри́стика; **~al** [-l] □ вы́мышленный; беллетристи́ческий.
fictitious [fik'tiʃəs] □ вы́мышленный; фикти́вный.
fiddle ['fidl] F **1.** скри́пка; **2.** игра́ть на скри́пке; **~stick** смычо́к.
fidelity [fi'deliti] ве́рность *f*, пре́данность *f*; то́чность *f*.
fidget ['fidʒit] F **1.** беспоко́йное состоя́ние; **2.** ёрзать, быть в волне́нии; приводи́ть в беспоко́йство; **~y** суетли́вый, беспоко́йный, не́рвный.
field [fi:ld] по́ле; луг; простра́нство; hold the **~** уде́рживать пози́ции; **~-glass** полево́й бино́кль *m*; **~-officer** штаб-офице́р; **~ of vision** по́ле зре́ния; **~-sports** *pl.* спорт на откры́том во́здухе.
fiend [fi:nd] дья́вол; злой дух; **~ish** ['fi:ndiʃ] □ дья́вольский; жесто́кий, злой.
fierce [fiəs] □ свире́пый, лю́тый; си́льный; **~ness** ['fiəsnis] свире́пость *f*, лю́тость *f*.
fif|teen ['fif'ti:n] пятна́дцать; **~teenth** [-θ] пятна́дцатый; **~th** [fifθ] **1.** пя́тый; **2.** пя́тая часть *f*; **~tieth** ['fiftiiθ] пятидеся́тый; **~ty** ['fifti] пятьдеся́т.
fig [fig] **1.** ви́нная я́года, инжи́р, смо́ква; **2.** F состоя́ние.
fight [fait] **1.** сраже́ние, бой; дра́ка; спор; борьба́; show **~** быть гото́вым к борьбе́; **2.** [*irr.*] *v/t.* боро́ться про́тив (P); отста́ивать [отстоя́ть]; *v/i.* сража́ться [срази́ться]; воева́ть; боро́ться; **~er** ['faitə] бое́ц; ✈ истреби́тель *m*; **~ing** ['faitiŋ] сраже́ние, бой; дра́ка; *attr.* боево́й.
figurative ['figjurətiv] □ перено́сный, метафори́ческий.
figure ['figə] **1.** фигу́ра; изображе́ние; ци́фра; диагра́мма; F цена́; **2.** *v/t.* изобража́ть [-рази́ть]; представля́ть себе́; вычисля́ть [вы́числить], рассчи́тывать [-ита́ть]; *v/i.* фигури́ровать.
filament ['filəmənt] ⚡ нить нака́ла; волокно́, волосо́к.
filbert ['filbət] ♀ лесно́й оре́х.
filch [filtʃ] [у]красть, [у-, с]тащи́ть (from у P).
file[1] [fail] **1.** ⊕ напи́льник; пи́лочка (для ногте́й); **2.** пили́ть, подпи́ливать [-ли́ть].
file[2] [~] **1.** регистра́тор; подши́тые бума́ги *f/pl.*; картоте́ка; **2.** регистри́ровать (докуме́нты) (*im*)*pf.*; подшива́ть к де́лу.
filial ['filjəl] □ сыно́вний, доче́рний.
filibuster ['filibʌstə] флибустье́р, пира́т.
fill [fil] **1.** наполня́ть(ся) [-о́лнить (-ся)]; [за]пломбирова́ть (зуб); удовлетворя́ть [-ри́ть]; *Am.* выполня́ть [вы́полнить] (зака́зы); **~** in заполня́ть [-о́лнить]; **2.** доста́ток; сы́тость *f*.
fillet ['filit] повя́зка (на го́лову); филе́(й) (мя́со) *n indecl.*
filling ['filiŋ] наполне́ние; погру́зка; (зубна́я) пло́мба; фарш, начи́нка; *mot.* **~** station бензи́новая коло́нка.
fillip ['filip] щелчо́к; толчо́к.
filly ['fili] молода́я кобы́ла.
film [film] **1.** плёнка; фильм; ды́мка; **~** cartridge кату́шка с плёнками; **2.** производи́ть киносъёмку (P); экранизи́ровать (*im*)*pf.*
filter ['filtə] **1.** фильтр, цеди́лка; **2.** [про]фильтрова́ть, проце́живать [-цеди́ть].
filth [filθ] грязь *f*; **~y** ['filθi] □ гря́зный, нечи́стый.
fin [fin] плавни́к (ры́бы); *sl.* рука́.
final ['fainl] **1.** □ заключи́тельный; оконча́тельный; **2.** *sport* фина́л.
financ|e [fi'næns] **1.** нау́ка о фина́нсах; **~s** *pl.* фина́нсы *m/pl.*; **2.** *v/t.* финанси́ровать (*im*)*pf.*; *v/i.* занима́ться фина́нсовыми опера́циями; **~ial** [fi'nænʃəl] □ фина́нсовый; **~ier** [-siə] финанси́ст.
finch [fintʃ] *zo.* зя́блик.

find [faind] [*irr.*] **1.** находи́ть [найти́]; счита́ть [счесть]; обрета́ть [обрести́]; заст(ав)а́ть; all found на всём гото́вом; **2.** нахо́дка; **~ing** ['faindiŋ] ⚖ пригово́р; *pl.* вы́воды.
fine[1] [fain] □ то́нкий, изя́щный; прекра́сный; высокопро́бный.
fine[2] [~] **1.** штраф; in ~ в о́бщем, сло́вом; наконе́ц; **2.** [о]штрафова́ть.
fineness ['fainnis] то́нкость *f*, изя́щество; острота́ (чувств).
finery ['fainəri] пы́шный наря́д; украше́ние.
finger ['fiŋgə] **1.** па́лец; **2.** тро́гать, перебира́ть па́льцами; **~-language** язы́к глухонемы́х; **~-print** дактилоскопи́ческий отпеча́ток.
finish ['finiʃ] **1.** *v/t.* конча́ть [ко́нчить]; заверша́ть [-ши́ть]; отде́л(ыв)ать; доеда́ть [дое́сть], допи́(ва́)ть; *v/i.* конча́ть(ся) [ко́нчить(ся)]; **2.** коне́ц; зако́нченность *f*; отде́лка; *sport* фи́ниш.
finite ['fainait] □ ограни́ченный, име́ющий преде́л.
fir [fə:] ель *f*, пи́хта; **~-cone** ['fə:koun] ело́вая ши́шка.
fire ['faiə] **1.** ого́нь *m*; be on ~ горе́ть; **2.** *v/t.* зажига́ть [заже́чь], поджига́ть [-же́чь]; [за]топи́ть (пе́чку); обжига́ть [обже́чь] (кирпичи́ и т. п.); *fig.* воспламеня́ть [-ни́ть]; *Am.* F увольня́ть [уво́лить]; *v/i.* стреля́ть [вы́стрелить]; **~-alarm** пожа́рная трево́га; **~-brigade,** *Am.* **~-department** пожа́рная кома́нда; **~-engine** [''faiər'endʒin] пожа́рная маши́на; **~-escape** [''faiəris'keip] пожа́рная ле́стница; **~-extinguisher** [-riks'tiŋgwiʃə] огнетуши́тель *m*; **~man** пожа́рный; кочега́р; **~place** ками́н; **~plug** пожа́рный кран, гидра́нт; **~proof** огнеупо́рный; **~-side** ме́сто о́коло ками́на; **~-station** пожа́рная ста́нция; **~wood** дрова́ *n/pl.*; **~works** *pl.* фейерве́рк.
firing ['faiəriŋ] стрельба́; отопле́ние.
firm [fə:m] **1.** □ кре́пкий, пло́тный, твёрдый; сто́йкий; насто́йчивый; **2.** фи́рма; **~ness** ['fə:mnis] твёрдость *f*.
first [fə:st] **1.** *adj.* пе́рвый; ра́нний; выдаю́щийся; ~ cost ✝ себесто́имость *f*; **2.** *adv.* сперва́, снача́ла; впервы́е; скоре́е; at ~ снача́ла; ~ of all пре́жде всего́; **3.** нача́ло; the ~ пе́рвое число́; from the ~ с са́мого нача́ла; **~-born** перве́нец; **~-class** первокла́ссный; **~ly** ['fə:stli] во-пе́рвых; **~-rate** первокла́ссный.
fish [fiʃ] **1.** ры́ба; F odd (или queer) ~ чуда́к; **2.** уди́ть ры́бу; выу́живать [вы́удить] (*a. fig.*); **~-bone** ры́бная кость *f*.
fisher|man ['fiʃəmən] рыба́к, рыболо́в; **~y** [-ri] рыболо́вство; ры́бный про́мысел.
fishing ['fiʃiŋ] ры́бная ло́вля; **~-line** ле́са́; **~-tackle** рыболо́вные принадле́жности *f/pl.*
fiss|ion ['fiʃən] ⚛ расщепле́ние; **~ure** ['fiʃə] тре́щина, рассе́лина.
fist [fist] кула́к; по́черк (шутли́во); **~icuffs** ['fistikʌfs] *pl.* кула́чный бой.
fit[1] [fit] **1.** □ го́дный, подходя́щий; здоро́вый; досто́йный; **2.** *v/t.* прила́живать [-ла́дить] (to к Д); подходи́ть [подойти́] к (Д); приспособля́ть [-спосо́бить] (for, to к Д); ~ out снаряжа́ть [-яди́ть]; снабжа́ть [-бди́ть]; ~ up соб(и)ра́ть, [с]монти́ровать; *v/i.* годи́ться; сиде́ть (о пла́тье); прила́живаться [-ла́диться]; приспособля́ться [-посо́биться]; **3.** ⊕ приго́нка; поса́дка.
fit[2] [fit] ⚕ припа́док, парокси́зм, при́ступ; поры́в; by ~s and starts поры́вами, уры́вками; give a p. a ~ поража́ть [порази́ть] (В), возмуща́ть [-ути́ть] (В).
fit|ful ['fitful] □ су́дорожный, поры́вистый; **~ness** [-nis] приго́дность *f*; **~ter** [-ə] меха́ник, монтёр; **~ting** [-iŋ] **1.** □ подходя́щий, го́дный; **2.** устано́вка; сбо́рка, монта́ж; приме́рка (пла́тья); **~s** *pl.* армату́ра.
five [faiv] **1.** пять; **2.** пятёрка.
fix [fiks] **1.** устана́вливать [-нови́ть]; укрепля́ть [-пи́ть]; остана́вливать [-нови́ть] (взгляд, внима́ние) (на П); *Am.* приводи́ть в поря́док; ~ o. s. устра́иваться [-ро́иться]; ~ up реша́ть [реши́ть]; организова́ть (*im*)*pf.*; ула́живать [ула́дить]; устра́ивать [-ро́ить]; *v/i.* затверде́(ва)ть; остана́вливаться [-нови́ться] (on на П); **2.** F диле́мма, затрудни́тельное положе́ние; **~ed** [fikst] (*adv.* **~edly** ['fiksidli]) неподви́жный; **~ture** ['fikstʃə] армату́ра; прибо́р, приспособле́ние; устано́вленная величина́; lighting ~ освети́тельный прибо́р.
fizzle ['fizl] [за]шипе́ть.
flabby ['flæbi] □ вя́лый; *fig.* слабохара́ктерный.
flag [flæg] **1.** флаг, зна́мя *n*; плита́; плитня́к; **2.** сигнализи́ровать фла́гом; украша́ть фла́гами; мости́ть пли́тами.
flagitious [flə'dʒiʃəs] □ престу́пный, гну́сный, позо́рный.
flagrant ['fleigrənt] □ сканда́льный; очеви́дный.
flag|staff флагшто́к; **~-stone** плита́ (для моще́ния).
flair [flɛə] чутьё, нюх.
flake [fleik] **1.** слой; **~s** *pl.* хло́пья *m/pl.*; **2.** па́дать хло́пьями; расслаиваться [-ло́иться].

flame [fleim] **1.** пла́мя *n*; ого́нь *m*; *fig.* пыл, страсть *f*; **2.** пламене́ть; пыла́ть.
flank [flæŋk] **1.** бок, сторона́; склон (горы́); ⚔ фланг; **2.** быть располо́женым сбо́ку, на фла́нге (Р); ~ (on) грани́чить (с Т), примыка́ть (к Д).
flannel ['flænl] флане́ль *f*; **~s** [-z] *pl.* флане́левые брю́ки *f/pl.*
flap [flæp] **1.** взмах (кры́льев); хлопо́к, шлепо́к; пола́; дли́нное у́хо (соба́ки и т. п.); **2.** *v/t.* маха́ть [махну́ть] (Т); взма́хивать [-хну́ть] (кры́льями); шлёпать [-пнуть], ударя́ть легко́; *v/i.* свиса́ть; развева́ться [-ве́яться].
flare [flɛə] **1.** горе́ть я́рким пла́менем; расширя́ться [-ши́риться]; ~ up вспы́хивать [-хнуть]; *fig.* разрази́ться гне́вом, вспыли́ть *pf.*; **2.** вспы́шка; сигна́льная раке́та; вспы́хивание.
flash [flæʃ] **1.** показно́й, безвку́сный, крича́щий; **2.** вспы́шка; *fig.* про́блеск; in a ~ в мгнове́ние о́ка; **3.** сверка́ть [-кну́ть]; вспы́хивать [-хнуть]; бы́стро пронести́сь; сро́чно передава́ть (по телефо́ну, телегра́фу); **~-light** *phot.* вспы́шка ма́гния; *Am.* карма́нный электри́ческий фона́рь *m*; **~y** □ показно́й, безвку́сный.
flask [flɑ:sk] фля́жка; флако́н.
flat [flæt] **1.** □ пло́ский; ро́вный; ску́чный; ⚕ вя́лый (о ры́нке); ♪ бемо́льный, мино́рный; прямо́й; ~ price станда́ртная цена́; fall ~ не име́ть успе́ха; sing ~ детони́ровать; **2.** пло́скость *f*; равни́на, низи́на; ♪ бемо́ль *m*; **~-iron** утю́г; **~ness** ['flætnis] пло́скость *f*; безвку́сица; ⚕ вя́лость *f*; **~ten** ['flætn] де́лать(ся) пло́ским, ро́вным.
flatter ['flætə] [по]льсти́ть (Д); **~er** [-rə] льстец (льсти́ца); **~y** [-ri] лесть *f*.
flavo(u)r ['fleivə] **1.** прия́тный вкус; арома́т; *fig.* при́вкус; **2.** приправля́ть [-ра́вить] (пи́щу); придава́ть за́пах, вкус (Д); **~less** [-lis] безвку́сный.
flaw [flɔ:] **1.** тре́щина, щель *f*; недоста́ток; поро́к; брак (това́ра); ⚓ шквал, поры́в ве́тра; **2.** поврежда́ть [-еди́ть]; [по]тре́скаться; **~less** ['flɔ:lis] □ безупре́чный.
flax [flæks] ⚘ лён.
flay [flei] сдира́ть ко́жу с (Р).
flea [fli:] блоха́.
fled [fled] *pt.* и *p. pt.* от **flee.**
flee [fli:] [*irr.*] [по]бежа́ть, спаса́ться бе́гством.
fleec|e [fli:s] **1.** руно́; ове́чья шерсть *f*; **2.** [о]стри́чь (овцу́); *fig.* обдира́ть [ободра́ть]; **~y** ['fli:si] покры́тый ше́рстью.
fleer [fliə] насмеха́ться [-ея́ться] (at над Т).
fleet [fli:t] **1.** □ бы́стрый; неглубо́кий; **2.** флот.
flesh [fleʃ] **1.** сыро́е мя́со; плоть *f*; мя́коть *f* (плода́); *fig.* по́хоть *f*; **2.** приуча́ть вку́сом кро́ви (соба́ку к охо́те); **~ly** ['fleʃli] пло́тский, теле́сный; **~y** [-i] мяси́стый; то́лстый.
flew [flu:] *pt.* от fly.
flexib|ility [fleksə'biliti] ги́бкость *f*; **~le** ['fleksəbl] □ ги́бкий, гну́щийся; *fig.* пода́тливый.
flicker ['flikə] **1.** мерца́ние; трепета́ние; **2.** мерца́ть; мелька́ть [-кну́ть].
flier *s.* flyer лётчик.
flight [flait] полёт, перелёт; стая́ (птиц); ⚔, ✈ звено́; бе́гство; ряд ступе́ней; put to ~ обраща́ть в бе́гство; **~y** ['flaiti] □ ве́треный, капри́зный.
flimsy ['flimzi] непро́чный, то́нкий.
flinch [flintʃ] уклоня́ться [-ни́ться] (from от Р).
fling ['fliŋ] **1.** бросо́к, швыро́к; жизнера́достность *f*; весе́лье; have one's ~ [по]весели́ться; **2.** [*irr.*] *v/i.* кида́ться [ки́нуться], броса́ться [бро́ситься]; *v/t.* кида́ть [ки́нуть], броса́ть [бро́сить]; распространя́ть [-ни́ть] (арома́т и т. п.); ~ open распа́хивать [-хну́ть] (окно́ и т. п.).
flint [flint] креме́нь *m*.
flip [flip] **1.** щелчо́к; **2.** щёлкать [щёлкнуть].
flippan|cy ['flipənsi] легкомы́слие, ве́треность *f*; **~t** □ легкомы́сленный, ве́треный.
flirt [flə:t] **1.** коке́тка; **2.** флиртова́ть; коке́тничать; **~ation** [flə:'teiʃən] флирт.
flit [flit] порха́ть [-хну́ть]; ю́ркать [юркну́ть]; (та́йно) переезжа́ть [перее́хать].
float [flout] **1.** поплаво́к; буй; паро́м; плот; пла́вательный по́яс; ломова́я теле́га; **2.** *v/t.* затопля́ть [-пи́ть]; наводня́ть [-ни́ть]; ⚓ снима́ть с ме́ли; ⚕ пуска́ть в ход (предприя́тие); *v/i.* пла́вать, [по]плы́ть (о предме́те); держа́ться на воде́.
flock [flɔk] **1.** пуши́нка; клочо́к; ста́до (ове́ц); ста́я; **2.** стека́ться [сте́чься]; держа́ться вме́сте.
flog [flɔg] [вы́]поро́ть, [вы́]сечь.
flood [flʌd] **1.** (*a.* ~-tide) прили́в, подъём воды́; наводне́ние, полово́дье, разли́в; **2.** поднима́ться [-ня́ться] (об у́ровне реки́), выступа́ть из берего́в; затопля́ть [-пи́ть]; наводня́ть [-ни́ть]; **~-gate** шлюз.
floor [flɔ:] **1.** пол; эта́ж; ⚒ гумно́; have the ~ *parl.* взять сло́во; **2.** настила́ть пол; вали́ть на́ пол; *fig.*

смущáть [смутúть]; **~ing** ['flɔ:riŋ] настúлка полóв; пол.
flop [flɔp] **1.** шлёпаться [-пнуться]; плю́хать(ся) [-хнуть(ся)]; бить (крыльями); *Am.* потерпéть фиáско; **2.** шлёпанье.
florid ['flɔrid] □ цветúстый (*a. fig.*).
florin [-in] флорúн (монéта).
florist ['flɔrist] торгóвец цветáми.
floss [flɔs] шёлк-сырéц.
flounce[1] [flauns] обóрка.
flounce[2] [~] бросáться [брóситься], рéзко двúгаться.
flounder[1] *zo.* ['flaundə] кáмбала.
flounder[2] [~] барáхтаться; [за]пýтаться (в словáх).
flour ['flauə] мукá.
flourish ['flʌriʃ] **1.** рóсчерк; цветúстое выражéние; ♪ туш; **2.** *v/i.* пы́шно растú; процветáть, преуспевáть; *v/t.* размáхивать (Т).
flout [flaut] насмехáться (at над Т).
flow [flou] **1.** течéние, потóк; струя́; прилúв; изобúлие; плáвность *f* (рéчи); **2.** течь; струúться; лúться.
flower [flauə] **1.** цветóк; цветéние; расцвéт; **2.** цвестú; **~y** [-ri] *fig.* цветúстый (стиль).
flown [floun] *p. pt.* от fly.
flu [flu:] = influenza F грипп.
fluctuat|e ['flʌktjueit] колебáться; быть неустóйчивым; **~ion** [flʌktju'eiʃən] колебáние; неустóйчивость *f*.
flue [flu:] дымохóд; ⊕ жаровáя трубá.
fluen|cy ['flu:ənsi] *fig.* плáвность *f*, бéглость *f* (рéчи); **~t** [-t] □ плáвный, бéглый; жúдкий; текýчий.
fluff [flʌf] пух, пушóк; **~y** ['flʌfi] пушúстый.
fluid ['flu:id] **1.** жúдкость *f*; **2.** жúдкий; текýчий.
flung [flʌŋ] *pt.* и *p. pt.* от fling.
flunk [flʌŋk] *Am.* F провалúться на экзáмене.
flunk(e)y ['flʌŋki] ливрéйный лакéй.
flurry ['flʌri] волнéние; суматóха.
flush [flʌʃ] **1.** внезáпный притóк; прилúв крóви, крáска (на лицé); прилúв (чувст); **2.** пóлный (до краёв); изобúлующий; **3.** *v/t.* затопля́ть [-пúть]; спускáть вóду в (П); *v/i.* течь; хлы́нуть *pf.*; [по-]краснéть.
fluster ['flʌstə] **1.** суетá, волнéние; **2.** [вз]волновáть(ся); возбуждáть (-ся) [-дúть(ся)].
flute [flu:t] **1.** ♪ флéйта; вы́емка (на колóнне); **2.** игрáть на флéйте.
flutter ['flʌtə] **1.** порхáние; трéпет, волнéние; **2.** *v/i.* махáть кры́льями; развевáться (по вéтру); порхáть [-хнýть].
flux [flʌks] *fig.* течéние; потóк; ⚕ патологúческое истечéние.
fly [flai] **1.** мýха; **2.** [*irr.*] летáть, [по]летéть; пролетáть [-етéть]; [по]спешúть; поднимáть [-ня́ть] (флаг); ✈ управля́ть (самолётом); ~ at набрáсываться [-брóситься] (с брáнью) на (В); **~ into** a passion вспылúть *pf.*
flyer ['flaiə] лётчик.
fly-flap ['flaiflæp] хлопýшка.
flying ['flaiiŋ] летáтельный; лётный; летýчий; ~ squad выезднáя полицéйская комáнда.
fly|-weight наилегчáйший вéс (о боксёре); **~-wheel** маховóе колесó.
foal [foul] **1.** жеребёнок; ослёнок; **2.** [о]жеребúться.
foam [foum] **1.** пéна; мы́ло (на лóшади); **2.** [вс]пéниться; взмы́ли(ва)ться (о лóшади); **~y** ['foumi] пéнящийся; взмы́ленный.
focus ['foukəs] **1.** центр; *phys.*, ⚕ фóкус; **2.** помещáть, быть в фóкусе; сосредотóчи(ва)ть (*a. fig.*).
fodder ['fɔdə] фурáж, корм (скотá).
foe [fou] враг.
fog [fɔg] **1.** густóй тумáн; мгла; замешáтельство; *phot.* вуаль *f*; **2.** [за]тумáнить; *fig.* напускáть (в глазá) тумáну; озадáчи(ва)ть; **~gy** ['fɔgi] □ тумáнный.
foible ['fɔibl] *fig.* слáбость *f*.
foil[1] [fɔil] фóльга; фон.
foil[2] [~] **1.** стáвить в тупúк; расстрáивать плáны (Р); **2.** рапúра.
fold[1] [fould] **1.** (*mst* sheep-~) загóн, овчáрня; *fig.* пáства; **2.** загоня́ть [загнáть] (овéц).
fold[2] [~] **1.** склáдка, сгиб; **2.** створ (двéри); ⊕ фальц; **3.** *v/t.* склáдывать [сложúть]; сгибáть [согнýть]; скрéщивать [-естúть] (рýки); **~er** ['fouldə] фальцóвщик; *Am.* брошю́ра.
folding ['fouldiŋ] складнóй; ствóрчатый; откиднóй; **~-camera** *phot.* складнóй аппарáт; **~-chair** складнóй стул; **~-door(s** *pl.*) двуствóрчатая дверь *f*; **~-screen** шúрма.
foliage ['fouliidʒ] листвá.
folk [fouk] нарóд, лю́ди *m/pl.*; **~lore** ['fouklɔ:] фольклóр; **~-song** нарóдная пéсня.
follow ['fɔlou] слéдовать (за Т *or* Д); следúть за (Т); [по]гнáться за (Т); занимáться [-ня́ться] (Т); ~ suit слéдовать примéру; **~er** ['fɔlouə] послéдователь(ница *f*) *m*; *pol.* попýтчик; поклóнник; **~ing** ['fɔlouiŋ] слéдующий; попýтный.
folly ['fɔli] безрассýдство, глýпость *f*, безýмие.
foment [fou'ment] класть припáрку (Д); подстрекáть [-кнýть].
fond [fɔnd] □ нéжный, любя́щий; be ~ of любúть (В).
fond|le ['fɔndl] [при]ласкáть; **~ness** [-nis] нéжность *f*, любóвь *f*.

font [fɔnt] купе́ль *f*; исто́чник.
food [fu:d] пи́ща; **~-stuffs** *pl.* съестны́е проду́кты *m/pl.*; **~-value** пита́тельность *f*.
fool [fu:l] **1.** дура́к, глупе́ц; make a ~ of a p. одура́чи(ва)ть кого́-либо; **2.** *v/t.* обма́нывать [-ну́ть]; ~ away упуска́ть [-сти́ть]; *v/i.* [по-] дура́читься; ~ about болта́ться зря.
fool|ery ['fu:ləri] дура́чество; **~-hardy** ['fu:lhɑ:di] □ безрассу́дно хра́брый; **~ish** ['fu:liʃ] □ глу́пый; **~ishness** [-nis] глу́пость *f*; **~-proof** несло́жный, безопа́сный.
foot [fut] **1.** (*pl.* feet) нога́, ступня́; фут (ме́ра); основа́ние; on ~ пешко́м; в ходу́; **2.** *v/t.* (*mst* ~ up) подсчи́тывать [-ита́ть]; ~ the bill заплати́ть по счёту; ~ it идти́ пешко́м; **~boy** паж; **~fall** по́ступь *f*; звук шаго́в; **~-gear** F *coll.* о́бувь *f*; чулки́ *m/pl.*; **~hold** *fig.* то́чка опо́ры.
footing ['futiŋ] опо́ра; основа́ние; ито́г столбца́ цифр; lose one's ~ оступа́ться [-пи́ться].
foot|lights *pl. thea.* ра́мпа; **~man** ['futmən] ливре́йный лаке́й; **~-path** тропи́нка; тротуа́р; **~print** след; **~-sore** со стёртыми нога́ми; **~step** стопа́; след; шаг; **~stool** скаме́ечка для ног; **~wear** *part. Am.* = ~-gear.
fop [fɔp] щёголь *m*, хлыщ.
for [fɔ:; fɔ:r; fɔ, fo, f] *prp. mst* для (Р); ра́ди (Р); за (В); в направле́нии (Р), к (Д); из-за (Р), по причи́не (Р), всле́дствие (Р); в тече́ние (Р), в продолже́ние (Р); ~ three days в тече́ние трёх дней; уже́ три дня; вме́сто (Р); в обме́н на (В); **2.** *cj.* так как, потому́ что, и́бо.
forage ['fɔridʒ] **1.** фура́ж; корм; **2.** фуражи́ровать.
foray ['fɔrei] набе́г, мародёрство.
forbad(e) [fə'beid] *pt.* от forbid.
forbear[1] [fɔ:'bɛə] [*irr.*] быть терпели́вым; возде́рживаться [-жа́ться] (from от Р).
forbear[2] ['fɔ:bɛə] пре́док; предше́ственник.
forbid [fə'bid] [*irr.*] запреща́ть [-ети́ть]; **~den** [-n] *p. pt.* от forbid; **~ding** [-iŋ] □ отта́лкивающий; угрожа́ющий.
forbor|e [fɔ:'bɔ:] *pt.* от forbear[1]; **~ne** [-n] *p. pt.* от forbear[1].
force [fɔ:s] **1.** си́ла; наси́лие, принужде́ние; смысл, значе́ние; armed ~s *pl.* вооружённые си́лы *f/pl.*; come in ~ вступа́ть в си́лу; **2.** заставля́ть [-а́вить], принужда́ть [-у́дить]; брать си́лой; ~ open взла́мывать [взлома́ть]; **~d** [-t]: ~ loan принуди́тельный заём; ~ landing вы́нужденная поса́дка; ~ march форси́рованный марш (похо́д); **~ful** □ си́льный, де́йственный.
forcible ['fɔ:səbl] □ наси́льственный; убеди́тельный; эффекти́вный.
ford [fɔ:d] **1.** брод; **2.** переходи́ть [вброд.]
fore [fɔ:] **1.** *adv.* впереди́; **2.** *adj.* пере́дний; **~bode** [fɔ:'boud] предвеща́ть; предчу́вствовать; **~boding** плохо́е предзнаменова́ние; предчу́вствие; **~cast 1.** ['fɔ:kɑ:st] предсказа́ние; **2.** [fɔ:'kɑ:st] [*irr.* (cast)] предска́зывать [-каза́ть]; **~father** пре́док; **~finger** указа́тельный па́лец; **~foot** пере́дняя нога́; **~go** [fɔ:'gou] [*irr.* (go)] предше́ствовать; **~gone** [fɔ:'gɔn, *attr.* 'fɔ:gɔn]: ~ conclusion зара́нее при́нятое реше́ние; **~ground** пере́дний план; **~head** ['fɔrid] лоб.
foreign ['fɔrin] иностра́нный; the ♀ Office министе́рство иностра́нных дел (в Ло́ндоне); ~ policy вне́шняя поли́тика; **~er** [-ə] иностра́нец (-нка).
fore|leg пере́дняя нога́; **~lock** чуб, прядь воло́с на лбу; **~man** ⚖ старшина́ прися́жных; деся́тник; проpа́б; **~most** пере́дний, передово́й; **~noon** у́тро; **~runner** предве́стник (-ица); **~see** [fɔ:'si:] [*irr.* (see)] предви́деть; **~sight** ['fɔ:sait] предви́дение; предусмотри́тельность *f*.
forest ['fɔrist] **1.** лес; **2.** заса́живать ле́сом.
forestall [fɔ:'stɔ:l] предупрежда́ть [-упреди́ть]; предвосхища́ть [-хи́тить].
forest|er ['fɔristə] лесни́к, лесни́чий; **~ry** [-tri] лесни́чество; лесово́дство.
fore|taste ['fɔ:teist] **1.** предвкуше́ние; **2.** предвкуша́ть [-уси́ть]; **~tell** [fɔ:'tel] [*irr.* (*tell*)] предска́зывать [-за́ть].
forfeit ['fɔ:fit] **1.** штраф; конфиска́ция; утра́та (пра́ва); фант; **2.** [по]плати́ться (Т); утра́чивать [-а́тить] (пра́во).
forgave [fə'geiv] *pt.* от forgive.
forge[1] [fɔ:dʒ] (*mst* ~ ahead) насто́йчиво продвига́ться вперёд.
forge[2] [~] **1.** ку́зница; **2.** кова́ть; подде́л(ыв)ать; **~ry** ['fɔ:dʒəri] подде́лка, подло́г.
forget [fə'get] [*irr.*] забы́(ва́)ть; **~ful** [-ful] □ забы́вчивый; **~-me-not** [-minɔt] незабу́дка.
forgiv|e [fə:giv] [*irr.*] проща́ть [прости́ть]; **~en** [fa'givn] *p. pt.* от ~e; **~eness** [-nis] проще́ние; **~ing** □ всепроща́ющий, снисходи́тельный.
forgo [fɔ:'gou] [*irr.* (go)] возде́рживаться [-жа́ться] от (Р), отка́зываться [-за́ться] от (Р).
forgot, ~ten [fə'gɔt(n)] *pt. a. p. pt.* от forget.

fork [fɔ:k] вилка; вилы *f/pl.*; ♪ камертóн; разветвлéние (дорóги).
forlorn [fə'lɔ:n] забрóшенный, несчáстный.
form [fɔ:m] **1.** фóрма; фигýра; бланк; *school* пáрта; класс; **2.** образóвывать(ся) [-овáть(ся)]; составля́ть [-áвить]; ⚔ [по]стрóить (-ся); [с]формировáть.
formal ['fɔ:məl] □ формáльный, официáльный; **~ity** [fɔ:'mæliti] формáльность *f*.
formation [fɔ:'meiʃən] образовáние; формировáние; ⚔ располoжéние, строй; систéма; строéние.
former ['fɔ:mə] прéжний, бы́вший; предшéствующий; **~ly** [-li] прéжде.
formidable ['fɔ:midəbl] □ стрáшный; громáдный; трýднопреодолúмый (о задáче).
formula ['fɔ:mjulə] фóрмула; ⚕ рецéпт; **~te** [-leit] формулúровать (*im*)*pf*., *pf*. *a*. [с-].
forsake [fə'seik] [*irr.*] оставля́ть [-áвить], покидáть [-úнуть].
forswear [fɔ:'swɛə] [*irr.* (swear)] отрекáться [-éчься] от (Р); **~ o. s.** нарушáть кля́тву.
fort [fɔ:t] ⚔ форт.
forth [fɔ:θ] *adv.* вперёд, дáльше; впредь; **~coming** предстоя́щий, грядýщий; **~with** *adv.* тотчáс, немéдленно.
fortieth ['fɔ:tiiθ] сороковóй; сороковáя часть *f*.
forti|fication [fɔ:tifi'keiʃən] фортификáция; укреплéние; **~fy** ['fɔ:tifai] ⚔ укрепля́ть [-пúть], сооружáть укреплéние (Р); *fig*. подкрепля́ть [-пúть] (фáктами); **~tude** [-tju:d] сúла дýха.
fortnight ['fɔ:tnait] две недéли *f/pl.*
fortress ['fɔ:tris] крéпость *f*.
fortuitous [fɔ:'tjuitəs] □ случáйный.
fortunate ['fɔ:tʃnit] счастлúвый, удáчный; **~ly** *adv.* к счáстью.
fortune ['fɔ:tʃən] судьбá; богáтство, состоя́ние; **~-teller** гадáлка.
forty ['fɔ:ti] сóрок.
forward ['fɔ:wəd] **1.** *adj.* передний; передовóй; развя́зный, дéрзкий; рáнний; **2.** *adv.* вперёд, дáльше; впредь; **3.** *sport* нападáющий; **4.** перес(ы)лáть; препровождáть [-водúть].
forwarding-agent экспедúтор.
forwent [fɔ:'went] *pt.* от **forego**.
foster ['fɔstə] воспúтывать [-итáть]; ходúть за (детьмú, больны́ми); *fig.* питáть (чýвство), лелéять (мысль); поощря́ть [-рúть]; благоприя́тствовать (Д).
fought [fɔ:t] *pt.* и *p. pt.* от **fight**.
foul [faul] **1.** □ гря́зный, отвратúтельный; бýрный (о погóде); гнóйный; зарáзный; бесчéстный; **run ~ of** стáлкиваться [столкнýться] с (Т); **2.** *sport* игрá прóтив прáвил; **3.** [за]пáчкать(ся); нечéстно игрáть.
found [faund] **1.** *pt.* и *p. pt.* от **find**; **2.** заклáдывать [заложúть] (фундáмент); оснóвывать [основáть]; учреждáть [-едúть]; ⊕ плáвить; отлú(вá)ть.
foundation [faun'deiʃən] фундáмент, оснóва.
founder ['faundə] **1.** основáтель(ница *f*) *m*, учредúтель(ница *f*) *m*; **2.** *v/i.* идтú ко днý.
foundry ['faundri] ⊕ литéйная; литьё.
fountain ['fauntin] истóчник; фонтáн; **~-pen** авторýчка, вéчное перó.
four [fɔ:] **1.** четы́ре; **2.** четвёрка; **~-square** квадрáтный; *fig*. устóйчивый; **~teen** ['fɔ:'ti:n] четы́рнадцать; **~teenth** [-θ] четы́рнадцатый; **~th** [fɔ:θ] **1.** четвёртый; **2.** чéтверть *f*.
fowl [faul] домáшняя птúца.
fox [fɔks] **1.** лисúца, лисá; **2.** [с]хитрúть; обмáнывать [-нýть]; **~y** ['fɔksi] хúтрый.
fraction ['frækʃən] дробь *f*; частúца.
fracture ['fræktʃə] **1.** трéщина, излóм; ⚕ перелóм; **2.** [с]ломáть (*a*. ⚕); раздробля́ть [-бúть].
fragile ['frædʒail] хрýпкий, лóмкий.
fragment ['frægmənt] облóмок, оскóлок; отры́вок.
fragran|ce ['freigrəns] аромáт; **~t** [-t] □ аромáтный.
frail [freil] □ хрýпкий; хúлый, болéзненный; **~ty** *fig*. хрýпкость *f*.
frame [freim] **1.** сооружéние; сруб, скелéт; телосложéние; рáмка, рáма; **~ of mind** настроéние; **2.** сооружáть [-удúть]; созд(ав)áть; вставля́ть в рáму; **~work** ⊕ рáма; сруб, óстов; *fig*. строй, рáмки *f/pl.*
franchise ['fræntʃaiz] ⚖ прáво учáствовать в вы́борах; привилéгия.
frank ['fræŋk] □ úскренний, откровéнный.
frankfurter ['fræŋkfətə] *Am.* сосúска.
frankness ['fræŋknis] откровéнность *f*.
frantic ['fræntik] (**~ally**) неистовый.
fratern|al [frə'tə:nl] □ брáтский; *adv.* по-брáтски; **~ity** [-niti] брáтство; óбщина; *Am. univ.* студéнческая организáция.
fraud [frɔ:d] обмáн, мошéнничество; **~ulent** ['frɔ:djulənt] □ обмáнный, мошéннический.
fray [frei] **1.** дрáка, столкновéние; **2.** изнáшивать(ся) [износúть(ся)].
freak [fri:k] капрúз, причýда; урóдец (в прирóде).

freckle ['frekl] веснушка.

free [fri:] 1. □ *com.* свобо́дный, во́льный; незави́симый; неза́нятый; беспла́тный; he is ~ to он во́лен (+ *inf.*); make ~ to *inf.* позволя́ть себе́; set ~ выпуска́ть на свобо́ду; 2. освобожда́ть [-боди́ть]; **~booter** ['fri:bu:tə] пира́т; **~dom** ['fri:dəm] свобо́да; ~ of a city зва́ние почётного граждани́на; **~holder** земе́льный со́бственник; **~mason** масо́н.

freez|e [fri:z] [*irr.*] *v/i.* замерза́ть [замёрзнуть]; засты́(ва́)ть; мёрзнуть; *v/t.* замора́живать [-ро́зить]; **~er** ['fri:zə] моро́женица; **~ing** 1. □ леденя́щий; 2. замора́живание; замерза́ние; ~ point то́чка замерза́ния.

freight [freit] 1. фрахт, груз; сто́имость перево́зки; 2. [по]грузи́ть; [за]фрахтова́ть; **~-car** *Am.* 🚃 това́рный ваго́н.

French [frentʃ] 1. францу́зский; take ~ leave уйти́ не прости́вшись; 2. францу́зский язы́к; the ~ францу́зы *pl.*; **~man** ['frentʃmən] францу́з; **~woman** ['frentʃwumən] францу́женка.

frenz|ied ['frenzid] взбешённый; **~y** [-zi] безу́мие, бе́шенство.

frequen|cy ['fri:kwənsi] частота́ (*a. phys.*); ча́стое повторе́ние; **~t** 1. [-t] □ ча́стый; 2. [fri'kwent] посеща́ть ча́сто.

fresh [freʃ] □ све́жий; но́вый; чи́стый; *Am.* F де́рзкий; ~ water пре́сная вода́; **~en** ['freʃn] освежа́ть [-жи́ть]; [по]свеже́ть; **~et** ['freʃit] полово́дье; *fig.* пото́к; **~man** [-mən] *univ. sl.* первоку́рсник; **~ness** [-nis] све́жесть *f.*

fret [fret] 1. волне́ние, раздраже́ние; ♪ лад (в гита́ре); 2. [о]беспоко́ить(ся), [вз]волнова́ть(ся); подта́чивать [-точи́ть], разъеда́ть [-е́сть]; **~ted instrument** стру́нный щипко́вый инструме́нт.

fretful ['fretful] □ раздражи́тельный, капри́зный.

friar ['fraiə] мона́х.

friction ['frikʃən] тре́ние (*a. fig.*).

Friday ['fraidi] пя́тница.

friend [frend] прия́тель(ница *f*) *m*, друг, подру́га; **~ly** [-li] дру́жеский; **~ship** [-ʃip] дру́жба.

frigate ['frigit] ⚓ фрега́т.

fright [frait] испу́г; *fig.* пу́гало, страши́лище; **~en** ['fraitn] [ис-]пуга́ть; вспу́гивать [-гну́ть]; **~ed** at и́ли of испу́ганный (Т); **~ful** [-ful] □ стра́шный, ужа́сный.

frigid ['fridʒid] □ холо́дный.

frill [fril] обо́рка.

fringe [frindʒ] 1. бахрома́; чёлка; кайма́; 2. отде́лывать бахромо́й; окаймля́ть [-ми́ть].

frippery ['fripəri] безделу́шки *f/pl.*; мишу́рные украше́ния *n/pl.*

frisk [frisk] 1. прыжо́к; 2. резви́ться; **~y** ['friski] □ ре́звый, игри́вый.

fritter ['fritə] 1. ола́дья; 2. ~ away растра́чивать по мелоча́м.

frivol|ity [fri'vɔliti] легкомы́слие; фриво́льность *f*; **~ous** ['frivələs] □ легкомы́сленный, пове́рхностный; пустя́чный.

frizzle ['frizl] жа́рить(ся) с шипе́нием.

fro [frou]: to and ~ взад и вперёд.

frock [frɔk] да́мское и́ли де́тское пла́тье; ря́са; (*mst* ~-coat) сюрту́к.

frog [frɔg] лягу́шка.

frolic ['frɔlik] 1. ша́лость *f*, весе́лье, ре́звость *f*; 2. резви́ться, [на]прока́зничать; **~some** [səm] □ игри́вый, ре́звый.

from [frɔm, frəm] *prp.* от (Р); из (Р); с (Р); по (Д); defend ~ защища́ть от (Р).

front [frʌnt] 1. фаса́д; пере́дняя сторона́; ⚔ фронт; in ~ of пе́ред (Т); впереди́ (Р); 2. пере́дний; 3. выходи́ть на (В) (об окне́) (*a.* ~ on, towards); **~al** ['frʌntl] *anat.* ло́бный; △ фаса́дный; фронта́льный; **~ier** ['frʌntjə] 1. грани́ца; 2. пограни́чный; **~ispiece** ['frʌntispi:s] *typ.* фронтиспи́с; △ фаса́д.

frost [frɔst] 1. моро́з; 2. побива́ть моро́зом (расте́ния); **~-bite** ⚕ отморо́женное ме́сто; **~y** ['frɔsti] □ моро́зный; *fig.* ледяно́й.

froth [frɔθ] 1. пе́на; 2. [вс-, за]пе́нить(ся); **~y** ['frɔθi] □ пе́нистый; *fig.* пусто́й.

frown [fraun] 1. хму́рый взгляд; нахму́ренные бро́ви *f/pl.*; 2. *v/i.* [на]хму́риться; [на]су́питься.

frow|zy, ~sy ['frauzi] за́тхлый, спёртый; неря́шливый.

froze [frouz] *pt.* от freeze; **~n** [-n] 1. *p. pt.* от freeze; 2. замёрзший; заморо́женный.

frugal ['fru:gəl] □ уме́ренный, скро́мный.

fruit [fru:t] 1. плод, фрукт; 2. плодоноси́ть, дава́ть плоды́; **~erer** ['fru:tərə] торго́вец фру́ктами; **~ful** ['fru:tful] □ плодови́тый, плодоро́дный; *fig.* плодотво́рный; **~less** [-lis] □ беспло́дный.

frustrat|e [frʌs'treit] расстра́ивать [-ро́ить] (пла́ны), де́лать тще́тным; **~ion** [frʌs'treiʃən] расстро́йство (пла́нов), круше́ние (наде́жд).

fry [frai] 1. жа́реное (ку́шанье); 2. [из]жа́рить(ся); **~ing-pan** ['fraiiŋpæn] сковорода́.

fudge [fʌdʒ] 1. вы́думка; пома́дка; 2. де́лать ко́е-ка́к.

fuel ['fjuəl] 1. то́пливо; 2. *mot.* горю́чее.

fugitive ['fju:dʒitiv] бегле́ц; бе́женец (-нка); 2. бе́глый; мимолётный.

fulfil(l) [ful'fil] выполня́ть [вы́-

полнить], осуществля́ть [-ви́ть]; **~ment** [-mənt] осуществле́ние, выполне́ние.

full [ful] 1. □ *com.* по́лный; це́лый; доро́дный; of ~ age соверше́ннолетний; 2. *adv.* вполне́; как раз; о́чень; 3. по́лность *f*; in ~ по́лностью; to the ~ в по́лной ме́ре; **~-dress** пара́дная фо́рма; **~-fledged** вполне́ опери́вшийся, ра́звитый.

ful(l)ness ['fulnis] полнота́, оби́лие.

fulminate ['fʌlmineit] сверка́ть [-кну́ть]; [за]греме́ть; ~ against [раз]громи́ть (B).

fumble ['fʌmbl] нащу́п(ыв)ать; [про]мя́млить; верте́ть в рука́х.

fume [fju:m] 1. пар, дым; испаре́ние; 2. оку́ривать [-ри́ть]; испаря́ться [-ри́ться].

fumigate ['fju:migeit] оку́ривать [-ри́ть].

fun [fʌn] весе́лье; заба́ва; make ~ of высме́ивать [вы́смеять] (B).

function ['fʌŋkʃən] 1. фу́нкция, назначе́ние; 2. функциони́ровать, де́йствовать; **~ary** [-əri] должностно́е лицо́.

fund [fʌnd] 1. запа́с; капита́л, фонд; ~s *pl.* госуда́рственные проце́нтные бума́ги *f/pl.*; 2. консолиди́ровать (*im*)*pf.*; фунди́ровать (*im*)*pf.*

fundament|al [fʌndə'mentl] □ основно́й, коренно́й, суще́ственный; **~als** *pl.* осно́вы *f/pl.*

funer|al ['fju:nərəl] 1. по́хороны *f/pl.*; 2. похоро́нный; **~eal** [fju:'niəriəl] □ тра́урный; мра́чный.

fun-fair ['fʌnfɛə] я́рмарка.

funnel ['fʌnl] воро́нка; ⚓, 🚂 дымова́я труба́.

funny ['fʌni] □ заба́вный, смешно́й; стра́нный.

fur [fə:] 1. мех; шку́ра; ~s *pl.* меха́ *m/pl.*, мехов́ые това́ры *m/pl.*, пушни́на; 2. подбива́ть ме́хом.

furbish ['fə:biʃ] [от]полирова́ть; ~ up подновля́ть [-ви́ть].

furious ['fjuəriəs] □ взбешённый.

furl [fə:l] уб(и)ра́ть (паруса́); скла́дывать [сложи́ть] (зо́нтик).

furlough ['fə:lou] 1. о́тпуск; 2. увольня́ть в о́тпуск (*mst* о солда́тах).

furnace ['fə:nis] горн, печь *f*; то́пка.

furnish ['fə:niʃ] снабжа́ть [снабди́ть] (with T); доставля́ть [-а́вить]; обставля́ть [-а́вить], меблирова́ть (*im*)*pf*.

furniture ['fə:nitʃə] ме́бель *f*, обстано́вка; обору́дование.

furrier ['fʌriə] меховщи́к.

furrow ['fʌrou] борозда́; колея́; жёлоб; морщи́на.

further ['fə:ðə] 1. да́льше, да́лее; зате́м; кро́ме того́; 2. соде́йствовать, спосо́бствовать (Д); **~ance** [-rəns] продвиже́ние (of P), соде́йствие (of Д); **~more** [-mɔ:] *adv.* к тому́ же, кро́ме того́.

furthest ['fə:ðist] са́мый да́льний.

furtive ['fə:tiv] □ скры́тый, та́йный.

fury ['fjuəri] неистовство, я́рость *f*.

fuse [fju:z] 1. пла́вка; ⚔ взрыва́тель *m*; ⚡ пла́вкий предохрани́тель *m*; 2. сплавля́ть(ся) [-а́вить(ся)]; ⚡ [рас]пла́вить(ся); ⚔ вставля́ть взрыва́тель в (B).

fusion ['fju:ʒən] пла́вка; *fig.* слия́ние.

fuss [fʌs] F 1. суета́; возбуждённое состоя́ние; 2. [за]суети́ться; [вз-]волнова́ться (about из-за P); надоеда́ть с пустяка́ми (Д).

fusty ['fʌsti] за́тхлый, спёртый; *fig.* старомо́дный, устаре́вший.

futile ['fju:tail] бесполе́зный, тще́тный; пусто́й.

future ['fju:tʃə] 1. бу́дущий; 2. бу́дущее, бу́дущность *f*; ~s *pl.* ✝ това́ры, закупа́емые заблаговре́менно.

fuzz [fʌz] 1. пух; пуши́нка; 2. покры́(ва́)ться пу́хом; разлета́ться [-лете́ться] (о пу́хе).

G

gab [gæb] F болтовня́; the gift of the ~ хорошо́ подве́шенный язы́к.

gabble ['gæbl] 1. бормота́ние, бессвя́зная речь *f*; 2. [про]бормота́ть; [за]гогота́ть.

gaberdine ['gæbədi:n] габарди́н.

gable ['geibl] ⚠ фронто́н, щипе́ц.

gad [gæd]: ~ about шля́ться, шата́ться.

gad-fly ['gædflai] *zo.* о́вод, слепе́нь *m*.

gag [gæg] 1. заты́чка, кляп; *parl.* прекраще́ние пре́ний; *Am.* острота́; 2. затыка́ть рот (Д); заста́вить замолча́ть; *pol.* заж(им)а́ть (кри́тику и т. п.).

gage [geidʒ] зало́г, закла́д; вы́зов.

gaiety ['geiəti] весёлость *f*.

gaily ['geili] *adv.* от gay ве́село; я́рко.

gain [gein] 1. при́быль *f*; вы́игрыш; за́работок; приро́ст; 2. выи́грывать [вы́играть]; приобрета́ть [-ести́]; **~ful** ['geinful] □ дохо́дный, вы́годный.

gait [geit] похо́дка.

gaiter ['geitə] гама́ша, ге́тра, кра́га.

gale [geil] шторм, си́льный ве́тер.

gall [gɔ:l] 1. ⚕ жёлчь *f*; жёлчность *f*; ссáдина; 2. раздражáть [-жи́ть]; [о]беспокóить.
gallant *mst* [gə'lænt] 1. □ галáнтный; внимáтельный; почти́тельный; 2. ['gælənt] *adj*. □ храбрый, дóблестный; *su*. кавалéр; **~ry** ['gæləntri] храбрость *f*; галáнтность *f*.
gallery ['gæləri] галерéя.
galley ['gæli] ⚓ галéра; **~-proof** грáнка.
gallon ['gælən] галлóн (мéра жи́дких и сыпу́чих тел; англ. = 4,54 л; ам. = 3,78 л).
gallop ['gæləp] 1. галóп; 2. скакáть (пускáть) галóпом.
gallows ['gælouz] *sg*. ви́селица.
gamble ['gæmbl] 1. азáртная игрá; рискóванное предприя́тие; 2. игрáть в азáртные и́гры; спекули́ровать (на би́рже); **~r** [-ə] картёжник, игрóк.
gambol ['gæmbəl] 1. прыжóк; 2. пры́гать, скакáть.
game [geim] 1. игрá; пáртия (игры́); дичь *f*; **~s** *pl*. состязáния *n/pl*.; и́гры *f/pl*.; 2. F охóтно готóвый (сдéлать чтó-либо); 3. игрáть на дéньги; **~ster** игрóк, картёжник.
gander ['gændə] гусáк.
gang [gæŋ] 1. бригáда; артéль *f*; смéна (рабóчих); шáйка, бáнда; 2. ~ up организовáть шáйку; **~-board** ⚓ схóдни *f/pl*.
gangway [-wei] прохóд мéжду рядáми (крéсел и т. п.); ⚓ схóдни *f/pl*.
gaol [dʒeil] тюрьмá; *s*. jail.
gap [gæp] пробéл; брешь *f*, щель *f*; *fig*. расхождéние (во взгля́дах).
gape [geip] разевáть рот; [по]глазéть; зия́ть.
garb [gɑ:b] наря́д, одея́ние.
garbage ['gɑ:bidʒ] (ку́хонные) отбрóсы *m/pl*.; му́сор.
garden ['gɑ:dn] 1. сад; огорóд; 2. занимáться садовóдством; **~er** садóвник, садовóд; **~ing** садовóдство.
gargle ['gɑ:gl] 1. полоскáть гóрло; 2. полоскáние для гóрла.
garish ['gɛəriʃ] □ кричáщий (о плáтье, крáсках); я́ркий.
garland ['gɑ:lənd] гирля́нда, венóк.
garlic ['gɑ:lik] ⚘ чеснóк.
garment ['gɑ:mənt] предмéт одéжды; *fig*. покрóв, одея́ние.
garnish ['gɑ:niʃ] 1. гарни́р; украшéние; 2. гарни́ровать (*im*)*pf*.; украшáть [укрáсить].
garret ['gærit] мансáрда.
garrison ['gærisn] ⚔ 1. гарнизóн; 2. стáвить (полк и т. п.) гарнизóном.
garrulous ['gæruləs] □ болтли́вый.
garter ['gɑ:tə] подвя́зка.
gas [gæs] 1. газ; F болтовня́; *Am*. F бензи́н, горю́чее; 2. выпускáть гáзы; отравля́ть гáзом; F болтáть, бахвáлиться; **~eous** ['geiziəs] газообрáзный.
gash [gæʃ] 1. глубóкая рáна, разрéз; 2. наноси́ть глубóкую рáну (Д).
gas|-lighter гáзовая зажигáлка; **~-mantle** кали́льная сéтка; **~-olene, ~oline** ['gæsoli:n] *mot*. газоли́н; *Am*. бензи́н.
gasp [gɑ:sp] задыхáться [задохну́ться]; лови́ть вóздух.
gas|sed [gæst] отрáвленный гáзом; **~-stove** гáзовая плитá; **~-works** *pl*. гáзовый завóд.
gate [geit] ворóта *n/pl*.; кали́тка; **~man** 🚂 стóрож; **~way** ворóта *n/pl*., вход; подворóтня.
gather ['gæðə] 1. *v/t*. соб(и)рáть; снимáть [снять] (урожáй); [на-, со]рвáть (о цветáх); *fig*. дéлать вы́вод; ~ speed набирáть скóрость; ускоря́ть ход; *v/i*. соб(и)рáться; 2. **~s** *pl*. сбóрки *f/pl*.; **~ing** собирáние; сбóрище, собрáние.
gaudy ['gɔ:di] □ я́ркий, кричáщий, безвку́сный.
gauge [geidʒ] 1. мéра; измери́тельный прибóр; масштáб; 🚂 ширинá колеи́; ⊕ шаблóн, лекáло; 2. измеря́ть [-éрить]; градуи́ровать (*im*)*pf*.; выверя́ть [вы́верить]; *fig*. оцéнивать [-ни́ть] (человéка).
gaunt [gɔ:nt] □ исхудáлый, измождённый; мрáчный.
ga(u)ntlet ['gɔ:ntlit] 1. *hist*. лáтная рукави́ца; рукави́ца (шофёра, фехтовáльная и т. п.); 2. run the ~ пройти́ сквозь стрóй; подвергáться рéзкой крити́ке.
gauze [gɔ:z] газ (матéрия); мáрля.
gave [geiv] *pt*. от give.
gawk [gɔ:k] F остолóп, рази́ня *m/f*; **~y** [gɔ:'ki] неуклю́жий. [стрый.]
gay [gei] □ весёлый; я́ркий, пё-
gaze [geiz] 1. внимáтельный взгляд; 2. при́стально глядéть.
gazette [gə'zet] 1. официáльная газéта; 2. опубликовáть в официáльной газéте.
gear [giə] 1. механи́зм; приспособлéния *n/pl*.; ⊕ шестерня́; зубчáтая передáча; *mot*. передáча; скóрость *f*; in ~ включённый, дéйствующий; 2. приводи́ть в движéние; включáть [-чи́ть]; **~ing** ⊕ зубчáтая передáча; привóд.
geese [gi:s] *pl*. от goose.
gem [dʒem] драгоцéнный кáмень *m*; *fig*. сокрóвище.
gender ['dʒendə] *gr*. род.
general ['dʒenərəl] 1. □ óбщий; обы́чный; повсемéстный; глáвный; генерáльный; ~ election всеóбщие вы́боры *m/pl*.; 2. ⚔ генерáл; **~ity** [dʒenə'ræliti] всеóбщность *f*; примени́мость ко

всему́; большинство́; **~ize** ['dʒenərəlaiz] обобща́ть [-щи́ть]; **~ly** [-li] вообще́; обы́чно.
generat|e ['dʒenəreit] порожда́ть [-роди́ть]; производи́ть [-вести́]; **~ion**; [dʒenə'reiʃən] поколе́ние; порожде́ние.
gener|osity [dʒenə'rɔsiti] великоду́шие; ще́дрость *f*; **~ous** ['dʒenərəs] □ великоду́шный; ще́дрый.
genial ['dʒi:njəl] □ тёплый, мя́гкий (кли́мат); до́брый, серде́чный.
genius ['dʒi:njəs] ге́ний; дух; одарённость *f*, гениа́льность *f*.
genteel [dʒen'ti:l] све́тский; элега́нтный.
gentle ['dʒentl] □ зна́тный; мя́гкий; кро́ткий; ти́хий; не́жный; сми́рный (о живо́тных); лёгкий (ве́тер); **~man** ['dʒentlmən] джентельме́н; господи́н; **~manlike, ~manly** [-li] воспи́танный; **~ness** ['dʒentlnis] мя́гкость *f*; доброта́.
gentry ['dʒentri] мелкопоме́стное дворя́нство.
genuine ['dʒenjuin] □ по́длинный; и́скренний; неподде́льный.
geography [dʒi'ɔgrəfi] геогра́фия.
geology [dʒi'ɔlədʒi] геоло́гия.
geometry [dʒi'ɔmitri] геоме́трия.
germ [dʒə:m] **1.** микро́б; заро́дыш; **2.** *fig.* зарожда́ться [-оди́ться].
German[1] ['dʒə:mən] **1.** герма́нский, неме́цкий; ~ silver ⊕ нейзи́льбер; **2.** не́мец, не́мка; неме́цкий язы́к.
german[2] [~]: brother ~ родно́й брат; **~e** [dʒə:'mein] уме́стный, подходя́щий.
germinate ['dʒə:mineit] дава́ть ростки́, прораста́ть [-расти́].
gesticulat|e [dʒes'tikjuleit] жестикули́ровать; **~ion** [-'tikju''leiʃən] жестикуля́ция.
gesture ['dʒestʃə] жест; ми́мика.
get [get] [*irr.*] **1.** *v/t.* дост(ав)а́ть; получа́ть [-чи́ть]; зараба́тывать [-бо́тать]; добы́(ва́)ть; заставля́ть [заста́вить]; I have got я име́ю; ~ one's hair cut [по]стри́чься; ~ by heart учи́ть наизу́сть; **2.** *v/i.* [с]де́латься, станови́ться [стать]; ~ ready [при]гото́виться; ~ about начина́ть ходи́ть (по́сле боле́зни); ~ abroad распростроня́ться [-ни́ться] (о слу́хах); ~ ahead продвига́ться вперёд; ~ at доб(и)ра́ться до (Р); ~ away уд(и)ра́ть, уходи́ть [уйти́]; отправля́ться [-а́виться]; ~ in входи́ть [войти́]; ~ on with a p. ужи́(ва́)ться с ке́м-либо; ~ out выходи́ть [вы́йти]; ~ to hear (know, learn) узн(ав)а́ть; ~ up вст(ав)а́ть; **~-up** [get'ʌp] мане́ра одева́ться; оформле́ние; *Am.* предприи́мчивость *f*.
ghastly ['gɑ:stli] ужа́сный; мёртвенно-бле́дный.
ghost [goust] при́зрак, привиде́ние; дух (*a. eccl.*); *fig.* тень *f*, лёгкий след; **~like** ['goustlaik], **~ly** [-li] похо́жий на привиде́ние, при́зрачный.
giant ['dʒaiənt] **1.** велика́н, гига́нт, исполи́н; **2.** гига́нтский, исполи́нский.
gibber ['dʒibə] говори́ть невня́тно.
gibbet ['dʒibit] **1.** ви́селица; **2.** ве́шать [пове́сить].
gibe [dʒaib] *v/t.* смея́ться над (Т); *v/i.* насмеха́ться (at над Т).
gidd|iness ['gidinis] ⚕ головокруже́ние; легкомы́слие; **~y** ['gidi] □ испы́тывающий головокруже́ние; легкомы́сленный.
gift [gift] дар, пода́рок; спосо́бность *f*, тала́нт (of к Д); **~ed** ['giftid] одарённый, спосо́бный, тала́нтливый.
gigantic [dʒai'gæntik] (**~ally**) гига́нтский, грома́дный.
giggle ['gigl] **1.** хихи́канье; **2.** хихи́кать [-кнуть].
gild [gild] [*irr.*] [по]золоти́ть.
gill [gil] *zo.* жа́бра.
gilt [gilt] **1.** позоло́та; **2.** позоло́ченный.
gin [dʒin] джин (напи́ток); ⊕ подъёмная лебёдка.
ginger ['dʒindʒə] **1.** имби́рь *m*; F воодушевле́ние; **2.** F подстёгивать [-стегну́ть], оживля́ть [-ви́ть]; **~bread** имби́рный пря́ник; **~ly** [-li] осторо́жный, ро́бкий.
Gipsy ['dʒipsi] цыга́н(ка).
gird [gə:d] [*irr.*] опоя́сывать(ся) [-сать(ся)]; окружа́ть [-жи́ть].
girder ['gə:də] ⊕ ба́лка, перекла́дина, подпо́рка.
girdle ['gə:dl] **1.** по́яс, куша́к; **2.** подпоя́сывать [-сать].
girl [gə:l] де́вочка, де́вушка; **~hood** ['gə:lhud] деви́чество; **~ish** □ деви́ческий.
girt [gə:t] *pt.* и *p. pt.* от gird.
girth [gə:θ] обхва́т, разме́р; подпру́га.
gist [dʒist] суть *f*, су́щность *f*.
give [giv] [*irr.*] **1.** *v/t.* да(ва́)ть; [по]дари́ть; причиня́ть [-ни́ть]; доставля́ть [-а́вить]; ~ birth to роди́ть; ~ away отд(ав)а́ть; F вы́да(ва́)ть, пред(ав)а́ть; ~ forth изд(ав)а́ть (за́пах и т. п.); объявля́ть [-ви́ть]; ~ in под(ав)а́ть; ~ up отка́зываться [-за́ться] от (Р); **2.** *v/i.* ~ (in) уступа́ть [-пи́ть]; ~ into, ~ (up)on выходи́ть на (В) (об о́кнах и т. п.); ~ out конча́ться [ко́нчиться]; обесси́леть *pf.*; [ис]по́ртиться; **~n** [givn] **1.** *p. pt.* от give; **2.** *fig.* да́нный; скло́нный (to к Д); пре́данный (to Д).
glaci|al ['gleisiəl] □ ледни́ковый; ледяно́й; леденя́щий; **~er** глётчер, ледни́к.
glad [glæd] □ дово́льный; ра́достный, весёлый; I am ~ я ра́д(а);

~ly охóтно, рáдостно; **~den** ['glædn] [об]рáдовать.
glade [gleid] прогáлина, прóсека.
gladness ['glædnis] рáдость *f*.
glamo|rous ['glæmərəs] обаятельный, очаровáтельный; **~(u)r** ['glæmə] **1.** очаровáние; **2.** очарóвывать [-ровáть].
glance [glɑ:ns] **1.** бы́стрый взгляд; **2.** скользи́ть [-зну́ть] (*mst* ~ aside, off); ~ at мéльком взгляну́ть на (В).
gland [glænd] железá.
glare [glɛə] **1.** ослепи́тельно сверкáть; при́стально смотрéть; **2.** при́стальный и́ли свирéпый взгляд; ослепи́тельный блеск.
glass [glɑ:s] **1.** стеклó; стакáн, рю́мка; зéркало; (a pair of) ~es *pl.* очки́ *n/pl.*; **2.** *attr.* стекля́нный; **~-shade** (стекля́нный) колпáк; абажу́р; **~y** ['glɑ:si] □ зеркáльный; безжи́зненный; стекля́нный.
glaz|e [gleiz] **1.** глазу́рь *f*, муравá; **2.** глази́ровать (*im*)*pf.*; застекля́ть [-ли́ть]; **~ier** ['gleiziə] стекóльщик.
gleam [gli:m] **1.** óтблеск; слáбый свет; *fig.* прóблеск; **2.** мерцáть, слáбо свети́ться.
glean [gli:n] *v/t. fig.* тщáтельно собирáть (фáкты, свéдения); *v/i.* подбирáть колóсья (пóсле жáтвы).
glee [gli:] ликовáние; ~ club клуб для хоровóго пéния.
glib [glib] □ глáдкий; бóйкий (о рéчи).
glid|e [glaid] **1.** скользи́ть, плáвно дви́гаться; ✈ [с]плани́ровать; **2.** плáвное движéние; **~er** ['glaidə] ✈ планёр.
glimmer ['glimə] **1.** мерцáние, ту́склый свет; *min.* слюдá; **2.** мерцáть, ту́скло свети́ть.
glimpse [glimps] **1.** мимолётный взгляд; мимолётное впечатлéние (of от Р); **2.** (у)ви́деть мéльком.
glint [glint] **1.** я́ркий блеск; **2.** я́рко блестéть; отражáть свет.
glisten ['glisn], **glitter** ['glitə] блестéть, сверкáть, сия́ть.
gloat [glout]: ~ (up)on, over пожирáть глазáми (В).
globe [gloub] шар; земнóй шар; глóбус.
gloom [glu:m], **~iness** ['glu:minis] мрак; мрáчность *f*; **~y** ['glu:mi] □ мрáчный; угрю́мый.
glori|fy ['glɔ:rifai] прославля́ть [-áвить]; восхваля́ть [-ли́ть]; **~ous** ['glɔ:riəs] □ великолéпный, чудéсный.
glory ['glɔ:ri] **1.** слáва; **2.** торжествовáть; горди́ться (in Т)
gloss [glɔs] **1.** внéшний блеск; глóсса; **2.** наводи́ть гля́нец на (В); ~ over прикрáшивать [-крáсить].
glossary ['glɔsəri] глоссáрий, словáрь *m* (в концé кни́ги).
glossy ['glɔsi] □ глянцеви́тый, лощёный.
glove [glʌv] перчáтка.
glow [glou] **1.** накаля́ться дóкраснá; горéть; тлеть; сия́ть; **2.** зной; накáл; зáрево; жар; румя́нец; **~-worm** светля́к, светлячóк.
glue [glu:] **1.** клей; **2.** [с]клéить.
glut [glʌt] пресыщéние; затовáривание (ры́нка).
glutton ['glʌtn] обжóра *m/f*; **~ous** [-əs] □ обжóрливый; **~y** [-i] обжóрство.
gnash [næʃ] [за]скрежетáть (зубáми).
gnat [næt] комáр.
gnaw [nɔ:] глодáть.
gnome [noum] гном, кáрлик.
go [gou] **1.** [*irr.*] *com.* ходи́ть, идти́ [пойти́]; проходи́ть [пройти́]; уходи́ть [уйти́]; éздить, [по]éхать; [с]дéлаться; рабóтать (о маши́не, сéрдце); let ~ пускáть [пусти́ть]; выпускáть из рук; ~ shares дели́ться пóровну; ~ to (*or* and) see заходи́ть [зайти́] к [Д], навещáть [-ести́ть]; ~ at набрáсываться [-рóситься] на (В); ~ between посрéдничать мéжду (Т); ~ by проходи́ть [пройти́]; руководи́ться (Т); ~ for идти́ [пойти́] за (Т); ~ for a walk дéлать прогу́лку; ~ in for an examination [про]экзаменовáться; ~ on продолжáть [-дóлжить]; идти́ дáльше; ~ through with доводи́ть до концá (В); ~ without обходи́ться [обойти́сь] без (Р); **2.** ходьбá, движéние; F мóда; энергия; on the ~ на ходу́; на ногáх; it is no ~ ничегó не подéлаешь; in one ~ срáзу; have a ~ at [по]прóбовать (В).
goad [goud] **1.** побуждáть [побуди́ть]; подстрекáть [-кну́ть]; **2.** стрекáло; *fig.* сти́мул, возбуди́тель *m.*
goal [goul] цель *f*; мéсто назначéния; *sport* ворóта *n/pl.*; гол; фи́ниш; **~-keeper** вратáрь *m.*
goat [gout] козёл, козá.
gobble [gɔbl] есть жáдно, бы́стро; **~r** [-ə] обжóра *m/f*; индю́к.
go-between ['goubitwi:n] посрéдник.
goblin ['gɔblin] гном, домовóй.
god бог (*eccl.*: ♀ Бог); божествó; *fig.* и́дол, куми́р; **~child** крéстник (-ица); **~dess** ['godis] боги́ня; **~-father** крёстный отéц; **~head** божествó; **~less** [-'lis] безбóжный; **~like** богоподóбный; **~liness** [-linis] нáбожность *f*; благочéстие; **~ly** [-li] благочести́вый; **~mother** крёстная мать *f*.
goggle [gɔgl] **1.** тарáщить глазá; **2.** (a pair of) **~s** *pl.* защи́тные очки́ *n/pl.*
going ['gouiŋ] **1.** иду́щий; дéйствующий; be ~ to *inf.* намéреваться, собирáться (+ *inf.*); **2.** ходьбá; ухóд; отъезд.

gold [gould] **1.** зóлото; **2.** золотóй; **~en** ['gouldən] золотóй; **~finch** *zo.* щегóл; **~smith** золотых дел мáстер.
golf [gɔlf] **1.** гольф; **2.** игрáть в гольф.
gondola ['gɔndələ] гондóла.
gone [gɔn] *p. pt.* от go; ушéдший, уéхавший; F безнадёжный, потéрянный; умéрший, покóйный.
good [gud] **1.** *com.* хорóший; дóбрый; гóдный, полéзный; ✝ кредитоспосóбный; ♀ Friday *eccl.* велúкая страстнáя пя́тница; be ~ at быть спосóбным к (Д); **2.** добрó, блáго; пóльза; ~s *pl.* товáр; that's no ~ э́то бесполéзно; for ~ навсегдá; **~by**(e) [gud'bai] **1.** до свидáния!, прощáйте!; **2.** прощáние; **~ly** ['gudli] миловúдный, приятный; значúтельный, изря́дный; **~natured** добродýшный; **~ness** [-nis] добротá; *int.* гóсподи!; **~will** доброжелáтельность *f.*
goody ['gudi] конфéта.
goose [gu:s], *pl.* geese [gi:s] гусь *m*, гусы́ня; портнóвский утю́г.
gooseberry ['gu:zbəri] крыжóвник (*no pl.*).
goose|-flesh, *Am.* **~-pimples** *pl. fig.* гусúная кóжа (от хóлода).
gore [gɔ:] **1.** запёкшаяся кровь *f*; **2.** забодáть *pf.*
gorge [gɔ:dz] **1.** пасть *f*, глóтка; ýзкое ущéлье; пресыщéние; **2.** [со]жрáть; ~ o. s. наж(и)рáться.
gorgeous ['gɔ:dʒəs] □ пы́шный, великолéпный.
gory ['gɔ:ri] □ окровáвленный; кровопролúтный.
gospel ['gɔspəl] евáнгелие.
gossip ['gɔsip] **1.** сплéтни *f/pl.*; сплéтник (-ица); **2.** [на]сплéтничать.
got [gɔt] *pt.* и *p. pt.* от get.
Gothic ['gɔθik] готúческий; *fig.* вáрварский.
gouge [gaudʒ] **1.** ⊕ долотó, стамéска; **2.** выдáлбливать [вы́долбить]; *Am.* F обмáнывать [-нýть].
gourd [guəd] ♀ ты́ква.
gout [gaut] ⚕ подáгра.
govern ['gʌvən] *v/t.* прáвить, управля́ть (Т); *v/i.* господ́ствовать; **~ess** [-is] гувернáнтка; **~ment** [-mənt] правúтельство; управлéние; губéрния; *attr.* правúтельственный; **~mental** [gʌvən'mentl] правúтельственный; **~or** ['gʌvənə] правúтель *m*; комендáнт; губернáтор; F отéц.
gown [gaun] **1.** (жéнское) плáтье; мáнтия; **2.** одé(вá)ть.
grab [græb] F **1.** схвáтывать [-атúть]; **2.** захвáт; ⊕ автоматúческий ковш, черпáк.
grace [greis] **1.** грáция, изя́щество; любéзность *f*; мúлость *f*, милосéрдие; Your ♀ Вáша Мúлость *f*; **2.** *fig.* украшáть [укрáсить]; удостáивать [-стóить]; **~ful** ['greisful] □ грациóзный, изя́щный; **~fulness** [-nis] грациóзность *f*, изя́щность *f*.
gracious ['greiʃəs] □ снисходúтельный; благосклóнный; мúлостивый.
gradation [grə'deiʃən] градáция, постепéнный перехóд.
grade [greid] **1.** стéпень *f*; грáдус; ранг; кáчество; *Am.* класс (шкóлы); 🚂 уклóн; **2.** [рас]сортировáть; ⊕ нивелúровать (*im*)*pf.*
gradua|l ['grædjuəl] □ постепéнный; послéдовательный; **~te 1.** [-eit] градуúровать (*im*)*pf.*, наносúть делéния; кончáть университéт; *Am.* кончáть (любóе) учéбное заведéние; **2.** [-it] *univ.* окóнчивший университéт с учёной стéпенью; **~tion** [grædju'eiʃən] градуирóвка (сосýда); *Am.* окончáние учéбного заведéния; *univ.* получéние учёной стéпени.
graft [grɑ:ft] **1.** ✔ черенóк; привúвка (растéния); *Am.* взя́тка; пóдкуп; **2.** ✔ привú(вá)ть (растéние); ⚕ пересáживать ткань; *Am.* давáть (брать) взя́тки.
grain [grein] зернó; хлéбные злáки *m/pl.*; крупúнка; *fig.* склóнность *f*, прирóда.
gramma|r ['græmə] граммáтика; ~ school срéдняя шкóла; *Am.* стáршие клáссы срéдней шкóлы; **~tical** [grə'mætikəl] □ грамматúческий.
gram(me) [græm] грамм.
granary ['grænəri] жúтница; амбáр.
grand [grænd] **1.** □ велúчественный; грандиóзный; велúкий; **2.** ♪ (*a.* ~ piano) роя́ль *m*; **~child** внук, внýчка; **~eur** ['grændʒə] грандиóзность *f*; велúчие.
grandiose ['grændious] □ грандиóзный; напы́щенный.
grandparents *pl.* дéдушка и бáбушка.
grange [greindʒ] фéрма.
grant [grɑ:nt] **1.** предоставля́ть [-áвить]; допускáть [-стúть]; даровáть (*im*)*pf.*; **2.** дар; субсúдия; дáрственный акт; take for ~ed считáть докáзанным.
granul|ate ['grænjuleit] [раз]дробúть; гранулúровать(ся) (*im*)*pf.*; **~e** ['grænju:l] зернó, зёрнышко.
grape [greip] виногрáд; **~-fruit** ♀ грéйпфрут.
graph [græf] диагрáмма, грáфик; **~ic(al** □) ['græfik, -ikəl] графúческий; нагля́дный; ~ arts *pl.* изобразúтельные искýсства *n/pl.*; **~ite** ['græfait] графúт.
grapple ['græpl]: ~ with борóться с (Т); *fig.* пытáться преодолéть (затруднéние).

grasp [grɑ:sp] **1.** хвата́ть [схвати́ть] (by за В); заж(им)а́ть (в руке́); хвата́ться [схвати́ться] (at за В); понима́ть [поня́ть]; **2.** спосо́бность восприя́тия; схва́тывание, кре́пкое сжа́тие; власть *f*.

grass [grɑ:s] трава́; па́стбище; send to ~ выгоня́ть на подно́жный корм; **~hopper** кузне́чик; **~-widow** F «соло́менная» вдова́; **~y** травяни́стый; травяно́й.

grate [greit] **1.** решётка; ⊕ гро́хот; **2.** [на]тере́ть (тёркой); [за]скрежета́ть (зуба́ми); ~ on *fig.* раздража́ть [-жи́ть] (В).

grateful ['greitful] □ благода́рный.

grater ['greitə] тёрка.

grati|fication [grætifi'keiʃən] вознагражде́ние; удовлетворе́ние; **~fy** ['grætifai] удовлетворя́ть [-ри́ть].

grating ['greitiŋ] **1.** □ скрипу́чий, ре́зкий; **2.** решётка.

gratitude ['grætitju:d] благода́рность *f*.

gratuit|ous [grə'tju(:)itəs] □ дарово́й, безвозме́здный; **~y** [-i] де́нежный пода́рок; чаевы́е.

grave [greiv] **1.** □ серьёзный, ве́ский; ва́жный; тяжёлый; **2.** моги́ла; **3.** [*irr.*] *fig.* запечатле́(ва́)ть; **~-digger** моги́льщик.

gravel ['grævəl] **1.** гра́вий; ⚕ мочево́й песо́к; **2.** посыпа́ть гра́вием.

graveyard кла́дбище.

gravitation [grævi'teiʃən] притяже́ние; тяготе́ние (*a. fig.*).

gravity ['græviti] серьёзность *f*, ва́жность *f*; тя́жесть *f*, опа́сность (положе́ния).

gravy ['greivi] (мясна́я) подли́вка.

gray [grei] се́рый.

graze [greiz] пасти́(сь); щипа́ть траву́; заде́(ва́)ть.

grease [gri:s] **1.** са́ло; сма́зка, сма́зочное вещество́; **2.** [gri:z] сма́з(ыв)ать.

greasy ['gri:zi] □ са́льный, жи́рный; ско́льзкий (о гря́зной доро́ге).

great [greit] □ *com.* вели́кий; большо́й; огро́мный; F восхити́тельный; великоле́пный; ~ grandchild пра́внук (-учка); **~coat** ['greit'kout] пальто́ *n indecl.*; **~ly** ['greitli] о́чень, си́льно; **~ness** [-nis] вели́чие, си́ла.

greed [gri:d] жа́дность *f*, а́лчность *f*; **~y** ['gri:di] □ жа́дный, а́лчный (of, for к Д).

Greek [gri:k] **1.** грек, греча́нка; **2.** гре́ческий.

green [gri:n] **1.** □ зелёный; незре́лый; *fig.* нео́пытный; **2.** зелёный цвет, зелёная кра́ска; мо́лодость *f*; лужа́йка; ~s *pl.* зе́лень *f*, о́вощи *m/pl.*; **~back** *Am.* банкно́та; **~grocer** зеленщи́к; **~house** тепли́ца, оранжере́я; **~ish** ['gri:niʃ] зеленова́тый; **~sickness** бле́дная не́мочь *f*.

greet [gri:t] приве́тствовать; кла́няться [поклони́ться] (Д); **~ing** ['gri:tiŋ] приве́тствие; приве́т.

grenade [gri'neid] ⚔ грана́та.

grew [gru:] *pt.* от grow.

grey [grei] **1.** □ се́рый; седо́й; **2.** се́рый цвет, се́рая кра́ска; **3.** де́лать(ся) се́рым; **~hound** борза́я (соба́ка).

grid [grid] решётка; се́тка; **~iron** [ра́шпер.]

grief [gri:f] го́ре, печа́ль *f*; come to ~ потерпе́ть неуда́чу, попа́сть в беду́.

griev|ance ['gri:vəns] оби́да; жа́лоба; **~e** [gri:v] горева́ть; огорча́ть [-чи́ть], опеча́ли(ва)ть; **~ous** ['gri:vəs] □ го́рестный, печа́льный.

grill [gril] **1.** ра́шпер; жа́реное на ра́шпере (мя́со и т. п.); **2.** жа́рить на ра́шпере; **~-room** ко́мната рестора́на, где мя́со жа́рится при пу́блике.

grim [grim] □ жесто́кий; мра́чный, злове́щий.

grimace [gri'meis] **1.** грима́са, ужи́мка; **2.** грима́сничать.

grim|e [graim] грязь *f*, са́жа (на ко́же); **~y** ['graimi] □ запа́чканный, гря́зный.

grin [grin] **1.** усме́шка; **2.** усмеха́ться [-хну́ться].

grind [graind] [*irr.*] **1.** [с]моло́ть; разма́лывать [-моло́ть]; растира́ть [растере́ть] (в порошо́к); [на]точи́ть; *fig.* зубри́ть; **2.** разма́лывание; тяжёлая, ску́чная рабо́та; **~stone** точи́льный ка́мень *m.*; жёрнов.

grip [grip] **1.** схва́тывание, зажа́тие, пожа́тие; рукоя́ть *f*; *fig.* тиски́ *m/pl.*; **2.** схва́тывать [схвати́ть] (*a. fig.*); овладева́ть внима́нием (Р).

gripe [graip] зажи́м; руко́ятка; ~s *pl.* ко́лики *f/pl.*

grisly ['grizli] ужа́сный.

gristle ['grisl] хрящ.

grit [grit] **1.** песо́к, гра́вий; F твёрдость хара́ктера, вы́держка; ~s *pl.* овся́ная крупа́; **2.** [за]скрежета́ть (Т).

grizzly ['grizli] **1.** се́рый; с про́седью; **2.** североамерика́нский се́рый медве́дь *m*, гри́зли *m indecl.*

groan [groun] о́хать [о́хнуть]; [за-] стона́ть.

grocer ['grousə] бакале́йщик; **~ies** [-riz] *pl.* бакале́я; **~y** [-ri] бакале́йная ла́вка; торго́вля бакале́йными това́рами.

groggy ['grɔgi] нетвёрдый на нога́х; ша́ткий.

groin [grɔin] *anat.* пах.

groom [grum] **1.** грум, ко́нюх; жени́х; **2.** ходи́ть за (ло́шадью); хо́лить; well- ~ed вы́холенный.

groove [gru:v] **1.** желобо́к, паз; *fig.* рути́на, привы́чка, колея́; **2.** де́лать вы́емку на (П).
grope [group] идти́ о́щупью; нащу́п(ыв)ать (*a. fig.*).
gross [grous] **1.** □ большо́й; ту́чный; гру́бый; † валово́й, бру́тто; **2.** ма́сса; гросс; in the ~ о́птом, гурто́м.
grotto ['grɔtou] пеще́ра, грот.
grouch [grautʃ] *Am.* F **1.** дурно́е настрое́ние; **2.** быть не в ду́хе; **~y** ['grautʃi] ворчли́вый.
ground[1] [graund] *pt.* и *p. pt.* от grind; ~ glass ма́товое стекло́.
ground[2] [graund] **1.** *mst* земля́, по́чва; уча́сток земли́; площа́дка; основа́ние; дно; **~s** *pl.* сад, парк (при до́ме); (кофе́йная) гу́ща; on the ~(s) of на основа́нии (Р); stand one's ~ удержа́ть свои́ пози́ции, прояви́ть твёрдость; **2.** класть на зе́млю; обосно́вывать [-нова́ть]; ⚡ заземля́ть [-ли́ть]; обуча́ть осно́вам предме́та; **~-floor** ни́жний эта́ж; **~less** [-lis] □ беспричи́нный, необосно́ванный; **~-staff** ✈ нелётный соста́в; **~work** фунда́мент, осно́ва.
group [gru:p] **1.** гру́ппа; фра́кция; **2.** (с)группирова́ть(ся); классифици́ровать (*im*)*pf*.
grove [grouv] ро́ща, лесо́к.
grovel ['grɔvl] *mst fig.* по́лзать, пресмыка́ться.
grow [grou] [*irr.*] *v/i.* расти́; выраста́ть [вы́расти]; [с]де́латься, станови́ться [стать]; *v/t.* ⚘ выра́щивать [вы́растить]; культиви́ровать (*im*)*pf.*; **~er** ['grouə] садово́д, плодово́д.
growl [graul] [за]рыча́ть; [за]ворча́ть.
grow|n [groun] *p. pt.* от grow; **~n-up** ['groun'ʌp] взро́слый; **~th** [grouθ] рост.
grub [grʌb] **1.** личи́нка; гу́сеница; **2.** вска́пывать [вскопа́ть]; выкорчёвывать [вы́корчевать]; **~by** ['grʌbi] чума́зый, неря́шливый.
grudge [grʌdʒ] **1.** недово́льство; за́висть *f*; **2.** [по]зави́довать в (П); неохо́тно дава́ть; [по]жале́ть.
gruff [grʌf] □ гру́бый.
grumble ['grʌmbl] [за]ворча́ть; [по]жа́ловаться; [за]грохота́ть; **~r** [-ə] *fig.* ворчу́н(ья).
grunt [grʌnt] хрю́кать [-кнуть].
guarant|ee [gærən'ti:] **1.** поручи́тель(ница *f*) *m*; гара́нтия; поруча́тельство; **2.** гаранти́ровать (*im*)*pf.*, руча́ться за (В); **~or** [gærən'tɔ] поручи́тель *m*; **~y** ['gærənti] гара́нтия.
guard [gɑ:d] **1.** стра́жа; ⚔ карау́л; 🚂 конду́ктор; *Am.* тюре́мщик; **~s** *pl.* гва́рдия; be off ~ быть недоста́точно бди́тельным; **2.** *v/t.* охраня́ть [-ни́ть]; сторожи́ть; защища́ть [защити́ть] (from от Р); *v/i.* [по]бере́чься, остерега́ться [-ре́чься] (against Р); **~ian** ['gɑ:djən] храни́тель *m*; ⚖ опеку́н; **~ianship** [-ʃip] охра́на; ⚖ опеку́нство.
guess [ges] **1.** дога́дка, предположе́ние; **2.** отга́дывать [-да́ть], уга́дывать [-да́ть]; *Am.* счита́ть, полага́ть.
guest [gest] го́сть(я *f*) *m*.
guffaw [gʌ'fɔ:] хо́хот.
guidance ['gaidəns] руково́дство.
guide [gaid] **1.** проводни́к, гид; ⊕ переда́точный рыча́г; Girl ♀s *pl.* ска́утки *f/pl.*; **2.** направля́ть [-ра́вить]; руководи́ть (Т); **~-book** путеводи́тель *m*; **~-post** указа́тельный столб.
guild [gild] цех, ги́льдия; организа́ция.
guile [gail] хи́трость *f*, кова́рство; **~ful** ['gailful] □ кова́рный; **~less** [-lis] □ простоду́шный.
guilt [gilt] вина́, вино́вность *f*; **~less** ['giltlis] □ невино́вный; **~y** ['gilti] □ вино́вный, винова́тый.
guise [gaiz] нару́жность *f*; ма́ска.
guitar [gi'tɑ:] ♪ гита́ра.
gulf [gʌlf] зали́в; про́пасть *f*.
gull [gʌl] **1.** ча́йка; глупе́ц; **2.** обма́нывать [-ну́ть]; [о]дура́чить.
gullet ['gʌlit] пищево́д; гло́тка.
gulp [gʌlp] **1.** жа́дно глота́ть; **2.** глото́к.
gum [gʌm] десна́; гу́мми *n indecl.*; клей; **~s** *pl. Am.* гало́ши *f/pl.*; **2.** скле́и(ва)ть; гумми́ровать (*im*)*pf*.
gun [gʌn] **1.** ору́дие, пу́шка; ружьё; *Am.* револьве́р; F big ~ *fig.* ва́жная персо́на, «ши́шка»; **2.** *Am.* охо́титься; **~boat** каноне́рка; **~man** *Am.* банди́т; **~ner** ⚔, ⚓ ['gʌnə] артиллери́ст, пулемётчик; **~powder** по́рох; **~smith** оруже́йный ма́стер.
gurgle ['gə:gl] [за]журча́ть, [за-]бу́лькать.
gush [gʌʃ] **1.** си́льный пото́к; ли́вень *m*; *fig.* излия́ние; **2.** хлы́нуть *pf.*; ли́ться пото́ком; *fig.* излива́ть чу́вства; **~er** ['gʌʃə] *fig.* челове́к, излива́ющий свои́ чу́вства; *Am.* нефтяно́й фонта́н.
gust [gʌst] поры́в (ве́тра).
gut [gʌt] кишка́; **~s** *pl.* вну́тренности *f/pl.*; F си́ла во́ли.
gutter ['gʌtə] водосто́чный жёлоб; сто́чная кана́ва.
guy [gai] **1.** пу́гало, чу́чело; *Am.* F па́рень *m*, ма́лый; **2.** издева́ться над (Т), осме́ивать [-ея́ть].
guzzle ['gʌzl] жа́дно пить; есть с жа́дностью.
gymnas|ium [dʒim'neizjəm] гимнасти́ческий зал; **~tics** [dzim'næstiks] *pl.* гимна́стика.
gyrate [dʒaiə'reit] враща́ться по кру́гу, дви́гаться по спира́ли.
gyroplane ['dʒaiəroplein] автожи́р.

H

haberdashery ['hæbədæʃəri] галантере́я; *Am.* мужско́е бельё.
habit ['hæbit] **1.** привы́чка; сложе́ние; сво́йство; **2.** оде́(ва́)ть; **~able** ['hæbitəbl] го́дный для жилья́; **~ation** [hæbi'teiʃən] жили́ще.
habitual [hə'bitjuəl] □ обы́чный, привы́чный.
hack [hæk] **1.** теса́ть; руби́ть [руб(а)ну́ть]; разбива́ть на куски́; **2.** наёмная ло́шадь *f*; моты́га.
hackneyed ['hæknid] *fig.* изби́тый, бана́льный.
had [hæd] *pt.* и *p. pt.* от have.
hag [hæg] (*mst fig.* old ~) ве́дьма.
haggard ['hægəd] □ измождённый, осу́нувшийся.
haggle [hægl] [с]торгова́ться.
hail [heil] **1.** град; о́клик; **2.** it ~s град идёт; *fig.* сы́паться гра́дом; приве́тствовать; ~ from происходи́ть из (Р); **~stone** гра́дина.
hair [hɛə] во́лос; **~-breadth** минима́льное расстоя́ние; **~-cut** стри́жка; **~-do** причёска; **~dresser** парикма́хер; **~less** ['hɛəlis] лы́сый, безволо́сый; **~pin** шпи́лька; **~-raising** стра́шный; **~splitting** крохобо́рство; **~y** [-ri] волоса́тый.
hale [heil] здоро́вый, кре́пкий.
half [hɑ:f] **1.** полови́на; ~ a crown полкро́ны; by halves ко́е-ка́к; go halves дели́ть попола́м; **2.** полу...; полови́нный; **3.** почти́; наполови́ну; **~-back** полузащи́тник; **~-breed** мети́с; гибри́д; **~-caste** челове́к сме́шанной ра́сы; **~-hearted** □ равноду́шный, вя́лый; **~-length** (*a.* ~ portrait) поясно́й портре́т; **~penny** ['heipni] полпе́нни *n indecl.*; **~-time** *sport* тайм, полови́на игры́; **~-way** на полпути́; **~witted** слабоу́мный.
halibut ['hælibət] па́лтус (ры́ба).
hall [hɔ:l] зал; холл, вестибю́ль *m*; *Am.* коридо́р; *univ.* общежи́тие для студе́нтов.
halloo [hə'lu:] крича́ть ату́; нау́ськ(ив)ать.
hallow ['hælou] освяща́ть [-яти́ть]; **~mas** [-mæs] *eccl.* день «всех святы́х».
halo ['heilou] *ast.* вене́ц; орео́л.
halt [hɔ:lt] **1.** прива́л; остано́вка; **2.** остана́вливать(ся) [-нови́ть(ся)]; де́лать прива́л; *mst fig.* колеба́ться; запина́ться [запну́ться].
halter ['hɔ:ltə] по́вод, недоу́здок.
halve [hɑ:v] **1.** дели́ть попола́м; **2.** ~s [hɑ:vz] *pl.* от half.
ham [hæm] о́корок, ветчина́.
hamburger ['hæmbə:gə] *Am.* (ру́бленая) котле́та.
hamlet ['hæmlit] дереву́шка.
hammer ['hæmə] **1.** молото́к, мо́лот; ♪ молото́чек; **2.** кова́ть мо́лотом; бить молотко́м; [по]стуча́ть; выко́вывать [вы́ковать].
hammock ['hæmək] гама́к, подвесна́я ко́йка.
hamper ['hæmpə] **1.** корзи́на с кры́шкой; **2.** [вос]препя́тствовать, [по]меша́ть (Д).
hand [hænd] **1.** рука́; по́черк; стре́лка (часо́в); рабо́чий; at ~ под руко́й; a good (poor) ~ at (не-) иску́сный в (П); ~ and glove в те́сной свя́зи; lend a ~ помога́ть [-мо́чь]; off ~ экспро́мтом; on ~ ✝ име́ющийся в прода́же, в распоряже́нии; on the one ~ с одно́й стороны́; on the other ~ с друго́й стороны́; ~-to-~ рукопа́шный; come to ~ получа́ться [-чи́ться]; прибы́(ва́)ть; **2.** ~ down оставля́ть пото́мству; ~ in вруча́ть [-чи́ть]; ~ over пере́д(ав)а́ть; **~-bag** да́мская су́мочка; **~bill** рекла́мный листо́к; **~-brake** ⊕ ручно́й то́рмоз; **~cuff** нару́чник; **~ful** ['hændful] горсть *f*; F «наказа́ние»; **~-glass** ручно́е зе́ркало.
handicap ['hændikæp] **1.** поме́ха; *sport* гандика́п; **2.** ста́вить в невы́годное положе́ние.
handi|craft [-krɑ:ft] ручна́я рабо́та, ремесло́; **~craftsman** куста́рь *m*; ремесленник; **~work** рукоде́лие; ручна́я рабо́та.
handkerchief ['hæŋkətʃi(:)f] носово́й плато́к; косы́нка.
handle [hændl] **1.** ру́чка, рукоя́тка; **2.** держа́ть в рука́х, тро́гать и́ли брать рука́ми; обходи́тся [обойти́сь] с (Т).
hand|made ручно́й рабо́ты; **~-set** *Am.* телефо́нная тру́бка; **~shake** рукопожа́тие; **~some** ['hænsəm] □ краси́вый; поря́дочный; **~work** ручна́я рабо́та; **~writing** по́черк; **~y** ['hændi] □ удо́бный; бли́зкий.
hang [hæŋ] **1.** [*irr.*] *v/t.* ве́шать [пове́сить]; подве́шивать [-ве́сить]; (*pt.* и *p. pt.* ~ed) ве́шать [пове́сить]; *v/i.* висе́ть; ~ about (*Am.* around) слоня́ться, окола́чиваться, шля́ться; ~ on прицепля́ться -[пи́ться] к (Д); *fig.* упо́рствовать; **2.** смысл, су́щность *f*.
hangar ['hæŋə] анга́р.
hang-dog присты́жённый, винова́тый (вид).
hanger ['hæŋə] ве́шалка (пла́тья); крючо́к, крюк; **~-on** *fig.* прихлеба́тель *m*.
hanging ['hæŋiŋ] ве́шание; пове́шение (казнь); ~s [-s] *pl.* драпиро́вки *f/pl.*
hangman ['hæŋmən] пала́ч.

hang-over F похмéлье.
hap|hazard ['hæp'hæzəd] **1.** случáйность *f*; at ~ наудáчу; **2.** случáйный; **~less** [-lis] □ злополýчный.
happen ['hæpən] случáться [-чи́ться], происходи́ть [произойти́]; окáзываться [-зáться]; he ~ed to be at home он случáйно оказáлся дóма; ~ (up)on, *Am.* ~ in with случáйно встрéтить; **~ing** ['hæpniŋ] слýчай, собы́тие.
happi|ly ['hæpili] счастли́во; к счáстью; **~ness** [-nis] счáстье.
happy ['hæpi] □ *com.* счастли́вый; удáчный.
harangue [hə'ræŋ] **1.** речь *f*; **2.** произноси́ть речь.
harass ['hærəs] [вс]тревóжить; изводи́ть [-вести́].
harbo(u)r ['hɑ:bə] **1.** гáвань *f*, порт; **2.** стать на я́корь; дать убéжище (Д); *fig.* затáивать [-и́ть]; **~age** [-ridʒ] убéжище, прию́т.
hard [hɑ:d] **1.** *adj. com.* твёрдый, жёсткий; крéпкий; трýдный; тяжёлый; *Am.* спиртнóй; ~ cash нали́чные *pl.* (дéньги); ~ currency устóйчивая валю́та; ~ of hearing тугóй нá ухо; **2.** *adv.* твёрдо; крéпко; си́льно; упóрно; с трудóм; ~ by бли́зко, ря́дом; ~ up в затрудни́тельном финáнсовом положéнии; **~-boiled** свáренный вкрутýю; бесчýвственный, чёрствый; *Am.* хладнокрóвный; **~en** ['hædn] дéлать(ся) твёрдым; [за-]твердéть; *fig.* закаля́ть(ся) [-ли́ть (-ся)]; **~-headed** практи́чный, трéзвый; **~-hearted** □ бесчýвственный; **~iness** вынóсливость *f*; **~ly** ['hɑ:dli] с трудóм; едвá; едвá ли; **~ness** [-nis] твёрдость *f* и т. д.; **~ship** [-ʃip] лишéние, нуждá; **~ware** скобянóй товáр; **~y** ['hɑ:di] □ смéлый, отвáжный; вынóсливый.
hare [hɛə] зáяц; **~-brained** рассéянный.
hark [hɑ:k] прислýш(ив)аться (to к Д); ~! чу!
harlot ['hɑ:lət] проститýтка.
harm [hɑ:m] **1.** вред, зло; оби́да; **2.** [по]вреди́ть (Д); **~ful** ['hɑ:mful] □ врéдный, пáгубный; **~less** [-lis] □ безврéдный, безоби́дный.
harmon|ic [hɑ:'mɔnik] (**~ally**, **~ious** □ [hɑ:'mounjəs]) гармони́чный, стрóйный; **~ize** ['hɑ:mənaiz] *v/t.* гармонизи́ровать (*im*)*pf.*; приводи́ть в гармóнию; *v/i.* гармони́ровать; **~y** [-ni] гармóния, созвýчие; соглáсие.
harness ['hɑ:nis] **1.** ýпряжь *f*, сбрýя; **2.** запрягáть [запря́чь].
harp [hɑ:p] **1.** áрфа; **2.** игрáть на áрфе; ~ (up)on завести́ волы́нку о (П).
harpoon [hɑ:'pu:n] гарпýн, острогá.
harrow ⚒ ['hærou] **1.** боронá; **2.** [вз]борони́ть; *fig.* [из]мýчить, [ис]терзáть.
harry ['hæri] разоря́ть [-ри́ть], опустошáть [-ши́ть].
harsh [hɑ:ʃ] □ рéзкий; жёсткий; стрóгий, сурóвый; тéрпкий.
hart [hɑ:t] *zo.* олéнь *m.*
harvest ['hɑ:vist] **1.** жáтва, убóрка (хлéба), сбор (я́блок и т. п.); урожáй; **2.** собирáть урожáй.
has [hæz] 3. *p. sg. pres.* от have.
hash [hæʃ] **1.** рýбленое мя́со; *fig.* пýтаница; **2.** [по]руби́ть, [по]кроши́ть (о мя́се).
hast|e [heist] поспéшность *f*, торопли́вость *f*; make ~ [по]спеши́ть; **~en** ['heisn] [по]торопи́ть(ся); **~y** ['heisti] □ поспéшный; вспы́льчивый; необдýманный.
hat [hæt] шля́па.
hatch [hætʃ] **1.** вы́водок; ⚓, ✈ люк; **2.** выси́живать [вы́сидеть] (цыпля́т и т. п.) (*a. fig.*); вылупля́ться из яйцá.
hatchet ['hætʃit] топóрик.
hatchway ['hætʃwei] ⚓ люк.
hat|e [heit] **1.** нéнависть *f*; **2.** ненави́деть; **~eful** ['heitful] □ ненави́стный; **~red** ['heitrid] нéнависть *f*.
haught|iness ['hɔ:tinis] надмéнность *f*, высокомéрие; **~y** [-ti] □ надмéнный, высокомéрный.
haul [hɔ:l] **1.** перевóзка; тя́га; **2.** [по]тянýть; таскáть, [по]тащи́ть; перевози́ть [-везти́].
haunch [hɔ:ntʃ] бедрó, ля́жка; зáдняя ногá.
haunt [hɔ:nt] **1.** появля́ться [-ви́ться] в (П) (о при́зраке); чáсто посещáть (мéсто); **2.** люби́мое мéсто; притóн; ~ed house дом с привидéнием.
have [hæv] **1.** [*irr.*] *v/t.* имéть; I ~ to do я дóлжен сдéлать; ~ one's hair cut стри́чься; he will ~ it that ... он настáивает на том, чтóбы (+ *inf.*); I had better go мне бы лýчше пойти́; I had rather go я предпочёл бы пойти́; ~ about one имéть при себé; **2.** *v/aux.* вспомогáтельный глагóл для образовáния перфéктной фóрмы: I ~ come я пришёл.
haven ['heivn] гáвань *f*; убéжище.
havoc ['hævək] опустошéние.
hawk [hɔ:k] **1.** я́стреб; **2.** торговáть вразнóс.
hawthorn ['hɔ:θɔ:n] ⚘ боя́рышник.
hay [hei] сéно; ~ fever сеннáя лихорáдка; **~cock**, **~stack** копнá сéна; **~loft** сеновáл.
hazard ['hæzəd] **1.** шанс; риск; **2.** рисковáть [-кнýть]; **~ous** ['hæzədəs] □ рискóванный.
haze [heiz] **1.** лёгкий тумáн, ды́мка; **2.** *Am.* зло подшýчивать над (Т)

hazel ['heizl] 1. ♣ орéшник; 2. кáрий (цвет); ~-**nut** лесной орéх.
hazy ['heizi] □ тумáнный; *fig.* смýтный.
he [hi:] 1. *pron. pers.* он; ~ who ... тот, кто ...; 2. ~-... пéред назвáнием живóтного обозначáет самцá.
head [hed] 1. *com.* головá; главá; начáльник; вождь *m*; изголóвье; лицевáя сторонá (монéты); come to a ~ назрé(вá)ть (о нарыве); *fig.* достигнуть критической стáдии; get it into one's ~ that ... забрáть себé в гóлову, что ...; 2. глáвный; 3. *v/t.* возглавлять; ~ off отклонять [-нить]; *v/i.* направляться [-áвиться]; ~ for держáть курс на (В); ~**ache** ['hedeik] головнáя боль *f*; ~-**dress** головнóй убóр; причёска; ~**ing** [-iŋ] заголóвок; ~**land** мыс; ~**light** 🚗 головнóй фонáрь *m*; *mot.* фáра; ~-**line** заголóвок; ~**long** *adj.* опромéтчивый; *adv.* опромéтчиво; очертя гóлову; ~**master** дирéктор шкóлы; ~-**phone** наýшник; ~**quarters** *pl.* ⚔ штаб-квартира; ~**strong** своевóльный, упрямый; ~**waters** *pl.* истóки *m/pl.*; ~**way**: make ~ дéлать успéхи; ~**y** ['hedi] □ стремительный; опьяняющий.
heal [hi:l] излéчивать [-чить], исцелять [-лить]; (*a.* ~ up) зажи(вá)ть.
health [helθ] здорóвье; ~**ful** ['helθful] □ целéбный; ~-**resort** курóрт; ~**y** ['helθi] □ здорóвый; полéзный.
heap [hi:p] 1. кýча, мáсса; грýда; 2. нагромождáть [-моздить]; нагружáть [-узить]; накоплять [-пить] (*a* ~ up).
hear [hiə] [*irr.*] [у]слышать; [по-]слýшать; ~**d** [hə:d] *pt.* и *p. pt.* от hear; ~**er** ['hiərə] слýшатель(ница *f*) *m*; ~**ing** [-iŋ] слух; ⚖ слýшание, разбóр дéла; ~**say** ['hiəsei] слух, молвá.
hearse [hə:s] катафáлк.
heart [hɑ:t] *com.* сéрдце; мýжество; суть *f*; сердцевина; ~**s** *pl.* чéрви *f/pl.* (кáрточная масть); *fig.* сéрдце, душá; by ~ наизýсть; out of ~ в уныннии; lay to ~ принимáть близко к сéрдцу; lose ~ терять мýжество; take ~ собрáться с дýхом; ~**ache** ['hɑ:teik] душéвная боль *f*; ~-**break** сильная печáль *f*; ~-**broken** убитый гóрем; ~**burn** изжóга; ~**en** ['hɑ:tən] ободрять [-рить]; ~**felt** искренний.
hearth [hɑ:θ] очáг (*a. fig.*).
heart|less ['hɑ:tlis] □ бессердéчный; ~**rending** душераздирáющий; ~**y** ['hɑ:ti] □ дрýжеский, сердéчный; здорóвый.
heat [hi:t] 1. *com.* жарá, жар; пыл; *sport* забéг, заплыв, заéзд; 2. нагрé(вá)ть(ся); топить; [раз]горячить; ~**er** ['hi:tə] ⊕ нагревáтель *m*; калорифер, радиáтор.
heath [hi:θ] мéстность, порóсшая вéреском; ♣ вéреск.
heathen ['hi:ðən] 1. язычник; 2. языческий.
heating ['hi:tiŋ] нагревáние; отоплéние; накáливание.
heave [hi:v] 1. подъём; волнéние (мóря); 2. [*irr.*] *v/t.* поднимáть [-нять]; [по]тянýть (якорь); *v/i.* вздымáться; напрягáться [-ячься].
heaven ['hevn] небесá *n/pl.*, нéбо; ~**ly** [-li] небéсный.
heaviness ['hevinis] тяжесть *f*; инéртность *f*; депрéссия.
heavy ['hevi] □ *com.* тяжёлый; обильный (урожáй); сильный (вéтер и т. п.); бýрный (о мóре); мрáчный; неуклюжий; ⚡ ~ current ток высóкого напряжéния; ~-**weight** *sport* тяжеловéс.
heckle ['hekl] прерывáть замечáниями (орáтора).
hectic ['hektik] ⚕ чахóточный; лихорáдочный, возбуждённый.
hedge [hedʒ] 1. изгородь *f*; 2. *v/t.* огорáживать изгородью; ограничи(ва)ть; *fig.* окружáть [-жить] (with T); *v/i.* уклоняться от прямóго отвéта; ~**hog** *zo.* ёж.
heed [hi:d] 1. внимáние, осторóжность *f*; take no ~ of не обращáть внимáния на (В); 2. обращáть внимáние на (В); ~**less** [-lis] □ небрéжный; необдýманный.
heel [hi:l] 1. пятка; каблýк; *Am. sl.* хам, подлéц; head over ~s, ~s over head вверх тормáшками; down at ~ *fig.* неряшливый; 2. прибивáть каблýк к (Д); слéдовать по пятáм за (Т).
heifer ['hefə] тёлка.
height [hait] высотá; вышинá; возвышенность *f*; верх; ~**en** ['haitn] повышáть [повысить]; усили(ва)ть.
heinous ['heinəs] □ отвратительный, ужáсный.
heir [ɛə] наслéдник; ~ apparent закóнный наслéдник; ~**ess** ['ɛəris] наслéдница; ~**loom** [-lu:m] наслéдство.
held [held] *pt.* и *p. pt.* от hold.
helicopter ['helikɔptə] вертолёт.
hell [hel] ад; *attr.* áдский; raise ~ скандáлить, безобрáзничать; ~**ish** ['heliʃ] □ áдский.
hello ['hʌ'lou, hə'lou] аллó!
helm [helm] ⚓ руль *m*, рулевóе колесó, штурвáл; *fig.* кормило.
helmet ['helmit] шлем.
helmsman ['helmzmən] ⚓ рулевóй; кóрмчий.
help [help] 1. *com.* пóмощь *f*; спасéние; mother's ~ бóнна 2. *v/t.* помогáть [помóчь] (Д); угощáть [уго-

сти́ть] (to T); ~ o. s. не церемо́ниться, брать (за столо́м); I could not ~ laughing я не мог не смея́ться; *v/i.* помога́ть [-мо́чь]; годи́ться; **~er** ['helpə] помо́щник (-ица); **~ful** ['helpful] □ поле́зный; **~ing** ['helpiŋ] по́рция; **~less** ['helplis] □ беспо́мощный; **~lessness** [-nis] беспо́мощность *f*; **~-mate** ['helpmeit], **~meet** [-mi:t] помо́щник (-ица); това́рищ, подру́га; супру́г(а).

helve [helv] ру́чка, рукоя́ть *f*.

hem [hem] **1.** рубе́ц, кро́мка; **2.** подруба́ть [-би́ть]; ~ in окружа́ть [-жи́ть].

hemisphere ['hemisfiə] полуша́рие.

hemlock ['hemlɔk] ⚘ болиголо́в.

hemp [hemp] конопля́, пенька́.

hemstitch ['hemstitʃ] ажу́рная стро́чка.

hen [hen] ку́рица; са́мка (пти́ца).

hence [hens] отсю́да; сле́довательно; a year ~ че́рез год; **~forth** ['hens'fɔ:θ], **~forward** ['hens'fɔ:wəd] с э́того вре́мени, впредь.

henpecked находя́щийся под башмако́м у жены́.

her [hə:, hə] её; ей.

herald ['herəld] **1.** ве́стник; **2.** возвеща́ть [-вести́ть], объявля́ть [-ви́ть]; ~ in вводи́ть [ввести́].

herb [hə:b] (целе́бная) трава́; (пря́ное) расте́ние; **~ivorous** [hə:'bivərəs] травоя́дный.

herd [hə:d] **1.** ста́до, гурт; *fig.* толпа́; **2.** *v/t.* пасти́ (скот); *v/i.* (*a.* ~ together) ходи́ть ста́дом; [с]толпи́ться; **~sman** ['hə:dzmən] пасту́х.

here [hiə] здесь, тут; сюда́; вот; ~'s to you! за ва́ше здоро́вье!

here|after [hiər'ɑ:ftə] **1.** в бу́дущем; **2.** бу́дущее; **~by** э́тим, настоя́щим; при сём; таки́м о́бразом.

heredit|ary [hi'reditəri] насле́дственный; **~y** [-ti] насле́дственность *f*.

here|in ['hiər'in] в э́том; здесь; при сём; **~of** э́того, об э́том; отсю́да, из э́того.

heresy ['herisi] е́ресь *f*.

heretic ['heritik] ерети́к (-и́чка).

here|tofore ['hiətu'fɔ:] пре́жде, до э́того; **~upon** вслед за э́тим, по́сле э́того; всле́дствие э́того; **~with** настоя́щим, при сём.

heritage ['heritidʒ] насле́дство; насле́дие (*mst fig.*).

hermit ['hə:mit] отше́льник, пусты́нник.

hero ['hiərou] геро́й; **~ic** [-'rouik] (**~ally**) герои́ческий, геро́йский; **~ine** ['herouin] герои́ня; **~ism** [-izm] герои́зм.

heron ['herən] *zo.* ца́пля.

herring ['heriŋ] сельдь *f*, селёдка.

hers [hə:z] *pron. poss.* её.

herself [hə:'self] сама́; себя́, -ся, -сь.

hesitat|e ['heziteit] [по]колеба́ться; запина́ться [запну́ться]; **~ion** [hezi'teiʃən] колеба́ние; запи́нка.

hew [hju:] [*irr.*] руби́ть; разруба́ть [-би́ть]; прокла́дывать [проложи́ть] (доро́гу); высека́ть [вы́сечь].

hey [hei] эй!

heyday ['heidei] *fig.* зени́т, расцве́т.

hicc|up, ['hikʌp] *a.* **~ough 1.** ико́та; **2.** ика́ть [икну́ть].

hid [hid], **hidden** ['hidn] *pt* и *p. pt.* от hide.

hide [haid] [*irr.*] [с]пря́тать(ся); скры́(ва́)ть(ся); **~-and-seek** игра́ в пря́тки.

hidebound ['heidbaund] *fig.* у́зкий, ограни́ченный.

hideous ['hidiəs] □ отврати́тельный, ужа́сный.

hiding-place потаённое ме́сто, убе́жище.

high [hai] **1.** *adj.* □ *com.* высо́кий; возвы́шенный; си́льный; вы́сший, верхо́вный; дорого́й (о цене́); с душко́м (мя́со); with a ~ hand своево́льно, вла́стно; ~ spirits *pl.* припо́днятое настрое́ние; ~ life вы́сшее о́бщество; ~ light основно́й моме́нт; ~ words гне́вные слова́ *n/pl.*; **2.** *adv.* высоко́; си́льно; **~-bred** поро́дистый; **~-brow** *Am. sl.* претенцио́зный интеллиге́нт; **~-class** первокла́ссный; **~-day** пра́здник; **~-grade** высокопроце́нтный; высокосо́ртный; **~-handed** своево́льный; повели́тельный; **~lands** *pl.* го́рная страна́; **~ly** ['haili] о́чень, весьма́; speak ~ of положи́тельно отзыва́ться о (П); **~-minded** возвы́шенный, благоро́дный; **~ness** ['hainis] возвы́шенность *f*; *fig.* высо́чество; **~-power**: ~ station мо́щная электроста́нция; **~-road** шоссе́ *n*, *indecl.*; гла́вная доро́га; **~-strung** очень чувстви́тельный; **~way** больша́я доро́га, шоссе́; *fig.* прямо́й путь *m*; **~wayman** разбо́йник.

hike [haik] F **1.** пешехо́дная экску́рсия; **2.** путеше́ствовать пешко́м; **~r** ['heikə] пешехо́дный путеше́ственник; стра́нник (-ица).

hilarious [hi'lɛəriəs] □ (шу́мно) весёлый.

hill [hil] холм, возвыше́ние; **~billy** *Am.* ['hilbili] челове́к из глухо́й стороны́; **~ock** ['hilək] хо́лмик; **~y** [-i] холми́стый.

hilt [hilt] рукоя́тка (са́бли и т. п.).

him [him] *pron. pers.* (ко́свенный паде́ж от he) его́, ему́; **~self** [him'self] сам; себя́, -ся, -сь.

hind [haind] **1.** лань *f*; **2.** ~ leg за́дняя нога́; **~er 1.** ['haində] *adj.* за́дний; **2.** ['hində] *v/t.* [по]мешáть, препя́тствовать (Д); **~most** сáмый зáдний.

hindrance ['hindrəns] помéха, препя́тствие.

hinge [hindʒ] **1.** пéтля; крюк; шарни́р; *fig.* стéржень *m*, суть *f*; **2.** ~ upon *fig.* зави́сеть от (P).

hint [hint] **1.** намёк; **2.** намекáть [-кнýть] (at на В).

hip [hip] бедрó; ♀ я́года шипóвника.

hippopotamus [hipə'pɔtəməs] гиппопотáм.

hire [haiə] **1.** наём, прокáт; **2.** нанимáть [наня́ть]; ~ out сдавáть в наём, давáть напрокáт.

his [hiz] *pron. poss.* егó, свой.

hiss [his] *v/i.* [про]шипéть; *v/t.* осви́стывать [-стáть].

histor|ian [his'tɔ:riən] истóрик; **~ic(al** □) [his'tɔrik, -rikəl] истори́ческий; **~y** ['histəri] истóрия.

hit [hit] **1.** удáр, толчóк; попадáние (в цель); *thea.*, ♪ успéх, боеви́к; **2.** [*irr.*] ударя́ть [удáрить]; поражáть [порази́ть]; попадáть [попáсть] в (цель и т. п.); *Am.* F прибы́(вá)ть в (В); ~ a p. a blow наноси́ть удáр (Д); F ~ it off with [по-]лáдить с (Т); ~ (up)on находи́ть [найти́] (В); нападáть [напáсть] на (В).

hitch [hitʃ] **1.** толчóк, рывóк; ⚓ пéтля, ýзел; *fig.* препя́тствие; **2.** подтáлкивать [-толкнýть]; зацепля́ть(ся) [-пи́ть(ся)], прицепля́ть (-ся) [-пи́ть(ся)]; **~-hike** *Am.* F *mot.* путешéствовать, пóльзуясь попýтными автомоби́лями.

hither ['hiðə] *lit.* сюдá; **~to** [-'tu:] *lit.* до сих пóр.

hive [haiv] **1.** ýлей; рой пчёл; *fig.* людскóй муравéйник; **2.** ~ up запасáть [-сти́]; жить вмéсте.

hoard [hɔ:d] **1.** запáс, склад; **2.** накопля́ть [-пи́ть]; запасáть [-сти́] (В); припря́т(ыв)ать.

hoarfrost ['hɔ:'frɔst] и́ней.

hoarse [hɔ:s] □ хри́плый, охри́пший.

hoary ['hɔ:ry] седóй; покры́тый и́неем.

hoax [houks] **1.** обмáн, мистификáция; **2.** подшýчивать [-ути́ть] над (Т), мистифици́ровать (*im*)*pf.*

hobble ['hɔbl] **1.** прихрáмывающая похóдка; **2.** *v/i.* прихрáмывать; *v/t.* [с]трenóжить (лóшадь).

hobby ['hɔbi] *fig.* конёк, люби́мое заня́тие.

hobgoblin ['hɔbgɔblin] домовóй.

hobo ['houbou] *Am.* F бродя́га *m.*

hod [hɔd] лотóк (для поднóса кирпичéй); коры́то (для и́звести).

hoe [hou] ⚒ **1.** моты́га; **2.** моты́жить; разрыхля́ть [-ли́ть] (моты́гой).

hog [hɔg] **1.** свинья́ (*a. fig.*); бóров; **2.** выгибáть спи́ну; кóротко подстригáть (гри́ву); **~gish** ['hɔgiʃ] □ сви́нский; обжóрливый.

hoist [hɔist] **1.** лебёдка; лифт; **2.** поднимáть [-ня́ть].

hold [hould] **1.** владéние; захвáт; власть *f*, влия́ние; ⚓ трюм; catch (*or* get, lay, take) ~ of схвáтывать [схвати́ть] (В); keep ~ of удéрживать [-жáть] (В); **2.** [*irr.*] *v/t.* держáть; выдéрживать [вы́держать]; остана́вливать [-нови́ть]; проводи́ть [-вести́] (собрáние и т. п.); завладé(вá)ть (внимáнием); занимáть [-ня́ть]; вмещáть [вмести́ть]; ~ one's own отстáивать свою пози́цию; ~ the line! *teleph.* не вéшайте трýбку; ~ over откладывать [отложи́ть]; ~ up поддéрживать [-жáть]; задéрживать [-жáть]; останови́ть с цéлью грабежá; **3.** *v/i.* останáвливаться [-нови́ться]; держáться (о погóде); ~ forth рассуждáть; разглагóльствовать; ~ good (*or* true) имéть си́лу; ~ off держáться поóдаль; ~ on держáться за (В); ~ to придéрживаться (Р); ~ up держáться пря́мо; **~er** ['houldə] арендáтор; владéлец; **~ing** [-iŋ] учáсток земли́; владéние; **~-over** *Am.* пережи́ток; **~-up** *Am.* налёт, ограблéние.

hole [houl] дырá, отвéрстие; я́ма; норá; F *fig.* затрудни́тельное положéние; pick **~s** in находи́ть недостáтки в (П).

holiday ['hɔlədi] прáздник; день óтдыха; óтпуск; **~s** *pl.* кани́кулы *f/pl.*

hollow ['hɔlou] **1.** □ пустóй, пóлый; впáлый, ввали́вшийся; **2.** пустотá; дуплó; лощи́на; **3.** выдáлбливать [вы́долбить].

holly ['hɔli] ♀ остроли́ст, пáдуб.

holster ['houlstə] кобурá.

holy ['houli] святóй, свящéнный; ~ water святáя водá; ♀ Week страстнáя недéля.

homage ['hɔmidʒ] почтéние, уважéние; do (*or* pay, render) ~ окáзывать почтéние (to Д).

home [houm] **1.** дом, жили́ще; рóдина; at ~ дóма; **2.** *adj.* домáшний; внýтренний; ♀ Office, *Am.* ♀ Departement министéрство внýтренних дел; ♀ Secretary мини́стр внýтренних дел; **3.** *adv.* домóй; hit (*or* strike) ~ попáсть в цель; **~-felt** прочýвствованный, сердéчный; **~less** ['houmlis] бездóмный; **~like** ую́тный; **~ly** [-li] *fig.* простóй, обы́денный; домáшний; некраси́вый; **~-made** домáшнего изготовлéния; **~sickness** тоскá по рóдине; **~stead** дом с учáстком земли́; усáдьба; **~ward**(s) [-wəd(s)] домóй.

homicide ['hɔmisaid] уби́йство; уби́йца *m/f.*

homogeneous [hɔmoˈdʒi:niəs] □ однорóдный.
hone [houn] **1.** оселóк, точи́льный кáмень *m*; **2.** [на]точи́ть.
honest [ˈɔnist] □ чéстный; **~y** [-i] чéстность *f*.
honey [ˈhʌni] мёд; my ~! дýшенька!; **~comb** [ˈhʌnikoum] сóты *m/pl.*; **~ed** [ˈhʌnid] медóвый; **~-moon 1.** медóвый мéсяц; **2.** проводи́ть медóвый мéсяц.
honorary [ˈɔnərəri] почётный.
hono(u)r [ˈɔnə] **1.** честь *f*; чéстность *f*; почёт; пóчесть *f*; Your ♀ вáша честь *f*; **2.** почитáть [-чти́ть]; удостáивать [-стóить]; ✝ плати́ть в срок (по вéкселю); **~able** [ˈɔnərəbl] □ почётный; благорóдный; почтéнный.
hood [hud] **1.** капюшóн; *mot.* капóт; **2.** покрывáть капюшóном.
hoodwink [ˈhudwiŋk] обмáнывать [-нýть].
hoof [hu:f] копы́то.
hook [hu:k] **1.** крюк, крючóк; багóр; серп; by ~ or by crook прáвдами и непрáвдами, так и́ли инáче; **2.** зацепля́ть [-пи́ть]; застёгивать(ся) [-стегнýть(ся)].
hoop [hu:p] **1.** óбруч; ⊕ обóйма, бýгель *m*, кольцó; **2.** набивáть óбручи на (В); скрепля́ть óбручем.
hooping-cough коклю́ш.
hoot [hu:t] **1.** крик совы́; ги́канье; **2.** *v/i.* [за]улюлю́кать, [за]ги́кать; *mot.* [за]гудéть; *v/t.* осви́стывать [-истáть].
hop [hɔp] **1.** ♀ хмель *m*; прыжóк; *sl.* танцевáльный вéчер; **2.** собирáть хмель; скакáть, пры́гать на однóй ногé.
hope [houp] **1.** надéжда; **2.** надéяться (for на В); ~ in полагáться [положи́ться] на (В); **~ful** [ˈhoupful] □ подаю́щий надéжды; надéющийся; **~less** [-lis] □ безнадёжный.
horde [hɔ:d] ордá; ватáга, шáйка.
horizon [hoˈraizn] горизóнт; *fig.* кругозóр.
horn [hɔ:n] рог; *mot.* гудóк; ♪ рожóк; ~ of plenty рог изоби́лия.
hornet [ˈhɔ:nit] *zo.* шéршень *m*.
horny [ˈhɔ:ni] □ мозóлистый.
horr|ible [ˈhɔrəbl] □ стрáшный, ужáсный, **~id** [ˈhɔrid] □ ужáсный; проти́вный; **~ify** [ˈhɔrifai] ужасáть [-снýть]; шоки́ровать; **~or** [ˈhɔrə] ýжас; отвращéние.
horse [hɔ:s] лóшадь *f*, конь *m*; кóзлы *f/pl.*; *sport* конь *m*; take ~ сесть на лóшадь; **~back**: on ~ верхóм; **~hair** кóнский вóлос; **~-laugh** F грýбый, грóмкий хóхот; **~man** [-mən] всáдник, верховóй; **~power** лошади́ная си́ла; **~-radish** ♀ хрен; **~shoe** подкóва.
horticulture [ˈhɔ:tikʌltʃə] садовóдство.
hose [houz] ✝ *coll.* чулки́ *m/pl.* (как назвáние товáра); шланг.
hosiery [ˈhouʒəri] ✝ чулóчные издéлия *n/pl.*, трикотáж.
hospitable [ˈhɔspitəbl] □ гостеприи́мный.
hospital [ˈhɔspitl] больни́ца, гóспиталь *m*; **~ity** [hɔspiˈtæliti] гостеприи́мство.
host [houst] хозя́ин; содержáтель гости́ницы; *fig.* мнóжество; **~s** of heaven *eccl.* áнгелы, си́лы небéсные.
hostage [ˈhɔstidʒ] залóжник (-ица).
hostel [ˈhɔstəl] общежи́тие; турбáза.
hostess [ˈhoustis] хозя́йка (*s.* host).
hostil|e [ˈhɔstail] враждéбный; **~ity** [hɔsˈtiliti] враждéбность *f*; враждéбный акт.
hot [hɔt] горя́чий; жáркий; пы́лкий; ~ dogs горя́чие соси́ски *f/pl.*; **~bed** парни́к; *fig.* очáг.
hotchpotch [ˈhɔtʃpɔtʃ] овощнóй суп; *fig.* вся́кая вся́чина.
hotel [ho(u)ˈtel] отéль *m*, гости́ница.
hot|headed опромéтчивый; **~-house** оранжерéя, тепли́ца; **~spur** вспы́лчивый человéк.
hound [haund] **1.** гóнчая собáка; *fig.* негодя́й, подлéц; **2.** трави́ть собáками.
hour [auə] час; врéмя; **~ly** [ˈauəli] [ежечáсный.]
house 1. [haus] *com.* дом; здáние; *parl.* палáта; *univ.* коллéдж; **2.** [hauz] *v/t.* поселя́ть [-ли́ть]; помещáть [-ести́ть]; приюти́ть *pf.*; *v/i.* помещáться [-ести́ться]; жить; **~-breaker** взлóмщик, громи́ла *m*; **~-check** *Am.* óбыск; **~hold** домáшнее хозя́йство; домочáдцы *m/pl.*; **~holder** главá семьи́; **~-keeper** экономка; **~keeping** домáшнее хозя́йство, домовóдство; **~warming** новосéлье; **~wife** хозя́йка; **~wifery** [ˈhauswifəri] домáшнее хозя́йство; домовóдство.
housing [ˈhauziŋ] снабжéние жили́щем; жили́щное строи́тельство.
hove [houv] *pt.* и *p. pt.* от heave.
hovel [ˈhɔvəl] навéс; лачýга, хибáрка.
hover [ˈhɔvə] пари́ть (о пти́це); *fig.* колебáться, не решáться.
how [hau] как?, каки́м óбразом?; ~ about ...? как обстои́т дéло с (Т)?; **~ever** [hauˈevə] **1.** *adv.* как бы ни; **2.** *cj.* однáко, тем не мéнее.
howl [haul] **1.** вой, завывáние; **2.** [за]вы́ть; **~er** [ˈhaulə] *sl.* грýбая оши́бка.
hub [hʌb] ступи́ца (колесá), втýлка; *fig.* центр (внимáния).
hubbub [ˈhʌbʌb] шум, гам.
huckster [ˈhʌkstə] мелочнóй торгóвец; бары́шник.

huddle ['hʌdl] **1.** сва́ливать в ку́чу, укла́дывать кое-ка́к; сверну́ться «кала́чиком»; ~ on надева́ть на́спех; **2.** ку́ча; су́толока, сумато́ха.
hue [hju:] отте́нок; ~ and cry пого́ня с кри́ками.
huff [hʌf] **1.** раздраже́ние; **2.** *v/t.* задира́ть; запу́гивать [-га́ть]; *v/i.* оскорбля́ться [-би́ться], обижа́ться [оби́деться].
hug [hʌg] **1.** объя́тие; **2.** обнима́ть [-ня́ть]; *fig.* быть приве́рженным, скло́нным к (Д).
huge [hju:dʒ] □ огро́мный, гига́нтский; **~ness** ['hju:dʒnis] огро́мность *f*.
hulk [hʌlk] *fig.* большо́й, неуклю́жий челове́к.
hull [hʌl] **1.** ⚘ шелуха́, скорлупа́; ко́рпус (корабля́); **2.** [на]шелуши́ть, [об]лущи́ть.
hum [hʌm] [за]жужжа́ть; напева́ть; F make things ~ вноси́ть оживле́ние в рабо́ту.
human ['hju:mən] **1.** □ челове́ческий; **~ly** по-челове́чески; **2.** F челове́к; **~e** [hju:'mein] □ гума́нный, челове́чный; **~itarian** [hjumæni'tɛəriən] филантро́п; **2.** гуманита́рный; гума́нный; **~ity** [hju'mæniti] челове́чество; гума́нность *f*; **~kind** ['hju:mən'kaind] людско́й род.
humble ['hʌmbl] **1.** □ скро́мный; поко́рный, смире́нный; **2.** унижа́ть [уни́зить]; смиря́ть [-ри́ть].
humble-bee ['hʌmblbi:] шмель *m*.
humbleness [-nis] скро́мность *f*; поко́рность *f*.
humbug ['hʌmbʌg] чепуха́; хвасту́н.
humdrum ['hʌmdrʌm] бана́льный, ску́чный.
humid ['hju:mid] сыро́й, вла́жный; **~ity** [hju'miditi] сы́рость *f*, вла́га.
humiliat|e [hju'milieit] унижа́ть [уни́зить]; **~ion** [hjumili'eiʃən] униже́ние.
humility [hju'militi] смире́ние; поко́рность *f*.
humming ['hʌmiŋ] F мо́щный; **~bird** *zo.* коли́бри *m/f indecl.*
humorous ['hju:mərəs] □ юмористи́ческий; коми́ческий.
humo(u)r ['hju:mə] **1.** ю́мор; шутли́вость *f*; настрое́ние; out of ~ не в ду́хе; **2.** потака́ть (Д); ублажа́ть [-жи́ть].
hump [hʌmp] **1.** горб; **2.** [с]го́рбить(ся).
hunch [hʌntʃ] **1.** горб; *Am.* подозре́ние; ломо́ть *m*; **2.** [с]го́рбить (-ся) (*a.* ~ out, up); **~back** горбу́н(ья).
hundred ['hʌndrəd] **1.** сто; **2.** со́тня; **~th** [-θ] со́тый; со́тая часть *f*; **~weight** це́нтнер.
hung [hʌŋ] *pt.* и *p.pt.* от hang.
Hungarian [hʌŋ'gɛəriən] **1.** венге́рец (-рка); **2.** венге́рский.
hunger ['hʌŋgə] **1.** го́лод; *fig.* жа́жда; **2.** *v/i.* голода́ть; быть голо́дным; *fig.* жа́ждать (for P).
hungry ['hʌŋgri] □ голо́дный.
hunk [hʌŋk] то́лстый кусо́к.
hunt [hʌnt] **1.** охо́та; по́иски *m/pl.* (for P); **2.** охо́титься на (В) *or* за (Т); трави́ть; ~ out *or* up отыскива́ть [-ка́ть]; ~ for *fig.* охо́титься за (Т), иска́ть (P *or* B); **~er** ['hʌntə] охо́тник; охо́тничья ло́шадь *f*; **~ing-ground** райо́н охо́ты.
hurdle ['hə:dl] препя́тствие, барье́р; **~-race** ска́чки с препя́тствиями; барье́рный бег.
hurl [hə:l] **1.** си́льный бросо́к; **2.** швыря́ть [-рну́ть], мета́ть [метну́ть].
hurricane ['hʌrikən] урага́н.
hurried ['hʌrid] □ торопли́вый.
hurry ['hʌri] **1.** торопли́вость *f*, поспе́шность *f*; **2.** *v/t.* [по]торопи́ть; поспе́шно посыла́ть; *v/i.* [по]спеши́ть (*a.* ~ up).
hurt [hə:t] **1.** поврежде́ние; **2.** [*irr.*] (*a. fig.*) причиня́ть боль; поврежда́ть [-еди́ть]; боле́ть (о ча́сти те́ла).
husband ['hʌzbənd] **1.** муж, супру́г; **2.** [с]эконо́мить, эконо́мно расхо́довать.
hush [hʌʃ] **1.** тишина́, молча́ние; **2.** ти́ше!; **3.** водворя́ть тишину́; ~ up зама́лчивать [замолча́ть]; *v/i.* успока́иваться [-ко́иться]; утиха́ть [ути́хнуть].
husk [hʌsk] **1.** ⚘ шелуха́; **2.** очища́ть от шелухи́, [на]шелуши́ть; **~y** ['hʌski] □ си́плый, охри́пший (го́лос); *Am.* ро́слый.
hustle ['hʌsl] **1.** *v/t.* толка́ть [-кну́ть]; [по]торопи́ть; понужда́ть [-ну́дить]; *v/i.* толка́ться [-кну́ться]; [по]торопи́ться; *part. Am.* бы́стро де́йствовать; **2.** толкотня́; *Am.* F энерги́чная де́ятельность *f*; ~ and bustle толкотня́ и шум.
hut [hʌt] хи́жина, хиба́рка; бара́к.
hutch [hʌtʃ] кле́тка (для кро́ликов и т. п.).
hybrid ['haibrid] 🕮 гибри́д, по́месь *f*; **~ize** ['haibridaiz] скре́щивать [-ести́ть] (расте́ния, живо́тных).
hydro... ['haidro...] 🕮 водо...; **~chloric** [-'klɔrik]: ~ acid соля́ная кислота́; **~gen** ['haidridʒən] ⚗ водоро́д; **~pathy** [hai'drɔpəθi] водолече́ние; **~phobia** ['haidrə-'foubiə] водобоя́знь *f*; **~plane** ['haidroplein] гидропла́н.
hygiene ['haidʒi:n] гигие́на.
hymn [him] **1.** церко́вный гимн; **2.** петь ги́мны.
hyphen ['haifən] **1.** дефи́с, соеди-

нительная чёрточка; **2.** писать через чёрточку.
hypnotize ['hipnətaiz] [за]гипнотизировать.
hypo|chondriac [haipo'kɔndriæk] ипохондрик; **~crisy** [hi'pɔkrəsi] лицемерие; **~crite** ['hipokrit] лицемер; **~critical** [hipo'kritikəl] □ лицемерный; **~thesis** [hai'pɔθisis] гипотеза, предположение.
hyster|ical [his'terikəl] □ истеричный; **~ics** [his'teriks] *pl.* истерика.

I

I [ai] *pers. pron.* я.
ice [ais] **1.** лёд; мороженое; **2.** замораживать [-розить]; покрывать льдом; глазировать *(im)pf.*; **~-age** ледниковый период; **~-bound** затёртый льдами; **~-box, ~-chest** холодильник, ледник; **~-cream** мороженое.
icicle ['aissikl] (ледяная) сосулька.
icing ['aisiŋ] сахарная глазурь *f*; ✈ обледенение.
icy ['aisi] □ ледяной.
idea [ai'diə] идея; понятие, представление; мысль *f*; **~l** [-l] **1.** □ идеальный; воображаемый; **2.** идеал.
identi|cal [ai'dentikəl] □ тождественный; одинаковый; **~fication** [ai'dentifi'keiʃən] отождествление; установление личности; **~fy** [-fai] отождествлять [-вить]; устанавливать личность (тождество) (P); **~ty** [-ti] тождественность *f*; **~** card удостоверение личности.
idiom ['idiəm] идиома; говор.
idiot ['idiət] идиот(ка); **~ic** [idi'ɔtik] (-ally) идиотский.
idle ['aidl] **1.** □ незанятый; безработный; ленивый; праздный; тщетный; ⊕ бездействующий, холостой; **~** hours *pl.* часы досуга; **2.** *v/t.* проводить (время) без дела (*mst* **~** away); *v/i.* лениться, бездельничать; **~ness** [-nis] праздность *f*, безделье; **~r** [-ə] бездельник (-ица), лентяй(ка).
idol ['aidl] идол; *fig.* кумир; **~atry** [ai'dɔlətri] идолопоклонство; обожание; **~ize** ['aidəlaiz] боготворить.
idyl(l) ['aidil] идиллия.
if [if] *cj.* если; если бы; (= whether) ли: **~** he knows знает ли он.
ignit|e [ig'nait] зажигать [-жечь]; загораться [-реться], воспламеняться [-ниться]; **~ion** [ig'niʃən] *mot.* зажигание; запал; *attr.* запальный.
ignoble [ig'noubl] □ низкий, позорный.
ignor|ance ['ignərəns] невежество; неведение; **~ant** [-rənt] невежественный; несведущий; **~e** [ig'nɔ:] игнорировать *(im)pf.*; ⚖ отвергать [-ергнуть].
ill [il] **1.** *adj.* больной, нездоровый; дурной; **2.** *adv.* едва ли; плохо, дурно; **3.** зло, вред.
ill|-advised неблагоразумный; **~-bred** невоспитанный.
illegal [i'li:gəl] □ незаконный.
illegible [i'ledʒəbl] □ неразборчивый.
illegitimate [ili'dʒitimit] □ незаконный; незаконнорождённый.
ill|-favo(u)red некрасивый; неприятный; **~-humo(u)red** в дурном настроении, не в духе.
illiberal [i'libərəl] □ ограниченный (о взглядах); скупой.
illicit [i'lisit] □ запрещённый (законом).
illiterate [i'litərit] □ **1.** неграмотный; **2.** необразованный человек; неуч.
ill|-mannered невоспитанный, грубый; **~-natured** □ дурного нрава, злобный.
illness ['ilnis] болезнь *f*.
ill|-timed несвоевременный, неподходящий; **~-treat** плохо обращаться с (T).
illumin|ate [i'lju:mineit] освещать [-етить], озарять [-рить]; просвещать [-етить]; проливать свет на (B); **~ating** [-neitiŋ] освещающий, осветительный; **~ation** [ilju:mi'neiʃən] освещение; иллюминация.
illus|ion [i'lu:ʒən] иллюзия, обман чувств; **~ive** [-siv], □ **~ory** □ обманчивый, иллюзорный.
illustrat|e ['iləstreit] иллюстрировать *(im)pf.*; пояснять [-нить]; **~ion** [iləs'treiʃən] иллюстрация; **~ive** ['iləstreitiv] □ иллюстративный.
illustrious [i'lʌstriəs] □ знаменитый.
ill-will недоброжелательность *f*.
image ['imidʒ] образ; изображение; отражение; подобие.
imagin|able [i'mædʒinəbl] □ вообразимый; **~ary** [-nəri] воображаемый; мнимый; **~ation** [imædʒi'neiʃən] воображение, фантазия; **~ative** [i'mæddʒinətiv] □ одарённый воображением; **~e** [i'mædʒin] воображать [-разить]; представлять [-авить] себе.
imbecile ['imbisail] **1.** □ слабоумный; **2.** глупец.
imbibe [im'baib] впитывать [впитать], вдыхать [вдохнуть]; *fig.* усваивать [усвоить] (идеи).

imbue [im'bju:] насыщáть [-ы́тить]; окрáшивать [окрáсить]; *fig.* наполня́ть [-óлнить].

imita|te ['imiteit] подражáть (Д); передрáзнивать [-ни́ть]; поддé-л(ыв)ать; **~tion** [imi'teiʃən] подражáние; поддéлка, суррогáт; *attr.* поддéльный, искýсственный.

immaculate [i'mækjulit] □ безукори́зненный; незапя́тнанный (*a. fig.*).

immaterial [imə'tiəriəl] □ несущéственный, невáжный; невещéственный.

immature [imə'tjuə] незрéлый; недорáзвитый.

immediate [i'mi:djət] □ непосрéдственный; ближáйший; безотлагáтельный; **~ly** [-li] *adv.* непосрéдственно; немéдленно.

immense [i'mens] □ огрóмный.

immerse [i'mə:s] погружáть [-узи́ть], окунáть [-нýть]; *fig.* ~ o. s. in погружáться [-узи́ться] в (В).

immigra|nt ['imigrənt] иммигрáнт(ка); **~te** [greit] иммигри́ровать (*im*)*pf.*; **~tion** [imi'greiʃən] иммигрáция.

imminent ['iminənt] □ грозя́щий, нави́сший.

immobile [i'moubail] неподви́жный.

immoderate [i'mɔdərit] неумéренный, чрезмéрный.

immodest [i'mɔdist] □ нескрóмный.

immoral [i'mɔrəl] □ безнрáвственный.

immortal [i'mɔ:tl] □ бессмéртный.

immovable [i'mu:vəbl] □ недви́жимый, неподви́жный; непоколеби́мый.

immun|e [i'mju:n] невосприи́мчивый (from к Д); иммýнный; **~ity** [-iti] освобождéние (от платежá); ⚕ иммунитéт, невосприи́мчивость *f* (from к Д); *pol.* иммунитéт.

imp [imp] бесёнок; шалуни́шка *m/f.*

impair [im'pɛə] ослабля́ть [-áбить]; [ис]пóртить; повреждáть [-еди́ть].

impart [im'pɑ:t] прид(ав)áть; перед(ав)áть (нóвости т. п.).

impartial [im'pɑ:ʃəl] □ беспристрáстный, непредвзя́тый; **~ity** ['impɑ:ʃi'æliti] беспристрáстность *f.*

impassable [im'pɑ:səbl] □ непроходи́мый, непроéзжий.

impassioned [im'pæʃənd] стрáстный, пы́лкий.

impassive [im'pæsiv] □ спокóйный, безмятéжный.

impatien|ce [im'peiʃəns] нетерпéние; **~t** [-t] □ нетерпели́вый.

impeach [im'pi:tʃ] порицáть; набрáсывать тень на (В).

impeccable [im'pekəbl] □ безупрéчный; непогреши́мый.

impede [im'pi:d] [вос]препя́тствовать (Д); [по]мешáть (Д).

impediment [im'pedimənt] помéха; задéржка.

impel [im'pel] принуждáть [-ýдить].

impend [im'pend] нависáть [-и́снуть]; надвигáться [-и́нуться].

impenetrable [im'penitrəbl] □ непроходи́мый; непроницáемый; *fig.* непостижи́мый.

imperative [im'perətiv] □ повели́тельный, влáстный; крáйне необходи́мый.

imperceptible [impə'septəbl] □ незамéтный.

imperfect [im'pə:fikt] □ непóлный; несовершéнный, дефéктный.

imperial [im'piəriəl] □ импéрский; императóрский; государственный.

imperil [im'peril] подвергáть опáсности.

imperious [im'piəriəs] □ влáстный; настоя́тельный; высокомéрный.

impermeable [im'pə:miəbl] непроницáемый.

impersonal [im'pə:snl] □ безли́чный.

impersonate [im'pə:səneit] олицетворя́ть [-ри́ть]; исполня́ть роль (Р).

impertinen|ce [im'pə:tinəns] дéрзость *f*; **~t** [-nənt] □ дéрзкий.

impervious [im'pə:viəs] □ непроницáемый, непроходи́мый; глухóй (to к Д).

impetu|ous [im'petjuəs] □ стреми́тельный; **~s** ['impitəs] дви́жущая си́ла.

impiety [im'paiəti] невéрие; неуважéние.

impinge [im'pindʒ] *v/i.* ударя́ться [удáриться] (on о В); покушáться [-уси́ться] (on на В).

impious ['impiəs] □ нечести́вый.

implacable [im'pleikəbl] □ неумоли́мый; непримири́мый.

implant [im'plɑ:nt] насаждáть [насади́ть]; внушáть [-ши́ть].

implement ['implimənt] **1.** инструмéнт; орýдие; принадлéжность *f*; **2.** выполня́ть [вы́полнить].

implicat|e ['implikeit] вовлекáть [-éчь], впýт(ыв)ать; заключáть в себé; **~ion** [impli'keiʃən] вовлечéние; вы́вод.

implicit [im'plisit] □ безоговóрочный; подразумевáемый.

implore [im'plɔ:] умоля́ть [-ли́ть].

imply [im'plai] подразумевáть; намекáть [-нýть] на (В); знáчить.

impolite [impo'lait] □ невéжливый, неучти́вый.

impolitic [im'pɔlitik] □ нецелесообрáзный.

import 1. ['impɔ:t] ввоз, и́мпорт; **~s** *pl.* ввози́мые това́ры *m/pl.*; **2.** [im'pɔ:t] ввози́ть [ввезти́], импорти́ровать (*im*)*pf.*; име́ть значе́ние; **~ance** [im'pɔ:təns] значи́тельность *f*, ва́жность *f*; **~ant** [-tənt] □ ва́жный, значи́тельный; **~ation** [impɔ:'teiʃən] ввоз, и́мпорт.

importun|ate [im'pɔ:tjunit] □ назо́йливый; **~e** [im'pɔ:tju:n] докуча́ть (Д), надоеда́ть [-е́сть] (Д).

impos|e [im'pouz] *v/t.* навя́зывать [-за́ть]; облага́ть [обложи́ть]; *v/i.* ~ upon производи́ть впечатле́ние на (В), импони́ровать (Д); **~ition** [impə'ziʃən] наложе́ние; обложе́ние.

impossib|ility [im'pɔsə'biliti] невозмо́жность *f*; невероя́тность *f*; **~le** [im'pɔsəbl] □ невозмо́жный; невероя́тный.

impost|or [im'pɔstə] обма́нщик; самозва́нец; **~ure** [im'pɔstʃə] обма́н, плутовство́.

impoten|ce ['impotəns] бесси́лие, сла́бость *f*; **~t** [-tənt] бесси́льный, сла́бый.

impoverish [im'pɔvəriʃ] доводи́ть до бе́дности; обедня́ть [-ни́ть].

impracticable [im'præktikəbl] □ неисполни́мый, неосуществи́мый.

impregnate ['impregneit] оплодотворя́ть [-ри́ть]; ⚗ насыща́ть [-ы́тить], пропи́тывать [-пита́ть].

impress 1. ['impres] отпеча́ток (*a. fig.*); *typ.* о́ттиск; **2.** [im'pres] отпеча́т(ыв)ать; запечатле́(ва́)ть; внуша́ть [-ши́ть] (on Д); производи́ть впечатле́ние на (В); **~ion** [im'preʃən] впечатле́ние; *typ.* о́ттиск; печа́тание; I am under the ~ that у меня́ впечатле́ние, что ...; **~ive** [im'presive] □ внуши́тельный, производя́щий впечатле́ние.

imprint 1. [im'print] запетчатле́(ва́)ть; отпеча́т(ыв)ать; **2.** ['imprint] отпеча́ток; *typ.* выходны́е све́дения *n/pl.*

imprison [im'prizn] заключа́ть в тюрьму́, заточа́ть [-чи́ть]; **~ment** [-mənt] заточе́ние, заключе́ние (в тюрьму́).

improbable [im'prɔbəbl] □ невероя́тный, неправдоподо́бный.

improper [im'prɔpə] □ неуме́стный; непристо́йный; непра́вильный.

improve [im'pru:v] *v/t.* улучша́ть [улу́чшить]; [у]соверше́нствовать; повыша́ть це́нность (Р); *v/i.* улучша́ться [улу́чшиться]; [у]соверше́нствоваться; ~ upon улучша́ть [улу́чшить] (В); **~ment** [-mənt] усоверше́нствование; улучше́ние.

improvise ['improvaiz] импровизи́ровать (*im*)*pf.*

imprudent [im'pru:dənt] □ неблагоразу́мный; неосторо́жный.

impuden|ce ['impjudəns] бессты́дство; де́рзость *f*; **~t** [-dənt] □ наха́льный; бессты́дный.

impuls|e ['impʌls], **~ion** [im'pʌlʃən] толчо́к; поры́в; ⚡ возбужде́ние.

impunity [im'pju:niti] безнака́занность *f*; with ~ безнака́занно.

impure [im'pjuə] □ нечи́стый; с при́месью.

imput|ation [impju'teiʃən] обвине́ние; **~e** [im'pju:t] вменя́ть [-ни́ть] (в вину́); припи́сывать [-са́ть] (Д/В).

in [in] **1.** *prp. com.* в, во (П or В); ~ number в коли́честве (Р), число́м в (В); ~ itself само́ по себе́; ~ 1949 в 1949-ом (в ты́сяча девятьсо́т со́рок девя́том) году́; cry out ~ alarm закрича́ть в испу́ге (*or* от стра́ха); ~ the street на у́лице; ~ my opinion по моему́ мне́нию, по-мо́ему; ~ English по-англи́йски; a novel ~ English рома́н на англи́йском языке́; ~ tens по десяти́; ~ the circumstances при да́нных усло́виях; a coat ~ velvet ба́рхатное пальто́ (*or* из ба́рхата); ~ this manner таки́м о́бразом; ~ a word одни́м сло́вом; ~ crossing the road переходя́ че́рез у́лицу; be ~ power быть у вла́сти; be engaged ~ reading занима́ться чте́нием; **2.** *adv.* внутри́; внутрь; be ~ for: a) быть обречённым на (что́-либо неприя́тное); b) I am ~ for an examination мне предстои́т экза́мен; F be ~ with быть в хоро́ших отноше́ниях с (Т).

inability [inə'biliti] неспосо́бность [*f.*]

inaccessible [inæk'sesəbl] □ недосту́пный; недосяга́емый.

inaccurate [in'ækjurit] □ нето́чный; неаккура́тный.

inactiv|e [in'æktiv] □ безде́ятельный; неде́йствующий; **~ity** [inæk'tiviti] безде́ятельность *f*; ине́ртность *f*.

inadequate [in'ædikwit] □ несоразме́рный; недоста́точный.

inadmissible [inəd'misəbl] недопусти́мый, неприе́млемый.

inadvertent [inəd'və:tənt] □ невнима́тельный; ненаме́ренный.

inalienable [in'eiliənəbl] □ неотъе́млемый.

inane [i'nein] □ бессмы́сленный; пусто́й.

inanimate [in'ænimit] □ неодушевлённый; безжи́зненный.

inapproachable [inə'proutʃəbl] недосту́пный, непристу́пный.

inappropriate [-priit] □ неуме́стный, несоотве́тствующий.

inapt [in'æpt] □ неспосо́бный; неподходя́щий.

inarticulate [inɑ:'tikjulit] □ нечленоразде́льный, невня́тный.

inasmuch [inəz'mʌtʃ]: ~ as *adv.* так как; ввиду́ того́, что.

inattentive [inə'tentiv] □ невнимáтельный.
inaugura|te [i'nɔ:gjureit] открывáть (выставку и т. п.); вводи́ть в дóлжность; **~tion** [inɔgju'reiʃən] вступлéние в дóлжность; (торжéственное) открытие.
inborn ['in'bɔ:n] врождённый; прирóдный.
incalculable [in'kælkjuləbl] □ неисчисли́мый, несчётный; ненадёжный (о человéке).
incandescent [inkæn'desnt] раскалённый; кали́льный.
incapa|ble [in'keipəbl] □ неспосóбный (of к Д *or* на В); **~citate** [inkə'pæsiteit] дéлать неспосóбным, непригóдным.
incarnate [in'kɑ:nit] воплощённый; олицетворённый.
incautious [in'kɔ:ʃəs] □ неосторóжный, опромéтчивый.
incendiary [in'sendjəri] **1.** поджигáтель *m*; *fig.* подстрекáтель *m*; **2.** зажигáтельный (*a.* ⚔); *fig.* подстрекáющий.
incense[1] ['insens] лáдан, фимиáм.
incense[2] [in'sens] [рас]серди́ть, приводи́ть в я́рость.
incentive [in'sentiv] побуди́тельный моти́в, побуждéние.
incessant [in'sesnt] □ непреры́вный.
incest ['insest] кровосмешéние.
inch [intʃ] дюйм (= 2,54 см); *fig.* пядь *f*; by **~**es мáло-помáлу.
inciden|ce ['insidəns] сфéра дéйствия; **~t** [-t] **1.** слу́чай, случáйность *f*; происшéствие; **2.** случáйный; прису́щий (to Д); **~tal** [insi'dentl] □ случáйный; побóчный; прису́щий (Д); **~ly** случáйно; мéжду прóчим.
incinerate [in'sinəreit] сжигáть [сжечь]; испепеля́ть [-ли́ть].
incis|e [in'saiz] надрéз(ыв)ать; дéлать надрéз на (П); **~ion** [in'siʒən] разрéз, надрéз; насéчка; **~ive** [in'saisiv] □ рéжущий; óстрый.
incite [in'sait] подстрекáть [-ну́ть]; побуждáть [-уди́ть]; **~ment** [-mənt] подстрекáтельство; побуждéние, сти́мул.
inclement [in'klemənt] сурóвый, холóдный.
inclin|ation [inkli'neiʃən] наклóн, откóс; отклонéние; наклóнность *f*, склóнность *f*; **~e** [in'klain] **1.** *v/i.* склоня́ться [-ни́ться]; **~** to *fig.* быть склóнным к (Д); *v/t.* склоня́ть [-ни́ть] (*a fig.*); располагáть [-ложи́ть]; **2.** наклóн; склóнность *f*.
inclose [in'klouz] *s.* enclose.
inclu|de [in'klu:d] заключáть [-чи́ть], содержáть (в себé); включáть [-чи́ть]; **~sive** [-siv] □ включáющий в себя́, содержáщий.
incoheren|ce [inko'hiərəns] несвя́зность *f*, непослéдовательность *f*; **~t** [-t] □ несвя́зный, непослéдовательный.
income ['inkəm] дохóд.
incommode [inkə'moud] [по]беспокóить.
incomparable [in'kɔmpərəbl] □ несравни́мый; несравнéнный.
incompatible [inkəm'pætəbl] □ несовмести́мый.
incompetent [in'kɔmpitənt] □ несвéдущий, неумéлый; ⚖ неправоспосóбный.
incomplete [inkəm'pli:t] □ непóлный; незакóнченный.
incomprehensible [in'kɔmpri''hensəbl] □ непоня́тный, непостижи́мый.
inconceivable [inkən'si:vəbl] □ невообрази́мый.
incongruous [in'kɔŋgruəs] □ неумéстный, нелéпый; несовмести́мый.
inconsequent(ial) [in'kɔnsikwənt, -'kwenʃəl] □ непослéдовательный.
inconsidera|ble [inkən'sidərəbl] □ незначи́тельный, невáжный; **~te** [-rit] □ неосмотри́тельный; необду́манный; невнимáтельный (к други́м).
inconsisten|cy [inkən'sistənsi] несовмести́мость *f*; **~t** [-tənt] □ несовмести́мый.
inconstant [in'kɔnstənt] □ непостоя́нный, неустóйчивый.
incontinent [in'kɔntinənt] □ несдéржанный; невоздéржанный.
inconvenien|ce [inkən'vi:njəns] **1.** неудóбство; беспокóйство; **2.** [по-] беспокóить; **~t** [-njənt] □ неудóбный, затрудни́тельный.
incorporat|e **1.** [in'kɔ:pəreit] объединя́ть(ся) [-ни́ть(ся)]; включáть [-чи́ть] (into в В); **2.** [-rit] соединённый, объединённый; **~ed** [-reitid] зарегистри́рованный (об óбществе; **~ion** [in'kɔ:pə''reiʃən] объединéние; регистрáция.
incorrect [inkə'rekt] □ неправильный; неисправный.
incorrigible [in'kɔridʒəbl] □ неисправи́мый.
increase **1.** [in'kri:s] увели́чи(ва)ть(ся); уси́ли(ва)ть(ся); **2.** ['inkri:s] рост; увеличéние; прирóст.
incredible [in'kredəbl] □ невероя́тный.
incredul|ity [inkri'dju:liti] недовéрчивость *f*; **~ous** [in'kredjuləs] □ недовéрчивый, скепти́ческий.
incriminate [in'krimineit] ⚖ инкримини́ровать (*im*)*pf*., обвиня́ть в преступлéнии.
incrustation [inkrʌs'teiʃən] корá, кóрка; ⊕ нáкипь *f*.
incub|ate ['inkjubeit] выводи́ть [вы́вести] (цыпля́т); **~ator** [-beitə] инкубáтор.
inculcate ['inkʌlkeit] внедря́ть [-ри́ть], вселя́ть [-ли́ть] (upon Д).

incumbent [in'kʌmbənt] возлóженный, (воз)лежáщий.
incur [in'kə:] подвергáться [-éргнуться] (Д); надéлать *pf.* (долгóв).
incurable [in'kjuərəbl] **1.** неизлечи́мый; **2.** страдáющий неизлечи́мой болéзнью.
incurious [in'kjuəriəs] □ нелюбопы́тный; невнимáтельный.
incursion [in'kə:ʃən] вторжéние.
indebted [in'detid] в долгý; *fig.* обя́занный.
indecen|cy [in'di:snsi] непристóйность *f*, неприли́чие; **~t** [-snt] □ неприли́чный.
indecisi|on [indi'siʒən] нерешительность *f*; колебáние; **~ve** [-saisiv] □ нереши́тельный; не решáющий.
indecorous [in'dekərəs] □ некорréктный; неприли́чный.
indeed [in'di:d] в сáмом дéле, действи́тельно; неужéли!
indefensible [indi'fensəbl] □ непригóдный для оборóны; *fig.* несостоя́тельный.
indefinite [in'definit] □ неопределённый; неограни́ченный.
indelible [in'delibl] □ неизглади́мый; несмывáемый.
indelicate [in'delikit] □ неделикáтный, нескрóмный.
indemni|fy [in'demnifai] возмещáть убы́тки (Р); обезопáсить *pf.*; компенси́ровать *(im)pf.*; **~ty** [-ti] гарáнтия от убы́тков; возмещéние, компенсáция.
indent [in'dent] **1.** зазýбривать [-ри́ть]; вырезáть [вы́резать]; предъявля́ть трéбование; † закáзывать товáры; **2.** трéбование; † закáз на товáры; óрдер; **~ation** [inden'teiʃən] зубéц; вы́резка; **~ure** [in'dentʃə] **1.** докумéнт, контрáкт, договóр; **2.** обя́зывать договóром.
independen|ce [indi'pendəns] незави́симость *f*, самостоя́тельность *f*; **~t** [-t] □ незави́симый, самостоя́тельный.
indescribable [indis'kraibəbl] □ неописýемый.
indestructible [-'strʌktəbl] □ неразруши́мый.
indeterminate [indi'tə:minit] □ неопределённый; нея́сный.
index ['indeks] **1.** и́ндекс, указáтель *m*; показáтель *m*; указáтельный пáлец; **2.** заноси́ть в и́ндекс.
India ['indjə] 'Индия; ~ rubber каучýк; рези́на; **~n** [-n] **1.** инди́йский; индéйский; ~ corn маи́с, кукурýза; **2.** инди́ец, индиáнка; (Red ~) индéец, индиáнка.
indicat|e ['indikeit] укáзывать [-зáть]; предпи́сывать [-сáть]; **~ion** [indi'keiʃən] указáние.
indict [in'dait] предъявля́ть обвинéние (for в П); **~ment** [-mənt] обвини́тельный акт.
indifferen|ce [in'difrəns] равнодýшие, безразли́чие; **~t** [-t] □ равнодýшный, беспристрáстный; незначи́тельный.
indigenous [in'didʒinəs] мéстный, тузéмный.
indigent ['indidʒənt] □ нуждáющийся.
indigest|ible [indi'dʒestəbl] □ неудобовари́мый; **~ion** [-tʃən] расстрóйство желýдка.
indign|ant [in'dignənt] □ негодýющий; **~ation** [indig'neiʃən] негодовáние; **~ity** [in'digniti] пренебрежéние, оскорблéние.
indirect [indi'rekt] □ непрямóй; окóльный; уклóнчивый.
indiscre|et [indis'kri:t] □ нескрóмный; неблагоразýмный; болтли́вый; **~tion** [-'kreʃən] нескрóмность *f*; неосмотри́тельность *f*; болтли́вость *f*.
indiscriminate [indis'kriminit] □ неразбóрчивый.
indispensable [indis'pensəbl] □ необходи́мый, обязáтельный.
indispos|ed [indis'pouzd] нездорóвый; **~ition** ['indispə''ziʃən] недомогáние, нездорóвье; нерасположéние (to к Д).
indistinct [indis'tiŋkt] □ нея́сный, неотчётливый; невня́тный.
indite [in'dait] выражáть в словáх; сочиня́ть [-ни́ть].
individual [indi'vidjuəl] **1.** □ ли́чный, индивидуáльный; характéрный; отдéльный; **2.** индиви́дуум; ли́чность *f*; **~ity** [-vidju'æliti] индивидуáльность *f*.
indivisible [indi'vizəbl] недели́мый.
indolen|ce ['indoləns] прáздность *f*; вя́лость *f*; **~t** [-t] □ прáздный; вя́лый.
indomitable [in'dɔmitəbl] □ упóрный; неукроти́мый.
indoor ['indɔ:] внýтренний; кóмнатный; **~s** ['in'dɔ:z] в дóме, внутри́ дóма.
indorse *s.* endorse.
induce [in'dju:s] побуждáть [-уди́ть]; вызывáть [вы́звать]; **~ment** [-mənt] побуждéние.
induct [in'dʌkt] водворя́ть [-ри́ть]; вводи́ть в дóлжность; **~ion** [in'dʌkʃən] вступлéние, введéние.
indulge [in'dʌldʒ] *v/t.* доставля́ть удовóльствие (Д with Т); баловáть; потвóрствовать (Д); *v/i.* ~ in a th. увлекáться [-éчься] (Т); пред(ав)áться (Д); **~nce** [-əns] снисхождéние; потвóрство; **~nt** [-ənt] □ снисходи́тельный; потвóрствующий.
industri|al [in'dʌstriəl] □ промы́шленный; производи́тельный; **~alist** [-ist] промы́шленник; **~ous**

[in'dʌstriəs] □ трудолюби́вый, приле́жный.

industry ['indəstri] промы́шленность *f*, инду́стрия; прилежа́ние.

inebriate 1. [in'i:briit] пья́ный; опьяне́вший; **2.** [-ieeit] опьяня́ть [-ни́ть].

ineffable [in'efəbl] □ невырази́мый.

ineffect|ive [ini'fektiv], **~ual** [-tjuəl] □ безрезульта́тный; недействи́тельный.

inefficient [ini'fiʃənt] □ неспосо́бный, неуме́лый; непроизводи́тельный.

inelegant [in'eligənt] □ грубова́тый, безвку́сный.

inept [i'nept] □ неуме́стный, неподходя́щий; глу́пый.

inequality [ini'kwɔliti] нера́венство; неодина́ковость *f*.

inequitable [in'ekwitəbl] приcтра́стный.

inert [i'nə:t] □ ине́ртный; вя́лый; ко́сный; **~ia** [i'nə:ʃiə], **~ness** [i'nə:tnis] ине́рция; вя́лость *f*.

inestimable [in'estiməbl] □ неоцени́мый.

inevitable [in'evitəbl] □ неизбе́жный, немину́емый.

inexact [inig'zækt] □ нето́чный.

inexhaustible [inig'zɔ:stəbl] □ неистощи́мый, неисчерпа́емый.

inexorable [in'eksərəbl] □ неумоли́мый, непрекло́нный.

inexpedient [iniks'pi:diənt] □ нецелесообра́зный.

inexpensive [iniks'pensiv] □ недорого́й, дешёвый.

inexperience [iniks'piəriəns] нео́пытность *f*; **~d** [-t] нео́пытный.

inexpert [ineks'pə:t] □ нео́пытный; неиску́сный, неуме́лый.

inexplicable [in'eksplikəbl] □ необъясни́мый, непоня́тный.

inexpressi|ble [iniks'presəbl] □ невырази́мый, неопису́емый; **~ve** [-siv] □ невырази́тельный.

inextinguishable [iniks'tiŋgwiʃəbl] □ неугаси́мый.

inextricable [in'ekstrikəbl] □ запу́танный; безвы́ходный.

infallible [in'fæləbl] □ безоши́бочный, непогреши́мый.

infam|ous ['infəməs] □ посты́дный, позо́рный, бесче́стный; **~y** [-mi] бесче́стье, позо́р; ни́зость *f*, по́длость *f*.

infan|cy ['infənsi] младе́нчество; **~t** [-t] младе́нец.

infanti|le ['infəntail], **~ne** [-tain] младе́нческий; инфанти́льный.

infantry ['infəntri] ⚔ пехо́та, инфанте́рия.

infatuate [in'fætjueit] вскружи́ть го́лову (Д); увлека́ть [-е́чь].

infect [in'fekt] заража́ть [-рази́ть]; **~ion** [in'fekʃən] инфе́кция, зара́за; зарази́тельность *f*; **~ious** [-ʃəs] □, **~ive** [-tiv] инфекцио́нный, зара́зный; зарази́тельный.

infer [in'fə:] де́лать вы́вод; подразумева́ть; **~ence** ['infərəns] вы́вод, заключе́ние; подразумева́емое.

inferior [in'fiəriə] **1.** ни́зший (по чи́ну); ху́дший, неполноце́нный; **2.** подчинённый; **~ity** [in'fiəri'ɔriti] бо́лее ни́зкое ка́чество (положе́ние, досто́инство); неполноце́нность *f*.

infernal [in'fə:nl] □ а́дский.

infertile [in'fə:tail] беспло́дный, неплодоро́дный.

infest [in'fest] *fig.* наводня́ть [-ни́ть]; be **~ed** with кише́ть (Т).

infidelity [infi'deliti] неве́рие; неве́рность *f* (to Д).

infiltrate [in'filtreit] *v/t.* пропуска́ть сквозь фильтр; *v/i.* проника́ть [-и́кнуть]; проса́чиваться [-сочи́ться].

infinit|e ['infinit] □ бесконе́чный, безграни́чный; **~y** [in'finiti] бесконе́чность *f*, безграни́чность *f*.

infirm [in'fə:m] □ не́мощный, дря́хлый; слабохара́ктерный; **~ary** [-əri] больни́ца; **~ity** [-iti] не́мощь *f*; недоста́ток.

inflame [in'fleim] воспламеня́ть (-ся) [-ни́ть(ся)]; ⚕ воспаля́ть(ся) [-ли́ть(ся)]; **~ed** [-d] воспалённый.

inflamma|ble [in'flæməbl] □ воспламеня́ющийся; огнеопа́сный; **~tion** [inflə'meiʃən] воспламене́ние; ⚕ воспале́ние; **~tory** [in'flæmətəri] поджига́тельский; воспали́тельный.

inflat|e [in'fleit] наду́(ва́)ть (га́зом, во́здухом); ✝ взду(ва́)ть; **~ion** [-ʃən] надува́ние; *fig.* напы́щенность *f*; инфля́ция.

inflexi|ble [in'fleksəbl] □ неги́бкий, негну́щийся; *fig.* непрекло́нный, непоколеби́мый; **~on** [-ʃən] изги́б; модуля́ция.

inflict [in'flikt] налага́ть [-ложи́ть]; наноси́ть [-нести́] (ра́ну и т. п.); причиня́ть [-ни́ть] (боль); **~ion** [infli'kʃən] наложе́ние и т. д.

influen|ce ['influəns] **1.** влия́ние, возде́йствие; **2.** возде́йствовать на (В) (*im*)*pf*., [по]влия́ть на (В); **~tial** [influ'enʃəl] □ влия́тельный.

influx ['inflʌks] впаде́ние (прито́ка); *fig.* наплы́в, прили́в.

inform [in'fɔ:m] *v/t.* информи́ровать (*im*)*pf*., уведомля́ть [уве́домить] (of о П); *v/i.* доноси́ть [-нести́] (against a p. на В); **~al** [-l] □ неофициа́льный; непринуждённый; **~ality** [infɔ:'mæliti] несоблюде́ние форма́льностей; отсу́тствие церемо́ний; **~ation** [infə'meiʃən] информа́ция, све́дения *n/pl.*; спра́вка; осведомле́ние;

~ative [in'fɔ:mətiv] информацио́нный.
infrequent [in'fri:kwənt] □ ре́дкий.
infringe [in'frindʒ] наруша́ть [-ру́шить] (*a.* ~ upon).
infuriate [in'fjuərieit] [вз]беси́ть.
infuse [in'fju:z] ⚕ вли(ва́)ть; *fig.* вселя́ть [-ли́ть]; наста́ивать [настоя́ть] (тра́вы и т. п.).
ingen|ious [in'dʒi:njəs] □ изобрета́тельный; **~uity** [indʒi'njuiti] изобрета́тельность *f*; **~uous** [in'dʒenjuəs] □ чистосерде́чный; просто́й, бесхи́тростный.
ingot ['iŋgət] сли́ток, брусо́к (мета́лла).
ingratitude [in'grætitju:d] неблагода́рность *f*.
ingredient [in'gri:diənt] составна́я часть *f*, ингредие́нт.
inhabit [in'hæbit] обита́ть, жить в (П); **~ant** [-itənt] жи́тель(ница *f*) *m*, обита́тель(ница *f*) *m*.
inhal|ation [inhə'leiʃən] вдыха́ние; ⚕ ингаля́ция; **~e** [in'heil] вдыха́ть [вдохну́ть].
inherent [in'hiərənt] □ прису́щий; прирождённый.
inherit [in'herit] насле́довать (*im*)*pf*.; унасле́довать *pf*.; **~ance** [-itəns] насле́дство; *biol.* насле́дственность *f*.
inhibit [in'hibit] [вос]препя́тствовать (Д); *biol.* [за]тормози́ть; **~ion** [inhi'biʃən] сде́рживание; *biol.* торможе́ние.
inhospitable [in'hɔspitəbl] □ негостеприи́мный.
inhuman [in'hju:mən] □ бесчелове́чный, нечелове́ческий.
inimitable [i'nimitəbl] □ неподража́емый; несравне́нный.
iniquity [i'nikwiti] несправедли́вость *f*; беззако́ние.
initia|l [i'niʃəl] **1.** □ нача́льный, первонача́льный; **2.** нача́льная бу́ква; **~s** *pl.* инициа́лы *m/pl.*; **~te 1.** [-iit] при́нятый (в о́бщество), посвящённый (в та́йну); **2.** [-ieit] вводи́ть [ввести́]; посвяща́ть [-вяти́ть]; положи́ть нача́ло (Д); **~tive** [i'niʃiətiv] инициати́ва, почи́н; **~tor** [-ieitə] инициа́тор.
inject [in'dʒekt] впры́скивать [-снуть].
injunction [in'dʒʌŋkʃən] прика́з; постановле́ние суда́.
injur|e ['indʒə] [по]вреди́ть по-; вреждáть [-еди́ть]; ра́нить (*im*)*pf*.; **~ious** [in'dʒuəriəs] □ вре́дный; оскорби́тельный; **~y** ['indʒəri] оскорбле́ние; поврежде́ние, ра́на.
injustice [in'dʒʌstis] несправедли́вость *f*.
ink [iŋk] **1.** черни́ла *n/pl.*; (*mst* printer's ~) типогра́фская кра́ска; **2.** ме́тить черни́лами; сади́ть кля́ксы на (В).

inkling ['iŋkliŋ] намёк (of на В); подозре́ние.
ink|pot черни́льница; **~stand** пи́сьменный прибо́р; **~y** ['iŋki] черни́льный.
inland ['inlənd] **1.** вну́тренняя террито́рия страны́; **2.** вну́тренний; **3.** [in'lænd] внутрь, внутри́ (страны́).
inlay [in'lei] **1.** [*irr.* (lay)] вкла́дывать [вложи́ть]; выстила́ть [вы́стлать]; покрыва́ть моза́икой; **2.** ['in'lei] моза́ика, инкруста́ция.
inlet ['inlet] у́зкий зали́в, бу́хта; входно́е (*or* вво́дное) отве́рстие.
inmate ['inmeit] сожи́тель(ница *f*) *m* (по ко́мнате).
inmost ['inmoust] глубоча́йший, сокрове́нный.
inn [in] гости́ница.
innate ['in'neit] □ врождённый, приро́дный.
inner ['inə] вну́тренний; **~most** [-moust] *s.* inmost.
innings ['iniŋz] о́чередь пода́чи мяча́.
innkeeper хозя́ин гости́ницы.
innocen|ce ['inosns] ⚖ невино́вность *f*; неви́нность *f*; простота́; **~t** [-snt] **1.** □ неви́нный; ⚖ невино́вный; **2.** простя́к, наи́вный челове́к.
innocuous [i'nɔkjuəs] □ безвре́дный, безоби́дный.
innovation [ino'veiʃən] нововведе́ние, но́вшество; нова́торство.
innuendo [inju'endou] ко́свенный намёк, инсинуа́ция.
innumerable [in'ju:mərəbl] □ бесчётный, бесчи́сленный.
inoculate [i'nɔkjuleit] де́лать приви́вку (Д), приви́(ва́)ть; *fig.* внуша́ть [-ши́ть].
inoffensive [inə'fensiv] безоби́дный, безвре́дный.
inoperative [in'ɔpərətiv] безде́ятельный; неде́йствующий.
inopportune [in'ɔpətju:n] □ несвоевре́менный, неподходя́щий.
inordinate [i'nɔ:dinit] □ неуме́ренный, чрезме́рный.
inquest ['inkwest] ⚖ сле́дствие, дозна́ние; coroner's ~ суде́бный осмо́тр тру́па.
inquir|e [in'kwaiə] узн(ав)а́ть; наводи́ть спра́вки (about, after, for о П; of у Р); ~ into иссле́довать (*im*)*pf*; **~ing** [-riŋ] □ пытли́вый; **~y** [-ri] спра́вка; рассле́дование, сле́дствие.
inquisit|ion [inkwi'ziʃən] рассле́дование; **~ive** [in'kwizitiv] □ любозна́тельный; любопы́тный.
inroad ['inroud] набе́г, наше́ствие; *fig.* посяга́тельство.
insan|e [in'sein] □ душевнобольно́й; безу́мный; **~ity** [in'sæniti] умопомеша́тельство; безу́мие.

insatia|ble [inˈseiʃiəbl] □, **~te** [-ʃiət] ненасы́тный, жа́дный.
inscribe [inˈskraib] впи́сывать [-са́ть]; надпи́сывать [-са́ть] (in, on В/Т *or* В на П); посвяща́ть [-яти́ть] (кни́гу).
inscription [inˈskripʃən] на́дпись *f*; посвяще́ние (кни́ги).
inscrutable [insˈkru:təbl] □ непостижи́мый, зага́дочный.
insect [ˈinsekt] насеко́мое; **~icide** [inˈsektisaid] сре́дство для истребле́ния насеко́мых.
insecure [insiˈkjuə] □ ненадёжный; небезопа́сный.
insens|ate [inˈsenseit] бесчу́вственный; бессмы́сленный; **~ible** [-əbl] □ нечувстви́тельный; потеря́вший созна́ние; незаме́тный; **~itive** [-itiv] нечувстви́тельный.
inseparable [inˈsepərəbl] □ неразлу́чный; неотдели́мый.
insert 1. [inˈsə:t] вставля́ть [-а́вить]; помеща́ть [-ести́ть] (в газе́те); **2.** [ˈinsə:t] вста́вка, вкла́дыш; **~ion** [inˈsə:ʃən] вста́вка; объявле́ние.
inside [ˈinˈsaid] **1.** вну́тренняя сторона́; вну́тренность *f*; изна́нка (оде́жды); **2.** *adj.* вну́тренний; **3.** *adv.* внутрь, внутри́; **4.** *prp.* внутри́ (Р).
insidious [inˈsidiəs] □ хи́трый, кова́рный.
insight [ˈinsait] проница́тельность *f*; интуи́ция.
insignia [inˈsigniə] *pl.* зна́ки отли́чия; значки́ *m/pl.*
insignificant [insigˈnifikənt] незначи́тельный.
insincere [insinˈsiə] нei͏́скренний.
insinuat|e [inˈsinjueit] инсинуи́ровать (*im*)*pf.*; намека́ть [-кну́ть] на (В); ~ o. s. *fig.* вкра́дываться [вкра́сться]; **~ion** [insinjuˈeiʃən] инсинуа́ция; вкра́дчивость *f*.
insipid [inˈsipid] безвку́сный, пре́сный.
insist [inˈsist] ~ (up)on: наста́ивать [-стоя́ть] на (П), утвержда́ть (В); **~ence** [-əns] насто́йчивость *f*; **~ent** [-ənt] □ насто́йчивый.
insolent [ˈinsələnt] □ на́глый.
insoluble [inˈsɔljubl] нераствори́мый; неразреши́мый.
insolvent [inˈsɔlvənt] несостоя́тельный (должни́к).
inspect [inˈspekt] осма́тривать [осмотре́ть]; инспекти́ровать; **~ion** [inˈspekʃən] осмо́тр; инспе́кция.
inspir|ation [inspəˈreiʃən] вдыха́ние; вдохнове́ние; воодушевле́ние; **~e** [inˈspaiə] вдыха́ть [вдохну́ть]; *fig.* вдохновля́ть [-ви́ть].
install [inˈstɔ:l] устана́вливать [-нови́ть]; вводи́ть в до́лжность; ⊕ [с]монти́ровать; **~ation** [instɔ:ˈleiʃən] устано́вка; устро́йство.
instalment [inˈstɔ:lmənt] очередно́й взнос (при рассро́чке); отде́льный вы́пуск (кни́ги).
instance [ˈinstəns] слу́чай; приме́р; тре́бование; ⚖ инста́нция; for ~ наприме́р.
instant [ˈinstənt] □ **1.** неме́дленный, безотлага́тельный; on the 10th ~ 10-го теку́щего ме́сяца; **2.** мгнове́ние, моме́нт; **~aneous** [instənˈteinjəs] □ мгнове́нный; **~ly** [ˈinstəntli] неме́дленно, то́тчас.
instead [inˈsted] взаме́н, вме́сто; ~ of вме́сто (Р).
instep [ˈinstep] подъём (ноги́).
instigat|e [ˈinstigeit] побужда́ть [-уди́ть]; подстрека́ть [-кну́ть]; **~or** [-ə] подстрека́тель(ница *f*) *m*.
instil(l) [inˈstil] влива́ть по ка́пле; *fig.* внуша́ть [-ши́ть] (into Д).
instinct [ˈinstiŋkt] инсти́нкт; **~ive** [inˈstiŋktiv] □ инстинкти́вный.
institut|e [ˈinstitju:t] нау́чное учрежде́ние, институ́т; **2.** учрежда́ть [-еди́ть]; устана́вливать [-нови́ть]; **~ion** [instiˈtju:ʃən] установле́ние; учрежде́ние, заведе́ние.
instruct [inˈstrʌkt] [на]учи́ть, обуча́ть [-чи́ть]; инструкти́ровать (*im*)*pf.*; **~ion** [inˈstrʌkʃən] обуче́ние; предписа́ние; инстру́кция; **~ive** [-tiv] □ поучи́тельный; **~or** [-tə] руководи́тель *m*, инстру́ктор; преподава́тель *m*.
instrument [ˈinstrumənt] инструме́нт; ору́дие (*a. fig.*); прибо́р, аппара́т; ⚖ докуме́нт; **~al** [instruˈmentl] □ слу́жащий сре́дством; инструмента́льный; **~ality** [-menˈtæliti] сре́дство, спо́соб.
insubordinate [insəˈbɔ:dnit] неподчиня́ющийся дисципли́не.
insufferable [inˈsʌfərəbl] □ невыноси́мый, нестерпи́мый.
insufficient [insəˈfiʃənt] недоста́точный.
insula|r [ˈinsjulə] □ островно́й; *fig.* за́мкнутый; **~te** [-leit] ⚡ изоли́ровать (*im*)*pf.*; **~tion** [insjuˈleiʃən] ⚡ изоля́ция.
insult 1. [ˈinsʌlt] оскорбле́ние; **2.** [inˈsʌlt] оскорбля́ть [-би́ть].
insur|ance [inˈʃuərəns] страхова́ние; *attr.* страхово́й; **~e** [inˈʃuə] [за]страхова́ть(ся).
insurgent [inˈsə:dʒənt] **1.** мяте́жный; **2.** повста́нец; мяте́жник.
insurmountable [insəˈmauntəbl] □ непреодоли́мый.
insurrection [insəˈrekʃən] восста́ние; мяте́ж.
intact [inˈtækt] нетро́нутый; неповреждённый.
intangible [inˈtændʒəbl] □ неосяза́емый; *fig.* неулови́мый.
integ|ral [ˈintigrəl] □ неотъе́млемый; це́лый; це́лостный; **~rate** [-greit] объединя́ть [-ни́ть]; интегри́ровать (*im*)*pf.*; **~rity** [inˈtegriti] че́стность *f*; це́лостность *f*.

intellect ['intilekt] ум, рассýдок; **~ual** [inti'lektjuəl] **1.** □ интеллектуáльный, ýмственный; **2.** интеллигéнт(ка); ~s *pl.* интеллигéнция.
intelligence [in'telidʒəns] ум, рассýдок, интеллéкт; Intelligence service развéдывательная слýжба, развéдка.
intellig|ent [in'telidʒənt] □ ýмный; смышлёный; **~ible** [-dʒəbl] □ понятный.
intemperance [in'tempərəns] неумéренность *f*; невоздéрж(ан)-ность *f*; пристрáстие к спиртны́м напи́ткам.
intend [in'tend] намеревáться; имéть в видý; ~ for предназначáть [-знáчить] для (Р).
intense [in'tens] □ си́льный; интенси́вный, напряжённый.
intensify [in'tensifai] уси́ли(ва)ть (-ся); интенсифици́ровать (*im*)*pf.*
intensity [in'tensiti] интенси́вность *f*, си́ла; я́ркость *f* (крáски).
intent [in'tent] **1.** □ стремя́щийся, склóнный (on к Д); внимáтельный, при́стальный; **2.** намéрение, цель *f*; to all ~s and purposes в сýщности; во всех отношéниях; **~ion** [in'tenʃən] намéрение; **~ional** [-l] □ намéренный, умы́шленный.
inter [in'tə:] предавáть земле́, [по-] хорони́ть.
inter... ['intə] *pref.* меж..., между...; пере...; взаимо...
interact [intər'ækt] дéйствовать друг на дрýга, взаимодéйствовать.
intercede [intə'si:d] ходáтайствовать.
intercept [-'sept] перехвáтывать [-хвати́ть]; прер(ы)вáть; преграждáть путь (Д); **~ion** [-pʃən] перехвáт(ывание); пересечéние.
intercess|ion [intə'seʃən] ходáтайство, заступничество; **~or** [-sə] ходáтай, застýпник.
interchange **1.** [intə'tʃeindʒ] *v/t.* чередовáть; обмéниваться [-ня́ться] (Т); *v/i.* чередовáться; **2.** ['intə'tʃeindʒ] обмéн; чередовáние, смéна.
intercourse ['intəkɔ:s] общéние, связь *f*; отношéния *n/pl.*; сношéния *n/pl.*
interdict **1.** [intə'dikt] запрещáть [-рети́ть]; лишáть прáва пóльзования; **2.** ['intədikt], **~ion** [intə'dikʃən] запрещéние.
interest ['intrist] **1.** *com.* интерéс; заинтересóванность *f* (in в П); вы́года; процéнты *m/pl.* (на капитáл); **2.** *com.* интересовáть; заинтересóвывать [-совáть]; **~ing** [-iŋ] □ интерéсный.
interfere [intə'fiə] вмéшиваться [-шáться]; [по]мешáть, надоедáть [-éсть] (with Д); **~nce** [-rəns] вмешáтельство; помéха.
interim ['intərim] **1.** промежýток врéмени; **2.** врéменный, промежýточный.
interior [in'tiəriə] **1.** □ внýтренний; **2.** внýтренность *f*; внýтренние óбласти страны́; *pol.* внýтренние делá *n/pl.*
interjection [intə'dʒekʃən] восклицáние; *gr.* междомéтие.
interlace [intəl'eis] переплетáть(ся) [-плести́(сь)].
interlock [intə'lɔk] сцепля́ть(ся) [-пи́ть(ся)].
interlocut|ion [intəlo'kju:ʃən] бесéда, диалóг; **~or** [intə'lɔkjutə] собесéдник.
interlope [intə'loup] вмéшиваться [-шáться]; **~r** [-ə] вмéшивающийся в чужи́е делá.
interlude ['intəlu:d] антрáкт; промежýточный эпизóд.
intermeddle [intə'medl] вмéшиваться [-шáться] (with, in в В); совáться не в своё дéло.
intermedia|ry [-'mi:diəri] **1.** = intermediate; посрéднический; **2.** посрéдник; **~te** [-'mi:djət] □ промежýточный; срéдний.
interment [in'tə:mənt] погребéние.
interminable [in'tə:minəbl] □ бесконéчный.
intermingle [intə'miŋgl] смéшивать(ся) [-шáть(ся)]; общáться.
intermission [-'miʃən] переры́в, пáуза, перемéна (в шкóле).
intermit [intə'mit] прер(ы)вáть (-ся); **~tent** [-ənt] □ преры́вистый; перемежáющийся.
intermix [intə'miks] перемéшивать(ся) [-шáть(ся)].
intern [in'tə:n] интерни́ровать (*im*)*pf.*
internal [in'tə:nl] □ внýтренний.
international [intə'næʃnl] □ междунарóдный, интернационáльный; ~ law междунарóдное прáво.
interpolate [in'tə:poleit] интерполи́ровать (*im*)*pf.*
interpose [intə'pouz] *v/t.* вставля́ть [-áвить], вводи́ть [ввести́]; *v/i.* станови́ться [стать] (between мéжду Т); вмéшиваться [-шáться] (в В).
interpret [in'tə:prit] объясня́ть [-ни́ть], растолкóвывать [-ковáть]; переводи́ть [-вести́] (ýстно); **~ation** [-''eiʃən] толковáние, интерпретáция, объяснéние; **~er** [-ə] перевóдчик (-ица).
interrogat|e [in'terogeit] допрáшивать [-роси́ть]; спрáшивать [спроси́ть]; **~ion** [-''geiʃən] допрóс; вопрóс; **~ive** [intə'rɔgətiv] □ вопроси́тельный.
interrupt [intə'rʌpt] прер(ы)вáть; **~ion** [-'rʌpʃən] переры́в.
intersect [intə'sekt] пересекáть(ся) [-сéчь(ся)]; скрéщивать(ся) [-ести́ть(ся)]; **~ion** [-kʃən] пересечéние.

intersperse [intə'spə:s] разбра́сывать [-броса́ть], рассыпа́ть [-ы́пать]; усе́ивать [усе́ять].
intertwine [intə'twain] сплета́ть (-ся) [-ести́(сь)].
interval ['intəvəl] промежу́ток, расстоя́ние, интерва́л; па́уза, переме́на.
interven|e [intə'vi:n] вме́шиваться [-ша́ться]; вступа́ться [-пи́ться]; **~tion** [-'venʃən] интерве́нция; вмеша́тельство.
interview ['intəvju:] **1.** свида́ние, встре́ча; интервью́ *n indecl.*; **2.** интервьюи́ровать *(im)pf.*, име́ть бесе́ду с (Т).
intestine [in'testin] **1.** вну́тренний; **2.** кишка́; **~s** *pl.* кишки́ *f/pl.*, кише́чник.
intima|cy ['intiməsi] инти́мность *f*, бли́зость *f*; **~te 1.** [-meit] сообща́ть [-щи́ть]; намека́ть [-кну́ть] на (В); **2.** [-mit] a) □ инти́мный, ли́чный; бли́зкий; b) бли́зкий друг; **~tion** [inti'meiʃən] сообще́ние; намёк.
intimidate [in'timideit] [ис]пуга́ть; запу́гивать [-га́ть].
into ['intu, intə] *prp.* в, во (В).
intolera|ble [in'tɔlərəbl] □ невыноси́мый, нестерпи́мый; **~nt** [-rənt] □ нетерпи́мый.
intonation [intou'neiʃən] интона́ция.
intoxica|nt [in'tɔksikənt] опьяня́ющий (напи́ток); **~te** [-keit] опьяня́ть [-ни́ть]; **~tion** [-''keiʃən] опьяне́ние.
intractable [in'træktəbl] □ неподатливый.
intrepid [in'trepid] неустраши́мый, бесстра́шный, отва́жный.
intricate ['intrikit] □ сло́жный, затрудни́тельный.
intrigue [in'tri:g] **1.** интри́га; любо́вная связь *f*; **2.** интригова́ть; [за]интригова́ть, [за]интересова́ть; **~r** [-ə] интрига́н(ка).
intrinsic(al □) [in'trinsik, -sikəl] вну́тренний; сво́йственный; суще́ственный.
introduc|e [intrə'dju:s] вводи́ть [ввести́]; представля́ть [-а́вить]; **~tion** [-'dʌkʃən] введе́ние; представле́ние; ♪ интроду́кция; **~tory** [-'dʌktəri] вступи́тельный, вво́дный.
intru|de [in'tru:d] вторга́ться [вто́ргнуться]; навя́зываться [-за́ться]; **~der** [-ə] проны́ра *m/f*; незва́ный гость *m*; **~sion** [-ʒən] вторже́ние; появле́ние без приглаше́ния; **~sive** [-siv] □ назо́йливый, навя́зчивый.
intrust [in'trʌst] *s.* entrust.
intuition [intju'iʃən] интуи́ция.
inundate ['inʌndeit] затопля́ть [-пи́ть], наводня́ть [-ни́ть].
inure [i'njuə] приуча́ть [-чи́ть] (to к Д).
invade [in'veid] вторга́ться [вто́ргнуться]; *fig.* овладе́(ва́)ть (Т); **~r** [-ə] захва́тчик, интерве́нт.
invalid 1. [in'vælid] недействи́тельный, не име́ющий зако́нной си́лы; **2.** ['invəli:d] a) нетрудоспосо́бный; b) инвали́д; **~ate** [in'vælideit] лиша́ть зако́нной си́лы, сде́лать недействи́тельным.
invaluable [in'væljuəbl] □ неоцени́мый.
invariable [in'vɛəriəbl] □ неизме́нный; неизменя́емый.
invasion [in'veiʒən] вторже́ние, набе́г; ⚖ посяга́тельство; ⚕ инва́зия.
inveigh [in'vei]: ~ against поноси́ть, [об]руга́ть (В).
invent [in'vent] изобрета́ть [-брести́]; выду́мывать [вы́думать]; **~ion** [in'venʃən] изобрете́ние; изобрета́тельность *f*; **~ive** [-tiv] □ изобрета́тельный; **~or** [-tə] изобрета́тель *m*; **~ory** ['invəntri] **1.** о́пись *f*, инвента́рь *m*; *Am.* переучёт това́ра, инвентариза́ция; **2.** составля́ть о́пись (Р); вноси́ть в инвента́рь.
inverse ['invə:s] □ перевёрнутый, обра́тный.
invert [in'və:t] перевёртывать [переверну́ть], переставля́ть [-а́вить].
invest [in'vest] вкла́дывать [вложи́ть] (капита́л); *fig.* облека́ть [обле́чь] (with Т); ⚔ обложи́ть *pf.* (кре́пость).
investigat|e [in'vestigeit] рассле́довать *(im)pf.*; разузн(ав)а́ть; иссле́довать *(im)pf.* **~ion** [investi'geiʃən] ⚖ сле́дствие; иссле́дование; **~or** [in'vestigeitə] иссле́дователь *m.*; ⚖ сле́дователь *m.*
invest|ment [in'vestmənt] вложе́ние де́нег, инвести́рование; вклад; **~or** [-ə] вкла́дчик.
inveterate [in'vetərit] закорене́лый; F зая́длый; застаре́лый.
invidious [in'vidiəs] □ вызыва́ющий вражде́бное чу́вство; ненави́стный; зави́дный.
invigorate [in'vigəreit] дава́ть си́лы (Д); воодушевля́ть [-ви́ть].
invincible [in'vinsəbl] □ непобеди́мый.
inviola|ble [in'vaiələbl] □ неруши́мый; неприкоснове́нный; **~te** [-lit] ненару́шенный.
invisible [in'vizəbl] неви́димый.
invit|ation [invi'teiʃən] приглаше́ние; **~e** [in'vait] приглаша́ть [-ласи́ть].
invoice ['invɔis] † накладна́я, факту́ра.
invoke [in'vouk] вызыва́ть [вы́звать] (ду́ха); взыва́ть [воззва́ть] о (П); приз(ы)ва́ть.
involuntary [in'vɔləntəri] □ нево́льный; непроизво́льный.

involve [in'vɔlv] включа́ть в себя́; вовлека́ть [-е́чь]; впу́т(ыв)ать.
invulnerable [in'vʌlnərəbl] □ неуязви́мый.
inward ['inwəd] **1.** вну́тренний; у́мственный; **2.** *adv.* (*mst* ~s [-z]) внутрь; вну́тренне; **3.** ~s *pl.* вну́тренности *f/pl.*
inwrought ['in'rɔ:t] во́тканный в мате́рию (об узо́ре); *fig.* те́сно свя́занный (with с Т).
iodine ['aiədi:n] йод.
IOU ['aiou'ju:] (= I owe you) долгова́я распи́ска.
irascible [i'ræsibl] □ раздражи́тельный.
irate [ai'reit] гне́вный.
iridescent [iri'desnt] ра́дужный, перели́вчатый.
iris ['aiəris] *anat.* ра́дужная оболо́чка (гла́за); ⚘ и́рис, каса́тик.
Irish ['aiəriʃ] **1.** ирла́ндский; **2.** the ~ ирла́ндцы *m/pl.* [ску́чный.]
irksome ['ə:ksəm] утоми́тельный,]
iron ['aiən] **1.** желе́зо; (*mst* flat-~) утю́г; ~s *pl.* око́вы *f/pl.*, кандалы́ *m/pl.*; **2.** желе́зный; **3.** [вы́]утю́жить, [вы́]гла́дить; **~clad 1.** покры́тый броне́й, брониро́ванный; **2.** броненосец; **~-hearted** *fig.* жестокосе́рдный.
ironic(al □) [aiə'rɔnik, -nikəl] ирони́ческий.
iron|ing ['aiəniŋ] **1.** гла́женье; ве́щи для гла́женья; **2.** глади́льный; **~mongery** скобяно́й това́р; **~mould** ржа́вое пятно́; **~works** *mst sg.* чугуноплави́льный и́ли железоде́лательный заво́д.
irony ['aiərəni] иро́ния.
irradiate [i'reidieit] озаря́ть [-ри́ть]; ⚕ облуча́ть [-чи́ть]; *phys.* испуска́ть лучи́; *fig.* распространя́ть [-ни́ть] (зна́ния и т. п.); пролива́ть свет на (В).
irrational [i'ræʃnl] неразу́мный; ⅍ иррациона́льный.
irreconcilable [i'rekənsailəbl] □ непримири́мый; несовмести́мый.
irrecoverable [iri'kʌvərəbl] □ непоправи́мый, невозвра́тный.
irredeemable [iri'di:məbl] □ невозвра́тимый; безысхо́дный; не подлежа́щий вы́купу.
irrefutable [i'refjutəbl] □ неопровержи́мый.
irregular [i'regjulə] □ непра́вильный (*a. gr.*); беспоря́дочный; нерегуля́рный.
irrelevant [i'relivənt] □ не относя́щийся к де́лу; неуме́стный.
irreligious [iri'lidʒəs] □ нерелигио́зный; неве́рующий.
irremediable [iri'mi:diəbl] □ непоправи́мый; неизлечи́мый.
irreparable [i'repərəbl] □ непоправи́мый.
irreproachable [iri'proutʃəbl] □ безукори́зненный, безупре́чный.
irresistible [iri'zistəbl] □ неотрази́мый; непреодоли́мый (о жела́нии и т. п.).
irresolute [i'rezəlu:t] □ нереши́тельный.
irrespective [iris'pektiv] □ безотноси́тельный (of к Д); незави́симый (of от Р).
irresponsible [iris'pɔnsəbl] □ безотве́тственный; невменя́емый.
irreverent [i'revərənt] □ непочти́тельный.
irrevocable [i'revəkəbl] □ безвозвра́тный.
irrigate ['irigeit] ороша́ть [ороси́ть].
irrita|ble ['iritəbl] □ раздражи́тельный; боле́зненно чувстви́тельный; **~nt** [-tənt] раздража́ющее сре́дство; **~te** [-teit] раздража́ть [-жи́ть]; **~tion** [iri'teiʃən] раздраже́ние.
irruption [i'rʌpʃən] набе́г, наше́ствие.
is [iz] 3. *p. sg. pres.* от be.
island ['ailənd] о́стров; **~er** [-ə] островитя́нин (-тя́нка).
isle [ail] о́стров; **~t** [ai'lit] островок.
isolat|e ['aisəleit] изоли́ровать; (*im*)*pf.*, отделя́ть [-ли́ть]; **~ion** [aisə'leiʃən] изоли́рование.
issue ['isju:] **1.** вытека́ние, излия́ние; вы́ход; пото́мство; спо́рный вопро́с; вы́пуск, изда́ние; исхо́д, результа́т; ~ in law разногла́сие о пра́вильности примене́ния зако́на; be at ~ быть в разногла́сии; быть предме́том спо́ра; point at ~ предме́т обсужде́ния; **2.** *v/i.* исходи́ть [изойти́] (from из Р); вытека́ть [вы́течь] (from из Р); происходи́ть [произойти́] (from от Р); *v/t.* выпуска́ть [вы́пустить], изд(ав)а́ть.
isthmus ['isməs] переше́ек.
it [it] *pron. pers.* он, она́, оно́; э́то.
Italian [i'tæljən] **1.** италья́нский; **2.** италья́нец (-нка); **3.** италья́нский язы́к.
italics [i'tæliks] *typ.* курси́в.
itch [itʃ] **1.** ⚕ чесо́тка; зуд; **2.** чеса́ться, зуде́ть; be ~ing to *inf.* горе́ть жела́нием (+ *inf.*).
item ['aitem] **1.** пункт, пара́граф; вопро́с (на пове́стке); но́мер (програ́ммы); **2.** *adv.* та́кже, то́же; **~ize** ['aitəmaiz] *part. Am.* перечисля́ть по пу́нктам.
iterate ['itəreit] повторя́ть [-ри́ть].
itinerary [i'tinərəri, ai't-] маршру́т, путь *m*; путеводи́тель *m.*
its [its] *pron. poss.* от it его́, её, свой.
itself [it'self] (сам *m*, сама́ *f*,) само́ *n*; себя́, -ся, -сь; себе́; in ~ само́ по себе́; by ~ само́ собо́й; отде́льно.
ivory ['aivəri] слоно́вая кость *f.*
ivy ['aivi] ⚘ плющ.

J

jab [dʒæb] F 1. толка́ть [-кну́ть]; ты́кать [ткнуть]; пыря́ть [-рну́ть]; 2. толчо́к, пино́к, (ко́лющий) уда́р.
jabber ['dʒæbə] болта́ть, тарато́рить.
jack [dʒæk] 1. па́рень *m*; вале́т (ка́рта); ⊕ домкра́т; ⚓ матро́с; флаг, гю́йс; 2. поднима́ть домкра́том; *Am. sl.* повыша́ть [-вы́сить] (це́ны); ~**ass** осёл; дура́к.
jacket ['dʒækit] жаке́т; ку́ртка; ⊕ чехо́л, кожу́х.
jack|-knife складно́й нож; ~**-of-all-trades** на все ру́ки ма́стер.
jade [dʒeid] кля́ча; *contp.* шлю́ха; неря́ха.
jag [dʒæg] зубе́ц; зазу́брина; дыра́, проре́ха; ~**ged** ['dʒægid], ~**gy** [-i] зубча́тый; зазу́бренный.
jail [dʒeil] тюрьма́; тюре́мное заключе́ние; ~**er** ['dʒeilə] тюре́мщик.
jam¹ [dzæm] варе́нье.
jam² [~] 1. сжа́тие, сжима́ние; ⊕ перебо́й; traffic ~ зато́р в у́личном движе́нии; *Am.* be in a ~ быть в затрудни́тельном положе́нии; 2. заж(им)а́ть; защемля́ть [-ми́ть]; набива́ть битко́м; загроможда́ть [-мозди́ть]; глуши́ть (радиопереда́чи).
jangle ['dʒæŋgl] издава́ть ре́зкие зву́ки; нестро́йно звуча́ть.
janitor ['dʒænitə] швейца́р; дво́рник.
January ['dʒænjuəri] янва́рь *m*.
Japanese [dʒæpə'ni:z] 1. япо́нский; 2. япо́нец (-нка); the ~ *pl.* япо́нцы *pl.*
jar [dʒɑ:] 1. кувши́н; ба́нка; ссо́ра; неприя́тный, ре́зкий звук; дребезжа́ние; 2. [за]дребезжа́ть; [по-] коро́бить; дисгармони́ровать.
jaundice ['dʒɔ:ndis] ⚕ желту́ха; жёлчность *f*; *fig.* за́висть *f*; ~**d** [-t] желту́шный; *fig.* зави́стливый.
jaunt [dʒɔ:nt] 1. увесели́тельная пое́здка, прогу́лка; 2. предпринима́ть увесели́тельную пое́здку и т. п.; ~**y** ['dʒɔ:nti] □ весёлый, бо́йкий.
javelin ['dʒævlin] копьё.
jaw [dʒɔ:] че́люсть *f*; ~**s** *pl.* рот, пасть *f*; ⊕ *mst pl.* губа́ (клеще́й); ~**-bone** челюстна́я кость *f*.
jealous ['dʒeləs] □ ревни́вый; зави́стливый; ~**y** [-i] ре́вность *f*; за́висть *f*.
jeep [dʒi:p] *Am.* ⚔ джип.
jeer [dʒiə] 1. насме́шка, глумле́ние; 2. насмеха́ться [-ея́ться], [по]глуми́ться (at над Т).
jejune [dʒi'dʒu:n] □ пре́сный; пусто́й, неинте́ресный.
jelly ['dʒeli] 1. желе́ *n indecl.*; сту́день *m*; 2. засты́(ва́)ть; ~**-fish** меду́за.
jeopardize ['dʒepədaiz] подверга́ть опа́сности.
jerk [dʒə:k] 1. рыво́к; толчо́к; подёргивание (му́скула); 2. ре́зко толка́ть и́ли дёргать; дви́гаться толчка́ми; ~**y** ['dʒə:ki] □ отры́вистый; ~ **ily** *adv.* рывка́ми.
jersey ['dʒə:zi] фуфа́йка; вя́заный жаке́т.
jest [dʒest] 1. шу́тка; насме́шка; 2. [по]шути́ть; насме́шничать; ~**er** ['dʒestə] шутни́к (-и́ца); шут.
jet [dʒet] 1. струя́ (воды́, га́за и т. п.); ⊕ жиклёр, форсу́нка; *attr.* реакти́вный; 2. бить струёй; выпуска́ть струёй.
jetty ['dʒeti] ⚓ при́стань *f*; мол; да́мба.
Jew [dʒu:] евре́й; *attr.* евре́йский.
jewel ['dʒu:əl] драгоце́нный ка́мень *m*; ~**(l)er** [-ə] ювели́р; ~**(le)ry** [-ri] драгоце́нности *f/pl.*
Jew|ess ['dʒu:is] евре́йка; ~**ish** [-iʃ] евре́йский.
jib [dʒib] ⚓ кли́вер.
jiffy ['dʒifi] F миг, мгнове́ние.
jig-saw *Am.* маши́нная ножо́вка; ~ puzzle составна́я карти́нка-зага́дка.
jilt [dʒilt] 1. коке́тка, обма́нщица; 2. увле́чь и обману́ть (о же́нщине).
jingle ['dʒiŋgl] 1. звон, звя́канье; 2. [за]звене́ть, звя́кать [-кнуть].
job [dʒɔb] 1. рабо́та, труд; де́ло; зада́ние; by the ~ сде́льно, поуро́чно; ~ lot ве́щи ку́пленные гурто́м по дешёвке ; ~ work сде́льная рабо́та; 2. *v/t.* брать (дава́ть) внаём; *v/i.* рабо́тать пошту́чно, сде́льно; быть ма́клером; ~**ber** ['dʒɔbə] занима́ющийся случа́йной рабо́той; сде́льщик; ма́клер; спекуля́нт.
jockey ['dʒɔki] 1. жоке́й; 2. обма́нывать [-ну́ть], наду́(ва́)ть.
jocose [dʒə'kous] шутли́вый, игри́вый.
jocular ['dʒɔkjulə] шутли́вый, юмористи́ческий.
jocund ['dʒɔkənd] □ весёлый, живо́й; прия́тный.
jog [dʒɔg] 1. толчо́к; тря́ская езда́; ме́дленная ходьба́; 2. *v/t.* толка́ть [-кну́ть]; *v/i.* (*mst* ~ along,) е́хать подпры́гивая, трясти́сь.
join [dʒɔin] 1. *v/t.* соединя́ть [-ни́ть], присоединя́ть [-ни́ть]; присоединя́ться [-ни́ться] к (Д); войти́ в компа́нию (Р); вступи́ть в чле́ны (Р); ~ battle вступа́ть в бой; ~ hands объединя́ться [-ни́ться]; бра́ться за́ руки; *v/i.*

соединя́ться [-ни́ться]; объединя́ться [-ни́ться]; ~ in with присоединя́ться [-ни́ться] к (Д); ~ up вступа́ть в а́рмию; 2. соедине́ние; то́чка (ли́ния, пло́скость) соедине́ния.

joiner ['dʒɔinə] столя́р; **~y** [-ri] столя́рничество.

joint [dʒɔint] 1. ме́сто соедине́ния; *anat.* суста́в; ⚘ у́зел; кусо́к мя́са для жа́рения; put out of ~ выви́хивать [вы́вихнуть]; 2. □ соединённый; о́бщий; ~ heir сонасле́дник; 3. соединя́ть [-ни́ть]; расчленя́ть [-ни́ть]; **~-stock** акционе́рный капита́л; ~ company акционе́рное о́бщество.

jok|e [dʒouk] 1. шу́тка, острота́; 2. *v/i.* [по]шути́ть; *v/t.* поддра́знивать [-ни́ть], **~er** ['dʒoukə] шутни́к (-и́ца); **~y** [-ki] □ шутли́вый; шу́точный.

jolly ['dʒɔli] весёлый, ра́достный; F преле́стный, сла́вный.

jolt [dʒoult] 1. трясти́ [тряхну́ть], встря́хивать [-хну́ть]; 2. толчо́к; тря́ска.

jostle ['dʒɔsl] 1. толка́ть(ся) [-кну́ть(ся)]; тесни́ть(ся); 2. толчо́к; толкотня́, да́вка (в толпе́).

jot [dʒɔt] 1. ничто́жное коли́чество, йо́та; 2. ~ down бе́гло наброса́ть, кра́тко записа́ть.

journal ['dʒə:nl] дневни́к; журна́л; *parl.* протоко́л заседа́ния; ⊕ ше́йка (ва́ла), ца́пфа; **~ism** ['dʒə:nlizm] журнали́стика.

journey ['dʒə:ni] 1. пое́здка, путеше́ствие; 2. путеше́ствовать; **~man** подмасте́рье; наёмник.

jovial ['dʒouviəl] весёлый, общи́тельный.

joy [dʒɔi] ра́дость *f*, удово́льствие; **~ful** ['dʒɔiful] □ ра́достный, весёлый; **~less** [-lis] □ безра́достный; **~ous** [-əs] □ ра́достный, весёлый.

jubil|ant ['dʒu:bilənt] лику́ющий; **~ate** [-leit] ликова́ть, торжествова́ть; **~ee** ['dʒu:bili:] юбиле́й.

judge [dʒʌdʒ] 1. судья́ *m*; арби́тр; знато́к, цени́тель; 2. *v/i.* суди́ть, посуди́ть *pf.*; быть арби́тром; *v/t.* суди́ть о (П); оце́нивать [-ни́ть]; осужда́ть [осуди́ть], порица́ть.

judg(e)ment ['dʒʌdʒmənt] пригово́р, реше́ние суда́; сужде́ние; рассуди́тельность *f*; мне́ние, взгляд.

judicature ['dʒu:dikətʃə] суде́йская корпора́ция; судоустро́йство; отправле́ние правосу́дия.

judicial [dʒu:'diʃəl] □ суде́бный; суде́йский; рассуди́тельный.

judicious [dʒu:'diʃəs] □ здравомы́слящий, рассуди́тельный; **~ness** [-nis] рассуди́тельность *f*.

jug [dʒʌg] кувши́н; F тюрьма́.

juggle ['dʒʌgl] 1. фо́кус, трюк; 2. жонгли́ровать; обма́нывать [-ну́ть]; **~r** [-ə] жонглёр; фо́кусник (-ица).

juic|e [dʒu:s] сок; **~y** ['dʒu:si] □ со́чный; F колори́тный; интере́сный.

July [dʒu'lai] ию́ль *m*.

jumble ['dʒʌmbl] 1. пу́таница, беспоря́док; 2. толка́ться; смё́шивать(ся) [-ша́ть(ся)]; дви́гаться в беспоря́дке; **~-sale** прода́жа вся́ких сбо́рных веще́й с благотвори́тельной це́лью.

jump [dʒʌmp] 1. прыжо́к; скачо́к; вздра́гивание (от испу́га); 2. *v/i.* пры́гать [-гнуть]; скака́ть [-кну́ть]; ~ at охо́тно приня́ть (предложе́ние, пода́рок), ухва́тываться [ухвати́ться] за (В); ~ to conclusions де́лать поспе́шные вы́воды; *v/t.* перепры́гивать [-гнуть]; **~er** ['dʒʌmpə] прыгу́н; скаку́н; дже́мпер; **~y** [-pi] не́рвный, легко́ вздра́гивающий.

junct|ion ['dʒʌŋkʃən] соедине́ние; 🚂 железнодоро́жный у́зел; **~ure** [-ktʃə] соедине́ние; стече́ние обстоя́тельств, положе́ние дел; (крити́ческий) моме́нт; at this ~ of things при подо́бном положе́нии дел.

June [dʒu:n] ию́нь *m*.

jungle ['dʒʌŋgl] джу́нгли *f/pl.*; густы́е за́росли *f/pl.*

junior ['dʒu:njə] 1. мла́дший; моло́же (to Р *or* чем И); 2. мла́дший.

junk [dʒʌŋk] □ джо́нка; *Am.* старьё; *sl.* хлам, отбро́сы *m/pl.*

juris|diction [dʒuəris'dikʃən] отправле́ние правосу́дия; юрисди́кция; **~prudence** ['dʒuərispru:dəns] юриспруде́нция, законове́дение.

juror ['dʒuərə] ⚖ прися́жный; член жюри́.

jury [-ri] ⚖ прися́жные *m/pl.*; жюри́ *n indecl.*; **~man** прися́жный; член жюри́.

just [dʒʌst] 1. □ *adj.* справедли́вый; пра́ведный; ве́рный, то́чный; 2. *adv.* то́чно, как раз, и́менно; то́лько что; пря́мо; ~ now сейча́с, сию́ мину́ту; то́лько что.

justice ['dʒʌstis] справедли́вость *f*; правосу́дие; судья́ *m*; court of ~ суд.

justification [dʒʌstifi'keiʃən] оправда́ние; реабилита́ция.

justify ['dʒʌstifai] опра́вдывать [-да́ть], извиня́ть [-ни́ть].

justly ['dʒʌstli] справедли́во.

justness [-nis] справедли́вость *f*.

jut [dʒʌt] (*a.* ~ out) выступа́ть; вы́да(ва́)ться.

juvenile ['dʒu:vinail] 1. ю́ный, ю́ношеский; 2. ю́ноша *m*, подро́сток.

K

kangaroo [kæŋgəˈru:] кенгуру́ *m/f. indecl.*
keel [ki:l] **1.** киль *m*; **2.** ~ over опроки́дывать(ся) [-и́нуть(ся)].
keen [ki:n] □ о́стрый; ре́зкий; проница́тельный; си́льный; be ~ on о́чень люби́ть (В), стра́стно увлека́ться (Т); **~ness** [ˈki:nnis] острота́; проница́тельность *f*.
keep [ki:p] **1.** содержа́ние; пропита́ние; for ~s F *part. Am.* навсегда́; **2.** [*irr.*] *v/t. com.* держа́ть; сохраня́ть [-ни́ть], храни́ть; содержа́ть; вести́ (кни́ги и т. п.); [с]держа́ть (сло́во и т. п.); ~ company with подде́рживать знако́мство с (Т); ~ waiting заставля́ть ждать; ~ away не подпуска́ть (from к Д); ~ a th. from a p. уде́рживать что́-либо от (Р); ~ in не выпуска́ть; оставля́ть (шко́льника) по́сле уро́ков; ~ on не снима́ть (шля́пы и т. п.); ~ up подде́рживать [-жа́ть]; **3.** *v/i.* держа́ться; уде́рживаться [-жа́ться] (from от Р); ост(ав)а́ться; не по́ртиться (о пи́ще); F или *Am.* жить, обрета́ться; ~ doing продолжа́ть де́лать; ~ away держа́ться в отдале́нии; ~ from возде́рживаться [-жа́ться] от (Р); ~ off держа́ться в отдале́нии от (Р); ~ on (talking) продолжа́ть (говори́ть); ~ to приде́рживаться (Р); ~ up держа́ться бо́дро; ~ up with держа́ться наравне́ с (Т), идти́ в но́гу с (Т).
keep|er [ˈki:pə] храни́тель *m*; сто́рож; **~ing** [ˈki:piŋ] хране́ние; содержа́ние; be in (out of) ~ with ... (не) согласова́ться с (Т); **~sake** [ˈki:pseik] пода́рок на па́мять.
keg [keg] бочо́нок.
kennel [ˈkenl] конура́.
kept [kept] *pt.* и *p. pt.* от keep.
kerb(stone) [ˈkə:b(stoun)] край тротуа́ра; бордю́рный ка́мень *m*.
kerchief [ˈkə:tʃif] (головно́й) плато́к; косы́нка.
kernel [ˈkə:nl] зерно́, зёрнышко; ядро́; *fig.* суть *f*.
kettle [ˈketl] ча́йник (для кипяче́ния воды́); котёл; **~drum** ♪ лита́вра; F зва́ный вече́рний чай.
key [ki:] **1.** ключ; код; ⊕ клин; шпо́нка; кла́виш(а); ♪ ключ, тона́льность *f*; *fig.* тон; **2.** запира́ть [запере́ть] (на ключ); ♪ настра́ивать [-ро́ить]; ~ up *fig.* придава́ть реши́мость (Д); be ~ed up *Am.* быть в взви́нченном состоя́нии; **~board** клавиату́ра; **~hole** замо́чная сква́жина; **~-note** тона́льность *f*; *fig.* основна́я мысль *f*; **~stone** ⚠ ключево́й ка́мень *m*.
kick [kik] **1.** уда́р (ного́й, копы́том); пино́к; F си́ла сопротивле́ния; **2.** *v/t.* ударя́ть [уда́рить] (ного́й); брыка́ть [-кну́ть]; ~ out *Am. sl.* вышвы́ривать [вы́швырнуть], выгоня́ть [вы́гнать]; *v/i.* брыка́ться [-кну́ться], ляга́ться [лягну́ться]; [вос]проти́виться; **~er** [ˈkikə] брыкли́вая ло́шадь *f*; футболи́ст.
kid [kid] **1.** козлёнок; ла́йка (ко́жа); F ребёнок; **2.** *sl.* поддра́знивать [-ни́ть].
kidnap [ˈkidnæp] похища́ть [-хи́тить] (люде́й); **~(p)er** [-ə] похити́тель-вымога́тель *m*.
kidney [ˈkidni] *anat.* по́чка; F тип, хара́ктер.
kill [kil] уби́(ва́)ть; бить (скот); *fig.* [по]губи́ть; *parl.* прова́ливать [-ли́ть] (законопрое́кт и т. п.); ~ off уничтожа́ть [-о́жить]; ~ time убива́ть вре́мя; **~er** [ˈkilə] уби́йца *m/f*.
kiln [kiln] обжига́тельная печь *f*.
kin [kin] семья́; родня́.
kind [kaind] **1.** □ до́брый, серде́чный, любе́зный; **2.** сорт, разнови́дность *f*; род; pay in ~ плати́ть нату́рой; **~-hearted** мягкосерде́чный, до́брый.
kindle [ˈkindl] зажига́ть(ся) [заже́чь(ся)]; воспламеня́ть [-ни́ть].
kindling [ˈkindliŋ] расто́пка.
kind|ly [ˈkaindli] до́брый; **~ness** [-nis] доброта́; до́брый посту́пок.
kindred [ˈkindrid] **1.** ро́дственный; **2.** кро́вное родство́.
king [kiŋ] коро́ль *m*; **~dom** [ˈkiŋdəm] короле́вство; ♀, *zo.* (расти́тельное, живо́тное) ца́рство; **~like** [-laik], **~ly** [-li] короле́вский; вели́чественный.
kink [kiŋk] изги́б; пе́тля; у́зел; *fig.* стра́нность *f*, причу́да.
kin|ship [ˈkinʃip] родство́; **~sman** [ˈkinzmən] ро́дственник.
kiss [kis] **1.** поцелу́й; **2.** [по]целова́ть(ся).
kit [kit] ка́дка; ра́нец; ⚔ ли́чное обмундирова́ние; **~-bag** ⚔ вещево́й мешо́к; ⊕ набо́р инструме́нтов.
kitchen [ˈkitʃin] ку́хня.
kite [kait] (бума́жный) змей.
kitten [ˈkitn] котёнок.
knack [næk] уда́чный приём; уме́ние, сноро́вка.
knapsack [ˈnæpsæk] ра́нец, рюкза́к.
knave [neiv] моше́нник; вале́т (ка́рта).
knead [ni:d] [с]меси́ть.
knee [ni:] коле́но; **~-cap** *anat.* коле́нная ча́шечка; **~l** [ni:l] [*irr.*]

станови́ться на коле́ни; стоя́ть на коле́нях (to пе́ред Т).
knell [nel] похоро́нный звон.
knelt [nelt] *pt.* и *p. pt.* от kneel.
knew [nju:] *pt.* и *p. pt.* от know.
knickknack ['niknæk] безделу́шка.
knife [naif] **1.** (*pl.* knives) нож; **2.** ре́зать, коло́ть ножо́м.
knight [nait] **1.** ры́царь *m*; *chess* конь *m*; **2.** возводи́ть в ры́цари; **~-errant** стра́нствующий ры́царь *m*; **~hood** ['naithud] ры́царство; **~ly** [-li] ры́царский.
knit [nit] [*irr.*] [с]вяза́ть; свя́зывать [-за́ть]; сраста́ться [срасти́сь]; ~ the brows хму́рить бро́ви; **~ting** ['nitiŋ] **1.** вяза́ние; **2.** вяза́льный.
knives [naivz] *pl.* от knife.
knob [nɔb] ши́шка; набалда́шник; ру́чка; кно́пка; голо́вка.
knock [nɔk] **1.** уда́р, стук; **2.** ударя́ть(ся) [уда́рить(ся)]; [по]стуча́ть(ся); F ~ about ры́скать по све́ту; ~ down сбива́ть с ног; ⊕ разбира́ть [-зобра́ть]; be ~ed down попада́ть под автомоби́ль и т. п.; ~ off work прекраща́ть рабо́ту; ~ off стря́хивать [-хну́ть], сма́хивать [-хну́ть]; ~ out вы́би(ва́)ть, выкола́чивать [вы́колотить]; *sport.* нокаути́ровать (*im*)*pf.*; **~-kneed** с вы́вернутыми внутрь коле́нями; *fig.* сла́бый; **~-out** нока́ут (*a.* ~ blow).
knoll [noul] холм, буго́р.
knot [nɔt] **1.** у́зел; сою́з, у́зы *f*/*pl.*; **2.** завя́зывать у́зел (или узло́м); спу́т(ыв)ать; **~ty** ['nɔti] узлова́тый; сучкова́тый; *fig.* затрудни́тельный.
know [nou] [*irr.*] знать; быть знако́мым с (Т); узн(ав)а́ть; [с]уме́ть; ~ French говори́ть по-францу́зски; come to ~ узн(ав)а́ть; **~ing** ['nouiŋ] □ ло́вкий, хи́трый; проница́тельный; **~ledge** ['nɔlidʒ] зна́ние; to my ~ по мои́м све́дениям; **~n** [noun] *p. pt.* от know; come to be ~ сде́латься изве́стным; make ~ объявля́ть [-ви́ть].
knuckle ['nʌkl] **1.** суста́в па́льца; **2.** ~ down, ~ under уступа́ть [-пи́ть]; подчиня́ться [-ни́ться].

L

label ['leibl] **1.** ярлы́к, этике́тка; **2.** накле́ивать ярлы́к на (В); *fig.* относи́ть к катего́рии (as Р).
laboratory [lə'bɔrətəri] лаборато́рия; ~ assistant лаборато́рный (-ная) ассисте́нт(ка).
laborious [lə'bɔ:riəs] □ тру́дный; стара́тельный.
labo(u)r ['leibə] **1.** труд; рабо́та; родовы́е му́ки *f*/*pl.*; hard ~ принуди́тельный труд; ♀ Exchange би́ржа труда́; **2.** рабо́чий; трудово́й; **3.** *v*/*i.* труди́ться, рабо́тать; прилага́ть уси́лия; *v*/*t.* выраба́тывать [вы́работать]; **~-creation** предоставле́ние рабо́ты; **~ed** вы́мученный; тру́дный; **~er** [-rə] рабо́чий.
lace [leis] **1.** кру́жево; шнуро́к; **2.** [за]шнурова́ть; окаймля́ть [-ми́ть] (кру́жевом и т. п.); хлеста́ть [-тну́ть], [вы́]поро́ть (*a.* ~ into *a p.*).
lacerate ['læsəreit] разрыва́ть [разорва́ть], раздира́ть [разодра́ть].
lack [læk] **1.** недоста́ток, нужда́; отсу́тствие (Р); **2.** испы́тывать недоста́ток, нужду́ в (П) he ~s money у него́ недоста́ток де́нег; be ~ing недост(ав)а́ть: water is ~ing недостаёт воды́; **~-lustre** ту́склый.
lacquer ['lækə] **1.** лак, политу́ра; **2.** [от]лакирова́ть.
lad [læd] па́рень *m*, ю́ноша *m*.
ladder ['lædə] ле́стница; ⚓ трап.
laden ['leidn] нагружённый; *fig.* обременённый.
lading ['leidiŋ] погру́зка; груз, фрахт.
ladle ['leidl] **1.** ковш; черпа́к; поло́вник; **2.** вычёрпывать [вы́черпнуть]; разли́(ва́)ть (суп) (*a.* ~ out).
lady ['leidi] да́ма; ле́ди *f. indecl.* (ти́тул); **~like** име́ющая мане́ры ле́ди; **~love** возлю́бленная; **~ship** [-ʃip]: your ~ ва́ша ми́лость *f.*
lag [læg] **1.** запа́здывать; отст(ав)а́ть (*a.* ~ behind); **2.** запа́здывание; отстава́ние.
laggard ['lægəd] ме́дленный, вя́лый челове́к.
lagoon [lə'gu:n] лагу́на.
laid [leid] *pt.* и *p. pt.* от lay; **~-up** лежа́чий (больно́й).
lain [lein] *p. pt.* от lie[2].
lair [lɛə] ло́говище, берло́га.
laity ['leiiti] миря́не *pl.*; профа́ны *m*/*pl.*
lake [leik] о́зеро.
lamb [læm] **1.** ягнёнок; **2.** [о]ягни́ться.
lambent ['læmbənt] игра́ющий, колыха́ющийся (о пла́мени).
lambkin ['læmkin] ягнёночек.
lame [leim] **1.** □ хромо́й; *fig.* неубеди́тельный; **2.** [из]уве́чить, [ис]кале́чить.
lament [lə'ment] **1.** стена́ние, жа́лоба; **2.** стена́ть; опла́к(ив)ать; [по]жа́ловаться; **~able** ['læməntəbl] жа́лкий; печа́льный; **~ation** [læmən'teiʃən] жа́лоба, плач.

lamp [læmp] ла́мпа; фона́рь *m*; *fig.* све́точ, свети́ло.
lampoon [læm'pu:n] **1.** памфле́т, па́сквиль *m*; **2.** писа́ть па́сквиль на (В).
lamp-post фона́рный столб.
lampshade абажу́р.
lance [lɑ:ns] **1.** пи́ка; острога́; **2.** пронза́ть пи́кой; вскрыва́ть ланце́том; **~-corporal** *Brit.* ⚔ ефре́йтор.
land [lænd] **1.** земля́, су́ша; страна́; **~s** *pl.* поме́стья *n/pl.*; **~** register поземе́льная кни́га; **2.** ⚓ выса́живать(ся) [вы́садить(ся)]; выта́скивать на бе́рег; ⚓ пристава́ть к бе́регу, прича́ли(ва)ть; ✈ приземля́ться [-ли́ться]; **~ed** ['lændid] земе́льный; **~holder** владе́лец земе́льного уча́стка.
landing ['lændiŋ] вы́садка; ✈ приземле́ние, поса́дка; **~** ground поса́дочная площа́дка; **~-stage** при́стань *f*.
land|lady хозя́йка (меблиро́ванных ко́мнат); поме́щица; **~lord** поме́щик; хозя́ин (кварти́ры, гости́ницы); **~mark** межево́й знак, ве́ха; ориенти́р; **~-owner** землевладе́лец; **~scape** ['lænskeip] ландша́фт, пейза́ж; **~slide** о́ползень *m*; *pol.* ре́зкое измене́ние (в распределе́нии голосо́в ме́жду па́ртиями).
lane [lein] тропи́нка; переу́лок.
language ['læŋgwidʒ] язы́к (речь); strong **~** си́льные выраже́ния *n/pl.*, брань *f*.
languid ['læŋgwid] □ то́мный.
languish ['læŋgwiʃ] [за]ча́хнуть; тоскова́ть, томи́ться.
languor ['læŋgə] апати́чность *f*; томле́ние; то́мность *f*.
lank ['læŋk] □ высо́кий и худо́й; прямо́й (о волоса́х); **~y** ['læŋki] □ долговя́зый.
lantern ['læntən] фона́рь *m*; **~-slide** диапозити́в.
lap [læp] **1.** пола́; коле́ни *n/pl.*; *fig.* ло́но; ⊕ накла́дка; перекры́тие; *sport.* круг; **2.** перекры́(ва́)ть; [вы́]лака́ть; жа́дно пить; плеска́ться.
lapel [lə'pel] отворо́т (пальто́ и т. п.).
lapse [læps] **1.** ход (вре́мени); оши́бка, опи́ска; (мора́льное) паде́ние; **2.** па́дать [упа́сть] (мора́льно); приня́ться за ста́рое; теря́ть си́лу (о пра́ве).
larceny ['lɑ:sni] ⚖ воровство́.
lard [lɑ:d] **1.** свино́е са́ло; **2.** [на-] шпигова́ть; **~er** ['lɑ:də] кладова́я.
large [lɑ:dʒ] □ большо́й, кру́пный; оби́льный; ще́дрый; at **~** на свобо́де; простра́нно, подро́бно; **~ly** ['lɑ:dʒli] в значи́тельной сте́пени; оби́льно, ще́дро; на широ́кую но́гу, в широ́ком масшта́бе; **~ness** [-nis] большо́й разме́р; широта́ (взгля́дов).
lark [lɑ:k] жа́воронок; *fig.* шу́тка, прока́за, заба́ва.
larva ['lɑ:və] *zo.* личи́нка.
larynx ['læ:riŋks] горта́нь *f*.
lascivious [lə'siviəs] □ похотли́вый.
lash [læʃ] **1.** плеть *f*; бич; реме́нь *m* (часть кнута́); уда́р (пле́тью и т. п.); ресни́ца; **2.** хлеста́ть [-тну́ть]; привя́зывать [-за́ть]; *fig.* бичева́ть.
lass, ~ie [læs, 'læsi] де́вушка, де́вочка.
lassitude ['læsitju:d] уста́лость *f*.
last[1] [lɑ:st] **1.** *adj.* после́дний; про́шлый; кра́йний; **~** but one предпосле́дний; **~** night вчера́ ве́чером; **2.** коне́ц; at **~** наконе́ц; **3.** *adv.* в после́дний раз; по́сле всех; в конце́.
last[2] [**~**] продолжа́ться [-до́лжиться]; [про]дли́ться; хвата́ть [-ти́ть]; сохраня́ться [-ни́ться].
last[3] [**~**] коло́дка.
lasting ['lɑ:stiŋ] □ дли́тельный, постоя́нный; про́чный.
lastly ['lɑ:stli] наконе́ц.
latch [lætʃ] **1.** щеко́лда, задви́жка; америка́нский замо́к; **2.** запира́ть [запере́ть].
late [leit] по́здний; запозда́лый; неда́вний; уме́рший, поко́йный; *adv.* по́здно; at (the) **~st** не поздне́е; of **~** за после́днее вре́мя; be **~** опа́здывать [опозда́ть]; **~ly** ['leitli] неда́вно; за после́днее вре́мя.
latent ['leitənt] □ скры́тый; 🕮 [latȇнтный.]
lateral ['lætərəl] □ боково́й; побо́чный, втори́чный.
lath [lɑ:θ] **1.** дра́нка; пла́нка; **2.** прибива́ть пла́нки к (Д).
lathe [leið] тока́рный стано́к.
lather ['lɑ:ðə] **1.** мы́льная пе́на; **2.** *v/t.* намы́ли(ва)ть; *v/i.* мы́литься, намы́ли(ва)ться; взмы́ли(ва)ться (о ло́шади).
Latin ['lætin] **1.** лати́нский язы́к; **2.** лати́нский.
latitude ['lætitju:d] *geogr.*, *ast.* широта́; *fig.* свобо́да де́йствий.
latter ['lætə] неда́вний; после́дний; **~ly** [-li] неда́вно; к концу́.
lattice ['lætis] решётка (*a.* **~-work**).
laud [lɔ:d] **1.** хвала́; **2.** [по]хвали́ть; **~able** ['lɔ:dəbl] □ похва́льный.
laugh [lɑ:f] **1.** смех; **2.** смея́ться; **~** at a p. высме́ивать [вы́смеять] (В), смея́ться над (Т); **~able** ['lɑ:fəbl] □ смешно́й; **~ter** ['lɑ:ftə] смех.
launch [lɔ:ntʃ] **1.** барка́с; мото́рная ло́дка; **2.** запуска́ть [-сти́ть]; спуска́ть [-сти́ть] (су́дно на́ воду); *fig.* пуска́ть в ход.
laund|ress ['lɔ:ndris] пра́чка; **~ry** [-ri] пра́чечная; бельё для сти́р-[ки.]
laurel ['lɔrəl] ⚘ лавр.

lavatory ['lævətəri] убóрная.
lavender ['lævində] ⚘ лавáнда.
lavish ['læviʃ] **1.** □ щéдрый, расточúтельный; **2.** расточáть [-чúть].
law [lɔ:] закóн; прáвило; ⚖ прáво; ⚖ юриспрудéнция; go to ~ начáть судéбный процéсс; lay down the ~ задавáть тон; **~-abiding** ⚖ законопослýшный, соблюдáющий закóн; **~-court** суд; **~ful** ['lɔ:ful] □ закóнный; **~less** ['lɔ:lis] □ беззакóнный.
lawn [lɔ:n] лужáйка, газóн; батúст [(ткань).]
law|suit ['lɔ:sju:t] судéбный процéсс; **~yer** ['lɔ:jə] юрúст; адвокáт.
lax [læks] □ вя́лый; рыхлый; небрéжный; неря́шливый; **~ative** ['læksətiv] слабúтельное.
lay[1] [lei] **1.** *pt.* от lie[2]; **2.** свéтский, мирскóй (не духóвный).
lay[2] [~] **1.** положéние, направлéние; **2.** [*irr.*] *v/t.* класть [положúть]; возлагáть [-ложúть; успокáивать [-кóить]; накры́(вá)ть (на стол); ~ before a p. предъявля́ть [-вúть] (Д); ~ in stocks запасáться [запастúсь] (of Т); ~ low опрокúдывать [-úнуть]; ~ open излагáть [изложúть]; откры́(вá)ть; ~ out выкла́дывать [вы́ложить]; разбú(вá)ть (сад, парк и т. п.); ~ up [на]копúть; прикóвывать к постéли; ~ with обклáдывать [обложúть] (Т); *v/i.* [с]нестúсь (о птúцах); держáть парú (*a.* ~ a wager).
layer ['leiə] слой, пласт, наслоéние.
layman ['leimən] миря́нин; неспециалúст, любúтель *m*.
lay|off приостанóвка производства; **~-out** план; разбúвка.
lazy ['leizi] □ ленúвый.
lead[1] [led] свинéц; ⚓ лот; грузúло; *typ.* шпóны *m/f pl.*
lead[2] [li:d] **1.** руковóдство; инициатúва; *sport.* лúдерство; *thea.* глáвная роль *f*; ⚡ ввóдный прóвод; **2.** [*irr.*] *v/t.* водúть, [по-] вестú; приводúть [-вестú]; склоня́ть [-нúть] (to к Д); руководúть (Т); ходúть [пойтú] с (Р *pl.*) (о кáрточной игрé); ~ on соблазня́ть [-нúть]; *v/t.* вестú; быть пéрвым ~ off нач(ин)áть, класть начáло.
leaden ['ledn] свинцóвый (*a. fig.*).
leader ['li:də] руководúтель(ница *f*) *m*; вождь *m*; передовáя статья́.
leading ['li:diŋ] **1.** руководя́щий; ведýщий; передовóй; выдающийся; **2.** руковóдство; ведéние.
leaf [li:f] (*pl.*: leaves) лист (⚘ *pl.*: лúстья); листвá; **~let** ['li:flit] листóвка; **~y** ['li:fi] покры́тый лúстьями.
league [li:g] **1.** лúга, сою́з; **2.** вступáть в сою́з; объединя́ть(ся) [-нúть(ся)].
leak [li:k] **1.** течь *f*; утéчка, **2.** давáть течь, пропускáть вóду; ~ out просáчиваться [-сочúться]; *fig.* обнарýжи(ва)ться; **~age** ['li:kidʒ] просáчивание; *fig.* обнарýжение (тáйны и т. п.); **~y** ['li:ki] с тéчью.
lean [li:n] **1.** [*irr.*] прислоня́ть(ся) [-нúть(ся)] (against к Д); опирáться [оперéться] (on на В) (*a. fig.*); наклоня́ть(ся) [-нúть(ся)]; **2.** тóщий, худóй.
leant [lent] *pt.* и *p. pt.* от lean.
leap [li:p] **1.** прыжóк, скачóк; **2.** [*a. irr.*] пры́гать [-гнуть], скакáть [скакнýть]; **~t** [lept] *pt.* и *p. pt.* от leap; **~-year** високóсный год.
learn [lə:n] [*a. irr.*] изучáть [-чúть], [на]учúться (Д); ~ from узн(ав)áть от (Р); **~ed** [lə:nid] □ учёный; **~ing** ['lə:niŋ] учéние; учёность *f*, эрудúция; **~t** [lə:nt] *pt.* и *p. pt.* от learn.
lease [li:s] **1.** арéнда; наём; **2.** сдавáть внаём, в арéнду; брать внаём, в арéнду.
least [li:st] *adj.* малéйший; наимéньший; *adv.* мéнее всегó, в наимéньшей стéпени; at (the) ~ по крáйней мéре.
leather ['leðə] **1.** кóжа; ремéнь *m*; **2.** (*a.* ~n) кóжаный.
leave [li:v] **1.** разрешéние, позволéние; óтпуск; **2.** [*irr.*] *v/t.* оставля́ть [-áвить]; покидáть [покúнуть]; предоставля́ть [-áвить]; *Am.* позволя́ть [-óлить]; ~ off бросáть [брóсить] (дéлать чтó-либо); *v/i.* уезжáть [уéхать]; уходúть [уйтú].
leaves [li:vz] *pl.* от leaf.
leavings ['li:viŋz] остáтки *m/pl.*; отбрóсы *m/pl.*
lecture ['lektʃə] **1.** доклáд; лéкция; наставлéние; **2.** *v/i.* читáть лéкции; *v/t.* отчúтывать [-итáть]; **~r** [-rə] доклáдчик (-ица); лéктор; *univ.* преподавáтель *m*.
led [led] *pt.* и *p. pt.* от lead.
ledge [ledʒ] вы́ступ, устýп; риф.
ledger ['ledʒə] ✝ гроссбýх, глáвная кнúга.
leech [li:tʃ] *zo.* пиявка.
leer [liə] **1.** взгляд úскоса; **2.** смотрéть, глядéть úскоса (at на В).
leeway ['li:wei] ⚓ дрейф; *fig.* make up for ~ навёрстывать упýщенное.
left[1] [left] *pt.* и *p. pt.* от leave; be ~ ост(ав)áться.
left[2] [~] **1.** лéвый; **2.** лéвая сторонá; **~-hander** левшá *m/f*.
leg [leg] ногá (от бедрá до ступнú); нóжка (столá и т. п.); штанúна.
legacy ['legəsi] наслéдство.
legal ['li:gəl] □ закóнный, легáльный; правовóй; **~ize** [-aiz] узакóни(ва)ть, легализовáть (*im*)*pf*.
legation [li'geiʃən] дипломатúческая мúссия.
legend ['ledʒənd] легéнда; нáдпись *f*; **~ary** [-əri] легендáрный.

leggings ['legiŋz] гамáши *f/pl.*, крáги *f/pl.*
legible ['ledʒəbl] □ разбóрчивый.
legionary ['li:dʒənəri] легионéр.
legislat|ion [ledʒis'leiʃən] законодáтельство; **~ive** ['ledʒisleitiv] законодáтельный; **~or** законодáтель *m.*
legitima|cy [li'dʒitiməsi] закóнность *f*; **~te 1.** [-meit] узакóни(ва)ть; **2.** [-mit] закóнный.
leisure ['leʒə] досýг; at your ~ когдá вам удóбно; **~ly** не спешá, спокóйно.
lemon ['lemən] лимóн; **~ade** [lemə'neid] лимонáд.
lend [lend] [*irr.*] одáлживать [одолжи́ть]; давáть взаймы́; *fig.* д(ав)áть, прид(ав)áть.
length [leŋð] длинá; расстоя́ние; продолжи́тельность *f*; отрéз (матéрии); at ~ подрóбно; go all ~s пойти́ на всё; **~en** ['leŋθən] удлиня́ть(ся) [-ни́ть(ся)]; **~wise** [-waiz] в длинý; вдоль; **~y** [-i] растя́нутый; многослóвный.
lenient ['li:niənt] □ мя́гкий; снисходи́тельный.
lens [lenz] ли́нза.
lent[1] [lent] *pt.* и *p. pt.* от **lend.**
Lent[2] [~] вели́кий пост.
less [les] **1.** (*comp.* от little) мéньший; **2.** *adv.* мéньше, мéнее; **3.** *prp.* без (Р).
lessen ['lesn] *v/t.* уменьшáть [умéньши́ть]; недооцéнивать [-ни́ть]; *v/i.* уменьшáться [умéньши́ться].
lesser ['lesə] мéньший.
lesson ['lesn] урóк; *fig.* give a ~ to a p. проучи́ть (В) *pf.*; предостережéние.
lest [lest] чтóбы не, как бы не.
let [let] [*irr.*] оставля́ть [-áвить]; сдавáть внаём; позволя́ть [-вóлить] (Д), пускáть [пусти́ть]; ~ alone остáвить в покóе; *adv.* не говоря́ ужé о ... (П); ~ down опускáть [-сти́ть]; *fig.* подводи́ть [-вести́]; ~ go выпускáть из рук; вы́кинуть из головы́ (мысль); ~ into посвящáть [-яти́ть] в (тáйну и т. п.); ~ off стреля́ть [вы́стрелить] из (Р); *fig.* выпáливать [вы́палить] (шýтку); ~ out выпускáть [вы́пустить]; ~ up *Am.* ослабé(вá)ть.
lethargy ['leθədʒi] летарги́я; апати́чность *f.*
letter ['letə] **1.** бýква; ли́тера; письмó; ~s *pl.* литератýра; учёность *f*; *attr.* пи́сьменный; to the ~ буквáльно; **2.** помечáть бýквами; дéлать нáдпись на (П); **~-case** бумáжник; **~-cover** конвéрт; **~ed** [-d] начи́танный, образóванный; **~-file** регистрáтор (пáпка); **~ing** [-riŋ] нáдпись *f*; тиснéние; **~press** текст в кни́ге (в отли́чие от иллюстрáций).

lettuce ['letis] салáт.
level ['levl] **1.** горизонтáльный; рóвный; одинáковый, рáвный, равномéрный; my ~ best всё, что в мои́х си́лах; **2.** ýровень *m*; ватерпáс, нивели́р; *fig.* масштáб; ~ of the sea ýровень мóря; on the ~ *Am.* чéстно, правди́во; **3.** *v/t.* вырáвнивать [вы́ровнять]; урáвнивать [-вня́ть]; сглáживать [сглáдить]; срáвнивать, [с]ровня́ть (с землёй); ~ up повышáть урáвнивая; *v/i.* ~ at прицéли(ва)ться в (В); **~-headed** уравновéшенный.
lever ['li:və] рычáг, вáга; **~age** [-ridʒ] подъёмная си́ла.
levity ['leviti] легкомы́слие, вéтренность *f.*
levy ['levi] **1.** сбор, взимáние (налóгов); ⚔ набóр (рéкрутов); **2.** взимáть (налóг); ⚔ наб(и)рáть.
lewd [lju:d] □ похотли́вый.
liability [laiə'biliti] отвéтственность *f* (*a.* ⚖); обязáтельство; задóлженность *f*; *fig.* подвéрженность *f*, склóнность *f*; liabilities *pl.* обязáтельства *n/pl.*; † долги́ *m/pl.*
liable ['laiəbl] □ отвéтственный (за В); обя́занный; подвéрженный; be ~ to быть предрасполóженным к (Д).
liar ['laiə] лгýн(ья).
libel ['laibəl] **1.** клеветá; **2.** [на-] клеветáть на (В).
liberal ['libərəl] **1.** □ щéдрый, оби́льный; *pol.* либерáльный; **2.** либерáл(ка); **~ity** [libə'ræliti] щéдрость *f*; либерáльность *f.*
liberat|e ['libəreit] освобождáть [-боди́ть]; **~ion** [libə'reiʃən] освобождéние; **~or** ['libəreitə] освободи́тель *m.*
libertine ['libətain] распýтник; вольнодýмец.
liberty [-ti] свобóда; вóльность *f*; бесцеремóнность *f*; be at ~ быть свобóдным.
librar|ian [lai'brεəriən] библиотéкарь *m*; **~y** ['laibrəri] библиотéка.
lice [lais] *pl.* от louse.
licen|ce, *Am.* **~se** ['laisəns] **1.** разрешéние, † лицéнзия; вóльность *f*; driving ~ води́тельские правá *n/pl.*; **2.** разрешáть [-ши́ть]; давáть прáво, патéнт на (В).
licentious [lai'senʃəs] □ распýщенный, безнрáвственный.
lick [lik] **1.** обли́зывание; **2.** лизáть [лизнýть]; обли́зывать [-зáть]; F [по]би́ть, [по]колоти́ть; ~ the dust быть повéрженным нáземь; быть уби́тым; ~ into shape привести́ в поря́док.
lid [lid] кры́шка; вéко.
lie[1] [lai] **1.** ложь *f*, обмáн; give the ~ обличáть во лжи; **2.** [со]лгáть.
lie[2] [~] **1.** положéние; направлéние; **2.** [*irr.*] лежáть; быть рас-

положенным, находиться; заключаться; ~ by оставаться без употребления; ~ down ложиться [лечь]; ~ in wait for поджидать (В).

lien ['liən] ⚖ право наложения ареста на имущество должника.

lieu [lju:]: in ~ of вместо (Р).

lieutenant [lef'tenənt, ⚓ and *Am.* lut-] лейтенант; **~-commander** капитан-лейтенант.

life [laif] жизнь *f*; образ жизни; биография; живость *f*; for ~ пожизненный; на всю жизнь; ~ sentence пожизненное заключение; **~-assurance** страхование жизни; **~-boat** спасательная лодка; **~-guard** лейб-гвардия; **~less** □ бездыханный, безжизненный; **~-like** словно живой; **~-long** пожизненный; **~-preserver** спасательный пояс; трость, налитая свинцом; **~-time** вся жизнь *f*, целая жизнь *f*.

lift [lift] 1. лифт; подъёмная машина; *phys.*, ✈ подъёмная сила; *fig.* возвышение; give a p. a ~ подвозить [-везти] кого-либо; 2. *v/t.* поднимать [-нять]; возвышать [-высить]; *sl.* [у]красть; *v/i.* возвышаться [-выситься]; подниматься [-няться].

light[1] [lait] 1. свет, освещение; огонь *m*; *fig.* светило; аспект; will you give me a ~ позвольте прикурить; put a ~ to зажигать [зажечь]; 2. светлый, ясный; 3. [*a. irr.*] *v/t.* зажигать [зажечь]; освещать [-етить]; *v/i.* (*mst* ~ up) загораться [-реться]; освещаться [-етиться].

light[2] [~] 1. *adj.* □ лёгкий, легковесный; незначительный; пустой, легкомысленный; ~ current ⚡ ток слабого напряжения; make ~ of относиться несерьёзно к (Д); 2. ~ on неожиданно натолкнуться на (В), случайно напасть на (В).

lighten ['laitn] освещать [-етить]; [по]светлеть; сверкать [-кнуть] (о молнии); делать(ся) более лёгким.

lighter ['laitə] зажигалка; запал; ⚓ лихтер.

light|headed легкомысленный; в бреду; **~-hearted** □ беззаботный; весёлый; **~house** маяк.

lighting ['laitiŋ] освещение.

light|-minded легкомысленный; **~ness** лёгкость *f*.

lightning [-niŋ] молния; **~-conductor**, **~-rod** громоотвод.

light-weight *sport* легковес.

like [laik] 1. похожий, подобный; равный; such ~ подобный тому, такой; F feel ~ хотеть (+ *inf.*); what is he ~? что он за человек?; 2. нечто подобное; ~s *pl.* склонности *f/pl.*, влечения *n/pl.*; his ~ ему подобные; 3. любить; [за-] хотеть; how do you ~ London? как вам нравится Лондон? I should ~ to know я хотел бы знать.

like|lihood ['laiklihud] вероятность *f*; **~ly** ['laikli] вероятный; подходящий; he is ~ to die он вероятно умрёт.

like|n ['laikən] уподоблять [-обить]; сравнивать [-нить]; **~ness** ['laiknis] сходство, подобие; **~wise** [-waiz] тоже, также; подобно.

liking ['laikiŋ] расположение (for к Д).

lilac ['lailək] 1. сирень *f*; 2. лиловый.

lily ['lili] лилия; ~ of the valley ландыш.

limb [lim] член, конечность *f*; ветка.

limber ['limbə] гибкий, мягкий.

lime [laim] известь *f*; ♀ лиметта (разновидность лимона); **~light** свет рампы; *fig.* центр общего внимания.

limit ['limit] граница, предел; off ~s вход воспрещён (надпись); be ~ed to ограничи(ва)ться (Т); **~ation** [limi'teiʃən] ограничение; ⚖ предельный срок; **~ed** ['limitid]: ~ (liability) company общество с ограниченной ответственностью; **~less** ['limitlis] □ безграничный.

limp [limp] 1. [за]хромать; 2. прихрамывание, хромота; 3. мягкий, нетвёрдый; слабый.

limpid ['limpid] прозрачный.

line [lain] 1. линия (*a.* 🚂, *tel.*); строка; черта, штрих; шнурок; леса (удочки); специальность *f*, занятие; ⚔ развёрнутый строй; ⚔ рубеж; ~s *pl.* стихи; ~ of conduct образ действия; hard ~s *pl.* неудача; in ~ with в согласии с (Т); stand in ~ *Am.* стоять в очереди; 2. *v/t.* разлиновывать [-новать]; класть на подкладку; ~ out набрасывать [-росать]; тянуться вдоль (Р).; *v/i.* ~ up выстраиваться [выстроиться] (в ряд).

linea|ge ['liniidʒ] родословная, происхождение; **~ment** [-mənt] черты (лица); очертание (гор); **~r** ['liniə] линейный.

linen ['linin] 1. полотно; *coll.* бельё; 2. полотняный.

liner ['lainə] пассажирский пароход или самолёт.

linger ['liŋgə] [по]медлить, [про-] мешкать; ~ over задерживаться [-жаться] на (П).

lingerie ['læ:nʒəri:] ✝ дамское бельё.

lining ['lainiŋ] подкладка; ⊕ обивка, облицовка, футеровка.

link [liŋk] 1. звено; связь *f*; соеди-

не́ние; *fig.* у́зы *f/pl.*; **2.** соединя́ть [-ни́ть]; смыка́ть [сомкну́ть]; примыка́ть [-мкну́ть].
linseed ['linsi:d] льняно́е се́мя *n*; ~ oil льняно́е ма́сло.
lion ['laiən] лев; **~ess** [-is] льви́ца.
lip [lip] губа́; край; F де́рзкая болтовня́; **~-stick** губна́я пома́да.
liquefy ['likwifai] превраща́ть(ся) в жи́дкость.
liquid ['likwid] **1.** жи́дкий; прозра́чный; ✝ легко́ реализу́емый; **2.** жи́дкость *f*.
liquidat|e ['likwideit] ликвиди́ровать *im(pf.)*; выпла́чивать [вы́платить] (долг); **~ion** [likwi'deiʃən] ликвида́ция; вы́плата до́лга.
liquor ['likə] жи́дкость *f*; (*a.* strong ~) спиртно́й напи́ток.
lisp [lisp] **1.** шепеля́вость *f*; ле́пет; **2.** шепеля́вить, сюсю́кать.
list [list] **1.** спи́сок, рее́стр, пе́речень *m*; крен (су́дна); **2.** вноси́ть в спи́сок; составля́ть спи́сок (Р); [на]крени́ться.
listen ['lisn] [по]слу́шать; прислу́ш(ив)аться; (to к Д); ~ in подслу́ш(ив)ать (to В); слу́шать ра́дио; **~er, ~er-in** [-ə'rin] слу́шатель(ница *f*) *m*.
listless ['listlis] апати́чный.
lit [lit] *pt.*и *p. pt.* от light[1].
literal ['litərəl] □ буква́льный, досло́вный.
litera|ry ['litərəri] □ литерату́рный; **~ture** ['litəritʃə] литерату́ра.
lithe [laið] ги́бкий.
lithography [li'θɔgrəfi] литогра́фия.
litigation [liti'geiʃən] тя́жба; спор.
litter ['litə] **1.** носи́лки *f/pl.*; подсти́лка (для скота́); помёт (припло́д); беспоря́док; **2.** подстила́ть [подостла́ть] (соло́му и т. п.); [о]щени́ться, [о]пороси́ться и т. п.; разбра́сывать в беспоря́дке.
little ['litl] **1.** *adj.* ма́ленький, небольшо́й; коро́ткий (о вре́мени); a ~ one малы́ш; **2.** *adv.* немно́го, ма́ло; **3.** пустя́к, ме́лочь *f*; a ~ немно́го; ~ by ~ ма́ло-пома́лу, постепе́нно; not a ~ нема́ло.
live 1. [liv] *com.* жить; существова́ть; ~ to see дожи́(ва́)ть до (Р); ~ down загла́живать [-ла́дить]; ~ out пережи́(ва́)ть; ~ up to a standard жить согла́сно тре́бованиям; **2.** [laiv] живо́й; жи́зненный; горя́щий; ⚔ боево́й, де́йствующий (снаря́д); ⚡ под напряже́нием; **~lihood** ['laivlihud] сре́дства к жи́зни; **~liness** [-nis] жи́вость *f*; оживле́ние; **~ly** ['laivli] живо́й; оживлённый.
liver ['livə] *anat.* пе́чень *f*; *cook.* печёнка.
livery ['livəri] ливре́я.
live|s [laivz] *pl.* от life; **~-stock** ['laivstɔk] живо́й инвента́рь *m*.
livid ['livid] ме́ртвенно бле́дный.
living ['liviŋ] **1.** □ живо́й; живу́щий, существу́ющий; **2.** сре́дства к жи́зни; жизнь *f*, о́браз жи́зни; **~-room** жила́я ко́мната.
lizard ['lizəd] я́щерица.
load [loud] **1.** груз; тя́жесть *f*, бре́мя *n*; заря́д; **2.** [на]грузи́ть; отягоща́ть [-готи́ть]; заряжа́ть [-яди́ть] (об ору́жии); *fig.* обременя́ть [-ни́ть]; **~ing** ['loudiŋ] погру́зка; груз; заря́дка.
loaf [loaf] **1.** (*pl.* loaves) хлеб, карава́й; **2.** безде́льничать; шата́ться, слоня́ться без де́ла.
loafer ['loufə] безде́льник; бродя́га *m*.
loam [loum] жи́рная гли́на; плодоро́дная земля́.
loan [loun] **1.** заём; on ~ взаймы́; **2.** дава́ть взаймы́, ссужа́ть [ссуди́ть].
lo(a)th [louθ] □ несклó́нный; **~e** [louð] пита́ть отвраще́ние к (Д); **~some** ['louðsəm] □ отврати́тельный.
loaves [louvz] *pl.* хле́бы *m/pl.*
lobby ['lɔbi] **1.** прихо́жая; *parl.* кулуа́ры *m/pl.*; *thea.* фойе́ *n indecl.*; **2.** *part. Am. parl.* пыта́ться возде́йствовать на чле́нов конгре́сса.
lobe [loub] ♀ *anat.* до́ля; мо́чка (у́ха).
lobster ['lɔbstə] ома́р.
local ['loukəl] **1.** □ ме́стный; ~ government ме́стное самоуправле́ние; **2.** ме́стное изве́стие; (*a.* ~ train) при́городный по́езд; **~ity** [lou'kæliti] ме́стность *f*, райо́н; окре́стность *f*; **~ize** ['loukəlaiz] локализова́ть *(im)pf.*; ограни́чивать распростране́ние (Р).
locat|e [lou'keit] *v/t.* определя́ть ме́сто (Р); располага́ть в определённом ме́сте; назнача́ть ме́сто для (Р); *Am.* отмеча́ть грани́цу (Р); be ~d быть располо́женным; *v/i.* поселя́ться [-ли́ться]; **~ion** [-ʃən] размеще́ние; определе́ние ме́ста; *Am.* местонахожде́ние.
lock [lɔk] **1.** замо́к; запо́р; зато́р; шлюз; ло́кон; пучо́к; **2.** *v/t.* запира́ть [запере́ть]; ⊕ [за]тормози́ть; ~ in запира́ть [запере́ть]; ~ up вложи́ть (капита́л) в тру́дно реализу́емые бума́ги; *v/i.* запира́ться [запере́ться]; замыка́ться [замкну́ться].
lock|er ['lɔkə] запира́ющийся шка́фчик; **~et** ['lɔkit] медальо́н; **~-out** лока́ут; **~smith** сле́сарь *m*; **~-up** вре́мя закры́тия (школ, магази́нов и т. п.);ареста́нтская ка́мера.
locomotive ['loukəmoutiv] **1.** дви́жущий(ся); **2.** (и́ли ~ engine) локо-

мотúв, паровóз, тепловóз, электровóз.

locust ['loukəst] саранчá.

lodestar путевóдная звездá.

lodg|e [lɔdʒ] **1.** сторóжка; (*mst* охóтничий) дóмик; (масóнская) лóжа; **2.** *v/t.* дать помещéние (Д); депонúровать (*im*)*pf.* (дéньги); по-д(ав)áть (жáлобу); *v/i.* квартировáть; застревáть [-ря́ть] (о пýле и т. п.); **~er** ['lɔdʒə] жилéц, жилúца; **~ing** ['lɔdʒiŋ] жилúще; **~s** *pl.* квартúра; кóмната (снимáемая).

loft [lɔft] чердáк; галерéя; **~y** ['lɔfti] □ высокомéрный; велúчественный.

log [lɔg] колóда; бревнó; ⚓ лаг; **~-cabin** бревéнчатая хúжина; **~gerhead** ['lɔgəhed]: be at **~s** быть в ссóре, ссóриться (with с Т).

logic ['lɔdʒik] лóгика; **~al** ['lɔdʒikəl] □ логúческий.

loin [lɔin] филéйная часть *f*; **~s** *pl.* пояснúца.

loiter ['lɔitə] слоня́ться без дéла; мéшкать.

loll [lɔl] сидéть разваля́сь; стоя́ть облокотя́сь.

lone|liness ['lounlinis] одинóчество; **~ly** [-li] □, **~some** [-səm] □ одинóкий.

long[1] [lɔŋ] **1.** дóлгий срок, дóлгое врéмя *n*; before ~ вскóре; for ~ надóлго; **2.** *adj.* длúнный; дóлгий; мéдленный; in the ~ run в концé концóв; be ~ мéдлить; дóлго длúться; **3.** *adv.* дóлго; ~ ago давнó; so ~! покá (до свидáния)!; **~er** дóльше; бóльше.

long[2] [~] стрáстно желáть, жáждать (for P), тосковáть (по Д).

long|-distance *attr.* дáльний; *sport* на длúнные дистáнции; **~evity** [lɔn'dʒeviti] долговéчность *f*.

longing ['lɔŋiŋ] **1.** □ тоскýющий; **2.** сúльное желáние, стремлéние (к Д), тоскá (по Д).

longitude ['lɔndʒitju:d] *geogr.* долготá.

long|shoreman ['lɔŋʃɔ:mən] портóвый грýзчик; **~sighted** дальнозóркий; **~-suffering** **1.** многострадáльный; долготерпелúвый; **2.** долготерпéние; **~-term** долгосрóчный; **~-winded** □ могýщий дóлго бежáть, не задыхáясь; многоречúвый.

look [luk] **1.** взгляд; выражéние (глаз, лицá); вид, нарýжность *f* (*a.* **~s** *pl.*); have a ~ at a th. посмотрéть на (В); ознакомля́ться [-кóмиться] с (Т); **2.** *v/i.* [по-] смотрéть (at на В); вы́глядеть; ~ for искáть (В *or* Р); ~ forward to предвкушáть [-усúть] (В); с рáдостью ожидáть (Р); ~ into исслéдовать (*im*)*pf.*; ~ out! берегúсь!, смотрú!; ~ (up)on *fig.* смотрéть как на (В), считáть за (В); *v/t.* ~ disdain смотрéть с презрéнием; ~ over не замечáть [-éтить]; просмáтривать [-мотрéть]; ~ up [по]искáть (в словарé и т. п.); навещáть [-естúть].

looker-on ['lukər'ɔn] зрúтель(ница *f*) *m*; наблюдáтель(ница *f*) *m*.

looking-glass зéркало.

look-out ['luk'aut] вид (на мóре и т. п.); вúды *m/pl.*, шáнсы *m/pl.*; that is my ~ э́то моё дéло.

loom [lu:m] **1.** ткáцкий станóк; **2.** маячить, неясно вырисóвываться.

loop [lu:p] **1.** (✈ мёртвая) пéтля; **2.** дéлать (✈ мёртвую) пéтлю; закрепля́ть пéтлей; **~hole** лазéйка (*a. fig.*); *fig.* увёртка; ⚔ бóйница, амбразýра.

loose [lu:s] **1.** □ *com.* свобóдный; неопределённый; простóрный; болтáющийся, шатáющийся; распýщенный (о нрáвах); несвя́занный; ры́хлый; **2.** освобождáть [-бодúть]; развя́зывать [-язáть]; **~n** ['lu:sn] ослабля́ть(ся) [-áбить (-ся)]; развя́зывать [-язáть]; разрыхля́ть [-лúть]; расшáтывать [-шатáть].

loot [lu:t] **1.** [о]грáбить; **2.** добы́ча, нагрáбленное добрó.

lop [lɔp] обрубáть [-бúть] (вéтки); **~-sided** кривобóкий; накренённый.

loquacious [lo'kweiʃəs] болтлúвый.

lord [lɔ:d] господúн, бáрин; лорд; повелúтель *m*; the ♀ госпóдь *m*; my ~ [mi'lɔ:d] милóрд (обращéние); the ♀'s prayer óтче наш (молúтва); the ♀'s Supper тáйная вéчеря; **~ly** ['lɔ:dli] высокомéрный; **~ship** ['lɔ:dʃip]: your ~ вáша свéтлость *f*.

lorry ['lɔri] 🚗 грузовúк; вагóн-платфóрма; подвóда; полóк.

lose [lu:z] [*irr.*] *v/t.* [по]теря́ть; упускáть [-стúть]; проúгрывать [-рáть]; ~ o. s. заблудúться *pf.*; *v/i.* [по]теря́ть; проúгрывать(ся) [-рáть(ся)]; отст(ав)áть (о часáх).

loss [lɔs] потéря, утрáта; урóн; убы́ток; прóигрыш; at a ~ в затруднéнии.

lost [lɔst] *pt.* и *p. pt.* от lose; be ~ пропадáть [-пáсть]; погибáть [-гúбнуть]; *fig.* растеря́ться *pf*.

lot [lɔt] жрéбий; ☤ вéщи продавáемые пáртией на аукциóне; ýчасть *f*, дóля; *Am.* учáсток землú; F мáсса, уйма; draw ~s бросáть жрéбий; fall to a p.'s ~ вы́пасть на дóлю когó-нибудь.

lotion ['louʃən] жúдкое косметúческое срéдство, жúдкий крем.

lottery ['lɔtəri] лотерéя.

loud [laud] □ грóмкий, звýчный; шýмный, криклúвый; *fig.* кричáщий (о крáсках).

lounge [laundʒ] **1.** сидéть развaля́сь; стоя́ть опира́ясь; 2. пра́здное времяпрепровожде́ние; дива́н; *thea.* фойе́ *n indecl.*

lour ['lauə] смотре́ть угрю́мо; [на]хму́риться.

lous|e [laus] (*pl.*: lice) вошь *f* (*pl.*: вши); **~y** ['lauzi] вши́вый; *fig.* парши́вый.

lout [laut] неуклю́жий, неотёсанный челове́к.

lovable ['lʌvəbl] □ привлека́тельный, ми́лый.

love [lʌv] 1. любо́вь *f*; влюблённость *f*; предме́т любви́; give (*or* send) one's ~ to a p. передава́ть, посыла́ть приве́т (Д); in ~ with влюблённый в (В); make ~ to уха́живать за (Т); 2. люби́ть; ~ to do де́лать с удово́льствием; **~-affair** любо́вная интри́га; **~ly** ['lʌvli] прекра́сный, чу́дный; **~r** ['lʌvə] любо́вник; возлю́бленный; люби́тель(ница *f*) *m.*

loving ['lʌviŋ] □ лю́бящий.

low[1] [lou] ни́зкий, невысо́кий; *fig.* сла́бый; ти́хий (о го́лосе); ни́зкий, непристо́йный; **~est bid** са́мая ни́зкая цена́, предло́женная на аукцио́не.

low[2] [~] 1. мыча́ние; 2. [за]мыча́ть.

lower[1] ['louə] 1. *compr.* от low[1]; ни́зший; ни́жний; 2. *v/t.* спуска́ть [-сти́ть] (ло́дку, па́рус); опуска́ть [-сти́ть] (глаза́); снижа́ть [-и́зить]; *v/i.* снижа́ться [-и́зиться] (о це́нах, зву́ке и т. п.); уменьша́ться [уме́ньши́ться].

lower[2] ['lauə] *s.* lour.

low|land ни́зменная ме́стность *f*, ни́зменность *f*; **~liness** ['loulinis] скро́мность *f*; **~ly** скро́мный; **~-necked** с ни́зким вы́резом; **~-spirited** пода́вленный, уны́лый.

loyal ['lɔiəl] □ ве́рный, лоя́льный; **~ty** [-ti] ве́рность *f*, лоя́льность *f*.

lozenge ['lɔzindʒ] табле́тка; ромб.

lubber ['lʌbə] у́вален *m.*

lubric|ant ['lu:brikənt] сма́зка; **~ate** [-keit] сма́з(ыв)ать (маши́ну); **~ation** [lu:bri'keiʃən] сма́зка.

lucid ['lu:sid] □ я́сный; прозра́чный.

luck [lʌk] уда́ча, сча́стье; good ~ счастли́вый слу́чай, уда́ча; bad ~, hard ~, ill ~ неуда́ча; **~ily** ['lʌkili] к сча́стью; **~y** ['lʌki] □ счастли́вый, уда́чный; принося́щий уда́чу.

lucr|ative ['lu:krətiv] □ при́быльный, вы́годный; **~e** ['lu:kə] бары́ш, при́быль *f*.

ludicrous ['lu:dikrəs] □ неле́пый, смешно́й.

lug [lʌg] [по]тащи́ть, [по]волочи́ть.

luggage ['lʌgidʒ] бага́ж; **~-office** 🚂 ка́мера хране́ния багажа́.

lugubrious [lu:gju:briəs] □ мра́чный.

lukewarm ['lu:kwɔ:m] теплова́тый; *fig.* равноду́шный.

lull [lʌl] 1. убаю́к(ив)ать; усыпля́ть [-пи́ть]; 2. вре́менное зати́шье; вре́менное успокое́ние.

lullaby ['lʌləbai] колыбе́льная пе́сня.

lumber ['lʌmbə] нену́жные громо́здкие ве́щи *f/pl.*; *Am.* пиломатериа́лы *m/pl.*; **~man** *Am.* лесопромы́шленник; лесору́б.

lumin|ary ['lu:minəri] свети́ло; **~ous** [-əs] □ светя́щийся, све́тлый; *fig.* пролива́ющий свет.

lump [lʌmp] 1. глы́ба, ком; *fig* чурба́н; кусо́к (са́хара и т. п.); in the ~ о́птом, гурто́м; ~ sum о́бщая су́мма; 2. *v/t.* брать огу́лом; сме́шивать в ку́чу; *v/i.* свёртываться в ко́мья; **~ish** ['lʌmpiʃ] неуклю́жий; тупоу́мный; **~y** ['lʌmpi] □ комкова́тый.

lunatic ['lu:nətik] 1. сумасше́дший, безу́мный; 2. психи́чески больно́й; ~ asylum психиатри́ческая больни́ца.

lunch(eon) ['lʌntʃ(ən)] 1. второ́й за́втрак; 2. [по]за́втракать.

lung [lʌŋ] лёгкое; (a pair of) **~s** *pl.* лёгкие *n/pl.*

lunge [lʌndʒ] 1. вы́пад, уда́р (рапи́рой, шпа́гой) 2. *v/i.* наноси́ть уда́р (at Д).

lurch [lə:tʃ] 1. [на]крени́ться; идти́ шата́ясь; 2. leave a. p. in the ~ поки́нуть кого́-нибудь в беде́, в тяжёлом положе́нии.

lure [ljuə] 1. прима́нка; *fig.* собла́зн; 2. примани́вать [-ни́ть]; *fig.* соблазня́ть [-ни́ть].

lurid ['ljuərid] мра́чный.

lurk [lə:k] скрыва́ться в заса́де; таи́ться.

luscious ['lʌʃəs] □ со́чный; при́торный.

lustr|e ['lʌstə] гля́нец; лю́стра; **~ous** ['lʌstrəs] □ глянцеви́тый.

lute[1] [lu:t, lju:t] ♪ лю́тня.

lute[2] [~] 1. зама́зка, масти́ка; 2. зама́зывать зама́зкой.

Lutheran ['lu:θərən] лютера́нский.

luxur|iant [lʌg'zjuəriənt] □ пы́шный; **~ious** [-riəs] □ роско́шный, пы́шный; **~y** ['lʌkʃəri] ро́скошь *f*; предме́т ро́скоши.

lye [lai] щёлок.

lying ['laiiŋ] 1. *p. pr.* от lie[1] и lie[2]; 2. *adj.* лжи́вый, ло́жный; лежа́щий; **~-in** [-'in] ро́ды *m/pl.*; ~ hospital роди́льный дом.

lymph [limf] ли́мфа.

lynch [lintʃ] расправля́ться самосу́дом с (Т); **~-law** ['lintʃlɔ:] самосу́д; зако́н Ли́нча.

lynx [links] *zo.* рысь *f*.

lyric ['lirik], **~al** [-ikəl] □ лири́ческий; **~s** *pl.* ли́рика.

M

macaroni [mækə'rouni] макаро́ны *f/pl.*

macaroon [mækə'ru:n] минда́льное пече́нье.

machin|ation [mæki'neiʃən] махина́ция, интри́га; ~s *pl.* ко́зни *f/pl.*; ~e [mə'ʃi:n] 1. маши́на; механи́зм; *attr.* маши́нный; ~ fitter сле́сарь-монта́жник; 2. подверга́ть маши́нной обрабо́тке; ~e-made сде́ланный механи́ческим спо́собом; ~ery [-əri] маши́нное обору́дование; ~ist [-ist] меха́ник; машини́ст.

mackerel ['mækrəl] *zo.* макре́ль *f.*

mackintosh ['mækintɔʃ] макинто́ш, плащ.

mad [mæd] □ сумасше́дший, поме́шанный; бе́шеный; *fig.* ди́кий; *Am.* взбешённый; go ~ сходи́ть с ума́; drive ~ своди́ть с ума́.

madam ['mædəm] мада́м *f indecl.*; суда́рыня.

mad|cap 1. сорвиголова́ *m/f*; 2. сумасбро́дный; ~den ['mædn] [вз]беси́ть; своди́ть с ума́.

made [meid] *pt.* и *p. pt.* от make.

made-up прихоро́шенный; гото́вый (об оде́жде); ~ of состоя́щий из (Р).

mad|house дом умалишённых; ~man сумасше́дший; ~ness ['mædnis] сумасше́ствие.

magazine [mægə'zi:n] склад боеприпа́сов; журна́л; ⊕, ⚔ магази́н.

maggot ['mægət] личи́нка.

magic ['mædʒik] 1. (*a.* ~al ['mædʒikəl] □) волше́бный; 2. волшебство́; ~ian [mə'dʒiʃən] волше́бник.

magistra|cy ['mædʒistrəsi] до́лжность судьи́; магистра́т; ~te [-trit] мирово́й судья́ *m.*

magnanimous [mæg'næniməs] □ великоду́шный.

magnet ['mægnit] магни́т; ~ic [mæg'netik] (~ally) магни́тный; магнети́ческий.

magni|ficence [mæg'nifisns] великоле́пие; ~ficent [-snt] великоле́пный; ~fy ['mægnifai] увели́чи(ва)ть; ~tude ['mægnitju:d] величина́; разме́ры *m/pl.*; ва́жность *f.*

mahogany [mə'hɔgəni] кра́сное де́рево.

maid [meid] деви́ца, де́вушка; го́рничная, служа́нка; old ~ ста́рая де́ва; ~ of honour фре́йлина; *Am.* подру́жка неве́сты.

maiden ['meidn] 1. деви́ца, де́вушка; 2. незаму́жняя; *fig.* де́вственный; *fig.* пе́рвый; ~ name де́вичья фами́лия; ~head, ~hood деви́чество; де́вственность *f*; ~ly [-li] деви́чий.

mail¹ [meil] кольчу́га.

mail² [~] 1. по́чта; *attr.* почто́вый; 2. *Am.* сдава́ть на по́чту; посыла́ть по́чтой; ~-bag почто́вая су́мка; ~man *Am.* почтальо́н.

maim [meim] [ис]кале́чить, [из-] уве́чить.

main [mein] 1. гла́вная часть *f*; ~s *pl.* ⚡ магистра́ль *f*; ⚡ сеть си́льного то́ка; *f*; in the ~ в основно́м; 2. гла́вный, основно́й; ~land ['meinlənd] матери́к; ~ly ['meinli] гла́вным о́бразом; бо́льшей ча́стью; ~spring *fig.* гла́вная дви́жущая си́ла; ~stay *fig.* гла́вная подде́ржка, опо́ра.

maintain [men'tein] подде́рживать [-жа́ть]; утвержда́ть [-рди́ть]; сохраня́ть [-ни́ть].

maintenance ['meintinəns] содержа́ние, сре́дства к существова́нию; подде́ржка; сохране́ние.

maize [meiz] ♀ маис, кукуру́за.

majest|ic [mə'dʒestik] (~ally) величественный; ~y ['mædʒisti] вели́чество; вели́чественность *f.*

major ['meidʒə] 1. ста́рший, бо́льший; ♪ мажо́рный; ~ key мажо́р; совершенноле́тний; 2. майо́р; *Am. univ.* гла́вный предме́т; ~-general генера́л-майо́р; ~ity [mə'dʒɔriti] совершенноле́тие; большинство́; чин майо́ра.

make [meik] 1. [*irr.*] *v/t. com.* [с]де́лать, производи́ть [-вести́]; [при-] гото́вить; составля́ть [-а́вить]; заключа́ть [-чи́ть] (мир и т. п.); заставля́ть [-ста́вить]; ~ good исправля́ть [-а́вить; [с]держа́ть (сло́во); do you ~ one of us? вы с на́ми? ~ a port входи́ть в порт, га́вань; ~ sure of удостоверя́ться [-ве́риться] в (П); ~ way уступа́ть доро́гу (for Д); ~ into превраща́ть [-рати́ть], переде́л(ыв)ать в (В); ~ out разбира́ть [разобра́ть]; выпи́сывать [вы́писать]; ~ over переда(ва́)ть; ~ up составля́ть [-а́вить] ула́живать [ула́дить] (о ссо́ре); [за]гримирова́ть; навёрстывать [наверста́ть] (вре́мя); = ~ up for (*v/i.*); ~ up one's mind реша́ться [-ши́ться]; 2. *v/i.* направля́ться [-а́виться] (for к Д); ~ away with отде́л(ыв)аться от (Р); ~ off уезжа́ть [уе́хать]; уходи́ть [уйти́]; ~ up for возмеща́ть [-ести́ть]; 3. тип, моде́ль *f*; изде́лие; ма́рка (фи́рмы); ~-believe притво́рство; предло́г; ~-shift заме́на; подру́чное сре́дство; ~-up соста́в; грим, косме́тика.

maladjustment ['mæləd'dʒʌstmənt] неуда́чное приспособле́ние.

maladministration ['mælədminis'treiʃən] плохо́е управле́ние.

malady ['mælədi] боле́знь *f.*
malcontent ['mælkəntent] **1.** недово́льный; **2.** недово́льный (челове́к).
male [meil] **1.** мужско́й; **2.** мужчи́на; саме́ц.
malediction [mæli'dikʃən] прокля́тие.
malefactor ['mælifæktə] злоде́й.
malevolen|ce [mə'levələns] злора́дство; недоброжела́тельность *f*; **~t** [-lənt] □ злора́дный; недоброжела́тельный.
malice ['mælis] зло́ба.
malicious [mə'liʃəs] □ зло́бный; **~ness** [-nis] зло́бность *f.*
malign [mə'lain] **1.** □ па́губный, вре́дный; **2.** [на]клевета́ть на (В); злосло́вить; **~ant** [mə'lignənt] □ зловре́дный; зло́бный, зло́стный; ⚕ злока́чественный; **~ity** [-niti] зло́бность *f*; па́губность *f*; ⚕ злока́чественность *f.*
malleable ['mæliəbl] ко́вкий; *fig.* пода́тливый.
mallet ['mælit] колоту́шка.
malnutrition ['mælnju:'triʃən] недоста́точное пита́ние.
malodorous ['mæ'loudərəs] □ злово́нный, воню́чий.
malt [mɔ:lt] со́лод; F пи́во.
maltreat [mæl'tri:t] ду́рно обраща́ться с (Т).
mammal ['mæməl] млекопита́ющее (живо́тное).
mammoth ['mæməθ] **1.** грома́дный; **2.** ма́монт.
man [mæn] **1.** (*pl.* men) челове́к; мужчи́на *m*; челове́чество; слуга́ *m*; фигу́ра (игры́); **2.** ⚔ ⚓ укомплекто́вывать соста́вом; ~ o. s. мужа́ться.
manage ['mænidʒ] *v/t.* управля́ть (Т), заве́довать (Т); стоя́ть во главе́ (Р); справля́ться [-а́виться] с (Т); обходи́ться [обойти́сь] (with (Т, without без Р); ~ to (+ *inf.*) [с]уме́ть ...; **~able** [-əbl] □ послу́шный, сми́рный; сгово́рчивый; **~ment** [-mənt] управле́ние, заве́дование; уме́ние спра́виться; **~r** [-ə] заве́дующий; дире́ктор; **~ress** [-əres] заве́дующая.
managing ['mænidʒiŋ] руководя́щий; делово́й.
mandat|e ['mændeit] манда́т; нака́з; **~ory** ['mændətəri] манда́тный; повели́тельный.
mane [mein] гри́ва; *fig.* ко́смы *f/pl.*
manful ['mænful] □ му́жественный.
mange [meindʒ] *vet.* чесо́тка.
manger ['meindʒə] я́сли *m/pl.*, корму́шка.
mangle ['mæŋgl] **1.** като́к (для белья́); **2.** [вы́]ката́ть (бельё); *fig.* искажа́ть [искази́ть].
mangy ['meindʒi] чесо́точный; парши́вый.
manhood ['mænhud] возмужа́лость *f*; му́жественность *f.*
mania ['meiniə] ма́ния; **~c** ['meiniæk] **1.** манья́к (-я́чка); **2.** поме́шанный.
manicure ['mænikjuə] **1.** маникю́р; **2.** де́лать маникю́р (Д).
manifest ['mænifest] **1.** □ очеви́дный, я́вный; **2.** ⚓ деклара́ция судово́го гру́за; **3.** *v/t.* обнару́живать; обнаро́довать *pf.*; проявля́ть [-ви́ть]; **~ation** ['mænifes'teiʃən] проявле́ние; манифеста́ция; **~o** [-'festou] манифе́ст.
manifold ['mænifould] □ **1.** разнообра́зный, разноро́дный; **2.** размножа́ть [-о́жить] (докуме́нты).
manipulat|e [mə'nipjuleit] манипули́ровать; **~ion** [mənipju'leiʃən] манипуля́ция; подтасо́вка.
man|kind [mæn'kaind] **1.** челове́чество; **2.** ['mænkaind] мужско́й род; **~ly** [-li] му́жественный.
manner ['mænə] спо́соб, ме́тод; мане́ра; о́браз де́йствий; **~s** *pl.* уме́ние держа́ть себя́; мане́ры *f/pl.*; обы́чаи *m/pl.*; in a ~ в не́которой сте́пени; **~ed** [-d] вы́чурный; **~ly** [-li] ве́жливый.
manoeuvre [mə'nu:və] **1.** манёвр; **2.** проводи́ть манёвры; маневри́ровать.
man-of-war вое́нный кора́бль *f.*
manor ['mænə] поме́стье.
mansion ['mænʃən] большо́й поме́щичий дом.
manslaughter ['mænslɔ:tə] непредумы́шленное уби́йство.
mantel [mæntl] облицо́вка ками́на; **~piece, ~shelf** по́лка ками́на.
mantle [mæntl] **1.** ма́нтия; *fig.* покро́в; **2.** *v/t.* оку́т(ыв)ать; покры́(ва́)ть; *v/i.* [по]красне́ть.
manual [-juəl] **1.** ручно́й; **2.** руково́дство (кни́га), уче́бник, спра́вочник.
manufactory [mænju'fæktəri] фа́брика.
manufactur|e [mænju'fæktʃə] **1.** произво́дство; изде́лие; **2.** выде́лывать [вы́делать], [с]фабрикова́ть; **~er** [-rə] фабрика́нт; заво́дчик; **~ing** [-riŋ] произво́дство, вы́делка; *attr.* фабри́чный, промы́шленный.
manure [mən'juə] **1.** удобре́ние; **2.** удобря́ть [-о́брить].
many ['meni] **1.** мно́гие, многочи́сленные; мно́го; ~ a ино́й; **2.** мно́жество; a good ~ поря́дочное коли́чество; a great ~ грома́дное коли́чество.
map [mæp] **1.** ка́рта; **2.** наноси́ть на ка́рту; ~ out [с]плани́ровать.
mar [mɑ:] искажа́ть [искази́ть]; [ис]по́ртить.
marble [mɑ:bl] **1.** мра́мор; **2.** распи́сывать под мра́мор.
March[1] [mɑ:tʃ] март.

march² [~] 1. ⚔ марш; похо́д; *fig.* разви́тие (собы́тий); 2. марширова́ть; *fig.* идти́ вперёд (*a.* ~ on).
marchioness ['mɑːʃənis] марки́за (ти́тул).
mare [mɛə] кобы́ла; ~'s nest иллю́зия; газе́тная у́тка.
margin ['mɑːdʒin] край; поля́ *n/pl.* (страни́цы); опу́шка (ле́са); ~al [-l] □ находя́щийся на краю́; ~ note заме́тка на поля́х страни́цы.
marine [mə'riːn] 1. морско́й; 2. солда́т морско́й пехо́ты; *paint.* морско́й вид (карти́на); ~r ['mærinə] моря́к, матро́с.
marital [mə'raitl] □ супру́жеский.
maritime ['mæritaim] примо́рский; морско́й.
mark¹ [mɑːk] ма́рка (де́нежная едини́ца).
mark² [~] 1. ме́тка, знак; балл, отме́тка (оце́нка зна́ний); фабри́чная ма́рка; мише́нь *f*; но́рма; a man of ~ выдаю́щийся челове́к; up to the ~ *fig.* на до́лжной высоте́; 2. *v/t.* отмеча́ть [-е́тить]; ста́вить расце́нку на (това́р); ста́вить отме́тку в (П); ~ off отделя́ть [-ли́ть]; ~ out расставля́ть указа́тельные зна́ки на (П); ~ time ⚔ отбива́ть шаг на ме́сте; ~ed [mɑːkt] □ отме́ченный; заме́тный.
market ['mɑːkit] 1. ры́нок, база́р; ✝ сбыт; in the ~ в прода́же; 2. привози́ть на ры́нок (для прода́жи); покупа́ть на ры́нке; прода́(ва́)ть; go ~ing ходи́ть на ры́нок; ~able [-əbl] □ хо́дкий.
marksman ['mɑːksmən] ме́ткий стрело́к.
marmalade ['mɑːməleid] (апельси́нное) варе́нье; мармела́д.
maroon [mə'ruːn] высáживать на необита́емом о́строве.
marquee [mɑː'kiː] шатёр.
marquis ['mɑːkwis] марки́з.
marriage ['mæridʒ] брак; сва́дьба; civil ~ гражда́нский брак; ~able [-əbl] дости́гший (-шая) бра́чного во́зраста; ~-lines *pl.* свиде́тельство о бра́ке.
married ['mærid] жена́тый; за́мужняя; ~ couple супру́ги *pl.*
marrow ['mærou] ко́стный мозг; *fig.* су́щность *f*; ~y [-i] костномозгово́й; *fig.* кре́пкий.
marry ['mæri] *v/t.* жени́ть; выдава́ть за́муж; *eccl.* сочета́ть бра́ком; жени́ться на (П), вы́йти за́муж за (В); *v/i.* жени́ться; вы́йти за́муж.
marsh [mɑːʃ] боло́то.
marshal ['mɑːʃəl] 1. ма́ршал; церемоннийме́йстер; *Am.* нача́льник поли́ции; 2. выстра́ивать [вы́строить] (войска́ и т. п.); торже́ственно вести́.
marshy ['mɑːʃi] боло́тистый, боло́тный.

mart [mɑːt] ры́нок; аукцио́нный зал.
marten ['mɑːtin] *zo.* куни́ца.
martial ['mɑːʃl] □ вое́нный; вои́нственный; ~ law вое́нное положе́ние.
martyr ['mɑːtə] 1. му́ченик (-ица); 2. за]му́чить (до́ смерти).
marvel ['mɑːvel] 1. ди́во, чу́до; 2. удивля́ться [-ви́ться]; ~lous ['mɑːvələs] □ изуми́тельный, удиви́тельный.
mascot ['mæskət] талисма́н.
masculine ['mɑːskjulin] мужско́й; му́жественный.
mash [mæʃ] 1. мешани́на; су́сло; 2. размина́ть [-мя́ть]; разда́вливать [-дави́ть]; ~ed potatoes *pl.* карто́фельное пюре́ *n indecl.*
mask [mɑːsk] 1. ма́ска; 2. [за]маскирова́ть; скры(ва́)ть; ~ed [-t]: ~ ball маскара́д.
mason ['meisn] ка́менщик; масо́н; ~ry [-ri] ка́менная (и́ли кирпи́чная) кла́дка; масо́нство.
masquerade [mæskə'reid] 1. маскара́д; 2. *fig.* притворя́ться [-ри́ться].
mass [mæs] 1. ма́сса; *eccl.* ме́сса; ~ meeting ма́ссовое собра́ние; 2. собира́ться толпо́й, собира́ть(ся) в ку́чу; ⚔ масси́ровать (*im*)*pf.*
massacre ['mæsəkə] 1. резня́, избие́ние; 2. выреза́ть [вы́резать] (людей).
massage ['mæsɑːʒ] 1. масса́ж; 2. масси́ровать.
massive ['mæsiv] масси́вный; кру́пный.
mast [mɑːst] ⚓ ма́чта.
master ['mɑːstə] 1. хозя́ин; господи́н; капита́н (су́дна); учи́тель *m*; ма́стер; *univ.* глава́ колле́джа; ♀ of Arts маги́стр иску́сств; 2. одоле́(ва́)ть; справля́ться [-а́виться] с (Т); овладе́(ва́)ть (Т); владе́ть (языко́м); 3. *attr.* мастерско́й; веду́щий; ~-builder строи́тель *m*; ~ful ['mɑːstəful] □ вла́стный; мастерско́й; ~key отмы́чка; ~ly [-li] мастерско́й; ~piece шеде́вр; ~ship [-ʃip] мастерство́; до́лжность учи́теля; ~y ['mɑːstəri] госпо́дство, власть *f*; мастерство́.
masticate ['mæstikeit] [с]жева́ть.
mastiff ['mæstif] англи́йский дог.
mat [mæt] 1. цино́вка, ро́гожа; 2. *fig.* спу́т(ыв)ать.
match¹ [mætʃ] спи́чка; ⚔ фити́ль *m.*
match² [~] 1. ро́вня́ *m/f*; матч, состяза́ние; вы́годный брак, па́ртия; be a ~ for быть ро́вней (Д); 2. *v/t.* [с]равня́ться с (Т); подбира́ть под па́ру; well ~ed couple хоро́шая па́ра; *v/i.* соотве́тствовать; сочета́ться; to ~ подходя́щий (по цве́ту, то́ну и т. п.); ~less ['mætʃlis] □ несравне́нный, беспodо́бный.
mate [meit] 1. това́рищ; сожи́тель

(-ница *f*) *m*; супру́г(а); саме́ц (са́мка); ⚓ помо́щник капита́на; 2. сочета́ть(ся) бра́ком.
material [mə'tiəriəl] 1. □ материа́льный; суще́ственный; 2. материа́л (*a. fig.*); мате́рия; вещество́.
matern|al [mə'tə:nl] □ матери́нский; **~ity** [-niti] матери́нство; (*mst* ~ hospital) роди́льный дом.
mathematic|ian [mæθimə'tiʃən] матема́тик; **~s** [-mæ'tiks] (*mst sg.*) матема́тика.
matriculate [mə'trikjuleit] приня́ть и́ли быть при́нятым в университе́т.
matrimon|ial [mætri'mounjəl] □ бра́чный; супру́жеский; **~y** ['mætrimǝni] супру́жество, брак.
matrix ['meitriks] ма́трица.
matron ['meitrən] заму́жняя же́нщина; эконо́мка; сестра́-хозя́йка (в больни́це).
matter ['mætə] 1. вещество́; материа́л; предме́т; де́ло; по́вод; what's the ~? что случи́лось?, в чём де́ло?; no ~ who ... всё равно́, кто ...; ~ of course само́ собо́й разуме́ющееся де́ло; for that ~ что каса́ется э́того; ~ of fact факт; 2. име́ть значе́ние; it does not ~ ничего́; **~-of-fact** факти́ческий; делово́й.
mattress ['mætris] матра́ц, тюфя́к.
matur|e [mə'tjuə] 1. □ зре́лый; вы́держанный; † подлежа́щий упла́те; 2. созре́(ва́)ть; вполне́ развива́ться; † наступа́ть [-пи́ть] (о сро́ке); **~ity** [-riti] зре́лость *f*; † срок платежа́ по ве́кселю.
maudlin ['mɔ:dlin] □ плакси́вый.
maul [mɔ:l] [рас]терза́ть; *fig.* жесто́ко критикова́ть.
mawkish ['mɔ:kiʃ] □ сентимента́льный; неприя́тный на вкус.
maxim ['mæksim] афори́зм; при́нцип; **~um** [-siməm] 1. ма́ксимум; вы́сшая сте́пень *f*; 2. максима́льный.
May[1] [mei] май.
may[2] [~] [*irr.*] (мода́льный глаго́л без инфинити́ва и прича́стий) [с]мочь; име́ть разреше́ние.
maybe ['meibi:] *Am.* мо́жет быть.
May-day ['meidei] пра́здник пе́рвого ма́я.
mayor [mɛə] мэр.
maz|e [meiz] лабири́нт; *fig.* пу́таница; be **~d** и́ли in a ~ быть расте́рянным; **~y** ['meizi] □ запу́танный.
me [mi:, mi] ко́свенный паде́ж от I: мне, меня́; F я.
meadow ['medou] луг.
meagre ['mi:gə] худо́й, то́щий; ску́дный.
meal [mi:l] еда́ (за́втрак, обе́д, у́жин); мука́.
mean[1] [mi:n] □ по́длый, ни́зкий; ска́редный.
mean[2] [~] 1. сре́дний; in the ~ time тем вре́менем; 2. середи́на; **~s** *pl.* состоя́ние, бога́тство; (*a. sg.*) сре́дство; спо́соб; by all ~s любо́й цено́й; коне́чно; by no ~s нисколько; отню́дь не ...; by ~s of посре́дством (P).
mean[3] [~] [*irr.*] намерева́ться; име́ть в виду́; хоте́ть сказа́ть, подразумева́ть; предназнача́ть [-зна́чить]; зна́чить; ~ well (ill) име́ть до́брые (плохи́е) наме́рения.
meaning ['mi:niŋ] 1. □ зна́чащий; 2. значе́ние; смысл; **~less** [-lis] бессмы́сленный.
meant [ment] *pt.* и *p. pt.* от mean.
mean|time, ~while тем вре́менем.
measles ['mi:zlz] *pl.* ⚕ корь *f*.
measure ['meʒə] 1. ме́ра; ме́рка; мероприя́тие; масшта́б; ♪ такт; ~ of capacity ме́ра объёма; beyond ~ непоме́рно; in a great ~ в большо́й сте́пени; made to ~ сде́ланный по ме́рке; 2. измеря́ть [-е́рить]; [с]ме́рить; снима́ть ме́рку с (P); **~less** [-lis] □ неизмери́мый; **~ment** [-mənt] разме́р; измере́ние.
meat [mi:t] мя́со; *fig.* содержа́ние; **~y** ['mi:ti] мяси́стый; *fig.* содержа́тельный.
mechanic [mi'kænik] меха́ник; ремесленник; **~al** [-nikəl] □ маши́нный; механи́ческий; машина́льный; **~ian** [mekə'niʃən] меха́ник; **~s** (*mst sg.*) меха́ника.
mechanize ['mekənaiz] механизи́ровать (*im*)*pf.*; ⚔ моторизова́ть (*im*)*pf.*
medal [medl] меда́ль *f*.
meddle [medl] (with, in) вме́шиваться [-ша́ться] (в В); **~some** [-səm] □ надое́дливый.
media|l ['mi:diəl] □, **~n** [-ən] сре́дний; среди́нный.
mediat|e ['mi:dieit] посре́дничать; **~ion** [mi:di'eiʃən] посре́дничество; **~or** ['mi:dieitə] посре́дник.
medical ['medikəl] □ медици́нский; враче́бный; ~ certificate больни́чный листо́к; медици́нское свиде́тельство; ~ man врач, ме́дик.
medicin|al [me'disinl] □ лека́рственный; целе́бный; **~e** ['med(i)sin] медици́на; лека́рство.
medi(a)eval [medi'i:vəl] □ средневеко́вый.
mediocre ['mi:dioukə] посре́дственный.
meditat|e ['mediteit] *v/i.* размышля́ть [-ы́слить]; *v/t.* обду́м(ывать (В); **~ion** [medi'teiʃən] размышле́ние; созерца́ние; **~ive** ['mediteitiv] □ созерца́тельный.
Mediterranean [meditə'reinjən] (и́ли ~ Sea) Средизе́мное мо́ре.
medium ['mi:diəm] 1. середи́на; сре́дство, спо́соб; ме́диум (у спири́тов); аге́нт; 2. сре́дний; уме́ренный.

medley ['medli] смесь *f*; ♪ попурри́ *n indecl.*
meek [mi:k] □ кро́ткий, мя́гкий; **~ness** ['miknis] кро́тость *f*, мя́гкость *f*.
meet [mi:t] [*irr.*] *v/t.* встреча́ть [-е́тить]; [по]знако́миться с (Т); удовлетворя́ть [-ри́ть] (тре́бования и т. п.); опла́чивать [-лати́ть] (долги́); go to ~ a p. идти́ навстре́чу (Д); *v/i.* [по]знако́миться; сходи́ться [сойти́сь], соб(и)ра́ться; ~ with испы́тывать [-пыта́ть] (В), подверга́ться [-ве́ргнуться] (Д); **~ing** ['mi:tiŋ] заседа́ние; встре́ча; ми́тинг, собра́ние.
melancholy ['melənkəli] **1.** уны́ние; грусть *f*; **2.** пода́вленный; уны́лый.
mellow ['melou] **1.** □ спе́лый; прия́тный на вкус; **2.** смягча́ть (-ся) [-чи́ть(ся)]; созре́(ва́)ть.
melo|dious [mi'loudjəs] □ мелоди́чный; **~dy** ['melədi] мело́дия.
melon ['melən] ⚘ ды́ня.
melt [melt] [рас]та́ять; [рас]пла́вить(ся); *fig.* смягча́ть(ся) [-чи́ть (-ся)].
member ['membə] член (*a. parl.*); **~ship** [-ʃip] чле́нство.
membrane ['membrein] плева́, оболо́чка; перепо́нка; ⊕ мембра́на.
memento [me'mentou] напомина́ние.
memoir ['memwɑ:] мемориа́лная статья́; ~s *pl.* мемуа́ры *m/pl.*
memorable ['memərəbl] □ незабве́нный.
memorandum [memə'rændəm] заме́тка; *pol.* мемора́ндум.
memorial [mi'mɔ:riəl] **1.** па́мятник; ~s *pl.* хро́ника; **2.** мемориа́льный.
memorize ['meməraiz] *part. Am.* зау́чивать наизу́сть.
memory ['meməri] па́мять *f*; воспомина́ние.
men [men] (*pl.* от man) лю́ди *m/pl.*; мужчи́ны *m/pl.*
menace ['menəs] **1.** угрожа́ть [-ози́ть], [по]грози́ть (Д; with Т); **2.** угро́за; опа́сность *f*.
mend [mend] **1.** *v/t.* исправля́ть [-а́вить]; [по]чини́ть; ~ one's ways исправля́ться [-а́виться]; *v/i.* улучша́ться [улу́чшиться]; поправля́ться [-а́виться]; **2.** почи́нка; on the ~ на попра́вку (о здоро́вье).
mendacious [men'deiʃəs] □ лжи́вый.
mendicant ['mendikənt] ни́щий; ни́щенствующий мона́х.
menial ['mi:niəl] *contp.* **1.** □ рабole-пный, лаке́йский; **2.** слуга́ *m*, лаке́й.
mental [mentl] □ у́мственный; психи́ческий; ~ arithmetic счёт в уме́; **~ity** [men'tæliti] спосо́бность мышле́ния; склад ума́.
mention ['menʃən] **1.** упомина́ние; **2.** упомина́ть [-мяну́ть] (В *or* о П); don't ~ it! не сто́ит!, не́ за что!
mercantile ['mə:kəntail] торго́вый, комме́рческий.
mercenary ['mə:sinəri] **1.** □ корыстный; наёмный; **2.** наёмник.
mercer ['mə:sə] торго́вец шёлком и ба́рхатом.
merchandise ['mə:tʃəndaiz] това́р (-ы *pl.*).
merchant ['mə:tʃənt] торго́вец, купе́ц; law ~ торго́вое пра́во; **~man** [-mən] торго́вое су́дно.
merci|ful ['mə:siful] □ милосе́рдный; **~less** [-lis] □ немилосе́рдный.
mercury ['mə:kjuri] ртуть *f*.
mercy [-si] милосе́рдие; сострада́ние; проще́ние; be at a p.'s ~ быть во вла́сти кого́-либо.
mere [miə] □ просто́й; сплошно́й; **~ly** то́лько, про́сто.
meretricious [meri'triʃəs] □ показно́й; мишу́рный; распу́тный.
merge [mə:dʒ] сли́(ва́)ть(ся) (in с Т); **~r** ['mə:dʒə] слия́ние, объедине́ние.
meridian [mə'ridiən] **1.** полу́денный; *fig.* вы́сший; **2.** по́лдень *m*; *geogr.* меридиа́н; *fig.* вы́сшая то́чка; расцве́т.
merit ['merit] **1.** заслу́га; досто́инство; make a ~ of a th. ста́вить что́-либо себе́ в заслу́гу; **2.** заслу́живать [-ужи́ть]; **~orious** [meri'tɔ:riəs] □ досто́йный награ́ды; похва́льный.
mermaid ['mə:meid] руса́лка, ная́да.
merriment ['merimənt] весе́лье.
merry ['meri] □ весёлый, ра́достный; make ~ весели́ться; **~-go-round** карусе́ль *f*; **~-making** весе́лье; пра́зднество.
mesh [meʃ] **1.** пе́тля; ~(es *pl.*) се́ти *f/pl.*; ⊕ be in ~ сцепля́ться [-пи́ться]; **2.** *fig.* опу́тывать сетя́ми; запу́таться в сетя́х.
mess[1] [mes] **1.** беспоря́док, пу́таница; неприя́тность *f*; каварда́к; make a ~ of a th. прова́ливать де́ло; **2.** *v/t.* приводи́ть в беспоря́док; *v/i.* F ~ about рабо́тать ко́е-ка́к.
mess[2] [~] ⚔ о́бщий стол; столо́вая.
message ['mesidʒ] сообще́ние; посла́ние; поруче́ние.
messenger ['mesindʒə] посы́льный; предве́стник.
met [met] *pt.* и *p. pt.* от meet.
metal ['metl] **1.** мета́лл; ще́бень *m*; **2.** мости́ть ще́бнем; **~lic** [mi'tælik] (~ally) металли́ческий; **~lurgy** ['metələ:dʒi] металлурги́я
meteor ['mi:tjə] метео́р; **~ology** [mi:tjə'rɔlədʒi] метеороло́гия.
meter ['mi:tə] счётчик; измери́тель *m.*

method ['meθəd] мéтод, спóсоб; систéма, порядок; **~ic**, *mst*. **~ical** □ [mi'θɔdik, -dikəl] систематический; методический, методичный.
meticulous [mi'tikjuləs] □ дотóшный; щепетильный.
metre ['mi:tə] метр.
metric ['metrik] (~ally) метрический; ~ system метрическая систéма.
metropoli|s [mi'trɔpəlis] столица; метропóлия; **~tan** [metrə'pɔlitən] столичный.
mettle [metl] темперáмент; пыл.
Mexican ['meksikən] 1. мексикáнский; 2. мексикáнец (-нка).
miauw [mi'au] [за]мяукать.
mice [mais] *pl.* мыши *f/pl.*
Michaelmas ['miklməs] Михáйлов день *m* (29 сентября).
micro... ['maikro] микро...
micro|phone ['maikrəfoun] микрофóн; **~scope** микроскóп.
mid [mid] срéдний; срединный; **~air**: in ~ высóкó в вóздухе; **~day** 1. пóлдень *m*; 2. полуденный.
middle [midl] 1. середина; 2. срéдний; ♀ Ages *pl.* срéдние векá *m/pl.*, средневекóвье; **~-aged** срéдних лет; **~-class** срéдняя буржуазия; **~man** посрéдник; **~-sized** срéдней величины; **~-weight** срéдний вéс (о бóксе); (боксёр) срéднего вéса.
middling ['midliŋ] посрéдственный.
middy ['midi] F = midshipman.
midge [midʒ] мóшка; **~t** ['midʒit] кáрлик; *attr.* миниатюрный.
mid|land ['midlənd] внутренняя часть страны; **~most** центрáльный; **~night** пóлночь *f*; **~riff** ['midrif] *anat.* диафрáгма; **~ship** мидель *m*; **~shipman** корабéльный гардемарин; **~st** [midst] середина; средá; in the ~ of среди (Р); in our ~ в нáшей средé; **~summer** середина лéта; **~way** на полпути; **~wife** акушéрка; **~wifery** ['midwifəri] акушéрство; **~winter** середина зимы.
mien [mi:n] мина (выражéние лицá).
might [mait] 1. мощь *f*; могущество; with ~ and main изо всех сил; 2. *pt.* и *p. pt.* от may; **~y** ['maiti] могущественный; громáдный.
migrat|e [mai'greit] мигрировать; **~ion** [-ʃən] миграция; перелёт; **~ory** ['maigrətəri] кочующий; перелётный.
mild [maild] □ мягкий; крóткий; слáбый (о напитке, табакé и т. п.).
mildew ['mildju:] ⚘ милдью *n indecl.*; плéсень *f*.
mildness ['maildnis] мягкость *f*; крóткость *f*.; умéренность *f*.
mile [mail] миля (= 1609,33 м).
mil(e)age ['mailidʒ] расстояние в милях.
milit|ary ['militəri] 1. □ вoéнный; вóинский; ♀ Government вoéнное правительство; 2. вoéнные; вoéнные влáсти *f/pl.*; **~ia** [mi'liʃə] милиция; ополчéние.
milk [milk] 1. молокó; powdered ~ молóчный порошóк; whole ~ цéльное молокó; 2. [вы]доить; **~maid** доярка; **~man** молóчник; **~sop** бесхарáктерный человéк, «тряпка»; **~y** ['milki] молóчный; ♀ Way Млéчный путь *m*.
mill[1] [mil] 1. мéльница; фáбрика, завóд; 2. [с]молóть; ⊕ [от]фрезеровáть (*im*)*pf*.
mill[2] [~] *Am.* (= 1/10 *cent*) милл (тысячная часть дóллара).
millepede ['milipi:d] *zo.* многонóжка.
miller ['milə] мéльник; ⊕ фрéзерный станóк; фрезерóвщик.
millet ['milit] ⚘ прóсо.
milliner ['milinə] модистка; **~y** [-ri] магазин дáмских шляп.
million ['miljən] миллиóн; **~aire** [miljə'nεə] миллионéр; **~th** ['miljənθ] 1. миллиóнный; 2. миллиóнная часть *f*.
mill-pond мéльничный пруд; **~stone** жёрнов.
milt [milt] молóки *f/pl.*
mimic ['mimik] 1. подражáтельный; 2. имитáтор; 3. пародировать (*im*)*pf*.; подражáть (Д); **~ry** [-ri] подражáние; *zo.* мимикрия.
mince [mins] 1. *v/t.* [из]рубить (мясо); he does not ~ matters он говорит без обиняков; *v/i.* говорить жемáнно; 2. рубленое мясо (*mst* ~d meat); **~meat** фарш из изюма, яблок и т. п.; **~-pie** пирóг (*s.* mincemeat).
mincing-machine мясорубка.
mind [maind] 1. ум, рáзум; мнéние; намéрение; охóта; пáмять *f*; to my ~ по моему мнéнию; out of one's ~ без умá; change one's ~ передум(ыв)ать; bear in ~ пóмнить, не забы(вá)ть; have a ~ to имéть желáние (+ *inf.*); have a th. on one's ~ беспокóиться о чём-либо; make up one's ~ решáться [-шиться]; 2. пóмнить; [по]забóтиться о (П); остерегáться [-рéчься] (Р); never ~! ничегó!; I don't ~ (it) я ничегó не имéю прóтив; would you ~ taking off your hat? будьте добры, снять шляпу; **~ful** ['maindful] □ (of) внимáтельный (к Д); забóтливый.
mine[1] [main] *pred.* мой *m*, моя *f*, моё *n*, мои *pl.*; 2. мои (родные) моя семья.
mine[2] [~] 1. рудник, копь *f*, шáхта; *fig.* истóчник; ⚔ мина; 2. добы(вá)ть; рыть; производить гóрные рабóты; ⚔ минировать

(*im*)*pf*.; подры́(ва́)ть; *fig*. подрыва́ть [подорва́ть]; **~r** ['mainə] горня́к, шахтёр.
mineral ['minərəl] **1.** минера́л; **~s** *pl*. минера́льные во́ды *f/pl*.; **2.** минера́льный.
mingle ['miŋgl] сме́шивать(ся) [-ша́ть(ся)].
miniature ['minjətʃə] **1.** миниатю́ра; **2.** миниатю́рный.
minim|ize ['minimaiz] доводи́ть до ми́нимума; *fig*. преуменьша́ть [-е́ньши́ть]; **~um** [-iməm] **1.** ми́нимум; **2.** минима́льный.
mining ['mainiŋ] го́рная промы́шленность *f*.
minister ['ministə] **1.** мини́стр; посла́нник; свяще́нник; **2.** *v/i*. соверша́ть богослуже́ние; [по-] служи́ть.
ministry ['ministri] служе́ние; министе́рство.
mink [miŋk] *zo*. но́рка.
minor ['mainə] **1.** мла́дший; ме́ньший; второстепе́нный; ♪ мино́рный; A ~ ля мино́р; **2.** несоверше́ннолетний; *Am. univ.* второстепе́нный предме́т; **~ity** [mai'nɔriti] несоверше́ннолетие; меньши́нство́.
minstrel ['minstrəl] менестре́ль *m*; **~s** *pl*. исполни́тели негритя́нских пе́сен.
mint [mint] ⚘ мя́та; моне́та; моне́тный двор; *fig*. «золото́е дно»; a ~ of money больша́я су́мма; **2.** [вы́-, от]чека́нить.
minuet [minju'et] ♪ менуэ́т.
minus ['mainəs] **1.** *prp*. без (P), ми́нус; **2.** *adj*. отрица́тельный.
minute **1.** [mai'nju:t] □ ме́лкий; незначи́тельный; подро́бный, дета́льный; **2.** ['minit] мину́та; моме́нт; **~s** *pl*. протоко́л; **~ness** [mai'nju:tnis] ма́лость *f*; то́чность *f*.
mirac|le ['mirəkl] чу́до; **~ulous** [mi'rækjuləs] □ чуде́сный.
mirage ['mirɑ:ʒ] мира́ж.
mire ['maiə] **1.** тряси́на; грязь *f*; **2.** завя́знуть в тряси́не.
mirror ['mirə] **1.** зе́ркало; **2.** отража́ть [отрази́ть].
mirth [mə:θ] весе́лье, ра́дость *f*; **~ful** ['mə:θful] □ весёлый, ра́достный; **~less** [-lis] □ безра́достный.
miry ['maiəri] то́пкий.
mis... [mis] *pref*. означа́ет непра́вильность и́ли недоста́ток, напр.: misadvise дать непра́вильный сове́т.
misadventure ['misəd'ventʃə] несча́стье; несча́стный слу́чай.
misanthrop|e ['mizənθroup], **~ist** [mi'zænθropist] мизантро́п, человеконенави́стник.
misapply ['misə'plai] злоупотребля́ть [-би́ть] (T); непра́вильно испо́льзовать.
misapprehend ['misæpri'hend] понима́ть оши́бочно.
misbehave ['misbi'heiv] ду́рно вести́ себя́.
misbelief ['misbi'li:f] заблужде́ние; е́ресь *f*.
miscalculate ['mis'kælkjuleit] ошиба́ться в расчёте; непра́вильно рассчи́тывать.
miscarr|iage ['mis'kæridʒ] неуда́ча; недоста́вка по а́дресу; вы́кидыш, або́рт; ~ of justice суде́бная оши́бка; **~y** [-ri] терпе́ть неуда́чу; сде́лать вы́кидыш.
miscellaneous [misi'leinjəs] □ сме́шанный; разносторо́нний.
mischief ['mistʃif] озорство́; прока́зы *f/pl*; вред; зло.
mischievous ['mistʃivəs] □ вре́дный; озорно́й, шаловли́вый.
misconceive ['miskən'si:v] непра́вильно понима́ть.
misconduct **1.** ['mis'kɔndəkt] дурно́е поведе́ние; плохо́е управле́ние; **2.** [-kən'dʌkt] пло́хо управля́ть (T); ~ o. s. ду́рно вести́ себя́.
misconstrue ['miskən'stru:] непра́вильно истолко́вывать.
miscreant ['miskriənt] негодя́й, злоде́й.
misdeed ['mis'di:d] злодея́ние.
misdemeano(u)r ['misdi'mi:nə] ⚖ суде́бно наказу́емый просту́пок.
misdirect ['misdi'rekt] неве́рно напра́вить; непра́вильно адресова́ть.
miser ['maizə] скупе́ц, скря́га *m/f*.
miserable ['mizərəbl] □ жа́лкий, несча́стный; убо́гий, ску́дный.
miserly ['maizəli] скупо́й.
misery ['mizəri] невзго́да, несча́стье, страда́ние; нищета́.
misfortune [mis'fɔ:tʃən] неуда́ча, несча́стье.
misgiving [mis'giviŋ] опасе́ние, предчу́вствие дурно́го.
misguide [mis'gaid] вводи́ть в заблужде́ние; непра́вильно напра́вить.
mishap ['mishæp] неуда́ча.
misinform ['misin'fɔ:m] непра́вильно информи́ровать.
misinterpret ['misin'tə:prit] неве́рно истолко́вывать.
mislay [mis'lei] [*irr*. (lay)] положи́ть не на ме́сто.
mislead [mis'li:d] [*irr*. (lead)] вводи́ть в заблужде́ние.
mismanage ['mis'mænidʒ] пло́хо управля́ть (T); [ис]по́ртить.
misplace ['mis'pleis] положи́ть не на ме́сто; *p.pt*. **~d** *fig*. неуме́стный.
misprint ['mis'print] **1.** непра́вильно печа́тать; сде́лать опеча́тку; **2.** опеча́тка.
misread ['mis'ri:d] [*irr*. (read)] чита́ть непра́вильно; непра́вильно истолко́вывать.
misrepresent ['misrepri'zent] представля́ть в ло́жном све́те.
miss[1] [mis] мисс, ба́рышня.

miss² [~] 1. про́мах; отсу́тствие; поте́ря; 2. *v/t.* упуска́ть [-сти́ть]; опа́здывать [-да́ть] на (В); прогляде́ть *pf.*, не заме́тить; не заста́ть до́ма; чу́вствовать отсу́тствие (кого́-либо); *v/i.* прома́хиваться [-хну́ться]; не попада́ть в цель.
missile ['misail] мета́тельный снаря́д; раке́та.
missing ['misiŋ] отсутствующий, недостающий; ⚔ бе́з вести пропа́вший; be ~ отсу́тствовать.
mission ['miʃən] ми́ссия, делега́ция; призва́ние; поруче́ние; *eccl.* миссионе́рская де́ятельность *f*; **~ary** ['miʃnəri] миссионе́р.
mis-spell ['mis'spel] [*a. irr.* (spell)] орфографи́чески непра́вильно писа́ть.
mist [mist] лёгкий тума́н; ды́мка.
mistake [mis'teik] 1. [*irr.* (take)] ошиба́ться [-би́ться]; непра́вильно понима́ть; принима́ть [-ня́ть] (for за (В); be ~n ошиба́ться [-би́ться]; 2. оши́бка; заблужде́ние; **~n** [ən] □ оши́бочный, непра́вильно по́нятый; неуме́стный.
mister ['mistə] ми́стер, господи́н (ста́вится перед фами́лией).
mistletoe ['misltou] ♣ оме́ла.
mistress ['mistris] хозя́йка до́ма; учи́тельница; мастери́ца; любо́вница; сокращённо: Mrs. ['misiz] ми́ссис, госпожа́ (ста́вится пе́ред фами́лией заму́жней же́нщины).
mistrust ['mis'trʌst] 1. не доверя́ть (Д); 2. недове́рие; **~ful** [-ful] □ недове́рчивый.
misty ['misti] □ тума́нный; нея́сный.
misunderstand ['misʌndə'stænd] [*irr.* (stand)] непра́вильно понима́ть; **~ing** [-iŋ] недоразуме́ние; размо́лвка.
misuse 1. ['mis'ju:z] злоупотребля́ть [-би́ть](Т); ду́рно обраща́ться с (Т); 2. [-'ju:s] злоупотребле́ние.
mite [mait] *zo.* клещ; ле́пта; малю́тка *m/f.*
mitigate ['mitigeit] смягча́ть [-чи́ть]; уменьша́ть [уме́ньши́ть].
mitre ['maitə] ми́тра.
mitten ['mitn] рукави́ца.
mix [miks] [с]меша́ть(ся); переме́шивать [-ша́ть]; враща́ться (в о́бществе); **~ed** переме́шанный, сме́шанный; разноро́дный; ~ up перепу́т(ыв)ать; be ~ed up with быть заме́шанным в (П); **~ture** ['mikstʃə] смесь *f.*
moan [moun] 1. стон; 2. [за]стона́ть.
moat [mout] крепостно́й ров.
mob [mɔb] 1. толпа́; чернь *f.* 2. [с]толпи́ться; напада́ть толпо́й на (В).
mobil|e ['moubail] подвижно́й; ⚔ моби́льный, подвижно́й; **~ization** [moubilai'zeiʃən] ⚔ мобилиза́ция; **~ize** ['moubilaiz] ⚔ мобилизова́ть (*im*)*pf.*;
moccasin ['mɔkəsin] мокаси́н (о́бувь инде́йцев).
mock [mɔk] 1. насме́шка; 2. подде́льный; мни́мый; 3. *v/t.* осме́ивать [-ея́ть]; *v/i.* ~ at насмеха́ться [-ея́ться] над (Т); **~ery** [-ri] насме́шка.
mode [moud] ме́тод, спо́соб; обы́чай; фо́рма; мо́да.
model [mɔdl] 1. моде́ль *f*; манеке́н; нату́рщик (-ица); *fig.* приме́р, образе́ц; *attr.* образцо́вый, приме́рный; 2. модели́ровать (*im*)*pf.*; [вы́]лепи́ть; оформля́ть [офо́рмить].
moderat|e 1. ['mɔdərit] □ уме́ренный; возде́ржанный; вы́держанный; 2. ['mɔdəreit] умеря́ть [уме́рить]; смягча́ть(ся) [-чи́ть(ся)]; **~ion** [mɔdə'reiʃən] уме́ренность *f*; воздержа́ние.
modern ['mɔdən] совреме́нный; **ize** [-aiz] модернизи́ровать (*im*)*pf.*
modest ['mɔdist] □ скро́мный; благопристо́йный; **~y** [-i] скро́мность *f.*
modi|fication [mɔdifi'keiʃən] видоизмене́ние; модифика́ция; **~fy** ['mɔdifai] видоизменя́ть [-ни́ть]; смягча́ть [-чи́ть].
modulate ['mɔdjuleit] модули́ровать.
moist [mɔist] вла́жный; **~en** ['mɔisn] увлажня́ть(ся) [-ни́ть(ся)]; **~ure** ['mɔistʃə] вла́жность; вла́га.
molar ['moulə] коренно́й зуб.
molasses [mə'læsiz] чёрная па́тока.
mole [moul] *zo.* крот; ро́динка; мол, да́мба.
molecule ['mɔlikju:l] моле́кула.
molest [mo'lest] приста́(ва́)ть к (Д).
mollify ['mɔlifai] успока́ивать [-ко́ить], смягча́ть [-чи́ть].
mollycoddle ['mɔlikɔdl] 1. не́женка *m/f.*; 2. изне́жи(ват)ь.
molten ['moultən] распла́вленный; лито́й.
moment ['moumənt] моме́нт, миг, мгнове́ние; = **~um**; **~ary** [-əri] □ momента́льный; кратковре́менный; **~ous** [mou'mentəs] □ ва́жный; **~um** [-təm] дви́жущая си́ла; *phys.* моме́нт.
monarch ['mɔnək] мона́рх; **~y** ['mɔnəki] мона́рхия.
monastery ['mɔnəstri] монасты́рь *m.*
Monday ['mʌndi] понеде́льник.
monetary ['mʌnitəri] моне́тный; валю́тный; де́нежный.
money ['mʌni] де́ньги *f/pl.*; readv ~ нали́чные де́ньги *f/pl*; **~-box** копи́лка; **~-changer** меня́ла *m*; **~-order** почто́вый де́нежный перево́д.
mongrel ['mʌŋgrəl] 1. *biol.* мети́с;

пóмесь *f*; дворня́жка; **2.** нечистокрóвный.
monitor ['mɔnitə] настáвник; ⚓ монитóр.
monk [mʌŋk] монáх.
monkey ['mʌŋki] **1.** обезья́на; ⊕ копрóвая бáба; **2.** F [по]дурáчиться; ~ with вози́ться с (Т); **~-wrench** ⊕ раздвижнóй гáечный ключ.
monkish ['mʌŋkiʃ] монáшеский.
mono|cle ['mɔnɔkl] монóкль *m*; **~gamy** [mɔ'nɔgəmi] единобрáчие; **~logue** [-lɔg] monолóг; **~polist** [mə'nɔpəlist] монополи́ст; **~polize** [-laiz] монополизи́ровать (*im*)*pf.*; *fig.* присвáивать себé (В); **~poly** [-li] монопóлия (Р); **~tonous** [mə'nɔtənəs] □ монотóнный; однозву́чный; **~tony** [-təni] монотóнность *f.*
monsoon [mɔn'su:n] муссóн.
monster ['mɔnstə] чудóвище; урóд; *fig.* и́зверг; *attr.* исполи́нский.
monstro|sity [mɔns'trɔsiti] чудóвищность *f*; урóдство; **~us** ['mɔnstrəs] □ урóдливый; чудóвищный.
month [mʌnθ] мéсяц; **~ly** ['mʌnθli] **1.** (еже)мéсячный; **2.** ежемéсячный журнáл.
monument ['mɔnjumənt] пáмятник; **~al** [mɔnju'mentl] □ монументáльный.
mood [mu:d] настроéние, расположéние ду́ха.
moody [mu:di] □ капри́зный; угрю́мый, уны́лый; не в ду́хе.
moon [mu:n] **1.** лунá, мéсяц; **2.** F проводи́ть врéмя в мечтáниях; **~light** лу́нный свет; **~lit** зали́тый лу́нным свéтом; **~struck** лунати́ческий.
Moor[1] [muə] мароккáнец (-нка); мавр(итáнка).
moor[2] [~] торфяни́стая мéстность, порóсшая вéреском.
moor[3] [~] ⚓ причáли(ва)ть; **~ings** ['muəriŋz] *pl.* ⚓ швартóвы *m/pl.*
moot [mu:t] : ~ point спóрный вопрóс.
mop [mɔp] **1.** швáбра; **2.** чи́стить швáброй.
mope [moup] хандри́ть.
moral ['mɔrəl] **1.** □ морáльный, нрáвственный; **2.** нравоучéние, морáль *f*; **~s** *pl.* нрáвы *m/pl.*; **~e** [mɔ'ra:l] *part.* ⚔ морáльное состоя́ние; **~ity** [mə'ræliti] морáль *f*, э́тика; **~ize** ['mɔrəlaiz] морализи́ровать.
morass [mə'ræs] болóто, тряси́на.
morbid ['mɔ:bid] □ болéзненный.
more [mɔ:] бóльше; бóлее; ещё; once ~ ещё раз; so much the ~ тем бóлее; no ~ бóльше не ...; **~over** [mɔ:'rouvə] сверх тогó, крóме тогó.
moribund ['mɔribʌnd] умирáющий.
morning ['mɔ:niŋ] у́тро; tomorrow ~ зáвтра у́тром; ~ **coat** визи́тка.
morose [mə'rous] □ угрю́мый.
morphia ['mɔ:fiə], **morphine** ['mɔ:fi:n] мóрфий.
morsel ['mɔ:səl] кусóчек.
mortal ['mɔ:tl] **1.** □ смéртный; смертéльный; **2.** смéртный, человéк; **~ity** [mɔ:'tæliti] смертéльность *f*; смéртность *f.*
mortar ['mɔ:tə] сту́пка; известкóвый раствóр; ⚔ морти́ра; миномёт.
mortgage ['mɔ:gidʒ] **1.** заклáд; ипотéка; закладнáя; **2.** заклáдывать [заложи́ть]; **~e** [mɔ:gə'dʒi:] кредитóр по закладнóй.
mortgag|er, ~or ['mɔ:gədʒə] должни́к по закладнóй.
morti|fication [mɔ:tifi'keiʃən] умерщвлéние (плóти); унижéние; **~fy** ['mɔ:tifai] умерщвля́ть [-рти́ть] (плоть); огорчáть [-чи́ть], унижáть [унизить].
morti|ce, ~se ['mɔ:tis] ⊕ гнездó шипá.
mortuary ['mɔ:tjuəri] мертвéцкая.
mosaic [mə'zeiik] мозáика.
moss [mɔs] мох; **~y** мши́стый.
most [moust] **1.** *adj.* □ наибóльший; **2.** *adv.* бóльше всегó; ~ beautiful сáмый краси́вый; **3.** наибóльшее коли́чество; бóльшая часть *f*; at (the) ~ сáмое бóльшее, не бóльше чем; **~ly** ['moustli] по бóльшей чáсти; глáвным óбразом; чáще всегó.
moth [mɔθ] моль *f*; мотылёк; **~-eaten** изъéденный мóлью.
mother ['mʌðə] **1.** мать *f*; **2.** относи́ться по-матери́нски к (Д); **~hood** ['mʌðəhud] матери́нство; **~-in-law** [-rinlɔ:] тёща; свекрóвь *f*; **~ly** [-li] матери́нский; **~-of-pearl** [-rəv'pə:l] перламу́тровый; **~-tongue** роднóй язы́к.
motif [mou'ti:f] моти́в.
motion ['mouʃən] **1.** движéние; ход; *parl.* предложéние; **2.** *v/t.* покáзывать жéстом; *v/i.* кивáть [кивну́ть] (to на В); **~less** [-lis] неподви́жный; **~-picture** *Am.* кино...; **~s** *pl.* фильм; кинó *n indecl.*
motive ['moutiv] **1.** дви́жущий; двигáтельный; **2.** пóвод, моти́в; **3.** побуждáть [-уди́ть]; мотиви́ровать (*im*)*pf.*; **~less** беспричи́нный.
motley ['mɔtli] разноцвéтный; пёстрый.
motor ['moutə] **1.** дви́гатель *m*, мотóр; = **~-car**; **2.** мотóрный; авто..., автомоби́льный; ~ mechanic, **~fitter** авторемóнтный мехáник; **3.** éхать (и́ли везти́) на автомоби́ле; **~-bicycle** мотоци́кл; **~-bus** автóбус; **~-car** автомоби́ль

m, F маши́на; **~-cycle** мотоци́кл; **~ing** ['moutəriŋ] автомоби́льное де́ло; автомоби́льный спорт; **~ist** [-rist] автомобили́ст(ка); **~lorry**, *Am.* **~truck** грузово́й автомоби́ль *m*, грузови́к.
mottled [mɔtld] кра́пчатый.
mould [mould] **1.** садо́вая земля́; по́чва; пле́сень *f*; фо́рма (лите́йная); шабло́н; склад, хара́ктер; **2.** отлива́ть в фо́рму; *fig.* [с]формирова́ть.
moulder ['mouldə] рассыпа́ться [-ы́паться].
moulding ['mouldiŋ] △ карни́з.
mouldy ['mouldi] запле́сневелый.
moult [moult] *zo.* [по]линя́ть.
mound [maund] на́сыпь *f*; холм; курга́н.
mount [maunt] **1.** гора́; ло́шадь под седло́м; **2.** *v/i.* восходи́ть [взойти́]; поднима́ться [-ня́ться]; сади́ться на ло́шадь; *v/t.* устана́вливать [-нови́ть] (ра́дио и т. п.), [с]монти́ровать; вставля́ть в ра́му (в опра́ву).
mountain ['mauntin] **1.** гора́; **2.** го́рный, наго́рный; **~eer** [maunti'niə] альпини́ст(ка); **~ous** ['mauntinəs] гори́стый.
mourn [mɔ:n] горева́ть; опла́к(ив)ать; **~er** ['mɔ:nə] скорбя́щий; **~ful** ['mɔ:nful] □ тра́урный; **~ing** ['mɔ:niŋ] тра́ур; плач; *attr.* тра́урный.
mouse [maus] (*pl.* mice) мышь *f*.
m(o)ustache [məs'tɑ:ʃ] усы́ *m/pl.*
mouth [mauθ], *pl.* **~s** [-z] рот, уста́ *n/pl.*; у́стье (реки́); вход (в га́вань); **~-organ** губна́я гармо́ника; **~piece** мундшту́к; *fig.* ру́пор.
move [mu:v] **1.** *v/t. com.* дви́гать [дви́нуть]; передвига́ть [-и́нуть]; тро́гать [тро́нуть]; вноси́ть [внести́] (предложе́ние); *v/i.* дви́гаться [дви́нуться]; переезжа́ть [перее́хать]; разви́(ва́)ться (о собы́тиях); идти́ [пойти́] (о дела́х); *fig.* враща́ться (в о́бществе и т. п.); ~ for a th. предлага́ть [-ложи́ть] что́-либо; ~ in въезжа́ть [въе́хать]; ~ on дви́гаться вперёд; **2.** движе́ние; перее́зд; ход (в игре́); *fig.* шаг; on the ~ на ходу́; make a ~ встать из-за стола́; предпринима́ть что́-либо; **~ment** ['mu:vmənt] движе́ние; ♪ темп, ритм; ♪ часть *f* (симфо́нии и т. п.); ⊕ ход (маши́ны).
movies ['mu:viz] *s. pl.* кино́ *n indecl.*
moving ['mu:viŋ] □ дви́жущийся; ~ staircase эскала́тор.
mow [mou] [*irr.*] [с]коси́ть; **~n** [-n] *p. pt.* от mow.
Mr ['mistə] *s.* mister.
Mrs ['misiz] *s.* mistress.
much [mʌtʃ] *adj.* мно́го; *adv.* мно́го, о́чень; I thought as ~ я так и ду́мал; make ~ of высоко́ цени́ть (В); I am not ~ of a dancer я нева́жно танцу́ю.
muck [mʌk] наво́з; *fig.* дрянь *f*.
mucus ['mju:kəs] слизь *f*.
mud [mʌd] грязь *f*; **~dle** [mʌdl] **1.** *v/t.* запу́тывать [-тать]; [с]пу́тать (*a.* ~ up, together); F опьяня́ть [-ни́ть]; *v/i.* халту́рить; де́йствовать без пла́на; **2.** F пу́таница, неразбери́ха; **~dy** ['mʌdi] гря́зный; **~-guard** крыло́.
muff [mʌf] му́фта; **~etee** [mʌfi'ti:] напу́льсник.
muffin ['mʌfin] сдо́бная бу́лка.
muffle ['mʌfl] глуши́ть, заглуша́ть [-ши́ть] (го́лос и т. п.); заку́т(ы-в)ать; **~r** [-ə] кашне́ *n indecl.*; *mot.* глуши́тель *m*.
mug [mʌg] кру́жка.
muggy ['mʌgi] ду́шный, вла́жный.
mulatto [mju'lætou] мула́т(ка).
mulberry ['mʌlbəri] ту́товое де́рево, шелкови́ца; ту́товая я́года.
mule [mju:l] мул; упря́мый челове́к; **~teer** [mju:li'tiə] пого́нщик му́лов.
mull[1] [mʌl] мусли́н.
mull[2] [~] *Am.*: ~ over обду́м(ы-в)ать; размышля́ть [-мы́слить].
mulled [mʌld]: ~ wine глинтве́йн.
multi|farious [mʌlti'fɛəriəs] □ разнообра́зный; **~form** ['mʌltifɔ:m] многообра́зный; **~ple** ['mʌltipl] **1.** ⅍ кра́тный; **2.** ⅍ кра́тное число́; многокра́тный; разнообра́зный; **~plication** [mʌltipli'keiʃən] умноже́ние; увеличе́ние; ~ table табли́ца умноже́ния; **~plicity** [-'plisiti] многочи́сленность *f*; разнообра́зие; **~ply** ['mʌltiplai] увели́чи(ва)ть(-ся); ⅍ умножа́ть [-о́жить]; **~tude** [-tju:d] мно́жество; ма́сса; толпа́; **~tudinous** [mʌlti'tju:dinəs] многочи́сленный.
mum [mʌm] ти́ше!
mumble [mʌmbl] [про]бормота́ть; с трудо́м жева́ть.
mummery ['mʌməri] пантоми́ма, маскара́д; *contp.* «представле́ние».
mumm|ify ['mʌmifai] мумифици́ровать; (*im*)*pf.*; **~y** ['mʌmi] му́мия.
mumps [mʌmps] *sg.* ⚕ сви́нка.
mundane ['mʌndein] □ мирско́й; све́тский.
municipal [mju'nisipəl] □ муниципа́льный; **~ity** [-nisi'pæliti] муниципалите́т.
munificen|ce [mju:'nifisns] ще́дрость *f*; **~t** [-t] ще́дрый.
murder ['mə:də] **1.** уби́йство; **2.** уби́(ва́)ть; *fig.* прова́ливать [-ли́ть] (пье́су и т. п.); **~er** [-rə] уби́йца; **~ess** [-ris] же́нщина-уби́йца; **~ous** [-rəs] □ уби́йственный.
murky ['mə:ki] □ тёмный; па́смурный.
murmur ['mə:mə] **1.** журча́ние; шо́рох (ли́стьев); ро́пот; **2.** [за-]журча́ть; ропта́ть.
murrain ['mʌrin] чума́ (рога́того скота́).

musc|le [mʌsl] му́скул, мы́шца; **~ular** ['mʌskjulə] му́скулистый; му́скульный.
Muse[1] [mju:z] му́за.
muse[2] [~] заду́м(ыв)аться (on над [Т).
museum [mju:'ziəm] музе́й.
mushroom ['mʌʃrum] **1.** гриб; **2.** расплю́щи(ва)ть(ся); *Am.* ~ up расти́ как грибы́.
music ['mju:zik] му́зыка; музыка́льное произведе́ние; но́ты *f/pl.*; set to ~ положи́ть на му́зыку; **~al** ['mju:zikəl] □ музыка́льный; мелоди́чный; ~ box шарма́нка; **~-hall** мю́зик-холл, эстра́дный теа́тр; **~ian** [mju:'ziʃən] музыка́нт (-ша); **~stand** пюпи́тр для нот; **~-stool** табуре́т для роя́ля.
musketry ['mʌskitri] руже́йный ого́нь *m*; стрелко́вая подгото́вка.
muslin ['mʌzlin] мусли́н (ткань).
mussel [mʌsl] ми́дия.
must [mʌst]: I ~ я до́лжен (+ *inf.*); I ~ not мне нельзя́; **2.** виногра́дное су́сло; пле́сень *f.*
mustache *Am.* усы́ *m/pl.*
mustard ['mʌstəd] горчи́ца.
muster ['mʌstə] **1.** смотр, осмо́тр; ⚔ сбор; **2.** проверя́ть [-е́рить].
musty ['mʌsti] за́тхлый.
muta|ble ['mju:təbl] □ изме́нчивый, непостоя́нный; **~tion** [mju:'teiʃən] измене́ние, переме́на.
mute [mju:t] **1.** □ немо́й; **2.** немо́й; стати́ст; **3.** надева́ть сурди́нку на (В).
mutilat|e ['mju:tileit] [из]уве́чить; **~ion** [-'eiʃən] уве́чье.
mutin|eer [mju:ti'niə] мяте́жник; **~ous** ['mju:tinəs] □ мяте́жный; **~y** [-ni] **1.** мяте́ж; **2.** поднима́ть мяте́ж.
mutter ['mʌtə] **1.** бормота́нье; ворча́ние; **2.** [про]бормота́ть; [за-] ворча́ть.
mutton [mʌtn] бара́нина; leg of ~ бара́нья но́жка; ~ chop бара́нья котле́та.
mutual ['mju:tjuəl] □ обою́дный, взаи́мный; о́бщий.
muzzle ['mʌzl] **1.** мо́рда, ры́ло; ду́ло, жерло́; намо́рдник; **2.** надева́ть намо́рдник (Д); *fig.* заста́вить молча́ть.
my [mai, *a.* mi] *pron. poss.* мой *m*, моя́ *f*, моё *n*; мои́ *pl.*
myrtle [mə:tl] ⚘ мирт.
myself [mai'self, mi-] *pron. refl.* **1.** себя́, меня́ самого́; -ся, -сь; **2.** (для усиле́ния) сам.
myster|ious [mis'tiəriəs] □ таи́нственный; **~y** [-ri] та́йна; та́инство.
mysti|c ['mistik] (*a.* **~al** [-ikəl] □) мисти́ческий; **~fy** [-tifai] мистифици́ровать (*im*)*pf.*; озада́чи(ва)ть.
myth [miθ] миф; мифи́ческое лицо́.

N

nab [næb] *sl.* схвати́ть на ме́сте преступле́ния.
nacre ['neikə] перламу́тр.
nag [næg] F **1.** кля́ча; **2.** прид(и)ра́ться к (Д).
nail [neil] **1.** *anat.* но́готь *m*; гвоздь *m*; **2.** заби́(ва́)ть гвоздя́ми, пригвожда́ть [-озди́ть], приби́(ва́)ть; *fig.* прико́вывать [-ова́ть].
naïve [nai'i:v, nɑ:'iv] □, **naive** [neiv] □ наи́вный; безыску́сственный.
naked ['neikid] □ наго́й, го́лый; я́вный; **~ness** [-nis] нагота́; обнажённость *f.*
name [neim] **1.** и́мя *n*; фами́лия; назва́ние; of (F by) the ~ of под и́менем (Р), по и́мени (И); in the ~ of во и́мя (Р); от и́мени (Р); call a p. ~s [об]руга́ть (В); **2.** наз(ы)ва́ть; дава́ть и́мя (Д); **~less** ['neimlis] □ безымя́нный; **~ly** [-li] и́менно; **~-plate** доще́чка с фами́лией; **~sake** тёзка *m/f.*
nap [næp] **1.** ворс; лёгкий сон; **2.** дрема́ть [вздремну́ть].
nape [neip] заты́лок.
napkin ['næpkin] салфе́тка; подгу́зник.
narcotic [nɑ:'kɔtik] **1.** (**~ally**) наркоти́ческий; **2.** нарко́тик.
narrat|e [næ'reit] расска́зывать [-за́ть]; **~ion** [-ʃən] расска́з; **~ive** ['nærətiv] **1.** □ повествова́тельный; **2.** расска́з.
narrow ['nærou] **1.** □ у́зкий; те́сный; ограни́ченный (об интелле́кте); **2.** **~s** *pl.* проли́в; **3.** су́живать(ся) [су́зить(ся)]; уменьша́ть (-ся) [уме́ньши́ть(ся)]; ограни́чи(ва)ть; **~-chested** узкогру́дый; **~-minded** □ ограни́ченный, у́зкий; недалёкий; **~ness** [-nis] у́зость *f.*
nasal ['neizəl] □ носово́й; гнуса́вый.
nasty ['nɑ:sti] □ проти́вный; неприя́тный; гря́зный; зло́бный.
natal ['neitl]: ~ day день рожде́ния.
nation ['neiʃən] на́ция.
national ['næʃnl] **1.** □ национа́льный, наро́дный; госуда́рственный; **2.** соотéчественник; по́дданный; **~ity** [næʃə'næliti] национа́льность *f*; по́дданство; **~ize** ['næʃnəlaiz] национализи́ровать (*im*)*pf.*; натурализова́ть (*im*)*pf.*
native ['neitiv] **1.** □ родно́й; ту-

зе́мный; ~ language родно́й язы́к; 2. уроже́нец (-нка); тузе́мец (-мка).
natural ['nætʃrəl] □ есте́ственный; ~ sciences есте́ственные нау́ки *f/pl.*; **~ist** [-ist] натурали́ст (в иску́сстве); естествоиспыта́тель *m*; **~ize** [-aiz] натуралызова́ть (*im*)*pf.*; **~ness** [-nis] есте́ственность *f.*
nature ['neitʃə] приро́да; хара́ктер.
naught [nɔ:t] ничто́; но́ль *m*; set at ~ пренебрега́ть [-бре́чь] (Т); **~y** ['nɔ:ti] □ непослу́шный, капри́зный.
nause|a ['nɔ:siə] тошнота́; отвраще́ние; **~ate** [-eit] *v/t.* тошни́ть; it ~s me меня́ тошни́т от э́того; внуша́ть отвраще́ние (Д); be ~d испы́тывать тошноту́; *v/i.* чу́вствовать тошноту́; **~ous** [-əs] □ тошнотво́рный.
nautical ['nɔ:tikəl] морско́й; морехо́дный.
naval ['neivəl] (вое́нно-)морско́й.
nave [neiv] ⚠ неф (це́ркви).
navel ['neivəl] пуп, пупо́к.
naviga|ble ['nævigəbl] □ судохо́дный; **~te** [-geit] *v/i.* управля́ть (су́дном, аэропла́ном); пла́вать (на су́дне); лета́ть (на аэропла́не); *v/t.* управля́ть (су́дном и т. д.); пла́вать по (Д); **~tion** [nævi'geiʃən] морехо́дство; навига́ция; **~tor** ['nævigeitə] мореплава́тель *m*; шту́рман.
navy ['neivi] вое́нный флот.
nay [nei] нет; да́же; бо́лее того́.
near [niə] 1. *adj.* бли́зкий; бли́жний; скупо́й; ~ at hand под руко́й; ~ silk полушёлк; 2. *adv.* по́дле; бли́зко, недалеко́; почти́; 3. *prp.* о́коло (Р), у (Р); 4. приближа́ться [-ли́зиться] к (Д); **~by** ['niə'bai] ря́дом; **~ly** ['niəli] почти́; **~ness** [-nis] бли́зость *f.*
neat [ni:t] □ чи́стый, опря́тный; стро́йный; иску́сный; кра́ткий; **~ness** ['ni:tnis] опря́тность *f* и т. д.
nebulous ['nebjuləs] □ о́блачный; тума́нный.
necess|ary ['nesisəri] 1. □ необходи́мый, ну́жный; 2. необходи́мое; **~itate** [ni'sesiteit] де́лать необходи́мым; **~ity** [-ti] необходи́мость *f*, нужда́.
neck [nek] ше́я; го́рлышко (буты́лки и т. п.); вы́рез (в пла́тье); ~ of land перешеек; ~ and ~ голова́ в го́лову; **~band** во́рот (руба́шки); **~erchief** ['nekətʃif] ше́йный плато́к; **~lace** [-lis] ожере́лье; **~tie** га́лстук.
née [nei] урождённая.
need [ni:d] 1. на́добность *f*; потре́бность *f*; нужда́; недоста́ток; be in ~ of нужда́ться в (П); 2. бе́дствовать; нужда́ться в (П); I ~ it мне э́то ну́жно; **~ful** ['ni:dful] □ ну́жный.
needle ['ni:dl] игла́, иго́лка; спи́ца (вяза́льная).
needless ['ni:dlis] □ нену́жный.
needlewoman швея́.
needy ['ni:di] □ нужда́ющийся; бе́дствующий.
nefarious [ni'feəriəs] бесче́стный.
negat|ion [ni'geiʃən] отрица́ние; **~ive** ['negətiv] 1. □ отрица́тельный; негати́вный *f*; 2. отрица́ние; *phot.* негати́в; 3. отрица́ть.
neglect [ni'glekt] 1. пренебреже́ние; небре́жность *f*; 2. пренебрега́ть [-бре́чь] (Т); **~ful** [-ful] □ небре́жный.
negligen|ce ['neglidʒəns] небре́жность *f*; **~t** [-t] □ небре́жный.
negotia|te [ni'gouʃieit] вести́ перегово́ры; догова́риваться [-вори́ться] о (П); F преодоле́(ва́)ть; **~tion** [nigouʃi'eiʃən] перегово́ры *m/pl.*; преодоле́ние (затрудне́ний); **~tor** [ni'gouʃieitə] лицо́, веду́щее перегово́ры.
negr|ess ['ni:gris] негритя́нка; **~o** ['ni:grou], *pl.* ~es [-z] негр.
neigh [nei] 1. ржа́ние; 2. [за]ржа́ть.
neighbo(u)r ['neibə] сосе́д(ка); **~hood** [-hud] сосе́дство; **~ing** [-riŋ] сосе́дний, сме́жный.
neither ['neiðə] 1. ни тот, ни друго́й; 2. *adv.* та́кже не; ~ ... nor ... ни ... ни...
nephew ['nevju:] племя́нник.
nerve [nə:v] 1. нерв; му́жество, хладнокро́вие; на́глость *f*; 2. придава́ть си́лы (хра́брости) (Д); **~less** ['nə:vlis] □ беcси́льный, вя́лый.
nervous ['nə:vəs] □ не́рвный; нерво́зный; си́льный; **~ness** [-nis] не́рвность *f*, нерво́зность *f*; эне́ргия.
nest [nest] 1. гнездо́ (*a. fig.*); 2. вить гнездо́; **~le** [nesl] *v/i.* удо́бно устро́иться; приж(им)а́ться (to, on, against к Д); *v/t.* приж(им)а́ть (го́лову).
net[1] [net] 1. сеть *f*; 2. расставля́ть се́ти; пойма́ть и́ли покры́ть се́тью.
net[2] [~] 1. не́тто *adj. indecl.*, чи́стый (вес, дохо́д); 2. приноси́ть (и́ли получа́ть) чи́стого дохо́да.
nettle [netl] 1. ⚘ крапи́ва; 2. обжига́ть крапи́вой; *fig.* уязвля́ть [-ви́ть].
network ['netwə:k] плетёнка; сеть *f* (желе́зных доро́г, радиоста́нций и т. п.).
neuter ['nju:tə] 1. *gr.* сре́дний; ⚘ беспо́лый; 2. сре́дний род; кастри́рованное живо́тное.
neutral ['nju:trəl] 1. □ нейтра́льный; сре́дний, неопределённый; 2. нейтра́льное госуда́рство; граждани́н нейтра́льного госуда́рства; **~ity** [nju'træliti] нейтралите́т; **~ize** ['nju:trəlaiz] нейтрализова́ть (*im*)*pf.*
never ['nevə] никогда́; совсе́м не; **~more** никогда́ бо́льше; **~theless** [nevəðə'les] тем не ме́нее; несмотря́ на э́то.

new [nju:] нóвый; молодóй (об овощáх); свéжий; **~-comer** новоприбы́вший; **~ly** ['nju:li] зáново, вновь; недáвно.
news [nju:z] нóвости *f/pl.*, извéстия *n/pl.*; **~-agent** газéтчик; **~-boy** газéтчик-разнóсчик; **~-monger** сплéтник (-ица); **~-paper** газéта; **~-print** газéтная бумáга; **~-reel** киножурнáл; **~stall,** *Am.* **~-stand** газéтный киóск.
New Year Нóвый год; **~'s Eve** канýн Нóвого гóда.
next [nekst] **1.** *adj.* слéдующий; ближáйший; ~ door to *fig.* чуть (ли) не, почти́; ~ to вóзле (Р); вслед за (Т); **2.** *adv.* потóм, пóсле; в слéдующий раз.
nibble [nibl] *v/t.* обгры́з(á)ть; [о]щипáть (*a. v/i.* ~ at); *v/i.* ~ at *fig.* прид(и)рáться к (Д).
nice [nais] □ прия́тный, ми́лый, слáвный; хорóшенький; тóнкий; привередливый; **~ty** ['naisiti] тóчность *f*; разбóрчивость *f*; *pl.* тóнкости *f/pl.*, детáли *f/pl.*
niche [nitʃ] ни́ша.
nick [nik] **1.** зарýбка; in the ~ of time как раз вó-время; **2.** сдéлать зарýбку в (П); поспéть вó-время на (В).
nickel [nikl] **1.** *min.* ни́кель *m*; *Am.* монéта в 5 цéнтов; **2.** [от]никелировáть.
nickname ['nikneim] **1.** прóзвище; **2.** да(вá)ть прóзвище (Д).
niece [ni:s] племя́нница.
niggard ['nigəd] скупéц; **~ly** [-li] скупóй, скáредный.
night [nait] ночь *f*, вéчер; by ~, at ~ нóчью, вéчером; **~-club** ночнóй клуб; **~fall** сýмерки *f/pl.*; **~-dress, ~gown** (жéнская) ночнáя сорóчка; **~ingale** ['naitiŋgeil] соловéй; **~ly** ['naitli] ночнóй; *adv.* нóчью; еженóщно; **~mare** кошмáр; **~-shirt** ночнáя рубáшка.
nil [nil] *particul. sport* ноль *m or* нуль *m*; ничегó.
nimble [nimbl] □ провóрный, лóвкий; живóй.
nimbus ['nimbəs] сия́ние, ореóл.
nine [nain] дéвять; **~pins** *pl.* кéгли *f/pl.*; **~teen** ['nain'ti:n] девятнáдцать; **~ty** ['nainti] девянóсто.
ninny ['nini] F простофи́ля *m/f.*
ninth [nainθ] **1.** девя́тый; **2.** девя́тая часть *f*; **~ly** ['nainθli] в-девя́тых.
nip [nip] **1.** щипóк; укýс; си́льный морóз; **2.** щипáть [щипнýть]; прищемля́ть [-ми́ть]; поби́ть морóзом; ~ in the bud пресекáть в зарóдыше.
nipper ['nipə] клешня́; (a pair of) **~s** *pl.* щипцы́ *m/pl.*
nipple [nipl] сосóк.
nitre ['naitə] ⚗ сели́тра.
nitrogen ['naitridʒən] азóт.
no [nou] **1.** *adj.* никакóй; in ~ time в мгновéние óка; ~ one никтó; **2.** *adv.* нет; **3.** отрицáние.
nobility [nou'biliti] дворя́нство; благорóдство.
noble ['noubl] **1.** □ благорóдный; знáтный; **2.** = **~man** титулóванное лицó, дворяни́н; **~ness** ['noublnis] благорóдство.
nobody ['noubədi] никтó.
nocturnal [nɔk'tə:nl] ночнóй.
nod [nɔd] **1.** кивáть головóй; дремáть, «клевáть нóсом»; **2.** кивóк головóй.
node [noud] ♀ ýзел; ⚕ нарóст, утолщéние.
noise [nɔiz] **1.** шум, гам; грóхот; **2.** ~ abroad разглашáть [-ласи́ть]; **~less** ['nɔizlis] □ бесшýмный.
noisome ['nɔisəm] врéдный; нездорóвый; зловóнный.
noisy ['nɔizi] □ шýмный; шумли́вый; *fig.* кричáщий (о крáсках).
nomin|al ['nɔminl] □ номинáльный; именнóй; ~ value номинáльная ценá; **~ate** ['nɔmineit] назначáть [-знáчить]; выставля́ть [вы́ставить] (кандидáта); **~ation** [nɔmi'neiʃən] выставлéние (кандидáта); назначéние.
non [nɔn] *prf.* не..., бес..., без...
nonage ['nounidʒ] несовершеннолéтие.
non-alcoholic безалкогóльный.
nonce [nɔns]: for the ~ тóлько для дáнного слýчая.
non-commissioned ['nɔnkə'miʃənd]: ~ officer сержáнт, ýнтер-офицéр.
non-committal уклóнчивый.
non-conductor ⚡ непроводни́к.
nonconformist ['nɔnkən'fɔ:mist] человéк не подчиня́ющийся óбщим прáвилам.
nondescript ['nɔndiskript] неопределённый; неопредели́мый.
none [nʌn] **1.** ничтó, никтó; ни оди́н; никакóй; **2.** нискóлько, совсéм не ...; ~ the less тем не мéнее.
nonentity [nɔ'nentiti] небытиé; ничтóжество (о человéке); фи́кция.
non-existence небытиé.
non-party ['nɔn'pɑ:ti] беспарти́йный.
non-performance неисполнéние.
nonplus [-'plʌs] **1.** замешáтельство; **2.** приводи́ть в замешáтельство.
non-resident не проживáющий в дáнном мéсте.
nonsens|e ['nɔnsəns] вздор, бессмы́слица; **~ical** [nɔn'sensikəl] □ бессмы́сленный.
non-skid ['nɔn'skid] приспособлéние прóтив буксовáния колёс.
non-stop безостанóвочный; ✈ беспосáдочный.
non-union не состоя́щий члéном профсою́за.
noodle ['nu:dl]: **~s** *pl.* лапшá.

nook [nuk] укрóмный уголóк; закоýлок.

noon [nu:n] пóлдень *m* (*a.* ~day, ~tide, ~time).

noose [nu:s] 1. пéтля; аркáн; 2. ловить арканом; вéшать [повéсить].

nor [nɔ:] и не; тáкже не; ни.

norm [nɔ:m] нóрма; стандáрт, образéц; **~al** ['nɔ:məl] □ нормáльный; **~alize** [-aiz] нормировáть (*im*)*pf*.; нормализовáть (*im*)*pf*.

north [nɔ:θ] 1. сéвер; 2. сéверный; 3. *adv*. ~ of к сéверу от (Р); **~-east** 1. сéверо-востóк; 2. сéверо-востóчный (*a*. **~-eastern** [-ən]); **~erly** ['nɔ:ðəli], **~ern** ['nɔ:ðən] сéверный; **~ward(s)** ['nɔ:θwəd(z)] *adv*. на сéвер; к сéверу; **~-west** 1. сéверо-зáпад; ⚓ норд-вéст; 2. сéверо-зáпадный (*a*. **~-western** [-ən]).

nose [nouz] 1. нос; нóсик (чáйника и т. п.); чутьё; нос (лóдки и т. п.); 2. *v/t*. [по]нюхать; разнюх(ив)ать; **~-dive** ✈ пикирóвка; **~gay** букéт цветóв.

nostril ['nɔstril] ноздря́.

nosy ['nouzi] F любопы́тный.

not [nɔt] не.

notable ['noutəbl] 1. □ достопримечáтельный; 2. выдающийся человéк.

notary ['noutəri] нотáриус (*a*. ~ public).

notation [nou'teiʃən] нотáция; зáпись *f*.

notch [nɔtʃ] 1. зарýбка; зазýбрина; 2. зарубáть [-бить]; зазýбри(ва)ть.

note [nout] 1. замéтка; зáпись *f*; примечáние; долговáя распи́ска; (дипломати́ческая) нóта; ♪ нóта; репутáция; внимáние; 2. замечáть [-éтить]; упоминáть [-мянýть]; (*a* ~ down) дéлать замéтки, запи́сывать [-сáть]; отмечáть [-éтить]; **~book** записнáя кни́жка; **~d** ['noutid] хорошó извéстный; **~-worthy** достопримечáтельный.

nothing ['nʌθiŋ] ничтó, ничегó; for ~ зря, дáром; bring (come) to ~ свести́ (сойти́) на нет.

notice ['noutis] 1. внимáние; извещéние, уведомлéние; предупреждéние; at short ~ без предупреждéния; give ~ предупреждáть об увольнéнии (и́ли об ухóде); извещáть [-ести́ть]; 2. замечáть [-éтить]; обращáть внимáние на (В); **~able** ['noutisəbl] □ достóйный внимáния; замéтный.

noti|fication [noutifi'keiʃən] извещéние, сообщéние; объявлéние; **~fy** ['noutifai] извещáть [-ести́ть], уведомля́ть [увéдомить].

notion ['nouʃən] поня́тие, представлéние; ~s *pl*. *Am*. галантерéя.

notorious [nou'tɔ:riəs] □ преслóвутый.

notwithstanding [nɔtwiθ'stændiŋ] несмотря́ на (В), вопреки́ (Д).

nought [nɔ:t] ничтó; ⅍ ноль *m* or нуль *m*.

nourish ['nʌriʃ] питáть (*a*. *fig*.); [на-, по]корми́ть; *fig*. [вз]лелéять (надéжду и т. п.); **~ing** [-iŋ] питáтельный; **~ment** [-mənt] питáние; пи́ща (*a*. *fig*.).

novel ['nɔvəl] 1. нóвый; необы́чный; 2. ромáн; **~ist** [-ist] романи́ст (áвтор); **~ty** ['nɔvəlti] нови́нка; новизнá.

November [no'vembə] ноя́брь *m*.

novice ['nɔvis] начинáющий; новичóк; *eccl*. послýшник (-ица).

now [nau] 1. тепéрь, сейчáс; тóтчас; just ~ тóлько что; ~ and again (и́ли then) от врéмени до врéмени; 2. *cj*. когдá, раз.

nowadays ['nauədeiz] в нáше врéмя.

nowhere ['nouwɛə] нигдé, никудá.

noxious ['nɔkʃəs] □ врéдный.

nozzle [nɔzl] нóсик (чáйника и т.п.); ⊕ соплó.

nucle|ar ['nju:kliə] я́дерный; ~ pile я́дерный реáктор; **~us** [-s] ядрó.

nude [nju:d] нагóй; *paint*. обнажённая фигýра.

nudge [nʌdʒ] F 1. подтáлкивать лóктем; 2. лёгкий толчóк лóктем.

nuisance [nju:sns] неприя́тность *f*; досáда; *fig*. надоéдливый человéк.

null [nʌl] невырази́тельный; недействи́тельный; ~ and void потеря́вший закóнную си́лу (о договóре); **~ify** ['nʌlifai] аннули́ровать (*im*)*pf*.; **~ity** [-ti] ничтóжность *f*; ничтóжество (о человéке); ⚖ недействи́тельность *f*.

numb [nʌm] 1. онемéлый, оцепенéлый; окоченéлый; 2. вызывáть онемéние (и́ли окоченéние) (Р).

number ['nʌmbə] 1. числó; нóмер; 2. [за]нумеровáть; насчи́тывать; **~less** [-lis] бесчи́сленный.

numera|l ['nju:mərəl] 1. и́мя числи́тельное; ци́фра; 2. числовóй; **~tion** [nju:mə'reiʃən] исчислéние; нумерáция.

numerical [nju:'merikəl] □ числовóй; цифровóй.

numerous ['nju:mərəs] □ многочи́сленный.

nun [nʌn] монáхиня; *zo*. синица-лазóревка.

nunnery ['nʌnəri] жéнский монасты́рь *m*.

nuptial ['nʌpʃəl] 1. брáчный, свáдебный; 2. **~s** [-z] *pl*. свáдьба.

nurse [nə:s] 1. корми́лица (*mst* wet-~); ня́ня (*a*. ~-maid); сидéлка (в больни́це); медици́нская сестрá; at ~ на попечéнии ня́ни; 2. корми́ть, вскáрмливать грýдью; ня́нчить; ухáживать за (Т); **~ry** ['nə:sri] дéтская (кóмната); ⚘ питóмник, рассáдник; ~ school дéтский сад.

nurs(e)ling ['nə:sliŋ] питóмец (-мица).

nurture ['nə:tʃə] **1.** пита́ние; воспита́ние; **2.** пита́ть; воспи́тывать [-та́ть].
nut [nʌt] оре́х; ⊕ га́йка; **~s** *pl.* ме́лкий у́голь *m*; **~cracker** щипцы́ для оре́хов; щелку́нчик; **~meg** ['nʌtmeg] муска́тный оре́х.
nutri|tion [nju:'triʃən] пита́ние; пи́ща; **~tious** [-ʃəs], **~tive** ['nju:tritiv] □ пита́тельный.
nut|shell оре́ховая скорлупа́; **in a ~** кра́тко, в двух слова́х; **~ty** ['nʌti] име́ющий вкус оре́ха; щегольско́й.
nymph [nimf] ни́мфа.

O

oaf [ouf] дурачо́к; неуклю́жий челове́к.
oak [ouk] дуб.
oar [ɔ:] **1.** весло́; **2.** *poet.* грести́; **~sman** ['ɔ:zmən] гребе́ц.
oasis [ou'eisis] оа́зис.
oat [out] овёс (*mst* **~s** *pl.*).
oath [ouθ] кля́тва; ⚔, ⚖ прися́га; руга́тельство.
oatmeal ['outmi:l] овся́нка (крупа́).
obdurate ['ɔbdjurit] □ закосне́лый.
obedien|ce [o'bi:djəns] послуша́ние, повинове́ние; **~t** [-t] □ послу́шный, поко́рный.
obeisance [o'beisəns] ни́зкий покло́н,264 реверáнс; почте́ние; **do ~** выража́ть почте́ние.
obesity [ou'bi:siti] ту́чность *f*, полнота́.
obey [o'bei] повинова́ться (*im*)*pf.* (Д); [по]слу́шаться (Р).
obituary [o'bitjuəri] некроло́г; спи́сок уме́рших.
object 1. ['ɔbdʒikt] предме́т, вещь *f*; объе́кт; *fig.* цель *f*, наме́рение; **2.** [əb'dʒekt] не люби́ть, не одобря́ть (Р); возража́ть [-рази́ть] (to про́тив Р).
objection [əb'dʒekʃən] возраже́ние; **~able** [-əbl] □ нежела́тельный; неприя́тный.
objective [ɔb'dʒektiv] **1.** □ объекти́вный; целево́й; **2.** ⚔ объе́кт, цель *f*.
object-lens *opt.* ли́нза объекти́ва.
obligat|ion [ɔbli'geiʃən] обяза́тельство; обя́занность *f*; **~ory** [ɔ'bligətəri] □ обяза́тельный.
oblig|e [ə'blaidʒ] обя́зывать [-за́ть]; принужда́ть [-у́дить]; **~ a p.** де́лать одолже́ние кому́-либо; **much ~d** о́чень благода́рен (-рна); **~ing** [-iŋ] □ услу́жливый, любе́зный.
oblique [o'bli:k] □ косо́й; око́льный; *gr.* ко́свенный.
obliterate [o'blitəreit] изгла́живать(ся) [-ла́дить(ся)]; вычёркивать [вы́черкнуть].
oblivi|on [o'bliviən] забве́ние; **~ous** [-əs] □ забы́вчивый.
obnoxious [əb'nɔkʃəs] □ неприя́тный, проти́вный, несно́сный.
obscene [ɔb'si:n] □ непристо́йный.
obscur|e [əb'skjuə] **1.** □ тёмный; мра́чный; нея́сный; неизве́стный; непоня́тный; **2.** затемня́ть [-ни́ть]; **~ity** [-riti] мрак, темнота́ и т. д.
obsequies ['ɔbsikwiz] *pl.* погребе́ние.
obsequious [əb'si:kwiəs] □ раболе́пный, подобостра́стный.
observ|able [əb'zə:vəbl] □ заме́тный; **~ance** [-vəns] соблюде́ние (зако́на, обря́да и т. п.); обря́д; **~ant** [-vənt] □ наблюда́тельный; **~ation** [ɔbzə'veiʃən] наблюде́ние; наблюда́тельность *f*; замеча́ние; **~atory** [əb'zə:vətri] обсервато́рия; **~e** [əb'zə:v] *v/t.* наблюда́ть; *fig.* соблюда́ть [-юсти́]; замеча́ть [-е́тить] (В); *v/i.* замеча́ть [-е́тить].
obsess [əb'ses] завладе́(ва́)ть (Т); **~ed by,** *a.* **with** одержи́мый (Т); пресле́дуемый (Т).
obsolete ['ɔbsoli:t, -səl-] устаре́лый.
obstacle ['ɔbstəkl] препя́тствие.
obstinate ['ɔbstinit] □ упря́мый.
obstruct [əb'strʌkt] [по]меша́ть (Д), затрудня́ть [-ни́ть]; загражда́ть [-ради́ть]; **~ion** [əb'strʌkʃən] препя́тствие, поме́ха; загражде́ние; обстру́кция; **~ive** [-tiv] меша́ющий; обструкцио́нный.
obtain [əb'tein] *v/t.* добы́(ва́)ть, доста́(ва́)ть; *v/i.* быть в обы́чае; **~able** [-əbl] † получа́емый; достижи́мый.
obtru|de [əb'tru:d] навя́зывать(ся) [-за́ть(ся)] (on Д); **~sive** [-siv] навя́зчивый.
obtuse [əb'tju:s] □ тупо́й (*a. fig.*).
obviate ['ɔbvieit] избега́ть [-ежа́ть] (Р).
obvious ['ɔbviəs] □ очеви́дный, я́сный.
occasion [ə'keiʒən] **1.** слу́чай; возмо́жность *f*; по́вод; причи́на; F собы́тие; **on the ~ of** по слу́чаю (Р); **2.** причиня́ть [-ни́ть]; дава́ть по́вод к (Д); **~al** [-ʒnl] □ случа́йный; ре́дкий.
Occident ['ɔksidənt] За́пад, стра́ны За́пада; **♀al** [ɔksi'dentl] □ за́падный.
occult [ɔ'kʌlt] □ окку́льтный, та́йный.
occup|ant ['ɔkjupənt] жи́тель(ница *f*) *m*; владе́лец (-лица); **~ation** [ɔkju'peiʃən] завладе́ние; ⚔ оккупа́ция; заня́тие, профе́ссия; **~y** ['ɔkjupai] занима́ть [заня́ть]; завладе́(ва́)ть (Т); оккупи́ровать (*im*)*pf*.
occur [ə'kə:] случа́ться [-чи́ться];

встреча́ться [-е́титься]; ~ to a p. приходи́ть в го́лову кому́; **~rence** [əˈkʌrəns] происше́ствие, слу́чай.
ocean [ˈouʃən] океа́н.
o'clock [əˈklɔk]: five ~ пять часо́в.
ocul|ar [ˈɔkjulə] □ глазно́й; **~ist** [ˈɔkjulist] окули́ст, глазно́й врач.
odd [ɔd] □ нечётный; непа́рный; ли́шний; разро́зненный; чудно́й, стра́нный; **~ity** [ˈɔditi] чудакова́тость *f*; **~s** [ɔdz] *pl.* нера́венство; разногла́сие; ра́зница; преиму́щество; гандика́п; ша́нсы *m/pl.*; be at ~ with не ла́дить с (Т); ~ and ends оста́тки *m/pl.*; то да сё.
odious [ˈoudiəs] ненави́стный; отврати́тельный.
odo(u)r [ˈoudə] за́пах; арома́т.
of [ov; *mst* əv, v] *prp.* о, об (П); из (Р); от (Р); ука́зывает на причи́ну, принадле́жность, объе́кт де́йствия, ка́чество, исто́чник; ча́сто соотве́тствует ру́сскому роди́тельному падежу́; think ~ a th. ду́мать о (П); ~ charity из милосе́рдия; die ~ умере́ть от (Р); cheat ~ обсчи́тывать на (В); the battle ~ Quebec би́тва под Кве́беком; proud ~ го́рдый (Т); the roof ~ the house кры́ша до́ма.
off [ɔ:f, ɔf] **1.** *adv.* прочь; far ~ далеко́; ча́ще всего́ перево́дится верба́льными приста́вками: go ~ уходи́ть [уйти́]; switch ~ выключа́ть [вы́ключить]; take ~ снима́ть [снять]; ~ and on от вре́мени до вре́мени; be well (badly) ~ быть зажи́точным (бе́дным), быть в хоро́шем (плохо́м) положе́нии; **2.** *prp.* с (Р), со (Р) (выража́ет удале́ние предме́та с пове́рхности); от (Р) (ука́зывает на расстоя́ние); **3.** *adj.* свобо́дный от слу́жбы (рабо́ты); да́льний, бо́лее удалённый; боково́й; пра́вый (о стороне́).
offal [ˈɔfəl] отбро́сы *m/pl.*; па́даль *f*; **~s** *pl.* потроха́ *m/pl.*
offen|ce, *Am.* **~se** [əˈfens] просту́пок; оби́да, оскорбле́ние; наступле́ние.
offend [əˈfend] *v/t.* обижа́ть [оби́деть], оскорбля́ть [-би́ть]; *v/i.* наруша́ть [-у́шить] (against В); **~er** оби́дчик; правонаруши́тель(ница *f*) *m*; first ~ престу́пник, суди́мый впервы́е.
offensive [əˈfensiv] **1.** □ оскорби́тельный, оби́дный; агресси́вный, наступа́тельный; проти́вный; **2.** наступле́ние.
offer [ˈɔfə] **1.** предложе́ние; **2.** *v/t.* предлага́ть [-ложи́ть]; приноси́ть в же́ртву; *v/i.* выража́ть гото́вность (+ *inf.*); [по]пыта́ться; явля́ться [яви́ться]; **~ing** [-riŋ] же́ртва; предложе́ние.
off-hand [ˈɔ:fˈhænd] *adv.* F бесцеремо́нно; без подгото́вки.
office [ˈɔfis] слу́жба, до́лжность *f*; конто́ра, канцеля́рия; *eccl.* богослуже́ние; ♀ министе́рство; **~r** [ˈɔfisə] должностно́е лицо́, чино́вник (-ица); ⚔ офице́р.
official [əˈfiʃəl] **1.** □ официа́льный; служе́бный; ~ channel служе́бный поря́док; ~ hours *pl.* служе́бные часы́ *m/pl.*; **2.** служе́бное лицо́, слу́жащий; чино́вник.
officiate [əˈfiʃieit] исполня́ть обя́занности (as Р).
officious [əˈfiʃəs] □ назо́йливый; официо́зный.
off|set возмеща́ть [-ести́ть]; **~shoot** побе́г; о́тпрыск; ответвле́ние; **~spring** о́тпрыск, пото́мок.
often [ˈɔ:fn; *a.* ˈɔ:ftən] ча́сто, мно́го раз.
ogle [ougl] **1.** стро́ить гла́зки (Д); **2.** влюблённый взгляд.
ogre [ˈougə] людое́д.
oil [ɔil] **1.** ма́сло (расти́тельное, минера́льное); нефть *f*; **2.** сма́з(ыв)ать; *fig.* подма́з(ыв)ать; **~cloth** клеёнка; **~skin** дождеви́к; **~y** [ˈɔili] □ масляни́стый, ма́сляный; *fig.* еле́йный.
ointment [ˈɔintmənt] мазь *f*.
O. K., okay [ˈouˈkei] F **1.** *pred.* всё в поря́дке, хорошо́; **2.** *int.* хорошо́!, ла́дно!, есть!
old [ould] *com.* ста́рый; (in times) of ~ в старину́; ~ age ста́рость *f*; **~-fashioned** [ˈouldˈfæʃənd] старомо́дный; **~ish** [ˈouldiʃ] старова́тый.
olfactory [ɔlˈfæktəri] *anat.* обоня́тельный.
olive [ˈɔliv] ♀ оли́ва; оли́вковый [цвет.]
ominous [ˈɔminəs] □ злове́щий.
omission [oˈmiʃən] упуще́ние; про́пуск.
omit [oˈmit] пропуска́ть [-сти́ть]; упуска́ть [-сти́ть].
omnipoten|ce [ɔmˈnipotəns] всемогу́щество; **~t** [-tənt] □ всемогу́щий.
on [ɔn] **1.** *prp. mst* на (П *or* В); ~ the wall на стене́; march ~ London марш на Ло́ндон; ~ good authority из достове́рного исто́чника; ~ the 1st of April пе́рвого апре́ля; ~ his arrival по его́ прибы́тии; talk ~ a subject говори́ть на те́му; ~ this model по э́тому образцу́; ~ hearing it услы́шав э́то; **2.** *adv.* да́льше; вперёд; да́лее; keep one's hat ~ остава́ться в шля́пе; have a coat ~ быть в пальто́; and so ~ и так да́лее (и т. д.); be ~ быть пу́щенным в ход, включённым (и т. п.).
once [wʌns] **1.** *adv.* раз; не́когда, когда́-то; at ~ сейча́с же; ~ for all раз навсегда́; ~ in a while и́зредка; this ~ на э́тот раз; **2.** *cj.* как то́лько.
one [wʌn] **1.** оди́н; еди́ный; еди́нственный; како́й-то; ~ day одна́жды; ~ never knows никогда́ не зна́ешь; **2.** (число́) оди́н; едини́ца;

the little ~s малыши́ *m/pl.*; ~ another друг дру́га; at ~ заодно́, сра́зу; ~ by ~ оди́н за други́м; I for ~ я со свое́й стороны́.
onerous ['ɔnərəs] □ обремени́тельный.
one|self [wʌn'self] *pron. refl.* -ся, -сь, (самого́) себя́; **~-sided** □ односторо́нний; **~-way**: ~ street у́лица односторо́ннего движе́ния.
onion ['ʌnjən] лук, лу́ковица.
onlooker ['ɔnlukə] зри́тель(ница *f*) *m*; наблюда́тель(ница *f*) *m*.
only ['ounli] 1. *adj.* еди́нственный; 2. *adv.* еди́нственно; то́лько; исключи́тельно; ~ yesterday то́лько вчера́; 3. *cj.* но; ~ that ... е́сли бы не то, что ...
onset ['ɔnset], **onslaught** [-slɔ:t] ата́ка, на́тиск, нападе́ние.
onward ['ɔnwəd] 1. *adj.* продвига́ющийся вперёд; 2. *adv.* вперёд; впереди́.
ooze [u:z] 1. ил, ти́на; 2. проса́чиваться [-сочи́ться]; ~ away убы́(ва́)ть.
opaque [ou'peik] □ непрозра́чный.
open ['oupən] 1. □ *com.* откры́тый; открове́нный; я́вный; ~ to досту́пный (Д); in the ~ air на откры́том во́здухе; 2. bring into the ~ обнару́жи(ва)ть; 3. *v/t.* откры́(ва́)ть; нач(ин)а́ть; *v/i.* откры́(ва́)ться; нач(ин)а́ться; ~ into откры́(ва́)ться в (В) (о две́ри); ~ on to выходи́ть на *or* в (В); **~-handed** ще́дрый; **~ing** ['oupniŋ] отве́рстие; нача́ло; откры́тие; **~-minded** *fig.* непредубеждённый.
opera ['ɔpərə] о́пера; **~-glass(es** *pl.*) бино́кль *m*.
operat|e ['ɔpəreit] *v/t.* управля́ть (Т); *part. Am.* приводи́ть в де́йствие; *v/i.* опери́ровать (*im*)*pf.*; ока́зывать влия́ние; рабо́тать; де́йствовать; **~ion** [ɔpə'reiʃən] де́йствие; ⚕, ⚔, ✝ опера́ция; проце́сс; be in ~ быть в де́йствии; **~ive** 1. ['ɔpərətiv] □ де́йствующий; действи́тельный; операти́вный (*a.* ⚕); 2. ['ɔpərətiv] (фабри́чный) рабо́чий; **~or** ['ɔpəreitə] опера́тор; телеграфи́ст(ка).
opinion [ə'pinjən] мне́ние; взгляд; in my ~ по-мо́ему.
opponent [ə'pounənt] оппоне́нт, проти́вник.
opportun|e ['ɔpətju:n] □ благоприя́тный; подходя́щий; своевре́менный; **~ity** [ɔpə'tju:niti] удо́бный слу́чай, возмо́жность *f*.
oppos|e [ə'pouz] противопоставля́ть [-ста́вить]; [вос]проти́виться (Д); **~ed** [-d] противопоста́вленный; be ~ to быть про́тив (Р); **~ite** ['ɔpəzit] 1. □ противополо́жный; 2. *prp., adv.* напро́тив, про́тив (Р); 3. противополо́жность *f*; **~ition** [ɔpə'ziʃən] сопротивле́ние; оппози́ция; контра́ст.
oppress [ə'pres] притесня́ть [-ни́ть], угнета́ть; **~ion** [-ʃən] притесне́ние, угнете́ние; угнетённость *f*; **~ive** [-siv] □ гнету́щий, угнета́ющий; ду́шный.
optic ['ɔptik] глазно́й, зри́тельный; **~al** [-tikəl] □ опти́ческий; **~ian** [ɔp'tiʃən] о́птик.
option ['ɔpʃən] вы́бор, пра́во вы́бора; ~ right пра́во преиму́щественной поку́пки; **~al** ['ɔpʃənl] □ необяза́тельный, факультати́вный.
opulence ['ɔpjuləns] бога́тство.
or [ɔ:] и́ли; ~ else и́наче; и́ли же.
oracular [ɔ'rækjulə] □ проро́ческий.
oral ['ɔ:rəl] □ у́стный; слове́сный.
orange ['ɔrindʒ] 1. апельси́н; ора́нжевый цвет; 2. ора́нжевый.
orat|ion [o'reiʃən] речь *f*; **~or** ['ɔrətə] ора́тор; **~ory** [-ri] красноре́чие; часо́вня.
orb [ɔ:b] шар; орби́та; *fig.* небе́сное свети́ло; держа́ва.
orchard ['ɔ:tʃəd] фрукто́вый сад.
orchestra ['ɔ:kistrə] ♪ орке́стр.
ordain [ɔ:'dein] посвяща́ть в духо́вный сан; предпи́сывать [-са́ть].
ordeal [ɔ:'di:l] *fig.* испыта́ние.
order ['ɔ:də] 1. поря́док; знак отли́чия; прика́з; ✝ зака́з; ранг; ⚔ строй; take (holy) ~s принима́ть духо́вный сан; in ~ to что́бы; in ~ that с тем, что́бы; make to ~ де́лать на зака́з; *parl.* standing ~s *pl.* пра́вила процеду́ры; 2. прика́зывать [-за́ть]; назнача́ть [-на́чить]; ✝ зака́зывать [-за́ть]; **~ly** [-li] 1. аккура́тный; споко́йный; регуля́рный; 2. ⚔ вестово́й, ордина́рец.
ordinance ['ɔ:dinəns] ука́з, декре́т.
ordinary ['ɔ:dnri] □ обыкнове́нный; зауря́дный.
ordnance ['ɔ:dnəns] ⚔, ⚓ артиллери́йские ору́дия *n/pl.*; артиллери́йское и техни́ческое снабже́ние.
ordure ['ɔ:djuə] наво́з; отбро́сы *m/pl*; грязь *f*.
ore ['ɔ:] руда́.
organ ['ɔ:gən] о́рган; го́лос; ♪ орга́н; **~grinder** шарма́нщик; **~ic** [ɔ:'gænik] (**~ally**) органи́ческий; **~ization** [ɔ:gənai'zeiʃən] организа́ция; **~ize** ['ɔ:gənaiz] организова́ть (*im*)*pf.*; **~izer** [-ə] организа́тор.
orgy ['ɔ:dʒi] о́ргия.
orient ['ɔ:rient] 1. восто́к; Восто́к, восто́чные стра́ны *f/pl.*; 2. ориенти́ровать (*im*)*pf.*; **~al** [ɔ:ri'entl] 1. □ восто́чный, азиа́тский; 2. жи́тель Восто́ка; **~ate** ['ɔ:rienteit] ориенти́ровать (*im*)*pf*.
orifice ['ɔrifis] отве́рстие; у́стье.
origin ['ɔridʒin] исто́чник; происхожде́ние; нача́ло.

original [ə'ridʒənl] **1.** □ первонача́льный; оригина́льный; по́длинный; **2.** оригина́л, по́длинник; чуда́к; **~ity** [əridʒi'næliti] оригина́льность *f*.

originat|e [ə'ridʒineit] *v/t*. дава́ть нача́ло (Д), порожда́ть [породи́ть]; *v/i*. происходи́ть [-изойти́] (from от Р); **~or** [-ə] созда́тель *m*; инициа́тор.

ornament 1. ['ɔ:nəmənt] украше́ние, орна́мент; *fig*. краса́; **2.** [-ment] украша́ть [укра́сить]; **~al** [ɔ:nə'mentl] □ декорати́вный.

ornate [ɔ:'neit] □ разукра́шенный; витиева́тый (стиль).

orphan ['ɔ:fən] **1.** сирота́ *m/f*.; **2.** осироте́лый (*a*. **~ed**); **~age** [-idʒ], **~-asylum** прию́т для сиро́т.

orthodox ['ɔ:θədɔks] □ правове́рный; *eccl*. правосла́вный.

oscillate ['ɔsileit] вибри́ровать; *fig*. колеба́ться.

ossify ['ɔsifai] [о]костене́ть.

ostensible [ɔs'tensəbl] □ очеви́дный.

ostentatio|n [ɔstən'teiʃən] хвастовство́; выставле́ние напока́з; **~us** [-ʃəs] □ показно́й.

ostler ['ɔslə] ко́нюх.

ostrich ['ɔstritʃ] *zo*. стра́ус.

other ['ʌðə] друго́й; ино́й; the ~ day на дня́х; the ~ morning неда́вно у́тром; every ~ day че́рез день; **~wise** [waiz] и́на́че; и́ли же.

otter ['ɔtə] *zo*. вы́дра.

ought [ɔ:t]: I ~ to мне сле́довало бы; you ~ to have done it вам сле́довало э́то сде́лать.

ounce [auns] у́нция (= 28,3 г).

our ['auə] *pron. poss*. **~s** ['auəz] *pron. poss. pred*. наш, на́ша, на́ше; на́ши *pl*.; **~selves** [auə'selvz] *pron*. **1.** *refl*. себя́, -ся, -сь; **2.** (для усиле́ния) (мы) са́ми.

oust [aust] выгоня́ть [вы́гнать], вытесня́ть [вы́теснить].

out [aut] **1.** *adv*. нару́жу; вон; до конца́; ча́сто перево́дится приста́вкой вы- : take ~ вынима́ть [вы́нуть]; be ~ with быть в ссо́ре с (Т); ~ and ~ соверше́нно; way ~ вы́ход; **2.** *parl*. the ~s *pl*. оппози́ция; **3.** † ~ size разме́р бо́льше норма́льного; **4.** *prp*. ~ of: из (Р); вне (Р); из-за (Р).

out... [~] пере...; вы...; рас...; про...; воз..., вз...; из...; **~balance** [aut'bæləns] переве́шивать [-ве́сить]; **~bid** [-'bid] [*irr*. (bid)] перебива́ть це́ну; **~-break** ['autbreik] взрыв, вспы́шка (гне́ва); (внеза́пное) нача́ло (войны́, эпиде́мии и т. п.); **~building** ['autbildiŋ] надво́рное строе́ние; **~burst** [-'bə:st] взрыв, вспы́шка; **~cast** [-kɑ:st] **1.** изгна́нник (-ица); па́рия *m/f*; **2.** и́згнанный; **~come** [-'kʌm] результа́т; **~cry** [-krai] вы́крик; проте́ст; **~do** [aut'du:] [*irr*. (do)] превосходи́ть [-взойти́]; **~door** ['autdɔ:] *adj*. (нахо́дящийся) вне до́ма и́ли на откры́том во́здухе; нару́жный; **~doors** ['aut'dɔ:z] *adv*. на откры́том во́здухе, вне до́ма.

outer ['autə] вне́шний, нару́жный; **~most** ['autəmoust] кра́йний.

out|fit [-fit] снаряже́ние; обмундиро́вка; обору́дование; **~going** [-gouiŋ] **1.** уходя́щий; исходя́щий (о бума́гах, пи́сьмах и т. п.); **2.** **~s** *pl*. расхо́ды *m/pl*.; **~grow** [aut'grou] [*irr*. (grow)] выраста́ть [вы́расти] из (пла́тья и т. п.); **~-house** [-haus] надво́рное строе́ние; фли́гель *m*.

outing ['autiŋ] (за́городная) прогу́лка.

out|last [aut'lɑ:st] продолжа́ться до́льше, чем ...; пережи́(ва́)ть; **~law** ['autlɔ:] **1.** челове́к вне зако́на; **2.** объявля́ть вне зако́на; **~lay** [-lei] изде́ржки *f/pl*.; **~let** [-let] выпускно́е отве́рстие; вы́ход; **~line** [-lain] **1.** (*a*. *pl*.) очерта́ние, ко́нтур; **2.** рисова́ть ко́нтур (Р); де́лать набро́сок (Р); **~live** [aut'liv] пережи́(ва́)ть; **~look** ['autluk] вид, перспекти́ва; то́чка зре́ния, взгляд; **~lying** [-laiiŋ] отдалённый; **~number** [aut'nʌmbə] превосходи́ть чи́сленостью; **~-post** [-poust] аванпо́ст; **~pouring** [-pɔ:riŋ] *mst pl*. излия́ние (чувств); **~put** [-put] вы́пуск; производи́тельность *f*; проду́кция.

outrage ['autreidʒ] **1.** гру́бое наруше́ние (on P); **2.** гру́бо наруша́ть (зако́н); **~ous** [aut'reidʒəs] □ неи́стовый; возмути́тельный.

out|right ['aut'rait] откры́то; сра́зу; вполне́; **~run** [aut'rʌn] [*irr*. (run)] перегоня́ть [-гна́ть], опережа́ть [-реди́ть]; *fig*. преступа́ть преде́лы (Р); **~set** ['autset] нача́ло; отправле́ние; **~shine** [aut'ʃain] [*irr*. (shine)] затмева́ть [-ми́ть]; **~side** ['aut'said] нару́жная сторона́; вне́шняя пове́рхность *f*; вне́шность *f*; кра́йность *f*; at the ~ в кра́йнем слу́чае; **2.** нару́жный, вне́шний; кра́йний; **3.** *adv*. нару́жу; снару́жи; на (откры́том) во́здухе; **4.** *prp*. вне (Р); **~sider** ['aut'saidə] посторо́нний (челове́к); **~skirts** ['autskə:ts] *pl*. окра́ина; **~spoken** [aut'spoukən] □ открове́нный; **~standing** ['autstændiŋ] выступа́ющий; *fig*. выдаю́щийся; неупла́ченный (счёт); **~stretch** [aut'stretʃ] протя́гивать [-тяну́ть]; **~strip** [-'strip] опережа́ть [-реди́ть]; превосходи́ть [-взойти́].

outward ['autwəd] **1.** вне́шний, пове́рхностный; **2.** *adv*. (*mst* **~s** [-z]) нару́жу; за преде́лы.

outweigh [aut'wei] превосходи́ть ве́сом; *fig.* переве́шивать [переве́сить].

oven ['ʌvn] (хле́бная) печь *f*; духо́вка.

over ['ouvə] **1.** *adv.* ча́ще всего́ перево́дится приста́вками глаго́лов: пере..., вы..., про...; сно́ва; вдоба́вок; сли́шком; ~ and above кро́ме того́; (all) ~ again сно́ва, ещё раз; ~ against напро́тив; ~ and ~ (again) то и де́ло; read ~ перечи́тывать [-чита́ть]; **2.** *prp.* над (Т); по (Д); за (В); вы́ше (Р); сверх (Р); че́рез (В); о(б) (П); **all ~ the** town по всему́ го́роду.

over ... ['ouvə] *pref.* как приста́вка, означа́ет: сверх...; над...; пере...; чрезме́рно; **~act** ['ouver'ækt] переи́грывать [-гра́ть] (роль); **~all** ['ouvərɔ:l] спецоде́жда; **~awe** [ouvər'ɔ:] держа́ть в благогове́йном стра́хе; **~balance** [ouvə'bæləns] теря́ть равнове́сие; переве́шивать [-ве́сить]; **~bearing** [-'bɛəriŋ] □ вла́стный; **~board** ['ouvəbɔ:d] ⚓ за́ борт, за бо́ртом; **~cast** ['ouvə'kɑ:st] па́смурный; **~charge** [ouvə'tʃɑ:dʒ] **1.** сли́шком высо́кая цена́; **2.** перегружа́ть [-узи́ть]; запра́шивать сли́шком высо́кую це́ну с (Р) (for за В); **~coat** [-kout] пальто́ *n indecl.*; **~come** [-'kʌm] [*irr.* (come)] преодоле́(ва́)ть, побежда́ть [-еди́ть]; **~crowd** [ouvə'kraud] переполня́ть [-о́лнить] (за́л и т. п.); **~do** [-'du:] [*irr.* (do)] пережа́ри(ва)ть (мя́со и т. п.); де́лать сли́шком усе́рдно, утри́ровать (*im*)*pf.*; **~draw** ['ouvə'drɔ:] [*irr.* (draw)] † превыша́ть [-вы́сить] (креди́т); **~dress** [-'dres] одева́ться сли́шком пы́шно; **~due** [-'dju:] просро́ченный; **~eat** [ouvər'i:t] [*irr.* (eat)]: ~ o. s. объеда́ться [объе́сться]; **~flow 1.** [ouvə'flou] [*irr.* (flow)] *v/t.* затопля́ть [-пи́ть]; *v/i.* перели́(ва́)ться; **2.** ['ouvəflou] наводне́ние; разли́в; **~grow** ['ouvə'grou] [*irr.* (grow)] заглуша́ть [-ши́ть] (о расте́ниях); расти́ сли́шком бы́стро; **~hang 1.** ['ouvə'hæŋ] [*irr.* (hang)] *v/i.* нависа́ть [-и́снуть]; **2.** ['ouvəhæŋ] свес; вы́ступ; **~haul** [ouvə'hɔ:l] [от]ремонти́ровать; **~head 1.** ['ouvə'hed] *adv.* над голово́й, наверху́; **2.** ['ouvəhed] *adj.* ве́рхний; † накладно́й; **3.** ~s *pl.* † накладны́е расхо́ды *m/pl.*; **~hear** [ouvə'hiə] [*irr.* (hear)] подслу́ш(ив)ать; неча́янно слы́шать; **~lap** [ouvə'læp] *v/t.* части́чно покрыва́ть; *v/i.* заходи́ть оди́н за друго́й; **~lay** [ouvə'lei] [*irr.* (lay)] ⊕ покры́(ва́)ть; **~load** [ouvə'loud] перегружа́ть [-узи́ть]; **~look** [ouvə'luk] обозре́(ва́)ть; прогля́дывать [-де́ть]; **~master** [ouvə'mɑ:stə] подчиня́ть себе́; **~much** ['ouvə'mʌtʃ] чрезме́рно; **~pay** [-'pei] [*irr.* (pay)] перепла́чивать [-лати́ть]; **~power** [ouvə'pauə] переси́ли(ва)ть; **~reach** [ouvə'ri:tʃ] перехитри́ть *pf.*; ~ o. s. брать сли́шком мно́го на себя́, сли́шком напряга́ть си́лы; **~ride** [-'raid] [*irr.* (ride)] перее́хать ло́шадью; *fig.* отверга́ть [-е́ргнуть]; **~run** [-'rʌn] [*irr.* (run)] перелива́ться че́рез край; **~sea** ['ouvə'si:] **1.** замо́рский; загран́ичный; **2.** (*a.* ~seas) за́ морем, за́ море; **~see** [-'si:] [*irr.* (see)] надзира́ть за (Т); **~seer** ['ouvəsiə] надзира́тель(ница *f*) *m*; **~shadow** [ouvə'ʃædou] броса́ть тень на (В); омрача́ть [-чи́ть]; **~sight** [-sait] недосмо́тр; **~sleep** ['ouvəsli:p] [*irr.* (sleep)] прос(ы)па́ть; **~spread** [ouvə'spred] [*irr.* (spread)] покры́(ва́)ть; **~state** ['ouvə'steit] преувели́чи(ва)ть; **~strain** [-'strein] **1.** переутомле́ние; **2.** переутомля́ть [-ми́ть]; **~take** [ouvə'teik] [*irr.* (take)] догоня́ть [догна́ть]; засти́гнуть враспло́х; **~tax** ['ouvə'tæks] обременя́ть чрезме́рным нало́гом; *fig.* сли́шком напряга́ть (си́лы и т. п.) **~throw 1.** [ouvə'θrou] [*irr.* (throw)] сверга́ть [све́ргнуть]; опроки́дывать [-и́нуть]; **2.** ['ouvəθrou] сверже́ние; ниспроверже́ние; **~time** ['ouvətaim] **1.** сверхуро́чные часы́ *m/pl.*; **2.** *adv.* сверхуро́чно.

overture ['ouvətjuə] ♪ увертю́ра; нача́ло (перегово́ров и т. п.); форма́льное предложе́ние.

over|turn [ouvə'tə:n] опроки́дывать [-и́нуть]; **~weening** [ouvə'wi:niŋ] высокоме́рный; **~whelm** [ouvə'welm] подавля́ть [-ви́ть]; переси́ли(ва)ть; **~work** [-wə:k] **1.** перегру́зка; переутомле́ние; **2.** [*irr.* (work)] переутомля́ть(ся) [-ми́ть(ся)]; **~wrought** ['ouvə'rɔ:t] переутомлённый; возбуждённый (о не́рвах).

owe [ouv] быть до́лжным (Д/В); быть обя́занным (Д/Т).

owing ['ouiŋ] до́лжный; неупла́ченный; ~ to *prp.* благодаря́ (Д).

owl [aul] сова́.

own [oun] **1.** свой, со́бственный; родно́й; **2.** my ~ моя́ со́бственность *f*; a house of one's ~ со́бственный дом; hold one's ~ сохраня́ть свои́ пози́ции; **3.** владе́ть (Т); призна́(ва́)ть (В); призна́(ва́)ться в (П).

owner ['ounə] владе́лец (-лица *f*); **~ship** [-ʃip] со́бственность *f*; пра́во со́бственности.

ox [ɔks], *pl.* **oxen** вол, бык.

oxid|e ['ɔksaid] ⚗ о́кись *f*; **~ize** ['ɔksidaiz] окисля́ть(ся) [-ли́ть(-ся)].

oxygen ['ɔksidʒən] ⚗ кислоро́д.

oyster ['ɔistə] у́стрица.

P

pace [peis] **1.** шаг; похóдка, пóступь *f*; темп; **2.** *v/t.* измеря́ть шагáми; *v/i.* [за]шагáть.
pacific [pə'sifik] (**~ally**) миролюби́вый; **♀** Ocean Ти́хий океáн; **~-ation** ['pæsifi'keiʃən] умиротворéние; усмирéние.
pacify ['pæsifai] умиротворя́ть [-ри́ть]; усмиря́ть [-ри́ть].
pack [pæk] **1.** пáчка; вьюк; свя́зка; ки́па; колóда (карт); свóра (собáк); стáя (волкóв); **2.** *v/t.* (*often* ~ up) упакóвывать [-ковáть]; заполня́ть [запóлнить], наби́(вá)ть; (*a.* ~ off) выпровáживать [вы́проводить]; ⊕ уплотня́ть [-ни́ть]; *v/i.* упакóвываться [-овáться]; (*often* ~ up) уклáдываться [уложи́ться]; **~age** ['pækidʒ] тюк; ки́па; упакóвка; мéсто (багажá); **~er** ['pækə] упакóвщик (-ица); **~et** ['pækit] пакéт; почтóвый парохóд; **~thread** бечёвка, шпагáт.
pact [pækt] пакт, договóр.
pad [pæd] **1.** мя́гкая проклáдка; блокнóт; **2.** подби(вá)ть, наби(вá)ть (вáтой и т. п.); **~ding** ['pædiŋ] наби́вочный материáл; *fig.* многословие.
paddle [pædl] **1.** веслó, гребóк; ⚓ лóпасть *f* (гребнóго колесá); **2.** грести́ гребкóм; плыть на байдáрке; **~-wheel** гребнóе колесó.
paddock ['pædək] вы́гон, загóн.
padlock ['pædlɔk] вися́чий замóк.
pagan ['peigən] **1.** язы́чник; **2.** язы́ческий.
page [peidʒ] **1.** паж; страни́ца; **2.** нумеровáть страни́цы (Р).
pageant ['pædʒənt] пы́шное (истори́ческое) зрéлище; карнавáльное шéствие.
paid [peid] *pt.* и *p. pt.* от pay.
pail [peil] ведрó, бадья́.
pain [pein] **1.** боль *f*; страдáние; наказáние; **~s** *pl.* (*often sg.*) старáния *n/pl.*; on ~ of под стрáхом (Р); be in ~ испы́тывать боль; take ~s [по]старáться; **2.** причиня́ть боль (Д); **~ful** ['peinful] □ болéзненный; мучи́тельный; **~less** [-lis] □ безболéзненный; **~staking** ['peinzteikiŋ] усéрдный, старáтельный.
paint [peint] **1.** крáска; румя́на *n/pl.*; **2.** [по]крáсить; [на]румя́нить(ся); **~-brush** кисть *f*; **~er** ['peintə] худóжник; маля́р; **~ing** ['peintiŋ] живопись *f*; карти́на; **~ress** [-tris] худóжница.
pair [pɛə] **1.** пáра; четá; a ~ of scissors нóжницы *f/pl.*; **2.** соединя́ть(ся) пó двое; спáривать(ся).
pal [pæl] *sl.* приятель(ница *f*) *m.*
palace ['pælis] дворéц.
palatable ['pælətəbl] вкýсный.
palate [-it] нёбо; вкус.
pale[1] [peil] **1.** □ блéдный; тýсклый; ~ ale свéтлое пи́во; **2.** [по]бледнéть.
pale[2] [~] кол; *fig.* предéлы *m/pl.*
paleness ['peilnis] блéдность *f.*
pall [pɔ:l] окýтывать покрóвом.
pallet ['pælit] солóменный тюфя́к.
palliat|e ['pælieit] облегчáть [-чи́ть] (болéзнь); *fig.* покры́(вá)ть; **~ive** ['pælietiv] паллиати́вный; смягчáющий.
pall|id ['pælid] □ блéдный; **~idness** [-nis], **~or** [-lə] блéдность *f.*
palm [pɑ:m] **1.** ладóнь *f*; ♀ пáльма; **2.** трóгать, глáдить ладóнью; пря́тать в рукé; ~ off on a p. всýчивать [-чи́ть] (Д); **~tree** пáльмовое дéрево.
palpable ['pælpəbl] □ осязáемый; *fig.* очеви́дный, я́вный.
palpitat|e ['pælpiteit] трепетáть; би́ться (о сéрдце); **~ion** [-ʃən] сердцебиéние.
palsy ['pɔ:lzi] **1.** парали́ч; *fig.* слáбость *f*; **2.** парализовáть (*im*)*pf.*
palter ['pɔ:ltə] [с]плутовáть; криви́ть душóй.
paltry ['pɔ:ltri] □ пустякóвый, ничтóжный.
pamper ['pæmpə] [из]баловáть, изнéжи(ва)ть.
pamphlet ['pæmflit] брошю́ра.
pan [pæn] кастрю́ля; сковородá.
pan... [~] *pref.* пан...; общe...
panacea [pænə'siə] панацéя, универсáльное срéдство.
pancake ['pænkeik] блин; олáдья.
pandemonium [pændi'mounjəm] 🕮 *fig.* «ад кромéшный».
pander ['pændə] **1.** потвóрствовать (to Д); свóдничать; **2.** свóдник (-ица).
pane [pein] (окóнное) cтеклó.
panegyric [pæni'dʒirik] панеги́рик, похвалá.
panel [pænl] **1.** ⚠ панéль *f*; филёнка; ⚖ спи́сок прися́жных заседáтелей; **2.** обшивáть панéлями (стéны).
pang [pæŋ] внезáпная óстрая боль *f*; **~s** *pl. fig.* угрызéния (сóвести).
panic ['pænik] **1.** пани́ческий; **2.** пáника.
pansy ['pænzi] ♀ аню́тины глáзки *m/pl.*
pant [pænt] задыхáться [задохнýться]; тяжелó дышáть; стрáстно желáть (for, after Р).
panties ['pæntiz] *Am.* F (a pair of ~) (дáмские) панталóны *m/pl.*
pantry ['pæntri] кладовáя; буфéтная (для посýды).
pants [pænts] *pl. Am.* и́ли P (a pair of ~) подштáнники *m/pl.*; штаны́ *m/pl.*

pap [pæp] ка́шка (для дете́й).
papal ['peipəl] □ па́пский.
paper ['peipə] **1.** бума́га; газе́та; обо́и *m/pl.*; нау́чный докла́д; доку́мент; **2.** о(б)кле́ивать обо́ями; ~**-bag** кулёк; ~**-clip**, ~**-fastener** скре́пка; ~**-hanger** обо́йщик; ~**-weight** пресс-папье́ *n indecl.*
pappy ['pæpi] кашицеобра́зный.
par [pɑ:] ра́венство; † номина́льная сто́имость *f*; at ~ альпа́ри; be on a ~ with быть наравне́, на одно́м у́ровне с (Т).
parable ['pærəbl] при́тча.
parachut|e ['pærəʃu:t] парашю́т; ~**ist** [-ist] парашюти́ст.
parade [pə'reid] **1.** выставле́ние напока́з; ⚔ пара́д; ⚔ плац (= ~-ground); ме́сто для гуля́нья; make a ~ of выставля́ть напока́з; **2.** выставля́ть напока́з; ⚔ выстра́ивать(ся) на пара́д.
paradise ['pærədais] рай.
paragon [-gən] образе́ц (соверше́нства, доброде́тели).
paragraph ['pærəgrɑ:f] абза́ц; пара́граф; газе́тная заме́тка.
parallel ['pærəlel] **1.** паралле́льный; **2.** паралле́ль *f* (*a. fig.*); *geogr.* паралле́ль *f*; without ~ несравни́мый; **3.** быть паралле́льным с (Т), проходи́ть паралле́льно (Д); сра́внивать [-ни́ть].
paraly|se ['pærəleiz] парализова́ть (*im*)*pf.*; ~**sis** [pə'rælisis] ⚕ парали́ч.
paramount ['pærəmaunt] верхо́вный, вы́сший; первостепе́нный.
parapet ['pærəpit] ⚔ бру́ствер; парапе́т, пери́ла *n/pl.*
paraphernalia [pærəfə'nei'ljə] *pl.* принадле́жности *f/pl.*
parasite ['pærəsait] паразит (*a. fig.*); *fig.* туне́ядец (-дка).
parasol [pærə'sɔl] зо́нтик (от со́лнца).
paratroops ['pærətru:ps] *pl.* ⚔ парашю́тно-деса́нтные войска́ *n/pl.*
parboil ['pɑ:bɔil] слегка́ прова́ривать.
parcel [pɑ:sl] **1.** паке́т; посы́лка; **2.** (*mst* ~ out) дели́ть на уча́стки; выделя́ть [вы́делить].
parch [pɑ:tʃ] иссуша́ть [-ши́ть]; опаля́ть [-ли́ть] (о со́лнце).
parchment [-mənt] перга́мент.
pardon [pɑ:dn] **1.** проще́ние; ⚖ поми́лование; **2.** проща́ть [прости́ть]; поми́ловать *pf.*; ~**able** [-əbl] □ прости́тельный.
pare [pɛə] [по]чи́стить (о́вощи и т. п.); обреза́ть [-ре́зать]; *fig.* уре́з(ыв)ать.
parent ['pɛərənt] роди́тель(ница *f*) *m*; *fig.* исто́чник; ~s *pl.* роди́тели *m/pl.*; ~**age** [-idʒ] происхожде́ние; ~**al** [pə'rentl] □ роди́тельский.
parenthe|sis [pə'renθisis], *pl.* ~ses [-si:z] вво́дное сло́во, вво́дное предложе́ние; *pl. typ.* (кру́глые) ско́бки *f/pl.*
paring ['pɛəriŋ] кожура́, ко́рка, шелуха́; ~s *pl.* обре́зки *m/pl.*; очи́стки *f/pl.*
parish ['pæriʃ] **1.** церко́вный прихо́д; прихожа́не *pl.*; (*a.* civil ~) гражда́нский о́круг; **2.** прихо́дский.
parity ['pæriti] ра́венство; равноце́нность *f.*
park [pɑ:k] **1.** парк; *mot.* стоя́нка; **2.** *mot.* ста́вить на стоя́нку; ~**ing** ['pɑ:kiŋ] *mot.* стоя́нка; *attr.* стоя́ночный.
parlance ['pɑ:ləns] спо́соб выраже́ния, язы́к.
parley [pɑ:li] **1.** перегово́ры *m/pl.*; **2.** вести́ перегово́ры.
parliament ['pɑ:ləmənt] парла́мент; ~**ary** [-'mentəri] парламента́рный, парла́ментский.
parlo(u)r ['pɑ:lə] приёмная; жила́я ко́мната; гости́ная; *Am.* зал, ателье́ *n indecl.*; ~**-maid** го́рничная.
parochial [pə'roukjəl] □ прихо́дский; *fig.* ме́стный; у́зкий, ограни́ченный.
parole [pə'roul] ⚔ паро́ль *m*; че́стное сло́во.
parquet ['pɑ:kei] парке́т; *thea.* пере́дние ряды́ парте́ра.
parrot ['pærət] **1.** попуга́й; **2.** повторя́ть как попуга́й.
parry ['pæri] отража́ть [отрази́ть], [от]пари́ровать (уда́р).
parsimonious [pɑ:si'mounjəs] □ бережли́вый, эконо́мный; скупо́й.
parsley ['pɑ:sli] ⚘ петру́шка.
parson [pɑ:sn] прихо́дский свяще́нник, па́стор.
part [pɑ:t] **1.** часть *f*, до́ля; уча́стие; *thea. a. fig.* роль *f*; ме́стность *f*; ♪ па́ртия; a man of ~s спосо́бный челове́к; take in good (bad) ~ хорошо́ (пло́хо) принима́ть (слова́ и т. п.); for my (own) ~ с мое́й стороны́; in ~ части́чно; on the ~ of со стороны́ (Р); **2.** *adv.* ча́стью, отча́сти; **3.** *v/t.* разделя́ть [-ли́ть]; ~ the hair де́лать пробо́р; *v/i.* разлуча́ться [-чи́ться], расст(ав)а́ться (with, from с Т).
partake [pɑ:'teik] [*irr.* (take)] принима́ть уча́стие; разделя́ть [-ли́ть].
partial ['pɑ:ʃəl] □ части́чный; пристра́стный; неравноду́шный (to к Д); ~**ity** [pɑ:ʃi'æliti) пристра́стие; скло́нность *f.*
particip|ant [pɑ:'tisipənt] уча́стник (-ица); ~**ate** [-peit] уча́ствовать (in в П); ~**ation** [-peiʃən] уча́стие.
particle ['pɑ:tikl] части́ца; крупи́ца.
particular [pə'tikjulə] **1.** □ осо́бенный; осо́бый; ча́стный; разбо́рчивый; **2.** подро́бность *f*, де-

та́ль *f*; in ~ в осо́бенности; **~ity** [pətikju'læriti] осо́бенность *f*; тща́тельность *f*; **~ly** [pə'tikjuləli] осо́бенно; чрезвыча́йно.

parting ['pɑ:tiŋ] **1.** разлу́ка; пробо́р; ~ of the ways *part. fig.* перепу́тье; **2.** проща́льный.

partisan [pɑ:ti'zæn] **1.** сторо́нник (-ица); ⚔ партиза́н; **2.** партиза́нский.

partition [pɑ:'tiʃən] **1.** разде́л; перегоро́дка; **2.** ~ off отделя́ть перегоро́дкой.

partly ['pɑ:tli] ча́стью, отча́сти.

partner['pɑ:tnə] **1.** уча́стник (-ица); ☨ компаньо́н(ка); партнёр(ша); **2.** ста́вить в па́ру; де́лать партнёром; быть партнёром; **~ship** [-ʃip] уча́стие; ☨ това́рищество, компа́ния.

part-owner совладе́лец.

part-time непо́лная за́нятость *f*; *attr.* не по́лностью за́нятый; ~ worker рабо́чий, за́нятый не по́лный рабо́чий день.

party ['pɑ:ti] па́ртия; отря́д; уча́стник (to в П); компа́ния; вечери́нка; ~ line *parl.* парти́йные директи́вы *f/pl.*; ~ ticket *Am.* парти́йная програ́мма.

pass ['pɑ:s] **1.** прохо́д; перева́л; па́спорт; про́пуск; беспла́тный биле́т; *univ.* посре́дственная сда́ча экза́мена; **2.** *v/i.* проходи́ть [пройти́]; прекраща́ться [-крати́ться]; умира́ть [умере́ть]; происходи́ть [-изойти́], случа́ться [-чи́ться]; переходи́ть [перейти́] (from ... to ... из [P] ... в [B] ...); име́ть хожде́ние; *cards* [с]пасова́ть; come to ~ случа́ться [-чи́ться]; ~ as, for счита́ться (T), слыть (T); ~ away исчеза́ть [-е́знуть]; умира́ть [умере́ть]; ~ by проходи́ть ми́мо; ~ into переходи́ть [перейти́] в (B); ~ off проходи́ть [пройти́] (о бо́ли и т. п.); ~ on идти́ да́льше; ~ out выходи́ть [вы́йти]; **3.** *v/t.* проходи́ть [пройти́]; проезжа́ть [-е́хать]; минова́ть (*im*)*pf.*; выде́рживать [вы́держать] (экза́мен); обгоня́ть [обогна́ть], опережа́ть [-реди́ть]; переправля́ть(ся) [-а́вить(ся)] че́рез (B); (*a.* ~ on) перед(ав)а́ть; выноси́ть [вы́нести] (пригово́р); проводи́ть [-вести́] (вре́мя); принима́ть [-ня́ть] (зако́н); **~able** ['pɑ:səbl] □ проходи́мый; ходя́чий (о деньга́х); посре́дственный, сно́сный.

passage ['pæsidʒ] прохо́д; тече́ние (вре́мени); перее́зд, перепра́ва; коридо́р; отры́вок (из кни́ги).

passenger ['pæsindʒə] пассажи́р; седо́к; **~-train** пассажи́рский по́езд.

passer-by ['pɑ:sə'bai] прохо́жий.

passion ['pæʃən] страсть *f*; гнев; ♀ *eccl.* кре́стные му́ки *f/pl.*; ♀ Week страстна́я неде́ля; **~ate** [-it] □ стра́стный.

passive ['pæsiv] □ пасси́вный; поко́рный.

passport ['pɑ:spɔ:t] па́спорт.

password [-wə:d] ⚔ паро́ль *m.*

past [pɑ:st] **1.** *adj.* про́шлый; мину́вший; for some time ~ за после́днее вре́мя; **2.** *adv.* ми́мо; **3.** *prp.* за (T); по́сле (P); ми́мо (P); свы́ше (P); half ~ two полови́на тре́тьего; ~ endurance нестерпи́мый; ~ hope безнадёжный; **4.** про́шлое.

paste [peist] **1.** те́сто; па́ста; клей; **2.** кле́ить, прикле́и(ва)ть; **~board** карто́н; *attr.* карто́нный.

pastel ['pæstel] пасте́ль *f.*

pasteurize ['pæstəraiz] пастеризова́ть (*im*)*pf.*

pastime ['pɑ:staim] времяпрепрово́ждение.

pastor ['pɑ:stə] па́стор; па́стырь *m*; **~al** [-rəl] пастора́льный; пасту́шеский.

pastry ['peistri] пиро́жное, пече́нье; **~-cook** конди́тер.

pasture ['pɑ:stʃə] **1.** па́стбище; вы́гон; **2.** пасти́(сь).

pat [pæt] **1.** похло́пывание; кружо́чек (ма́сла); **2.** похло́п(ыв)ать; **3.** кста́ти; во́-время.

patch [pætʃ] **1.** запла́та; клочо́к земли́; обры́вок; лоску́т; **2.** [за-] лата́ть, [по]чини́ть.

pate [peit] F башка́, голова́.

patent ['peitənt] **1.** я́вный; откры́тый; патенто́ванный; ~ fastener кно́пка (застёжка); ~ leather лакиро́ванная ко́жа; **2.** (*a.* letters ~ *pl.*) пате́нт; дипло́м; **3.** [за]патентова́ть; **~ee** [peitən'ti:] владе́лец пате́нта.

patern|al [pə'tə:nl] □ отцо́вский; оте́ческий; **~ity** [-niti] отцо́вство.

path [pɑ:θ], *pl.* **~s** [pɑ:ðz] тропи́нка, доро́жка.

pathetic [pə'θetik] (~ally) патети́ческий; тро́гательный.

patien|ce ['peiʃəns] терпе́ние; насто́йчивость *f*; **~t** [-t] **1.** □ терпели́вый; **2.** пацие́нт(ка).

patrimony ['pætriməni] родово́е поме́стье, во́тчина.

patrol [pə'troul] ⚔ **1.** патру́ль *m*; дозо́р; **2.** патрули́ровать.

patron ['peitrən] патро́н; покрови́тель *m*; клие́нт; **~age** ['pætrənidʒ] покрови́тельство; клиенту́ра; **~ize** [-naiz] покрови́тельствовать; снисходи́тельно относи́ться к (Д); постоя́нно покупа́ть у (P).

patter ['pætə] говори́ть скорогово́ркой; [про]бормота́ть; бараба́нить (о дожде́); топота́ть, семени́ть.

pattern ['pætən] **1.** образе́ц; моде́ль *f*; узо́р; **2.** де́лать по образцу́ (on P).

paunch [pɔ:ntʃ] брюшко́, пу́зо.
pauper ['pɔ:pə] ни́щий (-щая); **~ize** [-raiz] доводи́ть до нищеты́.
pause [pɔ:z] **1.** па́уза, переры́в, остано́вка; **2.** де́лать па́узу.
pave [peiv] [на]мости́ть; *fig.* прокла́дывать [проложи́ть] (путь); **~ment** ['peivmənt] тротуа́р, пане́ль *f*; мостова́я.
paw [pɔ:] **1.** ла́па; F рука́; **2.** тро́гать ла́пой; бить копы́том.
pawn [pɔ:n] **1.** зало́г, закла́д; *chess* пе́шка; in, at ~ в закла́де; **2.** закла́дывать [заложи́ть]; **~broker** ростовщи́к; **~shop** ломба́рд, ссу́дная ка́сса.
pay [pei] **1.** пла́та, упла́та; зарпла́та, жа́лованье; **2.** [*irr.*] *v/t.* [за]плати́ть; опла́чивать [оплати́ть]; вознагражда́ть [-ради́ть]; [с]де́лать (визи́т); ~ attention to обраща́ть внима́ние на (В); ~ down плати́ть нали́чными; *v/i.* окупа́ться [-пи́ться] (*a. fig.*); ~ for [у-, за]плати́ть за (В), опла́чивать [оплати́ть] (В); *fig.* [по]плати́ться за (В); **~able** ['peiəbl] подлежа́щий упла́те; **~-day** день вы́платы жа́лованья; **~ing** ['peiiŋ] вы́годный; **~master** казначе́й, касси́р; **~ment** [mənt] упла́та, платёж; **~roll** платёжная ве́домость *f*.
pea [pi:] ⚘ горо́х; горо́шина; **~s** *pl.* горох; *attr.* горо́ховый.
peace [pi:s] мир; споко́йствие; **~able** ['pi:səbl] □ миролюби́вый, ми́рный; **~ful** [-ful] □ ми́рный, споко́йный; **~maker** миротво́рец.
peach [pi:tʃ] пе́рсик; пе́рсиковое де́рево.
pea|cock ['pi:kɔk] павли́н; **~hen** [-hen] па́ва.
peak [pi:k] верши́на (горы́); козырёк (ке́пки); *attr.* максима́льный; вы́сший.
peal [pi:l] **1.** звон колоколо́в; раска́т (гро́ма); ~ of laughter взрыв сме́ха; **2.** разда́(ва́)ться; греме́ть; трезво́нить.
peanut ['pi:nʌt] земляно́й оре́х.
pear [pɛə] ⚘ гру́ша; гру́шевое де́рево.
pearl [pə:l] *coll.* же́мчуг; жемчу́жина *a. fig.*; *attr.* жемчу́жный; **~y** ['pə:li] как же́мчуг.
peasant ['pezənt] **1.** крестья́нин; **2.** крестья́нский; **~ry** [-ri] крестья́нство.
peat [pi:t] торф.
pebble ['pebl] голы́ш, га́лька.
peck [pek] **1.** пек, ме́ра сыпу́чих тел (= 9,087 ли́тра); *fig.* мно́жество; **2.** клева́ть [клю́нуть].
peculate ['pekjuleit] (незако́нно) растра́чивать [-ра́тить].
peculiar [pi'kju:ljə] □ своеобра́зный; осо́бенный; стра́нный; **~ity** [pikju:li'æriti] осо́бенность *f*; стра́нность *f*.
pecuniary [pi'kju:njəri] де́нежный.
pedagogue ['pedəgɔg] педаго́г, учи́тель(ница *f*) *m*.
pedal [pedl] **1.** педа́ль *f*; **2.** ножно́й; **3.** е́хать на велосипе́де; рабо́тать педа́лями.
peddle [pedl] торгова́ть вразно́с.
pedest|al ['pedistl] пьедеста́л (*a. fig.*); **~rian** [pi'destriən] **1.** пешехо́д; **2.** пешехо́дный.
pedigree ['pedigri:] родосло́вная.
pedlar ['pedlə] разно́счик, коробе́йник.
peek [pi:k] *Am.* **1.** ~ in загля́дывать [-яну́ть]; **2.** бе́глый взгляд.
peel [pi:l] **1.** ко́рка, ко́жица, шелуха́; **2.** (*a.* ~ off) *v/t.* снима́ть ко́жицу, ко́рку, шелуху́ с (Р); [по-] чи́стить (фру́кты, о́вощи); *v/i.* [об]лупи́ться, сходи́ть [сойти́] (о ко́же).
peep [pi:p] **1.** взгляд укра́дкой; **2.** взгля́дывать укра́дкой; *fig.* проявля́ться [-ви́ться]; [про]пища́ть; **~-hole** глазо́к (око́шечко).
peer [piə] **1.** [с]равня́ться с (Т); ~ at вгля́дываться [-де́ться] в (В); **2.** ро́вня *m/f.*; пэр; **~less** ['piəlis] □ несравне́нный.
peevish ['pi:viʃ] □ брюзгли́вый.
peg [pəg] **1.** ко́лышек; ве́шалка; ♪ коло́к; зажи́мка для белья́; *fig.* take a p. down a ~ сбива́ть спесь с кого́-либо; **2.** прикрепля́ть ко́лышком; отмеча́ть ко́лышками; ~ away, along F упо́рно рабо́тать; **~-top** юла́ (игру́шка).
pellet ['pelit] ша́рик; пилю́ля; дроби́нка.
pell-mell ['pel'mel] вперемё́шку.
pelt [pelt] **1.** ко́жа, шку́ра; **2.** *v/t.* обстре́ливать [-ля́ть]; забра́сывать [-роса́ть]; *v/i.* бараба́нить (о дожде́ и т. п.).
pen [pen] **1.** перо́; заго́н; **2.** [на-] писа́ть; [*irr.*] загоня́ть в заго́н.
penal [pi:nl] □ уголо́вный; кара́тельный; ~ servitude ка́торжные рабо́ты *f/pl.*; **~ize** ['pi:nəlaiz] нака́зывать [-за́ть]; **~ty** ['penlti] наказа́ние; ✝, *sport.* штраф; *attr.* штрафно́й.
penance ['penəns] эпитими́я.
pence [pens] *pl.* от penny.
pencil [pensl] **1.** каранда́ш; кисть *f* (живопи́сца); **2.** [на]рисова́ть; писа́ть карандашо́м; вычё́рчивать [вы́чертить].
pendant ['pendənt] куло́н, брело́к.
pending ['pendiŋ] **1.** ⚖ ожида́ющий реше́ния; **2.** *prp.* в продолже́ние (Р); (вплоть) до (Р).
pendulum ['pendjuləm] ма́ятник.
penetra|ble ['penitrəbl] □ прони́ца́емый; **~te** [-treit] проника́ть [-ни́кнуть] в (В); глубоко́ тро́гать; прони́зывать [-за́ть]; *fig.* вника́ть [вни́кнуть] в (В); **~tion** [peni'treiʃən] проника́ние; проница́тель-

ность *f*; **~tive** ['penitreitiv] □ проникающий; проницательный.
penholder ручка (для пера).
peninsula [pi'ninsjulə] полуостров.
peniten|ce ['penitəns] раскаяние; покаяние; **~t** **1.** □ раскаивающийся; **2.** кающийся грешник; **~tiary** [peni'tenʃəri] исправительный дом; *Am.* каторжная тюрьма.
penman ['penmən] писатель *m*; }
pen-name псевдоним. [писец.}
pennant ['penənt] ⚓ вымпел.
penniless ['penilis] □ без копейки.
penny ['peni] пенни *n indecl.*, пенс; *Am.* монета в 1 цент; **~weight** 24 грана (= 1,5552 гр).
pension **1.** ['penʃən] пенсия; **2.** увольнять на пенсию; давать пенсию (Д); **~ary**, **~er** ['penʃənəri, -ʃənə] пенсионер(ка).
pensive ['pensiv] □ задумчивый.
pent [pent] заключённый; **~-up** накопленный (о гневе и т. п.).
penthouse ['penthaus] навес.
penu|rious [pi'njuəriəs] скудный; скупой; **~ry** ['penjuri] нужда; недостаток.
people [pi:pl] **1.** народ; *coll.* люди *m/pl.*; население; **2.** заселять [-лить]; населять [-лить].
pepper ['pepə] **1.** перец; **2.** [по-, на-] перчить; **~mint** ⚘ мята; **~y** [-ri] □ наперченный; *fig.* вспыльчивый.
per [pə:] по (Д), через (В), посредством (Р); за (В), на (В), в (В); ~ cent процент.
perambulat|e [pə'ræmbjuleit] обходить [обойти], объезжать [-ехать]; **~or** ['præmbjuleitə] детская коляска.
perceive [pə'si:v] воспринимать [-нять]; ощущать [ощутить]; понимать [-нять].
percentage [pə'sentidʒ] процент; процентное отношение или содержание.
percepti|ble [pə'septəbl] □ ощутимый; **~on** [-ʃən] ощущение; восприятие.
perch [pə:tʃ] **1.** *zo.* окунь *m*; перч, мера длины (= 5.029 м); насест; **2.** садиться [сесть]; усаживаться [усесться]; сажать на насест.
percolate ['pə:kəleit] [про]фильтровать; процеживать [-цедить].
percussion [pə:'kʌʃən] удар.
perdition [pə:'diʃən] гибель *f*.
peregrination [perigri'neiʃən] странствование; путешествие.
peremptory [pə'remptəri] безапелляционный; повелительный, властный.
perennial [pə'renjəl] □ вечный, неувядаемый; ⚘ многолетний.
perfect **1.** ['pə:fikt] □ совершенный; законченный; **2.** [pə'fekt] [у]совершенствовать; завершать [-шить]; **~ion** [-ʃən] совершенство; *fig.* высшая степень *f*.

perfidious [pə'fidiəs] □ вероломный.
perfidy ['pə:fidi] вероломство.
perforate ['pə:fəreit] перфорировать (*im*)*pf*..
perform [pə'fɔ:m] исполнять [-олнить] (*a. thea.*); *thea.*, ♪ играть [сыграть] (роль, пьесу и т. п.), представлять [-авить]; **~ance** [əns] исполнение (*a. thea.*); *thea.* представление; *sport* достижение; **~er** [-ə] исполнитель(ница *f*) *m*.
perfume **1.** ['pə:fju:m] духи *m/pl.*; благоухание; **2.** [pə'fju:m] [на-] душить; **~ry** [-əri] парфюмерия.
perfunctory [pə'fʌŋktəri] □ *fig.* механический; поверхностный.
perhaps [pə'hæps, præps] может быть.
peril ['peril] **1.** опасность *f*; **2.** подвергать опасности; **~ous** [-əs] □ опасный.
period ['piəriəd] период; абзац; **~ic** [piəri'ɔdik] периодический; **~ical** [-dikəl] **1.** □ периодический; **2.** периодическое издание.
perish ['periʃ] погибать [-ибнуть]; [по]губить; **~able** ['periʃəbl] □ скоропортящийся; тленный.
periwig ['periwig] парик.
perjur|e ['pə:dʒə]: ~ o. s. лжесвидетельствовать; нарушать клятву; **~y** [-ri] лжесвидетельство; клятвопреступление.
perk [pə:k] F: *mst* ~ up *v/i.* задирать нос; *v/t.* ~ o. s. прихорашиваться.
perky ['pə:ki] □ дерзкий; самоуверенный.
permanen|ce ['pə:mənəns] постоянство; **~t** [-t] □ постоянный, неизменный.
permea|ble ['pə:miəbl] проницаемый; **~te** [-mieit] проникать [-икнуть], пропитывать [-итать].
permissi|ble [pə'misəbl] □ позволительный; **~on** [-ʃən] позволение, разрешение.
permit **1.** [pə'mit] разрешать [-шить], позволять [-волить]; допускать [-устить]; **2.** ['pə:mit] разрешение; пропуск.
pernicious [pə:'niʃəs] пагубный.
perpendicular [pə:pən'dikjulə] □ перпендикулярный.
perpetrate ['pə:pitreit] совершать [-шить] (преступление и т. п.).
perpetu|al [pə'petjuəl] постоянный, вечный; **~ate** [-jueit] увековечи(ва)ть.
perplex [pə'pleks] озадачи(ва)ть, сбивать с толку; **~ity** [-iti] озадаченность *f*; недоумение; затруднение.
perquisites ['pə:kwizits] *pl.* случайные доходы *m/pl.*
persecut|e ['pə:sikju:t] преследовать; **~ion** [pə:si'kju:ʃən] преследование.

persever|ance [pə:si'viərəns] настóйчивость *f*, упóрство; **~e** [-'viə] *v/i.* выдéрживать [вы́держать]; упóрно продолжáть (in B).
persist [pə'sist] упóрствовать (in в П); **~ence** [-əns] настóйчивость *f*; **~ent** [-ənt] □ настóйчивый.
person ['pə:sn] лицó, ли́чность *f*, осóба, человéк; **~age** [-idʒ] вáжная персóна; персонáж; **~al** [-l] □ ли́чный; **~ality** [pə:sə'næliti] ли́чность *f*; кóлкость *f*; **~ate** ['pə:səneit] игрáть роль (P); выдавáть себя́ за (B); **~ify** [pə:'sɔnifai] олицетворя́ть [-ри́ть], воплощáть [-лоти́ть]; **~nel** [pə:sə'nel] персонáл, ли́чный состáв.
perspective [pə'spektiv] перспекти́ва; ви́д.
perspicuous [pə'spikjuəs] □ я́сный.
perspir|ation [pə:spə'reiʃən] потéние; пот; **~e** [pəs'paiə] [вс]потéть.
persua|de [pə'sweid] убеждáть [убеди́ть]; склоня́ть [-ни́ть] (into к Д); **~sion** [-ʒən] убеждéние; убеди́тельность *f*; **~sive** [-siv] □ убеди́тельный.
pert [pə:t] □ дéрзкий; развя́зный.
pertain [pə:'tein] (to) принадлежáть (Д); относи́ться [отнести́сь] (к Д).
pertinacious [pə:ti'neiʃəs] □ упря́мый, неустýпчивый.
pertinent ['pə:tinənt] □ умéстный; относя́щийся к дéлу.
perturb [pə'tə:b] нарушáть [-ýшить] (спокóйствие); [о]беспокóить.
perus|al [pə'ru:zəl] внимáтельное прочтéние; **~e** [pə'ru:z] [про]читáть; внимáтельно прочи́тывать.
pervade [pə:'veid] распространя́ться [-ни́ться] по (Д) (о зáпахе и т. п.).
pervers|e [pə'və:s] □ превráтный, оши́бочный; ⚕ извращённый; **~ion** [-ʃən] ⚕ извращéние.
pervert 1. [pə'və:t] извращáть [-рати́ть]; совращáть [-рати́ть]; 2. ['pə:və:t] отстýпник (-ица).
pest [pest] *fig.* я́зва, бич; парази́т; **~er** ['pestə] докучáть (Д), надоедáть [-éсть] (Д).
pesti|ferous [pes'tifərəs] □ зарáзный; **~lence** ['pestiləns] чумá; **~lent** [-t] смертонóсный; **~lential** [pesti'lenʃəl] □ чумнóй; зловóнный.
pet [pet] 1. кóмнатное живóтное; люби́мец, бáловень *m*; 2. люби́мый; ~ dog кóмнатная собáчка, болóнка; ~ name ласкáтельное и́мя; 3. баловáть; ласкáть.
petition [pi'tiʃən] 1. прошéние, пети́ция; прóсьба; 2. [по]проси́ть; подавáть прошéние.
petrify ['petrifai] превращáть(ся) в кáмень; приводи́ть в оцепенéние.
petrol ['petrəl] *Brit. mot.* бензи́н.
petticoat ['petikout] ни́жняя ю́бка.
pettish ['petiʃ] □ оби́дчивый.
petty ['peti] □ мéлкий; мéлочный.
petulant ['petjulənt] раздражи́тельный.
pew [pju:] церкóвная скамья́.
pewter ['pju:tə] оловя́нная посýда.
phantasm ['fæntæzm] фантóм; иллю́зия.
phantom ['fæntəm] фантóм, при́зрак; иллю́зия.
Pharisee ['færisi:] фарисéй.
pharmacy ['fɑ:məsi] фармаци́я; аптéка.
phase [feiz] фáза; пери́од.
phenomen|on [fi'nɔminən], *pl.* **~a** [-nə] явлéние; феномéн.
phial ['faiəl] склянка, пузырёк.
philander ['fi'lændə] флиртовáть.
philanthropist [fi'lænθrəpist] филантрóп.
philologist [fi'lɔlədʒist] филóлог.
philosoph|er [fi'lɔsəfə] филóсоф; **~ize** [-faiz] филосóфствовать; **~y** [-fi] филосóфия.
phlegm [flem] мокрóта; флегмати́чность *f*.
phone [foun] F *s.* telephone.
phonetics [fo'netiks] *pl.* фонéтика.
phosphorus ['fɔsfərəs] фóсфор.
photograph ['foutəgrɑ:f] 1. фотогрáфия, сни́мок; 2. [с]фотографи́ровать; **~er** [fə'tɔgrəfə] фотóграф; **~y** [-fi] фотогрáфия (дéло).
phrase [freiz] 1. фрáза, выражéние; слог; 2. выражáть [вы́разить].
physic|al ['fizikəl] □ физи́ческий; телéсный; **~ian** [fi'ziʃən] врач; **~ist** ['fizisist] фи́зик; **~s** ['fiziks] *sg.* фи́зика.
physique [fi'zi:k] телосложéние.
pick [pik] 1. удáр (óстрым); вы́бор; киркá; 2. выбирáть [вы́брать]; ковыря́ть [-рнýть] в (П); соб(и)рáть (цветы́, плоды́); оглáдывать [оглодáть]; [по]клевáть; срывáть [сорвáть] (цветóк, фрукт); ~ out выбирáть [вы́брать]; ~ up соб(и)рáть; подбирáть [подобрáть]; поднимáть [-ня́ть]; заезжáть [заéхать] за (Т); **~-a-back** ['pikəbæk] (о дéтях) на спинé (отцá и т. п.); **~axe** киркá.
picket ['pikit] 1. кол; ⚔ сторожевáя застáва; стáчечный пикéт; 2. выставля́ть пикéты вокрýг (P); обноси́ть частоколóм.
picking ['pikiŋ] собирáние, отбóр и т. д. (*s. verb*); **~s** *pl.* остáтки *m/pl.*, объéдки *m/pl.*; *mst* **~s** *pl.* мéлкая пожи́ва.
pickle [pikl] 1. рассóл; *pl.* пи́кули *f/pl.*; F неприя́тности *f/pl.*; 2. [по-] соли́ть; **~d** herring солёная селёдка.

pick|lock ['pɪklɔk] отмычка; **~-pocket** карманный вор.
pictorial [pɪk'tɔːriəl] 1. иллюстрированный; изобразительный; 2. иллюстрированный журнал.
picture ['pɪktʃə] 1. картина; the ~s *pl.* кино *indecl.*; ~-gallery картинная галерея; ~ (post)card открытка с видом; 2. изображать [-разить]; описывать [-сать]; воображать [-разить]; **~sque** [pɪktʃə'resk] живописный.
pie [pai] паштет; пирог; торт.
piebald ['paibɔːld] пегий (о лошади).
piece [piːs] 1. кусок, часть *f*; обрывок, обломок; штука; ~ of advice совет; ~ of news новость *f*; by the ~ поштучно; give a ~ of one's mind высказывать своё мнение; take to ~s разбирать на части; 2. [по]чинить; соединять в одно целое, собирать из кусочков; **~meal** по частям, постепенно; **~work** сдельная работа.
pier [piə] устой; бык (моста); мол; волнолом; пристань *f*.
pierce [piəs] пронзать [-зить]; просверливать [-лить]; пронизывать [-зать].
piety ['paiəti] благочестие, набожность *f*.
pig [pig] свинья.
pigeon ['pidʒin] голубь *m*; **~-hole** 1. отделение (письменного стола и т. п.); 2. раскладывать по ящикам; откладывать в долгий ящик.
pig|headed ['pig'hedid] упрямый; **~-iron** чугун в болванках; **~skin** свиная кожа; **~sty** свинарник; **~tail** косичка, коса.
pike [paik] ⚔ копьё; пика; *zo.* щука.
pile [pail] 1. куча, груда; ⚡ батарея; костёр; штабель *m*; ~s *pl.* геморрой; 2. складывать [сложить]; сваливать в кучу.
pilfer ['pilfə] [у]воровать.
pilgrim ['pilgrim] паломник; **~age** ['pilgrimidʒ] паломничество.
pill [pil] пилюля.
pillage ['pilidʒ] 1. грабёж; 2. [о]грабить.
pillar ['pilə] столб, колонна; **~-box** почтовый ящик.
pillion ['piljən] *mot.* заднее сиденье.
pillory ['piləri] 1. позорный столб; 2. поставить к позорному столбу.
pillow ['pilou] подушка; **~-case, ~-slip** наволочка.
pilot ['pailət] 1. ✈ пилот; ⚓ лоцман; 2. ⚓ проводить [-вести]; ✈ пилотировать; **~-balloon** шар-пилот.
pimp [pimp] 1. сводник (-ица); 2. сводничать.
pimple [pimpl] прыщик.
pin [pin] 1. булавка; шпилька; кнопка; кегля; ♪ колок; 2. прикалывать [-колоть]; *fig.* пригвождать [-оздить].
pinafore ['pinəfɔː] передник.
pincers ['pinsəz] *pl.* клещи *f/pl.*; щипцы *m/pl.*
pinch [pintʃ] 1. щипок; щепотка (соли и т. п.); стеснённое положение, крайность *f*; 2. *v/t.* щипать [щипнуть]; прищемлять [-мить]; *v/i.* [по]скупиться; жать (об обуви).
pine [pain] 1. ♀ сосна; 2. [за]чахнуть; изны(ва)ть; **~-apple** ананас; **~-cone** сосновая шишка.
pinion ['pinjən] 1. оконечность птичьего крыла; перо (крыла); ⊕ шестерня; 2. подрезать крылья (Д); *fig.* связывать руки (Д).
pink [piŋk] 1. ♀ гвоздика; *fig.* высшая степень *f*; 2. розовый.
pinnacle ['pinəkl] ⌂ остроконечная башенка; вершина (горы); *fig.* верх.
pint [paint] пинта (= 0,47 литра).
pioneer [paiə'niə] 1. пионер; ⚔ сапёр; 2. прокладывать путь (for Д); руководить (кем-либо).
pious ['paiəs] □ набожный.
pip [pip] *vet.* типун; косточка, зёрнышко (плода); очко (на картах); звёздочка (на погоне).
pipe [paip] 1. труба; трубка; ♪ свирель *f*, дудка; бочка (для вина); 2. играть на свирели и т. п.; [за-] пищать; **~-layer** прокладчик труб; **~-line** трубопровод; нефтепровод; **~r** ['paipə] дудочник; волынщик.
piping ['paipiŋ]: 1. ~ hot очень горячий; 2. кант (на платье).
pique [piːk] 1. досада; 2. возбуждать [-удить] (любопытство); колоть [кольнуть], заде(ва)ть (самолюбие); ~ o. s. on чваниться (Т).
pira|cy ['paiərəsi] пиратство; нарушение авторского права; **~te** [-rit] 1. пират; нарушитель авторского права; 2. самовольно переиздавать.
pistol [pistl] пистолет.
piston ['pistən] ⊕ поршень *m*; **~-rod** шатун; **~-stroke** ход поршня.
pit [pit] 1. яма; шахта; оспина; *thea.* партер; *Am.* отдел товарной биржи; 2. складывать в яму (на зиму).
pitch [pitʃ] 1. смола; дёготь *m*; бросок; степень *f*; ♪ высота тона; ⚓ килевая качка; ⊕ наклон; 2. *v/t.* разби(ва)ть (палатку); метать [метнуть], бросать [бросить]; ♪ давать основной тон (Д); *v/i.* ⚔ располагаться лагерем; подвергаться качке; F ~ into набрасываться [-роситься] на (В).
pitcher ['pitʃə] кувшин.
pitchfork ['pitʃfɔːk] вилы *f/pl.*; ♪ камертон.
pitfall ['pitfɔːl] *fig.* ловушка.
pith [piθ] спинной мозг; сердцевина; *fig.* сущность *f*, суть *f*; **~y**

['piθi] с сердцеви́ной; энерги́чный.
pitiable ['pitiəbl] □ жа́лкий.
pitiful ['pitiful] □ жа́лостливый; жа́лостный; (*a. contp.*) жа́лкий.
pitiless ['pitilis] □ безжа́лостный.
pittance ['pitəns] ску́дное жа́лованье.
pity ['piti] **1.** жа́лость *f* (for к Д); it is a ~ жаль; **2.** [по]жале́ть.
pivot ['pivət] **1.** то́чка враще́ния; ⊕ сте́ржень *m* (*a. fig.*); штифт; **2.** враща́ться ([up]on вокру́г Р).
placable ['pleikəbl] □ кро́ткий, незлопа́мятный.
placard ['plækɑ:d] **1.** плака́т; **2.** раскле́и(ва)ть (объявле́ния); рекла́мировать плака́тами.
place [pleis] **1.** ме́сто; месте́чко, селе́ние; пло́щадь *f*; жили́ще; уса́дьба; до́лжность *f*, слу́жба; ~ of delivery ме́сто доста́вки; give ~ to уступа́ть ме́сто (Д); in ~ of вме́сто (Р); out of ~ неуме́стный; **2.** [по]ста́вить, класть [положи́ть]; размеща́ть [-сти́ть], помеща́ть [-сти́ть].
placid ['plæsid] □ споко́йный, безмяте́жный.
plagiar|ism ['pleidʒiərizm] плагиа́т; **~ize** [-raiz] незако́нно заи́мствовать (мы́сли и т. п.).
plague [pleig] **1.** бе́дствие, бич; чума́; **2.** [из]му́чить; F надоеда́ть [-е́сть] (Д).
plaid [plæd] шотла́ндка; плед.
plain [plein] **1.** □ просто́й; поня́тный; я́сный, я́вный; очеви́дный; обыкнове́нный; гла́дкий, ро́вный; **2.** *adv.* я́сно; разбо́рчиво; открове́нно; **3.** равни́на; пло́скость *f*; **~-clothes man** сы́щик; **~dealing** прямота́.
plaint|iff ['pleintif] исте́ц, исти́ца; **~ive** ['pleintiv] □ жа́лобный, зауны́вный.
plait [plæt, *Am.* pleit] **1.** коса́ (воло́с); **2.** заплета́ть [-ести́].
plan [plæn] **1.** план; **2.** составля́ть план; *fig.* намеча́ть [-е́тить]; намерева́ться.
plane [plein] **1.** пло́ский; **2.** пло́скость *f*; прое́кция; ✈ несу́щая пове́рхность *f*; самолёт; *fig.* у́ровень *m*; ⊕ руба́нок; **3.** [вы́]строга́ть; ✈ [с]плани́ровать.
plank [plæŋk] **1.** доска́, пла́нка; *Am. pol.* пункт парти́йной програ́ммы; **2.** настила́ть *или* обшива́ть до́сками; *sl.* ~ down выкла́дывать [вы́ложить] (де́ньги).
plant [plɑ:nt] **1.** расте́ние; ⊕ заво́д, фа́брика; **2.** сажа́ть [посади́ть] (расте́ние); устана́вливать [-нови́ть]; **~ation** [plæn'teiʃən] планта́ция; насажде́ние; **~er** ['plɑ:ntə] планта́тор.
plaque [plɑ:k] таре́лка (как стенно́е украше́ние); доще́чка.
plash [plæʃ] плеска́ть(ся) [-сну́ть].
plaster ['plɑ:stə] **1.** *pharm.* пла́стырь *m*; ⊕ штукату́рка; (*mst* ~ of Paris) гипс; **2.** [о]штукату́рить; накла́дывать пла́стырь на (В).
plastic ['plæstik] (~ally) пласти́ческий; ~ material пластма́сса.
plat [plæt] план, съёмка; уча́сток.
plate [pleit] **1.** пласти́нка; плита́; полоса́ (мета́лла); доще́чка с на́дписью; столо́вое серебро́; таре́лка; ⊕ листово́е желе́зо; **2.** покрыва́ть мета́ллом.
plat(t)en [plætn] ва́лик (пи́шущей маши́нки).
platform ['plætfɔ:m] перро́н, платфо́рма; трибу́на; площа́дка (ваго́на); полити́ческая програ́мма.
platinum ['plætinəm] *min.* пла́тина.
platitude [-titju:d] бана́льность *f*.
platoon [plə'tu:n] ⚔ взвод.
platter ['plætə] деревя́нная таре́лка.
plaudit ['plɔ:dit] рукоплеска́ния [*n/pl.*]
plausible ['plɔ:zəbl] □ правдоподо́бный.
play [plei] **1.** игра́; пье́са; ⊕ зазо́р; мёртвый ход; **2.** игра́ть [сыгра́ть] (в В, ♪ на П); свобо́дно дви́гаться (о механи́зме); ~ off *fig.* разы́грывать [-ра́ть]; стра́вливать [страви́ть] (against с Т); **~ed out** вы́дохшийся; **~bill** театра́льная афи́ша; **~er** ['pleiə] игро́к; актёр; **~er-piano** пиано́ла; **~fellow, ~mate** това́рищ игр, друг де́тства; партнёр; **~ful** ['pleiful] □ игри́вый; **~goer** театра́л; **~-ground** площа́дка для игр; **~-house** теа́тр; **~thing** игру́шка; **~wright** драмату́рг.
plea [pli:] оправда́ние, до́вод; мольба́; on the ~ (of *или* that ...) под предло́гом (Р *or* что ...).
plead [pli:d] *v/i.* обраща́ться к суду́; ~ for вступа́ться [-пи́ться] за (В); говори́ть за (В); ~ guilty признава́ть себя́ вино́вным; *v/t.* защища́ть [-ити́ть] (в суде́); приводи́ть в оправда́ние; **~er** ['pli:də] ⚖ защи́тник; **~ing** ['pli:diŋ] ⚖ защи́та.
pleasant [pleznt] □ прия́тный; **~ry** [-ri] шу́тка.
please [pli:z] [по]нра́виться (Д); угожда́ть [угоди́ть] (Д); if you ~ с ва́шего позволе́ния; изво́льте! ~ come in! войди́те пожа́луйста!; доставля́ть удово́льствие (Д); be ~d to do де́лать с удово́льствием; be ~d with быть дово́льным (Т); ~d [pli:zd] дово́льный.
pleasing ['pli:ziŋ] □ прия́тный.
pleasure ['pleʒə] удово́льствие, наслажде́ние; *attr.* увесели́тельный; at ~ по жела́нию.
pleat [pli:t] **1.** скла́дка; **2.** де́лать скла́дки на (П).

pledge [pledʒ] **1.** зало́г, закла́д; обе́т, обеща́ние; **2.** закла́дывать [заложи́ть]; руча́ться [поручи́ться] (Т); he ~d himself он связа́л себя́ обеща́нием.
plenary [pli:nəri] по́лный, плена́рный.
plenipotentiary [plenipə'tenʃəri] полномо́чный представи́тель *m*.
plentiful ['plentiful] □ оби́льный.
plenty [-ti] **1.** изоби́лие; доста́ток; изли́шек; ~ of мно́го (Р); **2.** F чрезвыча́йно; вполне́.
pliable ['plaiəbl] □ ги́бкий; *fig.* пода́тливый, мя́гкий.
pliancy ['plaiənsi] ги́бкость *f*.
pliers ['pleiəz] *pl.* плоскогу́бцы *m/pl*.
plight [plait] **1.** свя́зывать обеща́нием; помо́лвить *pf.*; **2.** (плохо́е) положе́ние.
plod [plɔd] (*a.* ~ along, on) таска́ться, [по]тащи́ться; корпе́ть (at над Т).
plot [plɔt] **1.** уча́сток земли́. деля́нка; за́говор; план; фа́була, сюже́т; **2.** *v/i.* составля́ть за́говор; [за]интригова́ть; *v/t.* наноси́ть [нанести́] (на ка́рту); *b. s.* замышля́ть [-ы́слить].
plough, *Am. a.* plow [plau] **1.** плуг; **2.** [вс]паха́ть; *fig.* [из]борозди́ть; ~share ле́мех.
pluck [plʌk] **1.** дёрганье; F сме́лость *f*, му́жество; потроха́ *m/pl.*; **2.** срыва́ть [сорва́ть] (цвето́к); ощи́пывать [-па́ть] (пти́цу); ~ at дёргать [дёрнуть] (В); хвата́ть(ся) [схвати́ть(ся)] за (В); ~ up courage собра́ться с ду́хом; ~y ['plʌki] сме́лый, отва́жный.
plug [plʌg] **1.** вту́лка; заты́чка; ⚡ ште́псель *m*; ~ socket ште́псельная розе́тка; **2.** *v/t.* затыка́ть [заткну́ть]; [за]пломбирова́ть (зуб).
plum [plʌm] сли́ва.
plumage ['plu:midʒ] опере́ние.
plumb [plʌm] **1.** вертика́льный; отве́сный; **2.** отве́с; лот; **3.** *v/t.* ста́вить по отве́су; измеря́ть ло́том; проника́ть вглубь (Р); *v/i.* рабо́тать водопрово́дчиком; ~er ['plʌmə] водопрово́дчик; ~ing [-iŋ] водопрово́д(ное де́ло).
plume [plu:m] **1.** перо́; плюма́ж; **2.** украша́ть плюма́жем; ~ o. s. on кичи́ться (Т).
plummet ['plʌmit] свинцо́вый отве́с; грузи́ло.
plump [plʌmp] **1.** *adj.* пу́хлый, по́лный; F □ реши́тельный; **2.** [по]толсте́ть; бу́хать(ся) [-хнуть (-ся)]; **3.** тяжёлое паде́ние; **4.** F *adv.* пря́мо, без обиняко́в.
plunder ['plʌndə] **1.** грабёж; награ́бленные ве́щи *f/pl.*; **2.** [о]гра́бить.
plunge [plʌndʒ] **1.** ныря́ть [нырну́ть]; окуна́ть(ся) [-ну́ть(ся)]; **2.** ныря́ние; погруже́ние; take the ~ де́лать реши́тельный шаг.
plurality [pluə'ræliti] мно́жество; большинство́; мно́жественность *f*.
plush [plʌʃ] плюш, плис.
ply [plai] **1.** слой; скла́дка; оборо́т; three-~ трёхсло́йный; **2.** *v/t.* засыпа́ть [засы́пать], забра́сывать [-роса́ть] (вопро́сами); *v/i.* курси́ровать; ~-wood фане́ра.
pneumatic [nju:'mætik] **1.** (~ally) пневмати́ческий; ~ post пневмати́ческая по́чта; **2.** пневмати́ческая ши́на.
pneumonia [nju:'mounjə] ⚕ воспале́ние лёгких.
poach [poutʃ] браконье́рствовать; ~ed egg яйцо́-пашо́т.
poacher ['poutʃə] браконье́р.
pocket ['pɔkit] **1.** карма́н; ✈ возду́шная я́ма; **2.** класть в карма́н; прикарма́ни(ва)ть; присва́ивать [-сво́ить]; подавля́ть [-ви́ть] (чу́вство); прогла́тывать [-лоти́ть] (оби́ду); **3.** карма́нный.
pod [pɔd] ♀ стручо́к; шелуха́.
poem ['pouim] поэ́ма; стихотворе́ние.
poet ['pouit] поэ́т; ~ess [-is] поэте́сса; ~ic(al □) [pou'etik, -tikəl] поэти́ческий; поэти́чный; ~ics [-tiks] *pl.* поэ́тика; ~ry ['pouitri] поэ́зия.
poignan|cy ['pɔi(g)nənsi] острота́; ~t [-t] о́стрый; *fig.* мучи́тельный.
point [pɔint] **1.** то́чка; пункт, смысл; суть де́ла; очко́; деле́ние (шкалы́); остриё, о́стрый коне́ц; 🚂 стре́лка; ~ of view то́чка зре́ния; the ~ is that ... де́ло в том, что ...; make a ~ of *ger.* поста́вить себе́ зада́чей (+ *inf.*); in ~ of в отноше́нии (Р); off the ~ не (относя́щийся) к де́лу; be on the ~ of *ger.* соб(и)ра́ться (+ *inf.*); win on ~s выи́грывать по пу́нктам; to the ~ к де́лу (относя́щийся); **2.** *v/t.* ~ one's finger пока́зывать па́льцем (at на В); заостря́ть [-ри́ть]; (*often* ~ out) ука́зывать [-за́ть]; ~ at направля́ть [-ра́вить] (ору́жие) на (В); *v/i.* ~ at ука́зывать [-за́ть] на (В); ~ to быть напра́вленным на (В); ~ed ['pɔintid] □ остроконе́чный; о́стрый; *fig.* ко́лкий; ~er ['pɔintə] указа́тель *m*; ука́зка; по́йнтер; ~less [-lis] пло́ский; бессмы́сленный.
poise [pɔiz] **1.** равнове́сие; оса́нка; **2.** *v/t.* уравнове́шивать [-е́сить]; держа́ть (го́лову и т. п.); *v/i.* находи́ться в равнове́сии; пари́ть.
poison ['pɔizn] **1.** яд, отра́ва; **2.** отравля́ть [-ви́ть]; ~ous [-əs] (*fig. a.*) ядови́тый.
poke [pouk] **1.** толчо́к, тычо́к; **2.** *v/t.* ты́кать [ткнуть]; толка́ть [-кну́ть]; сова́ть [су́нуть]; меша́ть кочерго́й; ~ fun at подшу́чивать [-шути́ть] над (Т); *v/i.* сова́ть нос

(into в В); искáть óщупью (for В) [or P).
poker ['poukə] кочергá.
poky ['pouki] тéсный; убóгий.
polar ['poulə] поля́рный; ~ **bear** бéлый медвéдь *m.*
pole [poul] пóлюс; шест; жердь *f*; кол; ♀ поля́к, пóлька; **~cat** *zo.* хорёк.
polemic [po'lemik] (*a.* **~al** [-mikəl] □) полеми́ческий.
pole-star Поля́рная звездá; *fig.* путевóдная звездá.
police [pə'li:s] **1.** поли́ция; **2.** поддéрживать поря́док в (П); **~-man** полицéйский; **~-station** полицéйский учáсток.
policy ['pɔlisi] поли́тика; ли́ния поведéния; страховóй пóлис.
Polish[1] ['pouliʃ] пóльский.
polish[2] ['pɔliʃ] **1.** полирóвка; *fig.* лоск; **2.** [на]полировáть; *fig.* утончáть [-чи́ть].
polite [pə'lait] □ вéжливый, благовоспи́танный; **~ness** [-nis] вéжливость *f.*
politic ['pɔlitik] □ полити́чный; расчётливый; **~al** [pə'litikəl] □ полити́ческий; госудáрственный; **~ian** [pɔli'tiʃən] поли́тик; **~s** ['pɔlitiks] *pl.* поли́тика.
poll [poul] **1.** голосовáние; подсчёт голосóв; спи́сок избирáтелей; **2.** *v/t.* получáть [-чи́ть] (голосá); *v/i.* [про]голосовáть; **~-book** спи́сок избирáтелей.
pollen ['pɔlin] ⚘ пыльцá.
poll-tax ['pɔltæks] подýшный налóг.
pollute [pə'lu:t] загрязня́ть [-ни́ть]; оскверня́ть [-ни́ть].
polyp(e) ['pɔlip] *zo.*, **~us** [-lipəs] ⚕ поли́п.
pommel ['pʌml] **1.** голóвка (эфéса шпáги); лукá (седлá), **2.** [по]би́ть; [по]колоти́ть.
pomp [pɔmp] пóмпа; великолéпие.
pompous ['pɔmpəs] □ напы́щенный.
pond [pɔnd] пруд.
ponder ['pɔndə] *v/t.* обдýм(ыв)ать; *v/i.* задýм(ыв)аться; **~able** [-rəbl] весóмый; **~ous** [-rəs] □ *fig.* тяжелoвéсный.
pontiff ['pɔntif] первосвящéнник.
pontoon [pɔn'tu:n] ⚔ понтóн; **~-bridge** понтóнный мост.
pony ['pouni] пóни *m indecl.* (лошáдка).
poodle [pu:dl] пýдель *m.*
pool [pu:l] **1.** лýжа; бассéйн; óмут; *cards* пýлька; ✝ пул; **2.** ✝ объединя́ть в óбщий фонд; склáдываться [сложи́ться] (with с Т).
poop [pu:p] ⚓ кормá.
poor [puə] □ бéдный, неимýщий; несчáстный; скýдный; плохóй; **~-house** богадéльня; **~-law** закóн о бéдных; **~ly** ['puəli] *adj.* нездорóвый; **~ness** ['puənis] бéдность *f.*
pop [pɔp] **1.** хлóпанье; F шипýчий напи́ток; **2.** *v/t.* совáть [сýнуть]; *v/i.* хлóпать [-пнуть] (о прóбке); [по]трéскаться (о каштáнах и т.п.); ~ in внезáпно появи́ться.
popcorn ['pɔpkɔ:n] *Am.* калёные зёрна кукурýзы.
pope [poup] (ри́мский) пáпа *m.*
poplar ['pɔplə] ⚘ тóполь *m.*
poppy ['pɔpi] ⚘ мак.
popula|ce ['pɔpjuləs] простонарóдье; **~r** [-lə] □ нарóдный; популя́рный; **~rity** [-'læriti] популя́рность *f.*
populat|e ['pɔpjuleit] населя́ть [-ли́ть]; **~ion** [pɔpju'leiʃən] населéние.
populous ['pɔpjuləs] □ многолю́дный.
porcelain ['pɔ:slin] фарфóр.
porch [pɔ:tʃ] подъéзд; пóртик; *Am.* верáнда.
pore [pɔ:] **1.** пóра; **2.** погружáться [-узи́ться] (over в В).
pork [pɔ:k] свини́на.
porous ['pɔ:rəs] □ пóристый.
porridge ['pɔridʒ] овся́ная кáша.
port [pɔ:t] **1.** гáвань *f*, порт; ⚓ лéвый борт; портвéйн; **2.** ⚓ брать налéво.
portable ['pɔ:təbl] портати́вный.
portal [pɔ:tl] портáл; тáмбур (дверéй).
portend [pɔ:'tend] предвещáть.
portent ['pɔ:tent] предвéстник, знáмение (плохóго); чýдо; **~ous** [pɔ:'tentəs] □ зловéщий; знаменáтельный.
porter ['pɔ:tə] привráтник, швейцáр; носи́льщик; пóртер (пи́во).
portion ['pɔ:ʃən] **1.** часть *f*; пóрция; *fig.* удéл, ýчасть *f*; **2.** дели́ть (на чáсти); наделя́ть [-ли́ть].
portly ['pɔ:tli] дорóдный; представи́тельный.
portmanteau [pɔ:t'mæntou] чемодáн.
portrait ['pɔ:trit] портрéт.
portray [pɔ:'trei] рисовáть портрéт с (Р); изображáть [-рази́ть]; опи́сывать [-сáть]; **~al** [-əl] рисовáние портрéта; изображéние; описáние.
pose [pouz] **1.** пóза; **2.** пози́ровать; стáвить в пóзу; [по]стáвить (вопрóс); ~ as выдавáть себя́ за (В).
position [pə'ziʃən] мéсто; положéние; пози́ция; состоя́ние; тóчка зрéния.
positive ['pɔzətiv] **1.** □ положи́тельный; пози́тивный; увéренный; самоувéренный; абсолю́тный; **2.** *gr.* положи́тельная стéпень *f*; *phot.* пози́тив.
possess [pə'zes] обладáть (Т); владéть (Т); *fig.* овладé(вá)ть (Т); be **~ed** быть одержи́мым; ~ o. s. of завладé(вá)ть (Т); **~ion** [-ʃən] владéние; обладáние; *fig.* одержи́мость *f*; **~or** [-sə] владéлец.
possib|ility [pɔsə'biliti] возмóжность *f*; **~le** ['pɔsəbl] □ возмóж-

ный; ~ly [-i] возмо́жно; if I ~ can е́сли у меня́ бу́дет возмо́жность *f*.
post [poust] **1.** по́чта; столб; до́лжность *f*; пост; *Am.* ~ exchange гарнизо́нный магази́н; **2.** *v/t.* отправля́ть по по́чте; раскле́и(ва)ть (афи́ши); расставля́ть [-а́вить]; well ~ed хорошо́ осведомлённый; *v/i.* [по]спеши́ть.
postage [-tidʒ] почто́вая опла́та; **~-stamp** почто́вая ма́рка.
postal ['poustəl] □ почто́вый; ~ order де́нежный почто́вый перево́д.
post-card откры́тка.
poster ['poustə] афи́ша, плака́т.
posterior [pɔs'tiəriə] **1.** □ после́дующий; за́дний; **2.** зад.
posterity [pɔs'teriti] пото́мство.
post-free без почто́вой опла́ты.
post-haste ['poust'heist] поспе́шно.
posthumous ['pɔstjuməs] □ посме́ртный; рождённый по́сле сме́рти отца́.
post|man почтальо́н; **~mark 1.** почто́вый ште́мпель *m*; **2.** [за-] штемпелева́ть; **~master** почтме́йстер.
post-mortem ['poust'mɔ:tem] **1.** посме́ртный; **2.** вскры́тие тру́па.
post|(-)office по́чта, почто́вая конто́ра; ~ box абоне́ментный почто́вый я́щик; **~-paid** франки́рованный.
postpone [poust'poun] отсро́чи(ва)ть; откла́дывать [отложи́ть]; **~ment** [-mənt] отсро́чка.
postscript ['pous(s)kript] постскри́птум.
postulate 1. ['pɔstjulit] постула́т; **2.** [-leit] ста́вить усло́вием; постули́ровать (*im*)*pf*.; [по]тре́бовать.
posture ['pɔstʃə] **1.** по́за; положе́ние; **2.** пози́ровать; ста́вить в по́зу.
post-war ['poust'wɔ:] послевое́нный.
posy ['pouzi] буке́т цвето́в.
pot [pɔt] **1.** горшо́к; котело́к; **2.** класть и́ли сажа́ть в горшо́к; заготовля́ть впрок.
potation [pou'teiʃən] питьё, напи́ток; (*part.* ~s *pl.*) попо́йка.
potato [pə'teitou] карто́фелина; **~es** *pl.* карто́фель *m*; F карто́шка.
pot-belly пу́зо; пуза́тый челове́к.
poten|cy ['poutənsi] си́ла, могу́щество; **~t** [-tənt] □ могу́щественный; кре́пкий; **~tial** [pə'tenʃəl] **1.** потенциа́льный, возмо́жный; **2.** потенциа́л.
pother ['pɔðə] сумато́ха; шум.
pot|-herb пря́ное расте́ние; **~house** каба́к.
potion ['pouʃən] ⚕ миксту́ра; зе́лье.
potter ['pɔtə] гонча́р; **~y** [-ri] гли́няные изде́лия *n/pl.*; гонча́рня.
pouch [pautʃ] **1.** су́мка (*a. biol.*); мешо́чек; **2.** прикарма́ни(ва)ть; класть в су́мку.
poultry ['poultri] дома́шняя пти́ца.
pounce [pauns] **1.** прыжо́к, наско́к; **2.** набра́сываться [-ро́ситься] ([up]on на В).
pound [paund] **1.** фунт; заго́н; ~ (sterling) фунт сте́рлингов (сокр. £ = 20 ш.); **2.** [ис]толо́чь; колоти́ть(ся); ~ at бомбардирова́ть.
pour [pɔ:] *v/t.* лить; ~ out нали́(ва́)ть; сыпать, насыпа́ть [насы́пать]; *v/i.* ли́ться; [по]сы́паться.
pout [paut] **1.** наду́тые гу́бы *f/pl.*; **2.** *v/t.* наду́(ва́)ть (гу́бы); *v/i.* [на-] ду́ться.
poverty ['pɔvəti] бе́дность *f*.
powder ['paudə] **1.** порошо́к; пу́дра; по́рох; **2.** [ис]толо́чь; [на-] пу́дрить(ся); посыпа́ть [посы́пать]; **~-box** пу́дреница.
power ['pauə] си́ла; мо́щность *f*; *pol.* держа́ва; власть *f*; ⚖ полномо́чие; ⅍ сте́пень *f*; **~-current** ток высо́кого напряже́ния; **~ful** [-ful] □ мо́щный, могу́щественный; си́льный; **~less** [-lis] бесси́льный; **~ plant** силова́я устано́вка; **~-station** электроста́нция.
pow-wow ['pau'wau] зна́харь (у инде́йцев) *m*; *Am.* шу́мное собра́ние.
practica|ble ['præktikəbl] □ осуществи́мый; проходи́мый (о доро́ге); **~l** [-kəl] □ практи́ческий; практи́чный; факти́ческий; ~ joke (гру́бая) шу́тка, проказа.
practice ['præktis] пра́ктика; упражне́ние, трениро́вка; привы́чка; обы́чай; put into ~ осуществля́ть [-ви́ть].
practise [~] *v/t.* применя́ть [-ни́ть]; занима́ться [-ня́ться] (Т); упражня́ться в (П); практикова́ть; *v/i.* упражня́ться; ~ (up)on злоупотребля́ть [-би́ть] (Т); **~d** [-t] о́пытный.
practitioner [præk'tiʃnə] практику́ющий врач.
praise [preiz] **1.** хвала́; **2.** [по]хвали́ть.
praiseworthy ['preizwə:ði] досто́йный похвалы́.
prance [prɑ:ns] станови́ться на дыбы́; гарцева́ть.
prank [præŋk] вы́ходка, прока́за.
prate [preit] **1.** пустосло́вие; **2.** пустосло́вить, болта́ть.
pray [prei] [по]моли́ться; [по]проси́ть; ~! прошу́ вас!
prayer [prɛə] моли́тва; про́сьба; Lord's ~ о́тче наш; **~-book** моли́твенник; **~ful** [-ful] □ богомо́льный.
pre... [pri:, pri] до...; пред...
preach [pri:tʃ] пропове́довать; **~er** ['pri:tʃə] пропове́дник.
preamble [pri:'æmbl] преа́мбула; вступле́ние.
precarious [pri'kɛəriəs] ненадёжный.
precaution [pri'kɔ:ʃən] предосторо́жность *f*.
precede [pri'si:d] предше́ствовать

(Д); **~nce, ~ncy** [-əns(i)] пе́рвенство,; преиму́щественное значе́ние; **~nt** ['presidənt] прецеде́нт.
precept ['pri:sept] наставле́ние; за́поведь *f*; **~or** [pri'septə] наста́вник.
precinct ['pri:siŋkt] преде́л; (полице́йский) уча́сток; (избира́тельный о́круг; **~s** *pl.* окре́стности *f/pl.*
precious ['preʃəs] **1.** □ драгоце́нный; **2.** F *adv.* о́чень; **~!** здо́рово!
precipi|ce ['presipis] про́пасть *f*; **~tate 1.** [pri'sipiteit] низверга́ть [-е́ргнуть]; [по]торопи́ть; ⚗ осажда́ть [осади́ть]; **2.** [-tit] a) □ опроме́тчивый; стреми́тельный; b) ⚗ оса́док; **~tation** [prisipi'teiʃən] низверже́ние; стреми́тельность *f*; оса́дки *m/pl.*; ⚗ осажде́ние; **~tous** [pri'sipitəs] □ круто́й; обры́вистый.
precis|e [pri'sais] □ то́чный; **~ion** [-'siʒən] то́чность *f*.
preclude [pri'klu:d] исключа́ть зара́нее; предотвраща́ть [-рати́ть] (В); [по]меша́ть (Д).
precocious [pri'kouʃəs] □ преждевре́менно разви́то́й.
preconceive ['pri:kən'si:v] представля́ть себе́ зара́нее; **~d** предвзя́тый. [предвзя́тое мне́ние.]
preconception ['pri:kən'sepʃən]
precursor [pri'kə:sə] предте́ча *m/f*; предше́ственник (-ица).
predatory ['predətəri] хи́щный.
predecessor ['pri:disesə] предше́ственник (-ица).
predestin|ate [pri:'destineit] предопределя́ть [-ли́ть]; **~ed** [-tind] предопределённый.
predicament [pri'dikəmənt] серьёзное затрудне́ние.
predicate ['predikit] предика́т.
predict [pri'dikt] предска́зывать [-за́ть]; **~ion** [-kʃən] предсказа́ние.
predilection [pri:di'lekʃən] скло́нность *f*, пристра́стие (for к Д).
predispos|e ['pri:dis'pouz] предрасполага́ть [-ложи́ть].
predomina|nce [pri'dɔminəns] госпо́дство, преоблада́ние; **~nt** [-nənt] □ преоблада́ющий; домини́рующий; **~te** [-neit] госпо́дствовать, преоблада́ть (over над Т).
pre-eminent [pri:'eminənt] □ выда́ющийся.
pre-emption [pri:'emʃən] (*a.* right of ~) преиму́щественное пра́во на поку́пку.
prefabricate ['pri:'fæbrikeit] изготовля́ть зара́нее (ча́сти стандáртного до́ма и т. п.).
preface ['prefis] **1.** предисло́вие; **2.** предпос(ы)ла́ть (Д with В); снабжа́ть предисло́вием.
prefect ['pri:fekt] префе́кт.
prefer [pri'fə:] предпочита́ть [-поче́сть]; повыша́ть [-ы́сить] (в чи́не); под(ав)а́ть (проше́ние); выдвига́ть [вы́двинуть] (тре́бование); **~able** ['prefərəbl] □ предпочти́тельный; **~ence** [rəns] предпочте́ние; **~ential** [prefə'renʃəl] □ предпочти́тельный; льго́тный.
prefix ['pri:fiks] пре́фикс, приста́вка.
pregnan|cy ['pregnənsi] бере́менность *f*; бога́тство (воображе́ния и т. п.); **~t** [-nənt] □ бере́менная; *fig.* чрева́тый; бога́тый.
prejud|ge ['pri:'dʒʌdʒ] осужда́ть, не вы́слушав; **~ice** ['predʒudis] **1.** предрассу́док; предубежде́ние; **2.** предубежда́ть [-беди́ть] (про́тив Р); наноси́ть уще́рб (Д); **~icial** [predʒu'diʃəl] па́губный.
prelate ['prelit] прела́т.
preliminar|y [pri'liminəri] **1.** □ предвари́тельный; вступи́тельный; **2.** подготови́тельное мероприя́тие.
prelude ['prelju:d] ♪ прелю́дия.
prematur|e [premə'tjuə] преждевре́менный.
premeditation [primedi'teiʃən] преднаме́ренность *f*.
premier ['premjə] **1.** пе́рвый; **2.** премье́р-мини́стр.
premises ['premisiz] *pl.* помеще́ние; дом (с пристро́йками).
premium ['pri:mjəm] награ́да, пре́мия; ✝ лаж; страхова́я пре́мия; at a ~ вы́ше номина́льной сто́имости; в большо́м спро́се.
premonit|ion [pri:mo'niʃən] предчу́вствие; предупрежде́ние.
preoccup|ied [pri'ɔkjupaid] озабо́ченный; **~y** [-pai] поглоща́ть внима́ние (Р); занима́ть ра́ньше (чем кто́-либо).
preparat|ion [prepə'reiʃən] приготовле́ние; подгото́вка; **~ory** [pri:pærətəri] □ предвари́тельный; подготови́тельный, приготови́тельный.
prepare [pri'pɛə] *v/t.* приготовля́ть [-то́вить]; [при]гото́вить; подготовля́ть [-то́вить]; *v/i.* [при]гото́виться; подготовля́ться [-то́виться] (for к Д); **~d** [-d] □ подгото́вленный; гото́вый.
prepondera|nce [pri'pɔndərəns] преоблада́ние; **~nt** [-rənt] □ преоблада́ющий; **~te** [-reit] име́ть переве́с; ~ over превосходи́ть [-взойти́] (В).
prepossess [pri:pə'zes] располага́ть к себе́; **~ing** [-iŋ] □ располага́ющий.
preposterous [pri'pɔstərəs] несообра́зный, неле́пый, абсу́рдный.
prerequisite ['pri:'rekwizit] предпосы́лка.
presage ['presidʒ] **1.** предзнаменова́ние; предчу́вствие; **2.** (*a.* [pri'seidʒ]) предзнаменова́ть, предвеща́ть; предчу́вствовать.
prescribe [pris'kraib] предпи́сы-

вать [-писа́ть]; ⚕ прописывать [-писа́ть].
prescription [pris'kripʃən] предписа́ние; ⚕ реце́пт.
presence [prezns] прису́тствие; ~ of mind прису́тствие ду́ха.
present[1] [preznt] 1. □ прису́тствующий; тепе́решний, настоя́щий; да́нный; 2. настоя́щее вре́мя; пода́рок; at ~ в да́нное вре́мя; for the ~ на э́тот раз.
present[2] [pri'zent] представля́ть [-а́вить]; преподноси́ть [-нести́]; под(ав)а́ть (проше́ние); [по]ста́вить (пье́су); одаря́ть [-ри́ть]; под(ав)а́ть.
presentation [prezen'teiʃən] представле́ние; подноше́ние; пода́ча.
presentiment [pri'zentimənt] предчу́вствие.
presently ['prezntli] вско́ре; сейча́с.
preservati|on [prezə'veiʃən] сохране́ние; сохра́нность *f*; **~ve** [pri'zə:vətiv] 1. предохрани́тельный; 2. предохрани́тельное сре́дство.
preserve [pri'zə:v] 1. сохраня́ть [-ни́ть]; предохраня́ть [-ни́ть]; заготовля́ть впрок (о́вощи и т.п.); 2. (*mst pl.*) консе́рвы *m/pl.* (*a. opt.*); варе́нье; запове́дник.
preside [pri'zaid] председа́тельствовать (over на П).
presiden|cy ['prezidənsi] президе́нтство; председа́тельство; **~t** [-dənt] президе́нт; председа́тель *m.*
press [pres] 1. печа́ть *f*, пре́сса; да́вка; ⊕ пресс; 2. *v/t.* жать; дави́ть; наж(им)а́ть; навя́зывать [-за́ть] (on Д); *Am.* [вы́]гла́дить; be **~ed** for time спеши́ть; *v/i.* дави́ть (on на В); ~ for наста́ивать [настоя́ть] на (П); ~ on [по]спеши́ть; ~ (up)on наседа́ть [-е́сть] на (В); **~ing** ['presiŋ] □ неотло́жный; **~ure** ['preʃə] давле́ние (*a. fig.*); сжа́тие.
presum|able [pri'zju:məbl] □ предположи́тельный; **~e** [pri'zju:m] *v/t.* предполага́ть [-ложи́ть]; *v/i.* полага́ть; осме́ли(ва)ться; ~ (up)on злоупотребля́ть [-би́ть] (Т); кичи́ться (Т).
presumpt|ion [pri'zʌmpʃən] самонаде́янность *f*; предположе́ние; **~ive** [-tiv] □ предполага́емый; **~uous** [-tjuəs] □ самонаде́янный.
presuppos|e [pri:sə'pouz] предполага́ть [-ложи́ть]; **~ition** ['pri:sʌpə'ziʃən] предположе́ние.
pretence [pri'tens] прете́нзия, тре́бование; притво́рство; предло́г.
pretend [pri'tend] притворя́ться [-ри́ться]; симули́ровать (*im*)*pf.*; претендова́ть (to на В).
pretension [pri'tenʃən] прете́нзия, притяза́ние (to на В).
pretentious [-ʃəs] претенцио́зный.
pretext ['pri:tekst] предло́г.
pretty ['priti] 1. □ хоро́шенький; прия́тный; 2. *adv.* дово́льно.
prevail [pri'veil] превозмога́ть [-мо́чь] (over В); преоблада́ть (over над Т *or* среди́ Р); ~ (up)on a p. to do убеди́ть кого́-нибудь что́-либо сде́лать; **~ing** [-iŋ] □ преоблада́ющий.
prevalent ['prevələnt] □ преоблада́ющий; широко́ распространённый.
prevaricat|e [pri'værikeit] отклоня́ться от прямо́го отве́та, увиливать [-льну́ть].
prevent [pri'vent] предотвраща́ть [-ати́ть]; [по]меша́ть (Д); предупрежда́ть [-упреди́ть]; **~ion** [pri'venʃən] предупрежде́ние; предотвраще́ние; **~ive** [-tiv] 1. □ предупреди́тельный; профилакти́ческий; 2. ⚕ профилакти́ческое сре́дство.
pre|view ['pri:vju:] предвари́тельный осмо́тр (фи́льма, мод и т. п.).
previous ['pri:vjəs] □ предыду́щий; преждевре́менный; предвари́тельный; ~ to до (Р); **~ly** пре́жде.
pre-war ['pri:wɔ:] довое́нный.
prey [prei] 1. добы́ча; же́ртва; beast (bird) of ~ хи́щный зверь *m* (хи́щная пти́ца); 2. ~ (up)on: (о)гра́бить; терза́ть; подта́чивать [-точи́ть].
price [prais] 1. цена́; 2. оце́нивать [-ни́ть]; назнача́ть це́ну (Д); **~less** ['praislis] бесце́нный.
prick [prik] 1. проко́л; уко́л; шип; 2. *v/t.* коло́ть [кольну́ть]; ~ up one's ears навостри́ть у́ши; *v/i.* коло́ться; **~le** [prikl] шип, колю́чка; **~ly** ['prikli] колю́чий.
pride [praid] 1. го́рдость *f*; take ~ in горди́ться (Т); 2. ~ o. s. горди́ться ([up]on Т).
priest [pri:st] свяще́нник.
prim [prim] □ чо́порный; натя́нутый.
prima|cy ['praiməsi] пе́рвенство; **~ry** [-ri] □ первонача́льный; основно́й; нача́льный; перви́чный.
prime [praim] 1. □ гла́вный; первонача́льный; перви́чный; основно́й; превосхо́дный; ~ cost † себесто́имость *f*; ♀ Minister премье́р-мини́стр; 2. *fig.* расцве́т; 3. *v/t.* снабжа́ть информа́цией; учи́ть гото́вым отве́там.
primer ['primə] буква́рь *m*; нача́льный уче́бник.
primeval [prai'mi:vəl] первобы́тный.
primitive ['primitiv] □ первобы́тный; примити́вный; основно́й.
primrose ['primrouz] ⚘ при́мула.
prince [prins] принц; князь *m*; **~ss** [prin'ses] принце́сса; княги́ня; княжна́.
principal ['prinsəpəl] 1. □ гла́вный, основно́й; 2. принципа́л,

главá; рéктор университéта; дирéктор шкóлы; основнóй капитáл.
principle ['prinsəpl] при́нцип; прáвило; причи́на, истóчник; **on ~** из при́нципа.
print [print] **1.** *typ.* печáть *f*; óттиск; шрифт; след; отпечáток; штамп; гравю́ра; произведéние печáти; ✝ набивнáя ткань *f*; **out of ~** распрóданный (о печáтном); **2.** [на]печáтать; *phot.* отпечáт(ыв)ать; *fig.* запечатлé(вá)ть (**on** на П); **~er** ['printə] печáтник.
printing ['printiŋ] печáтание; печáтное издáние; *attr.* печáтный; **~-ink** типогрáфская крáска; **~-office** типогрáфия.
prior ['praiə] **1.** предшéствующий (to Д); **2.** *adv.* **~ to** до (Р); **3.** *eccl.* настоя́тель *m*; **~ity** [prai'ɔriti] приоритéт; очерёдность *f*.
prism [prizm] при́зма.
prison ['prizn] тюрьмá; **~er** [-ə] заключённый; плéнный.
privacy ['praivəsi] уединéние; сохранéние в тáйне.
private ['praivit] **1.** □ чáстный; ли́чный; уединённый; конфиденциáльный; **2.** ⚔ рядовóй; **in ~** конфиденциáльно.
privation [prai'veiʃən] лишéние, нуждá.
privilege ['privilidʒ] **1.** привилéгия; **2.** давáть привилéгию (Д).
privy ['privi]: **~ to** посвящённый в (В); ♀ Council тáйный совéт; ♀ Councillor член тáйного совéта; ♀ Seal мáлая госудáрственная печáть *f*.
prize [praiz] **1.** прéмия, приз; ⚓ приз; трофéй; вы́игрыш; **2.** удостóенный прéмии; **3.** высокó ценúть; взлáмывать [взломáть]; **~-fighter** боксёр-профессионáл.
probab|ility [prɔbə'biliti] вероя́тность *f*; **~le** ['prɔbəbl] □ вероя́тный.
probation [prə'beiʃən] испытáние; испытáтельный стаж; ⚖ услóвное освобождéние.
probe [proub] ⚕ **1.** зонд; **2.** зонди́ровать.
probity ['proubiti] чéстность *f*.
problem ['prɔbləm] проблéма; ♞ задáча; **~atic(al** □) [prɔbli'mætik, -tikəl] проблемати́чный.
procedure [prə'si:dʒə] процеду́ра; óбраз дéйствия.
proceed [prə'si:d] отправля́ться дáльше; приступáть [-пи́ть] (to к Д); поступáть [-пи́ть]; продолжáть [-дóлжить] (with В); **~ from** исходи́ть (от Р); **~ing** [-iŋ] постýпок; **~s** *pl.* ⚖ судопроизвóдство; протокóлы *m/pl.*, труды́ *m/pl.*; **~s** ['prousi:dz] дохóд; вы́ручка, вы́рученная сýмма.
process **1.** ['prouses] процéсс; движéние, течéние; ход; спóсоб; **in ~** на ходý; **in ~ of construction** стрóящийся; **2.** [prə'ses] привлекáть к судý; ⊕ обрабáтывать [-бóтать]; **~ion** [-ʃən] процéссия.
proclaim [prə'kleim] провозглашáть [-ласи́ть]; объявля́ть [-ви́ть] (войнý и т. п.).
proclamation [prɔklə'meiʃən] воззвáние; объявлéние; проклами́ция.
proclivity [prə'kliviti] склóнность *f*.
procurat|ion [prɔkjuə'reiʃən] полномóчие, довéренность *f*; **~or** ['prɔkjuəreitə] повéренный.
procure [prə'kjuə] *v/t.* дост(ав)áть; *v/i.* свóдничать.
prod [prɔd] **1.** тычóк, толчóк; **2.** ты́кать [ткнуть]; толкáть [-кнýть]; *fig.* подстрекáть [-кнýть].
prodigal ['prɔdigəl] **1.** расточи́тельный; **~ son** блýдный сын; **2.** мот(óвка).
prodig|ious [prə'didʒəs] □ удиви́тельный; громáдный; **~y** ['prɔdidʒi] чýдо.
produc|e **1.** [prə'dju:s] предъявля́ть [-ви́ть]; представля́ть [-áвить]; производи́ть [-вести́]; [по]стáвить (фильм и т. п.); изд(ав)áть; **2.** ['prɔdju:s] продýкция; продýкт; **~er** [prə'dju:sə] производи́тель *m*; режиссёр *m*.
product ['prɔdəkt] продýкт, издéлие; **~ion** [prə'dʌkʃən] произвóдство; продýкция; постанóвка; (худóжественное) произведéние; **~ive** [prə'dʌktiv] □ производи́тельный, продукти́вный; плодорóдный; **~iveness** [-nis], **~ivity** [prɔdʌk'tiviti] продукти́вность *f*, производи́тельность *f*.
profan|e [prə'fein] **1.** □ мирскóй, свéтский; богохýльный; **2.** осквернн́ть [-ни́ть]; профани́ровать (*im*)*pf*.; **~ity** [prə'fæniti] богохýльство.
profess [prə'fes] исповéдовать (вéру); откры́то признавáть; заявля́ть [-ви́ть]; претендовáть на (В); *univ.* преподавáть; **~ion** [prə'feʃən] профéссия; заявлéние; вероисповéдание; **~ional** [-l] **1.** □ профессионáльный; **2.** специали́ст; профессионáл (*a. sport*); **~or** [-sə] профéссор.
proffer ['prɔfə] **1.** предлагáть [-ложи́ть]; **2.** предложéние.
proficien|cy [prə'fiʃənsi] óпытность *f*; умéние; **~t** [-ʃənt] **1.** □ умéлый; искýсный; **2.** мáстер, знатóк.
profile ['proufi:l] прóфиль *m*.
profit ['prɔfit] **1.** при́быль *f*; вы́года, пóльза; **2.** *v/t.* приноси́ть пóльзу (Д); *v/i.* **~ by** [вос]пóльзоваться (Т); извлекáть пóльзу из (Р); **~able** ['prɔfitəbl] □ при́быльный; вы́годный; полéзный; **~eer** [prɔfi'tiə] **1.** спекуля́нт; **2.** спеку-

ли́ровать; **~-sharing** уча́стие в при́были.
profligate ['prɔfligit] **1.** □ распу́тный; **2.** распу́тник.
profound [prə'faund] □ глубо́кий; основа́тельный; проникнове́нный.
profundity [prə'fʌnditi] глубина́.
profus|e [prə'fju:s] □ изоби́льный; ще́дрый; **~ion** [prə'fju:ʒən] изоби́лие.
progen|itor [prou'dʒenitə] прароди́тель(ница *f*) *m*; **~y** ['prɔdʒini] пото́мство.
program, ~me ['prougræm] программа.
progress **1.** ['prougres] прогре́сс; продвиже́ние; успе́хи *m/pl.*; be in ~ развива́ться; вести́сь; **2.** [prə'gres] продвига́ться вперёд; де́лать успе́хи; **~ion** [prə'greʃən] движе́ние вперёд; Ⱥ прогре́ссия; **~ive** [-siv] **1.** □ передово́й, прогресси́вный; прогресси́рующий; **2.** *pol.* член прогресси́вной па́ртии.
prohibit [prə'hibit] запреща́ть [-ети́ть]; препя́тствовать (Д); **~ion** [proui'biʃən] запреще́ние; **~ive** [prə'hibitiv] □ запрети́тельный.
project **1.** ['prɔdʒekt] прое́кт; план; **2.** [prə'dʒekt] *v/t.* броса́ть [бро́сить]; [с-, за]проекти́ровать; *v/i.* обду́мывать план; вы́да(ва́)ться; **~ile** [prə'dʒektail] снаря́д; **~ion** [prə'dʒekʃən] мета́ние; проекти́рование; прое́кт; вы́ступ; прое́кция; **~or** [-tə] ✝ проектиро́вщик; *opt.* прожéктор; волше́бный фона́рь *m.*
proletarian [proule'tɛəriən] **1.** пролета́рий; **2.** пролета́рский.
prolific [prə'lifik] (~ally) плодоро́дный; плодови́тый.
prolix ['prouliks] □ многосло́вный.
prologue ['proulɔg] проло́г.
prolong [prə'lɔŋ] продлева́ть [-ли́ть]; продолжа́ть [-до́лжить].
promenade [prɔmi'nɑ:d] **1.** прогу́лка; ме́сто для прогу́лки; **2.** прогу́ливаться [-ля́ться].
prominent ['prɔminənt] □ выступа́ющий; релье́фный; *fig.* выдаю́щийся.
promiscuous [prə'miskjuəs] □ разноро́дный; сме́шанный; неразбо́рчивый.
promis|e ['prɔmis] **1.** обеща́ние; **2.** обеща́ть (*im*)*pf.*, *pf. a.* [по-]; **~ing** [-iŋ] □ *fig.* подаю́щий наде́жды; **~sory** [-əri] заключа́ющий в себе́ обеща́ние; ~ note ✝ долгово́е обяза́тельство.
promontory ['prɔməntri] мыс.
promot|e [prə'mout] спосо́бствовать (*im*)*pf.*, *pf. a.* [по-] (Д); соде́йствовать (*im*)*pf.*, *pf. a.* [по-] (Д); выдвига́ть [вы́двинуть]; продвига́ть [-и́нуть]; повыша́ть по слу́жбе; ⚔ присво́ить зва́ние (Р); **~ion** [prə'mouʃən] повыше́ние (в чи́не и т. п.); продвиже́ние.
prompt [prɔmpt] **1.** □ бы́стрый; прово́рный; **2.** побужда́ть [-уди́ть]; внуша́ть [-ши́ть]; подска́зывать [-за́ть] (Д); суфли́ровать (Д); **~er** ['prɔmptə] суфлёр; **~ness** ['prɔmptnis] быстрота́; прово́рство.
promulgate ['prɔməlgeit] провозглаша́ть [-ласи́ть].
prone [proun] □ (лежа́щий) ничко́м; распростёртый; ~ to скло́нный к (Д).
prong [prɔŋ] зубе́ц (ви́лки); шпенёк.
pronounce [prə'nauns] произноси́ть [-нести́]; объявля́ть [-ви́ть].
pronunciation [-nʌnsi'eiʃən] произноше́ние.
proof [pru:f] **1.** доказа́тельство; про́ба. испыта́ние; *typ.* корректу́ра, про́бный о́ттиск; **2.** непроница́емый; недосту́пный; **~-reader** корре́ктор.
prop [prɔp] подпо́рка; опо́ра.
propaga|te ['prɔpəgeit] размножа́ть(ся) [-о́жить(ся)]; распространя́ть(ся) [-ни́ть(ся)]; **~tion** [prɔpə'geiʃən] размноже́ние; распростране́ние.
propel [prə'pel] продвига́ть вперёд; **~ler** [-ə] пропе́ллер, возду́шный винт; гребно́й винт.
propensity [prə'pensiti] скло́нность *f.*
proper ['prɔpə] □ сво́йственный, прису́щий; подходя́щий; пра́вильный; со́бственный; прили́чный; **~ty** [-ti] иму́щество, со́бственность *f*; сво́йство.
prophe|cy ['prɔfisi] проро́чество; **~sy** [-sai] [на]проро́чить.
prophet ['prɔfit] проро́к.
propi|tiate [prə'piʃieit] умилостивля́ть [уми́лостивить]; **~tious** [prə'piʃəs] □ благоскло́нный; благоприя́тный.
proportion [prə'pɔ:ʃən] **1.** пропо́рция; соразме́рность *f*; часть *f*; ~s *pl.* разме́ры *m/pl.*; **2.** соразмеря́ть [-ме́рить]; **~al** [-l] □ пропорциона́льный.
propos|al [prə'pouzəl] предложе́ние; план; **~e** [prə'pouz] *v/t.* предлага́ть [-ложи́ть]; ~ to o. s. ста́вить себе́ це́лью; *v/i.* де́лать предложе́ние (бра́ка); намерева́ться, предполага́ть; **~ition** [prɔpə'ziʃən] предложе́ние.
propound [prə'paund] предлага́ть на обсужде́ние.
propriet|ary [prə'praiətəri] со́бственнический; ча́стный; *pharm.* патенто́ванный; **~or** [-tə] владе́лец (-лица); **~y** [-ti] уме́стность *f*, присто́йность *f*; the proprieties *pl.* прили́чия *n/pl.*
propulsion [prə'pʌlʃən] ⊕ приво́д; движе́ние вперёд.
pro-rate [prou'reit] распределя́ть пропорциона́льно.

prosaic [prou'zeiik] (~**ally**) *fig.* прозаи́чный.
proscribe [pros'kraib] объявля́ть вне зако́на; запреща́ть [-ети́ть].
prose [prouz] **1.** про́за; **2.** прозаи́ческий; *fig.* прозаи́чный.
prosecut|e ['prɔsikju:t] проводи́ть [-вести́], [по]вести́; пресле́довать суде́бным поря́дком; ~**ion** [prɔsi'kju:ʃən] суде́бное пресле́дование; ~**or** ['prɔsikju:tə] ⚖ обвини́тель *m*; public ~ прокуро́р.
prospect 1. ['prɔspekt] перспекти́ва, вид (*a. fig.*); † предполага́емый покупа́тель *m* (клие́нт и т. п.); **2.** [prəs'pekt] ⚒ разве́д(ыв)ать (for на В); ~**ive** [prəs'pektiv] □ бу́дущий, ожида́емый; ~**us** [-təs] проспе́кт.
prosper ['prɔspə] *v/t.* благоприя́тствова́ть (Д); *v/i.* процвета́ть; преуспева́ть; ~**ity** [prɔs'periti] процвета́ние; благосостоя́ние; *fig.* расцве́т; ~**ous** ['prɔspərəs] □ благоприя́тный; состоя́тельный; процвета́ющий.
prostitute ['prɔstitju:t] **1.** проститу́тка; **2.** проституи́ровать (*im*)*pf.*; [о]бесче́стить.
prostrat|e 1. ['prɔstreit] распростёртый; пове́рженный; обесси́ленный; **2.** [prɔs'treit] поверга́ть ниц; унижа́ть [уни́зить]; истоща́ть [-щи́ть]; ~ o. s. па́дать ниц; ~**ion** [-ʃən] распростёртое положе́ние; изнеможе́ние.
prosy ['prouzi] □ *fig.* проза́ичный; бана́льный.
protect [prə'tekt] защища́ть [-ити́ть]; (пред)охраня́ть [-ни́ть] (from от Р); ~**ion** [prə'tekʃən] защи́та; ~**ive** [-tiv] защи́тный; предохрани́тельный; ~ duty покрови́тельственная по́шлина; ~**or** [-tə] защи́тник; ~**orate** [-tərit] протектора́т.
protest 1. ['proutest] проте́ст; опротестова́ние (ве́кселя); **2.** [prə'test] [за]протестова́ть; опротесто́вывать [-стова́ть] (ве́ксель).
Protestant ['prɔtistənt] **1.** протеста́нт(ка); **2.** протеста́нтский.
protestation [proutes'teiʃən] торже́ственное заявле́ние.
protocol ['proutəkɔl] протоко́л.
prototype [-taip] прототи́п.
protract [prə'trækt] тяну́ть (В *or* с Т); продолжа́ть [-до́лжить].
protru|de [prə'tru:d] выдава́ться нару́жу, торча́ть; ~**sion** [-ʒən] вы́ступ.
protuberance [prə'tju:bərəns] вы́пуклость *f*; опу́холь *f*.
proud [praud] □ го́рдый (of Т).
prove [pru:v] *v/t.* дока́зывать [-за́ть]; удостоверя́ть [-ве́рить]; испы́тывать [-пыта́ть]; *v/i.* ока́зываться [-за́ться].
provender ['prɔvində] корм.
proverb ['prɔvəb] посло́вица.
provide [prə'vaid] *v/t.* заготовля́ть [-то́вить]; снабжа́ть [-бди́ть]; обеспе́чи(ва)ть; ⚖ ста́вить усло́вием; *v/i.* запаса́ться [-сти́сь]; ~**d** (that) при усло́вии (что).
providen|ce ['prɔvidəns] провиде́ние; предусмотри́тельность *f*; ~**t** [-dənt] □ предусмотри́тельный; ~**tial** [prɔvi'denʃəl] □ провиденциа́льный.
provider [prə'vaidə] поставщи́к [(-и́ца).
provin|ce ['prɔvins] о́бласть *f*; прови́нция; *fig.* сфе́ра де́ятельности; ~**cial** [prə'vinʃəl] **1.** провинциа́льный; **2.** провинциа́л(ка).
provision [prə'viʒən] снабже́ние; обеспе́чение; ⚖ положе́ние (догово́ра и т. п.); ~**s** *pl.* прови́зия; ~**al** [-l] □ предвари́тельный; вре́менный.
proviso [prə'vaizou] усло́вие.
provocat|ion [prɔvə'keiʃən] вы́зов; провока́ция; раздраже́ние; ~**ive** [prə'vɔkətiv] вызыва́ющий (о поведе́нии и т. п.); провокацио́нный.
provoke [prə'vouk] [с]провоци́ровать; возбужда́ть [-буди́ть]; вызыва́ть [вы́звать]; [рас]серди́ть.
provost 1. ['prɔvest] ре́ктор; дека́н; **2.** [prə'vou] ⚔ офице́р вое́нной поли́ции.
prow [prau] ⚓ нос (су́дна).
prowess ['prauis] до́блесть *f*.
prowl [praul] кра́сться; броди́ть.
proximity [prɔk'simiti] бли́зость *f*.
proxy ['prɔksi] замести́тель *m*; полномо́чие; переда́ча го́лоса; дове́ренность *f*.
prude [pru:d] щепети́льная, стыдли́вая же́нщина.
pruden|ce ['pru:dəns] благоразу́мие; предусмотри́тельность *f*; осторо́жность *f*; ~**t** [-t] □ благоразу́мный; осторо́жный.
prud|ery ['pru:dəri] чрезме́рная стыдли́вость *f*; ~**ish** [-diʃ] □ чрезме́рно стыдли́вый.
prune [pru:n] **1.** чернosли́в; **2.** ✂ подреза́ть [-ре́зать], обреза́ть [обре́зать]; *fig.* сокраща́ть [-рати́ть].
prurient ['pruəriənt] □ похотли́вый.
pry [prai] **1.** подгля́дывать [-яде́ть]; ~ into сова́ть нос в (В); *Am.* ~ open вскры́(ва́)ть, взла́мывать [взлома́ть]; ~ up поднима́ть [-ня́ть]; **2.** рыча́г.
psalm [sɑ:m] псало́м.
pseudonym ['(p)sju:dənim] псевдони́м.
psychiatrist [sai'kaiətrist] психиа́тр.
psychic ['saikik], ~**al** [-kikəl] □ психи́ческий.
psycholog|ical [saikə'lɔdʒikəl] □ психологи́ческий; ~**ist** [sai'kɔlədʒist] психо́лог; ~**y** [-dʒi] психоло́гия.
pub [pʌb] F трактир, каба́к.

puberty ['pju:bəti] половáя зрéлость *f*.
public ['pʌblik] 1. □ публи́чный, общéственный; госудáрственный; коммунáльный; ~ house трактир; ~ law междунарóдное прáво; ~ spirit дух солидáрности, патриоти́зма; 2. пýблика; общéственность *f*; ~an ['pʌblikən] трактирщик; ~ation [pʌbli'keiʃən] опубликовáние; издáние; monthly ~ ежемéсячник; ~ity [pʌ'blisiti] глáсность *f*; реклáма.
publish ['pʌbliʃ] [о]публиковáть, изд(ав)áть; опубликóвывать [-ковáть]; оглашáть [-ласи́ть]; ~ing house издáтельство; ~er [-ə] издáтель *m*; ~s *pl.* издáтельство.
pucker ['pʌkə] 1. [с]мóрщить(ся); 2. морщи́на.
pudding ['pudiŋ] пýдинг; black ~ кровянáя колбасá.
puddle ['pʌdl] лýжа.
puerile ['pjuərail] □ ребя́ческий.
puff [pʌf] 1. дуновéние (вéтра); клуб (ды́ма); пухóвка; 2. *v/t.* надý(вá)ть; выпя́чивать [вы́пятить]; расхвáливать [-ли́ть], преувели́ченно реклами́ровать; ~ed eyes распýхшие глазá *m/pl.*; *v/i.* дуть поры́вами; пыхтéть; ~ away at попы́хивать (Т); ~ out надý(вá)ться; ~-paste слоёное тéсто; ~y ['pʌfi] запыхáвшийся; отёкший; одутловáтый.
pug [pʌg], ~-dog мопс.
pugnacious [pʌg'neiʃəs] драчли́вый.
pug-nosed ['pʌgnouzd] курнóсый.
puke [pju:k] рвóта.
pull [pul] 1. тя́га; рýчка (звонкá и т. п.); затя́жка (ды́мом); 2. [по-] тянýть; таскáть, [по]тащи́ть; выдёргивать [вы́дернуть]; дёргать [-рнуть]; ~ down сноси́ть [снести́] (здáние и т. п.); ~ out 🚂 отходи́ть [отойти́] (от стáнции); ⚕ ~ through выхáживать [вы́ходить]; поправля́ться [-áвиться] (от болéзни); ~ o. s. together взять себя́ в рýки; ~ up подтя́гивать [-янýть]; осáживать [осади́ть] (лошадéй); останáвливать(ся) [-нови́ть(ся)].
pulley ['puli] ⊕ блок; вóрот; ремённый шкив.
pulp [pʌlp] мя́коть плодá; пýльпа (зýба); ⊕ бумáжная мáсса.
pulpit ['pulpit] кáфедра (проповéдника).
pulpy ['pʌlpi] □ мя́гкий; мяси́стый.
puls|ate [pʌl'seit] пульси́ровать; би́ться; ~e [pʌls] пульс.
pulverize ['pʌlvəraiz] *v/t.* распыля́ть [-ли́ть]; размельчáть в порошóк; *v/i.* распыля́ться [-ли́ться].
pumice ['pʌmis] пéмза.
pump [pʌmp] 1. насóс; лёгкая бáльная тýфля; 2. качáть [качнýть] (насóсом); ~ up накáчивать [-чáть].
pumpkin ['pʌmpkin] ♀ ты́ква.
pun [pʌn] 1. каламбýр; 2. каламбýрить.
Punch[1] [pʌntʃ] полишинéль *m*.
punch[2] [~] 1. ⊕ кéрнер, пробóйник; компóстер; удáр кулакóм; 2. проби́(вá)ть (отвéрстия); [от-] штамповáть; бить кулакóм.
punctilious [pʌŋk'tiliəs] педанти́чный; щепети́льный до мелочéй.
punctual ['pʌŋktjuəl] □ пунктуáльный; ~ity [pʌŋktju'æliti] пунктуáльность *f*.
punctuat|e ['pʌŋktjueit] стáвить знáки препинáния; *fig.* перемежáть; ~ion [pʌŋktju'eiʃən] пунктуáция.
puncture ['pʌŋktʃə] 1. прокóл; ⚡ пробóй; 2. прокáлывать [-колóть]; получáть прокóл.
pungen|cy ['pʌndʒənsi] остротá, éдкость *f*; ~t [-t] óстрый, éдкий.
punish ['pʌniʃ] накáзывать [-зáть]; ~able [-əbl] □ наказýемый; ~ment [-mənt] наказáние.
puny ['pju:ni] □ крóхотный; тщедýшный.
pupil [pju:pl] *anat.* зрачóк; учени́к (-и́ца).
puppet ['pʌpit] марионéтка (*a. fig.*); ~show кýкольный теáтр.
puppy ['pʌpi] щенóк; *fig.* молокосóс; фат.
purchase ['pə:tʃəs] 1. покýпка, закýпка; приобретéние; ⊕ механи́зм для поднятия грýзов (рычáг; лебёдка и т. п.); *fig.* тóчка опóры; 2. покупáть [купи́ть]; приобретáть [-рести́]; ~r [-ə] покупáтель(ница *f*) *m*.
pure [pjuə] □ *com.* чи́стый; беспорóчный; беспри́месный; ~-bred ['pjuəbred] *Am.* чистокрóвный.
purgat|ive ['pə:gətiv] слаби́тельное; ~ory [-t(ə)ri] чисти́лище.
purge [pə:dʒ] 1. ⚕ слаби́тельное; *pol.* чи́стка; 2. очищáть [очи́стить]; *pol.* провод:ть чи́стку в (П).
purify ['pjuərifai] очищáть [очи́стить].
purity ['pjuəriti] чистотá; непорóчность *f*.
purl [pə:l] журчáть.
purlieus ['pə:lju:z] *pl.* окрéстности *f/pl.*
purloin [pə:'lɔin] [у]воровáть.
purple [pə:pl] 1. пурпýрный; багрóвый; 2. пýрпур; 3. turn ~ [по-] багровéть.
purport ['pə:pət] смысл, содержáние.
purpose ['pə:pəs] 1. намéрение, цель *f*; ýмысел; on ~ нарóчно; to the ~ кстáти; к дéлу; to no ~ напрáсно; 2. имéть цéлью; намеревáться [намéриться]; ~ful [-ful] □ умы́шленный; целеустремлённый; ~less [-lis] □ бесцéльный; ~ly [-li] нарóчно.
purr [pə:] [за]мурлы́кать.
purse [pə:s] 1. кошелёк; дéнежный приз; public ~ казнá; 2. подж(им)áть (гýбы); зажмýри(ва)ть (глазá).

pursuan|ce [pə'sju(:)əns]: in ~ of согла́сно (Д); ~t [-ənt]: ~ to согла́сно (Д).
pursu|e [pə'sju:] пресле́довать (В); занима́ться [заня́ться] (Т); продолжа́ть [-до́лжить]; ~er [-ə] пресле́дователь(ница *f*) *m*; ~it [pə'sju:t] пого́ня *f*; *mst* ~s *pl.* заня́тие.
purvey [pə:'vei] поставля́ть [-а́вить] (проду́кты); снабжа́ть [-бди́ть] (Т); ~or [-ə] поставщи́к.
pus [pʌs] ⚕ гной.
push [puʃ] 1. толчо́к; уда́р; давле́ние; напо́р; уси́лие; 2. толка́ть [-кну́ть]; наж(им)а́ть (на В); продвига́ть(ся) [-ви́нуть(ся)] (*a.* ~ on); притесня́ть [-ни́ть]; [по]торопи́ть; ~ one's way прота́лкиваться [протолка́ться]; ~-button ⚡ кно́пка (звонка́ и т. п.).
pussillanimous [pju:si'lænimǝs] □ малоду́шный.
puss(y) ['pus(i)] ко́шечка, ки́ска.
put [put] [*irr.*] 1. класть [положи́ть]; [по]ста́вить; сажа́ть [посади́ть]; зад(ав)а́ть (вопро́с, зада́чу и т. п.); сова́ть [су́нуть]; ~ across успе́шно проводи́ть (ме́ру); перевози́ть [-везти́]; ~ back ста́вить на ме́сто (обра́тно); ста́вить наза́д; ~ by откла́дывать [отложи́ть] (де́ньги); ~ down подавля́ть [-ви́ть] (восста́ние); запи́сывать [-са́ть]; заставля́ть замолча́ть; припи́сывать [-са́ть] (to Д); ~ forth проявля́ть [-ви́ть]; пуска́ть [пусти́ть] (побе́ги); пуска́ть в обраще́ние; ~ in вставля́ть [-а́вить]; всо́вывать [всу́нуть]; ~ off снима́ть [снять] (оде́жду); отде́л(ыв)аться от (Р with Т); отта́лкивать [оттолкну́ть]; откла́дывать [отложи́ть]; ~ on наде́(ва́)ть (пла́тье и т. п.); *fig.* принима́ть [-ня́ть] (вид); прибавля́ть [-а́вить]; ~ out выкла́дывать [вы́ложить]; протя́гивать [-тяну́ть]; выгоня́ть [вы́гнать]; [по]туши́ть (ого́нь); ~ through *teleph.* соединя́ть [-ни́ть] (to с Т); ~ to прибавля́ть [-ба́вить]; ~ to death казни́ть (*im*)*pf.*; ~ to the rack пыта́ть; ~ up [по-] стро́ить, возводи́ть [-вести́] (зда́ние); [по]ста́вить (пье́су); дава́ть прию́т (Д); 2. *v/i.*: ⚓ ~ off, ~ to sea уходи́ть в мо́ре; ~ in ⚓ заходи́ть в порт; up at остана́вливаться [останови́ться] в (П); ~ up with [по]мири́ться с (Т).
putrefy ['pju:trifai] (с)гнить.
putrid ['pju:trid] □ гнило́й; воню́чий; ~ity [pju:'triditi] гниль *f*.
putty ['pʌti] 1. (око́нная) зама́зка; 2. зама́з(ыв)ать (о́кна).
puzzle [pʌzl] 1. недоуме́ние; затрудне́ние; зага́дка; головоло́мка; 2. *v/t.* озада́чи(ва)ть; ста́вить в тупи́к; ~ out распу́т(ыв)ать; *v/i.* би́ться (over над Т); ~-headed ['pʌzl'hedid] бестолко́вый; сумбу́рный.
pygm|ean [pig'mi:ən] ка́рликовый; ~y ['pigmi] ка́рлик, пигме́й.
pyjamas [pə'dʒɑ:məz] *pl.* пижа́ма.
pyramid ['pirəmid] пирами́да; ~al [pi'ræmidl] пирамида́льный.
pyre ['paiə] погреба́льный костёр.
pyrotechnic [pairo'teknik] пиротехни́ческий; ~ display фейерве́рк.
Pythagorean [pai'θægə'ri:ən] пифаго́рейский.
pyx [piks] *eccl.* дарохрани́тельница.

Q

quack [kwæk] 1. зна́харь *m* (-рка); шарлата́н; кря́канье (у́ток); 2. шарлата́нский; 3. кря́кать [-кнуть]; ~ery ['kwækəri] шарлата́нство.
quadrangle [kwɔ'dræŋgl] четырёхуго́льник; шко́льный двор.
quadrennial [kwɔ'dreniəl] □ четырёхле́тний; происходя́щий раз в четы́ре го́да.
quadru|ped ['kwɔdruped] четвероно́гое живо́тное; ~ple ['kwɔdrupl] □ учетверённый; четверно́й.
quagmire ['kwægmaie] тряси́на, боло́то.
quail [kweil] дро́гнуть *pf.*; [с]тру́сить.
quaint [kweint] □ стра́нный, необы́чный.
quake [kweik] [за]трясти́сь; [за-] дрожа́ть; дро́гнуть *pf.*
Quaker ['kweikə] ква́кер.
quali|fication [kwɔlifi'keiʃən] квалифика́ция; сво́йство; ограниче́ние; ~fy ['kwɔlifai] *v/t.* квалифици́ровать (*im*)*pf.*; ограни́чи(ва)ть; смягча́ть [-чи́ть]; наз(ы)ва́ть (as Т); *v/i.* подгота́вливаться [-гото́виться] (for к Д); ~ty [-ti] ка́чество; сво́йство; досто́инство.
qualm [kwɔ:m, kwɑ:m] тошнота́; сомне́ние; присту́п малоду́шия.
quantity ['kwɔntiti] коли́чество; ⅍ величина́; мно́жество.
quarantine ['kwɔrənti:n] 1. каранти́н; 2. подверга́ть каранти́ну.
quarrel ['kwɔrəl] 1. ссо́ра, перебра́нка; 2. [по]ссо́риться; ~some [-səm] □ вздо́рный; приди́рчивый.
quarry ['kwɔri] 1. каменоло́мня; добы́ча (на охо́те) 2. добы́(ва́)ть (ка́мни); *fig.* [по]ры́ться.
quart [kwɔ:t] ква́рта (= 1,14 ли́тра).
quarter ['kwɔ:tə] 1. че́тверть *f*; че́тверть часа́; кварта́л; ме́сто, сторона́; поща́да; ~s *pl.* кварти́ра; ⚔ каза́рмы *f/pl.*; *fig.* исто́чники

m/pl.; from all ~s со всех сторо́н; **2.** дели́ть на четы́ре ча́сти; ⚔ расквартиро́вывать [-ирова́ть]; четвертова́ть (*im*)*pf.*; **~-day** день, начина́ющий кварта́л го́да; **~-deck** шка́нцы *m/pl.*; **~ly** [-li] **1.** кварта́льный; **2.** журна́л, выходя́щий ка́ждый кварта́л го́да; **~master** ⚔ квартирме́йстер.
quartet(te) [kwɔ:'tet] ♪ кварте́т.
quash [kwɔʃ] ⚖ аннули́ровать (*im*)*pf.*
quaver ['kweivə] **1.** дрожь *f*; ♪ трель *f*; **2.** вибри́ровать; говори́ть дрожа́щим го́лосом.
quay [ki:] на́бережная.
queasy ['kwi:zi] □ сла́бый (о желу́дке); тошнотво́рный.
queen [kwi:n] короле́ва; *chess* ферзь *m*; **~like, ~ly** ['kwi:nli] подоба́ющий короле́ве; ца́рственный.
queer [kwiə] стра́нный, эксцентри́чный.
quench [kwentʃ] утоля́ть [-ли́ть] (жа́жду); [по]туши́ть; охлажда́ть [охлади́ть].
querulous ['kweruləs] □ ворчли́вый.
query ['kwiəri] **1.** вопро́с; **2.** спра́шивать [спроси́ть]; подверга́ть сомне́нию.
quest [kwest] **1.** по́иски *m/pl.*; **2.** оты́скивать [-ка́ть], разы́скивать [-ка́ть].
question ['kwestʃən] **1.** вопро́с; сомне́ние; пробле́ма; beyond (all) ~ вне вся́кого сомне́ния; in ~ (лицо́, вопро́с,) о кото́ром идёт речь; call in ~ подверга́ть сомне́нию; that is out of the ~ об э́том не мо́жет быть и ре́чи; **2.** расспра́шивать [-роси́ть]; задава́ть вопро́с (Д); допра́шивать [-роси́ть]; подверга́ть сомне́нию; **~able** [-əbl] □ сомни́тельный; **~naire** [kestiə'nεə, kwestʃə'nεə] анке́та.
queue [kju:] **1.** о́чередь *f*, «хвост»; коса́ (воло́с); **2.** заплета́ть в ко́су; (*mst* ~ up) стоя́ть в о́череди.
quibble [kwibl] **1.** игра́ слов, каламбу́р; увёртка; **2.** [с]остри́ть; уклоня́ться [-ни́ться].
quick [kwik] **1.** живо́й; бы́стрый, ско́рый; прово́рный; о́стрый (слух и т. п.); **2.** чувстви́тельное ме́сто; to the ~ *fig.* за живо́е; до мо́зга косте́й; cut to the ~ заде́вать за живо́е; **~en** ['kwikən] *v/t.* ускоря́ть [-о́рить]; оживля́ть [-ви́ть]; *v/i.* ускоря́ться [-о́риться]; оживля́ться [-ви́ться]; **~ness** ['kwiknis] быстрота́; оживлённость *f*; сообрази́тельность *f*; **~sand** плыву́н, сыпу́чие пески́ *m/pl.*; **~silver** ртуть *f*; **~-witted** нахо́дчивый.
quiescen|ce [kwai'esns] поко́й; неподви́жность *f*; **~t** [-t] неподви́жный; *fig.* споко́йный.
quiet ['kwaiət] **1.** □ споко́йный, ти́хий; бесшу́мный; сми́рный; **2.** поко́й; тишина́; **3.** успока́ивать(ся), [-ко́ить(ся)]; **~ness** [-nis], **~ude** [-ju:d] тишина́; поко́й; споко́йствие.
quill [kwil] пти́чье перо́; ствол пера́; *fig.* перо́ (для письма́); игла́ (ежа́ и т. п.); **~ing** ['kwiliŋ] рюш (на пла́тье).
quilt [kwilt] **1.** стёганое одея́ло; **2.** [вы́]стега́ть.
quince [kwins] ❦ айва́.
quinine [kwi'ni:n, *Am.* 'kwainain] *pharm.* хини́н.
quintuple ['kwintjupl] пятикра́тный.
quip [kwip] сарка́зм; острота́; ко́лкость *f*.
quirk [kwə:k] = quibble, quip; причу́да; ро́счерк пера́; завито́к (рису́нка).
quit [kwit] **1.** покида́ть [-и́нуть]; оставля́ть [-а́вить]; give notice to ~ заявля́ть об ухо́де (с рабо́ты); **2.** свобо́дный, отде́лавшийся (of от Р).
quite [kwait] вполне́, соверше́нно, совсе́м; дово́льно; ~ a hero настоя́щий геро́й; ~ (so)!, ~ that! так!, соверше́нно ве́рно!
quittance ['kwitəns] квита́нция.
quiver ['kwivə] [за]дрожа́ть; [за-] трепета́ть.
quiz [kwiz] **1.** шу́тка; мистифика́ция; насме́шка; *part. Am.* опро́с, прове́рка зна́ний; **2.** подшу́чивать [-ути́ть] над (Т); *part. Am.* опра́шивать [опроси́ть].
quorum ['kwɔ:rəm] *parl.* кво́рум.
quota ['kwoutə] до́ля, часть *f*, кво́та.
quotation [kwou'teiʃən] цита́та; цити́рование; ✝ котиро́вка, курс.
quote [kwout] [про]цити́ровать; ✝ котирова́ть (*im*)*pf.*; дава́ть расце́нку на (В).

R

rabbi ['ræbai] равви́н.
rabbit ['ræbit] кро́лик.
rabble [ræbl] сброд; толпа́.
rabid ['ræbid] □ неи́стовый, я́ростный; бе́шеный.
rabies ['reibii:z] бе́шенство.
race [reis] **1.** ра́са; род; поро́да; состяза́ние в ско́рости; бег; го́нки *f/pl.*; (*mst* ~s *pl.*) ска́чки *f/pl.*; бега́ *m/pl.*; **2.** [по]мча́ться; состяза́ться в ско́рости; уча́ствовать в ска́чках и т. п.; **~-course** доро́жка; трек; **~r** ['reisə] уча́стник го́нок и́ли ска́чек (ло́шадь, автомоби́ль и т. п.).
racial ['reiʃəl] ра́совый.

rack [ræk] **1.** вéшалка; подстáвка; пóлка; стóйка; кормýшка; 🚂 luggage ~ сéтка для вещéй; **2.** класть в сéтку или на пóлку; пытáть; ~ one's brains ломáть себé гóлову; go to ~ and ruin погибáть [-и́бнуть]; разоря́ться [-ри́ться].
racket ['rækit] тéннисная ракéтка; шум, гам; *Am.* шантáж; **~eer** [ræki'tiə] *Am.* вымогáтель *m.*
racy ['reisi] □ характéрный; крéпкий; пикáнтный; колори́тный.
radar ['reidɑ:] радáр; ~ set радиолокáтор.
radian|ce ['reidiəns] сия́ние; **~t** [-t] □ лучи́стый; сия́ющий, лучезáрный.
radiat|e ['reidieit] излучáть [-чи́ть] (свет, теплó); **~ion** [reidi'eiʃən] излучéние; **~or** ['reidieitə] излучáтель *m*; ⚠, *mot.* радиáтор.
radical ['rædikəl] **1.** □ основнóй, кореннóй; фундаментáльный; радикáльный; **2.** *pol.* радикáл.
radio ['reidiou] **1.** рáдио *n indecl.*; ~ drama, ~ play радиопостанóвка; ~ set радиоприёмник; **2.** передавáть по рáдио; **~graph** [-grɑ:f] **1.** рентгéновский сни́мок; **2.** дéлать рентгéновский сни́мок с (Р); **~scopy** [reidi'ɔskəpi] исслéдование рентгéновскими лучáми; **~-telegram** радио(теле)грáмма.
radish ['rædiʃ] рéдька; (red) ~ реди́ска.
raffle [ræfl] **1.** *v/t.* разы́грывать в лотерéю; *v/i.* учáствовать в лотерéе; **2.** лотерéя.
raft [rɑ:ft] **1.** плот; парóм **2.** сплавля́ть [-áвить] (лес); **~er** ['rɑ:ftə] ⊕ стропи́ло.
rag [ræg] тря́пка; **~s** *pl.* тряпьё, вéтошь *f*; лохмóтья *m/pl.*
ragamuffin ['rægəmʌfin] оборвáнец; ýличный мáльчик.
rage [reidʒ] **1.** я́рость *f*, гнев; повáльное увлечéние; предмéт увлечéния; it is all the ~ э́то послéдний крик мóды; **2.** [вз]беси́ться; бушевáть.
ragged ['rægid] □ нерóвный; рвáный, понóшенный.
raid [reid] **1.** налёт; набéг; облáва; **2.** дéлать набéг, налёт на (В); вторгáться [вторгнуться] в (В).
rail [reil] **1.** пери́ла *n/pl.*; огрáда; 🚂 рельс; поперéчина; (main) ~ ⚓ пóручень *m*; run off the ~s сойти́ с рéльсов; **2.** éхать по желéзной дорóге; [вы́]ругáть, [вы́]брани́ть (at, against В).
railing ['reiliŋ] огрáда; пери́ла *n/pl.*
raillery ['reiləri] беззлóбная насмéшка, подшýчивание.
railroad ['reilroud] *part. Am.*, **railway** [-wei] желéзная дорóга.
rain [rein] **1.** дождь *m*; **2.** идти́ (о дождé); *fig.* [по]сы́паться; **~bow** рáдуга; **~coat** *Am.* дождеви́к, непромокáемое пальтó *n indecl.*; **~fall** коли́чество осáдков; **~-proof** непромокáемый; **~y** ['reini] □ дождли́вый.
raise [reiz] (*often* ~ up) поднимáть [-ня́ть]; воздвигáть [-ви́гнуть] (пáмятник и т. п.); возвышáть [-вы́сить]; воспи́тывать [-итáть]; вызывáть [вы́звать] (смех, гнев и т. п.); возбуждáть [-уди́ть] (чýвство); добы́(вá)ть (дéньги).
raisin [reizn] изю́минка; *pl.* изю́м.
rake [reik] **1.** грáбли *f/pl.*; кочергá; повéса *m*; распýтник; **2.** *v/t.* сгребáть [-ести́]; разгребáть [-ести́]; *fig.* ~ for тщáтельно искáть (В or Р).
rally ['ræli] **1.** вновь собирáть(ся); овладé(вá)ть собóй; **2.** *Am.* мáссовый ми́тинг; объединéние; съезд.
ram [ræm] **1.** барáн; тарáн; **2.** [про-] тарáнить; заби́(вá)ть.
rambl|e ['ræmbl] **1.** прогýлка (без цéли); **2.** броди́ть без цéли; говори́ть бессвя́зно; **~er** [-ə] праздношатáющийся; ползýчее растéние; **~ing** [-iŋ] бродя́чий; бессвя́зный; разбрóсанный; ползýчий.
ramify ['ræmifai] разветвля́ться [-етви́ться].
ramp [ræmp] скат, уклóн; **~ant** ['ræmpənt] стоя́щий на зáдних лáпах (о геральди́ческом живóтном); *fig.* необýзданный.
rampart ['ræmpɑ:t] вал.
ramshackle ['ræmʃækl] вéтхий.
ran [ræn] *pt.* от run.
ranch [ræntʃ] *Am.* скотовóдная фéрма.
rancid ['rænsid] □ прогóрклый.
ranco(u)r ['ræŋkə] злóба, затаённая враждá.
random ['rændəm] **1.** at ~ наугáд, наобýм; **2.** сдéланный (вы́бранный и т. д.) наугáд; случáйный.
rang [ræŋ] *pt.* от ring.
range [reindʒ] **1.** ряд; ли́ния (домóв); цепь *f* (гор); óбласть распространéния (растéний и т. п.); предéл, амплитýда; диапазóн (гóлоса); ⚔ дáльность дéйствия; стрéльбище; **2.** *v/t.* выстрáивать в ряд; стáвить в поря́дке; классифици́ровать (*im*)*pf.*; ⚓ плáвать, [по]плы́ть вдоль (Р); *v/i.* выстрáиваться в ряд; простирáться; броди́ть, ры́скать.
rank [ræŋk] **1.** ряд; ⚔ шерéнга; звáние, чин; категóрия; ~ and file рядовóй состáв; *fig.* людскáя мáсса; **2.** *v/t.* стрóить в шерéнгу; выстрáивать в ряд; классифици́ровать (*im*)*pf.*; *v/i.* стрóиться в шерéнгу; равня́ться (with Д); **3.** бýйный (о расти́тельности); прогóркльй (о мáсле); отъя́вленный.
rankle [ræŋkl] *fig.* мýчить, терзáть (об оби́де и т. п.); ~ in терзáть (В).
ransack ['rænsæk] [по]ры́ться в (П); [о]грáбить.
ransom ['rænsəm] **1.** вы́куп; **2.** выкупáть [вы́купить].

rant [rænt] **1.** деклама́ция; высокопа́рная речь *f*; **2.** говори́ть напы́щенно; [про]деклами́ровать; шу́мно весели́ться.

rap [ræp] **1.** лёгкий уда́р; стук (в дверь и т. п.); *fig.* not a ~ ни гроша́; **2.** ударя́ть [уда́рить]; [по-] стуча́ть.

rapaci|ous [rəˈpeiʃəs] □ жа́дный; хи́щный; **~ty** [rəˈpæsiti] жа́дность *f*; хи́щность *f*.

rape [reip] **1.** похище́ние; изнаси́лование; **2.** похища́ть [-и́тить]; [из]наси́ловать.

rapid [ˈræpid] **1.** □ бы́стрый, ско́рый; круто́й; **2.** **~s** *pl.* поро́ги *m/pl.*, стремни́ны *f/pl.*; **~ity** [rəˈpiditi] ско́рость *f*.

rapt [ræpt] восхищённый; увлечённый; **~ure** [ˈræptʃə] восто́рг, экста́з; go into **~s** приходи́ть в восто́рг.

rare [rɛə] □ ре́дкий; *phys.* разреже́нный.

rarefy [ˈrɛərifai] разрежа́ть(ся) [-еди́ть(ся)].

rarity [-riti] ре́дкость *f*.

rascal [ˈrɑːskəl] моше́нник; **~ity** [rɑːsˈkæliti] моше́нничество; **~ly** [ˈrɑːskəli] моше́ннический.

rash[1] [ræʃ] □ стреми́тельный; опроме́тчивый; необду́манный.

rash[2] [~] сыпь *f*.

rasp [rɑːsp] **1.** ра́шпиль *m*; скре́жет; **2.** подпи́ливать ра́шпилем; соскреба́ть [-ести́]; раздража́ть [-жи́ть].

raspberry [ˈrɑːzbəri] мали́на.

rat [ræt] кры́са; *sl.* изме́нник; smell a ~ чу́ять недо́брое.

rate [reit] **1.** но́рма; ста́вка; пропо́рция; сте́пень *f*; ме́стный нало́г; разря́д; ско́рость *f*; at any ~ во вся́ком слу́чае; ~ of exchange (валю́тный) курс; **2.** оце́нивать [-ни́ть], расце́нивать [-ни́ть]; [вы́-] брани́ть; ~ among счита́ться среди́ (P).

rather [rɑːðə] скоре́е; предпочти́тельно; верне́е; дово́льно; I had ~ ... я предпочёл бы ...

ratify [ˈrætifai] ратифици́ровать (*im*)*pf.*; утвержда́ть [-рди́ть].

rating [ˈreitiŋ] оце́нка; су́мма нало́га; ранг; класс.

ratio [ˈreiʃiou] 🕮 отноше́ние.

ration [ˈræʃən] **1.** рацио́н; паёк; **2.** снабжа́ть продово́льствием; нормирова́ть вы́дачу (P).

rational [ræʃnl] □ рациона́льный; разу́мный; **~ity** [ræʃˈnæliti] рациона́льность *f*; разу́мность *f*; **~ize** [ˈræʃnəlaiz] рационализи́ровать (*im*)*pf*.

ratten [rætn] саботи́ровать (*im*)*pf*.

rattle [rætl] **1.** треск; дребезжа́ние; трещо́тка (*a. fig.*); погрему́шка; **2.** [про]треща́ть; [за]дребезжа́ть; [за]греме́ть (T); говори́ть без у́молку; ~ off отбараба́нить *pf.*; **~snake** грему́чая змея́; **~trap** *fig.* ве́тхий экипа́ж, автомоби́ль и т. п.

rattling [ˈrætliŋ] *fig.* бы́стрый; великоле́пный.

raucous [ˈrɔkəs] □ хри́плый.

ravage [ˈrævidʒ] **1.** опустоше́ние; **2.** опустоша́ть [-ши́ть]; разоря́ть [-ри́ть].

rave [reiv] бре́дить (*a. fig.*), говори́ть бессвя́зно; нейстовствовать.

ravel [rævl] *v/t.* запу́т(ыв)ать; распу́т(ыв)ать; *v/i.* запу́т(ыв)аться; (*a.* ~ out) располза́ться по швам.

raven [reivn] во́рон.

raven|ing [ˈrævniŋ], **~ous** [-əs] прожо́рливый; хи́щный.

ravine [rəˈviːn] овра́г, лощи́на.

ravish [ˈræviʃ] приводи́ть в восто́рг; [из]наси́ловать; похища́ть [-и́тить]; **~ment** [-mənt] похище́ние; восхище́ние; изнаси́лование.

raw [rɔː] □ сыро́й; необрабо́танный; нео́пытный; обо́дранный; **~-boned** худо́й, костля́вый.

ray [rei] **1.** луч; *fig.* про́блеск; ⚕ ~ treatment облуче́ние.

raze [reiz] разруша́ть до основа́ния; сноси́ть [снести́] (зда́ние и т. п.); вычёркивать [вы́черкнуть].

razor [ˈreizə] бри́тва; **~-blade** ле́звие безопа́сной бри́твы.

re... [riː] *pref.* (придаёт сло́ву значе́ния:) сно́ва, за́ново, ещё раз, обра́тно.

reach [riːtʃ] **1.** преде́л досяга́емости; круг понима́ния, кругозо́р; о́бласть влия́ния; beyond ~ вне преде́лов досяга́емости; within easy ~ побли́зости; под руко́й; **2.** *v/t.* достига́ть [-и́гнуть] (P); доезжа́ть [дое́хать], доходи́ть [дойти́] до (P); простира́ться [-стере́ться] до (P); протя́гивать [-яну́ть]; дост(ав)а́ть до (P); *v/i.* протя́гивать ру́ку (for за T).

react [riˈækt] реаги́ровать; ~ upon each other взаимоде́йствовать; противоде́йствовать (against Д).

reaction [riˈækʃən] реа́кция; **~ary** [-ʃənəri] **1.** реакцио́нный; **2.** реакционе́р(ка).

read **1.** [riːd] [*irr.*] [про]чита́ть; изуча́ть [-чи́ть]; истолко́вывать [-кова́ть]; пока́зывать [-за́ть] (о прибо́ре); гласи́ть; ~ to a p. чита́ть кому́-нибудь вслух; **2.** [red] a) *pt.* и *p. pt.* от read 1.; b) *adj.* начи́танный; **~able** [ˈriːdəbl] □ интере́сный; чёткий; **~er** [ˈriːdə] чита́тель(ница *f*) *m*; чтец; ле́ктор; хрестома́тия.

readi|ly [ˈredili] *adv.* охо́тно; бы́стро; легко́; **~ness** [-nis] гото́вность *f*; подгото́вленность *f*.

reading [ˈriːdiŋ] чте́ние; ле́кция; толкова́ние, понима́ние; *parl.* чте́ние (законопрое́кта).

readjust [ˈriːəˈdʒʌst] сно́ва приводи́ть в поря́док; переде́л(ыв)ать;

~ment [-mənt] приведéние в порядок; передéлка.
ready ['redi] □ готóвый; склóнный; ⚕ налúчный; make (или get) ~ [при]готóвить(ся); **~-made** готóвый (о плáтье).
reagent [ri'eidʒənt] ⚗ реактúв.
real [riəl] □ действúтельный; реáльный; настоящий; ~ estate недвúжимость *f*; **~ity** [ri'æliti] действúтельность *f*; **~ization** [riəlai'zeiʃən] понимáние, осознáние; осуществлéние; ⚕ реализáция; **~ize** ['riəlaiz] представлять себé; осуществлять [-вúть]; осозн(ав)áть; реализовáть (*im*)*pf*.
realm [relm] королéвство; цáрство; сфéра.
realty ['riəlti] недвúжимое имýщество.
reap [ri:p] [с]жать (рожь и т. п.); *fig*. пож(ин)áть; **~er** ['ri:pə] жнец, жнúца.
reappear ['ri:ə'piə] появляться снóва.
rear [riə] **1.** *v/t*. воспúтывать [-тáть]; вырáщивать [вы́растить]; *v/i*. становúться на ды́бы; **2.** зáдняя сторонá; ⚔ тыл; at the ~ of, in (the) ~ of позадú (Р); **3.** зáдний; ты́льный; ⚔ тыловóй; **~-admiral** ⚓ контр-адмирáл; **~-guard** ⚔ арьергáрд.
re-arm ['ri:ɑ:m] перевооружáть(-ся) [-жúть(ся)].
reason [ri:zn] **1.** рáзум; рассýдок; основáние; причúна; by ~ of по причúне (Р); for this ~ поэ́тому; it stands to ~ that ... ясно, что ..., очевúдно, что ...; **2.** *v/i*. рассуждáть [-удúть]; заключáть [-чúть]; резюмúровать (*im*)*pf*.; *v/t*. ~ out продýмать до концá; ~ out of разубеждáть [-едúть] в (П); **~able** ['ri:znəbl] □ (благо)разýмный; умéренный; недорогóй.
reassure ['ri:ə'ʃuə] снóва уверять; успокáивать [-кóить].
rebate ['ri:beit] ⚕ скúдка; устýпка.
rebel **1.** [rebl] бунтовщúк (-úца); повстáнец; **2.** [~] (*a*. **~lious** [ri'beljəs]) мятéжный; **3.** [ri'bel] восст(ав)áть; бунтовáть [вз-ся]; **~lion** [ri'beljən] мятéж, восстáние; бунт.
rebirth ['ribə:θ] возрождéние.
rebound [ri'baund] **1.** отскáкивать [-скочúть]; **2.** рикошéт; отскóк.
rebuff [ri'bʌf] **1.** отпóр; рéзкий откáз; **2.** давáть отпóр (Д).
rebuild ['ri:'bild] [*irr*. (build)] восстанáвливать [-новúть] (здáние и т. п.).
rebuke [ri'bju:k] **1.** упрёк; вы́говор; **2.** упрекáть [-кнýть]; дéлать вы́говор (Д).
rebut [ri'bʌt] давáть отпóр (Д).
recall [ri'kɔ:l] **1.** отозвáние (депутáта, послá и т. п.); ⚕ отмéна; **2.** отзывáть [отозвáть]; призывáть обрáтно; отменять [-нúть]; напоминáть [-óмнить]; вспоминáть [-óмнить] (В); ⚕ брать (или трéбовать) обрáтно (капитáл); отменять [-нúть].
recapitulate [ri:kə'pitjuleit] резюмúровать (*im*)*pf*.
recast ['ri:'kɑ:st] [*irr*. (cast)] придавáть нóвую фóрму (Д); ⊕ отливáть зáново.
recede [ri'si:d] отступáть [-пúть]; удаляться [-лúться].
receipt [ri'si:t] **1.** распúска, квитáнция; получéние; рецéпт (кулинáрный); **~s** *pl*. прихóд; **2.** распúсываться [-сáться] на (П).
receiv|able [ri'si:vəbl] ⚕ неоплáченный (счёт); **~e** [ri'si:v] получáть [-чúть]; принимáть [-нять]; воспринимáть [-нять]; **~ed** [-d] общепрúзнанный; **~er** [-ə] получáтель(ница *f*) *m*; *teleph*. телефóнная трýбка; ⚖ судéбный исполнúтель *m*.
recent [ri:snt] □ недáвний; свéжий; нóвый; **~ly** [-li] недáвно.
receptacle [ri'septəkl] вместúлище.
reception [ri'sepʃən] получéние; приём; принятие.
receptive [ri'septiv] □ восприúмчивый (к Д).
recess [ri'ses] канúкулы *f*/*pl*.; перерыв; нúша; уединённое мéсто; **~es** *pl*. *fig*. тайникú *m*/*pl*.; **~ion** [-ʃən] удалéние; углублéние; ⚕ спад.
recipe ['resipi] рецéпт.
recipient [ri'sipiənt] получáтель (-ница *f*) *m*.
reciproc|al [ri'siprəkəl] взаúмный; обою́дный; эквиваléнтный; **~ate** [-keit] ⊕ двúгать(ся) взад и вперёд; обмéниваться [-няться] (услýгами и т. п.); **~ity** [resi'prɔsiti] взаúмность *f*.
recit|al [ri'saitl] чтéние, декламáция; повествовáние; ♪ концéрт (солúста); **~ation** [resi'teiʃən] декламáция; **~e** [ri'sait] [про]декламúровать; расскáзывать [-зáть].
reckless ['reklis] □ безрассýдный; опромéтчивый; беспéчный.
reckon ['rekən] *v/t*. исчислять [-чúслить]; причислять [-чúслить] (among к Д); считáть [счесть] за (В); *v/i*. предполагáть [-ложúть]; ~ (up)on *fig*. рассчúтывать на (В); **~ing** [-iŋ] подсчёт; счёт; расплáта.
reclaim [ri'kleim] исправлять [-áвить]; поднимáть [-нять] (целинý).
recline [ri'klain] откúдывать(ся) [-úнуть(ся)]; полулежáть.
recluse [ri'klu:s] отшéльник (-ица).
recogni|tion [rekəg'niʃən] опознáние; узнавáние; признáние (Р); **~ze** ['rekəgnaiz] узн(ав)áть; призн(ав)áть.

recoil [ri'kɔil] **1.** отскóк; ⚔ отдáча, откáт; **2.** отскáкивать [-скочи́ть]; откáтываться [-кати́ться].
recollect [rekə'lekt] вспоминáть [вспóмнить] (B); **~ion** [rekə'lekʃən] воспоминáние, пáмять *f* (of о П).
recommend [rekə'mend] рекомендовáть (*im*)*pf.*, *pf. a.* [по-]; **~ation** [rekəmen'deiʃən] рекомендáция.
recompense ['rekəmpəns] **1.** вознаграждéние; компенсáция; **2.** вознаграждáть [-ради́ть]; отплáчивать [отплати́ть] (Д).
reconcil|e ['rekənsail] примиря́ть [-ри́ть] (to с T); улáживать [улáдить]; **~e** o. s. примиря́ться [-ри́ться]; **~iation** ['rekənsili'eiʃən] примирéние.
recondition ['ri:kən'diʃən] [от]ремонти́ровать; переоборýдовать.
reconn|aissance [ri'kɔnisəns] ⚔ развéдка; **~oitre** [rekə'nɔitə] производи́ть развéдку; развéд(ы-в)ать.
reconsider ['ri:kən'sidə] пересмáтривать [-мотрéть].
reconstitute ['ri:kɔnstitju:t] восстанáвливать [-нови́ть].
reconstruct ['ri:kəns'trʌkt] восстанáвливать [-нови́ть]; перестрáивать [-стрóить]; **~ion** [-s'trʌkʃən] реконстрýкция; восстановлéние.
reconvert ['ri:kən'və:t] перестрáивать на ми́рный лад.
record **1.** ['rekɔ:d] зáпись *f*; *sport* рекóрд; ⚖ протокóл (заседáния и т. п.); place on ~ запи́сывать [-сáть]; граммофóнная пласти́нка; репутáция; ♀ Office госудáрственный архи́в; off the ~ *Am.* неофициáльно; on ~ зарегистри́рованный; **2.** [ri'kɔ:d] запи́сывать [-сáть]; [за]регистри́ровать; **~er** [ri'kɔ:də] регистрáтор; регистри́рующий прибóр.
recount [ri'kaunt] излагáть [изложи́ть] (подрóбно).
recoup [ri'ku:p] компенси́ровать (*im*)*pf.*, возмещáть [-ести́ть] (Д for B).
recourse [ri'kɔ:s] обращéние за пóмощью; прибéжище; have ~ to прибегáть к пóмощи (P).
recover [ri'kʌvə] *v/t.* получáть обрáтно; вернýть (себé) *pf.*; навёрстывать [-верстáть] (врéмя); *v/i.* оправля́ться [-áвиться] (*a.* ~ o. s.); **~y** [-ri] восстановлéние; выздоровлéние; возмещéние; ⚖ взыскáние.
recreat|e ['rekrieit] *v/t.* освежáть [-жи́ть]; развлекáть [-éчь]; *v/i.* освежáться [-жи́ться] (пóсле рабóты и т. п.) (*a.* ~ o. s.); развлекáться [-éчься]; **~ion** [rekri'eiʃən] óтдых; развлечéние.
recrimination [rikrimi'neiʃən] взаи́мное (и́ли встрéчное) обвинéние.
recruit [ri'kru:t] **1.** рéкрут, новобрáнец; *fig.* новичóк; **2.** [у]комплектовáть; [за]вербовáть (новобрáнцев).
rectangle ['rektæŋgl] прямоугóльник.
recti|fy ['rektifai] исправля́ть [-áвить]; выверя́ть [вы́верить]; ⚡ выпрямля́ть [вы́прямить]; **~tude** ['rektitju:d] прямотá, чéстность *f*.
rector ['rektə] рéктор; пáстор, свящéнник; **~y** [-ri] дом свящéнника.
recumbent [ri'kʌmbənt] □ лежáчий.
recuperate [ri'kju:pəreit] восстанáвливать си́лы; оправля́ться [опрáвиться].
recur [ri'kə:] возвращáться [-ратúться] (to к Д); приходи́ть снóва на ýм; происходи́ть вновь; **~rence** [ri'kʌrəns] повторéние; **~rent** [-rənt] □ повторя́ющийся; периоди́ческий; ⚕ возврáтный.
red [red] **1.** крáсный; ~ heat крáсное калéние; ~ herring *fig.* отвлечéние внимáния; ~ tape канцеля́рщина; **2.** крáсный цвéт; **~s** *pl.* (*part. pol.*) крáсные *pl.*
red|breast ['redbrest] мали́новка; **~den** [redn] [по]краснéть; **~dish** ['rediʃ] красновáтый.
redeem [ri'di:m] искупáть [-пи́ть]; выкупáть [вы́купить]; спасáть [-сти́]; **~er** [-ə] спаси́тель *m*.
redemption [ri'dempʃən] искуплéние; вы́куп; спасéние.
red-handed ['red'hændid]: take a p. ~ поймáть когó-либо на мéсте преступлéния.
red-hot накалённый дóкраснá; *fig.* взбешённый; горя́чий.
red-letter: ~ day прáздничный [день *m*.]
redness ['rednis] краснотá.
redolent ['redolənt] благоухáю[щий.]
redouble [ri'dʌbl] удвáивать(ся) [удвóить(ся)].
redound [ri'daund]: ~ to спосóбствовать (Д), помогáть [помóчь] (Д).
redress [ri'dres] **1.** исправлéние; ⚖ возмещéние; **2.** исправля́ть [-áвить]; заглáживать [-лáдить] (винý); возмещáть [-ести́ть].
reduc|e [ri'dju:s] понижáть [-и́зить]; снижáть [-и́зить]; доводи́ть [довести́] (to до P); уменьшáть [умéньши́ть]; сокращáть [-рати́ть]; урéз(ыв)ать; ~ to writing излагáть пи́сьменно; **~tion** [ri'dʌkʃən] снижéние (цен), ски́дка; уменьшéние; сокращéние; умéньшенная кóпия (карти́ны и т. п.).
redundant [ri'dʌndənt] □ изли́шний; чрезмéрный.
reed [ri:d] тростни́к; свирéль *f*.
reef [ri:f] риф, подвóдная скалá.
reek [ri:k] **1.** вонь *f*, зáтхлый зáпах; дым; пар; **2.** *v/i.* дыми́ться; (неприя́тно) пáхнуть (of T); испускáть пар.

reel [ri:l] 1. катушка; бобина; барабан, ворот; 2. *v/i.* [за]кружиться, [за]вертеться; шататься [шатнуться]; *v/t.* [на]мотать; ~ off разматывать [-мотать]; *fig.* отбарабанить *pf.*; ~ up наматывать на катушку.
re-elect ['ri:i'lekt] переизб(и)рать.
re-enter ['ri:'entə] входить снова в (В).
re-establish ['ri:is'tæbliʃ] восстанавливать [-новить].
refection [ri'fekʃən] закуска.
refer [ri'fə:]: ~ to *v/t.* приписывать [-сать] (Д); относить [отнести] (к Д); направлять [-равить] (к Д); передавать на рассмотрение (Д); *v/i.* ссылаться [сослаться] на (В); относиться [отнестись] к (Д); **~ee** [refə'ri:] *sport* судья *m*; **~ence** ['refrəns] справка; ссылка; рекомендация; упоминание; отношение; лицо, давшее рекомендацию; in ~ to относительно (Р); ~ book справочник; ~ library справочная библиотека; make ~ to ссылаться [сослаться] на (В).
referendum [refə'rendəm] референдум.
refill ['ri:'fil] наполнять снова; пополнять(ся) [-полнить(ся)].
refine [ri'fain] ⊕ очищать [очистить] рафинировать (*im*)*pf.*; делать(ся) более утончённым; ~ (up)on [у]совершенствовать; **~ment** [-mənt] очищение, рафинирование; отделка; усовершенствование; утончённость *f*; **~ry** [-əri] ⊕ очистительный завод.
reflect [ri'flekt] *v/t.* отражать [отразить]; *v/i.* ~ (up)on: бросать тень на (В); размышлять [-ыслить] о (П); отражаться [-разиться] на (В); **~ion** [ri'flekʃən] отражение; отсвет; размышление, обдумывание; *fig.* тень *f*; рефлексия.
reflex ['ri:fleks] 1. отражение; отсвет, отблеск; рефлекс; 2. рефлекторный.
reforest ['ri:fɔrist] снова засаждать лесом.
reform [ri'fɔ:m] 1. реформа; улучшение; 2. улучшать(ся) [улучшить(ся)]; реформировать (*im*)*pf.*; исправлять(ся); **~ation** [refə'meiʃən] преобразование; исправление (моральное); *eccl.* ♀ Реформация; **~atory** [ri'fɔ:mətəri] исправительное заведение; **~er** [-mə] реформатор.
refract|ion [ri'frækʃən] рефракция, преломление; **~ory** [-təri] □ упрямый; непокорный; ⊕ огнеупорный.
refrain [ri'frein] 1. *v/t.* сдерживать [-жать]; *v/i.* воздерживаться [-жаться] (from от Р); 2. припев, рефрен.
refresh [ri'freʃ] освежать [-жить]; подкреплять(ся) [-пить(ся)]; подновлять [-вить]; **~ment** [-mənt] подкрепление; закуска.
refrigerat|e [ri'fridʒəreit] замораживать [-розить]; охлаждать(ся) [охладить(ся)]; **~ion** [rifridʒə'reiʃən] замораживание; охлаждение.
refuel ['ri:'fjuəl] *mot.* заправляться горючим.
refuge ['refju:dʒ] убежище; **~e** [refju'dʒi:] беженец (-нка).
refulgent [ri'fʌldʒənt] лучезарный.
refund [ri'fʌnd] возмещать расходы (Д); возвращать [-ратить].
refusal [ri'fju:zəl] отказ.
refuse 1. [ri'fju:z] *v/t.* отказываться [-заться] от (Р); отказывать [-зать] в (П); отвергать [отвергнуть]; *v/i.* отказываться [-заться]; [за]артачиться (о лошади); 2. ['refju:s] брак ⊕; отбросы *m/pl.*; мусор.
refute [ri'fju:t] опровергать [-вергнуть].
regain [ri'gein] получать обратно; снова достигать.
regal [ri:gəl] □ королевский; царственный.
regale [ri'geil] *v/t.* угощать [угостить]; *v/i.* пировать; угощаться [угоститься] (on Т).
regard [ri'gɑ:d] 1. взгляд, взор; внимание; уважение; with ~ to по отношению к (Д); kind ~s сердечный привет; 2. [по]смотреть на (В); рассматривать (as как); [по]считаться с (Т); относиться [отнестись] к (Д); as ~s ... что касается (Р); **~ing** [-iŋ] относительно (Р); **~less** [-lis] *adv.* ~ of не обращая внимания на (В); не считаясь с (Т).
regenerate 1. [ri'dʒenəreit] перерождать(ся) [-одить(ся)]; возрождаться [-родиться]; ⊕ регенерировать; 2. [-rit] возрождённый.
regent ['ri:dʒənt] регент.
regiment ['redʒimənt] 1. полк; 2. формировать полк(и) из (Р); организовать (*im*)*pf.*; **~als** [redʒi'mentlz] *pl.* полковая форма.
region ['ri:dʒən] область *f*; район; **~al** [-l] □ областной; местный.
register ['redʒistə] 1. журнал (записей); реестр; официальный список; ♪ регистр; ⊕ заслонка; 2. регистрировать(ся) (*im*)*pf.*, *pf. a.* [за-]; заносить в список; ✉ посылать заказным.
registr|ar [redʒis'trɑ:] регистратор; служащий загса; **~ation** [redʒis'treiʃən] регистрация; **~y** ['redʒistri] регистратура; регистрация; регистрационная запись *f*; реестр.
regret [ri'gret] 1. сожаление; раскаяние; 2. [по]жалеть (that ... что ...); сожалеть о (П); горевать

о (П); раска́иваться [-ка́яться] в (П); **~ful** [-ful] □ по́лный сожале́ния; **~table** [-əbl] □ прискорбный.
regular ['regjulə] □ пра́вильный; регуля́рный (*a.* ⚔); форма́льный; **~ity** [regju'læriti] регуля́рность *f*.
regulat|e ['regjuleit] [у]регули́ровать, упоря́дочи(ва)ть; ⊕ [от]регули́ровать; **~ion** [regju'leiʃən] **1.** регули́рование; предписа́ние; **~s** *pl.* уста́в; **2.** *attr.* устано́вленный.
rehears|al [ri'hə:səl] *thea.*, ♪ репети́ция; **~e** [ri'hə:s] *thea.* [про]репети́ровать.
reign [rein] **1.** ца́рствование; *fig.* власть *f*; **2.** ца́рствовать; госпо́дствовать (*a. fig.*); *fig.* цари́ть.
reimburse [ri:im'bə:s] возвраща́ть [-рати́ть]; возмеща́ть расхо́ды (Д).
rein [rein] **1.** вожжа́; **2.** пра́вить (лошадьми́); сде́рживать [-жа́ть].
reinforce [ri:in'fɔ:s] подкрепля́ть [-пи́ть]; усили(ва)ть; **~ment** [-mənt] подкрепле́ние.
reinstate ['ri:in'steit] восстана́вливать [-нови́ть] (в права́х и т. п.).
reinsure ['ri:in'ʃuə] перестрахо́вывать [-ова́ть].
reiterate [ri:'itəreit] повторя́ть [-ри́ть] (*mst* многокра́тно).
reject [ri'dʒekt] отверга́ть [отве́ргнуть]; отка́зываться [-за́ться] от (Р); отклоня́ть [-ни́ть]; **~ion** [ri'dʒekʃən] отклоне́ние; отка́з.
rejoic|e [ri'dʒɔis] *v/t.* [об]ра́довать *v/i.* [об]ра́доваться (at, in Д); **~ing** [-iŋ] (ча́сто **~s** *pl.*) весе́лье; пра́зднование.
rejoin **1.** ['ri:'dʒɔin] сно́ва соединя́ться [-ни́ться] с (Т); сно́ва примыка́ть [-мкну́ть] к (Д); **2.** [ri'dʒɔin] возража́ть [-рази́ть].
rejuvenate [ri'dʒu:vineit] омола́живать(ся) [омолоди́ть(ся)].
relapse [ri'læps] **1.** рециди́в (⚕, ⚖); **2.** сно́ва впада́ть (в е́ресь, заблужде́ние и т. п.); сно́ва заболева́ть.
relate [ri'leit] *v/t.* расска́зывать [-за́ть]; приводи́ть в связь; *v/i.* относи́ться [отнести́сь]; **~d** [-id] ро́дственный (to с Т).
relation [ri'leiʃən] отноше́ние; связь *f*; родство́; ро́дственник (-ица); in **~** to по отноше́нию к (Д); **~ship** [-ʃip] родство́.
relative ['relətiv] **1.** □ относи́тельный; сравни́тельный (to с Т); усло́вный; **2.** ро́дственник (-ица).
relax [ri'læks] уменьша́ть напряже́ние (Р); смягча́ть(ся) [-чи́ть(-ся)]; де́лать(ся) ме́нее стро́гим; **~ation** [ri:læk'seiʃən] ослабле́ние; смягче́ние; о́тдых от рабо́т; развлече́ние.
relay [ri'lei] **1.** сме́на; *sport* эстафе́та; *attr.* эстафе́тный; **2.** *radio* трансли́ровать (*im*)*pf*.
release [ri'li:s] **1.** освобожде́ние; высвобожде́ние; избавле́ние; вы́пуск (фи́льма на прока́т и т. п.); **2.** освобожда́ть [-боди́ть]; высвобожда́ть [вы́свободить]; избавля́ть [-а́вить]; выпуска́ть [вы́пустить]; отпуска́ть [-сти́ть]; проща́ть [прости́ть] (долг).
relegate ['religeit] отсыла́ть [отосла́ть]; направля́ть [-ра́вить] (to к Д); ссыла́ть [сосла́ть].
relent [ri'lent] смягча́ться [-чи́ться]; **~less** [-lis] □ безжа́лостный.
relevant ['relivənt] уме́стный; относя́щийся к де́лу.
reliab|ility [rilaiə'biliti] надёжность *f*; про́чность *f*; **~le** [ri'laiəbl] □ надёжный; достове́рный.
reliance [ri'laiəns] дове́рие; уве́ренность *f*.
relic ['relik] пережи́ток; рели́квия; рели́кт; **~s** *pl.* оста́нки *m/pl.*
relief [ri'li:f] облегче́ние; по́мощь *f*; посо́бие; подкрепле́ние; сме́на (*a.* ⚔); ⚔ сня́тие оса́ды; релье́ф; **~** works *pl.* obще́ственные рабо́ты для безрабо́тных.
relieve [ri'li:v] облегча́ть [-чи́ть]; освобожда́ть [-боди́ть]; ока́зывать по́мощь (Д); выруча́ть [вы́ручить]; ⚔ снять оса́ду с (Р); сменя́ть [-ни́ть].
religion [ri'lidʒən] рели́гия.
religious [ri'lidʒəs] □ религио́зный; благогове́йный; добросо́вестный; *eccl.* мона́шеский.
relinquish [ri'liŋkwiʃ] оставля́ть [-а́вить] (наде́жду и т. п.); броса́ть [бро́сить] (привы́чку).
relish ['reliʃ] **1.** вкус; при́вкус; припра́ва; **2.** наслажда́ться [-лади́ться] (Т); получа́ть удово́льствие от (Р); придава́ть вкус (Д).
reluctan|ce [ri'lʌktəns] нежела́ние; нерасположе́ние; **~t** [-t] □ сопротивля́ющийся; неохо́тный.
rely [ri'lai]: **~** (up)on полага́ться [-ложи́ться] на (В), наде́яться на (В).
remain [ri'mein] ост(ав)а́ться; **~der** [-də] оста́ток.
remark [ri'mɑ:k] **1.** замеча́ние; заме́тка; **2.** замеча́ть [-е́тить]; выска́зываться [вы́сказаться] (on о П); **~able** [ri'mɑ:kəbl] □ замеча́тельный.
remedy ['remidi] **1.** сре́дство, лека́рство; ме́ра (for про́тив Р); **2.** исправля́ть [-а́вить]; выле́чивать [вы́лечить].
rememb|er [ri'membə] по́мнить; вспомина́ть [-о́мнить]; **~** me to ... переда́й(те) приве́т (Д); **~rance** [-brəns] воспомина́ние; па́мять *f*; сувени́р; **~s** *pl.* приве́т.
remind [ri'maind] напомина́ть [-о́мнить] (Д; of о П *or* В); **~er** [-ə] напомина́ние.
reminiscence [remi'nisns] воспомина́ние.
remiss [ri'mis] □ неради́вый;

невнима́тельный; вя́лый; **~ion** [ri'miʃən] проще́ние; отпуще́ние (грехо́в); освобожде́ние от упла́ты; уменьше́ние.

remit [ri'mit] отпуска́ть [-сти́ть] (грехи́); перес(ы)ла́ть (това́ры); уменьша́ть(ся) [уме́ньши́ть(ся)]; **~tance** [-əns] де́нежный перево́д.

remnant ['remnənt] оста́ток; пережи́ток.

remodel ['ri:mɔdl] перестра́ивать [[-стро́ить].

remonstra|nce [ri'mɔnstrəns] проте́ст; увеща́ние; **~te** [-treit] протестова́ть; увещева́ть, увеща́ть (with B).

remorse [ri'mɔ:s] угрызе́ния (*n*/*pl.*) со́вести; раска́яние; **~less** [-lis] □ безжа́лостный.

remote [ri'mout] □ отдалённый; да́льний; уединённый; **~ness** [-nis] отдалённость *f*.

remov|al [ri'mu:vəl] перее́зд; устране́ние; смеще́ние; ~ van фурго́н для перево́за ме́бели; **~e** [ri'mu:v] *v*/*t.* удаля́ть [-ли́ть]; уноси́ть [унести́]; передвига́ть [-и́нуть]; смеща́ть [смести́ть]; *v*/*i.* переезжа́ть [перее́хать]; **~er** [-ə] перево́зчик ме́бели.

remunerat|e [ri'mju:nəreit] вознагражда́ть [-ради́ть]; опла́чивать [оплати́ть]; **~ive** [ri'mju:nərətiv] □ хорошо́ опла́чиваемый, вы́годный.

renascence [ri'næsns] возрожде́ние; возобновле́ние.

rend [rend] [*irr.*] разрыва́ть(ся) [разорва́ть(ся)]; раздира́ть(ся) [разодра́ть(ся)].

render ['rendə] возд(ав)а́ть; ока́зывать [оказа́ть] (услу́гу и т. п.); представля́ть [-а́вить]; изобража́ть [-рази́ть]; [за]плати́ть (T for за B); ♪ исполня́ть [-о́лнить]; переводи́ть [-вести́] (на друго́й язы́к); раста́пливать [-топи́ть] (са́ло).

renew [ri'nju:] возобновля́ть [-нови́ть]; **~al** [-əl] возобновле́ние.

renounce [ri'nauns] отка́зываться [-за́ться] от (P); отрека́ться [-ре́чься] от (P).

renovate ['renoveit] восстана́вливать [-нови́ть]; освежа́ть [-жи́ть].

renown [ri'naun] *rhet.* изве́стность *f*; **~ed** [-d] *rhet.* знамени́тый.

rent[1] [rent] **1.** *pt.* и *p. pt.* от rend; **2.** проре́ха; дыра́.

rent[2] [~] **1.** аре́ндная пла́та; кварти́рная пла́та; ре́нта; **2.** нанима́ть [наня́ть] и́ли сда(ва́)ть (дом и т. п.); **~al** [rentl] аре́ндная пла́та.

renunciation [rinʌnsi'eiʃən] отрече́ние; отка́з (of от P).

repair[1] [ri'pɛə] **1.** почи́нка, ремо́нт; in (good) ~ в испра́вном состоя́нии; **2.** [по]чини́ть, [от]ремонти́ровать; исправля́ть [-а́вить].

repair[2]: ~ to отправля́ться [-а́виться] в (B).

reparation [repə'reiʃən] возмеще́ние; исправле́ние; *pol.* make ~s *pl.* плати́ть репара́ции.

repartee [repɑ:'ti:] нахо́дчивость *f*; остроу́мный отве́т.

repast [ri'pɑ:st] тра́пеза.

repay [*irr.* (pay)] [ri'pei] отпла́чивать [-лати́ть]; отдава́ть до́лг (Д); возвраща́ть [-рати́ть] (де́ньги); возмеща́ть [-ести́ть]; **~ment** [-mənt] возвра́т (де́нег); возмеще́ние.

repeal [ri'pi:l] **1.** аннули́рование; **2.** аннули́ровать (*im*)*pf.*; отменя́ть [-ни́ть].

repeat [ri'pi:t] **1.** повторя́ть(ся) [-ри́ть(ся)]; говори́ть наизу́сть; **2.** ♪ повторе́ние; знак повторе́ния; ✝ повто́рный зака́з.

repel [ri'pel] отта́лкивать [оттолкну́ть]; ⚔ отража́ть [-рази́ть]; отверга́ть [-е́ргнуть].

repent [ri'pent] раска́иваться [-ка́яться] (of в П); **~ance** [-əns] раска́яние; **~ant** [-ənt] ка́ющийся.

repetition [repi'tiʃən] повторе́ние; повторе́ние наизу́сть.

replace [ri:'pleis] ста́вить, класть обра́тно; заменя́ть [-ни́ть]; замеща́ть [-ести́ть] (кого́-либо); **~ment** [-mənt] замеще́ние.

replenish [ri'pleniʃ] пополня́ть [-о́лнить]; **~ment** [-mənt] пополне́ние (*a.* ⚔).

replete [ri'pli:t] напо́лненный; насы́щенный.

replica ['replikə] то́чная ко́пия.

reply [ri'plai] **1.** отве́т (to на B); **2.** отвеча́ть [-е́тить]; возража́ть [-рази́ть].

report [ri'pɔ:t] **1.** отчёт; сообще́ние; донесе́ние; докла́д; молва́, слух; свиде́тельство; звук (взры́ва и т. п.); **2.** сообща́ть [-щи́ть] (B *or* о П); доноси́ть [-нести́] о (П); докла́дывать [доложи́ть]; рапортова́ть (*im*)*pf.* о (П); **~er** [-ə] докла́дчик (-ица); репортёр(ша F).

repos|e [ri'pouz] **1.** о́тдых; поко́й; **2.** *v*/*t.* дава́ть о́тдых (Д); *v*/*i.* отдыха́ть [отдохну́ть] (*a.* ~ o. s.); поко́иться; быть осно́ванным (на П); **~itory** [ri'pɔzitəri] склад; храни́лище.

reprehend [repri'hend] де́лать вы́говор (Д).

represent [repri'zent] представля́ть [-а́вить]; изобража́ть [-рази́ть]; *thea.* исполня́ть роль (P); **~ation** [-zən'teiʃən] изображе́ние; представи́тельство; *thea.* представле́ние; **~ative** □ [repri'zentətiv] **1.** характе́рный; показа́тельный; представля́ющий (of B); *parl.* представи́тельный; **2.** представи́тель(ница *f*) *m*; House of ♀s *pl. Am. parl.* пала́та представи́телей.

repress [ri'pres] подавля́ть [-ви́ть]; **~ion** [ri'preʃən] подавле́ние.

reprimand ['reprimɑ:nd] **1.** вы́говор; **2.** де́лать вы́говор (Д).

reprisal [ri'praizəl] репрессáлия.

reproach [ri'proutʃ] **1.** упрёк; укóр; **2.** (~ a p. with a th.) упрекáть [-кнýть], укоря́ть [-ри́ть] (когó-либо в чём-либо).

reprobate ['reprobeit] распýтник; подлéц.

reproduc|e [ri:prə'dju:s] воспроизводи́ть [-извести́]; размножáться [-óжиться]; **~tion** [-'dʌkʃən] воспроизведéние; размножéние; репродýкция

reproof [ri'pru:f] порицáние; вы́говор.

reprove [ri'pru:v] порицáть; дéлать вы́говор (Д).

reptile ['reptail] пресмыкáющееся (живóтное).

republic [ri'pʌblik] респýблика; **~an** [-likən] **1.** республикáнский; **2.** республикáнец (-нка).

repudiate [ri'pju:dieit] отрекáться [-éчься] от (Р); отвергáть [-вéргнуть].

repugnan|ce [ri'pʌgnəns] отвращéние; нерасположéние; противорéчие; **~t** [-nənt] □ проти́вный, оттáлкивающий.

repuls|e [ri'pʌls] **1.** откáз; отпóр; **2.** ⚔ отражáть [отрази́ть]; оттáлкивать [оттолкнýть]; **~ive** [-iv] □ оттáлкивающий.

reput|able ['repjutəbl] □ почтéнный; **~ation** [repju:'teiʃən] репутáция; **~e** [ri'pju:t] óбщее мнéние; репутáция; **~ed** [ri'pju:tid] извéстный; предполагáемый; **be ~ed** (to be ...) слыть (за В).

request [ri'kwest] **1.** трéбование; прóсьба; ✝ спрос; in (great) ~ в (большóм) спрóсе; (*a. radio*) заявка; **2.** [по]проси́ть (В or Р or о П).

require [ri'kwaiə] нуждáться в (П); [по]трéбовать (Р); **~d** [-d] потрéбный; обязáтельный; трéбуемый; **~ment** [-mənt] трéбование; потрéбность *f.*

requisite ['rekwizit] **1.** необходи́мый; **2.** ~s *pl.* всё необходи́мое, нýжное; **~ion** [rekwi'ziʃən] **1.** официáльное предписáние; трéбование; ⚔ реквизи́ция; **2.** дéлать заявку на (В); ⚔ реквизи́ровать (*im*)*pf.*

requital [ri'kwaitl] вознаграждéние; возмéздие.

requite [ri'kwait] отплáчивать [-лати́ть] (Д for за В); вознаграждáть [-ради́ть]; [ото]мсти́ть за (В).

rescind [ri'sind] аннули́ровать (*im*)*pf.*

rescission [ri'siʒən] аннули́рование, отмéна.

rescue ['reskju:] **1.** освобождéние; спасéние; ⚖ незакóнное освобождéние; **2.** освобождáть [-боди́ть]; спасáть [-сти́]; ⚖ незакóнно освобождáть.

research [ri'sə:tʃ] изыскáние (*mst pl.*); исслéдование (наýчное).

resembl|ance [ri'zembləns] схóдство (to с Т); **~e** [ri'zembl] походи́ть на (В), имéть схóдство с (Т).

resent [ri'zent] обижáться [оби́деться] за (В); **~ful** [-ful] □ оби́женный; злопáмятный; **~ment** [-mənt] негодовáние; чýвство оби́ды.

reservation [rezə'veiʃən] оговóрка; скрывáние; *Am.* резервáция; заповéдник; резерви́рование; предвари́тельный закáз.

reserve [ri'zə:v] **1.** запáс; ✝ резéрвный фонд; ⚔ резéрв; сдéржанность *f*; скры́тность *f*; **2.** сберегáть [-рéчь]; приберегáть [-рéчь]; отклáдывать [отложи́ть]; резерви́ровать (*im*)*pf.*; оставля́ть за собóй; **~d** [-d] □ скры́тный; закáзанный заранée.

reside [ri'zaid] проживáть; ~ in быть присýщим (Д); **~nce** ['rezidəns] местожи́тельство; резидéнция; **~nt** [-dənt] **1.** проживáющий; живýщий; **2.** постоя́нный жи́тель *m*; резидéнт.

residu|al [ri'zidjuəl] остáточный; **~e** ['rezidju:] остáток; осáдок.

resign [ri'zain] *v/t.* откáзываться [-зáться] от (дóлжности, прáва); оставля́ть [-áвить] (надéжду); слагáть [сложи́ть] (обя́занности); уступáть [-пи́ть] (правá); ~ o. s. to покоря́ться [-ри́ться] (Д); *v/i.* уходи́ть в отстáвку; **~ation** [rezig'neiʃən] отстáвка; откáз от дóлжности; **~ed** [ri'zaind] □ покóрный, безрóпотный.

resilien|ce [ri'ziliəns] упрýгость *f*, эласти́чность *f*; **~t** [-t] упрýгий, эласти́чный.

resin ['rezin] **1.** смолá; **2.** [вы́]смоли́ть.

resist [ri'zist] сопротивля́ться (Д); противостоя́ть (Д); **~ance** [-əns] сопротивлéние; **~ant** [-ent] сопротивля́ющийся.

resolut|e ['rezəlu:t] □ реши́тельный; **~ion** [rezə'lu:ʃən] резолю́ция; реши́тельность *f*, реши́мость *f.*

resolve [ri'zɔlv] **1.** *v/t.* растворя́ть [-ори́ть]; *fig.* решáть [реши́ть]; разрешáть [-ши́ть]; *v/i.* решáть(ся) [реши́ть(ся)]; ~ (up)on решáться [-ши́ться] на (В); **2.** решéние; **~d** [-d] □ пóлный реши́мости.

resonant ['reznənt] □ звýчный; резони́рующий.

resort [ri'zɔ:t] **1.** прибéжище; курóрт; summer ~ дáчное мéсто; **2.** ~ to: прибегáть [-éгнуть] к (Д); чáсто посещáть (В).

resound [ri'zaund] [про]звучáть; оглашáть(ся) [огласи́ть(ся)]; отражáть [-рази́ть] (звук).

resource [ri'sɔ:s] ресýрс; срéдство; возмóжность *f*; нахóдчивость *f*; **~ful** [-ful] □ нахóдчивый.

respect [ri'spekt] **1.** уважéние; отношéние; почтéние (of к Д); **~s** *pl.* привéт, поклóн; **2.** *v/t.* уважáть, почитáть; **~able** [-əbl] □ почтéнный; представи́тельный; *part.* † соли́дный; **~ful** [-ful] □ почти́тельный; **~ing** [-iŋ] относи́тельно (Р); **~ive** [-iv] □ соответ́ственный; we went to our ~ places мы пошли́ по местáм; **~ively** [-ivli] и́ли; соответ́ственно.

respirat|ion [respə'reiʃən] дыхáние; вдох и вы́дох; **~or** ['respəreitə] респирáтор; противогáз.

respire [ris'paiə] дышáть; переводи́ть дыхáние.

respite ['respait] передь́шка; отсрóчка.

respond [ris'pɔnd] отвечáть [-éтить]; ~ to реаги́ровать на; отзывáться [отозвáться] на (В).

response [ris'pɔns] отвéт; *fig.* óтклик; óтзыв.

responsi|bility [rispɔnsə'biliti] ответ́ственность *f*; **~ble** [ris'pɔnsəbl] ответ́ственный (to пéред Т).

rest [rest] **1.** óтдых; покóй; лóже; опóра; **2.** *v/i.* отдыхáть [отдохнýть]; [по]лежáть; опирáться [оперéться] (on на В); *fig.* ~ (up)on оснóвываться [-овáться] на (П); *v/t.* давáть óтдых (Д).

restaurant ['restərɔ:ŋ] ресторáн.

restitution [resti'tju:ʃən] возврáт (об имýществе); восстановлéние; возмещéние убы́тков.

restive ['restiv] □ норови́стый (о лóшади); упря́мый.

restless ['restlis] непосéдливый; беспокóйный, неугомóнный; **~ness** [-nis] непосéдливость *f*; неугомóнность *f*.

restorat|ion [resto'reiʃən] реставрáция; восстановлéние; **~ive** [ris'tɔrətiv] укрепля́ющий, тони́ческий.

restore [ris'tɔ:] восстанáвливать [-нови́ть]; возвращáть [-рати́ть]; *paint.* реставри́ровать (*im*)*pf.*; ~ to health вылéчивать [вы́лечить].

restrain [ris'trein] сдéрживать [-жáть]; задéрживать [-жáть]; подавля́ть [-ви́ть] (чýвства); **~t** [-t] сдéржанность *f*; ограничéние; обуздáние.

restrict [ris'trikt] ограни́чи(ва)ть; **~ion** [ris'trikʃən] ограничéние.

result [ri'zʌlt] **1.** результáт; исхóд; **2.** проистекáть [-éчь] (from от, из Р); ~ in приводи́ть [-вести́] к (Д).

resum|e [ri'zju:m] возобновля́ть [-ви́ть]; получáть обрáтно; резюми́ровать (*im*)*pf.*; **~ption** [ri'zʌmpʃən] возобновлéние; продолжéние.

resurrection [rezə'rekʃən] воскресéние; воскрешéние (обы́чая и т. п.).

resuscitate [ri'sʌsiteit] воскрешáть [-еси́ть]; оживля́ть [-ви́ть].

retail 1. ['ri:teil] рóзничная продáжа; by ~ в рóзницу; *attr.* рóзничный; **2.** [ri:'teil] продавáть(ся) в рóзницу; **~er** [-ə] рóзничный торгóвец.

retain [ri'tein] удéрживать [-жáть]; сохраня́ть [-ни́ть].

retaliat|e [ri'tælieit] отплáчивать [-лати́ть] (тем же); **~ion** [ritæli'eiʃən] отплáта, возмéздие.

retard [ri'tɑ:d] задéрживать [-жáть]; замедля́ть [-éдлить]; запáздывать [запоздáть].

retention [ri'tenʃən] удержáние; сохранéние.

reticent ['retisənt] сдéржанный; молчали́вый.

retinue ['retinju:] сви́та.

retir|e [ri'taiə] *v/t.* увольня́ть в отстáвку; изымáть из обращéния; *v/i.* выходи́ть в отстáвку; удаля́ться [-ли́ться]; уединя́ться [-ни́ться]; **~ed** [-d] □ уединённый; отставнóй, в отстáвке; ~ pay пéнсия; **~ement** [-mənt] отстáвка; уединéние; **~ing** [-riŋ] скрóмный, застéнчивый.

retort [ri'tɔ:t] **1.** рéзкий (и́ли находчивый) отвéт; ⚗ ретóрта; **2.** отпари́ровать *pf.* (кóлкость); возражáть [-рази́ть].

retouch ['ri:tʌtʃ] дéлать попрáвки в (П); *phot.* ретуши́ровать (*im*)*pf.*

retrace [ri'treis] прослéживать до истóчника; ~ one's steps возвращáться по свои́м следáм (*a. fig.*).

retract [ri'trækt] отрекáться [отрéчься] от (Р); брать назáд (словá и т. п.); втя́гивать [втянýть].

retreat [ri'tri:t] **1.** отступлéние (*part.* ⚔); уединéние; пристáнище; ⚔ отбóй; ⚔ вечéрняя заря́; **2.** уходи́ть [уйти́]; удаля́ться [-ли́ться]; (*part.* ⚔) отступáть [-пи́ть].

retrench [ri'trentʃ] урéз(ыв)ать, сокращáть [-рати́ть] (расхóды).

retrieve [ri'tri:v] (снóва) находи́ть [найти́]; восстанáвливать [-нови́ть].

retro... ['retro(u), 'ri:tro(u)] обрáтно...; **~active** [retrou'æktiv] имéющий обрáтную си́лу; **~grade** ['retrougreid] **1.** ретрогрáдный; реакциóнный; **2.** регресси́ровать; **~gression** [retrou'greʃən] регрéсс, упáдок; **~spect** ['retrouspekt] взгляд на прóшлое; **~spective** [retrou'spektiv] □ ретроспекти́вный; имéющий обрáтную си́лу.

return [ri'tə:n] **1.** возвращéние; возврáт; † оборóт; дохóд, при́быль *f*; отдáча; результáт вы́боров; *attr.* обрáтный (билéт и т. п.); many happy ~s of the day поздравля́ю с днём рождéния; in ~ в обмéн (for на В); в отвéт; by ~ (of post) с обрáтной пóчтой; ~ ticket обрáтный билéт; **2.** *v/i.* возвращáться [-рати́ться]; вернýться *pf.*;

v/t. возвращáть [-ратúть]; вернýть *pf.*; отплáчивать [-латúть]; приносúть [-нестú] (дохóд); присылáть назáд; отвечáть [-éтить]; *parl.* изб(и)рáть. [воссоединéние.]
reunion ['ri:'ju:njən] собрáние;
revalorization [ri:væləraiˈzeiʃən] переоцéнка.
reveal [ri'vi:l] обнарýжи(ва)ть; откры́(вá)ть; **~ing** [-iŋ] обнарýживающий; показáтельный.
revel [revl] **1.** пировáть; упú(вá)ться (in T); **2.** пирýшка.
revelation [revi'leiʃən] откровéние; обнарýжéние; откры́тие.
revel|(l)er ['revlə] гулякá *m*; **~ry** [-ri] разгýл, кутёж.
revenge [ri'vendʒ] **1.** месть *f*; ревáнш; отмéстка; **2** [ото]мстúть за (B); **~ful** [-ful] □ мстúтельный.
revenue ['revinju:] (годовóй) дохóд; *pl.* дохóдные статьú *f/pl.*; ~ board, ~ office департáмент государственных сбóров.
reverberate [re'və:bəreit] отражáть(ся) [отразúть(ся)].
revere [ri'viə] уважáть, почитáть; **~nce** ['revərəns] **1.** почтéние; **2.** уважáть; благоговéть пéред (T); **~nd** [-d] **1.** почтéнный; **2.** *eccl.* преподóбие.
reverent(ial) ['revərənt, revə'renʃəl] почтúтельный; пóлный благоговéния.
reverie ['revəri] мечты́ *f/pl.*; мечтáтельность *f*.
revers|al [ri'və:səl] перемéна; обрáтный ход; отмéна; изменéние; **~e** [ri'və:s] **1.** обрáтная сторонá; перемéна; противоположное; **~s** *pl.* преврáтности *f/pl.*; **2.** □ обрáтный; противоположный; **3.** поворáчивать назáд; ⊕ давáть обрáтный ход; ⚖ отменять [-нúть]; **~ion** [ri'və:ʃən] возвращéние; *biol.* атавúзм.
revert [ri'və:t] возвращáться [-ратúться] (в прéжнее состояние úли к вопрóсу).
review [ri'vju:] **1.** обзóр; провéрка; ⚖ пересмóтр; ⚔, ⚓ смотр; обозрéние (журнáл); рецéнзия; **2.** пересмáтривать [-смотрéть]; писáть рецéнзию о (П); обозрé(вá)ть (B); ⚔, ⚓ производúть смотр (P).
revile [ri'vail] оскорблять [-бúть].
revis|e [ri'vaiz] пересмáтривать [-смотрéть]; исправлять [-áвить]; **~ion** [ri'viʒən] пересмóтр; ревúзия; исправленное издáние.
reviv|al [ri'vaivəl] возрождéние; оживлéние; **~e** [ri'vaiv] приходúть úли приводúть в чýвство; оживлять [-вúть]; ожú(вá)ть.
revocation [revə'keiʃən] отмéна, аннулúрование (закóна и т. п.).
revoke [ri'vouk] *v/t.* отменять [-нúть] (закóн и т. п.); *v/i.* дéлать ренóнс.
revolt [ri'voult] **1.** восстáние; мятéж; **2.** *v/i.* восст(ав)áть; *fig.* отпадáть [отпáсть] (from от P); *v/t.* *fig.* оттáлкивать [оттолкнýть].
revolution [revə'lu:ʃən] круговóе вращéние; ⊕ оборóт; *pol.* револю́ция; **~ary** [-əri] **1.** революциóнный; **2.** революционéр(ка); **~ize** [-aiz] революционизúровать (*im*)*pf*.
revolv|e [ri'vɔlv] *v/i.* вращáться; периодúчески возвращáться; *v/t.* вращáть; обдýм(ыв)ать; **~ing** [-iŋ] вращáющийся; поворóтный.
revulsion [ri'vʌlʃən] внезáпное изменéние (чувств и т. п.).
reward [ri'wɔ:d] **1.** нагрáда; вознаграждéние; **2.** вознаграждáть [-радúть]; награждáть [-радúть].
rewrite ['ri:'rait] [*irr.* (write)] перепúсывать [-сáть].
rhapsody ['ræpsədi] рапсóдия.
rheumatism ['ru:mətizm] ревматúзм.
rhubarb ['ru:bɑ:b] ⚘ ревéнь *m*.
rhyme [raim] **1.** рúфма; (рифмóванный) стих; without ~ or reason без смы́сла; **2.** рифмовáть(ся) (with, to с T).
rhythm [riðm] ритм; **~ic(al)** [-mik, -mikəl] ритмúчный, ритмúческий.
rib [rib] **1.** ребрó; **2.** ⊕ укреплять рёбрами.
ribald ['ribəld] грýбый, непристóйный.
ribbon ['ribən] лéнта; **~s** *pl.* клóчья *m/pl*.
rice [rais] рис.
rich [ritʃ] □ богáтый (in T); роскóшный; плодорóдный (о пóчве); жúрный (о пúще); пóлный (тон); густóй (о крáсках); ~ milk цéльное молокó; **~es** ['ritʃiz] *pl.* богáтство; сокрóвища *n/pl*.
rick [rik] ⚒ стог, скирд(á).
ricket|s ['rikits] рахúт; **~y** [-i] рахитúчный; шáткий.
rid [rid] [*irr.*] избавлять [-áвить] (of от P); get ~ of отдéл(ыв)аться от (P), избавляться [-áвиться] от (P).
ridden [ridn] **1.** *p. pt.* от ride; **2.** (в слóжных словáх) одержúмый (стрáхом, предрассýдками и т. п.), под влáстью (чегó-либо).
riddle [ridl] **1.** загáдка; решетó; **2.** изрешéчивать [-шетúть].
ride [raid] **1.** ездá верхóм; катáние; прогýлка; **2.** [*irr.*] *v/i.* éздить, [по]éхать (на лóшади, автомобúле и т. п.); катáться верхóм; *v/t.* éздить, [по]éхать на (П); катáть (на спинé); **~r** ['raidə] верховóй; наéздник (-ица) (в цúрке); всáдник (-ица).
ridge [ridʒ] гóрный кряж, хребéт; ⚠ конёк (кры́ши); ⚒ гря́дка.
ridicul|e ['ridikju:l] **1.** осмеяние, насмéшка; **2.** высмéивать [вы́-

смеять]; **~ous** [ri'dikjuləs] □ нелепый, смешной.
riding ['raidiŋ] верховая езда; *attr.* верховой.
rife [raif] □: ~ with изобилующий (Т).
riff-raff ['rifræf] подонки (общества) *m/pl.*
rifle [raifl] **1.** винтовка; **2.** [о]грабить; **~man** ⚔ стрелок.
rift [rift] трещина, расселина.
rig [rig] **1.** ⚓ оснастка; F наряд; **2.** оснащать [оснастить]; F наряжать [-ядить]; **~ging** ['rigiŋ] ⚓ такелаж, снасти *f/pl.*
right [rait] **1.** □ правильный, верный; правый; be ~ быть правым; put ~ приводить в порядок; **2.** *adv.* прямо; правильно; справедливо; как раз; ~ away сразу; ~ on прямо вперёд; **3.** право; справедливость *f*; the ~s *pl.* (of a story) настоящие факты *m/pl.*; by ~ of на основании (Р); on (*or* to) the ~ направо; **4.** приводить в порядок; выпрямлять(ся) [выпрямить(ся)]; **~eous** ['raitʃəs] □ праведный; **~ful** ['raitful] □ справедливый; законный.
rigid ['ridʒid] □ негнущийся, негибкий, жёсткий; *fig.* суровый; непреклонный; **~ity** [ri'dʒiditi] жёсткость *f*; непреклонность *f.*
rigo(u)r ['rigə] суровость *f*; строгость *f.*
rigorous [-rəs] □ суровый; строгий.
rim [rim] ободок; край; обод; оправа (очков).
rime [raim] иней; изморозь *f*; = rhyme.
rind [raind] кора, кожура; корка.
ring [riŋ] **1.** кольцо; круг; звон (колоколов); звонок; ✝, *sport* ринг; **2.** надевать кольцо на (В); (*mst* ~ in, round, about) окружать [-жить]; [*irr.*] [за]звучать; ~ the bell [по]звонить (у двери); звонить в колокол; ~ a p. up позвонить кому-нибудь по телефону; **~-leader** зачинщик (-ица); **~let** ['riŋlit] колечко; локон.
rink [riŋk] каток, скетинг-ринк.
rinse [rins] [вы]полоскать.
riot ['raiət] **1.** бунт; буйство; разгул; run ~ вести себя буйно; разгуливаться [-ляться]; **2.** принимать участие в бунте; предаваться разгулу; **~er** [-ə] бунтарь *m*; **~ous** [-əs] □ буйный, разгульный.
rip [rip] [рас]пороть(ся).
ripe [raip] □ зрелый (*a. fig.*); спелый; готовый; **~n** [raipn] созре(ва)ть, [по]спеть; **~ness** ['raipnis] спелость *f*; зрелость *f.*
ripple [ripl] **1.** рябь *f*, зыбь *f*; журчание; **2.** покрывать(ся) рябью; журчать.
rise [raiz] **1.** повышение; восход; подъём; выход (на поверхность); возвышенность *f*; происхождение; take (one's) ~ происходить [произойти]; **2.** [*irr.*] подниматься [-няться]; всходить [взойти]; вст(ав)ать; восст(ав)ать; нач(ин)аться; ~ to быть в состоянии справиться с (Т); **~n** [rizn] *p. pt.* от rise.
rising ['raiziŋ] вставание; возвышение; восстание; восход.
risk [risk] **1.** риск; run a (*or* the) ~ рисковать [-кнуть]; **2.** отваживаться на (В); рисковать [-кнуть] (Т); **~y** ['riski] □ рискованный.
rit|e [rait] обряд, церемония; **~ual** ['ritjuəl] **1.** ритуальный; **2.** ритуал.
rival ['raivəl] **1.** соперник (-ица); ✝ конкурент; **2.** соперничающий; **3.** соперничать с (Т); **~ry** [-ri] соперничество; соревнование.
rive [raiv] [*irr.*] раскалывать(ся) [расколоть(ся)].
river ['rivə] река; поток (*a. fig.*); **~side** берег реки; *attr.* прибрежный.
rivet ['rivit] **1.** заклёпка; **2.** заклёпывать [-лепать]; *fig.* приковывать [-овать] (В к Д).
rivulet ['rivjulit] ручей; речушка.
road [roud] дорога; путь *m*; *mst* ~s *pl.* ⚓ рейд (*a.* ~stead); **~ster** ['roudstə] дорожный велосипед; родстер (двухместный открытый автомобиль *m*); **~way** мостовая.
roam [roum] *v/t.* бродить по (Д); *v/i.* странствовать; скитаться.
roar [rɔ:] **1.** [за]реветь; [за]грохотать; ~ with laughter хохотать во всё горло; **2.** рёв; грохот; громкий хохот.
roast [roust] **1.** [из]жарить(ся); калить (орехи и т. п.); **2.** жареный; ~ meat жареное, жаркое.
rob [rɔb] [о]грабить; *fig.* лишать [-шить] (of Р); **~ber** ['rɔbə] грабитель *m*; **~bery** [-ri] грабёж.
robe [roub] мантия (судьи); ряса; халат.
robust [ro'bʌst] □ крепкий, здоровый.
rock [rɔk] **1.** скала; утёс; горная порода; ~ crystal горный хрусталь *m*; **2.** качать(ся) [качнуть(-ся)]; убаюк(ив)ать.
rocket ['rɔkit] ракета; *attr.* ракетный; **~-powered** с ракетным двигателем.
rocking-chair кресло-качалка.
rocky ['rɔki] каменистый; скалистый.
rod [rɔd] жезл; прут (*a.* ⊕); розга, розги; удочка; ⊕ шток; стержень *m*; род (мера длины, около 5-ти метров).
rode [roud] *pt.* от ride.
rodent ['roudənt] грызун.
rodeo [rou'deiou] *Am.* загон для клеймения скота; состязание ковбоев.

roe [rou] косу́ля; икра́; soft ~ моло́ки *n/pl.*
rogu|e [roug] жу́лик, моше́нник; **~ish** ['rougiʃ] жулнкова́тый, моше́ннический.
roister ['rɔistə] бесчи́нствовать.
rôle [roul] *thea.* роль *f* (*a. fig.*).
roll [roul] **1.** свёрток (мате́рии и т. п.); руло́н; кату́шка; рее́стр, спи́сок; раска́т (гро́ма); бу́лочка; **2.** *v/t.* ката́ть, [по]кати́ть; враща́ть; раска́тывать [-ката́ть] (те́сто); прока́тывать [-ката́ть] (мета́лл); ~ up свёртывать [сверну́ть]; ска́тывать [ската́ть]; *v/i.* ката́ться, [по]кати́ться; валя́ться (in в П); (о гро́ме) грохота́ть; ⚓ име́ть бокову́ю ка́чку; **~-call** ⚔ перекли́чка; **~er** ['roulə] ро́лик; вал; ~ skate конёк на ро́ликах.
rollick ['rɔlik] шу́мно весели́ться.
rolling ['rouliŋ] прока́тный; холми́стый; ~ mill ⊕ прока́тный стан.
Roman ['roumən] **1.** □ ри́мский; **2.** ри́млянин (-янка); *typ.* прямо́й све́тлый шрифт.
romance [rə'mæns] **1.** ♪ рома́нс; рома́н; **2.** *fig.* прикра́шивать действи́тельность; **3.** ♀ рома́нский; **~r** [-ə] романи́ст (а́втор).
romantic [ro'mæntik] (~ally) романти́чный; **~ism** [-tisizm] романти́зм, рома́нтика; **~ist** [-tisist] рома́нтик.
romp [rɔmp] **1.** возня́; сорвиголова́ *m/f*; **2.** вози́ться, шу́мно игра́ть.
röntgenogram [rɔnt'genəgræm] рентгеногра́мма.
rood [ru:d] че́тверть а́кра = 0,1 гекта́ра; распя́тие.
roof [ru:f] **1.** кры́ша; ~ of the mouth нёбо; **2.** [по]кры́ть (дом); **~ing** ['ru:fiŋ] **1.** кро́вельный материа́л; **2.** кро́вля; ~ felt кро́вельный толь *m.*
rook [ruk] **1.** грач; *chess* ладья́; *fig.* моше́нник; **2.** обма́нывать [-ну́ть].
room [ru:m] **1.** ко́мната; ме́сто; помеще́ние; простра́нство; **~s** *pl.* кварти́ра; ко́мнаты *f/pl.*; **2.** *Am.* жить квартира́нтом (-ткой); **~er** ['rumə] квартира́нт(ка), жиле́ц, жили́ца; **~mate** сожи́тель(ница *f*) *m*; **~y** ['rumi] □ просто́рный.
roost [ru:st] **1.** насе́ст; **2.** уса́живаться на насе́ст; *fig.* устра́иваться на́ ночь; **~er** ['ru:stə] пету́х.
root [ru:t] ко́рень *m*; strike ~ пуска́ть ко́рни; укореня́ться [-ни́ться]; ~ out вырыва́ть с ко́рнем (*a. fig.*); вы́искивать [вы́искать] (*a.* ~ up); **~ed** ['ru:tid] укорени́вшийся.
rope [roup] **1.** кана́т; верёвка; трос; ни́тка (же́мчуга, бус); F come to the end of one's ~ дойти́ до то́чки; know the **~s** *pl.* знать все ходы́ и вы́ходы; **2.** свя́зывать верёвкой; привя́зывать кана́том; (*mst* ~ off) оцепля́ть кана́том.
rosary ['rouzəri] *eccl.* чётки *f/pl.*
rose [rouz] **1.** ро́за; се́тка (на ле́йке); ро́зовый цвет; **2.** *pt.* от rise.
rosin ['rɔzin] канифо́ль *f.*
rostrum ['rɔstrəm] ка́федра; трибу́на.
rosy ['rouzi] □ ро́зовый; румя́ный; *fig.* ра́дужный.
rot [rɔt] **1.** гние́ние; гниль *f*; **2.** *v/t.* [с]гнои́ть; *v/i.* сгни(ва́)ть, [с]гнить.
rota|ry ['routəri] враща́тельный; ротацио́нный; **~te** [rou'teit] враща́ть(ся); чередова́ть(ся); **~tion** [rou'teiʃən] враще́ние; чередова́ние; **~tory** [rou'teitəri]: *s.* rotary; ⚡ многофа́зный.
rote [rout]: by ~ *fig.* механи́чески.
rotten [rɔtn] □ гнило́й; испо́рченный; F отврати́тельный.
rouge [ru:ʒ] **1.** румя́на *n/pl.*; **2.** [на-] румя́нить(ся).
rough [rʌf] **1.** □ гру́бый; шерша́вый; шерохова́тый; косма́тый; бу́рный; неделика́тный; ~ and ready сде́ланный ко́е-ка́к, на́спех; грубова́тый; **2.** буя́н; **3.** ~ it перебива́ться с трудо́м; **~cast 1.** ⊕ штукату́рка намётом; **2.** на́черно разрабо́танный; **3.** ⊕ штукату́рить намётом; **~en** ['rʌfən] де́лать(ся) гру́бым, шерохова́тым; **~ness** ['rʌfnis] шерохова́тость *f*; гру́бость *f*; **~shod**: ride ~ over обходи́ться гру́бо, суро́во с (Т).
round [raund] **1.** □ кру́глый; кругово́й; прямо́й, и́скренний; ~ trip *Am.* пое́здка ту́да и обра́тно; **2.** *adv.* круго́м, вокру́г; обра́тно; (*often* ~ about) вокру́г да о́коло; all the year ~ кру́глый год; **3.** *prp.* вокру́г, круго́м (Р); за (В *or* Т); по (Д); **4.** круг; цикл; тур (в та́нце); *sport* ра́унд; обхо́д; объе́зд; 100 **~s** ⚔ сто патро́нов; **5.** *v/t.* закругля́ть [-ли́ть]; огиба́ть [обогну́ть]; ~ up окружа́ть [-жи́ть]; *v/i.* закругля́ться [-ли́ться]; **~about** ['raundəbaut] **1.** око́льный; **2.** око́льный путь *m*; карусе́ль *f*; **~ish** ['raundiʃ] круглова́тый; **~-up** обла́ва.
rous|e [rauz] *v/t.* [раз]буди́ть; возбужда́ть [-уди́ть]; воодушевля́ть [-ви́ть]; ~ o. s. стряхну́ть лень; *v/i.* просыпа́ться [-сну́ться]; **~ing** ['rauziŋ] возбужда́ющий; бу́рный.
rout [raut] **1.** разгро́м; бе́гство; put to ~ разгроми́ть на́голову; обраща́ть в бе́гство; **2.** = put to ~; рыть ры́лом.
route [ru:t, ⚔ raut] путь *m*; ⚔ маршру́т.
routine [ru:'ti:n] **1.** заведённый поря́док; рути́на; **2.** рути́нный.
rove [rouv] скита́ться; броди́ть.
row[1] [rou] **1.** ряд; прогу́лка в ло́дке; **2.** грести́ (весло́м); пра́вить (ло́дкой).

row² [rau] F **1.** галдёж, гвалт; дра́ка; ссо́ра; **2.** задава́ть нагоня́й (Д).
row-boat ['roubout] гребна́я ло́дка.
rower ['rouə] гребе́ц (*wo*)*man*.
royal ['rɔiəl] □ короле́вский; великоле́пный; **~ty** [-ti] член короле́вской семьи́; короле́вская власть *f*; **~s** *pl.* а́вторский гонора́р.
rub [rʌb] **1.** тре́ние; растира́ние; *fig.* препя́тствие; **2.** *v/t.* тере́ть; протира́ть [-тере́ть]; натира́ть [натере́ть]; ~ out стира́ть [стере́ть]; ~ up [от]полирова́ть; освежа́ть [-жи́ть] (в па́мяти); *v/i.* тере́ться (against о В); *fig.* ~ along, on проби́(ва́)ться с трудо́м.
rubber ['rʌbə] каучу́к; рези́на; рези́нка; *cards* ро́ббер; **~s** *pl. Am.* гало́ши *f/pl.*; *attr.* рези́новый.
rubbish ['rʌbiʃ] му́сор; хлам; *fig.* вздор; глу́пости *f/pl.*
rubble [rʌbl] щё́бень *m*; ⚠ бут.
ruby ['ru:bi] руби́н; руби́новый цвет.
rudder ['rʌdə] ⚓ руль *m*; ✈ руль поворо́та.
rudd|iness ['rʌdinis] краснота́; румя́нец; **~y** ['rʌdi] я́рко-кра́сный; румя́ный.
rude [ru:d] □ неотёсанный; гру́бый; неве́жливый; *fig.* кре́пкий (о здоро́вье).
rudiment ['ru:diment] *biol.* рудиме́нт, зача́ток; **~s** *pl.* нача́тки *m/pl.*
rueful ['ru:ful] □ уны́лый, печа́льный.
ruff [rʌf] бры́жи *f/pl.*; *zo.* ёрш.
ruffian ['rʌfjən] грубия́н; хулига́н.
ruffle [rʌfl] **1.** манже́тка; рюш; сумато́ха; рябь *f*; **2.** [взъ]еро́шить (во́лосы); ряби́ть (во́ду); *fig.* наруша́ть споко́йствие (Р), [вс]трево́жить.
rug [rʌg] плед; ковёр, ко́врик; **~ged** ['rʌgid] □ неро́вный; шерохова́тый; суро́вый; пересечённый; ре́зкий.
ruin ['ruin] **1.** ги́бель *f*; разоре́ние; круше́ние (наде́жд и т. п.); *mst* **~s** *pl.* разва́лины *f/pl.*; **2.** [по]губи́ть; разоря́ть [-ри́ть]; разруша́ть [-у́шить]; [о]бесче́стить; **~ous** ['ruinəs] □ разори́тельный; губи́тельный.
rul|e [ru:l] **1.** пра́вило; уста́в; правле́ние; власть *f*; лине́йка; as a ~ обы́чно; **2.** *v/t.* управля́ть (Т); постановля́ть [-ви́ть]; [на]линова́ть; [раз]графи́ть; ~ out исключа́ть [-чи́ть]; *v/i.* госпо́дствовать; **~er** ['ru:lə] прави́тель(ница *f*) *m*; лине́йка.
rum [rʌm] ром; *Am.* спиртно́й напи́ток.
Rumanian [ru(:)'meinjən] **1.** румы́нский; **2.** румы́н(ка).
rumble ['rʌmbl] **1.** громыха́ние; гро́хот; (*Am.* ~-seat) откидно́е сиде́нье; **2.** [за]громыха́ть; [за-] грохота́ть; [за]греме́ть (о гро́ме).
rumina|nt ['ru:minənt] жва́чное живо́тное; **~te** [-neit] жева́ть жва́чку; *fig.* размышля́ть [-мы́слить].
rummage ['rʌmidʒ] **1.** распрода́жа ме́лочей (с благотвори́тельной це́лью); **2.** *v/t.* выта́скивать [вы́тащить]; переры́(ва́)ть; *v/i.* ры́ться.
rumo(u)r ['ru:mə] **1.** слух; молва́; **2.** it is ~ed ... хо́дят слу́хи ...
rump [rʌmp] огу́зок.
rumple [rʌmpl] [с]мять; [взъ]еро́шить (во́лосы, пе́рья и т. п.).
run [rʌn] **1.** [*irr.*] *v/i. com.* бе́гать, [по]бежа́ть; [по]те́чь; расплы́(ва́)ться (о кра́сках и т. п.); враща́ться, рабо́тать (о маши́не); гласи́ть; ~ across a p.ната́лкиваться [натолкну́ться] на (В); ~ away убега́ть [убежа́ть]; понести́ *pf.* (о ло́шади); ~ down сбега́ть [сбежа́ть]; остана́вливаться [-нови́ться (о часа́х и т. п.); истоща́ться [-щи́ться]; ~ dry иссяка́ть [-я́кнуть]; ~ for *parl.* выставля́ть свою́ кадидату́ру на (В); ~ into впада́ть [впасть] в (В); доходи́ть [дойти́] до (Р); встреча́ть [-е́тить]; ~ on продолжа́ться [-до́лжиться]; говори́ть без у́молку; ~ out, short конча́ться [ко́нчиться]; ~ through прочита́ть бе́гло; прома́тывать]-мота́ть]; ~ to достига́ть [-и́гнуть] (су́ммы); ~ up to доходи́ть [дойти́] до (Р); **2.** *v/t.* пробега́ть [-бежа́ть] (расстоя́ние); нали́(ва́)ть (во́ду и т. п.); вести́ (дела́); выгоня́ть в по́ле (скот); вонза́ть [-зи́ть]; управля́ть (конто́рой и т. п.); проводи́ть [-вести́] (Т, over по Д); ~ the blockade прорва́ть блока́ду; ~ down задавля́ть [-ви́ть]; *fig.* говори́ть пло́хо о (П); унижа́ть [уни́зить]; переутомля́ть [-ми́ть]; ~ over переезжа́ть [-е́хать], задавля́ть [-ви́ть]; прочита́ть бе́гло; ~ up взду(ва́)ть (це́ны); возводи́ть [-вести́] (зда́ние); ~ up a bill at [за]должа́ть (Д); **3.** бег; пробе́г; ход, рабо́та, де́йствие (маши́ны); тече́ние, ход (вре́мени); ряд; пое́здка, прогу́лка; ✝ спрос; управле́ние; *Am.* руче́й, пото́к; заго́н; па́стбище; разреше́ние по́льзоваться (of Т); the common ~ обыкнове́нные лю́ди *m/pl.*; *thea.* have a ~ of 20 nights идти́ два́дцать вечеро́в подря́д (о пье́се); in the long ~ со вре́менем; в конце́ концо́в.
run|about ['rʌnəbaut] лёгкий автомоби́ль *m*; **~away** бегле́ц; дезерти́р.
rung¹ [rʌŋ] *p. pt.* от ring.
rung² [~] ступе́нька.
run|let ['rʌnlit], **~nel** ['rʌnl] ручеёк; кана́ва.
runner ['rʌnə] бегу́н; по́лоз (у сане́й); побе́г (расте́ния); **~-up** [-'rʌp] занима́ющий второ́е ме́сто (в состяза́нии).

running ['rʌniŋ] **1.** бегу́щий; бего-во́й; теку́щий; two days ~ два дня подря́д; ~ fire ⚔ бе́глый ого́нь *m*; ~ hand бе́глый по́черк; **2.** бе́ганье; бег; бега́ *m/pl.*; де́йствие; **~-board** подно́жка.

runway ['rʌnwei] ✈ взлётно-поса́дочная полоса́.

rupture ['rʌptʃə] **1.** перело́м; раз-ры́в; ⚕ гры́жа; **2.** разрыва́ть [разорва́ть] (*a. fig.*); прор(ы)ва́ть.

rural ['ruərəl] □ се́льский, дере-ве́нский

rush [rʌʃ] **1.** ⚘ тростни́к, камы́ш; на́тиск; ✝ наплы́в (покупа́телей); ~ hours *pl.* часы́-пик; ⚔ пере-бе́жка; **2.** *v/i.* мча́ться; броса́ться [бро́ситься]; носи́ться, [по]нес-ти́сь; ~ into броса́ться необду́-манно в (В); ~ into print сли́шком поспе́шно выступа́ть в печа́ти; *v/t.* мчать; увлека́ть [увле́чь]; [по]торопи́ть; *fig.* ⚔ брать стреми́-тельным на́тиском.

russet ['rʌsit] кра́сно-кори́чневый.

Russia ['rʌʃə] Росси́я; **~n** [-n] **1.** ру́сский; **2.** ру́сский, ру́сская; ру́сский язы́к.

rust [rʌst] **1.** ржа́вчина; **2.** [за]ржа-ве́ть.

rustic ['rʌstik] **1.** (~ally) дереве́н-ский; просто́й; гру́бый; **2.** се́ль-ский жи́тель *m*.

rustle [rʌsl] **1.** [за]шелесте́ть; **2.** ше́лест, шо́рох.

rust|less ['rʌstlis] нержаве́ющий; **~y** ['rʌsti] заржа́вленный, ржа́-вый; порыже́вший.

rut [rʌt] колея́ (*a. fig.*); ⊕ фальц, жёлоб; *zo.* те́чка.

ruthless ['ru:θlis] □ безжа́лост-ный.

rutted ['rʌtid], **rutty** ['rʌti] изре́-занный колея́ми.

rye [rai] ⚘ рожь *f.*

S

sabotage ['sæbotɑ:ʒ] **1.** сабота́ж; **2.** саботи́ровать (В) (*a.* ~ on *a th.*) (*im*)*pf.*

sabre ['seibə] са́бля, ша́шка.

sack [sæk] **1.** грабёж; мешо́к, куль *m*; сак (пальто́); **2.** класть, ссыпа́ть в мешо́к; [о]гра́бить; F увольня́ть [уво́лить] (В); **~cloth, ~ing** ['sækiŋ] дерю́га, холст.

sacrament ['sækrəmənt] *eccl.* та́ин-ство, прича́стие.

sacred ['seikrid] □ свято́й; свя-щённый; ♪ духо́вный.

sacrifice ['sækrifais] **1.** же́ртва; жертвоприноше́ние; at a ~ ✝ себе́ в убы́ток; **2.** [по]же́ртвовать.

sacrileg|e ['sækrilidʒ] святота́т-ство, кощу́нство; **~ious** [sækri-'lidʒəs] □ святота́тственный.

sad [sæd] □ печа́льный, гру́стный; доса́дный; ту́склый.

sadden [sædn] [о]печа́лить(ся).

saddle [sædl] **1.** седло́; **2.** [о]сед-ла́ть; *fig.* взва́ливать [-ли́ть] (upon на В); обременя́ть [-ни́ть]; **~r** шо́р-ник.

sadism ['sɑ:dizm] сади́зм.

sadness ['sædnis] печа́ль *f*, грусть *f.*

safe [seif] **1.** □ невреди́мый; на-дёжный; безопа́сный; (бу́дучи) в безопа́сности; **2.** сейф, несгора́-емый шкаф; шкаф для прови́зии; **~-conduct** охра́нное свиде́тель-ство; **~guard 1.** охра́на; предо-сторо́жность *f*; защи́та; **2.** охра-ня́ть [-ни́ть]; защища́ть [-ити́ть].

safety ['seifti] **1.** безопа́сность *f*; надёжность *f*; **2.** безопа́сный; **~-pin** англи́йская була́вка; **~-razor** безопа́сная бри́тва.

saffron ['sæfrən] шафра́н.

sag [sæg] оседа́ть [осе́сть]; проги-ба́ться [-гну́ться]; обвиса́ть [-и́с-нуть]; ⚓ отклоня́ться от ку́рса.

sagacious [sə'geiʃəs] проница́тель-ный, прозорли́вый; **~ty** [sə'gæsiti] проница́тельность *f*, прозорли́-вость *f*.

sage [seidʒ] **1.** □ му́дрый; разу́м-ный; **2.** мудре́ц; ⚘ шалфе́й.

said [sed] *pt.* и *p. pt.* от say.

sail [seil] **1.** па́рус; пла́вание под паруса́ми; па́русное су́дно; **2.** *v/i.* идти́ под паруса́ми; пла́вать, [по-] плы́ть; отплы́(ва́)ть; носи́ться, [по]нести́сь (об облака́х); *v/t.* управля́ть (су́дном); пла́вать по (Д); **~-boat** *Am.* па́русная ло́дка; **~or** ['seilə] моря́к, матро́с; be a (good) bad ~ (не) страда́ть морско́й боле́знью; **~-plane** планёр.

saint [seint] **1.** свято́й; **2.** причис-ля́ть к ли́ку святы́х; **~ly** ['seintli] *adj.* свято́й.

sake [seik]: for the ~ of ра́ди (Р); for my ~ ра́ди меня́.

sal(e)able ['seiləbl] хо́дкий (това́р).

salad ['sæləd] сала́т.

salary ['lsæləri] **1.** жа́лованье; **2.** плати́ть жа́лованье (Д).

sale [seil] прода́жа; распрода́жа; аукцио́н; be for ~, be on ~ про-дава́ться.

sales|man продаве́ц; *Am.* комми-вояжёр; **~woman** продавщи́ца.

salient ['seiljənt] выдаю́щийся, выступа́ющий; вы́пуклый.

saline ['seilain] соляно́й; солёный.

saliva [sə'laivə] 🕮 слюна́.

sallow ['sælou] боле́зненный, жел-това́тый (о цве́те лица́).

sally ['sæli] **1.** ⚔ вы́лазка; ре́плика,

острота́; **2.** ⚔ де́лать вы́лазку; ~ forth, ~ out отправля́ться [-а́виться].
salmon ['sæmən] сёмга; ло́со́сь *m.*
saloon [sə'lu:n] зал; сало́н (на парохо́де); сало́н-ваго́н; *Am.* бар, пивна́я.
salt [sɔ:lt] **1.** соль *f*; *fig.* остроу́мие; old ~ быва́лый моря́к; **2.** солёный; жгу́чий; е́дкий; **3.** [по]соли́ть; заса́ливать [-соли́ть]; **~-cellar** соло́нка; **~petre** ['sɔ:ltpitə] сели́тра; **~y** ['sɔ:lti] солёный.
salubrious [sə'lu:briəs] □, **salutary** ['sæljutəri] □ благотво́рный; поле́зный для здоро́вья.
salut|ation [sælju'teiʃən] приве́тствие; **~e** [sə'lu:t] **1.** приве́тствие; ⚔ салю́т; ⚔ отда́ние че́сти; **2.** приве́тствовать; ⚔ салютова́ть (*im*)*pf.* (Д); ⚔ отдава́ть честь (Д).
salvage ['sælvidʒ] **1.** спасе́ние (иму́щества и́ли су́дна); спасённое иму́щество; подъём (затону́вших судо́в); **2.** спаса́ть [спасти́] (иму́щество от огня́, су́дно на мо́ре и т. п.).
salvation [sæl'veiʃən] спасе́ние; ♀ Army 'А́рмия спасе́ния.
salve[1] [sælv] = salvage.
salve[2] [sɑ:v] **1.** сре́дство для успокое́ния; **2.** успока́ивать [-ко́ить] (со́весть); сгла́живать [сгла́дить] (тру́дность).
salvo ['sælvou] (ору́дийный) залп; *fig.* взрыв аплодисме́нтов.
same [seim]: the ~ тот же са́мый; та же са́мая; то же са́мое; it is all the ~ to me мне всё равно́.
sample [sɑ:mpl] **1.** про́ба; обра́зчик, образе́ц; **2.** [по]про́бовать; отбира́ть образцы́ (Р).
sanct|ify ['sæŋktifai] освяща́ть [-яти́ть]; **~imonious** [sæŋkti'mounjəs] □ ха́нжеский; **~ion** ['sæŋkʃən] **1.** са́нкция; утвержде́ние; принуди́тельная ме́ра; **2.** санкциони́ровать (*im*)*pf.*; утвержда́ть [-рди́ть]; **~ity** [-titi] свя́тость *f*; **~uary** [-tjuəri] святи́лище; убе́жище.
sand [sænd] **1.** песо́к; **~s** *pl.* песча́ный пляж; о́тмель *f*; пески́ *m/pl.* (пусты́ни); **2.** посыпа́ть песко́м.
sandal [sændl] санда́лия.
sandwich ['sænwidʒ, -witʃ] **1.** бутербро́д, са́ндвич; **2.** просла́ивать [-сло́ить].
sandy ['sændi] песча́ный; песо́чный; песо́чного цве́та.
sane [sein] норма́льный; здра́вый; здравомы́слящий.
sang [sæŋ] *pt.* от sing.
sanguin|ary ['sæŋgwinəri] □ крова́вый; кровожа́дный; **~e** [-gwin] сангвини́ческий; оптимисти́ческий.
sanitary ['sænitəri] □ санита́рный; гигиени́ческий.
sanit|ation [sæni'teiʃən] оздоровле́ние; улучше́ние санита́рных усло́вий; санитари́я; **~y** ['sæniti] здра́вый ум.
sank [sæŋk] *pt.* от sink.
sap [sæp] **1.** сок (расте́ний); *fig.* жи́зненные си́лы *f/pl.*; ⚔ са́па; **2.** истоща́ть [-щи́ть]; подка́пывать [-копа́ть]; **~less** ['sæplis] худосо́чный; истощённый; **~ling** ['sæpliŋ] молодо́е деревцо́.
sapphire ['sæfaiə] *min.* сапфи́р.
sappy ['sæpi] со́чный; *fig.* си́льный.
sarcasm ['sɑ:kæzm] сарка́зм.
sardine [sɑ:'di:n] сарди́н(к)а.
sardonic [sɑ:'dɔnik] (**~ally**) сардони́ческий.
sash [sæʃ] куша́к, по́яс.
sash-window подъёмное окно́.
sat [sæt] *pt.* и *p. pt.* от sit.
satchel ['sætʃəl] (шко́льный) ра́нец.
sate [seit] насыща́ть [-ы́тить]; пресыща́ть [-ы́тить].
sateen [sæ'ti:n] сати́н.
satellite ['sætəlait] сателли́т (*a. astr.*); приспе́шник; *astr.* спу́тник.
satiate ['seiʃieit] пресыща́ть [-ы́тить]; насыща́ть [-ы́тить].
satin ['sætin] атла́с.
satir|e ['sætaiə] сати́ра; **~ist** ['sætərist] сати́рик; **~ize** [-raiz] высме́ивать [вы́смеять].
satisfaction [sætis'fækʃən] удовлетворе́ние.
satisfactory [sætis'fæktəri] удовлетвори́тельный.
satisfy ['sætisfai] удовлетворя́ть [-ри́ть]; утоля́ть [-ли́ть] (го́лод, любопы́тство и т. п.); выполня́ть [вы́полнить] (обяза́тельства); убежда́ть [убеди́ть].
saturate ['sætʃəreit] ⚗ насыща́ть [-ы́тить]; пропи́тывать [-ита́ть].
Saturday ['sætədi] суббо́та.
sauce [sɔ:s] **1.** со́ус; *fig.* припра́ва; F де́рзость *f*; **2.** приправля́ть со́усом; F [на]дерзи́ть (Д); **~pan** кастрю́ля; **~r** ['sɔ:sə] блю́дце.
saucy ['sɔ:si] □ F де́рзкий.
saunter ['sɔ:ntə] **1.** прогу́ливаться; флани́ровать; шата́ться; **2.** прогу́лка.
sausage ['sɔsidʒ] соси́ска, колбаса́.
savage ['sævidʒ] **1.** □ ди́кий; жесто́кий; свире́пый; **2.** дика́рь *m* (-а́рка); *fig.* ва́рвар(ка *f*); **~ry** [-ri] ди́кость *f*; жесто́кость *f*.
save [seiv] спаса́ть [спасти́]; избавля́ть [-а́вить] (from от Р); сберега́ть [-ре́чь]; откла́дывать [отложи́ть].
saving ['seiviŋ] **1.** □ спаси́тельный; сберега́тельный; **2.** спасе́ние; **~s** *pl.* сбереже́ния *n/pl.*
savings-bank сберега́тельная ка́сса.
saviour ['seivjə] спаси́тель *m*; ♀ Спаси́тель *m.*
savo(u)r ['seivə] **1.** вкус; F смак; *fig.* пика́нтность *f*; при́вкус; **2.** F смакова́ть; ~ of: отзыва́ться (Т); па́хнуть (Т); **~y** [-ri] □ вку́сный; пика́нтный; F сма́чный.

saw [sɔː] **1.** *pt.* от see; **2.** погово́рка; пила́; **3.** [*irr.*] пили́ть; **~dust** опи́лки *f/pl.*; **~-mill** лесопи́льный заво́д; **~n** [sɔːn] *p. pt.* от saw.

Saxon ['sæksn] **1.** саксо́нский; **2.** саксо́нец (-нка).

say [sei] **1.** [*irr.*] говори́ть [сказа́ть]; ~ grace чита́ть моли́тву (пе́ред едо́й); that is to ~ то́ есть, т. е.; you don't ~ so! неуже́ли!; I ~! послу́шай(те)!; he is said to be ... говоря́т, что он ...; **2.** речь *f*; сло́во; it is my ~ now о́чередь за мной тепе́рь говори́ть; **~ing** ['seiiŋ] погово́рка.

scab [skæb] струп (на я́зве); чесо́тка; *sl.* штрейкбре́хер.

scabbard ['skæbəd] но́жны *f/pl.*

scabrous ['skeibrəs] скабрёзный.

scaffold ['skæfəld] ⚠ леса́ *m/pl.*; подмо́стки *pl.*; эшафо́т; **~ing** [-iŋ] ⚠ леса́ *m/pl.*

scald [skɔːld] **1.** ожо́г (кипя́щей жи́дкостью); **2.** [о]шпа́рить; обва́ривать [-ри́ть].

scale[1] [skeil] **1.** чешу́йка (*coll.*: чешуя́); ви́нный ка́мень *m* (на зуба́х); на́кипь *f*, ока́лина (в котле́ и т. п.); (a pair of) **~s** *pl.* весы́ *m/pl.*; **2.** соскобля́ть чешую́ с (Р); ⊕ снима́ть ока́лину с (Р); шелуши́ться; чи́стить от ви́нного ка́мня; взве́шивать [-е́сить].

scale[2] [~] **1.** ле́стница; масшта́б; разме́р; шкала́; ♪ га́мма; *fig.* разме́р; **2.** взбира́ться [взобра́ться] (по ле́стнице и т. п.); ~ up увели́чивать по масшта́бу; ~ down уменьша́ть по масшта́бу.

scallop ['skɔləp] **1.** *zo.* гребешо́к (моллю́ск); **~s** *pl.* фесто́ны *m/pl.*; **2.** украша́ть фесто́нами.

scalp [skælp] **1.** скальп; **2.** скальпи́ровать (*im*)*pf.*, *pf. a.* [о-].

scaly ['skeili] чешу́йчатый; покры́тый на́кипью.

scamp [skæmp] **1.** безде́льник; **2.** рабо́тать кое-ка́к; **~er** [-ə] **1.** бежа́ть стремгла́в; уд(и)ра́ть; **2.** поспе́шное бе́гство; гало́п; *fig.* бе́глое чте́ние.

scandal ['skændl] сканда́л; позо́р; спле́тни *f/pl.*; **~ize** ['skændəlaiz] скандализи́ровать (*im*)*pf.*; **~ous** [-ləs] □ сканда́льный; клеветни́ческий.

scant, ~y [skænt, 'skænti] ску́дный; [ограни́ченный.]

scapegoat ['skeipgout] козёл отпуще́ния.

scapegrace [-greis] пове́са *m*, шалопа́й.

scar [skɑː] **1.** шрам; рубе́ц; **2.** *v/t.* покрыва́ть рубца́ми; *v/i.* [за]рубцева́ться.

scarc|e [skɛəs] недоста́точный; ску́дный; ре́дкий; **~ely** ['skɛəsli] едва́ ли; как то́лько, едва́; **~ity** [-siti] недоста́ток; дорогови́зна.

scare [skɛə] **1.** [на-, ис]пуга́ть; отпу́гивать [-гну́ть] (*a.* ~ away); **2.** па́ника; **~crow** пу́гало, чу́чело (*a. fig.*).

scarf [skɑːf] шарф; шаль *f*; га́лстук.

scarlet ['skɑːlit] **1.** а́лый цвет; **2.** а́лый; ~ fever ⚕ скарлати́на.

scarred [skɑːd] в рубца́х.

scathing ['skeiðiŋ] е́дкий; ре́зкий; *fig.* уничтожа́ющий.

scatter ['skætə] разбра́сывать [-броса́ть]; рассыпа́ть(ся) [-сы́пать(-ся)]; рассе́ивать(ся) [-е́ять(ся)].

scavenger ['skævindʒə] му́сорщик.

scenario [si'nɑːriou] сцена́рий.

scene [siːn] сце́на; ме́сто де́йствия; декора́ция; **~s** *pl.* кули́сы *f/pl.*; **~ry** ['siːnəri] декора́ции *f/pl.*; пейза́ж.

scent [sent] **1.** арома́т, за́пах; духи́ *m/pl.*; *hunt.* чутьё, нюх; **2.** [по-]чу́ять; [на]души́ть; **~less** ['sentlis] без арома́та, за́паха.

sceptic ['skeptik] ске́птик; **~al** [-tikəl] □ скепти́ческий.

scept|er, ~re ['septə] ски́петр.

schedule ['ʃedjuːl, *Am.* 'skedjuːl] **1.** табли́ца; гра́фик, пла́н; *Am.* расписа́ние поездо́в; **2.** составля́ть расписа́ние (Р); назнача́ть [назна́чить, намеча́ть [-е́тить].

scheme [skiːm] **1.** схе́ма; план; прое́кт; **2.** *v/t.* [за]проекти́ровать; *v/i.* интригова́ть.

schism ['sizm] схи́зма, раско́л.

scholar ['skɔlə] учёный; учени́к (-и́ца); **~ly** [-li] *adj.* учёный; **~ship** [-ʃip] учёность *f*, эруди́ция; *univ.* стипе́ндия.

scholastic [skə'læstik] (**~ally**) схоласти́ческий; шко́льный.

school [skuːl] **1.** шко́ла; класс (помеще́ние); at ~ в шко́ле; primary ~ нача́льная шко́ла; secondary ~ сре́дняя шко́ла; **2.** дисциплини́ровать (*im*)*pf.*; [вы́]шко́лить]; **~boy** шко́льник; **~fellow** шко́льный това́рищ; **~girl** шко́льница; **~ing** ['skuːliŋ] обуче́ние в шко́ле; **~master** учи́тель *m*; **~mate** *s.* schoolfellow; **~mistress** учи́тельница; **~room** кла́ссная ко́мната.

science ['saiəns] нау́ка; есте́ственные нау́ки *f/pl.*

scientific [saiən'tifik] [**~ally**] нау́чный; уме́лый.

scientist ['saiəntist] учёный; естестове́д.

scintillate ['sintileit] сверка́ть [-кну́ть]; мерца́ть.

scion ['saiən] побе́г (расте́ния); о́тпрыск, пото́мок.

scissors ['sizəz] *pl.* (a pair of ~) но́жницы *f/pl.*

scoff [skɔf] **1.** насме́шка; **2.** [по-]глуми́ться (at над Т).

scold [skould] **1.** сварли́вая же́нщина; **2.** [вы́]брани́ть.

scon(e) [skɔn, skoun] лепёшка.

scoop [skuːp] **1.** сово́к; черпа́к;

ковш; углубле́ние; сенсацио́нная но́вость (одно́й определённой газе́ты); 2. заче́рпывать [-пну́ть].
scooter ['sku:tə] *mot.* моторо́ллер; ⚓ ску́тер; самока́т (игру́шка).
scope [skoup] кругозо́р; разма́х; охва́т; просто́р.
scorch [skɔ:tʃ] *v/t.* обжига́ть [обже́чь]; опаля́ть [-ли́ть]; *v/i.* пали́ть; F бе́шено нести́сь.
score [skɔ:] 1. зару́бка; ме́тка; счёт (в игре́); два деся́тка; ♪ партиту́ра; ~s *pl.* мно́жество; run up ~s *pl.* де́лать долги́; on the ~ of по причи́не (P); what's the ~? како́в счёт? (в игре́); 2. отмеча́ть [-е́тить]; засчи́тывать [-ита́ть]; выи́грывать [вы́играть]; заби́ва́ть гол; оркестрова́ть *(im)pf.*; *Am.* [вы́]брани́ть.
scorn [skɔ:n] 1. презре́ние; 2. презира́ть [-зре́ть]; ~**ful** ['skɔ:nful] □ презри́тельный.
Scotch [skɔtʃ] 1. шотла́ндский; 2. шотла́ндский диале́кт; the ~ шотла́ндцы *m/pl.*; ~**man** ['skɔtʃmən] шотла́ндец.
scot-free ['skɔt'fri:] невреди́мый; ненака́занный.
scoundrel ['skaundrəl] негодя́й, подле́ц.
scour ['skauə] *v/t.* [по]чи́стить; отчища́ть [отчи́стить]; [вы́]мыть; смы(ва́)ть; ры́скать по (Д); *v/i.* ры́скать (*a.* ~ about).
scourge [skə:dʒ] 1. бич; бе́дствие; 2. бичева́ть; [по]кара́ть.
scout [skaut] 1. разве́дчик (*a.* ✈); Boy ♀s *pl.* бойска́уты *m/pl.*; ~ party ⚔ разве́дочный отря́д; 2. производи́ть разве́дку; отверга́ть с презре́нием.
scowl [skaul] 1. хму́рый вид; 2. [на]хму́риться.
scrabble ['skræbl] цара́пать; [вс]кара́бкаться; сгреба́ть [сгрести́].
scramble ['skræmbl] 1. [вс]кара́бкаться; [по]дра́ться (for за В); ~d eggs *pl.* яи́чница-болту́нья; 2. сва́лка, борьба́; кара́бканье.
scrap [skræp] 1. клочо́к; кусо́чек; лоскуто́к; вы́резка (из газе́ты); ⊕ лом; утильсырьё; ~s *pl.* оста́тки *m/pl.*; объе́дки *m/pl.*; 2. отдава́ть на слом; выбра́сывать [вы́бросить]; ~-**book** альбо́м для газе́тных вы́резок.
scrap|e [skreip] 1. скобле́ние; цара́пина; затрудне́ние; 2. скобли́ть; скрести́(сь); соскреба́ть [-ести́] (*mst* ~ off); отчища́ть [-и́стить]; заде́(ва́)ть; ша́ркать [-кнуть] (T); ска́редничать; ~**er** ['skreipə] скоба́ для чи́стки о́буви.
scrap|-heap сва́лка отбро́сов (и́ли ло́ма); ~-**iron** желе́зный лом.
scratch [skrætʃ] 1. цара́пина; *sport* черта́ ста́рта; 2. случа́йный; разношёрстный; *sport* без гандика́па; 3. [о]цара́пать; [по]чеса́ть; ~ out вычёркивать [вы́черкнуть].
scrawl [skrɔ:l] 1. кара́кули *f/pl.*; 2. писа́ть кара́кулями.
scream [skri:m] 1. вопль *m*; крик; 2. пронзи́тельно крича́ть; ~**y** [-i] крикли́вый; крича́щий (о кра́сках).
screech [skri:tʃ] пронзи́тельно крича́ть; взви́згивать [-гнуть].
screen [skri:n] 1. ши́рма; экра́н; щит; перегоро́дка; плете́нь *m*; ⚠ та́мбур; гро́хот, си́то; ⚔ прикры́тие; the ~ кино́ *n indecl.*; 2. прикры́(ва́)ть; заслоня́ть [-ни́ть]; *opt.* пока́зывать на экра́не; просе́ивать [-е́ять].
screw [skru:] 1. га́йка; винт; = screw-propeller; 2. приви́нчивать [-нти́ть] (*mst* ~ on); скрепля́ть винта́ми; *fig.* притесня́ть [-ни́ть]; ~ up [с]мо́рщить (лицо́); ~**driver** отвёртка; ~-**propeller** гребно́й винт.
scribble ['skribl] 1. кара́кули *f/pl.*; 2. [на]цара́пать.
scrimp [skrimp] *v/t.* уре́з(ыв)ать; *v/i.* [по]скупи́ться.
scrip [skrip] † квита́нция о подпи́ске на а́кции.
script [skript] рукопи́сный шрифт; *film* сцена́рий.
Scripture ['skriptʃə] свяще́нное писа́ние.
scroll [skroul] сви́ток (перга́мента); спи́сок; ⚠ завито́к (украше́ние).
scrub [skrʌb] 1. куст; ~s *pl.* куста́рник; по́росль *f*; 2. скрести́; чи́стить щёткой.
scrubby ['skrʌbi] низкоро́слый; захуда́лый.
scrup|le ['skru:pl] 1. сомне́ния *n/pl.*, колеба́ния *n/pl.*; 2. [по]стесня́ться; ~**ulous** ['skru:pjuləs] □ щепети́льный; добросо́вестный.
scrutin|ize ['skru:tinaiz] рассма́тривать [-мотре́ть]; тща́тельно проверя́ть; ~**y** ['skru:tini] испыту́ющий взгляд; то́чная прове́рка.
scud [skʌd] 1. гони́мые ве́тром облака́ *n/pl.*; стреми́тельный бег; 2. носи́ться, [по]нести́сь; скользи́ть [-зну́ть[.
scuff [skʌf] идти́, волоча́ но́ги.
scuffle ['skʌfl] 1. дра́ка; 2. [по-]дра́ться.
scullery ['skʌləri] помеще́ние при ку́хне для мытья́ посу́ды.
sculptor ['skʌlptə] ску́льптор, вая́тель *m*.
sculptur|e ['skʌlptʃə] 1. скульпту́ра; 2. [из]вая́ть; высека́ть [вы́сечь].
scum [skʌm] пе́на; на́кипь *f*; *fig.* подо́нки *m/pl.*
scurf [skə:f] пе́рхоть *f*.
scurrilous ['skʌriləs] гру́бый, непристо́йный.

scurry ['skʌri] бы́стро бе́гать; снова́ть (туда́ и сюда́).
scurvy ['skə:vi] ⚕ цинга́.
scuttle ['skʌtl] 1. ведёрко для у́гля; 2. уд(и)ра́ть; дезерти́ровать (*im*)*pf*.
scythe [saið] ⚒ коса́.
sea [si:] мо́ре; *attr.* морско́й; be at ~ *fig.* не знать, что де́лать; недоумева́ть; ~**board** бе́рег мо́ря; ~**faring** ['si:fɛəriŋ] морепла́вание; ~-**going** да́льнего пла́вания (о су́дне).
seal [si:l] 1. *zo.* тюле́нь *m*; печа́ть *f*; пло́мба; клеймо́; 2. запеча́т(ыв)ать; скрепля́ть печа́тью; опеча́т(ыв)ать; ~ up ⊕ гермети́чески уку́поривать; зама́з(ыв)ать; ~ (with lead) [за]пломби́ровать.
sea-level ['levl] у́ровень мо́ря.
sealing-wax сургу́ч.
seam [si:m] 1. шов (*a.* ⊕); рубе́ц; *geol.* просло́йка; 2. сши(ва́)ть; [из]борозди́ть.
seaman ['si:mən] моря́к; матро́с.
seamstress ['semstris] швея́.
sea-plane гидропла́н.
sear [siə] иссуша́ть [-ши́ть]; опаля́ть [-ли́ть]; ⚕ прижига́ть [-же́чь]; *fig.* притупля́ть [-пи́ть].
search [sə:tʃ] 1. по́иски *m/pl.*; о́быск; ро́зыск; in ~ of в по́исках (Р); 2. *v/t.* обы́скивать [-ка́ть]; зонди́ровать (ра́ну); прони́зывать [-за́ть]; *v/i.* разы́скивать [-ка́ть] (for В); ~ into проника́ть [-и́кнуть] в (В); ~**ing** [-iŋ] тща́тельный; испы́тующий; ~-**light** проже́ктор; ~-**warrant** докуме́нт на пра́во о́быска.
sea|-**shore** морско́й бе́рег; ~**sick** страда́ющий морско́й боле́знью; ~**side** побере́жье; взмо́рье; *attr.* примо́рский; ~ place, ~ resort морско́й куро́рт.
season ['si:zn] 1. вре́мя го́да; пери́од; сезо́н; out of ~ не во́время; with the compliments of the ~ с лу́чшими пожела́ниями к пра́зднику; 2. *v/t.* приправля́ть [-а́вить] (пи́щу); выде́рживать [вы́держать] (вино́, лес и т. п.); закаля́ть [-ли́ть] (to про́тив Р); ~-**able** [-əbl] ☐ своевре́менный; по сезо́ну; ~**al** ['si:zənl] ☐ сезо́нный; ~**ing** ['si:zniŋ] припра́ва; ~-**ticket** сезо́нный биле́т.
seat [si:t] 1. сиде́нье; стул; скамья́; ме́сто (в теа́тре и т. п.); поса́дка (на ло́шади); уса́дьба; подста́вка; 2. уса́живать [усади́ть]; снабжа́ть сту́льями; вмеща́ть [вмести́ть]; ~**ed** сидя́щий; be ~**ed** сиде́ть, сади́ться [сесть].
sea|-**urchin** морско́й ёж; ~**ward** ['si:wəd] *adj.* напра́вленный к мо́рю; *adv.* (*a.* ~*s*) к мо́рю; ~**weed** морска́я во́доросль *f*; ~**worthy** го́дный для морепла́вания.
secede [si'si:d] отка́лываться [отколо́ться], отпада́ть [отпа́сть] (от сою́за и т. п.).
secession [si'seʃən] раско́л; отпаде́ние; *hist.* вы́ход из сою́за (США); ~**ist** [-ist] отсту́пник (-ица).
seclu|**de** [si'klu:d] уединя́ть [-ни́ть]; ~**sion** [si'klu:ʒən] уедине́ние.
second ['sekənd] 1. ☐ второ́й; втори́чный; уступа́ющий (to Д); on ~ thoughts по зре́лом размышле́нии; 2. секу́нда; помо́щник; секунда́нт; ~*s pl.* ✝ това́р второ́го со́рта; 3. подде́рживать [-жа́ть]; подкрепля́ть [-пи́ть]; ~**ary** [-əri] ☐ втори́чный; второстепе́нный; побо́чный; ~-**hand** поде́ржанный; из вторы́х рук; ~**ly** [-li] во-вторы́х; ~-**rate** второсо́ртный; второразря́дный.
secre|**cy** ['si:krisi] скры́тность *f*; секре́тность *f*; ~**t** ['sikrit] 1. ☐ та́йный, секре́тный; скры́тный; 2. та́йна, секре́т; in ~ секре́тно, тайко́м; be in the ~ быть посвящённым в секре́т.
secretary ['sekrətri] секрета́рь *m*, секрета́рша; мини́стр.
secret|**e** [si'kri:t] (с)пря́тать; выделя́ть [вы́делить]; ~**ion** [-ʃən] секре́ция, выделе́ние; ~**ive** [-iv] скры́тный.
section ['sekʃən] сече́ние; разре́з; отре́зок; ⚕ вскры́тие, се́кция; отде́л; разде́л (кни́ги); ⚔ отделе́ние.
secular ['sekjulə] ☐ мирско́й, све́тский; веково́й.
secur|**e** [si'kjuə] 1. ☐ безопа́сный; надёжный; уве́ренный; 2. закрепля́ть [-пи́ть]; обеспе́чи(ва)ть; обезопа́сить *pf*; дост(ав)а́ть; ~**ity** [-riti] безопа́сность *f*; надёжность *f*; обеспе́чение; зало́г; ~**ities** *pl.* це́нные бума́ги *f/pl.*
sedate [si'deit] ☐ степе́нный; уравнове́шенный.
sedative ['sedətiv] *mst* ⚕ успока́ивающее сре́дство.
sedentary ['sedntəri] ☐ сидя́чий.
sediment ['sedimənt] оса́док.
sedition [si'diʃən] призы́в к бу́нту.
seditious [-ʃəs] ☐ бунта́рский.
seduc|**e** [si'dju:s] соблазня́ть [-ни́ть]; ~**tion** [si'dʌkʃən] собла́зн; ~**tive** [-tiv] ☐ соблазни́тельный.
sedulous ['sedjuləs] ☐ приле́жный.
see [si:] [*irr.*] *v/i.* [у]ви́деть; I ~ я понима́ю; ~ about a th. [по]забо́титься о (П); ~ through a p. ви́деть насквозь кого́-либо; ~ to присма́тривать [-смотре́ть] за (Т); *v/t.* [у]ви́деть; [по]смотре́ть (фильм, и т. п.); замеча́ть [-е́тить]; понима́ть [-ня́ть]; посеща́ть [-ети́ть]; ~ a p. home провожа́ть кого́-нибудь домо́й; ~ off провожа́ть [-води́ть]; ~ a th. through доводи́ть [довести́] что́-нибудь до конца́; ~ a p. through

помогáть [помóчь] (Д); live to ~ дожи́(вáт)ь до (P).
seed [si:d] 1. сéмя *n*; зернó; *coll.* семенá *n/pl.*; засéв; зёрнышко (я́блока и т. п.); потóмство; go to ~ пойти́ в семенá; *fig.* опускáться [-сти́ться]; 2. *v/t.* засевáть [засéять]; [по]сéять; *v/i.* пойти́ в сéмя; **~ling** ['si:dliŋ] ⚘ сéянец; **~s** *pl.* рассáда; **~y** ['si:di] напóлненный семенáми; потрёпанный, обноси́вшийся; F нездорóвый.
seek [si:k] [*irr.*] *mst fig.* [по]искáть (P); [по]пытáться; [по]старáться; ~ after добивáться (P).
seem [si:m] [по]казáться; **~ing** ['si:miŋ] □ кáжущийся; мни́мый; **~ly** [-li] подобáющий; пристóйный.
seen [si:n] *p. pt.* от see.
seep [si:p] просáчиваться [-сочи́ться]; протекáть [-éчь].
seer ['si(:)ə] прови́дец.
seesaw ['si:'sɔ:] 1. качéли *f/pl.*; качáние на доскé; 2. качáться на доскé.
seethe [si:ð] кипéть, бурли́ть.
segment ['segmənt] сегмéнт, отрéзок; дóля, дóлька.
segregate ['segrigeit] отделя́ть [-ли́ть].
seiz|e [si:z] хватáть [схвати́ть]; захвáтывать [захвати́ть]; ухвати́ться за (B) *pf.* (*a. fig.*); конфисковáть (*im*)*pf.*; *fig.* охвáтывать [-ти́ть] (о чу́встве); **~ure** ['si:ʒə] конфискáция; захвáт; ⚕ апоплекси́ческий удáр.
seldom ['seldəm] *adv.* рéдко, и́зредка.
select [si'lekt] 1. отбирáть [отобрáть]; подбирáть [подобрáть]; 2. отбóрный; и́збранный; **~ion** [si'lekʃən] вы́бор; подбóр; отбóр.
self [self] 1. *pron.* сам; себя́; ✝ или F = myself etc. я сам и т. д.; 2. *adj.* одноцвéтный; 3. *su.* (*pl.* **selves**, selvz) ли́чность *f*; **~-centred** эгоцентри́чный; **~-command** самообладáние; **~-conceit** самомнéние; **~-conceited** чванли́вый; **~-conscious** застéнчивый; **~-contained** самостоя́тельный; *fig.* зáмкнутый; **~-control** самооблáдание; **~-defence**: in ~ при самозащи́те; **~-denial** самоотречéние; **~-evident** очеви́дный; **~interest** своекоры́стие; **~ish** ['selfiʃ] □ эгоисти́чный; **~-possession** самооблáдание; **~-reliant** самоувéренный; **~-seeking** своекоры́стный; **~-willed** своевóльный.
sell [sel] [*irr.*] прод(ав)áть; торговáть; ~ off, ~ out ✝ распрод(ав)áть; **~er** ['selə] продавéц (-вщи́ца); good ~ ✝ хóдкий товáр.
semblance ['sembləns] подóбие; нару́жность *f*; вид.
semi... ['semi...] полу...; **~-final** полуфи́нал.
seminary ['seminəri] духóвная семинáрия; рассáдник (*fig.*).
sempstress [-stris] швея́.
senate ['senit] сенáт; *univ.* совéт.
senator ['senətə] сенáтор.
send [send] [*irr.*] пос(ы)лáть; отправля́ть [-áвить]; ~ for пос(ы)лáть за (T); ~ forth испускáть [-усти́ть]; изд(ав)áть; ~ up вызывáть повышéние (P); ~ word сообщáть [-щи́ть].
senil|e ['si:nail] стáрческий; **~ity** [si'niliti] стáрость *f*; дря́хлость *f*.
senior ['si:njə] 1. стáрший; ~ partner ✝ главá фи́рмы; 2. пожилóй человéк; стáрший; he is my ~ by a year он стáрше меня́ нá год; **~ity** [si:ni'ɔriti] старшинствó.
sensation [sen'seiʃən] ощущéние; чу́вство; сенсáция; **~al** [-ʃnl] □ сенсациóнный; сенсуáльный.
sense [sens] 1. чу́вство; ощущéние; смысл; значéние; in (out of) one's ~s *pl.* (не) в своём умé; bring one to his ~s *pl.* привести́ когó-либо в себя́; make ~ имéть смысл; быть поня́тным; 2. ощущáть [ощути́ть]; [по]чу́вствовать.
senseless ['senslis] □ бесчу́вственный; бессмы́сленный; бессодержáтельный; **~ness** [-nis] бесчу́вственность *f* и т. д.
sensibility [-i'biliti] чувстви́тельность *f*; тóчность *f* (прибóра).
sensible ['sensəbl] □ (благо)разу́мный; здравомы́слящий; ощути́мый, замéтный; be ~ of сознa(ва)́ть (B).
sensitiv|e ['sensitiv] □ чувстви́тельный (to к Д); **~ity** [-'tiviti] чувстви́тельность *f* (to к Д).
sensual ['sensjuəl] □ чу́вственный.
sensuous ['sensjuəs] □ чу́вственный; эстети́чный.
sent [sent] *pt.* и *p. pt.* от send.
sentence ['sentəns] 1. ⚖ приговóр; *gr.* предложéние; serve one's ~ отбывáть наказáние; 2. приговáривать [-говори́ть].
sententious [sen'tenʃəs] нравоучи́тели́ный; сентенциóзный.
sentient ['senʃənt] чу́вствующий.
sentiment ['sentimənt] чу́вство; настроéние; мнéние; мысль *f*; *s.* **~ality**; **~al** [senti'mentl] сентиментáльный; **~ality** [sentimen'tæliti] сентиментáльность *f*.
sentinel ['sentinl], **sentry** ['sentri] ⚔ часовóй; карау́льный.
separa|ble ['sepərəbl] □ отдели́мый; **~te** 1. ['seprit] □ отдéльный, осóбый; сепарáтный; 2. ['sepəreit] отделя́ть(ся) [-ли́ть(ся)]; разлучáть(ся) [-чи́ть(ся)]; расходи́ться [разойти́сь]; **~tion** [sepə'reiʃən] отделéние; разлучéние; разобщéние.
September [sep'tembə] сентя́брь *m*.

sepul|chre ['sepəlkə] *rhet.* гробни́ца; **~ture** ['sepəltʃə] погребе́ние.
sequel ['si:kwəl] продолже́ние; после́дствие.
sequen|ce ['si:kwəns] после́довательность *f*; **~t** [-kwənt] сле́дующий.
sequestrate [si'kwestreit] ⚖ секвестрова́ть *(im)pf.*; конфискова́ть *(im)pf.*
serenade [seri'neid] **1.** ♪ серена́да; **2.** петь серена́ду (Д).
seren|e [si'ri:n] □ безо́блачный (*a. fig.*); я́сный; безмяте́жный; Your ♀ Highness ва́ша све́тлость *f*; **~ity** [si'reniti] **1.** безмяте́жность *f*; безо́блачность *f*; **2.** ♀ све́тлость *f*.
serf [sə:f] крепостно́й; раб.
sergeant ['sɑ:dʒənt] ⚔ сержа́нт.
serial ['siəriəl] **1.** □ сери́йный; после́довательный; **2.** рома́н и́ли фильм в не́скольких частя́х.
series ['siəri:z] *pl.* се́рия; ряд.
serious ['siəriəs] □ серьёзный; be ~ серьёзно говори́ть; **~ness** [-nis] серьёзность *f*.
sermon ['sə:mən] про́поведь *f*.
serpent ['sə:pənt] змея́; **~ine** [-ain] изви́листый; змееви́дный.
servant ['sə:vənt] слуга́ *m/f*; служа́нка; служи́тель *m*; прислу́га.
serve [sə:v] **1.** *v/t.* [по]служи́ть (Д); под(ав)а́ть (обе́д, мяч в те́ннисе и т. п.); обслу́живать [-жи́ть]; вруча́ть [-чи́ть] (on Д); отбы́(ва́)ть (срок и т. п.); удовлетворя́ть [-ри́ть]; (it) ~s him right так ему́ и на́до; ~ out вы́да(ва́)ть, разд(ав)а́ть; *v/i.* [по]служи́ть (*a.* ⚔) (as Т); ~ at table прислу́живать за столо́м; **2.** *tennis*: пода́ча.
service ['sə:vis] **1.** слу́жба; обслу́живание; услу́га; (*a.* divine ~) богослуже́ние; сообще́ние; *tennis*: пода́ча (мяча́); the ~s *pl.* ⚔ а́рмия, флот и вое́нная авиа́ция; be at a p.'s ~ быть к чьи́м-либо услу́гам; **2.** *Am.* ⊕ [от]ремонти́ровать; **~able** ['se:visəbl] □ поле́зный; про́чный.
servil|e ['sə:vail] □ ра́бский; рабо-ле́пный; холо́пский; **~ity** [sə:viliti] ра́бство; раболе́пство.
servitude ['sə:vitju:d] ра́бство; penal ~ ка́торга.
session ['seʃən] се́ссия; заседа́ние.
set [set] **1.** [*irr.*] *v/t.* [по]ста́вить; класть [положи́ть]; помеща́ть [-ести́ть]; размеща́ть [-ести́ть]; сажа́ть [посади́ть] (насе́дку на я́йца); зад(ав)а́ть (уро́ки и т. п.); вставля́ть в ра́му (карти́ну и т. п.); уса́живать [усади́ть] (to за В); ⚕ вправля́ть [-а́вить] (ру́ку, но́гу); ~ a p. laughing [рас]смеши́ть кого́-нибудь; ~ sail пуска́ться в пла́вание; ~ one's teeth сти́снуть зу́бы; ~ aside откла́дывать [отложи́ть]; ~ store by высоко́ цени́ть (В); счита́ть ва́жным (В); ~ forth излага́ть [изложи́ть]; ~ off оттеня́ть [-ни́ть]; ~ up учрежда́ть [-еди́ть]; устра́ивать [-ро́ить]; **2.** *v/i. ast.* заходи́ть [зайти́], сади́ться [сесть]; засты́(ва́)ть; ~ about a th. принима́ться [-ня́ться] за что́-нибудь; ~ forth отправля́ться [-а́виться]; ~ (up)on нач(ин)а́ть (В); ~ out отправляться [-а́виться]; ~ to вступа́ть в бой; бра́ться [взя́ться] за (рабо́ту, еду́); ~ up for выдава́ть себя́ за (В); **3.** неподви́жный; устано́вленный; засты́вший (взгляд); твёрдый; ~ (up)on поглощённый (Т); ~ with опра́вленный (Т); hard ~ нужда́ющийся; ~ speech пригото́вленная ре́чь *f*; **4.** набо́р; компле́кт; прибо́р; се́рия; ряд; систе́ма; гарниту́р; серви́з (обе́денный и т. п.); (ра́дио)приёмник; круг (общества); *tennis*: сет; покро́й (пла́тья); *thea.* обстано́вка.
set|back ['set'bæk] неуда́ча; **~-down** отпо́р; **~-off** контра́ст; украше́ние.
setting ['setiŋ] опра́ва (камне́й); декора́ции и костю́мы; *fig.* окружа́ющая обстано́вка; захо́д (со́лнца); ♪ му́зыка на слова́.
settle ['setl] *v/t.* водворя́ть [-ри́ть]; приводи́ть в поря́док; успока́ивать [-ко́ить]; реша́ть [-и́ть] (вопро́с); ула́живать [-а́дить]; заселя́ть [-ли́ть]; опла́чивать [-ати́ть] (счёт); устра́ивать [-ро́ить] (дела́); *v/i.* (*often* ~ down) поселя́ться [-ли́ться]; водворя́ться [-ри́ться]; устра́иваться [-ро́иться]; уса́живаться [усе́сться]; приходи́ть к реше́нию; отста́иваться [-тоя́ться]; оседа́ть [осе́сть]; устана́вливаться [-нови́ться] (о пого́де); **~d** ['setld] постоя́нный; усто́йчивый; **~ment** ['setlmənt] реше́ние; урегули́рование; поселе́ние; ⚖ да́рственная за́пись *f*; **~r** ['setlə] поселе́нец.
set-to (кула́чный) бой; схва́тка.
seven ['sevn] семь; **~teen(th)** [-ti:n(θ)] семна́дцать(-тый); **~th** ['sevnθ] **1.** □ седьмо́й; **2.** седьма́я часть *f*; **~tieth** ['sevntiiθ] семидеся́тый; **~ty** ['sevnti] се́мьдесят.
sever ['sevə] разъединя́ть [-ни́ть]; разлуча́ть [-чи́ть]; [по]рва́ть(ся).
several ['sevrəl] не́сколько (Р); □ отде́льный; **~ly** в отде́льности.
severance ['sevərəns] разры́в; отделе́ние.
sever|e [si'viə] □ стро́гий, суро́вый; ре́зкий; си́льный; жесто́кий; е́дкий; кру́пный (убы́ток); **~ity** [si'veriti] стро́гость *f*; суро́вость *f*; жесто́кость *f*.
sew [sou] [*irr.*] [с]шить.
sewer ['sjuə] сто́чная труба́; **~age** ['sjuəridʒ] канализа́ция.

sew|ing ['souiŋ] шитьё; *attr.* швейный; **~n** [soun] *p. pt.* от sew.
sex [seks] пол.
sexton ['sekstən] церковный сторож, пономарь *m*; могильщик.
sexual ['seksjuəl] □ половой; сексуальный.
shabby ['ʃæbi] □ потёртый; жалкий; захудалый; подлый.
shack [ʃæk] *Am.* лачуга, хижина.
shackle ['ʃækl] **1.** ~s *pl.* кандалы *m/pl.*; оковы *f/pl.*; **2.** заковывать в кандалы.
shade [ʃeid] **1.** тень *f*; оттенок; абажур (для лампы); нюанс; тени *f/pl.* (в живописи); **2.** затенять [-нить]; омрачать [-чить]; [за-]штриховать; ♪ нюансировать (*im*)*pf.*; ~ off незаметно переходить (into в В).
shadow ['ʃædou] **1.** тень *f*; призрак; **2.** осенять [-нить]; (*mst* ~ forth) излагать туманно; следить тайно за (Т); **~y** [-i] тенистый; призрачный; смутный.
shady ['ʃeidi] тенистый; F тёмный, сомнительный; теневой.
shaft [ʃɑːft] древко; рукоятка; оглобля; *fig.* стрела (*a.* ⚘); ⊕ вал.
shaggy ['ʃægi] косматый; волосатый.
shake [ʃeik] **1.** [*irr.*] *v/t.* трясти (В *or* Т); тряхнуть (Т) *pf.*; встряхивать [-хнуть]; потрясать [-сти]; [по-]колебать; ~ hands пожать руку друг другу, обменяться рукопожатием; *v/i.* [за]трястись; [за]дрожать (with, at от Р); ♪ пускать трель; **2.** встряска; дрожь *f*; потрясение; ♪ трель *f*; **~-hands** *pl.* рукопожатие; **~n** ['ʃeikən] **1.** *p. pt.* от shake; **2.** *adj.* потрясённый.
shaky ['ʃeiki] □ нетвёрдый (на ногах); трясущийся; шаткий.
shall [ʃæl] [*irr.*] *v/aux.* вспом. глагол, образующий будущее (1-ое лицо единственного и множественного числа:) I shall do я буду делать, я сделаю.
shallow ['ʃælou] **1.** мелкий; *fig.* поверхностный; **2.** отмель *f*.
sham [ʃæm] **1.** притворный; поддельный; **2.** притворство; подделка; притворщик (-ица); **3.** *v/t.* симулировать (*im*)*pf.*; *v/i.* притворяться [-риться].
shamble ['ʃæmbl] волочить ноги; **~s** [-z] бойня.
shame [ʃeim] **1.** стыд; позор; for ~! стыдно!; put to ~ [при]стыдить; **2.** [при]стыдить; [о]срамить; **~-faced** ['ʃeimfeist] □ застенчивый; **~ful** ['ʃeimful] □ стыдный; позорный; **~less** ['ʃeimlis] □ бесстыдный.
shampoo [ʃæm'puː] **1.** шампунь *m*; мытьё головы; **2.** мыть шампунем.
shamrock ['ʃæmrɔk] ⚘ трилистник.
shank [ʃæŋk] голень *f*; ствол.
shanty ['ʃænti] хибарка, хижина.
shape [ʃeip] **1.** форма; образ; очертание; **2.** *v/t.* созд(ав)ать; придавать форму, вид (Д); *v/i.* [с]формироваться; **~less** ['ʃeiplis] бесформенный; **~ly** [-li] хорошо сложённый; приятной формы.
share [ʃɛə] **1.** доля, часть *f*; участие; акция; лемех, сошник (плуга); go ~s *pl.* делиться поровну; **2.** *v/t.* [по]делиться (Т); *v/i.* участвовать (in в П); **~holder** ✝ пайщик (-ица).
shark [ʃɑːk] акула; *fig.* мошенник.
sharp [ʃɑːp] **1.** □ *com.* острый (*a. fig.*); *fig.* отчётливый; крутой; едкий; кислый; резкий; пронзительный; колкий; F продувной; **2.** *adv.* круто; точно; look ~! живо!; **3.** ♪ диез; **~en** ['ʃɑːpən] [на-]точить; заострять [-рить]; **~er** ['ʃɑːpə] шулер; **~ness** ['ʃɑːpnis] острота; резкость *f* (и т. д.); **~-sighted** зоркий; **~-witted** остроумный.
shatter ['ʃætə] разбивать вдребезги; разрушать [-рушить] (надежды); расстраивать [-роить] (нервы, здоровье).
shave [ʃeiv] **1.** [*irr.*] [по]брить(ся); [вы]строгать (доску и т. п.); едва не задеть (В); **2.** бритьё; have a ~ [по]бриться; have a close ~ едва избежать опасности; **~n** ['ʃeivn] бритый.
shaving ['ʃeiviŋ] **1.** бритьё; **~s** *pl.* стружки *f/pl.*
shawl [ʃɔːl] шаль *f*; большой платок (на плечи).
she [ʃiː] **1.** она; **2.** женщина; **she-...** самка (животного): she-wolf волчица.
sheaf [ʃiːf] сноп; связка; пучок.
shear [ʃiə] **1.** [*irr.*] [о]стричь (овец); *fig.* обдирать как липку; **2.** ~s *pl.* (большие) ножницы *f/pl.*
sheath [ʃiːθ] ножны *f/pl.*; **~e** [ʃiːð] вкладывать в ножны; ⊕ обши(ва)ть.
sheaves [ʃiːvz] *pl.* от sheaf.
shed[1] [ʃed] [*irr.*] [по]терять (волосы, зубы); проли(ва)ть (слёзы, кровь); сбрасывать [сбросить] (одежду, кожу).
shed[2] [~] навес, сарай; ангар.
sheen [ʃiːn] блеск; отблеск.
sheep [ʃiːp] овца; **~-dog** овчарка; **~-fold** овчарня; **~ish** ['ʃiːpiʃ] □ глуповатый; робкий; **~skin** овчина; баранья кожа.
sheer [ʃiə] явный; полнейший; *Am.* прозрачный (о ткани); отвесный.
sheet [ʃiːt] простыня; лист (бумаги, железа); широкая полоса; ✝ таблица; ~ iron листовое железо; ~ lightning зарница.
shelf [ʃelf] полка; уступ; риф; on the ~ *fig.* сданный в архив.

shell [ʃel] **1.** скорлупа́; ра́ковина; щит (черепа́хи); ⚔ снаря́д; ги́льза; **2.** снима́ть скорлупу́ с (Р); [об]лущи́ть; обстре́ливать [-ля́ть]; **~-fish** моллю́ск; **~-proof** непробива́емый снаря́дами.
shelter [ˈʃeltə] **1.** прию́т, *fig.* кров; убе́жище (*a.* ⚔); **2.** *v/t.* дава́ть прию́т (Д), приюти́ть *pf.*; *v/i.* (*a.* take ~) укры́(ва́)ться; приюти́ться *pf.*
shelve [ʃelv] ста́вить на по́лку; *fig.* откла́дывать в до́лгий я́щик; увольня́ть [уво́лить].
shelves [ʃelvz] *pl.* от shelf.
shepherd [ˈʃepəd] **1.** пасту́х; па́стырь *m*; **2.** пасти́; направля́ть [-а́вить] (люде́й как ста́до).
sherbet [ˈʃə:bət] шербе́т.
shield [ʃi:ld] **1.** щит; защи́та; **2.** заслоня́ть [-ни́ть] (from от Р).
shift [ʃift] **1.** сме́на (на заво́де и т. п.); измене́ние; сдвиг; переме́на; уло́вка; make ~ ухитря́ться [-ри́ться]; [у]дово́льствоваться (with Т); **2.** *v/t.* [по]меня́ть; перемеща́ть [-мести́ть]; *v/i.* извора́чиваться [изверну́ться]; перемеща́ться [-мести́ться]; ~ for o. s. обходи́ться без по́мощи; **~less** [ˈʃiftlis] □ беспо́мощный; **~y** [ˈʃifti] □ *fig.* изворо́тливый, ло́вкий.
shilling [ˈʃiliŋ] ши́ллинг.
shin [ʃin] **1.** (или **~-bone**) го́лень *f*; **2.** ~ up вскара́бк(ив)аться.
shine [ʃain] **1.** сия́ние; свет; блеск, гля́нец, лоск; **2.** [*irr.*] сия́ть; свети́ть; блесте́ть; [от]полирова́ть; [по]чи́стить (о́бувь); *fig.* блиста́ть.
shingle [ˈʃiŋgl] га́лька; кро́вельная дра́нка; *Am.* вы́веска; **~s** *pl.* ⚕ опоя́сывающий лиша́й.
shiny [ˈʃaini] □ со́лнечный; лосня́щийся; блестя́щий.
ship [ʃip] **1.** су́дно, кора́бль *m*; **2.** грузи́ть на су́дно; перевози́ть [-везти́]; производи́ть поса́дку, нагру́зку (Р на су́дно); **~board**: ⚓ on ~ на корабле́; **~ment** [ˈʃipmənt] нагру́зка; погру́зка; **~-owner** владе́лец су́дна; **~ping** [ˈʃipiŋ] погру́зка; торго́вый флот, суда́ *n/pl.*; судохо́дство; *attr.* судохо́дный; **~wreck 1.** кораблекруше́ние; **2.** потерпе́ть кораблекруше́ние; **~-wrecked** потерпе́вший кораблекруше́ние; **~yard** верфь *f*.
shire [ˈʃaiə, ...ʃiə] гра́фство.
shirk [ʃə:k] уви́ливать [-льну́ть] от (Р); **~er** [ˈʃə:kə] прогу́льщик.
shirt [ʃə:t] мужска́я руба́шка, соро́чка; (*a.* **~-blouse**) блу́за.
shiver [ˈʃivə] **1.** дрожь *f*; **2.** [за]дрожа́ть; вздра́гивать [-ро́гнуть]; **~y** [-ri] дрожа́щий.
shoal [ʃoul] **1.** мелково́дье; мель *f*; стая, кося́к (ры́бы); **2.** ме́лкий; **3.** [об]меле́ть.
shock [ʃɔk] **1.** уда́р, толчо́к; потрясе́ние; копна́; ⚕ шок; **2.** *fig.* потряса́ть [-ясти́]; шоки́ровать; **~ing** [ˈʃɔkiŋ] □ потряса́ющий; сканда́льный; ужа́сный.
shod [ʃɔd] *pt.* и *p. pt.* от shoe.
shoddy [ˈʃɔdi] **1.** волокно́ из шерстяны́х тря́пок; *fig.* хлам; **2.** подде́льный; дрянно́й.
shoe [ʃu:] **1.** ту́фля; башма́к; полуботи́нок; подко́ва; **2.** [*irr.*] обу́(ва́)ть; подко́вывать [-кова́ть]; **~black** чи́стильщик сапо́г; **~blacking** ва́кса; **~horn** рожо́к (для о́буви); **~-lace**, *Am.* **~-string** шнуро́к для боти́нок; **~maker** сапо́жник; **~polish** *s.* shoeblacking.
shone [ʃɔn] *pt.* и *p. pt.* от shine.
shook [ʃuk] *pt.* от shake.
shoot [ʃu:t] **1.** стрельба́; ⚘ росто́к, побе́г; **2.** [*irr.*] *v/t.* стреля́ть; застрели́ть *pf.*; расстре́ливать [-ля́ть]; снима́ть [снять], засня́ть *pf.* (фильм); *v/i.* стреля́ть [вы́стрелить]; дёргать (о бо́ли); (*a.* ~ along, past) проноси́ться [-нести́сь]; промелькну́ть *pf.*; промча́ться *pf.*; ⚘ расти́ (бы́стро); ~ ahead ри́нуться вперёд; **~er** [ˈʃu:tə] стрело́к.
shooting [ˈʃu:tiŋ] стрельба́; охо́та; ~ star па́дающая звезда́.
shop [ʃɔp] **1.** ла́вка, магази́н; мастерска́я; talk ~ говори́ть в о́бществе о свое́й профе́ссии; **2.** де́лать поку́пки (*mst* go ~ping); **~keeper** ла́вочник (-ица); **~man** ла́вочник; продаве́ц; **~-steward** цехово́й ста́роста *m*; **~-window** витри́на.
shore [ʃɔ:] **1.** бе́рег; взмо́рье, побере́жье; on ~ на́ берег, на берегу́; подпо́рка; **2.** ~ up подпира́ть [-пере́ть].
shorn [ʃɔ:n] *p. pt.* от shear.
short [ʃɔ:t] коро́ткий; кра́ткий; невысо́кий (рост); недоста́точный; непо́лный; отры́вистый, сухо́й (отве́т); песо́чный (о пече́нье); in ~ вкра́тце; come (или fall) ~ of име́ть недоста́ток в (П); не достига́ть [-и́чь] *or* [-и́гнуть] (Р); не опра́вдывать [-да́ть] (ожида́ний); cut ~ прер(ы)ва́ть; fall (или run) ~ истоща́ться [-щи́ться], иссяка́ть [-я́кнуть]; stop ~ of не доезжа́ть [дое́хать], не доходи́ть [дойти́] до (Р); **~age** [ˈʃɔ:tidʒ] нехва́тка; **~coming** недоста́ток; изъя́н; **~cut** сокраще́ние доро́ги; **~-dated** † краткосро́чный; **~en** [ˈʃɔ:tn] *v/t.* сокраща́ть [-рати́ть]; укора́чивать [-роти́ть]; *v/i.* сокраща́ться [-рати́ться]; укора́чиваться [-роти́ться]; **~ening** [-iŋ] жир для те́ста; **~hand** стеногра́фия; **~ly** [ˈʃɔ:tli] *adv.* вско́ре; ко́ротко; **~ness** [-nis] коро́ткость *f*; кра́ткость *f*; **~-sighted** близору́кий; **~-term** краткосро́чный; **~-winded** страда́ющий оды́шкой.

shot [ʃɔt] 1. *pt.* и *p. pt.* от shoot; 2. вы́стрел; ядро́ (пу́шки); дробь *f*, дроби́нка (*mst* small ~); стрело́к; *sport* ядро́ (для толка́ния); уда́р; *phot.* сни́мок; ⚕ инъе́кция; have a ~ сде́лать попы́тку; F not by a long ~ отню́дь не; ~-**gun** дробови́к.
should [ʃud, ʃəd] *pt.* от shall.
shoulder [ˈʃouldə] 1. плечо́; усту́п, вы́ступ; 2. взва́ливать на пле́чи; *fig.* брать на себя́; ⚔ брать к плечу́ (ружьё); ~-**blade** лопа́тка (*anat.*).
shout [ʃaut] 1. крик; во́зглас; 2. [за]крича́ть [кри́кнуть]; [на]крича́ть (at на В).
shove [ʃʌv] 1. толчо́к; 2. пиха́ть [пихну́ть]; толка́ть [-кну́ть].
shovel [ˈʃʌvl] 1. лопа́та, сово́к; 2. копа́ть [копну́ть]; сгреба́ть лопа́той.
show [ʃou] 1. [*irr.*] *v/t.* пока́зывать [-за́ть]; выставля́ть [вы́ставить]; проявля́ть [-ви́ть]; дока́зывать [-за́ть]; ~ in вводи́ть [ввести́]; ~ up изоблича́ть [-чи́ть]; *v/i.* пока́зываться [-за́ться]; проявля́ться [-ви́ться]; ~ off пуска́ть пыль в глаза́; 2. зре́лище; вы́ставка; ви́димость *f*; пока́зывание; ~-**case** витри́на.
shower [ˈʃauə] 1. ли́вень *m*; душ; 2. ли́ться ли́внем; ороша́ть [ороси́ть]; поли́(ва́)ть; *fig.* осыпа́ть [осы́пать]; ~**y** [ˈʃauəri] дождли́вый.
show|n [ʃoun] *p. pt.* от show; ~-**room** вы́ставочный зал; ~-**window** *Am.* витри́на; ~**y** [ˈʃoui] □ роско́шный; эффе́ктный.
shrank [ʃræŋk] *pt.* от shrink.
shred [ʃred] 1. лоскуто́к, клочо́к; кусо́к; 2. [*irr.*] ре́зать, рвать на клочки́; F [ис]кромса́ть.
shrew [ʃru:] сварли́вая же́нщина.
shrewd [ʃru:d] проница́тельный; хи́трый.
shriek [ʃri:k] 1. пронзи́тельный крик, вопль *m*; 2. [за]вопи́ть.
shrill [ʃril] 1. □ пронзи́тельный; 2. пронзи́тельно крича́ть, [за]визжа́ть.
shrimp [ʃrimp] *zo.* креве́тка; *fig.* сморчо́к.
shrine [ʃrain] ра́ка; святы́ня.
shrink [ʃriŋk] [*irr.*] сокраща́ться [-рати́ться]; усыха́ть [усо́хнуть]; сади́ться [сесть] (о мате́рии, ше́рсти); устраша́ться [-ши́ться] (from, at P); ~**age** [ˈʃriŋkidʒ] сокраще́ние; уса́дка; усу́шка.
shrivel [ˈʃrivl] смо́рщи(ва)ть(ся); съёжи(ва)ться.
shroud [ʃraud] 1. са́ван; *fig.* покро́в; 2. завёртывать в са́ван; оку́т(ыв)ать (*a. fig.*).
shrub [ʃrʌb] куст; ~**s** *pl.* куста́рник.
shrug [ʃrʌg] 1. пож(им)а́ть (плеча́ми); 2. пожима́ние (плеча́ми).
shrunk [ʃrʌŋk] *pt.* и *p. pt.* от shrink (*a.* ~en).
shudder [ˈʃʌdə] 1. вздра́гивать [-ро́гнуть]; содрога́ться [-гну́ться]; 2. дрожь *f*; содрога́ние.
shuffle [ˈʃʌfl] 1. ша́ркать [-кнуть] (при ходьбе́); волочи́ть (но́ги); [с]тасова́ть (ка́рты); виля́ть (лука́вить); ~ off свали́ть с себя́ (отве́тственность); 2. ша́рканье; тасова́ние (карт); увёртка.
shun [ʃʌn] избега́ть [-ежа́ть] (P); остерега́ться [-ре́чься] (P).
shunt [ʃʌnt] 1. 🚂 маневри́ровать; ⚡ шунти́ровать; *fig.* откла́дывать [отложи́ть]; 2. 🚂 стре́лка; перево́д на запа́сный путь; ⚡ шунт.
shut [ʃʌt] [*irr.*] 1. закры́(ва́)ть(ся), затворя́ть(ся) [-ри́ть(ся)]; ~ down прекраща́ть рабо́ту; ~ up! замолчи́!; 2. закры́тый; ~**ter** [ˈʃʌtə] ста́вень *m*; *phot.* затво́р.
shuttle [ˈʃʌtl] ⊕ челно́к; ~ **train** при́городный по́езд.
shy [ʃai] 1. пугли́вый; засте́нчивый; 2. [ис]пуга́ться (at P).
shyness [ˈʃainis] засте́нчивость *f*.
Siberian [saiˈbiəriən] 1. сиби́рский; 2. сибиря́к (-я́чка).
sick [sik] 1. больно́й (of T); чу́вствующий тошноту́; уста́вший (of от P); be ~ for тоскова́ть по (Д *or* П); ~**en** [ˈsikn] *v/i.* заболе́(ва́)ть; [за]ча́хнуть; ~ at чу́вствовать отвраще́ние к (Д); *v/t.* де́лать больны́м; вызыва́ть тошноту́ у (P); ~**fund** больни́чная ка́сса.
sickle [ˈsikl] серп.
sick|-leave о́тпуск по боле́зни; ~**ly** [ˈsikli] боле́зненный; тошното́рный; нездоро́вый (кли́мат); ~**ness** (-nis) боле́знь *f*; тошнота́.
side [said] 1. *com.* сторона́; бок; край; ~ by ~ бок о́ бок; take ~ with примыка́ть к стороне́ (P); 2. *attr.* боково́й; побо́чный; 3. ~ with стать на сто́рону (P); ~**board** буфе́т; ~-**car** *mot.* коля́ска мотоци́кла; ~-**light** боково́й фона́рь *m*; ~**long** *adv.* вкось; *adj.* косо́й; боково́й; ~-**path** тротуа́р; ~-**stroke** пла́вание на боку́; ~-**track** 1. 🚂 запасно́й путь *m*; 2. переводи́ть (по́езд) на запа́сный путь; ~**walk** *Am.* тротуа́р; ~**ward** (-**s**) [ˈsaidwədz], ~**ways** в сто́рону; вкось; бо́ком.
siding [ˈsaidiŋ] 🚂 ве́тка.
sidle [ˈsaidl] подходи́ть (*и́ли* ходи́ть) бочко́м.
siege [si:dʒ] оса́да; lay ~ to осажда́ть [осади́ть].
sieve [si:v] си́то.
sift [sift] просе́ивать [-е́ять]; *fig.* [про]анализи́ровать.
sigh [sai] 1. вздох; 2. вздыха́ть [вздохну́ть].

sight [sait] **1.** зре́ние; вид; взгляд; зре́лище; прице́л; ~s *pl.* достопримеча́тельности *f/pl.*; catch ~ of уви́деть *pf.*, заме́тить *pf.*; lose ~ of потеря́ть из ви́ду; **2.** уви́деть *pf.*; вы́смотреть *pf.*; прице́ли(ва)ться (at в В); **~ly** ['saitli] краси́вый; прия́тный на вид; **~-seeing** ['sait-si:iŋ] осмо́тр достопримеча́тельностей.
sign [sain] **1.** знак; при́знак; симпто́м; вы́веска; in ~ of в знак (Р); **2.** *v/i.* подава́ть зна́к (Д); *v/t.* подпи́сывать [-са́ть].
signal ['signl] **1.** сигна́л; **2.** □ выдаю́щийся, замеча́тельный; **3.** [про]сигнализи́ровать; **~ize** ['signəlaiz] отмеча́ть [-е́тить].
signat|ory ['signətəri] **1.** подписа́вший; **2.** сторона́, подписа́вшая (догово́р); ~ powers *pl.* держа́вы-уча́стницы (догово́ра); **~ure** ['signitʃə] по́дпись *f.*
sign|board вы́веска; **~er** ['sainə] лицо́, подписа́вшее како́й-либо докуме́нт.
signet ['signit] печа́тка.
signific|ance [sig'nifikəns] значе́ние; **~ant** [-kənt] □ значи́тельный, многозначи́тельный; характе́рный (of для Р); **~ation** [signifi'keiʃən] значе́ние; смысл.
signify ['signifai] зна́чить, означа́ть; выка́зывать [вы́казать].
signpost указа́тельный столб.
silence ['sailəns] **1,** молча́ние; безмо́лвие; ~! молча́ть!; **2.** заста́вить молча́ть; заглуша́ть [-ши́ть]; **~r** [-ə] глуши́тель *m.*
silent ['sailənt] □ безмо́лвный; молчали́вый; бесшу́мный.
silk [silk] **1.** шёлк; **2.** шёлковый; **~en** ['silkən] □ шелкови́стый; **~worm** шелкови́чный червь *m*; **~y** ['silki] шелкови́стый.
sill [sil] подоко́нник; поро́г.
silly ['sili] □ глу́пый, дура́шливый.
silt [silt] **1.** ил; **2.** засоря́ть(ся) и́лом (*mst* ~ up).
silver ['silvə] **1.** серебро́; **2.** сере́бряный; **3.** [по]серебри́ть; **~y** [-ri] серебри́стый.
similar ['similə] □ схо́дный (с Т), похо́жий (на В); подо́бный; **~ity** [simi'læriti] схо́дство; подо́бие.
simile ['simili] сравне́ние (как ритори́ческая фигу́ра).
similitude [si'militju:d] подо́бие; о́браз; схо́дство.
simmer ['simə] ме́дленно кипе́ть (и́ли кипяти́ть).
simper ['simpə] **1.** жема́нная улы́бка; **2.** жема́нно улыба́ться.
simple ['simpl] □ просто́й; несло́жный; простоду́шный; **~-hearted** наи́вный; **~ton** [-tən] простак.
simpli|city [sim'plisiti] простота́; простоду́шие; **~fy** [-fai] упроща́ть [-ости́ть].
simply ['simpli] про́сто; несло́жно.
simulate ['simjuleit] симули́ровать (*im*)*pf.*, притворя́ться [-ори́ться].
simultaneous [siməl'teinjəs] □ одновре́ме́нный.
sin [sin] **1.** грех; **2.** согреша́ть [-ши́ть], греши́ть.
since [sins] **1.** *prp.* с (Р); **2.** *adv.* с тех пор; ... тому́ наза́д; **3.** *cj.* с тех пор, как; так как; поско́льку.
sincer|e [sin'siə] □ и́скренний; **~ity** [sin'seriti] и́скренность *f.*
sinew ['sinju:] сухожи́лие; *fig. mst* ~s *pl.* физи́ческая си́ла; **~y** [-jui] му́скулистый; си́льный.
sinful ['sinful] □ гре́шный.
sing [siŋ] [*irr.*] [с]петь; воспе́(ва́)ть; ~ing bird пе́вчая пти́ца.
singe [sindʒ] опаля́ть [-ли́ть].
singer ['siŋə] певе́ц, певи́ца.
single ['siŋgl] **1.** □ еди́нственный; одино́чный; одино́кий; холосто́й, незаму́жняя; ~ entry проста́я бухгалте́рия; in ~ file гусько́м; **2.** одино́чная игра́ (в те́ннисе); **3.** ~ out отбира́ть [отобра́ть]; **~-breasted** однобо́ртный (пиджа́к); **~-handed** самостоя́тельно, без посторо́нней по́мощи; **~t** ['siŋglit] те́льная фуфа́йка; **~-track** одноколе́йный.
singular ['siŋgjulə] необыча́йный; стра́нный; еди́нственный; **~ity** [siŋgju'læriti] необыча́йность *f.*
sinister ['sinistə] злове́щий.
sink [siŋk] **1.** [*irr.*] *v/i.* опуска́ться [-сти́ться]; [по-, у]тону́ть; погружа́ться [-узи́ться]; *v/t.* затопля́ть [-пи́ть]; [вы́]рыть (коло́дец); прокла́дывать [проложи́ть] (тру́бы); помеща́ть невы́годно (капита́л); зама́лчивать [замолча́ть] (фа́кты); **2.** ра́ковина (водопрово́дная); **~ing** [-iŋ] ⚕ внеза́пная сла́бость *f*; ~ fund амортизацио́нный фонд.
sinless ['sinlis] безгре́шный.
sinner ['sinə] гре́шник (-ица).
sinuous ['sinjuəs] □ изви́листый.
sip [sip] **1.** ма́ленький глото́к; **2.** пить ма́ленькими глотка́ми.
sir [sə:] су́дарь *m* (обраще́ние); ♀ сэр (ти́тул).
siren ['saiərin] сире́на.
sirloin ['sə:lɔin] филе́й.
sister ['sistə] сестра́; **~hood** [-hud] се́стринская о́бщи́на; **~-in-law** [-rinlɔ:] неве́стка; золо́вка; свояче́ница; **~ly** [-li] се́стринский.
sit [sit] [*irr.*] *v/i.* сиде́ть; заседа́ть; *fig.* быть располо́женным; ~ down сади́ться [сесть]; *v/t.* сажа́ть [посади́ть] (на я́йца).
site [sait] местоположе́ние; уча́сток (для строи́тельства).
sitting ['sitiŋ] заседа́ние; **~-room** гости́ная.
situat|ed ['sitjueitid] располо́женный; **~ion** [sitju'eiʃən] положе́ние; ситуа́ция; до́лжность *f.*

six [siks] 1. шесть; 2. шестёрка; **~teen** ['siks'ti:n] шестна́дцать; **~teenth** [-θ] шестна́дцатый; **~th** [siksθ] 1. шесто́й; 2. шеста́я часть *f*; **~tieth** ['sikstiiθ] шестидеся́тый; **~ty** ['siksti] шестьдеся́т.
size [saiz] 1. разме́р, величина́; форма́т; но́мер (о́буви и т. п.); 2. сортирова́ть по разме́рам; ~ **up** определя́ть величину́ (Р); ... **~d** [-d] ... разме́ра.
siz(e)able ['saizəbl] поря́дочного разме́ра.
sizzle ['sizl] [за]шипе́ть.
skat|e [skeit] 1. конёк (*pl.*: коньки́); (= roller-~) конёк на ро́ликах; 2. ката́ться на конька́х; **~er** ['skeitə] конькобе́жец (-жка).
skein [skein] мото́к пря́жи.
skeleton ['skelitn] скеле́т, о́стов; карка́с; *attr.* ⚔ недоукомплекто́ванный (полк и т. д.); ~ **key** отмы́чка.
sketch [sketʃ] 1. эски́з, набро́сок; 2. де́лать набро́сок (Р); рисова́ть эски́зы.
ski [ʃi:, *Am.* ski:] 1. (*pl.* ~ *или* ~s) лы́жа; 2. ходи́ть на лы́жах.
skid [skid] 1. тормозно́й башма́к; буксова́ние; ✈ хвостово́й костыль *m*; 2. *v/t.* [за]тормози́ть; *v/i.* буксова́ть.
skilful ['skilful] □ иску́сный, уме́лый.
skill [skil] мастерство́, уме́ние; **~ed** квалифици́рованный; иску́сный.
skim [skim] 1. снима́ть [снять] (на́кипь, сли́вки и т. п.); [по-] нести́сь по (Д), скользи́ть [-зну́ть] по (Д); просма́тривать [-смотре́ть]; ~ **over** бе́гло прочи́тывать; 2. ~ **milk** снято́е молоко́.
skimp [skimp] ску́дно снабжа́ть; уре́з(ыв)ать; [по]скупи́ться (**in** на В); **~y** ['skimpi] □ ску́дный; у́зкий.
skin [skin] 1. ко́жа; шку́ра; кожура́; оболо́чка; 2. *v/t.* сдира́ть ко́жу, шку́ру, кору́ с (Р); ~ **off** F снима́ть [снять] (перча́тки, чулки́ и т. п.); *v/i.* зажи́(ва́)ть (о ра́не) (*a.* ~ **over**); **~-deep** пове́рхностный; **~flint** скря́га *m*; **~ny** ['skini] то́щий.
skip [skip] 1. прыжо́к; ⚒ бадья́; 2. *v/i.* [по]скака́ть; *fig.* переска́кивать [-скочи́ть] (**from** с [Р]), **to** на [В]); *v/t.* пропуска́ть [-сти́ть] (страни́цу и т. п.).
skipper ['skipə] шки́пер, капита́н.
skirmish ['skə:miʃ] 1. ⚔ перестре́лка; сты́чка; 2. перестре́ливаться.
skirt [skə:t] 1. ю́бка; пола́; край, окра́ина; 2. окаймля́ть [-ми́ть]; идти́ вдоль кра́я (Р); быть располо́женным на окра́ине (Р).
skit [skit] сати́ра, паро́дия; **~tish** ['skitiʃ] □ игри́вый, коке́тливый.
skittle ['skitl] ке́гля; **play (at) ~s** *pl.* игра́ть в ке́гли; **~-alley** кегельба́н.
skulk [skʌlk] скрыва́ться; пря́таться; кра́сться; **~er** ['skʌlkə] скрыва́ющийся; прогу́льщик.
skull [skʌl] че́реп.
sky [skai] не́бо (*eccl.*: небеса́); **~lark** 1. жа́воронок; 2. выки́дывать шту́ки; **~light** ве́рхний свет; све́тлый люк; **~line** горизо́нт; очерта́ние (на фо́не не́ба); **~-scraper** небоскрёб; **~ward(s)** ['skaiwəd(z)] к не́бу.
slab [slæb] плита́; пласти́на.
slack [slæk] 1. неради́вый; расхля́банный; сла́бый; ме́дленный; ненатя́нутый (о пово́дьях и т. п.); (*a.* ✝) вя́лый; 2. ⚓ слабина́ (кана́та); ✝ засто́й; **~s** *pl.* свобо́дные (рабо́чие) брю́ки *f/pl.*; 3. = **~en**; = **slake**; **~en** ['slækn] ослабля́ть [-а́бить]; [о]сла́бнуть; замедля́ть [-е́длить]; ло́дырничать.
slag [slæg] шлак, ока́лина.
slain [slein] *p. pt.* от **slay**.
slake [sleik] утоля́ть [-ли́ть] (жа́жду); гаси́ть (и́звесть).
slam [slæm] 1. хло́панье; (в ка́рточной игре́) шлем; 2. хло́пать [-пнуть] (Т); захло́пывать(ся) [-пнуть(ся)].
slander ['slɑ:ndə] 1. клевета́; 2. [на]клевета́ть; **~ous** [-rəs] □ клеветни́ческий.
slang [slæŋ] слэнг; жарго́н.
slant [slɑ:nt] 1. склон, укло́н; *Am.* то́чка зре́ния; 2. *v/t.* класть ко́со; направля́ть вкось; *v/i.* лежа́ть ко́со; **~ing** ['slɑ:ntiŋ] *adj.* □ косо́й; **~wise** [-waiz] *adv.* ко́со.
slap [slæp] 1. шлепо́к; ~ **in the face** пощёчина; 2. шлёпать [-пнуть].
slash [slæʃ] 1. уда́р сплеча́; разре́з; вы́рубка; 2. руби́ть [рубану́ть] (са́блей); [по]ра́нить (ножо́м); [ис]полосова́ть [полосну́ть] (кнуто́м и т. п.).
slate [sleit] 1. сла́нец, ши́фер; гри́фельная доска́; 2. крыть ши́ферными пли́тами; **~-pencil** гри́фель *m*.
slattern [slætən] неря́ха (же́нщина).
slaughter ['slɔ:tə] 1. убо́й (скота́); резня́, кровопроли́тие; 2. [за]ре́зать (дома́шнее живо́тное); **~-house** бо́йня.
Slav [slɑ:v] 1. славяни́н (-я́нка); 2. славя́нский.
slave [sleiv] 1. раб(ы́ня); *attr.* ра́бский; 2. рабо́тать как ка́торжник.
slaver ['slævə] 1. слю́ни *f/pl.*; 2. [за]слюня́вить; пуска́ть слю́ни.
slav|ery ['sleivəri] ра́бство; **~ish** [-viʃ] □ ра́бский.
slay [slei] [*irr.*] уби́(ва́)ть.
sled [sled], **~ge**[1] [sledʒ] са́ни *f/pl.*; сала́зки *f/pl.*
sledge[2] [~] кузне́чный мо́лот.
sleek [sli:k] 1. □ гла́дкий, прили́-

занный; хо́леный; 2. пригла́живать [-гла́дить]; ~ness [sli:knis] гла́дкость *f*.

sleep [sli:p] 1. [*irr.*] *v/i.* спать; ~(up-)on отложи́ть до за́втра; *v/t.* дава́ть (кому́-нибудь) ночле́г; ~ away прос(ы)па́ть; 2. сон; ~**er** [-ə] спя́щий; 🚃 шпа́ла; F спа́льный ваго́н; ~**ing** [-iŋ]: ~ partner компаньо́н, не уча́ствующий акти́вно в дела́х; ~**ing-car(riage)** 🚃 спа́льный ваго́н; ~**less** [-lis] □ бессо́нный; ~-**walker** луна́тик; ~**y** [-i] □ со́нный, за́спанный.

sleet [sli:t] 1. дождь со сне́гом и́ли гра́дом; 2. it ~s идёт дождь со сне́гом; ~**y** ['sli:ti] сля́котный.

sleeve [sli:v] рука́в; ⊕ му́фта; вту́лка.

sleigh [slei] са́ни *f/pl.*; сала́зки *f/pl.*

sleight [slait] (*mst* ~ of hand) ло́вкость *f* (рук); фо́кусничество.

slender ['slendə] □ стро́йный; то́нкий; ску́дный.

slept [slept] *pt.* и *p. pt.* от sleep.

sleuth [slu:θ] соба́ка-ище́йка; *fig.* сы́щик.

slew [slu:] *pt.* от slay.

slice [slais] 1. ло́мтик; то́нкий слой; часть *f*; 2. ре́зать ло́мтиками.

slick [slik] F гла́дкий; *Am.* хи́трый; ~**er** *Am.* ['slikə] жу́лик.

slid [slid] *pt.* и *p. pt.* от slide.

slide [slaid] 1. [*irr.*] скользи́ть [-зну́ть]; ката́ться по льду; вдвига́ть [-и́нуть], всо́вывать [всу́нуть] (into в В); let things ~ относи́ться ко всему́ спустя́ рукава́; 2. скольже́ние; ледяна́я гора́ и́ли доро́жка; о́ползень *m*; накло́нная пло́скость *f*; ⊕ сала́зки *f/pl.*; диапозити́в; ~-**rule** логарифми́ческая лине́йка.

slight [slait] 1. □ то́нкий, хру́пкий; незначи́тельный; сла́бый; 2. пренебреже́ние; 3. пренебрега́ть [-бре́чь] (Т); трети́ровать.

slim|e [slaim] слизь *f*; ли́пкий ил; ~**y** ['slaimi] сли́зистый; вя́зкий.

sling [sliŋ] 1. (руже́йный) реме́нь *m*; рога́тка; праща́; ⚕ повя́зка; 2. [*irr.*] швыря́ть [швырну́ть]; ве́шать через плечо́; подве́шивать [-е́сить].

slink [sliŋk] [*irr.*] кра́сться.

slip [slip] 1. [*irr.*] *v/i.* скользи́ть [-зну́ть]; поскользну́ться *pf.*; выскольза́ть [вы́скользнуть] (*a.* ~ away); буксова́ть (о колёсах); ошиба́ться [-би́ться]; *v/t.* сова́ть [су́нуть]; спуска́ть [спусти́ть] (соба́ку); выпуска́ть [вы́пустить] (стрелу́); ~ a p.'s memory ускольза́ть из па́мяти (Р); ~ on (off) наде́(ва́)ть (сбра́сывать [сбро́сить]); 2. скольже́ние; полоса́; про́мах; оши́бка; опи́ска; опеча́тка; комбина́ция (бельё); ⚓ э́ллинг, ста́пель *m*; на́волочка; give a p. the ~ ускольза́ть [-зну́ть] от (Р); ~**per** ['slipə] ко́мнатная ту́фля, ~s *pl.* щлёпанцы *m/pl.*; ~**pery** [slipəri] □ ско́льзкий; ненадёжный; ~**shod** ['slipʃɔd] неря́шливый; небре́жный; ~**t** [slipt] *pt.* и *p. pt.* от slip.

slit [slit] 1. разре́з; щель *f*; 2. [*irr.*] разреза́ть в длину́.

sliver ['slivə] ще́пка, лучи́на.

slogan [slougən] ло́зунг, деви́з.

sloop [slu:p] ⚓ шлюп.

slop [slɔp]: 1. лу́жа; ~s *pl.* жи́дкая пи́ща; ~s *pl.* помо́и *m/pl.*; 2. проли́(ва́)ть; расплёскивать(ся) [-еска́ть(ся)].

slope [sloup] 1. накло́н, склон, скат; 2. клони́ться; име́ть накло́н.

sloppy ['slɔpi] □ мо́крый (о доро́ге); жи́дкий (о пи́ще); неря́шливый.

slot [slɔt] щель *f*; паз.

sloth [slouθ] лень *f*, ле́ность *f*; *zo.* лени́вец.

slot-machine автома́т (для прода́жи папиро́с и т. п.).

slouch [slautʃ] 1. [с]суту́литься; неуклю́же держа́ться; свиса́ть [сви́снуть]; 2. суту́лость *f*; ~ hat мя́гкая шля́па.

slough[1] [slau] боло́то; топь *f*.

slough[2] [slʌf] сбро́шенная ко́жа (змей).

sloven ['slʌvn] неря́ха *m/f*; ~**ly** [-li] неря́шливый.

slow [slou] 1. □ ме́дленный; медли́тельный; тупо́й; вя́лый; be ~ отст(ав)а́ть (о часа́х); 2. (*a.* ~ down, up, off) замедля́ть(ся) [заме́длить (-ся)]; ~**coach** тугоду́м; отста́лый челове́к; ~-**worm** *zo.* медяни́ца.

sludge [slʌdʒ] *f*; отсто́й; ти́на.

slug [slʌg] 1. слизня́к; *Am.* F жето́н для телефо́нных автома́тов; 2. *Am.* F [от]тузи́ть.

slugg|ard ['slʌgəd] лежебо́ка *m/f.*; ~**ish** ['slʌgiʃ] □ ме́дленный, вя́лый.

sluice [slu:s] 1. шлюз; 2. отводи́ть шлю́зом; шлюзова́ть (*im*)*pf.*; обли́(ва́)ть (over В).

slum [slʌm] *mst* ~s *pl.* трущо́ба.

slumber ['slʌmbə] 1. (*a.* ~s *pl.*) сон; 2. дрема́ть; спать.

slump [slʌmp] 1. ре́зкое паде́ние (цен, спро́са); 2. ре́зко па́дать; тяжело́ опуска́ться (на стул и т. п.).

slung [slʌŋ] *pt.* и *p. pt.* от sling.

slunk [slʌŋk] *pt.* и *p. pt.* от slink.

slur [slə:] 1. слия́ние (зву́ков); *fig.* пятно́ (на репута́ции); ♪ ли́га; 2. *v/t.* сли(ва́)ть (слова́); ~ over зама́зы(ва)ть; ♪ игра́ть лега́то.

slush [slʌʃ] сля́коть *f*; та́лый снег.

sly [slai] □ хи́трый; лука́вый; on the ~ тайко́м.

smack [smæk] 1. (при́)вкус; за́пах; чмо́канье; зво́нкий поцелу́й; *fig.*

оттéнок; 2. отзывáться [отозвáться] (of T); пáхнуть (of T); имéть прúвкус (of P); чмóкать [-кнуть] (губáми); хлóпать [-пнуть] (T); шлёпать [-пнуть].

small [smɔ:l] *com.* мáленький, небольшóй; мéлкий; незначúтельный; ~ change мéлочь *f*; ~ fry мéлкая рыбёшка; мелюзгá; ~ of the back *anat.* пояснúца; **~-arms** *pl.* ручнóе огнестрéльное орýжие; **~ish** [smɔ:liʃ] довóльно мáленький; **~pox** *pl.* ⚕ óспа; **~-talk** лёгкий, бессодержáтельный разговóр.

smart [smɑ:t] 1. □ рéзкий, сúльный (удáр); сурóвый (о наказáнии); лóвкий; остроýмный; щеголевáтый; нарядный; 2. боль *f*; 3. болéть (о чáсти тéла); страдáть; **~-money** компенсáция за увéчье; отступны́е дéньги *f/pl.*; **~ness** ['smɑ:tnis] нарядность *f*; элегáнтность *f*; лóвкость *f*.

smash [smæʃ] 1. *v/t.* сокрушáть [-шúть] *a. fig.*; разбивáть вдрéбезги; *v/i.* разбú(вá)ться; стáлкиваться [столкнýться] (into с T); † [о]банкрóтиться; 2. битьё вдрéбезги; столкновéние (поездóв и т. п.); **~-up** катастрóфа; банкрóтство.

smattering ['smætəriŋ] повéрхностное знáние.

smear [smiə] 1. пятнó; мазóк; 2. [на]мáзать, измáз(ыв)ать.

smell [smel] 1. зáпах; обоняние; 2. [*irr.*] обонять (B); [по]чýять (B); (*a.* ~ at) [по]нюхать (B); ~ of пáхнуть (T).

smelt[1] [smelt] *pt.* и *p. pt.* от smell.

smelt[2] [~] выплавлять [вы́плавить] (метáлл).

smile [smail] 1. улы́бка; 2. улыбáться [-бнýться].

smirch [smə:tʃ] *rhet.* [за]пятнáть.

smirk [smə:k] ухмыляться [-льнýться].

smite [smait] [*irr.*] поражáть [поразúть]; ударять [удáрить]; разбú(вá)ть (неприятеля); разрушáть [-рýшить].

smith [smiθ] кузнéц.

smithereens ['smiðə'ri:nz] *pl.* оскóлки *m/pl.*; черепкú *m/pl.*; (in)to ~ вдрéбезги.

smithy ['smiði] кýзница.

smitten ['smitn] 1. *p.pt.* от smite; 2. поражённый (with T); очарóванный (with T).

smock [smɔk] 1. украшáть обóрками; 2. **~-frock** рабóчий халáт.

smoke [smouk] 1. дым; have a ~ покурúть *pf.*; 2. курúть; [на-]дымúть; [за]дымúться; выкýривать [вы́курить] (*a.* ~ out); **~-dried** копчёный; **~r** ['smoukə] курящий; 🚃 F вагóн для курящих; отделéние для курящих; **~-stack** 🚃 ⚓ дымовáя трубá.

smoking ['smoukiŋ] курящий; курúтельный (о кóмнате); **~-compartment** отделéние для курящих.

smoky [-ki] ды́мный; закоптéлый.

smooth [smu:ð] 1. □ глáдкий; *fig.* плáвный; спокóйный; вкрáдчивый, льстúвый; 2. приглáживать [-лáдить]; разглáживать [-лáдить]; *fig.* (*a.* ~ over) смягчáть [-чúть], смáз(ыв)ать; **~ness** ['smu:ðnis] глáдкость *f* и т. д.

smote [smout] *pt.* от smite.

smother ['smʌðə] [за]душúть.

smoulder ['smouldə] тлеть.

smudge [smʌdʒ] 1. [за]пáчкать(ся); 2. грязное пятнó.

smug [smʌg] самодовóльный.

smuggle ['smʌgl] занимáться контрабáндой; протáскивать контрабáндой; **~r** [-ə] контрабандúст(ка).

smut [smʌt] 1. сáжа, ýгольная пыль *f* и т. п.; грязное пятнó; непристóйности *f/pl.*; ⚘ головня; 2. [за-]пáчкать.

smutty ['smʌti] □ грязный.

snack [snæk] лёгкая закýска; **~-bar** закýсочная.

snaffle ['snæfl] трéнзель *m*.

snag [snæg] коряга; сучóк; облóманный зуб; *fig.* препятствие.

snail [sneil] *zo.* улúтка.

snake [sneik] *zo.* змея.

snap [snæp] 1. щёлк, треск; застёжка; хрустящее печéнье; дéтская кáрточная игрá; *fig.* энергúчность *f*; cold ~ внезáпное похолодáние; 2. *v/i.* [с]ломáться; щёлкать [-кнуть]; ухвáтываться [ухватúться] (at за B); огрызáться [-знýться] (at на B); [по]рвáться; цáпать [цáпнуть] (at B); *v/t.* защёлкивать [защелкнýть]; *phot.* дéлать моментáльный снúмок (P); ~ out отрéзать *pf.*; ~ up подхвáтывать [-хватúть]; **~fastener** кнóпка (застёжка); **~pish** ['snæpiʃ] □ раздражúтельный; **~py** ['snæpi] F энергúчный; живóй; **~shot** *phot.* моментáльный снúмок.

snare [snɛə] 1. силóк; *fig.* ловýшка; западня; 2. поймáть в ловýшку.

snarl [snɑ:l] 1. рычáние; 2. [про-]рычáть; *fig.* огрызáться [-знýться].

snatch [snætʃ] 1. рывóк; хватáние; обры́вок; кусóчек; 2. хватáть [схватúть]; ~ at хватáться [схватúться] за (B); ~ up подхвáтывать [-хватúть].

sneak [sni:k] 1. *v/i.* крáсться; *v/t.* F стащúть *pf.*, укрáсть *pf.*; 2. трус; ябедник (-ица); **~ers** ['sni:kəz] *pl.* тéннисные тýфли *f/pl*; тáпочки *f/pl.*

sneer [sniə] 1. усмéшка; насмéшка; 2. насмéшливо улыбáться; [по-]глумúться (at над T).

sneeze [sni:z] 1. чихáнье; 2. чихáть [чихнýть].

snicker ['snikə] ти́хо ржа́ть; хихи́кать [-кнуть].
sniff [snif] фы́ркать [-кнуть] (в знак презре́ния); [за]сопе́ть; [по-] ню́хать.
snigger ['snigə] пода́вленный смешо́к.
snip [snip] **1.** обре́зок; надре́з; **2.** ре́зать но́жницами.
snipe [snaip] стреля́ть из укры́тия.
snippy ['snipi] F отры́висто-гру́бый; надме́нный.
snivel ['snivl] [за]хны́кать; F распуска́ть со́пли.
snob [snɔb] сноб; **~bery** ['snɔbəri] снοби́зм.
snoop [snu:p] *Am.* **1.** сова́ть нос в чужи́е дела́; **2.** проны́ра *m/f.*
snooze [snu:z] F **1.** лёгкий, коро́ткий сон; **2.** дрема́ть, вздремну́ть *pf.*
snore [snɔ:] [за]храпе́ть.
snort [snɔ:t] фы́ркать [-кнуть]; [за]храпе́ть (о ло́шади).
snout [snaut] ры́ло; мо́рда.
snow [snou] **1.** снег; **2.** it ~s снег идёт; be ~ed under быть занесённым сне́гом; **~-drift** сне́жный сугро́б; **~y** ['snoui] □ сне́жный; белосне́жный.
snub [snʌb] **1.** *fig.* оса́живать [осади́ть]; **2.** вы́говор; **~-nosed** курно́сый.
snuff [snʌf] **1.** ню́хательный таба́к; **2.** снима́ть нага́р (со свечи́); (*a.* take ~) ню́хать таба́к; **~le** ['snʌfl] гнуса́вить, говори́ть в нос.
snug [snʌg] □ ую́тный; доста́точный; **~gle** ['snʌgl] (ла́сково) прижи(им)а́ть(ся) (to к Д).
so [sou] так; ита́к; таки́м о́бразом; I hope ~ я наде́юсь; are you tired? ~ I am вы уста́ли? — да; you are tired, ~ am I вы уста́ли и я то́же; ~ far до сих пор.
soak [souk] *v/t.* [на]мочи́ть; впи́тывать [впита́ть]; *v/i.* промока́ть; пропи́тываться [-пита́ться]; проса́чиваться [-сочи́ться].
soap [soup] **1.** мы́ло; soft ~ жи́дкое мы́ло; **2.** намы́ли(ва)ть; **~-box** мы́льница; импровизи́рованная трибу́на; **~y** ['soupi] □ мы́льный.
soar [sɔ:] высо́ко лета́ть; пари́ть; ✈ [с]плани́ровать.
sob [sɔb] **1.** рыда́ние; **2.** [за]рыда́ть, разрыда́ться *pf.*
sober ['soubə] **1.** □ тре́звый; уме́ренный; **2.** вытрезвля́ть [вы́трезвить]; **~ness** [-nis], **~sobriety** [sou'braiəti] тре́звость *f.*
so-called ['soukɔ:ld] так называ́емый.
sociable ['souʃəbl] **1.** □ общи́тельный; дру́жеский; **2.** *Am.* вечери́нка.
social ['souʃəl] **1.** □ обще́ственный; социа́льный; све́тский; ~ service социа́льное учрежде́ние; **2.** вечери́нка; **~ize** [-aiz] социализи́ровать (*im*)*pf.*
society [sə'saiəti] о́бщество; компа́ния (торго́вая); обще́ственность *f*; объедине́ние.
sociology [sousi'ɔlədʒi] социоло́гия.
sock [sɔk] носо́к; сте́лька.
socket ['sɔkit] впа́дина (глазна́я); углубле́ние; ⚡ патро́н (электри́ческой ла́мпочки); ⊕ му́фта.
soda ['soudə] со́да; со́довая вода́; **~-fountain** сифо́н.
sodden ['sɔdn] промо́кший.
soft [sɔft] □ *com.* мя́гкий; не́жный; ти́хий; нея́ркий; кро́ткий; изне́женный; придуркова́тый; ~ drink *Am.* F безалкого́льный напи́ток; **~en** ['sɔfn] смягча́ть(ся) [-чи́ть(ся)].
soggy ['sɔgi] сыро́й; пропи́танный водо́й.
soil [sɔil] **1.** по́чва, земля́; грязь *f*; пятно́; **2.** [за]па́чкать(ся).
sojourn ['sɔdʒə:n, 'sʌdʒ-] **1.** пребыва́ние; **2.** (вре́менно) прожива́ть.
solace ['sɔləs] **1.** утеше́ние; **2.** утеша́ть [уте́шить].
sold [sould] *pt.* и *p. pt.* от sell.
solder ['sɔ(l)də] **1.** спа́йка; **2.** пая́ть, запа́ивать [запая́ть].
soldier ['souldʒə] солда́т; **~like, ~ly** [-li] во́инский; во́инственный; **~y** [-ri] солда́ты *m/pl.*
sole[1] [soul] □ еди́нственный; исключи́тельный.
sole[2] [~] **1.** подо́шва; подмётка; **2.** ста́вить подмётку к (Д).
solemn ['sɔləm] □ торже́ственный; ва́жный; **~ity** [sə'lemniti] торже́ственность *f*; **~ize** ['sɔləmnaiz] [от]пра́здновать; торже́ственно отмеча́ть.
solicit [sə'lisit] [по]хода́тайствовать; выпра́шивать [вы́просить]; прист(ав)а́ть (к мужчи́не на у́лице); **~ation** [səlisi'teiʃən] хода́тайство; насто́йчивая про́сьба; **~or** [sə'lisitə] ⚖ стря́пчий; пове́ренный; *Am.* аге́нт фи́рмы; **~ous** [-əs] □ забо́тливый; ~ of стремя́щийся к (Д); **~ude** [-ju:d] забо́тливость *f*, забо́та.
solid ['sɔlid] **1.** □ твёрдый; про́чный; сплошно́й; масси́вный; ⅍ простра́нственный, куби́ческий; *fig.* соли́дный; надёжный; единогла́сный; сплочённый; a ~ hour це́лый час; ~ tire масси́вная ши́на; **2.** твёрдое те́ло; **~arity** [sɔli'dæriti] солида́рность *f*; **~ify** [sə'lidifai] [за]тверде́ть; де́лать твёрдым; **~ity** [-ti] твёрдость *f*; про́чность *f.*
soliloquy [sə'liləkwi] моноло́г; разгово́р с сами́м собо́й.
solit|ary ['sɔlitəri] □ одино́кий; уединённый; отде́льный; **~ude** [-tju:d] одино́чество; уединённое ме́сто.

solo ['soulou] со́ло *n indecl.*; ✈ одино́чный полёт; **~ist** ['soulouist] соли́ст(ка).
solu|ble ['sɔljubl] раствори́мый; разреши́мый; **~tion** [sə'lu:ʃən] растворе́ние; реше́ние; ⊕ раство́р; рези́новый клей.
solv|e [sɔlv] реша́ть [реши́ть], разреша́ть [-ши́ть]; **~ent** [-vənt] **1.** растворя́ющий; † платёжеспосо́бный; **2.** раствори́тель *m.*
somb|er, ~re ['sɔmbə] □ мра́чный.
some [sʌm, səm] не́кий; како́й-то; како́й-нибудь; не́сколько; не́которые; о́коло (P); ~ 20 miles миль два́дцать; in ~ degree, to ~ extent до изве́стной сте́пени; **~body** ['sʌmbədi] кто́-то; кто́-нибудь; **~how** [-hau] ка́к-то; ка́к-нибудь; ~ or other так и́ли и́наче; **~one** [~wʌn] *s.* somebody.
somer|sault ['sʌməsɔ:lt], **~set** [-set] кувырка́ние; turn ~s *pl.* кувырка́ться, turn a ~ кувыркну́ться *pf.*
some|thing ['sʌmθiŋ] что́-то; что́-нибудь; кое-что́; ~ like приблизи́тельно; что-то вро́де (P): **~time** [-taim] **1.** когда́-то; не́когда; **2.** бы́вший, пре́жний; **~times** иногда́; **~what** [-wɔt] слегка́, немно́го; до не́которой сте́пени; **~where** [-wɛə] где́-то, куда́-то; где́-нибудь, куда́-нибудь.
son [sʌn] сын (*pl.*: сыновья́; *fig. pl.*: сыны́).
song [sɔŋ] пе́сня; рома́нс; F for a mere ~ за бесце́нок; **~-bird** пе́вчая пти́ца; **~ster** ['sɔŋstə] певе́ц; пе́вчая пти́ца.
son-in-law зять *m.*
sonorous [sə'nɔ:rəs] □ зву́чный.
soon [su:n] ско́ро, вско́ре; ра́но; охо́тно; as (*or* so) ~ as как то́лько; **~er** ['su:nə] скоре́е; no ~ ... than едва́ ..., как; no ~ said than done ска́зано — сде́лано.
soot [su:t] **1.** са́жа; ко́поть *f*; **2.** покрыва́ть са́жей.
sooth|e [su:ð] успока́ивать [-ко́ить]; утеша́ть [уте́шить]; **~sayer** ['su:θseiə] предсказа́тель(ница *f*) *m.*
sooty ['su:ti] □ закопчённый; чёрный как са́жа.
sop [sɔp] **1.** обмакну́тый (в подли́вку и т. п.) кусо́к хле́ба и т. п.; *fig.* взя́тка; **2.** обма́кивать [-макну́ть]; нама́чивать [-мочи́ть].
sophist|icate [so'fistikeit] извраща́ть [-рати́ть]; подде́л(ыв)ать; лиша́ть наи́вности; **~icated** [-id] извращённый, искажённый; лишённый наи́вности; искушённый; **~ry** ['sɔfistri] софи́стика.
soporific [soupə'rifik] усыпля́ющее, снотво́рное сре́дство.
sorcer|er ['sɔ:sərə] волше́бник; **~ess** [-ris] волше́бница; ве́дьма; **~y** [-ri] волшебство́.

sordid ['sɔ:did] □ гря́зный; убо́гий.
sore [sɔ:] **1.** □ чувстви́тельный; боле́зненный; больно́й, воспалённый; оби́женный; ~ throat боль в го́рле; **2.** боля́чка; я́зва (*a. fig.*).
sorrel ['sɔ:rəl] **1.** гнедо́й (о ло́шади); **2.** гнеда́я ло́шадь *f.*
sorrow ['sɔrou] **1.** го́ре, печа́ль *f*; **2.** горева́ть, печа́литься; **~ful** ['sɔrouful] □ печа́льный, ско́рбный.
sorry ['sɔri] □ по́лный сожале́ния; (I am) (so) ~! мне о́чень жаль!; винова́т!; I am ~ for you мне вас жаль.
sort [sɔ:t] **1.** род, сорт; people of all ~s *pl.* всевозмо́жные лю́ди *m/pl.*; ~ of F как бу́дто; be out of ~s *pl.* быть не в ду́хе; пло́хо чу́вствовать себя́; **2.** сортирова́ть; ~ out рассортиро́вывать [-ирова́ть].
sot [sɔt] го́рький пья́ница *m.*
sough [sau] **1.** ше́лест; **2.** [за-] шелесте́ть.
sought [sɔ:t] *pt.* и *p. pt.* от seek.
soul [soul] душа́.
sound [saund] **1.** □ здоро́вый, кре́пкий, про́чный; здра́вый; норма́льный; † платёжеспосо́бный; ⚖ зако́нный; **2.** звук, шум; звон; зонд; проли́в; пла́вательный пузы́рь *m* (у ры́бы); **3.** звуча́ть (*a. fig.*); разд(ав)а́ться; зонди́ровать (*a. fig.*); измеря́ть глубину́ (P); выслу́шивать [вы́слушать] (больно́го); **~ing** ['saundiŋ] ⚓ проме́р глубины́ ло́том; зонди́рование; **~less** [-lis] □ беззву́чный; **~ness** [-nis] здоро́вье и т. д.; **~-proof** звуконепроница́емый.
soup [su:p] суп.
sour ['sauə] **1.** □ ки́слый; *fig.* угрю́мый; раздражи́тельный; **2.** *v/t.* [за]кваси́ть; *fig.* озлобля́ть [озло́бить]; *v/i.* закиса́ть [-и́снуть]; прокиса́ть [-и́снуть].
source [sɔ:s] исто́к; исто́чник (*mst fig.*), ключ, родни́к.
sour|ish ['sauəriʃ] □ кислова́тый; **~ness** [-nis] кислота́; *fig.* го́речь *f*; раздражи́тельность *f.*
souse [saus] [за]соли́ть; [за]маринова́ть; ока́чивать [окати́ть].
south [sauθ] **1.** юг; **2.** ю́жный; **~-east 1.** юго-восто́к; **2.** юго-восто́чный (*a.* ~-eastern).
souther|ly ['sʌðəli], **~n** ['sʌðən] ю́жный; **~ner** [-ə] южа́нин, южа́нка; *Am.* жи́тель(ница) ю́жных шта́тов.
southernmost [-moust] са́мый ю́жный.
southward, ~ly ['sauθwəd, -li], **~s** [-dz] *adv.* к ю́гу, на юг.
south|-west 1. юго-за́пад; **2.** юго-за́падный (*a.* ~-westerly, ~-western); **~-wester** юго-за́падный ве́тер; ⚓ зюйдве́стка.

souvenir ['su:vəniə] сувени́р.
sovereign ['sɔvrin] **1.** □ верхо́вный; сувере́нный; превосхо́дный; **2.** мона́рх; сoveréн (моне́та в оди́н фунт сте́рлингов); **~ty** [-ti] верхо́вная власть *f*; суверените́т.
soviet ['souviet] **1.** сове́т; **2.** сове́тский.
sow[1] [sau] *zo.* свинья́, свинома́тка; ⊕ чу́шка.
sow[2] [sou] [*irr.*] [по]се́ять; засева́ть [засе́ять]; **~n** [soun] *p. pt.* от sow[2].
spa [spɑ:] куро́рт (с минера́льными во́дами); целе́бные во́ды *f/pl.*
space [speis] **1.** простра́нство; ме́сто; промежу́ток; срок; *attr.* косми́ческий; **2.** *typ.* набира́ть в разря́дку.
spacious ['speiʃəs] □ просто́рный; обши́рный; вмести́тельный.
spade [speid] лопа́та; **~s** пи́ки *f/pl.* (ка́рточная масть).
span [spæn] **1.** пролёт (мо́ста́); коро́ткое расстоя́ние и́ли вре́мя; *Am.* па́ра лошаде́й (воло́в и т. п.); **2.** стро́ить мост че́рез (В); измеря́ть [-е́рить].
spangle ['spæŋgl] **1.** блёстка; **2.** украша́ть блёстками; *fig.* усе́ивать [усе́ять].
Spaniard ['spænjəd] испа́нец (-нка).
Spanish ['spæniʃ] испа́нский.
spank [spæŋk] F **1.** шлёпать [-пнуть]; отшлёп(ыв)ать; **2.** шлепо́к; **~ing** ['spæŋkiŋ] све́жий (ве́тер).
spar [spɑ:] **1.** ⚓ ранго́утное де́рево; ✈ лонжеро́н; **2.** бокси́ровать (в трениро́вке); *fig.* [по]спо́рить, препира́ться.
spare [spɛə] **1.** □ запасно́й; ли́шний, свобо́дный; ску́дный; худоща́вый; скро́мный; ~ time свобо́дное вре́мя *n*; **2.** ⊕ запасна́я часть *f*; **3.** [по]щади́ть; [по]жале́ть; [с]бере́чь; уделя́ть [-ли́ть] (вре́мя); избавля́ть [-а́вить] от (Р).
sparing ['spɛəriŋ] □ уме́ренный; бережли́вый; ску́дный.
spark [spɑ:k] **1.** и́скра; щёголь *m*; **2.** [за]и́скриться; **~(ing)-plug** *mot.* запа́льная свеча́.
sparkle ['spɑ:kl] **1.** и́скра; сверка́ние; **2.** [за]и́скриться, [за]сверка́ть; sparkling wine шипу́чее вино́.
sparrow ['spærou] воробе́й.
sparse [spɑ:s] □ ре́дкий; разбро́санный.
spasm [spæzm] спа́зма, су́дорога; **~odic(al** □) [spæz'mɔdik, -dikəl] су́дорожный.
spat [spæt] **1.** ге́тра; **2.** *pt.* и *p.pt.* от spit.
spatter ['spætə] бры́згать [-знуть]; расплёскивать [-плеска́ть].
spawn [spɔ:n] **1.** икра́; *fig. contp.* отро́дье; **2.** мета́ть икру́; *contp.* [рас]плоди́ться.
speak [spi:k] [*irr.*] *v/i.* говори́ть; [по]говори́ть (with, to с Т); разгова́ривать; ~ out, ~ up выска́зываться [вы́сказаться]; говори́ть гро́мко; *v/t.* выска́зывать [вы́сказать]; говори́ть [сказа́ть] (пра́вду и т. п.); **~er** ['spi:kə] ора́тор; *parl.* спи́кер (председа́тель пала́ты); **~ing-trumpet** ру́пор.
spear [spiə] **1.** копьё; дро́тик; острога́; **2.** пронза́ть копьём; бить острого́й (ры́бу).
special ['speʃəl] **1.** □ специа́льный; осо́бенный; осо́бый; э́кстренный; **2.** специа́льный корреспонде́нт; э́кстренный по́езд; **~ist** [-ist] специали́ст; **~ity** [speʃi'æliti] осо́бенность *f*; специа́льность *f*; **~ize** ['speʃəlaiz] специализи́ровать(ся) (*im*)*pf.* (в П *or* по Д); **~ty** ['speʃəlti] *s.* speciality.
specie ['spi:ʃi:] зво́нкая моне́та; **~s** ['spi:ʃi:z] вид; разнови́дность *f*.
speci|fic [spi'sifik] (~ally) характе́рный; осо́бенный; определённый; **~fy** [-fai] специфици́ровать (*im*)*pf.*; то́чно определя́ть; **~men** [-min] образе́ц; обра́зчик; экземпля́р.
specious ['spi:ʃəs] □ благови́дный; показно́й.
speck [spek] **1.** пя́тнышко; кра́пинка; **2.** [за]пятна́ть; **~le** ['spekl] **1.** пя́тнышко; **2.** испещря́ть [-ри́ть]; [за]пятна́ть.
spectacle ['spektəkl] зре́лище; **~s** *pl.* очки́ *n/pl.*
spectacular [spek'tækjulə] □ эффе́ктный, импоза́нтный.
spectator [spek'teitə] зри́тель(ница *f*) *m*.
spect|er ['spektə] при́зрак; **~ral** ['spektrəl] □ при́зрачный; **~re** *s.* ~er.
speculat|e ['spekjuleit] размышля́ть [-ы́слить]; ✝ спекули́ровать (in Т); **~ion** [spekju'leiʃən] размышле́ние; предположе́ние; ✝ спекуля́ция; **~ive** ['spekjulətiv] □ умозри́тельный; спекуляти́вный; **~or** [-leitə] ✝ спекуля́нт.
sped [sped] *pt.* и *p. pt.* от speed.
speech [spi:tʃ] речь *f*; го́вор; **~less** ['spi:tʃlis] □ безмо́лвный.
speed [spi:d] **1.** ско́рость *f*, быстрота́; *mot.* ход, ско́рость *f*; good ~! всего́ хоро́шего!; **2.** [*irr.*] *v/i.* [по]спеши́ть; идти́ поспе́шно; успева́ть (в заня́тиях); *v/t.* ~ up ускоря́ть [-о́рить]; **~-limit** допуска́емая ско́рость *f* (езды́); **~ometer** [spi:'dɔmitə] *mot.* спидо́метр; **~y** ['spi:di] □ бы́стрый.
spell [spel] **1.** (коро́ткий) пери́од; промежу́ток вре́мени; рабо́чее вре́мя *n*; ча́ры *f/pl.*; обая́ние; **2.** [*a. irr.*] писа́ть, чита́ть по бу́квам; писа́ть пра́вильно; означа́ть [означи́ть]; **~bound** *fig.* очаро́ванный;

~er ['spelə] *part. Am.* буква́рь *m*; **~ing** [-iŋ] правописа́ние; **~ing-book** буква́рь *m*.
spelt [spelt] *pt.* и *p. pt.* от spell.
spend [spend] [*irr.*] [по]тра́тить, [из]расхо́довать (де́ньги); проводи́ть [-вести́] (вре́мя); истоща́ть [-щи́ть]; **~thrift** ['spendθrift] мот (-о́вка), расточи́тель(ница *f*) *m*.
spent [spent] **1.** *pt.* и *p. pt.* от spend. **2.** *adj.* истощённый.
sperm [spə:m] спе́рма; кашало́т.
spher|e [sfiə] шар; земно́й шар; небе́сная сфе́ра; гло́бус; *fig.* сфе́ра; круг, по́ле де́ятельности; среда́; **~ical** ['sferikəl] □ сфери́ческий.
spice [spais] **1.** спе́ция, пря́ность *f*; *fig.* соль *f*; при́вкус; **2.** приправля́ть [-а́вить].
spick and span ['spikən'spæn] щегольско́й, с иго́лочки.
spicy ['spaisi] □ пря́ный; пика́нтный.
spider ['spaidə] *zo.* пау́к.
spigot ['spigət] *Am.* кран (бо́чки).
spike [spaik] **1.** остриё; шип, гвоздь *m* (на подо́шве); ♆ ко́лос; **2.** прибива́ть гвоздя́ми; снабжа́ть шипа́ми; пронза́ть [-зи́ть].
spill [spil] **1.** [*irr.*] *v/t.* проли́(ва́)ть; рассыпа́ть [-ы́пать]; F выва́ливать [вы́валить] (седока́); *v/i.* проли́(ва́)ться; **2.** F паде́ние.
spilt [spilt] *pt.* и *p. pt.* от spill.
spin [spin] **1.** [*irr.*] [с]прясть; [с]сучи́ть (кана́т и т. п.); крути́ться; [за]кружи́ть(ся); ~ a yarn расска́зывать небыли́цы; ~ along ката́ться, [по]кати́ться; **2.** круже́ние; бы́страя езда́.
spinach ['spinidʒ] ♆ шпина́т.
spinal ['spainl] спинно́й; ~ column спинно́й хребе́т; ~ cord, ~ marrow спинно́й мозг.
spindle ['spindl] веретено́.
spine [spain] *anat.* спинно́й хребе́т, позвоно́чный столб; колю́чка.
spinning|-mill пряди́льная фа́брика; **~-wheel** пря́лка.
spinster ['spinstə] ста́рая де́ва; ⚖ незаму́жняя (же́нщина).
spiny ['spaini] колю́чий.
spiral ['spaiərəl] **1.** □ спира́льный; ~ staircase винтова́я ле́стница; **2.** спира́ль *f*.
spire ['spaiə] шпиль *m*; шпиц; остроконе́чная верши́на.
spirit ['spirit] **1.** *com.* дух; привиде́ние; смысл; воодушевле́ние; спирт; **~s** *pl.* (high припо́днятое, low пода́вленное) настрое́ние; спиртны́е напи́тки *m/pl.*; **2.** ~ away, off таи́нственно похища́ть; **~ed** [-id] □ живо́й; сме́лый; энерги́чный; **~less** [-lis] □ вя́лый; ро́бкий; безжи́зненный.
spiritual ['spiritjuəl] □ духо́вный; одухотворённый; религио́зный; **~ism** [-izm] спирит(уал)и́зм.
spirituous ['spiritjuəs] спиртно́й, алкого́льный.
spirt [spə:t] *s.* spurt.
spit [spit] **1.** ве́ртел; слюна́; плево́к; *fig.* подо́бие; **2.** [*irr.*] плева́ть [плю́нуть]; треща́ть (об огне́); шипе́ть (о ко́шке); мороси́ть.
spite [spait] **1.** зло́ба, злость *f*; in ~ of не смотря́ на (В); **2.** досажда́ть [досади́ть]; **~ful** ['spaitful] зло́бный.
spitfire ['spitfaiə] вспы́льчивый челове́к.
spittle ['spitl] слюна́; плево́к.
spittoon [spi'tu:n] плева́тельница.
splash [splæʃ] **1.** бры́зги *f/pl.* (*mst* **~es** *pl.*); плеск; **2.** бры́згать [-знуть]; плеска́ть(ся) [-сну́ть].
splayfoot ['spleifut] косола́пый.
spleen [spli:n] *anat.* селезёнка; хандра́.
splend|id ['splendid] □ блестя́щий; великоле́пный, роско́шный; **~o(u)r** [-də] блеск; великоле́пие, ро́скошь *f*; пы́шность *f*.
splice [splais] ⚓ сплета́ть [-ести́] (кана́ты), спле́сни(ва)ть.
splint [splint] **1.** ⚕ лубо́к; **2.** накла́дывать лубо́к на (В); **~er** ['splintə] **1.** оско́лок; лучи́на; зано́за; **2.** расщепля́ть(ся) [-пи́ть(ся)].
split [split] **1.** тре́щина; щель *f*; *fig.* раско́л; **2.** расщеплённый; раско́лотый; **3.** [*irr.*] *v/t.* раска́лывать [-коло́ть]; расщепля́ть [-пи́ть]; ~ hairs вдава́ться в то́нкости; ~ one's sides with laughing надрыва́ться от сме́ха; *v/i.* раска́лываться [-коло́ться]; ло́паться [ло́пнуть]; **~ting** ['splitiŋ] ужа́сный (о головно́й бо́ли); оглуши́тельный.
splutter ['splʌtə] *s.* sputter.
spoil [spɔil] **1.** (*a.* **~s** *pl.*) награ́бленное добро́, добы́ча; *pol. part. Am.* **~s** system распределе́ние госуда́рственных должносте́й за услу́ги; **2.** [*irr.*] [ис]по́ртить; [по]губи́ть; [ис]по́ртиться (о пи́ще); [из]балова́ть (ребёнка).
spoke [spouk] **1.** *pt.* от speak; **2.** спи́ца (колеса́); ступе́нька, перекла́дина; **~n** ['spoukən] *p. pt.* от speak; **~sman** ['spouksmən] представи́тель *m*.
sponge [spʌndʒ] **1.** гу́бка; **2.** *v/t.* вытира́ть и́ли мыть гу́бкой; ~ up впи́тывать гу́бкой; *v/i.* жить на чужо́й счёт; **~-cake** бискви́т; **~r** ['spʌndʒə] прижива́льщик (-лка).
spongy ['spʌndʒi] гу́бчатый.
sponsor ['spɔnsə] **1.** покрови́тель (-ница *f*) *m*; поручи́тель(ница *f*) *m*; крёстный оте́ц, крёстная мать *f*; *Am.* абоне́нт радиорекла́мы; **2.** руча́ться [поручи́ться] за (В); быть крёстным отцо́м (крёстной ма́терью) у (Р).
spontane|ity [spɔntə'ni:iti] непо-

сре́дственность *f*; самопроизво́льность *f*; **~ous** [spɔn'teinjəs] □ непосре́дственный; непринуждённый; самопроизво́льный.
spook [spu:k] привиде́ние.
spool [spu:l] **1.** шпу́лька; **2.** нама́тывать на шпу́льку.
spoon [spu:n] **1.** ло́жка; **2.** че́рпать ло́жкой; **~ful** ['spu:nful] ло́жка (ме́ра).
sport [spɔ:t] **1.** спорт; **~s** *pl.* спорти́вные и́гры *f/pl.*; *attr.* спорти́вный; *fig.* игру́шка; развлече́ние, заба́ва; *sl.* молоде́ц; **2.** *v/i.* игра́ть, весели́ться, резви́ться; *v/t.* F щеголя́ть [-льну́ть] (Т); **~ive** ['spɔ:tiv] □ игри́вый; весёлый; **~sman** ['spɔ:tsmən] спортсме́н.
spot [spɔt] **1.** *com.* пятно́; кра́пинка; ме́сто; on the ~ на ме́сте; сра́зу, неме́дленно; **2.** нали́чный; подлежа́щий неме́дленной упла́те; **3.** [за]пятна́ть; ⚔ обнару́жи(ва)ть; F опозн(ав)а́ть; **~less** ['spɔtlis] □ безупре́чный; незапя́тнанный; **~light** проже́ктор; *fig.* центр внима́ния; **~ty** ['spɔti] пятни́стый; кра́пчатый; прыщева́тый.
spouse [spauz] супру́г(а).
spout [spaut] **1.** струя́; но́сик (ча́йника и т. п.); водосто́чная труба́; **2.** выпуска́ть струёй (В); би́ть струёй; F ора́торствовать.
sprain [sprein] **1.** растяже́ние (свя́зок); **2.** растя́гивать [-яну́ть]; вы́вихнуть *pf.*
sprang [spræŋ] *pt.* от spring.
sprawl [sprɔ:l] растя́гивать(ся) [-яну́ть(ся)]; разва́ливаться [-ли́ться] (в кре́сле); ⚘ бу́йно разраста́ться.
spray [sprei] **1.** водяна́я пыль *f*; бры́зги *f/pl.*; пульвериза́тор, распыли́тель *m* (*a.* **~er**); **2.** распыля́ть [-ли́ть]; обры́зг(ив)ать.
spread [spred] **1.** [*irr.*] *v/t.* (*a.* ~ out) расстила́ть [разостла́ть]; распространя́ть [-ни́ть]; нама́з(ыв)ать (Т); ~ the table накры́(ва́)ть на стол; *v/i.* простира́ться [простере́ться]; распространя́ться [-ни́ться]; **2.** *pt.* и *p. pt.* от spread 1.; **3.** распростране́ние; протяже́ние.
spree [spri:] весе́лье; ша́лость *f*; кутёж.
sprig [sprig] ве́точка, побе́г; *fig.* о́тпрыск; ⊕ шти́фтик; гво́здик.
sprightly ['spraitli] оживлённый, весёлый.
spring [spriŋ] **1.** прыжо́к, скачо́к; родни́к, ключ; (*a.* **~***time*) весна́; ⊕ пружи́на, рессо́ра; *fig.* моти́в; **2.** [*irr.*] *v/t.* взрыва́ть [взорва́ть]; вспу́гивать [-гну́ть] (дичь); ~ a leak ⚓ дава́ть течь (о корабле́); ~ a th. (up)on a p. неожи́данно сообщи́ть (В/Д); *v/i.* пры́гать [-гнуть]; вска́кивать [вскочи́ть]; ⚘ появля́ться [-ви́ться] (о по́чках); ~ up возника́ть [-и́кнуть]; **~-board** трампли́н; **~tide** весна́; ~ tide сизиги́йный прили́в; **~y** ['spriŋi] □ упру́гий.
sprinkl|e ['spriŋkl) бры́згать [-знуть]; [о]кропи́ть; **~ing** [-iŋ] лёгкий дождь *m*; а ~ немно́го.
sprint [sprint] *sport* **1.** спринт (бег на коро́ткую диста́нцию); **2.** бе́гать на ско́рость.
sprite [sprait] эльф.
sprout [spraut] **1.** пуска́ть ростки́; всходи́ть [взойти́] (о семена́х); отра́щивать [отрасти́ть]; **2.** ⚘ росто́к, побе́г.
spruce¹ [spru:s] □ щеголева́тый; наря́дный.
spruce² [~] ⚘ ель *f*.
sprung [sprʌŋ] *pt.* и *p. pt.* от spring.
spry [sprai] *part. Am.* живо́й; сообрази́тельный; прово́рный.
spun [spʌn] *pt.* и *p. pt.* от spin.
spur [spə:] **1.** шпо́ра; *fig.* побужде́ние; act on the ~ of the moment де́йствовать под влия́нием мину́ты; **2.** пришпо́ри(ва)ть; побужда́ть [-уди́ть].
spurious ['spuəriəs] □ подде́льный, подло́жный.
spurn [spə:n] отверга́ть с презре́нием; отта́лкивать [оттолкну́ть] (ного́й).
spurt [spə:t] **1.** наддава́ть хо́ду; бить струёй; выбра́сывать [вы́бросить] (пла́мя); **2.** струя́; поры́в ве́тра; рыво́к; *sport* спурт.
sputter ['spʌtə] **1.** бры́зги *f/pl.*; шипе́ние; **2.** [за]шипе́ть (об огне́); бры́згать слюно́й; говори́ть бессвя́зно.
spy [spai] **1.** шпио́н(ка); та́йный аге́нт; **2.** шпио́нить, следи́ть (on за Т); **~-glass** подзо́рная труба́.
squabble ['skwɔbl] **1.** перебра́нка, ссо́ра; **2.** [по]вздо́рить.
squad [skwɔd] брига́да; отря́д; ⚔ отделе́ние; гру́ппа, кома́нда; **~ron** ['skwɔdrən] ⚔ эскадро́н; ✈ эскадри́лья; ⚓ эска́дра.
squalid ['skwɔlid] □ убо́гий.
squall [skwɔ:l] **1.** шквал; вопль *m*; крик; **2.** [за]вопи́ть.
squander ['skwɔndə] прома́тывать [-мота́ть]; расточа́ть [-чи́ть].
square [skwɛə] **1.** □ квадра́тный; прямоуго́льный; пра́вильный; ро́вный; то́чный; прямо́й, че́стный; недвусмы́сленный; ~ measure квадра́тная ме́ра; 2 feet ~ 2 фу́та в квадра́те; **2.** квадра́т; прямоуго́льник; пло́щадь *f*; **3.** *v/t.* де́лать прямоуго́льным; опла́чивать [оплати́ть] (счёт); согласо́вывать [-сова́ть]; *v/i.* согласо́вываться [-сова́ться]; сходи́ться [сойти́сь]; **~-toes** F педа́нт.
squash [skwɔʃ] **1.** фрукто́вый напи́ток; разда́вленная ма́сса; F толчея́; **2.** разда́вливать [-дави́ть].
squat [skwɔt] **1.** призе́мистый;

2. сидеть на корточках; **~ter** ['skwɔːtə] *Am.* поселившийся самовольно в незанятом доме, на незанятой земле.
squawk [skwɔːk] **1.** пронзительный крик (птицы); **2.** пронзительно кричать.
squeak [skwiːk] [про]пищать; *sl.* доносить [донести].
squeal [skwiːl] [за]визжать; *s.* squeak.
squeamish ['skwiːmiʃ] □ щепетильный; обидчивый; привередливый; брезгливый.
squeeze [skwiːz] **1.** сж(им)ать; стискивать [-снуть]; выжимать [выжать]; *fig.* вымогать (from у Р); **2.** сжатие; пожатие; давление; давка; **~r** ['skwiːzə] выжималка.
squelch [skweltʃ] F хлюпать; раздавливать ногой; *fig.* подавлять [-вить].
squint [skwint] косить (глазами); [со]щуриться.
squire ['skwaiə] **1.** сквайр (титул); **2.** сопровождать (даму).
squirm [skwəːm] F изви(ва)ться, [с]корчиться.
squirrel [skwirəl, *Am.* 'skwəːrəl] белка.
squirt [skwəːt] **1.** струя; шприц; F выскочка *m/f*; **2.** пускать струю (Р); бить струёй.
stab [stæb] **1.** удар (чем-либо острым); **2.** *v/t.* закалывать [заколоть]; *v/i.* наносить удар (at Д).
stabili|ty [stə'biliti] устойчивость *f*; прочность *f*; **~ze** ['stæbilaiz] стабилизировать (*im*)*pf.*
stable[1] ['steibl] □ стойкий; устойчивый.
stable[2] [~] **1.** конюшня; хлев; **2.** ставить в конюшню (или в хлев).
stack [stæk] **1.** стог (сена и т. п.); штабель *m*; труба (парохода); куча; **2.** складывать в стог и т. д.; нагромождать [-моздить].
stadium ['steidiəm] *sport* стадион; ⚕ стадия.
staff [stɑːf] **1.** посох; жезл; древко; ⚔ штаб; *attr.* штабной; ♪ нотная линейка; служебный персонал; **2.** снабжать персоналом.
stag [stæg] *zo.* олень-самец.
stage [steidʒ] **1.** подмостки *m/pl.*; сцена; эстрада; стадия; перегон; этап; **2.** [по]ставить (пьесу), инсценировать (*im*)*pf.*; **~-coach** дилижанс; **~-manager** режиссёр.
stagger ['stægə] **1.** *v/i.* шататься [(по)шатнуться]; *v/t.* потрясать [-ясти]; поражать [поразить]; **2.** шатание.
stagna|nt ['stægnənt] □ стоячий (о воде); *fig.* косный; **~te** [-neit] застаиваться [застояться]; *fig.* [за-]коснеть.
staid [steid] □ солидный, уравновешенный.
stain [stein] **1.** пятно; ⊕ протрава; **2.** [за]пачкать; [за]пятнать; ⊕ протравливать [-равить] (дерево); [по]красить; **~ed glass** цветное стекло; **~less** ['steinlis] незапятнанный; нержавеющий (о стали); *fig.* безупречный.
stair [stɛə] ступенька; **~s** *pl.* лестница; **~case**, *Am.* **~way** лестница; лестничная клетка.
stake [steik] **1.** кол; ставка, заклад (в пари); **~s** *pl.* приз; be at ~ быть поставленным на карту (*a. fig.*); **2.** подпирать (или огораживать) кольями; ставить на карту; ~ **out**, off отмечать вехами.
stale [steil] □ несвежий; выдохшийся; спёртый (воздух); избитый.
stalk [stɔːk] **1.** стебель *m*, черенок; *hunt.* подкрадывание; **2.** *v/i.* важно шествовать, гордо выступать; *v/t.* подкрадываться [-расться] к (Д).
stall [stɔːl] **1.** стойло; прилавок; киоск, ларёк; *thea.* место в партере; **2.** ставить в стойло; застревать [-рять] (в снегу и т. п.); ✈ терять скорость.
stallion ['stæljən] жеребец.
stalwart ['stɔːlwət] рослый, дюжий; стойкий.
stamina ['stæminə] выносливость *f.*
stammer ['stæmə] **1.** заикаться [-кнуться]; запинаться [запнуться]; **2.** заикание.
stamp [stæmp] **1.** штамп, штемпель *m*; печать *f* (*a. fig.*); клеймо; (почтовая, гербовая) марка; топанье; **2.** [от]штамповать; [за]штемпелевать; [за]клеймить; топать ногой.
stampede [stæm'piːd] **1.** паническое бегство; **2.** обращать(ся) в паническое бегство.
stanch [stɑːntʃ] **1.** останавливать кровотечение из (Р); **2.** верный, лояльный.
stand [stænd] **1.** [*irr.*] *v/i. com.* стоять; постоять *pf.*; простаивать [-стоять]; останавливаться [-новиться]; держаться; устоять *pf.*; ~ against [вос]противиться, сопротивляться (Д); ~ aside [по]сторониться; ~ back отступать [-пить]; ~ by присутствовать; *fig.* быть наготове; поддерживать [-жать] (В); ~ for быть кандидатом (Р); стоять за (В); значить; ~ off отодвигаться [-инуться] от (Р); ~ out выделяться [выделиться] (against на П); ~ over оставаться нерешённым; ~ to держаться (Р); ~ up вст(ав)ать, подниматься [-няться]; ~ up for защищать [-итить]; **2.** *v/t.* [по]ставить; выдерживать [выдержать], выносить [вынести]; F угощать [угостить] (Т); **3.** остановка; сопротивление; точка зрения; ки-

бск; позиция; место; подставка; трибуна; make a ~ against сопротивляться (Д).

standard ['stændəd] 1. знамя *n*, флаг, штандарт; норма, стандарт; образец; уровень *m*; 2. стандартный; образцовый; **~ize** [-aiz] нормировать (*im*)*pf*.

stand-by ['stænd'bai] опора.

standing ['stændiŋ] 1. □ стоящий; стойчий; постоянный; ~ orders *pl.* устав; *parl.* правила процедуры; 2. стояние; положение; продолжительность *f*; **~-room** место для стоящих (пассажиров, зрителей).

stand|-offish сдержанный; **~point** точка зрения; **~still** бездействие; мёртвая точка; **~-up**: ~ collar стоячий воротничок.

stank [stæŋk] *pt.* от stink.

stanza ['stænzə] строфа, станс.

staple ['steipl] 1. главный продукт; главная тема; 2. основной.

star [stɑ:] 1. звезда (*a. fig.*); *fig.* судьба; **~s** and stripes *pl. Am.* национальный флаг США; 2. украшать звёздами; играть главную роль; предоставлять главную роль (Д).

starboard ['stɑ:bəd] ⚓ 1. правый борт; 2. класть руль направо.

starch [stɑ:tʃ] 1. крахмал; *fig.* чопорность *f*; 2. [на]крахмалить.

stare [steə] 1. пристальный взгляд; 2. смотреть пристально; таращить глаза (at на В).

stark [stɑ:k] окоченелый; совершенный; *adv.* совершенно.

star|ry ['stɑ:ri] звёздный; как звёзды; **~-spangled** [-'spæŋgld] усеянный звёздами; ~ banner *Am.* национальный флаг США.

start [stɑ:t] 1. вздрагивание; отправление; ✈ взлёт; *sport* старт; начало; *fig.* преимущество; get the ~ of a p. получить преимущество перед кем-либо; 2. *v/i.* вздрагивать [-рогнуть]; вскакивать [вскочить]; отправляться в путь; *sport* стартовать (*im*)*pf*.; нач(ин)аться; ✈ взлетать [-ететь]; *v/t.* пускать [пустить] (в ход); *sport* давать старт (Д); *fig.* нач(ин)ать; учреждать [-едить]; вспугивать [-гнуть]; побуждать [-удить] (a p. doing кого-либо делать); **~er** ['stɑ:tə] *mot.* стартер; *sport* стартер, Ғ стартёр; *fig.* инициатор.

startl|e [stɑ:tl] поражать [поразить]; вздрагивать [-рогнуть]; **~ing** ['stɑ:tliŋ] поразительный.

starv|ation [stɑ:'veiʃən] голод; голодание; **~e** [stɑ:v] голодать; умирать с голоду; морить голодом; ~ for *fig.* жаждать (Р).

state [steit] 1. состояние; положение; государство (*pol. a.* ♀); штат; *attr.* государственный; in ~ с помпой; 2. заявлять [-вить]; констатировать (*im*)*pf*.; [с]формулировать; излагать [изложить]; **~ly** величавый, величественный; **~ment** утверждение; заявление; официальный отчёт; † ~ of account извлечение (или выписка) из счёта; **~room** парадный зал; ⚓ отдельная каюта (на пароходе); **~sman** ['steitsmən] государственный (*Am. a.* политический) деятель *m*.

static ['stætik] статический; стационарный.

station ['steiʃən] 1. место, пост; станция; вокзал; остановка; ⚓ военно-морская база; 2. [по]ставить, помещать [-естить]; ⚔ размещать [-естить]; **~ary** ['steiʃnəri] □ неподвижный; стационарный; **~ery** [~] канцелярские принадлежности *f/pl.*; **~-master** 🚂 начальник станции.

statistics [stə'tistiks] статистика.

statu|ary ['stætjuəri] скульптурный; **~e** [-ju:] статуя, изваяние.

stature ['stætʃə] рост, стан, фигура.

status ['steitəs] положение, состояние; статус.

statute ['stætju:t] статут; закон; законодательный акт; устав.

staunch [stɔ:ntʃ] *s.* stanch.

stave [steiv] 1. клёпка (бочарная); перекладина; строфа; 2. [*irr.*] (*mst* ~ in) проламывать [-ломить], разби(ва)ть (бочку и т. п.); ~ off предотвращать [-вратить].

stay [stei] 1. ⚓ штаг; опора, поддержка; остановка; пребывание; **~s** *pl.* корсет; 2. *v/t.* поддерживать [-жать]; задерживать [-жать]; *v/i.* ост(ав)аться; останавливаться [-новиться], жить (at в П); *sport* проявлять выносливость; **~er** ['steiə] выносливый человек; *sport* стайер; ~ race велосипедная гонка за лидером.

stead [sted]: in ~ of вместо (Р); **~fast** ['stedfəst] стойкий, непоколебимый.

steady ['stedi] 1. □ устойчивый; установившийся; твёрдый; равномерный; степенный; 2. делать (-ся) устойчивым; приходить в равновесие.

steal [sti:l] [*irr.*] *v/t.* [у]воровать, [у]красть; *v/i.* красться, прокрадываться [-расться].

stealth [stelθ]: by ~ украдкой, тайком; **~y** ['stelθi] □ тайный; бесшумный.

steam [sti:m] 1. пар; испарение; 2. *attr.* паровой; 3. *v/i.* выпускать пар; плавать [по]плыть, (о пароходе); *v/t.* варить на пару; парить; выпаривать [выпарить]; **~er** ['sti:mə] ⚓ пароход; **~y** ['sti:mi] □ парообразный; насыщенный парами.

steel [sti:l] 1. сталь *f*; 2. стальной

(*a.* ~у); *fig.* жестóкий; **3.** покрывáть стáлью; *fig.* закалять [-лить].
steep [sti:p] **1.** крутóй; F невероятный; **2.** погружáть [-узить] (в жидкость); пропитывать [-итáть]; *fig.* погружáться [-узиться] (in в В).
steeple ['sti:pl] шпиль *m*; колокóльня; **~-chase** скáчки с препятствиями.
steer¹ [stiə] кастрированный бычóк.
steer² [~] прáвить рулём; управлять (Т); водить, [по]вести ((сýдно); **~age** ['stiəridʒ] ⚓ управлéние рулём; срéдняя пáлуба; **~sman** ['stiəzmən] рулевóй.
stem [stem] **1.** ствол; стéбель *m*; *gr.* оснóва; ⚓ нос; **2.** задéрживать [-жáть]; сопротивляться (Д).
stench [stentʃ] зловóние.
stencil ['stensl] трафарéт.
stenographer [ste'nɔgrəfə] стенографист(ка).
step¹ [step] **1.** шаг; похóдка; ступéнька; поднóжка; *fig.* мéра; постýпок; tread in the ~s of *fig.* идти по стопáм (Р); ~s *pl.* стремянка; **2.** *v/i.* шагáть [шагнýть]; ступáть [-пнýть]; ходить, идти [пойти]; ~ out бóдро шагáть; *v/t.* измерять шагáми (*a.* ~ out); ~ up продвигáть [-инуть].
step² [~]: **~daughter** пáдчерица; **~-father** ['stepfɑ:ðə] óтчим; **~-mother** мáчеха; **~son** пáсынок.
steppe [step] степь *f.*
stepping-stone *fig.* трамплин.
steril|e ['sterail] бесплóдный; стерильный; **~ity** [ste'riliti] бесплóдие; стерильность *f*; **~ize** ['sterilaiz] стерилизовáть (*im*)*pf.*
sterling ['stə:liŋ] полновéсный; полноцéнный; † стéрлинговый.
stern [stə:n] **1.** □ стрóгий, сурóвый; неумолимый; **2.** ⚓ кормá; **~ness** ['stə:nnis] стрóгость *f*, сурóвость *f*; **~-post** ⚓ ахтерштéвень *m.*
stevedore ['sti:vidɔ:] ⚓ грýзчик.
stew [stju:] **1.** [с]тушить(ся); **2.** тушёное мясо; F беспокóйство.
steward [stjuəd] эконóм; управляющий; ⚓, ✈ стюард, бортпроводник; распорядитель *m*; **~ess** ['stjuədis] ⚓, ✈ стюардéсса, бортпроводница.
stick [stik] **1.** пáлка; трость *f*; прут; пóсох; **2.** [*irr.*] *v/i.* приклéи(ва)ться, прилипáть [-липнуть]; застревáть [-рять]; завязáть [-язнуть]; торчáть (дóма и т. п.); ~ to придéрживаться [-жáться] (Р); ~ at nothing не останáвливаться ни перед чéм; ~ out, ~ up торчáть; стоять торчкóм; *v/t.* вкáлывать [вколóть]; втыкáть [воткнýть]; приклéи(ва)ть; расклéи(ва)ть; F терпéть, вытерпеть *pf.*
sticky ['stiki] □ липкий, клéйкий.
stiff [stif] □ жёсткий, негибкий; тугóй; трýдный; окостенéлый; натянутый; **~en** ['stifn] дéлать (-ся) жёстким и т. д.; окостенé(вá)ть; **~necked** ['stif'nekt] упрямый.
stifle ['staifl] [за]душить; задыхáться [задохнýться].
stigma ['stigmə] *eccl.* стигмáт; *fig.* пятнó, клеймó; **~tize** [-taiz] [за-] клеймить.
still [stil] **1.** *adj.* тихий; неподвижный; **2.** *adv.* ещё, всё ещё; **3.** *cj.* всё же, однáко; **4.** успокáивать [-кóить]; **5.** дистиллятор; **~-born** мертворождённый; **~-life** натюрмóрт; **~ness** ['stilnis] тишинá.
stilt [stilt] ходýля; **~ed** ['stiltid] ходýльный, высокопáрный.
stimul|ant ['stimjulənt] **1.** ⚕ возбуждáющее срéдство; **2.** ⚕ стимулирующий, возбуждáющий; **~ate** [-leit] возбуждáть [-удить]; поощрять [-рить]; **~ation** [stimju'leiʃən] возбуждéние; поощрéние; **~us** ['stimjuləs] стимул.
sting [stiŋ] **1.** жáло; укýс (насекóмого); óстрая боль *f*; *fig.* кóлкость *f*; **2.** [*irr.*] [у]жáлить; жéчь (-ся)(о крапиве); уязвлять [-вить]; **~iness** ['stindʒinis] скáредность *f*; **~y** ['stindʒi] скáредный, скупóй.
stink [stiŋk] **1.** вонь *f*; **2.** [*irr.*] вонять.
stint [stint] **1.** ограничéние; предéл; **2.** урéз(ыв)ать; ограничи(ва)ть; [по]скупиться на (В).
stipend ['staipend] жáлованье, оклáд (*mst* священника).
stipulat|e ['stipjuleit] стáвить услóвием; обуслóвливать [-вить]; **~ion** [stipju'leiʃən] услóвие; клáузула, оговóрка.
stir [stə:] **1.** шевелéние; суетá, сумафóха; движéние; *fig.* оживлéние; **2.** шевелить(ся) [-льнýть (-ся)]; [по]мешáть (чай и т. п.); [вз]волновáть; ~ up возбуждáть [-удить]; размéшивать [-шáть].
stirrup ['stirəp] стрéмя *n* (*pl.:* стременá).
stitch [stitʃ] **1.** стежóк (о шитьé); пéтля (о вязáнии); ⚕ шов; **2.** [с]шить, прошить(вá)ть.
stock [stɔk] **1.** ствол; опóра; рýчка; лóжа (винтóвки); инвентáрь *m*; запáс; † сырьё; live ~ живóй инвентáрь *m*; скот; † основнóй капитáл; фóнды *m/pl.*; *Am.* áкция, áкции; ~s *pl.* госудáрственный долг; ~s *pl.* ⚓ стáпель *m*; † take ~ of дéлать переучёт (Р); *fig.* критически оцéнивать; **2.** имéющийся в запáсе (или наготóве); избитый, шаблóнный; **3.** оборýдовать (хозяйство); снабжáть [-бдить]; † имéть на склáде.
stockade [stɔ'keid] частокóл.
stock|-breeder животновóд; ~

broker биржевóй мáклер; ~ **exchange** фóндовая бúржа; **~holder** *Am.* акционéр.

stockinet ['stɔkinet] трикотáж.

stocking ['stɔkiŋ] чулóк.

stock|-jobber биржевóй спекулянт, мáклер; **~-taking** переучёт товáра; провéрка инвентарá; *fig.* обзóр результáтов; **~y** ['stɔki] кореáстый.

stoic ['stouik] **1.** стóик; **2.** стоúческий.

stoker ['stoukə] кочегáр; истопнúк.

stole [stoul] *pt.* от steal; **~n** ['stoulən] *p. pt.* от steal.

stolid ['stɔlid] □ флегматúчный; бесстрáстный; тупóй.

stomach ['stʌmək] **1.** желýдок; живóт; *fig.* охóта (for к Д); **2.** перевáривать [-варúть] (*a. fig.*); *fig.* сносúть [снестú].

stone [stoun] **1.** кáмень *m*; кóсточка (плодá); **2.** кáменный; **3.** облицóвывать камнáми; забрáсывать камнáми; вынимáть кóсточки из (Р); **~-blind** совсéм слепóй; **~ware** гончáрные издéлия *n/pl.*

stony ['stouni] кáменный; каменúстый; *fig.* кáменный.

stood [stud] *pt.* и *p. pt.* от stand.

stool [stu:l] табурéтка; ⚕ стул; **~-pigeon** *Am.* провокáтор.

stoop [stu:p] **1.** *v/i.* наклонáться [-нúться], нагибáться [нагнýться]; [с]сутýлиться; унижáться [унúзиться] (to до Р); снисходúть [снизойтú]; *v/t.* [с]сутýлить; **2.** сутýлость *f*; *Am.* верáнда.

stop [stɔp] **1.** *v/t.* затыкáть [заткнýть] (*a.* ~ up); задéл(ыв)ать; [за]пломбировáть (зуб); преграждáть [-градúть]; удéрживать [-жáть]; прекращáть [-кратúть]; останáвливать [-новúть]; ~ **it!** брось!; *v/i.* перест(ав)áть; останáвливаться [-новúться]; прекращáться [-кратúться]; кончáться [кóнчиться]; **2.** останóвка; пáуза; задéржка; ⊕ стóпор; упóр; ♪ клáпан; ♪ лад (стрýнного инструмéнта); ♪ педáль *f* (оргáна); *gr.* (*a.* full ~) тóчка; **~-gap** затычка; подрýчное срéдство; **~page** ['stɔpidʒ] задéржка, останóвка; прекращéние рабóты; ⊕ засорéние; **~per** ['stɔpə] прóбка; **~ping** ['stɔpiŋ] (зубнáя) плóмба.

storage ['stɔ:ridʒ] хранéние; склад.

store [stɔ:] **1.** запáс; склад; амбáр; *fig.* изобúлие; *Am.* лáвка; **~s** *pl.* припáсы *m/pl.*; универмáг; **in ~** нaготóве; про запáс; **2.** снабжáть [снабдúть]; запасáть [-стú]; хранúть на склáде; **~house** склад; *fig.* сокрóвищница; **~-keeper** кладовщúк; *Am.* лáвочник.

stor(e)y ['stɔ:ri] этáж.

stork [stɔ:k] áист.

storm [stɔ:m] **1.** бýря; ⚓ *a.* шторм; ⚔ штурм; **2.** бушевáть, свирéпствовать (*a. fig.*); it **~s** бýря бушýет; ⚔ штурмовáть; **~y** □ бýрный; штормовóй; áростный.

story ['stɔ:ri] расскáз; пóвесть *f*; *thea.* фáбула; F ложь *f*.

stout [staut] **1.** □ крéпкий, прóчный, плóтный; тýчный; отвáжный; **2.** крéпкое пúво.

stove [stouv] печь *f*, пéчка; (кýхонная) плитá.

stow [stou] уклáдывать [уложúть] (о грýзе и т. п.); **~away** ⚓ безбилéтный пассажúр, «зáяц».

straddle ['strædl] расставлáть [-áвить] (нóги); ходúть, расставлáя нóги; стоáть, расстáвив нóги; сидéть верхóм на (П).

straggl|e ['strægl] отст(ав)áть; идтú вразбрóд; быть разбрóсанным; **~ing** [-iŋ] разбрóсанный (о домáх и т. п.); беспорáдочный.

straight [streit] **1.** *adj.* прямóй; прáвильный; чéстный; *Am.* неразбáвленный; put ~ приводúть в порáдок; **2.** *adv.* прáмо; срáзу; **~en** ['streitn] выпрямлáть(ся) [вы́прямить(ся)]; ~ out приводúть в порáдок; **~forward** ['fɔ:wəd] □ чéстный, прямóй, откровéнный.

strain [strein] **1.** порóда; плéмя *n*; ⊕ деформáция; напряжéние; растяжéние (*a.* ⚕); ♪ *mst* **~s** *pl.* напéв, мелóдия; влечéние (of к Д); **2.** *v/t.* натáгивать [натянýть]; (*a.* ⊕) напрягáть [-áчь]; процéживать [-едúть]; переутомлáть [-мúть]; ⊕ деформúровать (*im*)*pf.*, сгибáть [согнýть]; ⚕ растáгивать [-янýть]; *v/i.* напрягáться [-áчься]; тянýться (after за Т); тянýть изо всех сил (at В); [по]старáться; **~er** ['streinə] дуршлáг; сúто; фильтр.

strait [streit] пролúв; **~s** *pl.* затруднúтельное положéние; ~ **waistcoat** смирúтельная рубáшка; **~ened** ['streitnd] стеснённый.

strand [strænd] **1.** бéрег (морскóй); прядь *f*; **2.** сесть на мель; be **~ed** *fig.* быть без средств.

strange [streindʒ] □ чужóй; чýждый; стрáнный; **~r** ['streindʒə] чужезéмец (-мка); чужóй (человéк); посторóнний (человéк).

strangle ['stræŋgl] [у]давúть.

strap [stræp] **1.** ремéнь *m*; лáмка; штрúпка; ⊕ крепúтельная плáнка; **2.** стáгивать ремнём; порóть ремнём.

stratagem ['strætidʒəm] стратагéма, (воéнная) хúтрость *f*.

strateg|ic [strə'ti:dʒik] (**~ally**) стратегúческий; **~y** ['strætidʒi] стратéгия.

strat|um ['streitəm], *pl.* **~a** [-tə] *geol.* пласт; слой (óбщества).

straw [strɔ:] **1.** солóма; солóминка; **2.** солóменный; ~ vote *Am.*

неофициа́льное про́бное голосова́ние; **~berry** клубни́ка; (*a.* wild ~) земляни́ка.
stray [strei] **1.** сбива́ться с пути́; заблуди́ться *pf.*; отби́(ва́)ться (from от Р); блужда́ть; **2.** (*a.* ~ed) заблуди́вшийся; бездо́мный; случа́йный; **3.** отби́вшееся живо́тное; беспризо́рник (-ница).
streak [stri:k] **1.** прослойка; поло́ска; *fig.* черта́; **2.** проводи́ть по́лосы на (П).
stream [stri:m] **1.** пото́к; руче́й; струя́; **2.** *v/i.* [по]те́чь; струи́ться; развева́ться; **~er** ['stri:mə] вы́мпел; дли́нная ле́нта; транспара́нт; столб (се́верного сия́ния); *typ.* кру́пный газе́тный заголо́вок.
street [stri:t] у́лица; *attr.* у́личный; **~-car** *Am.* трамва́й.
strength [streŋθ] си́ла; кре́пость *f* (материа́ла); on the ~ of в си́лу (Р); на основа́нии (Р); **~en** ['streŋθən] *v/t.* уси́ли(ва)ть; укрепля́ть [-пи́ть]; *v/i.* уси́ли(ва)ться.
strenuous ['strenjuəs] □ си́льный; энерги́чный; напряжённый.
stress [stres] **1.** давле́ние; напряже́ние; ударе́ние; **2.** подчёркивать [-черкну́ть]; ста́вить ударе́ние на (П).
stretch [stretʃ] **1.** *v/t.* натя́гивать [-яну́ть]; растя́гивать [-яну́ть]; вытя́гивать [вы́тянуть]; раски́дывать [-ки́нуть]; протя́гивать [-яну́ть] (*mst* ~ out); *fig.* преувели́чи(ва)ть; *v/i.* тяну́ться; растя́гиваться [-яну́ться]; натя́гиваться [-яну́ться]; **2.** растя́гивание; напряже́ние; протяже́ние; натя́жка; преувеличе́ние; простра́нство; промежу́ток вре́мени; **~er** ['stretʃə] носи́лки *f/pl.*
strew [stru:] [*irr.*] посыпа́ть [посы́пать]; разбра́сывать [-роса́ть].
stricken ['strikən] *p. pt.* от strike.
strict [strikt] то́чный; стро́гий; **~ness** ['striktnis] то́чность *f*; стро́гость *f*.
stridden ['stridn] *p. pt.* от stride.
stride [straid] **1.** [*irr.*] шага́ть [шагну́ть]; ~ over переша́гивать [-гну́ть]; **2.** большо́й шаг.
strident ['straidnt] □ скрипу́чий.
strike [straik] **1.** ста́чка; забасто́вка; be on ~ бастова́ть; **2.** [*irr.*] *v/t.* ударя́ть [уда́рить]; высека́ть [вы́сечь] (ого́нь); [от]чека́нить; спуска́ть [-сти́ть] (флаг); поража́ть [порази́ть]; находи́ть [найти́]; подводи́ть [-вести́] (бала́нс); заключа́ть [-чи́ть] (сде́лку); принима́ть [-ня́ть] (по́зу); наноси́ть [нанести́] (уда́р); ~ up завя́зывать [-за́ть] (знако́мство); *v/i.* [про]би́ть (о часа́х); [за]бастова́ть; ⚓ сесть на мель; ~ home *fig.* попада́ть в са́мую то́чку; **~r** ['straikə] забасто́вщик (-ица).
striking ['straikiŋ] □ порази́тельный; замеча́тельный; уда́рный.
string [striŋ] **1.** верёвка; бечёвка; тетива́ (лу́ка); ♪ струна́; ни́тка (бус); ~s *pl.* ♪ стру́нные инструме́нты *m/pl.*; pull the ~s быть закули́сным руководи́телем; **2.** [*irr.*] натя́гивать стру́ны на (В); напряга́ть [-ря́чь]; *Am.* завя́зывать [завяза́ть]; нани́зывать [-за́ть]; *Am. sl.* води́ть за́ нос; **~-band** стру́нный орке́стр.
stringent ['strindʒənt] стро́гий; то́чный; обяза́тельный; стеснённый (в деньга́х).
strip [strip] **1.** сдира́ть [содра́ть] (*a.* ~ off); обдира́ть [ободра́ть]; разде́(ва́)ть(ся); *fig.* лиша́ть [-ши́ть] (of P); [о]гра́бить; ⊕ разбира́ть [разобра́ть] (на ча́сти); ⚓ разоружа́ть [-жи́ть] (су́дно); **2.** полоса́; ле́нта.
stripe [straip] полоса́; ⚔ наши́вка.
strive [straiv] [*irr.*] [по]стара́ться; стреми́ться (for к Д); **~n** [-n] *p. pt.* от strive.
strode [stroud] *pt.* от stride.
stroke [strouk] **1.** уда́р (*a.* ⚕); взмах; штрих, черта́; ⊕ ход (по́ршня); ~ of luck уда́ча; **2.** [по]гла́дить; приласка́ть *pf.*
stroll [stroul] **1.** прогу́ливаться [-ля́ться]; **2.** прогу́лка.
strong [strɔŋ] □ *com.* си́льный; про́чный; кре́пкий; о́стрый; твёрдый; **~hold** кре́пость *f*; *fig.* опло́т; **~-willed** реши́тельный; упря́мый.
strop [strɔp] **1.** реме́нь для пра́вки бритв; **2.** пра́вить (бри́тву).
strove [strouv] *pt.* от strive.
struck [strʌk] *pt.* и *p. pt.* от strike.
structure ['strʌktʃə] структу́ра, строй; устро́йство; ⚠ строе́ние, сооруже́ние.
struggle ['strʌgl] **1.** боро́ться; вся́чески стара́ться; би́ться (with над Т); ~ through с трудо́м пробива́ться; **2.** борьба́.
strung [strʌŋ] *pt.* и *p. pt.* от string.
strut [strʌt] **1.** *v/i.* ходи́ть го́голем; *v/t.* ⊕ подпира́ть [-пере́ть]; **2.** ва́жная похо́дка; ⊕ подпо́рка.
stub [stʌb] **1.** пень *m*; оку́рок; огры́зок; **2.** выкорчёвывать [вы́корчевать]; ударя́ться [уда́риться] (ного́й) (against о В).
stubble ['stʌbl] жнивьё.
stubborn ['stʌbən] □ упря́мый; неподатливый; упо́рный.
stuck [stʌk] *pt.* и *p. pt.* от stick; **~-up** F высокоме́рный.
stud [stʌd] **1.** гвоздь *m* (для украше́ния); за́понка; ко́нный заво́д; **2.** оби́(ва́)ть (гвоздя́ми); усе́ивать [усе́ять] (with T); **~-horse** племенно́й жеребе́ц.
student ['stju:dənt] студе́нт(ка).
studied ['stʌdid] обду́манный;

преднаме́ренный; изы́сканный; де́ланный.
studio ['stju:diou] сту́дия; ателье́ *n indecl.*; мастерска́я.
studious ['stju:djəs] □ приле́жный, стара́тельный, усе́рдный.
study ['stʌdi] **1.** изуче́ние; нау́чное заня́тие; нау́ка; заду́мчивость *f*; кабине́т; *paint.* этю́д, эски́з; **2.** учи́ться (Д); изуча́ть [-чи́ть]; иссле́довать (*im*)*pf.*
stuff [stʌf] **1.** материа́л; вещество́; мате́рия; F дря́нь *f*; чепуха́; **2.** *v/t.* наби́(ва́)ть; заби́(ва́)ть; начиня́ть [-ни́ть]; засо́вывать [засу́нуть]; *v/i.* объеда́ться [объе́сться]; **~ing** ['stʌfiŋ] наби́вка (поду́шки и т. п.); начи́нка; **~y** ['stʌfi] □ спёртый, ду́шный.
stultify ['stʌltifai] выставля́ть в смешно́м ви́де; своди́ть на не́т.
stumble ['stʌmbl] **1.** спотыка́ние; запи́нка; **2.** спотыка́ться [-ткну́ться]; запина́ться [запну́ться]; **~ upon** натыка́ться [наткну́ться] на (В).
stump [stʌmp] **1.** пень *m*; обру́бок; оку́рок; **2.** *v/t.* F ста́вить в тупи́к; **~ the country** агити́ровать по стране́; *v/i.* тяжело́ ступа́ть; **~y** ['stʌmpi] □ призе́мистый.
stun [stʌn] оглуша́ть [-ши́ть] (*a. fig.*); *fig.* ошеломля́ть [-ми́ть].
stung [stʌŋ] *pt.* и *p. pt.* от sting.
stunk [stʌŋk] *pt.* и *p. pt.* от stink.
stunning ['stʌniŋ] F сногсшиба́тельный.
stunt[1] [stʌnt] *Am.* F трюк; ✈ фигу́ра вы́сшего пилота́жа.
stunt[2] [~] заде́рживать рост (Р); **~ed** ['stʌntid] ча́хлый.
stup|efy ['stju:pifai] изумля́ть [-ми́ть]; поража́ть [порази́ть]; **~endous** [stju:'pendəs] □ изуми́тельный; **~id** ['stju:pid] □ глу́пый, тупо́й; **~idity** [stju'piditi] глу́пость *f*; **~or** ['stju:pə] оцепене́ние.
sturdy ['stə:di] си́льный, кре́пкий; здоро́вый.
stutter ['stʌtə] заика́ться [-кну́ться]; запина́ться [запну́ться].
sty [stai] свина́рник; ячме́нь *m* (на глазу́).
style [stail] **1.** стиль *m*; слог; мо́да; фасо́н; ти́тул; **2.** титулова́ть (*im*)*pf.*
stylish ['stailiʃ] □ мо́дный; элега́нтный; **~ness** [-nis] элега́нтность *f*.
suave [sweiv] учти́вый; мя́гкий.
sub... [sʌb] *mst* под...; суб...
subdivision ['sʌbdi'viʒən] подразделе́ние.
subdue [səb'dju:] подчиня́ть [-ни́ть]; покоря́ть [-ри́ть]; подавля́ть [-ви́ть].
subject ['sʌbdʒikt] **1.** подчинённый; подвла́стный; *fig.* **~ to** подлежа́щий (Д); **2.** *adv.* **~ to** при усло́вии (Р); **3.** по́дданный; предме́т; сюже́т; (*a.* **~ matter**) те́ма; **4.** [səb'dʒekt] подчиня́ть [-ни́ть]; *fig.* подверга́ть [-е́ргнуть]; **~ion** [səb'dʒekʃən] покоре́ние; подчине́ние.
subjugate ['sʌbdʒugeit] порабоща́ть [-боти́ть].
sublease ['sʌb'li:s], **sublet** ['sʌb'let] [*irr.* (let)] сдать на права́х субаре́нды
sublime [[sə'blaim] □ возвы́шенный.
submachine ['sʌbmə'ʃi:n]: **~ gun** автома́т.
submarine ['sʌbməri:n] **1.** подво́дный; **2.** ⚓ подво́дная ло́дка.
submerge [sʌb'mə:dʒ] погружа́ть (-ся) [-узи́ть(ся)]; затопля́ть [-пи́ть].
submiss|ion [səb'miʃən] подчине́ние; поко́рность *f*; представле́ние (докуме́нта и т. п.); **~ive** [səb'misiv] □ поко́рный.
submit [səb'mit] подчиня́ть(ся) [-ни́ть(ся)] (Д); представля́ть [-а́вить] (на рассмотре́ние).
subordinate **1.** [sə'bɔ:dnit] подчинённый; *gr.* прида́точный; **2.** [~] подчинённый (-ённая); **3.** [sə'bɔ:dineit] подчиня́ть [-ни́ть].
suborn [sʌ'bɔ:n] подкупа́ть [-пи́ть].
subscribe [səb'skraib] *v/t.* подпи́сывать [-са́ть]; [по]же́ртвовать; *v/i.* присоединя́ться [-ни́ться] (to к Д); подпи́сываться [-са́ться] (to на В; † for на В); абони́роваться (to на В); **~r** [-ə] подпи́счик (-чица); абоне́нт(ка).
subscription [səb'skripʃən] подпи́ска (на журна́л и́ли на заём); абонеме́нт.
subsequent ['sʌbsikwənt] □ после́дующий; **~ly** впосле́дствии.
subservient [səb'sə:vient] раболе́пный; соде́йствующий (to Д).
subsid|e [səb'said] спада́ть [спасть] (о температу́ре); убы́(ва́)ть (о воде́); утиха́ть [ути́хнуть], уле́чься *pf.*; **~iary** [səb'sidjəri) **1.** □ вспомога́тельный; **2.** филиа́л; **~ize** ['sʌbsidaiz] субсиди́ровать (*im*)*pf.*; **~y** [-di] субси́дия.
subsist [səb'sist] существова́ть; жить (on, by Т); **~ence** [-əns] существова́ние; сре́дства к существова́нию.
substance ['sʌbstəns] су́щность *f*, суть *f*; содержа́ние; вещество́; иму́щество.
substantial [səb'stænʃəl] □ суще́ственный, ва́жный; про́чный; веще́ственный; состоя́тельный; пита́тельный.
substantiate [səb'stænʃieit] дока́зывать справедли́вость (Р); подтвержда́ть [-рди́ть].
substitut|e ['sʌbstitju:t] **1.** заменя́ть [-ни́ть]; замеща́ть [-ести́ть] (for В); **2.** замести́тель(ница *f*) *m*; за-

ме́на; суррога́т; **~ion** [sʌbsti'tju:ʃən] заме́на; замеще́ние.
subterfuge ['sʌbtəfju:dʒ] увёртка, отгово́рка.
subterranean [sʌbtə'reinjən] □ [подзе́мный.]
subtle ['sʌtl] □ то́нкий; неулови́мый; утончённый; **~ty** [-ti] то́нкость *f*; неулови́мость *f*.
subtract [səb'trækt] ⅍ вычита́ть [вы́честь].
suburb ['sʌbə:b] при́город; предме́стье; **~an** [sə'bə:bən] при́городный.
subver|sion [sʌb'və:ʃən] ниспроверже́ние; **~sive** [-siv] *fig.* подрывно́й; разруши́тельный; **~t** [sʌb'və:t] ниспроверга́ть [-е́ргнуть]; разруша́ть [-у́шить].
subway ['sʌbwei] тонне́ль *m* (*a.* тунне́ль); *Am.* метро́(полите́н) *n indecl.*
succeed [sək'si:d] [по]сле́довать за (Т); быть пре́емником (Р); достига́ть це́ли; преуспе́(ва́)ть.
success [sək'ses] успе́х; уда́ча; **~ful** [sək'sesful] □ успе́шный; уда́чный; уда́чливый; **~ion** [-'seʃən] после́довательность *f*; непреры́вный ряд; пре́емственность *f*; in ~ оди́н за други́м; подря́д; **~ive** [-'sesiv] □ после́дующий; после́довательный; **~or** [-'sesə] пре́емник (-ица); насле́дник (-ица).
succo(u)r ['sʌkə] **1.** по́мощь *f*; **2.** приходи́ть на по́мощь (Д).
succulent ['sʌkjulənt] со́чный.
succumb [sə'kʌm] уступа́ть [-пи́ть] (to Д); не вы́держивать [вы́держать] (to Р); быть побеждённым.
such [sʌtʃ] тако́й; *pred.* тако́в, -á и т. д.; ~ a man тако́й челове́к; ~ as тако́й, как ...; как наприме́р.
suck [sʌk] **1.** соса́ть; выса́сывать [вы́сосать] (*a.* ~ out); вса́сывать [всоса́ть] (*a.* ~ in); **2.** соса́ние; **~er** ['sʌkə] сосуно́к; ⚘, *zo.* присо́ска, присо́сок; *Am.* проста́к; **~le** ['sʌkl] корми́ть гру́дью; **~ling** ['sʌkliŋ] грудно́й ребёнок; сосу́н(о́к).
suction ['sʌkʃən] **1.** вса́сывание; **2.** *attr.* вса́сывающий.
sudden ['sʌdn] □ внеза́пный; all of a ~ внеза́пно, вдруг.
suds [sʌdz] *pl.* мы́льная вода́.
sue [sju:] *v/t.* пресле́довать суде́бным поря́дком; ~ out выхлопа́тывать [вы́хлопота́ть]; *v/i.* возбужда́ть иск (for о П).
suéde [sweid] за́мша.
suet [sjuit] по́чечное са́ло.
suffer ['sʌfə] *v/i.* [по]страда́ть (from от Р *or* Т); *v/t.* [по]терпе́ть; сноси́ть [снести́]; **~ance** [-rəns] попусти́тельство; **~er** [-rə] страда́лец (-лица); **~ing** [-riŋ] страда́ние.
suffice [sə'fais] хвата́ть [-ти́ть], быть доста́точным.
sufficien|cy [sə'fiʃənsi] доста́точность *f*; доста́ток; **~t** [-ənt] □ доста́точный.
suffocate ['sʌfəkeit] души́ть, удуша́ть [-ши́ть]; задыха́ться [задохну́ться].
suffrage ['sʌfridʒ] избира́тельное [пра́во.]
suffuse [sə'fju:z] зали́(ва́)ть слеза́ми); покры́(ва́)ть (кра́ской).
sugar ['ʃugə] **1.** са́хар; **2.** са́харный; **~y** [-ri] са́харный (*a. fig.*); *fig.* при́торный, слаща́вый.
suggest [sə'dʒest] внуша́ть [-ши́ть]; подска́зывать [-за́ть]; наводи́ть на мысль о (П); [по]сове́товать; предлага́ть [-ложи́ть]; **~ion** [-ʃən] внуше́ние; сове́т, предложе́ние; намёк; **~ive** [-iv] □ наводя́щий на размышле́ние; соблазни́тельный; двусмы́сленный.
suicide ['sjuisaid] самоуби́йца *m/f*; самоуби́йство.
suit [sju:t] **1.** проше́ние; набо́р; (*a.* ~ of clothes) костю́м; (ка́рточная) масть *f*; ⚖ тя́жба; иск; **2.** *v/t.* приспоса́бливать [-осо́бить] (to, with к Д); соотве́тствовать (Д); удовлетворя́ть [-ри́ть]; быть (кому́-либо) к лицу́ (*a.* with a p.); устра́ивать [-ро́ить]; подходи́ть [подойти́] (Д); ~ed подходя́щий; *v/i.* годи́ться; **~able** ['sju:təbl] □ подходя́щий; соотве́тствующий; **~-case** чемода́н; **~e** [swi:t] сви́та; набо́р; ♪ сю́ита; (и́ли ~ of rooms) анфила́да ко́мнат; гарниту́р (ме́бели); **~or** ['sju:tə] уха́живатель *m*; ⚖ исте́ц; проси́тель(ница *f*) *m*.
sulk [sʌlk] **1.** [на]ду́ться; быть не в ду́хе; **2.** ~s [-s] *pl.* плохо́е настрое́ние; **~y** ['sʌlki] □ наду́тый, угрю́мый.
sullen ['sʌlən] угрю́мый, мра́чный; серди́тый.
sully ['sʌli] *mst fig.* [за]пятна́ть.
sulphur ['sʌlfə] ⚗ се́ра; **~ic** [sʌl'fjuərik] се́рный.
sultriness ['sʌltrinis] духота́, зной.
sultry ['sʌltri] □ ду́шный, зно́йный.
sum [sʌm] **1.** су́мма; ито́г; *fig.* содержа́ние; су́щность; ~s *pl.* арифме́тика; **2.** (*a.* ~ up) ⅍ скла́дывать [сложи́ть]; *fig.* подводи́ть ито́г.
summar|ize ['sʌməraiz] сумми́ровать (*im*)*pf.*; резюми́ровать (*im*-)*pf.*; **~y** [-ri] **1.** □ кра́ткий; сокращённый; ⚖ дисциплина́рный; **2.** (кра́ткое) изложе́ние, резюме́ *n indecl.*
summer ['sʌmə] ле́то; **~(l)y** [-ri, -li] ле́тний.
summit ['sʌmit] верши́на (*a. fig.*); преде́л; верх.
summon ['sʌmən] соз(ы)ва́ть (собра́ние и т. п.); ⚖ вызыва́ть [вы́звать] (в суд); приз(ы)ва́ть; **~s** [-z] вы́зов (в суд); суде́бная пове́стка; ⚔ предложе́ние сда́ться.

sumptuous ['sʌmptjuəs] роско́шный; пы́шный.
sun [sʌn] **1.** со́лнце; **2.** со́лнечный; **3.** гре́ть(ся) на со́лнце; **~burn** ['sʌnbə:n] зага́р.
Sunday ['sʌndi] воскресе́нье.
sun|-dial со́лнечные часы́ *m/pl.*; **~-down** *Am.* зака́т, захо́д со́лнца.
sundries ['sʌndriz] *pl.* вся́кая вся́чина; ✝ разные расхо́ды *m/pl.*
sung [sʌŋ] *p. pt.* от sing.
sun-glasses *pl.* тёмные очки́ *n/pl.*
sunk [sʌŋk] *p. pt.* от sink.
sunken [sʌŋkən] *fig.* впа́лый.
sun|ny ['sʌni] □ со́лнечный; **~rise** восхо́д со́лнца; **~set** захо́д со́лнца, зака́т; **~shade** зо́нт(ик) от со́лнца; **~shine** со́лнечный свет; in the ~ на со́лнце; **~stroke** ⚕ со́лнечный уда́р; **~up** ['sʌnʌp] *Am.* восхо́д со́лнца.
sup [sʌp] [по]у́жинать.
super... ['sju:pə] *pref.*: пере..., пре...; сверх...; над...; супер...; **~abundant** [sju:pərə'bʌndənt] □ изоби́льный; **~annuate** [sju:pə'rænjueit] переводи́ть на пе́нсию; *fig.* сдава́ть в архи́в; **~d** престаре́лый; устаре́лый.
superb [sju'pə:b] роско́шный, прекра́сный.
super|charger ['sju:pətʃɑ:dʒə] ⊕ нагнета́тель *m*; **~cilious** [sju:pə'siliəs] □ высокоме́рный; **~ficial** [sju:pə'fiʃəl] □ пове́рхностный; **~fine** ['sju:pə'fain] чрезме́рно утончённый; вы́сшего со́рта; **~fluity** [sju:pə'fluiti] изоби́лие, изли́шек; изли́шество; **~fluous** [sju'pə:fluəs] □ изли́шний; **~heat** [sju:pə'hi:t] ⊕ перегре́(ва́)ть; **~intend** [sju:prin'tend] надзира́ть за (Т); заве́довать (Т); **~intendent** [-ənt] надзира́тель *m*; заве́дующий; управдо́м.
superior [sju'piəriə] **1.** □ вы́сший; ста́рший (по чи́ну); лу́чший; превосхо́дный; превосходя́щий (to B); **2.** ста́рший, нача́льник; *eccl.* настоя́тель *m*, (*mst* lady ~) настоя́тельница; **~ity** [sjupiəri'ɔriti] превосхо́дство.
super|lative [sju'pə:lətiv] **1.** □ высоча́йший; велича́йший; **2.** превосхо́дная сте́пень *f*; **~numerary** [sju:pə'nju:mərəri] **1.** сверхшта́тный; **2.** сверхшта́тный рабо́тник; *thea.* стати́ст; **~scription** [sju:pə'skripʃən] на́дпись *f*; **~sede** [-si:d] заменя́ть [-ни́ть]; вытесня́ть [вы́теснить]; *fig.* обгоня́ть [обогна́ть]; **~stition** [-'stiʃən] суеве́рие; **~stitious** [-'stiʃəs] суеве́рный; **~vene** [sju:pə'vi:n] добавля́ться [-а́виться]; неожи́данно возника́ть; **~vise** ['sju:pəvaiz] надзира́ть за (Т); **~vision** [sju:pə'viʒən] надзо́р; **~visor** ['sju:pəvaizə] надзира́тель *m*.
supper ['sʌpə] у́жин; the (Lord's) ♀ та́йная ве́черя.
supplant [sə'plɑ:nt] вытесня́ть [вы́теснить] (В).
supple ['sʌpl] ги́бкий; пода́тливый.
supplement **1.** ['sʌplimənt] добавле́ние, дополне́ние; приложе́ние; **2.** [-'ment] дополня́ть [допо́лнить]; **~al** [sʌpli'mentl] □, **~ary** [-təri] дополни́тельный, доба́вочный.
suppliant ['sʌpliənt] проси́тель (-ница *f*) *m*.
supplicat|e ['sʌplikeit] умоля́ть (for о П); **~ion** [sʌpli'keiʃən] мольба́; про́сьба.
supplier [sə'plaiə] поставщи́к (-и́ца).
supply [sə'plai] **1.** снабжа́ть [-бди́ть] (with Т); поставля́ть [-а́вить]; доставля́ть [-а́вить]; возмеща́ть [-ести́ть]; замеща́ть [-ести́ть]; **2.** снабже́ние; поста́вка; запа́с; вре́менный замести́тель *m*; *pl.* продово́льствие; припа́сы *m/pl.*; ✝ предложе́ние; *mst pl. parl.* ассигнова́ния *n/pl.* (утверждённые парла́ментом).
support [sə'pɔ:t] **1.** подде́ржка; опо́ра; **2.** подпира́ть [-пере́ть]; подде́рживать [-жа́ть]; содержа́ть (семью́ и т. п.).
suppose [sə'pouz] предполага́ть [-ложи́ть]; полага́ть; F ~ we do so? а е́сли мы э́то сде́лаем?
supposed [sə'pouzd] □ предполага́емый; **~ly** [-zidli] предположи́тельно; я́кобы.
supposition [sʌpə'ziʃən] предположе́ние.
suppress [sə'pres] подавля́ть [-ви́ть]; запреща́ть [-ети́ть] (газе́ту); сде́рживать [-жа́ть] (смех, гнев и т. п.); **~ion** [sə'preʃən] подавле́ние и т. д.
suppurate ['sʌpjuəreit] гнои́ться.
suprem|acy [sju'preməsi] превосхо́дство; верхо́вная власть *f*; **~e** [sju'pri:m] □ верхо́вный; вы́сший; кра́йний.
surcharge [sə:'tʃɑ:dʒ] **1.** перегружа́ть [-узи́ть]; **2.** ['sə:tʃa:dʒ] перегру́зка; припла́та, допла́та (за письмо́ и т. п.); надпеча́тка.
sure [ʃuə] □ *com.* ве́рный; уве́ренный; безопа́сный; надёжный; to be ~! *Am.* ~! безусло́вно, коне́чно; **~ly** ['ʃuəli] несомне́ннс; наве́рно; **~ty** [-ti] пору́ка; поручи́тель *m*.
surf [sə:f] прибо́й.
surface ['sə:fis] **1.** пове́рхность *f*; **2.** пове́рхностный.
surfeit ['sə:fit] **1.** изли́шество; пресыще́ние; **2.** пресыща́ть(ся) [-ы́тить(ся)] (on Т); переeда́ть [перее́сть] (on P).
surge [sə:dʒ] **1.** волна́; **2.** вздыма́ться (о во́лна́х); *fig.* [вз]волнова́ться.

surg|eon ['sə:dʒen] хиру́рг; **~ery** ['sə:dʒəri] хирурги́я; хирурги́ческий кабине́т.

surgical ['sə:dʒikəl] □ хирурги́ческий.

surly [sə:li] □ угрю́мый; гру́бый.

surmise ['sə:maiz] **1.** предположе́ние, дога́дка; **2.** [sə:'maiz] предполага́ть [-ложи́ть].

surmount [sə:'maunt] преодоле́(ва́)ть, превозмога́ть [-мо́чь].

surname ['sə:neim] фами́лия; про́звище.

surpass [sə:'pɑ:s] перегоня́ть [-гна́ть]; превосходи́ть [-взойти́]; **~ing** [-iŋ] превосхо́дный.

surplus ['sə:pləs] **1.** изли́шек; оста́ток; **2.** изли́шний; доба́вочный, приба́вочный.

surprise [sə'praiz] **1.** удивле́ние; неожи́данность *f*, сюрпри́з; *attr.* неожи́данный; ⚔ внеза́пный; **2.** удивля́ть [-ви́ть]; застава́ть врасплох.

surrender [sə'rendə] **1.** сда́ча; капитуля́ция; **2.** *v/t.* сда(ва́)ть; отка́зываться [-за́ться] от (Р); *v/i.* сд(ав)а́ться (*a.* ~ o. s.).

surround [sə'raund] окружа́ть [-жи́ть]; **~ing** [-iŋ] окружа́ющий; **~ings** [-iŋz] *pl.* окре́стности *f/pl.*

surtax ['sə:tæks] доба́вочный нало́г.

survey 1. [sə:'vei] обозре́(ва́)ть; осма́тривать [осмотре́ть]; *surv.* межева́ть; **2.** ['sə:vei] осмо́тр; обзо́р; *fig.* обсле́дование; *surv.* межева́ние; *attr.* обзо́рный; **~or** [sə:'veiə] землеме́р; *Am.* инспе́ктор.

surviv|al [sə'vaivəl] выжива́ние; пережи́ток; **~e** [sə'vaiv] *v/t.* пережи́(ва́)ть; выжива́ть по́сле (Р); *v/i.* остава́ться в живы́х, вы́жи(ва́)ть; **~or** [-ə] оста́вшийся в живы́х.

susceptible [sə'septəbl] □ восприи́мчивый (to к Д); оби́дчивый; be ~ of допуска́ть [-сти́ть] (В).

suspect [səs'pekt] **1.** подозрева́ть, заподо́зривать [-до́зрить] (of в П); сомнева́ться [усомни́ться] в (по́длинности и т. п.); полага́ть; **2.** подозри́тельный; подозрева́емый.

suspend [səs'pend] ве́шать [пове́сить]; приостана́вливать [-нови́ть]; откла́дывать [отложи́ть]; вре́менно прекраща́ть; **~ed** подвесно́й; **~ers** [-əz] *pl. Am.* подтя́жки *f/pl.*; подвя́зки *f/pl.*

suspens|e [səs'pens] напряжённое внима́ние; состоя́ние неизве́стности; be in ~ быть нерешённым; **~ion** [səs'penʃən] подве́шивание; прекраще́ние; вре́менная отста́вка; ~ bridge вися́чий мост.

suspici|on [səs'piʃən] подозре́ние; *fig.* чу́точка; **~ous** [-əs] □ подозри́тельный.

sustain [səs'tein] подпира́ть [-пере́ть]; подде́рживать [-жа́ть]; подтвержда́ть [-рди́ть]; выде́рживать [вы́держать]; выноси́ть [вы́нести], испы́тывать [испыта́ть].

sustenance ['sʌstinəns] пи́ща; сре́дства к существова́нию.

svelte [svelt] стро́йный.

swab [swɔb] **1.** шва́бра; ⚕ мазо́к; **2.** (*a.* ~ down) мы́ть шва́брой.

swaddle ['swɔdl] [с-, за]пелена́ть; swaddling clothes *pl.* пелёнки *f/pl.*

swagger ['swægə] ва́жничать; чва́ниться; [по]хва́стать (*a.* -ся).

swallow ['swɔlou] **1.** *zo.* ла́сточка; глото́к; **2.** глота́ть; прогла́тывать [-лоти́ть].

swam [swæm] *pt.* от **swim.**

swamp [swɔmp] **1.** боло́то, топь *f*; **2.** затопля́ть [-пи́ть], зали́(ва́)ть; **~y** ['swɔmpi] боло́тистый.

swan [swɔn] ле́бедь *m.* (*poet. a. f.*).

swap [swɔp] F **1.** обме́нивать(ся) [-ня́ть(ся)]; [по]меня́ть; **2.** обме́н.

sward [swɔ:d] газо́н; дёрн.

swarm [swɔ:m] **1.** рой (пчёл); стая (птиц); толпа́; **2.** рои́ться (о пчёлах); кише́ть (with T).

swarthy ['swɔ:ði] сму́глый.

swash [swɔʃ] плеска́ть [-сну́ть]; плеска́ться.

swath [swɔ:θ] ✓ проко́с.

swathe [sweið] [за]бинтова́ть; заку́т(ыв)ать.

sway [swei] **1.** колеба́ние; кача́ние; влия́ние; **2.** кача́ть(ся) [качну́ть(-ся)]; [по]колеба́ться; име́ть влия́ние на (В); властвова́ть над (Т).

swear [swɛə] [*irr.*] [по]кля́сться (by T); заставля́ть покля́сться (to в П); *b. s.* [вы́]руга́ться.

sweat [swet] **1.** пот; поте́ние; **2.** [*irr.*] *v/i.* [вс]поте́ть; исполня́ть тяжёлую рабо́ту; *v/t.* заставля́ть поте́ть; эксплуати́ровать; выделя́ть [вы́делить] (вла́гу); **~y** ['sweti] по́тный.

Swede [swi:d] шве́д(ка).

Swedish ['swi:diʃ] шве́дский.

sweep [swi:p] **1.** [*irr.*] мести́, подмета́ть [-ести́]; [по]чи́стить; проноси́ться [-нести́сь] (*a.* ~ past, along); *fig.* увлека́ть [-е́чь] (*a.* ~ along); ⚔ обстре́ливать [-ля́ть]; **2.** подмета́ние; разма́х; взмах; трубочи́ст; make a clean ~ (of) отде́л(ыв)аться (от Р); **~er** ['swi:pə] мете́льщик; **~ing** ['swi:piŋ] □ стреми́тельный; широ́кий, разма́шистый; огу́льный; **~ings** [-z] *pl.* му́сор.

sweet [swi:t] **1.** □ сла́дкий; све́жий; души́стый; ми́лый; have a ~ tooth быть сластёной; **2.** конфе́та; **~s** *pl.* сла́дости *f/pl.*, сла́сти *f/pl.*; **~en** ['swi:tn] подсла́щивать [-ласти́ть]; **~heart** возлю́бленный (-енная); **~ish** ['swi:tiʃ] сладкова́тый; **~meat** конфе́та; **~ness** ['swi:tnis] сла́дость *f*.

swell [swel] **1.** [*irr.*] *v/i.* [о]пу́хнуть; разду́(ва́)ться; набуха́ть [-у́хнуть];

нарастáть [-сти́] (о звýке); *v/t.* раздý(вá)ть; увели́чи(ва)ть; **2.** F щегольско́й; шика́рный; великолéпный; **3.** вы́пуклость *f*; о́пухоль *f*; ⚓ мёртвая зыбь *f*; F щёголь *m*; свéтский человéк; **~ing** ['sweliŋ] о́пухоль *f*.
swelter ['sweltə] томи́ться от жары́.
swept [swept] *pt.* и *p. pt.* от sweep.
swerve [swəːv] **1.** отклоня́ться от прямо́го пути́; (вдруг) сворáчивать в стóрону; **2.** отклонéние.
swift [swift] □ бы́стрый, скóрый; **~ness** ['swiftnis] быстротá.
swill [swil] **1.** помóи *m/pl.*; пóйло; **2.** [про]полоскáть; [вы́]лакáть.
swim [swim] **1.** [*irr.*] плáвать, [по-] плы́ть; перепль́і(вá)ть; my head **~s** у меня́ головá крýжится; **2.** плáвание; be in the ~ быть в кýрсе дéла.
swindle ['swindl] **1.** обмáнывать [-нýть], надý(вá)ть; **2.** обмáн, надувáтельство.
swine [swain] (*sg. mst fig.*) свинья́; сви́ньи *f/pl.*
swing [swiŋ] **1.** [*irr.*] качáть(ся) [качнýть(ся)]; [по]колебáть(ся); размáхивать (рукáми); болтáть (ногáми); висéть; F быть повéшенным; **2.** качáние, колебáние; размáх; взмах; ритм; качéли *f/pl.*; in full ~ в пóлном разгáре; **~-door** дверь, открывáющаяся в любýю стóрону.
swinish ['swainiʃ] □ сви́нский.
swipe [swaip] **1.** ударя́ть сплечá; **2.** удáр сплечá.
swirl [swəːl] **1.** кружи́ть(ся) в водоворóте; клуби́ться; **2.** водоворóт; кружéние; ви́хрь *m*.
Swiss [swis] **1.** швейцáрский; **2.** швейцáрец (-рка); the ~ *pl.* швейцáрцы *m/pl.*
switch [switʃ] **1.** прут; 🚂 стрéлка; ⚡ выключáтель *m*; фальши́вая косá; **2.** хлестáть [-стнýть]; 🚂 маневри́ровать; ⚡ переключáть [-чи́ть] (*often* ~ over) (*a. fig.*); *fig.* переменя́ть направлéние (P); ~ on ⚡ включáть [-чи́ть]; ~ off выключáть [вы́ключить]; **~-board** ⚡ коммутáтор.
swollen ['swoulən] *p. pt.* от swell.
swoon [swuːn] **1.** óбморок; **2.** пáдать в óбморок.
swoop [swuːp] **1.** (*a.* ~ down), устремля́ться вниз (на добы́чу и т. п.); налетáть [-етéть] (on на B); **2.** налёт, внезáпное нападéние.
sword [sɔːd] шпáга; меч.
swordsman ['sɔdzmən] фехтовáльщик.
swore [swɔː] *pt.* от swear.
sworn [swɔːn] *p. pt.* от swear.
swum [swʌm] *p. pt.* от swim.
swung [swʌŋ] *pt.* и *p. pt.* от swing.
sycophant ['sikofənt] льстец.
syllable ['siləbl] слог.
symbol ['simbəl] си́мвол, эмблéма; знак; **~ic(al** □) [sim'bɔlik, -əl] символи́ческий; **~ism** ['simbəlizm] символи́зм.
symmetr|ical [si'metrikəl] □ симметри́чный; **~y** ['simitri] симметри́я.
sympath|etic [simpə'θetik] (~ally) сочýвственный; симпати́чный; ~ strike забастóвка солидáрности; **~ize** ['simpəθaiz] [по]сочýвствовать (with Д); симпатизи́ровать (with Д); **~y** [-θi] сочýвствие (with к Д); симпáтия (for к Д).
symphony ['simfəni] симфóния.
symptom ['simptəm] симптóм.
synchron|ize ['siŋkrənaiz] *v/i.* совпадáть по врéмени; *v/t.* синхронизи́ровать (*im*)*pf.*; устанáвливать одноврéмéнность (собы́тий); сверя́ть [свéрить] (часы́); **~ous** [-nəs] □ синхрóнный.
syndicate **1.** ['sindikit] синдикáт; **2.** [-keit] синдици́ровать (*im*)*pf.*
synonym ['sinənim] синóним; **~ous** [si'nɔniməs] синоними́ческий.
synopsis [si'nɔpsis] конспéкт; синóпсис.
synthe|sis ['sinθisis] си́нтез; **~tic(al** □) [sin'θetik, -tikəl] синтети́ческий.
syringe ['sirindʒ] **1.** шприц; **2.** спринцевáть.
syrup ['sirəp] сирóп; пáтока.
system ['sistim] систéма; **~atic** [sistə'mætik] (~ally) системати́ческий.

T

tab [tæb] вéшалка; пéтелька; ⚔ петли́ца (на воротникé).
table ['teibl] **1.** стол; óбщество за столóм; плитá; дощéчка; табли́ца; тáбель *m*; ~ of contents оглавлéние; **2.** класть на стол; представля́ть [-áвить] (предложéние и т. п.); **~-cloth** скáтерть *f*; **~-spoon** столóвая лóжка.
tablet ['tæblit] дощéчка; блокнóт; таблéтка; кусóк (мы́ла и т. п.).
taboo [tə'buː] **1.** табý *n indecl.*; запрещéние, запрéт; **2.** подвергáть табý; запрещáть [-ети́ть]; **3.** запрещённый.
tabulate ['tæbjuleit] располагáть в ви́де табли́ц.
tacit ['tæsit] □ молчали́вый (о соглáсии и т. п.); подразумевáемый; **~urn** ['tæsitəːn] □ молчали́вый, неразговóрчивый.
tack [tæk] **1.** гвóздик с ширóкой

шля́пкой; кно́пка (канцеля́рская); стежо́к; ⚓ галс; *fig.* полити́ческая ли́ния; **2.** *v/t.* прикрепля́ть гвоздиками или кно́пками; смётывать [смета́ть]; присоединя́ть [-ни́ть], добавля́ть [-а́вить] (to, on к Д); *v/i.* ⚓ повора́чивать на друго́й галс; *fig.* меня́ть полити́ческий курс.

tackle ['tækl] **1.** принадле́жности *f/pl.*; снасть *f*; ⊕, ⚓ та́ли *f/pl.*; **2.** энерги́чно бра́ться за (В); би́ться над (Т).

tact [tækt] такт, такти́чность *f*; **~ful** ['tæktful] □ такти́чный.

tactics ['tæktiks] та́ктика.

tactless ['tæktlis] □ беста́ктный.

taffeta ['tæfitə] тафта́.

tag [tæg] **1.** ярлычо́к, этике́тка; ушко́ (сапога́); *fig.* изби́тая фра́за; **2.** прикрепля́ть ярлы́к, ушко́ к (Д).

tail [teil] **1.** хвост; коса́ (воло́с); пола́, фа́лда; обра́тная сторона́ (моне́ты); **2.** *v/t.* снабжа́ть хвосто́м; отруба́ть хвост (щеня́т); высле́живать [вы́следить]; *v/i.* тяну́ться дли́нной верени́цей; ~ off отст(ав)а́ть; **~-coat** фрак; **~-light** *mot.*, 🚃 за́дний фона́рь *m*; ✈ хвостово́й ого́нь *m*.

tailor ['teilə] **1.** портно́й; **2.** портня́жничать; [с]шить; **~-made** сши́тый на зака́з.

taint [teint] **1.** поро́к; пятно́ позо́ра; зара́за; испо́рченность *f*; **2.** [за]пятна́ть; [ис]по́ртить(ся); ⚕ заража́ть(ся) [зарази́ть(ся)].

take [teik] **1.** [*irr.*] *v/t.* брать [взять]; принима́ть [-ня́ть]; [съ]есть, [вы́-]пить; занима́ть [заня́ть] (ме́сто); *phot.* снима́ть [снять]; отнима́ть [-ня́ть] (вре́мя); I ~ it that я полага́ю, что ...; ~ the air выходи́ть на во́здух; ✈ отлета́ть [-ете́ть]; ~ fire загора́ться [-ре́ться]; ~ in hand бра́ться [взя́ться] за (В), предпринима́ть [-ня́ть]; ~ pity on сжа́литься *pf.* над (Т); ~ place случа́ться [-чи́ться], происходи́ть [произойти́]; ~ rest отдыха́ть [отдохну́ть]; ~ a seat сади́ться [сесть]; ~ a view выска́зывать свою́ то́чку зре́ния; ~ a walk [по]гуля́ть, прогу́ливаться [-ля́ться]; ~ down снима́ть [снять]; запи́сывать [-са́ть]; ~ for принима́ть [-ня́ть] за (В); ~ from брать [взять] у (Р); отнима́ть [отня́ть] у (Р) *or* от (Р); ~ in обма́нывать [-ну́ть]; принима́ть [-ня́ть] (го́стя); получа́ть (газе́ту и т. п.); ~ off снима́ть [снять] (оде́жду); ~ out вынима́ть [вы́нуть]; ~ to pieces разбира́ть [разобра́ть] (на ча́сти); ~ up бра́ться [взя́ться] за (В); занима́ть [заня́ть], отнима́ть [отня́ть] (ме́сто, вре́мя); **2.** *v/i.* [по]де́йствовать; име́ть успе́х; ~ after походи́ть на (В); ~ off уменьша́ться [уме́ньши́ться]; ✈ взлета́ть [-ете́ть]; оторва́ться от земли́; ~ over принима́ть до́лжность (from от Р); ~ to пристрасти́ться к (Д) *pf.*; привяза́ться к (Д) *pf.*; that won't ~ with me э́тим меня́ не возьмёшь; **3.** уло́в (ры́бы); (театра́льный) сбор; **~s** *pl.* бары́ши́ *m/pl.*; **~n** ['teikən] *p. pt.* от take; be ~ ill заболе́(ва́)ть; **~-off** ['tei'kɔf] карикату́ра; подража́ние; ✈ взлёт.

taking ['teikiŋ] **1.** □ привлека́тельный; зара́зный; **2.** **~s** [-z] *pl.* ✝ бары́ши́ *m/pl.*

tale [teil] расска́з, по́весть *f*; вы́думка; спле́тня.

talent ['tælənt] тала́нт; **~ed** [-id] тала́нтливый.

talk [tɔ:k] **1.** разгово́р; бесе́да; слух; **2.** [по]говори́ть; разгова́ривать; [по]бесе́довать; [на]спле́тничать; **~ative** ['tɔ:kətiv] болтли́вый; **~er** ['tɔ:kə] **1.** говору́н(ья), болту́н(ья); собесе́дник (-ница).

tall [tɔ:l] высо́кий; F невероя́тный; ~ order чрезме́рное тре́бование; ~ story *Am.* F неправдоподо́бный расска́з, небыли́ца.

tallow ['tælou] топлёное са́ло (для свече́й).

tally ['tæli] **1.** би́рка; ко́пия, дублика́т; опознава́тельный ярлы́к; **2.** отмеча́ть [-е́тить]; подсчи́тывать [-ита́ть]; соотве́тствовать (with Д).

tame [teim] **1.** □ ручно́й, приручённый; поко́рный; пасси́вный; ску́чный; **2.** прируча́ть [-чи́ть]; смиря́ть [-ри́ть].

tamper ['tæmpə]: ~ with вме́шиваться [-ша́ться] в (В); неуме́ло вози́ться с (Т); подде́л(ыв)ать (В); стара́ться подкупи́ть (В).

tan [tæn] **1.** зага́р; корьё, толчёная дубо́вая кора́; **2.** рыжева́то-кори́чневый; **3.** [вы́]дуби́ть (ко́жу); загора́ть.

tang [tæŋ] ре́зкий при́вкус; налёт.

tangent ['tændʒənt] ⩘ та́нгенс; go (*a.* fly) off at a ~ внеза́пно отклоня́ться (от те́мы и т. п.).

tangible ['tændʒəbl] □ осяза́емый, ощути́мый.

tangle ['tæŋgl] **1.** пу́таница, неразбери́ха; **2.** запу́т(ыв)ать(ся).

tank [tæŋk] **1.** цисте́рна; бак; ⚔ танк, *attr.* та́нковый; **2.** налива́ть в бак.

tankard ['tæŋkəd] высо́кая кру́жка.

tannery ['tænəri] коже́венный заво́д.

tantalize ['tæntəlaiz] [за-, из]му́чить.

tantrum ['tæntrəm] F вспы́шка гне́ва или раздраже́ния.

tap[1] [tæp] **1.** вту́лка; кран; F сорт, ма́рка (напи́тка); **2.** вставля́ть кран в (бо́чку); де́лать проко́л (для выпуска́ния жи́дкости) у

(больно́го); дела́ть надре́з на (де́реве для получе́ния со́ка); выпра́шивать де́ньги у (Р).
tap² [~] **1.** [по]стуча́ть; хло́пать [-пнуть]; **2.** лёгкий стук; шлепо́к; **~-dance** чечётка.
tape [teip] тесьма́; *sport* фи́нишная ле́нточка; телегра́фная ле́нта; red ~ бюрократи́зм, канцеля́рщина; **~-measure** ['teipmeʒə] руле́тка.
taper ['teipə] **1.** то́нкая восковая свеча́; **2.** *adj.* су́живающийся к концу́; кони́ческий; **3.** *v/i.* су́живаться к концу́; *v/t.* заостря́ть [-ри́ть].
tape-recorder магнитофо́н.
tapestry ['tæpistri] гобеле́н.
tape-worm ⚕ соли́тёр.
tap-room ['tæprum] пивна́я.
tar [tɑ:] **1.** дёготь *m*; смола́; **2.** обма́зывать дёгтем; [вы́]смоли́ть.
tardy ['tɑ:di] □ медли́тельный; запозда́лый, по́здний.
tare¹ [tɛə] та́ра; ски́дка на та́ру.
tare² [~] ⚘ посевна́я ви́ка.
target ['tɑ:git] цель *f*; мише́нь (*a. fig.*); ~ practice стрельба́ по мише́ням.
tariff ['tærif] тари́ф.
tarnish ['tɑ:niʃ] **1.** *v/t.* лиша́ть бле́ска (мета́лл); *fig.* [о]поро́чить; *v/i.* [по]тускне́ть (о мета́лле); **2.** ту́склость *f*; *fig.* пятно́.
tarry¹ ['tæri] ме́длить, ме́шкать; ~ for ждать (В *or* Р), дожида́ться (Р).
tarry² ['tɑ:ri] вы́мазанный дёгтем.
tart [tɑ:t] **1.** сла́дкая ватру́шка; **2.** ки́слый, те́рпкий; е́дкий; *fig.* ко́лкий.
task [tɑ:sk] **1.** зада́ча; уро́к; take to ~ призыва́ть к отве́ту; отчи́тывать [-ита́ть]; **2.** дава́ть зада́ние (Д); обременя́ть [-ни́ть], перегружа́ть [-узи́ть].
tassel ['tæsl] ки́сточка (украше́ние).
taste [teist] **1.** вкус; скло́нность *f* (for к Д); про́ба; **2.** [по]про́бовать (на вкус), отве́д(ыв)ать; *fig.* испы́тывать [-пыта́ть]; ~ sweet быть сла́дким на вкус; **~ful** ['teistful] □ (сде́ланный) со вку́сом; **~less** [-lis] □ безвку́сный.
tasty ['teisti] □ F вку́сный; прия́тный.
tatter ['tætə] **1.** изна́шивать(ся) в лохмо́тья; рва́ть(ся) в кло́чья; **2.** **~s** *pl.* лохмо́тья *n/pl.*; кло́чья *m/pl.* (*sg.* клок).
tattle ['tætl] **1.** болтовня́; **2.** [по-] болта́ть; [по]суда́чить.
tattoo [tə'tu:] **1.** ⚔ сигна́л вече́рней зари́; татуиро́вка; **2.** тату́ировать (*im*)*pf*.
taught [tɔ:t] *pt.* и *p. pt.* от teach.
taunt [tɔ:nt] **1.** насме́шка, «шпи́лька»; **2.** говори́ть ко́лкости (Д); [съ]язви́ть.
taut [tɔ:t] ⚓ ту́го натя́нутый; вполне́ испра́вный (о корабле́).
tavern ['tævən] таве́рна.
tawdry ['tɔ:dri] □ мишу́рный, безвку́сный.
tawny ['tɔ:ni] рыжева́то-кори́чневый.
tax [tæks] **1.** нало́г (on на В); *fig.* напряже́ние; бре́мя *n*; испыта́ние; **2.** облага́ть нало́гом; ⚖ такси́ровать (*im*)*pf.*; определя́ть разме́р (издéржек, штра́фа и т. п.); чрезме́рно напряга́ть (си́лы); подверга́ть испыта́нию; ~ a p. with a th. обвиня́ть [-ни́ть] кого́-либо в чём-либо; **~ation** [tæk'seiʃən] обложе́ние нало́гом; взима́ние нало́га; ⚖ такса́ция.
taxi ['tæksi] **1.** = **~-cab** такси́ *n indecl.*; **2.** е́хать в такси́; ✈ рули́ть.
taxpayer ['tækspeiə] налогопла́тельщик.
tea [ti:] чай.
teach [ti:tʃ] [*irr.*] [на]учи́ть, обуча́ть [-чи́ть]; преподава́ть; **~able** ['ti:tʃəbl] □ спосо́бный к уче́нию; подлежа́щий обуче́нию; **~er** ['ti:tʃə] учи́тель(ница *f*) *m*, преподава́тель (-ница *f*) *m*.
team [ti:m] упря́жка (лошаде́й и т. п.); *sport* кома́нда; брига́да, арте́ль *f* (рабо́чих); **~ster** ['ti:mstə] возни́ца *m*; **~-work** совме́стная рабо́та; согласо́ванная рабо́та.
teapot ['ti:pɔt] ча́йник (для зава́рки).
tear¹ [tɛə] **1.** [*irr.*] дыра́, проре́ха; **2.** [по]рва́ть(ся); разрыва́ть(ся) [разорва́ть(ся)]; *fig.* раздира́ть (-ся); [по]мча́ться.
tear² [tiə] слеза́ (*pl.* слёзы).
tearful ['tiəful] □ слезли́вый; по́лный слёз (о глаза́х).
tease [ti:z] **1.** зади́ра *m/f*; челове́к, лю́бящий дразни́ть; **2.** F дразни́ть; задира́ть (В); прист(ав)а́ть к (Д).
teat [ti:t] сосо́к.
technic|al ['teknikəl] □ техни́ческий; **~ality** [tekni'kæliti] техни́ческая сторона́ де́ла; техни́ческая дета́ль *f*; **~ian** [tek'niʃən] те́хник.
technique [tek'ni:k] те́хника.
technology [tek'nɔlədʒi] техноло́гия; техни́ческие нау́ки *f/pl.*
tedious ['ti:diəs] □ ску́чный, утоми́тельный.
tedium ['ti:diəm] ску́ка.
tee [ti:] мише́нь *f* (в и́грах); ме́тка для мяча́ (в го́льфе).
teem [ti:m] изоби́ловать, кише́ть (with Т).
teens [ti:nz] *pl.* во́зраст от трина́дцати до девятна́дцати лет.
teeth [ti:θ] *pl.* от tooth; **~e** [ti:ð]: the child is teething у ребёнка проре́заются зу́бы.
teetotal(l)er [ti:'toutlə] тре́звенник.
telegram ['teligræm] телегра́мма.
telegraph ['teligrɑ:f] **1.** телегра́ф; **2.** телеграфи́ровать (*im*)*pf.*; **3.** *attr.*

телегра́фный; **~ic** [teli'græfik] (~ally) телегра́фный; **~y** [ti'legrəfi] телеграфи́я.

telephon|e ['telifoun] **1.** телефо́н; **2.** телефони́ровать (*im*)*pf.*; **~ic** [teli'fɔnik] (~ally) телефо́нный; **~y** [ti'lefəni] телефони́я; телефони́рование.

telephoto ['teli'foutou] *phot.* телефотогра́фия.

telescope ['teliskoup] **1.** телеско́п; **2.** скла́дывать(ся) [сложи́ть(ся)] (подо́бно телеско́пу); вреза́ться друг в дру́га (о ваго́нах при круше́нии).

televis|ion ['teli'viʒən] телеви́дение; **~or** [-vaizə] телеви́зор.

tell [tel] [*irr.*] *v/t.* говори́ть [сказа́ть]; расска́зывать [-за́ть]; уверя́ть [уве́рить]; отлича́ть [-чи́ть]; ~ a p. to do a th. веле́ть кому́-либо что́-либо де́лать; ~ off F [вы́]брани́ть, «отде́л(ыв)ать»; *v/i.* ска́зываться [сказа́ться]; выделя́ться [вы́делиться]; расска́зывать [-за́ть] (about о П); **~er** ['telə] расска́зчик; касси́р (в ба́нке); **~ing** ['teliŋ] □ многоговоря́щий, многозначи́тельный; **~tale** ['telteil] спле́тник (-ица); болту́н(ья); доно́счик (-ица); ⊕ предупреди́тельное сигна́льное приспособле́ние.

temper ['tempə] **1.** умеря́ть [уме́рить]; смягча́ть [-чи́ть]; ⊕ отпуска́ть [-сти́ть]; закаля́ть [-ли́ть] (*a fig.*); **2.** хара́ктер; настрое́ние; раздраже́ние, гнев; ⊕ о́тпуск (мета́лла); **~ament** [-rəmənt] темпера́мент; **~amental** [tempərə'mentl] □ темпера́ментный; **~ance** ['tempərəns] уме́ренность *f*; **~ate** [-rit] □ уме́ренный, возде́ржанный; **~ature** ['tempritʃə] температу́ра.

tempest ['tempist] бу́ря; **~uous** [tem'pestjuəs] □ бу́рный, бу́йный.

temple ['templ] храм; *anat.* висо́к.

tempor|al ['tempərəl] □ вре́менный; мирско́й, све́тский; **~ary** [-rəri] □ вре́менный; **~ize** [-raiz] стара́ться вы́играть вре́мя; приспособля́ться к обстоя́тельствам.

tempt [tempt] искуша́ть [-уси́ть], соблазня́ть [-ни́ть]; привлека́ть [-е́чь]; **~ation** [temp'teiʃən] искуше́ние, собла́зн; **~ing** [-tiŋ] □ зама́нчивый, соблазни́тельный.

ten [ten] **1.** де́сять; **2.** деся́ток.

tenable ['tenəbl] про́чный; ⚔ обороноспосо́бный.

tenaci|ous [ti'neiʃəs] □ упо́рный; це́пкий; вя́зкий; **~ty** [ti'næsiti] це́пкость *f*; сто́йкость *f*, упо́рство.

tenant ['tenənt] нанима́тель(ница *f*) *m*; аренда́тор; жи́тель(ница *f*) *m*.

tend [tend] *v/i.* име́ть скло́нность (to к Д); клони́ться; направля́ться [-ра́виться]; *v/t.* [по]забо́титься о (П); уха́живать, [по]смотре́ть за (Т); ⊕ обслу́живать [-и́ть]; **~ance** ['tendəns] уха́живание (of за Т); присмо́тр (of за Т); **~ency** [-si] тенде́нция; накло́нность *f*.

tender ['tendə] **1.** □ *com.* не́жный; мя́гкий; сла́бый (о здоро́вье); чувстви́тельный; ла́сковый; чу́ткий; **2.** (официа́льное) предложе́ние; зая́вка (*part.* ✝); 🚂 те́ндер; ⚓ посы́льное су́дно; плаву́чая ба́за; legal ~ зако́нное платёжное сре́дство; **3.** предлага́ть [-ложи́ть]; представля́ть [-а́вить] (докуме́нты); приноси́ть [-нести́] (извине́ние, благода́рность); **~foot** F нови́чо́к; **~ness** [-nis] не́жность *f*.

tendon ['tendən] *anat.* сухожи́лие.

tendril ['tendril] ⚘ у́сик.

tenement ['tenimənt] снима́емая кварти́ра; ~ house многокварти́рный дом.

tenor ['tenə] ♪ те́нор; тече́ние, направле́ние; укла́д (жи́зни); о́бщий смысл (ре́чи и т. п.).

tens|e [tens] **1.** *gr.* вре́мя *n*; **2.** □ натя́нутый; возбуждённый; напряжённый; **~ion** ['tenʃən] напряже́ние (*a.* ⚡); натяже́ние; *pol.* напряжённость *f*; натя́нутость *f*.

tent[1] [tent] **1.** пала́тка, тент; **2.** размеща́ть в пала́тках; жить в пала́тках.

tent[2] [~] **1.** тампо́н; **2.** вставля́ть тампо́н в (В).

tentacle ['tentəkl] *zo.* щу́пальце.

tentative ['tentətiv] □ про́бный; эксперимента́льный; **~ly** в ви́де о́пыта.

tenth [tenθ] **1.** деся́тый; **2.** деся́тая часть *f*.

tenure ['tenjuə] владе́ние; пребыва́ние (в до́лжности); срок владе́ния.

tepid ['tepid] □ теплова́тый.

term [tə:m] **1.** преде́л; срок; семе́стр; те́рмин; ⚖ член; ⚖ се́ссия; день упла́ты аре́нды и т. п.; ~s *pl.* усло́вия; be on good (bad) ~s быть в хоро́ших (плохи́х) отноше́ниях; come to ~s прийти́ к соглаше́нию; **2.** выража́ть [вы́разить]; наз(ы)ва́ть; [на]именова́ть.

termina|l ['tə:minl] **1.** □ заключи́тельный; коне́чный; семестро́вый; **2.** коне́чный пункт; коне́чный слог; экза́мен в конце́ семе́стра; ⚡ зажи́м; *Am.* 🚂 коне́чная ста́нция; **~te** [-neit] конча́ть(ся) [ко́нчить(ся)]; **~tion** [tə:mi'neiʃən] оконча́ние; коне́ц.

terminus ['tə:minəs] 🚂 коне́чная ста́нция.

terrace ['terəs] терра́са; на́сыпь *f*; ряд домо́в; **~d** [-t] располо́женный терра́сами.

terrestrial [ti'restriəl] □ земно́й; *zo.* сухопу́тный.

terrible ['terəbl] □ ужа́сный, стра́шный.

terri|fic [tə'rifik] (~ally) ужаса́ющий; F великоле́пный; **~fy** ['terifai] *v/t.* ужаса́ть [-сну́ть].
territor|ial [teri'tɔ:riəl] **1.** □ территориа́льный; земе́льный; ♀ Army, Force территориа́льная а́рмия; **2.** ⚔ солда́т территориа́льной а́рмии; **~y** ['teritəri] террито́рия; о́бласть *f*; сфе́ра.
terror ['terə] у́жас; терро́р; **~ize** [-raiz] терроризова́ть (*im*)*pf*.
terse [tə:s] □ сжа́тый, вырази́тельный (стиль).
test [test] **1.** испыта́ние; крите́рий; про́ба; ана́лиз; ⚗ реакти́в; *attr.* испыта́тельный; про́бный; **2.** подверга́ть испыта́нию, прове́рке, (⚗) де́йствию реакти́ва.
testify ['testifai] дава́ть показа́ние, свиде́тельствовать (to в по́льзу Р, against про́тив Р, on о П).
testimon|ial [testi'mounjəl] аттеста́т; рекоменда́тельное письмо́; **~y** ['testimeni] у́стное показа́ние; пи́сьменное свиде́тельство.
test-tube ⚗ проби́рка.
testy ['testi] □ вспы́льчивый, раздражи́тельный.
tether ['teðə] **1.** при́вязь *f* (живо́тного); come to the end of one's ~ дойти́ до то́чки; **2.** привя́зывать [-за́ть] (живо́тное).
text [tekst] текст; те́ма (про́поведи); **~book** уче́бник, руково́дство.
textile ['tekstail] **1.** тексти́льный; **2.** ~s *pl.* тексти́льные изде́лия *n/pl.*; ткани *f/pl.*
texture ['tekstʃə] ткань *f*; ка́чество тка́ни; строе́ние, структу́ра (ко́жи и т. п.).
than [ðæn,ðən] чем, не́жели.
thank [θæŋk] **1.** [по]благодари́ть (В); ~ you благодарю́ вас; **2.** ~s *pl.* спаси́бо!; ~s to благодаря́ (Д); **~ful** ['θæŋkful] □ благода́рный; **~less** [-lis] □ неблагода́рный; **~sgiving** [θæŋksgiviŋ] благода́рственный моле́бен.
that [ðæt, ðət] **1.** *pron.* тот, та, то; те *pl.*; (*a.* э́тот и т. д.); кото́рый и т. д.; **2.** *cj.* что; что́бы.
thatch (θætʃ] **1.** соло́менная и́ли тростнико́вая кры́ша; **2.** крыть соло́мой и́ли тростнико́м.
thaw [θɔ:] **1.** о́ттепель *f*; та́яние; **2.** *v/i.* [рас]та́ять; отта́ивать [отта́ять]; *v/t.* раста́пливать [растопи́ть] (снег и т. п.).
the [ði:; пе́ред гла́сными ði; пе́ред согла́сными ðə] **1.** определённый член, арти́кль; **2.** *adv.* ~ ... ~ ... чем ..., тем ...
theatr|e ['θiətə] теа́тр; *fig.* аре́на; ~ of war теа́тр вое́нных де́йствий; **~ic(al** □) [θi'ætrik, -trikəl] театра́льный (*a. fig.*); сцени́ческий.
theft [θeft] воровство́, кра́жа.
their [ðεə] *pron. poss.* (от they) их; свой, своя́, своё, свои́ *pl.*; **~s** [ðεəz] *pron. poss. pred.* их, свой и т. д.
them [ðem, ðəm] *pron. pers.* (ко́свенный паде́ж от they) их, им.
theme [θi:m] те́ма, предме́т (разгово́ра и т. п.); шко́льное сочине́ние.
themselves [ðem'selvz] *pron. refl.* себя́, -ся; *emphasis* са́ми.
then [ðen] **1.** *adv.* тогда́; пото́м, зате́м; **2.** *cj.* тогда́, в тако́м слу́чае; зна́чит; **3.** *adj.* тогда́шний.
thence *lit.* [ðens] отту́да; с того́ вре́мени; *fig.* отсю́да, из э́того.
theolog|ian [θiə'loudʒiən] богосло́в; **~y** [θi'ɔlədʒi] богосло́вие.
theor|etic(al □) [θiə'retik, -tikəl] теорети́ческий; **~ist** ['θiərist] теоре́тик; **~y** ['θiəri] тео́рия.
there [ðεə] там, туда́; ~! вот!, ну!; ~ is, ~ are [ðə'riz, ðə'rɑ:] есть, име́ется, име́ются; **~about(s)** ['ðεərəbaut(s)] побли́зости; о́коло э́того, приблизи́тельно; **~after** [ðεər'ɑ:ftə] с э́того вре́мени; **~by** ['ðεə'bai] посре́дством э́того; таки́м о́бразом; **~fore** ['ðεəfɔ:] поэ́тому; сле́довательно; **~upon** ['ðεərə'pɔn] по́сле того́, вслед за те́м; вследствие того́.
thermo|meter [θə'mɔmitə] термо́метр, гра́дусник; **~s** ['θə:mɔs] (*or* ~ flask, ~ bottle) те́рмос.
these [ði:z] *pl.* от this.
thes|is ['θi:sis], *pl.* **~es** [-si:z] те́зис; диссерта́ция.
they [ðei] *pron. pers.* они́.
thick [θik] **1.** □ *com.* то́лстый; густо́й; пло́тный; хри́плый (го́лос); F глу́пый; ~ with гу́сто покры́тый (Т); **2.** ча́ща; *fig.* гу́ща; in the ~ of в са́мой гу́ще (Р); в разга́ре (Р); **~en** ['θikən] [по]толсте́ть; сгуща́ть(ся) [сгусти́ть(ся)]; учаща́ться [участи́ться]; **~et** ['θikit] ча́ща; за́росли *f/pl.*; **~-headed** тупоголо́вый, тупоу́мный; **~ness** ['θiknis] толщина́; пло́тность *f*; сгущённость *f*; **~-set** ['θik'set] гу́сто наса́женный; корена́стый; **~-skinned** (*a. fig.*) толстоко́жий.
thie|f [θi:f], *pl.* ~ves [θi:vz] вор; **~ve** [θi:v] *v/t.* [у]кра́сть; *v/i.* ворова́ть.
thigh [θai] бедро́.
thimble ['θimbl] напёрсток.
thin [θin] **1.** □ *com.* то́нкий; худо́й, худоща́вый; ре́дкий; жи́дкий; in a ~ house в полупусто́м за́ле (теа́тра); **2.** де́лать(ся) то́нким, утонча́ть(ся) [-чи́ть(ся)]; [по]реде́ть; [по]худе́ть.
thing [θiŋ] вещь *f*; предме́т; де́ло; ~s *pl.* ли́чные ве́щи *f/pl.*; бага́ж; оде́жда; принадле́жности *f/pl.*; the ~ (не́что) са́мое ва́жное, ну́жное; ~s are going better положе́ние улучша́ется.

think [θiŋk] [*irr.*] *v/i.* [по]ду́мать (of, about о П); мы́слить; полага́ть; вспомина́ть [вспо́мнить] (of о П); намерева́ться (+ *inf.*); приду́м(ыв)ать (of В); *v/t.* счита́ть [счесть]; ~ much of быть высо́кого мне́ния о (П).
third [θə:d] **1.** тре́тий; **2.** треть *f.*
thirst [θə:st] **1.** жа́жда; **2.** жа́ждать (for, after Р) (*part. fig.*); **~y** ['θəsti] □ томи́мый жа́ждой; I am ~ я хочу́ пить.
thirt|een ['θə:ti:n] трина́дцать; **~eenth** ['θə:'ti:nθ] трина́дцатый; **~ieth** ['θə:tiiθ] тридца́тый; **~y** ['θə:ti] три́дцать.
this [ðis] *pron. demonstr.* (*pl.* these) э́тот, э́та, э́то; э́ти *pl.*; ~ morning сего́дня у́тром.
thistle ['θisl] ⚘ чертополо́х.
thong [θɔŋ] реме́нь *m*; плеть *f.*
thorn [θɔ:n] ⚘ шип; колю́чка; *fig.* ~ s *pl.* те́рния *n/pl.*; **~y** ['θɔ:ni] колю́чий; *fig.* тяжёлый, терни́стый.
thorough ['θʌrə] □ основа́тельный; соверше́нный; **~ly** *adv.* основа́тельно, доскона́льно; соверше́нно; **~bred 1.** чистокро́вный; **2.** чистокро́вное живо́тное; **~fare** прохо́д; прое́зд; гла́вная арте́рия (го́рода); **~going** радика́льный.
those [ðouz] *pl.* от that.
though [ðou] *conj.* хотя́; да́же е́сли бы, хотя́ бы; *adv.* тем не ме́нее; одна́ко; всё-таки; as ~ как бу́дто, сло́вно.
thought [θɔ:t] **1.** *pt.* и *p. pt.* от think; **2.** мысль *f*; мышле́ние; размышле́ние; забо́та; внима́тельность *f*; **~ful** ['θɔ:tful] □ заду́мчивый; глубокомы́сленный; забо́тливый; внима́тельный (of к Д); **~less** ['θɔ:tlis] □ беспе́чный; необду́манный; невнима́тельный (of к Д).
thousand ['θauzənd] ты́сяча; **~th** ['θauzən(t)θ] **1.** ты́сячный; **2.** ты́сячная часть *f.*
thrash [θræʃ] [с]молоти́ть; [по]би́ть; F побежда́ть [-еди́ть] (в состяза́нии); ~ out тща́тельно обсужда́ть (вопро́с и т. п.); *s.* thresh; **~ing** ['θræʃiŋ] молотьба́; побо́и *m/pl.*, F взбу́чка.
thread [θred] **1.** ни́тка, нить *f*; *fig.* нить *f*; ⊕ (винтова́я) резьба́, наре́зка; **2.** продева́ть ни́тку в (иго́лку); нани́зывать [-за́ть] (бу́сы); ⊕ нареза́ть [-е́зать]; **~bare** ['θredbɛə] потёртый, изно́шенный; *fig.* изби́тый.
threat [θret] угро́за; **~en** ['θretn] *v/t.* [при]грози́ть, угрожа́ть (Д with Т); *v/i.* грози́ть.
three [θri:] **1.** три; **2.** тро́йка; **~fold** ['θri:fould] тройно́й; *adv.* втройне́; **~pence** ['θrepəns] три пе́нса (моне́та); **~-score** ['θri:'skɔ:] шестьдеся́т.
thresh [θreʃ] ⚒ [с]молоти́ть; *s.* thrash; ~ out *fig.* = thrash out.
threshold ['θreʃ(h)ould] поро́г.
threw [θru:] *pt.* от throw.
thrice [θrais] три́жды.
thrift [θrift] бережли́вость *f*, эконо́мность *f*; **~less** ['θriftlis] □ расточи́тельный; **~y** ['θrifti] □ эконо́мный, бережли́вый.
thrill [θril] **1.** *v/t.* [вз]волнова́ть; приводи́ть в тре́пет, [вз]будора́жить; *v/i.* [за]трепета́ть (with от Р); [вз]волнова́ться; **2.** тре́пет; глубо́кое волне́ние; не́рвная дрожь *f*; **~er** ['θrilə] сенсацио́нный рома́н (*mst* детекти́вный).
thrive [θraiv] [*irr.*] процвета́ть; преуспева́ть; разраста́ться; **~n** ['θrivn] *p. pt.* от thrive.
throat [θrout] го́рло, гло́тка; clear one's ~ отка́шливаться [-ляться].
throb [θrɔb] **1.** пульси́ровать; си́льно би́ться; **2.** пульса́ция; бие́ние; *fig.* тре́пет.
throes [θrouz] *pl.* му́ки *f/pl.*; аго́ния; родовы́е му́ки *f/pl.*
throne [θroun] трон, престо́л.
throng [θrɔŋ] **1.** толпа́, толчея́; **2.** [с]толпи́ться; заполня́ть [-о́лнить] (о толпе́).
throttle ['θrɔtl] **1.** [за]души́ть (за го́рло); ⊕ дроссели́ровать; **2.** ⊕ дро́ссель *m.*
through [θru:] **1.** че́рез (В); сквозь (В); по (Д); *adv.* наскво́зь; от нача́ла до конца́; **2.** прямо́й, беспереса́дочный (по́езд и т. п.); сквозно́й (биле́т); **~out** [θru:'aut] **1.** *prp.* че́рез (В); по всему́, всей ...; **2.** повсю́ду; во всех отноше́ниях.
throve [θrouv] *pt.* от thrive.
throw [θrou] **1.** [*irr.*] броса́ть [бро́сить], кида́ть [ки́нуть], мета́ть [метну́ть]; ~ over перебра́сывать [-бро́сить]; покида́ть [-и́нуть] (друзе́й); ~ up изверга́ть [-е́ргнуть]; вски́дывать [вски́нуть]; **2.** бросо́к; броса́ние; **~n** [-n] *p. pt.* от throw.
thru *Am.* = through.
thrum [θrʌm] бренча́ть, тре́нькать.
thrush [θrʌʃ] дрозд.
thrust [θrʌst] **1.** толчо́к; уда́р; ⊕ распо́р; end ~ осево́е давле́ние; **2.** [*irr.*] толка́ть [-кну́ть]; ты́кать [ткнуть]; ~ o. s. into *fig.* втира́ться [втере́ться] в (В); ~ upon a p. навя́зывать [-за́ть] (Д).
thud [θʌd] **1.** глухо́й звук; **2.** па́дать с глухи́м зву́ком.
thug *Am.* [θʌg] уби́йца *m*, головоре́з.
thumb [θʌm] **1.** большо́й па́лец (руки́); **2.** захва́тывать [захвата́ть], загрязня́ть [-ни́ть] (па́льцами); **~tack** *Am.* чертёжная кно́пка.
thump [θʌmp] **1.** глухо́й стук; тяжёлый уда́р; **2.** наноси́ть тяжёлый уда́р (Д).

thunder ['θʌndə] **1.** гром; **2.** [за-] греме́ть; it ~s гром греми́т; *fig.* мета́ть гро́мы и мо́лнии; **~bolt** уда́р мо́лнии; **~clap** уда́р гро́ма; **~ous** ['θʌndərəs] □ грозово́й; громово́й, оглуша́ющий; **~-storm** гроза́; **~-struck** сражённый уда́ром мо́лнии; *fig.* как гро́мом поражённый.

Thursday ['θə:zdi] четве́рг.

thus [ðʌs] так, таки́м о́бразом.

thwart [θwɔ:t] **1.** ба́нка (скамья́ для гребца́); **2.** меша́ть исполне́нию (жела́ний и т. п.), расстра́ивать [-ро́ить].

tick [tik] **1.** *zo.* клещ; креди́т, счёт; ти́канье; тик (мате́рия); **2.** *v/i.* ти́кать; *v/t.* брать и́ли отпуска́ть в креди́т; ~ off отмеча́ть «пти́чкой»; F проб(и)ра́ть, отде́л(ыв)ать.

ticket ['tikit] **1.** биле́т; ярлы́к; удостовере́ние; квита́нция; *Am.* спи́сок кандида́тов па́ртии; **2.** прикрепля́ть ярлы́к к (Д); **~office,** *Am.* **~-window** биле́тная ка́сса.

tickl|e ['tikl] [по]щекота́ть; **~ish** [-iʃ] □ щекотли́вый.

tidal ['taidl]: ~ wave прили́вная волна́.

tide [taid] **1.** low ~ отли́в; high ~ прили́в; *fig.* тече́ние; **2.** *fig.* ~ over преодоле́(ва́)ть.

tidings ['taidiŋz] *pl.* но́вости *f/pl.*, изве́стия *n/pl.*

tidy ['taidi] **1.** опря́тный, аккура́тный; значи́тельный; **2.** приб(и)ра́ть; приводи́ть в поря́док.

tie [tai] **1.** связь *f*; га́лстук; ра́вный счёт (голосо́в и́ли очко́в); ничья́; ⊕ скре́па; *pl.* у́зы *f/pl.*; **2.** *v/t.* завя́зывать [-за́ть]; свя́зывать [-за́ть]; *v/i.* игра́ть вничью́; сравня́ть счёт.

tier [tiə] ряд; я́рус.

tie-up связь *f*; сою́з; *Am.* прекраще́ние рабо́ты и́ли у́личного движе́ния.

tiger ['taigə] тигр.

tight [tait] □ пло́тный, компа́ктный; непроница́емый; туго́й; ту́го натя́нутый; те́сный; F подвы́пивший; F ~ place *fig.* затрудни́тельное положе́ние; **~en** ['taitn] стя́гивать(ся) [стяну́ть(ся)] (*a.* ~ up); затя́гивать [-яну́ть]; подтя́гивать [-яну́ть]; **~-fisted** скупо́й; **~ness** ['taitnis] пло́тность *f* и т. д.; **~s** [taits] *pl.* трико́ *n indecl.*

tigress ['taigris] тигри́ца.

tile [tail] **1.** черепи́ца; ка́фель *m*, изразе́ц; **2.** крыть черепи́цей и т. д.

till [til] **1.** де́нежный я́щик, ка́сса (в прила́вке); **2.** *prp.* до (Р); **3.** *cj.* пока́; **4.** ⚒ возде́л(ыв)ать (В); [вс]паха́ть; **~age** ['tilidʒ] па́шня; обрабо́тка земли́.

tilt [tilt] **1.** накло́нное положе́ние, накло́н; уда́р копьём; **2.** наклоня́ть(ся) [-ни́ть(ся)]; опроки́дывать(ся) [-и́нуть(ся)]; би́ться на ко́пьях; ~ against боро́ться с (Т).

timber ['timbə] **1.** лесоматериа́л, строево́й лес; ба́лка; **2.** пло́тничать; столя́рничать; стро́ить из де́рева.

time [taim] **1.** вре́мя *n*; пери́од; пора́; раз; такт; темп; at the same ~ в то же вре́мя; for the ~ being пока́, на вре́мя; in (*or* on) ~ во́время; **2.** (уда́чно) выбира́ть вре́мя для (Р); назнача́ть вре́мя для (Р); хронометри́ровать (*im*)*pf.*; **~ly** ['taimli] своевре́менный; **~-piece** часы́ *m/pl.*; **~-table** 🚂 расписа́ние.

timid ['timid] □, **timorous** ['timərəs] □ ро́бкий.

tin [tin] **1.** о́лово; (*a.* **~-plate**) жесть *f*; жестя́нка; **2.** [по]луди́ть; [за-] консерви́ровать (в жестя́нках).

tincture ['tiŋktʃə] **1.** ⚕ тинкту́ра; *fig.* отте́нок; **2.** окра́шивать [окра́сить].

tinfoil ['tin'fɔil] фо́льга.

tinge [tindʒ] **1.** слегка́ окра́шивать; *fig.* придава́ть отте́нок (Д); **2.** лёгкая окра́ска; *fig.* отте́нок.

tingle ['tiŋgl] испы́тывать и́ли вызыва́ть пока́лывание (в онеме́вших чле́нах), пощи́пывание (на моро́зе), зуд, звон в уша́х и т. п.

tinker ['tiŋkə] **1.** луди́льщик; **2.** неуме́ло чини́ть (at В); вози́ться (at с Т).

tinkle ['tiŋkl] звя́кать [-кнуть].

tin-plate ['tin'pleit] (бе́лая) жесть *f.*

tinsel ['tinsəl] блёстки *f/pl.*; мишура́.

tinsmith ['tinsmiθ] жестя́н(щ)ик.

tint [tint] **1.** кра́ска; отте́нок, тон; **2.** слегка́ окра́шивать.

tiny ['taini] □ о́чень ма́ленький, кро́шечный.

tip [tip] **1.** (то́нкий) коне́ц; наконе́чник; ко́нчик; чаевы́е *pl.*; ча́стная информа́ция; намёк; лёгкий толчо́к; **2.** снабжа́ть наконе́чником; опроки́дывать [-и́нуть]; дава́ть на чай (Д); дава́ть ча́стную информа́цию (Д).

tipple ['tipl] пья́нствовать; вы́пи(ва́)ть, пить.

tipsy ['tipsi] подвы́пивший.

tiptoe ['tip(')tou]: on ~ на цы́почках.

tire [taiə] **1.** о́бод колеса́; *mot.* ши́на; **2.** утомля́ть [-ми́ть]; уст(ав)а́ть; **~d** [-d] уста́лый; **~less** ['taiəlis] неутоми́мый; **~some** [-səm] утоми́тельный; надое́дливый; ску́чный.

tiro ['taiərou] новичо́к.

tissue ['tisju:] ткань *f* (*a. biol.*); *fig.* сплете́ние (лжи и т. п.); **~-paper** [-'peipə] шёлковая бума́га; папиро́сная бума́га.

titbit ['titbit] лáкомый кусóчек; *fig.* пикáнтная нóвость *f.*
titillate ['titileit] [по]щекотáть.
title ['taitl] заглáвие; тúтул; звáние; ⚖ прáво сóбственности (to на B); ~d титулóванный.
titter ['titə] **1.** хихúканье; **2.** хихúкать [-кнуть].
tittle ['titl] малéйшая частúца; to a ~ тютелька в тютельку; **~-tattle** [-tætl] сплéтни *f/pl.*, болтовня́.
to [tu:, tu, tə] *prp.* (укáзывает на направлéние движéния, цель): к (Д); в (В); на (В); (укáзывает на лицó, по отношéнию к котóрому чтó-либо происхóдит, и соответствует рýсскому дáтельному падежý): ~ me *etc.* мне и т. д.; ~ and fro *adv.* взад и вперёд; (частúца, слýжащая показáтелем инфинитúва): ~ work рабóтать; I weep ~ think of it я плáчу, дýмая об э́том.
toad [toud] жáба; **~stool** погáнка (гриб); **~y** ['toudi] **1.** подхалúм; **2.** подхалúмничать пéред (Т).
toast [toust] **1.** гренóк; тост; **2.** приготовля́ть гренкú; поджáри(ва)ть; *fig.* грéть(ся) (у огня́); пить за чьё-либо здорóвье, пить за (В).
tobacco [tə'bækou] табáк; **~nist** [tə'bækənist] торгóвец табáчными издéлиями.
toboggan [tə'bɔgən] **1.** салáзки *f/pl.*; **2.** катáться на салáзках (с горы́).
today [tə'dei] сегóдня; в нáше врéмя.
toe [tou] **1.** пáлец (на ногé); носóк (чулкá, башмакá); **2.** касáться носкóм (P).
together [tə'geðə] вмéсте; друг с дрýгом; подря́д, непреры́вно.
toil [tɔil] **1.** тяжёлый труд; **2.** усúленно трудúться; идтú с трудóм.
toilet ['tɔilit] туалéт (одевáние и костю́м); убóрная; **~-table** туалéтный стóлик.
toilsome ['tɔilsəm] □ трýдный, утомúтельный.
token ['toukən] знак; примéта; подáрок на пáмять; ~ money биллóнные дéньги *f/pl.*
told [tould] *pt.* и *p. pt.* от tell.
tolera|ble ['tɔlərəbl] □ терпúмый; снóсный; **~nce** [-rəns] терпúмость *f*; **~nt** [-rənt] □ терпúмый; **~te** [-reit] [по]терпéть, допускáть [-стúть]; **~tion** [tɔlə'reiʃən] терпúмость *f*; допущéние.
toll [toul] пóшлина; *fig.* дань *f*; **~-bar, ~-gate** застáва (где взимáется пóшлина).
tom [tɔm]: ~ cat кот.
tomato [tə'mɑ:tou, *Am.* tə'meitou], *pl.* **~es** [-z] помидóр, томáт.
tomb [tu:m] могúла; надгрóбный пáмятник.
tomboy ['tɔmbɔi] сорванéц (о дéвочке).
tomfool ['tɔm'fu:l] шут; дурáк.
tomorrow [tə'mɔrou] зáвтра.
ton [tʌn] (metric) тóнна (= 1000 кг).
tone [toun] **1.** тон (♪, *paint.*, *fig.*); интонáция; **2.** придавáть желáтельный тон (звýку, крáске); настрáивать [-рóить] (инструмéнт).
tongs [tɔŋz] *pl.* щипцы́ *m/pl.*, клещú *f/pl.*
tongue [tʌŋ] язы́к; hold one's ~ держáть язы́к за зубáми; **~-tied** ['tʌŋtaid] косноязы́чный; молчалúвый.
tonic ['tɔnik] **1.** (~ally) тонúческий (*a.* ♪); укрепля́ющий; **2.** ♪ основнóй тон; ⚕ укрепля́ющее срéдство.
tonight [tə'nait] сегóдня вéчером.
tonnage ['tʌnidʒ] ⚓ тоннáж; грузоподъёмность *f*; грузовáя пóшлина.
tonsil ['tɔnsl] *anat.* глáнда, миндáлина.
too [tu:] тáкже, тóже; слúшком; óчень.
took [tuk] *pt.* от take.
tool [tu:l] (рабóчий) инструмéнт; орýдие (*a. fig.*)
toot [tu:t] **1.** звук рожкá, гудóк; **2.** трубúть в рожóк.
tooth [tu:θ] (*pl.* teeth) зуб; **~ache** зубнáя боль *f*; **~-brush** зубнáя щётка; **~less** ['tu:θlis] □ беззýбый; **~pick** зубочúстка; **~some** ['tu:θsəm] вкýсный.
top [tɔp] **1.** вéрхняя часть *f*; верхýшка, вершúна (горы́); макýшка (головы́, дéрева); верх (автомобúля, лéстницы, странúцы); волчóк; at the ~ of one's voice во весь гóлос; on ~ наверхý; **2.** вы́сший, пéрвый; максимáльный (о скóрости и т. п.); **3.** покры́(вá)ть (свéрху); *fig.* превышáть [-ы́сить]; быть во главé (P).
toper ['toupə] пья́ница *m/f.*
top-hat F цилúндр (шля́па).
topic ['tɔpik] тéма, предмéт; **~al** ['tɔpikəl] мéстный; злободнéвный.
topmost ['tɔpmoust] сáмый вéрхний; сáмый вáжный.
topple ['tɔpl] опрокúдывать(ся) [-úнуть(ся)] (*a.* ~ over).
topsyturvy ['tɔpsi'tə:vi] □ вверх дном; шúворот-навы́ворот.
torch [tɔtʃ] фáкел; electric ~ кармáнный электрúческий фонáрь *m*; **~-light** свет фáкела; ~ procession фáкельное шéствие.
tore [tɔ:] *pt.* от tear.
torment **1.** ['tɔ:ment] мучéние, мýка; **2.** [tɔ:'ment] [из-, за]мýчить; изводúть [известú].
torn [tɔ:n] *p. pt.* от tear.
tornado [tɔ:'neidou] торнáдо *m indecl.*, смерч; ураráн *a. fig.*
torpedo [tɔ:'pi:dou] **1.** торпéда; **2.**

торпедировать (*im*)*pf*.; *fig*. взрывать [взорвать].
torpid ['tɔ:pid] □ онемелый, оцепенелый; вялый, апатичный; **~ity** [tɔ:'piditi], **torpor** ['tɔ:pə] оцепенение; апатия.
torrent ['tɔrənt] поток (*a. fig*.).
torrid ['tɔrid] жаркий, знойный.
tortoise ['tɔ:təs] *zo*. черепаха.
tortuous ['tɔ:tjuəs] □ извилистый; *fig*. уклончивый, неискренний.
torture ['tɔ:tʃə] **1.** пытка; **2.** пытать, [из-, за]мучить.
toss [tɔs] **1.** метание, бросание; толчок, сотрясение; (*a*. ~-up) бросание монеты (в орлянке); **2.** бросать [бросить]; беспокойно метаться (о больном); вскидывать [-инуть] (голову); подбрасывать [-росить] (*mst* ~ up); ~ (up) играть в орлянку; *sport* разыгрывать ворота.
tot [tɔt] F маленький ребёнок, малыш.
total ['toutl] **1.** □ полный, абсолютный; тотальный; общий; **2.** целое, сумма; итог; **3.** подводить итог, подсчитывать [-итать]; составлять в итоге; равняться (Д); **~itarian** [toutæli'tɛəriən] тоталитарный; **~ity** [tou'tæliti] вся сумма, всё количество.
totter ['tɔtə] идти неверной походкой; шататься [(по)шатнуться].
touch [tʌtʃ] **1.** осязание; прикосновение; *fig*. соприкосновение, общение; чуточка; примесь *f*; лёгкий приступ (болезни); ♪ туше *n indecl.*; штрих; **2.** трогать [тронуть] (В) (*a. fig*.); прикасаться [-коснуться], притрагиваться [-тронуться] к (Д); *fig*. касаться [коснуться] (Р), затрагивать [-ронуть] (В) (тему и т. п.); be **~ed** *fig*. быть тронутым; быть слегка помешанным; ~ up отдел(ыв)ать, поправлять [-авить] (несколькими штрихами); ~ at ⚓ заходить [зайти] в (порт); **~ing** ['tʌtʃiŋ] трогательный; **~stone** пробирный камень *m*, оселок; *fig*. пробный камень *m*; **~y** ['tʌtʃi] □ обидчивый; слишком чувствительный.
tough [tʌf] **1.** жёсткий; вязкий; упругий; выносливый; трудный; **2.** *Am*. хулиган; **~en** ['tʌfn] делать(ся) жёстким, плотным и т. д.; **~ness** ['tʌfnis] жёсткость *f* и т. д.
tour [tuə] **1.** круговое путешествие; турне *n indecl.*; тур, объезд; **2.** совершать путешествие или турне по (Д); путешествовать (through по Д); **~ist** ['tuərist] турист(ка); ~ agency бюро путешествий.
tournament [-nəmənt] турнир.
tousle ['tauzl] взъероши(ва)ть, растрёпывать [-репать].
tow [tou] ⚓ **1.** буксирный канат, трос; буксировка; take in ~ брать на буксир; **2.** буксировать; тянуть (баржу) на бечеве.
towards [tə'wɔ:dz, tɔ:dʒ] *prp*. (указывает на направление к предмету, отношение к чему-либо) по направлению к (Д); к (Д), по отношению к (Д); для (Р).
towel ['tauəl] полотенце.
tower ['tauə] **1.** башня; вышка; *fig*. опора; **2.** возвышаться [-ыситься] (above, over над Т) (*a. fig*.).
town [taun] **1.** город; **2.** *attr*. городской; ~ council городской совет; ~ hall ратуша; **~sfolk** ['taunzfouk], **~speople** [-pi:pl] горожане *m/pl*.; **~sman** ['taunzmən] горожанин; согражданин.
toxi|c(al □) ['tɔksik, -sikəl] ядовитый; **~n** ['tɔksin] токсин.
toy [tɔi] **1.** игрушка; забава; безделушка; **2.** *attr*. игрушечный; **3.** играть; забавляться; флиртовать; **~book** детская книга с картинками.
trace [treis] **1.** след; черта; постромка; **2.** [на]чертить; выслеживать [выследить] (В); прослеживать [-едить] (В); *a. fig*. [с]калькировать.
tracing [treisiŋ] чертёж на кальке.
track [træk] **1.** след; просёлочная дорога; тропинка; беговая дорожка; 🚂 колея, рельсовый путь *m*; **2.** следить за (Т); прослеживать [-едить] (В); ~ down, ~ out выслеживать [выследить] (В).
tract [trækt] трактат; брошюра; пространство, полоса (земли, воды).
tractable ['træktəbl] сговорчивый; поддающийся обработке.
tract|ion ['trækʃən] тяга; волочение; ~ engine тягач; **~or** [træ'ktə] ⊕ трактор.
trade [treid] **1.** профессия; ремесло; торговля; **2.** торговать (in Т; with с Т); обменивать [-нять] (for на В); ~ on использовать (*im*)*pf*.; **~-mark** фабричная марка; **~-price** оптовая цена; **~r** ['treidə] торговец; торговое судно; **~sman** ['treidzmən] торговец, лавочник; ремесленник; **~(s)-union** ['treid(z)'ju:njən] профсоюз; **~wind** ⚓ пассатный ветер.
tradition [trə'diʃən] традиция; предание; старый обычай; **~al** □ традиционный.
traffic [træfik] **1.** движение (уличное, железнодорожное и т. п.); торговля; ~ jam затор уличного движения; **2.** торговать.
traged|ian (trə'dʒi:diən] автор трагедии; трагик; **~y** ['trædʒidi] трагедия.
tragic(al □) ['trædʒik, -dʒikəl] трагический, трагичный.

trail [treil] **1.** след; тропа́; **2.** *v/t.* таска́ть, [по]тащи́ть, [по]волочи́ть; идти́ по сле́ду (Р); *v/i.* таска́ться, [по]тащи́ться; ♀ свиса́ть [сви́снуть]; **~er** ['treilə] *mot.* прице́п.
train [trein] **1.** по́езд; шлейф (пла́тья); цепь *f*, верени́ца; хвост (коме́ты, павли́на); сви́та, толпа́ (покло́нников); by ~ по́ездом; **2.** воспи́тывать [-та́ть]; приуча́ть [-чи́ть]; [на]тренирова́ть(ся); ⚔ обуча́ть [-чи́ть]; [вы́]дрессирова́ть.
trait [treit] черта́ (лица́, хара́ктера).
traitor ['treitə] преда́тель *m*, изме́нник.
tram [træm] *s.* ~-car, ~way; **~-car** ['træmkɑ:] ваго́н трамва́я.
tramp [træmp] **1.** бродя́га *m*; (до́лгое) путеше́ствие пешко́м; звук тяжёлых шаго́в; **2.** тяжело́ ступа́ть; тащи́ться с трудо́м; F то́пать; бродя́жничать; **~le** ['træmpl] топта́ть; тяжело́ ступа́ть; поп(и)ра́ть (В); ~ down зата́птывать [-топта́ть].
tramway ['træmwei] трамва́й.
trance [trɑ:ns] ⚕ транс; экста́з.
tranquil ['træŋkwil] □ споко́йный; **~lity** [træŋ'kwiliti] споко́йствие; **~lize** ['træŋkwilaiz] успока́ивать (-ся) [-ко́ить(ся)].
transact [træn'zækt] проводи́ть [-вести́] (де́ло), соверша́ть [-ши́ть]; **~ion** [-'zækʃən] де́ло, сде́лка; веде́ние, отправле́ние (де́ла); **~s** *pl.* труды́ *m/pl.*, протоко́лы *m/pl.* (нау́чного о́бщества).
transatlantic ['trænzət'læntik] трансатланти́ческий.
transcend [træn'send] переступа́ть преде́лы (Р); превосходи́ть [-взойти́], превыша́ть [-вы́сить].
transcribe [træns'kraib] перепи́сывать [-са́ть]; *gr.*, ♪ транскриби́ровать (*im*)*pf*.
transcript ['trænskript] ко́пия; **~ion** [træn'skripʃən] перепи́сывание; ко́пия; *gr.*, ♪ транскри́пция.
transfer 1. [træns'fə:] *v/t.* переноси́ть [-нести́], перемеща́ть [-мести́ть]; перед(ав)а́ть; переводи́ть [-вести́] (в друго́й го́род, на другу́ю рабо́ту); *v/i. Am.* переса́живаться [-се́сть]; **2.** ['trænsfə:] перено́с; переда́ча; трансфе́рт; перево́д; *Am.* переса́дка; **~able** [træns'fə:rəbl] предоста́вленный с пра́вом переда́чи; допуска́ющий переда́чу.
transfigure [træns'figə] видоизменя́ть [-ни́ть]; преобража́ть [-рази́ть].
transfix [-'fiks] пронза́ть [-зи́ть]; прока́лывать [-коло́ть]; **~ed** *fig.* прико́ванный к ме́сту (with от Р).
transform (-'fɔ:m] превраща́ть [-врати́ть]; преобразо́вывать [-зова́ть]; **~ation** [-fə'meiʃən] преобразова́ние; превраще́ние; ⚡ трансформа́ция.
transfuse [-'fu:z] перели́(ва́)ть; ⚕ де́лать перелива́ние (кро́ви); *fig.* перед(ав)а́ть (свой энтузиа́зм и т. п.).
transgress (-'gres] *v/t.* преступа́ть [-пи́ть], наруша́ть [-у́шить] (зако́н и т. п.); *v/i.* [со]греши́ть; **~ion** [-'greʃən] просту́пок; наруше́ние (зако́на и т. п.); **~or** [-'gresə] (право)наруши́тель(ница *f*) *m*; гре́шник (-ица).
transient ['trænʃənt] **1.** *s.* transitory; **2.** *Am.* прое́зжий (-жая).
transition [træn'siʒən] перехо́д; перехо́дный пери́од.
transitory ['trænsitəri] □ мимолётный, скороте́чный, скоропреходя́щий.
translat|e [trɑ:ns'leit] переводи́ть [-вести́] (from с Р, into на В); *fig.* перемеща́ть [-мести́ть]; **~ion** [trɑ:ns'leiʃən] перево́д.
translucent [trænz'lu:snt] просве́чивающий; полупрозра́чный.
transmigration [trænzmai'greiʃən] переселе́ние.
transmission [trænz'miʃən] переда́ча (*a.* ⊕); пересы́лка; ⊕ трансми́ссия; *radio* переда́ча; трансля́ция; *opt.* пропуска́ние.
transmit [trænz'mit] отправля́ть [-а́вить]; пос(ы)ла́ть; перед(ав)а́ть (*a. radio*); *opt.* пропуска́ть [-сти́ть]; **~ter** [-ə] переда́тчик (*a. radio*); *tel.* микрофо́н.
transmute [trænz'mju:t] превраща́ть [-рати́ть].
transparent [træns'pɛərənt] □ прозра́чный.
transpire [-'paiə] испаря́ться [-ри́ться]; проса́чиваться [-сочи́ться]; *fig.* обнару́жи(ва)ться.
transplant [-'plɑ:nt] переса́живать [-сади́ть]; *fig.* переселя́ть [-ли́ть].
transport 1. [træns'pɔ:t] перевози́ть [-везти́]; перемеща́ть [-мести́ть]; *fig.* увлека́ть [-е́чь], восхища́ть [-ити́ть]; **2.** ['trænspɔ:t] тра́нспорт; перево́зка; тра́нспортное (-ные) сре́дство (-ства *n/pl.*); be in **~s** быть вне себя́ (of от Р); **~ation** [trænspɔ:'teiʃən] перево́зка.
transpose [træns'pouz] перемеща́ть [-мести́ть]; переставля́ть [-а́вить] (слова́ и т. п.); ♪ транспони́ровать (*im*)*pf*.
transverse ['trænzvə:s] □ попере́чный.
trap [træp] **1.** лову́шка, западня́; капка́н; **2.** расставля́ть лову́шки; лови́ть в лову́шку; *fig.* замани́ть в лову́шку; **~-door** ['træpdɔ:] люк; опускна́я дверь *f*.
trapeze [trə'pi:z] трапе́ция.
trapper ['træpə] охо́тник, ста́вящий капка́ны.

trappings ['træpiŋz] *pl.* ко́нская (пара́дная) сбру́я; пара́дный мунди́р.

traps [træps] *pl.* F ли́чные ве́щи *f/pl.*; бага́ж.

trash [træʃ] хлам; отбро́сы *m/pl.*; *fig.* дрянь *f*; макулату́ра (о кни́ге); вздор, ерунда́; **~y** ['træʃi] □ дрянно́й.

travel ['trævl] **1.** *v/i.* путеше́ствовать; е́здить, [по]е́хать; передвига́ться [-и́нуться]; распространя́ться [-ни́ться] (о све́те, зву́ке); *v/t.* объезжа́ть [-е́здить, -е́хать]; проезжа́ть [-е́хать] (... км в час и т. п.); **2.** путеше́ствие; ⊕ ход; (пере)движе́ние; **~(l)er** [-ə] путеше́ственник (-ица).

traverse ['trævə:s] **1.** пересека́ть [-се́чь]; проходи́ть [пройти́] (В); **2.** попере́чина; ⚠, ⚔ тра́верс.

travesty ['trævisti] **1.** паро́дия; искаже́ние; **2.** пароди́ровать; искажа́ть [исказить].

trawler ['trɔ:lə] тра́льщик.

tray [trei] подно́с; лото́к.

treacher|ous ['tretʃərəs] □ преда́тельский, вероло́мный; ненадёжный; **~y** [-ri] преда́тельство, вероло́мство.

treacle ['tri:kl] па́тока.

tread [tred] **1.** [*irr.*] ступа́ть [-пи́ть]; ~ down зата́птывать [затопта́ть]; **2.** по́ступь *f*, похо́дка; ступе́нька; *mot.* проте́ктор; **~le** ['tredl] педа́ль *f* (велосипе́да); подно́жка (шве́йной маши́ны).

treason ['tri:zn] изме́на; **~able** [-əbl] □ изме́ннический.

treasure ['treʒə] **1.** сокро́вище; **2.** храни́ть; высо́ко́ цени́ть; **~r** [-rə] казначе́й.

treasury ['treʒəri] казначе́йство; сокро́вищница.

treat [tri:t] **1.** *v/t.* обраба́тывать [-бо́тать]; ⚕ лечи́ть; угоща́ть [угости́ть] (to Т); обраща́ться [обрати́ться] с (Т), обходи́ться [обойти́сь] с (Т); *v/i.* ~ of име́ть предме́том, обсужда́ть [-уди́ть] (В); ~ with вести́ перегово́ры с (Т); **2.** удово́льствие, наслажде́ние; угоще́ние; **~ise** ['tri:tiz] тракта́т; **~ment** ['tri:tmənt]; обрабо́тка (Т); лече́ние; обраще́ние (of с Т); **~y** ['tri:ti] догово́р.

treble ['trebl] **1.** □ тройно́й, утро́енный; **2.** тройно́е коли́чество; ♪ ди́скант; **3.** утра́ивать(ся) [утро́ить(ся)].

tree [tri:] де́рево; родосло́вное де́рево; (сапо́жная) коло́дка.

trefoil ['trefɔil] трили́стник.

trellis ['trelis] **1.** решётка; ⚘ шпале́ра; **2.** обноси́ть решёткой; сажа́ть (расте́ния) шпале́рой.

tremble ['trembl] [за]дрожа́ть, [за-] трясти́сь (with от Р).

tremendous [tri'mendəs] □ стра́шный, ужа́сный; F грома́дный.

tremor ['tremə] дрожа́ние.

tremulous ['tremjuləs] □ дрожа́щий; тре́петный, ро́бкий.

trench [trentʃ] **1.** кана́ва; ⚔ транше́я, око́п; **2.** рыть рвы, транше́и и т. п.; вска́пывать [вскопа́ть]; ~ (up)on посяга́ть [-гну́ть] на (В); **~ant** ['tren(t)ʃənt] □ ре́зкий, ко́лкий.

trend [trend] **1.** направле́ние (*a. fig.*); *fig.* тече́ние; напра́вленность *f*; **2.** отклоня́ться [-ни́ться] (to к Д) (о грани́це и т. п.); име́ть тенде́нцию (towards к Д).

trespass ['trespəs] **1.** нару́шать грани́цы (on Р); соверша́ть просту́пок; злоупотребля́ть [-би́ть] (on Т); **2.** наруше́ние грани́ц; злоупотребле́ние ([up]on Т); **~er** [-ə] наруши́тель грани́ц; правонаруши́тель *m*.

tress [tres] ло́кон; коса́.

trestle ['tresl] ко́злы *f/pl.*; подста́вка.

trial ['traiəl] испыта́ние; о́пыт, про́ба; ⚖ суде́бное разбира́тельство; суд; on ~ на испыта́нии, на испыта́ние; под судо́м; give *a. p.* a ~ нанима́ть кого́-либо на испыта́тельный срок; ~ ... *attr.* про́бный, испыта́тельный.

triang|le ['traiæŋgl] треуго́льник; **~ular** [trai'æŋgjulə] □ треуго́льный.

tribe [traib] пле́мя *n*; *contp.* компа́ния.

tribun|al [trai'bju:nl] суд; трибуна́л; **~e** ['tribju:n] трибу́на; трибу́н.

tribut|ary ['tribjutəri] **1.** □ платя́щий дань; *fig.* подчинённый; спосо́бствующий; **2.** да́нник (-ица); *geogr.* прито́к; **~e** ['tribju:t] дань *f*; подноше́ние.

trice [trais]: in a ~ мгнове́нно.

trick [trik] **1.** шту́ка, ша́лость *f*; фо́кус, трюк; уло́вка; сноро́вка; **2.** обма́нывать [-ну́ть]; наду́(ва́)ть; иску́сно украша́ть; **~ery** ['trikəri] надува́тельство; проде́лка.

trickle ['trikl] те́чь стру́йкой; сочи́ться.

trick|ster ['trikstə] обма́нщик; **~y** ['triki] □ хи́трый; мудрёный, сло́жный, тру́дный.

tricycle ['traisikl] трёхколёсный велосипе́д.

trifl|e ['traifl] **1.** пустя́к; ме́лочь *f*; a ~ *fig.* немно́жко; **2.** *v/i.* [по]шути́ть; занима́ться пустяка́ми; *v/t.* ~ away зря тра́тить; **~ing** ['traifliŋ] пустя́чный, пустяко́вый.

trig [trig] **1.** опря́тный; наря́дный; **2.** наряжа́ть [-яди́ть]; [за]тормози́ть.

trigger ['trigə] ⚔ спусково́й крючо́к; ⊕ соба́чка, защёлка.

trill [tril] **1.** трель *f*; **2.** выводи́ть трель.

trim [trim] **1.** □ наря́дный; приведённый в поря́док; **2.** наря́д;

поря́док; состоя́ние гото́вности; ⚓ (пра́вильное) размеще́ние гру́за; 3. приводи́ть в поря́док; (~ up) подреза́ть [-е́зать], подстрига́ть [-и́чь]; отде́л(ыв)ать (пла́тье); ⚓ уравнове́шивать [-е́сить] (су́дно); **~ming** ['trimiŋ] *mst* ~s *pl.* отде́лка (на пла́тье); припра́ва, гарни́р.

trinket ['triŋkit] безделу́шка; брело́к; ~s *pl. contp.* финтифлю́шки *f/pl.*

trip [trip] 1. путеше́ствие; пое́здка; экску́рсия; спотыка́ние; *fig.* обмо́лвка, оши́бка; 2. *v/i.* идти́ легко́ и бы́стро; спотыка́ться [споткну́ться]; обмо́лвиться *pf.*; *v/t.* подставля́ть но́жку (Д).

tripartite ['trai'pɑ:tait] тро́йственный; состоя́щий из трёх часте́й.

tripe [traip] *cook.* рубе́ц.

triple ['tripl] тройно́й; утро́енный; **~ts** ['triplits] *pl.* тро́йня *sg.*

tripper [tripə] F экскурса́нт(ка).

trite [trait] □ бана́льный, изби́тый.

triturate ['tritjəreit] растира́ть в порошо́к.

triumph ['traiəmf] 1. триу́мф; торжество́; 2. пра́здновать побе́ду, триу́мф; торжествова́ть, восторжествова́ть *pf.* (over над Т); **~al** [trai'ʌmfəl] триумфа́льный; **~ant** [-fənt] □ победоно́сный; торжеству́ющий.

trivial ['triviəl] □ обы́денный; ме́лкий, пусто́й; тривиа́льный.

trod [trɔd] *pt.* от tread; **~den** ['trɔdn] *p. pt.* от tread.

troll [troul] напева́ть.

troll(e)**y** ['trɔli] вагоне́тка; 🚂 дрези́на; *Am.* трамва́й.

trollop ['trɔləp] *contp.* неря́ха *m/f*; проститу́тка.

trombone [trɔm'boun] ♪ тромбо́н.

troop [tru:p] 1. толпа́; отря́д; ⚔ кавалери́йский и́ли та́нковый взвод; *Am.* эскадро́н; 2. дви́гаться или собира́ться толпо́й; ~ away, ~ off удаля́ться [-ли́ться]; **~er** ['tru:pə] (рядово́й) кавалери́ст; рядово́й-танки́ст; **~s** *pl.* войска́ *n/pl.*

trophy ['troufi] трофе́й, добы́ча.

tropic ['trɔpik] тро́пик; ~s *pl.* тро́пики *m/pl.* (зо́на); **~**(**al** □) [~, -pikəl] тропи́ческий.

trot [trɔt] 1. рысь (ло́шади); бы́стрый ход (челове́ка); 2. бе́гать ры́сью; пуска́ть ры́сью; [по]спеши́ть.

trouble ['trʌbl] 1. беспоко́йство; волне́ние; забо́ты *f/pl.*, хло́поты *f/pl.*; затрудне́ния *n/pl.*; го́ре, беда́; take ~ утружда́ться; 2. [по-] беспоко́ить(ся); [по]проси́ть; утружда́ть [-уди́ть]; don't ~! не труди́тесь!; **~some** [-səm] тру́дный; причиня́ющий беспоко́йство.

trough [trɔf] коры́то, корму́шка; квашня́; жёлоб.

trounce [trauns] F [по]би́ть, [вы́-]поро́ть.

troupe [tru:p] *thea.* тру́ппа.

trousers ['trauzəz] *pl.* брю́ки *f/pl.*

trout [traut] форе́ль *f.*

trowel ['trauəl] лопа́тка (штукату́ра).

truant ['tru:ənt] 1. лентя́й; прогу́льщик; учени́к, прогуля́вший уро́ки; 2. лени́вый; пра́здный.

truce [tru:s] переми́рие.

truck [trʌk] 1. вагоне́тка; теле́жка; *Am.* грузови́к; 🚂 (откры́тая) това́рная платфо́рма; ме́на; товарообме́н; 2. перевози́ть на грузовика́х; вести́ менову́ю торго́влю; обме́нивать [-ня́ть]; **~-farmer** *Am.* огоро́дник.

truckle ['trʌkl] раболе́пствовать.

truculent ['trʌkjulənt] свире́пый; гру́бый.

trudge [trʌdʒ] идти́ с трудо́м; таска́ться, [по]тащи́ться.

true [tru:] ве́рный; пра́вильный; настоя́щий; it is ~ пра́вда; come ~ сбы́(ва́)ться; ~ to nature то́чно тако́й, как в нату́ре.

truism ['tru:izm] трюи́зм.

truly ['tru:li] правди́во; лоя́льно; пои́стине; то́чно; yours ~ пре́данный (-ная) вам.

trump [trʌmp] 1. ко́зырь *m*; 2. козыря́ть [-рну́ть]; бить ко́зырем; ~ up выду́мывать [вы́думать]; **~ery** ['trʌmpəri] мишура́; дрянь *f.*

trumpet ['trʌmpit] 1. труба́; 2. [за-, про]труби́ть; *fig.* возвеща́ть [-ести́ть].

truncheon ['trʌntʃən] ⚒ (ма́ршальский) жезл; дуби́нка (полице́йского).

trundle ['trʌndl] ката́ть(ся), [по-]кати́ть(ся).

trunk [trʌŋk] ствол (де́рева); ту́ловище; хо́бот (слона́); доро́жный сунду́к; **~-call** *teleph.* вы́зов по междугоро́дному телефо́ну; **~-line** 🚂 магистра́ль *f*; *teleph.* междугоро́дная ли́ния.

truss [trʌs] 1. свя́зка; большо́й пук; ⚕ банда́ж; ⚠ стропи́льная фе́рма; 2. увя́зывать в пуки́; скру́чивать ру́ки (Д); ⚠ свя́зывать [-за́ть]; укрепля́ть [-пи́ть].

trust [trʌst] 1. дове́рие; ве́ра; отве́тственное положе́ние; † креди́т; трест; on ~ в креди́т; на ве́ру; 2. *v/t.* доверя́ть, [по]ве́рить (Д); вверя́ть [вве́рить], доверя́ть [-е́рить] (Д with В); *v/i.* полага́ться [положи́ться] (in, to на В); наде́яться (in, to на В); **~ee** [trʌs'ti:] ⚖ опеку́н; попечи́тель *m*; **~ful** ['trʌstful] □, **~ing** ['trʌstiŋ] □ дове́рчивый; **~worthy** [-wə:ði] заслу́живающий дове́рия.

truth [tru:θ] пра́вда; и́стина; **~ful** ['tru:θful] □ правди́вый; ве́рный.

try [trai] 1. испы́тывать [испыта́ть]; [по]про́бовать; [по]пыта́ться; [по]стара́ться; утомля́ть [-ми́ть]; ⚖ суди́ть; ~ on примеря́ть [-е́рить] (на себя́); 2. попы́тка; **~ing** ['traiiŋ] □ тру́дный; тяжёлый; раздража́ющий.

tub [tʌb] ка́дка; лоха́нь *f*; бадья́; F ва́нна.

tube [tju:b] труба́, тру́бка; F метро́ *n indecl.* (в Ло́ндоне).

tuber ['tju:bə] ⚘ клу́бень *m*; **~culous** [tju:'bə:kjuləs] ⚕ туберкулёзный.

tubular ['tju:bjulə] □ тру́бчатый, цилиндри́ческий.

tuck [tʌk] 1. скла́дка, сбо́рка (на пла́тье); 2. де́лать скла́дки; подбира́ть под себя́; запря́т(ыв)ать; ~ up подвёртывать [-верну́ть] (подо́л); засу́чивать [-чи́ть] (рукава́).

Tuesday ['tju:zdi] вто́рник.

tuft [tʌft] пучо́к (травы́); хохоло́к; боро́дка кли́нышком.

tug [tʌg] 1. рыво́к; гуж; ⚓ букси́р; 2. тащи́ть с уси́лием; дёргать [дёрнуть] (изо всех сил); ⚓ букси́ровать.

tuition [tju'iʃən] обуче́ние.

tulip ['tju:lip] тюльпа́н.

tumble ['tʌmbl] 1. *v/i.* па́дать [упа́сть] (споткну́вшись); кувырка́ться [-кну́ться]; опроки́дываться [-и́нуться]; мета́ться (в посте́ли); *v/t.* приводи́ть в беспоря́док, [по]мя́ть; 2. паде́ние; беспоря́док; **~-down** [-daun] полуразру́шенный; **~r** [-ə] акроба́т; бока́л, (высо́кий) стака́н.

tumid ['tju:mid] □ распу́хший; *fig.* напы́щенный.

tumo(u)r ['tju:mə] о́пухоль *f*.

tumult ['tju:mʌlt] шум и кри́ки; бу́йство; душе́вное возбужде́ние; **~uous** [tju'mʌltjuəs] шу́мный, бу́йный; возбуждённый.

tun [tʌn] больша́я бо́чка.

tuna ['tju:nə] туне́ц.

tune [tju:n] 1. мело́дия, моти́в; тон; строй; звук; in ~ настро́енный (роя́ль); в тон; out of ~ расстро́енный (роя́ль); не в тон; 2. настра́ивать [-ро́ить] (инструме́нт); ~ in *radio* настра́ивать приёмник (to на В); **~ful** ['tju:nful] □ мелоди́чный, гармони́чный; **~less** ['tju:nlis] □ немелоди́чный.

tunnel ['tʌnl] 1. тунне́ль *m* (*a.* тонне́ль *m*); ⚒ што́льня; 2. проводи́ть тунне́ль че́рез (В).

turbid ['tə:bid] му́тный; тума́нный.

turbulent ['tə:bjulənt] бу́рный; бу́йный, непоко́рный.

tureen [tə'ri:n, tju'r-] супова́я ми́ска.

turf [tə:f] 1. дёрн; торф; ко́нный спорт, ска́чки *f/pl.*; 2. обдерня́ть [-ни́ть]; **~y** ['tə:fi] покры́тый дёрном, дерни́стый; торфяно́й.

turgid ['tə:dʒid] □ опу́хший; *fig.* напы́щенный.

Turk [tə:k] ту́рок, турча́нка.

turkey ['tə:ki] индю́к, инде́йка.

Turkish ['tə:kiʃ] 1. туре́цкий; 2. туре́цкий язы́к.

turmoil ['tə:mɔil] шум, сумато́ха; беспоря́док.

turn [tə:n] 1. *v/t.* враща́ть, верте́ть; повора́чивать [поверну́ть]; обора́чивать [оберну́ть]; точи́ть (на тока́рном станке́); превраща́ть [-рати́ть]; направля́ть [-ра́вить]; ~ a corner заверну́ть за́ угол; ~ down отверга́ть [-е́ргнуть] (предложе́ние); загиба́ть [загну́ть]; ~ off закры́(ва́)ть (кран); выключа́ть [вы́ключить]; ~ on откры́(ва́)ть (кран); включа́ть [-чи́ть]; ~ out выгоня́ть [вы́гнать]; увольня́ть [уво́лить]; выпуска́ть [вы́пустить] (изде́лия); ~ over перевёртывать [-верну́ть]; *fig.* пере-д(ав)а́ть (дове́ренность и т. п.); ~ up поднима́ть вверх; 2. *v/i.* враща́ться, верте́ться; повора́чиваться [поверну́ться]; [с]де́латься, станови́ться [стать]; превраща́ться [-врати́ться]; ~ about обёртываться [оберну́ться]; ⚔ повора́чиваться круго́м; ~ in заходи́ть мимохо́дом; F ложи́ться спать; ~ out ока́зываться [-за́ться]; ~ to принима́ться [-ня́ться] за (В); обраща́ться [обрати́ться] к (Д); ~ up появля́ться [-ви́ться]; случа́ться [-чи́ться]; ~ upon обраща́ться [обрати́ться] про́тив (Р); 3. *su.* оборо́т; поворо́т; изги́б; переме́на; о́чередь *f*; услу́га; оборо́т (ре́чи); F испу́г; at every ~ на ка́ждом шагу́, постоя́нно; by и́ли in ~s по о́череди; it is my ~ моя́ о́чередь *f*; take ~s де́лать поочерёдно; does it serve your ~? э́то вам подхо́дит?, э́то вам годи́тся?; **~coat** перебе́жчик, хамелео́н *fig.*; **~er** ['tə:nə] то́карь *m*; **~ery** [-ri] тока́рное ремесло́; тока́рные изде́лия *n/pl.*

turning ['tə:niŋ] поворо́т (у́лицы и т. п.); враще́ние; тока́рное ремесло́; **~-point** *fig.* поворо́тный пункт; перело́м.

turnip ['tə:nip] ⚘ ре́па.

turn|key ['tə:nki:] тюре́мщик; **~-out** ['tə:n'aut] ⚒ вы́пуск проду́кции; **~over** ['tə:nouvə] ⚒ оборо́т; **~pike** шлагба́ум; **~stile** турнике́т.

turpentine ['tə:pəntain] скипида́р.

turpitude ['tə:pitju:d] позо́р; ни́зость *f*.

turret ['tʌrit] ба́шенка; ✈ туре́ль *f*; ⚔, ⚓ оруди́йная ба́шня.

turtle ['tə:tl] *zo.* черепа́ха.

tusk [tʌsk] клык (слона́, моржа́).

tussle ['tʌsl] 1. борьба́, дра́ка; 2. (упо́рно) боро́ться, [по]дра́ться.

tussock ['tʌsək] ко́чка.

tutelage ['tju:tilidʒ] опеку́нство; опе́ка.

tutor ['tju:tə] 1. домашний учитель *m*; репетитор; ⚖ опекун; 2. обучать [-чить]; наставлять [наставить].
tuxedo [tʌk'si:dou] *Am.* смокинг.
twaddle ['twɔdl] 1. пустая болтовня; 2. пустословить.
twang [twæŋ] 1. звук натянутой струны; (*mst* nasal ~) гнусавый выговор; 2. звенеть (о струне); гнусавить.
tweak [twi:k] щипать [щипнуть].
tweezers ['twi:zəz] *pl.* пинцет.
twelfth [twelfθ] двенадцатый.
twelve [twelv] двенадцать.
twent|ieth ['twentiiθ] двадцатый; **~y** ['twenti] двадцать.
twice [twais] дважды; вдвое.
twiddle ['twidl] вертеть (в руках); играть (T); *fig.* бездельничать.
twig [twig] веточка, прут.
twilight ['twailait] сумерки *f/pl.*
twin [twin] 1. близнец; двойник; парная вещь *f*; 2. двойной; парный.
twine [twain] 1. бечёвка, шпагат, шнурок; 2. [с]вить; [с]плести; обви(ва)ть(ся).
twinge [twindʒ] приступ боли.
twinkle ['twiŋkl] 1. мерцание; мигание; мелькание; 2. [за]мерцать; [за]сверкать; мигать [мигнуть].
twirl [twə:l] 1. кручение; вращение; 2. вертеть; закручивать [-утить].
twist [twist] 1. кручение; скручивание; сучение; изгиб; поворот; вывих; 2. [с]крутить; [с]сучить; [с]вить(ся); сплетать(ся) [-ести(сь)].
twit [twit]: ~ a p. with a th. попрекать [-кнуть] кого-либо (T).
twitch [twitʃ] 1. подёргивание, судорога; 2. дёргать(ся) [дёрнуть (-ся)].
twitter ['twitə] 1. щебет; 2. [за-] щебетать; чирикать [-кнуть]; be in a ~ дрожать.
two [tu:] 1. два, две; двое; пара; in ~ надвое, пополам; 2. двойка; in ~s попарно; **~fold** ['tu:fould] 1. двойной; 2. *adv.* вдвое; **~pence** ['tʌpəns] два пенса; **~-storey** двухэтажный; **~-way** двусторонний; ~ plug двойной штепсель *m*.
tyke [taik] дворняжка; шустрый ребёнок.
type [taip] тип; типичный представитель *m*; *typ.* литера; шрифт; true to ~ типичный; set in ~ *typ.* наб(и)рать; **~write** [*irr.* (write)] писать на машинке; **~writer** пишущая машинка.
typhoid ['taifɔid] ⚕ (*a.* ~ fever) брюшной тиф.
typhoon [tai'fu:n] тайфун.
typhus ['taifəs] ⚕ сыпной тиф.
typi|cal ['tipikəl] □ типичный; **~fy** [-fai] служить типичным примером для (P); **~st** ['taipist] переписчик (-чица) (на машинке), машинистка; shorthand ~ стенографист(ка).
tyrann|ic(al □) [ti'rænik, -ikəl] тиранический; **~ize** ['tirənaiz] тиранить; **~y** [-ni] тирания, деспотизм.
tyrant ['taiərənt] тиран, деспот.
tyre ['taiə] шина (колеса).
tyro ['taiərou] новичок.

U

ubiquitous [ju:'bikwitəs] □ вездесущий.
udder ['ʌdə] вымя *n.*
ugly ['ʌgli] □ безобразный; дурной; противный.
ulcer ['ʌlsə] 🕮 язва; **~ate** [-reit] изъязвлять(ся) [-вить(ся)]; **~ous** [-rəs] изъязвлённый; язвенный.
ulterior [ʌl'tiəriə] □ более отдалённый; *fig.* дальнейший; скрытый (мотив и т. п.).
ultimate ['ʌltimit] □ последний; конечный; максимальный; **~ly** [-li] в конце концов.
ultimo ['ʌltimou] *adv.* истёкшего месяца
ultra[1] ['ʌltrə] крайний.
ultra[2]... [~...] *pref.* сверх..., ультра-...
umbel ['ʌmbəl] ⚘ зонтик.
umbrage ['ʌmbridʒ] обида; *poet.* тень *f*, сень *f*.
umbrella [ʌm'brelə] зонтик.
umpire ['ʌmpaiə] 1. посредник; третейский судья *m*; *sport* судья *m*; 2. быть (третейским) судьёй; быть посредником.
un... [ʌn...] *pref.* (придаёт отрицательное или противоположное значение) не..., без...
unable ['ʌn'eibl] неспособный; be ~ не быть в состоянии, не [с]мочь.
unaccountable ['ʌnə'kauntəbl] □ необъяснимый; безответственный.
unaccustomed ['ʌnə'kʌstəmd] не привыкший; непривычный.
unacquainted [-'kweintid]: ~ with незнакомый с (T); не знающий (P).
unadvised ['ʌnəd'vaizd] □ неблагоразумный; необдуманный.
unaffected ['ʌnə'fektid] □ непритворный, искренний; не(за)тронутый (by T).
unaided ['ʌn'eidid] лишённый помощи; без посторонней помощи.
unalterable [ʌn'ɔ:ltərəbl] □ неизменный.

unanim|ity [ju:nə'nimiti] единодýшие; **~ous** [ju:'nænimәs] □ единодýшный, единоглáсный.
unanswerable [ʌn'ɑ:nsәrәbl] □ неопровержи́мый.
unapproachable [ʌnә'proutʃәbl] □ непристýпный; недостýпный.
unapt [ʌ'næpt] □ неподходя́щий; неспосóбный, неумéлый.
unasked ['ʌn'ɑ:skt] непрóшенный.
unassisted ['ʌnә'sistid] без пóмощи.
unassuming ['ʌnә'sju:miŋ] скрóмный, непритязáтельный.
unattractive ['ʌnә'træktiv] □ непривлекáтельный.
unauthorized ['ʌn'ɔ:θәraizd] неразрешённый; неправомóчный.
unavail|able ['ʌnә'veilәbl] не имéющийся в распоряжéнии; **~ing** [-liŋ] бесполéзный.
unavoidable [ʌnә'vɔidebl] □ неизбéжный.
unaware ['ʌnә'weә] не знáющий, не подозревáющий (of P); be ~ of ничегó не знать о (П); не замечáть [-éтить] (P); **~s** [-z] неожи́данно, врасплóх; нечáянно.
unbacked [ʌn'bækt] *fig.* не имéющий поддéржки.
unbalanced ['ʌn'bælәnst] неуравновéшенный.
unbearable [ʌn'bɛәrәbl] □ невыноси́мый.
unbecoming ['ʌnbi'kʌmiŋ] □ неподходя́щий; не идýщий к лицý; неприли́чный.
unbelie|f ['ʌnbi'li:f] невéрие; **~vable** ['ʌnbi'li:vәbl] □ невероя́тный; **~ving** [-iŋ] □ невéрующий.
unbend ['ʌn'bend] [*irr.* (bend)] выпрямля́ть(ся) [вы́прямить(ся)]; станови́ться непринуждённым; **~ing** [-iŋ] □ негнýщийся; *fig.* непреклóнный.
unbias(s)ed ['ʌn'baiәst] □ беспристрáстный.
unbind ['ʌn'baind] [*irr.* (bind)] развя́зывать [-зáть]; *fig.* освобождáть [-боди́ть].
unblushing [ʌn'blʌʃiŋ] бессты́дный.
unbosom [ʌn'buzәm] поверя́ть [-éрить] (тáйну); ~ o. s. изливáть дýшу.
unbounded [ʌn'baundid] □ неограни́ченный; беспредéльный.
unbroken ['ʌn'broukn] неразби́тый; не поби́тый (рекóрд); непреры́вный.
unbutton ['ʌn'bʌtn] расстёгивать [расстегнýть].
uncalled [ʌn'kɔ:ld]: ~-for непрóшенный; неумéстный.
uncanny [ʌn'kæni] □ жýткий, сверхъестéственный.
uncared ['ʌn'kɛәd]: ~-for забрóшенный.
unceasing [ʌn'si:siŋ] □ непрекращáющийся, безостанóвочный.
unceremonious ['ʌnseri'mounjәs] □ бесцеремóнный.
uncertain [ʌn'sә:tn] □ неувéренный; неопределённый; неизвéстный; **~ty** [-ti] неувéренность *f*; неизвéстность *f*; неопределённость *f*.
unchang|eable [ʌn'tʃeindʒәbl] □, **~ing** [-iŋ] неизмéнный; неизменя́емый.
uncharitable [ʌn'tʃæritәbl] □ немилосéрдный.
unchecked ['ʌn'tʃekt] беспрепя́тственный; непровéренный.
uncivil ['ʌn'sivl] □ невéжливый; **~ized** ['ʌn'sivilaizd] нецивилизóванный.
uncle ['ʌŋkl] дя́дя *m.*
unclean ['ʌn'kli:n] □ нечи́стый.
unclose ['ʌn'klouz] откры́(вá)ть (-ся).
uncomfortable [ʌn'kʌmfәtәbl] □ неудóбный; нелóвкий.
uncommon [ʌn'kɔmәn] □ необыкновéнный; замечáтельный.
uncommunicative ['ʌnkә'mju:nikeitiv] необщи́тельный, неразговóрчивый.
uncomplaining ['ʌnkәm'pleiniŋ] □ безрóпотный.
uncompromising [ʌn'kɔmprәmaiziŋ] □ бескомпроми́ссный.
unconcern ['ʌnkәn'sә:n] беззабóтность *f*; беспéчность *f*; **~ed** [-d] □ беззабóтный; беспéчный.
unconditional ['ʌnkәn'diʃnl] □ безоговóрочный, безуслóвный.
unconquerable [ʌn'kɔŋkәrәbl] □ непобеди́мый.
unconscionable [ʌn'kɔnʃnәbl] □ бессóвестный.
unconscious [ʌn'kɔnʃәs] □ бессознáтельный; потеря́вший сознáние; be ~ of не созн(ав)áть (P); **~ness** [-nis] бессознáтельность *f*.
unconstitutional ['ʌnkɔnsti'tju:ʃnl] □ противорéчащий конститýции.
uncontrollable [ʌnkәn'troulәbl] □ неудержи́мый; не поддаю́щийся контрóлю.
unconventional ['ʌnkәn'venʃәnl] □ чýждый услóвности; необы́чный; нешаблóнный.
uncork ['ʌn'kɔ:k] откýпори(ва)ть.
uncount|able ['ʌn'kauntәbl] бесчи́сленный; **~ed** [-tid] несчётный.
uncouple ['ʌn'kʌpl] расцепля́ть [-пи́ть].
uncouth [ʌn'ku:θ] неуклю́жий.
uncover [ʌn'kʌvә] откры́(вá)ть (лицó и т. п.); снимáть кры́шку с (P); обнажáть [-жи́ть] (гóлову).
unct|ion ['ʌŋkʃәn] помáзание; мазь *f*; **~uous** ['ʌŋktjuәs] □ масляни́стый; *fig.* елéйный.
uncult|ivated ['ʌn'kʌltiveitid] невоздéланный; некультýрный.
undamaged ['ʌn'dæmidʒd] неповреждённый.

undaunted [ʌn'dɔ:ntid] □ неустраши́мый.
undeceive ['ʌndi'si:v] выводи́ть из заблужде́ния.
undecided ['ʌndi'saidid] □ нерешённый; нереши́тельный.
undefined ['ʌndi'faind] □ неопределённый.
undeniable [ʌndi'naiəbl] □ неоспори́мый; несомне́нный.
under ['ʌndə] **1.** *adv.* ни́же; внизу́, вниз; **2.** *prp.* под (В, Т); ни́же (Р); ме́ньше (Р); при (П); **3.** *pref.* ниже..., под..., недо...; **4.** ни́жний; ни́зший; **~bid** ['ʌndə'bid] [*irr.* (bid)] предлага́ть бо́лее ни́зкую це́ну чем (И); **~brush** [-brʌʃ] подле́сок; **~carriage** [-'kæridʒ] шасси́ *n indecl.*; **~clothing** [-klouðiŋ] ни́жнее бельё; **~cut** [-kʌt] сбива́ть це́ны; подреза́ть [-е́зать]; **~done** [-dʌn] недожа́ренный; **~estimate** [-r'estimeit] недооце́нивать [-и́ть]; **~fed** [-fed] истощённый от недоеда́ния; **~go** [-'gou] [*irr.* (go)] испы́тывать [испыта́ть]; подверга́ться [-е́ргнуться] (Д); **~graduate** [-'grædjuit] студе́нт(ка) после́днего ку́рса; **~ground** ['ʌndəgraund] **1.** подзе́мный; подпо́льный; **2.** метро́(полите́н) *n indecl.*; подпо́лье; **~hand** [-hænd] **1.** та́йный, закули́сный; **2.** *adv.* та́йно, «за спино́й»; **~lie** [ʌndə'lai] [*irr.* (lie)] лежа́ть в основа́нии (Р); **~line** [-'lain] подчёркивать [-черкну́ть]; **~ling** [-liŋ] подчинённый; **~mine** [ʌndə'main] [за]мини́ровать (*im*)*pf.*; подка́пывать [-копа́ть] (*a. fig.*); *fig.* подрыва́ть [подорва́ть]; **~most** ['ʌndəmoust] са́мый ни́жний; ни́зший; **~neath** [ʌndə'ni:θ] **1.** *prp.* под (Т/В); **2.** *adv.* вниз, внизу́; **~privileged** [-'privilidʒd] лишённый привиле́гий; **~rate** [ʌndə'reit] недооце́нивать [-и́ть]; **~-secretary** ['ʌndə'sekrətəri] замести́тель мини́стра (в Англии и США); **~sell** [-'sel] [*irr.* (sell)] ✝ продава́ть дешёвле други́х; **~signed** [-'saind] нижеподписа́вшийся; **~stand** [ʌndə'stænd] [*irr.* (stand)] *com.* понима́ть [поня́ть]; подразумева́ть (by под Т); make o. s. understood уме́ть объясни́ться; an understood thing решённое де́ло; **~standable** [-əbl] поня́тный; **~standing** [-iŋ] понима́ние; соглаше́ние; взаимопонима́ние; **~state** ['ʌndə'steit] преуменьша́ть [-ме́ньши́ть]; **~stood** [ʌndə'stud] *pt.* и *p. pt.* от understand; **~take** [ʌndə'teik] [*irr.* (take)] предпринима́ть [-ня́ть]; бра́ть на себя́; обя́зываться [-за́ться]; **~taker** **1.** [ʌndə'teikə] предпринима́тель *m*; **2.** ['ʌndəteikə] содержа́тель похоро́нного бюро́; **~taking** **1.** [ʌndə'teikiŋ] предприя́тие; обяза́тельство; **2.** ['ʌndəteikiŋ] похоро́нное бюро́; **~tone** [-toun]: in an ~ вполго́лоса; **~value** [-'vælju:] недооце́нивать [-и́ть]; **~wear** [-wɛə] ни́жнее бельё; **~wood** [-wud] подле́сок; **~write** [-rait] [*irr.* (write)] подпи́сывать поли́с морско́го страхова́ния; принима́ть в страхо́вку; **~writer** [-raitə] морско́й страхо́вщик.
undeserved ['ʌndi'zə:vd] □ незаслу́женный.
undesirable [-'zaiərəbl] □ нежела́тельный; неудо́бный, неподходя́щий.
undisciplined [ʌn'disiplind] недисциплини́рованный.
undisguised ['ʌndis'gaizd] □ незамаскиро́ванный; я́вный.
undo ['ʌn'du:, ʌn'du:] [*irr.* (do)] уничтожа́ть [-о́жить] (сде́ланное); развя́зывать [-за́ть]; расстёгивать [расстегну́ть]; расторга́ть [-о́ргнуть] (догово́р и т. п.); **~ing** [-iŋ] уничтоже́ние; ги́бель *f*; развя́зывание; расстёгивание и т. д.
undoubted [ʌn'dautid] □ несомне́нный, бесспо́рный.
undreamt [ʌn'dremt]: ~-of невообрази́мый, неожи́данный.
undress ['ʌn'dres] **1.** дома́шний костю́м; **2.** разде́(ва́)ть(ся); **~ed** ['ʌn'drest] неоде́тый; невы́деланный (о ко́же).
undue ['ʌn'dju:] □ неподходя́щий; чрезме́рный; ненадлежа́щий; ещё не подлежа́щий опла́те.
undulat|e ['ʌndjuleit] быть волни́стым, волнообра́зным; **~ion** [ʌndju'leiʃən] волнообра́зное движе́ние; неро́вность пове́рхности.
unearth ['ʌn'ə:θ] вырыва́ть из земли́; *fig.* раска́пывать [-копа́ть]; **~ly** [ʌn'ə:θli] неземно́й; стра́нный, ди́кий.
uneas|iness [ʌn'i:zinis] беспоко́йство; трево́жность *f*; стесне́ние; **~y** [ʌn'i:zi] □ беспоко́йный, трево́жный; стеснённый (о движе́ниях и т. п.).
uneducated ['ʌn'edjukeitid] необразо́ванный; невоспи́танный.
unemotional ['ʌni'mouʃnl] □ пасси́вный; бесстра́стный; сухо́й *fig.*
unemploy|ed ['ʌnim'plɔid] безрабо́тный; неза́нятый; **~ment** [-'plɔimənt] безрабо́тица.
unending [ʌn'endiŋ] □ несконча́емый, бесконе́чный.
unendurable ['ʌnin'djuərəbl] нестерпи́мый.
unengaged ['ʌnin'geidʒd] неза́нятый; свобо́дный.
unequal ['ʌn'i:kwəl] □ нера́вный; неро́вный; **~led** [-d] непревзойдённый.
unerring ['ʌn'ə:riŋ] □ непогреши́мый; безоши́бочный.

unessential ['ʌni'senʃəl] □ несущéственный (to для P).
uneven ['ʌn'i:vn] □ нерóвный; шероховáтый (*a. fig.*).
uneventful ['ʌni'ventful] □ без осóбых событий.
unexampled [ʌnig'zɑ:mpld] беспримéрный.
unexpected ['ʌniks'pektid] □ неожиданный.
unfailing [ʌn'feiliŋ] □ неизмéнный; неисчерпáемый.
unfair ['ʌn'fɛə] □ несправедливый; нечéстный (о спортсмéне, игрé и т. п.).
unfaithful ['ʌn'feiθful] □ невéрный, верoлóмный; неточный.
unfamiliar ['ʌnfə'miljə] незнакóмый; непривычный.
unfasten ['ʌn'fɑ:sn] открепля́ть [-пи́ть]; расстёгивать [расстегну́ть]; **~ed** [-d] расстёгнутый; неприкреплённый.
unfavo(u)rable ['ʌn'feivərəbl] □ неблагоприятный; невыгодный.
unfeeling [ʌn'fi:liŋ] □ бесчу́вственный.
unfinished ['ʌn'finiʃt] незакóнченный.
unfit 1. ['ʌn'fit] □ негóдный, неподходящий; 2. [ʌn'fit] дéлать непригóдным.
unfix ['ʌn'fiks] открепля́ть [-пи́ть]; дéлать неустóйчивым.
unfledged ['ʌn'fledʒd] неоперившийся (*a. fig.*).
unflinching [ʌn'flintʃiŋ] □ неуклóнный.
unfold [ʌn'fould] развёртывать(ся) [-вернуть(ся)]; откры́(вá)ть (тáйну и т. п.).
unforced ['ʌn'fɔ:st] □ непринуждённый.
unforgettable ['ʌnfə'getəbl] □ незабвéнный.
unfortunate [ʌn'fɔ:tʃnit] 1. несчáстный; неудáчный; неудáчливый; 2. неудáчник (-ица); **~ly** [-li] к несчáстью; к сожалéнию.
unfounded ['ʌn'faundid] □ необоснóванный; неосновáтельный.
unfriendly ['ʌn'frendli] недружелюбный; неприветливый.
unfurl [ʌn'fə:l] развёртывать [развернýть].
unfurnished ['ʌn'fə:niʃt] немеблирóванный.
ungainly [ʌn'geinli] нескладный.
ungenerous ['ʌn'dʒenərəs] □ не великодушный, не щéдрый.
ungentle ['ʌn'dʒentl] □ неделикáтный, неучтивый.
ungodly [ʌn'gɔdli] □ безбóжный.
ungovern|able [ʌn'gʌvənəbl] □ неукротимый; распýщенный.
ungraceful ['ʌn'greisful] □ неизящный, неграциóзный.
ungracious ['ʌn'greiʃəs] □ немилостивый.
ungrateful [ʌn'greitful] □ неблагодáрный.
unguarded ['ʌn'gɑ:did] □ неохраняемый; неосторóжный; незащищённый.
unguent ['ʌŋgwənt] мазь *f*.
unhampered ['ʌn'hæmpəd] беспрепятственный.
unhandsome [ʌn'hænsəm] □ некрасивый.
unhandy [ʌn'hændi] □ неудóбный; нелóвкий.
unhappy [ʌn'hæpi] □ несчáстный.
unharmed ['ʌn'hɑ:md] благополýчный; невредимый.
unhealthy [ʌn'helθi] □ нездорóвый, болéзненный; врéдный.
unheard-of [ʌn'hə:dɔv] неслыханный.
unhesitating [ʌn'heziteitiŋ] □ неколéблющийся, решительный.
unholy [ʌn'houli] безбóжный; дьявольский.
unhonoured ['ʌn'ɔnəd] не уважáемый; неоплáченный.
unhope|d-for [ʌn'houpt'fɔ:] неожиданный; **~ful** [-ful] не подающий надéжды, безнадёжный.
unhurt ['ʌn'hə:t] невредимый, цéлый.
uniform ['ju:nifɔ:m] 1. □ однообрáзный; однорóдный; 2. фóрма, мундир; 3. дéлать однообрáзным; обмундирóвывать [-ровáть]; **~ity** [ju:ni'fɔ:miti] единообрáзие, однообрáзие.
unify ['ju:nifai] объединять [-нить]; унифицировать (*im*)*pf*.
unilateral ['ju:ni'lætərəl] одностирóнний.
unimaginable [ʌni'mædʒinəbl] □ невообразимый.
unimportant ['ʌnim'pɔ:tənt] □ невáжный.
uninformed ['ʌnin'fɔ:md] несвéдущий; неосведомлённый.
uninhabit|able ['ʌnin'hæbitəbl] негóдный для жилья; **~ed** [-tid] нежилóй; необитáемый.
uninjured ['ʌn'indʒəd] неповреждённый, невредимый.
unintelligible ['ʌnin'telidʒəbl] □ непонятный.
unintentional ['ʌnin'tenʃnl] □ непреднамéренный, неумышленный.
uninteresting ['ʌn'intristiŋ] □ неинтерéсный, безынтерéсный.
uninterrupted ['ʌnintə'rʌptid] □ непрерывный, беспрерывный.
union ['ju:njən] объединéние; соединéние (*a.* ⊕); союз, федерáция; профсоюз; 2 Jack британский национáльный флаг; **~ist** [-ist] член профсоюза.
unique [ju:'ni:k] единственный в своём рóде; бесподóбный.
unison ['ju:nizn] ♪ унисóн; *fig.* соглáсие.

unit ['ju:nit] ⚔ часть *f*, подразделéние; ⚓ единица; ⊕ агрегáт; **~e** [ju:'nait] соединя́ть(ся) [-ни́ть(-ся)]; объединя́ть(ся) [-ни́ть(ся)]; **~y** ['ju:niti] единéние; еди́нство.
univers|al [juni'və:sl] □ всеóбщий; всеми́рный; универсáльный; **~ality** [ju:nivə:'sæliti] универсáльность *f*; **~e** ['ju:nivə:s] мир, вселéнная; **~ity** [juni'və:siti] университéт.
unjust ['ʌn'dʒʌst] □ несправедли́вый; **~ified** [ʌn'dʒʌstifaid] неоправ́данный.
unkempt ['ʌn'kempt] нечёсаный; неопря́тный.
unkind [ʌn'kaind] □ недóбрый.
unknown ['ʌn'noun] **1.** неизвéстный; ~ to me *adv.* тáйно от меня́; **2.** незнакóмец (-мка).
unlace ['ʌn'leis] расшнурóвывать [-овáть].
unlawful ['ʌn'lɔ:ful] □ незакóнный.
unlearn ['ʌn'lə:n] разу́чиваться [(-и́ться].
unless [ən'les, ʌn'les] *cj.* éсли ... не.
unlike ['ʌn'laik] **1.** непохóжий на (В); **2.** *prp.* в отли́чие от (Р); **~ly** [ʌn'laikli] неправдоподóбный; невероя́тный.
unlimited [ʌn'limitid] безграни́чный, неограни́ченный.
unload ['ʌn'loud] выгружáть [вы́грузить], разгружáть [-узи́ть]; ⚔ разряжáть [-яди́ть].
unlock ['ʌn'lɔk] отпирáть [отперéть]; **~ed** [-t] незáпертый.
unlooked-for [ʌn'lukt'fɔ:] неожи́данный, непредви́денный.
unlovely ['ʌn'lʌvli] некраси́вый, непривлекáтельный.
unlucky [ʌn'lʌki] □ неудáчный, несчастли́вый.
unman ['ʌn'mæn] лишáть му́жественности.
unmanageable [ʌn'mænidʒəbl] □ тру́дно поддаю́щийся контрóлю; непокóрный.
unmarried ['ʌn'mærid] неженáтый, холостóй; незаму́жняя.
unmask ['ʌn'mɑ:sk] снимáть мáску с (Р); *fig.* разоблачáть [-чи́ть].
unmatched ['ʌn'mætʃt] бесподóбный.
unmeaning [ʌn'mi:niŋ] □ бессмы́сленный.
unmeasured [ʌn'meʒəd] неизмéренный; неизмери́мый.
unmeet ['ʌn'mi:t] неподходя́щий.
unmentionable [ʌn'menʃnəbl] невырази́мый; нецензу́рный.
unmerited ['ʌn'meritid] незаслу́женный.
unmindful [ʌn'maindful] □ забы́вчивый; невнимáтельный (of к Д).
unmistakable ['ʌnmis'teikəbl] □ несомнéнный; легкó узнавáемый.
unmitigated [ʌn'mitigeitid] несмягчённый; *fig.* абсолю́тный.
unmounted ['ʌn'mauntid] пéший; неопрáвленный (драгоцéнный кáмень); не смонти́рованный.
unmoved ['ʌn'mu:ved] нетрóнутый.
unnamed ['ʌn'neimd] безымя́нный; неупомя́нутый.
unnatural [ʌn'nætʃrəl] □ неестéственный; противоестéственный.
unnecessary [ʌn'nesisəri] □ нену́жный, изли́шний.
unnerve ['ʌn'nə:v] лишáть прису́тствия ду́ха.
unnoticed ['ʌn'noutist] незамéченный.
unobjectionable ['ʌnəb'dʒekʃnəbl] □ безукори́зненный.
unobserved ['ʌnəb'zə:vd] □ незамéченный.
unobtainable ['ʌnəb'teinəbl]: ~ thing вещь, котóрой нельзя́ достáть и́ли получи́ть.
unoccupied ['ʌn'ɔkjupaid] незáнятый.
unoffending ['ʌnə'fendiŋ] безоби́дный.
unofficial ['ʌnə'fiʃəl] □ неофициáльный.
unopposed ['ʌnə'pouzd] не встречáющий сопротивлéния.
unostentatious ['ʌnɔstən'teiʃəs] □ скрóмный; не показнóй.
unpack ['ʌn'pæk] распакóвывать [-овáть].
unpaid ['ʌn'peid] неуплáченный, неоплáченный.
unparalleled [ʌn'pærəleld] несравнéнный, беспримéрный.
unpeople ['ʌn'pi:pl] обезлю́дить *pf.*
unpleasant [ʌn'pleznt] □ неприя́тный; **~ness** [-nis] неприя́тность *f*.
unpolished ['ʌn'pɔliʃt] неотполирóванный; *fig.* неотёсанный.
unpolluted ['ʌnpə'lu:tid] незапя́тнанный, непорóчный.
unpopular ['ʌn'pɔpjulə] □ непопуля́рный, нелюби́мый.
unpracti|cal ['ʌn'præktikəl] □ непракти́чный; **~sed** [-tist] неóпытный; неприменённый.
unprecedented [ʌn'presidəntid] □ беспрецедéнтный; беспримéрный.
unprejudiced [ʌn'predʒudist] □ непредубеждённый, беспристрáстный.
unprepared ['ʌnpri'pɛəd] □ неподготóвленный; без подготóвки.
unpreten|ding ['ʌnpri'tendiŋ] □, **~tious** [-ʃəs] □ скрóмный, без претéнзий.
unprincipled ['ʌn'prinsəpld] беспринци́пный; безнрáвственный.
unprofitable [ʌn'prɔfitəbl] невы́годный; нерентáбельный.
unproved ['ʌn'pru:vd] недокáзанный.

unprovided ['ʌnprə'vaidid] не обеспе́ченный, не снабжённый (with T); ~-for непредви́денный.
unprovoked ['ʌnprə'voukt] □ ниче́м не вы́званный.
unqualified ['ʌn'kwɔlifaid] □ неквалифици́рованный; безогово́рочный.
unquestionable [ʌn'kwestʃənəbl] □ несомне́нный, неоспори́мый.
unravel [ʌn'rævəl] распу́т(ыв)ать; разга́дывать [-да́ть].
unready ['ʌn'redi] □ негото́вый.
unreal ['ʌn'riəl] □ ненастоя́щий; нереа́льный.
unreasonable [ʌn'ri:znəbl] □ не(благо)разу́мный; безрассу́дный; непоме́рный.
unrecognizable ['ʌn'rekəgnaizəbl] □ неузнава́емый.
unredeemed ['ʌnri'di:md] □ неиспо́лненный (об обеща́нии); невы́купленный (закла́д); неопла́ченный (долг).
unrefined ['ʌnri'faind] неочи́щенный.
unreflecting ['ʌnri'flektiŋ] □ легкомы́сленный, не размышля́ющий.
unregarded ['ʌnri'gɑ:did] не при́нятый в расчёт.
unrelenting [ʌnri'lentiŋ] □ безжа́лостный.
unreliable ['ʌnri'laiəbl] ненадёжный.
unrelieved ['ʌnri'li:vd] □ необлегчённый; не получа́ющий по́мощи.
unremitting [ʌnri'mitiŋ] □ беспреры́вный; неосла́бный.
unreserved ['ʌnri'zə:vd] □ открове́нный; невозде́ржанный; безогово́рочный.
unresisting ['ʌnri'zistiŋ] □ не сопротивля́ющийся.
unrest ['ʌn'rest] беспоко́йство, волне́ние.
unrestrained ['ʌnris'treind] □ несде́ржанный; необу́зданный.
unrestricted ['ʌnris'triktid] □ неограни́ченный.
unriddle [ʌn'ridl] разга́дывать [-да́ть].
unrighteous [ʌn'raitʃəs] □ непра́ведный; несправедли́вый.
unripe ['ʌn'raip] незре́лый, неспе́лый.
unrival(l)ed [ʌn'raivəld] непревзойдённый; без сопе́рника.
unroll ['ʌn'roul] развёртывать [-верну́ть].
unruffled ['ʌn'rʌfld] гла́дкий (о мо́ре и т. п.); невозмути́мый.
unruly [ʌn'ruli] непоко́рный.
unsafe ['ʌn'seif] □ ненадёжный, опа́сный.
unsal(e)able ['ʌn'seiləbl] неходово́й (това́р); непрода́жный.
unsanitary ['ʌn'sænitəri] негигиени́чный; антисанита́рный.
unsatisfactory ['ʌnsætis'fæktəri] □ неудовлетвори́тельный.
unsavo(u)ry ['ʌn'seivəri] □ невку́сный; непривлека́тельный.
unsay ['ʌn'sei] [*irr.* (say)] брать наза́д (ска́занное).
unscathed ['ʌn'skeiðd] невреди́мый.
unschooled ['ʌn'sku:ld] необу́ченный; недисциплини́рованный.
unscrew ['ʌn'skru:] отви́нчивать (-ся) [-нти́ть(ся)].
unscrupulous [ʌn'skru:pjuləs] □ беспринци́пный; бессо́вестный; неразбо́рчивый (в сре́дствах).
unsearchable [ʌn'sə:tʃəbl] □ непостижи́мый, необъясни́мый.
unseasonable [ʌn'si:znəbl] □ несвоевре́менный.
unseemly [ʌn'si:mli] неподоба́ющий; непристо́йный.
unseen ['ʌn'si:n] неви́димый; неви́данный.
unselfish ['ʌn'seilfiʃ] □ бескоры́стный.
unsettle ['ʌn'setl] приводи́ть в беспоря́док; расстра́ивать [-ро́ить]; ~d [-d] неустро́енный; неустанови́вшийся; не решённый; неопла́ченный (счёт).
unshaken ['ʌn'ʃeikən] непоколе́бленный.
unshaven ['ʌn'ʃeivn] небри́тый.
unship ['ʌn'ʃip] сгружа́ть с корабля́.
unshrink|able ['ʌn'ʃriŋkəbl] не садя́щийся при сти́рке (о мате́рии); ~ing [-iŋ] □ непоколеби́мый, бесстра́шный.
unsightly [ʌn'saitli] непригля́дный.
unskil|ful ['ʌn'skilful] □ неуме́лый, неиску́сный; ~led ['ʌn'skild] неквалифици́рованный.
unsoci|able [ʌn'souʃəbl] необщи́тельный.
unsolder ['ʌn'sɔldə] распа́ивать [-пая́ть].
unsolicited ['ʌnsə'lisitid] непро́шенный, невостре́бованный.
unsophisticated ['ʌnsə'fistikeitid] безыску́ственный; бесхи́тростный.
unsound ['ʌn'saund] □ нездоро́вый; испо́рченный; необосно́ванный.
unsparing [ʌn'spɛəriŋ] □ беспоща́дный; ще́дрый.
unspeakable [ʌn'spi:kəbl] □ невырази́мый.
unspent ['ʌn'spent] неистра́ченный; неутомлённый.
unstable ['ʌn'steibl] □ нетвёрдый, неусто́йчивый; *phys.*, ⚗ нестойкий.
unsteady ['ʌn'stedi] □ *s.* unstable; ша́ткий; непостоя́нный.
unstring ['ʌn'striŋ] [*irr.* (string)] снима́ть стру́ны с (P); распуска́ть

[-усти́ть] (бу́сы и т. п.); расшáтывать [-шатáть] (не́рвы).
unstudied ['ʌn'stʌdid] есте́ственный, непринуждённый.
unsubstantial ['ʌnsəb'stænʃəl] □ нереáльный; несуще́ственный.
unsuccessful ['ʌnsək'sesful] □ неудáчный, безуспе́шный; неудáчливый.
unsuitable ['ʌn'sju:təbl] □ неподходя́щий.
unsurpassable ['ʌnsə'pɑ:səbl] □ не могу́щий быть превзойдённым.
unsuspect|ed ['ʌnsəs'pektid] неподозревáемый; неожи́данный; **~ing** [-iŋ] неподозревáющий (of о П).
unsuspicious ['ʌnsəs'piʃəs] □ неподозревáющий; не вызывáющий подозре́ний.
unswerving [ʌn'swə:viŋ] □ неуклóнный.
untangle['ʌn'tæŋgl]распу́т(ыв)ать.
untarnished ['ʌn'tɑ:niʃt] неопорóченный.
unthink|able ['ʌn'θiŋkəbl] невообрази́мый; немы́слимый; **~ing** [-iŋ] □ опромéтчивый.
unthought ['ʌn'θɔ:t](и́ли **~-of**) неожи́данный.
untidy [ʌn'taidi] □ неопря́тный, неаккурáтный; неу́бранный.
untie ['ʌn'tai] развя́зывать [-зáть].
until [ən'til, ʌn'til] **1.** *prp.* до (Р); **2.** *cj.* (до тех пор) покá ... (не) ...
untimely [ʌn'taimli] несвоевре́менный.
untiring [ʌn'taiəriŋ] □ неутоми́мый.
untold ['ʌn'tould] нерасскáзанный; несчётный.
untouched ['ʌn'tʌtʃt] нетрóнутый (*a. fig.*); *phot.* неретуши́рованный.
untried ['ʌn'traid] неиспы́танный; ⚖ недопрóшенный.
untroubled ['ʌn'trʌbld] беспрепя́тственный; ненару́шенный.
untrue ['ʌn'tru:] □ непрáвильный; неве́рный.
untrustworthy ['ʌn'trʌstwə:ði] □ не заслу́живающий дове́рия.
unus|ed **1.** ['ʌn'ju:zd] неупотреби́тельный; не бы́вший в употребле́нии; неиспóльзованный; **2.** ['ʌn'ju:st] непривы́кший (to к Д); **~ual** [ʌn'ju:ʒuəl] □ необыкнове́нный, необы́чный.
unutterable [ʌn'ʌtərəbl] □ невырази́мый.
unvarnished ['ʌn'vɑ:niʃt] *fig.* неприкрáшенный.
unvarying [ʌn'vɛəriiŋ] □ неизменя́ющийся, неизме́нный.
unveil [ʌn'veil] снимáть покрывáло с (Р); откры́(вá)ть (пáмятник, тáйну).
unwanted ['ʌn'wɔntid] нежелáнный; нену́жный.
unwarrant|able [ʌn'wɔrəntəbl] □ недопусти́мый; **~ed** [-tid] ниче́м не опрáвданный; негаранти́рованный.
unwary [ʌn'wɛəri] □ необду́манный, неосторóжный.
unwholesome ['ʌn'houlsəm] нездорóвый, неблаготвóрный.
unwieldy [ʌn'wi:ldi] □ неуклю́жий; громóздкий.
unwilling ['ʌn'wiliŋ] □ несклóнный, нерасполóженный.
unwise ['ʌn'waiz] □ неразу́мный.
unwitting [ʌn'witiŋ] □ невóльный, непреднаме́ренный.
unworkable [ʌn'wə:kəbl] неприме́нимый, негóдный для рабóты.
unworthy [ʌn'wə:ði] □ недостóйный.
unwrap ['ʌn'ræp] развёртывать (-ся) [-верну́ть(ся)].
unyielding [ʌn'ji:ldiŋ] □ неподáтливый, неусту́пчивый.
up [ʌp] **1.** *adv.* вверх, наве́рх; вверху́, наверху́; вы́ше; *fig.* be ~ to the mark быть на дóлжной высотé (нау́ки и т. п.); be ~ against a task стоя́ть пе́ред задáчей; ~ to вплоть до (Р); it is ~ to me (to do) мне прихóдится (де́лать); what's ~? *sl.* что случи́лось?, в чём де́ло?; **2.** *prp.* вверх по (Д); по направле́нию к (Д); вдоль по (Д); ~ the river вверх по рекé; **3.** *adj.* ~ train пóезд, иду́щий в гóрод; **4.** *su.* the ~s and downs *fig.* преврáтности судьбы́; **5.** *vb.* F поднимáть [-ня́ть]; повышáть [-ы́сить]; вст(ав)áть.
up|braid [ʌp'breid] [вы́]брани́ть; **~bringing** ['ʌpbriŋiŋ] воспитáние; **~heaval** [ʌp'hi:vl] переворóт; **~hill** ['ʌp'hil] (иду́щий) в гóру; *fig.* тяжёлый; **~hold** [ʌp'hould] [*irr.* (hold)] поддéрживать [-жáть]; приде́рживаться (взгля́да) **~holster** [ʌp'houlstə] оби́(вá)ть (ме́бель); [за]драпировáть (кóмнату); **~holsterer** [-rə] обóйщик; драпирóвщик; **~holstery** [-ri] ремеслó драпирóвщика и́ли обóйщика.
up|keep ['ʌpki:p] содержáние; стóимость содержáния; **~land** ['ʌplənd] нагóрная странá; **~lift** **1.** ['ʌplift] (духóвный) подъём; **2.** [ʌp'lift] поднимáть [-ня́ть]; возвышáть [-ы́сить].
upon [ə'pɔn] *s.* on.
upper ['ʌpə] ве́рхний; вы́сший; **~most** [-moust] сáмый ве́рхний; наивы́сший.
up|raise [ʌp'reiz] возвышáть [-ы́сить]; **~right** ['ʌp'rait] **1.** □ прямóй, вертикáльный; *adv. a.* стоймя́; **2.** стóйка; (*a.* ~ piano) пиани́но *n indecl.*; **~rising** [ʌp'raiziŋ] восстáние.
uproar ['ʌprɔ:] шум, гам, волне́-

ние; **~ious** [ʌp'rɔːriəs] □ шу́мный, бу́йный.
up|root [ʌp'ruːt] искореня́ть [-ни́ть]; вырыва́ть с ко́рнем; **~set** [ʌp'set] [*irr.* (set)] опроки́дывать(ся) [-и́нуть(ся)]; расстра́ивать [-ро́ить]; выводи́ть из (душе́вного) равнове́сия; **~shot** ['ʌpʃɔt] развя́зка; заключе́ние; **~side** ['ʌpsaid] *adv.*: ~ down вверх дном; **~stairs** ['ʌp'stɛəz] вверх (по ле́стнице), наве́рх(у́); **~start** ['ʌpstɑːt] вы́скочка *m/f*; **~stream** ['ʌp'striːm] вве́рх по тече́нию; **~turn** [ʌp'təːn] переве́ртывать [переверну́ть]; **~ward(s)** ['ʌpwəd(z)] вверх, наве́рх.
urban ['əːbən] городско́й; **~e** [əː'bein] □ ве́жливый; изы́сканный.
urchin ['əːtʃin] постре́л, мальчи́шка *m.*
urge [əːdʒ] 1. понужда́ть [-у́дить]; подгоня́ть [подогна́ть] (*often* ~ on); 2. стремле́ние, толчо́к *fig.*; **~ncy** ['əːdʒənsi] настоя́тельность *f*; сро́чность *f*; насто́йчивость *f*; **~nt** ['əːdʒənt] □ сро́чный; настоя́тельный, насто́йчивый.
urin|al ['juərinl] писсуа́р; **~ate** [-rineit] [по]мочи́ться; **~e** [-rin] моча́.
urn [əːn] у́рна.
us [ʌs; əs] *pron. pers.* (ко́свенный паде́ж от we) нас, нам, на́ми.
usage ['juːzidʒ] употребле́ние; обы́чай.
usance ['juːzəns] ✝: bill at ~ ве́ксель на срок, устано́вленный торго́вым обы́чаем.
use 1. [juːs] употребле́ние; примене́ние; по́льзование; по́льза; привы́чка; (of) no ~ бесполе́зный; 2. [juːz] употребля́ть [-би́ть]; по́льзоваться (T); воспо́льзоваться (T) *pf.*; испо́льзовать (*im*)*pf.*; обраща́ться [обрати́ться] с (T), обходи́ться [обойти́сь] с (T); I **~d** [juːs(t)] to do я, быва́ло, ча́сто де́лал; **~d** [juːst]: ~ to привы́кший к (Д); **~ful** ['juːsful] □ поле́зный; приго́дный; **~less** ['juːslis] □ бесполе́зный; неприго́дный, него́дный.
usher ['ʌʃə] 1. капельди́нер; швейца́р; при́став (в суде́); 2. проводи́ть [-вести́] (на ме́сто); вводи́ть [ввести́].
usual ['juːʒuəl] □ обыкнове́нный, обы́чный.
usurer ['juːʒərə] ростовщи́к.
usurp [juː'zəːp] узурпи́ровать (*im*)*pf.*; **~er** [juː'zəːpə] узурпа́тор.
usury ['juːʒuri] ростовщи́чество.
utensil [juː'tensl] (*mst pl.* ~s) посу́да, у́тварь *f*; принадле́жность *f*.
utility [juː'tiliti] поле́зность *f*; вы́годность *f*; public ~ коммуна́льное предприя́тие; *pl.* предприя́тия обще́ственного по́льзования; коммуна́льные услу́ги *f/pl.*
utiliz|ation [juːtilai'zeiʃən] испо́льзование, утилиза́ция; **~e** ['juːtilaiz] испо́льзовать (*im*)*pf.*, утилизи́ровать (*im*)*pf*.
utmost ['ʌtmoust] кра́йний, преде́льный.
utter ['ʌtə] 1. □ *fig.* по́лный; кра́йний; абсолю́тный; 2. изд(ав)а́ть (зву́ки); выража́ть слова́ми; **~ance** [-rəns] выраже́ние; произнесе́ние; выска́зывание; **~most** [-moust] кра́йний; преде́льный.

V

vacan|cy ['veikənsi] пустота́; вака́нсия, свобо́дное ме́сто; пробе́л; рассе́янность *f*; **~t** ['veikənt] □ неза́нятый, вака́нтный; пусто́й; рассе́янный (взгляд и т. п.).
vacat|e [və'keit, *Am.* 'veikeit] освобожда́ть [-боди́ть] (дом и т. п.); покида́ть [-и́нуть], оставля́ть [-а́вить] (до́лжность); упраздня́ть [-ни́ть]; **~ion** [və'keiʃən, *Am.* vei'keiʃən] оставле́ние; кани́кулы *f/pl.*; о́тпуск.
vaccin|ate ['væksineit] ⚕ приви́(ва́)ть; **~ation** [væksi'neiʃən] ⚕ приви́вка; **~e** ['væksiːn] ⚕ вакци́на.
vacillate ['væsileit] колеба́ться.
vacuum ['vækjuəm] *phys.* ва́куум; пустота́; ~ cleaner пылесо́с; ~ flask, ~ bottle те́рмос.
vagabond ['vægəbənd] 1. бродя́га *m*; 2. бродя́жничать.
vagrant ['veigrənt] 1. бродя́га *m*; праздноша́тающийся; 2. стра́нствующий; бродя́чий.
vague [veig] неопределённый, нея́сный, сму́тный.
vain [vein] □ тще́тный, напра́сный; пусто́й, су́етный; тщесла́вный; in ~ напра́сно, тще́тно; **~glorious** [vein'glɔːriəs] тщесла́вный; хвастли́вый.
valediction [væli'dikʃən] проща́ние; проща́льная речь *f*.
valet ['vælit] 1. камерди́нер; 2. служи́ть камерди́нером.
valiant ['væljənt] □ *rhet.* хра́брый, до́блестный.
valid ['vælid] ⚖ действи́тельный, име́ющий си́лу; ве́ский, обосно́ванный; **~ity** [və'liditi] действи́тельность *f* и т. д.
valley ['væli] доли́на.
valo(u)r ['vælə] *rhet.* до́блесть *f*.

valuable ['væljuəbl] **1.** □ це́нный; **2.** ~s *pl.* це́нности *f/pl.*
valuation [vælju'eiʃən] оце́нка (иму́щества).
value ['vælju:] **1.** це́нность *f*; цена́; ✝ сто́имость *f*; ✝ валю́та; значе́ние; **2.** оце́нивать [-и́ть] (В); [о-] цени́ть (В); дорожи́ть (Т); ~**less** ['vælju:lis] ничего́ не сто́ящий.
valve ['vælv] ⊕ кла́пан, ве́нтиль *m*; *radio* электро́нная ла́мпа.
van [væn] фурго́н; 🚃 бага́жный или това́рный ваго́н; ⚔ аванга́рд.
vane [vein] флю́гер; крыло́ (ветряно́й ме́льницы); ло́пасть *f* (винта́); лопа́тка (турби́ны).
vanguard ['vængɑ:d] ⚔ аванга́рд.
vanish ['væniʃ] исчеза́ть [-е́знуть].
vanity ['væniti] су́етность *f*; тщесла́вие; ~ bag да́мская су́мочка.
vanquish ['væŋkwiʃ] побежда́ть [-еди́ть].
vantage ['vɑ:ntidʒ] преиму́щество.
vapid ['væpid] □ безвку́сный, пре́сный; *fig.* ску́чный.
vapor|ize ['veipəraiz] испаря́ть(ся) [-ри́ть(ся)]; ~**ous** [-rəs] парообра́зный; (*mst fig.*) тума́нный.
vapo(u)r ['veipə] **1.** пар; пары́; тума́н; *fig.* химе́ра, фанта́зия; **2.** бахва́литься.
varia|ble ['vɛəriəbl] □ непостоя́нный, изме́нчивый; переме́нный; ~**nce** [-riəns] разногла́сие; ссо́ра; be at ~ расходи́ться во мне́ниях; находи́ться в противоре́чии; ~**nt** [-riənt] **1.** ино́й; различный; **2.** вариа́нт; ~**tion** [vɛəri'eiʃən] измене́ние; отклоне́ние; ♪ вариа́ция.
varie|d ['vɛərid] □ *s.* various; ~**gate** ['vɛərigeit] де́лать пёстрым; разнообра́зить; ~**ty** [və'raiəti] разнообра́зие; многосторо́нность *f*; разнови́дность *f*; ряд, мно́жество; ~ show варьете́ *n indecl.*
various ['vɛəriəs] ра́зный; разли́чный; разнообра́зный.
varnish ['vɑ:niʃ] **1.** лак; оли́фа; лакиро́вка (*a. fig.*); *fig.* прикра́са; **2.** [от]лакирова́ть; придава́ть лоск (Д); *fig.* прикра́шивать [-ра́сить] (недоста́тки).
vary ['vɛəri] изменя́ть(ся) [-ни́ть (-ся)]; ра́зниться; расходи́ться [разойти́сь] (о мне́ниях); разнообра́зить.
vase [vɑ:z] ва́за.
vast [vɑ:st] □ обши́рный, грома́дный.
vat [væt] чан; бо́чка, ка́дка.
vault [vɔ:lt] **1.** свод; склеп; подва́л, по́греб; *sport* прыжо́к (с упо́ром); **2.** выводи́ть свод над (Т); перепры́гивать [-гнуть].
vaunt [vɔ:nt] [по]хва́статься (of Т).
veal [vi:l] теля́тина; *attr.* теля́чий.
veer [viə] меня́ть направле́ние (о ве́тре); *fig.* изменя́ть взгля́ды и т. п.
vegeta|ble ['vedʒitəbl] **1.** о́вощ; ~s *pl.* зе́лень *f*, о́вощи *m/pl.*; **2.** расти́тельный; овощно́й; ~**rian** [vedʒi'tɛəriən] **1.** вегетариа́нец (-нка); **2.** вегетариа́нский; ~**te** ['vedʒiteit] *fig.* прозяба́ть.
vehemen|ce ['vi:iməns] си́ла; стреми́тельность *f*; стра́стность *f*; ~**t** [-t] стреми́тельный; стра́стный.
vehicle ['vi:ikl] экипа́ж, пово́зка (и любо́е друго́е сре́дство тра́нспорта и́ли передвиже́ния); *fig.* сре́дство выраже́ния (мы́слей); проводни́к (зара́зы и т. п.).
veil [veil] **1.** покрыва́ло; вуа́ль *f*; *fig.* заве́са; **2.** закрыва́ть покрыва́лом, вуа́лью; *fig.* [за]маскирова́ть.
vein [vein] ве́на; жи́ла (*a.* ⚒); *fig.* [жи́лка; настрое́ние.]
velocity [vi'lɔsiti] ско́рость *f*.
velvet ['velvit] ба́рхат; *attr.* ба́рхатный; ~**y** [-i] ба́рхатный (*fig.*); бархати́стый.
venal ['vi:nl] прода́жный, подкупно́й (*a.* подку́пный).
vend [vend] прод(ав)а́ть; ~**er**, ~**or** ['vendə] продаве́ц.
veneer [və'niə] **1.** фане́ра; **2.** обкле́ивать фане́рой; *fig.* придава́ть (Д) вне́шний лоск.
venera|ble ['venərəbl] □ почте́нный; ~**te** [-reit] благогове́ть пе́ред (Т); ~**tion** [venə'reiʃən] благогове́ние, почита́ние.
venereal [vi'niəriəl] венери́ческий.
Venetian [vi'ni:ʃən] венециа́нский; ~ blind жалюзи́ *n indecl.*
vengeance ['vendʒəns] месть *f*, мще́ние.
venison ['venzn] оле́нина.
venom ['venəm] (*part.* змеи́ный) яд (*a. fig.*); ~**ous** [-əs] □ ядови́тый (*a. fig.*).
vent [vent] **1.** отве́рстие; отду́шина; give ~ to изли́(ва́)ть (В); **2.** *fig.* изли́(ва́)ть (В), дава́ть вы́ход (Д).
ventilat|e ['ventileit] прове́три(ва)ть; [про]вентили́ровать; *fig.* обсужда́ть [-уди́ть], выясня́ть [вы́яснить] (вопро́с); ~**ion** [venti'leiʃən] прове́тривание; вентиля́ция; *fig.* выясне́ние, обсужде́ние (вопро́са).
venture ['ventʃə] **1.** риско́ванное предприя́тие; спекуля́ция; at a ~ науга́д, науда́чу; **2.** рискова́ть [-кну́ть] (Т); отва́жи(ва)ться на (В) (*a.* ~ upon); ~**some** [-səm] □, **venturous** [-rəs] □ сме́лый; риско́ванный.
veracious [və'reiʃəs] правди́вый.
verb|al ['və:bəl] □ слове́сный; у́стный; *gr.* глаго́льный; ~**iage** ['və:biidʒ] многосло́вие; ~**ose** [və:'bous] □ многосло́вный.
verdant ['və:dənt] □ зелене́ющий, зелёный.

verdict ['vǝ:dikt] ⚖ верди́кт; пригово́р (прися́жных) (*a. fig.*).
verdigris ['vǝ:digris] ярь-медя́нка.
verdure ['vǝ:dʒǝ] зе́лень *f*.
verge [vǝ:dʒ] 1. край; кайма́ (вокру́г клу́мбы); *fig.* грань *f*; **on the ~ of** на гра́ни (P); **2.** клони́ться (to к Д); приближа́ться [-ли́зиться] (to к Д); ~ (up)on грани́чить с (T).
veri|fy ['verifai] проверя́ть [-е́рить]; подтвержда́ть [-рди́ть]; **~table** ['veritǝbl] ☐ настоя́щий, и́стинный.
vermin ['vǝ:min] *coll.* вреди́тели *m/pl.*, парази́ты *m/pl.*; **~ous** ['vǝ:minǝs] кише́щий парази́тами.
vernacular [vǝ'nækjulǝ] **1.** ☐ наро́дный (о выраже́нии); родно́й (о языке́); ме́стный (о диале́кте); **2.** наро́дный язы́к; ме́стный диале́кт; жарго́н.
versatile ['vǝ:sǝtail] ☐ многосторо́нний; подвижно́й.
verse [vǝ:s] стих; стихи́ *m/pl.*; поэ́зия; строфа́; **~d** [vǝ:st] о́пытный, све́дущий.
versify ['vǝ:sifai] *v/t.* перелага́ть на стихи́; *v/i.* писа́ть стихи́.
version ['vǝ:ʃǝn] вариа́нт; ве́рсия; перево́д.
vertebral ['vǝ:tibrǝl] позвоно́чный.
vertical ['vǝ:tikǝl] ☐ вертика́льный; отве́сный.
vertig|inous [vǝ:'tidʒinǝs] ☐ головокружи́тельный.
verve [vɛǝv] жи́вость *f* (изображе́ния); разма́х.
very ['veri] **1.** *adv.* о́чень; **the ~ best** са́мое лу́чшее; **2.** *adj.* настоя́щий, су́щий; са́мый (как усиле́ние); **the ~ same** тот са́мый; **the ~ thing** и́менно то, что ну́жно; **the ~ thought** уже́ одна́ мысль *f*, сама́ мысль *f*; **the ~ stones** да́же ка́мни *m/pl.*; **the veriest rascal** после́дний негодя́й.
vesicle ['vesikl] пузырёк.
vessel ['vesl] сосу́д; су́дно, кора́бль *m*.
vest [vest] **1.** жиле́т; нате́льная фуфа́йка; вста́вка (в пла́тье); **2.** *v/t.* облека́ть [-е́чь] (with T); *v/i.* переходи́ть во владе́ние (in P).
vestibule ['vestibju:l] вестибю́ль *m*.
vestige ['vestidʒ] след.
vestment ['vestment] одея́ние; *eccl.* облаче́ние, ри́за.
vestry ['vestri] *eccl.* ри́зница; **~man** [-mǝn] член прихо́дского управле́ния.
veteran ['vetǝrǝn] **1.** ветера́н; быва́лый солда́т; **2.** *attr.* ста́рый, о́пытный.
veterinary ['vetnri] **1.** ветерина́р (*mst* ~ surgeon); **2.** ветерина́рный.
veto ['vi:tou] **1.** ве́то *n indecl.*; **2.** налага́ть ве́то на (B).
vex [veks] досажда́ть [досади́ть], раздража́ть [-жи́ть]; **~ation** [vek'seiʃǝn] доса́да, неприя́тность *f*; **~atious** [-ʃǝs] доса́дный.
via ['vaiǝ] че́рез (B) (на пи́сьмах и т. п.).
vial ['vaiǝl] пузырёк, буты́лочка.
viands ['vaiǝndz] *pl.* я́ства *n/pl.*
vibrat|e [vai'breit] [по]колеба́ться, вибри́ровать; **~ion** [-ʃǝn] вибра́ция.
vice [vais] **1.** поро́к; недоста́ток; ⊕ тиски́ *m/pl.*; **2.** *pref.* ви́це...; **~roy** ['vaisroi] ви́це-коро́ль *m*.
vice versa ['vaisi'vǝ:sǝ] наоборо́т.
vicinity [vi'siniti] окре́стность *f*; бли́зость *f*.
vicious ['viʃǝs] ☐ поро́чный; зло́й.
vicissitude [vi'sisitju:d] : *mst* **~s** *pl.* превра́тности *f/pl.*
victim ['viktim] же́ртва; **~ize** [-timaiz] де́лать свое́й же́ртвой; [за]му́чить.
victor ['viktǝ] победи́тель *m*; **~ious** [vik'tɔ:riǝs] ☐ победоно́сный; **~y** ['viktǝri] побе́да.
victual ['vitl] **1.** *v/i.* запаса́ться прови́зией; *v/t.* снабжа́ть прови́зией; **2.** *mst* **~s** *pl.* продово́льствие, прови́зия; **~ler** ['vitlǝ] поставщи́к продово́льствия.
video ['vidiou] *adj.* телевизио́нный.
vie [vai] сопе́рничать.
view [vju:] **1.** вид (of на B); по́ле зре́ния, кругозо́р; взгляд; наме́рение; осмо́тр; **in ~ of** ввиду́ (P); **on ~** (вы́ставленный) для обозре́ния; **with a ~ to** *or* **of** + *ger.* с наме́рением (+ *inf.*); **have in ~** име́ть в виду́; **2.** осма́тривать [осмотре́ть]; рассма́тривать [-мотре́ть]; [по]смотре́ть на (B); **~point** то́чка зре́ния.
vigil|ance ['vidʒilǝns] бди́тельность *f*; **~ant** [-lǝnt] ☐ бди́тельный.
vigo|rous ['vigǝrǝs] ☐ си́льный, энерги́чный; **~(u)r** ['vigǝ] си́ла, эне́ргия.
vile [vail] ☐ ме́рзкий, ни́зкий.
vilify ['vilifai] поно́сить, [о]черни́ть.
village ['vilidʒ] село́, дере́вня; *attr.* се́льский, дереве́нский; **~r** [-ǝ] се́льский (-кая) жи́тель(ница *f*) *m*.
villain ['vilǝn] злоде́й, негодя́й; **~ous** [-ǝs] злоде́йский; по́длый; **~y** [-i] злоде́йство; по́длость *f*.
vim [vim] F эне́ргия, си́ла.
vindic|ate ['vindikeit] отста́ивать [отстоя́ть] (пра́во и т. п.); реабилити́ровать (*im*)*pf.*; опра́вдывать [-да́ть]; **~tive** [vin'diktiv] ☐ мсти́тельный.
vine [vain] виногра́дная лоза́; **~gar** ['vinigǝ] у́ксус; **~-growing** виногра́дарство; **~yard** ['vinjǝd] виногра́дник.

vintage ['vintidʒ] сбор виногра́да; вино́ (из сбо́ра определённого го́да).

violat|e ['vaiəleit] наруша́ть [-у́шить], преступа́ть [-пи́ть] (кля́тву, зако́н и т. п.); [из]наси́ловать; **~ion** [vaiə'leiʃən] наруше́ние; изнаси́лование.

violen|ce ['vaiələns] неи́стовство; наси́лие; **~t** [-t] □ неи́стовый; я́ростный; наси́льственный.

violet ['vaiəlit] фиа́лка; фиоле́товый цвет.

violin [vaiə'lin] ♪ скри́пка.

viper ['vaipə] гадю́ка.

virago [vi'reigou] сварли́вая же́нщина.

virgin ['vəːdʒin] **1.** де́вственница; *poet. a. eccl.* де́ва; **2.** □ де́вственный (*a.* **~al**); **~ity** [vəː'dʒiniti] де́вственность *f.*

viril|e ['virail] возмужа́лый; му́жественный; **~ity** [vi'riliti] му́жество; возмужа́лость *f.*

virtu ['vəːtuː] понима́ние то́нкостей иску́сства; article of ~ худо́жественная ре́дкость *f*; **~al** ['vəːtjuəl] □ факти́ческий; **~e** ['vəːtjuː] доброде́тель *f*; досто́инство; in ~ of посре́дством (P); в си́лу (P); **~ous** ['vəːtjuəs] □ доброде́тельный; целому́дренный.

virulent ['virulənt] вируле́нтный (яд); опа́сный (о боле́зни); *fig.* зло́бный.

visa ['viːzə] *s.* visé.

viscount ['vaikaunt] вико́нт.

viscous ['viskəs] □ вя́зкий; тягу́чий (о жи́дкости).

visé ['viːzei] **1.** ви́за; **2.** визи́ровать (*im*)*pf.*, *pf. a.* [за-].

visible ['vizəbl] □ ви́димый; ви́дный; *fig.* я́вный, очеви́дный; *pred.* is he ~? принима́ет ли он?

vision ['viʒən] зре́ние; вид; виде́ние; *fig.* проница́тельность *f*; **~ary** ['viʒənəri] **1.** при́зрачный; фантасти́ческий; мечта́тельный; **2.** прови́дец (-дица); мечта́тель(ница *f*) *m.*

visit ['vizit] **1.** *v/t.* навеща́ть [-ести́ть]; посеща́ть [-ети́ть]; осма́тривать [-мотре́ть]; *fig.* постига́ть [-и́гнуть] *or* [-и́чь]; *v/i.* де́лать визи́ты; гости́ть; **2.** посеще́ние, визи́т; **~ation** [vizi'teiʃən] официа́льное посеще́ние; *fig.* испыта́ние, ка́ра; **~or** ['vizitə] посети́тель (-ница *f*) *m*, го́сть(я *f*) *m*; инспе́ктор.

vista ['vistə] перспекти́ва; вид.

visual ['vizjuəl] □ зри́тельный; нагля́дный; опти́ческий; **~ize** [-aiz] нагля́дно представля́ть себе́, мы́сленно ви́деть.

vital ['vaitl] □ жи́зненный; насу́щный, суще́ственный; живо́й (стиль); **~s**, ~ parts *pl.* жи́зненно ва́жные о́рганы *m/pl.*; **~ity** [vai'tæliti] жизнеспосо́бность *f*, жи́зненность *f*, живу́честь *f*; **~ize** ['vaitəlaiz] оживля́ть [-ви́ть].

vitamin(e) ['vaitəmin] витами́н.

vitiate ['viʃieit] [ис]по́ртить; де́лать недействи́тельным.

vivaci|ous [vi'veiʃəs] □ живо́й, оживлённый; **~ty** [-'væsiti] жи́вость *f*, оживлённость *f.*

vivid ['vivid] □ *fig.* живо́й, я́ркий.

vivify ['vivifai] оживля́ть [-ви́ть].

vixen ['viksn] лиси́ца-са́мка.

vocabulary [və'kæbjuləri] слова́рь *m*, спи́сок слов; запа́с слов.

vocal ['voukəl] □ голосово́й; звуча́щий; ♪ вока́льный.

vocation [vou'keiʃən] призва́ние; профе́ссия; **~al** [-l] □ профессиона́льный.

vociferate [vou'sifəreit] гро́мко крича́ть, горла́нить.

vogue [voug] мо́да; популя́рность *f.*

voice [vɔis] **1.** го́лос; give ~ to выража́ть [вы́разить] (В); **2.** выража́ть [вы́разить] (слова́ми).

void [vɔid] **1.** пусто́й; лишённый (of P); недействи́тельный; **2.** пустота́; ва́куум; **3.** ⚖ опорожня́ть [-ро́жнить]; де́лать недействи́тельным.

volatile ['vɔlətail] ⚗ лету́чий (*a. fig.*); *fig.* изме́нчивый.

volcano [vɔl'keinou] (*pl.*: volcanoes) вулка́н.

volition [vou'liʃən] волево́й акт, хоте́ние; во́ля.

volley ['vɔli] **1.** залп; *fig.* град (упрёков и т. п.); **2.** стреля́ть за́лпами; сы́паться гра́дом; *fig.* испуска́ть [-усти́ть] (кри́ки, жа́лобы).

voltage ['voultidʒ] ⚡ напряже́ние.

voluble ['vɔljubl] речи́стый, многоречи́вый.

volum|e ['vɔljum] том; объём; ёмкость *f*, вмести́тельность *f*; *fig.* си́ла, полнота́ (зву́ка и т. п.); **~inous** [və'ljuːminəs] □ объёмистый; многото́мный; обши́рный.

volunt|ary ['vɔləntəri] □ доброво́льный; доброво́льческий; **~eer** [vɔlən'tiə] **1.** доброво́лец; **2.** *v/i.* вызыва́ться [вы́зваться] (for на В); идти́ доброво́льцем; *v/t.* предлага́ть [-ложи́ть] (свою́ по́мощь и т. п.).

voluptu|ary [və'lʌptjuəri] сладостра́стник, сластолю́бец; **~ous** [-s] сладостра́стный; (*of people*) сластолюби́вый.

vomit ['vɔmit] **1.** рво́та; **2.** [вы́-] рвать: he ~s его́ рвёт; *fig.* изверга́ть [-е́ргнуть].

voraci|ous [vo'reiʃəs] □ прожо́рливый, жа́дный; **~ty** [vo'ræsiti] прожо́рливость *f.*

vortex ['vɔːteks] *mst fig.* водоворо́т; *mst fig.* вихрь *m.*

vote [vout] **1.** голосова́ние; баллотиро́вка; (избира́тельный) го́лос; пра́во го́лоса; во́тум; реше́ние; cast a ~ отдава́ть го́лос (for за В; against про́тив Р); **2.** *v/i.* голосова́ть (*im*)*pf.*, *pf. a.* [про-] (for за В; against про́тив Р); *v/t.* голосова́ть (*im*)*pf.*, *pf. a.* [про-]; **~r** ['voutə] избира́тель(ница *f*) *m.*

voting... ['voutiŋ] избира́тельный.

vouch [vautʃ]: ~ for руча́ться [поручи́ться] за (В); **~er** ['vautʃə] расписка; оправда́тельный докуме́нт; поручи́тель *m*; **~safe** [vautʃ'seif] удоста́ивать [-сто́ить] (В/Т).

vow [vau] **1.** обе́т, кля́тва; **2.** *v/t.* [по]кля́сться в (П).

vowel ['vauəl] гла́сный (звук).

voyage [vɔidʒ] **1.** путеше́ствие (мо́рем); **2.** путеше́ствовать (по́ морю).

vulgar ['vʌlgə] □ гру́бый, вульга́рный; по́шлый; широко́ распространённый; ~ tongue наро́дный язы́к; **~ize** [-raiz] опошля́ть [опо́шлить]; вульгаризи́ровать (*im*)*pf.*

vulnerable ['vʌlnərəbl] □ *fig.* уязви́мый.

vulture ['vʌltʃə] *zo.* стервя́тник; *fig.* хи́щник.

W

wad [wɔd] **1.** клочо́к ва́ты, ше́рсти и т. п.; пыж; **2.** набива́ть и́ли подбива́ть ва́той; забива́ть пыжо́м; **~ding** ['wɔdiŋ] наби́вка, подби́вка.

waddle ['wɔdl] ходи́ть вперева́лку.

wade [weid] *v/t.* переходи́ть вброд; *v/i.* проб(и)ра́ться (through по Д *or* че́рез В).

wafer ['weifə] обла́тка; ва́фля.

waffle ['wɔfl] *part. Am.* ва́фля.

waft [wɑ:ft] **1.** дунове́ние (ве́тра); струя́ (за́паха); **2.** носи́ть(ся), [по-] нести́(сь) (по во́здуху).

wag [wæg] **1.** шутни́к; **2.** маха́ть [махну́ть] (Т), виля́ть [вильну́ть] (Т); ~ one's finger грози́ть па́льцем.

wage [weidʒ] **1.** вести́ (войну́); **2.** *mst* **~s** ['weidʒiz] *pl.* за́работная пла́та.

waggish ['wægiʃ] □ шаловли́вый; заба́вный, коми́чный.

waggle ['wægl] F пома́хивать (Т); пока́чивать(ся).

wag(g)on ['wægən] пово́зка, теле́га; F де́тская коля́ска; 🚂 *Brit.* ваго́н-платфо́рма; **~er** [-ə] во́зчик.

waif [weif] беспризо́рник; бездо́мный челове́к; бро́шенная вещь *f.*

wail [weil] **1.** вопль *m*; вой (ве́тра); причита́ние; **2.** [за]вопи́ть; вы́ть, завы́(ва́)ть; причита́ть.

waist [weist] та́лия; ⚓ шкафу́т; **~coat** ['weiskout, 'weskət] жиле́т.

wait [weit] *v/i.* жда́ть (for В *or* Р), ожида́ть (for Р), подожда́ть *pf.* (for В *or* Р); (ча́сто: ~ at table) прислу́живать [-жи́ть] (за столо́м); ~ (up)on прислу́живать (Д); ~ and see занима́ть выжида́тельную пози́цию; *v/t.* выжида́ть [вы́ждать] (В); ~ dinner подожда́ть с обе́дом (for В); **~er** ['weitə] официа́нт.

waiting ['weitiŋ] ожида́ние; **~-room** приёмная; 🚂 зал ожида́ния.

waitress ['weitris] официа́нтка.

waive [weiv] отка́зываться [-за́ться] от (пра́ва и т. п.); **~r** ['weivə] ⚖ отка́з (от пра́ва, тре́бования).

wake [weik] **1.** ⚓ кильва́тер; **2.** [*irr.*] *v/i.* бо́дрствовать; (*mst* ~ up) просыпа́ться [просну́ться], пробужда́ться [-уди́ться]; *v/t.* [раз]буди́ть, пробужда́ть [-уди́ть]; возбужда́ть [-уди́ть] (жела́ния и т. п.); **~ful** ['weikful] □ бессо́нный; бди́тельный; **~n** ['weikən] *s.* wake 2.

wale [weil] полоса́, рубе́ц.

walk [wɔ:k] **1.** *v/i.* ходи́ть, идти́ [пойти́] (пешко́м); [по]гуля́ть; появля́ться [-ви́ться] (о привиде́нии); *v/t.* прогу́ливать (ло́шадь и т. п.); обходи́ть [обойти́]; **2.** ходьба́; похо́дка; прогу́лка пешко́м; тропа́, алле́я; ~ of life обще́ственное положе́ние; профе́ссия.

walking ['wɔ:kiŋ] **1.** ходьба́; **2.** гуля́ющий; ходя́чий; ~ tour экску́рсия пешко́м; **~-stick** трость *f.*

walk|-out ['wɔ:k'aut] *Am.* забасто́вка; **~-over** лёгкая побе́да.

wall [wɔ:l] **1.** стена́; сте́нка (сосу́да); **2.** обноси́ть стено́й; ~ up заде́л(ыв)ать (дверь и т. п.).

wallet ['wɔlit] бума́жник.

wallflower ⚘ желтофио́ль *f*; *fig.* де́вушка, оста́вшаяся без кавале́ра (на балу́).

wallop ['wɔləp] F [по]би́ть, [по-, от]колоти́ть.

wallow ['wɔlou] валя́ться, бара́xтаться.

wall|-paper ['wɔ:lpeipə] обо́и *m/pl.*; **~-socket** ⚡ ште́псельная розе́тка.

walnut [-nət] ⚘ гре́цкий оре́х.

walrus ['wɔ:lrəs] *zo.* морж.

waltz [wɔ:ls] **1.** вальс; **2.** вальси́ровать.

wan [wɔn] □ бле́дный; изнурённый; ту́склый.

wand [wɔnd] (волшéбная) пáлочка.
wander [ˈwɔːndə] бродить; стрáнствовать; блуждáть (тáкже о взгля́де, мы́слях и т. п.).
wane [wein] **1.** убывáние (луны́); **2.** уменьшáться [умéньшиться]; убы́(вá)ть, быть на ущéрбе (о лунé); подходи́ть к концу́.
wangle [ˈwæŋgl] *sl.* ухитря́ться получи́ть.
want [wɔnt] **1.** недостáток (of P *or* в П); нуждá; потрéбность *f*; бéдность *f*; **2.** *v/i.* be **~ing**: he is **~ing** in patience емý недостаёт терпéния; **~** for нуждáться в (П); *v/t.* [за]хотéть (P *a.* B); [по]желáть (P *a.* B); нуждáться в (Д); he **~s** energy емý недостаёт энéргии; what do you **~**? что вам нýжно?; **~ed** (в объявлéниях) трéбуется, ⚖ разы́скивается.
wanton [ˈwɔntən] **1.** □ рéзвый; произвóльный; бýйный (о рóсте); похотли́вый; распýтный; **2.** резви́ться.
war [wɔː] **1.** войнá; *fig.* борьбá; make **~** вести́ войнý ([up]on с T); **2.** *attr.* воéнный; **3.** воевáть.
warble [ˈwɔːbl] издавáть трéли; [с]пéть (о пти́цах).
ward [wɔːd] **1.** опекáемый; райóн (гóрода); (больни́чная) палáта; (тюрéмная) кáмера; **~s** *pl.* борóдка (ключá); **2.** **~** (off) отражáть [отрази́ть], отвращáть [-рати́ть] (удáр); **~er** [ˈwɔːdə] тюрéмщик; **~robe** [ˈwɔːdroub] гардерóб; **~** trunk чемодáн-шкáф.
ware [wɛə] (в слóжный словáх) посýда; **~s** *pl.* товáр(ы *pl.*).
warehouse **1.** [ˈwɛəhaus] товáрный склад; пакгáуз; **2.** [-hauz] помещáть в склад; храни́ть на склáде.
warfare [ˈwɔːfɛə] войнá, ведéние войны́.
wariness [ˈwɛərinis] осторóжность *f*.
warlike [ˈwɔːlaik] вои́нственный.
warm [wɔːm] **1.** □ тёплый (*a. fig.*); *fig.* горя́чий; **2.** согревáние; **3.** [на-, со]грéть, нагрé(вá)ть(ся), согрé(вá)ть(ся) (*a.* **~** up); **~th** [-θ] теплó; теплотá (*a. fig.*).
warn [wɔːn] предупреждáть [-редить] (of, against о П); предостерегáть [-стерéчь] (of, against от P); **~ing** [ˈwɔːniŋ] предупреждéние; предостережéние.
warp [wɔːp] [по]корóбить(ся) (о дéреве); *fig.* извращáть [-рати́ть], искажáть [исказить] (взгля́ды и т. п.).
warrant [ˈwɔrənt] **1.** правомóчие; ручáтельство; ⚖ довéренность *f*; **~** of arrest прикáз об арéсте; **2.** оправдывать [-дáть]; ручáться [поручи́ться] за (B); ✝ гаранти́ровать (*im*)*pf.*; **~y** [-i] гарáнтия; ручáтельство.
warrior [ˈwɔriə] *poet.* боéц, вóин.
wart [wɔːt] бородáвка; нарóст (на стволé дéрева).
wary [ˈwɛəri] □ осторóжный.
was [wɔz, wəz] *pt.* от be.
wash [wɔʃ] **1.** *v/t.* [вы́]мыть; обмы́(вá)ть; промы́(вá)ть; [вы́]стирáть; *v/i.* [вы́]мы́ться; стирáться (о матéрии); плескáться; **2.** мытьё; сти́рка; бельё (для сти́рки); прибóй; помóи *m/pl.*; *pharm.* примóчка; **~able** [ˈwɔʃəbl] (хорошó) стирáющийся; **~-basin** [ˈwɔʃbeisn] таз; умывáльная рáковина; **~-cloth** тря́почка для мытья́; **~er** [ˈwɔʃə] мóйщик (-ица); промывáтель *m*; стирáльная маши́на; ⊕ шáйба, проклáдка; **~(er)woman** прáчка; **~ing** [ˈwɔʃiŋ] **1.** мытьё; сти́рка; бельё (для сти́рки); **2.** стирáльный; стирáющийся; **~y** [ˈwɔʃi] жи́дкий, водяни́стый.
wasp [wɔsp] осá.
wastage [ˈweistidʒ] изнáшивание; потéри утéчкой, усýшкой и т. п.
waste [weist] **1.** пусты́ня; потéря; изли́шняя трáта; отбрóсы *m/pl.*; ⊕ отхóды *m/pl.*; угáр; lay **~** опустошáть [-ши́ть]; **2.** пусты́нный; невозде́ланный; опустошённый; **3.** *v/t.* расточáть [-чи́ть] (дéньги и т. п.); [по]теря́ть (врéмя); опустошáть [-ши́ть]; изнуря́ть [-ри́ть] (органи́зм); *v/i.* истощáться [-щи́ться]; **~ful** [ˈweistful] □ расточи́тельный; **~-paper**: **~** basket корзи́на для бумáги.
watch [wɔtʃ] **1.** стрáжа; стóрож; ⚓ вáхта; (кармáнные или нарýчные) часы́ *m/pl.*; **2.** *v/i.* [по]караýлить (over B); стоя́ть на стрáже; бóдрствовать; **~** for выжидáть [вы́ждать] (B); *v/t.* [по]сторожи́ть; наблюдáть, следи́ть за (T); выжидáть [вы́ждать]; **~-dog** сторожевóй пёс; **~ful** [ˈwɔtʃful] □ бди́тельный; **~maker** часовщи́к; **~man** [-mən] (ночнóй) стóрож; **~word** парóль *m*; лóзунг.
water [ˈwɔːtə] **1.** водá; **~s** *pl.* вóды *f/pl.*; drink the **~s** пить целéбные вóды; *attr.* водянóй; вóдный; водо...; **2.** *v/t.* орошáть [ороси́ть]; [на]пои́ть (живóтных); поли́(вá)ть; (*a.* **~** down) разбавля́ть водóй; *fig.* чересчýр смягчáть; *v/i.* слези́ться; ходи́ть на водопóй; набирáть вóду (о кораблé); **~fall** водопáд; **~-gauge** водомéр.
watering [ˈwɔːtəriŋ]: **~-can**, **~-pot** лéйка; **~-place** водопóй; вóды *f/pl.*, курóрт с минерáльными вóдами; морскóй курóрт.
water|-level ýровень воды́; ⊕ ватерпáс; **~man** [ˈwɔːtəmən] лóдочник, перевóзчик; **~proof** **1.** непромокáемый; **2.** непромокáемый плащ *m*; **3.** придавáть водонепроницáемость (Д); **~shed**

водораздéл; бассéйн реки́; **~-side** бéрег; *attr.* располóженный на берегу́; **~tight** водонепроницáемый; *fig.* выдéрживающий кри́тику; **~-way** вóдный путь *m*; фарвáтер; **~works** *pl., a. sg.* водопровóдная стáнция; **~y** ['wɔːtəri] водяни́стый (*a. fig.*).
wattle ['wɔtl] **1.** плетéнь *m*; **2.** [с]плести́; стрóить из плетня́.
wave (weiv) **1.** волнá; знак (рукóй); зави́вка (причёски); **2.** *v/t.* [по-] махáть, дéлать знак (Т); зави́(вá)ть (вóлосы); ~ a p. away дéлать знак комý-либо, чтóбы он удали́лся; ~ aside *fig.* отмáхиваться [-хнýться] от (Р); *v/i.* развевáться (о знамёнах); волновáться (о ни́ве); качáться (о вéтке); ви́ться (о волосáх); **~-length** длинá волны́.
waver ['weivə] [по]колебáться; колыхáться [-хнýться] (о плáмени); дрóгнуть (о войскáх) *pf.*
wavy ['weivi] волни́стый.
wax[1] [wæks] **1.** воск; сургу́ч; ушнáя сéра; *attr.* восковóй; **2.** [на-] вощи́ть.
wax[2] [~] [*irr.*] прибы́(вá)ть (о лунé).
wax|en ['wæksən] (*mst fig.*) восковóй; *fig.* мя́гкий как воск; **~y** ['wæksi] □ восковóй; похóжий на воск.
way [wei] *mst* дорóга, путь *m*; сторонá, направлéние; мéтод; срéдство; обы́чай, привы́чка; óбласть *f*, сфéра; состоя́ние; отношéние; (*a.* ~s *pl.*) óбраз (жи́зни, мы́слей); ~ in, out вход, вы́ход; this ~ сюдá; by the ~ кстáти, мéжду прóчим; по дорóге; by ~ of рáди (Р); в кáчестве (Р); on the ~ в пути́; по дорóге; out of the ~ находя́щийся в сторонé; необы́чный; необыкновéнный; under ~ ⚓ на ходу́ (*a. fig.*); give ~ уступáть [-пи́ть] (Д); have one's ~ добивáться своегó; настáивать на своём; lead the ~ идти́ во главé; покáзывать примéр; **~-bill** накладнáя; спи́сок пассажи́ров; **~farer** пу́тник; **~lay** [wei'lei] [*irr.* (lay)] подстерегáть [-рéчь]; **~side 1.** обóчина; **2.** придорóжный; **~ward** ['weiwəd] □ своенрáвный; капри́зный.
we [wiː, wi] *pron. pers.* мы.
weak [wiːk] □ слáбый; **~en** ['wiːkən] *v/t.* ослабля́ть [-áбить]; *v/i.* [о]слабéть; **~ly** [-li] хи́лый; *adv.* слáбо; **~-minded** ['wiːk'maindid] слабоу́мный; **~ness** [-nis] слáбость [*f.*]
weal[1] [wiːl] блáго.
weal[2] [~] *s.* wale.
wealth [welθ] богáтство; изоби́лие; **~y** ['welθi] □ богáтый.
wean [wiːn] отнимáть от груди́; отучáть [-чи́ть] (from, of от Р).
weapon ['wepən] ору́жие; *fig.* срéдство (самозащи́ты).
wear [wɛə] **1.** [*irr.*] *v/t.* носи́ть (одéжду); (*a.* ~ away, down, off) стирáть [стерéть], изнáшивать [износи́ть]; *fig.* изнуря́ть [-ри́ть], истощáть [-щи́ть] (*mst* ~ out); *v/i.* носи́ться (о плáтье); ~ on мéдленно тяну́ться (о врéмени); **2.** ношéние, нóска (одéжды); одéжда, плáтье; (*a.* ~ and tear, *part.* ⊕) изнóс, изнáшивание; be the ~ быть в мóде.
wear|iness ['wiərinis] устáлость *f*; утомлённость *f*; **~isome** [-səm] □ утоми́тельный; **~y** ['wiəri] **1.** □ утомлённый; утоми́тельный; **2.** утомля́ть(ся) [-ми́ть(ся)].
weasel ['wiːzl] *zo.* лáска.
weather ['weðə] **1.** погóда; **2.** *v/t.* вывéтривать [вы́ветрить]; выдéрживать [вы́держать] (бу́рю) (*a. fig.*); подвергáть атмосфéрному влия́нию; *v/i.* вывéтриваться [вы́ветриться]; подвергáться атмосфéрному влия́нию; **~-beaten, ~-worn** обвéтренный; закалённый (о человéке); повреждённый бу́рями.
weav|e [wiːv] [*irr.*] [со]ткáть; [с]плести́; *fig.* сочиня́ть [-ни́ть]; **~er** ['wiːvə] ткач, ткачи́ха.
web [web] ткань *f*; паути́на; (плáвательная) перепóнка; **~bing** ['webiŋ] ткáная тесьмá.
wed [wed] выдавáть зáмуж; жени́ть (*im*)*pf.*; сочетáть брáком; **~ding** ['wediŋ] **1.** свáдьба; **2.** свáдебный.
wedge [wedʒ] **1.** клин; **2.** закрепля́ть кли́ном; раскáлывать при пóмощи кли́на; (*a.* ~ in) вкли́нивать(ся) [-ни́ть(ся)]; ~ o. s. in вти́скиваться [вти́снуться].
wedlock ['wedlɔk] брак.
Wednesday ['wenzdi] средá (день).
wee [wiː] крóшечный, мáленький.
weed [wiːd] **1.** сóрная травá, сорня́к; **2.** [вы́]полóть; **~s** [-z] *pl.* вдóвий трáур; **~y** ['wiːdi] зарóсший сóрной травóй; F *fig.* долговя́зый, тóщий.
week [wiːk] недéля; by the ~ понедéльно; this day ~ недéлю томý назáд; чéрез недéлю; **~-day** бу́дний день *m*; **~-end** нерабóчее врéмя от суббóты до понедéльника; **~ly** ['wiːkli] **1.** еженедéльный; недéльный; **2.** еженедéльник.
weep [wiːp] [*irr.*] [за]плáкать; покрывáться кáплями; **~ing** ['wiːpiŋ] плаку́чий (об и́ве, берёзе).
weigh [wei] *v/t.* взвéшивать [-éсить] (*a. fig.*); ~ anchor поднимáть я́корь; ~ed down отягощённый; *v/i.* вéсить; взвéшиваться [-éситься]; *fig.* имéть вес, значéние; ~ (up)on тяготéть над (Т).
weight [weit] **1.** вес; тя́жесть *f*; ги́ря; *sport* штáнга; брéмя *n*; вли-

я́ние; **2.** отягоща́ть [-готи́ть]; *fig.* обременя́ть [-ни́ть]; **~y** ['weiti] □ тяжёлый; *fig.* ва́жный, ве́ский.

weird [wiəd] таи́нственный; роково́й; F стра́нный, непоня́тный.

welcome ['welkəm] **1.** приве́тствие; you are ~ to *inf.* я охо́тно позволя́ю вам (+ *inf.*); (you are) ~ не́ за что!; ~! добро́ пожа́ловать!; **2.** жела́нный; прия́тный; **3.** приве́тствовать (*a. fig.*); раду́шно принима́ть.

weld [weld] ⊕ сва́ривать(ся) [-и́ть (-ся)].

welfare ['welfɛə] благосостоя́ние; ~ work рабо́та по улучше́нию бытовы́х усло́вий населе́ния.

well[1] [wel] **1.** коло́дец; родни́к; *fig.* исто́чник; пролёт (ле́стницы); ⊕ бурова́я сква́жина; **2.** хлы́нуть *pf.*; бить ключо́м.

well[2] [~] **1.** хорошо́; ~ off состоя́тельный; I am not ~ мне нездоро́вится; **2.** *int.* ну! *or* ну, ...; **~-being** благополу́чие; **~-bred** благовоспи́танный; **~-favo(u)red** привлека́тельный; **~-mannered** с хоро́шими мане́рами; **~-timed** своевре́менный; **~-to-do** [-tə'du:] состоя́тельный, зажи́точный; **~-worn** поно́шенный; *fig.* изби́тый.

Welsh [welʃ] **1.** уэ́льский, валли́йский; **2.** валли́йский язы́к; the ~ валли́йцы *m/pl.*

welt [welt] рант (на о́буви); полоса́ (от уда́ра кнуто́м и т. п.).

welter ['weltə] **1.** сумато́ха, сумбу́р; **2.** валя́ться, бара́хтаться.

wench [wentʃ] де́вка, (крестья́нская) де́вушка.

went [went] *pt.* от **go.**

wept [wept] *pt.* и *p. pt.* от **weap.**

were [wə:, wə] *pt. pl.* от **be.**

west [west] **1.** за́пад; **2.** за́падный; **3.** *adv.* к за́паду, на за́пад; ~ of к за́паду от (Р); **~erly** ['westəli], **~ern** ['westən] за́падный; **~ward(s)** ['westwəd(z)] на за́пад.

wet [wet] **1.** дождли́вая пого́да; мокрота́; **2.** мо́крый; вла́жный, сыро́й; дождли́вый; **3.** [*irr.*] [на-] мочи́ть, нама́чивать [-мочи́ть]; увлажня́ть [-ни́ть].

wether ['weðə] кастри́рованный бара́н.

wet-nurse ['wetnə:s] корми́лица.

whale [weil] кит; **~bone** ['weilboun] кито́вый ус; **~r** ['weilə] китобо́йное су́дно; китоло́в.

whaling ['weiliŋ] охо́та на кито́в.

wharf [wɔ:f] (това́рная) при́стань *f*; на́бережная.

what [wɔt] **1.** что?; ско́лько ...?; **2.** то, что; что; ~ about ...? что но́вого о ...?; ну, как ...?; ~ for? заче́м?; ~ a blessing! кака́я благода́ть!; **3.** ~ with ... ~ with отча́сти от (Р) ... отча́сти от (Р); **~(so)ever** [wɔt(sou)'evə] како́й бы ни; что бы ни; there is no doubt whatever нет никако́го сомне́ния.

wheat [wi:t] пшени́ца.

wheel [wi:l] **1.** колесо́; гонча́рный круг; *mot.* руль *m*; **2.** ката́ть, [по-] кати́ть (коля́ску и т. п.); е́хать на велосипе́де; опи́сывать круги́; повора́чивать(ся) [поверну́ть(ся)]; ⚔ заходи́ть фла́нгом; ⚔ right ~! ле́вое плечо́ вперёд — марш!; **~barrow** та́чка; **~-chair** кре́сло на колёсах (для инвали́да); **~ed** [wi:ld] колёсный, на колёсах.

wheeze [wi:z] дыша́ть с при́свистом.

when [wen] **1.** когда́?; **2.** *conj.* когда́, в то вре́мя как, как то́лько; тогда́ как.

whence [wens] отку́да.

when(so)ever [wen(sou)'evə] вся́кий раз когда́; когда́ бы ни.

where [wɛə] где, куда́; from ~ отку́да; **~about(s) 1.** ['wɛərə'baut(s)] где?, о́коло како́го ме́ста?; **2.** ['wɛərəbaut(s)] местонахожде́ние; **~as** [wɛər'æz] тогда́ как; поско́льку; **~by** [wɛə'bai] посре́дством чего́; **~fore** ['wɛəfɔ:] почему́?; **~in** [wɛər'in] в чём; **~of** [wɛər'ɔv] из кото́рого; о кото́ром; о чём; **~upon** [wɛərə'pɔn] по́сле чего́; **~ver** [wɛər'evə] где бы ни, куда́ бы ни; **~withal** [-wi'ðɔ:l] необходи́мые сре́дства *n/pl.*

whet [wet] [на]точи́ть (на оселке́).

whether ['weðə] ... ли; ~ or no так и́ли ина́че; во вся́ком слу́чае.

whetstone ['wetstoun] точи́льный ка́мень *m*.

whey [wei] сы́воротка.

which [witʃ] **1.** кото́рый?; како́й?; **2.** кото́рый; что; **~ever** [-'evə] како́й уго́дно, како́й бы ни ...

whiff [wif] **1.** дунове́ние, струя́ (во́здуха); дымо́к; затя́жка (при куре́нии); **2.** пуска́ть клубы́ (ды́ма); попы́хивать (Т).

while [wail] **1.** вре́мя *n*, промежу́ток вре́мени; for a ~ на вре́мя; F worth ~ сто́ящий затра́ченного труда́; **2.** ~ away проводи́ть [-вести́] (вре́мя); **3.** (*a.* whilst [wailst]) пока́, в то вре́мя как; тогда́ как.

whim [wim] при́хоть *f*, капри́з.

whimper ['wimpə] [за]хны́кать.

whim|sical ['wimzikəl] □ прихотли́вый, причу́дливый; **~sy** ['wimzi] при́хоть *f*; причу́да.

whine [wain] [за]скули́ть; [за]хны́кать.

whip [wip] **1.** *v/t.* хлеста́ть [-стну́ть]; [вы́]сечь; сби(ва́)ть (сли́вки, я́йца и т. п.); *pol.* ~ in созы(ва́ть]; ~ up расшеве́ливать [-ли́ть]; подстёгивать [-стегну́ть]; *v/i.* ю́ркать [юркну́ть]; трепа́ться (о па́русе); **2.** кнут (*a.* riding-~) хлыст; ку́чер; *parl.* организа́тор па́ртии.

whippet *zo.* ['wipit] гóнчая собáка.
whipping ['wipiŋ] подстёгивание (кнутóм); взбýчка; **~-top** волчóк.
whirl [wə:l] **1.** вихревóе движéние; вихрь *m*; кружéние; **2.** кружи́ть(ся); **~-pool** водоворóт; **~-wind** вихрь *m*.
whisk [wisk] **1.** вéничек, метёлочка; мутóвка; **2.** *v/t.* сби(вá)ть (сли́вки и т. п.); смáхивать [-хнýть]; помáхивать (хвостóм); *v/i.* ю́ркать [юркнýть]; **~ers** ['wiskəz] *pl. zo.* усы́ (кóшки и т. п.) *m/pl.*; бакенбáрды *f/pl.*
whisper ['wispə] **1.** шёпот; **2.** шептáть [шепнýть].
whistle ['wisl] **1.** свист; свистóк; **2.** свистáть, свистéть [сви́стнуть].
white [wait] **1.** *com.* бéлый; блéдный; F чéстный; неви́нный, чи́стый; ~ heat бéлое калéние; ~ lie неви́нная (*or* святáя) ложь *f*; **2.** бéлый цвет; белизнá; белóк (глáза, яйцá); бели́ла *n/pl.*; **~n** ['waitn] [по]бели́ть; [по]белéть; **~ness** ['waitnis] белизнá; **~wash** **1.** побéлка; **2.** [по]бели́ть; *fig.* обеля́ть [ли́ть].
whither *lit.* ['wiðə] кудá.
whitish ['waitiʃ] бел(ес)овáтый.
Whitsun ['witsn] *eccl.* трóица.
whittle ['witl] строгáть и́ли оттáчивать ножóм; *fig.* ~ away свести́ на нет.
whiz(z) [wiz] свистéть (о пýлях и т. п.).
who [hu:] *pron.* **1.** кто?; **2.** котóрый; кто; тот, кто ...; *pl.*: те, кто.
whoever [hu:'evə] *pron.* кто бы ни ...; котóрый бы ни ...
whole [houl] **1.** □ цéлый, весь; невреди́мый; ~ milk цéльное молокó; **2.** цéлое; всё *n*; итóг; (up)on the ~ в цéлом; в óбщем; **~-hearted** □ и́скренний, от всегó сéрдца; **~sale** **1.** (*mst* ~ trade) оптóвая торгóвля; **2.** оптóвый; *fig.* в бóльших размéрах; ~ dealer оптóвый торгóвец; **3.** óптом; **~some** [houlsəm'] □ полéзный, здорóвый.
wholly ['houli] *adv.* целикóм, всецéло.
whom [hu:m] *pron.* (вини́тельный падéж от who) когó и т. д.; котóрого и т. д.
whoop [hu:p] **1.** ги́канье; **2.** ги́кать [ги́кнуть]; **~ing-cough** ['hu:piŋkɔf] ⚕ коклю́ш.
whose [hu:z] (роди́тельный падéж от who) чей *m*, чья *f*, чьё *n*, чьи *pl.*; *rel. pron. mst*: котóрого, котóрой: ~ father отéц котóрого ...
why [wai] **1.** почемý?, отчегó?, зачéм?; **2.** да ведь ...; что же...
wick [wik] фити́ль *m*.
wicked ['wikid] □ злой, злóбный; безнрáвственный; **~ness** [-nis] злóбность *f*; безнрáвственность *f*.
wicker ['wikə] прýтья для плетéния; ~ basket плетёная корзи́нка; ~ chair плетёный стул.
wicket ['wikit] кали́тка; ворóтца *n/pl.* (в кри́кете).
wide [waid] *a.* □ *and adv.* ширóкий; простóрный; далёкий; ширóкó; далекó, далёко (of от P); ~ awake бди́тельный; осмотри́тельный; 3 feet ~ три фýта в ширинý, ширинóй в три фýта; **~n** ['waidn] расширя́ть(ся) [-и́рить (-ся)] **~-spread** широкó распространённый.
widow ['widou] вдовá; *attr.* вдóвий; **~er** [-ə] вдовéц.
width [widθ] ширинá; широтá.
wield [wi:ld] *lit.* владéть (T); имéть в рукáх.
wife [waif] женá; **~ly** ['waifli] свóйственный женé.
wig [wig] пари́к.
wild [waild] **1.** □ ди́кий; бýрный; бýйный; run ~ расти́ без присмóтра; talk ~ говори́ть не дýмая; **2.** ~, ~s [-z] ди́кая мéстность *f*; дéбри *f/pl.*; **~cat** *zo.* ди́кая кóшка; *fig.* недобросóвестное рискóванное предприя́тие; *attr.* рискóванный; нелегáльный; **~erness** ['wildənis] пусты́ня, ди́кая мéстность *f*; **~-fire**: like ~ с быстротóй мóлнии.
wile [wail] *mst* ~s *pl.* хи́трость *f*; улóвка.
wil(l)ful ['wilful] □ упря́мый, своевóльный; преднамéренный.
will [wil] **1.** вóля; си́ла вóли; желáние; завещáние; with a ~ энерги́чно; **2.** [*irr.*] *v/aux.*: he ~ come он придёт; he ~ do it он э́то сдéлает; он хóчет э́то сдéлать; он обы́чно э́то дéлает; **3.** завещáть (*im*)*pf.*; [по]желáть, [за]хотéть; ~ o. s. заставля́ть [-стáвить] себя́.
willing ['wiliŋ] □ охóтно готóвый (to на B *or* + *inf.*); **~ness** [nis] готóвность *f*.
will-o-the-wisp ['wiləðəwisp] блуждáющий огонёк.
willow ['wilou] ⚘ и́ва.
wily ['waili] □ хи́трый, ковáрный.
win [win] [*irr.*] *v/t.* вы́игрывать [вы́играть]; одéрживать [-жáть] (побéду); получáть [-чи́ть]; снискáть *pf.*; (to do) склоня́ть [-ни́ть] (сдéлать); ~ a p. over склони́ть когó-либо на свою́ стóрону; *v/i.* вы́игрывать [вы́играть]; одéрживать побéду.
wince [wins] вздрáгивать [вздрóгнуть].
winch [wintʃ] лебёдка; вóрот.
wind[1] [wind, *poet.* waind] **1.** вéтер; дыхáние; ⚕ гáзы *m/pl.*; ♪ духовы́е инструмéнты *m/pl.*; **2.** заставля́ть запыхáться; давáть перевести́ дух; [по]чýять.
wind[2] [waind] [*irr.*] *v/t.* намáтывать [намотáть]; обмáтывать [об-

мотáть]; обви́(вá)ть; ~ up заводи́ть [завести́] (часы́); † ликвиди́ровать (im)pf.; закáнчивать [закóнчить] (дéло, прéния и т. п.); v/i. намáтываться [намотáться]; обви́(вá)ться.
wind|bag ['windbæg] sl. болту́н, пустозвóн; **~fall** пáданец; бурелóм; fig. неожи́данное счáстье.
winding ['waindiŋ] 1. изги́б, изви́лина; намáтывание; ⚡ обмóтка; 2. изви́листый; спирáльный; ~ stairs pl. винтовáя лéстница; **~-sheet** сáван.
wind-instrument ['windinstrumənt] ♪ духовóй инструмéнт.
windlass ['windləs] ⚓ брáшпиль m; ⊕ вóрот.
windmill [-mil] ветрянáя мéльница.
window ['windou] окнó; витри́на; **~-dressing** декори́рование витри́ны; fig. покáз в лу́чшем ви́де.
wind|pipe ['windpaip] anat. трахéя; **~-screen** mot. ветровóе стеклó.
windy ['windi] □ вéтреный; fig. несерьёзный; многослóвный.
wine [wain] винó; **~press** винодéльный пресс.
wing [wiŋ] 1. крылó; co. рукá; ✈, ⚔ авиапóлк, Am. авиабригáда; ⚔ фланг; ⚠ фли́гель m; thea. **~s** pl. кули́сы f/pl.; take ~ полетéть pf.; on the ~ на летý; 2. fig. окрылять [-ли́ть]; ускоря́ть [-óрить]; [по]летéть.
wink [wiŋk] 1. моргáние; миг; F not get a ~ of sleep не смыкáть глаз; 2. моргáть [-гнýть], мигáть [мигнýть]; ~ at подми́гивать [-гнýть] (Д); смотрéть сквозь пáльцы на (В).
win|ner ['winə] победи́тель(ница f) m; призёр; **~ning** ['winiŋ] 1. вы́игрывающий; побеждáющий; fig. привлекáтельный (a. **~some** [-səm]); 2. **~s** pl. вы́игрыш.
wint|er ['wintə] 1. зимá; attr. зи́мний; 2. проводи́ть зи́му, [пере-, про]зимовáть; **~ry** ['wintri] зи́мний; холóдный; fig. непривéтливый.
wipe [waip] вытирáть [вы́тереть]; утирáть [утерéть]; ~ out fig. смы(вá)ть (позóр); уничтожáть [-óжить].
wire ['waiə] 1. прóволока; прóвод; F телегрáмма; 2. монти́ровать проводá на (П); телеграфи́ровать (im)pf.; скрепля́ть и́ли свя́зывать прóволокой; **~drawn** ['waiə'drɔ:n] тóнкий, казуисти́ческий; **~less** ['waiəlis] 1. □ беспрóволочный; attr. рáдио...; 2. рáдио n indecl.; on the ~ по рáдио; ~ (message) радиогрáмма; ~ (telegraphy) беспрóволочный телегрáф, радиотелеграфи́я; ~ operator ради́ст; ~ pirate радиозáяц; ~ (set) радиоприёмник; 2. передавáть по рáдио; **~-netting** прóволочная сéтка.
wiry ['waiəri] прóволочный; fig. жи́листый; вынóсливый.
wisdom ['wizdəm] му́дрость f; ~ tooth зуб му́дрости.
wise [waiz] 1. му́дрый; благоразу́мный; **~crack** Am. удáчное и́ли саркасти́ческое замечáние; 2. óбраз, спóсоб.
wish [wiʃ] 1. желáние; пожелáние; 2. [по]желáть (Р) (a. ~ for); ~ well (ill) (не) благоволи́ть (к Д); **~ful** ['wiʃful] □ желáющий, жáждущий; тоскли́вый.
wisp [wisp] пучóк (солóмы, сéна и т. п.).
wistful ['wistful] □ задýмчивый, тоскли́вый.
wit [wit] 1. остроýмие; рáзум (a. **~s** pl.); остря́к; be at one's ~'s end быть в тупикé; 2. to ~ тó есть, а и́менно.
witch [witʃ] колдýнья, вéдьма; fig. чародéйка; **~craft** ['witʃkrɑ:ft] колдовствó.
with [wið] с (Т), со (Т); от (Р); у (Р); при (П); ~ a knife ножóм, ~ a pen перóм и т. д.
withdraw [wið'drɔ:] [irr. (draw)] v/t. отдёргивать [-рнуть]; брать назáд; изымáть [изъя́ть] (кни́гу из продáжи, дéньги из обращéния); v/i. удаля́ться [-ли́ться]; ретировáться (im)pf.; ⚔ отходи́ть [отойти́]; **~al** [-əl] отдёргивание; изъя́тие; удалéние; ⚔ отхóд.
wither ['wiðə] v/i. [за]вя́нуть; [по-]блёкнуть; v/t. иссушáть [-ши́ть].
with|hold [wið'hould] [irr. (hold)] удéрживать(ся) [-жáть(ся)]; откáзывать [-зáть] в (П); скры(вá)ть (from от Р); **~in** [-'in] 1. lit. adv. внутри́; 2. prp. в (П), в предéлах (Р); внутри́ (Р); ~ doors в дóме; ~ call в предéлах слы́шимости; **~out** [-'aut] 1. lit. adv. вне, снару́жи; 2. prp. без (Р); вне (Р); **~stand** [-'stænd] [irr. (stand)] противостоя́ть (Д).
witness ['witnis] 1. свидéтель(ница f) m; очеви́дец (-дица); bear ~ свидéтельствовать (to, of о П); in ~ of в доказáтельство (Р); 2. свидéтельствовать о (П); засвидéтельствовать (В) pf.; быть свидéтелем (Р); заверя́ть [-éрить] (пóдпись и т. п.).
wit|ticism ['witisizm] острóта, шýтка; **~ty** ['witi] □ остроýмный.
wives [waivz] pl. от wife.
wizard ['wizəd] волшéбник, маг.
wizen(ed) ['wizn(d)] вы́сохший; смóрщенный.
wobble ['wɔbl] качáться [качнýться]; ковыля́ть [-льнýть].
woe [wou] гóре, скорбь f; ~ is me! гóре мне!; **~begone** ['woubigɔn] удручённый гóрем; мрáчный;

~ful ['wouful] □ скóрбный, гóрестный; жáлкий.
woke [wouk] *pt.* от **wake**; **~n** ['woukən] *p. pt.* от wake.
wolf [wulf] **1.** волк; **2.** пожирáть с жáдностью; **~ish** ['wulfiʃ] вóлчий; хи́щный.
wolves [wulvz] *pl.* от wolf 1.
woman ['wumən] **1.** жéнщина; **2.** жéнский; ~ doctor жéнщина-врач; ~ student студéнтка; **~hood** [-hud] жéнский пол; жéнственность *f*; **~ish** [-iʃ] □ женоподóбный, бáбий; **~kind** [-'kaind] *coll.* жéнщины *f/pl.*; **~like** [-laik] женоподóбный; **~ly** [-li] жéнственный.
womb [wu:m] *anat.* мáтка; чрéво (мáтери); *fig.* лóно.
women ['wimin] *pl.* от **woman**; **~folk** [-fouk] жéнщины *f/pl.*
won [wʌn] *pt.* и *p. pt.* от win.
wonder ['wʌndə] **1.** удивлéние, изумлéние; чýдо; дикóвина; **2.** удивля́ться [-ви́ться] (at Д); I ~ (мне) интерéсно знать; **~ful** [-ful] □ удиви́тельный, замечáтельный.
won't [wount] не бýду и т. д.; не хочý и т. д.
wont [~] **1.** be ~ имéть обыкновéние; **2.** обыкновéние, привы́чка; **~ed** привы́чный.
woo [wu:] ухáживать за (Т); [по-] свáтаться за (В).
wood [wud] лес; дéрево, лесоматериáл; дровá *n/pl.*; *attr.* леснóй; деревя́нный; дровянóй; ♪ деревя́нные духовы́е инструмéнты *m/pl.*; **~cut** гравю́ра на дéреве; **~-cutter** дровосéк; гравёр по дéреву; **~ed** ['wudid] леси́стый; **~en** ['wudn] деревя́нный; *fig.* безжи́зненный; **~man** [-mən] лесни́к; лесорýб; **~pecker** ['pekə] дя́тел; **~-winds** [-windz] деревя́нные духовы́е инструмéнты *m/pl.*; **~work** деревя́нные издéлия *n/pl.*; деревя́нные чáсти *f/pl.* (строéния); **~y** ['wudi] леси́стый; *fig.* деревяни́стый.
wool [wul] шерсть *f*; *attr.* шерстянóй; **~-gathering** ['wulgæðəriŋ] витáние в облакáх; **~(l)en** ['wulin] **1.** шерстянóй; **2.** шерстянáя матéрия; **~ly** ['wuli] **1.** покры́тый шéрстью; шерсти́стый; си́плый; **2.** wollies *pl.* шерстяны́е вéщи *f/pl.*
word [wə:d] **1.** *mst* слóво; разговóр; вéсть *f*; сообщéние; ⚔ парóль *m*; **~s** *pl.* ♪ словá (пéсни) *n/pl.*; *fig.* крýпный разговóр; **2.** выражáть словáми; формули́ровать (*im*)*pf.*, *pf. a.* [с-]; **~ing** ['wə:diŋ] формулирóвка; **~-splitting** софи́стика; буквоéдство.
wordy ['wə:di] □ многословный; словéсный.
wore [wɔ:] *pt.* от wear 1.
work [wə:k] **1.** рабóта; труд; дéло; заня́тие; произведéние, сочинéние; *attr.* рабóто...; рабóчий; **~s** *pl.* механи́зм; строи́тельные рабóты *f/pl.*; завóд; мастерски́е *f/pl.*; be in (out of) ~ имéть рабóту (быть безрабóтным); set to ~ брáться за рабóту; **~s** council произвóдственный совéт; **2.** *v/i.* рабóтать; занимáться [-ня́ться]; дéйствовать; *v/t.* [*irr.*] обрабáтывать [-бóтать]; отдéл(ыв)ать; [*regular vb.*] разрабáтывать [-бóтать] (рудни́к и т. п.); приводи́ть в дéйствие; ~ one's way проби́(вá)ться; ~ off отрабáтывать [-бóтать]; отдéл(ыв)аться от (Р); ✝ распрод(ав)áть; ~ out решáть [реши́ть] (задáчу); разрабáтывать [-бóтать] (план) [*a. irr.*]; ~ up отдéл(ыв)ать; взбудорáжи(ва)ть; подстрекáть [-нýть] на (В).
work|able ['wə:kəbl] □ примени́мый; выполни́мый; пригóдный для рабóты; **~aday** ['wə:kədai] бýдничный; **~day** бýдний (*or* рабóчий) день *m*; **~er** ['wə:kə] рабóчий; рабóтник (-ица); **~-house** рабóтный дом; *Am.* исправи́тельный дом; **~ing** ['wə:kiŋ] **1.** рабóта, дéйствие; разрабóтка; обрабóтка; **2.** рабóтающий; рабóчий; дéйствующий.
workman ['wə:kmən] рабóчий; рабóтник; **~like** [-laik] искýсный; **~ship** мастерствó (ремéсленника); отдéлка (рабóты).
work|shop ['wə:kʃɔp] мастерскáя; цех; **~woman** рабóтница.
world [wə:ld] *com.* мир, свет; *attr.* мировóй; всеми́рный; *fig.* a ~ of мнóжество, кýча (Р); bring (come) into the ~ рождáть [роди́ть] (рождáться [роди́ться]); champion of the ~ чемпиóн ми́ра.
wordly ['wə:ldli] мирскóй; свéтский; **~-wise** ['wə:ldli'waiz] óпытный, бывáлый.
world-power мировáя держáва.
worm [wə:m] **1.** червя́к, червь *m*; ⚕ глист; **2.** вывéдывать [вы́ведать], выпы́тывать [вы́пытать] (out of у Р); ~ o. s. *fig.* вкрáдываться [вкрáсться] (into в В); **~eaten** источенный червя́ми; *fig.* устарéлый.
worn [wɔ:n] *p. pt.* от wear 1; **~-out** [wɔ:n'aut] изнóшенный; *fig.* измýченный.
worry ['wʌri] **1.** беспокóйство; тревóга; забóта; **2.** беспокóить(ся); надоедáть [-éсть] (Д); прист(ав)áть к (Д); [за]мýчить.
worse [wə:s] хýдший; *adv.* хýже; сильнéе; from bad to ~ всё хýже и хýже; **~n** ['wə:sn] ухудшáть(ся) [ухýдшить(ся)].
worship ['wə:ʃip] **1.** культ; почитáние; поклонéние; богослужéние; **2.** поклоня́ться (Д); почитáть; обожáть; **~per** [-ə] поклóнник (-ица); почитáтель(ница *f*) *m*.

worst [wə:st] **1.** (са́мый) ху́дший, наиху́дший; *adv.* ху́же всего́; **2.** одерживать верх над (Т), побежда́ть [-еди́ть].
worsted ['wustid] **1.** *attr.* камво́льный; **2.** га́рус; камво́льная пря́жа.
worth [wə:θ] **1.** сто́ящий; заслу́живающий; be ~ заслу́живать, сто́ить; **2.** цена́, сто́имость *f*; це́нность *f*; досто́инство; **~less** ['wə:θlis] □ ничего́ не сто́ящий; **~-while** ['wə:θ'wail] F сто́ящий; be ~ име́ть смысл; be not ~ не сто́ить труда́; **~y** ['wɔ:ði] □ досто́йный (of P); заслу́живающий (of B).
would [wud] (*pt.* от will) *v/aux.*: he ~ do it он сде́лал бы э́то; он обы́чно э́то де́лал; **~-be** ['wudbi] мни́мый; так называ́емый; самозва́нный.
wound[1] [wu:nd] **1.** ра́на, ране́ние; **2.** ра́нить (*im*)*pf.*; *fig.* заде́(ва́)ть.
wound[2] [waund] *pt.* и *p. pt.* от wind.
wove ['wouv] *pt.* от weave; **~n** ['wouvn] *p. pt.* от weave.
wrangle ['ræŋgl] **1.** препира́ния *n/pl.*, **2.** препира́ться.
wrap [ræp] **1.** *v/t.* (ча́сто ~ up) завёртывать [заверну́ть]; обёртывать [оберну́ть] (бума́гой); заку́т(ыв)ать; оку́т(ыв)ать (*a. fig.*); be ~ped up in быть погружённым в (В); *v/i.* ~ up заку́т(ыв)аться; **2.** обёртка; шаль *f*; плед; **~per** ['ræpə] обёртка; хала́т, капо́т; бандеро́ль *f*; суперобло́жка (кни́ги); **~ping** ['ræpiŋ] упако́вка; обёртка.
wrath [rɔ:θ] гнев.
wreath [ri:θ], *pl.* **~s** [ri:ðz] вено́к; гирля́нда; *fig.* кольцо́, коле́чко (ды́ма); **~e** [ri:ð] [*irr.*] *v/t.* сви(ва́)ть; сплета́ть [сплести́]; *v/i.* обви́(ва́)ться; клуби́ться.
wreck [rek] **1.** ⚓ обло́мки су́дна; круше́ние, ава́рия; разва́лина (о челове́ке); **2.** разруша́ть [-у́шить]; [по]топи́ть (су́дно); be ~ed потерпе́ть ава́рию, круше́ние; *fig.* разруша́ться [-у́шиться] (о пла́нах); **~age** ['rekidʒ] обло́мки (су́дна и т. п. по́сле круше́ния); круше́ние; крах; **~er** ['rekə] граби́тель разби́тых судо́в; рабо́чий авари́йной кома́нды и́ли ремо́нтной брига́ды.
wrench [rentʃ] **1.** дёрганье; скру́чивание; вы́вих; *fig.* тоска́, боль *f*; искаже́ние; ⊕ га́ечный ключ; **2.** вывёртывать [вы́вернуть]; выви́хивать [вы́вихнуть]; *fig.* искажа́ть [искази́ть] (факт, и́стину); ~ open взла́мывать [взлома́ть].
wrest [rest] вырыва́ть [вы́рвать] (from у P) (*a. fig.*); истолко́вывать в свою́ по́льзу; **~le** ['resl] *mst sport* боро́ться; **~ling** [-liŋ] борьба́.
wretch [retʃ] негодя́й; несча́стный.
wretched ['retʃid] □ несча́стный; жа́лкий.
wriggle ['rigl] изви́(ва́)ться (о червяке́ и т. п.); ~ out of уклоня́ться [-ни́ться] от (Р).
wright [rait]: ship~ кораблестрои́тель *m*; cart~ каре́тник; play~ драмату́рг.
wring [riŋ] [*irr.*] скру́чивать [-у-ти́ть]; лома́ть (ру́ки); (*a.* ~ out) выжима́ть [вы́жать] (бельё и т. п.); вымога́ть (from у P).
wrinkle ['riŋkl] **1.** морщи́на; скла́дка; **2.** [с]мо́рщить(ся).
wrist [rist] запя́стье; ~ watch ручны́е (*or* нару́чные) часы́ *m/pl.*
writ [rit] ⚖ предписа́ние, пове́стка; Holy ♀ Свяще́нное писа́ние.
write [rait] [*irr.*] [на]писа́ть; ~ up подро́бно опи́сывать; дописывать [-са́ть]; восхваля́ть в печа́ти; **~r** ['raitə] писа́тель(ница *f*) *m*; письмоводи́тель *m.*
writhe [raið] [с]ко́рчиться (от бо́ли).
writing ['raitiŋ] **1.** писа́ние; (литерату́рное) произведе́ние, сочине́ние; (*a* hand~) по́черк; докуме́нт; in ~ пи́сьменно; **2.** пи́сьменный; пи́счий; **~-case** несессе́р для пи́сьменных принадле́жностей; **~-paper** почто́вая (*or* пи́счая) бума́га.
written ['ritn] **1.** *p. pt.* от write; **2.** [пи́сьменный.
wrong [rɔŋ] **1.** □ непра́вильный, оши́бочный; не тот (,кото́рый ну́жен); be ~ быть непра́вым; go ~ уклоня́ться от пра́вильного пути́; не получа́ться [-чи́ться], срыва́ться [сорва́ться] (о де́ле); *adv.* непра́вильно, не так; **2.** неправота́; непра́вильность *f*; оби́да; несправедли́вость *f*; зло; **3.** поступа́ть несправедли́во с (Т); причиня́ть зло (Д); обижа́ть [оби́деть]; **~doer** злоде́й(ка); **~ful** ['rɔŋful] □ незако́нный (посту́пок); несправедли́вый.
wrote [rout] *pt.* от write.
wrought [rɔ:t] *pt.* и *p. pt.* от work 2 [irr.]: ~ goods гото́вые изде́лия *n/pl.*; ~ iron ⊕ сва́рочное желе́зо.
wrung [rʌŋ] *pt.* и *p. pt.* от wring.
wry [rai] □ криво́й, перєко́шенный; искажённый.

X

X-ray ['eks'rei] **1.** ~s *pl.* рентге́новские лучи́ *m/pl.*; **2.** просве́чивать рентге́новскими луча́ми; **3.** рентге́новский.
xylophone ['zailɔfoun] ♪ ксилофо́н.

Y

yacht [jɔt] ⚓ **1.** я́хта; **2.** плы́ть на я́хте; **~ing** ['jɔtiŋ] я́хтенный спорт.
yankee ['jæŋki] F америка́нец, я́нки *m indecl.*
yap [jæp] **1.** тя́вкать [-кнуть]; *Am. sl.* болта́ть.
yard [jɑ:d] ярд (о́коло 91 см); двор; лесно́й склад; **~stick** изме́рительная лине́йка длино́й в 1 ярд; *fig.* ме́рка, «арши́н».
yarn [jɑ:n] **1.** пря́жа; F *fig.* расска́з; (фантасти́ческая) исто́рия; **2.** F расска́зывать ска́зки, небыли́цы.
yawn [jɔ:n] **1.** зево́та; **2.** зева́ть [зевну́ть]; *fig.* зия́ть.
year [jə:, jiə] год (*pl.* года́, го́ды, лета́ *n/pl.*); **~ly** ежего́дный.
yearn [jə:n] томи́ться, тоскова́ть (for, after по Д).
yeast [ji:st] дро́жжи *f/pl.*
yell [jel] **1.** пронзи́тельный крик; **2.** пронзи́тельно крича́ть, [за]вопи́ть.
yellow ['jelou] **1.** жёлтый; F трусли́вый; ~ press жёлтая пре́сса, бульва́рная пре́сса; **2.** [по]желте́ть; [за]желти́ть; **~ed** пожелте́вший; **~ish** ['jelouiʃ] желтова́тый.
yelp [jelp] **1.** лай, визг; **2.** [за]визжа́ть, [за]ла́ять.
yes [jes] **1.** да; **2.** согла́сие.
yesterday ['jestədi] вчера́.
yet [jet] **1.** *adv.* ещё, всё ещё; уже́; до сих пор; да́же; тем не ме́нее; **as ~** пока́, до сих пор; **not ~** ещё не(т); **2.** *cj.* одна́ко, всё же, несмотря́ на э́то.
yield [ji:ld] **1.** *v/t.* приноси́ть [-нести́] (плоды́, урожа́й, дохо́д и т. п.); сда(ва́)ть; *v/i.* уступа́ть [-пи́ть] (to Д); подд(ав)а́ться; сд(ав)а́ться; **2.** урожа́й, (урожа́йный) сбор; ✝ вы́ход; дохо́д; **~ing** ['ji:ldiŋ] □ *fig.* усту́пчивый.
yoke [jouk] **1.** ярмо́ (*a. fig.*); па́ра запряжённых воло́в; коромы́сло; *fig.* и́го; **2.** впряга́ть в ярмо́; *fig.* спа́ри(ва)ть; подходи́ть друг к дру́гу.
yolk [jouk] желто́к.
yonder ['jɔndə] *lit.* **1.** вон тот, вон та и т. д.; **2.** *adv.* вон там.
you [ju:, ju] *pron. pers.* ты, вы; тебя́, вас; тебе́, ва́м (ча́сто to ~) и т. д.
young [jʌŋ] **1.** □ молодо́й; ю́ный; **2.** the ~ молодёжь *f*; *zo.* детёныши *m/pl.*; with ~ супоро́с(н)ая, сте́льная и т. п.; **~ster** ['jʌŋstə] F подро́сток, ю́ноша *m.*
your [jɔ:, juə] *pron. poss.* твой *m*, твоя́ *f*, твоё *n*, твои́ *pl.*; ваш *m*, ва́ша *f*, ва́ше *n*, ва́ши *pl.*; **~s** [jɔ:z, juəz] *pron. poss. absolute form* твой *m*, твоя́ *f* и т. д.; **~self** [jɔ:'self], *pl.* **~selves** [-'selvz] сам *m*, сама́ *f*, само́ *n*, са́ми *pl.*; себя́, -ся.
youth [ju:θ] *coll.* молодёжь *f*; ю́ноша *m*; мо́лодость *f*; **~ful** ['ju:θful] □ ю́ношеский; моложа́вый.
yule [ju:l] *lit.* свя́тки *f/pl.*

Z

zeal [zi:l] рве́ние, усе́рдие; **~ot** ['zelət] ревни́тель *m*; **~ous** ['zeləs] □ рья́ный, усе́рдный, ре́вностный.
zenith ['zeniθ] зени́т (*a. fig.*).
zero ['ziərou] нуль *m* (*a.* ноль *m*); нулева́я то́чка.
zest [zest] **1.** пика́нтность *f*, «изю́минка»; F наслажде́ние, жар; **2.** придава́ть пика́нтность (Д), де́лать пика́нтным.
zigzag ['zigzæg] зигза́г.
zinc [ziŋk] **1.** цинк; **2.** оцинко́вывать [-ова́ть].
zip [zip] свист (пу́ли); F эне́ргия; ~ fastener = **~per** ['zipə] (застёжка-)мо́лния.
zone [zoun] зо́на (*a. pol.*); по́яс; райо́н.
zoolog|ical [zouə'lɔdʒikəl] □ зоологи́ческий; **~y** [zou'ɔlədʒi] зооло́гия.

APPENDIX

Grammatical Tables

Грамматические таблицы

Conjugation and Declension

The following two rules relative to the spelling of endings in Russian inflected words must be observed:

1. **Stems terminating in г, к, х, ж, ш, ч, щ are never followed by ы, ю, я, but by и, у, а.**

2. **Stems terminating in ц are never followed by и, ю, я, but by ы, у, а.**

Besides these, a third spelling rule, dependent on phonetic conditions, viz. position of stress, is likewise important:

3. **Stems terminating in ж, ш, ч, щ, ц can be followed by an о in the ending only if the syllable in question bears the stress; otherwise, i. e. in unstressed position, е is used instead.**

A. Conjugation

Prefixed forms of the perfective aspect are represented by adding the prefix in square brackets, e. g.: [про]чита́ть = чита́ть *impf.*, прочита́ть *pf.*

Personal endings of the present (and perfective future) tense:

1st conjugation:	**-ю (-у)**	**-ешь**	**-ет**	**-ем**	**-ете**	**-ют (-ут)**
(stressed)		**(-ёшь)**	**(-ёт)**	**(-ём)**	**(-ёте)**	
2nd conjugation:	**-ю (-у)**	**-ишь**	**-ит**	**-им**	**-ите**	**-ят (-ат)**

***Reflexive*:**

1st conjugation:	**-юсь (-усь)**	**-ешься**	**-ется**	**-емся**	**-етесь**	**-ются (-утся)**
2nd conjugation:	**-юсь (-усь)**	**-ишься**	**-ится**	**-имся**	**-итесь**	**-ятся (-атся)**

Suffixes and endings of the other verbal forms:

imp.	**-й(те)**	**-и(те)**	**-ь(те)**	
reflexive	**-йся (-йтесь)**	**-ись (-итесь)**	**-ься (-ьтесь)**	
	m	***f***	***n***	***pl.***
p.pr.a.	**-щий(ся)**	**-щая(ся)**	**-щее(ся)**	**-щие(ся)**
p.pr.p.	**-мый**	**-мая**	**-мое**	**-мые**
short form	**-м**	**-ма**	**-мо**	**-мы**
g.pr.	**-я(сь), after ж, ш, ч, щ: -а(сь)**			
pt.	**-л**	**-ла**	**-ло**	**-ли**
refl.	**-лся**	**-лась**	**-лось**	**-лись**
p.pt.a.	**-вший(ся)**	**-вшая(ся)**	**-вшее(ся)**	**-вшие(ся)**

p.pt.p.	-нный -тый	-нная -тая	-нное -тое	-нные -тые
short form	-н -т	-на -та	-но -то	-ны -ты
g.pt.	-в, -вши(сь)			

Stress:

a) There is *no change of stress unless the final syllable of the infinitive is stressed*, i. e. in all forms of the respective verb stress remains invariably on the root syllable accentuated in the infinitive, e. g.: пла́кать. The forms of пла́кать correspond to paradigm [3], except for the stress, which is always on пла́-. The imperative of such verbs also differs from the paradigms concerned: it is in **-ь(те)** provided their stem ends in **one consonant** only, e. g.: пла́кать — пла́чь(те), ве́рить — ве́рь(те); and in **-и(те)** (unstressed!) in cases of **two and more consonants** preceding the imperative ending, e. g.: по́мнить — по́мни(те). Verbs with a vowel stem termination, however, generally form their imperative in **-й(те)**: успоко́ить — успоко́й(те).

b) The prefix вы- in perfective verbs always bears the stress: вы́полнить (but *impf.*: выполня́ть). Imperfective (iterative) verbs with the suffix **-ыв-/-ив-** are always stressed on the syllable preceding the suffix: пока́зывать (but *pf.* показа́ть), спра́шивать (but *pf.* спроси́ть).

c) In the past participle passive of verbs in **-а́ть (-я́ть)**, there is usually a shift of stress back onto the root syllable as compared with the infinitive (see paradigms [1]—[4], [6], [7], [28]). With verbs in **-е́ть** and **-и́ть** such a shift may occur as well, very often in agreement with a parallel accent shift in the 2nd p. sg. present tense, e. g.: [про]смотре́ть: [про]смотрю́, смо́тришь — просмо́тренный; see also paradigms [14] — [16] as against [13]: [по]мири́ть: [по]мирю́, -и́шь — помирённый. In this latter case the short forms of the participles are stressed on the last syllable throughout: -ённый: -ён, -ена́, -ено́, -ены́. In the former examples, however, stress remains on the same root syllable as in the long form: -'енный: -'ен, -'ена, -'ено, -'ены.

Any details differingf rom the following paradigms and not explained in the foregoing notes are either mentioned in special remarks attached to the individual paradigms or, if not, pointed out after the entry word itself.

Verbs in -ать

1 [про]**чита́ть**

pr. [*ft.*]	[про]чита́ю, -а́ешь, -а́ют
imp.	[про]чита́й(те)
p.pr.a.	чита́ющий
p.pr.p.	чита́емый
g.pr.	чита́я
pt.	[про]чита́л, -а, -о, -и
p.pt.a.	[про]чита́вший
p.pt.p.	прочи́танный
g.pt.	прочита́в(ши)

2 [по]**трепа́ть**
(with л after б, в, м, п, ф)

pr. [*ft.*]	[по]треплю́, -е́плешь, -е́плют
imp.	[по]трепли́(те)
p.pr.a.	тре́плющий
p.pr.p.	—
g.pr.	трепля́
pt.	[по]трепа́л, -а, -о, -и
p.pt.a.	[по]трепа́вший
p.pt.p.	потрёпанный
g.pt.	потрепа́в(ши)

3 [об]**глода́ть**
(with changing consonant:
г, д, з > ж
к, т > ч
х, с > ш
ск, ст > щ)

pr. [*ft.*]	[об]гложу́, -о́жешь, -о́жут
imp.	[об]гложи́(те)
p.pr.a.	гло́жущий
p.pr.p.	—
g.pr.	гложа́
pt.	[об]глода́л, -а, -о, -и
p.pt.a.	[об]глода́вший
p.pt.p.	обгло́данный
g.pt.	обглода́в(ши)

4 [по]**держа́ть**
(with preceding ж, ш, ч, щ)

pr. [*ft.*]	[по]держу́, -е́ржишь, -е́ржат
imp.	[по]держи́(те)
p.pr.a.	держа́щий
p.pr.p.	—
g.pr.	держа́
pt.	[по]держа́л, -а, -о, -и
p.pt.a.	[по]держа́вший
p.pt.p.	поде́ржанный
g.pt.	подержа́в(ши)

Verbs in -авать

5 **дава́ть**
(*st.* = -ешь, -ет, *etc.*)

pr. [*ft.*]	даю́, даёшь, даю́т
imp.	дава́й(те)
p.pr.a.	даю́щий
p.pr.p.	дава́емый
g.pr.	дава́я
pt.	дава́л, -а, -о, -и
p.pt.a.	дава́вший
p.pt.p.	—
g.pt.	—

Verbs in -евать

6 [на]**малева́ть**
(*e.* = -ю́, -ёшь, *etc.*)

pr. [*ft.*]	[на]малю́ю, -ю́ешь, -ю́ют
imp.	[на]малю́й(те)
p.pr.a.	малю́ющий
p.pr.p.	малю́емый
g.pr.	малю́я
pt.	[на]малева́л, -а, -о, -и
p.pt.a.	[на]малева́вший
p.pt.p.	намалёванный
g.pt.	намалева́в(ши)

Verbs in -овать (and in -евать with preceding ж, ш, ч, щ, ц)

7 [на]**рисова́ть**
(*e.* = -ю́, -ёшь, *etc.*)

pr. [*ft.*]	[на]рису́ю, -у́ешь, -у́ют
imp.	[на]рису́й(те)
p.pr.a.	рису́ющий
p.pr.p.	рису́емый
g.pr.	рису́я
pt.	[на]рисова́л, -а, -о, -и
p.pt.a.	[на]рисова́вший
p.pt.p.	нарисо́ванный
g.pt.	нарисова́в(ши)

Verbs in -еть

8 [по]**жале́ть**

pr. [*ft.*]	[по]жале́ю, -е́ешь, -е́ют
imp.	[по]жале́й(те)
p.pr.a.	жале́ющий
p.pr.p.	жале́емый
g.pr.	жале́я
pt.	[по]жале́л, -а, -о, -и
p.pt.a.	[по]жале́вший
p.pt.p.	...ённый (*e.g.* одолённый)
g.pt.	пожале́в(ши)

9 [с]**горе́ть**

pr. [*ft.*]	[с]горю́, -и́шь, -я́т
imp.	[с]гори́(те)
p.pr.a.	горя́щий
p.pr.p.	—
g.pr.	горя́
pt.	[с]горе́л, -а, -о, -и
p.pt.a.	[с]горе́вший
p.pt.p.	...е́нный (*e.g.* презре́нный)
g.pt.	сгоре́в(ши)

10 [по]**терпе́ть**

pr. [*ft.*]	[по]терплю́, -е́рпишь, -е́рпят
imp.	[по]терпи́(те)
p.pr.a.	терпя́щий
p.pr.p.	терпи́мый
g.pr.	терпя́
pt.	[по]терпе́л, -а, -о, -и
p.pt.a.	[по]терпе́вший
p.pt.a.	...енный (*e.g.* претерпенный)
g.pt.	потерпе́в(ши)

11 [по]**лете́ть**
(with changing consonant:
д, з > ж
к, т > ч
х, с > ш
ск, ст > щ)

pr. [*ft.*]	[по]лечу́, -ети́шь, -етя́т
imp.	[по]лети́(те)
p.pr.a.	летя́щий
p.pr.p.	—
g.pr.	летя́
pt.	[по]лете́л, -а, -о, -и

p.pt.a.	[по]летéвший
p.pt.p.	...енный (*e. g.* вéрченный)
g.pt.	полетéв(ши)

Verbs in -ерéть

12	[по]**терéть** (*st.* = -ешь, -ет, *etc.*)
pr. [*ft.*]	[по]трý, -трёшь, -трýт
imp.	[по]три́(те)
p.pr.a.	трýщий
p.pr.p.	—
g.pr.	—
pt.	[по]тёр, -рла, -о, -и
p.pt.a.	[по]тёрший
p.pt.p.	[по]тёртый
g.pt.	потерéв *or* потёрши

Verbs in -ить

13	[по]**мири́ть**
pr. [*ft.*]	[по]мирю́, -ри́шь, -ря́т
imp.	[по]мири́(те)
p.pr.a.	миря́щий
p.pr.p.	мири́мый
g.pr.	миря́
pt.	[по]мири́л, -а, -о, -и
p.pt.a.	[по]мири́вший
p.pt.p.	помирённый
g.pt.	помири́в(ши)

14	[на]**корми́ть** (with л after б, в, м, п, ф)
pr. [*ft.*]	[на]кормлю́, -óрмишь, -óрмят
imp.	[на]корми́(те)
p.pr.a.	кóрмящий
p.pr.p.	корми́мый
g.pr.	кормя́
pt.	[на]корми́л, -а, -о, -и
p.pt.a.	[на]корми́вший
p.pt.p.	накóрмленный
g.pt.	накорми́в(ши)

15	[по]**проси́ть** (with changing consonant: д, з > ж; к, т > ч; х, с > ш; ск, ст > щ)
pr. [*ft.*]	[по]прошý, -óсишь, -óсят
imp.	[по]проси́(те)
p.pr.a.	прося́щий
p.pr.p.	проси́мый
g.pr.	прося́
pt.	[по]проси́л, -а, -о, -и
p.pt.a.	[по]проси́вший
p.pt.p.	попрóшенный
g.pt.	попроси́в(ши)

16	[на]**точи́ть** (with preceding ж, ш, ч, щ)
pr. [*ft.*]	[на]точý, -óчишь, -óчат
imp.	[на]точи́(те)
p.pr.a.	точáщий
p.pr.p.	точи́мый
g.pr.	точá
pt.	[на]точи́л, -а, -о, -и
p.pt.a.	[на]точи́вший
p.pt.p.	натóченный
g.pt.	наточи́в(ши)

Verbs in -оть

17	[рас]**колóть**
pr. [*ft.*]	[рас]колю́, -óлешь, -óлют
imp.	[рас]коли́(те)
p.pr.a.	кóлющий
p.pr.p.	—
g.pr.	кóля
pt.	[рас]колóл, -а, -о, -и
p.pt.a.	[рас]колóвший
p.pt.p.	раскóлотый
g.pt.	расколóв(ши)

Verbs in -уть

18	[по]**дýть**
pr. [*ft.*]	[по]дýю, -ýешь, -ýют
imp.	[по]дýй(те)
p.pr.a.	дýющий
p.pr.p.	—
g.pr.	дýя
pt.	[по]дýл, -а, -о, -и
p.pt.a.	[по]дýвший
p.pt.p.	дýтый
g.pt.	подýв(ши)

19	[по]**тянýть**
pr. [*ft.*]	[по]тянý, -я́нешь, -я́нут
imp.	[по]тяни́(те)
p.pr.a.	тя́нущий
p.pr.p.	—
g.pr.	—
pt.	[по]тянýл, -а, -о, -и
p.pt.a.	[по]тянýвший
p.pt.p.	[по]тя́нутый
g.pt.	потянýв(ши)

20	[со]**гнýть** (*st.* = -ешь, -ет, *etc.*)
pr. [*ft.*]	[со]гнý, -нёшь, -нýт
imp.	[со]гни́(те)
p.pr.a.	гнýщий
p.pr.p.	—
g.pr.	—

pt.	[со]гну́л, -а, -о, -и
p.pt.a.	[со]гну́вший
p.pt.p.	[со́]гну́тый
g.pt.	согну́в(ши)

21	[по]**ту́хнуть** (-г- = -г- instead of -х- throughout)
pr. [*ft.*]	[по]ту́хну, -нешь, -нут
imp.	[по]ту́хни(те)
p.pr.a.	ту́хнущий
p.pr.p.	—
g.pr.	—
pt.	[по]ту́х, -хла, -о, -и
p.pt.a.	[по]ту́хший
p.pt.p.	...нутый (*e. g.* дости́гнутый)
g.pt.	поту́хши

Verbs in -ыть

22	[по]**кры́ть**
pr. [*ft.*]	[по]кро́ю, -о́ешь, -о́ют
imp.	[по]кро́й(те)
p.pr.a.	кро́ющий
p.pr.p.	—
g.pr.	кро́я
pt.	[по]кры́л, -а, -о, -и
p.pt.a.	[по]кры́вший
p.pt.p.	[по]кры́тый
g.pt.	покры́в(ши)

23	[по]**плы́ть** (*st.* = -ешь, -ет, *etc.*)
pr. [*ft.*]	[по]плыву́, -вёшь, -ву́т
imp.	[по]плыви́(те)
p.pr.a.	плыву́щий
p.pr.p.	—
g.pr.	плывя́
pt.	[по]плы́л, -а́, -о, -и
p.pt.a.	[по]плы́вший
p.pt.p.	...ы́тый (*e.g.* проплы́тый)
g.pt.	поплы́вши

Verbs in -зти, -зть, (-сти)

24	[по]**везти́** (-с[т]- = -с[т]- instead of -з- throughout) (*st.* = -ешь, -ет, *etc.*)
pr. [*ft.*]	[по]везу́, -зёшь, -зу́т
imp.	[по]вези́(те)
p.pr.a.	везу́щий
p.pr.p.	везо́мый
g.pr.	везя́
pt.	[по]вёз, -везла́, -о́, -и́
p.pt.a.	[по]вёзший
p.pt.p.	повезённый
g.pt.	повёзши

Verbs in -сти, -сть

25	[по]**вести́** (-т- = -т- instead of -д- throughout) (*st.* = -ешь, -ет, *etc.*)
pr. [*ft.*]	[по]веду́, -дёшь, -ду́т
imp.	[по]веди́(те)
p.pr.a.	веду́щий
p.pr.p.	ведо́мый
pt.	[по]вёл, -вела́, -о́, -и́
p.pt.a.	[по]ве́дший
p.pt.p.	поведённый
g.pt.	поведя́

Verbs in -чь

26	[по]**вле́чь** (г/ж = г instead of к, and ж instead of ч) (-б- = -б- instead of к/ч) (*st.* = -ешь, -ет, *etc.*)
pr. [*ft.*]	[по]влеку́, -ечёшь, -еку́т
imp.	[по]влеки́(те)
p.pr.a.	влеку́щий
p.pr.p.	влеко́мый
g.pr.	—
pt.	[по]влёк, -екла́, -о́, -и́
p.pt.a.	[по]влёкший
p.pt.p.	повлечённый
g.pt.	повлёкши

Verbs in -ять

27	[рас]**та́ять** (*e.* = -ю́, -ёшь, -ёт, *etc.*)
pr. [*ft.*]	[рас]та́ю, -а́ешь, -а́ют
imp.	[рас]та́й(те)
p.pr.a.	та́ющий
p.pr.p.	—
g.pr.	та́я
pt.	[рас]та́ял, -а, -о, -и
p.pt.a.	[рас]та́явший
p.pt.p.	...янный (*e. g.* обла́янный)
g.pt.	раста́яв(ши)

28	[по]**теря́ть**
pr. [*ft.*]	[по]теря́ю, -я́ешь, -я́ют
imp.	[по]теря́й(те)
p.pr.a.	теря́ющий
p.pr.p.	теря́емый
g.pr.	теряя
pt.	[по]теря́л, -а, -о, -и
p.pt.a.	[по]теря́вший
p.pt.p.	поте́рянный
g.pt.	потеря́в(ши)

B. Declension

Noun

a) Succession of the six cases (horizontally): nominative, genitive, dative, accusative, instrumental and prepositional in the singular and (thereunder) the plural. *With nouns denoting animate beings (persons and animals) there is a coincidence of endings in the accusative and genitive both singular and plural of the masculine, but only in the plural of the feminine and neuter genders.* This rule also applies, of course, to adjectives as well as various pronouns and numerals that must in syntactical connections agree with their respective nouns.

b) Variants of the following paradigms are pointed out in notes added to the individual declension types or, if not, mentioned after the entry word itself.

Masculine nouns:

1	ви́д	—	-а	-у	—	-ом	о -е
		-ы	-ов	-ам	-ы	-ами	о -ах

Note: Nouns in -ж, -ш, -ч, -щ have in the *g/pl.* the ending -ей.

2	реб	-ёнок	-ёнка	-ёнку	-ёнка	-ёнком	о -ёнке
		-я́та	-я́т	-я́там	-я́т	-я́тами	о -я́тах

3	слу́ча	-й	-я	-ю	-й	-ем	о -е
		-и	-ев	-ям	-и	-ями	о -ях

Notes: Nouns in -ий have in the *prpos/sg.* the ending -ии.
When *e.*, the ending of the *instr/sg.* is -ём, and of the *g/pl.* -ёв.

4	про́фил	-ь	-я	-ю	-ь	-ем	о -е
		-и	-ей	-ям	-и	-ями	о -ях

Note: When *e.*, the ending of the *instr/sg.* is -ём.

Feminine nouns:

5	рабо́т	-а	-ы	-е	-у	-ой (-ою)	о -е
		-ы	—	-ам	-ы	-ами	о -ах

Note: In the *g/pl.* with many nouns having two final stem consonants -о- or -е- is inserted between these (cf. p. 15 and entry words concerned).

6	неде́л	-я	-и	-е	-ю	-ей (-ею)	о -е
		-и	-ь	-ям	-и	-ями	о -ях

Notes: Nouns in -ья have in the *g/pl.* the ending -ий (unstressed) or -е́й (stressed), the latter being also the termination of nouns in -е́я. Nouns in -я with preceding vowel terminate in the *g/pl.* in -й (for -ий see also No. 7).
When *e.*, the ending of the *instr/sg.* is -ёй (-ёю).
For the insertion of -е-, -о- in the *g/pl.* cf. note with No. **5**.

7	áрми	-я	-и	-и	-ю	-ей (-ею)	об -и
		-и	-й	-ям	-и	-ями	об -ях
8	тетрáд	-ь	-и	-и	-ь	-ью	о -и
		-и	-ей	-ям	-и	-ями	о -ях

Neuter nouns:

9	блю́д	-о	-а	-у	-о	-ом	о -е
		-а	—	-ам	-а	-ами	о -ах

Note: For the insertion of -о-, -е- in the *g/pl.* cf. note with No. 5.

10	пóл	-е	-я	-ю	-е	-ем	о -е
		-я́	-éй	-я́м	-я́	-я́ми	о -я́х

Note: Nouns in -ье have in the *g/pl.* the ending -ий. Besides, they do not shift their stress.

11	жили́щ	-е	-а	-у	-е	-ем	о -е
		-а	—	-ам	-а	-ами	о -ах
12	желáни	-е	-я	-ю	-е	-ем	о -и
		-я	-й	-ям	-я	-ями	о -ях
13	врéм	-я	-ени	-ени	-я	-енем	о -ени
		-енá	-ён	-енáм	-енá	-енáми	о -енáх

Adjective

(also ordinal numbers, etc.)

Notes

a) Adjectives in -ский have no predicative (short) forms.

b) Variants of the following paradigms have been recorded with the individual entry words. See also p. 15.

		m	*f*	*n*	*pl.*	
14	бéл	-ый (-óй)	-ая	-ое	-ые	long form
		-ого	-ой	-ого	-ых	
		-ому	-ой	-ому	-ым	
		-ый (-ого)	-ую	-ое	-ые (-ых)	
		-ым	-ой (-ою)	-ым	-ыми	
		о -ом	о -ой	о -ом	о -ых	
		—*	-á	-о(*a.*: -ó)	-ы (*a.*: -ы́)	short form
15	си́н	-ий	-яя	-ее	-ие	long form
		-его	-ей	-его	-их	
		-ему	-ей	-ему	-им	
		-ий (-его)	-юю	-ее	-ие (-их)	
		-им	-ей (-ею)	-им	-ими	
		о -ем	о -ей	о -ем	о -их	
		-(ь)*	-я́	-е	-и	short form
16	стрóг	-ий	-ая	-ое	-ие	long form
		-ого	-ой	-ого	-их	
		-ому	-ой	-ому	-им	
		-ий (-ого)	-ую	-ое	-ие (-их)	
		-им	-ой (-ою)	-им	-ими	
		о -ом	о -ой	о -ом	о -их	
		—*	-á	-о	-и	short form

17	**тóщ**	**-ий**	**-ая**	**-ее**	**-ие**	long form
		-его	-ей	-его	-их	
		-ему	-ей	-ему	-им	
		-ий (-его)	-ую	-ее	-ие (-их)	
		-им	-ей (-ею)	-им	-ими	
		о -ем	о -ей	о -ем	о -их	
		—	-á	-е(ó)	-и	short form
18	**олéн**	**-ий**	**-ья**	**-ье**	**-ьи**	
		-ьего	-ьей	-ьего	-ьих	
		-ьему	-ьей	-ьему	-ьим	
		-ий(-ьего)	-ью	-ье	-ьи (-ьих)	
		-ьим	-ьей (-ьею)	-ьим	-ьими	
		об -ьем	об -ьей	об -ьем	об -ьих	
19	**дя́дин**	**—**	**-а**	**-о**	**-ы**	
		-а	-ой	-а	-ых	
		-у	-ой	-у	-ым	
		— (-а)	-у	-о	-ы (-ых)	
		-ым	-ой (-ою)	-ым	-ыми	
		о -ом**	о -ой	о -ом	о -ых	

* In the masculine short form of many adjectives having two final stem consonants -о- or -е- is inserted between these (cf. p. 15 and entry words concerned).

** Masculine surnames in -ов, -ев, -ин, -ын have the ending -е.

Pronoun

20	**я**	меня́	мне	меня́	мной (мнóю)	обо мне
	мы	нас	нам	нас	нáми	о нас
21	**ты**	тебя́	тебé	тебя́	тобóй (тобóю)	о тебé
	вы	вас	вам	вас	вáми	о вас
22	**он**	егó	емý	егó	им	о нём
	онá	её	ей	её	éю (ей)	о ней
	онó	егó	емý	егó	им	о нём
	они́	их	им	их	и́ми	о них

Note: After prepositions the oblique forms receive an н-prothesis, e.g.: для негó, с нéю (ней).

23	**кто**	когó	комý	когó	кем	о ком
	что	чегó	чемý	что	чем	о чём

Note: In combinations with ни-, не- a preposition separates such compounds, e.g. ничтó: ни от чегó, ни к чемý.

24	**мой**	моегó	моемý	мой (моегó)	мои́м	о моём
	моя́	моéй	моéй	мою́	моéй (моéю)	о моéй
	моё	моегó	моемý	моё	мои́м	о моём
	мои́	мои́х	мои́м	мои́ (мои́х)	мои́ми	о мои́х
25	**наш**	нáшего	нáшему	наш (нáшего)	нáшим	о нáшем
	нáша	нáшей	нáшей	нáшу	нáшей (нáшею)	о нáшей
	нáше	нáшего	нáшему	нáше	нáшим	о нáшем
	нáши	нáших	нáшим	нáши (нáших)	нáшими	о нáших

26	**чей**	чьего́	чьему́	чей (чьего́)	чьим	о чьём
	чья	чьей	чьей	чью	чьей (чье́ю)	о чьей
	чьё	чьего́	чьему́	чьё	чьим	о чьём
	чьи	чьих	чьим	чьи (чьих)	чьи́ми	о чьих
27	**э́тот**	э́того	э́тому	э́тот (э́того)	э́тим	об э́том
	э́та	э́той	э́той	э́ту	э́той (э́тою)	об э́той
	э́то	э́того	э́тому	э́то	э́тим	об э́том
	э́ти	э́тих	э́тим	э́ти (э́тих)	э́тими	об э́тих
28	**тот**	того́	тому́	тот (того́)	тем	о том
	та	той	той	ту	той (то́ю)	о той
	то	того́	тому́	то	тем	о том
	те	тех	тем	те (тех)	те́ми	о тех
29	**сей**	сего́	сему́	сей (сего́)	сим	о сём
	сия́	сей	сей	сию́	сей (се́ю)	о сей
	сие́	сего́	сему́	сие́	сим	о сём
	сии́	сих	сим	сии́ (сих)	си́ми	о сих
30	**сам**	самого́	самому́	самого́	сами́м	о само́м
	сама́	само́й	само́й	самоё	само́й (само́ю)	о само́й
	само́	самого́	самому́	само́	сами́м	о само́м
	са́ми	сами́х	сами́м	сами́х	сами́ми	о сами́х
31	**весь**	всего́	всему́	весь (всего́)	всем	обо всём
	вся	всей	всей	всю	всей (все́ю)	обо всей
	всё	всего́	всему́	всё	всем	обо всём
	все	всех	всем	все (всех)	все́ми	обо всех
32	**не́сколько**	не́скольких	не́скольким	не́сколько (не́скольких)	не́сколькими	о не́скольких

Numeral

33	**оди́н**	одного́	одному́	оди́н (одного́)	одни́м	об одно́м
	одна́	одно́й	одно́й	одну́	одно́й (одно́ю)	об одно́й
	одно́	одного́	одному́	одно́	одни́м	об одно́м
	одни́	одни́х	одни́м	одни́ (одни́х)	одни́ми	об одни́х

34	**два**	**две**	**три**	**четы́ре**
	двух	двух	трёх	четырёх
	двум	двум	трём	четырём
	два (двух)	две (двух)	три (трёх)	четы́ре (четырёх)
	двумя́	двумя́	тремя́	четырьмя́
	о двух	о двух	о трёх	о четырёх

35	**пять**	**пятна́дцать**	**пятьдеся́т**	**сто**	**со́рок**
	пяти́	пятна́дцати	пяти́десяти	ста	сорока́
	пяти́	пятна́дцати	пяти́десяти	ста	сорока́
	пять	пятна́дцать	пятьдеся́т	сто	со́рок
	пятью́	пятна́дцатью	пятью́десятью	ста	сорока́
	о пяти́	о пятна́дцати	о пяти́десяти	о ста	о сорока́

86	**две́сти**	**три́ста**	**четы́реста**	**пятьсо́т**
	двухсо́т	трёхсо́т	четырёхсо́т	пятисо́т
	двумста́м	трёмста́м	четырёмста́м	пятиста́м
	две́сти	три́ста	четы́реста	пятьсо́т
	двумяста́ми	тремяста́ми	четырьмяста́ми	пятьюста́ми
	о двухста́х	о трёхста́х	о четырёхста́х	о пятиста́х
87	**о́ба**	**о́бе**	**дво́е**	**че́тверо**
	обо́их	обе́их	двои́х	четверы́х
	обо́им	обе́им	двои́м	четверы́м
	о́ба (обо́их)	о́бе (обе́их)	дво́е (двои́х)	че́тверо (четве-ры́х)
	обо́ими	обе́ими	двои́ми	четверы́ми
	об обо́их	об обе́их	о двои́х	о четверы́х

American and British Geographical Names

Американские и британские географические названия

A

Aberdeen (æbə'di:n) г. Абердин.
Adelaide ('ædəleid) г. Аделаида.
Aden ('eidn) г. 'Аден.
Africa ('æfrikə) 'Африка.
Alabama (ælə'bɑ:mə) Алабáма.
Alaska (ə'læskə) Аляска.
Albany ('ɔ:lbəni) 'Олбани.
Alleghany ('æligeini) **1.** Аллегáны *pl.* (горы); **2.** Аллегéйни (река).
America (ə'merikə) Амéрика.
Antilles (æn'tili:z) Антильские островá.
Antwerp ('æntwə:p) Антвéрпен.
Arabia (ə'reibjə) Арáвия.
Argentina (ɑ:dʒən'ti:nə) Аргентина.
Arizona (æri'zounə) Аризóна.
Arkansas ('ɑ:kənsɔ: штат в США, ɑ:'kænsəs река в США) Аркáнзáс.
Ascot ('æskət) г. 'Эскот.
Asia ('eiʃə) 'Азия; ~ *Minor* Мáлая 'Азия.
Auckland ('ɔ:klənd) г. 'Окленд (порт в Новой Зеландии).
Australia (ɔ:s'treiljə) Австрáлия.
Austria ('ɔ:striə) 'Австрия.
Azores (ə'zɔ:z) Азóрские островá.

B

Bahamas (bə'hɑ:məz) Багáмские островá.
Balkans ('bɔ:lkənz): *the* ~ Балкáны.
Baltic Sea ('bɔ:ltik'si:) Балтийское мóре.
Baltimore ('bɔ:ltimɔ:) г. Бáлтимор.
Barents Sea ('bɑ:rənts'si:) Бáренцово мóре.
Bavaria (bə'vɛəriə) Бавáрия.
Belfast ('belfɑ:st) г. Бéлфаст (столица Северной Ирландии).
Belgium ('beldʒəm) Бéльгия.
Bengal (beŋ'gɔ:l) Бенгáлия.
Berlin ('bə:'lin, bə:'lin) г. Берлин.
Bermudas (bə[:]'mju:dəz) Бермýдские островá.
Birmingham ('bə:miŋəm) г. Бирмингем.
Biscay ('biskei): *Bay of* ~ Бискáйский залив.
Black Sea ('blæk'si:) Чёрное мóре.
Boston ('bɔstən) г. Бостóн.
Brazil (brə'zil) Бразилия.
Brighton ('braitn) г. Брáйтон.
Bristol ('bristl) г. Бристóль (порт и торговый город на юге Англии).
Britain ('britən) (*Great* Велико-) Британия; *Greater* ~ Великобритáния с колóниями, Британская импéрия.
Brooklyn ('bruklin) Брýклин.
Brussels ('brʌslz) г. Брюссéль.
Burma ('bə:mə) Бирма.
Bulgaria (bʌl'gɛəriə) Болгáрия.
Byelorussia (bjelou'rʌʃə) Белорýссия.

C

Calcutta (kæl'kʌtə) г. Калькýтта.
California (kæli'fɔ:njə) Калифóрния.
Cambridge ('keimbridʒ) г. Кéмбридж.
Canada ('kænədə) Канáда.
Canary (kə'nɛəri): ~ *Islands* Канáрские островá.
Canterbury ('kæntəbəri) г. Кéнтербери.
Capetown ('keiptaun) г. Кéйптаун.
Cardiff ('kɑ:dif) г. Кáрдифф.
Caribbean Sea (kæ'ribi:ən'si:) Карибское мóре.
Carolina (kærə'lainə) Каролина (*North* Сéверная, *South* 'Южная).
Ceylon (si'lɔn) о-в Цейлóн.
Chesterfield ('tʃestəfi:ld) г. Чéстерфильд.
Cheviot ('tʃeviət): ~ *Hills* Чевиóтские гóры.
Chicago (ʃi'kɑ:gou, *a.* ʃi'kɔ:gou) г. Чикáго.
Chile ('tʃili) Чили.
China ('tʃainə) Китáй.
Cincinnati (sinsi'næti) г. Цинциннáти.
Cleveland ('kli:vlənd) г. Кливленд.
Clyde (klaid) р. Клáйд.
Colorado (kɔlə'rɑ:dou) Колорáдо.
Columbia (kə'lʌmbiə) Колýмбия (река, город, адм. округ).
Connecticut (kə'nektikət) Коннéктикут (река и штат в США).
Cordilleras (kɔ:di'ljɛərəz) Кордильéры (горы).
Coventry ('kɔvəntri) г. Кóвентри.
Cyprus ('saiprəs) о-в Кипр.

D

Dakota (də'koutə) Дакóта (*North* Сéверная, *South* 'Южная).
Denmark ('denmɑ:rk) Дáния.
Danube ('dænju:b) р. Дунáй.
Delhi ('deli) г. Дéли.
Detroit (də'trɔit) г. Детрóйт.
Dover ('douvə) г. Дувр.
Dublin ('dʌblin) г. Дýблин.
Dunkirk (dʌn'kə:k) г. Дюнкéрк.

E

Edinburgh ('edinbərə) г. 'Эдинбург.
Egypt ('i:dʒipt) Еги́пет.
Eire ('εərə) 'Эйре.
England ('iŋglənd) 'Англия.
Erie ('iəri): *Lake* ~ óзеро 'Эри.
Eton ('i:tn) г. 'Итон.
Europe ('juərəp) Еврóпа.

F

Falkland ('fɔ:klənd): ~ *Islands* Фолклéндские островá.
Florida ('flɔridə) Флори́да.
Folkestone ('foukstən) г. Фóлкстон.
France (frɑ:ns) Фрáнция.

G

Galveston(e) ('gælvistən) г. Гáлвестон.
Geneva (dʒi'ni:və) г. Женéва.
Georgia ('dʒɔ:dʒiə) Джóрджия (штат в США).
Germany ('dʒə:məni) Гермáния.
Gettysburg ('getizbə:g) г. Гéттисберг.
Ghana (gɑ:nə) Гáна.
Glasgow ('glɑ:sgou) г. Глáзго.
Gloucester ('glɔstə) г. Глóстер.
Greenwich ('grinidʒ) г. Гри́н(в)ич.
Guernsey ('gə:nzi) о-в Гéрнси.
Guiana (gi'ɑ:nə) Гвиáна.
Guinea ('gini) Гвинéя.

H

Haiti ('heiti) Гаи́ти.
Halifax ('hælifæks) г. Гáлифакс.
Harwich ('hæridʒ) г. Хáридж.
Hawaii (hɑ:'waii) о-в Гавáйи.
Hebrides ('hebridi:z) Гебри́дские островá.
Heligoland ('heligoulænd) о-в Гéльголанд.
Hindustan (hindu'stæn, -'stɑ:n) Индостáн.
Hollywood ('hɔliwud) г. Гóлливуд.
Hudson ('hʌdsn) р. Гýдзóн.
Hull (hʌl) г. Гулль.
Hungary ('hʌŋgəri) Вéнгрия.
Huron ('hjuərən): *Lake* ~ óзеро Гýрóн.

I

Iceland ('aislənd) Ислáндия.
Idaho ('aidəhou) Айдáхо.
Illinois (ili'nɔi) 'Иллинóйс.
India ('indjə) 'Индия.
Indiana (indi'ænə) Индиáна.
Iowa ('aiouə) 'Айова.
Irak, Iraq (i'rɑ:k) Ирáк.
Iran (iə'rɑ:n) Ирáн.
Ireland ('aiələnd) Ирлáндия.
Italy ('itəli) Итáлия.

J

Jersey ('dʒə:zi) **1.** о-в Джéрси; **2.** ~ *City* г. Джéрси-Си́ти.

K

Kansas ('kænzəs) Кáнзáс.
Karachi (kə'rɑ:tʃi) г. Карáчи.
Kashmir (kæʃ'miə) Кашми́р.
Kentucky (ken'tʌki) Кентýкки.
Kenya ('ki:njə, 'kenjə) Кéния.
Klondike ('klɔndaik) Клóндайк.
Korea (ko'riə) Корéя.

L

Labrador ('læbrədɔ:) п-в Лабрадóр.
Lancaster ('læŋkəstə) г. Лáнкáстер.
Leeds (li:dz) г. Лидс.
Leicester ('lestə) Лéстер.
Lincoln ('liŋkən) г. Линкольн.
Liverpool ('livəpu:l) г. Ли́верпýл(ь).
London ('lʌndən) г. Лóндон.
Los Angeles (lɔs'ændʒili:z) г. Лос-'Анжелос.
Louisiana (lu[:]i:zi'ænə) Луизиáна.

M

Mackenzie (mə'kenzi) р. Макéнзи.
Madras (mə'dræs) г. Мадрáс.
Maine (mein) Мэн (штат в США).
Malta ('mɔ:ltə) о-в Мáльта.
Manchester ('mæntʃistə) г. Мáнчестер.
Manhattan (mæn'hætən) Манхáттан.
Manitoba (mæni'toubə) Манитóба.
Maryland ('merilənd, *Brt.* mεəri-) Мэ́риленд.
Massachusetts (mæsə'tʃu:sets) Массачýсетс.
Melbourne ('melbən) г. Мéльбурн.
Miami (mai'æmi) г. Майáми.
Michigan ('miʃigən) Ми́чиган (штат в США); *Lake* ~ óзеро Ми́чиган.
Milwaukee (mil'wɔ:ki[:]) г. Милуóки.
Minneapolis (mini'æpəlis) г. Миннеáполис.
Minnesota (mini'soutə) Миннесóта.

Mississippi (misi'sipi) Миссиси́пи (река и штат).
Missouri (mi'zuəri, *Brt.* mi'suəri) Миссу́ри (река и штат).
Montana (mɔn'tɑ:nə) Монта́на (штат в США).
Montreal (mɔntri'ɔ:l) г. Монреа́ль.
Moscow ('mɔskou) г. Москва́.
Munich ('mju:nik) г. Мю́нхен.
Murray ('mʌri) р. Му́ррей (Ма́рри).

N

Natal (nə'tæl) Ната́ль.
Nebraska (ni'bræskə) Небра́ска (штат в США).
Nevada (ne'vɑ:də) Нева́да (штат в США).
Newcastle ('nju:kɑ:sl) г. Ньюка́сл.
Newfoundland (nju:'faundlənd, ⚓ nju:fənd'lænd) о-в Ньюфаундле́нд.
New Hampshire (nju:'hæmpʃiə) Нью-Хэ́мпшир (штат в США).
New Jersey (nju:'dʒə:zi) Нью-Дже́рси (штат в США).
New Mexico (nju:'meksikou) Нью-Ме́ксико (штат в США).
New Orleans (nju:'ɔ:liənz) г. Но́вый Орлеа́н.
New York ('nju:'jɔ:k) Нью-Йо́рк (город и штат).
New Zealand (nju:'zi:lənd) Но́вая Зела́ндия.
Niagara (nai'ægərə) р. Ниага́ра, ~ *Falls* Ниага́рские водопа́ды.
Nigeria (nai'dʒiəriə) Ниге́рия.
Northampton (nɔ:'θæmptən) Нортге́мптон.
Norway ('nɔ:wei) Норве́гия.
Nottingham ('nɔtiŋəm) Но́ттингем.

O

Oceania (ouʃi'einiə) Океа́ния.
Ohio (ou'haiou) Ога́йо (река и штат).
Oklahoma (ouklə'houmə) Оклахо́ма (штат в США).
Ontario (ɔn'tɛəriou) Онта́рио; *Lake* ~ о́зеро Онта́рио.
Oregon ('ɔrigən) Орего́н (штат в США).
Orkney ('ɔ:kni): ~ *Islands* Оркне́йские острова́.
Ottawa ('ɔtəwə) г. Отта́ва.
Oxford ('ɔksfəd) г. 'Оксфорд.

P

Pakistan ('pɑ:kis'tɑ:n) Пакиста́н.
Paris ('pæris) г. Пари́ж.
Pennsylvania (pensil'veinjə) Пенсильва́ния (штат в США).
Philadelphia (filə'delfjə) г. Филаде́льфия.
Philippines ('filipi:nz) Филиппи́ны.
Pittsburg(h) ('pitsbə:g) г. Пи́тсбург.
Plymouth ('plimәθ) г. Пли́мут.
Poland ('poulənd) По́льша.
Portsmouth ('pɔ:tsmeθ) г. По́ртсмут.
Portugal ('pɔ:tjugəl) Португа́лия.
Punjab (pʌn'dʒɑ:b) Пенджа́б.

Q

Quebec (kwi'bek) Квебе́к.

R

Rhine (rain) р. Рейн.
Richmond ('ritʃmənd) г. Ри́чмонд.
Rhode Island (roud'ailənd) Род-'Айленд (штат в США).
Rhodes (roudz) о-в Ро́дос.
Rhodesia (rou'di:ziə) Роде́зия.
Rome (roum) г. Рим.
Russia ('rʌʃə) Росси́я.

S

Scandinavia (skændi'neivjə) Скандина́вия.
Scotland ('skɔtlənd) Шотла́ндия.
Seattle (si'ætl) г. Сиэ́тл.
Seoul (soul) г. Сеу́л.
Sheffield ('ʃefi:ld) г. Ше́ффилд.
Shetland ('ʃetlənd): *the* ~ *Islands* Шетла́ндские острова́.
Siberia (sai'biəriə) Сиби́рь.
Singapore (siŋgə'pɔ:) г. Сингапу́р.
Soudan (su[:]'dæn) Суда́н.
Southampton (sauθ'æmptən) г. Саутге́мптон.
Spain (spein) Испа́ния.
St. Louis (snt'luis) г. Сент-Лу́ис.
Stratford ('strætfəd): ~ on Avon г. Стра́тфорд-на-'Эйвоне.
Sweden ('swi:dn) Шве́ция.
Switzerland ('switsələnd) Швейца́рия.
Sydney ('sidni) г. Си́дней.

T

Tennessee (tene'si:) Теннесси́ (река и штат в США).
Texas ('teksəs) Теха́с (штат в США).
Thames (temz) р. Те́мза.
Toronto (tə'rɔntou) г. Торо́нто.
Trafalgar (trə'fælgə) Трафальга́р.
Transvaal ('trænzvɑ:l) Трансваа́ль.
Turkey ('tə:ki) Ту́рция.

U

Utah ('ju:tɑ:) 'Юта (штат в США).

V

Vancouver (væn'ku:və) г. Ванку́вер.
Vermont (və:'mɔnt) Вермо́нт (штат в США).

Vienna (vi'enə) г. Ве́на.
Virginia (və'dʒinjə) Вирги́ния (штат в США).

W

Wales (weilz) Уэ́льс.
Washington ('wɔʃiŋtən) Ва́шингто́н (город и штат в США).
Wellington ('weliŋtən) г. Ве́ллингтон (столица Новой Зеландии).
West Virginia ('westvə'dʒinjə) За́падная Вирги́ния (штат в США).
Winnipeg ('winipeg) Ви́ннипег (город и озеро в Канаде).
Wisconsin (wis'kɔnsin) Виско́нсин (река и штат в США).
Worcester ('wustə) г. Ву́стер.
Wyoming (wai'oumiŋ) Вайо́минг (штат в США).

Y

York (jɔ:k) Йорк.
Yugoslavia ('ju:gou'slɑ:viə) Югосла́вия.

Наиболее употребительные сокращения, принятые в СССР

Current Russian Abbreviations

авт. (автóбус) (motor) bus
Азербайджáнская ССР (Совéтская Социалистúческая Респýблика) Azerbaijan S.S.R. (Soviet Socialist Republic)
акад. (акадéмик) academician
АН СССР (Акадéмия наýк Сою́за Совéтских Социалистúческих Респýблик) Academy of Sciences of the U.S.S.R. (Union of Soviet Socialist Republics)
Армя́нская ССР (Совéтская Социалистúческая Респýблика) Armenian S.S.R. (Soviet Socialist Republic)
арх. (архитéктор) architect
АССР (Автонóмная Совéтская Социалистúческая Респýблика) Autonomous Soviet Socialist Republic
АТС (автоматúческая телефóнная стáнция) telephone exchange

б-ка (библиотéка) library
БССР (Белорýсская Совéтская Социалистúческая Респýблика) Byelorussian S.S.R. (Soviet Socialist Republic)
БСЭ (Большáя Совéтская Энциклопéдия) Big Soviet Encyclopedia

в. (век) century
вв. (векá) centuries
ВВА (Воéнно-воздýшная акадéмия) Air Force College
ВВС (Воéнно-воздýшные сúлы) Air Forces
ВЛКСМ (Всесою́зный Лéнинский Коммунистúческий Сою́з Молодёжи) Leninist Young Communist League of the Soviet Union
вм. (вмéсто) instead of
ВС (Верхóвный Совéт) Supreme Soviet
ВСХВ (Всесою́зная сельскохозя́йственная вы́ставка) Agricultural Fair of the U.S.S.R.
втуз (вы́сшее технúческое учéбное заведéние) technical college, institute of technology
вуз (вы́сшее учéбное заведéние) university, college
ВЦИК (Всероссúйский Центрáльный Исполнúтельный Комитéт) All-Russian Central Executive Committee
ВЦСПС (Всесою́зный Центрáльный Совéт Профессионáльный Сою́зов) the All-Union Central Council of Trade Unions
ВЧК (Всероссúйская Чрезвычáйная Комúссия по борьбé с контрреволю́цией, саботáжем и спекуля́цией) All-Russian Special Committee for the Suppression of Counter-Revolution, Sabotage, and Black Marketeering (*historical*)

г (грамм) gram(me)
г. **1.** (год) year; **2.** (гóрод) city
га (гектáр) hectare
гг. (гóды) years
ГДР (Гермáнская Демократúческая Респýблика) German Democratic Republic
г-жа (госпожá) Mrs.
глав... in compounds (глáвный)
главврáч (глáвный врач) head physician
г-н (господúн) Mr.
гос... in compounds (государственный)
Госбáнк (госудáрственный банк) State Bank
Гослитиздáт (Госудáрственное издáтельство худóжественной литератýры) State Publishing House for Literature
Госполитиздáт (Госудáрственное издáтельство политúческой литератýры) State Publishing House for Political Literature

ГПУ (Госуда́рственное полити́ческое управле́ние) G.P.U. Political State Administration (*historical*)
гр. (граждани́н) citizen
Грузи́нская ССР (Сове́тская Социалисти́ческая Респу́блика) Georgian S.S.R. (Soviet Socialist Republic)
ГСО (Гото́в к санита́рной оборо́не) Ready to do medical service
ГТО (Гото́в к труду́ и оборо́не) Ready to work and defend
ГУМ (Госуда́рственный универса́льный магази́н) department store
ГУС (Госуда́рственный учёный сове́т) State Advisory Board of Scholars

Детги́з (Госуда́рственное изда́тельство де́тской литерату́ры) State Publishing House for Children's Books
дир. (дире́ктор) director
ДКА (Дом Кра́сной 'Армии) House of the Red Army
доб. (доба́вочный) additional
Донба́сс (Доне́цкий бассе́йн) Donets Basin
доц. (доце́нт) lecturer, instructor
д-р (до́ктор) doctor

ж. д. (желе́зная доро́га) railroad, railway
ж.-д. (железнодоро́жный) relating to railroads *or* railways

завко́м (заводско́й комите́т) works council
загс (отде́л за́писей а́ктов гражда́нского состоя́ния) registrar's (registry) office

и др. (и други́е) etc.
им. (и́мени) called
и мн. др. (и мно́гие други́е) and many (much) more
и пр., и проч. (и про́чее) etc.
и т. д. (и так да́лее) and so on
и т. п. (и тому́ подо́бное) etc.

к. (копе́йка) kopeck
Каза́хская ССР (Сове́тская Социалисти́ческая Респу́блика) Kazak S.S.R. (Soviet Socialist Republic)
кв. **1.** (квадра́тный) square; **2.** (кварти́ра) apartment, flat
кг (килогра́мм) kg (kilogram[me])
КИМ (Коммунисти́ческий интернациона́л молодёжи) Communist Youth International
Кирги́зская ССР (Сове́тская Социалисти́ческая Респу́блика) Kirghiz S.S.R. (Soviet Socialist Republic)
км/час (киломе́тров в час) km/h (kilometers per hour)
колхо́з (коллекти́вное хозя́йство) collective farm, kolkhoz
комсомо́л (Коммунисти́ческий Сою́з Молодёжи) Young Communist League
коп. (копе́йка) kopeck
КПСС (Коммунисти́ческая па́ртия Сове́тского Сою́за) C.P.S.U. (Communist Party of the Soviet Union)
куб. (куби́ческий) cubic

Латви́йская ССР (Сове́тская Социалисти́ческая Респу́блика) Latvian S.S.R. (Soviet Socialist Republic)
Лито́вская ССР (Сове́тская Социалисти́ческая Респу́блика) Lithuanian S.S.R. (Soviet Socialist Republic)
л. с. (лошади́ная си́ла) h.p. (horse power)

МВД (Министе́рство вну́тренних дел) Ministry of Internal Affairs
МГУ (Моско́вский госуда́рственный университе́т) Moscow State University
МГФ (Моско́вская городска́я филармо́ния) Moscow Municipal Philharmonic Hall
Молда́вская ССР (Сове́тская Социалисти́ческая Респу́блика) Moldavian S.S.R. (Soviet Socialist Republic)
м. пр. (ме́жду про́чим) by the way, incidentally; among other things
МТС (маши́нно-тра́кторная ста́нция) machine and tractor station (*hist.*)
Музги́з (Музыка́льное госуда́рственное изда́тельство) State Publishing House for Music
МХАТ (Моско́вский худо́жественный академи́ческий теа́тр) Academic Artists' Theater, Moscow

напр. (наприме́р) for instance

НКВД (Наро́дный комиссариа́т вну́тренних дел) People's Commissariat of Internal Affairs (*1935 to 1946; since 1946* МВД, *cf.*)
№ (но́мер) number
н. ст. (но́вый стиль) new style (*Gregorian calendar*)
н. э. (на́шей э́ры) A. D.
нэп (но́вая экономи́ческая поли́тика) New Economic Policy

о. (о́стров) island
обл. (о́бласть) region; province, sphere, field (*fig.*)
о-во (о́бщество) society
ОГИЗ (Объедине́ние госуда́рственных изда́тельств) Union of the State Publishing Houses
оз. (о́зеро) lake
ОНО (отде́л наро́дного образова́ния) Department of Popular Education
ООН (Организа́ция Объединённых На́ций) United Nations Organization
отд. (отде́л) section, (отделе́ние) department

п. (пункт) point, paragraph
п. г. (про́шлого го́да) of last year
пер. (переу́лок) lane, alleyway, side street
пл. (пло́щадь *f*) square; area (*a.* ℞); (*living*) space
п. м. (про́шлого ме́сяца) of last month
проф. (профе́ссор) professor

р. **1.** (река́) river; **2.** (ру́бль *m*) r(o)uble
райко́м (райо́нный комите́т) district committee (*Sov.*)
РСФСР (Росси́йская Сове́тская Федерати́вная Социалисти́ческая Респу́блика) Russian Soviet Federative Socialist Republic

с. г. (сего́ го́да) (of) this year
след. (сле́дующий) following
см (сантиме́тр) cm. (centimeter)
с. м. (сего́ ме́сяца) (of) this month
см. (смотри́) see
совхо́з (сове́тское хозя́йство) state farm
ср. (сравни́) cf. (compare)
СССР (Сою́з Сове́тских Социалисти́ческих Респу́блик) U.S.S.R. (Union of Soviet Socialist Republics)
ст. **1.** (ста́нция) station; **2.** (стани́ца) Cossack village
стенгазе́та (стенна́я газе́та) wall newspaper
стр. (страни́ца) page
ст. ст. (ста́рый стиль) old style (*Julian calendar*)
с. х. (се́льское хозя́йство) agriculture
с.-х. (сельскохозя́йственный) agricultural
с. ч. (сего́ числа́) this day's
США (Соединённые Шта́ты Аме́рики) U.S.A. (United States of America)

т (то́нна) ton
т. **1.** (това́рищ) comrade; **2.** (том) volume
Таджи́кская ССР (Сове́тская Социалисти́ческая Респу́блика) Tadzhik S.S.R. (Soviet Socialist Republic)
ТАСС (Телегра́фное Аге́нтство Сове́тского Сою́за) TASS (Telegraph Agency of the Soviet Union)
т-во (това́рищество) company, association
т. г. (теку́щего го́да) of the current year
т. е. (то́ есть) i. e. (that is)
тел. (телефо́н) telephone
тел. комм. (телефо́нный коммута́тор) telephone switchboard
т. к. (та́к как) *cf.* так
т. м. (теку́щего ме́сяца) instant
т. наз. (так называ́емый) so-called
тов. *s.* т. 1.
торгпре́дство (торго́вое представи́тельство) trade agency of the U.S.S.R.
тролл. (тролле́йбус) trolley bus
тт. (тома́) volumes
Туркме́нская ССР (Сове́тская Социалисти́ческая Респу́блика) Turkmen S.S.R. (Soviet Socialist Republic)
тыс. (ты́сяча) thousand

Узбе́кская ССР (Сове́тская Социалисти́ческая Респу́блика) Uzbek S.S.R. (Soviet Socialist Republic)
ул. (у́лица) street
УССР (Украинская Сове́тская Социалисти́ческая Респу́блика) Ukrainian S.S.R. (Soviet Socialist Republic)
Учпедги́з (Госуда́рственное изда́тельство учёбно-педагоги́ческой литерату́ры) State Publishing House for Educational Books

ФРГ (Федерати́вная Респу́блика Герма́нии) Federal Republic of Germany

ЦИК (Центра́льный Исполни́тельный Комитéт) Central Executive Committee (*Sov.*); *cf.* ЦК
ЦК (Центра́льный Комитéт) Central Committee
ЦПКиО (Центра́льный парк культу́ры и о́тдыха) Central Park for Culture and Recreation

ч. (час) hour, (часть) part
ЧК (Чрезвыча́йная коми́ссия ...) Cheka (*predecessor*, *1917—22*, of the ГПУ, *cf.*)

Эсто́нская ССР (Сове́тская Социалисти́ческая Респу́блика) Estonian S.S.R. (Soviet Socialist Republic)

Current American and British Abbreviations

Наиболее употребительные сокращения, принятые в США и Великобритании

A

A.B.C. *American Broadcasting Company* Америка́нская радиовеща́тельная корпора́ция.

A-bomb *atomic bomb* а́томная бо́мба.

A.C. *alternating current* переме́нный ток.

A/C *account (current)* контокорре́нт, теку́щий счёт.

acc(t). *account* отчёт; счёт.

A.E.C. *Atomic Energy Commission* Коми́ссия по а́томной эне́ргии.

AFL-CIO *American Federation of Labor & Congress of Industrial Organizations* Америка́нская федера́ция труда́ и Конгре́сс произво́дственных профсою́зов, АФТ/КПП.

A.F.N. *American Forces Network* радиосе́ть америка́нских войск (в Европе).

Ala. *Alabama* Алаба́ма (штат в США).

Alas. *Alaska* Аля́ска (территория в США).

a.m. *ante meridiem* (лат. = *before noon*) до полу́дня.

A.P. *Associated Press* Ассо́шиэйтед пресс.

A.R.C. *American Red Cross* Америка́нский Кра́сный Крест.

Ariz. *Arizona* Аризо́на (штат в США).

Ark. *Arkansas* Арка́нза́с (штат в США).

A.R.P. *Air-Raid Precautions* гражда́нская ПВО (противовозду́шная оборо́на).

B

B.A. *Bachelor of Arts* бакала́вр филосо́фии.

B.B.C. *British Broadcasting Corporation* Брита́нская радиовеща́тельная корпора́ция.

B/E *Bill of Exchange* ве́ксель *m*, тра́тта.

B.E.A.C. *British European Airways Corporation* Брита́нская корпора́ция европе́йских возду́шных сообще́ний.

Benelux *Belgium, Netherlands, Luxemburg* экономи́ческий и тамо́женный сою́з, БЕНИЛЮКС.

B.F.B.S. *British Forces Broadcasting Service* радиовеща́тельная организа́ция брита́нских вооружённых сил.

B.L. *Bachelor of Law* бакала́вр пра́ва.

B/L *bill of lading* коносаме́нт; тра́нспортная накладна́я.

B.M. *Bachelor of Medicine* бакала́вр медици́ны.

B.O.A.C. *British Overseas Airways Corporation* Брита́нская корпора́ция трансокеа́нских возду́шных сообще́ний.

B.O.T. *Board of Trade* министе́рство торго́вли (в Англии).

B.R. *British Railways* Брита́нская желе́зная доро́га.

Br(it). *Britain* Великобрита́ния; *British* брита́нский, англи́йский.

Bros. *brothers* бра́тья *pl.* (в названиях фирм).

B.S.A. *British South Africa* Брита́нская 'Южная 'Африка.

B.T.U. *British Thermal Unit(s)* брита́нская теплова́я едини́ца.

B.U.P. *British United Press* информацио́нное аге́нтство „Бри́тиш Юна́йтед Пресс".

C

c. 1. *cent(s)* цент (американская монета); **2.** *circa* приблизи́тельно, о́коло; **3.** *cubic* куби́ческий.

C/A *current account* теку́щий счёт.

Cal(if). *California* Калифо́рния (штат в США).

Can. *Canada* Кана́да; *Canadian* кана́дский.

C.C. *continuous current* постоя́нный ток.

C.I.C. *Counter Intelligence Corps* слу́жба контрразве́дки США.

C.I.D. *Criminal Investigation Division* кримина́льная поли́ция.

c.i.f. *cost, insurance, freight* цена́, включа́ющая сто́имость, расхо́ды по страхова́нию и фрахт.

c/o *care of* че́рез, по а́дресу (надпись на конвертах).

Co. 1. *company* о́бщество, компа́ния; **2.** (в США и Ирландии также) *County* о́круг.

C.O.D. *cash* (ам. *collect.*) *on delivery* нало́женный платёж, упла́та при доста́вке.
Col. *Colorado* Колора́до (штат в США).
Conn. *Connecticut* Конне́ктикут (штат в США).
c.w.o. *cash with order* нали́чный расчёт при вы́даче зака́за.
cwt. *hundredweight* це́нтнер.

D

d. *penny* (*pence pl.*) (условное обозначение английской монеты) пе́нни (пе́нс[ы] *pl.*).
D.C. 1. *direct current* постоя́нный ток; **2.** *District of Columbia* федера́льный о́круг Колу́мбия (с американской столицей).
Del. *Delaware* Де́лавэр (штат в США).
Dept. *Department* отде́л; управле́ние; министе́рство; ве́домство.
disc(t). *discount* ски́дка; диско́нт, учёт векселе́й.
div(d). *dividend* дивиде́нд.
dol. *dollar* до́ллар.
doz. *dozen* дю́жина.
D.P. *Displaced Person* перемещённое лицо́.
d/p *documents against payment* докуме́нты за нали́чный расчёт.
Dpt. *Department* отде́л; управле́ние; министе́рство; ве́домство.

E

E. 1. *East* восто́к; *Eastern* восто́чный; **2.** *English* англи́йский.
E. & O.E. *errors and omissions excepted* исключа́я оши́бки и про́пуски.
E.C.E. *Economic Commission for Europe* Экономи́ческая коми́ссия ООН для Евро́пы.
ECOSOC *Economic and Social Council* Экономи́ческий и социа́льный сове́т ООН.
EE., E./E. *errors excepted* исключа́я оши́бки.
e.g. *exempli gratia* (лат. = *for instance*) напр. (наприме́р).
Enc. *enclosure(s)* приложе́ние (-ния).
E.R.P. *European Recovery Program(me)* програ́мма „восстановле́ния Евро́пы“, т. наз. „план Ма́ршалла“.
Esq. *Esquire* эсква́йр (титул дворянина, должностного лица; обычно ставится в письме после фамилии).

F

f. 1. *farthing* (брит. монета) че́тверть пе́нса, фа́ртинг; **2.** *fathom* морска́я саже́нь f; **3.** *feminine* же́нский; *gram.* же́нский род; **4.** *foot* фут, *feet* фу́ты; **5.** *following* сле́дующий.
FBI *Federal Bureau of Investigation* федера́льное бюро́ рассле́дований (в США).
FIFA *Fédération Internationale de Football Association* Междунаро́дная федера́ция футбо́льных о́бществ, ФИФА.
Fla. *Florida* Флори́да (штат в США).
F.O. *Foreign Office* министе́рство иностра́нных дел.
fo(l). *folio* фо́лио *indecl. n* (формат в пол-листа); лист (бухгалтерской книги).
f.o.b. *free on board* фра́нко-борт, ФОБ.
f.o.q. *free on quay* фра́нко-на́бережная.
f.o.r. *free on rail* фра́нко-ре́льсы, фра́нко желе́зная доро́га.
f.o.t. *free on truck* фра́нко ж.-д. платфо́рма; фра́нко-грузови́к.
f.o.w. *free on waggon* фра́нко-ваго́н.
fr. *franc(s)* фра́нк(и).
ft. *foot* фут, *feet* фу́ты.

G

g. 1. *gram(me)* грамм; **2.** *guinea* гине́я (денежная единица = 21 шиллингу).
Ga. *Georgia* Гео́ргия (штат в США).
G.A.T.T. *General Agreement on Tariffs and Trade* 'Общее соглаше́ние по тамо́женным тари́фам и торго́вле.
G.I. *government issue* казённый; госуда́рственная со́бственность f; *fig.* америка́нский солда́т.
G.M.T. *Greenwich Mean Time* сре́днее вре́мя по гри́нвичскому меридиа́ну.
gns. *guineas* гине́и.
gr. *gross* бру́тто.
gr.wt. *gross weight* вес бру́тто.
Gt.Br. *Great Britain* Великобрита́ния.

H

h. *hour(s)* час(ы́).
H.B.M. *His (Her) Britannic Majesty* Его́ (Её) Брита́нское Вели́чество.
H-bomb *hydrogen bomb* водоро́дная бо́мба.
H.C. *House of Commons* пала́та о́бщин (в Англии).
hf. *half* полови́на.
H.L. *House of Lords* пала́та ло́рдов (в Англии).
H.M. *His (Her) Majesty* Его́ (Её) Вели́чество.
H.M.S. 1. *His (Her) Majesty's Service* на слу́жбе Его́ (Её) Вели́чества; ✉ служе́бное де́ло; **2.** *His (Her)*

Majesty's Ship корáбль англи́йского вое́нно-морскóго флóта.
H.O. *Home Office* министе́рство внýтренних дел (в Англии).
H.P., h.p. *horse-power* лошади́ная си́ла (единица мощности).
H.Q., Hq. *Headquarters* штаб.
H.R. *House of Representatives* палáта представи́телей (в США).
H.R.H. *His (Her) Royal Highness* Егó (Её) Королéвское Высóчество.
hrs. *hours* часы́.

I

Ia. *Iowa* 'Айова (штат в США).
Id. *Idaho* Айдáхо (штат в США).
I.D. *Intelligence Department* развéдывательное управлéние.
i.e. *id est* (лат. = *that is to say*) т. е. (тó есть).
Ill. *Illinois* 'Иллинóйс (штат в США).
I.M.F. *International Monetary Fund* Междунарóдный валю́тный фонд ООН.
in. *inch(es)* дю́йм(ы).
Inc. **1.** *Incorporated* обьединённый; зарегистри́рованный как корпорáция; **2.** *Including* включи́тельно; **3.** *Inclosure* приложéние.
Ind. *Indiana* Индиáна (штат в США).
I.N.S. *International News Service* Междунарóдное телегрáфное агéнтство.
inst. (лат. = *instant*) с. м. (сегó мéсяца).
Ir. *Ireland* Ирлáндия; *Irish* ирлáндский.

J

J.P. *Justice of the Peace* мировóй судья́ *m.*
Jr. *junior* млáдший.

K

Kan(s). *Kansas* Кáнзáс (штат в США).
k.o. *knock(ed) out* спорт.: нокáут; *fig.* (окончательно) раздéлаться с кéм-либо.
Ky. *Kentucky* Кентýкки (штат в США).

L

l. *litre* литр.
£ *pound sterling* фунт стéрлингов.
La. *Louisiana* Луизиáна (штат в США).
£A *Australian pound* австрали́йский фунт (денежная единица).
lb. *pound* фунт (мера веса).
L/C *letter of credit* аккредити́в.
£E *Egyptian pound* еги́петский фунт (денежная единица).
L.P. *Labour Party* лейбори́стская пáртия.
LP *long-playing* долгоигрáющий; ~ *record* долгоигрáющая пласти́нка.
Ltd. *limited* с ограни́ченной ответственностью.

M

m. **1.** *male* мужскóй; **2.** *metre* метр; **3.** *mile* ми́ля; **4.** *minute* минýта.
M.A. *Master of Arts* маги́стр филосóфии.
Man. *Manitoba* Манитóба (провинция Канады).
Mass. *Massachusetts* Массачýсетс (штат в США).
M.D. *medicinae doctor* (лат. = *Doctor of Medicine*) дóктор медици́ны.
Md. *Maryland* Мэ́риленд (штат в США).
Me. *Maine* Мэн (штат в США).
mg. *milligramme* миллигрáмм.
Mich. *Michigan* Ми́чигáн (штат в США).
Minn. *Minnesota* Миннесóта (штат в США).
Miss. *Mississippi* Миссиси́пи (штат в США).
mm. *millimetre* миллимéтр.
Mo. *Missouri* Миссýри (штат в США).
M.O. *money order* дéнежный перевóд по пóчте.
Mont. *Montana* Монтáна (штат в США).
MP, M.P. **1.** *Member of Parliament* член парлáмента; **2.** *Military Police* вое́нная поли́ция.
m.p.h. *miles per hour* (столько-то) миль в час.
Mr. *Mister* ми́стер, господи́н.
Mrs. *Mistress* ми́ссис, госпожá.
MS. *manuscript* рýкопись f.
M.S. *motorship* теплохóд.

N

N. *North* сéвер; *Northern* сéверный.
N.A.A.F.I. *Navy, Army, and Air Force Institutes* вое́нно-торгóвая слýжба ВМС (вое́нно-морски́х сил), ВВС (вое́нно-воздýшных сил) и сухопýтных войск.
NATO *North Atlantic Treaty Organization* Североатланти́ческий сою́з, НАТО.
N.C. *North Carolina* Сéверная Кароли́на (штат в США).
N.Dak. *North Dakota* Сéверная Дакóта (штат в США).
N.E. *Northeast* северо-востóк.
Neb. *Nebraska* Небрáска (штат в США).
Nev. *Nevada* Невáда (штат в США).
N.H. *New Hampshire* Нью-Хэ́мпшир (штат в США).
N.J. *New Jersey* Нью-Джéрси (штат в США).

N.Mex. *New Mexico* Нью-Ме́ксико (штат в США).
nt.wt. *net weight* вес не́тто, чи́стый вес.
N.W. *Northwestern* се́веро-за́падный.
N.Y. *New York* Нью-Йо́рк (штат в США).
N.Y.C. *New York City* Нью-Йо́рк (го́род).

O

O. 1. *Ohio* Ога́йо (штат в США); **2.** *order* поруче́ние, зака́з.
o/a *on account of* за (чей-либо) счёт.
O.E.E.C. *Organization of European Economic Co-operation* Организа́ция европе́йского экономи́ческого сотру́дничества.
O.H.M.S. *On His (Her) Majesty's Service* состоя́щий на короле́вской (госуда́рственной или вое́нной) слу́жбе; ✉ служе́бное де́ло.
O.K. *all correct* всё в поря́дке, всё пра́вильно; утверждено́, согласо́вано.
Okla. *Oklahoma* Оклахо́ма (штат в США).
Ore(g). *Oregon* Орего́н (штат в США).

P

p.a. *per annum* (лат.) в год; ежего́дно.
Pa. *Pennsylvania* Пенсильва́ния (штат в США).
P. A. A. *Pan American Airways* Панамерика́нская авиакомпа́ния.
P.C. 1. *post-card* почто́вая ка́рточка, откры́тка; **2.** *police constable* полице́йский.
p.c. *per cent* проце́нт, проце́нты.
pd. *paid* упла́чено; опла́ченный.
Penn(a). *Pennsylvania* Пенсильва́ния (штат в США).
per pro(c). *per procurationem* (лат. = *by proxy*) по дове́ренности.
p.m. *post meridiem* (лат. = *after noon*) ... часо́в (часа́) дня.
P.O. 1. *Post Office* почто́вое отделе́ние; **2.** *postal order* де́нежный перево́д по по́чте.
P.O.B. *Post Office Box* почто́вый абонеме́нтный я́щик.
p.o.d. *pay on delivery* нало́женный платёж.
P.O.S.B. *Post Office Savings Bank* сберега́тельная ка́сса при почто́вом отделе́нии.
P.S. *Postscript* постскри́птум, припи́ска.
P.T.O., p.t.o. *please turn over* см. н/об. (смотри́ на оборо́те).
PX *Post Exchange* вое́нно-торго́вый магази́н.

Q

quot. *quotation* котиро́вка.

R

R.A.F. *Royal Air Force* вое́нно-возду́шные си́лы Великобрита́нии.
ref(c). *reference* ссы́лка, указа́ние.
regd. *registered* зарегистри́рованный; ✉ заказно́й.
reg. ton *register ton* реги́стровая то́нна.
ret. *retired* изъя́тый из обраще́ния; вы́купленный, опла́ченный.
Rev. *Reverend* преподо́бный.
R.I. *Rhode Island* Род-'Айленд (штат в США).
R.N. *Royal Navy* англи́йский вое́нно-морско́й флот Великобрита́нии.
R.P. *reply paid* отве́т опла́чен.
R.R. *Railroad Am.* желе́зная доро́га.

S

S. *South* юг; *Southern* ю́жный.
s. 1. *second* секу́нда; **2.** *shilling* ши́ллинг.
S.A. 1. *South Africa* 'Южная 'Африка; **2.** *South America* 'Южная Аме́рика; **3.** *Salvation Army* 'Армия спасе́ния.
S.C. 1. *South Carolina* 'Южная Кароли́на (штат в США); **2.** *Security Council* Сове́т Безопа́сности ООН.
S.Dak. *South Dakota* 'Южная Дако́та (штат в США).
S.E. 1. *Southeast* юго-восто́к; *Southeastern* юго-восто́чный; **2.** *Stock Exchange* фо́ндовая би́ржа (в Лондоне).
sh. *shilling* ши́ллинг.
Soc. *society* о́бщество.
sov. *sovereign* сове́рен (золотая монета в один фунт стерлингов).
Sq. *Square* пло́щадь f.
sq. *square...* квадра́тный.
S.S. *steamship* парохо́д.
St. *Station* ста́нция; вокза́л.
St. Ex. Stock Exchange фо́ндовая би́ржа.
stg. *sterling* фунт сте́рлингов.
suppl. *supplement* дополне́ние, приложе́ние.
S.W. *Southwest* юго-восто́к; *Southwestern* юго-восто́чный.

T

t. *ton* то́нна.
T.D. *Treasury Department* министе́рство фина́нсов (в США).
Tenn. *Tennessee* Теннесси́ (штат в США).
Tex. *Texas* Теха́с (штат в США).
T.M.O. *telegraphic money order* де́нежный перево́д по телегра́фу.
T.O. *Telegraph (Telephone) Office* телегра́фное (телефо́нное) отделе́ние.
T.U. *Trade Union* тред-юнио́н, профессиона́льный сою́з.

T.U.C. *Trade Unions Congress* конгрéсс (британских) тред-юниóнов.

U

U.K. *United Kingdom* Соединённое Королéвство (Англия, Шотландия, Уэльс и Северная Ирландия).
U.N. *United Nations* Объединённые Нáции.
UNESCO *United Nations Educational, Scientific, and Cultural Organization* Организáция Объединённых Нáций по вопрóсам просвещéния, наýки и культýры, ЮНЕСКО.
U.N.S.C. *United Nations Security Council* Совéт Безопáсности ООН.
U.P. *United Press* телегрáфное агéнтство „Юнáйтед Пресс".
U.S.(A.) *United States (of America)* Соединённые Штáты (Амéрики).
Ut. *Utah* 'Юта (штат в США).

V

Va. *Virginia* Виргúния (штат в США).
VE-day *Victory in Europe-day* День побéды в Еврóпе (над Германией в 1945).
viz. *videlicet* (лат.) а úменно.
vol. *volume* том.
vols. *volumes* томá *pl.*
Vt. *Vermont* Вермóнт (штат в США).

W

W. *West* зáпад; *Western* зáпадный.
Wash. *Washington* Вáшингтóн (штат в США).
W.D. *War Department* воéнное министéрство США.
W.F.T.U. *World Federation of Trade Unions* Всемúрная федерáция профессионáльных союзов, ВФП.
W.H.O. *World Health Organization* Всемúрная организáция здравоохранéния, ВОЗ.
W.I. *West Indies* Вест-'Индия.
Wis. *Wisconsin* Вискóнсин (штат в США).
W.O. *War Office* (британское) воéнное министéрство.
wt. *weight* вес.
W.Va. *West Virginia* Зáпадная Виргúния (штат в США).
Wyo. *Wyoming* Вайóминг (штат в США).

X

Xmas *Christmas* рождествó.

Y

yd(s). *yard(s)* ярд(ы).
Y.M.C.A. *Young Men's Christian Association* Христиáнская ассоциáция молодых людéй.
Y.W.C.A. *Young Women's Christian Association* Христиáнская ассоциáция (молодых) дéвушек.

Числительные — Numerals

Количественные
Cardinals

0 ноль & нуль *m* naught, zero, cipher
1 оди́н *m*, одна́ *f*, одно́ *n* one
2 два *m/n*, две *f* two
3 три three
4 четы́ре four
5 пять five
6 шесть six
7 семь seven
8 во́семь eight
9 де́вять nine
10 де́сять ten
11 оди́ннадцать eleven
12 двена́дцать twelve
13 трина́дцать thirteen
14 четы́рнадцать fourteen
15 пятна́дцать fifteen
16 шестна́дцать sixteen
17 семна́дцать seventeen
18 восемна́дцать eighteen
19 девятна́дцать nineteen
20 два́дцать twenty
21 два́дцать оди́н *m* (одна́ *f*, одно́ *n*) twenty-one
22 два́дцать два *m/n* (две *f*) twenty-two
23 два́дцать три twenty-three
30 три́дцать thirty
40 со́рок forty
50 пятьдеся́т fifty
60 шестьдеся́т sixty
70 се́мьдесят seventy
80 во́семьдесят eighty
90 девяно́сто ninety
100 сто (а и́ли one) hundred
200 две́сти two hundred
300 три́ста three hundred
400 четы́реста four hundred
500 пятьсо́т five hundred
600 шестьсо́т six hundred
700 семьсо́т seven hundred
800 восемьсо́т eight hundred
900 девятьсо́т nine hundred
1000 (одна́) ты́сяча *f* (а и́ли one) thousand
60 140 шестьдеся́т ты́сяч сто со́рок sixty thousand one hundred and forty
1 000 000 (оди́н) миллио́н *m* (а и́ли one) million
1 000 000 000 (оди́н) миллиа́рд *or* биллио́н *m* milliard, *Am.* billion

Порядковые
Ordinals

1st пе́рвый first
2nd второ́й second
3rd тре́тий third
4th четвёртый fourth
5th пя́тый fifth
6th шесто́й sixth
7th седьмо́й seventh
8th восьмо́й eighth
9th девя́тый ninth
10th деся́тый tenth
11th оди́ннадцатый eleventh
12th двена́дцатый twelfth
13th трина́дцатый thirteenth
14th четы́рнадцатый fourteenth
15th пятна́дцатый fifteenth
16th шестна́дцатый sixteenth
17th семна́дцатый seventeenth
18th восемна́дцатый eighteenth
19th девятна́дцатый nineteenth
20th двадца́тый twentieth
21st два́дцать пе́рвый twenty-first
22nd два́дцать второ́й twenty-second
23rd два́дцать тре́тий twenty-third
30th тридца́тый thirtieth
40th сороково́й fortieth
50th пятидеся́тый fiftieth
60th шестидеся́тый sixtieth
70th семидеся́тый seventieth
80th восьмидеся́тый eightieth
90th девяно́стый ninetieth
100th со́тый (one) hundredth
200th двухсо́тый two hundredth
300th трёхсо́тый three hundredth
400th четырёхсо́тый four hundredth
500th пятисо́тый five hundredth
600th шестисо́тый six hundredth
700th семисо́тый seven hundredth
800th восьмисо́тый eight hundredth
900th девятисо́тый nine hundredth
1000th ты́сячный (one) thousandth
60 140th шестьдеся́т ты́сяч сто сороково́й sixty thousand one hundred and fortieth
1 000 000th миллио́нный millionth

Русские меры длины и веса

Russian Measures and Weights

In the U.S.S.R. the metric system is in force since January 1st, 1927. Hence measures and weights are in accordance with the international metric system.

Moreover the following old Russian measures and weights are occasionally still used within the Soviet Union:

1. Мéры длины́. Long measures

1 верстá (verst) = 500 сажéням (сажéнь, fathom) = 1500 арши́нам (arshin) = 1066.78 m.

1 арши́н (arshin) = 2.333 фýта (фут, foot) = 16 вершкáм (вершóк, vershock) = 28 дю́ймам (дюйм, inch) = 0.71 m.

2. Квадрáтные мéры. Square measures

1 квадрáтная верстá (square verst) = 104.167 десяти́ны (dessiatine) = 250 000 квадрáтным сажéням (square sagene)

1 десяти́на (dessiatine) = 2400 кв. сажéням (square sagene) = 109.254 acres

3. Мéры объёма. Cubic measures

куби́ческий фут (cubic foot); куби́ческая сажéнь (cubic sagene); куби́ческий арши́н (cubic arshin)

4. Хлéбные мéры. Dry measures

1 чéтверть (chetvert) = 2 осьми́нам (осьми́на, osmina, eighth) = 4 полуосьми́нам (poluosmina) = 8 четверикáм (четвери́к, chetverik) = 64 гáрнцам (гáрнец, garnetz) = 209.9 l.

5. Мéры жи́дкостей. Liquid measures

1 ведрó (bucket) = 10 крýжкам (крýжка, mug) = 100 чáркам (чáрка, cup, gin-glas) = 12.30 l.

6. Мéры мáссы (вéса). Weights

1 пуд (pood) = 40 фýнтам (фунт, pound) = 1280 лóтам (small weight) = 16.38 kg.

1 лот (small weight) = 3 золотникáм (золотни́к, zolotnick) = 288 дóлям (дóля, dolya)

Валю́та. Currency

1 рубль (rouble) = 100 копéйкам (копéйка, copeck)

American and British Measures and Weights

Американские и британские меры длины и веса

1. Ме́ры длины́

1 **line (l.)** ли́ния = 2,12 мм
1 **inch (in.)** дюйм = 2,54 см
1 **foot (ft.)** фут = 30,48 см
1 **yard (yd.)** ярд = 91,44 см

2. Морски́е ме́ры

1 **fathom (f., fm.)** морска́я саже́нь = 1,83 м
1 **cable('s) length** ка́бельтов = 183 м, в США = 120 морски́м саже́ням = 219 м
1 **nautical mile (n. m.)** *or* **1 knot** морска́я ми́ля = 1852 м

3. Квадра́тные ме́ры

1 **square inch (sq. in.)** квадра́тный дюйм = 6,45 кв. см
1 **square foot (sq. ft.)** квадра́тный фут = 929,03 кв. см
1 **square yard (sq. yd.)** квадра́тный ярд = 8 361,26 кв. см
1 **square rod (sq. rd.)** квадра́тный род = 25,29 кв. м
1 **rood (ro.)** руд = 0,25 а́кра
1 **acre (a.)** акр = 0,4 га
1 **square mile (sq. mi.)** квадра́тная ми́ля = 259 га

4. Ме́ры объёма

1 **cubic inch (cu. in.)** куби́ческий дюйм = 16,387 куб. см
1 **cubic foot (cu. ft.)** куби́ческий фут = 28 316,75 куб. см
1 **cubic yard (cu. yd.)** куби́ческий ярд = 0,765 куб. м
1 **register ton (reg. ton)** реги́стровая то́нна = 2,832 куб. м

5. Ме́ры ёмкости

Ме́ры жи́дких и сыпу́чих тел

1 **British** *or* **Imperial gill (gl., gi.)** станда́ртный и́ли англи́йский джилл = 0,142 л
1 **British** *or* **Imperial pint (pt.)** станда́ртная и́ли англи́йская пи́нта = 0,568 л
1 **British** *or* **Imperial quart (qt.)** станда́ртная и́ли англи́йская ква́рта = 1,136 л
1 **British** *or* **Imp. gallon (Imp. gal.)** станда́ртный и́ли англи́йский галло́н = 4,546 л

6. Ме́ры сыпу́чих тел

1 **British** *or* **Imperial peck (pk.)** станда́ртный и́ли англи́йский пек = 9,086 л
1 **Brit.** *or* **Imp. bushel (bu., bus.)** станда́ртный и́ли англи́йский бу́шель = 36,35 л
1 **Brit.** *or* **Imperial quarter (qr.)** станда́ртная и́ли англи́йская че́тверть = 290,8 л

7. Ме́ры жи́дких тел

1 **Brit.** *or* **Imperial barrel (bbl., bl.)** станда́ртный и́ли англи́йский ба́ррель = 1,636 гл

Америка́нские ме́ры жи́дких и сыпу́чих тел

Ме́ры сыпу́чих тел

1 **U.S. dry pint** америка́нская суха́я пи́нта = 0,551 л
1 **U.S. dry quart** америка́нская суха́я ква́рта = 1,1 л
1 **U.S. dry gallon** америка́нский сухо́й галло́н = 4,4 л
1 **U.S. peck** америка́нский пек = 8,81 л
1 **U.S. bushel** америка́нский бу́шель = 35,24 л

Ме́ры жи́дких тел

1 **U.S. liquid gill** америка́нский джилл (жи́дкости) = 0,118 л
1 **U.S. liquid pint** америка́нская пи́нта (жи́дкости) = 0,473 л
1 **U.S. liquid quart** америка́нская ква́рта (жи́дкости) = 0,946 л
1 **U.S. liquid gallon** америка́нский галло́н (жи́дкости) = 3,785 л
1 **U.S. barrel** америка́нский ба́ррель = 119 л
1 **U.S. barrel petroleum** америка́нский ба́ррель не́фти = 158,97 л

8. Торго́вые ме́ры ве́са

1 **grain (gr.)** гран = 0,0648 г
1 **dram (dr.)** дра́хма = 1,77 г
1 **ounce (oz.)** у́нция = 28,35 г
1 **pound (lb.)** фунт = 453,59 г
1 **quarter (qr.)** че́тверть = 12,7 кг, в США = 11,34 кг
1 **hundredweight (cwt.)** це́нтнер = 50,8 кг, в США = 45,36 кг
1 **stone (st.)** стон = 6,35 кг
1 **ton (tn., t.)** = 1016 кг (тж long ton: tn. l.), в США = 907,18 кг (тж short ton: tn. sh.)